THE Destruction OF THE European Jews

RAUL HILBERG received his doctorate in Public Law and Government at Columbia University. He was a member of the War Documentation Project in the Federal Records Center at Alexandria, Virginia, and subsequently taught at Hunter College and the University of Puerto Rico. Since 1956 he has been in the Department of Political Science at the University of Vermont.

THE Destruction OF THE European Jews

by Raul Hilberg

WITH A NEW POSTSCRIPT BY THE AUTHOR

New Viewpoints
A Division of Franklin Watts, Inc.
New York, 1973

First NEW VIEWPOINTS edition published 1973 by Franklin Watts, Inc.

Manufactured in the United States of America.

Preface

To begin with, a word should be said about the scope of this book. Lest one be misled by the word "Jews" in the title, let it be pointed out that this is not a book about the Jews. It is a book about the people who destroyed the Jews. Not much will be read here about the victims. The focus is placed on the perpetrators.

The following chapters will describe the vast organization of the Nazi machinery of destruction and the men who performed important functions in this machine. They will reveal the correspondence, memoranda, and conference minutes which were passed from desk to desk as the German bureaucracy made its weighty and drastic decisions to destroy, utterly and completely, the Jews of Europe. They will deal with the administrative and psychological obstacles which blocked action from time to time, and they will show how these impediments were cleared away.

On the other hand, there will be no emphasis on the effects of the German measures upon Jewry in Europe and elsewhere. We shall not dwell on Jewish suffering, nor shall we explore the social characteristics of ghetto life or camp existence. Insofar as we may examine Jewish institutions, we will do so primarily through the eyes of the Germans: as tools which were used in the destruction process. In short, this study does not encompass the internal developments of Jewish organization and Jewish social structure. That is Jewish history. It is concerned with the storm that caused the wreckage. That is a part of Western history. The history of the West has at times been shaped by the Jews. It has been changed no less – and perhaps more so – by those who have acted against the Jews, for when I do something to another, I also do something to myself.

The total import of the German measures has not yet been explored; the destruction of the European Jews has not yet been absorbed as a historical event. This does not mean a general denial that millions of people have disappeared, nor does it imply a serious doubt that masses of these people were shot in ditches and gassed in camps. But acknowledgment of a fact does not signify its acceptance in an academic sense. Unprecedented occurrences of such magnitude are accepted academically only when they are studied as tests of existing conceptions about force, about relations between cultures, about society as a whole. Only a generation ago, the incidents described in this book would have been considered improbable, infeasible, or even inconceivable. Now they have happened. The destruction of the Jews was a process of extremes. That, precisely, is why it is so important as a group phenomenon. That is why it can serve as a test of social and political theories. But to perform such tests, it is not enough to know that the Jews have been destroyed; one must also grasp how this deed was done. That is the story to be told in this book.

Acknowledgments

My work was begun in 1948; it was accomplished with considerable help. A great many people gave me counsel and assistance. Some of them furthered decisively the achievement of the final result.

From the outset I have been indebted to Professor Hans Rosenberg of Brooklyn College. I must credit him with comments which convinced me that this project had to be undertaken.

The late Franz Neumann of Columbia University introduced me to the indispensable Nuremberg material. He then placed me on the staff of a research organization to examine the document collections at Alexandria, Virigina.

Professor William T. R. Fox of Columbia University gave me much encouragement during a difficult period. His many acts of kindness, freely extended again and again, brought me a degree and an award, as well as grants and teaching positions.

The late Dr. Philip Friedman of Columbia University and the YIVO Institute also went out of his way to express concern for me and my work. At the same time, my father shared with me his patience and his sense of literary balance.

My old friend Eric Marder stood by for a decade while the work was under way. Throughout these years I drew extensively on his penetrating insights in the shaping of the book.

Shortly before the end of the effort, Mr. Frank C. Petschek interested himself in the manuscript. He read it line by line. Then he offered in a singular gesture to make possible its appearance in print.

When this study was first conceived, it was intended as the first word on a difficult subject. Now that the job is done, let it be received in that spirit.

RAUL HILBERG

BURLINGTON, VERMONT
October 25, 1960

Table of Contents

INTRODUCTION

I / *Precedents*

The German destruction of the European Jews was a tour de force; the Jewish collapse under the German assault was a manifestation of failure. Both of these phenomena were the final product of an earlier age.

Anti-Jewish policies and anti-Jewish actions did not have their beginning in 1933. For many centuries, and in many countries, the Jews have been victims of destructive action. What was the object of these activities? What were the aims of those who persisted in anti-Jewish deeds? Throughout Western history, three consecutive policies have been applied against Jewry in its dispersion.

The first anti-Jewish policy started in the fourth century after Christ in Rome.[1] In the early 300's, during the reign of Constantine, the Christian Church gained power in Rome, and Christianity became the state religion. From this period, the state carried out Church policy. For the next twelve centuries, the Catholic Church prescribed the measures that were to be taken with respect to the Jews. Unlike the pre-Christian Romans, who claimed no monopoly on religion and faith, the Christian Church insisted upon acceptance of Christian doctrine.

For an understanding of Christian policy toward Jewry, it is essential to realize that the Church pursued conversion not so much for the sake of aggrandizing its power (the Jews have always been few in number) but because of the conviction that it was the duty of true believers to save unbelievers from the doom of eternal hellfire. Zealousness in the pursuit of conversion was an indication of the depth of faith. The Christian religion was not one of many religions, like other religions. It was the true religion, the only religion. Those who were not in its fold were either ignorant or in error. The Jews could not accept Christianity.

In the very early stages of the Christian faith, many Jews regarded Christians as members of a Jewish sect. The first Christians, after all, still observed the Jewish law. They had merely added a few nonessential practices, such as baptism, to their religious life. But this view was changed abruptly when Christ was elevated to Godhood. The Jews have only one God. That God is indivisible. He is a jealous God and admits of no other gods. He is not Christ, and Christ is not He. Christianity and Judaism have since been irreconcilable. An acceptance of Christianity has since signified an abandonment of Judaism.

In antiquity and in the Middle Ages, Jews did not abandon Judaism lightly. With patience and persistence, the Church attempted to convert obstinate Jewry, and for twelve hundred years, the theological argument was fought without interruption. The Jews were not convinced. Gradually the Church began to back its words with force. The Papacy did not permit pressure to be put on individual Jews; Rome never permitted forceful conversions.[2] However, the clergy did use pressure on the whole. Step by step, but with ever widening effect, the

1. Pre-Christian Rome had no anti-Jewish policy. Rome had crushed the independent Jewish state of Judea, but the Jews *in* Rome enjoyed equality under the law. They could execute wills, enter into valid marriages with Romans, exercise the rights of guardianship, and hold office. Otto Stobbe, *Die Juden in Deutschland während des Mittelalters* (Leipzig, 1902), p. 2.

Church adopted "defensive" measures against its passive victims. Christians were "protected" from the "harmful" consequences of intercourse with Jews by rigid laws against intermarriage, by prohibitions of discussions about religious issues, by laws against domicile in common abodes. The Church "protected" its Christians from the "harmful" Jewish teachings by burning the Talmud and by barring Jews from public office.[3]

These measures, which we shall discuss more fully in a moment, were precedent-making destructive activities. How little the Church had accomplished its aim is revealed by the treatment of that relative handful of Jews who succumbed to the Christian religion. The clergy was not sure of its success – hence the widespread practice, in the Middle Ages, of identifying proselytes as former Jews,[4] hence the inquisition of new Christians suspected of heresy,[5] hence the issuance in Spain of certificates of "purity" (*limpieza*) signifying purely Christian ancestry, and the specification of half new Christians, quarter new Christians, one-eighth new Christians, etc.[6]

The failure of conversion had far-reaching consequences. The unsuccessful Church began to look upon the Jews as a special group of people, different from Christians, deaf to Christianity, and dangerous to the Christian faith. In 1542, a reform leader and founder of a new church, Martin Luther, wrote the following lines.

> And if there were a spark of common sense and understanding in them, they would truly have to think like this: O my God, it does not stand and go well with us; our misery is too great, too long, too hard; God has forgotten us, etc. I am no Jew, but I do not like to think in earnest about such brutal wrath of God against this people, for I am terrified at the thought which cuts through my body and soul: What is going to happen with the eternal wrath in hell against all false Christians and unbelievers?[7]

In short, if *he* were a Jew, he would have accepted Christianity long ago.

A people cannot suffer for fifteen hundred years and still think of itself as the chosen people. But this people was blind. It had been stricken by the wrath of God. He had struck them "with frenzy, blindness, and raging heart, with the eternal fire, of which the Prophets say: The wrath of God will hurl itself outward like a fire that no one can smother."[8]

2. This prohibition had one weakness: once converted, even though forcibly, a Jew was forbidden to return to his faith. Guido Kisch, *The Jews in Medieval Germany* (Chicago, 1949), pp. 201–2.

3. Actually, non-Jews who wish to become Jews face formidable obstacles. See Louis Finkelstein, "The Jewish Religion: Its Beliefs and Practices," in Finkelstein (ed.), *The Jews: Their History, Culture, and Religion,* (New York, 1949), II, 1376.

4. Kisch, *Jews in Medieval Germany,* p. 315.

5. *Ibid.*

6. Cecil Roth, "Marranos and Racial Anti-Semitism – A Study in Parallels," *Jewish Social Studies,* II (1940), 239–48. New Christian doctors were accused of killing patients; a Toledo tribunal handed down a decision in 1449 to the effect that new Christians were ineligible for public office; and in 1604 new Christians were barred from the University of Coimbra (*ibid.*). Anyone who was a descendant of Jews or Moors was also ineligible to serve in the "Militia of Christ," Torquemada's army, which tortured and burned "heretics" Franz Helbing, *Die Tortur – Geschichte der Folter im Kriminalverfahren aller Völker und Zeiten* (Berlin, 1902), p. 118.

7. Martin Luther, *Von den Jueden und Jren Luegen* (Wittenberg, 1543), p. Aiii2. Page numbers in the original edition of Luther's book are placed on the bottom of every second or fourth page, as follows: A, Aii, Aiii, B, Bii, Biii, to Z, Zii, Ziii, starting over with a, aii, aiii. In order to identify quotations more closely, I have inserted arabic numerals in my footnotes, thus: Aiii2, Aiii3, etc.

8. Luther, *Von den Jueden,* p. diii. The reference to frenzy is an inversion. Frenzy, etc., is one of the punishments for deserting the one and only God.

The Lutheran manuscript was published at a time of increasing hatred for the Jew. Too much had been invested in twelve hundred years of conversion policy. Too little had been gained. From the thirteenth to the sixteenth centuries, the Jews of England, France, Germany, Spain, Bohemia, and Italy were presented with ultimatums which gave them no choice but one: conversion or expulsion.

Expulsion is the second anti-Jewish policy in history. To be sure, in its origin, that policy presented itself only as an alternative – moreover, as an alternative which was left to the Jews. But long after the separation of church and state, long after the state had ceased to carry out church policy, expulsion and exclusion remained the goal of anti-Jewish activity.

The anti-Semites of the nineteenth century, who divorced themselves from religious aims, espoused the emigration of the Jews. The anti-Semites hated the Jews with a feeling of righteousness and reason, as though they had acquired the antagonism of the church like speculators buying the rights of a bankrupt corporation. With this hatred, the post-ecclesiastic enemies of Jewry also took the idea that the Jews could not be changed, that they could not be converted, that they could not be assimilated, that they were a finished product, inflexible in their ways, set in their notions, fixed in their beliefs.

The expulsion and exclusion policy was adopted by the Nazis and remained the goal of all anti-Jewish activity until 1941. That year marks a turning point in anti-Jewish history. In 1941, the Nazis found themselves in the midst of a total war. Several million Jews were incarcerated in ghettos. Emigration was impossible. A last-minute project to ship the Jews to the African island of Madagascar had fallen through. The "Jewish problem" had to be "solved" in some other way. At this crucial time, the idea of a "territorial solution" emerged in Nazi minds; the "territorial solution," or "the final solution of the Jewish question in Europe," as it became known, envisaged the death of European Jewry. The European Jews were to be killed. That is the third anti-Jewish policy in history.

To summarize: Since the fourth century after Christ, there have been three anti-Jewish policies: conversion, expulsion, and annihilation. The second appeared as an alternative to the first, and the third emerged as an alternative to the second.

The destruction of the European Jews between 1933 and 1945 appears to us now as an unprecedented event in history. Indeed, in its dimensions and total configuration, nothing like it had ever happened before. Five million people were killed as a result of an organized undertaking in the short space of a few years. The operation was over before anyone could grasp its enormity, let alone its implications for the future.

Yet if we analyze that singularly massive upheaval, we discover that most of what happened in those twelve years had already happened before. The Nazi destruction process did not come out of a void; it was the culmination of a cyclical trend.[9] We have observed the trend in the three successive goals of anti-Jewish administrators. The missionaries of Christianity had said in effect: You have no right to live among us as Jews. The secular rulers who followed had proclaimed: You have no right to live among us. The German Nazis at last decreed:

9. A regular trend is unbroken (for instance, an increase of population); a cyclical trend is observed in some of the recurring phenomena. We may speak, for example, of a set of wars that become progressively more destructive, depressions that decline in severity, etc.

You have no right to live.

These progressively more drastic goals brought in their wake a slow and steady growth of anti-Jewish action and anti-Jewish thinking. The process began with the attempt to drive the Jews into Christianity. The development was continued in order to force the victims into exile. It was finished when the Jews were driven to their deaths. The German Nazis, then, did not discard the past; they built upon it. They did not begin a development; they completed it. In the deep recesses of anti-Jewish history, we shall find many of the administrative and psychological tools with which the Nazis implemented their destruction process. In the hollows of the past, we shall also discover the roots of the characteristic Jewish response to an outside attack.

The significance of the historical precedents will most easily be understood in the administrative sphere. The destruction of the Jews was an administrative process, and the annihilation of Jewry required the implementation of systematic administrative measures in successive steps. There are not many ways in which a modern society can, in short order, kill a large number of people living in its midst. This is an efficiency problem of the greatest dimensions, one which poses uncounted difficulties and innumerable obstacles. Yet, in reviewing the documentary record of the destruction of the Jews, one is almost immediately impressed with the fact that the German administration knew what it was doing. With an unfailing sense of direction and with an uncanny pathfinding ability, the German bureaucracy found the shortest road to the final goal.

We know, of course, that the very nature of a task determines the form of its fulfilment. Where there is the will, there is also the way, and if the will is only strong enough, the way will be found. But what if there is no time to experiment? What if the task must be solved quickly and efficiently? A rat in a maze, which has only one path to the goal, learns to choose that path after many trials. Bureaucrats, too, are sometimes caught in a maze, but they cannot afford a trial run. There may be no time for hesitations and stoppages. That is why past performance is so important, that is why past experience is so essential. Necessity is said to be the mother of invention, but if precedents have already been formed, if a guide has already been constructed, invention is no longer a necessity. The German bureaucracy could draw upon such precedents and follow such a guide, for the German bureaucrats could dip into a vast reservoir of administrative experience, a reservoir which church and state had filled in fifteen hundred years of destructive activity.

In the course of its attempt to convert the Jews, the Catholic Church had taken many measures against the Jewish population. These measures were designed to "protect" the Christian community from Jewish teachings and, not incidentally, to weaken the Jews in their "obstinacy." It is characteristic that as soon as Christianity became the state religion of Rome, in the fourth century A.D., Jewish equality of citizenship was ended. "The Church and the Christian state, concilium decisions and imperial laws, henceforth worked hand in hand to persecute the Jews."[10] Table 1 compares the basic anti-Jewish measures of the Catholic Church and the modern counterparts enacted by the Nazi regime.[11]

10. Stobbe, *Die Juden in Deutschland,* p. 2.

11. The list of Church measures is taken in its entirety from J. E. Scherer, *Die Rechtsverhältnisse der Juden in den deutsch-österreichischen Ländern* (Leipzig, 1901), pp. 39–49. Only the first date of each measure is listed in Table 1.

Table 1 / *Canonical and Nazi Anti-Jewish Measures*

Canonical Law	Nazi Measure
Prohibition of intermarriage and of sexual intercourse between Christians and Jews, Synod of Elvira, 306	Law for the Protection of German Blood and Honor, September 15, 1935 (RGB1 I, 1146.)
Jews and Christians not permitted to eat together, Synod of Elvira, 306	Jews barred from dining cars (Transport Minister to Interior Minister, December 30, 1939, Document NG-3995.)
Jews not allowed to hold public office, Synod of Clermont, 535	Law for the Re-establishment of the Professional Civil Service, April 7, 1933 (RGB1 I, 175.)
Jews not allowed to employ Christian servants or possess Christian slaves, 3d Synod of Orleans, 538	Law for the Protection of German Blood and Honor, September 15, 1935 (RGB1 I, 1146.)
Jews not permitted to show themselves in the streets during Passion Week, 3d Synod of Orleans, 538	Decree authorizing local authorities to bar Jews from the streets on certain days (i.e., Nazi holidays), December 3, 1938 (RGB1 I, 1676.)
Burning of the Talmud and other books, 12th Synod of Toledo, 681	Book burnings in Nazi Germany
Christians not permitted to patronize Jewish doctors, Trulanic Synod, 692	Decree of July 25, 1938 (RGB1 I, 969.)
Christians not permitted to live in Jewish homes, Synod of Narbonne, 1050	Directive by Göring providing for concentration of Jews in houses, December 28, 1938 (Borman to Rosenberg, January 17, 1939, PS-69.)
Jews obliged to pay taxes for support of the Church to the same extent as Christians, Synod of Gerona, 1078	The "Sozialausgleichsabgabe" which provided that Jews pay a special income tax in lieu of donations for Party purposes imposed on Nazis, December 24, 1940 (RGB1 I, 1666.)
Prohibition of Sunday work, Synod of Szabolcs, 1092	
Jews not permitted to be plaintiffs, or witnesses against Christians in the Courts, 3d Lateran Council, 1179, Canon 26	Proposal by the Party Chancellery that Jews not be permitted to institute civil suits, September 9, 1942 (Bormann to Justice Ministry, September 9, 1942, NG-151.)
Jews not permitted to withhold inheritance from descendants who had accepted Christianity, 3d Lateran Council, 1179, Canon 26	Decree empowering the Justice Ministry to void wills offending the "sound judgment of the people," July 31, 1938 (RGB1 I, 937.)
The marking of Jewish clothes with a badge, 4th Lateran Council, 1215, Canon 68 (Copied from the legislation by Caliph Omar II [634–44], who had decreed that Christians wear blue belts and Jews, yellow belts.)	Decree of September 1, 1941 (RGB1 I, 547.)
Construction of new synogogues prohibited, Council of Oxford, 1222	Destruction of synagogues in entire Reich, November 10, 1938 (Heydrich to Göring, November 11, 1938, PS-3058.)
Christians not permitted to attend Jewish ceremonies, Synod of Vienna, 1267	Friendly relations with Jews prohibited, October 24, 1941 (Gestapo directive, L-15.)
Jews not permitted to dispute with simple Christian people about the tenets of the Catholic religion, Synod of Vienna, 1267	

TABLE 1 / *Canonical and Nazi Anti-Jewish Measures (Continued)*

CANONICAL LAW	NAZI MEASURE
Compulsory ghettos, Synod of Breslau, 1267	Order by Heydrich, September 21, 1939 (PS-3363.)
Christians not permitted to sell or rent real estate to Jews, Synod of Ofen, 1279	Decree providing for compulsory sale of Jewish real estate, December 3, 1938 (RGBl I, 1709.)
Adoption by a Christian of the Jewish religion or return by a baptized Jew to the Jewish religion defined as a heresy, Synod of Mainz, 1310	Adoption by a Christian of the Jewish religion places him in jeopardy of being treated as a Jew, Decision by Oberlandesgericht Königsberg, 4th Zivilsenat, June 26, 1942 (*Die Judenfrage* [*Vertrauliche Beilage*], November 1, 1942, pp. 82–83.)
Sale or transfer of Church articles to Jews prohibited, Synod of Lavour, 1368	
Jews not permitted to act as agents in the conclusion of contracts between Christians, especially marriage contracts, Council of Basel, 1434, Sessio XIX	Decree of July 6, 1938, providing for liquidation of Jewish real estate agencies, brokerage agencies, and marriage agencies catering to non-Jews (RGBl I, 823.)
Jews not permitted to obtain academic degrees, Council of Basel, 1434, Sessio XIX	Law against Overcrowding of German Schools and Universities, April 25, 1933 (RGBl I, 225.)

No summation of the canonical law can be as revealing as a description of the Rome ghetto, maintained by the Papal State until the occupation of the city by the Royal Italian Army in 1870. A German journalist who visited the ghetto in its closing days published such an account in the *Neue Freie Presse*.[12] The ghetto consisted of a few damp, dark, and dirty streets, into which 4700 human creatures had been packed tightly (*eingepfercht*).

To rent any house or business establishment outside of the ghetto boundaries, the Jews needed the permission of the Cardinal Vicar. Acquisition of real estate outside the ghetto was prohibited. Trade with industrial products or books was prohibited. Higher schooling was prohibited. The professions of lawyer, druggist, notary, painter, and architect were prohibited. A Jew could be a doctor, provided that he confined his practice to Jewish patients. No Jew could hold office. Jews were required to pay taxes like everyone else and, in addition, the following: (1) a yearly stipend for the upkeep of the Catholic officials who supervised the Ghetto Finance Administration and the Jewish community organization; (2) a yearly sum of 5250 lira to the Casa Pia for missionary work among Jews; (3) a yearly sum of 5250 lira to the Cloister of the Converted for the same purpose. In return, the Papal State expended a yearly sum of 1500 lira for welfare work. But no state money was paid for education or the care of the sick.

The papal regime in the Rome ghetto gives us an idea of the cumulative effect of the canonical law. *This* was its total result. Moreover, the policy of the Church gave rise not only to ecclesiastical regulations; for more than a thousand years, the will of the Church was also enforced by the state. The decisions of the synods and councils became basic guides for state action. Every medieval state copied the canonical law and elaborated upon it.

12. Carl Eduard Bauernschmid in *Neue Freie Presse*, May 17, 1870, reprinted in *Allgemeine Zeitung des Judenthums* (Leipzig), July 19, 1870, pp. 580–82.

Thus there arose an "international medieval Jewry law" which, in fact, continued to develop until the eighteenth century. The governmental refinements and elaborations of the clerical regime may briefly be noted in Table 2, which shows also the Nazi versions.

These are some of the precedents which were handed down to the Nazi bureaucratic machine. To be sure, not all the lessons of the past were still remembered in 1933; much had been obscured by the passage of time. That is particularly true of negative principles, such as the avoidance of riots and pogroms. In 1406, the state sought to make profits from mob violence in the Jewish quarter of Vienna. Christians suffered greater losses in this pogrom than Jews, because the Jewish pawnshops, which went up in smoke during the great ghetto fire, contained the possessions of the very people who

TABLE 2 / *Pre-Nazi and Nazi Anti-Jewish Measures*

PRE-NAZI STATE DEVELOPMENT	NAZI MEASURE
Per capita protection tax (*der goldene Opferpfennig*) imposed upon Jews by King Ludwig the Bavarian, 1328–1337 (Stobbe, *Die Juden in Deutschland*, p. 31.)	
The property of Jews slain in a German city considered as public property, "because the Jews with their possessions belong to the Reich chamber," provision in the 14th-century code *Regulae juris "Ad decus"* (Kisch, *Jews in Medieval Germany*, pp. 360–61, 560–61.)	13th Ordinance to the Reich Citizenship Law providing that the property of a Jew be confiscated after his death, July 1, 1943 (RGB1 I, 372.)
Confiscation of Jewish claims against Christian debtors at the end of the 14th-century in Nuremberg (Stobbe, *Die Juden in Deutschland*, p. 58.)	11th Ordinance to the Reich Citizenship Law, November 25, 1941 (RGB1 I, 722.)
"Fines": for example, the Regensburg fine for "killing Christian child," 1421 (*Ibid.*, pp. 77–79.)	Decree for the "Atonement Payment" by the Jews, November 12, 1928 (RGB1 I, 1579.)
Marking of documents and personal papers identifying possessor or bearer as a Jew (Zosa Szajkowski, "Jewish Participation in the Sale of National Property during the French Revolution," *Jewish Social Studies*, 1952, p. 291n.)	Decree providing for identification cards, July 23, 1938 (RGB1 I, 922.) Decree providing for marking of passports, October 5, 1938 (RGB1 I, 1342.)
Ca. 1800, the Jewish poet Ludwig Börne had to have his passport marked "Jud" von Frankfurt," (Heinrich Graetz, *Volkstümliche Geschichte der Juden* [Berlin-Vienna, 1923], III, 373–74.)	
Marking of houses, special shopping hours, and restrictions of movement, 17th century, Frankfurt (*Ibid.*, pp. 387–88.)	Marking of Jewish apartments (*Jüdisches Nachrichtenblatt* [Berlin], April 17, 1942.) Decree providing for movement restrictions, September 1, 1941 (RGB1 I, 547.)
Compulsory Jewish names in 19th-century bureaucratic practice (Leo M. Friedman, "American Jewish Names," *Historica Judaica* [October, 1944], p. 154.)	Decree of January 5, 1937 (RGB1 I, 9.) Decree of August 17, 1938 (RGB1 I, 1044.)

were rioting in the streets.[13] This experience was all but forgotten when, in November, 1938, Nazi mobs surged once more into Jewish shops. The principal losers now were German insurance companies, who had to pay German owners of the damaged buildings for the broken window glass.[14] A historical lesson had to be learned all over again.

If some old discoveries had to be made anew, it must be stressed that many a new discovery had not even been fathomed of old. The administrative precedents, created by church and state, were in themselves incomplete. The destructive path, charted in past centuries, was an interrupted path. The anti-Jewish policies of conversion and expulsion could carry destructive operations only up to a point. These policies were not only goals; they were also limits, before which the bureaucracy had to stop and beyond which it could not pass. Only the removal of these restraints could bring the development of destructive operations to its fullest potentiality. That is why the Nazi administrators became improvisers and innovators; that is also why the German bureaucracy under Hitler did infinitely more damage in twelve years than the Catholic Church was capable of in twelve centuries.

The administrative precedents, however, are not the only historical determinants with which we are concerned. In a Western society, destructive activity is not just a technocratic phenomenon. The problems arising in a destruction process are not only administrative but also psychological. A Christian is commanded to choose good and to reject evil. The greater his destructive task, therefore, the more potent are the moral obstacles in his way. These obstacles must be removed – the internal conflict must somehow be resolved. One of the principal means through which the perpetrator will attempt to clear his conscience is by clothing his victim in a mantle of evil, by portraying the victim as an object that must be destroyed.

In recorded history, we find many such portraits. Invariably, they are floating – effusively, like clouds – through the centuries and over the continents. Whatever their origins and whatever their destinations, the function of these stereotypes is always the same. They are used as justifications for destructive thinking; they are employed as excuses for destructive action.

The Nazis needed such a stereotype. They required just such an image of the Jew. It is therefore of no little significance that, when Hitler came to power, the image was already there. The model was already fixed. When Hitler spoke about the Jew, he could speak to the Germans in familiar language. When he reviled his victim, he resurrected a medieval conception. When he shouted his fierce anti-Jewish attacks, he awakened his Germans as if from slumber to a long-forgotten challenge. How old, precisely, are these charges? Why did they have such an authoritative ring?

The picture of the Jew which we encounter in Nazi propaganda and Nazi correspondence had been drawn several hundred years before. Martin Luther had already sketched the main outlines of that portrait, and the Nazis, in their time, had little to add to it. We shall look here at a few excerpts from Luther's book *About the Jews and Their Lies.* In doing so, let it be stressed that Luther's ideas were shared by others in his century, and that the mode of his expression was the style of his times. His work is

13. Otto Stowasser, "Zur Geschichte der Wiener Geserah," *Vierteljahrschrift für Sozial- und Wirtschaftsgeschichte,* XVI (1922), 117.
14. See pp. 26–28.

cited here only because he was a towering figure in the development of German thought, and the writing of such a man is not to be forgotten in the unearthing of so crucial a conceptualization as this. Luther's treatise about the Jews was addressed to the public directly, and, in that pouring recital, sentences descended upon the audience in a veritable cascade. Thus the passage:

> Herewith you can readily see how they understand and obey the fifth commandment of God, namely, that they are thirsty bloodhounds and murderers of all Christendom, with full intent, now for more than fourteen hundred years, and indeed they were often burned to death upon the accusation that they had poisoned water and wells, stolen children, and torn and hacked them apart, in order to cool their temper secretly with Christian blood.[15]

And:

> Now see what a fine, thick, fat lie that is when they complain that they are held captive by us. It is more than fourteen hundred years since Jerusalem was destroyed, and at this time it is almost three hundred years since we Christians have been tortured and persecuted by the Jews all over the world (as pointed out above), so that we might well complain that they had now captured us and killed us – which is the open truth. Moreover, we do not know to this day which devil has brought them here into our country; we did not look for them in Jerusalem.[16]

Even now no one held them here, Luther continued. They might go whenever they wanted to. For they were a heavy burden, "like a plague, pestilence, pure misfortune in our country." They had been driven from France, "an especially fine nest," and the "dear Emperor Charles" drove them from Spain, "the best nest of all." And this year, they were expelled from the entire Bohemian town, including Prague, "also a very fine nest" – likewise from Regensburg, Magdeburg, and other towns.[17]

> Is this called captivity, if one is not welcome in land or house? Yes, they hold us Christians captive in our country. They let us work in the sweat of our noses, to earn money and property for them, while they sit behind the oven, lazy, let off gas, bake pears, eat, drink, live softly and well from our wealth. They have captured us and our goods through their accursed usury; mock us and spit on us, because we work and permit them to be lazy squires who own us and our realm; they are therefore our lords, we their servants with our own wealth, sweat, and work. Then they curse our Lord, to reward us and to thank us. Should not the devil laugh and dance, if he can have such paradise among us Christians, that he may devour through the Jews – his holy ones – that which is ours, and stuff our mouths and noses as reward, mocking and cursing God and man for good measure.
>
> They could not have had in Jerusalem under David and Solomon such fine days on their own estate as they have now on ours – which they rob and steal daily. But still they complain that we hold them captive. Yes, we have and hold them in captivity, just as I have captured my calculum, my blood heaviness, and all other maladies . . .[18]

What have the Christians done, asks Luther, to deserve such a fate? "We do not call their women whores, do not curse them, do not steal and dismember their children, do not poison their water. We do not thirst after their blood." It was not otherwise than Moses had said. God had struck them with frenzy, blindness, and raging heart.[19]

This is Luther's picture of the Jews.

15. Luther, *Von den Jueden,* p. diii3.
16. *Ibid.,* pp. diii3, diii4.
17. *Ibid.,* pp. diii4, e.
18. *Ibid.,* p. e2.
19. *Ibid.,* p. eii.

First, they want to rule the world.[20] Second, they are arch-criminals, killers of Christ and all Christendom.[21] Third, he refers to them as a "plague, pestilence, and pure misfortune."[22] That Lutheran portrait of Jewish world rule, Jewish criminality, and the Jewish plague has often been repudiated. But, in spite of denial and exposure, the charges have survived. In four hundred years the picture has not been changed.

In 1895 the Reichstag was discussing a measure, proposed by the anti-Semitic faction, for the exclusion of foreign Jews. The speaker, Ahlwardt, belonged to that faction. We reproduce here a few excerpts from his speech:[23]

> It is quite clear that there is many a Jew among us, of whom one cannot say anything bad. If one designates the whole of Jewry as harmful one does so in the knowledge that the racial qualities of this people are such that in the long run they cannot harmonize with the racial qualities of the Germanic peoples, and that every Jew who at this moment has not done anything bad may nevertheless under the proper conditions do precisely that, because his racial qualities drive him to do it.
>
> Gentlemen, in India there was a certain sect, the Thugs, who elevated the act of assassination to an act of policy. In this sect, no doubt, there were quite a few people who personally never committed a murder, but the English in my opinion have done the right thing when they exterminated [*ausrotteten*] this whole sect, without regard to the question whether any particular member of the sect already had committed a murder or not, for in the proper moment every member of the sect would do such a thing.

Ahlwardt pointed out that the anti-Semites were fighting the Jews not because of their religion but because of their race. He then continued:

> The Jews accomplished what no outer enemy has accomplished: they have driven the people from Frankfurt into the suburbs. And that's the way it is wherever Jews congregate in large numbers. Gentlemen, the Jews are indeed beasts of prey . . .
>
> Mr. Rickert [another deputy who had opposed the exclusion of the Jews] started by saying that we already had too many laws, and that's why we should not concern ourselves with a

20. Emperor Frederick II, excluding Jews from public office, stated, in 1237: "Faithful to the duties of a Catholic prince, we exclude Jews from public office so they will not abuse official power for the oppression of Christians." Kisch, *Jews in Medieval Germany*, p. 149.

21. The following is a passage from a fifteenth-century German lawbook, the municipal code of Salzwedel, par. 83,2: "Should a Jew assault a Christian or kill him, the Jew may not make any reply, he must suffer in silence what the law appoints, for he has no claim on Christendom and is God's persecutor and a murderer of Christendom." Kisch, *Jews in Medieval Germany*, p. 268. Kisch points out that earlier German lawbooks contained no such discrimination.

The poisoned wells legend (fourteenth century) and the ritual murders legend (thirteenth century) were both condemned by the Popes. Scherer, *Die Rechtsverhältnisse der Juden*, pp. 36–38. On the other hand, the thirteenth-century Castilian law code "El Sentenario," Partita VII, Tit. 24, Ley 2, makes reference to the capital crime of crucifying Christian children or wax figures on Holy Friday. Scherer, *Die Rechtsverhältnisse der Juden*, pp. 50–51. As for the legal view of usury, see Kisch, *Jews in Medieval Germany*, pp. 191–97.

22. The Fourth Lateran Council expressly called upon the secular powers to "exterminate" (*exterminare*) all heretics. Kisch, *Jews in Medieval Germany*, p. 203. This provision was the basis for a wave of stake burnings during the inquisitions.

The story of the tenth plague, the slaying of the first-born, has given rise to the ritual murder legend, in accordance with which Jews kill Christian children at Passover time to use their blood in matzos. See also the provision in the "Sentenario" in which the tenth plague is combined with the Gospels to produce the crucifixion of children.

23. Reichstag *Stenographische Berichte*, 53. Sitzung, March 6, 1895, pp. 1296 ff. To Paul Massing belongs the credit for discovering this speech and including it in his book, *Rehearsal for Destruction* (New York, 1949).

new anti-Jewish code. That is really the most interesting reason which has ever been advanced against anti-Semitism. We should leave the Jews alone because we have too many laws?! Well, I think, if we would do away with the Jews [*die Juden abschaffen*], we could do away with half the laws which we have now on the books.

Then, Deputy Rickert said that it is really a shame – whether he actually said that I don't know because I could not take notes – but the sense of it was that it was a shame that a nation of 50 million people should be afraid of a few Jews. [Rickert had cited statistics to prove that the number of Jews in the country was not excessive.] Yes, gentlemen, Deputy Rickert would be right, if it were a matter of fighting with honest weapons against an honest enemy; then it would be a matter of course that the Germans would not fear a handful of such people. But the Jews, who operate like parasites, are a different kind of problem. Mr. Rickert, who is not as tall as I am, is afraid of a single cholera germ – and, gentlemen, the Jews are cholera germs.

(*Laughter*)

Gentlemen, it is the infectiousness and exploitative power of Jewry which is involved. . . .

Ahlwardt then called upon the deputies to wipe out "these beasts of prey" (*Rotten Sie diese Raubtiere aus*) and continued:

If it is now pointed out – and that was undoubtedly the main point of the two previous speakers – that the Jew is human too, then I must reject that totally. The Jew is no German. If you say that the Jew is born in Germany, is raised by German nurses, has obeyed the German laws, has had to become a soldier – and what kind of soldier, we don't want to talk about that –

(*Laughter in the right section*)

has fulfilled all his duties, has had to pay taxes, too, then all of that is not decisive for nationality, but only the race out of which he was born [*aus der er herausgeboren ist*] is decisive. Permit me to use a banal analogy, which I have already brought out in previous speeches: a horse which is born in a cowbarn is still no cow. (*Stormy laughter.*) A Jew who is born in Germany, is still no German; he is still a Jew. . . .

Ahlwardt then remarked that this was no laughing matter but deadly serious business.

It is necessary to look at the matter from this angle. We do not even think of going so far as, for instance, the Austrian anti-Semites in the Reichsrath, that we demand an appropriation to reward everybody who shoots a Jew [*dass wir ein Schussgeld für die Juden beantragen wollten*], or that we should decide that whoever kills a Jew, inherits his property. (*Laughter, uneasiness.*) That kind of thing we do not intend here; that far we do not want to go. But we do want a quiet and common sense separation of the Jews from the Germans. And to do that, it is first of all necessary that we close the hatch, so that more of them cannot come in.

It is remarkable that two men, separated by a span of three hundred and fifty years, can still speak the same language. Ahlwardt's picture of the Jews is in its basic features a replica of the Lutheran portrait. The Jew is still (1) an enemy, who has accomplished what no external enemy has accomplished: he has driven the people of Frankfurt into the suburbs; (2) a criminal, a thug, a beast of prey, who commits so many crimes that his elimination would enable the Reichstag to cut the criminal code in half; and (3) a plague, or, more precisely, a cholera germ. Under the Nazi regime, these conceptions of the Jew were expounded and repeated in an almost endless flow of speeches, posters, letters, and memoranda. Hitler himself preferred to look upon the Jew as an enemy, a menace, a dangerous cunning foe. This is what he said in a speech delivered in 1940, as he reviewed his "struggle for power":

It was a battle against a satanical power which had taken possession of our entire people, which had grasped in its hands all key positions of scientific, intellectual, as well as political and economic life, and which kept watch over the entire nation from the vantage of these key positions. It was a battle against a power which, at the same time, had the influence to combat with the law every man who attempted to take up battle against them and every man who was ready to offer resistance to the spread of this power. At that time, all-powerful Jewry declared war on us. . . .[24]

Gauleiter Julius Streicher emphasized the contention that the Jews were criminal. The following is an excerpt from a typical Streicher speech to the Hitler youth. It was made in 1935.

Boys and girls, look back to a little more than ten years ago. A war – the World War – had whirled over the peoples of the earth and had left in the end a heap of ruins. Only one people remained victorious in this dreadful war, a people of whom Christ said its father is the devil. That people had ruined the German nation in body and soul.

But then Hitler arose and the world took courage in the thought that now the human race might be free again from this people which has wandered about the world for centuries and millenia, marked with the sign of Cain.

Boys and girls, even if they say that the Jews were once the chosen people, do not believe it, but believe us when we say that the Jews are not a chosen people. Because it cannot be that a chosen people should act among the peoples as the Jews do today.

A chosen people does not go into the world to make others work for them, to suck blood. It does not go among the peoples to chase the peasants from the land. It does not go among the peoples to make your fathers poor and drive them to despair. A chosen people does not slay and torture animals to death. A chosen people does not live by the sweat of others. A chosen people joins the ranks of those who live because they work. Don't you ever forget that.

Boys and girls, for you we went to prison. For you we have always suffered. For you we had to accept mockery and insult, and became fighters against the Jewish people, against that organized body of world criminals, against whom already Christ had fought, the greatest anti-Semite of all times.[25]

A number of Nazis, including the chief of the German SS and Police Himmler, the jurist and *Generalgouverneur* of Poland Hans Frank, and Justice Minister Thierack, inclined to the view that the Jews were a lower species of life, a kind of vermin, which upon contact infected the German people with deadly diseases. Himmler once cautioned his SS generals not to tolerate the stealing of property which had belonged to dead Jews. "Just because we exterminated a bacterium," he said, "we do not want, in the end, to be infected by that bacterium and die of it."[26] Frank frequently referred to the Jews as "lice." When the Jews in his Polish domain were killed, he announced that now a sick Europe would become healthy again.[27] Justice Minister Thierack once wrote the following letter to a worried Hitler:

A full Jewess, after the birth of her child, sold her mother's milk to a woman doctor, and concealed the fact that she was a Jewess. With this milk, infants of German blood were fed in a children's clinic. The accused is charged with fraud. The purchasers of the milk have suffered damage, be-

24. Speech by Hitler, German press, November 10–11, 1940.

25. Speech by Streicher, June 22, 1935, M-1.

26. Speech by Himmler, October 4, 1943, PS-1919.

27. Generalgouvernement Health Conference, July 9, 1943, Frank Diary, PS-2233. Remarks by Frank recorded verbatim.

cause the mother's milk of a Jewess cannot be considered food for German children. The impudent conduct of the accused is also an insult. However, there has been no formal indictment in order to spare the parents — who do not know the facts — unnecessary worry. I will discuss the race-hygienic aspects of the case with the Reich Health Chief.[28]

The twentieth-century Nazis, like the nineteenth-century anti-Semites and the sixteenth-century clerics, regarded the Jews as hostile, criminal, and parasitical. But there is also a difference between the recent writings and the older scripts which requires explanation. In the Nazi and anti-Semitic speeches we discover references to race. That formulation does not appear in sixteenth-century books. Conversely, in Luther's work there is repeated mention of God's scorn, thunder and lightning worse than Sodom and Gomorrah, frenzy, blindness, and raging heart. Such language disappeared in the nineteenth-century.

There is, however, a close functional relationship between Luther's references to divine blows and Ahlwardt's reliance upon race characteristics, for both Luther and Ahlwardt tried to show that the Jew could not be changed, that a Jew remained a Jew. "What God does not improve with such terrible blows, that we shall not change with words and deeds."[29] There was some evil in the Jew that even the fires of God, burning high and hot, could not extinguish. In Ahlwardt's time these evil qualities — fixed and unchangeable — are traced to a definite cause. The Jew "cannot help himself" because his racial qualities drive him to commit antisocial acts. We can see, therefore, that even the race idea fits into a trend of thought. Let us examine the function of the race conception a little more closely.

Anti-Jewish racism had its beginning in the second half of the seventeenth century, when the "Jewish caricature" first appeared in cartoons.[30] These caricatures were the first attempt to discover race characteristics in the Jew. However, racism acquired a "theoretical" basis only in the nineteenth-century. The racists of the nineteenth-century stated explicitly that cultural characteristics, good or bad, were the product of physical characteristics. Physical attributes did not change; hence social behavior patterns also had to be immutable. In the eyes of the anti-Semite, the Jews therefore became a "race."[31]

We should emphasize, however, that there is a functional difference between American racism and German racism. The American racist identifies a racial group, for instance, Negroes, and attributes to that group social behavior patterns. The German racist does the opposite. He identifies a group with ethnic characteristics and attributes to such a group a racial quality. In the American scheme, racism is indispensable. Without the claim that physical characteristics, such as skin color, give rise to spiritual qualities, the American racist would run into serious difficulties. In the German scheme, racism has a reinforcement function only. The Jew is bad. That is because he has bad blood. That is why he is bad. In the following chapters, we shall therefore pay little attention to German race theory; we will concern ourselves primarily with the picture of the Jew which race

28. Thierack to Hitler, April, 1943, NG-1656. The expert in charge of the case was Ministerialrat Dr. Malzan.

29. Luther, *Von den Jueden*, p. Aiii2.

30. Eduard Fuchs, *Die Juden in der Karikatur* (Munich, 1921), pp. 160–61.

31. For a Nazi discussion of race, including such formulations as "racial substance" (*Rassekern*), "superior race" (*Hochrasse*), and "racial decline" (*Rasseverfall*), see Konrad Dürre, "Werden und Bedeutung der Rassen," *Die Neue Propyläen-Weltgeschichte* (Berlin, 1940), pp. 89–118.

theory was designed to maintain: the concepts of world Jewish conquest, Jewish criminality, and Jewish parasitical existence. These ideas arose before race theory and, dormant, they are still with us today.

In this book we shall deal mainly with the perpetrators, with the administrative and psychological determinants which made possible the annihilation of five million people. The success of that destruction process depended, however, not only on its perpetrators but also on its victims. We are not going to discuss the Jewish catastrophe in all of its ramifications. A great deal that happened to the Jewish community was without effect upon the perpetrators; some of the long-range effects have yet to be felt in full. But the immediate reactions of the European Jews affected the progress of the destruction process and its ultimate success; whether the Jews resisted or submitted was a matter of considerable importance to German agencies which were engaged in anti-Jewish action.

The Jewish reaction pattern is older than the precedents which we have just discussed. The Jews have responded to force in a typical fashion for almost two thousand years. ("Jews," in this context, refers only to the "exiled," "dispersed," or "ghetto" Jews, not the Palestine or Israel Jews.) It is significant that in the first century after Christ, when the Jews of Palestine were fighting their war against the Roman conquerors, the Jewish colony in the Egyptian city of Alexandria, which was under Roman domination, had already unlearned the art of revolt. Similarly, in the twentieth-century, the European Jews surrendered to their fate only a few years before Palestine Jewry hurled back Arab invaders by force of arms. Therefore the "Jewish reaction pattern" is confined to the pattern which was formed in exile, by the Diaspora, in the ghetto. What is this pattern? It is indicated in the following diagram:

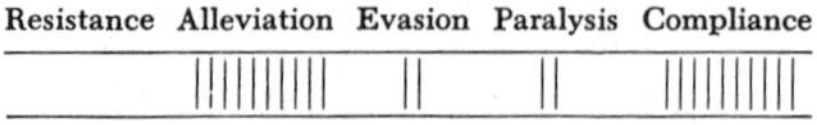

Resistance	Alleviation	Evasion	Paralysis	Compliance
	|||||||||	||	||	|||||||||

Preventive attack, armed resistance, and revenge are almost completely absent in two thousand years of Jewish ghetto history. Instances of violent opposition, which may be found in one or another history book, are atypical and episodic. The critical period of the 1930's and 1940's is marked by that same absence of physical opposition.

On the other hand, alleviation attempts are typical and instantaneous responses by the Jewish community. Under the heading of alleviation are included petitions, protection payments, ransom arrangements, anticipatory compliance, relief, rescue, salvage, reconstruction – in short, all those activities which are designed to avert danger, or, in the event that force has already been used, to diminish its effects. Let us give a few illustrations.

The ancient city of Alexandria, Egypt, was divided into five districts: α, β, γ, δ, and ε. The Jews were heavily concentrated in the Delta (waterfront section), but they had residences also in other parts of town. In A.D. 38, Emperor Caligula wanted to be worshipped as a half-god. The Jews refused to pay him the desired respect. Thereupon, riots broke out in Alexandria. The Jews were driven into the Delta, and the mob took over abandoned apartments. Equality of rights was temporarily abolished, the food supply to the Delta was cut off, and all exits were sealed. From time to time, a centurion of Roman cavalry penetrated into Jewish homes on the pretext of searching for arms. Under these conditions, which have a peculiarly modern flavor, the Jews sent a delegation to Rome, in order to petition the Emperor Caligula for relief.

The delegation included the famous philosopher Philo, who disputed about the matter in Rome with an anti-Jewish public figure, Apion.[32] That is one of the earliest examples of Jewish petition diplomacy. More than nineteen hundred years later, in 1942, a delegation of Bulgarian Jews was petitioning for a very similar purpose. In that rather typical appeal, the Jews were attempting to ward off ejection from their homes.[33]

Sometimes the Jews attempted to buy protection with money. In 1384, when much Jewish blood was flowing in Franken, the Jews sought to ransom themselves. Arrangements for payment were made with speed. The city of Nuremberg collected the enormous sum of 80,000 guilders. King Wenzel got his share of 15,000 guilders from that amount. The representatives of the King, who participated in negotiations with other cities, received 4,000 guilders. Net profit to the city: over 60,000 guilders, or 190,000 thaler.[34] The Jews in Nazi-occupied Europe, from the Netherlands to the Caucasus, made identical attempts to buy safety from death with money and valuables.[35]

One of the most sagacious alleviation reactions in the Jewish arsenal is anticipatory compliance. In this type of alleviation attempt, the victim foresees the danger and combats it by doing the very thing demanded of him. But he does so *before* he is confronted by ultimatums. He is, therefore, giving in on his own terms. In a sense, this is the action of a man who – sensing a fatal blow – wounds himself. With this wound he seeks to demonstrate that the blow is unnecessary. In recent times the most commonplace manifestation of anticipatory compliance has been the organized attempt by world Jewry to shift its occupational distribution from professional and commercial activity to engineering, skilled labor, and agricultural work. This movement, which in Germany was known as *Berufsumschichtung* ("occupational shift"), has sometimes been referred to as an attempt to channel the Jews into "useful" activities. Apart from the usefulness of agricultural labor in Palestine, the movement was, however, no more than an anticipatory compliance with quota systems, job discriminations, and other anti-Jewish measures in the economic field. In Poland, after the Nazi invasion, this *Berufsumschichtung* was carried to the extent of a *ghetto-directed* mobilization of forced labor, in anticipation of and for the prevention of a *German-directed* labor system.[36]

The alleviations which follow disaster are developed to a very high degree in the Jewish community. Relief, rescue, and salvage are old Jewish institutions. The relief committees and subcommittees formed by "prominent" Jews (the "Prominente"), which are so typical of the United Jewish Appeal machinery today, were commonplace in the nineteenth-century. Already during the 1860's, collections for Russian Jews were conducted in Germany on a fairly large scale.[37] Reconstruction – that is to say, the rebuilding of Jewish life, whether in new surroundings or, after abatement of persecution, in the old home – has been a matter of automatic adjustment for hundreds of years. Reconstruction is identical with the continuity of Jewish life. The bulk of any general Jewish history book is devoted to the story of the constant shifts, the recurring readjustments, the

32. Graetz, *Volkstümliche Geschichte der Juden*, I, 600–609.

33. See p. 481.

34. Stobbe, *Die Juden in Deutschland*, pp. 57–58.

35. See pp. 370, 472–73, 503–4, 509, 543–48, 664.

36. See p. 163.

37. See, for example, list of contributions in *Allgemeine Zeitung des Judenthums* (Leipzig), November 2, 1869, pp. 897 ff.

endless rebuilding of the Jewish community. For the years following 1945, the historians will have to write one of their biggest chapters on Jewish reconstructive effort.

Next in our scale is the reaction of evasion, of flight. In our diagram, the evasive reaction is not marked as strongly as the alleviation attempts. By that we do not mean the absence of flight, concealment, and hiding in the Jewish response pattern; we mean, rather, that the Jews have placed less hope, less expectation, less reliance, upon these devices. It is true that the Jews have always wandered from country to country. But they have rarely done so because the restrictions of a regime became too burdensome. Jews have migrated chiefly for two reasons, expulsion and economic depression. Jews have rarely run from a pogrom. They have lived through it. The Jewish tendency has been not to run from, but to survive with, anti-Jewish regimes. It is a fact, now confirmed by many documents, that the Jews made an attempt to live with Hitler. In many cases they failed to escape while there was still time, more often still, they failed to step out of the way when the killers were already upon them.

Paralysis occurs when the obstacles to resistance, to alleviation attempts, and to flight are just as formidable as the difficulties of co-operation. The result of such a balance of forces is inactivity. (We should bear in mind that inactivity or passivity is a reaction which influences the perpetrator and affects his decisions. It is a zero which enters into his calculations.) The reaction actually occurs rarely. But paralysis afflicted world Jewry in 1941 and 1942, just when the destruction process in Europe entered into its killing phase. The Jews all over the world looked on helplessly while disaster overtook the European Jews. The same reaction occurred in occupied Poland and occupied Russia, when the victims gazed into the open graves, unable to resist, unable to speak, unable to flee, and unable to jump in.

The last reaction on the scale is compliance. To the Jews, compliance with anti-Jewish laws or orders has always been equivalent to survival. The restrictions have been petitioned against and sometimes evaded, but when those attempts have been unsuccessful, automatic compliance has been the normal course of action. Compliance has been carried to the greatest lengths and to the most drastic situations. In seventeenth-century Frankfurt, on September 1, 1614, a mob under the leadership of a certain Vincenz Fettmilch attacked the Jewish quarter in order to kill and plunder. Many Jews fled to the cemetery. There they huddled together and prayed, dressed in the ritual shrouds of the dead and waiting for the killers.[38] This example is particularly pertinent because the voluntary assembly at graves was repeated many times during the Nazi killing operations of 1941.

The Jewish reactions to force have always been alleviation and compliance. We shall notice the re-emergence of this pattern time and again in the next few hundred pages. However, before we pass on, it should be empha-

38. Graetz, *Volkstümliche Geschichte der Juden*, III, 388–89. The mob permitted them to flee. The Jews returned to their homes two months later, under imperial protection. Fettmilch was torn to pieces by four horses upon orders of the authorities—the Emperor did not like pogroms. In Erfurt, during the fourteenth-century, a mob was permitted by the city council to kill 100 Jews. When the crowds began to threaten the remaining 3000 Jews, the victims fled to their apartments, blocked the entrances, and then set fire to their own homes, burning themselves to death in the holocaust. Ludwig Count Ütterodt, *Gunther Graf von Schwarzenburg—Erwählter Deutscher König* (Leipzig, 1862), p. 33n.

sized again that the term "Jewish reactions" refers only to ghetto Jews. This reaction pattern was born in the ghetto and it will die there. It is part and parcel of ghetto life. It applies to *all* ghetto Jews, assimilationists and Zionists, the capitalists and the socialists, the unorthodox and the religious ones.

One other point has to be understood. The alleviation-compliance response dates, as we have seen, to pre-Christian times. It has its beginnings with the Jewish philosophers and historians, Philo and Josephus, who bargained in behalf of Jewry with the Romans and who cautioned the Jews not to attack, in word or deed, any other people. The Jewish reaction pattern assured the survival of Jewry during the Church's massive conversion drive. The Jewish policy once more assured to the embattled community a foothold and a chance for survival during the period of expulsion and exclusion.

If, therefore, the Jews have always played along with an attacker, they have done so with deliberation and calculation, in the knowledge that their policy would result in least damage and least injury. The Jews knew that measures of destruction were self-financing or even profitable up to a certain point but that beyond that limit they could be costly. As one historian put it: "One does not kill the cow one wants to milk."[39] In the Middle Ages the Jews carried out vital economic functions. Precisely in that usury so much complained of by Luther and his contemporaries there was an important catalyst for the development of a more complex economic system. In modern times, too, Jews have pioneered in trade, in the professions, and in the arts. Among some Jews the conviction grew that Jewry was "indispensable."

In the early 1920's, one Hugo Bettauer wrote a fantasy novel entitled *Die Stadt ohne Juden* ("The City without Jews").[40] This highly significant novel, published only eleven years before Hitler came to power, depicts an expulsion of the Jews from Vienna. The author shows how Vienna cannot get along without its Jews. Ultimately, the Jews are recalled. That was the mentality of Jewry, and of Jewish leadership, on the eve of the destruction process. When the Nazis took over in 1933, the old Jewish reaction pattern set in again, but this time the results were catastrophic. The German bureaucracy was not slowed by Jewish pleading; it was not stopped by Jewish indispensability. Without regard to cost, the bureaucratic machine, operating with accelerating speed and ever-widening destructive effect, proceeded to annihilate the European Jews. The Jewish community, unable to switch to resistance, increased its co-operation with the tempo of the German measures, thus hastening its own destruction.

We see, therefore, that both perpetrators and victims drew upon their age-old experience in dealing with each other. The Germans did it with success. The Jews did it with disaster.

39. Stowasser, "Zur Geschichte der Wiener Geserah," p. 106.

40. Hugo Bettauer, *Die Stadt ohne Juden—Ein Roman von übermorgen* (Vienna, 1922).

II / *Antecedents*

The first chapter has dealt with historical parallels, with events and patterns of pre-Nazi times which were repeated in the years 1933-45. These events were the precedents of the destruction process. Now we turn to a description of the climate in which the destruction process began. The activities which were designed to create this climate we shall call the antecedents.

The specific question to which we shall address ourselves in this chapter is simply this: What was the state of readiness for anti-Jewish action in 1933? We know that the antagonistic conception of Jewry, the portrait in which the Jew was painted as an enemy, a criminal, and a parasite, was already quite old. We know also that administrative action against European Jewry had been taken even earlier. Jewry law was a product of medieval times. We know, third, that an administrative apparatus capable of efficient operations on a complicated level had been developed in Germany for centuries. Hitler thus did not have to originate any propaganda. He did not have to invent any laws. He did not have to create a machine. He *did* have to rise to power. A bureaucratic body, like an inanimate object, is subject to inertia. A bureaucracy at rest tends to remain at rest; a bureaucracy in motion tends to continue in motion. It has to be started. It has to be stopped. In 1933 the missing push was applied, and the ball started to roll. The machinery of destruction was activated. The destruction process was set into motion.

There is an inherent relationship between the force necessary to start such a process and the opposition which asserts itself against the operation. The greater the opposition, the stronger the required force. The less the opposition, the weaker the force. It is significant that the German administration needed no pressure, no prodding, no reminders. The bureaucrats wanted only the authority, the backing, the signal from above. The German bureaucracy was so sensitive a mechanism that in the right climate it began to function almost by itself.

The organization which assigned to itself the task of activating the bureaucratic machine was the German Nazi party, the Nationalsozialistische Deutsche Arbeiter Partei (NSDAP). The party was organized soon after the First World War by Adolf Hitler. In those days the party drew up a program, dated February 24, 1920, which contained only three points that dealt with Jews. Those articles were the sum total of policy guidance which the party supplied to the bureaucracy. The paragraphs are as follows:

> 4. Only a member of the community [*Volksgenosse*] can be a citizen. Only a person with German blood, regardless of his religious adherence, can be a member of the community. No Jew may therefore be a member of the community.
>
> 5. Whoever is not a citizen should live only as a guest in Germany, under the law applicable to foreigners.
>
> 8. Every immigration of non-Germans is to be prevented. We demand that all non-Germans who have migrated to Germany since August 2, 1914, be forced to leave the Reich immediately.[1]

Paragraph 17 provided for the expropriation of real property for com-

1. Text in Ludwig Münz, *Führer durch die Behörden und Organisationen* (Berlin, 1939), p. 3.

munity purposes. This provision, which troubled the propertied supporters of the Nazi party, was authoritatively interpreted by Hitler to mean that only Jewish property was involved.[2] All that this program demanded, therefore, was that no Jews be permitted to enter the country, that Jews who had immigrated since the start of World War I be obliged to leave the country, that those who remained enjoy only such rights as were granted to foreigners. As an afterthought, and to save himself embarrassment, Hitler also called for the expropriation of Jewish land. Finally, the program contained a hidden provision that, in defining the concept of "Jew," the bureaucracy was to keep in mind that if a Jew was converted, he was still a Jew.

As Göring, the number-two Nazi, informed us after the war, the program had been drawn up by very "simple people." Neither Hitler nor Göring had participated in the drafting. The "Jewish press," however, had attacked the party immediately. The party had "fought back." In the course of this propaganda war "many a harsh word" had been said against the Jews, but, in Göring's opinion, the Jewish side had produced the greater volume of invective.[3] In any case, the party was not very influential until it seized power. At that point, on January 30, 1933, the wishes of the party became the wishes of the people; the leader of the party became the leader of the Reich;[4] and the program of the party became the first blueprint for action.

A blueprint does not mean a complete plan of action. The party program contained no hint of the measures which were taken in the next several years. There was no hint of total expropriation, no indication of ghetto formation, no reference of any kind to deportations or killing operations. The program was just a guide pointing in a certain direction, and only knowing interpreters could find that route. Thus, when the party came to power, the bureaucracy was given only a bare signpost for its first step. For subsequent measures, the bureaucrats had to rely on their own imagination.

Now it might still be asked whether it is possible that the German bureaucracy began to draft destructive measures as a matter of course, without threats, without debates, and without directives. It is true that the Nazi party itself did not think that the mere "seizure of power" was sufficient to produce spontaneous bureaucratic action. For this reason, the party launched a three-pronged needling campaign. With anti-Jewish propaganda, an anti-Jewish boycott, and minor violence against individual Jews, the party sought to convey to the bureaucrats that the people wanted action. However, if we closely examine the dates of this provocative activity (end of March, 1933) and the date of the first anti-Jewish decree (April 7, 1933), we discover that the precipitatory campaign was largely superfluous. The bureaucracy had already gone to work. It needed no prodding.[5] The party ex-

2. *Ibid.*, p. 4.

3. Testimony by Göring, *Trial of the Major War Criminals*, IX, 273.

4. From 1933 to 1934, Hindenburg was President and Hitler was Chancellor. When Hindenburg died in 1934, Hitler became "Führer und Reichskanzler." The title "Chancellor" was dropped later.

5. On March 6, 1933, the *Staatssekretär* in the Ministry for Economy, Bang (a party man), wrote to the Chief of the Reich Chancellery, Lammers, to suggest some anti-Jewish action (a ban on immigration of Eastern Jews and the revocation of name changes). Bang specified that he was writing unofficially, in his private capacity. Lammers sent the suggestions to Interior Minister Frick, March 9, 1933, adding a suggestion of his own (deportation of Eastern Jews of foreign nationality). Frick replied to Lammers, March 15, 1933, that the proposals had been passed on to subordinate offices in the Interior Ministry.

hortations were little more than a nuisance which imported difficulties from home and abroad.

The impression abroad was decidedly unfavorable. A boycott movement was started against German exports and was supported by Jews and non-Jews alike. By March 27, 1933, Vice Chancellor von Papen was forced to write a letter to the Board of Trade for German-American Commerce, in which he pointed out that the number of "excesses" against Americans was "less than a dozen," that hundreds of thousands of Jews remained unmolested, that the big Jewish publishing houses were still in business, that there was no St. Bartholomew Night, etc., etc.[6]

In June, 1933, the German Foreign Minister, von Neurath, visited London. In his report to Reich President von Hindenburg, the Foreign Minister noted that he could hardly recognize London. The Jewish question had come up again and again, and no counter-arguments were of any avail. The Englishmen had declared that in judging this matter they were guided only by sentiment (*gefühlsmässig*). This point was made to von Neurath by the English King himself in a "very earnest conversation." In international conferences von Neurath had noted that many governments were represented by people who were well-known Jews as a kind of protest.[7]

Another difficulty was created by the undisciplined behavior of party members. Many Jews were mistreated and a few were killed. In Bavaria, the police arrested several members of a uniformed party formation, the Schutzstaffeln (SS), for the mistreatment of Jews. The SS office in the city of Aschaffenburg thereupon claimed that no member of the SS could be arrested by a policeman. This assertion was so novel that the Bavarian Minister of Justice, Dr. Hans Frank, himself a top Nazi, questioned the claim and asked the Bavarian Minister President (Siebert) to discuss the matter with SS Chief Himmler and with Himmler's superior, SA Chief Röhm.[8]

Shortly after this incident, a few killings took place in the Bavarian concentration camp of Dachau. The victims were two Germans and a Jew (Dr. Delwin Katz). Himmler and Röhm requested that proceedings against the responsible SS men be quashed for "state-political" reasons. Bavarian Staatsminister of the Interior Wagner (another party man) agreed but expressed the hope that in future such requests would not be put to him again. Writing to Frank, Wagner asked the Justice Minister to quash the proceedings in the concentration camp, "which houses, as is known, almost exclusively criminal characters" (*das bekanntlich fast ausschliesslich Verbrechernaturen beherbergt*).[9]

Still another consequence of the

Correspondence in document NG-902. The first suggestion by Bang (immigration ban) was superfluous. The name revocations were decreed five years later (See p. 119). The ejection of Polish Jews was also attempted in 1938 (See p. 258). The boycott manifesto of the party, dated March 29, 1933, confined itself to a demand for a numerus clausus (quota) in the universities and professions. Text of manifesto in document L-199. By 1938, the exclusion of Jews from universities and professions was virtually complete.

6. Von Papen to Board of Trade of German-American Commerce, March 27, 1933, D-635. *New York Times,* March 29, 1933. For molestation of Americans, see report by U.S. Consul General Messersmith to the Secretary of State, March 14, 1933, L-198. Similar to the Papen letter is the telegram of the Cologne branch of the American Chamber of Commerce in Germany to the U.S. Chamber of Commerce, March 25, 1933, RC-49.

7. Von Neurath to von Hindenburg, June 19, 1933, Neurath-11.

8. Frank to Bavarian Staatsminister of the Interior Adolf Wagner, September 6, 1933, D-923. The SS was then part of the larger party formation, the SA.

9. Wagner to Frank, November 29, 1933, D-926.

party's activities made itself felt in the economic sector. The party's agitation, particularly the party-directed boycott, had unforeseeably disturbed the delicate balance of the German business world. On August 20, 1935, an interministerial conference on the economic effects of party action was held in the office of Reichsbankpräsident Schacht. The conference was attended by Interior Minister Frick, Finance Minister von Krosigk, Justice Minister Dr. Gürtner, Education Minister Rust, several *Staatssekretäre*, and Staatsminister Adolf Wagner in his capacity as the party's representative.[10]

Schacht opened the discussion by pointing out that the "unlawful" activity against Jewry would soon have to end (*dass das gesetzlose Treiben gegen das Judentum bald ein Ende nehmen müsse*), or else, he, Schacht, would not be able to cope with his task of economic rearmament. To give a few examples, the boycott chief Streicher was trying to force German firms to dismiss their Jewish representatives in foreign countries. Now, it could not be forgotten, Schacht continued, that these Jewish representatives were "especially skilful." When the Jewish agent of Alliance Insurance in Egypt was subjected to party chicanery, he simply quit and took the business with him. The English had captured the market. Another example: In many cities, including Leipzig, Jews were not allowed in public baths. How was that going to work out during the Leipzig exhibition? Furthermore, this "unlawful activity" (*gesetzlose Treiben*) had provoked counteraction abroad. A French importer had annulled a large order he had placed with Salamander Shoes. The Bosch firm had lost its entire South American market. It was often said that one could do without the Jewish business, but whoever maintained that view, said Schacht, simply did not know the world. The Jews were needed even for importations, for the trade with rare products, needed by the armed forces, was in Jewish hands.

This did not mean, Schacht said, that all "single actions" (*Einzelaktionen*) against Jews were to be condemned. For example, he could see no objections to the display of signs reading "Jews not wanted." Such signs could often be found in the United States, too. The case of barring Jews from the resort town of Bad Tölz was more doubtful. The party's ejection of Jews from Langenschwalbach was an "extremely doubtful" case. But utterly impossible was the case which had occurred in Arnswalde. There the director of the local Reichsbank office, one of Schacht's own men, had bought something from a Jew who had served as a sergeant in the war and who had received the Iron Cross. Thereupon, Streicher had displayed the picture of the *Reichsbankrat* on three public bulletin boards,[11] and under the picture had appeared the words: Whoever buys from a Jew is a traitor to the people (*Volksverräter*). Schacht had immediately protested to the local party official and had demanded an apology to be displayed on the same bulletin boards. Then Schacht had sent a copy of his protest to the highest regional party authority, Gauleiter Kube. Schacht's wishes had not been satisfied; consequently, he had ordered that the local Reichsbank office be closed. But Schacht was especially disappointed that Gauleiter Kube had not found it necessary to send a reply.

Minister of the Interior Frick was the next speaker. He too was of the

10. Summary of Schacht conference on Jewish matters, held August 20, 1935, dated August 22, 1935, NG-4067. The Reichsbank, a government institution, was the central bank.

11. *Stürmerkästen* – used by Streicher to publicize the more defamatory materials in his paper.

opinion that "wild single actions" (*wilde Einzelaktionen*) against Jews would have to stop. His ministry was already working on a number of decrees. The Jewish question was going to be solved in a perfectly legal manner.

Staatsminister Wagner, the party's representative, spoke next. He too was against these "wild" actions. But the people would stop spontaneously, he said, as soon as they noticed that the Reich government was taking measures against the Jews.

A representative of the Propaganda Ministry then put in that, from his standpoint, nothing was wrong with Streicher's condemnation of the *Reichsbankrat* who had made a purchase from a Jew.

Schacht replied with indignation that he simply had never heard of such an idea. As a non-party member he had a right to buy where he pleased. He knew of no laws to the contrary. The Propaganda Ministry's representative evidently did not know that even government offices were placing orders with Jews. The Arnswalde incident was "a case of the highest perfidy and meanness" (*ein Fall höchster Perfidie und Gemeinheit*).

At the conclusion of the meeting, the conferees made the following decisions: Some law was to be enacted to prevent the establishment of new Jewish enterprises; the government was to make an effort to place its orders only with German enterprises; Wagner was to submit some party suggestions for more laws. Needless to say, these resolutions were not very important. The decision on new Jewish enterprises was deadwood; the placement of business orders with German firms was decreed later;[12] and the additional party suggestions did not materialize.

It is important to stress, at this point, what Schacht was protesting against and what he was trying to do. Schacht did *not* oppose anti-Jewish action. He opposed "wild" party measures. He preferred the "legal" way – that is, certainty instead of uncertainty. It was uncertainty which hurt business. Schacht never opposed anti-Jewish decrees;[13] to the contrary, he welcomed them and was impatient when they were not issued quickly enough,[14] for, basically, he wanted "clarity" in order that he might cope with the business mechanism.

On October 4, 1935, even Streicher declared that the Jewish question was being solved, "piece by piece," in a legal manner. Whoever, said Streicher, recognized the tremendous importance of these decrees would not allow himself to be dragged into ridiculous chicanery. "We don't smash any windows and we don't smash any Jews. We don't have to do that. Whoever engages in single actions [*Einzelaktionen*] of that kind is an enemy of the state, a provocateur, or even a Jew [*oder gar ein Jude*].[15] But in November, 1938, something happened which completely upset the applecart.

Certain sections of the party became restless and suddenly started a riot which had far more serious consequences than the "wild" actions of 1933. It must be remembered that this outburst occurred in the sixth year of the Nazi regime. There was no longer any need to remind the bureaucracy of the "people's wishes." The destruction process was well under way. Anti-

12. See p. 63.

13. Interrogation of Hjalmar Schacht, October 17, 1945, PS-3729. In this testimony, Schacht pointed out that the anti-Jewish decrees were "not important enough to risk a break" with Hitler.

14. Schacht to Frick, October 30, 1935, protesting against delays in the issuance of certain anti-Jewish implementing regulations, NG-4067.

15. Speech by Streicher before German Labor Front mass meeting, October 4, 1935, M-35. The German Labor Front was a party organization.

Jewish decrees by the dozen had already been published or were in preparation. Today we know the real reason for these riots; the party, apart from the SS formation, no longer had important functions in Jewish affairs. This was true especially of the uniformed brownshirts (the SA) and the propaganda apparatus. The 1938 riots were a bid for power. The party men wanted to play a role in the actual implementation of the anti-Jewish destruction process, but they failed miserably. Here is the story.

On November 9, 1938, a minor German Foreign Office official, Legationsrat vom Rath, was assassinated by a Jew, Herschel Grynzpan, in the German Embassy in Paris. This was not the first assassination of its kind. About three years before, a Jewish rabbinical student had fatally shot the leader of the Swiss branch of the Nazi party.[16] The Swiss assassination did not have any repercussions, but the Paris incident was seized upon as an opportunity for party action. In the evening of November 9, 1938, the Propaganda Minister, Dr. Josef Goebbels, told a group of party leaders in Munich that riots had started against Jews in the districts of Kurhessen and Magdeburg-Anhalt. Upon his suggestion, said Goebbels, the Führer (Hitler) had thereupon decided that, in the event the riots spread spontaneously throughout the Reich, they were not to be discouraged. The party leaders listened attentively. To them, Goebbels' statement had only one meaning: the party was not to appear outwardly as the architect of the demonstrations, but was to organize and execute them.[17]

The riots spread with lightning speed. The SA formation sent out its brigades to burn down systematically all Jewish synagogues in the country.[18] The black-uniformed SS and the regular police had not been notified. But late in the same evening, Gruppenführer Wolff, Chief of Himmler's Personal Staff, was still in his office, attending a conference. A call came at 11:15 P.M. to the effect that Goebbels had ordered a pogrom. Wolff immediately contacted Himmler. The chief of the SS and Police arrived at 1 A.M., November 10, and ordered his forces into action to prevent large-scale looting and, incidentally, to fill his concentration camps with 20,000 Jews.[19] Having attended to the needs of the hour, Himmler dictated a file memorandum, in which he expressed his personal reactions to the Goebbels pogrom. The memorandum read somewhat as follows: "The order was given by the Propaganda Directorate, and I suspect that Goebbels, in his craving for power, which I noticed long ago, and also in his empty-headedness [*Hohlköpfigkeit*] started this action just at a time when the foreign political situation is very grave. . . . When I asked the Führer about it, I had the impression that he did not know anything about these events."[20]

The Himmler reaction appears to

16. David Frankfurter, "I Kill a Nazi Gauleiter," *Commentary,* February, 1950, pp. 133–41. The assassinated Nazi, Wilhelm Gustloff, actually was not a *Gauleiter* but a *Landesgruppenleiter*. A *Gauleiter* was a party regional chief within the Reich; a *Landesgruppenleiter* was the party leader of German citizens in a foreign country.

17. Report by chief of the Party Court Walter Buch to Hermann Göring, February 13, 1939, PS-3063.

18. See six reports by *SA-Brigaden,* dated November 10 and November 11, 1938, on destruction of synagogues, PS-1721.

19. Affidavit by Hauptsturmführer Luitpold Schallermeier, July 5, 1946, SS(A)-5. For SS ranks, see chart, Appendix II. Schallermeier was Wolff's personal assistant.

A reference to 20,000 arrests is made in the report by Security Police Chief Heydrich to Göring, November 11, 1938, PS-3058. Heydrich's position is explained on p. 128.

20. Affidavit by Schallermeier, July 5, 1946, SS(A)-5.

have been relatively mild. After all, he too had something to gain from the action, although he generally preferred to make his own decisions. But the reaction of the other top Nazis was not so indifferent. When Economy Minister Funk (Schacht's successor) heard about the riots, he called up the Propaganda Minister on the telephone and spoke to him in the following vein: "Are you crazy, Goebbels? To make such a mess of things [*Schweinereien*]! One has to be ashamed to be a German. We are losing our whole prestige abroad. I am trying, day and night, to conserve the national wealth, and you throw it willy-nilly out of the window. If this thing does not stop immediately, you can have the whole filthy mess [*werfe ich den ganzen Dreck hin*]."[21]

The number-two Nazi, Göring, was completely unaware of what was going on, because, at the time of the instigation of the riot, he was on board a train. The news was communicated to him upon his arrival on the Berlin railway platform. Göring lost no time in complaining to Hitler that Goebbels was very irresponsible, that the effects on the economy, especially the "spirit of conservation," would be disastrous, etc. Hitler "made some apologies for Goebbels" but agreed that such events were not to be repeated. Later the same day (November 10) Göring and Hitler had a second conference. This time Goebbels was also present. The propaganda chief began "his usual talk." This was not the first murder committed by a Jew; such things could not be tolerated, and so forth. Then Goebbels suggested something which stunned Göring. The Jews were to pay a fine. "Indeed, he wished that each *Gau* [party district] should collect such a fine, and he named an almost incredibly high sum." Göring countered that such a procedure was utterly impossible. Since Herr Goebbels was also the *Gauleiter* (regional party chief) of Berlin, and since he had a large number of Jews right in his own *Gau*, he was obviously "the most interested party." If such measures were to be taken, the state would have to collect the money. Hitler agreed, and after some discussion "this way and that," the sum of one billion reichsmark was agreed upon.[22]

Goebbels was defeated. His hopes were dashed to the ground, and his cravings for power were left unsatisfied. The morsel had been taken right out of his mouth. From now on, we shall have little to say about Goebbels. While he made a few attempts at a comeback, his role in the destruction of the Jews was never again of paramount importance. As *Gauleiter* of Berlin, he was to have some say in the deportation of Jews from the capital; as Propaganda Minister and chief of the party's Propaganda Office, he remained the principal dispenser of words. But even this function he had to share with others; and, in the meantime, the Propaganda Minister was a

21. Affidavit by Louise Funk, November 5, 1945, Funk-3. Affiant, the wife of the Economy Minister, claims to have overheard the conversation. Whether Funk, a former *Staatssekretär* in the Propaganda Ministry, expressed such strong sentiments to his former boss may be open to some question. Mrs. Funk is, however, the only living witness.

22. Testimony by Göring, *Trial of the Major War Criminals*, IX, 276–78. At the official rate of exchange, one billion reichsmark equalled $400,000,000.

In neighboring Italy, Foreign Minister Ciano noted in his diary an interesting private comment on the "fine" by Benito Mussolini: "The Duce is critical of the German decision to impose a fine of a thousand million marks. He agrees with reprisals of a personal nature but considers the valuation of vom Rath's life at seven thousand million lire to be excessive. Or rather absurd." Galeazzo Ciano, *Ciano's Hidden Diary 1937–1938* (New York, 1953), entry for November 13, 1938, p. 194. We shall have more to say about the "fine" in the chapter on expropriation.

very unpopular personality in the German bureaucracy, for he had saddled the bureaucrats with a host of undesirable problems.

First on the list of unfavorable repercussions was the foreign reaction. Comments in the foreign press were critical, international negotiations were jarred, and the creeping boycott of German goods was intensified.

Ambassador Dieckhoff, in Washington, wrote to the Foreign Office that he hoped that "the storm at present sweeping across the United States will subside again in the foreseeable future and that we shall be able to work again." Until November 10 a large proportion of the American people had still remained aloof from the anti-German campaign. Now this was no longer the case. The outcry came not only from the Jews but from all camps and classes, including even the German-American camp. "What particularly strikes me," continued the German ambassador, "is the fact that, with few exceptions, the respectable patriotic circles, which are thoroughly anti-Communist, and, for the greater part, anti-Semitic in their outlook, also begin to turn away from us. The fact that the Jewish newspapers write still more excitedly than before and that the Catholic bishops' campaign against Germany is waged more bitterly than before is not surprising; but that men like Dewey, Hoover, Hearst, and many others who have hitherto maintained a comparative reserve and have even, to some extent, expressed sympathy toward Germany, are now publicly adopting so violent and bitter an attitude against her is a serious matter. . . . In the general atmosphere of hate, the idea of boycotting German goods has received new fuel, and trade negotiations cannot be considered at the moment."[23] Such reports poured into the Foreign Office from all over the world.[24]

But if the diplomats received a few jolts, the sharpest disappointments were reserved for the exporters, the armament experts, and all those interested in the supply of foreign currency. German trade had, for some time, suffered from organized boycotts in foreign countries. Still, the boycott movement had been confined largely to the consumer level; it was not, of course, directed against Jewish firms in Germany; and it did not have many non-Jewish followers. The riots changed all that. For the first time the boycott movement gained many adherents among retailers, distributors, and importers.

This meant, in practice, large-scale cancellations of contracts, particularly in France, England, the United States, Canada, and Yugoslavia. The Armament-Economy Staff of the Armed Forces reported that many companies had lost 20 per cent to 30 per cent of their export business. Among the hardest hit were leather goods and toy manufacturers. One toy enterprise lost all its business in England; another lost all its outlets in the United States. Because of the elimination of Jewish firms in Germany, much of the foreign exchange which these firms had earned was also sacrificed. Thus one company whose Jewish owner had been arrested was unable under new "Aryan" management to procure a contract, in the amount of 600,000 reichsmark, which had already been negotiated before the pogrom. Most painful, however, was the severance of old connections between "Aryan" firms in Germany and

23. Dieckhoff to Foreign Office, November 14, 1938, *Akten zur Deutschen Auswärtigen Politik, 1918–1945*, Ser. D, Vol. IV, No. 501. In English translation, also in *Documents on German Foreign Policy, 1918–1945,* same series, same volume, same document number.

24. See, for example, the report by the German Legation in Uruguay (signed Langmann) to the Foreign Office, November 11, 1938, NG-3235.

"Aryan" firms in foreign countries. The Germans simply could not understand why non-Jewish enterprises should have felt compelled to join in the boycott. Yet this is what happened. In Holland, one of the largest Dutch trading companies, Stockies en Zoonen, Amsterdam, which had represented in the Netherlands such German firms as Krupp, Ford (German branch), DKW, and BMW, terminated all its German contracts and took over the representation of English firms.[25]

Clearly, the first consequence of the pogrom was the loss of much good will abroad. The second result was the damage to property at home.[26]

On November 12, 1938, two days after the riots, Göring called a conference to survey the damage and to discuss measures to deal with it. The conference was attended by Economy Minister Funk, Propaganda Minister Goebbels, Finance Minister von Krosigk, representative of the German insurance companies Hilgard, Chief of the Security Police Heydrich, Chief of the Order Police Daluege, representative of the Foreign Office Woermann, and many other interested parties.[27] In his opening remarks Göring emphasized that he had had "enough of these demonstrations. They don't harm the Jew," he said, "but me, because I am the authority ultimately responsible for the co-ordination of the German economy. If today a Jewish shop is destroyed, if goods are thrown into the street, the insurance company will pay for the damages, which the Jew does not even have. . . . It is insane to clear out and burn a Jewish warehouse, then have a German insurance company make good for the loss. And the goods which I need desperately, whole bales of clothing and what-not, are being burned, and I miss them everywhere. I may as well burn the raw materials before they arrive."

After the opening remarks, Hilgard, the insurance expert, was called in. His recital is vaguely reminiscent of the medieval *Klosterneuburger Chronik*, which had grudgingly admitted that the damages caused by a mob in the Jewish quarter of Vienna had hurt Christians more than Jews, for the damage had been done to Christian property in the Jewish pawnshops. Now, in 1938, Hilgard unfolded a similar story. Windows which were insured for about $6,000,000 had been smashed. At least half this amount would have to be produced in foreign exchange, for the expensive window panes were manufactured in Belgium. What was more, the windows of Jewish shops belonged not to the Jewish storekeepers but to the German house owners. The problem was similar in the case of consumer goods looted in stores. Damage in the Margraf jewelry store alone was reported at $1,700,000.

Göring interrupted at this point: "Daluege and Heydrich, you'll have to get me this jewelry through raids, staged on a tremendous scale!" Heydrich replied that recovery might not be so easy. Things had been thrown into the street. "The crowd was naturally rushing to pick up minks, skunks, etc. It will be very difficult to recover that. Even children have filled their pockets, just for fun." Then Heydrich

25. Report by Armament-Economy Staff IIb (*Wehrwirtschaftsstab/IIb*), December 21, 1938, Wi/1.149a. The Armament-Economy Staff was a forerunner of the *Wirtschafts-Rüstungsamt* (Wi Rü), which is discussed on pp. 178n, 179, 234–35.

26. Incomplete reports indicated the following damage: 815 shops destroyed; 171 houses set on fire; 191 synagogues burned out; 14 cemetery chapels, community halls, and similar buildings demolished. Twenty thousand Jews were arrested; thirty-six were killed; another thirty-six were seriously injured. Heydrich to Göring, November 11, 1938, PS-3058.

27. Minutes of Göring conference, November 12, 1938, PS-1816. The minutes are divided into seven parts. Three parts (II, IV, and VI) are missing.

added sarcastically, for the benefit of Goebbels: "It is suggested that the Hitler Youth is not to be employed and to participate in such actions without the Party's consent."

Hilgard, continuing his account, said that the total damage in property would be about 25,000,000 reichsmark. Heydrich suggested that, if the loss in consumer goods, lost taxes, and other indirect losses were added, the damage would be measured in the hundreds of millions. He added that 7500 stores had been ransacked. Daluege elaborated that, in many cases, the goods in stores were not the property of the store owners, but were still owned by the German wholesalers.

HILGARD: We will have to pay for them too.

GÖRING (*to Heydrich*): I wish you had killed two hundred Jews, and not destroyed such values.

HEYDRICH: Thirty-five were killed.

In the end, the conferees decided upon the following regulation of damage claims – that is, they apportioned the damage in the following way: (1) The uninsured losses of Jewish property remained Jewish losses. Jewelry, furs, or any other loot was not returned to the Jewish owners. To the extent that anything was recovered, the items were confiscated by the state.[28] (2) Insured property of the Germans (mainly window glass and shipments of consumer goods) had to be made good by the insurance companies. (3) Insured losses of Jewish property were dealt with as follows: the Jewish insurance claims were confiscated by the Reich (the State); the companies were directed to make payments to the government; the Jewish property owners, in turn, were ordered to repair the damage "for the restoration of the street appearance."[29] However, a subsequent decree allowed the Jews to deduct the cost of repairs from payments toward the billion mark fine.[30] The net effect of these regulations, therefore, was to place the burden of the insured damage upon the insurance companies.

Hilgard admitted that the companies would have to make payments, lest public confidence in German insurance be destroyed. But he had hoped for a government refund in secret. Göring, however, would not "dream" of it; that would be a "present." Still, in the course of the conference, Hilgard received a promise that something would be done for the "small" companies – of course, only in cases where it was "absolutely necessary." At this point there is a gap in the conference record, but in Part V of the proceedings Göring pointed out that "after all is said and done, there will remain some profit for the insurance companies, since they wouldn't have to make good for all the damage. Mr. Hilgard, you may enjoy yourself."

HILGARD: I have no reason for that – the fact that we won't have to pay for all the damage is called profit!

GÖRING: Just a moment! If you are compelled under the law to pay five million, and all of a sudden there appears an angel in my somewhat corpulent form before you, and tells you that you keep one million, why cannot that be called a profit? I should actually split with you, or whatever you'd call it; I can see it looking at you, your whole body grins. You made a big profit.

(*Remark*: Let's initiate a tax for damages resulting from public disturbances, to be paid by the insurance companies.)

Hilgard rejoined that, in his view, "the honorable German merchant" was still footing the bill. The insurance companies were still the losers. "That is so, and that will remain so, and nobody can tell me differently."

28. See directive by Darmstadt State Police (Gestapo), December 7, 1938, D-183.

29. Decree, signed by Göring, November 12, 1938, RGBl I, 1581.

30. Decree, signed by von Krosigk, November 21, 1938, RGBl I, 1638.

GÖRING: Then why don't you take care that a few windows less are smashed! You belong to the people, too!

A third problem which arose from the Goebbels pogrom was the destruction of synagogues. Compared with the foreign repercussions and the insurance claims, this was a relatively minor problem. Since Göring had no use for synagogues, he did not regard them as German property. But the ruins were in the way. After much correspondence on this problem, the Church Ministry hit upon the solution of invoking the building code in order to saddle the Jewish communities with the rubble clearance.[31]

The fourth matter to be dealt with was the possibility of Jewish actions in the courts. The Justice Ministry took care of this problem by issuing a decree that Jews of German nationality would have no legal claims in any case arising from the "occurrences" of November 8–10.[32] The foreign Jews who had suffered injury or damage naturally had recourse to diplomatic intervention and claims against the state. Göring could find no way out of this dilemma, although he was annoyed that "the minute the Itzig has left Poland, he should be treated like a Pole!". When the Foreign Office representative put in that one had to deal with countries like the United States, which was in a position to retaliate, Göring replied that the United States was a "gangster state" and that German investments there should have been liquidated long ago. "But you are right, Mr. Woermann, the matter has to be considered."[33]

The fifth problem was, in some respects, the most difficult of all. In the course of the riots, many acts had been committed which were crimes under the penal code. Personal belongings had been stolen (without subsequent delivery to the state), women had been assaulted, men had been killed. On January 23-26, 1939, Justice Minister Gürtner called the prosecutors of the highest courts into conference to discuss the problem. Staatssekretär Freisler (second highest man in the Justice Ministry) explained that the problem was twofold: prosecution of party members and prosecution of non-party members. As for the non-party men, the judicial machinery could act at once, without "shouting about its work all over the place." Gürtner remarked that only the "big crumbs" should be prosecuted. Rape, for instance, would have to be dealt with. Minor matters, such as the appropriation of a few cans of food, would, on the other hand, have to be quashed. Oberstaatsanwalt Joel (a prosecutor) agreed that it was not necessary to prosecute anyone for taking a pair of underdrawers. Furthermore, one would have to take into account that the temptation was great, the need was present, and the instigation was clear. With regard to party members, action could only be taken after their expulsion from the Party, since there was a presumption that they had acted upon orders.[34]

In February, 1939, the Supreme Party Court met in order to decide the cases of thirty men who had committed "excesses." In his report to Göring, Chief Party Judge Buch pointed to the extenuating circumstance that the pogrom had been not spontaneous but organized. Twenty-six of the defendants had killed Jews. Not one of

31. Circular by Church Ministry, probably March, 1939, NG-26. See also correspondence in documents NG-2088, NG-2089, and NG-2090.

32. Decree, signed by Stuckart, Hess, Schlegelberger, and Reinhardt, March 18, 1939, RGBl I, 614.

33. Minutes of Göring conference, November 12, 1938, PS-1816.

34. Summary of Judicial Conference, January 23-26, 1939 (signed Leimer), NG-1566. See also summary of Judges Conference, February 1, 1939, NG-629.

these party men was expelled. In behalf of all twenty-six, the Justice Minister was urged to quash proceedings in the criminal courts. In all these cases the court had found no "ignoble" motives. Even if the men had acted without orders, they understood that the purpose of the pogrom was vengeance. Either they had been ordered to kill or they had been carried away by their feelings of hatred; consequently, expulsion and prosecution were not justified. Four men who had assaulted women were expelled from the party and handed over to the courts. Moral crimes could not be justified by the pogrom. In these cases the men had used the riot only as a pretext for their actions.[35]

The entire German bureaucracy, including most party leaders, reacted to the Goebbels pogrom with a feeling of annoyance and vexation. The impact of these events abroad, the damage to property, the synagogue ruins in every major German city, the claims by foreign Jews, and, finally, the problem of "excesses" were more than anybody had bargained for. At the conclusion of the conference, held on November 12, Göring declared: "Once and for all, I want to eliminate individual acts" (*Einzelaktionen*). Shortly afterward, at a conference of *Gauleiter*, Göring reiterated his opposition to pogroms. The riots, he said, gave way to "baser instincts" and had undesirable foreign repercussions besides.[36]

The November pogrom was the last occasion for violence against Jews in German streets. In September, 1941, when, at the behest of the Propaganda Ministry, a decree was issued for the marking of Jews with a yellow star, the chief of the Party Chancellery, Bormann, issued instructions to make sure that there would be no repetition of the November "demonstrations." It would be beneath the dignity of the "movement," said Bormann, if its members were to molest individual Jews (*wenn ihre Angehörigen sich an einzelnen Juden vergreifen würden*). Such actions, he concluded, "are and remain strictly prohibited."[37]

The one reason for the revulsion and even horror which the entire leadership – save Goebbels – felt for pogroms and street violence was the realization that these "actions" could not be controlled. When the mob was turned loose, things inevitably got out of hand. The pogroms were too expensive and, in the last analysis, accomplished nothing. The party's activities during the 1930's consequently had only one effect on the German bureaucracy. Every bureaucrat, in and out of the party, was henceforth convinced that measures against Jews had to be taken *systematically* and that the amateurish handling of the situation by Goebbels and other agitators was to be avoided under all circumstances. From now on, the Jews were going to be dealt with in a "legal" fashion – that is to say, in an orderly way that would allow for proper and thorough planning of each measure, by means of memoranda, correspondence, and conferences. Henceforth, the pros and cons of each measure were weighed carefully; hasty action was precluded. The bureaucracy had taken over. It is the bureaucratic destruction process which, in its step-by-step manner, finally led to the annihilation of five million victims.

How, in the meantime, did the *Jews* react to all this violence? Curiously enough, the Jewish reaction to the

35. Buch to Göring, February 13, 1939, PS-3063. In later chapters, we shall meet again this basic distinction between "idealistic" and "selfish" motives.

36. Affidavit by Dr. Siegfried Uiberreither (*Gauleiter*, Styria), February 27, 1946, Göring-38.

37. Instructions by Amtsleiter Ruberg of the *Auslands-Organisation* (the party's Foreign Organization), September 20, 1941, enclosing Bormann order, NG-1672.

party's excesses paralleled, in crucial respects, the responses by the German bureaucracy. Like Vice Chancellor Papen, the Jewish organizations hurried to protest against demonstrations and "atrocity propaganda" in foreign countries. The organization of Jewish war veterans attacked the emigrants as people who had "deserted" their fellow Jews and who were now "shooting arrows from secure hiding places" to the detriment of Germany and the German Jews.[38]

The Central-Verein deutscher Staatsbürger jüdischen Glaubens, central agency of assimilationist Jews, declared with indignation: "Nobody can rob us of our German fatherland. . . . In that we fight this battle, we carry out a German, not a selfish-Jewish, fight."[39] The Jews were convinced that they were going to have hard times but that their position would not become untenable. "One may condemn us to hunger, but one cannot condemn us to starve." (*Man kann uns zum Hungern verurteilen, aber nicht zum Verhungern.*)[40] Like Schacht, the Jews were waiting for the implementation of decrees that would put an end to uncertainty and define their status. "One can live under any law." (*Man kann unter jedem Gesetz leben.*)[41]

In the beginning of April, 1933, at the time of the first wave of party propaganda, boycott, and violence, and at the moment when the first anti-Jewish decree was published, a controversy developed between two wings of the Jewish community. This polemic is characteristic of all that is to be said. The *Central-Verein Zeitung,* organ of the assimilationists, had published an editorial, born out of despair, which contained Goethe's famous line of frustrated love: "If I love you, what business is it of yours?" The Zionist paper *Jüdische Rundschau* thereupon published a reply which stated with defiance: "If I love you, then it *is* your business. The German people should know: a historical alliance, hundreds of years old, cannot be severed so simply."[42] But it *was* severed. The bureaucracy cut, link by link, the ties between the German and Jewish communities. Already in June, the Zionist paper, all hope gone, made its last appeal:

> The National Socialists, in their demonstrations, designate the Jews as "enemies of the state." That designation is incorrect. The Jews are not enemies of the state. The German Jews desire and wish for the rise of Germany, for which they have always invested, to the best of their knowledge, all their resources, and that is what they wish to continue to do.[43]

By 1939 even the reproachful appeal had vanished. The Jewish community leadership in its officially approved publication had only one word of advice for its readers: the fulfilment with the greatest exactitude of all official orders and directives.[44] The Jews had their laws.

38. Press release by Reichsbund jüdischer Frontsoldaten, containing telegram sent to U.S. Embassy, in *Kölnische Volkszeitung,* March 27, 1933, RC-49.

39. *Central-Verein Zeitung,* March 23, 1933, in Hans Lamm, "Über die Innere und Äussere Entwicklung des Deutschen Judentums im Dritten Reich," (Erlangen, 1951; mimeographed), pp. 143, 176n. Also, Zionist declaration in *Jüdische Rundschau,* March 17, 1933, in Lamm, "Deutsches Judentum," pp. 143, 176n.

40. Ismar Elbogen in *Central-Verein Zeitung,* April 6, 1933, quoted by Lamm, "Deutsches Judentum," pp. 144, 176n.

41. From a statement by Georg Kareski, an "extreme Jewish nationalist," quoted by Lamm, "Deutsches Judentum," pp. 147–48.

42. *Jüdische Rundschau,* with quotation of *Central-Verein Zeitung* editorial, April 13, 1933, in Lamm, "Deutsches Judentum," pp. 152–53, 177n.

43. *Jüdische Rundschau,* June 27, 1933, in Lamm, "Deutsches Judentum," pp. 157, 177n.

44. *Jüdisches Nachrichtenblatt* (Berlin), September 5, 1939.

III / *Scope and Organization*

In the opening observations we have encountered two concepts which have not yet been explained, the "destruction process" and the "machinery of destruction." These formulations are basic tools of analysis. They enable us to see the destruction of the Jews not merely as a monolithic, non-transparent, and impenetrable event but as a series of operations which fall into a definite pattern.

The term "destruction process" is a reference to an administrative development with certain component parts.[1] The destruction of the Jews did not proceed from a basic plan. No bureaucrat in 1933 could predict what kind of measures would be taken in 1935, nor was it possible in 1935 to foretell decisions made in 1938. The destruction process was a step-by-step operation, and the administrator could seldom see more than one step ahead.

The steps of the destruction process were introduced in the following order: At first the concept of "Jew" was defined; then the expropriatory operations were inaugurated; third, the Jews were concentrated in ghettos; finally, the decision was made to annihilate European Jewry. Mobile killing units were sent to Russia, while in the rest of Europe the victims were deported to killing centers. The chronological development may therefore be summarized as follows:

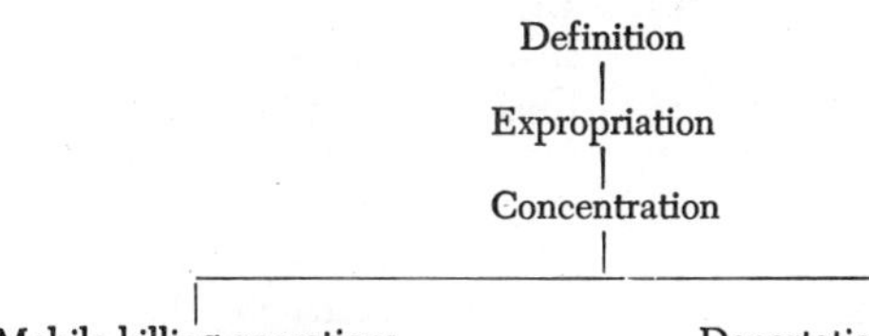

The concept "destruction process" excludes the Party actions discussed in the previous chapter. Schacht and Frick called these party activities *Einzelaktionen* ("isolated actions"). The *Einzelaktionen* were without administrative significance. They fell into no administrative pattern. They accomplished no administrative objective. They did not constitute a step in an administrative process. That is why, after 1938, they vanished completely in Germany and occurred only rarely in occupied territory.

The definition of the Jews appears to be a relatively harmless measure, in comparison with the bloody riots of 1938; yet its significance is much greater, for the definition of the victim was an essential requisite for further action. The measure itself did not harm anyone. But it had administrative continuity. That is the chief difference between a pogrom and a destruction process. A pogrom results in some damage to property and injuries to people, and that is all. It does not call for further action. On the other hand, a measure in a destruction process never stands alone. It may not always do damage, but it always has consequences. Each step of a destruc-

1. First suggested in an affidavit by Dr. Rudolf Kastner, September 13, 1945, PS-2605.

tion process contains the seed of the next step.

The destruction process straddled two policies: emigration (1933–40) and annihilation (1941–45). In spite of this change of policies, the administrative continuity of the destruction process was unbroken, and the reason for that phenomenon is to be found in the fact that the three steps introduced before 1940 (definition, expropriation, and concentration) served not only as inducements to emigrations but also as steppingstones to a killing operation:

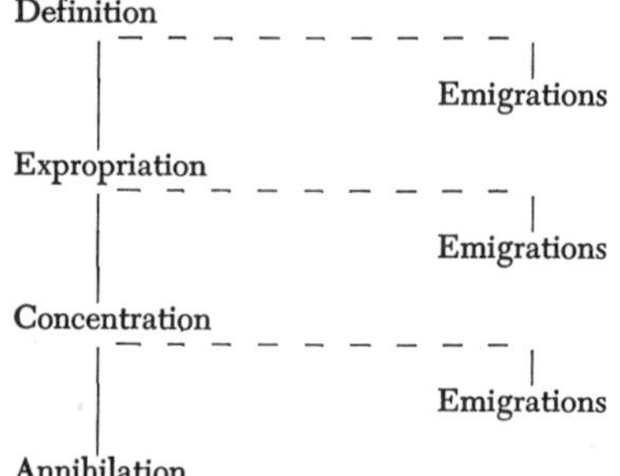

The path to annihilation leads directly through these age-old steps.

Although we are dealing with a single administrative development, there is an important difference between the two phases. Until 1940 the destruction process was revocable; after 1940 it was irrevocable. A ghetto can still be disbanded, but the dead cannot be raised. It is significant that, in spite of this difference, no change in personnel was necessary. The same machinery was used, although, of course, different offices achieved prominence. There was only one change in the approach to the operations: the destruction process I was public; the destruction process II was secret. Decrees, ordinances, and pronouncements had given way to concealed operations.

Now we come to our second concept. Who carried out the destruction process? What kind of machinery was employed for these tasks? The term "machinery or destruction" implies that no single agency was charged with the whole operation. Even though some agencies had supervisory functions in the implementation of certain measures, no office directed or co-ordinated the entire process. "Machinery" is therefore a designation for a very decentralized apparatus rather than a single organization.

Let us now consider for a moment how large that apparatus had to be. In 1933, the Jews were almost completely emancipated and almost completely integrated into the German community. The severance of Jew from German was, consequently, a very complex operation. There was hardly an agency, an office, or an organization which did not, at one time or other, have an interest in anti-Jewish measures. If we were to enumerate the public and private agencies which may be called the "German government" and those agencies which may be called the "machinery of destruction," we would discover that we are dealing with identical offices.

However, the designations "German government" and "machinery of destruction" do refer to different roles, since "government" is the more inclusive term. It implies the totality of administrative functions in a society. "Destruction" is only one very specialized administrative activity. What may be a powerful agency in the government may not be a vital part of the machinery of destruction, and, conversely, what may be a key agency in the destructive apparatus may not be an important link in the governmental structure. In short, when we speak of the machinery of destruction, we refer to German government in one of its special roles. How, then, was that government organized? How may we portray its structure?

The German administrative apparatus consisted of a Führer (Adolf Hitler) and four distinct hierarchical groups,[2] the ministerial bureaucracy, the armed forces, industry, and the party. Their detailed organization is shown in Tables 3–7.

The civil service and the military have, for centuries, been considered the two pillars of the German state. The modern civil service and the modern German army have their origins in the mid-seventeenth century; and the growth of these two bureaucracies, not merely as administrative machines but also as hierarchies with their own traditions, values, and policies, is in a sense synonymous and identical with the rise of the modern German state. The business sector became a political factor, on a par with the older organizations, only in the nineteenth century. The party was the youngest hierarchy in the Nazi government; it was barely ten years old in 1933. But the party already had a vast bureaucracy, competing with the other hierarchies and, in some areas, threatening their prerogatives. In spite of the different historical origins of these four bureaucracies and in spite of their different interests, all four could agree on the destruction of the Jews. The co-operation of these hierarchies was, in fact, so complete that we may truly speak of their fusion into a machinery of destruction.

The specific contribution of each hierarchy can be assessed roughly along jurisdictional lines. The ministerial bureaucracy, staffed with civil servants, was the chief implementer of anti-Jewish decrees during the early stages of the destruction process. The ministerial civil service wrote the decrees and regulations which defined the concept of "Jew," which provided for the expropriation of Jewish property, and which affected the ghettoization of the Jewish community in Germany. Thus the civil servant set the course and the direction of the entire process. This was his most important function in the destruction of the Jews. But the civil service also had a surprisingly large role in the later, more drastic anti-Jewish operations. The Foreign Office negotiated with Axis states for the deportation of Jews to killing centers; the German railways took care of the transport; the police, completely merged with the party's SS, was engaged extensively in killing operations.

The army was drawn into the destruction process after the outbreak of war by virtue of its control over vast territories in eastern and western Europe. Military units and offices had to participate in all measures, including the killing of Jews by special mobile units and the transport of Jews to the death camps.

Industry and finance had an important role in the expropriations, in the forced labor system, and even in the gassing of the victims.

The party concerned itself with all questions which involved delicate problems of German-Jewish relations (half-Jews, Jews in mixed marriage, etc.) and generally pushed for drastic action. It was not an accident that the military arm of the party, the SS (which was amalgamated with the Interior Ministry's police), carried out the most drastic operations of all, the killing operations.

Each hierarchy contributed to the

2. The four hierarchical groups were first recognized by Franz Neumann, *Behemoth* (2d ed.; New York, 1944), pp. 365–99, 468–70. The charts of the ministerial bureaucracy, the business sector, and the regional machinery are based in part on an organization chart certified by Frick, PS-2905. The organization of the armed forces prior to 1938 is described by Gisevius in *Trial of the Major War Criminals*, XII, 197. The armed forces after reorganization are described by Brauchitsch in his affidavit of November 7, 1945, PS-3703. The party chart is based on an affidavit by Franz Xaver Schwarz (Party Treasurer), November 16, 1945, PS-2903.

TABLE 3 / *Ministerial Bureaucracy**

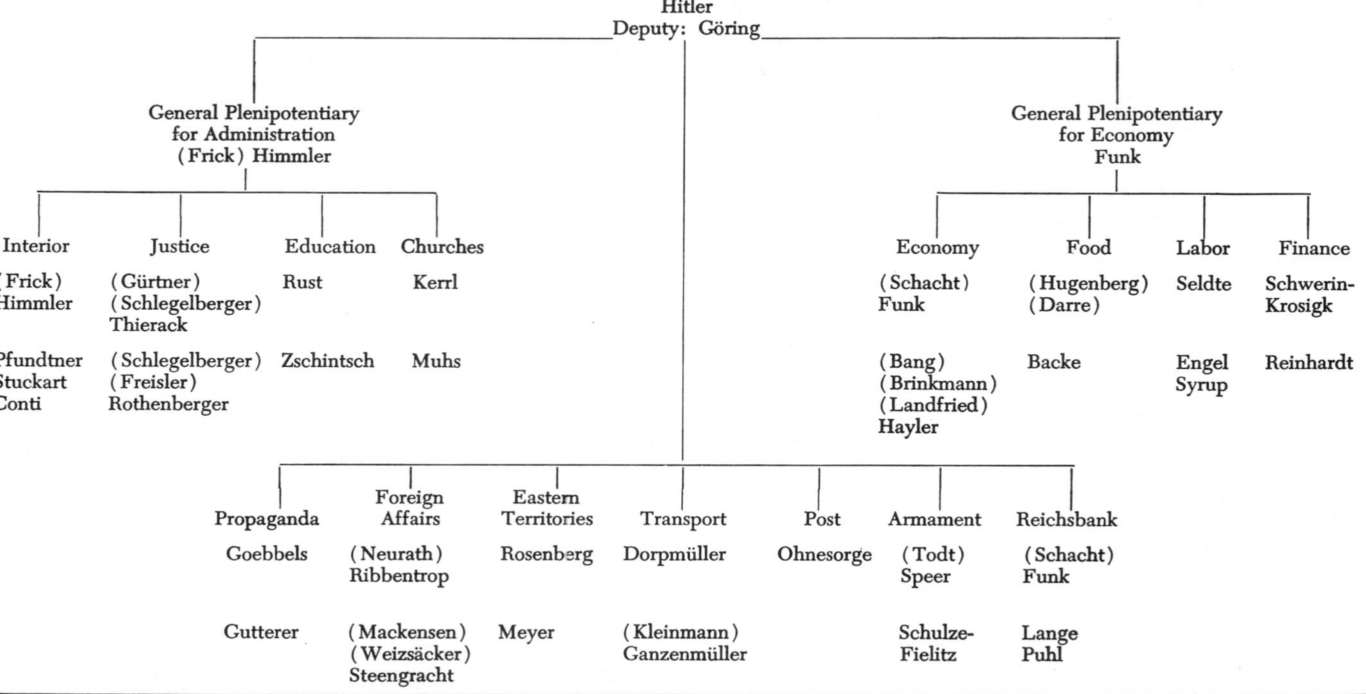

*Predecessors of last incumbents placed in parentheses. Ministers and *Staatssekretäre* (Undersecretaries) separated by line space. The Reich Chancellery (not shown) was placed between Hitler and the ministries for liaison purposes.

TABLE 4 / *The Armed Forces*

TO JANUARY, 1938
(NAVY, AIR FORCE OMITTED)

War Ministry	Armed Forces Office in War Ministry
Feldmarschall von Blomberg	Generaloberst Keitel
Commander in Chief of the Army	**Chief of the General Staff**
Generaloberst von Fritsch	Generaloberst Beck

AFTER REORGANIZATION

Commander in Chief of the Armed Forces	Chief, High Command of the Armed Forces (*Oberkommando der Wehrmacht* or OKW)
Hitler	Feldmarschall Keitel

Commander in Chief of the Army	Chief, High Command of the Army	Commander in Chief of the Navy	Chief, Directorate of Naval Warfare	Commander in Chief of the Air Force	Chief, General Staff of the Air Force
von Brauchitsch (succeeded by Hitler)	Halder (succeeded by Zeitzler and Guderian)	Räder (succeeded by Doenitz)	Schniewindt (succeeded by Fricke)	Göring	Jeschonnek (succeeded by Korten and Kreipe)

TABLE 5 / *Business*

Planning				War Production: Allocations, Priorities, etc.		"Rationalization" and Efficiency Problems	Business Practices and Miscellaneous Matters
	Office of the Four-Year Plan Göring——Kehrl Deputy: Körner	Planning Office		Armanent Ministry Speer			Reich Economic Chamber (*Reichswirtschaftskammer*) Pietzsch
Hermann Göring Works	Main Trusteeship Office East	Business Groups (*Geschäftsgruppen*)	General Plenipotentiaries (*Generalbevollmächtigte*)	Main Committees (*Hauptausschüsse*)	Industrial Rings (*Industrieringe*)	Trade Associations (*Reichsvereinigungen*)	Reich Groups (*Reichsgruppen*)
Pleiger	Winkler	Food: Backe Forests: Alpers Prices: Fischböck Etc.	Labor: Sauckel Chemical Industry: Krauch Etc.	Weapons:, Zangen Etc.	(Each member of a ring produced components of the final product, e.g., ball bearings)	Iron: Röchling Coal: Pleiger Etc.	Industry: Zangen Trade: Hayler Etc. (The regional machinery of the Reich Chamber consisted of the Chambers of Commerce and Industry)

Table 6 / *Party**

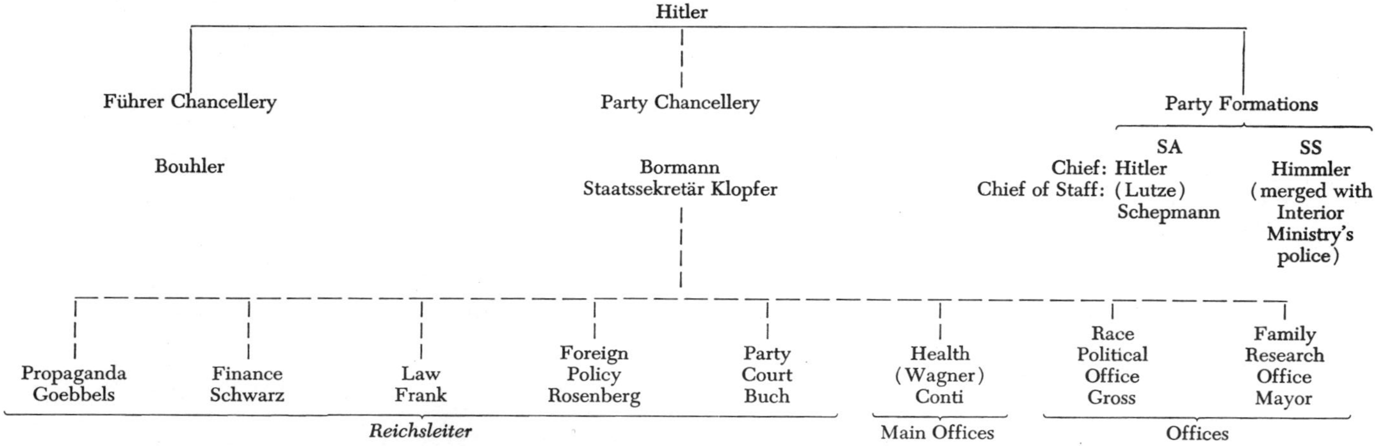

Hitler

Führer Chancellery

Bouhler

Party Chancellery

Bormann
Staatssekretär Klopfer

Party Formations

SA
Chief: Hitler
Chief of Staff: (Lutze) Schepmann

SS
Himmler (merged with Interior Ministry's police)

Reichsleiter

Propaganda
Goebbels

Finance
Schwarz

Law
Frank

Foreign Policy
Rosenberg

Party Court
Buch

Main Offices

Health
(Wagner) Conti

Offices

Race Political Office
Gross

Family Research Office
Mayor

*Broken lines indicate position of Party Chancellery as clearing house for reports to Hitler and as channel of directives from Hitler. All party agencies were responsible to Hitler. Not all of them are listed.

TABLE 7 / *Regional Machinery*

State	State	Party	Party
14 *Reichsstatthalter* ("Regents") in non-Prussian *Länder*	13 *Oberpräsidenten* in Prussian Provinces	11 *Reichsstatthalter* and *Gauleiter* in *Reichsgaue* (These areas were incorporated into the Reich under the Nazi regime; the *Reichsstatthalter* and *Gauleiter* in each *Reichsgau* was *one* person)	31 *Gauleiter* in non-Prussion *Länder* and Prussian provinces (The territory of a *Gau* was not necessarily identical with the area of a *Land* or province)
	Regierungspräsidenten		*Kreisleiter*
	Landräte (rural); *Bürgermeister* (cities)		*Ortsgruppenleiter*

destruction process not only administrative measures but also administrative characteristics. The civil service infused the other hierarchies with its sure-footed planning and bureaucratic thoroughness. From the army the machinery of destruction acquired its military precision, discipline, and callousness. Industry's influence was felt in the great emphasis upon accounting, penny-saving, and salvage, as well as in the factory-like efficiency of the killing centers. Finally, the party contributed to the entire apparatus an "idealism," a sense of "mission," and a notion of "history-making." Thus the four bureaucracies were merged not only in action but also in their thinking.

To summarize: the destruction process and the machinery of destruction are the two axes upon which our whole account will hinge. This scheme defines automatically the scope and organization of our project. We shall have to analyze the whole process, from the definition of the victim to the killing operations, and in the course of this analysis we shall consider the actions of all participating agencies. Since these agencies frequently co-operated in implementing individual administrative measures, our study will be focused on the steps of the destruction process, starting with the definition.

			Machinery of Destruction			
			Civil Service	Army	Industry	Party
Steps of the Destruction Process	I	Definition				
		Expropriation				
		Concentration				
	II	Mobile killing operations				
		Deportations				
		Killing center operations				

THE DESTRUCTION PROCESS I

IV / *Definition*

A destruction process is a series of administrative measures which must be aimed at a definite group. The German bureaucracy knew with whom it had to deal: the target of its measures was Jewry. But what, precisely, was Jewry? Who was a member of that group? The answer to this question had to be worked out by an agency which dealt with general problems of administration – the Interior Ministry. In the course of the definition-making, several other offices from the civil service and the party became interested in the problem. For purposes of orientation, therefore, Tables 8–10 show the structure of the Interior Ministry and of the two agencies which, throughout the years, were most closely concerned with the general aspects of anti-Jewish action, the judicial machinery and the Reich Chancellery.

The problem of defining the Jews was by no means simple; in fact, it was a stumbling block for an earlier generation of anti-Semites. Hellmut von Gerlach, one of the anti-Semitic deputies in the Reichstag during the 1890's, explained in his memoirs why the sixteen anti-Semitic members of the legislature had never proposed an anti-Jewish law; they could not find a workable definition of the concept of Jew. All had agreed upon the jingle:

> Never mind to whom he prays,
> The rotten mess is in the race.
> [*Was er glaubt ist einerlei*
> *In der Rasse liegt die Schweinerei.*]

But how to define race in a law? The anti-Semites had never been able to come to an agreement about that question. That is why "everybody continued to curse the Jews, but nobody introduced a law against them."[1] The

1. Hellmut von Gerlach, *Von Rechts nach Links* (Zurich, 1937), pp. 111–13. The author, an anti-Semitic deputy, quit the faction in disgust.

Table 8 / *The Interior Ministry**

Minister	Dr. Wilhelm Frick†
Staatssekretär in Charge	Hans Pfundtner‡
Constitution and Law	Staatssekretär Dr. Wilhelm Stuckart§
Deputy	Ministerialdirigent Hering
Constitution	Ministerialrat Medicus
Administrative Law	Ministerialrat Dr. Hoche
Citizenship Law	Ministerialrat Dr. Hubricht
Naturalization	Oberregierungsrat Dr. Duckart
International Law	Ministerialrat Globke
Race	Ministerialrat Lösener
Name Changes	Ministerialrat Globke
Health	Staatssekretär Dr. Leonardo Conti
Public Health	Ministerialdirektor Dr. Cropp
Eugenics and Race	Ministerialdirigent Dr. Linden

*For more elaborate charts and descriptions of the Ministry, see Hans Pfundtner (ed.), *Dr. Wilhelm Frick und sein Ministerium* (Munich, 1937); affidavit by Hans Globke, November 14, 1947, NG-3540; organization chart of the Interior Ministry, 1938, NG-3462; organization chart of the Interior Ministry, 1943, in *Taschenbuch für Verwaltungsbeamte*, 1943, PS-3475.

†Frick was succeeded in 1943 by Himmler.

‡Pfundtner resigned in 1943; his position was left vacant.

§Stuckart was appointed in 1935; his predecessor was Staatssekretär Grauert.

‖Conti was also appointed in 1935; his predecessor was Ministerialdirektor Dr. Gütt.

"simple" people who wrote the Nazi Party program in 1920 did not supply a definition either; they simply pointed out that a member of the community could only be a person of "German blood, without regard to confession."

When the Interior Ministry drafted its first anti-Jewish decree for the dismissal of Jewish civil servants, it was confronted by the same problem which had troubled the anti-Semites and the early Nazis. But the bureaucrats of the

TABLE 9 / *The Judicial Machinery**

JUSTICE MINISTRY

	1933-41	1941-42	1942-45
Minister:	Gürtner	Schlegelberger (acting)	Thierack
Staatssekretär:	Schlegelberger	Rothenberger	Klemm

	I	Personnel and Organization	Letz
	II	Training	Segelken
Criminal	III	Penal Code	Schäfer
	IV	Criminal Law (Procedure)	Engert
	V	Prisons	Marx
Civil	VI	Civil Law	Altstötter
		Deputy	Hesse
		Race Experts	Rexroth, Meinhof
	VII	Trade and International Law	Quassowski
	VIII	Pensions	Schneller

COURTS

Ordinary Courts (Each court divided into criminal and civil sections)	Extraordinary Courts (Prosecution of political crimes)
Reichsgericht	*Volksgerichtshof* ("People's Court")
Oberlandesgerichte	
Landgerichte	
Amtsgerichte	*Sondergerichte* ("Special Courts")

*Organization chart of Reich government (certified by Frick), PS-2905; organization chart of Division VI, February, 1944, NG-917; affidavit by Rothenberger, February 12, 1947, NG-776. For titles of judges and prosecutors, see document NG-2252.

TABLE 10 / *The Reich Chancellery**

Chief of the Chancellery	Hans Heinrich Lammers
Staatssekretär	Kritzinger
A. Administration, Propaganda, Education, Public Health	Meerwald
B. Four-Year Plan, Reichsbank, Transport, Agriculture	Willuhn
C. Finance, Budget, Labor, Audit, Civil Service Matters	Killy
D. Foreign Affairs, Occupied Areas in Eastern Europe	Stutterheim
E. Interior, Police, Justice, Armed Forces, Party	Ficker

*Organization chart of the Reich Chancellery, NG-3811; affidavit by Dr. Otto Meissner (Chief, *Präsidialkanzlei*) on role and powers of Lammers, May 15, 1947, NG-1541; affidavit by Hans Heinrich Lammers on his career, April 26, 1947, NG-1364; affidavit by Fredrich Wilhelm Kritzinger on his career, April 25, 1947, NG-1363.

Interior Ministry attacked the problem systematically, and soon they found the answer.

The decree of April 7, 1933,[2] provided that officials of "non-Aryan descent" were to be retired. The term "non-Aryan descent" was defined in the regulation of April 11, 1933,[3] as a designation for any person who had a Jewish parent or a Jewish grandparent; the parent or grandparent was presumed to be Jewish if he (or she) belonged to the Jewish religion.

The phraseology of this definition is such that it could not be said to have run counter to the stipulations of the party program. The ministry had divided the population into two categories: "Aryans," who were people with no Jewish ancestors (i.e., pure "German blood"), and "non-Aryans," who were all persons, Jewish or Christian, who had at least one Jewish parent or grandparent. It should be noted that the definition is in no sense based on racial criteria, such as blood type, curvature of the nose, or other physical characteristics. Nazi commentators, for propagandistic reasons, called the decrees "racial laws" (*Rassengesetze*),[4] and non-German writers, adopting this language, have also referred to these definitions as "racial."[5] But it is important to understand that the sole criterion for categorization into the "Aryan" or "non-Aryan" group was religion – to be sure, not the religion of the person involved but, in any case, the religion of his ancestors. After all, the Nazis were not interested in the "Jewish nose." They were interested in the "Jewish influence."

The 1933 definition (known as the *Arierparagraph*) did give rise to difficulties. One problem arose from the use of the terms "Aryan" and "non-Aryan," which had been chosen in order to lend to the decrees a racial flavor.[6] Foreign nations, notably Japan, were offended by the general implication that non-Aryans were inferior to Aryans. On November 15, 1934, representatives of the Interior Ministry and the Foreign Office, together with the chief of the party's Race-Political Office, Dr. Gross, discussed the adverse effect of the *Arierparagraph* upon Far Eastern policy. The conferees had no solution.

The Foreign Office reported that its missions abroad had explained the German policy of distinguishing between the *types* of races, rather than the *qualities* of the races (*Verschiedenartigkeit der Rassen*, rather than *Verschiedenwertigkeit der Rassen*). According to this view, each race produced its own social characteristics, but the characteristics of one race were not necessarily inferior to those of other races. In short, racial "type" comprised physical and spiritual qualities, and German policy attempted no more than the promotion of conditions which would permit each race to develop in its own way. However, this explanation did not quite satisfy the Far East states, who still felt that the catch-all term "non-Aryan" placed them into the same category with Jews.[7]

There was another difficulty which reached into the substance of the

2. RGBl I, 175.
3. RGBl I, 195.
4. For example, the commentary by Wilhelm Stuckart and Rolf Schiedmair, *Rassen- und Erbpflege in der Gezetzgebung des Reiches* (5th ed.; Leipzig, 1944).
5. One Jewish historian went so far as to call the medieval practice of identifying new Christians as former Jews "racial." See Cecil Roth, "Marranos and Racial Antisemitism – A Study in Parallels," *Jewish Social Studies*, 1940, pp. 239–48.

6. Actually, the term "Aryan," like "Semitic," is not even a race designation. At best, it is a term for a linguistic-ethnic group.
7. Circular letter by Pfundtner, February 9, 1935, NG-2292. Bülow-Schwante (Foreign Office) to missions and consulate abroad, May 17, 1935, enclosing circular letter by the Ministry of Interior, April 18, 1935, NG-3942.

measure. The term "non-Aryan" had been defined in such a way as to include not only full Jews — that is to say, persons with four Jewish grandparents — but also three-quarter Jews, half-Jews, and one-quarter Jews. Such a definition was considered necessary in order to eliminate from official positions all persons who, even in the slightest degree, might have been carriers of the "Jewish influence." Nevertheless, it was recognized that the term "non-Aryan," aside from embracing the full Jews, included also a number of persons whose inclusion in subsequent, more drastic measures would result in difficulties. In order to narrow the application of subsequent decrees to exclude such persons, a definition of what was actually meant by "Jew" became necessary.

At the beginning of 1935 the problem received some attention in party circles. One of the meetings was attended by Dr. Wagner, then *Reichsärzteführer* (chief medical officer of the party), Dr. Gross (Race-Political Office), and Dr. Blome, at that time secretary of the medical association, later Deputy *Reichsärzteführer*. Dr. Blome spoke out against a special status for part-Jews. He did not want a "third race." Consequently, he proposed that all quarter-Jews be considered Germans and that all half-Jews be considered Jews. Reason: "Among half-Jews, the Jewish genes are notoriously dominant."[8] This view later became party policy, but the party never succeeded in imposing that policy on the Interior Ministry, where the decisive decrees were written.

On the occasion of the Nuremberg party rally, Hitler ordered, on September 13, 1935, that a decree be written — in two days — under the title "Law for the Protection of German Blood and Honor." Two experts of the Interior Ministry, Ministerialrat Medicus and Ministerialrat Lösener, were thereupon summoned to Nuremberg by plane. When they arrived, they found Staatssekretäre Pfundtner and Stuckart, Ministerialrat Seel (civil service expert of the Interior Ministry), Ministerialrat Sommer (a representative of the Führer's Deputy Hess), and several other gentlemen in the police headquarters, drafting a law. Interior Minister Frick and Reichsärzteführer Wagner shuttled between Hitler's quarters and the police station with drafts. In the midst of the commotion, to the accompaniment of music and marching feet, and in a setting of flags, the new decree was hammered out. The law no longer dealt with "non-Aryans" but with "Jews." It prohibited marriages and extramarital intercourse between Jews and citizens of "German or related blood," the employment in Jewish households of female citizens of "German or related blood" under the age of 45, and the raising by Jews of the Reich flag.[9] None of the terms used were defined in the decree.

On the evening of September 14, Frick returned to his villa from a visit to Hitler and told the exhausted experts to get busy with a draft of a Reich Citizenship Law. The *Staatssekretäre* and *Ministerialräte* now went to work in the music room of Frick's villa, to write a citizenship law. Soon they ran out of paper and requisitioned old menu cards. By 2:30 A.M. the citizenship law was finished. It provided that only persons of "German or related blood" could be citizens. Since "citizenship" in Nazi Germany implied nothing, no interest attaches to the drafting of this decree, except insofar as the civil servants stuck in a provision to the effect that "full Jews" could not be citizens. This implied a new

8. Affidavit by Dr. Kurt Blome, January 17, 1946. NO-1710.

9. Law for the Protection of German Blood and Honor, September 15, 1935, RGBl I, 1146.

categorization, differentiating between Germans and part-Jews, on the one hand, and such persons, regardless of religion, who had four Jewish grandparents, on the other hand. Hitler saw this implication immediately and crossed out the provision.[10]

The attitudes of the party and of the civil service toward part-Jews had now emerged quite clearly. The party "combatted" the part-Jew as a carrier of the "Jewish influence;" the civil service wanted to protect in the part-Jew "that part which is German."[11] The final definition was written in the Interior Ministry, and so it is not surprising that the party view did not prevail.

The authors of the definition were Staatssekretär Dr. Stuckart and his expert in Jewish affairs, Dr. Lösener. Stuckart was then a young man of 33. He was a Nazi, a believer in Hitler and Germany's destiny. He was also regarded as a party man. There is a difference between these two concepts. Everyone was presumed to be, and was accepted as, a Nazi unless by his own conduct he insisted otherwise. But not everyone was regarded as a party man. Only those people were party men who held positions in the party, who owed their positions to the party, or who represented the party's interests in disagreements between the party and other hierarchies. Stuckart was in the party (he had even joined the SS in an honorary capacity); he had risen to power more quickly than other people; and he knew what the party wanted. But in this last respect Stuckart was not an all-out party man; he refused to go along with the party in the definition business.

Stuckart's expert on Jewish affairs, Dr. Bernhard Lösener, had been transferred to the Interior Ministry after long service in the customs administration. Definitions and Jewish affairs were an entirely new experience to him; yet he became an efficient "expert" in his new assignment. Ultimately he drafted, or helped draft, 27 anti-Jewish decrees.[12] He is the prototype of other "experts" in Jewish matters, whom we shall meet in the Finance Ministry, in the Labor Ministry, in the Foreign Office, and in many other agencies.

The two men had an urgent task to perform. The terms "Jew" and "German" had already been used in a decree which contained criminal sanctions. There was no time to be lost. The final text of the definition corresponds in substance to a memorandum written by Lösener and dated November 1, 1935.[13] Lösener dealt in his memorandum with the critical problem of the half-Jews. He rejected the party's proposal to equate half-Jews with full-Jews. In the first place, Lösener argued, such a categorization would strengthen the Jewish side. "In principle, the half-Jew should be regarded as a more serious enemy than the full Jew because, in addition to Jewish characteristics, he possesses so many Germanic ones which the full Jew lacks." Second, the equation would result in an injustice. Half-Jews could not emigrate and could not compete with full Jews for jobs with Jewish employers. Third, there was the need of the armed forces, which would be deprived of a potential 45,000 men. Fourth, a boycott against half-Jews was impractical (the German people would not go along). Fifth, half-Jews had performed meritorious services (recital

10. The history of the two laws is taken from the affidavit by Dr. Bernard Lösener, February 24, 1948, NG-1944-A. Final version of the Reich Citizenship Law, dated September 15, 1935, in RGBl I, 1146.

11. See letter by Stuckart, March 16, 1942, NG-2586-I.

12. See list compiled by Lösener in his affidavit of February 28, 1948, NG-1944-A.

13. Stuckart to Foreign Minister von Neurath, November 1, 1935, enclosing Lösener memorandum, NG-3941.

of names). Sixth, there were many marriages between Germans and half-Jews. Suppose, for example, that Mr. Schmidt finds out, after ten years of marriage, that his wife is half-Jewish—a fact which, presumably, all half-Jewish wives keep secret?

In view of all these difficulties, Lösener proposed that the half-Jews be sorted into two groups.[14] There was no practical way of sorting half-Jews individually, according to their political convictions. But there was an automatic way of dealing with that problem; Lösener proposed that only those half-Jews be counted as Jews who belonged to the Jewish religion or who were married to a Jewish person.

The Lösener proposal was incorporated into the First Regulation to the Reich Citizenship Law, dated November 14, 1935.[15] In its final form, the automatic sorting method separated the "non-Aryans" into the following categories: Everyone was defined as a Jew who (1) descended from at least three Jewish grandparents (full Jews and three-quarter Jews), or (2) descended from two Jewish grandparents (half-Jews) and (*a*) belonged to the Jewish religious community on September 15, 1935, or joined the community on a subsequent date, *or* (*b*) was married to a Jewish person on September 15, 1935, or married one on a subsequent date, *or* (*c*) was the offspring of a marriage contracted with a three-quarter or a full Jew after the Law for the Protection of German Blood and Honor had come into force (September 15, 1935, *or* (*d*) was the offspring of an extramarital relationship with a three-quarter or a full Jew, and was born out of wedlock after July 31, 1936. For the determination of the status of the grandparents, the presumption remained that the grandparent was Jewish if he or she belonged to the Jewish religious community.

Defined *not* as a Jew but as an individual of "mixed Jewish blood" was (1) any person who descended from two Jewish grandparents (half-Jewish), but who (*a*) did not adhere (or adhered no longer) to the Jewish religion on September 15, 1935, and who did not join it at any subsequent time, *and* (*b*) was not married (or was married no longer) to a Jewish person on September 15, 1935, and who did not marry such a person at any subsequent time (such half-Jews were called *Mischlinge* of the first degree), and (2) any person descended from one Jewish grandparent (*Mischling* of the second degree). The designations "*Mischling* of the first degree" and "*Mischling* of the second degree" were not contained in the decree of November 14, 1935, but were added in a later ruling by the Ministry of Interior.[16]

In practice, therefore, Lösener had split the non-Aryans into two groups, *Mischlinge* and Jews. The *Mischlinge* were no longer subjected to the destruction process. They remained non-Aryans under the earlier decrees and continued to be affected by them, but subsequent measures were, on the whole, taken only against "Jews." Henceforth, the *Mischlinge* were left out.[17]

The administration of the Lösener decree, and of the *Arierparagraph* which preceded it, was a complicated procedure which is interesting because it affords a great deal of insight into the Nazi mentality. In the first place, both decrees were based on descent: the religious status of the grandparents. For that reason, it was necessary to *prove* descent. In this respect,

14. The nature of these arguments is quite interesting, since they could have been used equally well to argue against all anti-Jewish measures.

15. RGBl I, 1333.

16. Stuckart, *Rassenpflege,* p. 17.

17. For summary of anti-*Mischling* measures from 1933 to 1944, see pp. 268, 273n, 274.

the decrees affected not only "non-Aryans;" *everybody* who wanted to be employed by the Reich, or in the party, had to search for the records of his ancestors. An applicant for a position (and, in many cases, an office holder) required seven documents: his own birth or baptismal certificate, the certificates of his two parents, and the certificates of all four grandparents.[18]

Prior to 1875-76, births were registered only by churches.[19] Thus the churches were drawn into the administration of the very first measure of the destruction process. They did their part of the job as a matter of course. Oddly enough, however, the office holders themselves were not prepared to offer their full co-operation. As late as 1940, the chief of the party's foreign organization had to remind his personnel to submit the documents. Most employees in the office had simply ignored an earlier directive for submission of records, without even giving an excuse or explanation for failure to comply.[20] Of course, in part at least, the lack of prompt compliance was simply due to the difficulty of procuring the necessary papers.

Even in the early thirties, a whole new profession of licensed "family researchers" (*Sippenforscher* or *Familienforscher*) had appeared on the scene, to assist applicants and office holders in finding documents. The Sippenforscher compiled *Ahnentafeln* ("ancestor charts"), which listed parents and grandparents. Sometimes it was necessary to do research on great-grandparents also. Such procedures, however, were limited to two types of cases: (1) applications for service in such party formations as the SS, which, in the case of officers, required proof of non-Jewish descent from 1750, and (2) attempts to show that a Jewish grandparent was actually the offspring of Christian parents. This latter procedure was possible, because a grandparent was only *presumed* to be Jewish if he (or she) belonged to the Jewish religion. In the same way, inquiry into the status of the great-grandparents could be used to the detriment of an applicant. For if it were shown that a Christian grandparent had actually been the child of Jews, the grandparent would be considered a Jew, and a "downward" classification would result.[21]

The final decision about the correctness of the facts was made by the agency which had to pass on the applicant, but in doubtful cases a party office on family research (the *Sippenamt*) rendered expert opinions for the guidance of agency heads. There was, in that connection, a very interesting category of doubtful cases: the offspring of extramarital relationships. The status of these individuals raised a peculiar problem. How was one to classify someone whose descent could not be determined? This problem was divided into two parts: individuals with Jewish mothers and individuals with German mothers.

In cases of offspring of unmarried Jewish mothers, the *Reichssippenamt* ("Family Research Office") presumed that any child born *before* 1918 had a Jewish father and that any child born *after* 1918 had a Christian father. The reason for this presumption was a Nazi hypothesis known as the "emancipation theory," according to which Jews did not mix with Germans before 1918. However, after 1918 the Jews had the opportunity to pursue the systematic

18. For detailed specifications, see, for example, the Merkblatt für den Abstammungsnachweis of the Reichsfilmkammer, October, 1936, G-55.

19. *Pfarrämter*. After 1875–76, registrations were performed by the state's *Standesämter*. *Reichsfilmkammer Merkblatt*, October, 1936. G-55.

20. Order by Gauleiter Bohle, May 31, 1940, NG-1672.

21. Stuckart, *Rassenpflege*, p. 16.

disintegration (*Zersetzung*) of the German people (*Volkskörper*). This activity included the fostering of extramarital relationships. In commenting upon this theory, Amtsgerichtsrat ("Judge") Klemm of the party's Legal Office pointed out that it was quite true that Jews were guilty of this practice but that, after all, the practice was intended only to violate German *woman.* It could hardly be assumed that a Jewish woman undertook pregnancy in order to harm the German *man.* According to the criteria used by the *Reichssippenamt,* complained Klemm, a Jewish mother could simply refuse to tell the office who the father was, and her child would automatically become a *Mischling* of the first degree.[22] Klemm's comments were probably quite correct. This was perhaps the only Nazi theory which worked to the complete advantage of a number of full Jews.

The "emancipation theory" does not seem to have been applied to the offspring of unwed German mothers. The reason was simple: the Party's *Reichssippenamt* rarely, if ever, got such cases. If it had gotten them, just about all of Germany's illegitimate children born after 1918 would have been classified as *Mischlinge* of the first degree. But since the Party did not get the cases, the illegitimate offspring of a German mother remained a German, with all the rights and obligations of a German in Nazi Germany. However, there were a few instances when a Jew or *Mischling* had acknowledged paternity of a German mother's child. In some of these cases, persons who had been classified as *Mischlinge* went to court, pointing out that the legal father was not the actual father and that, therefore, there was ground for reclassification. For such cases, the Justice Ministry laid down the rule that the courts were not to inquire into the motives of the person who had acknowledged fatherhood and that they were to reject any testimony by the mother, "who is only interested in protecting her child from the disadvantages of Jewish descent."[23]

The cumbersome task of proving descent was not the only problem which complicated the administration of the decrees. Although the definition appeared to be airtight, in the sense that – given the facts – it should have been possible at once to determine whether an individual was a German, a *Mischling,* or a Jew, there were in fact several problems of interpretation. Consequently, we find a whole number of administrative and judicial decisions which were designed to make the definition more precise.

The principal problem of interpretation hinged on the provision in the Lösener decree according to which half-Jews were classified as *Mischlinge* of the first degree if they did not belong to the Jewish religion and were not married to a Jewish person on or after September 15, 1935. There was no legal difficulty in determining whether a person was married; marriage is a clearly defined legal concept. But the determination of criteria for adherence to the Jewish religion was not so simple. Whether a half-Jew was to be classified as a Jew or a *Mischling* of the first degree ultimately depended on the answer to the question: Did the man regard himself as a Jew?

In 1941 the Reichsverwaltungsgericht (Reich Administrative Court) received a petition from a half-Jew who had not been raised as a Jew and who had never been affiliated with any syna-

22. Amtsgerichtsrat Klemm, "Spricht eine Vermutung für die Deutschblütigkeit des nicht feststellbaren Erzeugers eines von einer Jüdin ausserehelich geborenen Kindes?" *Deutsches Recht,* 1942, p. 850, and *Die Judenfrage* (*Vertrauliche Beilage*), July 1, 1942, pp. 50–51.

23. Directive by Ministry of Justice, May 24, 1941. *Deutsche Justiz,* 1941, p. 629.

gogue. Nevertheless, the court classified the petitioner as a Jew because there was evidence that, on various occasions since 1914, he had designated *himself* as a Jew in filling out forms and official documents, and he had failed to correct the impression of the authorities that he was a Jew. Toleration of a presumption was sufficient conduct for the purpose of classification as a Jewish person.[24]

In a later decision the Reichsgericht (highest court in Germany) ruled that conduct was not enough; the attitude disclosed by the conduct was decisive. The particular case concerned a young woman, half-Jewish, who had married a half-Jew (*Mischling* of the first degree). The marriage consequently did not place her into the Jewish category. Now, however, there was the matter of her religion.[25] The evidence showed that in 1923 and 1924 she had had Jewish religious instruction upon the insistence of her Jewish father. In subsequent years she accompanied her father to the synagogue, once a year, on Jewish high holy days. After her father died in 1934, she discontinued visits to the synagogue, but, in asking for a job in the Jewish community organization, she listed her religion as Jewish. Until 1938, moreover, she was entered as a member of a synagogue. The court decided that she was *not* Jewish. The evidence showed that she had resisted her father's attempt to have her formally accepted with prayer and blessing into the Jewish religion. She had visited the synagogue not for religious reasons but only in order to please her father. In asking for a position with the Jewish community organization, she was motivated not by a feeling of Jewishness but solely by economic considerations. As soon as she discovered her entry in the Jewish community list, she requested that her name be struck out.[26]

The attitude and intention of the individual was decisive in another case, which is very interesting from a psychological point of view. A half-Jew who had married a German woman in 1928 had thereupon ceased to be a member of his synagogue. In 1941 the Jewish community organization in Berlin, which was then performing important functions in the destruction process, suddenly demanded information about the man's personal finances, and when this information was refused, the Jewish community went to court, claiming that the defendant had quit his synagogue but not his religion. The court rejected the Jewish organization's argument, pointing out that the Jewish religious community had no legal personality and no public law status. Consequently, any man who had quit his synagogue had quit his religion at the same time, unless there was evidence that he still regarded himself as a Jew. There was no such evidence in this case. To the contrary, the defendant had provided proof of his membership in party organizations, and in every other respect the court was satisfied that this man had intended to sever his connections with Jewry when he stepped out of the synagogue.

This decision was one of the few which was assailed by the party's Race-Political Office. A lawyer of that office, Dr. Schmidt-Klevenow, referring to the fact that the Jewish community itself had claimed the defendant to be a member, asked whether the court had to be "more pontifical than the pontiff (*päpstlicher als der Papst*)."[27]

24. Decision of the Reichsverwaltungsgericht, June 5, 1941. *Deutsches Recht,* p. 2413; also in *Die Judenfrage* (*Vertrauliche Beilage*), February 1, 1942, pp. 11–12.

25. In the Jewish practice, the *mother's* religion is decisive in determining the religion of the half-Jewish child.

26. Decision of the Reichsgericht/3. Strafsenat, August 13, 1942. *Deutsches Recht,* 1943, p. 80, and *Die Judenfrage* (*Vertrauliche Beilage*), February 1, 1943, pp. 11-12.

From all these decisions, the judiciary's concern with half-Jews is quite evident. This concern was the product of a desire to balance the protection of the German community against the destruction of the Jews. When a person was both German and Jewish by parental descent, the judges had to determine which element was dominant in the man. To do this, they only had to be a little more precise than Lösener had been in asking the question of how the individual had classified himself.

The court interpretations of the Lösener decree illustrate once more that there is nothing "racial" in the basic design of the definition. In fact, there are a few very curious cases in which a person with *four* German grandparents was classified as a Jew because he belonged to the Jewish religion. In its decision one court pointed out that Aryan treatment was to be accorded to persons who had the "racial" requisites "but that in cases when the individual involved feels bound to Jewry in spite of his Aryan blood, and shows this fact externally, his attitude is decisive."[28] In another decision, by the Reich Finance Court, it was held that an Aryan who adhered to the Jewish religion was to be treated as a Jew for the duration of his adherence to the Jewish faith. According to the court, an individual "who is racially a non-Jew, but who openly claims membership in the Jewish community, belongs to the community and therefore has placed himself in the ranks of the Jews."[29]

Even while the judiciary closed the loopholes of the Lösener definition by making it more precise, it became necessary, in an increasing number of cases, to make exceptions on behalf of individuals whose categorization into a particular group was considered unjust. In creating the *Mischlinge,* Lösener had constructed a so-called third race, that is, a group of people who for administrative purposes were neither Jews nor Germans. The *Mischlinge* suffered from three discriminations: (1) they were excluded from the civil service and the party; (2) they were restricted in the army to service as common soldiers; and (3) they could not marry Germans without official consent.[30]

Because of these discriminations, pressure for exceptional treatment, was applied by colleagues, superiors, friends, and relatives. Consequently, in 1935 a procedure was instituted for the reclassification of a *Mischling* into a higher category, i.e., *Mischling* of the first degree to *Mischling* of the second degree, or *Mischling* of the second degree to German, or *Mischling* of the first degree to German. This procedure was known as *Befreiung* ("liberation"). There were two kinds, "pseudo-liberations" and "genuine liberations" (*unechte Befreiungen* and *echte Befreiungen*). The pseudo-liberation was a reclassification based upon a clarification of the facts or of the law. It was achieved by showing, for example, that an allegedly Jewish grandfather was not really Jewish, or that a presumed adherence to the Jewish religion had not existed. The "real liberation,"

27. Decision of an Amtsgericht, affirmed on appeal, reported in *Deutsches Recht,* 1941, pp. 1552-53. Summary of case with comment by Schmidt-Klevenow in *Die Judenfrage* (*Vertrauliche Beilage*), September 1, 1941, pp. 61-63.

28. Decision by Oberlandesgericht Königsberg, 4. Zivilsenat, June 26, 1942, in *Die Judenfrage* (*Vertrauliche Beilage*), November 1, 1942, pp. 82-83.

29. Decision by the Reichsfinanzhof, February 11, 1943. *Reichssteuerblatt,* 1943, p. 251, and *Die Judenfrage* (*Vertrauliche Beilage*), April 15, 1943, pp. 30-31. This case, as well as the case cited above, concerned individuals who had accepted the Jewish religion upon marriage to a Jewish woman.

30. Later, *Mischlinge* were denied admission to the bar and suffered from discriminations in the schools.

however, was granted upon showing the applicant's "merit."[31] Applications for real liberations were routed through the Interior Ministry and the Reich Chancellery to Hitler if the petitioner was a civilian, and through the Army High Command and the Führer Chancellery if the petitioner was a soldier.[32]

The recipients of this favor were sometimes high officials. Ministerialrat Killy of the Reich Chancellery, a man who performed significant functions in the destruction of the Jews, was a *Mischling* of the second degree. His wife was a *Mischling* of the first degree. He had joined the party and had entered the Reich Chancellery without telling anyone about his origin. When the decree of April 7, 1933 (*Arierparagraph*), was issued, Killy informed Lammers about the state of affairs and offered to resign. Lammers thought the situation quite grave because of Killy's wife but advised Killy not to resign. Thereupon, Lammers spoke to Hitler, who agreed to Killy's continuing service. Then on Christmas Eve in 1936, while the Killy family was sitting around the tree and opening gifts, a courier brought a special present: a *Befreiung* for Killy and his children.[33]

The "liberations" increased in volume to such an extent that on July 20, 1942, Lammers informed the Highest Reich Authorities of Hitler's desire to cut down on their number. The applications had been handled too "softly" (*weichherzig*). Hitler did not think that the blameless conduct of a *Mischling* was sufficient ground for his "liberation"; the *Mischling* had to show "positive merit," which might be proved if, for example, without awareness of his ancestry he had fought for the party uninterruptedly and for many years, prior to 1933.[34]

Lest we leave the impression that the tendency to equate *Mischlinge* with Germans was unopposed, we should point out that there was another tendency to eliminate the "third race" by reclassifying *Mischlinge* of the second degree as Germans and transforming all *Mischlinge* of the first degree into Jews. This pressure, which came from party circles and the police, reached its zenith in 1942; however, it never succeeded.

Thus we find that the Lösener definition remained the basis of categorization throughout the destruction process. Even though some different definitions were later adopted in some occupied countries and Axis states, the basic concept of these early decrees remained unchanged.

In summary, here is a recapitulation of the terms and their meanings:

Non-Aryans:

- *Mischlinge* of the second degree:
  Persons with one Jewish grandparent
- *Mischlinge* of the first degree:
  Persons with two Jewish grandparents who did not belong to the Jewish religion and were not married to a Jewish person on September 15, 1935
- Jews:
  Persons with two Jewish grandparents, if they belonged to the Jewish religion or were married to a Jewish person on September 15, 1935, and persons with three or four Jewish grandparents

31. Stuckart, *Rassenpflege,* pp. 18-19.

32. Affidavit by Blome, January 17, 1946, NO-1719.

33. For Killy's adventures, see his testimony in Case No. 11, transcript pp. 23,235–23,267.

34. Lammers to Highest Reich Authorities, July 20, 1942, NG-4819. The Lammers letter was based on remarks by Hitler at the dinner table. See Henry Picker (ed.), *Hitler's Tischgespräche im Führerhauptquartier 1940–1942* (Berlin, 1951), entries for May 10, 1942, and July 1, 1942, pp. 303, 313.

V / *Expropriation*

The first step in the destruction process consisted only of a set of definitions. However, that step was very important. It amounted to creating a target which could be bombarded at will. The Jews were trapped at this range. Initially, they could still emigrate, but later they could only brace themselves for what was to come.

In the course of the next few years the machinery of destruction was turned on Jewish "wealth." In increasing numbers, one Jewish family after another discovered that it was impoverished. More and more was taken from the Jews; less and less was given in return. The Jews were deprived of their professions, their enterprises, their financial reserves, their wages, their claims upon food and shelter, and, finally, their last personal belongings, down to underwear, gold teeth, and women's hair. We shall refer to this process as "expropriation."

The expropriation machinery cut across all four major hierarchical groups. The organizations which were in the forefront of the expropriatory operations will be found in the civil service and in the business sector. Some of these agencies, including the Office of the Four-Year Plan and the Ministries for Finance, Economy, Labor, Food, and Agriculture, are described in Tables 11–15.

TABLE 11 / *Office of the Four-Year Plan**

Göring	
Personal Adviser	Ministerialdirektor Gritzbach
Staatssekretär	Körner
Deputy of the *Staatssekretär*	Ministerialdirigent Marotzke
Top Experts	Ministerialdirektor Wohlthat
	Ministerialdirektor Gramsch
	Gerichtsassessor Dr. Hahn
Generaldirektor in charge of Hermann Göring Works	Staatssekretär Pleiger

*Organization chart of the Reich government, 1945, certified by Frick, PS-2905, and information gathered from documents to be cited in the text.

TABLE 12 / *Finance Ministry**

Minister	Schwerin von Krosigk
Staatssekretär	Fritz Reinhardt
Customs Inspector	Hossfeld (transferred to SS and Police)
General Finance Bureau	Ministerialdirigent Bayrhoffer
Administration of Securities	Patzer
Liaison to Main Trusteeship Office East	Dr. Casdorf
I. Reich Budget	Ministerialdirektor von Manteuffel
Armed-SS Budget	Ministerialrat Rademacher
II. Customs and Sales Taxes	Ministerialdirektor Dr. Wucher
III. Property and Income Taxes	Ministerialdirektor Dr. Hedding
Anti-Jewish Fine	Dr. Uhlich
IV. Salaries and Pensions of Civil Servants	Ministerialdirektor Wever

Table 12 / *Finance Ministry* (Continued)*

V. International Finance	Ministerialdirektor Dr. Berger
Economic Warfare	Dr. Schwandt
Enemy Property	Baenfer
VI. Administration	Ministerialdirektor Maass
Organization	Ministerialdirektor Groth
Enemy Property Administration	Ministerialrat Dr. Maedel
Reich Main Treasury	Fiebig
Tax Court	Regierungsrat Mirre

*Ludwig Münz, *Führer durch Behörden und Organisationen* (Berlin, 1939), p. 112; organization chart of Finance Ministry, July 10, 1943, NG-4397; organization chart of Reich government, 1945, certified by Frick, PS-2905.

Table 13 / *Economy Ministry**

Minister	[Schacht] Funk
Staatssekretär	[Bang, Brinkmann, Landfried] Hayler
Staatssekretär for Special Purposes	Posse
I. Personnel and Administration	Illgner
II. Economic Organization and Industry	[Hannecken, Kehrl] Ohlendorf
III. Foreign Trade	[Jagwitz] Kirchfeld
IV. Credits and Banks	[Klucki] Riehle
V. Mines	Gabel

*Based on the organization chart of the Reich government, 1945, certified by Frick, PS-2905. Last office holders in right column; predecessors in brackets.

Table 14 / *Labor Ministry**

Minister	Seldte
Staatssekretär	Syrup
Staatssekretär	Engel
I. General	Börger
II. Labor Insurance	Zschimmer
III. Wages	Vacant
IV. City Planning and Construction Police	Durst
V. Unemployment Assistance	Beisigel
VI. European Office for Labor Allocation	Timm

*See note to Table 13.

Table 15 / *Food and Agriculture Ministry**

Minister	[Hugenberg, Darre] Backe (acting)
Staatssekretär	Willikens
Staatssekretär	Riecke
General	Schulenburg
Markets and Agricultural Production	Moritz
Farm Labor and Credit	Lorenz
Trade Policy	Walter
Peasantry	Manteuffel
State Agricultural Property	Kummer
Settlement of New Areas	Hiege
The Village	Rheinthaler

*See note to Table 13.

1 / Dismissals

The very first expropriation measures were designed to break that "satanical power" which, in Hitler's words, had "grasped in its hands all key positions of scientific and intellectual as well as political and economic life, and which kept watch over the entire nation from the vantage of these key positions."[1] In short, the initial economic measures were directed against Jews who held positions of any kind in the four governing hierarchies of Nazi Germany.

The non-Aryan population (Jews and *Mischlinge*) in 1933 was about 600,000, or 1 per cent of Germany's total population. The number of non-Aryans in government service was in the neighborhood of 5000, or 0.5 per cent of the total government personnel.[2] These non-Aryans were deprived of their positions in consequence of the Law for the Re-establishment of the Professional Civil Service. The law was dated April 7, 1933,[3] and signed by Hitler, Frick (Interior), and von Krosigk (Finance). The sequence of signatures tells us that the decree was drafted by the appropriate experts in the Interior Ministry and that the competent experts in the Finance Ministry were consulted before publication.

In substance, the law provided for the compulsory retirement of non-Aryan officials, although there were some exceptions to this rule. The non-Aryan clause did *not* apply to officials who had served in the government since August 1, 1914, or who had fought at the front for Germany or one of Germany's allies in World War I, or whose fathers or sons had been killed on the German side during that war. The nature of these exceptions appears to reflect a feeling that loyalty ought to be rewarded with loyalty. Moreover, those who were subject to retirement were entitled to a pension if they had completed ten years of service.[4]

These, then, were the provisions of the first decree designed to inflict actual harm upon the Jews. It was a mild decree. But the destruction process was a development which began with mild measures and ended with drastic action. The victims never remained in one position for long. There were always changes, and the changes were always for the worse. Let us examine what happened to this law.

The exemption clauses were soon made ineffectual. One of the paragraphs in the decree provided that anyone could be retired from the civil service if such separation would further the "simplification of administration." According to Ministerialdirigent Hubrich of the Interior Ministry, this paragraph was used extensively to eliminate non-Aryans who were old officials, veterans, or relatives of deceased veterans. There were no restrictions upon the payment of pensions to officials retired in that fashion.[5] Finally, the decree of November 14, 1935, which defined the concept of "Jew," stipulated that all remaining Jewish civil servants (excepting only teachers in Jewish schools)

1. Speech by Hitler, German press, November 10–11, 1940.

2. For detailed statistics, see "Statistisches Reichsamt," *Statistik des Deutschen Reichs*, CDLI, Pt. 5, "Die Glaubensjuden im Deutschen Reich," 29, 61, 66. See also Erich Rosenthal, "Trends of the Jewish Population in Germany, 1910-1939," *Jewish Social Studies*, 1944, pp. 255–57; and Institute of Jewish Affairs, *Hitler's Ten-Year War on the Jews* (New York, 1943), p. 7.

The number of government employees who were Jews by religion was about 4000. In public education (all three levels) there were 1832; in the judiciary, 286; in the railway and postal administrations, 282; in all other agencies, including the armed forces, 1545.

3. RGBl I, 175.

4. Affidavit by Dr. Georg Hubrich (*Ministerialdirigent*, Interior Ministry), November 21, 1947, NG-3567.

5. Affidavit by Hubrich, November 21, 1947, NG-3567.

were to be removed by December 31, 1935. Officials retired under this decree were granted pensions only if they had served as front-line soldiers in the First World War.[6]

The Jews had now been ousted from the civil service, but the regulation of the pension system was far from perfect (see Table 16). Something had to be straightened out here. To the bureaucrats this meant, of course, that some pensions would have to be cut out. For a long time nothing was done about the matter; then in November, 1939, Staatssekretär Pfundtner proposed to Chief of the Reich Chancellery Lammers a complex regulation for the reduction of pension payments to Jews.[7] Reichspostminister ("Minister for Postal Affairs") Ohnesorge commented that the draft was too complicated. "I consider it undesirable," he wrote, "that the administrative apparatus should be burdened with additional difficulties on account of the Jews, of all people."

Moreover, it was "quite likely" (*durchaus denkbar*) that the Jews who were still in the country – most of whom were "doing nothing" anyhow (*untätig herumlungern*) – would be incarcerated in protective custody, security arrest, "or the like" for the duration of the war. Consequently, one could prepare for this eventuality in the pension field right now, by withdrawing all pension provisions for Jews and by granting payments only on a revocable basis or on a basis of need.[8] These lines, which were written in 1939, indicate how quickly the German bureaucracy – even in the Postal Ministry – could develop some drastic thoughts in connection with such a minor matter as pensions. Incarcerations "and the like" soon became a reality. The pensions, however, remained untouched. The problem did not reemerge until the Jews were killed.

Unlike the civil service ousters, the dismissals from the armed forces posed no particular difficulty. In the first place, the army in 1933 was a comparatively small organization whose size was limited by treaty to 100,000 men. Second, the military had always discriminated against Jews. As late as 1910 no Jew could become a career officer in the Prussian Army unless he changed his religion or unless he was a doctor.[9] Consequently, the status of non-Aryans in the armed forces could be regulated by a single decree, issued on May 21, 1935, and signed by Hitler, War Minister Feldmarschall von Blomberg, and Interior Minister Frick.[10] The law provided that "Aryan" descent was a prerequisite for active service in the

TABLE 16 / *Regulation of Pension System*

	1933	"Simplification"	1935
Veterans		pension	pension
Surviving relatives		pension	no pension
Service before 1914		pension	no pension
Ten-year service	pension		
Less than ten years	no pension		

6. RGBl I, 1333. The *Mischlinge* were not affected by the decree of November 14, 1935. Insofar as they had survived under the excepting clauses of the law of April 7, 1933, the *Mischlinge* could therefore continue in office.

7. Pfundtner to Lammers, November 17, 1939, NG-358.

8. *Reichspostminister* to Minister of Interior, November 30, 1939, NG-358.

9. "Die Juden im deutschen Heere," *Allgemeine Zeitung des Judentums* (Berlin, November 25, 1910), pp. 556–59.

10. RGBl I, 609.

armed forces; however, there was a provision for "exceptions," to be agreed upon by the Interior Ministry and the War Ministry, and another clause which provided that service of non-Aryans in wartime could be regulated by special directives. It must be remembered that this law was published several months *before* the Interior Ministry defined the term "Jew." One of the reasons for splitting the non-Aryans into *Mischlinge* and Jews was to enable the armed forces to make use of the *Mischling* cannon fodder.

In the party there were no dismissals because the party had no Jews. However, the party – or, to be more precise, the propaganda apparatus in the party – was keenly interested in the elimination of Jews who held positions which, in a broad sense, could serve a propagandistic purpose. When Goebbels, the party's propaganda chief, formed his Propaganda Ministry, he began to issue decrees. One of the first measures was the decree of October 4, 1933, which directed the newspapers to remove all non-Aryan editors.[11] Other regulations which followed assured the ouster of Jewish musicians, artists, writers, and so on, by excluding them from the guilds ("chambers"). No artist could practice unless he was a member of one of the Goebbels-controlled guilds.

The most interesting and also the most complicated dismissal process occurred in the business sector. Business was no single hierarchy but a conglomeration of organizations. Since there was no office that could direct all enterprises to remove their Jewish employees, each company had to make its own decision about its own Jews. In the business sector the Jews therefore felt themselves safe. They did not think that purely private organizations would join in the destruction process without compulsion. The following is an illustration from I. G. Farben.

11. RGBl I, 713.

In July, 1933, a DuPont delegation visited I. G. Farben in Germany. The DuPont representatives held many conferences with I. G. Farben officials, and in the course of these talks one of the DuPont men had a conversation with one of the many Jews who had helped build the I. G. Farben empire. The Jewish official was Dr. Karl von Weinberg, Deputy Chairman of the Verwaltungsrat. The Verwaltungsrat was an assembly of I. G. Farben "elder statesmen" who had no actual power but whose advice was considered weighty.[12] This was the American businessman's impression of von Weinberg:

> Following luncheon, we visited Dr. Carl von Weinberg, who is now 73 years old and who comes to the office daily for consultation with the active members of the I.G. Dr. von Weinberg also discussed the situation in Germany, and although he is a Jew, has given the movement his full stamp of approval. He stated further that all his money is invested in Germany and he does not have one pfennig outside the country. We spoke of the proposed increase in collaboration with I.G., to which he was in hearty agreement. In touching upon I.G.'s interest in the U.S.A., Dr. von Weinberg indicated that I.G. was very well pleased with the investment, and by suggestion gave us to understand that they had no intention of retiring from that market.[13]

But even men like von Weinberg lasted only a little longer than the Jewish civil servants. In I. G. Farben almost all Jewish executives were dropped by 1937.[14] On August 1, 1942, an informed

12. For list of Verwaltungsrat members, see affidavit by Hermann Baessler, July, 1947, NI-7957.

13. Homer H. Ewing, E. I. DuPont De Nemours and Co., Wilmington, Delaware, to Wendell R. Swint, Director, Foreign Relations Department of DuPont, July 17, 1933, NI-9784.

14. Affidavit by Baessler, July 17, 1947, NI-7957.

ex-diplomat, Ulrich von Hassel, noted in his diary: "The old Weinberg sits at 81 years in a concentration camp."[15]

The dismissals in the business sector were all the more remarkable because of two obstacles that German enterprises had to overcome, employment contracts and efficiency problems. The long-term employment contracts with Jews posed a legal difficulty. Since there was no decree directing business firms to dismiss their Jewish personnel or freeing the companies from the obligation of employment assumed in the contracts, many cases actually came to court. In the courts the German enterprises usually attempted to justify the dismissals on the ground that there was party pressure or on the ground that some clause in the employment contract, however remote, was applicable to the case.[16]

Just how far these attempts were pursued is illustrated by a case decided by the highest court in the country, the Reichsgericht. A defendant movie company (German) claimed that it was entitled to fire a Jewish stage manager with whom it had concluded a long-term contract, because of a clause in that contract which provided for termination of employment in the case of "sickness, death, or similar causes rendering the stage manager's work impossible." The Reichsgericht held that the clause was "unqualifiedly applicable" (*unbedenklich anwendbar*) on the ground that the "racial characteristics" of the plaintiff amounted to sickness and death.[17] In the thinking of Germany's highest judges, the Jews had already ceased to be living organisms. They were dead matter that could no longer contribute to the growth of a German business.

The second obstacle to the removal of the Jews from German enterprises was the matter of efficiency. There was a strong conviction that in certain posts (such as sales positions in the export trade) Jews were ideal,[18] or even irreplaceable. This notion led I. G. Farben and several other enterprises which had branches abroad to transfer Jewish personnel to foreign countries. In that way the Jews were out of Germany and all problems seemed to be solved. However, even this solution was only temporary, for invariably the major enterprises decided on the "gradual reduction" of their Jewish representatives abroad.[19]

As the dismissals gained momentum, the conditions under which the Jews were fired became worse. The later a Jew was removed, the less his severance pay, settlement, or pension.[20] The process was well under way before the ministerial bureaucracy stepped in. Early in 1938 the Interior Ministry prepared a decree which defined the term "Jewish enterprise." The decree, dated June 14, 1938,[21] was to form the basis for the compulsory transfer of Jewish firms into German hands. The definition, however, was very broad. A business was considered Jewish not only if it was owned by Jews but also if a legal representative or board member was a Jew. A branch of a German business was considered Jewish if a manager of the branch was a Jew. Such a definition was ample incentive for the firing of Jewish directors, Prokuristen

15. Ulrich von Hassel, *Vom Andern Deutschland* (Zurich, 1946), p. 273.

16. See Ernst Fraenkel, *The Dual State* (New York, 1941), pp. 92, 95; for arguments in dissolution of partnerships, see pp. 90, 91.

17. Decision by Reichsgericht, June 17, 1936, cited by Fraenkel, *The Dual State,* pp. 95-96.

18. See summary of the Schacht conference, p. 21.

19. See summary of meeting of I. G. Farben Commercial Committee, von Schnitzler presiding, October 17, 1937, NI-4862.

20. Statement by Hugo Zinsser, member of the Vorstand of the Dresdner Bank, November 17, 1945, NI-11864.

21. RGBl I, 627.

(managers with powers to represent the firm), or branch managers, insofar as such executives were still in office. In November, 1938, the ministries stepped in again. The decree of November 12, 1938,[22] signed by Göring, directed German firms to dismiss *all* their Jewish managers by the end of the year. Dismissal could be effected after six weeks' notice. After expiration of such notice, the Jewish manager had no further financial claim upon his employer.

Thus the expropriations began with the slow but thorough purge of Jews from the machinery of destruction. This, in Nazi eyes, was the logical beginning. Before one could dominate the Jews, it was obviously necessary to eliminate their "domination." However, the dismissals constituted only a grazing attack on the Jewish community. In the course of this attack only a few thousand individuals became casualties. The major centers of Jewish "power," the citadels of Jewish "domination," the symbols of Jewish "exploitation," were the independent Jewish enterprises, from the myriads of small stores to the few major companies that might have qualified for the title "big business." The Jewish business establishments fell into the hands of German business firms in a process of transfer known as "Aryanization" (*Arisierung*).

2 / Aryanizations

Today we are accustomed to hearing and reading about "nationalization"; we should, therefore, make a clear-cut distinction between "nationalization" and "Aryanization." In nationalization the government takes private property and returns some form of compensation. In the case of "Aryanization" private German enterprises bought private Jewish enterprises. The Aryanizations were divided into two phases: (1) the so-called voluntary Aryanizations (January, 1933, to November, 1938), which were transfers in pursuance of "voluntary" agreements between Jewish sellers and German buyers, and (2) the "compulsory Aryanizations" (after November, 1938), which were transfers in pursuance of state orders compelling the Jewish owners to sell their property.

The word "voluntary" belongs in quotation marks because no sale of Jewish property under the Nazi regime was voluntary in the sense of a freely negotiated contract in a free society. The Jews were under pressure to sell. The longer they chose to wait, the greater the pressure and the smaller the compensation. This does not mean that the Jews were entirely powerless; Aryanization was perhaps the only phase of the destruction process in which the Jews had some maneuverability, some opportunity for playing German against German, and some occasion for delaying tactics. But it was a dangerous game. Time was against the Jews.

The tendency to hold out or to give in was not a measure of size. The large Jewish enterprises presented more formidable obstacles to German buyers, but they were also more "tempting morsels." The more weapons a Jewish enterprise had at its disposal, the greater the forces arrayed against it. The speed with which a Jewish business was sold was therefore no indication of the owner's resources; it was only a clue to his expectations and fears. Sometimes an owner would sell part of his holdings, only to cling desperately to the remainder. Sometimes he would sell everything at once. We have a few interesting examples of quick sales in territories occupied by the Germans in 1938 and 1939. The Germans marched into Austria in March, 1938, into the Sudetenland of Czechoslovakia in Octo-

22. RGBl I, 1580.

ber, 1938, into Bohemia-Moravia (the Protektorat) in March, 1939. There are instances when sell-outs in these areas preceded the entry of German troops. Jewish fear, in short, was operative before the pressure could be applied.

In Austria the most important pre-Anschluss negotiations were carried out between the Rothschild-controlled Österreichische Kreditanstalt and the German I. G. Farben company. The subject of the negotiations was a Kreditanstalt subsidiary, the Pulverfabrik Skodawerke-Wetzler A. G. The talks were begun originally with a view to the joint construction of a new plant in Austria; however, in the course of the discussions the I. G. Farben plenipotentiary, Ilgner, demanded sale by the Kreditanstalt of 51 per cent of its Pulverfabrik holdings to the I. G.[1] The Kreditanstalt could not accede to this demand because Austria, a small country, offered few investment possibilities. In other words, the Kreditanstalt could not use the schillinge which I. G. Farben offered in payment to acquire as good a holding as the prosperous Pulverfabrik.[2]

Nevertheless, negotiations continued. In February, 1938, a month before the Anschluss, the Kreditanstalt agreed to a merger of the Pulverfabrik with another Austrian chemical concern (the Carbidwerk Deutsch-Matrei A.G.). The merger was to be carried out under the "patronage" of I. G. Farben, so that the new company could be controlled by the German firm.[3] This understanding is psychologically significant, for it means that the Kreditanstalt had agreed, however reluctantly, to permit I. G. Farben to control its industrial base. Although the proposed merger did not provide for the complete elimination of the Rothschild interests, such an aim was clearly envisaged by the German negotiators. According to the I. G. Farben officials who reported on the matter in April, 1938, the discussions were in fact continued after the initial accord had been reached, and the talks were broken off only when the German Army marched into Austria.[4]

What happened after the Anschluss? Vorstand member Rothenberg of the Kreditanstalt was taken for a ride by uniformed brownshirts (SA) and thrown out of a moving automobile.[5] Engineer Isidor Pollack, who had built the Pulverfabrik into a major concern and who was its *Generaldirektor,* met with a violent end. One day in April, 1938, the SA paid him a visit in his home in order to "search" his house. During the "search" he was trampled to death.[6] In the meantime, the German businessmen went about their business. The Kreditanstalt was gobbled up by the giant Deutsche Bank, and its subsidiary, the Pulverfabrik, fell to I. G. Farben.[7]

As in the case of Austria, Jewish interests in Prague were selling out before the Czechoslovak state was crushed. In February, 1939, a month before the German march into Prague,

1. Affidavit by Dr. Franz Rothenberg, September 13, 1947, NI-10997. Rothenberg, a Jew, was a Vorstand member of the Kreditanstalt. The Vorstand corresponds roughly to the management (president and vice-presidents) of an American company.

2. Affidavit by Dr. Josef Joham, September 13, 1947, NI-10998. Affiant was another Vorstand member of the Kreditanstalt.

3. I. G. Farbenindustrie A. G. (signed Häfliger and Krüger) to Staatssekretär Keppler, April 9, 1938, NI-4024.

4. *Ibid.*

5. Affidavit by Rothenberg, September 13, 1947, NI-10997.

6. *Ibid.* Also, affidavit by Joham, September 13, 1947, NI-10998.

7. Affidavit by Georg von Schnitzler, March 10, 1947, NI-5194; von Schnitzler, a Vorstand member of the I. G., was chairman of the I. G. Commercial Committee. To gain complete control of the Pulverfabrik, the I. G. had to buy out the interest of the Deutsche Bank.

the Jewish-controlled Böhmische Escompte Bank passed into the hands of the German Dresdner Bank. Like the Kreditanstalt officials, the leading Jewish directors of the Böhmische Escompte Bank did not profit much from the sale. Directors Dr. Feilchenfeld and Dr. Lob died in a killing center; Director Dr. Kantor was hanged.[8]

The Kreditanstalt and Böhmische Escompte Bank are both cases in which the threat was felt across the border and reaction came before the Germans were in a position to use force. The Jews anticipated the force and complied with it in advance. We shall call this reaction anticipatory compliance, and we shall meet with it time and again.

Those Jewish enterprises which chose to wait for further developments were subjected to a broad pressure which was designed to increase their readiness to sell at the lowest possible price. This pressure was applied not against any particular Jewish firm but against Jewish business as a whole. Mainly, an attempt was made to cut off the Jewish companies from their customers and their suppliers. The alienation of the customer was to be carried out by means of an anti-Jewish boycott; the severance of supplies was to be accomplished through a series of allocation measures. These efforts, it must be emphasized, were not compulsory Aryanization procedures; they were designed only to facilitate voluntary transfers.

The boycott was initially organized by the party, which established a boycott committee on March 29, 1933. Its membership was as follows:[9]

Julius Streicher, Chairman
Robert Ley, German Labor Front
Adolf Hühnlein, SA
Heinrich Himmler, SS
Reinhold Muchow, Nazi Party Factory Cells
Hans Oberlindober, Nazi Party Organization for Care of War Victims
Jakob Spenger, Nazi League for Public Officials
Walter Darre, Party Chief for Agricultural Matters
Dr. von Renteln, Party Leader for the Middle Class
Dr. Hans Frank, Party Legal Chief
Dr. Gerhard Wagner, Party Health Chief
Willy Körber, Hitler Youth
Dr. Achim Gercke, Party Information Department

The committee carried out its work by calling mass meetings which were addressed by such personalities as Streicher and Goebbels, and by placing in front of Jewish stores "defensive guards" assigned by the brown-shirted SA and the black-uniformed SS. The guards were ordered only to "inform" the public that the proprietor of the establishment was a Jew.[10] Sometimes the information was conveyed by smearing the show windows with the word *Jude*.[11]

It should be pointed out that the party's boycott committee launched its campaign not so much in order to facilitate the purchase of Jewish firms by German concerns as to remind the ministries of the "popular" hostility against Jewry and thus to influence the civil service in taking action against the Jews. However, the boycott had distinct economic effects which were not overlooked but intensified and widened.

8. Interrogation of Engineer Jan Dvoracek (Zivno Bank), November 22, 1946, NI-11870. Also, affidavit by Dvoracek, February 2, 1948, NI-14348.

9. Announcement by the Central Committee for Defense against Jewish Horror and Boycott, March 29, 1933, PS-2156.

10. Order signed by Streicher, March 31, 1933, PS-2154.

11. When Austria was occupied, German stores in Vienna sometimes found it necessary to mark their establishments *Arisches Geschäft* ("Aryan Store"). Gauleiter Bürckel (Vienna) to Hess, March 26, 1938, PS-3577.

We have already seen that at the conclusion of the Schacht conference on August 20, 1935, it was decided to withhold all public contracts from Jewish firms.[12] This decision was implemented by amending the Directive of the Reich Cabinet Concerning Awards of Public Contracts.[13] At the same time, the boycott was made compulsory not only for Reich agencies but also for Reich employees. Upon the initiative of the Interior Ministry, it was ruled that civil servants could no longer receive subsidies for services obtained from Jewish physicians, lawyers, dentists, hospitals, drugstores, and – by suggestion of the Justice Ministry – also from maternity homes and funeral parlors.[14] The compulsory boycott applied also to party members. In one particular case a party member, Dr. Kurt Prelle, was hauled before a party court because his wife had, without his knowledge, bought 10 pfennige worth of picture postcards in a store owned by a Jew named Cohn. Prelle was expelled by the party court and, upon request of the deputy of the Führer (Hess), was also to be forbidden to practice his profession as a notary because there was doubt whether he was ready to support and defend the National Socialist state at all times.[15]

That efforts should have been made to enforce the boycott among party members, civil servants, and Reich agencies is not surprising, for the "movement" and the Reich were supposed to be in the vanguard of political action. They were to set the example, and the people were to follow. Actually, the boycott never became airtight because there was an economic need for Jewish goods and services which German firms could not always meet. In the middle thirties, therefore, an attempt was made to isolate the Jewish producer from his customers and his suppliers alike. If he could not buy, he could not produce; if he could not produce, he could not sell. The raw-material supply could be shut off in three ways: (1) voluntary refusal by German suppliers to sell to Jews; (2) action by cartels, in which raw material quotas of Jewish members could be cut or eliminated; and (3) the downward adjustment of foreign currency allocations by the state (with a view to depriving Jewish producers of imported materials). Necessarily, these were cumbersome and by no means fully effective controls, but they were invoked as part of the general scheme to depress the price of Jewish firms.[16]

As a result of allocation control, boycott, and the Jewish apprehension that more was still to come, many Jewish

12. See p. 22.

13. Instructions by Reich Propaganda Ministry, enclosing the amended directive, March 26, 1938, G-61.

14. Pfundtner to Highest Reich Authorities, May 19, 1936, NG-2612. Stuckart to Highest Reich Authorities, September 9, 1936, NG-2612.

15. Decree ordering investigation of Prelle, signed by Staatssekretär Dr. Schlegelberger of the Justice Ministry, December 6, 1938, NG-901. See also investigation order signed by Schlegelberger concerning another notary, Dr. Wolfgang Rotmann, who bought cigars in a Jewish store, June 3, 1939, NG-901.

16. See letter by Rohde to Steinbrinck (internal correspondence, Flick steel concern), November 22, 1937, NI-1880. Rohde reported that the Jewish steel enterprise Rawack and Grünfeld was no longer authorized to purchase ores, "which should certainly influence the market value of [Rawack and Grünfeld] shares."

See also the circular letter by *Wirtschaftsgruppe Eisenschaffende Industrie* ("Economy Group Iron-Producing Industry") to *Fach-* and *Fachuntergruppen* and member firms, January 13, 1938, NI-8058. Also, *Wirtschaftsgruppe Gross- Ein- und Ausfuhrhandel/Fachgruppe Eisen- und Stahlhandel* ("Economy Group Large Import and Export Trade/Branch Group Iron and Steel Trade") to member firms and the *Wirtschaftsgruppe Eisenschaffende Industrie,* March 28, 1938, NI-8059. Germany was an importer of iron ore.

businessmen were ready to sell their holdings. There was now a "market." German enterprises by the thousands were surveying the country in search of suitable Jewish firms. In German business parlance, the Jewish enterprises had now become *Objekte* ("objects"). Since it was not always easy to find an *Objekt,* the process of searching became a specialized business in itself. The institutions which specialized in this business were the banks. It was a lucrative activity. The banks collected threefold profits from the Aryanization transactions: (1) commissions (ca. 2 per cent of the sales price) for work done in bringing together buyers and sellers, (2) interest on loans extended to buyers, and (3) profits from subsequent business contracted between the bank and the Aryanized firm. (Such business usually derived from a provision in the contract between prospective buyer and bank, pursuant to which the buyer was to designate the bank as "principal banking connection" for his newly acquired firm.)[17] Moreover, the banks were not only agents — steering *Objekte* to interested buyers — they were buyers themselves, and they missed no opportunity to buy out a Jewish bank or some choice industrial shares. Every type of German business was in the scramble, but the banks were in the very midst of it.

Jewish casualties in the Aryanization boom were heavy, but by the beginning of 1938 there were signs of a general weakening in the German business sector. Jewish holdouts survived their own fears and German pressure. In May, 1938, an official of the Dresdner Bank complained that there were more Jewish enterprises than German buyers. It was especially difficult to find buyers for the large Jewish holdouts. In analyzing this reversal of the trend, the Dresdner Bank expert drew only one major conclusion: the price had to come down.[18]

To decrease the price of Jewish "objects," direct pressure was needed; in order to apply direct pressure upon Jewish enterprises, competition among buyers had to cease. In the words of an economic journal: "The temptation to swallow a formerly strong [Jewish] competitor, or even to snap such a delicious morsel from under the nose of another [German] competitor, must surely have led to overvaluation in many cases."[19] With the elimination of buyers' competition, the Jewish owner would face either one German negotiator or a united front.

The means by which such concerted action was brought about was the buyers' agreement, of which there were two types: one covered the purchase of one Jewish enterprise by several buyers acting together; the other provided for the allocation of several Jewish enterprises to specific buyers. The first type of agreement is exemplified by a contract concluded on November 30, 1937, by Mitteldeutsche Stahlwerke (Flick) and L. Possehl and Company, for the purchase of shares of the Jewish firm Rawack & Grünfeld on a fifty-fifty basis. The agreement provided that after the purchase and before January 1, 1943, neither party could dispose of its shares without the consent of the other. After January 1, 1943, neither party could dispose of its shares unless it offered half its package to the other party.[20] The Flick-

17. See report on Aryanizations by Böhmische Escompte Bank (Dresdner Bank subsidiary), signed by Kanzler and Stilz, August 6, 1941, NI-13463. For a "principal banking connection" clause, see contract between Böhmische and Oswald Pohl, October 5, 1940, NI-12319. The Böhmische, originally under Jewish control, had been Aryanized itself.

18. Memorandum by Dr. P. Binder, May 7, 1938, NI-6906.

19. *Der Volkswirt,* XII (September 9, 1938), 2409.

Possehl agreement is typical of the purchases of single Jewish firms.

When several parties were interested in several *Objekte*, it was customary to assign one *Objekt* to each purchaser. For example, on March 23, 1939, the Dresdner Bank, Deutsche Bank, and Kreditanstalt der Deutschen agreed to parcel out three Jewish-controlled banks: the Dresdner Bank was to acquire the Böhmische Escompte Bank; the Deutsche Bank was to purchase the Böhmische Union Bank; and the Kreditanstalt der Deutschen was to take over the Länderbank.[21] Both types of agreements were designed to deprive the Jewish owners of a chance to bargain. As a general rule, Jews affected by such agreements could sell at the buyer's price or not sell at all.

On April 26, 1938, the ministerial bureaucracy took another decisive step for the depression of price levels. Henceforth, a contract for the transfer of a business from a Jew to a German would require official approval.[22] A month after this decree was issued, Regierungsrat Dr. Gotthardt of the Economy Ministry explained to a Dresdner Bank official the purpose and effect of the measure. According to Gotthardt, purchasers had in the past paid not only for the plant value of an enterprise but also for such intangibles as "good will" (trademarks, reputation, sales contracts, and other factors enhancing the value). From now on, buyers were no longer to pay for "good will," because nowadays non-Aryan concerns *had no good will.* Furthermore, the German purchaser was to deduct from the purchase price such sums as he might have to pay *after* transfer for the unilateral breach of contracts, including employment contracts, contracts with Jewish wholesalers, etc. In general, therefore, the Economy Ministry would give its approval only to such contracts which provided for the payment of 66⅔ per cent to 75 per cent of the original value.[23]

The choice presented to the Jewish owners was now clear-cut: they could sell at prescribed terms, or they could wait for further developments. No Jew thought that further developments would ease the situation, but a few, owners of some of the most powerful firms, were ready to face the future.

In the central German coal belt which stretches into Czechoslovakia three Jewish families, in control of vast properties, were determined to hold out, come what might. These three families, who were unwilling to give up their holdings for any price in German currency, were the Rothschilds, the Weinmanns, and the Petscheks. The battle which they put up was not a Jewish battle; rather, there were three separate struggles waged for three separate interests in a vain attempt to live through, if not with, Nazism. The determination to resist the pressure of buyers was born of the conviction that the losses resulting from the clash would be smaller than the sacrifice that was inherent in the sale of the shares,

20. Agreement between Mittelstahl and Possehl, November 30, 1937, NI-1944.

21. Summary of bank discussion held on March 21, 1939, in the building of the Czech Ministry of Commerce (signed by Kiesewetter), March 23, 1939, NI-13394. The list of participants was as follows:

Dr. Köster, German Economy Ministry; Dr. Schickedanz, Office of the Reichskommissar in the Sudentenland; Dr. Rasche, Dresdner Bank; Freiherr von Lüdinghausen, Dresdner Bank; Dr. Rösler, Deutsche Bank; Pohle, Deutsche Bank; Osterwind, Deutsche Bank; Dr. Werner, Vereinigte Finanzkontore, Berlin; Kiesewetter, Kreditanstalt der Deutschen; Dr. Baumann, Kreditanstalt der Deutschen; Pulz, Kreditanstalt der Deutschen. The conference was held in Prague, barely a week after German troops had marched into the city. The Dresdner Bank had already swallowed its morsel.

22. Decree of April 26, 1938, RGBl I, 415.

23. Memorandum by Dr. P. Binder (Dresdner Bank) May 23, 1938, NI-6906.

for these Jews measured their resources not in the current market value of the stocks but in production statistics, plant capacity, ore and coal reserves. The Rothschilds, Weinmanns, and Petscheks were prepared to fight with weapons not available to poor Jews, weapons such as foreign holding corporations and the argument of "indispensability." The German side, on its part, was aware of the difficulties. The Germans knew that the Aryanization of these enterprises would require concentrated pressure and ruthless tactics unprecedented in the history of German business. This pressure and this ruthlessness were supplied, in part, by a unique industrial institution, the Hermann Göring Works.

The Göring Works were formed in the early days of the Nazi regime by Hermann Göring and a few of his ace troubleshooters as a Reich-owned enterprise. Göring acquired mines and land by a very simple method. He presented to practically every major steel producer an ultimatum to transfer some of its property to Göring.[24] He had a simple argument to justify this method: the Göring Works were operated not for profit, but in the "state-political interest" for the benefit of the Reich. Such persuasive arguments, when offered by the number-two man in Germany, proved to be irresistible. When Germany began to expand in 1938, the Göring Works naturally wanted to expand too. Its great opportunities were in the acquisition of major non-German enterprises in the new territories. It is, therefore, hardly surprising that Göring should have cast a longing eye on the properties of Messrs. Rothschild, Weinmann, and Petschek. He elected himself as chief Aryanizer of major Jewish concerns: "The Aryanization of all the larger establishments naturally is to be my lot."[25] Göring thus became the driving force behind the coalition of businessmen and ministerial officials who were sent, like infantry men, into the conference rooms to do battle with the Jews.

One of these battles had to be fought with the Rothschilds. The family was spread out in several countries. There was a Baron Rothschild in Vienna (Louis), another baron in Prague (Eugene), a third in Paris (Dr. Alphons). The Rothschild investments were similarly dispersed, for the family had been careful not to place all its eggs in one basket. In addition, the holdings were intertwined. Thus the Vienna Rothschild had interests in Czechoslovakia; the Prague Rothschild held properties in France; and so on. This setup gave the Rothschild family a certain resilience. One could not strike at the whole empire at once, and one could not attack any part of it without incurring the danger of countermeasures from other strongholds of the structure.

In Czechoslovakia, near Moravska Ostrava, the Rothschilds owned a major steel enterprise in which the Germans were interested: the Witkowitz Bergbau- und Eisenhütten Gewerkschaft. In February, 1937, more than two years *before* the fall of Czechoslovakia, the Rothschilds transferred ownership of the Witkowitz shares to the Alliance Assurance Company of London. Alliance Assurance in turn issued bearer certificates, expressed in units, which represented the actual participation in the capital of Witkowitz.[26] These units were owned by the Rothschilds and by a friendly group, the Gutmanns. This was the first move which was to make life difficult for the Nazis, for Alliance Assurance was a British firm, and the Rothschilds now

24. Memorandum by Flick (steel industrialist), December 5, 1939, NI-3338.

25. Göring in conference of November 12, 1938, PS-1816.

26. Affidavit by Leonard Keesing (Rothschild interests), March 19, 1948, NI-15625.

looked upon Witkowitz as British property. In March, 1938, the Germans marched into Austria. Two days after the Anschluss, the Vienna Rothschild (Baron Louis) was arrested.[27] This was the first move which was to make life difficult for the Rothschilds. Baron Louis was not released, and soon it became evident that he was being held as a hostage. His arrest was probably the first employment of the exit-visa method of Aryanization.

On December 29, 1938, the Länderbank Wien A. G. sent to the Reichswerke A. G. für Erzbergbau und Eisenhütten "Hermann Göring" an expert valuation report on Witkowitz. The valuation had been made on December 31, 1935, and the Länderbank pointed out that, in view of subsequent Czech currency devaluation as well as plant improvement, the present value was higher.[28] In February, 1939, a month before the invasion of Czechoslovakia, the Prague Rothschild (Eugene), who had in the meantime become a French citizen, went to London "to obtain support from the British government for the sale of Witkowitz to the Czechoslovak government."[29] A Czech negotiator, Dr. Preiss, who was president of the largest Czech financial institution, the Zivnostenska Banka (Zivno Bank), was also present. The negotiators discussed a tentative price of £10,000,000 in British currency.[30] (We might note in passing that this sum was identical to the amount promised by the British to the Czechoslovak government in compensation for the Munich agreement.) At any rate, in March the Germans occupied the rest of Czechoslovakia, including Witkowitz, and the negotiations fell through.

27. *Ibid.*

28. Länderbank Wien to Hermann Göring Works, attention Attorney Spick, December 29, 1938, NI-5697.

29. Affidavit by Keesing, March 19, 1948, NI-15625.

30. *Ibid.*

The next move was made by the Germans. Preparations were made to buy Witkowitz. On March 23, 1939, a week after the occupation of Czechoslovakia, the chief of the industrial division of the Economy Ministry, Kehrl, empowered Dr. Karl Rasche, a Vorstand member of the Dresdner Bank, and Dr. Jaroslav Preiss, president of the Zivno Bank and the very same man who had one month previously negotiated in behalf of the Czechoslovak government, to enter into negotiations with the Rothschilds for the purchase of the property in behalf of the Reich. In his authorization Kehrl mentioned that foreign exchange could be made available.[31]

On March 27, 1939, a German delegation arrived in Paris and met with the Rothschild group. The participating negotiators included the following representatives:[32]

German: Dr. Rasche (Dresdner Bank)
Prasident Preiss (Zivno Bank)
Direktor Wolzt (Vorstand member, Länderbank Wien)

Jewish: Baron Eugene Rothschild (Prague-Paris)
Baron Alphons Rothschild (Paris)
Baron Willi Gutmann
Direktor Keesing
Direktor Schnabel
Generaldirektor Federer (Chairman of the *Aufsichtsrat,* or Board of Directors, Witkowitz)

At the outset of the conference the German group made an offer. For the transfer of the Witkowitz interests, including the subsidiary Bergwerks Aktiebolaget Freja in Stockholm (iron mines, capitalization skr 2,600,000),[33] the Germans offered 1,341,000,000

31. Kehrl to Rasche, March 23, 1939, NI-13407.

32. The attendance list and the account of the meeting is taken from the German conference summary enclosed in a letter by Wolzt to Rasche, April 1, 1939, NI-14473.

Czech crowns. This sum was to be paid in Czech currency, except for a small part payable in foreign exchange.[34]

Before the collapse of Czechoslovakia, 1,341,000,000 Czech crowns had been worth approximately £10,000,000. But this was no longer true; the Czech currency, like Czechoslovakia itself, was imprisoned. Czech crowns were useless to the Rothschilds. Such a large amount of money could not be reinvested, nor could it be sold to anyone in England, the United States, Switzerland, etc., without great loss. The Rothschild group consequently rejected the offer, demanding instead the payment of £10,000,000 in sterling. The Rothschild-Gutmann representatives pointed out that the seller of the shares was a British corporation, namely, the Alliance Assurance Company. This British corporation, the Rothschilds explained, did not discriminate between the nationalities of the various owners. It paid dividends to all owners (holders of bearer certificates) in one currency, pounds sterling.[35]

The meeting was adjourned, and on the next day the negotiators met again. The second get-together was a little more explosive. The Germans learned for the first time that the far-flung Rothschild apparatus had gone into action. Various Witkowitz accounts deposited in Swiss, Dutch, and American banks had been attached – that is to say, court orders had been obtained to prevent the payment of money from such accounts, pending a clarification of legal rights. A credit of £200,000 to Freja had been blocked.

The Germans were indignant. Under the Reich currency laws, all *Inländer* ("resident nationals") had to offer their foreign holdings to the Reich in exchange for marks; the Rothschild move was a violation of the law which would bring penalties. Baron Eugene Rothschild (the Prague Rothschild) thereupon asked for a counteroffer. The Germans offered £2,750,000 in sterling. This was an offer which the Rothschilds could discuss, and after some haggling the price was upped to £3,600,000 in sterling; in other words, the Germans were to get Witkowitz and its Swedish subsidiary Freja, while the Rothschilds were to get a little over a third of the sterling they had asked for, and Baron Louis.

In order to ransom Baron Louis, part of the transfers had to be made *before* his release. Accordingly, the Rothschild machinery was set into motion with a flood of letters and telegrams to Kuhn, Loeb and Company, the Bank of Manhattan, Coha-Bank, Nederlandschen Handels Mij, Amstelbank, Blankart et Cie, and other financial institutions, to lift attachments and hold at the disposal of the Germans moneys and securities, on condition "that Louis Rothschild shall have freely left Germany over the Swiss or French frontier on or before May 4."[36] On the German side, Kehrl (Economy Ministry) sent letters to Rasche, authorizing him to negotiate with Baron Louis, and

33. Memorandum in files of Hermann Göring Works, March 31, 1944, NG-2887. Skr 2,600,000 equaled $628,000 or £113,000 at March, 1939, cable rates of exchange.

34. The Germans offered foreign currency to those owners who were considered foreigners under the Reich currency laws. The currency law of December 12, 1938, RGB1 I, 1734, defined a foreigner as a non-resident alien *or* emigrant who had assets in the Reich.

35. The availability of this currency derived from the sale by Witkowitz of virtually all its output – steel plates – to the British Navy. Memorandum by Regierungsbaurat Teuber, June 22, 1939, NI-9043.

36. See Dr. Karl von Lewinski (German attorney retained by the Rothschilds) to Regierungsrat Dr. Britsch ("trustee" in charge of Rothschild matters in the Economy Ministry), April 25, 1939, NI-15550. Also, Keesing (in Paris) to Bankhaus S. M. von Rothschild in Vienna (under German control), April 28, 1939, NI-15550.

to the Gestapo Office in Vienna, requesting permission for a meeting between Rasche and Rothschild.[37]

After the release of Louis Rothschild the Germans moved to complete arrangements for transfer. On June 15, 1939, a group of armament experts met to discuss the inclusion of Witkowitz into the Panzer program. Some of the participants expressed some doubts about entrusting armament secrets to Witkowitz. The Aryanization would have to be completed and the necessary personnel changes made from top to bottom before Witkowitz could be considered German.[38] A week later it turned out that Witkowitz expected to fulfil orders from the British Navy until the end of the year.[39]

In the meantime, however, Direktor Rasche of the Dresdner Bank was shuttling between Paris and Berlin to conclude the agreement.[40] In Prague the Czech financial authorities (Finance Minister Kalfus of the "autonomous" Czech administration) were protesting that the Germans planned to cover the purchase price with foreign currency belonging to the "Protektorat."[41] That is to say, Minister Kalfus had discovered that the Czechs were to pay for the enterprise.

In July, the final agreement was drawn up. The parties agreed to the transfer of 80 of the 100 bearer certificates for a price of £3,200,000. The vendor was entitled to offer, and the purchaser was obliged to accept, the remaining 20 shares at a price of £400,000. The profits of the business year 1938 were to be collected by the buyer.[42] These were the terms which, in substance, had been agreed upon in March. The contract was to enter into operation by the end of September.[43] This too had been agreed upon in March.[44] The Germans were happy. On July 13 the agreement was signed in Basel;[45] on August 2, Rasche sent a letter to Gruppenführer Wolff, chief of the Personal Staff of SS and Police Chief Himmler, in which the Dresdner Bank expressed its appreciation for the assistance rendered by the police (arrest of Baron Louis) in bringing down the price.[46] Then, suddenly, there was a snag.

On September 1, 1939, the war broke out, and the agreement could not enter into operation. According to the postwar account by Direktor Keesing, the Rothschilds' financial expert, the contract had purposely been drafted by the Rothschilds in such a way that transfer of title was not to take place until certain payments and conditions were satisfied. The object of these provisions, according to Keesing, was the frustration of the transfer upon the outbreak of the war.[47]

We do not know what was in the minds of the Rothschilds. We do not know whether this financial empire was endowed with prophetic insights which enabled it to predict accurately

37. Kehrl to Rasche, April 14, 1939, NI-13792. Kehrl to *Staatspolizeileitstelle* in Vienna, April 14, 1939, NI-13790.

38. Memorandum by Regierungsbaurat Teuber on conference of military armament officials under chairmanship of Oberstleutnant Nagel, June 15, 1939, NI-9043.

39. Memorandum by Teuber, June 22, 1939, NI-9043.

40. Summary of Dresdner Bank Vorstand meeting, Götz presiding, June 29, 1939, NI-1395. Also, Vorstand meeting of July 7, 1939, NI-15368.

41. Memorandum by Herbeck (Vorstand member, Dresdner Bank), June 23, 1939, NI-14474.

42. Text of contract (undated), in NI-15551.

43. Summary of Vorstand meeting, Dresdner Bank, July 7, 1939, NI-15368.

44. See memorandum on Paris conference, April 1, 1939, NI-14473.

45. Herbeck to Rasche, July 13, 1939, NI-15547.

46. Rasche to Wolff, August 2, 1939, NI-13669.

47. Affidavit by Leonard Keesing, March 19, 1948, NI-15625.

the time when war was to start. We *do* know that the transaction was a painful one for the Rothschilds, and it is therefore likely that, in their choice between relinquishment of title for 36 per cent of just compensation and retention of title in the hope that after the destruction of the Hitler regime possession would be regained, the Rothschilds oscillated from one alternative to the other until war made the decision for them. Thus, in September, 1939, the owners of the Witkowitz Works leaned back to find out who would last longer, the Nazi regime or the Rothschilds. But the waiting was not a very tranquil and peaceful proposition.

In November, 1939, the Germans attempted to secure the shares of the Freja Works by an action in a Swedish court. They failed.[48] In January, 1940, the Witkowitz Works, now no longer producing for the British Navy, were placed under the "supervision" of a board consisting of the following members:[49]

Dr. Delius, Hermann Göring Works
Karl Hermann Frank, Staatssekretär, Protektorat Administration
Generaldirektor Pleiger, Hermann Göring Works
Generaldirektor Raabe, Hermann Göring Works
Dr. Rasche, Dresdner Bank
Dr. Rheinländer Reichsstelle für Wirtschaftsausbau (Construction Planning Office, Four-Year Plan)
Generalmajor Weigand, Armament Inspectorate, Prague

Göring was now in the saddle. However, the Germans still wanted to make an agreement. The Witkowitz Works were English, and the Germans, though at war, still expected to come to terms with England. In short, physical possession did not solve the problem for them. Accordingly, in March, 1940, Dr. Rasche wrote to the president of the Swedish subsidiary Freja, Mr. Sune Wetter, suggesting new negotiations.[50] In April, Rasche went to Stockholm to threaten drastic measures. If the Rothschilds were not prepared to negotiate on neutral soil, the Witkowitz Works would be "leased" to a German concern (Hermann Göring Works), to be run for the latter's account. Thus the owners would be deprived of all war profits, and, in addition, claims against Freja would be instituted, this time "in a different direction."[51] But the Rothschilds were not prepared to negotiate. Then, in June, 1940, France fell.

On the day of the armistice, the Dresdner Bank asked the High Command of the Army for a special pass to enable Rasche to travel to France. Reason: there was a rumor that the Freja stocks were located somewhere in Paris and could be seized.[52] The shares were, in fact, located in the Paris Rothschild bank.[53] The Rothschilds began to weaken. England was fighting a single-handed battle against Germany and Italy; the Nazi regime seemed more secure than it had been at any time, since it had, so far, met the test of war and emerged victorious everywhere.

In December, 1940, the Foreign Division of the Reichsbank called the chairman of the Vorstand of the Dresdner Bank, Götz, to report that an American bank had inquired, on be-

48. Affidavit by Leo F. Spitzer (General Counsel, Witkowitzer Bergbau), October 15, 1948, NI-15678.

49. Order by the *Reichsprotektor* in Prague (von Neurath), January 15, 1940, NI-15347.

50. Rasche to Sune Wetter, March 11, 1940, NI-13654.

51. Sune Wetter (Stockholm) to Oskar Federer (London), April 6, 1940, NI-13637.

52. G. Stiller (Secretariat, Dr. Rasche) to *Generalquartiermeister/Passierscheinhauptstelle* ("General Quartermaster/Main Pass Section"), June 24, 1940, NI-1853.

53. File note, Dresdner Bank, July 2, 1940, NI-1832.

half of the Rothschilds, whether the Germans were interested in a resumption of negotiations about Witkowitz.[54] Rasche was a bit surprised that the Rothschilds took this step. He was no longer so eager for negotiations, but he suggested that talks be held in Spain.[55] These discussions apparently did not take place either, but, for the moment, neither side made an aggressive move. As late as June, 1941, the Freja Works made regular shipments of iron ore to Witkowitz, as though there were no expropriations and no war.[56]

Early in 1941 a grotesque incident occurred. We may recall that there were 100 bearer certificates signifying ownership of the British corporation which, in turn, owned the Witkowitz shares. These Witkowitz shares numbered 223,312.[57] Fourteen thousand had been handed over to the Germans as part of the ransom arrangement for Louis Rothschild's release; 43,300 (a considerable parcel) had been left behind in Paris when Baron Eugene fled from the Germans. These shares were lying in a depot at Nevers, guarded by a French official (Jannicot, Director, Administration of Property and General Revenue Office, Department Seine) and a Rothschild representative. On January 8, 1941, a group of Germans (the *Devisenschutzkommando*, or "Currency Squad") arrived at the depot, shoved the Frenchmen aside physically, and removed the shares. The Vichy government, considerably annoyed, countered this move by sequestering (blocking with a view to confiscation) all Rothschild properties in France.[58] The Germans retreated, offering to purchase the shares for a suitable sum.[59] (This was part of a plan to get hold of a majority, or all, of the 223,000 shares; however, the scheme was not very practical, because only the 43,300 shares discovered in Paris were actually "within reach" [*greifbar*].)[60]

As a result, the Göring Works continued in possession of the enterprise without owning it. In a memorandum dated March 31, 1944, the Witkowitz Works are listed as part of the Göring complex with the notation: "no capital participation – operational connection only."[61] Notwithstanding the fact that the connection was "operational" only, the Göring Works pocketed the profits, which amounted during the business year 1941 to 2,400,000 reichsmark.[62] And that is the history of the Witkowitz "Aryanization."

We can see now the advance of techniques which marks the pre-Rothschild and Rothschild phases of "voluntary" Aryanizations. The pre-Rothschild arsenal contained the following principal weapons: (1) boycott, (2) allocation control, (3) buyers' agreements, (4) elimination of "good will" by decree. The Witkowitz Aryanization reveals, in addition, the following methods: (5) negotiation by plenipotentiary (Dresdner Bank), (6)

54. Götz to Rasche, December 21, 1940, NI-13292.

55. Rasche to Götz, December 28, 1940, NI-13292.

56. G. Stiller (Secretariat, Dr. Rasche) to Assessor Zöppke (Legal Division, Foreign Office), June 21, 1941, NI-1557.

57. Note by Stiller, February 3, 1943, NI-2643.

58. Affidavit by Yvonne Delree Kandelafte, March 19, 1948, NI-15552. Affiant was private secretary to Baron Eugene. Jannicot to Director General for Registration, Administration of Property, and Revenue (Vichy), January 11, 1941, NI-15537.

59. Marotzke (Office of the Four-Year Plan) to *Militärbefehlshaber Frankreich/Verwaltungsstab* ("Military Commander France/-Administration"), copy to Dr. Rasche, November 6, 1941, NI-2647.

60. Note by Stiller, February 3, 1943, NI-2643.

61. Reichswerke Hermann Göring/Montanblock to Economy Ministry/Main Division III/Division 5 – Foreign Currency, March 31, 1944, NG-2887.

62. Pleiger to Göring, December 5, 1941, NI-15575.

exit-visa restriction, (7) attempted stealing of shares, (8) operation of the enterprise and collection of the profits.

The Rothschild case, however, is not the best example of the effectiveness of German operative techniques. For practical purposes Göring had accomplished his aim, but he did fail to complete the transaction. There was no final transfer, and Witkowitz was not entered in the books as a German plant. Undoubtedly, this reluctance is traceable only to the fact that the Rothschilds had succeeded in making Witkowitz an English enterprise. The British flag stopped the Germans from installing themselves as the new owners of the firm.

In the cases of Weinmann and Petschek the transfer was completed. Extraordinary pressure had to be applied against both of these families; the Reich itself finally stepped in, confiscated the enterprises, and sold them at a profit to the interested buyers. Yet it must be emphasized that these "confiscations" were not part of any general confiscatory process. They were entirely individual measures which were taken only after the German negotiators, using all their tools and all their tricks, had gotten nowhere. In short, these "confiscations" were imposed as a sort of penalty for the obstinancy and the unco-operative attitude of the Jewish owners. The "provocations" in each case were not identical – the Weinmanns petitioned, the Petscheks defied. But their fate in the end was the same. Survival in Nazi Germany could not be assured by insisting upon one's rights.

The party most interested in the Weinmann and Petschek properties was the same which had acquired Witkowitz: the Hermann Göring Works. The Göring Works were originally and primarily a coal and steel concern. (These two branches could often be found in the same German enterprise. Steel corporations were always on the lookout for a "coal base"; that is, they were interested in the acquisition of sufficient coal mines to assure a dependable supply for the manufacture of steel.) Since the Göring Works were operated in the "state-political interest," it was not difficult for Göring to obtain Economy Minister Funk's agreement that all soft coal mines in the Sudeten area (annexed from Czechoslovakia in October, 1938) should belong to his concern.[63]

To integrate the Sudeten coal mines into the Göring enterprise, a new corporation, the Sudetenländische Bergbau A. G., Brüx (abbreviated Subag), was formed on June 10, 1939. Significantly, the first meeting of this Göring subsidiary was held, not in the Sudetenland in Brüx, but in Berlin in the offices of the Dresdner Bank.[64] The reason for this location was obvious. The properties of the Subag had not yet been acquired. The Aryanization still had to be carried out by the Dresdner Bank. The mines in question were still owned by the Weinmann and Petschek families.

The smaller, but older, of the two concerns were the Weinmann enterprises, with headquarters in Aussig, Sudetenland. The value of these enterprises was a subject of dispute from the beginning. Table 17 shows the discrepancy of the estimates.[65] It will be

63. Funk to Staatssekretär Körner, April 13, 1939, NI-12512.

64. Minutes of first Aufsichtsrat meeting, June 10, 1939, NI-13910. Generaldirektor Pleiger was elected chairman; other members were Unterstaatssekretär von Hannecken (Economy Ministry), Ing. Wolfgang Richter, Kehrl (Economy Ministry – Industry), Gabel (Economy Ministry – Mines), Ministerialrat Mundt, Dr. Rasche, Delius (Göring Works), and Ing. Nathow. For articles of incorporation, dated June 12, 1939, see NI-13641.

65. Dresdner Bank to Ministerialdirigent Nasse (Finance Ministry), listing par value of the stocks, February 10, 1939, NI-13719. Finance Ministry memorandum, listing per-

TABLE 17 / *The Weinmann Enterprises*
(*Values in Thousands*)

Enterprise	Par Value of Stocks Held by Weinmanns		Weinmann Estimate of Market Value		German Estimate of Market Value	
	Crowns	Dollars	Crowns	Dollars	Crowns	Dollars
Brucher Kohlenwerke A. G. (100 per cent Weinmann)	100,000	3,500	100,000–119,000	3,500–4,165	40,000–50,000	1,400–1,750
Westböhmischer Bergbau Aktienverein (40 per cent Weinmann)	50,000	1,750	60,000–70,000	2,100–2,450	42,500	1,477.5
Total	150,000	5,250	160,000–189,000	5,600–6,615	83,000–92,500	2,900–3,877.5

noted that the Germans offered only about half the amount wanted by the Weinmanns. The reason for that rather low valuation was to be found in the fact that the principal Weinmann enterprise, the Brucher Kohlenwerke, had for ten years been operated at a loss.[66] There are various ways of figuring out the value of a corporation. One method is to estimate plant value and "good will" (marketability of the product). That is evidently what the Weinmanns did. Another method is to project past earnings (or losses) into the future, measuring the value in terms of such past performance. That is what the Germans did.

There was another difficulty which was even more important: the problem of foreign exchange. If the Germans had at least made their offer in pounds or dollars, the Weinmanns might have been happy. But the offer was made in a captive currency, Czech crowns. The Weinmanns had neglected to do what the Rothschild family had done. They had not established a British, Swiss, or American corporation to hold their property; in fact, during the summer of 1938, *before* the German invasion of Czechoslovakia, the Weinmann financial expert, Geiringer, had given assurances to Sudeten German interests that the enterprises would not be sold to the Czechs for foreign exchange or anything else.[67] The Weinmanns had taken only one precautionary measure. In 1936, they had made a loan to the Czech government which was repayable in foreign currency.[68] However, in March, 1939, there was no longer a Czech government and, so far as the Germans were concerned, there was no longer a Czech state. The loan served only to excite German interest about the question of where the foreign currency which the Czech government had promised might come from. For that reason and also because no agreement had been reached on the Aryanization of the Weinmann holdings, one of the Weinmanns (Hans), caught by the invasion in Prague, was not allowed to leave. Unlike Louis Rothschild, he was free, but to "guarantee readiness to negotiate [*Kaution für Verhandlungsbereitschaft*]" he was not given a passport.[69]

To get Hans Weinmann out of Prague, Fritz Weinmann (in Paris) paid 20,000 Swiss francs for "a real passport." Then Hans Weinmann suddenly took off surreptitiously, without any passport. When Rasche and Ansmann, the two Dresdner Bank Aryanization experts, arrived in Paris on May 25, 1939, to discuss with Fritz Weinmann and his finance expert Dr. Geiringer the purchase of the enterprises, Fritz started the discussion by demanding his 20,000 francs back.[70] Apparently encouraged by Hans' escape, Fritz Weinmann then demanded payment for his mines in foreign currency. To back his claim, he recited the following

centage interests, February 17, 1939, NI-15635. Memorandum by Ansmann (Aryanization expert, Dresdner Bank), discussing differences of estimates, April 18, 1939, NI-15607.

According to the financial expert of the Weinmann group, Geiringer, the value of the Weinmann holdings in 1938 was between 200 and 250 million crowns, or $7,000,000 to $8,750,000 at the March, 1938, rate of exchange. Affidavit by Ernest Geiringer, October 15, 1948, NI-15679. Geiringer was a director of the Österreichische Kreditanstalt, Vienna.

66. Memorandum by Ansmann, April 19, 1939, NI-15607.

67. Reinhold Freiherr von Lüdinghausen (industrialist of the Sudeten area) to Rasche, enclosing summary of a conference attended by Sudeten German bankers and industrialists, July 28, 1938, NI-13399.

68. Affidavit by Geiringer, October 15, 1948, NI-15679.

69. Memorandum by Ansmann, April 18, 1939, NI-15607.

70. Summary of Weinmann conference prepared by the German negotiators, May 26, 1939, NI-15629.

reasons: First, he was entitled to foreign exchange because he had rendered important services to the German people (*das Deutschtum*). With what seemed to the Germans "unheard-of impudence," he then "began to discuss National Socialism, whose principles he had espoused even before Hitler [*In ungewöhnlich frecher Weise zog er dann über den Nationalsozialismus her, dessen Grundsätze er schon vor Hitler vertreten habe*]." The mining headquarters of "Aussig would simply be inconceivable without him, then or now [*Aussig sei weder früher noch jetzt ohne ihn denkbar*]." Finally, Weinmann reminded the Germans that in 1938 he had not sold his property to the Czechs because the local Sudeten German interests had not wanted him to. This could be proved by such leading Sudeten personalities as Richter, Schickedanz, Henlein, and last, but not least, Göring himself.

The Fritz Weinmann speech did not have the intended effect upon the Germans. The Dresdner Bank officials were annoyed. Rasche and Ansmann pointed out that their understanding of Weinmann's services was quite different, and they reiterated that his solution to the payment problem (foreign exchange) was "utterly out of the question." The German negotiators then declared that the illegal emigration of Hans had created a new situation; the entire Weinmann property might now be confiscated.

Fritz Weinmann thereupon played his last card. There were some exports by a company in which he had a financial interest; the foreign exchange received from the sale of these exports, he promised, would never find its way back to Germany. This was a weak defense, and the conference broke up. Weinmann had lost.

In September, 1939, the Economy Ministry ordered the sale of the Weinmann enterprises for the benefit of the Reich.[71] In October the Dresdner Bank was busy collecting the shares deposited in various banks.[72] Gradually, the Hermann Göring Works – through its subsidiary, the Subag – moved in. The Finance Ministry was not altogether happy with the sale of the Weinmann holdings to the Göring Works because the Subag paid only about 60 per cent of the value, as determined by the Economy Ministry's experts.[73] It is true that the Göring Works were "Reich-owned"; nevertheless, they were financially autonomous. What Göring retained for his enterprises, the Reich could not use in its budget. In other words, Göring had cheated the Reich out of 40 per cent.

What had brought about this rapid development, in which the Weinmanns lost not only the physical possession of their enterprises but their claim to ownership as well? The Weinmanns were completely subservient. Fritz Weinmann claimed that he was indispensable. He did not hesitate to call himself a Nazi. Of course, we would be very much mistaken to take these petitions literally. Fritz Weinmann was no more a Nazi than he was indispensable; he was merely acting out an ancient Jewish reaction pattern, and he was doing it more fervently than his Jewish colleagues.

In 1941 the Weinmann family came to the United States. Fritz Weinmann became Frederick Wyman. Hans remained Hans, but his son Charles "soon became a part of the American industrial pattern." In an account printed by the *New York Times* on January 4, 1953, there is no mention of the fact that the Weinmanns were

71. Memorandum dated September 21, 1939, in files of Westböhmische Bergbau Aktien-Verein, NI-15623.

72. Dresdner Bank to Economy Ministry/Division II, attention Assessor Scheidemann, October 16, 1939, NI-15624.

73. Memorandum by Finance Ministry, March, 1941, NI-15638.

Jews whose property had been Aryanized. Instead, the impression is created that they lost their mines because they lent financial support to the Czech government. In fact, the article does not mention the word "Jew." It does mention that Charles Wyman, the son of Hans, was already a member of various firms and that he was "also a leader in the Unitarian Church." The article goes on: "How well the Wymans have fitted into the American pattern is probably best illustrated by the names Charles and his wife, Olga, gave their three children. They are John Howard, Thomas Michael and Virginia Ann."[74] That indeed is adaptability.

The Dresdner Bank and the Economy Ministry responded to the Weinmann approach quickly and decisively. The petitioning by Fritz Weinmann merely smoothed the way to complete confiscation, for in the German mind the Weinmann appeal was construed not as subservience (which it was) but as mockery (which it was not intended to be). The idea that a Jew should be indispensable or that he might even hold National Socialist ideas could only be treated as an insult, for if it were otherwise, the entire rationale of the destruction process would collapse.

The last of the Aryanization histories to discuss is that of the Petschek enterprises. The Petschek properties were owned by two families: the sons of Julius Petschek and the sons of Ignaz Petschek. Both families operated coal mines in Germany and Czechoslovakia. (A list of these holdings may be found in Table 18.)[75]

The Aryanization of the Petschek "complex" was entrusted to two negotiators, Friedrich Flick's Central Steel Works (*Mittelstahl*) and the Dresdner Bank. The division of work was territorial. Friedrich Flick was impowered to negotiate for the transfer of the Julius and Ignaz Petschek properties in Germany; the Dresdner Bank was the plenipotentiary for mines in Czechoslovakia.[76] This division reflects a certain preference for "territorial solutions." The central German mines had to be Aryanized first.

The two Petschek groups, for their part, were not united. They competed with "and even opposed" each other.[77] When the threat of Aryanization confronted the two families, they reacted in contrasting patterns.

The Julius Petscheks were in an excellent bargaining position. They had created a British dummy corporation which, in turn, was controlled by an American dummy. The entire setup was "obscure" to the Germans. It seemed to the Flick negotiators that the Julius Petscheks had actually *sold* the mines to foreign interests but that the Petschek group had retained an option to repurchase. At any rate, nothing could be proved.[78] Then, suddenly,

74. Robert H. Fetridge, "Along the Highways and Byways of Finance," *New York Times*, January 4, 1953, p. F3.

75. German holdings of both Petschek groups listed in Finance Ministry memorandum, September 26, 1938, NG-4034. Value of Julius Petschek German holdings in Finance Ministry report of October 26, 1938, NG-4033. Value of Ignaz Petschek German holdings in conference summary (signed Wohlthat), August 2, 1938, NG-2398. Czech holdings of Julius Petschek group listed in Finance Ministry memorandum, September 26, 1938, NG-4034. Value of Julius Petschek Czech holdings in Finance Ministry memorandum, February 17, 1939, NI-15635. Ignaz Petschek Czech holdings and their value in letter by Dresdner Bank to Ministerialdirigent Nasse, February 25, 1939, NI-13719. The lists and figures do *not* include many minor holdings.

76. Göring to Flick, February 1, 1938, NI-899. Dresdner Bank to Ministerialdirigent Nasse, February 10, 1939, NI-13719. Gerischtsassessor Dr. Hahn (Office of the Four-Year Plan) to *Oberfinanzpräsident* in Berlin, attention Regierungsrat Dr. Müller, and Ministerialrat Gebhardt (Finance Ministry), February 10, 1939, NI-10086.

77. Memorandum by Finance Ministry, September 26, 1938, NG-4034.

without giving the Germans time to become organized, the Julius Petschek group offered to sell out. The Petscheks explained that they wanted to dissolve their interests in Germany; hence, they would accept only foreign exchange. To back up their claim, they pointed to immunity from Aryanization by reason of their foreign arrangements.[79] cate formed by Winterschall A. G., I. G., Farben, and Flick's own Mitteldeutsche Stahlwerke took over the Julius Petschek German mines. The syndicate was represented by Flick; Petschek was represented by the United Continental Corporation, New York. Under the terms of the contract, the purchasers acquired 24,000,000

TABLE 18 / *The Petschek Enterprises*

Julius Petschek (headquarters in Prague)	Germany: Anhaltische Kohlenwerke A. G., Halle; Werschen-Weissenfelder Braunkohlen A. G., Halle	RM $	24,012,000 9,604,800
	Czechoslovakia (Sudeten): Nordböhmische Kohlenwerke A. G., Brüx; Brüxer Kohlen-Bergbau Gesellschaft	Cr. $	200–243 mill. 7 mill.–8,505,000
Ignaz Petschek (headquarters in Aussig)	Germany: Öhriger Bergbau A. G.; Preussengrube A. G.; Niederlausitzer Kohlenwerke A. G.; Hubertus Braunkohle A. G.; "Ilse" Bergbau A. G.; "Eintracht" A. G.; Etc.	RM $	200,000,000 80,000,000
	Czechoslovakia (Sudeten): Britannia A. G., Falkenau; Vereinigte Britannia A. G., Seestadt; (Majority of) Duxer Kohlengesellschaft A. G., Teplitz-Schönau	Cr. $	36,700,000 1,286,500

Flick speculated that the Petscheks feared war or a similar catastrophe,[80] but he acted quickly. "By order of Generalfeldmarschall Göring," a syndi- reichsmark worth of stock for 11,718,250 reichsmark. However, payment was made in foreign exchange, which was made available by the Economy Ministry "at the express wish of Generalfeldmarschall Göring." The dollar price was $4,750,000. The contract was signed on May 21, 1938.[81]

78. Memorandum by Steinbrinck (Flick representative), January 10, 1938, NI-3254.

79. Memorandum by Steinbrinck, January 10, 1938, NI-3254.

80. Memorandum by Flick, January 19, 1938, NI-784.

81. Memorandum by Finance Ministry, September 26, 1938, NG-4034. Report by

After this fast work, the Dresdner Bank had no trouble with the Julius Petschek enterprises in the Sudetenland. Less than a year later the Dresdner Bank, acting on behalf of the Reich, had acquired the mines, which were worth 200–243 million crowns, for 70 million crowns (Czech currency) plus coal deliveries. Only the money had to be paid immediately; the deliveries were to be spaced over a period of five years. Präsident Kehrl of the Economy Ministry was overjoyed with the transaction ("extraordinarily satisfactory and advantageous"). He thought that the Reich could always get rid of the property for double the purchase price.[82] But when the Dresdner Bank presented its bill for its troubles, the faces of the Reich officials fell. The commission was 4 per cent instead of the usual 2 per cent. Since the Dresdner Bank had advanced its own funds to make the purchase, the Reich also had to pay interest at 6½ per cent. After a dispute with the Finance Ministry it was agreed that in future deals the commission would be 2 per cent and the interest 5½ per cent.[83] Moreover, there was no 100 per cent profit in the sale of the mines because the purchaser of the Julius Petschek Sudeten properties was of course the Subag, Hermann Göring subsidiary.[84]

Although the Julius Petscheks had rid themselves of their mines only at great loss, they had moved quickly and adroitly. Behind their demands they had employed just the right amount of pressure. That is why they were remarkably successful in comparison with other Jewish negotiators. The Germans realized this fact and regretted it as soon as the Ignaz Petschek Aryanizations had run their course.

Unlike their cousins, the sons of Ignaz Petschek decided to hold on to their property. This decision was, for the Germans, a very serious matter because the Petschek mines were a major part of the central German coal industry. In the beginning of January, 1938, Göring set up a commission for "the solution of the Petschek problem." The commission had the following members:[85]

Staatssekretär Posse, Economy Ministry
Staatssekretär Keppler, Office of the Four-Year Plan
Staatssekretär Pleiger, Hermann Göring Works
Flick, in his capacity as industrial expert
Sauckel, as the local *Gauleiter*

Flick was to be the principal negotiator. This choice is of interest for two reasons: In the first place, Flick was not a disinterested expert; he was the biggest industrialist in the area, and he had a personal stake in the outcome of the discussions. (As we have seen, Flick was to profit from the Aryanization of the *Julius* Petschek parcel.)

Flick is interesting also because he was no stranger to the Petscheks and the Petscheks were not strangers to him. Like Flick, old Ignaz Petschek was a self-made man. Starting as a *Prokurist* (assistant to a director with power to represent the firm) in the Weinmann enterprises, Ignaz had become independent and had acquired one mine after another. Friedrich Flick had served in an *Aufsichtsrat* of a Petschek company. Later he was to

Oberregierungsrat Dr. Müller and Tax Inspector Krause to *Oberfinanzpräsident* in Berlin, October 26, 1938, NG-4033.

82. Finance Ministry memorandum, February 17, 1939, NI-15635.

83. Finance Ministry memorandum, March 13, 1939, NI-15637. In 1940, the Dresdner Bank offered to accept a lump sum for services rendered in the Weinmann and Petschek Aryanizations in the amount of 300,000 reichsmark. Dresdner Bank (signed Andre and Rasche) to the Vorstand of the Subag, July 16, 1940, NI-15665.

84. Dresdner Bank to Ministerialrat Gebhardt (Finance Ministry), March 30, 1940, NI-14756.

85. Memorandum by Steinbrinck, January 5, 1938, NI-3252.

head his own industrial empire, the Mitteldeutsche Stahlwerke. Flick and Petschek remained in touch with each other, and just before Ignaz Petschek's death in 1934, Flick sent him birthday greetings on the occasion of his seventy-fifth birthday. "I was on most friendly terms with old Ignaz Petschek at all times," said Flick after the war.[86]

How could a man function properly on behalf of the Reich if he had such interest in the Petschek property and such relations with the Petschek family? So far as Flick's desire for personal acquisition was concerned, Göring was confident that he could deal with any competitor by invoking the Reich interest. As we shall see, this calculation proved correct. The personal relations between Flick and the Petschek family were to prove no obstacle to the Aryanization. Even in its early days the destruction process was a powerful transformer of relationships and attitudes.

On January 10, 1938, Flick's deputy, Steinbrinck, wrote a memorandum in which he noted that the Ignaz Petschek group was not willing to sell its property or to exchange the mines for other holdings. In view of that situation, "one would have to consider the possible employment of force or Reich intervention [*muss man gegebenenfalls Gewaltmassnahmen oder staatliche Eingriffe ins Auge fassen*]."[87]

This remark is significant. One rarely finds such a naked expression of Nazi philosophy, even in secret documents. In this case, the remark is doubly significant, for in the same memorandum there is a clear implication that, even if the Petscheks were willing to sell out for reichsmark, there would not be enough capital to pay for the property. Four interested parties – namely, I. G. Farben, the Vereinigte Stahlwerke, the Hermann Göring Works, and the Dresdner Bank – were ready to invest less than half the funds necessary to pay for the Petschek stocks at *par* value.[88]

In the meantime, the Ignaz Petscheks were beginning to set up dummy corporations in Switzerland and Holland.[89] No time could be lost, for with the passage of the months the Ignaz Petscheks would scatter their holdings among foreign corporations, a process which the Germans called *Einneblung*, or "fogging in." On January 19, 1938, the leader of the Ignaz Petschek group, Karl, was summoned to the Economy Ministry, where he declared to Staatssekretär Posse and the assembled German officials: "You want war, gentlemen; I am prepared."[90]

The Germans looked for a way to open the attack. In June a Flick lawyer submitted a memorandum on possible legal action against the Petscheks. There was no possibility for such action, complained the lawyer, for there was no law compelling a Jew to sell his property. And he enclosed a draft of such a law as his only solution.[91] Then in July things began to move.

On July 22, an interministerial conference was called to discuss the Petschek problem – the only such conference concerned with a single Jewish family of which we have a record.[92] The following officials participated:

Ministerialdirektor Wohlthat (Chairman), Office of Four-Year Plan

86. Testimony by Flick, Case No. 5, tr. p. 3242.

87. Memorandum by Steinbrinck, January 10, 1938, NI-3254.

88. *Ibid.*

89. *Ibid.*

90. File note by Steinbrinck, January 19, 1938, NI-3249.

91. Dr. Hugo Dietrich to Direktor Steinbrinck, June 20, 1938, NI-898.

92. Summary of Petschek conference (signed Wohlthat), August 2. 1938, NG-2398. The office of the *Oberfinanzpräsident* in Berlin was a regional office of the Finance Ministry. The *Reichskommissar* for Coal was an agency of the Office of the Four-Year Plan.

Gerichtsassessor Dr. Hahn, Office of Four-Year Plan
Oberregierungsrat Dr. Müller, *Oberfinanzpräsident*, Berlin
Steuerinspektor Krause, *Oberfinanzpräsident*, Berlin
Legationsrat Altenburg, Foreign Office
Konsul Dr. Kalisch, Foreign Office
Oberregierungsrat Dr. Gotthardt, Economy Ministry
Bergrat Ebert, Economy Ministry
Dr. Lintl, *Reichskommissar* for Coal
Amtsgerichtsrat Herbig, Justice Ministry

Wohlthat opened the discussion by pointing out that Göring had ordered the Aryanization of the Ignaz Petschek properties in Germany. The value of these properties was 200,000,000 reichsmark. The representative of the Justice Ministry explained that there was no basis for legal action under any anti-Jewish decrees; then, as the conference went on, the representatives of the ministries all agreed that funds for the purchase of the property were simply not available. The representative of the Coal Commissar stressed the importance of the Petschek coal for the economy. He wanted immediate Aryanization. Everyone agreed, however, that no measures could be taken that would throttle production in the Petschek coal mines. The Finance Ministry offered a partial solution: one could always claim taxes. In fact, research had already disclosed that the Petscheks owed 30,000,000 reichsmark to the Reich. The conferees then considered alternate solutions: replacement of Jewish directors in subsidiaries of the Petschek combine on the ground that the Jews were a danger to the community, dissolution of the Petschek-controlled East Elbian Lignite Syndicate (wholesale trade organizations), etc.

The tax claims proved to be the lever which toppled the Petschek empire. In October, 1938, the Germans, marching into the Czechoslovak Sudetenland, took possession of the Ignaz Petschek headquarters in Aussig, with a view to discovering further tax delinquencies. Matters were going so well that in a conference of Finance, Economy, and Mittelstahl officials Steinbrinck advised the suspension of negotiations on the ground that "the Petscheks were not yet soft enough [*Die Petscheks seien noch nicht weich genug*]."[93] From the government of the short-lived, amputated Czech state (October, 1938, to March, 1939), help came in response to a German request. Czech Foreign Minister Chvalkowski declared his readiness to co-operate in the investigation in every respect, "since the Czech state too had been defrauded by the Petscheks."[94]

By June, 1939, the Finance Ministry had increased its claim from 30,000,000 marks to 300,000,000 marks. The entire Petschek property in Germany would now be insufficient to pay the taxes claimed by the Reich.[95] The Finance Ministry was jubilant. On June 26 the Finance Ministry's Ministerialrat Gebhardt stated that his Ministry's position was now "stronger than ever." Speaking to Steinbrinck, Gebhardt called it "unshakable." In other words, after all the troubles with plenipotentiaries and committees, the Finance Ministry had done the job singlehandedly. Gebhardt's happiness was clouded by only one thought; it was unfortunate, he said, that the Reich had made a deal with the *Julius* Petschek group so hastily. Undoubted-

93. Hahn to Oberregierungsrat Müller and Ministerialrat Gebhardt, February 10, 1939, NI-10086. During the same meeting Dr. Rasche of the Dresdner Bank made an attempt to take over the functions of the Finance Ministry by offering to negotiate the tax claims with the Petscheks. Gebhardt declined on the ground that such an arrangement would bring the other great banks into "ill humor." *Ibid.*

94. *Ibid.*

95. File note by Steinbrinck, June 12, 1939, NI-3364.

ly, that concern had also engaged in "irregular business activities."[96]

The Ignaz Petschek enterprises were now sold by the Reich for whatever the traffic would bear. The central German mines were taken over by Göring and Flick, but only after a nasty swap of mines between the Göring Works and Mittelstahl, under the terms of which the *Reichsmarschall* received the decidedly better bargain in the "state-political interest."[97]

The Czech mines, captured in the meantime by the Dresdner Bank without any difficulty at all, were transferred to an *Auffanggesellschaft,* that is to say, a company formed for the explicit purpose of taking over Aryanized property. The company in question, the Egerländer Bergbau A. G., was Reich-owned because the Czech mines too had been confiscated by the Reich in partial satisfaction of the tax claim. However, the Egerländer Bergbau was sold to private interests controlled by the industrial family Seebohm.[98]

The fate of the Ignaz Petscheks was the same as the fate of the Weinmanns, and this was true even though the Weinmanns had argued and petitioned, while Karl Petschek had "declared war." The answer to the riddle is that both the Weinmanns and the Petscheks were pursuing strategies which led inevitably to a showdown. In the final encounter, neither family could defend itself. The Weinmanns were playing a very old game, and their performance was not unskilful. But they were maneuvering without a base. The Ignaz Petschek group stood fast, since they were literally too big for bargaining. Their battle, however, was inevitably lost, for they were fighting alone against the total power of the German state.

The "penalty" confiscations of the Weinmann and Ignaz Petschek enterprises mark the close of the "voluntary" Aryanizations. Of course, "voluntary" in this connection means only that the Weinmanns and the Petscheks still had an opportunity to bargain with the Germans. So long as such an opportunity existed – no matter how adverse the conditions and how strong the pressure – the process was considered a voluntary one. The involuntary or forced Aryanization (*Zwangsarisierung* or *Zwangsentjudungsverfahren*) was characterized by the complete absence of a Jewish negotiator. In such a proceeding the Jewish owner was represented by a "trustee"; i.e., both parties in the negotiations were German.

There were two reasons for the introduction of the involuntary scheme of Aryanizations. One was the impatience of the ministries. With compulsory procedures, the process could be speeded up, termination dates could be set, and the over-all completion of the transfers could be envisaged within those time limits. The other reason was more important: the ministerial bureaucracy wanted to have a say in the distribution of the Jewish enterprises.

One of the major effects of the Aryanizations was an increasing concentration within the business sector. We have seen that there was no tendency to break up Jewish enterprises among small buyers. There was no decartellization. Similarly, it happened only rarely that a major Jewish business was taken over by several German firms acting as a buying syndicate or *Auffanggesellschaft.* Most often the German buyer was bigger than the

96. File note by Steinbrinck, June 26, 1939, NI-10139.

97. Memorandum by Flick, December 5, 1939, NI-3338. This remarkably candid account of Flick's relations with Göring was read to the Vorstand members of one of Flick's subsidiaries, Harpen.

98. Memorandum by Direktor Andre (Dresdner Bank), November 5, 1940, NI-13944. Memorandum for Vorstand meeting, Dresdner Bank, by Direktor Busch, November 7, 1940, NI-6462.

Jewish seller. In short, the Aryanizations had altered the structure of German business in such a way as to accentuate the power of already powerful firms. This means that the business sector as a whole, represented as it was by powerful industrialists, had become more formidable in its dealings with the other hierarchies.

In their attitude toward the distribution problem, however, the party and the ministries did not manage to form a united front. In fact, disagreements cut clearly across the two hierarchies. Most of the party officials and the Interior Ministry became defenders of the small businessman, whereas the Economy Ministry, the Finance Ministry, and, ultimately, a very decisive party voice (Göring) lined up with big business in what was called the "liberal" point of view. The issue was fought out in a great debate, one which was to be dwarfed only by another controversy in the 1940's about the status of the *Mischlinge*. The debate was precipitated in the course of the Interior Ministry's publication of three administrative measures which were obviously preparatory steps in the development of an involuntary Aryanization process.

On April 26, 1938, the Interior Ministry ordered all Jews to register their property.[99] Characteristically, the work of registration was entrusted to regional offices which were not answerable to competing ministries: the Regierungspräsidenten in Prussia and Bavaria; the Police President in Berlin; the Reichsstatthalter in Thüringen, Hessen, Schaumburg-Lippe, Hamburg, and Lippe; the Kreishauptmänner in Saxony; the Ministries of State in Mecklenburg and Anhalt; the Reichskommissare in the Saar and in Austria.

Another decree of the same date provided that contracts involving transfer of a business from a Jew to a German required the approval of the "higher administrative offices" (*Höhere Verwaltungsbehörden*).[100] Ordinarily, the term *Höhere Verwaltungsbehörden* comprised only the regional offices of general administration, of the kind which were entrusted with the registrations. In this case, however, the Economy Ministry, the party regional economic advisors (*Gauwirtschaftsberater* and *Kreiswirtschaftsberater*), the local Chambers of Commerce, and the competent industrial associations all got into the picture.[101] Everyone wanted the veto power in the final transaction.

On June 14, 1938, the Interior Ministry took the third preparatory measure: the definition of a Jewish enterprise.[102] This decree provided that a business was Jewish if the proprietor was a Jew, if a partner was a Jew, or if, on January 1, 1938, one of the Vorstand or Aufsichtsrat members was a Jew. Also considered Jewish was a business in which Jews had more than one-fourth of the shares or more than one-half of the votes, or which was factually under predominantly Jewish influence. A branch of a Jewish business was declared Jewish, and a branch of a non-Jewish business was considered Jewish, if the manager of the branch was a Jew.

On the very day of the issuance of the business definition decree, June 14, 1938, Interior Minister Frick opened the debate by proposing the introduction of compulsory Aryanization.[103] Frick suggested that Jewish enterprises

99. RGBl I, 414.

100. RGBl I, 415.

101. Memorandum by Dr. P. Binder, May 23, 1938, NI-6906.

102. RGBl I, 627. Drafts of the decree were circulated, after an interministerial conference and before publication, to Göring; the Labor, Economy, Finance, and Justice Ministries; the Foreign Office; the Reich Chancellery; and the Deputy of the Führer (Hess). See circular letter by Stuckart, April 30, 1938, NG-3938. The decree was signed by Frick (Interior), Hess, Funk (Economy), and Gürtner (Justice).

be transferred to the Reich in return for bonds and sold by the Reich, on credit basis, to suitable middle-class buyers. The rights of non-Jewish creditors were to be largely cut out; so far as Frick was concerned, Aryan creditors who to that day had kept up business relations with Jews deserved no consideration anyhow.

In a reply dated August 23, 1938, Minister of Finance von Krosigk, noting the Interior Ministry's preference for the middle class, stated that – on principle – important enterprises should be taken over by financially strong concerns, and that enterprises in overcrowded branches should be liquidated. The Finance Minister expressed his opposition to the Reich's extension of credit to buyers ("the credit of the Reich must not be impaired") and to the cancellation of debts owed to non-Jewish creditors. His reply concluded that, if compulsory transfers of Jewish property were desired, it would be best to set up time limits in which the Jews would be required to dispose of their business.[104]

The final word in this debate was said by Göring in the conference of November 12, 1938:

> It is easily understood that strong attempts will be made to get all these [Jewish] stores into the hands of party members . . . I have witnessed terrible things in the past; little chauffeurs of *Gauleiters* have profited so much by these transactions, they have now about half a million. You gentlemen know it. Is that correct? *(Assent)* Of course, things like that are impossible . . . We shall insist upon it that the Aryan taking over the establishment is experienced in the business and knows his job. Generally speaking, he will have to pay for the store with his own money.[105]

That was the end of the debate.

From July to December, 1938, the ministerial bureaucracy wiped out in six consecutive blows the remaining structure of Jewish business and self-employed activity. The decrees (*a*) set termination dates for the operation of commercial services, doctors' offices, lawyers' offices, and retail establishments; (*b*) provided for trustee administration (by appointees of the Economy Ministry) of retail establishments, industrial enterprises, real estate, and agricultural properties. It is noteworthy that these measures proceeded from the assumption that small Jewish firms, particularly in "overcrowded" fields, were to be liquidated entirely. Only efficient enterprises or businesses with a high plant value were found worthy of transfer into Aryan hands.[106]

The first decree, dated July 6, 1938,[107] dealt with commercial services.

103. Frick to Oberregierungsrat Hallwachs (Office of the Four-Year Plan), Ministerialbürodirektor Reinecke (Economy Ministry), SS-Oberführer Klopfer (Party Chancellery), SS-Untersturmführer Regierungsrat Dr. Tanzmann (Security Police), June 14, 1938, NG-3937.

104. Von Krosigk to Frick, Göring, Hess, Ribbentrop, Lammers, Funk, and Heydrich, August 23, 1938, NG-3937. See also Finance Ministry memorandum of July 16, 1938, NG-4031. For Economy Ministry's attitude, see memorandum by Dr. Binder (Dresdner Bank) on his discussion with Regierungsrat Dr. Gotthardt, May 23, 1938, NI-6906. Also, Binder to Götz, May 30, 1938, NI-6906. Götz was chairman of the Vorstand (board) and chairman of the Aufsichtsrat (president) of the Dresdner Bank.

105. Minutes of conference, November 12, 1938, PS-1816.

106. Figures are available only for Austria. Before the Anschluss, there were 25,898 Jewish enterprises (not including doctors' and lawyers' offices) in the country. By the end of 1939, 21,143 had been liquidated. The percentages of liquidations in individual branches were as follows:

Artisan trades	87%
Sales	83%
Travel and shipping	82%
Banks	81%
Industrial	26%
Agricultural	2%

Krakauer Zeitung, December 2, 1939, p. *Wirtschafts-Kurier.*

It provided for the termination, by December 31, 1938, of Jewish business activities in the following: guard services, credit information bureaus, real estate agencies, brokerage agencies, visitors' guides, marriage agencies catering to non-Jews and peddling. No compensation was provided for any financial losses resulting from cessation of business.

The second decree was enacted on July 25, 1938.[108] In pursuance of this measure, licenses were withdrawn from Jewish physicians. However, the Interior Ministry was empowered to issue permits restricting the practice of Jewish doctors to the treatment of Jews. That was no more than a re-enactment of canonical law, but modern innovation was the provision that leases for apartments rented by Jewish physicians were terminable at the option of either landlord or tenant. The decree was signed by Hitler, Frick (Interior), Hess (Führer Deputy), Gürtner (Justice), and Reinhardt (*Staatssekretär*, Finance Ministry).[109]

On September 27, 1938, a decree signed by Hitler, Gürtner, Frick, Hess, and Reinhardt provided for the elimination of all Jewish lawyers, effective December 31.[110]

These three measures, it must be emphasized, were straight liquidation decrees. Under the terms of these laws, there was no transfer of enterprises from Jews to Germans. Only the customers, patients, and clients were transferred to German patronage.

On the occasion of the November riots, Hitler and Göring had a discussion about fines and similar matters. One of the products of this discussion was Hitler's decision to undertake the "economic solution" of the Jewish problem; in other words, he wanted all remaining Jewish enterprises to be Aryanized. Characteristically for Hitler, his motivation was not at all economic. He wanted a quick Aryanization – particularly of the department stores – because he did not think that Aryan customers, notably officials and government employees who could shop only between 6 and 7 P.M., obtained adequate service.[111] Whatever the logic of this reasoning, the remedy was applied immediately.

On November 12, 1938, retail establishments were ordered to cease all business activity by December 31.[112] In elaboration of this decree, the ordinance of November 23, 1938,[113] signed by Staatssekretär Brinkmann (Economy Ministry) and Reichminister Gürtner (Justice Ministry), ordered that the entire Jewish retail trade, including shops, mail order houses, department stores, etc., be dissolved and liquidated as a matter of principle. The Jewish owners were forbidden to sell their stock to consumers. All goods were to be offered to the competent branch group or association (*Fachgruppe* or *Zweckvereinigung*). Prices were to be fixed by experts appointed by the presidents of the competent Chambers of Commerce. In other words, the German consumer was to

107. RGBl I, 823.

108. RGBl I, 969.

109. The Jewish doctors, whose practice was restricted to Jews, were deprived not only of their business but also of their title. They were henceforth called *Krankenbehandler*. Jewish dentists were deprived of their licenses by the decree of January 17, 1939, RGBl I, 47.

110. RGBl I, 1403. Lawyers, whose practice was restricted to Jews, were called *Konsulenten*. Patent agents had already been removed by the decree of April 22, 1933, signed by Hindenburg, Hitler, and Frick, RGBl I, 217. Tax advisors had been eliminated by the decree of May 6, 1933, signed by Hitler and Gürtner, RGBl I, 257.

111. Testimony by Göring, *Trial of the Major War Criminals*, IX, 278.

112. RGBl I, 1580. Wholesale establishments remained outside of the compulsory Aryanization process.

113. RGBl I, 1642.

get nothing out of this deal; the German competitor was to get the bargain. To hurry matters along, the Economy Ministry was empowered to appoint liquidators, and it could grant in special cases the right of transfer (Aryanization) to a German buyer. The Jewish owners of handicraft shops, however, were simply to be struck off the register and their licenses confiscated.

On December 3, 1938, the last and most important measure was enacted.[114] This decree, which was signed by Funk and Frick, dealt with industrial enterprises, real estate, and securities. With respect to Jewish industrial firms, the measure provided that the owners could be ordered to sell or liquidate within a definite time. A "trustee" could be appointed to effect the sale or liquidation. The trustees were to be appointed by the Economy Ministry, but they were to be "supervised" by the top regional officials of the Reich. To conduct a sale, the trustees had to have the permission also of those agencies which exercised a veto power in these matters (the *Gau* economic advisors, Chambers of Commerce, and industrial associations). As a negotiator, the authority of a trustee replaced any legally required power of attorney.

The decree provided, further, that a Jew could be ordered to sell his land, forest, or real estate properties. In these holdings, too, trustees could be appointed to make the sale. However, as we shall see, the real estate Aryanizations lagged for several years because in many cases the Jews had mortgaged their houses to the "roof antenna."[115] Finally, the decree ordered the Jews to deposit all stocks, bonds, and other securities at the regional offices of the Finance Ministry. Deposits and titles were to be marked as Jewish. Disposal of securities henceforth required the authorization of the Economy Ministry.

That was the "economic solution." We might note that these decrees did *not* solve all problems. To begin with, they were not in effect in the so-called Protektorat of Bohemia and Moravia, where the Dresdner Bank and its cohorts were busy with "voluntary" Aryanizations.[116] Second, the laws did not apply to foreign Jewish enterprises in the Reich. The attempt to cover foreigners was made, but it did not succeed. Under the registration decree of April 26, the foreign Jews had been ordered to register their domestic property. The decree also contained a phrase which was in part administrative, in part propagandistic. The phrase was to the effect that the registered properties would be used in accord with the necessities of the German economy. In consequence of these provisions, the United States, Great Britain, France, Belgium, Switzerland, Poland, Latvia, Lithuania, and Czechoslovakia protested. All of these countries except Belgium and Poland also had treaties with Germany which specifically prohibited the parties to take the properties of each other's nationals without adequate compensation.

As a result of these protests, Staatssekretär Weizsäcker of the Foreign Office pointed out that an indiscriminate application of the principle of "utilization" would have serious political consequences disproportionate to any advantages gained.[117] This opinion was

114. RGBl I, 1709.

115. The average mortgage was 75 per cent. See the *Deutsche Volkswirt*, July 29, 1938, pp. 2142-43.

116. The Protektorat decree of June 21, 1939 (signed by Reichsprotektor von Neurath), stipulated that the transfer of a Jewish business was permissible only with special written authorization. In addition, the *Reichsprotektor* empowered himself to appoint trustees "in cases which seem approprite to him." *Verordnungsblatt des Reichsprotektors in Böhmen und Mähren,* 1939, p. 45.

confirmed by Lammers, the Chief of the Reich Chancellery, after a discussion with Ribbentrop, Frick, and Hitler. The four men had considered the interesting question – pregnant with implications for future policy – whether Jews of foreign nationality should be treated as foreigners or as Jews. It was decided that, as a matter of principle, they should be treated as Jews, but that exceptions might be necessary in individual cases, for reasons of foreign policy.[118] The upshot of these discussions was Göring's grudging decision to exempt the foreign Jews from forced Aryanizations. As he put it during the conference of November 12, 1938: "We shall try to induce them through slight, and then through stronger pressure, and through clever maneuvering to let themselves be pushed out voluntarily."[119]

The party was not quite satisfied with the "solution" to the Aryanization problem, because the "middle class" or the "little chauffeurs of *Gauleiter*" – which ever way one wished to look at the matter – were left out in the cold. In the *Gau* Franken, Streicher's district, the party decided upon its own economic solution. On the eve of the November decrees, suspecting that no time was to be lost, the offices of Gauleiter Streicher went to work. One Jew after another was called in and made to sign a paper transferring his real estate to the city of Fürth, the *Gau*, or some other worthy purchaser. From the Jewish community organization the city of Fürth acquired 100,000 reichsmark worth of property for 100 reichsmark. From a private person the city took 20,000 reichsmark worth of real estate for 180 reichsmark, and so on. Jew after Jew filed in, and document after document was signed.

Now, however, there was a difficulty because some court officers refused to enter the transactions in the real estate book (*Grundbuch*), a step which was required to make the deal legal. One of the judges, Amtsgerichtsrat Leiss, was willing to go ahead. He reasoned that "the question of freedom of will was perhaps dubious but that every action in life was governed by some influence or other." But Leiss wanted to put the circumstances of the transaction into writing. Furthermore, some of the judicial officials insisted that Gauleiter Streicher be entered as purchaser for such properties as were transferred to the *Gau* ("party district"), because the *Gau* as such had no "legal personality." The party men decided that the name of the *Gauleiter* had to be "left out of this" and entered the name of Deputy Gauleiter Holz as a trustee." Staatssekretär Schlegelberger of the Justice Ministry had no objection to this procedure, and the party officials explained in their defense that "the *Gau* Franken had made special contributions in the Jewish question and that therefore it was entitled to special rights."[120]

If the party had its grievances, the Reich had more cause for complaint. For when all was said and done, the major profit accrued neither to the party nor to the Reich but to private business interests: the purchasers of Jewish enterprises and the competitors of liquidated firms. This was true un-

117. Weizsäcker to Brinkmann (*Staatssekretär*, Economy Ministry), June, 1938, NG-3802.

118. Lammers to Hess, July 21, 1938, NG-1526.

119. Minutes of Göring conference, November 12, 1938, PS-1816.

120. The story of the Franken Aryanizations is taken from the memorandum by Oberstaatsanwalt Joel, February 15, 1939, NG-616. A special commission was appointed by Göring to look into these transactions. For its report, see document PS-1757. An unpublished decree, signed by Göring and dated December 10, 1939, invalidated all irregular Aryanizations concluded after November 1, 1938, NG-1520.

der involuntary Aryanization no less than under voluntary Aryanization. The idea that one special class should have all the profit from a measure taken for the "good of the people" was a distasteful one, even for Göring. Consequently, it was decided that the new owners would have to part with some of their gains.

First, there was the problem of bridging the gap between purchase price and actual value. It seemed to Göring that the trustees were not supposed to serve the Jews. They were appointed to serve the state. As he saw it, the trustees were to fix the amount to be paid to the Jewish owner for his property. "Naturally," he said, "this amount is to be set as low as possible." But in turning over the property to a German buyer, the trustee was to collect the highest possible price – the actual value. The difference was to be pocketed by the Reich.[121] That is why Göring did not want "little chauffeurs" among the purchasers. However, the scheme did not work out, since the German buyers were not disposed to pay more under forced Aryanization than they had paid under voluntary Aryanization. As a consequence, the enterprises were actually sold for as "little as possible," and the Reich had to collect the difference from the purchasers instead of the trustees. That was not so easy.

Under the decree of December 3, 1939,[122] the beneficiaries of Jewish property were made liable to the payment of an "equalization" tax in the amount of the supposed difference between purchase price and actual value. The tax affected only those purchasers whose transactions had been subject to official approval under the decrees of April 26 and December 3 – in short, no Aryanization concluded *prior* to April 26, 1938. On February 6, 1941, a circular order by the Economy Minister retroactively subjected the pre-1938 transactions to the same levy. However, the Ministry decided not to be "petty" in the enforcement of the tax.[123] That the enforcement was not "petty" is shown by the following figures, indicating the meager "equalization" receipts during three fiscal years:[124]

1942	RM	34,530,483.87
1943	RM	9,156,161.17
1944 (estimate)	RM	5,000,000.00

In addition to this tax, the acquisitors of Jewish enterprises had to undergo still another tribulation, the removal of Jewish trademarks and firm names. This measure was demanded first by Göring during the conference of November 12, 1938. Pointing out that many Aryans had been so "clever" as to keep the Jewish designations, Göring stressed that many of these Aryanized firms had been looted during the November riots by mistake. From now on, the "names of former Jewish firms shall have to disappear completely, and the German shall have to come forward with his or his firm's name. . . . All that is obvious."[125]

But the matter was not so obvious to the German businessman. A trademark or a firm name that sold goods was an asset, and an asset was worth money. True, the Aryan buyers had not paid for this particular type of asset, for that was part of "good will" and Jews were not supposed to have any "good will," but then again, no one

121. Minutes of conference of November 12, 1938, PS-1816.

122. RGBl I, 1709.

123. *Der Deutsche Volkswirt*, February 28, 1941, XV, 820-21. For detailed instructions, see *Dienstnachrichten des Reichsbauernführer*, 1941, p. 418, NG-1678.

124. Liquidation Administration of the German Finance Ministry (signed Dr. Siegert) to Control Commission of Germany/-British Element/Finance Division, November 14, 1946, NG-4904. There is no indication of any receipts prior to fiscal year 1942.

125. Minutes of conference, November 12, 1938, PS-1816.

likes to lose something valuable just because he did not pay for it. Accordingly, the merchants and industrialists were not satisfied when, under the decree of December 3, 1938, the trustees were empowered to remove Jewish firm names, and they were even less gratified by the decree of March 27, 1941,[126] which required every purchaser of a Jewish enterprise which still carried the name of the Jewish owner to remove such name within four months. To make himself absolutely clear, the Justice Minister (who was responsible for this measure) pointed out in an explanatory instruction that the names of *all* former Jewish owners had to be removed, whether such names sounded Jewish or not, whether they were whole or abbreviated.[127] That regulation gave rise to petitions, correspondence, and conferences.

On April 18, 1941, the Rosenthal-Porzellan A. G. sent a letter to Goebbels, with a request that the honored *Reichsminister* persuade the Ministry of Justice to make an exception for the name "Rosenthal," since in this case "it was not a question of a name, but a symbol of a product [*Sachbegriff*]." The founder of the firm, Generaldirektor Geheimrat Philipp Rosenthal (a Jew) had retired in 1933, and the Rosenthal family had never controlled more than 20 per cent of the shares. The name itself had been for fifty years a recognized trademark all over the world, and particularly in foreign countries where "Rosenthal" had become the symbol of the "epitome in quality" of porcelain. Moreover, the firm name *had* already been changed in 1938 from "Porzellanfabrik Philipp Rosenthal A. G." to "Rosenthal-Porzellan A. G."[128]

The Propaganda Ministry sent the petition with a favorable recommendation to the Justice Ministry.[129] Encouraged, the porcelain firm deluged the Justice Ministry with additional memoranda which pointed out among other things that the Vorstand of the company had been fully Aryanized by 1933, that the Aufsichtsrat had been cleared of Jews by 1934, that the *Generaldirektor* had died, to be replaced by his fully Aryan widow during that same year, and that the Rosenthal family had transferred its shares to Aryan interests by 1936.[130] The Justice Ministry gave in. It decided that the order did not apply to the firm because, under the decree of June 14, 1938, defining a Jewish business, Rosenthal was not a Jewish enterprise![131]

The case of Rosenthal is particularly interesting, because the Aryans who had taken over the enterprise and its name were the kind of people who inserted anti-Jewish advertisements in the press. The case is significant also for its postwar implications. The new management was right when it claimed that the name "Rosenthal" was known abroad. After the war, the firm shipped its china to many a Jewish department store in New York which, in turn, sold

126. RGB1 I, 177.

127. *Allgemeine Verfügung des Reichsjustizministers*, March 27, 1941, *Deutsche Justiz*, Heft 15/16, p. 459.

128. Rosenthal-Porzellan A. G. to Goebbels, April 18, 1941, G-64.

129. Ministerialdirigent Dr. Schmidt-Leonhardt to Ministry of Justice, April 26, 1941, G-64.

130. Rosenthal-Porzellan A. G. / Vorstand (signed Klaas and Zöllner) to Justice Ministry, May 27, 1941, G-64. Rosenthal-Porzellan A. G. / Vorstand to Justice Ministry, June 7, 1941, G-64.

131. Justice Ministry (signed Quassowski) to Rosenthal-Porzellan A. G./Vorstand, August 25, 1941, G-64. Schmidt-Leonhardt to Goebbels, July 10, 1941, G-64. Under the June 14, 1938, decree a business was Jewish if, in *1938*, one-fourth of the shares were in Jewish hands or if, on January 1, 1938, a Jew was a member of the Vorstand or Aufsichtsrat.

the merchandise to many a Jewish customer who was under the impression that he was buying a Jewish product.

The Rosenthal method of obtaining individual exemption did not satisfy the business sector. The businessmen wanted to do away with the ordinance altogether. On May 29, 1941, representatives of the ministries and of business met to discuss the problem. In his opening remarks, the chairman, Ministerialrat Kühnemann of the Justice Ministry explained that the purpose of the decree was to smother the Jewish firm names, so that the German merchant could in future sell his wares without these "reminders of the supremacy of Jewish business sense in the German economy." The representative of the Reichsgruppe Industrie ("Reich industrial association"), Dr. Gerder, proposed without ado that the decree be postponed until the end of the war; Oberregierungsrat von Coelln of the Economy Ministry supported him, so did Kammergerichtsrat Dr. Heinemann of the Agriculture Ministry and Dr. Grosse of the Reich Chamber of Commerce. Only the Party Chancellery (Staatsanwalt von Kaldenberg) supported the chairman.[132]

In subsequent correspondence, too, the weight of opinion was against the Justice Ministry. The Reichsgruppe Industrie wanted wholesale exceptions for all famous firm names. One business representative, Hunke, writing to the Propaganda Ministry, pointed out that the decree had a fatal defect. The ordinance affected only those firms which had taken over Jewish enterprises. What would prevent some little porcelain factory in Thüringen from registering a world-famous name such as "Rosenthal" as soon as the owners of that name were divested of its use? The "quickest" firms would be rewarded, whereas the primary object of the ordinance – the "extinction" of the names of former Jewish owners – would remain unfulfilled.[133] The whole decree was simply impossible. Nobody wanted it. Only the Party Chancellery continued in its support of the harassed Justice Ministry. The Party Chancellery wanted an extension of the decree to cover *all* Jewish names, the names of freemasons, non-Germanic (*artfremde*) trademarks, etc.[134] The result of the controversy was the complete defeat of the Justice Ministry. In September, it was decided that nothing further would be done about the removal of Jewish names during the war.[135]

As we review the Aryanizations, we find that the business sector had swallowed a great many Jewish enterprises and that it had benefited from a large number of forced liquidations. We have no over all figures showing the extent of these gains; we know only that the purchaser of a Jewish business rarely paid more than 75 per cent of its value and that often he paid less than 50 per cent. We know also that the German beneficiaries of Jewish liquidations invested little or nothing. The profit to the business sector must therefore be reckoned in the billions of reichsmark.

What about the Reich? What about Göring's pronouncements that the Reich, and only the Reich, was entitled to profit from the Aryanizations? The Finance Ministry had few receipts indeed. Apart from a few major penalty confiscations (which did not yield so

132. Summary of firm names conference (signed Sünner), May 29, 1941, G-59.

133. *Präsident des Werberates der deutschen Wirtschaft* (signed Hunke) to Propaganda Ministry, July 11, 1941, G-59.

134. Party Chancellery to Justice Ministry, July 16, 1941, G-59.

135. Regierungsrat Dr. Hilleke (Propaganda Ministry) to *Präsident des Werberates der deutschen Wirtschaft,* September 22, 1941, G-59. Announcement by the Economy Ministry, *Ministerialblatt des Reichswirtschaftsministeriums,* January 14, 1942, p. 15.

much when the purchaser was Göring), and apart from the Aryanization equalization tax (which did not yield much, either), the ministry registered no receipts at all. But, indirectly, the Reich did take a huge bite out of the leftovers of Jewish property values. It collected the vast amounts of cash and other liquid assets which the Jews had acquired in the course of the Aryanizations as payment for their enterprises. That money was confiscated by the Finance Ministry in pursuance of two property taxes, the so-called Reich Flight Tax and the so-called Penance Payment.

3 / Property Taxes

The flight tax was first decreed on December 8, 1931,[1] more than one year *before* Hitler came to power. Originally, the measure affected all emigrating Reich nationals who on January 31, 1931, had property worth more than 200,000 reichsmark or whose income during the calendar year 1931 was more than 20,000 reichsmark. On May 18, 1934, the effect of the decree was widened by making it applicable to all emigrating Reich nationals who on January 31, 1931 (or any time thereafter), owned property worth more than 50,000 reichsmark or who in 1931 (or any subsequent year) earned more than 20,000 reichsmark.[2]

"Property" included all values taxable under the regular property tax laws, plus such assets (ordinarily not taxable) as shares in personal partnerships and certain Reich loans. The tax consisted of one-fourth of the current value of the property (that is, value at time of emigration). There were no exemptions and no allowable deductions. The eligible emigrant had to pay a full fourth of his current taxable assets. What did this mean? Simply this. A Jew whose taxable property on January 1, 1931, was worth 60,000 reischmark and who at the time of his emigration, say in 1938, still owned 16,000 reichsmark paid a tax of 4000 reichsmark. A Jew whose taxable property never rose above a value of 50,000 reichsmark but whose income during the single year 1932 was 25,000 reichsmark paid a fourth of whatever taxable property assets he had at time of emigration; if these assets were 5000 reichsmark, he paid 1250 reichsmark.[3]

Obviously the amendment introduced in 1934, and the administrative rules enacted for the implementation of this decree, reflected not only a change of effect but also a change of purpose. The original measure was designed to *deter* emigration, particularly the emigration of well-to-do people who desired to take their wealth out of the country in the form of commodity shipments or money transfers. The amended measure was designed to *take advantage* of emigration – this time, the emigration of Jews who were leaving the country in order to begin life anew abroad. This change is illustrated by the following figures showing receipts for five fiscal years, one pre-Nazi year, four Nazi years.[4]

1932/33	RM	1,000,000
1935/36	RM	45,000,000
1936/37	RM	70,000,000
1937/38	RM	81,000,000
1938/39	RM	342,000,000

1. RGBl I, 699, pp. 731-33.
2. RGBl I, 392.

3. For details of administration of this law, see Heinz Cohn, *Auswanderungsvorschriften für Juden in Deutschland* (Berlin, 1938), pp. 61–68.

4. *Deutsche Bank* (published by the Deutsche Bank / Volkswirtschaftliche Abteilung), May 30, 1939, pp. 144-45. In German practice, fiscal year 1938 (or 1938-39) means the year beginning on April 1, 1938. In American practice, fiscal year 1938 means the year ending June 30, 1938. The value of the reichsmark, in dollars, will vary according to the criteria used. If an American wanted free reichsmark, he had to pay for the mark the official price (rate) set by the German government: $1 = RM 2.40.

Although we have no data for fiscal years 1933–34, 1934–35, and 1939–40, we can make some estimates for these periods on the basis of emigration statistics. On such a basis, the Finance Ministry should have collected approximately 50,000,000 reichsmark during fiscal years 1933–34 and 1934–35, and roughly 300,000,000 reichsmark during fiscal year 1939–40 (the last significant emigration year).[5] The total yield of the Reich Flight Tax was consequently in the neighborhood of 900,000,000 reichsmark.

We have already examined some of the circumstances which led to the implementation of the second property tax, the "Atonement Payment" (*Sühneleistung*) imposed upon the Jews after the assassination of Gesandtschaftsrat vom Rath in Paris. We have seen that after a struggle between Göring and Goebbels, the Finance Ministry instead of the party was designated as recipient of the fine. During the argument, Hitler, Göring, and Goebbels had also fixed the amount of the tax: the round sum of a billion reichsmark. The collection of that sum posed an interesting problem.

A tax collector can never tell in advance precisely how much revenue a certain tax will yield. A tax is almost always expressed as a fixed percentage of income, property, or property turnover values. If income, property values, or property turnover changes from one fiscal year to the next, so does the tax yield. In order to predict revenue collection, it is therefore necessary to make some complicated calculations. The Finance Ministry had an even more difficult task than that. Instead of starting with a tax and calculating the revenue, it had to start with a precise amount and determine the tax. There was no precedent to be guided by. In no previous fiscal year had taxes been imposed on Jews specifically. (The Reich Flight Tax was paid only by emigrants.)

The Finance Ministry knew that an income tax would not do, since the income of the Jews was declining too fast. The only way in which such a sum could be collected was in the form of a property tax. But this required a knowledge of how much property the Jews still had in their possession. The Finance Ministry *knew* how much Jewish property was available. Only a few months before the November fine was decreed the Interior Ministry, with that foresight borne out of a conviction that sooner or later all Jewish property would be German, had ordered the Jews to register their property.

The decree of April 26, 1938,[6] which we have already mentioned as a preparatory measure in the Aryanizations, required all Jews (other than foreign Jews) to evaluate and report their domestic and foreign property. Foreign Jews had to report only their domestic property. Movable objects used by the individual and home furnishings did not have to be included unless they were luxuries. The property had to be evaluated at current and usual prices. It had to be reported if its value was over 5000 reichsmark. In pursuance of this decree (which was in effect in the Old Reich and Austria) the following property values were registered:[7] 135,750 Jews of German nationality reported 7,050,000,000 reichsmark; 9,567 foreign Jews reported 415,000,000

5. Emigration statistics for the Old Reich (boundaries of 1937) in Hans Lamm, "Über die Innere und Äussere Entwicklung des Deutschen Judentums im Dritten Reich" (Erlangen, 1951; mimeographed), p. 223. Emigration statistics for Austria can be calculated from report by Statistical Office, *Reichsgau* Vienna, December 15, 1939, PS-1949.

6. RGBl I, 414.

7. Wiehl (Foreign Office/Political Trade Division) to German missions and consulates abroad, January 25, 1939, NG-1793.

reichsmark; 2,269 stateless Jews reported 73,500,000 reichsmark; the total reported was thus 7,538,500,000 reichsmark. With such figures at its disposal, the Finance Ministry could arrive at a tax rate without much difficulty.

On November 12, 1938, Göring proclaimed the "fine."[8] Nine days later, on November 21, the Finance Ministry was ready with its implementation decree,[9] which made liable all Jews (except foreign Jews) who had reported their property under the decree of April 26, 1938. Valuations were to be adjusted to November 12. It was estimated that between April 26 and November 12 about two billion reichsmark of the registered assets had passed into German possession.[10] The finance officials had to assume that a large number – if not all – of the sellers had already left the country. After deducting these two billion, and after making another adjustment for the property of the foreign Jews (four hundred million), property worth at least five billion reichsmark was left to be taxed. The "fine" to be paid by each liable Jew was consequently fixed at 20 per cent of his registered property, due in four installments, on December 15, 1938, February 15, 1939, May 15, 1939, and August 15, 1939. The finance offices were empowered to require payment of a security by Jews wishing to emigrate.

On December 10, 1938, the Finance Ministry issued unpublished supplementary instructions to its regional machinery.[11] These instructions reveal more clearly how the fine was designed to confiscate Jewish liquid assets. The finance offices were requested to take note of payment offices set up by the Economy Ministry for the purchase of valuables and art objects. Since payments would be made also from accounts in foreign countries, notification of such money transfers could be expected from the Foreign Exchange Office of the Economy Ministry. Securities were to be accepted, if quoted on official exchange lists, at the rate of exchange stated there. Preference was to be given to shares first, bonds next, and Reich loans last. Acceptance of such securities was to be considered as a privilege extended to the Jew. He was therefore obliged to pay the stock exchange turnover tax. Actually, of course, the provision for acceptance of securities was not a "privilege" at all. It was a necessity because of the depletion of Jewish cash reserves and because the Finance Ministry could not afford to allow the Jews to "throw" their securities into the market, "thus spoiling the market for the Reich loan."[12]

As the cash, art objects, foreign exchange, and securities began to roll in, the Finance Ministry became worried that the rate of 20 per cent had been fixed too low. Accordingly, another installment of 5 per cent was added, payable on November 15, 1939.[13] With this installment the Ministry overshot the mark, as revealed by the following totals:[14]

8. RGBl I, 1579.

9. RGBl I, 1638.

10. Speech by Economy Minister Funk, November 15, 1938, PS-3545.

11. Finance Ministry instructions, December 10, 1938, NG-4902.

12. Testimony by Finance Minister Schwerin von Krosigk, Case No. 11, tr. p. 23292. Schacht pointed out after the war that about one-third of the *first* installment had to be accepted "in kind." Interrogation of Hjalmar Schacht, July 11, 1945, PS-3724.

13. Decree of October 19, 1939, RGBl I, 2059.

14. Liquidation Administration of former German Finance Ministry (signed Siegert) to Control Commission of Germany/British Element/Finance Division, November 14, 1946, NG-4904.

Fiscal year 1938	RM	498,514,808
Fiscal year 1939	RM	533,126,504
Fiscal year 1940	RM	94,971,184
Total	RM	1,126,612,496

The "Reich Flight Tax" and the "Jewish Atonement Payment" are summarized in Table 19. The two taxes yielded a total of two billion reichsmark. The combined yield during the fiscal year 1938 (RM 841,000,000) represented nearly 5 per cent of total revenues (RM 17,690,000,000) of that year.[15] Fiscal 1938 (April 1, 1938, to March 31, 1939) was a year of mobilization. The shortage of funds was "critical." As the Finance Ministry collected the Jewish money, it was poured immediately into the funnels of armament spending.[16]

Although the two billion reichsmark constituted the greatest profit registered by the Reich in the entire European destruction process, the amount was less than a third of the assets reported by the Jews in 1938. From the 7,500,000,000 reichsmark registered in that year, the Reich received only the leftovers. This fact became clear when the Finance Ministry discovered that in some cases the "ridiculous counter-value" received by the Jews for their Aryanized property was insufficient to pay the property taxes.[17]

TABLE 19 / *"Reich Flight Tax" and "Jewish Atonement Payment"*

	"Flight Tax"	"Atonement Payment"
Liability	All emigrating Reich nationals who had property of more than RM 50,000 on January 1, 1931 (or any time thereafter) or an income of more than RM 20,000 in 1931 (or any year thereafter)	All Jews (other than foreign Jews) who had registered property of more than RM 5000
Amount of tax	25 per cent of taxable property	25 per cent of registered property
Yield	RM 900,000,000	RM 1,100,000,000

4 / Blocked Money

Now we might ask: Suppose a Jew sold his property and paid his taxes and, after these ruinous procedures, still had some money left? Could he take it to the bank, exchange it for dollars, and travel to America? The answer is, of course, no.

In the first place, there was a view that all Jewish capital in Germany really belonged to the German people, because the Jews could not have acquired it honestly.[1] In other words, the Jews could not be permitted to transfer any money abroad, for, if they still had any money, the Reich wanted to confiscate it eventually. A second and more formidable reason was this: If emigrating Jews were to be permitted to salvage any of their resources, the Reich would be forced to expend foreign currency for mere reichsmark. And that was out of the question. Ever since 1931, strict exchange controls had regulated all transactions in foreign currency. Under the law, every German was obliged to offer to the Reichs-

15. Fiscal 1938 revenue total from *Deutsche Bank,* May 30, 1939, pp. 144-45.

16. Summary by Wörmann (Foreign Office/Political Division) of a speech by Göring to ministers, *Staatssekretäre,* and generals, dated November 19, 1938, PS-3575. Interrogation of Schacht, July 11, 1945, PS-3724.

17. Affidavit by Ministerialrat Walter Donandt, May 20, 1948, Krosigk-24. Donandt was personal advisor to Finance Minister von Krosigk.

1. Foreign Office notes (signed by Staatssekretär Weizsäcker) to German embassies in London, Paris, Rome, Washington, and Warsaw, and to German legations in Belgrade, Bucharest, Budapest, Prague, and Sofia, July 8, 1938, NG-3702.

bank any foreign currency at his disposal, even including claims expressed in foreign currency. Thus if an exporter sold some goods abroad, he was paid in reichsmark, and the Reich collected the dollars, pounds, francs, or whatever.

The purpose of this mobilization of foreign exchange was to insure that whatever foreign funds were available would be spent only for essential imports. Any diversion of such reserves to enable Jewish emigrants to establish life anew abroad was the last thing anybody thought of doing. Yet something of the sort *had* to be done if the emigration of the Jews was to be furthered. Foreign countries were loath to accept any Jews, let alone poor Jews.[2] The exchange controls were, therefore, one of the principal stumbling blocks to rapid emigration. The problem could be solved in two ways only: through financial support by fellow Jews abroad, and through exceptional, roundabout, and forbidden currency transfers. To the extent that foreign Jewish assistance failed, the salvaging of money became an absolute prerequisite for any emigration program.

Following is a list of twelve methods used by the Jews to transfer money abroad. That there were at least twelve of these avenues is in itself a telling indication of the German dilemma.

1. The so-called *Freigrenze* ("free currency zone"). Each emigrant, including a Jew, was permitted to take out of the country the sum of 10 reichsmark in foreign currency (at the official exchange rate), and twice that amount if the point of destination was a country with which Germany had no border. In other words, a family of three traveling to the United States could take along $24.[3]

2. The *Warenfreigrenze* ("free goods zone"). An emigrant was also permitted to remove goods in the amount of 1000 reichsmark. For the calculation of the price, the sales value at the point of destination rather than market value in the Reich was decisive.[4]

3. Each emigrant could also take out of the country his *personal belongings,* including furniture; however, emigrants were required to submit to the authorities lists of all items intended for removal.[5] The purpose of the lists was to screen the shipments, with a view to preventing the export of jewelry and valuables. There was, of course, a tendency to smuggle such items out of the country, but the bureaucracy did its best to frustrate transfers of that sort. On February 21, 1939, the Jews were directed to surrender their gold, platinum, silver, precious stones, and art objects to purchasing offices of the Economy Ministry, "compensation to be fixed by the ministry."[6]

4. Another way of disposing of moneys before emigration was the purchase of *railway and ship accommodations* in reichsmark. This method was altogether permissible, but foreign steamship lines were not always willing to accept German currency. For example, the Italian line Lloyd Triestino required payment of half the fare in foreign exchange.[7]

5. The *Altreu,* or *Allgemeine Treuhandstelle für die Jüdische Auswande-*

2. See report by Albrecht (Foreign Office/Legal Division) to Himmler on immigration restrictions affecting Jews in the United States, Canada, Guatemala, El Salvador, Brazil, Ecuador, Bolivia, the South African Union, and Palestine, November 10, 1937, NG-3236.

3. Implementation decree to the Currency Law, December 22, 1938, RGBl I, 1851. The ten-mark limit resulted from successive reductions. It was in effect from 1934.

4. Cohn, *Auswanderungsvorschriften,* p. 35.

5. Currency Law, December 12, 1938, RGBl I, 1734, par. 58.

6. RGBl I, 279.

7. *New York Times,* July 6, 1939, p. 14.

rung ("General Trusteeship Office for Jewish Emigration") was an exchange office which was set up in order to convert reichsmark into foreign currency (other than Palestine currency) at a 50 per cent loss to the Jew. Complicated schedules governed the administration of this procedure. Up to October, 1937, the upper limit was 8000 reichsmark; the maximum was then pushed up, in some cases, to 50,000 reichsmark. In 1938, however, new applications were no longer accepted.[8]

6. Jews emigrating to Palestine were given a special opportunity to remove their capital by the so-called *Haavara* agreement. This agreement was concluded by the German Reich and the Jewish Agency for Palestine. In form, it was a modified clearing arrangement. Under its terms a Jewish "capitalist" who wanted to emigrate to Palestine was permitted to make a contract with a German exporter for the transfer of goods from Germany to Palestine. The German exporter was paid with funds drawn from the blocked account of the emigrating Jew. The emigrant received his Palestine currency from the Jewish Agency upon arrival in Palestine. In short, the channels were as follows:[9]

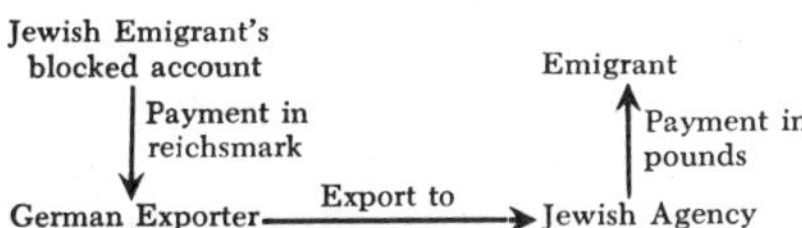

The Jewish Agency and the exporters were just as satisfied with this arrangement as the emigrants themselves. German goods poured into Palestine and, after a while, the Haavara clearing agreement was supplemented by a barter agreement providing for the exchange of Palestine oranges for German timber, wrapping paper, motor cars, pumps, agricultural machinery, etc.[10] It seemed as though the economic relations between Nazi Germany and the Jewish community in Palestine were excellent. Naturally, there was some dissatisfaction in the Nazi Party, the Foreign Office's Germany Referat (which was to deal with Jewish matters), and, last but not least, the Palestine Germans, who complained that their interests had been neglected utterly in favor of the Jews.[11] Nevertheless, this interesting arrangement survived.

7. *Aryanization payments* in foreign currency. Only rich Jews who had foreign nationality or who controlled foreign enterprises could benefit from this method.

8. The *sale of blocked reichsmark.* An emigrant who did not take his money along automatically lost that money to a blocked account (*Sperrguthaben*) over which he could exercise no control. The blocked accounts were under the supervision of the Devisenstellen, which were administratively part of the offices of the Oberfinanzpräsidenten (regional offices of the Finance Ministry) but which received directives from the Economy Ministry.[12] The Devisenstellen were empowered to permit the exploitation of blocked accounts for only three major purposes: (1) to grant credit to a German, (2) to make insurance payments, and (3) to

8. Cohn, *Auswanderungsvorschriften,* pp. 37-39.

9. Foreign Office memorandum, March 10, 1938, NG-1889.

10. Summary of interministerial conference in the offices of the Economy Ministry, September 22, 1937, NG-4075.

11. Correspondence and conferences, 1937 to 1938, in documents NG-1889, NG-4075, and NG-3580.

12. Currency Law, December 12, 1938, RGBl I, 1734. Implementation decree by the Economy Minister, December 22, 1938, RGBl I, 1851. The Currency Law and the implementation ordinance are codifications of earlier regulations. For complete compilation – with expert comment – of currency regulations to 1939, see Regierungsrat Hans Gurski and Regierungsrat Friedrich Schulz (eds.), *Devisengesetz* (Berlin, 1941).

acquire real estate. These provisions were, of course, intended not for the benefit of the emigrating Jews but for non-Jewish foreigners interested in making such investments. However, the fact that blocked marks, or *Sperrmark,* were released for *some* purpose gave them at least *some* value. In fact, some Jews were able to sell their blocked holdings at an exchange rate of 20 cents per *Sperrmark* or even a little better – that is, at a loss of not more than 50 per cent.[13] Those Jews who did not sell their *Sperrmark* accounts lost the accounts when, in the course of later confiscations, they were gobbled up by the Finance Ministry.

9. The *smuggling out of currency* in contravention of the law was practiced by some poor Jews who had only a little money and who wanted to exchange it quickly, without middle men. Since money smuggled out in cash had to be smuggled back to be of use to anyone except a souvenir hunter, the exchange rate of such transactions was only 10 to 13 cents per mark.[14] The Czech crown, which was worth 3.43 cents before the Germans marched into Prague, was sold in New York banks a week later for less than 1 cent.[15]

10. Another illicit but common transaction was a *private arrangement* for which three Jewish parties were needed: an emigrating Jew with German currency, a destitute Jewish family which remained behind, and a foreign relative of the destitute family willing to extend help. Under the agreement, the emigrant gave his reichsmark to the poor family and later collected the intended gift dollars (or pounds or francs) from the helping relatives abroad.

11. Since, under the currency law, foreign holdings belonging to German nationals had to be reported to the Reich, the *retention of foreign holdings* was equivalent to a currency transfer. Obviously, there were only two ways of keeping foreign investments – by not reporting them or by obtaining permission to keep them. Both methods were rare.

12. Since many Jews were so poor that they could not even afford to pay for their fare, Security Police Chief Heydrich decided upon some unconventional forms of relief by means of a typical *Heydrich method.* During the conference of November 12, 1938, Heydrich explained it this way: "Through the Jewish Kultusgemeinde [Jewish community organization in Vienna] we extracted a certain amount of money from the rich Jews who wanted to emigrate. By paying this amount, and an additional sum in foreign exchange [drawn from Jewish accounts in foreign countries], they made it possible for a number of poor Jews to leave. The problem was not to make the rich Jews leave but to get rid of the Jewish mob." Göring was not enthusiastic about this procedure: "But, children, did you ever think this through? It doesn't help us to extract hundreds of thousands from the Jewish mob. Have you ever thought of it that this procedure may cost us so much foreign currency that in the end we won't be able to hold on?" Heydrich, in his defense, said, "Only what the Jew has had in foreign currency."[16]

The problem of the poor Jews was so great that it received attention from many quarters. Toward the end of 1938, Reichsbank Präsident Schacht,

13. Edward J. Condlon, "Shoppers for Foreign Exchange Benefit As Stocks Here Increase," *New York Times,* March 19, 1939, pp. 1, 5.

14. *Ibid.*

15. *Ibid.*

16. Minutes of Göring conference, November 12, 1938, PS-1816. See also summary of Heydrich's remarks at a meeting of the committee of the *Reichszentrale für die jüdische Auswanderung,* held on February 11, 1939, in *Akten zur Deutschen Auswärtigen Politik 1918-1945,* Ser. D, Vol. V, Doc. 665.

then no longer Economy Minister but still a powerful figure, went to London with a plan for the emigration of some 150,000 Jews. The Jews were to leave their assets behind, and their resettlement was to be financed by a foreign syndicate. This foreign group was to advance 1½ billion mark, to be repaid (with interest) by the Reich in the form of "additional exports" over a long period of time.[17] Schacht's motivation, and that of his backers, seems to have run along the following lines: First, the scheme was a way of combatting the foreign propaganda which accused Germany of robbing the Jews of all property, turning them out destitute. (At that very time, the Germans were making identical charges with respect to the treatment of Sudeten-Germans in Czechosolovakia.)[18]

A more important reason was Schacht's conviction that Germany would ultimately profit more from "additional exports" than from the unindemnified taking of Jewish property. The additional exports, after all, were going to create many new consumers of German goods. Once a customer, always a customer; once a market, always a market. The exports would in the long run pay for themselves; Schacht was convinced of that. On the other hand, if war should interrupt the exports, all problems would be solved immediately. The Jews would be out; the Jewish assets would be in. Either way, Germany could not lose.

The Schacht scheme did not materialize, in part at least because of the opposition of the German Foreign Office. Ribbentrop saw no reason why the Jews should be permitted to transfer, in one form or another, what he regarded as stolen German property.[19] Behind this reasoning there was a grievance which had nothing to do with the Jews. The negotiations were being conducted in London by Schacht himself, and the Foreign Office was shut out. Its jurisdiction was ignored. Rankled by this procedure, the Foreign Minister expressed his disapproval of the whole idea.[20] Property *and* Jews remained behind.[21]

17. Unterstaatssekretär Wörmann (Foreign Office/Political Division) to Foreign Minister Ribbentrop, Staatssekretär Weizsäcker, Deputy Chief of Political Division, Chiefs of Legal Division, Culture Division, Economy Division, and *Referat Deutschland* (all in Foreign Office), November 14, 1938, NG-1522. Ambassador Dirksen (London) to Foreign Office, December 16, 1938, *Akten zur Deutschen Auswärtigen Politik 1933-1945*, Ser. D, Vol. V, Doc. 661. The Schacht plan was *not* intended to help the "capitalists" in the Haavara manner. The intent was to finance the emigration of the poor Jews with the funds of the rich, in the process getting rid of both.

18. Prof. Freiherr von Freytag-Loringhoven to Vortragender Legationsrat Geheimrat Dr. Albrecht (Foreign Office), July 26, 1938, NG-3443. Von Freytag-Loringhoven had written an article about the Czechs and was embarrassed by countercharges against Germany. He asked the Foreign Office for an explanation. Albrecht replied, on August 9, 1938 (NG-3443): "Any representation of the actual facts must refrain from confessing that the position of German foreign exchange does not permit that emigrating Jews transfer their property at home for the corresponding value abroad."

19. Staatssekretär von Weizsäcker (Foreign Office) to German missions abroad, July 8, 1938, NG-3702.

20. Weizsäcker to Ribbentrop, Wörmann (chief, Political Division), Deputy Chief of Political Division, Chief of Trade-Political Division, Chief of *Referat* Germany, December 20, 1938, NG-1521. Weizsäcker to Ribbentrop, etc., January 4, 1939, NG-1518. A few days later Ribbentrop agreed to the "quiet" organization of the emigration, provided that the Foreign Office could participate. Weizsäcker memorandum, January 13, 1939, NG-1532. Nothing came of the matter.

21. About half the 800,000 Jews in the Reich-Protektorat area emigrated. Report by SS statistician Korherr, March 23, 1943, NO-5194.

5 / Introduction of Forced Labor and Wage Regulations

In 1939 the remaining Jewish community, shrunken to half its original size, was already impoverished. The capitalists had lost their capital; the professionals had lost their professions; and ordinary workers by the thousands were turned out by firms which had formerly been Jewish but which were now German. The personnel force, too, was "Aryanized."[1]

That was not all. The remaining Jews were less able to sustain themselves with hard labor than were those who had emigrated. The Jews who were left behind had less capacity for survival, since the emigration had drawn off the younger elements and had left a large surplus of women. In the old Reich (1933 boundaries), the percentage of Jews over forty had changed from 47.7 in 1933 to 73.7 in 1939.[2] The percentage of women had risen from 52.2 in 1933 to 57.7 in 1939.[3] In short, the Jewish community had acquired the characteristics of a large family of dependents. But a relief campaign was the last solution in the minds of the bureaucrats.

Under the decree of March 29, 1938, Jewish relief institutions were deprived of their tax exemptions.[4] On November 19, 1938, a decree signed by Frick, von Krosigk, and Labor Minister Seldte stipulated that, in principle, Jews were to be excluded from public relief.[5] During the following year the destitute Jews were pushed into hard menial labor.

In a decree published on March 4, 1939, the president of the Reich Labor Exchange (*Reichsanstalt für Arbeitsvermittlung*), Staatssekretär Syrup, in agreement with the Economy Ministry and the Food and Agriculture Ministry, established the principle that unemployed Jews be put to work in construction and reclamation projects, segregated from non-Jewish laborers.[6] In the beginning of 1941, about 30,000 Jews were working, in groups, on hard labor projects.[7] The remaining employable Jews were laboring in factories and in the growing network of Jewish community organizations. A few professionals were eking out a living as *Krankenbehandler* and *Konsulenten,* catering to the community's health and legal needs.

Since the Jews had already lost their positions, their property, and their money, they lost themselves in the hope that henceforth they would be left alone if only they worked hard and minded their own business – after all, the Jewish "citadels of power" had been smashed and the looting was over. Nevertheless, the bureaucracy could not stop in the middle. The destruction process had to continue. Whereas, before 1939, anti-Jewish measures were aimed at investments, the wartime decrees dealt with income. From now on, the bureaucracy took from the Jews their earnings. The income expropriations yielded much less than the property confiscations, but to the Jews the new measures were more serious. Poor people spend a larger proportion of their income on necessities than rich

1. See, for example, the letter by the I. G. Farben trustees in the I. Petschek mines at Falkenau (signed Kersten and Prentzel) to Regierungsrat Dr. Hoffmann of the Economy Ministry, on *Säuberungsaktion* ("cleansing action"), resulting in dismissal of 209 employees, January 18, 1939, NI-11264.

2. From figures in *Jüdisches Nachrichtenblatt,* Berlin, November 10, 1939.

3. From figures in "Die Juden und jüdischen Mischlinge im Dritten Reich," *Wirtschaft und Statistik,* XX, 84.

4. RGBl I, 360.

5. RGBl I, 1694.

6. Text in Jewish Black Book Committee, *The Black Book* (New York, 1946), p. 506.

7. Report by Kaiser (Reich Chancellery) to Reichskabinettsrat Dr. Killy (also in the Reich Chancellery), January 9, 1941, NG-1143.

people do, and very poor people spend all their income on necessities. In the step-by-step manner of the bureaucratic destruction process, the Jews were deprived of an ever increasing slice of their bare necessities. Survival became more and more difficult.

It is characteristic that just as in the case of Jewish property, so also in the matter of Jewish income: the business sector had the first pick. First, Jewish wages were reduced. What was left was taxed.

The formulation of a wage policy for Jews was begun in the Labor Ministry at the end of 1939, upon the principle that German labor laws should be modified so as to exclude certain payments to Jews.[8] While the ministerial bureaucrats discussed the details of the proposed measure, industry began to take measures of its own. A number of firms refused to pay wages for legal holidays, and Jewish employees countered by going to court. The Labor Court in Kassel naturally held for the companies, reasoning that Jews had "no inner tie" to the performance of labor, that to a Jew labor was only a commodity, and that a Jew had no loyalty to his employer. Hence a Jew was not entitled to receive pay for holidays.[9]

At the beginning of 1940 the draft of a law regulating wage payments to Jews was drawn up in the Labor Ministry. The draft provided that Jews be deprived of pay for holidays, family and children's allowances, birth or marriage subsidies, death benefits, bonuses, anniversary gifts, compensatory payments in the event of accidents, and – in cases of workers far from their homes – all but one yearly allowance for travel pay to visit family members.[10] The proposed decree met with a number of objections, chiefly because it contained an enumeration of exceptions rather than a positive principle (such as the rule that Jews be paid only for work actually performed).[11] These objections hurt the jurisdictional pride of the Labor Minister, and therefore he decided to implement his ideas by issuing the appropriate instructions to his regional offices, without waiting for the concurrence of other ministries.[12]

At the end of the year the Labor Ministry was invited by the Interior Ministry to attend a conference on the labor status of the Jews. Accepting the invitation, Staatssekretär Syrup, writing in behalf of the Labor Ministry, added the following words: "I consider it self-evident that I am in charge of formulating all questions concerning labor laws, also with regard to Jews so long as Jews continue to be employed privately."[13]

The conference was held under the chairmanship of the Interior Ministry's Jewish expert, Ministerialrat Lösener. One of those present (Göring's representative) declared that he wanted only a ruling to the effect that the Jews had a separate labor status. The proposed decree did not interest him at all. The conferees thereupon compromised on two decrees, one to establish the principle, the other to contain the details.[14]

8. Labor Minister Seldte to Chief of the Reich Chancellery Lammers, April 16, 1940, NG-1143.

9. Dietrich Wilde, "Der Jude als Arbeitnehmer," *Die Judenfrage*, July 15, 1940, p. 95. The identical conclusion was reached by Staatssekretär Stuckart of the Interior Ministry in his proposal to Lammers, April 30, 1940, NG-1143.

10. Seldte to Lammers, April 16, 1940, NG-1143.

11. Stuckart to Lammers, April 30, 1940, NG-1143.

12. Staatssekretär Syrup to Interior Ministry, January 3, 1941, NG-1143. For detailed regional rulings, see Oberregierungsrat Hans Küppers, "Die vorläufige arbeitsrechtliche Behandlung der Juden," *Reichsarbeitsblatt*, Part V, pp. 106-10.

13. Syrup to Interior Ministry, January 3, 1941, NG-1143.

14. Kaiser to Killy, January 9, 1941, NG-1143.

The principle of separate labor status was finally promulgated in the decree of October 3, 1941, signed by Staatssekretär Körner of the Office of the Four-Year Plan.[15] The Labor Ministry's implementation decree, dated October 31, 1941, and signed by Staatssekretär Engel,[16] provided that Jews had only the right to be paid for work actually done. Then it listed the payments to which Jews were not entitled – and which they had not been receiving for quite some time anyhow. But the decree contained also several new provisions which were important: Jews had to accept every job assigned to them by the labor offices; Jews had to be employed in groups; Jewish youths between fourteen and eighteen could be employed at all hours; Jewish invalids (except war invalids) had to accept all assignments. In summary, industry had been given the right of almost unlimited exploitation: to pay minimum wages for maximum work.

6 / Special Income Taxes

The Finance Ministry now had the job of taxing Jewish wages (or what was left of them). The idea of a special Jewish income tax actually originated at the end of 1936, when the first drafts were drawn up in the Interior Ministry. Hitler himself wanted this tax for punitive reasons, for 1936 was the year of the first assassination of a Nazi leader by a Jew (the Landesgruppenleiter Wilhelm Gustloff in Switzerland). The income tax was desired as a kind of penalty.[1] A subsequent draft prepared by the Referat Blühme in the Finance Ministry actually provided for a fluctuating tax increase, correlated with the conduct of Jews as public enemies,[2] but the punitive idea was dropped when the Justice Ministry objected to the measure as legally unsound and politically dangerous, particularly because of the possibility of retaliations against German minorities abroad (a typical Nazi fear).[3] Göring too did not like the decree, although he used the penalty idea for his so-called fine after the assassination of the second Nazi, vom Rath.[4]

Nothwithstanding all the objections, the early tax correspondence did come up with some results. One of these was the abolition, in 1938, of income tax exemptions for Jewish children.[5] In the words of the tax decree of 1939, which re-enacted the provision, "children" were persons who were not Jews.[6] The reason for specifying the status of the child, rather than the status of the wage earner, was to insure that a Christian father of a Jewish child would not get a rebate and that a Jewish father of a *Mischling* child would retain the exemption. In short, this measure was aimed at parents whose children were classified as Jews.[7]

15. RGBl I, 675.

16. RGBl I, 681.

1. Staatssekretär Reinhardt (Finance Ministry) to Foreign Office, attention Amtsrat Hofrat Schimke; Economy Ministry, att. Ministrialbürodirektor Reinecke; Propaganda Ministry, att. Regierungsrat Braekow; Deputy of the Führer (Hess), att. Hauptdienstleiter Reinhardt; Plenipotentiary of the Four-Year Plan (Göring); and Staatssekretär Lammers (Reich Chancellery), February 9, 1937, enclosing letter by Stuckart dated December 18, 1936, NG-3939.

2. Memorandum by Zülow and Kühne (Finance Ministry/Div. III), April 25, 1938, NG-4030.

3. Reinhardt letter, enclosing Stuckart correspondence, February 9, 1937, NG-3939.

4. Memorandum by Zülow and Kühne, April 25, 1938, NG-4030.

5. Reinhardt letter, February 9, 1937, enclosing letter by Prof. Dr. Hedding (Finance Ministry) to Staatssekretär Stuckart, dated January 17, 1937, NG-3939. Reinhardt to Foreign Office, November 27, 1937, NG-3939. Tax Law of 1938, RGBl I, 129, p. 135.

6. Decree of February 17, 1939, RGBl I, 284.

7. In 1938, the bureaucrats in the Finance Ministry were very enthusiastic about the idea of abolishing tax exemptions. Among the

The early correspondence contained also a proposed tax justification which was different from the punitive idea. That justification, first mentioned by Stuckart, lingered in the minds of the bureaucrats long after the measure itself had been shelved. Stuckart had reasoned that Jews did not make contributions to Nazi charitable and relief organizations. In lieu of such contributions, he argued, the Jews should pay a special income tax[8] This brilliant idea could not be wasted; on August 5, 1940, the proposal was translated into action, not against the Jews but against the Poles who were then being imported in increasing numbers into the Reich. The tax was called *Sozialausgleichsabgabe* ("Social Equalization Tax"). It was a 15 per cent special income tax with an exemption of 39 reichsmark per month. The contribution was levied on top of the regular income tax.[9] After the measure had been decreed against the Poles, it was extended to the people for whom it was originally intended, the Jews. This was accomplished by the decree of December 24, 1940, signed by Staatssekretär Reinhardt of the Finance Ministry.[10]

7 / Starvation Measures

The economic strangulation of the Jewish community did not stop with wage cutting and tax increases. After all the deductions the Jews still had a little income which the bureaucrats looked upon as a bundle of Jewish claims upon German goods and services. This was bad enough. But since the Jews had only a few marks, they had to claim with these marks what they needed most – food. And food was not just a commodity. In German, food is called "means of life" (*Lebensmittel*). In World War I the German Army had gone hungry; in World War II food was looted from all areas of occupied Europe, to be distributed in Germany under a careful rationing system. It is therefore hardly surprising that the German bureaucracy began to impose restrictions on the distribution of food articles to Jewish purchasers. The Jews were not to get their share.

Rationing was the responsibility of the Food and Agriculture Ministry. Every three or four weeks the Ministry sent rationing instructions to the regional food offices (*Provinzialernährungsämter* in Prussia and *Landesernährungsämter* in other provinces). On the regional level, the food offices sometimes supplemented these instructions in accordance with local supplies.

The food supply was divided into four categories: (1) unrationed foods: (2) basic rations for normal consumers; (3) supplementary rations for heavy workers and night workers, children, pregnant women and nursing mothers, and sick persons and invalids; (4) special allotments of rationed foods when in plentiful supply, or of unrationed but generally unavailable foods when available. (These varied from time to time and from place to place.) The Agriculture Ministry proceeded in its restrictions upon Jewish food purchasers in the characteristic step-by-step manner. Starting with special allotments, the ministry worked itself up to supplementary rations, finally cutting basic rations and unrationed foods.

On December 1, 1939, Acting Min-

---

proposals was a suggestion to deprive blinded Jewish war veterans of the dog tax exemption generally enjoyed by the war blind. Memorandum by Zülow and Kühne, April 25, 1938, NG-4030.

8. Reinhardt letter, February 9, 1937, enclosing Stuckart proposal, NG-3939.

9. RGBl I, 1077.

10. RGBl I, 1666. For details of implementation, see Ministerialrat Josef Oermann (Finance Ministry), *Die Sozialausgleichsabgabe* (2d ed.; Berlin, 1944).

ister of Food Backe instructed the regional food offices to deprive Jews of the special food allocations for the ration period December 18, 1939, to January 14, 1940. As a result, Jews were to receive less meat, less butter, no cocoa, and no rice. Coupons were to be invalidated before the issuance of the ration cards. In case of doubt as to whether the ration holder was a Jew, the police or party offices could be consulted. The instructions were not to be published in the press.[1] The instructions for the next ration period (January 15 to February 4, 1940) again provided for cutting of special rations, this time in meat and legumes.[2]

The regional food offices did not apply these instructions uniformly. Either confused or overeager, they cut into the supplementary rations of children, heavy workers, and the incapacitated, and even into the basic rations of normal consumers. On March 11, 1940, the regional food offices were reminded that basic rations and differentials for children, etc., were not to be touched. The specially alloted rations, however, were to be cut. Similarly, unrationed foods which were generally unavailable and which were distributed only from time to time by means of customers' lists were to be taken from the Jews. For the current period, the unrationed items included poultry, game fish, and smoked foods.

The clarification order then enumerated for the guidance of the food offices the following procedural rules and recommendations: All ration cards held by Jews were to be stamped with a *J*. Special ration coupons could be invalidated by the *J*. Household ration cards were to be exchanged for travel and restaurant coupons only in cases of absolute necessity; Jews could make their short trips without food. Finally, the food offices were empowered to set aside special shopping hours for Jews in order to make sure that Aryan purchasers were not "inconvenienced." In effect, this provision insured that items sold on a first-come-first-served basis never reached Jewish customers.[3] Shopping hours for Jews were fixed in Vienna between 11 A.M. and 1 P.M. and between 4 P.M. and 5 P.M., in Berlin between 4 P.M. and 5 P.M. only, and in Prague between 3 P.M. and 5 P.M.[4]

In spite of the clarification order of March 11, 1940, mistakes on the regional level continued. One such mistake resulted in a somewhat bizzare incident. Berlin received a shipment of real coffee (i.e., *Bohnenkaffee* rather than *Ersatzkaffee*). The population had to register for the coffee and, in the absence of any prohibitions, five hundred Jews were among the registrants. When the food office discovered the registrations, it struck the Jews off the lists and imposed fines on them for disturbing the public order. One Jew brought the case into a local court (Amtsgericht). The food office argued that the Jews should have known that they were not entitled to coffee, but the court overruled the Food Office on the ground that a fine could not be based on an "artificial interpretation of the law [*gekünstelten Auslegung des Gesetzes*]." When a new Justice Minister, Thierack, took over in 1942, he discussed the case in the first of his famous "instructions to the judges [*Richterbriefe*]." This is what Thierack said:

> The decision of the Amtsgericht borders in form and content on delib-

1. Backe to regional food offices, December 1, 1939, NI-13359.

2. Food Ministry (signed Narten) to regional food offices, January 3, 1940, NG-1651.

3. Narten to regional food offices, March 11, 1940, NI-14581.

4. Boris Shub (Institute of Jewish Affairs), *Starvation over Europe* (New York, 1943), p. 61.

> erate embarrassment [*Blosstellung*] of a German administrative body vis-à-vis Jewry. The judge should have asked himself with what satisfaction the Jew received the decision of this court, which certified to him and his five hundred racial comrades in a twenty-page argument his right and his victory over a German office, not to speak of the reaction of the people's sound instinct [*gesundes Volksempfinden*] to that impertinent and presumptuous behavior of the Jews.[5]

The Jews who "won" the case were, incidentally, deported to a killing center immediately.[6] No more coffee for these Jews.

In 1941, determined to close every loophole, the Agriculture Ministry took measures against the shipment of parcels from foreign countries. These parcels supplemented the diet of Jews who were fortunate enough to have helping friends and relatives in neutral states. But the ministry could not bear the thought that Jews should receive food twice, from their relatives and from the German people. Accordingly, the Food Ministry requested the customs administration of the Finance Ministry to send weekly reports to the food offices of parcels known or suspected to be intended for Jews. The contents were then subtracted from the food rations.[7]

Gradually the ministry became more stringent in its instructions to the food offices. Item after item was reduced or taken off entirely. On June 26, 1942, the Food and Agriculture Ministry invited representatives of the Party Chancellery, the Reich Chancellery, the Office of the Four-Year Plan, and the Propaganda Ministry to meet in conference for a final review of the question of food supplies for Jews.[8]

Judging from the official summary,[9] the conference was remarkably smooth. All proposals were adopted unanimously. The conferees were informed that, in accordance with instructions by the Food Ministry, Jews were no longer receiving cakes. Moreover, a number of food offices had already prohibited the distribution of white bread and rolls. All those present agreed that it would be "appropriate" to direct all food offices to withhold white bread and rolls from Jews. Next, the conferees learned that the ministry had already instructed the food offices not to distribute any egg cards to Jews. The representatives at the conference thought that it would be "justifiable" (*vertretbar*) to exclude Jews also from the purchase of all meats.

Third, the bureaucrats were unanimous in the belief that it would be "correct" (*richtig*) to lift the equality of treatment still enjoyed by Jewish children. (Until now, Jewish children had received the same supplementary quantities of bread, meat, and butter given to German children.) Accordingly, it was decided to cut these supplementary rations. That would have given to Jewish children the rations of adult German consumers. However, since that was still too much, the bureaucrats agreed to decrease the rations of Jewish children to the level of rations given to Jewish adults. Consequently, if Jewish adults lost their meat cards, so would Jewish children. Since Jewish children had enjoyed equality also in milk distribution, it was thought

5. Richterbrief No. 1 (signed Thierack), October 1, 1942, NG-295.

6. Dr. Hugo Nothmann (Jewish survivor) in Lamm, *Über die Entwicklung des deutschen Judentums,* p. 312.

7. Finance Ministry (signed Seidel) to *Oberfinanzpräsidenten,* April 20, 1941, NG-1292.

8. Food and Agriculture Ministry (signed Moritz) to Ministerialdirektor Klopfer (Party Chancellery), Reichskabinettsrat Willuhn (Reich Chancellery), Ministerialdirektor Gramsch (Office of the Four-Year Plan), and Ministerialdirektor Berndt (Propaganda Ministry), June 26, 1942, NG-1890.

9. Conference summary, dated July 1, 1942, NG-1890.

proper to change the milk ration too. Henceforth, Jewish children were to receive not whole milk but skimmed milk. Aryan children, to their third birthday, received ¾ liter daily; to their sixth year, ½ liter; and from the age of six to their fourteenth birthday, ¼ liter of whole milk. Jewish children were to receive milk only to their sixth birthday, and the maximum quantity even for the smallest children was not to exceed ½ liter of skimmed milk.

Next the bureaucrats scrutinized the rations of pregnant women, nursing mothers, and sick persons. The representative of the Agriculture Ministry pointed out that Jewish mothers had already been taken care of by a directive in April, 1942, and that the Staatssekretär for Health in the Interior Ministry (Dr. Conti) had directed doctors not to prescribe for Jewish patients and invalids any supplementary rations whatever. It was agreed that the Conti order be reinforced by a directive to the food offices.

Finally, the conferees considered that it would be "correct" to strike supplementary rations for long-hour workers, night workers, and heavy workers. Until now, these supplementary rations had been granted to Jews for reasons of efficiency, but, only lately, experience had shown again that work done by Jews was in no sense as valuable as work performed by Germans. The distribution of supplementary rations to Jewish laborers had provoked ill humor among large sections of German labor. Nevertheless, it might be necessary to give to Jews exposed to poisons ½ liter of skimmed milk a day. This exception would affect particularly the Jewish workers in powerhouses (in Berlin alone, approximately 6000). In this connection, the conferees were reminded that Berlin had already stricken supplementary rations for Jewish workers some time ago.

At the conclusion of the conference, it was noted that Staatssekretär for Health Dr. Conti was not represented and that, as a result, no one present could judge "expertly" whether the proposed ration cuts did not go "too far" in weakening the Jews physically, thus promoting epidemics and threatening the Aryan population as well. Consequently, it was decided to seek the agreement of Staatssekretär Conti before putting the ration cuts into effect. Second, it was noted that Plenipotentiary for Labor Sauckel was not represented either, and therefore it was decided to seek his advice too, this time from the viewpoint of work efficiency.

It appears that neither Staatssekretär Dr. Conti nor Labor Plenipotentiary Sauckel had any special objections, for the instructions to the regional food offices, dated September 18, 1942,[10] did not alleviate the drastic decisions of the June 29 conference. In one respect, the regulations of September 18 reached even further: there was a new restriction in the matter of food parcels, something that must have bothered the ministry very much. Heretofore, food parcels addressed to Jews had been opened in order to charge the contents against the rations of the recipient. Now there were so many prohibited items that any package found to contain contraband, such as coffee or perhaps a salami, was to be transferred by the customs administration to the food offices, for distribution to German hospitals or other big consumers.[11]

10. Instructions by Staatssekretär Riecke, September 18, 1942, NG-452.

11. In the Protektorat of Bohemia and Moravia, the Czech Ministry of Land and Forestry of the "autonomous" Czech administration quickly followed suit. In two consecutive orders Jews were barred from the purchase of all meats, eggs, white bread and rolls, milk (except a ¼ liter for children under six), all fruits and vegetables (whether fresh, dried, or canned), nuts, wines, fruit

Since 1942 was the year of mass deportations, ever smaller numbers of Jews remained within the frontiers of the Reich. By 1943 the rationing problem was so simplified that in Vienna the Jewish Council handed out a single meal a day at its headquarters at Kleine Pfarrgasse 8. The food was available until 1 P.M.; Jews working in forced labor could get their meal until 7 P.M.[12] And thus, with a few strokes of the pen, the bureaucracy had reduced a once-prosperous community, with accumulated know-how and far-flung investments, to a band of starving forced laborers asking for their meager meal at the end of the day.

juices, syrups, marmalades, jams, cheeses, candies, fish, and poultry in any state of preparation. Circular order by Protektorat Land Ministry (signed Oberembt), December 1, 1942, *Die Judenfrage* (*Vertrauliche Beilage*), February 15, 1943, pp. 14-15. Announcement by Protektorat Land Ministry (signed Hruby), December 2, 1942, *Die Judenfrage* (*Vertrauliche Beilage*), February 1, 1943, p. 10.

12. *Jüdisches Nachrichtenblatt* (Vienna), May 17, 1943.

VI / *Concentration*

1 / The Reich-Protektorat Area

The third step of the destruction process was the concentration of the Jewish community. Concentration comprised, in Germany, two developments: the crowding of the Jews into large cities and the separation of the Jews from the German population. The urbanization process was a consequence of the anti-Jewish economic measures discussed in the previous chapter; the ghettoization process was deliberately planned, measure for measure.

Even before the Nazis came to power, the Jewish community in Germany had already been highly urbanized, but after 1933 a further crowding into the cities became noticeable. Isolated Jewish families departed from villages to towns. From there the stream continued to Berlin, Vienna, Frankfurt, and other large population centers.[1] Taking the area of the Old Reich and Austria as a whole, the percentage of Jews living in cities with populations of more than 100,000 rose from 74.2 in 1933 to 82.3 in 1939.[2] The census of May 17, 1939, revealed a Jewish population of 330,892. More than two-thirds of this number lived in ten cities, as follows:[3]

Vienna	91,480
Berlin	82,788
Frankfurt	14,461
Breslau	11,172
Hamburg	10,131
Cologne	8,539
Munich	5,050
Leipzig	4,477
Mannheim	3,024
Nuremberg	2,688
	233,810

More than half the Jews lived in two cities, Vienna and Berlin.

To repeat: the Germans did not plan this movement. The migration was caused mainly by the gradual impoverishment of the Jewish community, which gave rise to increasing intra-Jewish dependence, particularly the dependence of poor Jews upon Jewish relief organizations. At least one mayor, the *Oberbürgermeister* of Frankfurt, made inquiries of his police chief whether the influx of country Jews into his city could not somehow be stopped. The police chief replied that "unfortunately" he had no legal means of doing so.[4]

Unlike the uncontrolled movement of the Jews into the cities, the ghettoization of the Jewish community (i.e., its isolation from the surrounding German population) was directed, step by step, by the bureaucracy. Ghettoization does not mean that Jewish districts, complete with walls, were set up in the cities of the Reich and the Bohemian-Moravian Protektorat. Such districts were later established in Poland and Russia to the east, but the Jewish community in Germany *was* subjected to conditions which had many characteristics of the ghetto. These characteristics are reflected in five steps of the ghettoization process: (1) the severance of social contacts between Jews and Germans, (2) housing restrictions, (3) movement regulations, (4) identification measures, and (5) the institu-

1. Georg Flatow, "Zur Lage der Juden in den Kleinstädten," *Jüdische Wohlfahrtspflege und Sozialpolitik*, 1934, pp. 237-45.

2. "Die Juden und jüdischen Mischlinge," *Wirtschaft und Statistik*, XX, 86.

3. *Ibid.*

4. *Polizeipräsident*, Frankfurt am Main, to Oberbürgermeister Staatsrat Dr. Krebs, June 8, 1936, G-113.

tion of Jewish administrative machinery.

The severance of social contacts was the first step toward Jewish isolation. In a country where members of a minority group enjoy close personal relations with the dominant group, drastic segregation measures will not be successful until these relations are dissolved and until a certain distance is established between the two groups. The dissolution of social relations began with the dismissals of Jews from the civil service and industry, and with the Aryanization or liquidation of Jewish business establishments. However, these measures were primarily economic. Their social consequences were incidental.

We shall now be concerned with calculated measures against the mixing of Jews and Germans. These specific, anti-mixing decrees fell into two categories, one based on the assumption that the Germans were too friendly with the Jews and that such friendships therefore, had to be prohibited in the interest of German purity and National Socialist ideals. The other category was based on the opposite assumption that the Germans were so hostile to the Jews that segregation measures were required for the maintenance of public order. There is a simple explanation for this contradictory reasoning. The former category comprised measures which, for their *administrative* effectiveness, had to be enforced against Germans; the latter consisted only of injunctions against Jews.

The earliest anti-mixing decree was the above mentioned Law for the Protection of German Blood and Honor,[5] which prohibited marriages as well as extramarital relationships between Jews and citizens of German or similar blood.[6] Since any intermarriage contracted *after* the decree's entry into force was considered null and void, the parties to such a marriage were automatically guilty of extramarital intercourse as well. Under the penalty provisions, both man and woman could be punished by penitentiary sentences for entering into an intermarriage, but only the *man* (whether he was Jew or German) could be sent to jail for extramarital intercourse. It was Hitler's wish that the *woman* (Jewish or German) be immune from prosecution for intercourse.

We do not know the reason for Hitler's insistence upon this exemption. It may have been a sense of chivalry or, more likely, the belief that women (even German women) were very weak individuals without wills of their own. At any rate, neither the judiciary nor the Security Police were happy with the exemption. During a judicial conference it was therefore decided to heed Hitler's wish in the literal sense only. No German would be punished for intercourse with a Jew (or for *Rassenschande* [race defilement], as that crime became known), but if she were trapped into telling a lie during the proceedings against the man, she could be sent to jail for perjury.[7] Gruppenführer Heydrich of the Security Police on his part decided that a Jewish woman could not remain free if her German partner went to jail. Such an arrangement went against his grain,

5. Signed by Hitler, Frick, Gürtner, Hess, and dated September 15, 1935, RGBl I, 1146.

6. The decree also prohibited the employment by Jews of German women under forty-five years of age in households. In 1938 the Party Chancellery proposed an amendment to the law with a view to extending the prohibition to receptionists, models, etc. The Interior Ministry replied that it was already overwhelmed with work in anti-Jewish legislation. The proposal was not important enough to warrant the necessary drafting. Pfundtner to Hess, May 25, 1938, NG-347. By November of that year the party proposal was obsolete. Hering to Justice Ministry, December 12, 1938, NG-347.

7. Summary of judicial conference, February 1, 1939, NG-629.

Hitler order or no Hitler order. Accordingly, he issued secret instructions to his State Police and Criminal Police offices to follow up the lawful conviction of a German man for *Rassenschande* with the immediate arrest of his Jewish woman partner, who was to be spirited away to a concentration camp.[8]

Other modifications in the direction of more severity were proposed in connection with the *Mischlinge*. Just what was the status of *Mischlinge* under the Law for the Protection of German Blood and Honor? The law obviously mentioned only Jews and Germans. The definition of the concept of Jew had not yet been perfected, and the *Mischlinge* did not yet exist as a group. However, as soon as this "third race" was created, it became evident that the *Mischlinge* – as persons who were neither Jews nor citizens of "German or related blood" – were actually a bridge between the Jewish and German communities. A *Mischling* could marry anybody, and he could have extramarital relations with anybody. Since this situation was very awkward, it had to be modified. So far as marriages were concerned, certain prohibitions were put into the way of the *Mischling*. (These modifications are listed in Table 20.[9] To understand the regulation of *Mischling* marriages, it may be useful to recall that the *Mischling* of the first degree was a person with *two* Jewish grandparents, who did not belong to the Jewish religion and who was not married to a Jewish person on the target date of September 15, 1935. The *Mischling* of the second degree had only *one* Jewish grandparent.)

These regulations isolated the *Mischling* of the first degree. Except by official permission, he was not allowed to marry anyone but another *Mischling* of the first degree. Curiously enough, however, the *Mischling* of the first degree was unhampered in his extramarital relations. He could not commit *Rassenschande*, whether he chose a Jewish or a German partner.[10] Needless to say, attempts were made to close this loophole. In 1941, Hitler himself requested an amendment to the Blood and Honor Law which would have prohibited the extramarital relations of a *Mischling* of the first degree with a

8. Heydrich to Gestapo and Kripo offices, June 12, 1937, NG-326.

9. Wilhelm Stuckart and Rolf Schiedmair, *Rassen- und Erbpflege in der Gesetzgebung des Reiches* (5th ed.; Leipzig 1944), pp. 46-48. *Die Judenfrage* (*Vertrauliche Beilage*), April 25, 1941, pp. 22-24.

10. *Die Judenfrage* (*Vertrauliche Beilage*), April 25, 1941, pp. 22–24.

TABLE 20 / *Regulation of "Mischling" Marriages*

PERMITTED MARRIAGES	
German	German
Mischling of the second degree	German
Mischling of the first degree	*Mischling* of the first degree
Jew	Jew
PROHIBITED EXCEPT BY SPECIAL CONSENT	
Mischling of the first degree	German
Mischling of the first degree	*Mischling* of the second degree
Mischling of the first degree	Jew (*Mischling* automatically became a Jew)
PROHIBITED	
German	Jew
Mischling of the second degree	Jew
Mischling of the second degree	*Mischling* of the second degree

German.[11] But, after a conference and much discussion, the matter was dropped with Hitler's consent.[12] Apparently the bureaucracy was not confident that it could enforce such a prohibition.

This brings us to a consideration of the enforcement of the *Rassenschande* decree in general. Just how successful was it? If the repetition of an illegal act is a criterion of the enforcibility of a law, the bureaucracy had tough going. In 1942 not fewer than sixty-one Jews were convicted of *Rassenschande* in the Old Reich. (This figure naturally includes only Jewish men, not women.) It compares with fifty-seven convictions for passport fraud and fifty-six convictions for currency violations.[13] Why, then, this continuing need for associations between Jews and Germans? We must understand that the Blood and Honor Law caught a great many mixed couples, who had intended to be married, before they had an opportunity to carry out their plans. Such a couple had three choices. It could separate – that was the aim of the decree. Alternatively, the couple could emigrate. Third, it could "live in sin."

The alternative of emigration was, incidentally, considered an offense. There is at least one case when a German who became a Jew in 1932 in order to marry a Jewish woman, and who subsequently emigrated to Czechoslovakia, where he married her, was caught after the occupation of Czechoslovakia and convicted of *Rassenschande*. The defendant argued that he was a Jew, but the court rejected that argument. He also argued the general legal principle that a law subjects people to its provisions only within the territorial jurisdiction. The law had no language indicating its applicability to German citizens living abroad. But the court held that the defendant had violated the law by leaving the country for the purpose of doing something contrary to its stipulations. His emigration was part of the total offense. He had therefore violated the law when he was still within German frontiers.[14]

One reason, then, for the large number of convictions was the unwillingness of mixed couples to separate in the face of a blanket marriage prohibition. There was, however, still another reason why the statistics were a little high. *Rassenschande* cases were almost always treated harshly by the courts. There were no mitigating circumstances, and there was no need for elaborate proof. The burden was entirely on the defense. An accused could not claim, for example, that he was unaware of the status of his woman partner; in fact, the Reichsgericht held that any German man wishing to have extramarital intercourse with *any* woman had the legal duty of inspecting her papers (*Ariernachweis*) to make sure that she was not Jewish under the law. He had to be especially careful with half-Jewish women, who might either be Jewish (prohibited relationship) or *Mischling* of the first degree (permitted relationship), depending on complex legal questions relating to religious adherence.[15] The accused was helpless also against the assertion of un-

11. Pfundtner to Deputy of the Führer, Justice Ministry, and Security Police, May 7, 1941, NG-1066.

12. Summary of *Mischling* conference, May 13, 1941, NG-1066. Lammers to Interior Ministry, September 25, 1941, NG-1066.

13. Justice Ministry (signed Grau) to *Präsident* of Reichsgericht, *Präs.* Volksgerichtshof, *Oberlandesgerichtspräsidenten, Oberreichsanwälte* at the Reichsgericht and Volksgerichtshof, and *Generalstaatsanwälte,* April 4, 1944, NG-787.

14. Decision by the Reichsgericht, December 5, 1940, *Deutsche Justiz,* 1941, p. 225. Also, *Die Judenfrage* (*Vertrauliche Beilage*), March 10, 1941, pp. 15–16.

15. Decision by Reichsgericht, November 26, 1942, *Deutsches Recht,* 1943, p. 404. Discussed also in *Die Judenfrage* (*Vertrauliche Beilage*), April 15, 1943, p. 31.

proved allegations. Needless to say, extramarital intercourse is not easily proved, but in the German courts the barest indications of a friendly relationship could suffice for a strong presumption. The most flagrant example of such a case, "which kicked up a lot of dust in the judiciary,"[16] was the accusation against Lehmann Katzenberger, chief of the Jewish Community in Nuremberg.

The facts of this case were as follows: In 1932, Katzenberger owned a wholesale shoe establishment in Nuremberg. He was then a prosperous man, fifty-nine years old, the father of grown-up children. During that year, a young unmarried German woman, twenty-two years of age, arrived in Nuremberg to manage a photography business in Katzenberger's building. Her father asked Katzenberger to look after her. In the course of the years Katzenberger helped the young lady with her problems, occasionally lending her some money and giving her little presents. This friendship continued after the girl was married, and after the war had broken out. One day the woman, Mrs. Irene Seiler, was summoned by the District Party Office (*Kreisleitung*) and warned to discontinue the acquaintance. She promised to do so, but shortly thereafter Katzenberger was arrested, to be tried for *Rassenschande* in the criminal chamber of an ordinary court. Katzenberger was then in his late sixties; Mrs. Seiler was over thirty.

The prosecutor who had charge of the case, Hermann Markl, considered the matter quite routine. He looked forward to a "moderate" sentence. (Under the Blood and Honor Law, a man convicted of *Rassenschande* could be sentenced to any term in prison.) However, the presiding justice of the local *special* court (Sondergericht, with jurisdiction in political cases) heard of the proceeding and immediately became interested in it. According to prosecutor Markl, this justice, Landgerichtsdirektor Dr. Rothaug, had a "choleric" disposition. He was an obstinate and tough fanatic who inspired fear even in his prosecutors. When the Katzenberger case came to his attention, he ordered the transfer of the proceedings to his court. In the words of another prosecutor, Dr. Georg Engert, Justice Rothaug "drew" the case into his court, for he was determined not to miss this opportunity to sentence a Jew to death.

The proceedings in Rothaug's special court turned out to be a show trial. He goaded witnesses. When the defense attorney proved testimony to be false, he was dismissed with the ruling that the witness had simply made a mistake. Rothaug frequently broke in with insulting remarks about the Jews. When Katzenberger wanted to speak, the judge cut him off. In his final plea Katzenberger tried to reiterate his innocence and in this connection reproached Rothaug for harping on the Jews and forgetting that he, Katzenberger, was a human being. Then Katzenberger brought up the name of Frederick the Great. Rothaug broke in immediately to object to the "besmirching" of the great name of the great Prussian king, especially by a Jew.

On March 13, 1942, Landgerichtsdirektor Dr. Rothaug, joined by Landgerichtsräte Dr. Ferber and Dr. Hoffmann, gave his decision. He summarized the "evidence" as follows:

> So it is said that the two had approached each other sexually [*geschlechtliche Annäherungen*] in various ways, including also intercourse. They are alleged to have kissed each other, sometimes in the apartment of Mrs. Seiler, at other times in Katzenberger's business premises. Seiler is alleged to

16. Affidavit by Dr. Georg Engert (Prosecutor, Nuremberg), January 18, 1947, NG-649.

> have sat on Katzenberger's lap and Katzenberger, with intent to have sexual satisfaction, is said to have stroked her thigh over [not under] her clothes. On such occasions Katzenberger is alleged to have pressed Seiler close and to have placed his head on her bosom.

Seiler admitted that she had kissed Katzenberger, but playfully. Rothaug dismissed the playful motive by pointing out that she had accepted money from Katzenberger. She was therefore "accessible" (*zugänglich*). Pronouncing sentence, Rothaug condemned Katzenberger to death and sent Mrs. Seiler to prison for perjury.[17]

After pronouncement of judgment there was one more incident in the case. Though the time was March, 1942, and in Russia a great spring offensive was being prepared, the commander of the German armed forces and Führer of the German Reich, Adolf Hitler, had heard of the decision and protested that his injunction against sentencing the woman had not been heeded. No woman, said Hitler, could be sentenced for *Rassenschande*. He was quickly informed that Mrs. Seiler had been imprisoned not for *Rassenschande* but for lying on oath. This explanation mollified Hitler.[18]

In June, Katzenberger was put to death, but a short time thereafter Mrs. Seiler, having served six months of her sentence, was released.[19]

The Katzenberger case was symptomatic of an attempt to break friendly relations between Jews and Germans. We must keep in mind that Lehmann Katzenberger was president of the Jewish Community in Nuremberg (tenth largest in the Reich), that before Rothaug had a chance to rule on the case Katzenberger had been accused before an ordinary court, and that before Katzenberger was accused Mrs. Seiler had been warned by the party to discontinue her acquaintance with the Jewish leader. The Katzenberger case is thus not without administrative significance; it was part of an attempt to isolate the Jewish community. We find confirmation of this fact in an order issued by the Security Police headquarters (*Reichssicherheitshauptamt*) on October 24, 1941, to all Gestapo offices. It reads as follows:

> Lately it has repeatedly become known that, now as before, Aryans are maintaining friendly relations with Jews and that they show themselves with them conspicuously in public. In view of the fact that these Aryans still do not seem to understand the elementary basic principles of National Socialism, and because their behavior has to be regarded as disrespect towards measures of the state, I order that in such cases the Aryan party is to be taken into protective custody temporarily for educational purposes, and that in serious cases they be put into a concentration camp, grade I, for a period of up to three months. The Jewish party is in any case to be taken into protective custody until further notice and to be sent to a concentration camp.[20]

Needless to say, Security Police proceedings were entirely extra-judicial.

17. This account is based on the following materials: Affidavit by Oberstaatsanwalt (prosecutor) Dr. Georg Engert, January 18, 1947, NG-649. Affidavit by Staatsanwalt Hermann Markl, January 23, 1947, NG-681. Affidavit by Irene Seiler, March 14, 1947, NG-1012. Paul Ladiges (brother-in-law of Mrs. Seiler) to "Justizministerium Nürnberg" (U.S. Military Tribunal in Nuremberg), November 23, 1946, NG-520. Judgment of the special court at Nürnberg-Fürth in the case against Lehmann Katzenberger and Irene Seiler, signed by Rothaug, Ferber, and Hoffmann, March 13, 1942, NG-154.

18. Lammers to SS-Gruppenführer Schaub (adjutant of the Führer), March 28, 1942, NG-5170.

19. Letter by Ladiges, November 23, 1946, NG-520.

20. Circular by State Police Office in Nürnberg-Fürth (signed Dr. Grafenberger), enclosing order from Berlin, November 3. 1941, L-152.

They involved no confrontation in a court, ordinary or extraordinary. The order was designed to deter relationships which could not always be classified as *Rassenschande* (namely, friendly relations between Jews and Germans, particularly manifest, open friendliness as shown by conversation in the streets or visits to homes).[21] There was, perhaps, some apprehension that the toleration of such friendliness might encourage some Germans to offer Jews sanctuary in the deportation roundups; but that fear was unfounded, for when the hour of decision came, few Germans made any move to protect their Jewish friends.

The Blood and Honor Law and the order by Security Police Chief Heydrich were designed to sever close personal relations – whether passionate or platonic – between Jews and Germans. These two measures had to be directed not only at the Jewish party but also at the German. That is why these injunctions were rationalized as measures against a kind of heresy. The German who left the country in order to marry his Jewish girl friend was guilty of heresy; he could not claim that he was a Jew. Similarly, the German who stopped in the street to talk to an old Jewish acquaintance was also guilty of a lack of understanding of and respect for Nazi "principles."[22]

Of course, ghettoization went a little further than that. An attempt was made to keep Germans and Jews apart as long as possible and as much as possible. These measures could be taken only by barring Jews at certain times from certain places. The rationalization for these decrees was that the Germans did not like the Jews, that Aryans were "inconvenienced" by the presence of Jews, and that therefore the Jews had to be kept out or kept away.

The most important of these antimixing ordinances were the Law against Overcrowding of German Schools of April 25, 1933, which reduced the number of Jews in higher institutions to the proportion of Jews in the population,[23] and the subsequent decrees culminating in the complete expulsion of Jews from German schools in November, 1938. From that date, Jews were permitted to attend only Jewish schools.[24]

Although the school segregation measures created a very serious problem for the Jewish community, they provoked less discussion and less controversy in the upper levels of the German bureaucracy than the orders per-

21. An awkward situation was created for the churches when baptized Jews turned up for services. The Protestant churches made their stand "courageously." No pastor, writes Lutheran Bishop Lilje, "ever thought of turning these people away." Hanns Lilje (Bishop of Hanover), "Resurgence of Faith," *Life*, May 10, 1954, p. 123. Cardinal Bertram issued instructions that the "conduct of special services [*die Abhaltung von Sondergottesdiensten*]" was to be "weighed" only in the event of "major difficulties," such as the staying away or ostentatious departure from the services by civil servants, party comrades, etc. *Mitteilungen zur Weltanschaulichen Lage*, April 15, 1942, pp. 13–17, EAP 250-c-10/5.

22. At certain times during the Middle Ages, mixed couples who had had intercourse were judged guilty of superharlotry (*ueberhure*) and burned (or buried) alive. At that time, too, the guilty Christian was deemed to have denied his faith (*ungelouben*), in other words, to have committed heresy. Guido Kisch, *The Jews in Medieval Germany* (Chicago, 1949), pp. 205–7, 465–68.

23. Decree of April 25, 1933, signed by Hitler and Frick, RGB1 I, 255. The law excepted from the quota all non-Aryans who had at least one German grandparent, or whose fathers had fought for Germany at the front in World War I.

24. German press, November 16, 1938. *Mischlinge* of the first degree were ejected from the schools in 1942; *Mischlinge* of the second degree were permitted to continue their schooling, provided their presence did not contribute to overcrowding. *Die Judenfrage* (*Vertrauliche Beilage*), March 1, 1943, pp. 17–19.

taining to Jewish traveling on trains. Propaganda Minister Goebbels came to the conference of November 12, 1938, well prepared with proposals for travel regulations. Here is an excerpt from the discussion:

Goebbels: It is still possible today for a Jew to share a compartment in a sleeping car with a German. Therefore, we need a decree by the Reich Ministry for Transport stating that separate compartments shall be available for Jews; in cases where compartments are filled up, Jews cannot claim a seat. They will be given a separate compartment only after all Germans have secured seats. They will not mix with Germans, and if there is no room, they will have to stand in the corridor.

Göring: In that case, I think it would make more sense to give them separate compartments.

Goebbels: Not if the train is overcrowded!

Göring: Just a moment. There'll be only one Jewish coach.

Goebbels: Suppose, though, there aren't many Jews going on the express train to Munich, suppose there are two Jews on the train and the other compartments are overcrowded. These two Jews would then have a compartment all for themselves. Therefore, I say, Jews may claim a seat only after all Germans have secured a seat.

Göring: I'd give the Jews one coach or one compartment. And should a case like you mention arise and the train be overcrowded, believe me, we won't need a law. We'll kick him out and he'll have to sit all alone in the toilet all the way!

Goebbels: I don't agree; I don't believe in this. There ought to be a law. . . .[25]

More than a year passed before the Transport Minister issued a directive on Jewish travel: "In the interest of the maintenance of order in the passenger trains," Jews of German nationality and stateless Jews were barred from the use of all sleepers and dining cars on all railway lines within "Greater Germany." However, the directive did not introduce separate compartments, an arrangement which the Transport Minister considered impractical.[26] Not until July, 1942, were Jews barred from waiting rooms and restaurants in railway stations. This measure, however, was ordered not by the Transport Ministry but by the Security Police.[27] The Transport Ministry did not concern itself with the compartment problem anymore.

The school and railway ordinances were accompanied by many other measures which were designed to alleviate "over-crowding," to promote the "convenience" of the German population, and to maintain the "public order." We have already noted the special shopping hours introduced by the Food and Agriculture Ministry.[28] At the insistence of Propaganda Minister Goebbels and Security Police Chief Heydrich, Jews were barred from resorts and beaches.[29] Hospitalized Jews were transferred to Jewish institutions, and the services of Aryan barbershops were no longer extended to Jews.[30]

The anti-mixing decrees constituted the first phase of the ghettoization proc-

25. Minutes of conference of November 12, 1938, PS-1816.

26. Transport Minister (Dorpmüller) to Interior Minister, December 30, 1939, NG-3995. The compartments on European trains are laid out as follows:

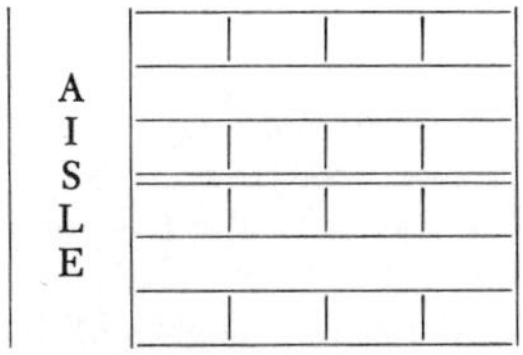

A
I
S
L
E

Third-class compartments hold eight; second and first-class compartments seat six.

27. *Die Judenfrage* (*Vertrauliche Beilage*), March 1, 1943, pp. 17–19.

28. See p. 102.

29. Minutes of conference of November 12, 1938, PS-1816.

30. *Die Judenfrage* (*Vertrauliche Beilage*), March 1, 1943, pp. 17–19.

ess. Most were drafted in the 1930's, and their aim was limited to social separation of Jews and Germans. In the second phase, the bureaucracy attempted a physical concentration by setting aside special Jewish housing accommodations. This type of ghettoization measure is always a very difficult administrative problem, because people have to change apartments.

Before any serious move was made in the housing field, Göring brought up a very fundamental question in the conference of November 12, 1938: Should Jews be crowded into ghettos or only into houses? Turning to Security Police Chief Heydrich, who was proposing all sorts of movement restrictions and insignia for Jews, Göring said:

> But my dear Heydrich, you won't be able to avoid the creation of ghettos on a very large scale, in all cities. They will have to be created.[31]

Heydrich replied very emphatically:

> As for the question of ghettos, I would like to make my position clear right away. From the point of view of the police, I don't think a ghetto, in the form of a completely segregated district where only Jews would live, can be put up. We could not control a ghetto where Jews congregate amid the whole Jewish people. It would remain a hideout for criminals and also for epidemics and the like. We don't want to let the Jews live in the same house with the German population; but today the German population, their blocks or houses, force the Jew to behave himself. The control of the Jew through the watchful eye of the whole population is better than having him by the thousands in a district where I cannot properly establish a control over his daily life through uniformed agents.[32]

The "police point of view" is most interesting in two respects. Heydrich looked upon the whole German population as a kind of auxiliary police force. They were to make sure that the Jew "behaved" himself; they were to watch all Jewish movements and to report anything that might be suspicious. Interesting also is Heydrich's prediction of epidemics. Of course, epidemics are not necessary concomitants of ghetto walls; but they do occur when housing deteriorates, when medical services are inadequate, and, above all, when the food supply is shut off. In the Polish ghettos Heydrich's predictions came true. The control mechanism in the Polish ghettos *was* weak, and epidemics *did* break out. Göring heeded Heydrich's advice, and on December 28, 1939, he issued a directive that Jews be concentrated in houses rather in districts.[33]

Now that the moving was to start, one other question had to be resolved — the problem of mixed marriage. In the Blood and Honor Law the bureaucracy had prohibited the formation of *new* intermarriages, but that law did not affect *existing* intermarriages. Under the marriage law, intermarriages were subject to the same regulations as other marriages: no divorce could be granted unless one of the parties had done something wrong or unless the parties had been separated for at least three years.

Only one provision affecting intermarriages had been written into the marriage law of 1938. Under that provision the Aryan party to a mixed marriage could obtain a divorce if he (or she) could convince the court that after the introduction of the Nuremberg laws he had obtained such enlightenment about the Jewish question that he was now convinced that if he had only had such enlightenment before the intermarriage had occurred,

31. Minutes of conference of November 12, 1938, PS-1816.

32. Minutes of conference of November 12, 1938, PS-1816.

33. Enclosed in letter from Bormann to Rosenberg, January 17, 1939, PS-69.

he would never have entered into it. That conviction, of course, had to be proven to the satisfaction of the court. Moreover, the Aryan party was given only until the end of 1939 to institute a divorce proceeding on such a ground.[34] Apparently only a few Germans took advantage of this cumbersome – and potentially embarrassing – procedure. In 1939 there were still about 30,000 intermarried couples in the Reich-Protektorat area; that is, almost one out of every ten Jews lived in an intermarriage.[35] The problem now facing the bureaucracy was what to do with these 30,000 intermarried couples. Should they too be moved into special Jewish houses?

The Göring directive of December 28, 1938, solved this problem by dividing the intermarried couples into two categories: a "privileged" and an "unprivileged" category. (The classification criteria are indicated in Table 21.)[36]

TABLE 21 / *Classification of Intermarriages*

	CHILDREN NOT RAISED AS JEWS ("MISCHLINGE" OF THE FIRST DEGREE)	CHILDREN RAISED IN JEWISH RELIGION	CHILDLESS
Jewish wife – German husband	privileged	not privileged	privileged
Jewish husband – German wife	privileged	not privileged	not privileged

It should be noted that the decisive factor for the classification of all intermarried couples with children was the religious status of the child. If the offspring was not raised in the Jewish religion, he was a *Mischling* of the first degree. As such, he was liable for induction into the armed forces or into the Labor Service. Göring did not want such *Mischlinge* to be "exposed to Jewish agitation" in houses occupied by Jews; hence he exempted all couples with such children. In the case of childless couples the Jewish wife of a German husband was considered privileged, possibly because the household belonged to the German spouse. On the other hand, the German wife of a Jewish husband was liable to be moved into a Jewish house. Göring hoped that these German wives would divorce their husbands and "return" to the German community.[37] Judging from partial statistics,[38] the privileged couples outnumbered the unprivileged intermarriages nearly three to one, and the reason for that ratio is not hard to find. The large majority of mixed couples did not raise their children in the Jewish religion.

It should be emphasized that the housing exemption granted to couples in privileged mixed marriage was extended with few modifications to wage and food regulations. Moreover, in 1941–44 the Jews in mixed marriage, including those in *unprivileged* mixed marriage, were *not* subjected to deportation. That phenomenon was a characteristic of the step-by-step destruction process. Once a group was taken out of the circle of victims for the purpose of one measure, it was immune to subsequent measures as well.

34. See comment by Dietrich Wilde and Dr. Krekau in "Auflösung von Mischehen nach Par. 55 EheG.," *Die Judenfrage (Vertrauliche Beilage)*, May 15, 1943, pp. 33–36.

35. Exact figures for the end of 1938 are not available, but on December 31, 1942, the number of Jews in intermarriage was still 27,744. Report by SS-Statistician Korherr, April 19, 1943, NO-5193.

36. Bormann to Rosenberg, January 17, 1939, PS-69.

37. Bormann to Rosenberg, January 17, 1939, PS-69.

38. Korherr report, April 19, 1943, NO-5193.

Or, to put it another way, if the privilege was upheld in the matter of changing apartments, it was also upheld in the application of more drastic measures. However, we shall have occasion to deal with that subject more thoroughly in the next chapter, for, just as the party was dissatisfied with the exemption of *Mischlinge* of the first degree, so the party men challenged the privilege of mixed marriage, which was in large measure an outgrowth of the *Mischling* concept.

The actual implementation of the housing restrictions was a very slow process. A great many Jewish families had to be evicted, but eviction was no solution so long as these Jewish families had no place to go. It was practicable only if the homeless family could be quartered in another Jewish household or if there was a vacancy in a house designated for Jewish occupancy. The very first eviction regulation against Jews is to be found in the decree of July 25, 1938,[39] which allowed German landlords to terminate leases for Jewish doctors' apartments. The year 1938 was, moreover, a period of very loose court interpretation of tenancy regulations and leases. During that year many Jews emigrated and, consequently, there were vacancies. In a decision dated September 16, 1938, a Berlin court went so far as to rule that the tenancy laws did not apply to Jews at all. Inasmuch as Jews were not members of the people's community (*Volksgemeinschaft*), they could not be members of the housing community (*Hausgemeinschaft*).[40] This decision anticipated matters a bit, but in effect it was put into a decree dated April 30, 1939, and signed by Hitler, Gürtner, Krohn (Deputy of the Labor Minister), Hess, and Frick.[41] The decree provided that Jews could be evicted by a German landlord if the landlord furnished a certificate showing that the tenant could live somewhere else. At the same time, the decree provided that homeless Jewish families had to be accepted as tenants by other Jews still in possession of their apartments.

Now the crowding of Jews into *Judenhäuser* could begin. Selecting the houses and steering the Jews into them was the job of the local housing authorities (*Wohnungsämter*). In larger cities the *Wohnungsämter* had special divisions for the movement of Jews (*Judenumsiedlungsabteilungen*). By 1941 the movement had evidently progressed far enough to entrust the remaining apartment allocations to the Jewish community organization, which kept a close watch on vacancies or space in the *Judenhäuser*. Needless to say, the Jewish bureaucrats worked under the close supervision of the State Police (Gestapo).[42]

The housing restrictions were not intended to be the only constraint upon the Jews. Almost contemporaneously with the housing regulations, the bureaucracy tightened Jewish movements and communications. In September, 1939, shortly after the outbreak of war, the local police offices ordered the Jews off the streets after 8 P.M. The Reich Press Chief instructed the newspapers to justify this restriction with the explanation that "Jews had often taken advantage of the blackout to molest Aryan women."[43] On November

39. RGBl I, 1146.

40. Decision by Amtsgericht Berlin-Schöneberg, September 16, 1938, *Juristische Wochenschrift*, 1938, p. 3405. Reported by Ernst Fraenkel, *The Dual State* (New York, 1941), p. 93.

41. RGBl I, 864.

42. Circular note by *Fachgruppe* ("Association") of Painters, Administrators, and Agents in Real Estate to *Bezirksgruppe* ("Local Group") Vienna-Lower Austria, June 14, 1941, Occ E 6a-15. Reichsbaurat Walter Uttermöhle in *Die Judenfrage* (*Vertrauliche Beilage*), September 1, 1941, pp. 63–64.

43. Instructions by the Reich Press Chief (Brammer Material), September 15, 1939, NG-4697.

28, 1939, Security Police Chief Heydrich signed a decree in which he authorized the *Regierungspräsidenten* in Prussia, Bavaria, and the Sudeten area, the Mayor of Vienna, the *Reichskommissar* in the Saar, and the competent authorities in other areas to impose movement restrictions on Jews — the prohibition not only to appear in public at certain times but also to enter certain areas at all times.[44] The police president of Berlin thereupon declared certain areas to be forbidden zones.[45] The police president of Prague (Charvat) forbade Jews to change their address or to leave the city limits, except for purposes of emigration.[46] On July 17, 1941, Charvat also forbade the Jews to enter the woods at Prague.[47] By a decree of September 1, 1941 (a fundamental measure, to be discussed later in full), Jews were forbidden to leave the boundary of their residential districts without carrying written permission of the local police authority. (Jews in mixed marriage were exempted from this restriction.)[48] The ghetto began to take shape.

Movement *within* the cities was regulated still more by orders concerning the use of city transportation by Jews. In Prague the police president forbade to Jews the use of trolleys and buses in his decree of December 12, 1941.[49] In the Reich area, including Austria, the Transport Ministry ruled on September 18, 1941, that Jews could use city transportation at all times except during rush hours — in principle, Jews were to take seats only when there were no German standees.[50]

On March 24, 1942, Chief Security Police Heydrich, in agreement with the Transport Ministry and the Postal Ministry, issued an order which sharply restricted the right of Jews to use public transportation, including subways, street cars, and buses. Henceforth, the Jews required police permits (issued by the local Order Police) for use of any such transportation. Permits were to be granted to workers if they could prove that the distance from home to their place of work was seven kilometers (a little over four miles) or one hour. Sick persons or invalid workers could obtain permits for relatively shorter distances. School children were to be given a permit, provided that their distance was at least five kilometers (over three miles) or one hour each way, rain or shine. Lawyers and doctors (*Konsulenten* and *Krankenbehandler*) could obtain a permit for any distance.[51]

At the same time, communications were cut still more by withdrawal of the right to use telephones. In 1941, private telephones were ripped out of Jewish apartments. This measure was followed by a prohibition to use public telephones except for conversations with Aryans. Finally, this permission was withdrawn, and all telephone booths were marked with signs reading "Use by Jews prohibited."[52]

These elaborate restrictions were reinforced by an elaborate system of

44. RGBl I, 1676.

45. Decree of December 3, 1938; text in Institute of Jewish Affairs, *Hitler's Ten-Year War*, pp. 22–23.

46. *Jüdisches Nachrichtenblatt* (Prague), November 8, 1940.

47. *Jüdisches Nachrichtenblatt* (Prague), July 25, 1941.

48. RGBl I, 547.

49. *Jüdisches Nachrichtenblatt* (Prague), December 12, 1941.

50. "Benutzung der Verkehrsmittel durch Juden," *Die Judenfrage* (*Vertrauliche Beilage*), December 10, 1941, pp. 78–79.

51. Regierungspräsident/Führungsstab Wirtschaft in Wiesbaden to Chambers of Commerce in area, May 12, 1942, enclosing Heydrich directive of March 24, 1942, L-167. *Jüdisches Nachrichtenblatt* (Berlin), April 17, 1942.

52. Propaganda Ministry (signed Wächter and Berndt) to all *Gauleiter*, Chiefs of Propaganda Offices and Propaganda Chiefs with *Gauleiter*, undated, probably end of 1941, G-44. Mimeographed notice of Vorstand

identifications. The first element in this system was identification in personal documents. Identification papers are an important ingredient of any police state system; in the case of Jews the document requirements were especially stringent.

The decree of July 23, 1938,[53] prepared by the Interior and Justice Ministries, required all Jews of German nationality to apply (stating that they were Jews) for identification cards. The cards had to be asked for by December 31, 1938. Jews over fifteen years of age had to carry their cards with them at all times. In dealings with party or ministerial offices Jews were to indicate that they were Jews and were to show their cards without being asked to do so.

Jews who were about to emigrate also had to obtain passports. At first, nothing in a passport indicated whether the bearer was a Jew — apparently no one thought of making any changes in passports issued to Jews or held by Jews until action was initiated by officials of a foreign country. That country was Switzerland. After the Austrian Anschluss many Jews had taken advantage of a German-Swiss agreement for the abolition of the visa requirement to cross into Switzerland. On June 24, 1938, the chief of the Federal Swiss Police, Heinrich Rothmund, protested to the German Legation in Bern against what he called the "inundation" (*Überflutung*) of Switzerland by Viennese Jews, for whom, he said, the Swiss had no more use than Germany did.[54]

On August 10 the Swiss Minister in Berlin looked up the chief of the Political Division of the German Foreign Office to tell him that the flow of Jews to Switzerland had reached "extraordinary proportions." In one day forty-seven Jews had arrived in Basel alone. The Swiss government was decidedly against the "Judaification" (*Verjudung*) of their country, which is something the Germans could understand. Under the circumstances, the Swiss were now considering the reimposition of visa controls.[55] On August 31, Bern denounced the visa agreement. Three days later, however, the Swiss police chief (Rothmund) informed the German Minister in Bern that he was ready to compromise: the Swiss government would be willing to restrict its visa requirement to German *Jews* if the passports would indicate clearly that their holders were Jews. This condition was accepted after some haggling about "reciprocity" (i.e., visa requirements for Swiss Jews, which the Swiss were reluctant to accept).[56] On September 26, Rothmund went to Berlin. On September 29 a treaty was signed which provided that the Reich would undertake to mark *all* passports of its Jews (whether traveling to Switzerland or not) with a sign identifying the bearers as Jews.[57] A few days

---

of Jüdische Kultusgemeinde (Berlin), November 14, 1941, G-229. *Jüdisches Nachrichtenblatt* (Prague), February 13, 1942. *Die Judenfrage* (*Vertrauliche Beilage*), March 1, 1943, pp. 17–19.

53. RGBl I, 922.

54. *Akten zur Deutschen Auswärtigen Politik 1918–1945,* Ser. D, Vol. V, Document 642 (footnote).

55. Memorandum by Wörmann (Chief, Polit. Div. in For. Off.), August 10, 1938, *Akten,* Ser. D, Vol. V, Doc. 642.

56. *Akten,* Ser. D, Vol. V, Doc. 643 (footnote).

57. Ministerialrat Krause (passport official, Security Police) to Foreign Office, attention Vortragender Legationsrat Rödiger, October 3, 1938, enclosing text of German-Swiss agreement, *Akten,* Ser. D, Vol. V, Doc. 643 (with footnotes). The agreement was signed by Dr. Best, Krause, Kröning, and Rödiger for the German side, and by Rothmund and Kappeler for the Swiss. The Swiss Bundesrat approved the agreement on October 4, 1938. Ratifications were exchanged on the following November 11. Under the agreement, the German government reserved the right to impose visa requirements on Swiss Jews. Whether this provision was carried into operation, we do not know.

after this agreement had been negotiated, a passport decree was drafted.

The decree, dated October 5, 1938,[58] and signed by the head of the administrative office of the Security Police, Ministerialdirigent Best,[59] provided that all German passports held by Jews be stamped with a large red *J*. In a letter to Vortragender Legationsrat Rödiger of the Legal Division of the Foreign Office, dated October 5, 1938,[60] Best requested that passports of Jews residing abroad be stamped whenever the documents were presented to consulates or missions for renewal or some other purpose, and that lists be made of Jews abroad who did not respond to invitations to have their passports stamped.

On October 11, Rödiger wrote to the German diplomatic and consular representatives abroad,[61] repeating and elaborating on these requests. Specifically, invitations were to be issued to holders of passports valid for over six months; other Jews were to have their passports stamped only when they presented them; no charge was to be made for the entry; and so on. These instructions have significance because they extended the identification system to tens of thousands of emigrated Jews in countries later occupied by the Germans.

The document-stamping did not stop with passports. We have seen that on March 11, 1940, the Food and Agriculture Ministry directed that ration cards belonging to Jews be marked with a *J* for identification.[62] On September 18, 1942, Staatssekretär Riecke of the Food and Agriculture Ministry ordered that ration cards issued to Jews be marked obliquely and throughout with the word *Jude*.[63]

The second part of the identification system consisted of the assignment of Jewish names. This idea was first considered by Staatssekretär Bang of the Economy Ministry, who proposed to Lammers a revocation of name changes granted since November, 1918.[64] Jews who had adopted German names would thus have to revert to their old names. The Bang proposal slept for a long time, but on January 5, 1938, it was put into effect. The decree of that date[65] provided that name changes granted before January 30, 1933, could be revoked.

The revocation order was followed by the decree of August 17, 1938,[66] drafted by Ministerialrat Globke, name expert of the Interior Ministry, and signed by Staatssekretär Stuckart and Justice Minister Gürtner. This decreee stipulated that Jewish men had to add to their regular first name the middle name Israel, and Jewish women the name Sara, unless they already had a first name included in an approved list of the Interior Ministry. The approved list – which, incidentally, had to be used for the naming of newly born children – was also drawn up by expert Globke.[67]

In compiling his list, Globke neces-

58. RGBl I, 1342.

59. Competence to make regulations concerning passports, police control, registration, and identification was given to the Interior Ministry by the decree of May 11, 1937, signed by Hitler, Frick, Staatssekretär von Mackensen (Foreign Office), Staatssekretär Reinhardt (Finance Ministry), and Staatssekretär Schlegelberger (Justice Ministry), RGBl I, 589.

60. Best to Rödiger, October 5, 1938, NG-3366.

61. Rödiger to missions and consulates abroad, October 11, 1938, NG-3366.

62. Narten to food offices, March 11, 1940, NI-14581.

63. Riecke to food offices, September 18, 1942, NG-1292.

64. Bang to Lammers, March 6, 1933, NG-902.

65. RGBl I, 9.

66. RGBl I, 1044. Authorship of the decree is stated by Lösener in his affidavit of February 24, 1948, NG-1944-A.

67. Affidavit by Lösener, February 24, 1948, NG-1944-A. The complete list is in the decree of August 18, 1938, *Ministerial-Blatt*

sarily had to omit Hebrew names which in the popular mind (*Volksbewusstsein*) were no longer regarded as alien first names because they had been completely Germanized (*eingedeutscht*). Hence he omitted such names as Adam, Daniel, David, Michael, and Raphael for men, and Anna, Debora, Esther, Eva, and Ruth for women. Instead, he supplied (for boys) Faleg, Feibisch, Feisel, Feitel, Feiwel, and Feleg, plus (for girls) Scharne, Scheindel, Scheine, Schewa, Schlämche, Semche, Simche, Slowe, and Sprinzi, as well as many other distortions and figments of the imagination. The name changes and new names had to be recorded in birth and marriage certificates by the local Order Police. The new designations henceforth appeared not only in personal documents of Jews, but also in court records and all official correspondence dealing with individually named Jews.

The third component of the identification system was the outward marking of persons and apartments. Outward marking was designed to set off, visually, the Jews from the rest of the population. An indirect marking process had already started in the middle thirties. It was customary in Germany, especially in the big cities, to hoist the red-white-black flag from the windows on holidays (more ardent Nazis put color pictures of Hitler in their windows), to wear Nazi insignia and swastika armbands, and to give the "German salute" – the *deutscher Gruss* (outstretched arm and "Heil Hitler"). All these manifestations of membership in the German community were successively denied to Jews. The Blood and Honor Law[68] prohibited Jews to display the Reich colors and expressly permitted the Jews to display the Zionist blue-white-blue flag; the decree of November 14, 1935,[69] regulated the use of insignia, medals, titles, etc.; finally, a ruling of the Justice Ministry, dated November 4, 1937,[70] deprived those Jews who were prone to give the "German salute" of a chance to hide their identity.

Direct marking was first proposed by Heydrich in the conference of November 12, 1938. As Heydrich outlined his proposal, chairman Göring, who was not only Germany's first industrialist but also its first designer of uniforms, suggested hopefully, "A uniform?" Not to be deterred, Heydrich answered, "An insignia."[71] However, Hitler opposed the marking of the Jews at that time, and Göring disclosed the decision at the *Gauleiter* conference of December 6, 1938.[72]

The marking of the Jews was first applied in Poland, where, it was felt, the Hitler prohibition was not in force. And it is characteristic of the development of the destruction process that, in spite of the veto by the highest authority of the Reich, recurrent suggestions for introducing the measure in Greater Germany were circulated in the ministerial offices of the bureaucracy. On July 30, 1941, Staatssekretär and SS-Gruppenführer Karl Hermann Frank of the Protektorate administration in Prague urgently requested in a letter to Lammers that he be permitted to mark the Jews in Bohemia-Moravia.[73] Lammers forwarded the request to the Interior Ministry.[74] Stuckart replied on August 14, 1941, raising the question whether the decree could be applied

des Reichs- und Preussischen Ministeriums des Innern, 1938, p. 1346.

68. September 15, 1935, RGBl I, 1146.

69. RGBl I, 1341.

70. *Deutsche Justiz,* 1937, p. 1760.

71. Minutes of conference of November 12, 1938, PS-1816.

72. Stuckart to Lammers, August 14, 1941, NG-1111. The reason for Hitler's opposition is something of a mystery. Probably Hitler objected to the marking on aesthetic grounds.

73. Lammers to Frank, August 10, 1941, NG-1111.

74. *Ibid.*

to the entire Reich-Protektorat area. However, he wanted first to have the opinion of the Foreign Office and of the Labor Ministry.[75]

At this point, on August 20, 1941, the Propaganda Ministry seized the initiative and requested Hitler to change his mind. Hitler agreed.[76] Having scored this success, the Propaganda Ministry circulated the news and invited the interested ministries to a conference,[77] which was held under the chairmanship of Staatssekretär Gutterer of the Propaganda Ministry. The Interior Ministry's expert on Jewish affairs (Ministerialrat Lösener), who attended this meeting, said after the war: "I had assumed that as usual it would be a small conference of the participating experts." Instead, there were speeches. "Then there was applause, not like in a conference – but as if it were an election campaign."[78] However, in the end, the drafting of the decree was entrusted to Lösener.[79]

In its final form the decree – dated September 1, 1941[80] provided that Jews six years or over were to appear in public only when wearing the Jewish star. According to specification, the star had to be as large as the palm of a hand. Its color had to be black, the background yellow, and for the center of the star the decree prescribed the black inscription *Jude*. The victim was to sew the star tightly on the left front of his clothing. Jews in privileged mixed marriage were exempt.

The party feared that the star decree would result in renewed violence, and Bormann issued circulars warning party members not to molest Jews.[81] Children especially were to be cautioned. But there is no record of violence. In fact, there is a story of a little girl who went out of her way to greet politely a Jewish community worker; she said, "Heil Hitler, Mr. Jew."[82]

The Security Police, in the meantime, extended the marking to apartments: in 1942 the Jews were ordered to paste the star on their doors, in black print on white paper.[83]

The whole identification system, with its personal documents, specially assigned names, and conspicuous tagging in public, was a powerful weapon in the hands of the police. First, the system was an auxiliary device which facilitated the enforcement of residence and movement restrictions. Second, it was an independent control measure in that it enabled the police to pick up any Jew, anywhere, anytime. Third, and perhaps most important, identification had a paralyzing effect on its victims. The system induced the Jews to be even more docile, more responsive to command than before. The wearer of the star was exposed; he thought that all eyes were fixed upon him. It was as though the whole population had become a police force, watching him and guarding his actions. No Jew, under those conditions, could resist, escape, or hide without first ridding himself of the conspicuous tag, the revealing middle name, the tell-tale ration card, passport, and identification papers. Yet the riddance of these burdens was dangerous, for the victim could be recognized and denounced. Few Jews took the chance. The vast

75. Stuckart to Lammers, August 14, 1941, NG-1111.

76. Unterstaatssekretär Luther (Foreign Office/Division Germany) to Staatssekretär Weizsäcker of the Foreign Office, September 19, 1941, Doc. Weizsäcker-488.

77. *Ibid.*

78. Testimony by Lössener, Case No. 11, tr. pp. 7636–38.

79. Affidavit by Lösener, February 24, 1948, NG-1944-A.

80. RGBl I, 547.

81. See the previously mentioned Bormann directive in NG-1672.

82. Account by Dr. Hugo Nothmann (Jewish survivor) in Hans Lamm, "Über die Entwicklung des deutschen Judentums," (mimeographed, 1951), p. 313.

83. *Jüdisches Nachrichtenblatt* (Berlin), April 17, 1942.

majority wore the star and, wearing it, were lost.

We have now seen how, in consecutive steps, the Jewish community was isolated socially, crowded into special houses, restricted in its movements, and exposed by a system of identification. This process, which we have called ghettoization, was completed with the institution of a Jewish administrative apparatus through which the Germans exercised a stranglehold on the Jewish population. For our understanding of how the Jews were ultimately destroyed it is essential to know the origins of the Jewish bureaucratic machine. The Jews had created that machine themselves.

Early in 1933 the Jewish community organization was still decentralized. Each city had its own Jewish administration which controlled the hospitals, ran the Jewish schools, and kept up the synagogues. The community organization was run as a business, and each community had a Vorstand, filled with prominent businessmen. In March, 1933, the *Kommerzienräte, Geheimräte, Justizräte*, and all other "Prominente" serving in the Jewish communal network were called together by the chairman of the Vorstand of the Berlin Jewish Community, Direktor Heinrich Stahl, for the purpose of forming a national organization, a kind of holding company.

The purpose of the national organization, however, was intended to be not so much financial as political. The organization, to be called *Reichsvertretung der Juden in Deutschland* ("Reich Representation of the Jews in Germany"), was to enter into an "open debate" (*offene Aussprache*), a "dignified controversy" (*Auseinandersetzung . . . mit Waffen der Vornehmheit*) with the Nazis on the subject of anti-Semitism and the Jewish future in Germany.[84] At the end of 1933 this organization was activated and placed under the chairmanship of Rabbi Leo Baeck and the deputy chairmanship of Direktor Stahl.[85] The *Reichsvertretung* had few occasions for dignified controversy but increasing opportunities for education, training, emigration work, care of the sick, and relief. On July 4, 1939, the *Reischsvertretung* was taken over, lock, stock, and barrel, by the Security Police, and it was converted into something that its founders had not imagined in their wildest dreams.

The decree of July 4, 1939,[86] was drafted by Ministerialrat Lösener and a fellow expert, Rolf Schiedermair.[87] It was signed by Interior Minister Frick, Deputy of the Führer Hess, Minister of Education Rust, and Minister for Church Affairs Kerrl. The decree changed the name of the organization from *Reichsvertretung* ("Reich Representation") to *Reichsvereinigung* ("Reich Association"). The territorial jurisdiction of the organization was confined to the Old Reich (including the Sudeten area but excluding Austria and the Protektorat.)[88]

The subjects of the *Reichsvereinigung* were all Jews, not merely Jews by religion, but all persons classified as Jews by the definition decree. The responsibility of the *Reichsvereinigung* for the upkeep of Jewish schools and financial support of poor Jews was affirmed. So far, little change. However, the decree had another provision which proved to be of great importance: the Interior Ministry (by which was meant the Security Police) was empowered to assign additional tasks to the *Reichsvereinigung*. This provision turned the Jewish administrative machine into a

84. Lamm, "Über die Entwicklung des deutschen Judentums," pp. 98–99.

85. *Ibid.*, pp. 99–100.

86. RGB1 I, 1097.

87. Affidavit by Lösener, February 24, 1948, NG-1944-A.

88. The structure of the Jewish community organization at the end of 1939 is indicated in Tables 22–23.

tool for the destruction of the Jews. The network of Jewish communal organizations had thus become, without change of personnel, an integral part of the machinery of destruction.

The additional tasks were not assigned all at once but were imposed upon the Jewish apparatus gradually.

TABLE 22 / *Jewish Community Organization, 1939**

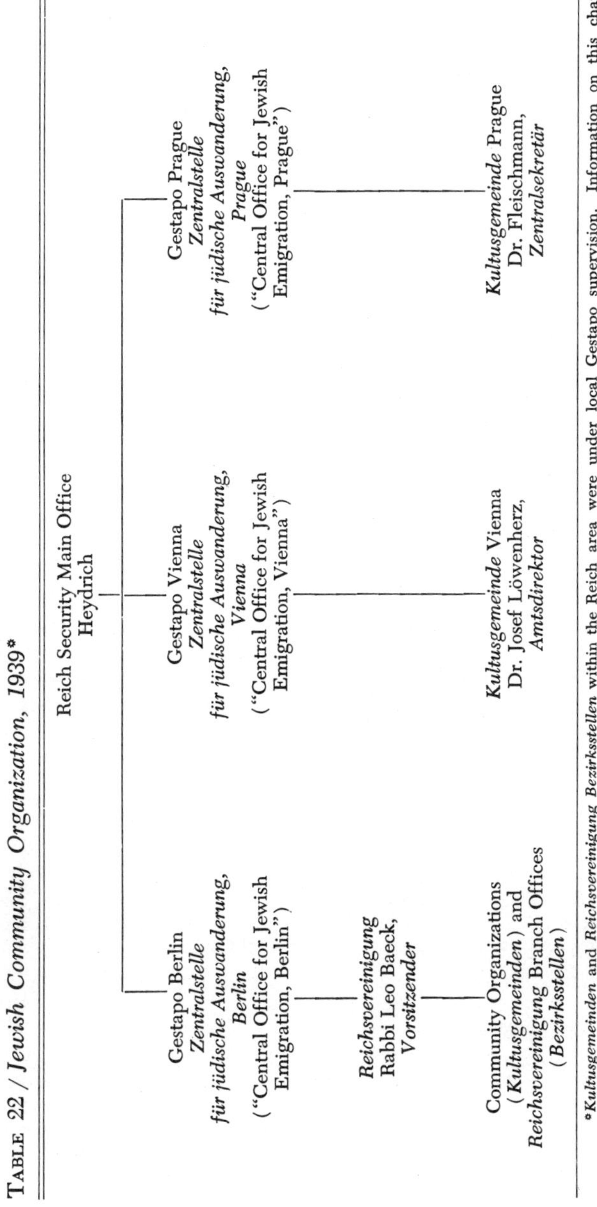

**Kultusgemeinden* and *Reichsvereinigung Bezirksstellen* within the Reich area were under local Gestapo supervision. Information on this chart based on documents in the YIVO Institute, New York City.

The community publications (*Jüdisches Nachrichtenblatt*) became channels for informing the Jews of German decrees and orders; the statistical experts of the community machine kept the Gestapo informed of births, deaths, and demographic changes of all sorts; the Jewish apartment experts concentrated the Jews in specially selected Judenhäuser. At the end of 1941 an important transformation took place in the functions of those German offices which had previously expedited Jewish emigration. Without change of personnel or even of their title, the Gestapo central offices for Jewish Emigration were entrusted with the job of deporting the Jews to camps in the East where the victims were to die. Following in the footsteps of the Gestapo, the emigration divisions of the Jewish organizations without change of personnel or designation undertook the task of preparing lists of Jewish deportees, of notifying the families involved, and of sending the Jewish police (called *Ordnungsdienst*) to round up the victims.

In watching this transformation, we have to keep in mind that the *Reichsvereinigung* and the *Kultusgemeinden* were *not* puppets picked by the Germans to control the more unruly elements of the Jewish population. The Germans had not created the *Reichsvereinigung*; they had taken it over. The Germans had not deposed or installed any Jewish leaders. Rabbi Leo

TABLE 23 / *The "Reichsvereinigung," 1939**

Function		Official
Chairman of the Vorstand		Rabbi Dr. Leo Baeck
Deputy Chairman		Heinrich Stahl
Vorstand Members		Dr. Paul Eppstein Moritz Henschel Philipp Kozower Dr. Arthur Lilienthal Dr. Julius Seligsohn
Finance and Communities		Dr. Arthur Lilienthal
Finance		Paul Meyerheim
Communities		Dr. Arthur Lilienthal
Migration		Dr. Paul Eppstein
Information, Statistics, Emigration of Women		Dr. Cora Berliner
Passage, Finance, Administration		Victor Löwenstein
Counseling and Planning		Dr. Julius Seligsohn
Emigration to Palestine	(Representatives in Germany of Jewish Agency for Palestine)	Erich Gerechter and Dr. Ludwig Jacobi
Pre-Emigration Preparations		
Vocational Training and Re-training		Dr. Conrad Cohn
Agriculture		Martin Gerson
Commerce and the Professions, Apartment Problems		Philipp Kozower
Schools		Paula Fürst
Teachers		Ilse Cohn
Teaching of Languages		Ilse Cohn
Welfare		Dr. Conrad Cohn
General Welfare Problems		Hannah Kaminski
Health		Dr. Walter Lustig

**Jüdisches Nachrichtenblatt* (Berlin), July 21, 1939. As listed in the *Jüdisches Nachrichtenblatt*, all Jewish officials carried the middle name Israel or Sara. The *Jüdisches Nachrichtenblatt* was the official publication of the *Reichsvereinigung*. There was also a *Jüdisches Nachrichtenblatt* in Vienna, published there by the Jewish community, and another *Jüdisches Nachrichtenblatt* in Prague.

Baeck, Direktor Stahl, Dr. Hirsch, and all the others *were* the Jewish leaders. The Germans controlled the Jewish leadership, and that leadership, in turn, controlled the Jewish community. This system was foolproof. Truly, the Jewish communal organizations had become a self-destructive machine.

The concentration of the Jews marks the close of the preliminary phase of the destruction process in the Reich-Protektorat area, and the fatal effects of this preliminary phase were manifested in two phenomena. One was the relationship of perpetrators and victims. When the bureaucracy stood at the threshold of most drastic action, the Jewish community was reduced to utter compliance with orders and directives. The other manifestation of the German strangulation regime was the ever widening gap between births and deaths in the Jewish community: its birth rate was plunging toward zero; the death rate was climbing steadily to unheard of heights (see Table 24).[89] The Jewish community was a dying organism.

Table 24 / *Births and Deaths of Jews in Old Reich (Not Including Austria and Protektorat)*

Year	Births	Deaths	Population at End of Year
1940	396	6,199	ca. 200,000
1941	351	6,249	ca. 150,000
1942	239	7,657	[after deportations] 51,327
1940–42	986	20,105	

2 / Poland

When the German Army moved into Poland in September, 1939, the destruction process was already well within its concentration stage. Polish Jewry was therefore immediately threatened. The concentration was carried out with much more drastic dispatch than had been dared in the Reich-Protektorat region. The newly occupied Polish territory was, in fact, an area of experimentation. Within a short time the machinery of destruction in Poland overtook and outdid the bureaucracy in Berlin.

There were three reasons for this development. One is to be found in the personnel composition of the German administration in Poland. As we shall see, that administration had a large number of party men in its ranks. It was less careful, less thorough, less "bureaucratic" than the administration in the Reich.

Another, more important reason for the unhesitating action in the East was the German conception of the Pole and of the Polish Jew. In German eyes a Pole naturally was lower than a German and a Polish Jew lower (if such a thing was possible) than a German Jew. The Polish Jew was on the bottom of the German scale – the Germans referred to eastern Jewry as "subhumanity" (*Untermenschtum*). In dealing with eastern peoples, both Poles and Jews, the bureaucracy could be less considerate and more drastic. In Germany, the bureaucracy was concerned with the rights and privileges of Germans. It was careful to deflect destructive measures from the German population. Much thought was given to such problems as couples in mixed marriage, the disruption of German-

89. SS-Statistician Korherr to Himmler, March 27, 1943, NO-5194. Mass deportations started in September, 1941.

Jewish business relationships, and so on. In Poland such problems simply did not exist, for it did not matter that a Pole was hurt in consequence of a measure aimed at the Jews. Similarly, the bureaucracy in Germany made some concessions to Jews who had fought in the World War, who had served for many years in the civil service, or who had done something else for Germany. In Poland such considerations did not apply.

The third and most important reason for the special treatment of the Polish Jews was the weight of their numbers. Ten per cent of the Polish population was Jewish; out of 33,000,000 people, 3,300,000 were Jews. When Germany and the USSR divided Poland in September, 1939, 2,000,000 of these Jews were suddenly placed under German domination. Warsaw alone had about 400,000 Jews – that is to say, almost as many Jews as had lived in Germany in 1933, and more Jews than remained in the entire Reich-Protektorat area at the end of 1939. The uprooting and segregation of so many Jews posed altogether different problems and gave rise to altogether different solutions. Thus the concentration in Poland was not confined to a system of composite restrictions such as those discussed in the first section of this chapter. Instead, the bureaucracy in Poland resurrected the medieval ghetto, shut off entirely from the rest of the world.

It may be recalled that the introduction of the destruction process in Germany was preceded by *Einzelaktionen*, short, violent outbursts against individual Jews; in Austria too, for a brief period after the Anschluss there were a few *Einzelaktionen.* When the German Army moved east, these *Einzelaktionen* occurred also in Poland. As in the case of the Reich and Austria, the violence had the function of convincing both the authorities and the victims of the need for law and order. Just as in Germany, the *Einzelaktionen* were started by party elements and curbed by the authority having responsibility for the administration of the area. The party elements in Poland were the Armed SS (*Waffen-SS*), military party formations which fought as integral units in the armed forces. The initial governing authority was the army.

The first reports of violence arrived a few days after the outbreak of war. In one locality, a member of the army's Secret Field Police and an SS-man drove fifty Jews, who had been employed in the repair of a bridge all day, into a synagogue and shot them down without any reason whatever (*in einer Synagoge zusammengetrieben und grundlos zusammengeschossen*). After a long correspondence in which it was pointed out that the SS-man had been aroused by Polish atrocities and had acted in "youthful initiative" (*jugendlichen Draufgängertum*), the punishment of both culprits was fixed at three years.[1]

A few days after this incident the commander of the Fourteenth Army, Wilhelm List, had to issue an order to prohibit the looting of property, burning of synagogues, raping of women, and shooting of Jews.[2] But even after the end of hostilities the *Einzelaktionen* continued. On October 10, 1939, Chief of the General Staff Halder made a cryptic remark in his diary: "Jewish massacres – discipline!"[3] During the following month the army began to collect systematically the evidence of SS atrocities. It may be pointed out that

1. Diary of Chief of the General Staff Halder, September 10, 1939, NOKW-3140. Army memorandum, September 13, 1939, D-421. *Oberkriegsgerichtsrat* 3d Army (signed Lipski) to *Oberstkriegsgerichtsrat* in Office of *Generalquartiermeister*, September 14, 1939, D-421.

2. Order by List, September 18, 1939, NOKW-1621.

3. Halder diary, October 10, 1939, NOKW-3140.

the army was concerned not so much with the Jews as with the attempt to build up a case against the SS in general; hence the army memoranda dealing with anti-Jewish *Einzelaktionen* are filled also with other complaints against the SS, all mixed up together.

On November 23, 1939, General der Artillerie Petzel, commander of the newly formed Army District XXI in Poznan, reported an incident which had taken place in the town of Turck on September 30. A number of SS trucks filled with SS-men and under the command of a senior SS officer had driven through the town. The SS-men had been armed with horsewhips and had used those weapons freely, whipping passers-by on their heads without discrimination. Apparently a number of ethnic Germans had also been horsewhipped. The party had then driven up to a synagogue, had crowded the Jews into the building, and had forced the victims to crawl, singing, under the benches. The Jews had then been obliged to drop their pants to be whipped. In the course of this whipping, the memorandum continued, one Jew had in fright moved his bowels. The SS-men had thereupon forced the victim to smear the dirt on the faces of other Jews. Dropping the Jews, the report continued with a complaint against a Goebbels representative who had apparently made a victory speech in which he had managed to laud the SS without even mentioning the army.[4]

In February, 1940, the army commander in Poland (Blaskowitz) compiled a long list of complaints for presentation to the Commander-in-Chief of the Army (von Brauchitsch). The report contained altogether thirty-three items, each one of which was a separate complaint. Item 7, for example, dealt with a search that had been carried out on December 31, 1939, in the bitter cold, at night, on the street. The Jews, particularly the women, had been forced to undress as the police had pretended to look for gold. Another complaint (item 8) mentioned that an SS lieutenant, Untersturmführer Werner, was living with a Jewish actress, Johanna Epstein of Warsaw, in an apartment under an assumed name — a clear case of *Rassenschande* committed by an SS officer. Item 31 was a description of a whipping orgy in Nasielek. This orgy had lasted all night and had affected 1600 Jews. Item 33, which was reserved for the end, discussed the case of two policemen who had dragged two teen-age Jewish girls out of bed. One of the girls had been raped in a Polish cemetery. The other girl, who had become ill, had been told by the policemen that they would get her some other time and that they would pay her 5 zloty. However, that portion of the report which, to us, is by far the most interesting is its conclusion. "It is a mistake," noted Generaloberst Blaskowitz, "to massacre some 10,000 Jews and Poles, as is being done at present; for — so far as the mass of the population is concerned — this will not eradicate the idea of a Polish state, nor will the Jews be exterminated."[5]

The complaint by Blaskowitz echoed the words which Schacht had spoken five years earlier. Like Schacht, the general was not outraged by the idea of drastic action, but only by the amateurish way in which the SS attempted to deal with such a massive body as 2,000,000 Jews. Actually, the "professionals" in the SS had already taken the situation in hand.

On September 19, 1939, Security Police Chief Heydrich met with Ge-

4. High Command of the Army/Chief of the Replacement Army (Fromm) to High Command of the Armed Forces, November 30, 1939, enclosing report of General der Artillerie Petzel, dated November 23, 1939, D-419.

5. Notes for an oral report prepared by Blaskowitz, February 6, 1940, NO-3011.

neralquartiermeister Wagner of the Army High Command to discuss some Polish problems. The two officials agreed upon a "cleanup once and for all," of "Jews, intelligentsia, clergy, nobility."[6] On the next day word came from the commander-in-chief of the army that "the ghetto idea exists in broad outline; details are not yet clear."[7] However, within another twenty-four hours, on September 21, 1939 (just one week before the conclusion of the Polish campaign), Heydrich sent a detailed concentration plan to his mobile units roaming in Poland, the *Einsatzgruppen*.[8]

The Heydrich plan was grandiose in its design. The introductory statement, which referred to an "ultimate goal," has given rise to interpretations that Heydrich had already in 1939 considered the killing operations which started two years later. Blaskowitz too had used the word "extermination," though sarcastically. Indeed, such hints and ambiguities multiplied in speeches and correspondence after 1939, but these rumblings were mere forerunners; as yet the drastic idea had not been accepted as feasible by any German, with the possible exception only of Hitler himself and his second in command, Göring. The mysterious "goal" to which Heydrich referred in the opening paragraph of his order is clarified by another passage in the same document where he spoke of the "emigration of the Jews" which "must be completed later." The gigantic concentration which Heydrich outlined in his directive was designed to facilitate a forced emigration plan. As we shall find out later, Heydrich, as well as some other people, Nazis and non-German Europeans, had formed the fantastic idea of shipping millions of Jews to the African island of Madagascar. This plan fell through, and the Jews were shipped to killing centers instead.

Part I of the concentration order provided that the Jews were to be ejected from the territories of Danzig, West Prussia, Poznan, and Eastern Upper Silesia. These areas later became incorporated territory, that is, territory integrated into the administration of the Reich. The Jews from these areas were to be shoved into the interior of Poland, a territory later known as the "General Government."[9] The Jews in the General Government were to be concentrated in cities. Only such cities were to be chosen as concentration points which were located at railroad junctions or at least along a railroad. On principle, all Jewish communities of less than five hundred were to be dissolved and transferred to the nearest concentration center.

In Part II of the order Heydrich directed that a council of Jewish elders (*Ältestenrat*, also *Judenrat*) composed of influential persons and rabbis was to be set up in each Jewish community. The councils were to be made fully responsible (in the literal sense of the word) for the exact execution of all instructions. They were to take an improvised census of the Jews in their area; they were to be made personally responsible for the evacuation of the Jews from the countryside to the concentration points, for the maintenance of the Jews during transport, and for housing upon arrival. There was no objection against Jews taking with them their movable possessions. The reason to be given for the concentration was that the Jews had participated deci-

6. Halder diary, September 10, 1939, NOKW-3140.

7. Halder diary, September 20, 1939, NOKW-3140.

8. Heydrich to *Einsatzgruppen*, copies to Army High Command (OKH), Staatssekretär Naumann in Office of Four-Year Plan, Staatssekretär Stuckart of the Interior Ministry, Staatssekretär Landfried of the Economy Ministry, and Chief of Civil Administration in the Occupied Territories, September 21, 1939, PS-3363.

9. See map on opposite page.

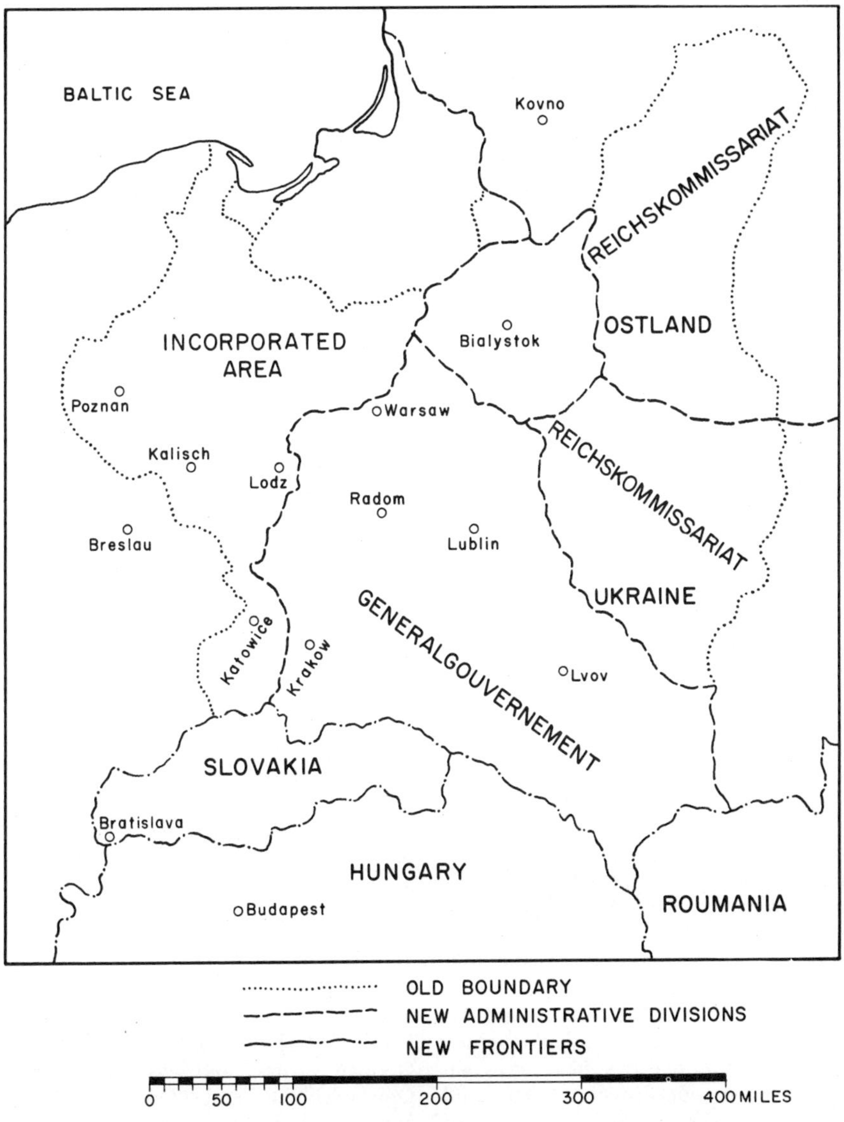

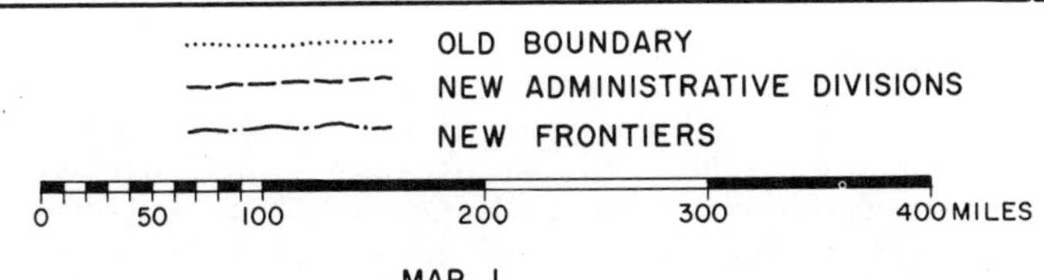

MAP I

POLAND UNDER GERMAN OCCUPATION

sively in sniper attacks and plundering.

It is interesting to note that the army wanted no part in the execution of this plan. During the Heydrich-Wagner discussion of September 19, 1939, the army quartermaster-general had insisted that the military authorities be notified of all activities by the SS and Police but that the "cleanup" take place after the withdrawal of the army and the transfer of power to the civilian administration – that is, not before early December.[10] In view of the army's early abdication of power in Poland, this demand could easily be fulfilled. This time the army did not have to dirty its hands with such business. In 1941, as we shall see, the military could no longer extricate itself from its assigned role in the destruction of the European Jews, but in Poland the concentration process was placed squarely into the laps of the newly formed civil administration.

In discussing the administration of occupied Poland, we have to distinguish between the authorities in the territories incorporated into the Reich and the so-called "General Government" (*Generalgouvernement*). The administrative structure in the incorporated territories was not distinguishable from the territorial organization in Germany itself. Two new *Reichsgaue* had been carved out of the conquered incorporated territory: Danzig-West Prussia and the Wartheland. A *Reichsgau* was a territorial unit which combined the features of a Prussian province (or non-Prussian *Land*) and a party district (*Gau*). The chief of this territorial unit was a regional Reich official (*Reichsstatthalter*) who was at the same time a regional party official (*Gauleiter*).

The *Reichsstatthalter* and *Gauleiter* of Danzig-West Prussia was a man called Forster. Inasmuch as Forster had already been the *Gauleiter* of the "Free City" of Danzig, the appointment resulted in a widening of his functions. The *Reichsstatthalter* and *Gauleiter* of the Wartheland, Greiser, had previously been the president of the Danzig senate. In that office he had distinguished himself by introducing the whole gamut of anti-Jewish legislation long before the arrival of German troops. The "Free City" had enacted a Law for Blood and Honor, decrees for the removal of Jewish doctors and lawyers, and a systematic Aryanization program. Approximately 3000 of Danzig's 10,000 Jews had emigrated before the war.[11] After Danzig had been overrun, Senatspräsident Greiser, who was out of a job, was shifted south to become the chief executive of the Wartheland. Unlike his colleague Forster, who had only some tens of thousands of Jews, Greiser had several hundred thousand. His role in the concentration, the deportations, and even the killing operations therefore became crucial.

In addition to the two *Reichsgaue* the incorporated territory contained also two smaller units which were parceled out to neighboring Reich provinces. The province of East Prussia annexed some territory in this process, and Silesia became Great Silesia. However, Great Silesia was a cumbersome administrative unit, and thus, in January, 1941, the *Grossgau* was divided into two *Gaue*: Lower Silesia (seat Breslau), which contained only old German territory and was governed by Oberpräsident and Gauleiter Karl Hanke, and Upper Silesia (seat Katowice), which consisted mostly of incorporated territory and which was placed under Oberpräsident and Gauleiter Fritz Bracht.[12]

10. Halder diary, September 19, 1939, NOKW-3140.

11. F. Redlin, "Danzig löst die Judenfrage," *Die Judenfrage*, January 26, 1939, p. 5. Greiser had worked in close co-operation with the German Foreign Office. Weizsäcker via Wörmann to Erdmannsdorff, October 17, 1938, NG-5334.

Counterclockwise, the new administrative units, with their chief executives and the number of Polish Jews brought under their jurisdiction, were therefore as follows:

East Prussia (Koch) ....a few thousand
Danzig West-Prussia (Forster)..30-40,000
Wartheland (Greiser) 400,000
Silesia (Wagner) ....ca. 120,000
Upper Silesia (Bracht)

East and south of the incorporated territories the Germans created a new type of territorial administration, first known as the "General Government in Poland" and later referred to simply as the "General Government" (*Generalgouvernement*). In 1939, this region held approximately 1,400,000 Jews. The principal difference between the incorporated areas and the *Generalgouvernement* was the degree of centralization in the bureaucratic machinery. The *Reichsstatthalter* was primarily a co-ordinator; thus the regional offices of the various ministries took all their functional instructions (*fachliche Anweisungen*) from Berlin and were subject only to territorial orders from the *Reichsstatthalter* or *Oberpräsident* in accordance with the following formula:

Hitler ⟶ *Reichsstatthalter*
↓ ↓
Ministry ⟶ Regional Office

The horizontal arrows represent functional authority, the vertical arrows territorial authority.

In the *Generalgouvernement* this closed diagram did not apply. Generalgouverneur Hans Frank did not have ministerial offices; he had main divisions (*Hauptabteilungen*) which were responsible only to him:

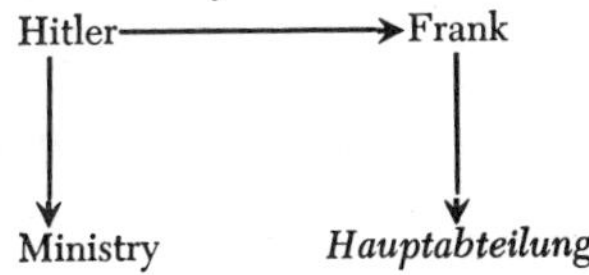

Frank as *Generalgouverneur* had more authority than a *Reichsstatthalter* or an *Oberpräsident*. He also had more prestige, for he was a *Reichsminister* without portfolio, a *Reichsleiter* of the party, the president of the German Academy of Law – in short, a top Nazi in every respect.

When Frank came to Poland, he brought with him a retinue of party dignitaries who occupied some of his *Hauptabteilungen*:[13]

Generalgouverneur, Hans Frank
Deputy (to May, 1940), Reichsminister Seyss-Inquart
Staatssekretär, Dr. Buhler
Deputy *Staatssekretär*, Dr. Boepple
Higher SS and Police Leader (from April, 1942) *Staatssekretär*, Security, SS-Obergruppenführer Krüger (replaced in 1943 by Koppe)
Main Divisions
- Interior, Ministerialrat Dr. Siebert (Losacker)
- Justice, Ministerialrat Wille
- Education, Hofrat Watzke
- Propaganda, Oberregierungsrat Ohlenbusch
- Railways (*Ostbahn*), Präsident Gerteis
- Postal Service, Präsident Lauxmann
- Construction, Präsident Bauder
- Forests, Oberlandforstmeister Dr. Eissfelt
- *Emissionsbank*, Reichsbankdirektor (ret.) Dr. Paersch
- Economy, Ministerialdirigent Dr. Emmerich
- Food and Agriculture, SS-Brigadeführer Körner (Naumann)
- Labor, Reichshauptamtsleiter Dr. Frauendorfer
- Finance, Finanzpräsident Spindler (Sendowsky)
- Health, Obermedizinalrat Dr. Walbaum (Teitge)

The regional network of the *Generalgouvernement* administration closely

12. *Krakauer Zeitung*, January 28, 1941, p. 1.

13. Dr. Max Freiherr du Prel (ed.), *Das Generalgouvernement* (Würzburg, 1942), pp. 375-80. Also *Krakauer Zeitung* (passim) and the Frank diary, PS-2233.

paralleled the regional machinery in the Reich, but the titles varied somewhat, as Table 25 shows.

The *Gouverneur* was originally called *Distriktchef*, but the new title was conferred as a boost to morale.[14] There were four *Gouverneure* in Poland in 1939; after the outbreak of war with Russia, the German Army overran Galicia, and this area became the fifth district of the *Generalgouvernement* in August, 1941. (The names of the *Gouverneure* and of their administrative deputies are listed in Table 26.)[15] It may be noted that, as a rule, the *Gouverneur* was a party man but that his *Amtschef* was a civil servant – the *Generalgouvernement* administra-

TABLE 25 / *Reich and General Government Regional Machinery*

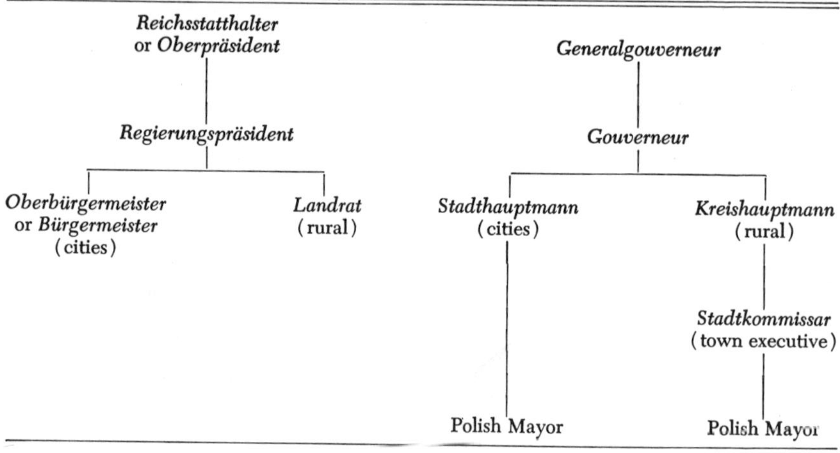

TABLE 26 / *The Gouverneure*

Krakow
Gouverneur: SS-Brigadeführer Dr. Wächter (SS-Brigadeführer Dr. Wendler, von Burgsdorff)
Amtschef: Ministerialrat Wolsegger (Dr. Eisenlohr)

Lublin
Gouverneur: Oberstarbeitsführer Zörner
Amtschef: Landrat Dr. Schmige (Oberregierungsrat Engler)

Radom
Gouverneur: Reichsamtsleiter Dr. Karl Lasch (Unterstaatssekretär Kundt)
Amtschef: Oberregierungsrat Dr. Egen

Warsaw
Gouverneur: Hauptamtsleiter SA-Brigadeführer Dr. Fischer
Amtschef: Reichsamtsleiter Landgerichtsdirektor Barth (Reichshauptstellenleiter Staatsanwalt Dr. Hummel)

Galicia
Gouverneur: Dr. Lasch (SS-Brigadeführer Dr. Wächter)
Amtschef: Regierungsrat Dr. Losacker

14. Summary of discussion between Frank and Dr. Wächter (*Gouverneur*, Warsaw), November 10, 1939, Frank diary, PS-2233.

15. Compiled from: Dr. Max Freiherr du Prel, *Das Deutsche Generalgouvernement in Polen* (Krakow, 1940), pp. 87, 100–101, 147,

tion combined party initiative on the top with bureaucratic thoroughness on the bottom.

Generalgouverneur Hans Frank was a moody autocrat who displayed sentimentality and brutality. He was a jurist who often used the eloquent and precise language of the law, but he was also a party man who could address the mob in the language of the street. In his castle in Krakow, Frank behaved like a cultured ruler who entertained his guests by playing Chopin's piano music. In the conference room, however, he was one of the principal architects of the destruction process in Poland. He was powerful but vain. The party treasurer (*Reichsschatzmeister*), Schwarz, once referred to him as "*König* Frank" which means "King Frank" or "the royal Frank."[16]

The *Generalgouverneur* was an uneasy king. He did not fear the Poles and much less the Jews, but he fought a desperate battle with certain personalities in Berlin who wanted to rob him of his authority and his power. Frank never tired of pointing out that he was an absolute dictator responsible only to Hitler, that the *Generalgouvernement* was his private preserve, and that no one was permitted to do anything in this preserve unless he took orders from the castle in Krakow. "As you know," he said, "I am a fanatic of the unity of administration."[17] "Unity of administration" meant that no one holding an office in the *Generalgouvernement* was supposed to take orders from anyone but Frank. The attempt by Berlin agencies to give instructions to offices in the *Generalgouvernement* Frank called *hineinregieren* (to "reign into" his domain). He did not tolerate that. But the unity of administration was actually a fiction, at least so far as three agencies were concerned.

The first exception was the army; Frank had no authority over the troops. The authority was held exclusively by a general who was called, successively, *Oberbefehlshaber Ost* (Generaloberst Blaskowitz), *Militärbefehlshaber im Generalgouvernement* (General der Kavallerie Kurt Freiherr von Gienanth) and, ultimately, *Wehrkreisbefehlshaber im Generalgouvernement* (Gienanth and General der Infantrie Hännicke). The army controlled not only its troops but also war production, which was in the hands of the *Rüstungsinspektion,* or Armament Inspectorate (Generalleutnant Schindler). The relation between Gienanth and Schindler is illustrated in the following diagram.

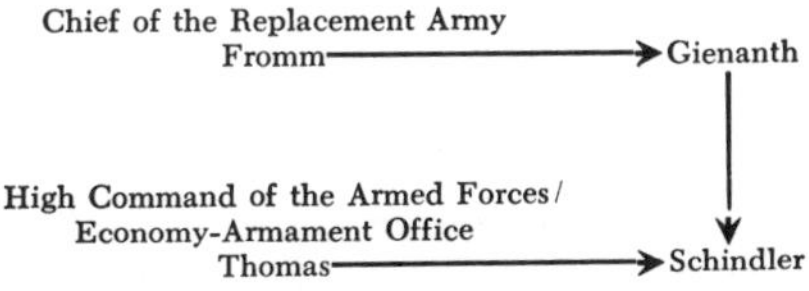

Chief of the Replacement Army
Fromm ——→ Gienanth
↓
High Command of the Armed Forces/
Economy-Armament Office
Thomas ——→ Schindler

Gienanth and Schindler had subordinate but not unimportant functions in the destruction process.

The second exception to Frank's unity of administration was the railway system. Although Frank had a Main Division Railways under the direction of Präsident Gerteis, that official was also the *Generaldirektor* of the *Ostbahn,* which in turn was run by the *Reichsbahn.* The *Ostbahn* operated the confiscated Polish State Railways in the *Generalgouvernement,*[18] and its key personnel consisted of 9000 Germans.[19] However, the railway had taken over, in addition to the Polish equipment,

200; du Prel, *Das Generalgouvernement* (Würzburg, 1942), pp. 375–80; *Krakauer Zeitung* (passim).

16. Berger (chief of SS Main Office) to Himmler, July 2, 1941, NO-29. The *Generalgouvernement* was sometimes called (in joke) *Frankreich.*

17. Summary of conference of party men in the GG, March 18, 1942, Frank diary, PS-2233.

18. Reichsbahnrat Dr. Peicher, "Die Ostbahn," in du Prel, *Das Generalgouvernement,* pp. 80–86.

19. *Ibid.*

about 40,000 railway employees.[20] By the end of 1943 the *Ostbahn* was still run by 9000 Germans, but by that time it employed 145,000 Poles plus a few thousand Ukrainians.[21] These statistics are not without significance, because the railway administration was to play a crucial role in the concentrations, and a decisive one in the deportations.

The third and most important exception to Frank's absolute authority was the SS and Police, the apparatus of Heinrich Himmler. What was the Himmler apparatus and how did it assert its authority in the *Generalgouvernement?*

Himmler himself was a school teacher, and among his chief lieutenants there were a number of other schoolteachers. Power-hungry and pedantic, Himmler was forever on the lookout for corruption in his own ranks and, more particularly, in the ranks of his rivals. He was interested in a great many things; in fact, his interests ran the whole gamut of foreign affairs, internal administration, armament production, the resettlement of populations, the conduct of the war, and of course the destruction of the Jews. He could talk about those subjects at great length, and he often held his audience for three hours at a stretch. (It may be added that the audience consisted of his own SS generals.) Above all, Himmler's power rested on his independence. This is a fact of utmost importance. Himmler was not part of any hierarchy, but he had his footholds in every hierarchy. In our charts of the machinery of destruction,[22] he is, perforce, placed between two hierarchies, the ministerial bureaucracy and the party. Himmler received most of his funds from the Finance Ministry and recruited most of his men from the party. Both fiscally and in its personnel structure, the SS and Police were consequently a civil service-party amalgamation.[23]

20. Oberlandgerichtsrat Dr. Weh, "Das Recht des Generalgouvernements," *Deutsches Recht*, 1940, pp. 1393–1400. In April, 1940, German railway personnel included 9298 in the *Generalgouvernement* and 47,272 in the incorporated territories, while the Polish employees numbered 36,640 in the *Generalgouvernement* and 33,967 in incorporated territory. Transport Ministry to OKH/Transport, April 11, 1940, H 12/101.2, p. 219. The *Ostbahn* was confined to the *Generalgouvernement.* It did *not* administer the railways in the incorporated areas.

21. Speech by Frank before air force officers, December 14, 1943, Frank diary, PS-2233.

22. See pp. 34, 37.

23. Originally, the SS was part of the party formation SA. See order by Röhm (SA commander), November 6, 1933, SA-13. The police were a decentralized apparatus, placed under Himmler in 1936. Himmler was henceforth the *Reichsführer-SS und Chef der deutschen Polizei.* Decree of June 17, 1936, RGB1 I, 487. The SS (party sector) consisted of 700,000 men on December 31, 1943. It reached nearly 800,000 on June 30, 1944. Most of these men were organized into field units for combat. SS-Statistician Korherr to Himmler, September 19, 1944, NO-4812. Only 39,415 SS-men were in the administrative apparatus: the main offices and their regional machinery. Memorandum, Statistical Office of the SS, June 30, 1944, D-878.

The police were divided into Security Police and Order Police. The former (composed of Gestapo and Criminal Police) had no more than 65,000 men. Affidavit by Schellenberg (Security Police), November 21, 1945, PS-3033. The latter were several hundred thousand strong. If air raid wardens, fire brigades, and foreign auxiliary policemen are added, the total strength of the Order Police at the end of 1942 was 2,800,000. SS-Oberst-Gruppenführer Daluege (chief of the Order Police) to Chief of Himmler's Personal Staff Wolff, February 28, 1943, NO-2861.

The Armed SS (*Waffen-SS*), which were fighting as combat units, and the police forces were paid for by the Reich. The bill for the *Waffen-SS* alone was RM 657,000,000 during fiscal year 1943. Summary of conference between Finance Ministry and SS officials, NG-5516. But, to finance some of his "special" projects, Himmler drew funds also from the party (Party Treasurer Schwarz). Berger to Himmler, July 2, 1941, NO-29. In addition, he received contributions from industry. Von Schröder to Himmler, enclosing 1,100,000

The SS and Police operated centrally through main offices, the chiefs of which were directly responsible to Himmler, and regionally through Higher SS and Police Leaders (*Höhere SS- und Polizeiführer*) who were also directly responsible to Himmler.

The central organization consisted of twelve main offices (see Table 27).[24]

TABLE 27 / *The Main Offices*

Office	Chief
SS-Hauptamt (SSHA) ("SS Main Office")	(Wittje) Berger
Reichssicherheitshauptamt (RSHA) ("Reich Security Main Office")	Heydrich (Kaltenbrunner)
Hauptamt Ordnungspolizei ("Main Office Order Police")	Dalüge (Wünnenberg)
Chef des Persönlichen Stabes RF-SS ("Chief of Himmler's Personal Staff")	Wolff
SS Wirtschafts-Verwaltungshauptamt (WVHA) ("Economic-Administrative Main Office")	Pohl
SS Personal Hauptamt ("Personnel")	Schmitt
Hauptamt SS-Gericht ("SS-Court")	Breithaupt
SS-Führungshauptamt ("Operational Main Office")	Jüttner
Dienststelle Heissmeyer (Services to families of SS men)	Heyssmeyer
Stabshauptamt des Reichskommissars für die Festigung des deutschen Volkstums ("Staff Main Office of the *Reichskommissar* for Strengthening of Germandom")	Greifelt
Hauptamt Volksdeutsche Mittelstelle (VOMI) ("Welfare Main Office for Ethnic Germans")	Lorenz
Rasse- und Siedlungshauptamt (RuSHA) ("Race and Resettlement Main Office")	Hofmann (Hildebrandt)

The regional organization was topped by more than thirty Higher SS and Police Leaders. (The number varied from time to time.) The five with jurisdiction in Poland were: *Generalgouvernement*, Krüger (Koppe); Danzig-West Prussia, Hildebrandt; Wartheland, Koppe; East Prussia, Rediess (Sporrenberg); Silesia, Schmauser. The regional machinery of the main offices was co-ordinated by the Higher SS and Police Leaders, in accordance with the usual functional-territorial pattern:

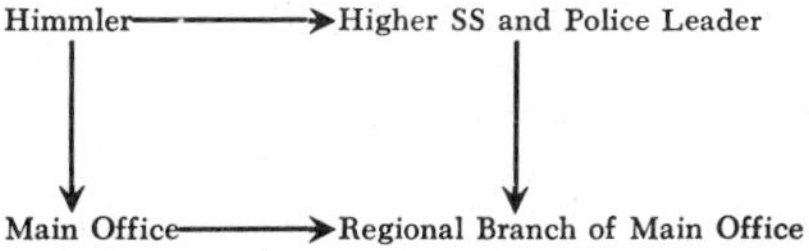

Himmler →	Higher SS and Police Leader
↓	↓
Main Office →	Regional Branch of Main Office

We shall be concerned primarily with the regional machinery of two main offices: the Main Office Order Police and the Reich Security Main Office (RSHA). These two *Hauptämter* had three types of regional ma-

reichsmark, September 21, 1943, EC-453. Other sources of income, such as the SS industries, special arrangements for the looting of Jewish property, and the hiring out of Jewish slave labor will be mentioned later.

24. From *Organisationsbuch der NSDAP*, 1943, pp. 417–29, PS-2640. Names of officials were taken from several documents. The functions of each main office will be explained later.

chinery, one in the Reich, another in occupied territories, the third in areas undergoing invasion (see Table 28).

In the *Generalgouvernement* the two key police officials were: BdO (in succession): Oberg, Katzman, Diehm. Each SS and Police Leader disposed over a *Kommandeur der Ordnungspolizei* (KdO) and a *Kommandeur der Sicherheitspolizei und des Sicherheitsdienstes* (KdS). Command relations consequently looked like this:

TABLE 28 / *Regional Machinery of Order Police and RSHA*

	REICH	OCCUPIED TERRITORY	INVADED AREAS
Order Police	*Inspekteur der Ordnungspolizei* ("Inspector of Order Police") IdO	*Befehlshaber der Ordnungspolizei* ("Commander of Order Police") BdO	*Truppenverbände* ("troop units") organized in police regiments and police battalions
RSHA	*Inspekteur der Sicherheitspolizei und des Sicherheitsdienstes* ("Inspector of Security Police and Security Service") IdS	*Befehlshaber der Sicherheitspolizei und des Sicherheitsdienstes* ("Commander of Security Police and Security Service") BdS	Mobile units organized in *Einsatzgruppen* (battalion size) and *Einsatzkommandos* (company size)

cession): Becker, Riege, Winkler, Höring; BdS (in succession): Streckenbach, Schöngarth, Bierkamp. The police organization in the *Generalgouvernement* was highly centralized, and the centralization was carried down from the *Generalgouverneur* level to the *Gouverneur* level. That is, corresponding to the five *Gouverneure*, the Himmler organization maintained five SS and Police Leaders: Krakow (in succession): Zech, Scherner, Thier; Lublin (in succession): Globocnik, Sporrenberg; Radom (in succession): Katzman, Böttcher; Warsaw (in succession): Moder, Wigand, von Sammern, Stroop, Geibel; Galicia (in succession): Oberg, Katzman, Diehm.

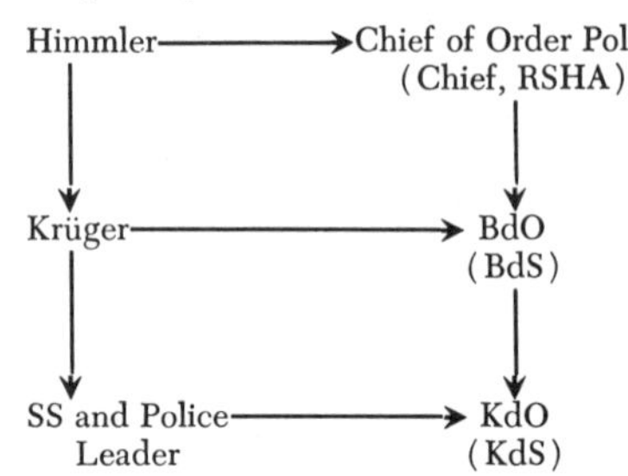

To Frank, this was an incomplete picture. He imagined himself in front of Krüger as a kind of supreme territorial chief:

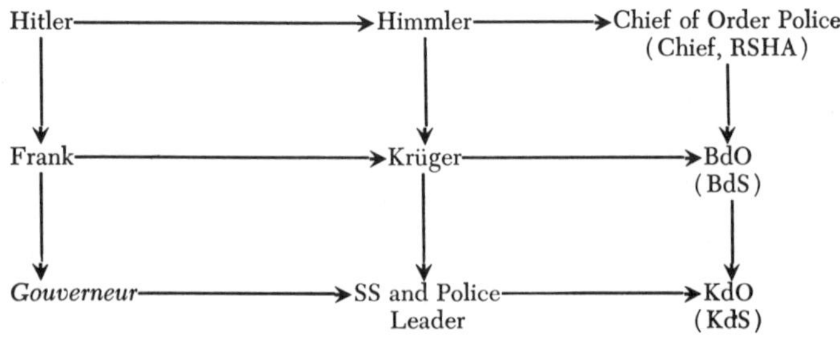

To make sure of such a relationship, Frank had in fact appointed Krüger his *Staatssekretär* for Security.[25] The new title was intended not as an honor but as a device to insure that Krüger would take orders from Frank. Himmler, of course, regarded such a relationship as an absurdity. Just as Frank was a "fanatic" of territorial centralization, Himmler was a fanatic of functional centralization. From *his* men Himmler demanded 100 per cent accountability to himself.

Thus from the very beginning Frank and Himmler were enemies, and it is not accidental that this friction should find its first target in the Jews, for, also from the very beginning, the Himmler apparatus claimed primary authority in Jewish matters throughout Poland – and that was a big claim. We can understand the basis for this assertion of jurisdiction if we examine the closing stages of the concentration process in the Reich-Protektorat area. In the enforcement of movement restrictions and indentification measures, and particularly in the direction of Jewish administrative machinery, the SS and Police emerged gradually as the most important control mechanism. As the destruction process proceeded into its more drastic phases, it began to take on more and more characteristics of a police operation. Movement control, roundups, concentration camps – all these are police functions.

In the Reich-Protektorat area the rise of the SS and Police was imperceptible. The increasing importance of the Himmler apparatus in the home area grew out of the natural development of the destruction process. In Poland, however, the destruction process was introduced in its concentration stage. The immediate entry of the SS and Police on a very high level of policy formation was therefore conspicuous, and troublesome. In fact, we have noted that Security Police Chief Heydrich issued his ghettoization order on September 21, 1939, *before* the civil administration had a chance to organize itself. That means that in Jewish matters Himmler was not only independent of, but ahead of Frank. The destruction process in Poland was thus to be carried out by these two men. It is characteristic that, as enemies and rivals, Himmler and Frank competed only in ruthlessness. The competition did not benefit the Jews; it helped to destroy them.

The Expulsions

As we have seen, the Heydrich plan for the concentration of the Polish Jews was divided into two phases. In the course of the first phase, approximately 600,000 Jews were to be shifted from the incorporated territories to the *Generalgouvernement;* the Jewish population of the *Generalgouvernement* was therefore to be raised from about 1,400,000 to 2,000,000. The second part of the Heydrich directive stipulated that these 2,000,000 Jews be crowded into closed quarters – the ghettos.

Since the army had insisted that the "cleanup" be postponed until after the transfer of jurisdiction from military to civilian authority, the first phase could not begin immediately.[26] Arrangements were consequently made to set aside, after November 15, 1939, the entire railway network of the *Generalgouvernement* (the *Ostbahn*) for the purpose of resettling the Jews.[27] Just before the mass resettlement was to begin, the *Generalgouvernement's* Higher SS and Police Leader, Krüger, announced at

25. Summary of *Generalgouvernement* police conference, April 21, 1942, Frank diary, PS-2233.

26. Notwithstanding SS assurances, a few movements took place in September. See army correspondence, September 12–24, 1939, NOKW-129.

27. Summary of *Generalgouvernement* police conference under the chairmanship of Frank, October 31, 1939, Frank diary, PS-2233.

a meeting of main division chiefs and *Gouverneure* that, in addition to the Jews, the Poles of the incorporated territory were to be sent into the *Generalgouvernement.* Altogether, 1,000,000 Poles and Jews were to be moved in by spring, at the rate of 10,000 a day.[28]

By December 1, a little behind schedule, the trains started to roll into the *Generalgouvernement.*[29] Hardly had these movements begun when the evacuation program was expanded still more. Not only Jews and Poles from the incorporated territories, but also Jews and Gypsies from the Reich, were to be dispatched to the *Generalgouvernement* – the Reich with all its incorporated territories was to be cleared of Jews, Poles, and Gypsies alike. The depopulated regions of the incorporated areas were to be filled with ethnic Germans "returning," by special arrangements with Russia, from the Baltic states and the other territories allocated to the Soviet sphere. A vast movement had started. Train after train moved into the *Generalgouvernement* without prior notification or planning. The transports were sent farther and farther east, until someone got the idea that the Lublin district was to be turned into a Jewish reserve, or *Judenreservat.*

At first Frank took all these movements in stride. An unsigned memorandum, dated January, 1940, and probably written by Frank, speaks of the whole idea in very nonchalant terms. Altogether, Frank was prepared to receive 1,000,000 Jews (600,000 from the incorporated areas; 400,000 from the Reich). The sojourn of the Jews in his "kingdom" was to be temporary, at any rate. "After the victory" an evacuation of several million Jews, "possibly to Madagascar," would create plenty of room. Frank was not even worried about the Poles who were being sent into his *Generalgouvernement* in increasing numbers. "After the victory" the "superfluous Poles" could be sent farther east, perhaps to Siberia, as part of a "reorganization" of the entire eastern European area.[30]

Himmler's grandiose resettlement plans did not long remain in force: Frank took a closer look at the situation and became fightened. The uninterrupted and never ending flow of Jews, Poles, and Gypsies into his limited area became a *Lebensfrage,* the central question for his administration, particularly the administration of the Lublin district, which could no longer stand the strain.[31]

In the first two months of the program about 200,000 Poles and Jews had been shoved into the *Generalgouvernement.* Their number included 6000 Jews from Vienna, Prague, Moravska Ostrava (Protektorat), and Stettin.[32] The Stettin transport had been so brutal that, to everyone's embarrassment, it was widely commented on in the foreign press.[33] On February 12, 1940, Frank went to Berlin and protested against the manner in which transports were shoved down his throat.[34]

In the presence of Reichsführer-SS Himmler, Reichsstatthalter Forster and Greiser, and Oberpräsidenten Koch

28. Summary of conference under chairmanship of Frank, November 8, 1939, Frank diary, PS-2233.

29. Summary of conference of *Generalgouvernement Amtsleiter,* December 8, 1939, Frank diary, PS-2233.

30. Materials for submission to the Committee of Nationality Law of the Academy of German Law (unsigned), January, 1940, PS-661. Frank was president of the academy.

31. Frank speech to *Kreishauptmänner* and *Stadthauptmänner* in the Lublin district, March 4, 1940, Frank diary, PS-2233.

32. Heydrich memorandum (undated), NO-5150.

33. See letter by Lammers to Hitler, March 28, 1940, enclosing a report received by the Reich Chancellery, NG-2490. Also, instructions by the *Reichspressechef* to German press (Brammer material), February 15, 1940, NG-4698.

34. Summary of Göring conference on eastern problems, February 12, 1940, EC-305.

and Wagner, the chairman of the conference (Göring) declared that henceforth no transports were to be sent to the *Generalgouvernement* without prior notification of the *Generalgouverneur.* Koch (East Prussia) pointed out that no Jews had been sent from his districts to the *Generalgouvernement.* Forster (Danzig-West Prussia) announced that he had virtually no Jews left; only 1,800 remained. Greiser Wartheland) reported that after the evacuation of 87,000 Jews and Poles he still had 400,000 Jews and 3,700,000 Poles. Wagner (Silesia) requested that 100,000 to 120,000 Jews, plus 100,000 "unreliable" Poles in his area, be deported. Himmler thereupon pointed out that room would have to be made in the incorporated territories for 40,000 Reich Germans, 70,000 Baltic Germans, 130,000 Wolhynian Germans, and 30,000 Lublin Germans. The last group was to get out of Lublin because that district was to become a Jewish reserve.[35]

Although Göring had ruled only that the *Generalgouvernement* had to be *notified* of arriving transports, Frank went home with the firm conviction that he had been given absolute veto power over all incoming transports.[36] This interpretation proved to be correct, for on March 23, 1940, Göring ordered all evacuations stopped. Henceforth, transports could proceed only with Frank's permission.[37] Reichsstatthalter Greiser of the Wartheland, who had 400,000 Jews in his *Gau,* protested vehemently. He understood that Göring might have issued such a ruling on account of the Stettin "case," but the *Feldmarschall* (Göring) could not have meant the Wartheland, for on February 12, 1940, Frank had already promised to Greiser that the 200,000 Jews of the city of Lodz would be taken into the *Generalgouvernement.* He was dismayed to hear of this turnabout, etc.[38] But Frank had carried away his victory. On March 11, Himmler thanked the *Staatssekretär* of the Transport Ministry, Kleinmann, for his co-operation, and with these thanks the evacuation program came to an end.[39]

At this point, however, Frank decided upon a little evacuation program of his own. His resettlements were to take place *within* the *Generalgouvernement.* In particular, Frank wanted to remove the Jewish population from his capital, Krakow. Addressing his main division chiefs on April 12, 1940, the *Generalgouverneur* described conditions in the city as scandalous. German generals "who commanded divisions" were forced, because of the apartment shortage, to live in houses which also contained Jewish tenants. The same applied to higher officials, and such conditions were "intolerable." By November 1, 1940, the city of Krakow with its 60,000 Jews had to become *judenfrei* – free of Jews. Only about 5000 or at most 10,000, skilled Jewish workers might be permitted to remain. If the Reich could bring hundreds of thousands of Jews into the *Generalgouvernement,* he reasoned, surely there had to be room for 50,000 more from Krakow. The Jews would be permitted to take along all their property, "except of course stolen property." Then the Jewish quarter would be cleansed so that German people would be able to live there and breathe "German air."[40]

35. Summary of conference attended by Göring, Frank, Koch, Forster, Greiser, Wagner, and Himmler, February 12, 1940, EC-305.

36. Frank speech to Lublin officials, March 4, 1940, Frank diary, PS-2233.

37. Summary of interministerial conference in Berlin, April 1, 1940, *Dokumenty i Materialy,* III, 167-68.

38. *Ibid.*

39. Himmler to Kleinmann, March 11, 1940, NO-2206.

40. Summary of conference of main division chiefs, April 12, 1940, Frank diary, PS-2233. The Jewish population of Krakow had

The Krakow expulsions were divided into two phases, voluntary and involuntary. Up to August 15, 1940, the Jews of the city were given an opportunity to move with all their possessions to any city of their choice within the *Generalgouvernement*. *Gouverneure* were instructed to accept these Jews. All those still in Krakow after midnight of August 15 were to be subjected to "organized" expulsion, with limited luggage, to cities of the administration's choice.[41]

By means of an "intensive persuasion campaign against the Jewish Council [*intensives Einwirken auf den Judenrat*]," it was possible to effect the "voluntary" removal of 23,000 Jews.[42] On the last day of the voluntary phase Frank made a speech in which he repeated that it was simply intolerable to permit the representatives of the Greater German Reich of Adolf Hitler to be established in a city which was "crawling" with Jews to such an extent that a "decent person" could not step into the street. The Krakow expulsions, Frank continued, were meant as a signal: the Jews of all Europe had to "disappear" (*verschwinden*). Obviously Frank was thinking of Madagascar.[43]

The involuntary phase was put into effect immediately. Through notifications sent to affected families via the Jewish Council, another 9000 Jews were expelled by mid-September. The total number expelled was now 32,000.[44] In spite of these drastic measures, the apartment situation in the city did not improve to the expected extent. For one thing, it was discovered that the Jews had been housed "tightly" (i.e., Jewish apartments had been overcrowded); furthermore, the Jewish dwellings were so dilapidated as to be unacceptable for German habitation.[45] Nevertheless, or perhaps because of these results, the expulsions continued. On November 25, 1940, the *Gouverneur* of the Krakow district ordered another 11,000 Jews to leave. These evacuations were conducted alphabetically. All those whose names began with *A* to *D* were to report on December 2, 1940, the *E* to *J* group on December 4, etc.[46] This measure brought the total number of evacuees to 43,000, close to the goal that Frank had envisaged. The remaining Krakow Jews were crowded into a closed ghetto, the *Judenwohnbezirk*, in the Podgorce section of the city.[47]

And thus, so far as Frank was concerned, the evacuation program was over. He had accepted 200,000 Jews and Poles from the incorporated territories; he had "cleared" his own city of Krakow; the Jewish population in the incorporated territories had dropped from about 600,000 to 500,000, while the Jewish population in the *Generalgouvernement* had increased from about 1,400,000 to 1,500,000. Even with the shift of 43,000 Jews from Krakow to other parts of the *Generalgouvernement*, and with the countless thousands moved in minor shifts from the countryside into towns and from towns to cities, the concentration process had not actually transformed the existing pattern of population distribution.

It is an odd fact, but true, that from a purely administrative point of view it was easier to deport Jews to killing centers than to shift them into over-

actually risen to 80,000 since September, 1939. Dr. Dietrich Redecker, "Deutsche Ordnung kehrt im Ghetto ein," *Krakauer Zeitung*, March 13, 1940.

41. *Krakauer Zeitung*, August 6, 1940, *Generalgouvernement* page.

42. *Krakauer Zeitung*, December 31, 1940/January 1, 1941, GG page.

43. *Krakauer Zeitung*, August 17, 1940.

44. *Krakauer Zeitung*, December 31, 1940/January 1, 1941, GG page.

45. *Ibid.*

46. Apenszlak (ed.), *The Black Book of Polish Jewry* (New York, 1943), pp. 80–81.

47. Announcement by the *Stadthauptmann* of Krakow (Schmid) in *Krakauer Zeitung*, March 23, 1941, p. 18.

crowded ghettos. The death camps were equipped with installations for the immediate killing of all arrivals and the disposal of their corpses; the ghettos, however, increased in density until they threatened the surrounding cities with epidemics.

Nevertheless, there were people (notably Himmler) who could see no valid objection to the overstuffing of Jewish quarters. On June 25, 1940, Frank wrote a letter to Lammers in which he said that he was plagued by constant rumors from Danzig and the Wartheland capital of Poznan to the effect that new plans were afoot to send many thousands of Jews and Poles into the *Generalgouvernement.* Such a movement, Frank informed Lammers, was utterly out of the question, especially since the armed forces were expropriating large tracts of land for the purpose of holding maneuvers.[48]

At the beginning of July, Frank was jubilant again. On July 12, 1940, he informed his main division chiefs that the Führer himself had decided that no more transports of Jews would be sent into the *Generalgouvernement;* instead, the entire Jewish community in the Reich, the Protektorat, *and* the *Generalgouvernement* was to be transported in the "shortest time imaginable," immediately upon the conclusion of a peace treaty, to an African or American colony. The general thinking, he said, centered on Madagascar, which France was to cede to Germany for that very purpose. With an area of 500,000 square kilometers, Frank explained, the island (incidentally, mostly jungle) could easily hold several million Jews. "I have intervened on behalf of the Jews of the *Generalgouvernement,*" he continued, "so that those Jews too may profit from the advantages of starting a new life on new soil." That proposal, Frank concluded, had been accepted in Berlin, so that the entire *Generalgouvernement* administration could look forward to a "colossal unburdening."[49]

Radiant with pleasure, Frank repeated his speech in the Lublin district, which had been threatened most with overflowing transports of Jewish evacuees. As soon as maritime transport was restored, he said, the Jews would be removed, "piece by piece, man by man, mrs. by mrs., miss by miss [*Stück um Stück, Mann um Mann, Frau um Frau, Fräulein um Fräulein*]." Having produced *Heiterkeit* in his audience (the term used by German protocol experts for amusement registered by an official audience), Frank predicted that Lublin too would become a "decent" and "human" city for German men and women.[50]

But Frank's jubilation was premature. No peace treaty was concluded with France, and no African island was set aside for the Jews. Frank was stuck with his Jews, and once more the pressure of new expulsions was to trouble his administration.

On October 2, 1940, Frank met with other officials in Hitler's apartment. The *Reichsstatthalter* of Vienna, von Schirach, mentioned that he had 50,000 Jews which Frank had to take off his hands; the *Generalgouverneur* replied that this was utterly impossible. Thereupon, the *Oberpräsident* of East Prussia, Erich Koch, put in that until now he had deported neither Jews nor Poles, but now the time had arrived when the *Generalgouvernement* had better accept these people. Again Frank protested that it was utterly impossible to receive such masses of Poles and Jews; there simply was no room for them. At this point Hitler remarked that he

48. Frank to Lammers, June 25, 1940, NG-1627.

49. Frank to main division chiefs, July 12, 1940, Frank diary, PS-2233.

50. Frank speech to Lublin officials, July 25, 1940, Frank diary, PS-2233.

was quite indifferent to the population density of the *Generalgouvernement,* that so far as he was concerned the *Generalgouvernement* was only a "huge Polish labor camp [*ein grosses polnisches Arbeitslager*]."[51]

Once more Frank averted the threatened stream, although he could not prevent some Poles and a trickle of Vienna Jews crossing his borders. Finally, on March 25, 1941, Krüger announced that no more transports would be sent to the *Generalgouvernement.*[52] From now on the pressure was no longer on Frank; instead, it hit the administration of the incorporated territories.

In September, 1941, mass deportations began in the Reich. They did not end until the destruction process was over. The object of these movements was not emigration but the annihilation of the Jews. As yet, however, there were no killing centers in which the victims could be gassed to death, and so it was decided that, pending the construction of death camps, the Jews were to be dumped into ghettos of the incorporated territories and the occupied Soviet areas farther east. The target city in the incorporated territories was the ghetto of Lodz.

On September 18, 1941, Himmler addressed a letter to Reichsstatthalter Greiser on the proposed evacuations. The Führer desired, wrote Himmler, that the Old Reich and the Protektorat be "liberated from the Jews" as soon as possible. Himmler was therefore planning "as a first step" to transport the Jews to incorporated territory, with a view to shipping them farther east next spring. He intended to quarter 60,000 Jews in the Lodz ghetto, which, as he "heard," had enough room. Looking forward to Greiser's co-operation, Himmler closed with the remark that he was entrusting Gruppenführer Heydrich with the task of carrying out these Jewish migrations.[53]

Although there is a gap in the correspondence, we may deduce from subsequent letters that Greiser had succeeded in reducing the figure of 60,000 migrants to 20,000 Jews and 5000 Gypsies. But even this reduced total came as a shock to the local authorities. A representative of the *Oberbürgermeister* (mayor) of Lodz (the city was renamed "Litzmannstadt") protested immediately to the *Regierungspräsident* of the area, the honorary SS-Brigadeführer Uebelhoer.[54]

In his protest Oberbürgermeister Ventzki announced that he would divest himself of every responsibility for the consequences of the measure. Then he recited some reasons for his attitude: The ghetto had originally held 160,400 people in an area of 4.13 square kilometers. The population had now declined to 144,000 owing to deaths and departures to forced labor camps, but there was more than a corresponding decline of area, to 3.41 square kilometers. Density was now 59,917 persons per square kilometer. The 144,000 inhabitants lived in 2000 houses with 25,000 rooms, that is, 5.8 persons per room.

Within the ghetto, said Ventzki, large factories were producing vital materials needed by the Reich (figures cited), but only starvation rations were coming into the ghetto. Lack of coal had impelled the inmates to tear out doors, windows, and floors to feed the

51. Memorandum by Bormann on conference in Hitler's apartment, October 2, 1940, USSR-172. See also Lammers to von Schirach, December 3, 1940, PS-1950.

52. Summary of GG conference, March 25, 1941, Frank diary, PS-2233.

53. Himmler to Greiser, copies to Heydrich and the Higher SS and Police Leader in the Wartheland, Gruppenführer Koppe, September 18, 1941, Himmler Files, Folder No. 94.

54. *Oberbürgermeister* of Lodz (signed Ventzki) to Uebelhoer, September 24, 1941, Himmler Files, Folder No. 94. Honorary members of the SS wore uniforms but had no SS functions.

fires in the stoves. The arrival of an additional 20,000 Jews and 5000 Gypsies would increase the population density to 7 persons per room. The newcomers would have to be housed in factories, with the result that production would be disrupted. Starvation would increase and epidemics would rage unchecked. The digging of additional ditches for the disposal of feces would lead to an increase in the number of flies which would ultimately plague the German quarter. The Gypsies, as born agitators and arsonists, would start a conflagration, etc. Uebelhoer forwarded this report to Himmler, underlining some of the conclusions in a letter of his own.[55]

Heydrich's way of dealing with these protests was to cable Uebelhoer to the effect that the transports would begin to arrive on schedule in accordance with arrangements concluded with the Transport Ministry.[56] Himmler wrote a more conciliatory letter to the unhappy *Regierungspräsident*. "Naturally," he began, "it is not pleasant to get new Jews. But I should like to ask you in all cordiality to show for these things the same natural understanding which has been extended by your *Gauleiter*." The objections had obviously been drawn up by some subordinate in an expert manner, but Himmler could not recognize them. War production was nowadays the favorite reason for opposing anything at all. No one had demanded that the Jews be quartered in factories. Since the ghetto population had declined, it could increase again. As for the Gypsy arsonists, Himmler advised Uebelhoer to announce that for every fire in the ghetto ten Gypsies would be shot. "You will discover," said Himmler, "that the Gypsies will be the best firemen you ever had."[57]

Uebelhoer was now truly aroused. He wrote a second letter to Himmler in which he explained that a representative of the Reich Security Main Office, Sturmbannführer Eichmann, had been in the ghetto and with Gypsy-like horse-trading manners had completely misrepresented to the *Reichsführer-SS* the true state of affairs. Uebelhoer then made a constructive suggestion: he requested Himmler to send the Jews to Warsaw rather than to Lodz. Uebelhoer had read in a Berlin newspaper that the Warsaw Ghetto in the *Generalgouvernement* still had dance halls and bars. He had seen the pictures in the *Berliner Illustrierte*. Conclusion: Warsaw was the place for the 20,000 Jews and 5000 Gypsies.[58]

This time Himmler replied in a gruff tone. "Mr. *Regierungspräsident*, read your letter once again. You have adopted the wrong tone. You have obviously forgotten that you have addressed a superior." Henceforth, all communications from Uebelhoer's office would not be accepted.[59] Heydrich wrote his own letter to Greiser, protesting specifically against the remarks concerning SS-comrade Eichmann, whom Uebelhoer had accused of the gypsy-like horse-trading manners.[60]

On October 16 the first transports began to arrive. By November 4 twenty transports had dumped 20,000 Jews into the ghetto: 5000 from Vienna, 5000 from Prague, 4200 from Berlin, 2000 from Cologne, 1100 from Frankfurt, 1000 from Hamburg, 1000 from Düs-

55. Uebelhoer to Himmler, October 4, 1941, Himmler Files, Folder No. 94.

56. Heydrich to Himmler, October 18, 1941, enclosing his telegram to Uebelhoer, Himmler Files, Folder No. 94.

57. Himmler to Uebelhoer, October 10, 1941, Himmler Files, Folder No. 94.

58. Uebelhoer to Himmler, October 9, 1941, Himmler Files, Folder No. 94.

59. Himmler to Uebelhoer, October 9, 1941, Himmler Files, Folder No. 94. This letter was actually dispatched *before* Himmler's first reply.

60. Heydrich to Greiser, October 11, 1941, Himmler Files Folder No. 94.

seldorf, and 500 from the occupied principality of Luxembourg. (The Gypsies arrived too).[61] So crowded was the ghetto that many of the newcomers had to be quartered in the factories.[62]

On October 28, Greiser wrote a friendly letter to Himmler. The *Gauleiter* had talked to the *Regierungspräsident.* Uebelhoer had succumbed to his "famous temper." But the *Regierungspräsident* was an old Nazi who had always done his job. He had done everything to bring this action to a successful conclusion.[63]

Himmler replied that he had received Greiser's letter. "As everyone knows, I bear no grudges [*Ich bin bekanntlich nicht nachtragend*]." The good Uebelhoer was to take a vacation and rest his nerves; then all would be forgiven.[64] Indeed, the incident was soon forgotten, for on July 28, 1942, Uebelhoer had had occasion to thank Himmler for a birthday gift: a porcelain figure with the inscription "Standard bearer of the SS."[65]

The expulsions were over and the situation was stabilized.

Ghetto Formation

From the fall of 1939 to the fall of 1941, three expulsion movements had taken place from west to east: (1) Jews (and Poles) from the incorporated territories to the *Generalgouvernement,* (2) Jews (and Gypsies) from the Reich-Protektorat area to the *Generalgouvernement,* (3) Jews (and Gypsies) from the Reich-Protektorat area to the incorporated territories. These movements are significant not so much for their numerical extent as for their psychological mainsprings. They are evidence of the terrific tensions which then convulsed the entire bureaucracy. The period 1939-41 was a time of transition from the forced emigration program to the "final solution" policy. At the height of this transition phase, transports were pushed from west to east in efforts to arrive at "intermediary" solutions. In the *Generalgouvernement* the nervousness was greatest because 1,500,000 Jews were already in the area and there was no possibility of pushing them farther east.

If the expulsions were regarded as temporary measures toward intermediary goals, the second part of the Heydrich program, which provided for the concentration of the Jews in closed ghettos, was intended to be no more than a makeshift device in preparation for the ultimate mass emigration of the victims. In the incorporated territories the administration looked forward only to the expulsion of its Jews to the *Generalgouvernement,* and the *Generalgouverneur* was waiting only for a "victory" which would make possible the forced relocation of all his Jews to the African colony of Madagascar. We can understand, therefore, in what spirit this ghettoization was approached. During the first six months there was little planning and much confusion. The administrative preliminaries were finished quickly enough, but the actual formation of the ghettos was tardy and slow. Thus the walls around the giant ghetto of Warsaw were not closed until autumn of 1940. The Lublin ghetto was not established until April, 1941.

The preliminary steps of the ghettoization process consisted of marking, movement restrictions, and the creation of Jewish control organs. The first two of these steps gave rise to no difficulties at all.

61. Report by Hauptmann der Schutzpolizei Künzel, November 13, 1941, *Dokumenty i Materialy,* III, 203–6.

62. Armament Inspectorate XXI to OKW/Economy-Armament Office, December 12, 1941, Wi/ID 1.14.

63. Greiser to Himmler, October 28, 1941, Himmler Files, Folder No. 94.

64. Himmler to Greiser, November, 1941, Himmler Files, Folder No. 94.

65. Uebelhoer to Himmler, July 29, 1942, Himmler Files, Folder No. 94.

In the *Generalgouvernement,* Frank ordered that all "Jews and Jewesses" who had reached the age of twelve be forced to wear a white armband with a blue Jewish star.[66] His order was carried out by the decree of November 23, 1939.[67] In the incorporated territories a few *Regierungspräsidenten* imposed markings of their own. For the sake of uniformity, Reichsstatthalter Greiser of the Wartheland ordered that all Jews in his *Reichsgau* wear a four-inch (ten-centimeter) yellow star sewed on the front *and* back of their clothes.[68] The Jews took to the stars immediately. In Warsaw, for example, the sale of armbands became a regular business; there were ordinary armbands of cloth and fancy plastic armbands which were washable.[69]

In conjunction with the marking decrees, the Jews were forbidden to move freely. By *Generalgouvernement* decree of December 11, 1939, signed by the Higher SS and Police Leader Krüger, Jews were forbidden to change residence, except within the locality, and they were forbidden to enter the streets between 9 P.M. and 5 A.M.[70] Under the decree of January 26, 1940, the Jews were prohibited also from using the railways, except for authorized trips.[71]

The most important, and ultimately also the most troublesome, of the preliminary steps in the ghettoization process was the establishment of Jewish councils – *Judenräte.* According to the *Generalgouvernement* decree of November 28, 1939,[72] every Jewish community with a population of up to 10,000 had to elect a *Judenrat* of twelve members, and every community with more than 10,000 people had to elect a *Judenrat* of twenty-four.[73] Who served in the *Judenräte,* and what was their function?

It is significant that, in Poland just as in the Reich, the *Judenräte* were filled with prewar Jewish community leaders. To be sure, there were some reshuffles. "Dark horses" took over the two largest ghettos. Adam Czerniakow, chairman of the Warsaw *Judenrat,* was a "Polish-speaking" (as opposed to Yiddish-speaking) Zionist, an engineer, and a "litttle-known leader in the Artisans' Union."[74] Chaim Rumkowski, "Eldest of the Jews" in Lodz, was a businessman who had apparently stepped out of obscurity to become a benevolent despot and ghetto dictator.[75] But on the whole, there were no significant changes in personnel. The major change was one of function.

66. Summary of discussion between Frank and Krakow's Gouverneur Dr. Wächter, November 10, 1939, Frank diary, PS-2233.

67. *Verordnungsblatt des Generalgouverneurs,* 1939, p. 61.

68. Order by *Regierungspräsident* in Kalisz (Übelhör), December 11, 1939, amending his instructions of November 14, 1939, *Dokumenty i Materialy,* III, 23.

69. "Warschaus Juden ganz unter sich," *Krakauer Zeitung,* December 4, 1940, *Generalgouvernement* page.

70. *Verordnungsblatt des Generalgouverneurs,* 1939, p. 231.

71. *Verordnungsblatt des Generalgouverneurs* I, 1940, p. 45.

72. *Verordnungsblatt des Generalgouverneurs,* 1939, p. 72.

73. For statistical compilation of Jewish population in eastern European cities, see Peter-Heinz Seraphim, *Das Judentum im osteuropäischen Raum* (Essen, 1938), pp. 713–18.

74. Bernard Goldstein, *The Stars Bear Witness* (New York, 1949), p. 35. The author, a survivor, was a leader of the non-Zionist and Yiddish-speaking Jewish Socialist *Bund.* Czerniakow was a member of the prewar community council. In Warsaw all old councilmen became members of the new *Judenrat.* New faces in the Warsaw *Judenrat* were additions brought in by Czerniakow. Actual "elections" never took place. See Jonas Turkow, *Azoy is es gewen* (Buenos Aires, 1948), pp. 47–49, as reproduced in English translation by Philip Friedman (ed.), *Martyrs and Fighters* (New York, 1954), pp. 68–69.

75. See Solomon Bloom, "Dictator of the Lodz Ghetto," *Commentary,* February, 1949, p. 114.

The traditional role of the Jewish community machinery – to educate the children in the schools, to feed the hungry in the soup kitchens, and to help the sick in its hospitals – was now supplemented by another, quite different function: the transmission of German directives and orders to the Jewish population, the use of Jewish police to enforce German will, the deliverance of Jewish property, Jewish labor, and Jewish lives to the German enemy. The Jewish councils, in the exercise of their historic function, continued until the end to make desperate attempts to alleviate the suffering and to stop the mass dying in the ghettos. But at the same time, the councils responded to German demands with automatic compliance and invoked German authority to compel the community's obedience. Thus the Jewish leadership both saved and destroyed its people – saving some Jews and destroying others, saving the Jews at one moment and destroying them at the next. Some leaders broke under this power; others became intoxicated with it.

As time passed by, the Jewish councils became increasingly impotent in their efforts to cope with the welfare portion of their task, but they made themselves felt all the more in their implementation of Nazi decrees. With the growth of the destructive function of the *Judenräte*, many Jewish leaders felt an almost irresistible urge to look like their German masters. In March, 1940, a Nazi observer in Krakow was struck by the contrast between the poverty and filth in the Jewish quarter and the businesslike luxury of the Jewish community headquarters, which was filled with beautiful charts, comfortable leather chairs, and heavy carpets.[76] In Warsaw the Jewish oligarchy took to wearing boots.[77] In Lodz the ghetto "dictator" Rumkowski printed postage stamps bearing his likeness and made speeches which contained expressions such as "my children," "my factories," and "my Jews."[78] From the inside, then, it seemed already quite clear that the Jewish leaders had become rulers, reigning and disposing over the ghetto community with a finality that was absolute. On the outside, however, it was not yet clear to whom these absolute rulers actually belonged.

Under the *Generalgouvernement* decree of November 28, 1939, the *Judenräte* were placed under the *Stadthauptmänner* (in the cities) and the *Kreishauptmänner* (in the country districts). Similarly, in the incorporated territories the *Judenräte* were responsible to the *Bürgermeister* in cities and to the *Landräte* in the country (see Table 29).

Under the decree of November 28 the authority of the regional offices over the *Judenräte* was unlimited. The members of a *Judenrat* were held personally responsible for the execution of all instructions. In fact, the Jewish leaders were so fearful and tremulous in the presence of their German overlords that the Nazi officials merely had to signal their desire. As Frank pointed out in a moment of satisfaction and complacency: "The Jews step forward and receive orders [*die Juden treten an und empfangen Befehle*]."[79] But this arrangement did not remain unchallenged.

76. Dr. Dietrich Redecker, "Deutsche Ordnung kehrt im Ghetto ein," *Krakauer Zeitung*, March 13, 1940.

77. Emanuel Ringelblum, *Notitsn fun Varshever Ghetto* (Warsaw, 1952), p. 291, as quoted in English translation by Friedman, *Martyrs and Fighters*, pp. 81–82. Ringelblum, a historian, was killed by the Germans. His notes were found after the war.

78. Solomon Bloom, "Dictator of the Lodz Ghetto," *Commentary*, February, 1949, pp. 113, 115.

79. Verbatim minutes of interview of Frank by correspondent Kleiss of *Völkischer Beobachter*, February 6, 1940, Frank diary, PS-2233.

Table 29 / *German Controls over Jewish Councils*

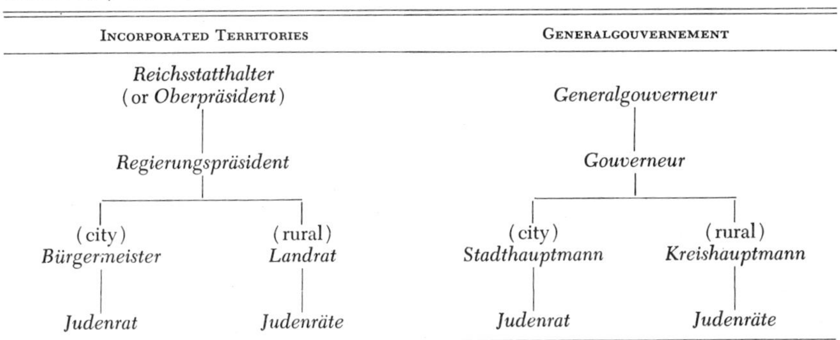

On May 30, 1940, at a meeting in Krakow, the SS and Police made a bid for power over the *Judenräte*. Opening the attack, the commander of the Security Police and Security Service units in the *Generalgouvernement*, Brigadeführer Streckenbach, informed his civilian colleagues that the Security Police were "very interested" in the Jewish question. That was why, he said, the Jewish councils had been created. Now, he had to admit that local authorities, by close supervision of the councils' activities, had gained something of an insight into Jewish methods, etc. But, as a result of this arrangement, the Security Police had been partly edged out, while all sorts of agencies had stepped into the picture. For example, in the matter of labor procurement everyone was planlessly approaching the *Judenräte*.

This problem required a clear "solution." First, it would have to be "decided" who was in charge of the *Judenräte*: the *Kreishauptmann*, the *Gouverneur*, the *Stadthauptmann*, or possibly even the *Sicherheitspolizei* (the Security Police). If Streckenbach recommended his Security Police, he did so for "functional reasons." Sooner or later, he said, all questions pertaining to Jewish matters would have to be referred to the Security Police, especially if the contemplated action required "executive enforcement" (*Exekutiveingriff*). Experience had shown, furthermore, that only the Security Police had a long-range view of conditions affecting Jewry. All this did not mean in the least that the Security Police desired to skim off the cream, so to speak. The Security Police were not interested in Jewish property; they were receiving all their money from Germany and did not desire to enrich themselves. Streckenbach would therefore propose that the Jewish councils "and thereby Jewry as a whole" be placed under the supervision of the Security Police, that all demands upon Jewry be handled by the Security Police. If the Jewish communities were to be further exploited as much as they already had been, then one day the *Generalgouvernement* would have to support millions of Jews. After all, the Jews were very poor; there were no rich Jews in the *Generalgouvernement*, only a "Jew proletariat." He would therefore welcome the transfer of power to the Security Police. To be sure, the Security Police were by no means eager to shoulder this additional burden, but experience had shown that the present arrangement was not "functional."

At the conclusion of this speech, Frank remained silent. The *Gouver-*

neur of Lublin, Zörner, gave an account of conditions in his district. Since Frank had not spoken, the *Gouverneur* ventured to suggest only that the Security Police could not handle the *Judenräte* because of insufficient numerical strength. After Zörner had finished, the *Gouverneur* of Krakow, Wächter, made a speech in which he alluded to Streckenbach's remarks by pointing out that in Jewish matters the civil administration could not get along without the Security Police and that, conversely, the Security Police could not act without the civil apparatus. Cautiously, Wächter suggested that perhaps the two bodies could co-operate. Finally, Frank spoke up. In terse legal language he rejected Streckenbach's suggestions. "The police," he said, "are the armed force of the Reich government for the maintenance of order in the interior. . . . The police have no purpose in themselves."[80]

The opening move by the police had failed; yet the challenge had been made, and for the next few years the struggle over the Jews was to continue unabated. Ultimately the police emerged victorious, but their prize was a heap of corpses.

The three preliminary steps – marking, movement restrictions, and the establishment of Jewish control machinery – were taken in the very first few months of civil rule. But then a full year passed before the actual formation of the ghettos began in earnest. Ghetto formation, that is to say, the creation of closed Jewish districts, was a decentralized process. The initiative in each city and town was taken by the competent *Kreishauptmann* or *Stadthauptmann,* and in the case of major ghettos only, by a *Gouverneur* or by Frank himself.

The very first ghettos appeared in the incorporated territories during the winter of 1939–40.[81] The first major ghetto was created in the city of Lodz in April, 1940.[82] During the following spring the ghetto-formation process spread slowly to the *Generalgouvernement.* The Warsaw ghetto was created in October, 1940;[83] the smaller ghettos in the Warsaw district were formed in the beginning of 1941.[84] For the Jews remaining in the city of Krakow, a ghetto was established in March, 1941.[85] The Lublin ghetto was formed in April, 1941.[86] The double ghetto of Radom, shaped into two separate districts, was finished that same month.[87] The ghetto of Kielce, in the Radom district, also came into existence at that time.[88] In August, 1941, the *Generalgouvernement* acquired its fifth district, Galicia, an area which the German Army had wrested from Soviet occupation. The Galician capital, Lvov (Lemberg), became the site of Poland's third-largest ghetto in December, 1941.[89] The ghetto-formation process in the *Generalgouvernement* was, on the whole, completed by the end of that year.[90] Only a few ghettos remained to be set up in 1942.[91]

80. Summary of police meeting with verbatim remarks by Frank, May 30, 1940, Frank diary. PS-2233.

81. Philip Friedman, "The Jewish Ghettos in the Nazi Era," *Jewish Social Studies,* 1954, p. 80. Friedman believes the very first ghetto was established at Tulisszkow, Wartheland, in December, 1939, or January, 1940.

82. Documents in *Dokumenty i Materialy,* III, 35–49.

83. *Krakauer Zeitung,* October 16, 1940, *Generalgouvernement* page.

84. *Generalgouvernement* conference, January 15, 1941, Frank diary, PS-2233.

85. *Krakauer Zeitung,* March 23, 1941, p. 18.

86. Proclamation by Gouverneur Zörner of Lublin, March 24, 1941, in *Krakauer Zeitung,* March 30, 1941, p. 8.

87. *Krakauer Zeitung,* April 6, 1941, p. 5.

88. *Krakauer Zeitung,* April 8, 1941, p. 6.

89. *Krakauer Zeitung,* November 15, 1941, p. 5.

90. Armament Inspectorate *Generalgouvernement* to OKW/Wi Rü/Rü IIIA, report covering July 1, 1940, to December 31, 1941, dated May 7, 1942, pp. 102–3, Wi/ID 1.2.

Although the creation of the closed districts did not proceed from any order or basic plan, the procedure was remarkably similar in all cities. This should hardly be surprising, for the problems of ghetto formation were largely the same everywhere. Let us look at the first major ghetto-forming operation, which was the prototype of all subsequent operations: the establishment of the Lodz ghetto.

On December 10, 1939, the *Regierungspräsident* in Kalisz, Uebelhoer, appointed a "working staff" to make preparations for the formation of the ghetto. Uebelhoer himself took over the chairmanship; he appointed his representative in Lodz, Oberregierungsrat Dr. Moser, as deputy. The working staff also included members of the party, the offices of the city, the Order Police, the Security Police, the Death Head Formation of the SS, and Lodz Chamber of Industry and Commerce, and the Financial Office in Lodz. The preparations were to be made in secret; the moving was to be sudden and precise (*schlagartig*). As we shall see, this secrecy was needed in order to assure the hurried abandonment of a lot of Jewish property, which could then be conveniently confiscated.

Uebelhoer did not look upon the ghetto as a permanent institution. "The creation of the ghetto," he said in his order, "is, of course, only a transition measure. I shall determine at what time and with what means the ghetto – and thereby also the city of Lodz – will be cleansed of Jews. In the end, at any rate, we must burn out this bubonic plague [*Endziel muss jedenfalls sein, dass wir diese Pestbeule restlos ausbrennen*]."[92]

The working staff selected a slum quarter, the Baluty area, as the ghetto site. The district already contained 62,000 Jews, but more than 100,000 Jews who lived in other parts of the city and its suburbs had to be moved in.[93] On February 8, 1940, the *Polizeipräsident* of Lodz, Brigadeführer Schäfer, issued his sudden and precise orders. Poles and ethnic Germans had to leave the ghetto site by February 29.[94] The Jews had to move into the ghetto in batches; every few days the *Polizeipräsident* published a moving schedule affecting a certain quarter of the city. All Jews living in that quarter had to move into the ghetto within the time allotted. The first batch had to vacate its apartments between February 12 and February 17;[95] the last batch moved in on April 30. Then days later, on May 10, Polizeipräsident Schäfer issued the order which closed off the ghetto population from the rest of the world. "Jews," he ordered, "must not leave the ghetto, as a matter of principle. This prohibition applies also to the Eldest of the Jews [Rumkowski] and to the chiefs of the Jewish police . . . Germans and Poles," he continued, "must not enter the ghetto as a matter of principle." Entry permits could be issued only by the *Polizeipräsident*. Even within the ghetto, Jews were not allowed freedom of movement; from 7 P.M. to 7 A.M. they were not permitted to be on the streets.[96]

91. Friedman, "Jewish Ghettos," *Jewish Social Studies*, 1954, p. 83.

92. Uebelhoer to Greiser, Party District Lodz, Representative of the *Regierungspräsident* in Lodz (Moser), City Administration of Lodz, *Polizeipräsident* of Lodz, Order Police in Lodz, Security Police in Lodz, Lodz Chamber of Industry and Commerce, and Finance Office in Lodz, December 10, 1939, *Dokumenty i Materialy*, III, 26–31.

93. Statistical report on the Lodz ghetto, apparently prepared by the Jewish Council for the German administration, and covering the period May 1, 1940 to June 30, 1942, Lodz Ghetto Collection No. 58.

94. Order by Schäfer, February 8, 1940, *Dokumenty i Materialy*, III, 35–37.

95. Police order, February 8, 1940, *Dokumenty i Materialy*, III 38–49.

After the movements had been completed, the Germans threw a fence around the ghetto. The fence was manned by a detachment of the Order Police.[97] The more intriguing job of secret police work was entrusted to the Security Police. That organization consisted of two branches: State Police (Gestapo) and Criminal Police (*Kripo*). The State Police, as their title implies, concerned themselves with enemies of the state. Since the Jews were enemies par excellence, the State Police established an office within the ghetto. The Criminal Police was competent in the handling of common crimes. A Criminal Police detachment of twenty men was consequently attached to the Order Police which guarded the ghetto. The function of the detachment was to prevent smuggling. But the arrangement irked the Criminal Police; like their colleagues of the Gestapo, the Criminal Police men wanted to be *inside* the ghetto. Accordingly, Kriminal Inspektor Bracken drafted a memorandum in which he set forth the reason for the urgent necessity of moving his detachment across the fence. "In the ghetto," he said, "'live, at any rate, about 250,000 Jews, all of whom have more or less criminal tendencies." Hence the necessity for "constant supervision" by officials of the Criminal Police.[98] The detachment moved in.

As Regierungspräsident Uebelhoer had predicted, the ghetto was a transitional measure, but the transition did not lead to emigrations; it led to annihilation. The inmates of the Lodz ghetto either died there or were deported to a killing center. For reasons which we shall explain later, the liquidation of the ghetto took a very long time. When it was finally broken up in August, 1944, it had existed for four years and four months. This was a record unequalled by any ghetto in Nazi Europe.

Across from the border of the incorporated territories, in the *Generalgouvernement,* Gouverneur Fischer of the Warsaw district proposed, as early as November 7, 1939, that the Warsaw Jews (whose number he estimated at 300,000) be incarcerated in a ghetto. Frank gave his immediate consent to the proposal,[99] but the plan was premature. The administrative obstacles were formidable; the emigration policy was still in force; and the military offices in the city – to whom, in the meantime, the Jews were appealing for intervention – were apparently opposed to the whole idea.[100] In February, 1940, the proposal was renewed by the SS and Police, only to be opposed on administrative grounds by the civilian offices in Warsaw.[101] But the project was far from dead.

On September 6, 1940, pressure was applied from still another quarter. During a discussion held on that date between Frank and the medical chief of the *Generalgouvernement,* Obermedizinalrat Dr. Walbaum, the medical chief presented statistics of the increas-

96. Order by Schäfer, May 10, 1940, *Dokumenty i Materialy,* III, 83–84.

97. The order Police had two branches, *Schutzpolizei* (in cities) and *Gendarmerie* (in rural areas). The units guarding the ghetto belonged to the *Schutzpolizei.* For instructions to the *Schutzpolizei* detachments to "shoot on sight," see order by commander of Lodz *Schutzpolizei,* Oberst der Polizei Keuck, April 11, 1941, *Dokumenty i Materialy,* III, 86–87.

98. Memorandum by Kriminal Inspektor Bracken, May 19, 1940, *Dokumenty i Materialy,* III, 92–94; also, memorandum by the chief of the Criminal Police in Lodz, Kriminaldirektor Zirpins, October 23, 1940, *Dokumenty i Materialy,* III, 100–101.

99. Summary of discussion between Fischer and Frank, November 7, 1939, Frank diary, PS-2233.

100. Concerning the Jewish appeal, see J. S. Hertz (ed.), *Zygelboim Buch* (New York, 1947), pp. 131–35, as quoted by Friedman, *Martyrs and Fighters,* pp. 25–28; also Goldstein, *The Stars Bear Witness,* pp. 36–38.

101. Report by SS and Police Leader in Warsaw (Stroop), May 16, 1943, PS-1061.

ing incidence of spotted fever among Jews. According to Walbaum, the Jews were spreading the disease to the non-Jewish population; he concluded that, to relieve the situation, it was of the greatest importance to take "health-political" measures, i.e., the incarceration of the Jews in a closed ghetto.[102] On September 12, 1940, Frank announced during a conference of main division chiefs that 500,000 Jews in the city of Warsaw were posing a threat to the whole population. The Jews could no longer be permitted to "roam around." They would have to be brought into a ghetto.[103]

We may note in passing that as a quarantine the ghetto was not very effective. As the typhus epidemic soared within the ghetto, the Poles outside of the ghetto were affected too. On December 16, 1941, more than a year after the creation of the ghetto, Amtschef Dr. Hummel of the Warsaw district reported 2405 typhus cases inside the ghetto and 1092 cases outside the ghetto walls (including 503 sick Poles in the city and 589 cases in the rest of the district).[104] However, as an excuse for the establishment of the ghetto, the Jewish typhus cases were more important even than Jewish criminality and the Jewish drive for world power. In February, 1941, the chief of the Migration Section, in the Interior Division of the office of the Warsaw *Gouverneur,* Reichsamtsleiter Schön, listed three reasons for the ghettoization. His reasons, in order of importance, were the epidemics, Jewish black-market activity and price gouging, and "political and moral" reasons.[105] In March the Medical Division in the office of the Warsaw *Gouveneur,* in co-operation with the Propaganda Division of the district, launched a propaganda campaign directed at the Polish population. The two divisions had devised a slogan which they circulated on posters, in newspapers, in movies, and in schools. the slogan was "Jews-Lice-Typhus" (*Juden-Läuse-Fleckfieber*).[106]

We need not discuss the details of the ghetto formation in Warsaw, because they are quite similar to the administrative measures which had been taken in Lodz. After the Warsaw ghetto had been closed, *Stadthauptmänner* and *Kreishauptmänner* in all parts of the *Generalgouvernement* followed suit. In town after town, local officials passed through the same three-stage process. They selected the location of the ghetto; they issued the sudden (*schlagartige*) movement orders; and they sealed off the finished ghetto. There were, of course, some variations. A number of small Jewish communities were incarcerated in ghetto towns; that is, whole towns became ghettos.[107] The larger communities were crowded into closed-off city districts, each of which became a city within a city.

As may be seen from the statistics in Table 30, a ghetto was usually a tightly packed slum area, without parks, empty lots, or open spaces.[108]

102. Summary of discussion between Frank, Dr. Walbaum, and Warsaw District Health Chief Dr. Franke, September 6, 1940, Frank diary, PS-2233.

103. Summary of conference of main division chiefs, September 12, 1940, Frank diary, PS-2233.

104. Summary of *Generalgouvernement* conference, December 16, 1941, Frank diary, PS-2233.

105. *Krakauer Zeitung,* February 7, 1941, *Generalgouvernement* page.

106. *Krakauer Zeitung,* March 25, 1941, p. 5; April 23, 1941, p. 5.

107. For description of such a ghetto-town, see Gustav Andraschko, "Das fiel uns auf in Szydlowiec . . .!" *Krakauer Zeitung,* June 21, 1941, pp. 6–7.

108. The Warsaw statistics were taken from the archives of the Jewish Historical Institute, Warsaw, by Isaiah Trunk, and published by him in an article entitled "Epidemics in the Warsaw Ghetto," *YIVO Annual of Jewish Social Science,* VIII, p. 87. The figures on apartment density in the Warsaw ghetto are confirmed by Stroop (SS and Police Leader

In spite of its small size, a ghetto which was placed in the middle of a metropolis invariably created traffic problems. In Warsaw trolley lines had to be rerouted;[109] in Lodz the city administration had to install a new bus line which skirted the ghetto;[110] while in Lublin, Stadthauptmann Sauermann had to build a detour road around the Jewish quarter.[111] Traffic problems also determined, to a large extent, the method of sealing a ghetto. Only a few cities, such as Warsaw, Krakow, Radom, and Neu-Sandez surrounded their ghettos with massive medieval-like walls and built-in gates.[112] Some ghettos, such as Lodz, were only fenced in with barbed wire. Still others, including Lublin, could not be sealed at all.

While not every ghetto could be closed completely, no Jew was permitted to remain outside its boundaries. There were no exceptions. Jews in mixed marriage with their Polish spouses and *Mischlinge* of all degrees were pushed into the ghettos.[113] On February 26, 1941, the First Secretary of the Soviet Embassy, Bogdanov, inquired why certain nationals of the Soviet Union were forced to live in certain places. Unterstaatssekretär Wörmann of the Foreign Office replied that the nationals involved were Jews (*dass es sich um Juden handele*) and that Jews of Soviet nationality were receiving the same treatment as Jews of other nationalities.[114]

TABLE 30 / *Densities in the Ghettos of Warsaw and Lodz*

	City of Warsaw, March, 1941	"Aryan" Warsaw	Ghetto of Warsaw	Ghetto of Lodz, September, 1941
Population	1,365,000	920,000	445,000	144,000
Area (square miles)	54.6	53.3	1.3	1.6
Rooms	284,912	223,617	61,295	25,000
Persons per room	4.8	4.1	7.2	5.8

By the end of 1941 almost all Jews in the incorporated territories and the *Generalgouvernement* were living in ghettos. What happened inside these Jewish quarters? We are not going to discuss here the complex changes which the institution of the ghetto imported into the Jewish communities; that is a subject which belongs to Jewish history, not to the history of the anti-Jewish destruction process. In this book we

in Warsaw) in a report to Krüger, May 16, 1943, PS-1061. Stroop mentions 27,000 apartments with an average of 2½ rooms each. Lodz statistics from report by Ventzki to Übelhör, September 24, 1941, Himmler Files, Folder No. 94.

109. *Krakauer Zeitung*, November 27, 1941, *Generalgouvernement* page.

110. Office of the Mayor of Lodz (Dr. Marder) to Office of the *Regierungspräsident* in Lodz, July 4, 1941, *Dokumenty i Materialy*, III 177–79.

111. Report by Sauermann in conference attended by Frank, October 17, 1941, Frank diary, PS-2233.

112. Photograph of Radom Wall in *Krakauer Zeitung*, November 20, 1940, *Generalgouvernement* page. Photograph of Krakow Wall in *Krakauer Zeitung*, May 18, 1941, p. 5.

113. Representative of the *Regierungspräsident* in Lodz (signed Moser) to *Polizeipräsident* in Lodz, August 26, 1940, enclosing letter by *Reichsstatthalter's* office in Wartheland (signed Coulon) to Representative of *Regierungspräsident* in Lodz, August 6, 1940, *Dokumenty i Materialy*, III, 172.

114. Unterstaatssekretär Wörmann (chief, Political Division) via deputy chief of Political Division to Section V of the Division (Soviet affairs), February 24, 1941, NG-1514. However, the release of Soviet Jews was under consideration; see report by Representative of Foreign Office in *Generalgouvernement* (Wühlisch) to Foreign Office, February 7, 1941, NG-1528.

shall be interested in the ghetto only as a control mechanism in the hands of the German bureaucracy. To the Jews the ghetto was a way of life; to the Germans it was an administrative measure. We have to discuss that measure and understand how it worked.

To begin with, the Germans did not stop with the fencing-in or walling-in of the Jewish quarters. This was not the end of concentration but the starting point for the institution of tighter controls over the Jewish community. The administrative structure of the German control machinery and of the Jewish councils was enlarged, and the functions of both German and Jewish offices were increased. In Lodz and Warsaw, particularly, brand-new machinery was built into the German apparatus.

The Lodz Jewish Council was placed under a "Food and Economic Office Ghetto" (*Ernährungs- und Wirtschaftsstelle Ghetto*). Originally, this office regulated only economic questions affecting the ghetto. Soon, however, its title was changed to *Ghettoverwaltung Litzmannstadt* ("Ghetto Administration, Lodz"), and with that change of title there was also a change of function. The office took charge of all ghetto affairs. The place of the *Ghettoverwaltung* in the local governmental structure is indicated in Table 31.[115]

TABLE 31 / *German Controls over the Lodz Ghetto*

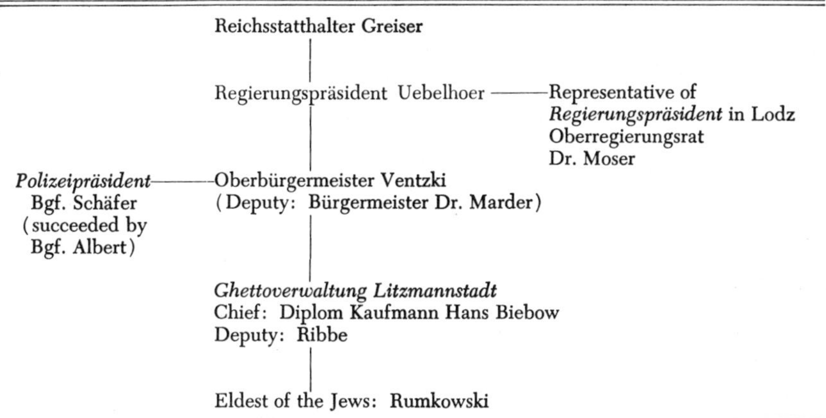

In Warsaw the administrative changes were more far-reaching. The direction of the ghetto was entrusted to a *Kommissar* who was answerable only to the *Gouverneur*. The flow of goods to and from the ghetto was regulated by a public law corporation known as the *Transferstelle*, which operated under the supervision of the *Kommissar* (see Table 32).[116]

While the expansion of the German control apparatus was confined, on the whole, to the two largest ghettos – Warsaw, with 470,000 Jews, and Lodz with 160,000 – the growth of the Jewish

115. For appointment of Diplom Kaufmann Hans Biebow as chief of the *Ghettoverwaltung* and other personnel questions, see Biebow to DAF Ortsgruppe Rickmers, April 30, 1940, and Biebow to Bürgermeister Dr. Marder, November 12, 1940, *Dokumenty i Materialy*, III, 253, 256–57. *Diplom Kaufmann* was the title of a graduate from a school of business administration.

116. *Krakauer Zeitung*, May 1, 1941, p. 6; May 18, 1941, p. 6; May 21, 1941, p. 5. *Der jüdische Wohnbezirk* ("District of Jewish residence"), was the euphemism used by the Germans in Warsaw for "ghetto."

TABLE 32 / *German Controls over the Warsaw Ghetto*

Gouverneur Dr. Fischer

|

Kommissar für den jüdischen Wohnbezirk — Transferstelle
Auerswald — Bischoff

|

Chairman of the Jewish Council
Czerniakow

bureaucracy could be observed in all ghettos. Each chairman of a *Judenrat* became, de facto, a mayor. (*One Judenrat* chairman, Czerniakow of Warsaw, even held the title of mayor.) Each *Judenrat* had to perform the functions of a city council. The entire Jewish apparatus was now composed of city administrators; moreover, viewed internally, the ghettos were not cities but city-states, and totalitarian ones at that. Each *Judenrat* operated large economic enterprises (in the case of Lodz, all economic enterprises). Each *Judenrat* had the power to impress labor. During the deportations, it became clear that each *Judenrat* also held powers of life and death.

Measured in its powers to regulate and interfere with the life of the inhabitants, the Jewish bureaucracy of the Lodz ghetto was probably the most totalitarian of all ghetto bureaucracies. The following is a list of the offices which operated under the Lodz *Judenrat* in 1940:[117]

- The Eldest of the Jews
- Council of Elders with the Eldest of the Jews
- Central Bureau *(Zentrale)*
  - Central Negotiations Office *(Zentral-Verhandlungsstelle)*
  - Correspondence Division (*Präsidialabteilung*)
  - Personnel Bureau
  - Main Treasury and Bookkeeping
  - Information Office
  - Cemetery Division
  - Rabbinical Office
  - Bureau of the Eldest of the Jews for the Children's Colony
- Registration and Records
  - Registration Office
  - Records Office
  - Statistical Division
- Police Headquarters (*Ordnungsdienst Kommando)*
  - Law Division
  - 4 Precincts
  - 2 Reserves (Mobile)
  - Auxiliary Police (*Hilfsordnungsdienst* or "Hido")
  - Sanitation Control
  - Price Enforcement
  - Special Commando *(Sonderkommando)*
- Fire-fighting Division
- Main Post Office and Post Office Branch
- Control Commission for German and Polish Property in the Ghetto
- Housing Division
- Finance Division
  - Rent Office
  - Tax Office
  - Executor's Office *(Vollstreckungsstelle)*
  - Bank (Main Building and Branch)
  - Purchasing Office for Valuables and Clothes
- Economy Division
  - Real Estate Administration
  - Janitor Division
  - Chimney Sweeps
  - Technical Renovation

117. Based upon organization chart of the Jewish Council in the Lodz ghetto, August 20, 1940, Wi/ID 1.40. The records of the Lodz Jewish Council and its divisions (in Yiddish) are preserved in the Lodz ghetto collection in the YIVO Institute, New York City. For a description of the Lodz ghetto offices, see also the article by Bendet Hershkovitch, "The Ghetto in Litzmannstadt (Lodz)," in the *YIVO Annual of Jewish Social Science*, 1950, V, 85–122.

Garbage and Sewage Disposal (*Müll- und Fäkalienabfuhr*)
Warehouses
Sales Office for Household Items

Agricultural Division (Main Office and Branch)

School Division

Central Bureau for Labor
4 Tailors' Divisions
2 Carpenters' Divisions
1 Shoemakers' Division
1 Textile Workers' Division

Public Works Division
Work Assignment Office
Construction Office

Supply Division
Receiving Station
Central Bureau
Auditing Office
Main Depot
Vegetable Depot
Coal Depot
Dairy Depot
Meat Depot
Meat Cold Storage Depot
Cigarette and Tobacco Depot
Community Bakery
36 Food Distribution Points
17 Stores for Sale of Milk, Butter, and Foods Purchasable upon Doctor's Prescription
14 Butcher Shops

Welfare Division
Relief Division (Money and Products)
Nursery
2 Orphanages
Home for the Aged
Invalids' Home
Collecting Point for Homeless People
Public Kitchens
Children's Colony
Children's Sanatorium

Health Division
Central Bureau
4 Hospitals
4 Dispensaries
Dental Clinic
Central Drug Store and 6 Branch Drug Stores
2 Ambulance Units
Laboratory
Laboratory for Bacteriological Examination
Disinfection Division

The Jewish machinery in Lodz reflected, in its very organization, the peculiar dual role of the ghetto in the destruction process. The survival function of the ghetto is illustrated primarily by the three divisions on the bottom of the list: health, welfare, and supply. The destructive function is recognized most clearly in the Central Bureau, the Registration and Records Office, and, above all, in the police. It is characteristic that the office which was most openly destructive in its function, the police, followed the German model even in its organization. A close look at the structure of the ghetto police reveals that it was divided into a kind of Order Police (complete with precincts, reserves, auxiliaries, and sanitation control) and a kind of Security Police: a price-control force which had criminal functions, and a *Sonderkommando* which had Gestapo functions. In one respect the Lodz ghetto machine was more advanced even than its Nazi prototype: the *Judenrat* had no separate justice department; the only legal office in the ghetto was incorporated into its police.[118]

Since ghettoization combined territorial confinement with absolute subjugation, the Jewish community was no longer an integrated whole. Each ghetto was on its own. Even so, the isolation was not complete. Although no one, not even the chairman of a *Judenrat,* was allowed to leave a ghetto, some contacts with the outside world remained. Telephone connections were not entirely cut off. Banking services were linked with outside financial institutions. A postal service was operated in the ghettos for the dispatch and receipt of parcels and letters.[119] During the deportations, some ghettos

118. For Warsaw ghetto machinery, see Apenszlak, *The Black Book of Polish Jewry,* p. 224. A description of the Warsaw ghetto police is given by Mary Berg, *Warsaw Ghetto* (New York, 1945), pp. 41–46.

were able to dispatch runners who climbed over walls and fences with uncensored messages to other ghettos and to the outside world. Similarly, spies ascertained the true destination of the special trains hauling away millions of deportees. Nevertheless, in spite of these gaps in the structure, most of the ghetto communities remained paralyzed — so deep-rooted was the thinking of the past, so strong the strangulation of the present.

Confiscations

In the Reich-Protektorat area the expropriations preceded the concentration process. Insofar as any sequence of steps is recognizable, the bureaucracy thought first of expropriations and only later of ghettoization measures. The opposite was true in Poland. The destruction process was introduced into Poland with the elaborate Heydrich concentration plan. This plan became the focal point of anti-Jewish action in the Polish territories, and expropriatory measures were conceived and carried out only in terms of the ghettoization process. They were a part of the institution of the ghetto.

The economic destruction in Poland comprised three operations: confiscation of property, conscription of labor, and deprivation of food. In Germany the gains from property expropriations far outweighed the proceeds from labor and food measures, for the Jewish community in Germany had a great deal of capital but relatively few people. In Poland that situation was just reversed. The Polish Jewish community had little capital but more people; therefore the confiscatory process in Poland was not so important as forced labor and the starvation regime. Still, we shall pay some attention to the property confiscations because they did pose some interesting problems to the German bureaucracy.

The first problem arose when Göring decided to do all the confiscating in Poland. For this purpose he set up the Main Trusteeship Office East (*Haupttreuhandstelle Ost*), which had its headquarters in Berlin, in the Office of the Four-Year Plan.[120] The Main Trusteeship Office East immediately set up branches in Danzig (*Reichsgau* Danzig-West Prussia), Poznan (Wartheland), Zichenau (East Prussia), Katowice (Silesia), and Krakow (*Generalgouvernement*).[121] The head of the Main Trusteeship Office was the retired Bürgermeister Max Winkler.[122]

The creation of an office with headquarters in Berlin and competence in the *Generalgouvernement* was a violation of Frank's sacred rule of the unity of administration; it was an act of *hineinregieren* ("reigning into" his territorial sphere) and therefore intolerable. Accordingly, Frank countered the Göring move by setting up his own trusteeship office under Ministerialrat Dr. Plodeck.[123] Göring decided not to make an issue of the matter.[124] Henceforth, there were *two* trusteeship offices

119. Ghetto post offices in fact used their own rubber stamps with Hebrew-lettered inscriptions. However, Jewish post office employees were not permitted to touch a German postage stamp with their rubber stamps, lest the swastika or Hitler portrait on the postage stamp be covered with the Hebrew letters of the rubber stamp. A few envelopes with Hebrew letters over German postage stamps are said to exist; such envelopes were not sent out but kept for stamp-collecting purposes. M. Markowicz, "Das Postwesen im Ghetto," *Aufbau* (New York), July 28, 1950, p. 34.

120. Announcement (signed Göring), November 1, 1939, *Deutscher Reichsanzeiger und Preussischer Staatsanzeiger*, No. 260.

121. *Ibid.*

122. Winkler had previously been the Reich's Chief Trustee. Affidavit by Winkler, September 9, 1947, NI-10727.

123. The office was set up on November 15, two weeks after the establishment of the Main Trusteeship Office East. See Plodeck, "Die Treuhandverwaltung im Generalgouvernement," in duPrel, *Das Generalgouvernement* (Würzburg, 1942), pp. 110–14.

in Poland: one, under Winkler, with jurisdiction in the incorporated territories, the other, under Plodeck, with functions in the *Generalgouvernement.* It goes without saying that neither of these offices bought anything. The trusteeship offices confiscated property and sold it to interested buyers in accordance with certain priority criteria. The proceeds from such sales in the incorporated territories accrued to the Reich, while the profit in the *Generalgouvernement* was retained by the Krakow administration.

To pave the way for smooth and efficient confiscations, both offices took certain preliminary steps. In the incorporated territories only one such measure was enacted: the decree of September 17, 1940, signed by Göring, for the sequestration of Jewish property. The object of that decree was to prohibit the owners of sequestered property to dispose over it in any way.[125]

The administration of the *Generalgouvernement* was more elaborate in its preparatory work. By November, 1939, the chief of the Foreign Currency and Trade Division of the *Generalgouvernement* had ordered all Jewish deposits and accounts in banks to be blocked. The Jewish depositor was permitted to withdraw only 250 zloty (RM 125 or $50) weekly, or a larger amount if needed for the upkeep of his business. At the same time, Jews had to deposit all cash reserves in excess of 2000 zloty (RM 1000 or $400), while debtors of Jews had to make all payments in excess of 500 zloty (RM 250 or $100) into the blocked account.[126] Needless to say, this measure discouraged the sale of Jewish property. The discouragement was turned into a prohibition with the sequestration decree of January 24, 1940, signed by Generalgouverneur Frank.[127] On the same day the *Generalgouvernement* administration enacted a registration decree. This measure, unlike the Reich decree of April 26, 1938, required the registration of all kinds of property, including even clothes, cooking utensils, furniture, and, of course, jewelry. Moreover, no allowances were made for small amounts.[128]

The actual confiscatory process was divided into three phases. During the first phase, prior to ghettoization, the confiscations were confined to skimming off the cream. It was during this phase that the trusteeship offices and some of their unauthorized competitors plundered warehouses and requisitioned fine homes.[129] The second phase was pivotal and crucial; it was the phase which was tied to the ghettoization process.

As the Jews moved into the ghetto, they left most of their property behind. That "abandoned" property was confiscated. It can readily be understood now that the choice of the ghetto location was of utmost importance to the success of the operation. As a rule the preferred ghetto site was a slum, for in that way the better houses, apartments, and furniture were left behind. But this solution also had its difficulties, because the slums were often filled with warehouses and factories – Thus it was discovered during the formation

124. Testimony by Bühler (*Staatssekretär, Generalgouvernement*), in *Trial of the Major War Criminals,* XII, 67.

125. RGB1 I, 1270. The decree was a trifle late.

126. *Krakauer Zeitung,* November 26/27, 1939, *Wirtschafts-Kurier* page. See also draft directive by OKH/GenQu/Z(W), mid-September, 1939, Wi/I .121.

127. *Verordnungsblatt des Generalgouverneurs* I, 23.

128. *Ibid.,* p. 31.

129. For unauthorized competition, see letter by Brigadeführer Schäfer to Lodz press, January 17, 1940, *Dokumenty i Materialy,* III, 63–64. Schäfer authorized the Jews to demand official papers from requisitioners and to call the police, if necessary.

of the Lodz ghetto that the largest textile warehouses lay within the proposed ghetto boundaries. Naturally, the local merchants were disturbed. "It could hardly have been intended," wrote one of these commercial men, "to leave these enormous values in the ghetto district. So far as at all possible, these things will have to be seized and stored in yards outside the ghetto."[130] Almost equally important were the sudden and precise (*schlagartige*) moving schedules, which were designed to stun the Jews into leaving most of their movables behind. The Jews were given no time to prepare for the transport of all their possessions into the ghetto, and they did not have time to find adequate storage space in the overcrowded ghetto districts.[131]

During the third phase of the confiscations the trusteeship offices reached *into* the ghettos to administer property or to haul out valuables. This phase was not very productive, because the agencies looked upon the ghettos as transitory institutions; it was obviously easier to seize everything upon the liquidation of the ghettos than to search them for hidden property. That is why we shall have to say something more about the confiscations in the deportation chapter.[132]

Undoubtedly the most interesting part of the confiscatory process was the distribution of the property to buyers. It is characteristic of the entire destruction process that it was easier to take away Jewish property than to determine who should get it; there were always many takers for things to be had for nothing, and Poland was no exception.

The incorporated territories in particular had a major distribution problem. The territories were the scene of huge upheavals. Jews were being sent into the ghettos. Poles were being expelled, Reich Germans – whether officials or fortune hunters – were arriving by the thousands, and ethnic German resettlers from the Baltic states and Volhynia were coming too. In addition, we must not forget the local ethnic Germans, who felt that they had first claim on everything. The distribution of the confiscated properties in the incorporated territories was therefore a very complex business.

The Jewish and Polish enterprises were subjected to a truly gigantic liquidation process. It was estimated that in 1930 the incorporated territories held 76,000 minor firms, 9000 medium enterprises, and 294 major concerns.[133] It did not take long before the Main Trusteeship Office, in close co-operation with the industrial associations (*Reichsgruppen*) separated the wheat from the chaff. In the Lodz area alone, 43,000 non-manufacturing firms were reduced to 3000.[134] The liquidated companies had been in possession of tremendous stocks of raw materials and finished products which were rapidly channeled through the confiscatory machine. The raw materials and half-

130. Unsigned memorandum dated January 16, 1940, *Dokumenty i Materialy*, III, 52–54.

131. See order by Gouverneur Zörner for establishment of the Lublin ghetto, March 24, 1941, *Krakauer Zeitung*, March 30, 1941, p. 8. Zörner directed the Jews to offer their excess properties to the branch office of the Trusteeship Division in Lublin.

132. It should be pointed out that Polish property too was confiscated. In the incorporated territories the Germans confiscated Polish land, real estate, enterprises, and, above all, the properties "abandoned" by Poles who had been shoved into the *Generalgouvernement*. See decree of Septembr 17, 1940, RGBl I, 1270. In the *Generalgouvernement* Polish properties were subject to confiscation only in cases of "political or economic necessity." See Dr. Helmut Seifert (Trusteeship Division, *Generalgouvernement*) in *Krakauer Zeitung*, October 11, 1942, p. 11.

133. "Die Haupttreuhandstelle Ost," *Frankfurter Zeitung*, February 22, 1941, NI-3742.

134. "Textilzentrum Litzmannstadt," *Donauzeitung* (Belgrade), January 14, 1942, p. 6; also *Frankfurter Zeitung*, February 22, 1941, NI-3742.

finished items were seized by the army (Oberbefehlshaber Ost / Plenipotentiary for Raw-Materials Seizure Generalmajor Bührmann) for delivery to war industries.[135] The army thus killed two birds with one stone: it relieved shortages of raw materials and it profited from the sale of the materials to industry. To dispose of the finished products, the Main Trusteeship Office East set up an "Administration and Disposal Company" (*Verwaltungs- und Verwertungsgesellschaft*) which, as its title implies, first seized, then sold the Jewish goods.[136]

The surviving enterprises were the subject of the greatest interest in Himmler's *Stabshauptamt für die Festigung deutschen Volkstums* ("Staff Main Office for the Strengthening of Germandom"). The *Stabshauptamt* was one of the twelve main offices of the SS and Police. Its primary task was to Germanize newly occupied territories by strengthening the local German elements and by encouraging the settlement of German newcomers. Hence the *Stabshauptamt* was eager to assure the distribution of enterprises to German residents and German settlers, as distinguished from absentee Reich German investors. As soon as the Main Trusteeship Office came into existence, the chief of the *Stabshauptamt*, Brigadeführer Greifelt, dispatched a liaison man (Obersturmbannführer Galke) to Winkler. Next, Greifelt insisted (successfully) upon the right to veto the appointment of any trustee or the conclusion of any sale.[137] (Trustees were frequently interested buyers—hence this precaution). Finally, Himmler and Winkler agreed that the ethnic Germans were to obtain the enterprises for the price of the machinery and inventory only. No other values were to be paid for and no debts were to be assumed.[138]

The Main Trusteeship Office East was now in a straitjacket. Winkler was particularly anxious to rid himself of the burdensome necessity of submitting every trustee appointment and every sales contract to Greifelt for approval, but for such riddance Winkler had to pay a price. On July 29, 1940, he made a new agreement with Greifelt which provided for the sale of enterprises in accordance with a rigid priority and preference scheme. Winkler and Greifelt set up four priority groups of prospective buyers:

Group I (top priority) consisted of Reich Germans (*Reichsdeutsche,* citizens of Germany) and ethnic Germans who had resided in the incorporated territories on December 31, 1938.

Group II included all ethnic German resettlers.

Group III comprised Reich Germans and ethnic Germans who had given up their residence in the incorporated territories after October 1, 1918 (when the territories became Polish), all Danzig Germans, and Germans from Western Germany evacuated to the incorporated territories because of war conditions.

Group IV (lowest priority) consisted of all other interested German buyers.

Within each group, first preference was to be given to soldiers *(Kriegsteilnehmer)* and the survivors of ethnic Germans "murdered" by the Poles, second preference to loyal (*bewährte*) party members and big families, third preference to survivors of fallen soldiers, and last preference to all other persons.[139]

135. Office of the *Regierungspräsident* in Kalisz (signed Weihe) to *Oberbürgermeister* in Lodz, *Polizeipräsident* in Lodz, *Oberbürgermeister* in Kalisz, *Landräte,* and *Regierungspräsident Aussenstelle* in Lodz (Moser), March 4, 1940, *Dokumenty i Materialy,* III, 67–68.

136. Polizeipräsident Schäfer (Lodz) to newspapers in Lodz, January 17, 1940, *Dokumenty i Materialy,* III, 63–64.

137. Affidavit by Winkler, August 15, 1947, NO-5261.

138. Himmler-Winkler agreement, February 20, 1940, NG-2042.

139. Agreement between Greifelt and

The first preference for veterans was a bit difficult to implement, since Germany was just beginning to fight its war. Enterprises therefore had to be reserved for the prospective veterans. This was done by the formation of so-called *Auffanggesellschaften* (literally "catch companies") which took over Jewish and Polish enterprises for the purpose of running them and expanding them, pending the return of the soldiers from the wars. The Main Trusteeship Office East sank millions of reichsmark into these companies to enable them to perform their "trusteeship" functions.[140]

The ethnic Germans who bought enterprises also needed money. Accordingly, the *Stabshauptamt* set up two credit institutions which operated in the agricultural sphere, the *Deutsche Ansiedlungsgesellschaft* (DAG) and the *Deutsche Umsiedlungstreuhandgesellschaft* (DUT).[141] For other buyers in need of funds there was credit also from German banks. The ubiquitous Dresdner Bank set up a subsidiary, the "Ostbank A. G.," with headquarters in Poznan. The Ostbank specialized in substantially the same business as its parent company – the "reprivatization" of Polish and Jewish enterprises under trusteeship.[142]

We should say a word or two about apartments and furniture, for, in the incorporated territories, not only enterprises but also homes were in demand. Nominally, the Main Trusteeship Office East had complete charge of vacant apartments and their contents; actually, self-help played a considerable role in the distribution process. Obviously, the Germans and Poles ejected from the proposed ghetto sites had to move into vacated Jewish apartments. Resettlers, too, wanted to be settled quickly. Officials plundered the better Jewish homes in order to furnish new offices. For the sake of order, the local civil servants were later directed to report their holdings of Jewish furniture to the Main Trusteeship Office East.[143] The remaining furniture, which was confiscated by the Main Trusteeship Office, was to be distributed in accordance with the same criteria applied to enterprises. The furniture was simply included in the Winkler-Greifelt agreement.[144]

The confiscatory process in the *Generalgouvernement* duplicated the situation in the incorporated territories, except for the fact that the ethnic Germans did not have official backing. The local Germans consequently felt the competition of the Reich Germans more keenly. The big German firms were ready to gobble up every worthwhile *Objekt* in Poland. Even in July, 1939, more than a month before the outbreak of war, I. G. Farben had prepared a report entitled "The Most Important Chemical Firms in Poland."[145]

Winkler, 1940, NO-5149. The administration of agricultural properties (Polish and Jewish) was transferred entirely to the *Stabshauptamt*. Greifelt-Winkler agreement, *ibid.* Affidavit by Greifelt, July 1, 1947, NO-4715. Polish and Jewish real estate in the territory of the former "Free State" of Danzig were confiscated by Oberbürgermeister Lippke on behalf of the city. This move was based on an "ordinance" which the "Free City" had hurriedly passed on September 4, 1939 (four days after the German occupation). See memorandum by Maass (Finance Ministry), August 14, 1941, on Danzig conference of May 27, 1941, NG-1669.

140. In Upper Silesia, the *Auffanggesellschaft für Kriegsteilnehmerbetriebe im Regierungsbezirk Kattowitz, GmbH* received an initial amount of RM 5,000,000. *Krakauer Zeitung*, March 23, 1941, p. 14.

141. Affidavit by Standartenführer Herbert Hübner (*Stabshauptamt* representative in the Warthegau), May 29, 1947, NO-5094.

142. *Ostbank* report of 1941 for the stockholders, NI-6881.

143. Staatssekretär Stuckart to *Regierungspräsidenten* in the incorporated territories, June 12, 1940, NG-2047.

144. Document NO-5149.

145. I. G. Farben report, July 28, 1939, NI-9155. Only one of these firms, that of

The over-all picture is indicated by some statistics for the district of Warsaw: During the summer of 1942, 913 non-agricultural enterprises in the district were administered by 208 "trustees"; according to nationality, the "trustees" were 70 Reich Germans, 51 ethnic Germans, 85 Poles, 1 Russian, and 1 Ukrainian.[146]

A novel situation was introduced into the administration of the Jewish real estate which was confiscated by the state but not sold to private interests. In the city of Warsaw, 4000 Jewish-owned houses had been expropriated on both sides of the ghetto boundary. Outside the ghetto the real estate was placed under 241 German "plenipotentiaries" who in turn bossed 1200 Polish "administrators." Within the ghetto the trusteeship administration consisted of 25 German "main plenipotentiaries," 57 Jewish "plenipotentiaries," and 450 Jewish "house administrators."[147] Business undertakings which were subject to complete liquidation posed only the problem of the disposal of their inventory. The *Generalgouvernement* administration solved that problem by installing in each city or rural district a "reliable" German wholesale or import firm which had complete authority to sell the goods and which guaranteed that nothing would find its way into the black market.[148]

Unfortunately, we do not know the total profit from the sale of Jewish property in Poland.[149] We do know, however, that the Germans were not quite satisfied with the extent of their loot. They suspected that the Jews had hidden the bulk of their valuables in the ghetto enclosures So long, therefore, as the Jewish ghettos remained in existence, the German confiscations could not be completed. The looters had to wait, and during that waiting period tension mounted.

Already in 1940, several agencies busied themselves with the task of "discovering" hidden ghetto treasures. Such activities led to accusations of "sabotage" and "corruption." In Lodz a Criminal Police detachment had established itself inside the ghetto. From this vantage point the detachment hauled out so many goods, gold, and valuables that the *Ghettoverwaltung* complained of "sabotage."[150] On October 23, 1940, the Criminal Police and the *Ghettoverwaltung* made an agreement to the effect that all goods confiscated by the detachment in the ghetto would be delivered to the *Ghettoverwaltung.* On its part the *Ghettoverwaltung* declared that it would have no objection if Criminal Police personnel "reflected" upon certain items and wished to buy them at appraised prices.[151]

The SS and Police was not so considerate when the shoe was on the other foot. Himmler hated vices, and the vice which he hated most was corruption.

Dr. M. Szpilfogel, was Jewish-owned. For its rapid acquisition by the I. G., see documents NI-8457, NI-2749, NI-1093, NI-8380, NI-1149, NI-8373, NI-8397, NI-8378, NI-707, NI-8388, NI-7371, NI-6738, and NI-7367.

146. The *Gouverneur* of the district of Warsaw (Fischer) to the *Staatssekretär, Generalgouvernement,* report for June and July, 1942, dated August 15, 1942, on pp. 12–13, Occ E 2-3.

147. *Die Judenfrage,* March 10, 1941, p. 35.

148. Summary of remarks by Ministerialdirigent Dr. Emmerich in *Generalgouvernement* economic conference under chairmanship of Frank, October 31, 1940, Frank diary, PS-2233.

149. According to Winkler, the Main Trusteeship Office East collected RM 1,500,000,-000. But this figure includes the value of Polish as well as Jewish properties, and it gives no clue to the confiscations in the *Generalgouvernement.* Affidavit by Winkler, September 9, 1947, NI-10727.

150. Memorandum by Kriminal Oberassistent Richter, undated (probably fall of 1940), *Dokumenty i Materialy,* III, 96–98.

151. Memorandum by Kriminaldirektor Zirpins (chief of Criminal Police in Lodz) on his discussion with Biebow, October 23, 1940. *ibid.,* pp. 100–101.

On March 5, 1942, Himmler, Bormann, and Lammers met with Frank to discuss informally (*kameradschaftlich*) certain problem matters (*Fragenkomplexe*). The purpose of the discussion was to clear up these problems "without bothering the Führer with these things." Violently on the defensive, Frank spoke in a "theatrical manner" about his work and about corruption. Allegedly he was the chief corruptionist (*Oberkorruptionist*). He would not stand for such accusations. Himmler then spoke in a disparaging manner about the entire *Generalgouvernement* administration and remarked that an "impossible" situation had been created because of purchases by private persons in the ghettos. Himmler continued by pointing out that Fräulein Frank, the sister of the *Generalgouverneur,* had personally conducted negotiations with the Jews, that the "castle" (Frank's headquarters) was stuffed with items from the ghetto, that these items had been obtained at "arbitrary" prices, etc. Next, Himmler brought up the "immense corruption" (*Riesenkorruption*) of Gouverneur Dr. Lasch of Radom, and Frank countered by demanding the withdrawal of SS and Police Leader Globocnik of Lublin.[152] (Incidentally, both Lasch and Globocnik became casualties in the Himmler-Frank war.) In the meantime, the trusteeship offices looked forward to the second – and major – haul upon the liquidation of the ghetto system. As we shall see, they were to be disappointed.

Labor Exploitation

The expropriatory process in Poland had three components. Since the Polish Jews were a poor people, the confiscations were fiscally and otherwise the least important part of the expropriations. We may be certain that the 800,000 Jews of the Reich, Austria, and the Protektorat owned more property than the 2,500,000 Jews in the incorporated territories and the *Generalgouvernement.* To the Germans, the economic importance of Polish Jewry was expressed in its numbers: two and one half million people are an important productive factor. This was especially true in Poland, where the Jews constituted an unusually high percentage of the available skilled labor.

The initial impact of the war upon Poland had produced a large number of unemployed. The whole economy was disrupted. Thus, at the beginning of the occupation, 2,150,000 people were out of work, while 6,420,000 (comprising the unemployed and their dependents) were directly affected by the upheaval.[153] There was no need for a forced labor system during that period, but, to the Germans, the sight of thousands of Jews "milling around" (*herumlungernde Juden*) was a challenge that had to be met right away. Even during the first few weeks of the occupation, military and civilian offices seized the Jews in the streets and forced them to clear rubble, fill anti-tank ditches, shovel snow, and perform all sorts of other emergency tasks.[154]

On October 26, 1939, the *Generalgouvernement* administration established this kind of forced labor as a general principle. A decree of that date provided that Jews were liable to forced labor in "forced labor troops" (*Zwangsarbeitertroups*).[155] The forced labor troops or Jewish columns (*Judenkolonnen*) were the very first form of labor utilization in Poland. Whenever

152. Memorandum by Himmler, March 5, 1942, NG-3333.

153. Report by Armament Economy Inspectorate Ober-Ost (comprising all of occupied Poland), October 28, 1939, Wi/ID 1.49.

154. *Krakauer Zeitung*, February 4/5, 1940, GG page; May 19/20, 1940, GG page.

155. *Verordnungsblatt des Generalgouverneurs,* 1939, p. 6.

Jews were needed by a particular agency, they were picked up in the street, organized into columns, and put to work. At the end of the working day the Jews were released, and next day the same procedure started all over again. That was all there was to it.[156] But then an astonishing thing happened.

We may recall that, in pursuance of the November 28 decree, *Judenräte* were formed all over Poland. In Warsaw the newly established *Judenrat* decided to do something about the forced labor columns. This decision was "its first major action" undertaken "on its own initiative." We quote from the account of a highly placed Jewish survivor: "In an attempt to mitigate the terror aroused by the press gangs which seized people at random in the streets, the *Judenrat* offered to provide labor battalions at specified times and in specified numbers for the use of the German authorities. The Germans agreed to this plan."[157] In other words, the Warsaw *Judenrat*, in one of the most conspicuous examples of anticipatory compliance, had offered to make the forced labor system more efficient. Naturally the Germans agreed. On December 12, 1939, Krüger signed a decree which empowered the *Judenräte* to organize forced labor columns for the use of any agency which needed them.[158]

Henceforth, each office in need of labor made its wishes known to the *Judenrat*, either directly or indirectly through the Police, the competent *Kreishauptmann*, or the local *Stadthauptmann*. Now some order had been introduced into the system. Over the desks of *Judenrat* officials charts with straight lines moving diagonally upward indicated the increasing utilization of the forced labor columns.[159] A German eyewitness reported: "Today in the *Generalgouvernement*, one can see Jewish troops, spades on shoulders, marching without any German escort through the countryside. At the head of the column marches likewise a Jew."[160] Generalgouverneur Frank praised the Jews condescendingly for their diligence, as though he had reformed them: "They work very well [*sehr brav*], yes, they are even eager about it [*ja sie drängen sich dazu*], and they feel rewarded when they are permitted to work in the 'castle.' Here we do not know the typical Eastern Jew; our Jews work."[161]

Nevertheless, a few problems remained unsolved. Some agencies ignored the new system and continued to seize Jews in the streets.[162] The Higher SS and Police Leader in the *Generalgouvernement*, Krüger, proposed the compilation of a *Zentralkartei*, a central register listing all Jews in the *Generalgouvernement*, with their occupation, age, sex, and other vital statistics.[163] Behind this demand lurked the police desire to seize the entire forced system.[164] But Frank conceded

156. Nothing else was considered feasible at the time. See report by Krüger in GG conference of December 8, 1939, Frank diary, PS-2233.

157. Goldstein, *The Stars Bear Witness*, p. 35.

158. *Verordnungsblatt des Generalgouverneurs*, 1939, pp. 246–48.

159. See report by Dr. Dietrich Redecker about the Krakow *Judenrat* in *Krakauer Zeitung*, March 13, 1940.

160. "Die Juden im Generalgouvernement," *Die Judenfrage*, August 1, 1940, pp. 107–08.

161. Verbatim minutes of interview of Frank by correspondent Kleiss of the *Völkischer Beobachter*, February 6, 1940, Frank diary, PS-2233.

162. See letter of Stadthauptmann Schmid of Krakow to the Krakow *Judenrat*, May 8, 1940, in *Gazeta Zydowska* (Krakow), July 23, 1940. Schmid requested the *Judenrat* to report all cases of wild labor impressments.

163. Krüger in summary of conference of December 8, 1939, Frank dairy, PS-2233.

164. The demand was brought up again during the very conference in which Security Police Commander Streckenbach asked for control over the *Judenräte*. Summary of con-

no special jurisdiction to the SS and Police. Since Krüger already had his fingers in the pie, Frank agreed only that in labor procurement matters the *Stadt-* and *Kreishauptmänner* would work "in closest contact" with the Security Police and Security Service.[165] Toward the end of 1940 the Main Division Labor of the *Generalgouvernement* started to compile a *Zentralkartei*,[166] but it is doubtful that this register was ever used for the recruitment of labor columns.

Notwithstanding these impairments in efficiency, the labor columns remained a very cheap source of manpower. There was no uniform wage policy. Payments were erratic and were granted, if at all, as a matter of grace. The city of Krakow reimbursed the *Judenrat* for the columns it furnished. This lump-sum method of payment enabled the *Judenrat* to force the poorest Jews to "work off" money received from community relief or food eaten in public kitchens.[167] The army agreed to pay two zloty to each man per day (2 zloty = 1 reichsmark = 40 cents). In a peculiar spirit of righteousness the army also insisted that the Jewish councils match these payments with a like amount. But many agencies used labor columns gratuitously, placing the burden of payment entirely upon the *Judenräte*. What did the *Judenräte* do in this situation? The Warsaw *Judenrat*, faced with the necessity of disbursing large sums to its forced laborers, solved its financial problem in the following way: Notices to report for work were sent to all Jews on a rotation basis, but the rich and influential Jews were permitted to buy their way out of the labor columns. With the money thus collected, the *Judenrat* could make some payments to forced laborers and their families.[168]

The columns were the first form of labor utilization; they were suitable only for day-to-day emergency work and for some construction projects. As time passed, there grew out of the labor columns a new and more permanent type of forced labor, the labor camps.[169]

Labor camps were set up for the purpose of employing Jews on a larger scale in more formidable projects. The first proposal for a large-scale project came, significantly, from Reichsführer-SS and Chief of the German Police Heinrich Himmler. In February, 1940, Himmler suggested to Commander-in-Chief of the Army von Brauchitsch the construction of an enormous anti-tank ditch along the newly formed frontiers of the east, facing the Red Army. For the building of this line Himmler dreamed of using all the Polish Jews.[170]

In the course of further planning the Himmler line was trimmed a bit. The ditch was confined to the Bug-San gap, a stretch of territory without a river to hold up a Red advance. The project required the employment not of millions of Jews, as originally envisaged,

ference of May 30, 1940, Frank diary, PS-2233.

165. *Ibid.*

166. Reichshauptamtsleiter Dr. Frauendorfer, "Aufgaben und Organisation der Abteilung Arbeit im Generalgouvernement," *Reichsarbeitsblatt*, 1941, Part V, pp. 67–71.

167. Dr. Dietrich Redecker in *Krakauer Zeitung*, March 13, 1940.

168. Goldstein, *The Stars Bear Witness*, pp. 35–36.

169. However, the labor columns continued in existence even after the ghettos were closed off. In several ghettos passes were issued to enable the columns to leave and return daily. See article in *Krakauer Zeitung* entitled "Jüdisches Wohnviertel auch in Kielce," April 8, 1941, p. 6. In addition to the labor columns, a handful of individuals were employed by army installations outside the ghettos. This was known as *Kleineinsatz* (small-scale labor utilization). See memorandum by *Militärbefehlshaber im Generalgouvernement/Chef des Generalstabes*, October 15, 1942, NOKW-132.

170. Halder diary, February 5, 1940, and February 24, 1940, NOKW-3140.

but only of a few thousand. Labor camps were set up at Belzec and Plazow and a few other locations. By October, 1940, the project was nearing its end.[171]

However, the Himmler line was only the beginning. The Lublin district administration launched a major river-regulation and canalization project which used 10,000 Jews in forty-five camps (over-all director, Regierungsbaurat Haller).[172] In the Warsaw district a similar land-restoration program was started in 1941. About 25,000 Jews were required for that project.[173] In the incorporated territories labor camps dotted the landscape of Upper Silesia. The largest Silesian camp was Markstedt. It had 3000 Jewish inmates.[174] The Warthegau too had big plans for the "outside employment" (*Ausseneinsatz*) of Jews, and in 1940 camps were set up in Pabianice and Löwenstadt.[175]

At first the inmates of camps were used only in outdoor projects, such as the digging of anti-tank ditches, canalization and river regulation, road and railroad construction, and so on. Later on, industrial enterprises moved into some of the camps, and camps were built near major plants. Camp labor thus became a permanent institution, no longer dependent on projects. What effect the industrialization of Jewish labor had on the deportations will be discussed in a following chapter.

171. *Gouverneur* Lublin/Interior Division/Population and Welfare to *Generalgouvernement* Main Division Interior/Population and Welfare (attention Dr. Föhl), October 21, 1940, *Dokumenty i Materialy*, I, 220-21.

172. *Krakauer Zeitung*, December 17, 1940, *Generalgouvernement* page.

173. *Ibid.*, April 18, 1941, p. 5.

174. Affidavit by Rudolf Schönberg (Jewish survivor), July 21, 1946, PS-4071.

175. Office of the *Regierungspräsident* in Lodz (signed Regierungsrat von Herder) to *Ghettoverwaltung* in Lodz, October 28, 1940, enclosing summary of conference held under chairmanship of Moser on October 18, 1940, *Dokumenty i Materialy*, III, 102–4.

Like the labor columns, Jewish camp workers were recruited by the *Judenräte*.[176] Like the columns, the camp groups were furnished complete with Jewish "supervisors" (*Aufseher*) and "group leaders" (*Judengruppenführer*); furthermore, the proper behavior of the forced laborer was insured by keeping a record of the family members he left behind. In conformity with this hostage policy, the German administration in Lodz decided that "out-employment" would be reserved primarily for heads of families.[177] Consequently, it was not necessary to divert large police forces for the guarding of the camps and of the Jewish work parties. The meager SS and Police regulars were supplemented by ethnic German police auxiliaries,[178] hired guards of the *Wach- und Schliessgesellschaft* ("Watchmen's Association"),[179] SA-men, army men, members of the *Organisation Todt* (the Reich agency in charge of construction),[180] and Polish work foreman.[181]

176. Berg, *Warsaw Ghetto*, pp. 51, 94–95.

177. Von Herder to *Ghettoverwaltung*, October 28, 1940, enclosing conference summary of October 18, 1940, *Dokumenty i Materialy*, III, 102–4. The conference was attended by Regierungsvizepräsident Dr. Moser, Regierungsrat Baur, Polizeipräsident Albert, Bürgermeister Dr. Marder, Dr. Moldenhower, Chief of Ghettoverwaltung Biebow and Regierungsrat von Herder.

178. *Krakauer Zeitung*, December 17, 1940, *Generalgouvernement* page. Ethnic German auxiliaries in the *Generalgouvernement* were organized into the Selbstschutz (self-defense force), placed under the command of the BdO (Order Police), and the *Sonderdienst* (Special Service), originally controlled by the *Kreishauptmänner* but later taken over by the commander of the Order Police. *Krakauer Zeitung*, May 21, 1940; August 16, 1940; April 9, 1941, *Generalgouvernement* page; Frank diary, PS-2233. The Himmler line project was guarded in part by the Sonderkommando Dirlewanger, a special SS unit composed of unreliables (Globocnik to Berger), August 5, 1941, NO-2921.

179. Labor Ministry memorandum, May 9, 1941, NG-1368.

180. Affidavit by Schönberg (survivor), July 21, 1946, PS-4071.

The cost of the labor camps was very low. All camps were primitive. No comforts were allowed. No clothes were issued. Food was supplied in some camps by the nearest *Judenrat* and in other camps by the civil administration, but the chief ingredients of the workers' diet were only bread, watery soup, potatoes, margarine, and meat leftovers. Working from dawn to dusk, seven days a week, the Jews were driven to collapse. A survivor reports that even small camps, with no more than 400 to 500 inmates, had approximately twelve dead every day.[182]

The financial aspects of the camps were not very complicated. Reich agencies were not required to pay any wages, and public employers were therefore free to exploit their Jewish workers without limit. Private enterprises were not "entitled" to Jewish labor. In the *Generalgouvernement* private enterprises did not enter into the camps before 1942. In the incorporated territories the Reich Labor Trustees (one in each *Reichsgau*) directed the enterprises to pay wages, at rates considerably lower than prevailing wages for German workers. However, not even the reduced wage was paid wholly to the Jewish camp inmate; the bulk of the money was kept by the regional offices of the Reich for the "upkeep" of the camps. As a rule, the *Reichsstatthalter* and *Oberpräsident* could make a profit in the transaction.[183]

Because camp labor was so cheap, it did not always occur to the bureaucracy to return Jewish workers to their ghettos at the conclusion of a project. Many a Jewish camp laborer never saw his community again. When he was no longer needed in one camp, he was simply shifted to another. A report by a local Lublin official revealed the whole attitude of the bureaucracy toward Jewish camp labor. In October, 1940, the Belzec labor camp was broken up. Thousands of Jews were to be sent elsewhere. One train left with 920 Jews for the town of Hrubieschow, but the official who reported the matter did not even know whether the guards were SS men or members of the ethnic German auxiliary, the *Selbstschutz*. When the train arrived in Hrubieschow only 500 Jews were aboard; the other 400 were missing. "Since they could not very well have been shot in such large numbers," wrote this official, "I have heard suspicions that perhaps these Jews had been released against payment of some kind of money." The second train, carrying another 900 Jews, he continued, had arrived in Radom intact. Most of the Jews on the second train were Lublin residents. It would be very difficult, he concluded, to get them back.[184]

The labor exploitation regime in Poland consisted of three parts: (1) the forced labor columns, which were only a makeshift device but which persisted because of their low cost; (2) the labor camps, which were an offshoot of the labor columns but which soon overshadowed the colmuns in importance; and (3) the ghetto labor system. Not until the development of ghetto labor did the Germans utilize fully the vast reserves of Jewish manpower.

Essentially, there were two kinds of ghetto labor utilization: the municipal workshop system and employment by private enterprises. Municipal work-

181. *Krakauer Zeitung*, December 17, 1940, *Generalgouvernement* page.

182. Affidavit by Schönberg, July 21, 1946, PS-4071.

183. For detailed regulations by the labor trustees, see the Labor Ministry memorandum of May 9, 1941, NG-1368.

184. *Gouverneur* Lublin/Interior Division/ Population and Welfare to *Generalgouvernement* Main Division Interior/Population and Welfare, attention Dr. Föhl, October 21, 1940, *Dokumenty i Materialy*, I, 220–21.

shops, the prevalent form of ghetto employment, were actually run by the *Judenräte* under the close supervision of the control organs. The largest workshop ghetto was located in Lodz.[185] Private enterprises, too, calculated that the utilization of ghetto labor for substandard pay would cut production costs so much that profits would be enormous. These calculations were entirely correct. Companies such as the ethnic German firm Többens and the Danzig concern Schulz, both of which moved into the Warsaw ghetto, became major enterprises within a few short years.[186] Poles and Jews were also in business and in some cases seemed to have established partnerships with Germans.[187] The German administration did not prohibit such Jewish business activity; on the contrary, investments were encouraged by the release of blocked accounts.[188]

Labor utilization was far more complete in the workshop ghettos than in the private enterprise ghettos, since in the workshop ghettos labor was conscripted. In Lodz, for example, the "Eldest of the Jews" Rumkowski was empowered to "recruit all Jews for unpaid labor."[189] In Opole regimentation was carried so far that the entire Jewish population was divided for housing purposes into labor groups. All carpenters were assigned to live in one section, all tailors in another, etc.[190]

Whereas the workshop ghettos forced their inmates into rigid living patterns, the private enterprise ghettos tossed their victims into an economic jungle. The Warsaw ghetto, for example, had a formidable upper class composed of bureaucrats, traders, and speculators. These privileged groups were large enough to be conspicuous. They frequented nightclubs, ate in expensive restaurants, and rode in man-drawn rikshas.[191] The Germans photographed these institutions and spread the news of ghetto prosperity.[192] But there was little prosperity in the Warsaw ghetto. The private enterprises employed only a small portion of the population;[193] there was not enough work; the crowded and starving masses had to fight fiercely for every bit of space and every piece of bread. A German newspaperman who visited the ghetto described the situation as follows: "Everything that has an office in this Jew ghetto – and above all a great deal of police – makes a prosperous impression; whoever can work has something to eat, and whoever can trade manages quite well, but for those who cannot integrate themselves into this process nothing is done."[194]

The two ghetto systems had one

185. Memorandum by Technischer Kriegsverwaltungsintendant Merkel on conversation with Biebow, March 18, 1941, Wi/ID 1.40.

186. Goldstein, *The Stars Bear Witness*, pp. 88–90; *Krakauer Zeitung*, September 3, 1941, p. 5; April 24, 1942, p. 5.

187. Goldstein, *The Stars Bear Witness*, pp. 88–90.

188. Proclamation by the *Kommissar für den jüdischen Wohnbezirk* (signed Auerswald), August 1, 1941, *Amtlicher Anzeiger für das Generalgouvernement*, 1941, p. 1329. Private Jewish firms operated not only in the Warsaw ghetto. See letter by Jewish *Kultusgemeinde*/Office of the President in Sosnowice, Upper Silesia, to David Passermann Füllfeder-Reparaturwerkstatt Sosnowitz, March 21, 1941, in Natan Eliasz Szternfinkel (ed.), *Zaglada Zydow Sosnowca* (Katowice, 1946), pp. 63–64.

189. Office of the *Oberbürgermeister* (signed Schiffer) to Rumkowski, April 30, 1940, *Dokumenty i Materialy*, III, 74–75.

190. *Krakauer Zeitung*, August 26, 1942, p. 5.

191. Goldstein, *The Stars Bear Witness*, p. 91. Berg, *Warsaw Ghetto*, pp. 55, 65, 87, 111.

192. Photographs of rikshas in *Krakauer Zeitung*, May 18, 1941, p. 5, and in *Donauzeitung* (Belgrade), November 22, 1941, p. 8.

193. *Rüstungsinspektion* GG to OKW/Wi Rü/Rü IIIA, covering July 1, 1940 to December 31, 1941, dated May 7, 1942, pp. 102–3, Wi/ID 1.2.

194. Carl W. Gilfert, "Ghetto Juden und Ungeziefer gehören zusammen" ("Ghetto Jews and Vermin Belong Together"), *Donauzeitung* (Belgrade), November 22, 1941, p. 8.

thing in common: both supplied very cheap labor. Ghetto production was typical cheap labor production: uniforms, ammunition boxes, leather and straw and wooden shoes, metal gadgets and metal finishing work, brushes, brooms, baskets, mattresses, containers, toys, and the repair of old furniture and of old clothes.[195] The chief customers for these goods were the armed forces, the SS and Police agencies helping ethnic Germans (*Stabshauptamt* and *Volksdeutsche Mittelstelle*), the labor service organizations such as the ethnic German *Baudienst* in the *Generalgouvernement,* and many private firms. Gradually, however, the army emerged as the most important purchaser of ghetto products, crowding out other buyers. The ghettos thus became an integral part of the war economy, and this development was to cause considerable difficulty during the deportations. The Germans came to depend on the output of the Jewish labor force. Generalgouverneur Frank himself recognized that dependence, for on September 12, 1940, just after he had ordered the creation of the Warsaw ghetto, he added the following remarks to his speech in secret conference:

> As for the rest, the Jews in the *Generalgouvernement* are not always decrepit creatures [*verlotterte Gestalten*] but a necessary skilled labor component of the total structure of Polish life. . . . We can teach the Poles neither the energy nor the ability to take the place of the Jews [*Wir können den Polen weder die Tatkraft noch die Fähigkeit beibringen, an Stelle der Juden zu treten*]. That is why we are forced to permit these skilled Jewish laborers to continue in their work.[196]

Indeed, the Jews had a powerful motivation to labor diligently. In their indispensability they saw their chance for survival.

Food Controls

The survival of the ghetto population depended, in the first instance, upon the supply of food and fuel. By decreasing and choking off the food supply, the Germans were able to turn the ghettos into death traps. And that is what they did.

With the establishment of the ghettos, Jews could no longer buy food in the open market. Aside from certain devious purchases on the black market, smuggling, and food growing in the ghettos — all of which amounted to very little — the only food supply was purchased by the *Judenräte.* The food came in at the very same place at which manufactured products went out: at the check points (*Umschlagplätze*) established by the respective *Transferstelle, Ghettoverwaltung,* or municipal administration. The Germans therefore had a very clear view of how much food was shipped into the ghetto, and since food allocations were made in bulk for weekly or monthly periods, the temptation to scale down the quantities — which on paper looked formidable — was irresistible. German food policy in Poland was very simple. As much as could possibly be looted was sent to Germany. The Poles were to be kept alive. The Jews, automatically placed on the bottom, were suspended between life and death.

On October 25, 1940, in Lodz, a number of local officials under the

195. *Krakauer Zeitung,* January 23, 1942, p. 5; April 10, 1942, p. 5; April 24, 1942, p. 5; June 10, 1942, p. 5; July 24, 1942, p. 5. On Lodz ghetto, described by Biebow as "Europe's greatest tailor workshop" and "Germany's biggest workshop," see memorandum by Merkel, March 18, 1941, Wi/ID 1.40; and Part II of report by *Rüstungsinspektion* XXI, covering October 1, 1940 to December 31, 1941, pp. 33–34, and Anlage 6, Wi/ID 1.20.

196. Verbatim remarks by Frank in conference of main division chiefs, September 12, 1942, Frank diary, PS-2233.

chairmanship of Regierungsvizepräsident Dr. Moser discussed the whole question of supplying the ghetto with food. Dr. Moser pointed out that the ghetto, "that is, the Jew community," was a most unwelcome institution but a necessary evil. The Jews, most of whom were living a useless life at the expense of the German people, had to be fed; that in this connection they could not be considered normal consumers in the framework of the food economy required no comment. The quantities, Moser continued, would have to be determined by the *Ghettoverwaltung* after consultations with food experts. As for the quality of the food, Moser explained that "preferably the most inferior merchandise" should be diverted from normal trade channels and delivered to the ghetto. The prices charged by the food growers would have to be controlled very closely, for it seemed natural that the price level would have to be brought into harmony with the quality of the "more or less dubious merchandise."[197]

Translated into statistics, the Moser policy meant that for purposes of food allocation the Lodz Ghetto was considered a prison. Deliveries were to assure a prison diet. Actually, in 1941 the food supply fell *below* the prison level.[198] Table 33 shows deliveries for a period of seven months.[199]

The statistics are psychologically misleading. To be understood properly, each figure has to be divided by approximately 150,000, which gives the monthly ration for the individual. Ninety-eight tons of meat are thus reduced to less than 1½ pounds per individual; 192,520 eggs amount to little more than 1 egg per individual, and 793 tons of potatoes equal 12 pounds per individual. That is not very much food for a whole month. Moreover, the statistics do not indicate the quality of the food. They do not reveal the German policy of shipping to the ghetto damp, rotten, or frozen potatoes and "dubious" merchandise of so-called *B*- and *C*- quality.

In the *Generalgouvernment,* too, there was a reluctance to supply the Jews with food. It seems that for a brief period right after the establishment of the Warsaw ghetto food deliveries were stopped altogether, and stocks were so low that Frank seriously entertained the thought of disbanding the ghetto as a means of easing the food situation.[200] Even after the supply had to some degree been regularized, Gouverneur Dr. Fischer, fearful of the consequences of starvation, asked that allocations be increased. Main Division Chief of Food and Agriculture, Naumann naturally turned down the request. He could not possibly ship an additional 10,000 tons of wheat into the Warsaw ghetto, nor could the meat ration be increased. However, he thought it might be possible to send some eggs and some quantities of sugar, fat, and marmalade. Frank thereupon voiced his opinion that no increases could be granted to Jews. Such a thing was utterly inconceivable to him.[201]

197. Summary of Lodz ghetto conference (signed by Palfinger of the *Ernährungs- und Wirtschaftsstelle Ghetto*), October 25, 1940, *Dokumenty i Materialy,* III, 241–42. The *Ernährungs- und Wirtschaftsstelle Ghetto* was later transformed into the *Ghettoverwaltung.*

198. Biebow to Gestapo Lodz (attention Kommissar Fuchs), March 4, 1942, *Dokumenty i Materialy,* III, 232–35.

199. Oberbürgermeister Ventzki of Lodz, enclosing report with statistics, to Regierungspräsident Uebelhoer, September 24, 1941, Himmler Files, Folder No. 94.

200. Summary of *Generalgouvernement* conference, January 15, 1941, Frank diary, PS-2233.

201. Summary of *Generalgouvernement* conference, October 15, 1941, Frank diary, PS-2233. The ghetto Jews tried to increase the food supply by devious methods of food smuggling and by the conversion of vacant lots to vegetable patches. Berg, *Warsaw Ghetto,* pp. 59–62, 86, 112, 116, 130–31, 134; Goldstein, *The Stars Bear Witness,* pp. 75–78.

To make matters worse for the Jewish population, there were not one but *two* food controls. The first was the outside control which was in the hands of the Germans and which determined the total supply of food available to

TABLE 33 / *The Lodz Ghetto Food Supply (1941, in Metric tons)**

Items	January 30–February 26	February 27–March 26	March 27–April 30	May 1–28	May 29–June 29	June 30–August 3	August 4–31
Bread	892	142					
Flour	838	1,736	2,438	1,202	1,312	1,560	1,210
Meat	98	126	76	82	104	84	36
Fat	38	49	55	85	70	71	65
Milk (liters)	72,850	69,338	142,947	118,563	187,772	230,856	181,760
Cheese					1		
Eggs (pieces)					192,520	190,828	14,000
Fish					15		
Potatoes	794	1,596	3,657	916	1,067	346	1,576
Vegetables	700	2,772	3,532	2,324	672	679	3,507
Salt	90	169	132	55	105	198	97
Sugar	48	48	48	48	211	256	229
Coffee mixture	15	35	61	56	19	7	12
Artificial honey	76	36	37	36	35	43	36
Marmalade					1	1	1
Miscellaneous foods	160	171	149	132	186	148	98
Fodder	1	8	34	10	21	13	17
Hay	3	3			3	5	18
Straw	3	19	9	15	35	36	11
Charcoal	175	28	17	25	10	49	42
Coal	2,826	2,395	997	622	723	871	634

*Blank spaces indicate no deliveries.

the ghetto inhabitants. The second system was instituted within the ghetto by the *Judenräte.* The inside control determined how much of the available supply was distributed to individual Jews. From the very beginning, the interior controls were such as to promote the well-being of some people at the expense of others. When the food supply is very limited, unequal distribution means disaster for the unfortunate victims. Inequality was in evidence everywhere.

Even in such a tightly compartmentalized, totalitarian economy as that of the Lodz ghetto, favoritism, stealing, and corruption went wild. Originally, the Lodz ghetto had party-controlled soup kitchens. There were *Bund* kitchens for socialists, Zionist kitchens for Zionists, etc. This impossible situation was remedied by the "nationalization" of the soup kitchens. But those who worked in the kitchens not only ate their fill but also appropriated food for profit.

Aside from the soup kitchens, the ghetto also had food stores which were "co-operatives." In these "co-operatives" a part of each food shipment was distributed at fixed prices, but the rest was sold under the counter. Under such conditions only the rich could eat. The "co-operatives," too, were consequently nationalized, but those who handled the food continued to enjoy good living conditions. Finally, the Lodz ghetto had its built-in "legalized" corruption. The ghetto distributed supplementary rations (so-called talons) to heavy laborers, physicians, pharmacists, and instructors. But by far the biggest supplementary rations were made available to officials and their families. On top of everything, the weekly supplements were posted in the windows of the stores, where starving people could see what they were deprived of.[202]

In the "free" economy of the Warsaw ghetto the amount of food a man ate depended on the amount of money he could spend. The poorest sections of the population depended on soup kitchens and begging.[203] Employed groups could buy inadequate quantities of rationed products. (Ration cards were distributed by the *Judenrat* upon payment of monthly fees.)[204] Only "capitalists" could afford to sustain themselves on a steady diet of smuggled foods at the black market prices (Figures listed are price per pound in June, 1941):[205]

Potatoes	3 zloty
Rye bread	8 zloty
Horse meat	9 zloty
Groats	11 zloty
Corn bread	13 zloty
Beans	14 zloty
Sugar	16 zloty
Lard	35 zloty

Since the daily wage in a workshop was

202. This description of the Lodz food controls is taken from the article by Bendet Hershkovitch, "The Ghetto in Litzmannstadt (Lodz)," *YIVO Annual of Jewish Social Science,* V (1950), 86–87, 104–5. Incoming food parcels were consumed by the ghetto police. Food smuggling and parcel post packages were not tolerated, because the Eldest of the Jews Rumkowski wanted his Jews to depend entirely upon his rations. *Ibid.,* p. 96.

203. Soup kitchens were operated by the so-called Jewish Self-Help (*Jüdische Selbsthilfe*) and, until the end of 1941, also by the American Joint Distribution Committee. On Self-Help, see survivors' reports in Friedman, *Martyrs and Fighters,* pp. 77–78, 80. On expenditures of the Joint Distribution Committee, see reports of that organization (*Aiding Jews Overseas*) for 1939, 1940, and 1941.

204. One zloty at first, 3½ zloty by March, 1942. Michael Mazur and Polish Underground report in Friedmann, *Martyrs and Fighters,* pp. 71–73.

205. From Isaiah Trunk, "Epidemics in the Warsaw Ghetto," *YIVO Annual of Jewish Social Science,* VIII, 94. Trunk's statistics are taken from Ringelblum Archives No. 1193; other black market prices in Berg, *Warsaw Ghetto,* pp. 59–60, 86, 116, 130–31.

20-35 zloty,[206] black market food was seldom available for workers and practically unavailable for non-workers. It was difficult to eat in this ghetto inflation.

Very gradually at first, but more rapidly later on, the effects of the food constriction became visible. The overcrowding, the lack of medical supplies, and the poor hygienic conditions now combined with food shortages to produce enormous typhus epidemics. The summer epidemics of 1941 in the Warthegau ghettos took on such vast proportions that *Bürgermeister* and *Landräte* clamored for the dissolution of the ghettos and the transfer of 100,000 inmates to the overcrowded Lodz ghetto. The chief of the *Ghettoverwaltung* in Lodz, Biebow, vigorously opposed this suggestion and warned that the "frivolous" transfer of such masses of people into his ghetto would be devastating.[207] On July 24, 1941, Regierungspräsident Uebelhoer prohibited the transfer of any sick Jews from the small Warthegau ghettos into Lodz.[208] On August 16, 1941, Uebelhoer ordered drastic measures in the stricken Warthegau ghettos: the victims of the epidemic were to be completely isolated; entire houses were to be evacuated and filled with sick Jews.[209]

The situation in the Warsaw ghetto also deteriorated. The Warsaw epidemics started in the synagogues and other institutional buildings which housed thousands of homeless people.[210] During the winter of 1941–42, the sewage pipes froze. The toilets could no longer be used, and human excrement was dumped with garbage into the streets.[211] To combat the typhus epidemic the Warsaw *Judenrat* organized disinfection brigades, subjected people to "steaming action" (*porowka*), set up quarantine stations, hospitalized serious cases, and as a last resort instituted "house blockades" imprisoning in their homes the sick and the healthy alike.[212] The one useful article, serum, was almost unavailable. A single tube of anti-typhus medicine cost several thousand zloty.[213]

All over the incorporated territories and the *Generalgouvernement* the ghetto hunger raged unchecked. A primitive struggle for survival began. On March 21, 1942, the Propaganda Division of the Warsaw district reported laconically:

> The death figure in the ghetto still hovers around 5000 per month. A few days ago, the first case of hunger-cannibalism was recorded. In a Jewish family the man and his three children died within a few days. From the flesh of the child who died last – a twelve-year-old boy – the mother ate a piece. To be sure, this could not save her either, and she herself died two days later.[214]

The ghetto Jews were fighting for life with their last ounce of strength. People collapsed at work and in the streets. Hungry beggars snatched food from

206. Berg, *Warsaw Ghetto*, pp. 130–31.

207. Memorandum by Biebow, June 3, 1941, *Dokumenty i Materialy*, III, 184.

208. Dr. Marder (Office of the *Oberbürgermeister*) to *Ghettoverwaltung*, July 26, 1941, *Dokumenty i Materialy*, III, 186.

209. Uebelhoer to *Landräte, Oberbürgermeister in Kalisz, and Polizeipräsident in Lodz*, August 16, 1941, *Dokumenty i Materialy*, III, 187.

210. Goldstein, *The Stars Bear Witness*, p. 73.

211. Berg, *Warsaw Ghetto*, p. 117.

212. Trunk, "Epidemics in the Warsaw Ghetto," pp. 107–12. In June, 1941, the number of blockaded houses in the ghetto was 179. Trunk, citing Ringelblum Archives No. 223, at p. 107.

213. Berg, *Warsaw Ghetto*, p. 85.

214. *Generalgouvernement*/Main Division Propaganda, consolidated weekly reports by the district propaganda divisions for March, 1942 (marked "Top Secret–to be destroyed immediately"), report by the Warsaw Division, March 21, 1942, Occ E 2-2. See also reports by a survivor and the Polish underground in Friedman, *Martyrs and Fighters*, pp. 59, 62–63.

the hands of the shoppers.[215] Corpses were lying on the sidewalk, covered with newspapers, pending the arrival of cemetery carts.[216]

Toward the end of the winter in 1942 the Gestapo office in Lodz, oblivious to all that was going on, sent a letter to the chief of the *Ghettoverwaltung*, Biebow, suggesting that the Lodz ghetto was receiving too much food and that such food allocations could not be justified. In an angry reply Biebow pointed to the epidemic and to the collapsing workers producing war materials for the German Army, and concluded by asking the Gestapo to stop this "time-consuming "correspondence.[217] In a letter to Oberbürgermeister Ventzki, Biebow pointed out, on April 19, 1943, that the food supply to the ghetto could no longer guarantee the continuation of producion. For months the Jews had received no butter, no margarine, and no milk. In the soup kitchens, vegetables of *B*- and *C*- quality had been cooked in water with a little oil. No fat and no potatoes had been added to the soup. The total expenditure for food had now dropped to 30 pfennige (12 cents) per person per day. No Jewish labor camp and no prison had hitherto managed with so little.[218]

The ghetto starvation regime produced something more than the death of individuals; it spelled the doom of a community. These two effects are intrinsically different. The death of an individual occurs every day. The death of a community is an event which happens much more rarely in history. What precisely had happened to the Jewish community in Poland during the concentration stage? The answer is partially indicated in the following statistics. In 1938 the *monthly* average death rate among the Jews of Lodz was 0.09 per cent. In 1941 the *monthly* death rate jumped to 0.63 per cent. During the first six months of 1942 it was 1.49 per cent. In March, 1942, it was as high as 1.72 per cent.[219] In absolute figures, the Lodz Jews (original population 160,000) had 29,561 dead and about 1300 live births from May 1, 1940, to June 30, 1942.[220]

The implication of these figures is quite clear. Assuming a steady monthly death rate of 1.5 per cent and an absence of a significant number of births, a community of 150,000 shrinks to 1000 in just 25½ years. We know that the Lodz ghetto conditions were duplicated in practically all the other ghettos of occupied Poland. The small Warthegau ghettos probably fared even worse. The Warsaw ghetto was little better. The Warsaw Jewish community (470,000 people) had 44,630 deaths in 1941,[221] and 37,462 deaths during the first nine months of 1942.[222] The death-birth ratio in the ghetto was about 45:1.[223] From these partial statistics we may calculate that in the whole of occupied Poland 500,000 to 600,000 Jews died in ghettos and labor camps.[224] During their short period of

215. Friedman, *Martyrs and Fighters*, pp. 56–57.

216. Goldstein, *The Stars Bear Witness*, p. 74.

217. Biebow to Gestapo Office Lodz (att. Kommissar Fuchs), March 4, 1942, *Dokumenty i Materialy*, III, 243–45.

218. Biebow to Oberbürgermeister Ventzki, April 19, 1943, *Dokumenty i Materialy*, III, 245–48.

219. Statistics from Lodz Ghetto Collection, No. 58, p. 23.

220. *Ibid.*, pp. 23, 26.

221. Apenszlak, *The Black Book of Polish Jewry*, pp. 55–56. On p. 199 the figure of 47,428 is cited. Possibly this figure includes 1940 deaths in the ghetto.

222. *Gouverneur* of Warsaw (signed Hummel) to *Staatssekretär, Generalgouvernement*, report for October and November, 1942, dated December 10, 1942, p. 6, Occ E 2-3.

223. Report by Warsaw propaganda division, March 21, 1942, Occ E 2-2.

224. This rough calculation is affirmed by the statistics of SS Statistician Korherr in his report to Himmler, April 19, 1943, NO-5193. Korherr lists a combined total of 762,593

existence the ghettos accounted for the death of *one-fifth* of the Polish Jews. In the perspective of history this is a very fast rate of disappearance. But the pace was not quick enough for the German machinery of destruction. The Nazis could not wait for a whole generation; they could not "entrust" the task of "solving the Jewish problem" to a future generation. They had to "solve the problem," in one way or another, right then and there.

Jewish dead and emigrants, as of December 31, 1942, in the incorporated territories (including the Bialystok district, added in August, 1941) and the *Generalgouvernement* (including the Galician district, added in August, 1941). Biaylstok and Galicia lost approximately 100,000 Jews as result of the mobile killing operations to be described in the next chapter. Another 100–150,000 Jews escaped from these areas before the arrival of the Germans.

THE DESTRUCTION PROCESS II

VII / *Mobile Killing Operations*

So far, we have considered the preliminary phase of the destruction process — the definition of the Jews, the expropriation of their property, and their concentration into ghettos. The completion of these measures brought the German bureaucracy to a dividing line, and the step across this dividing line inaugurated the killing phase. All measures during that phase were taken upon Hitler's orders to kill the European Jews.

In German correspondence the killing phase was referred to as the "final solution of the Jewish question." The word "final" in this context has a double meaning: In its narrow sense, it meant that the aim of the destruction process had now been clarified. During the concentration stage it was still conceivable to shove the Jews out of Europe to some other continent or to let them languish in ghettos. The decision to take measures for the total annihilation of European Jewry shut out any such alternative. In this sense the direction and aim of the destruction process were finalized. But the phrase "final solution" has a wider, more significant meaning. In Himmler's words, it meant that the Jewish problem would never have to be solved again. Definitions, expropriations, and concentrations can be undone. Killings cannot. The killing phase was irreversible; hence it gave to the entire destruction process its character of finality.

How was the killing phase brought about? Basically, we are dealing with two of Hitler's decisions. One order was given in the spring of 1941, during the planning of the invasion of the USSR; it provided that small units of the SS and Police be dispatched to Soviet territory, where they were to move from town to town to kill all Jewish inhabitants on the spot. This method may be called the "mobile killing operations." Shortly after the mobile operations had begun in the occupied Soviet territories, Hitler handed down his second order. That decision doomed the rest of European Jewry. Unlike the Russian Jews, who were overtaken by mobile units, the Jewish population of central, western, and southeastern Europe was transported to killing centers. In short (outside Russia), the mobile operations were reversed. Instead of moving the killers to the victims, the victims were brought to the killers. This second method, the central killing operations, will be discussed in the subsequent two chapters, which deal with the deportations and the killing center operations, respectively.

1 / Preparations

When the German Wehrmacht — the armed forces — attacked the USSR on June 22, 1941, the invading armies were accompanied by small mechanized killing units of the SS and Police which were tactically subordinated to the field commanders but otherwise free to go about their special business. The mobile killing units were operating in the front-line areas under a special arrangement and in a unique partnership with the German Army. To understand what made this partnership work, it is necessary to have a closer look at the two participants: the German Wehrmacht and the Reich Security Main Office of the SS and Police.

The Wehrmacht was one of the four independent hierarchies in the machinery of destruction. Unlike the party, the civil service agencies, and the business enterprises, the armed forces had no major role to play in the preliminary phase of the destruction process; but in the inexorable development of the process every segment of organized German society was drawn into the destructive work. We may recall that even in 1933 the Wehrmacht was interested in the definition of "Jews." Later the army was affected by the expropriation of Jewish enterprises producing war materials. In Poland the Generals narrowly escaped from an entanglement in the concentration process. Now, with the onset of the mobile killing operations, the armed forces found themselves suddenly in the very center of the holocaust.

The Wehrmacht's involvement began on the top level of the High Command structure and spread from there to the field. (The central features of the military machine are shown in Table 34.)[1] It will be noted that the *Oberster Befehlshaber der Wehrmacht* was in charge of the commanders-in-chief (*Oberbefehlshaber*) of the three services; however, there was *no* corresponding chain of command running from the OKW to the OKH, the OKM, and the OKL. The OKW, as well as the three other high commands, were essentially staff organizations, each of which carried out planning functions within its sphere of jurisdiction. Thus the integration of the mobile killing units into the invading army groups was accomplished only after extensive negotiations with the OKW and the OKH.

The territorial organization of the army is shown in Table 35. This table distinguishes between three types of territorial command: the Reich itself, occupied territories, and newly invaded areas. Broadly speaking, the military authority over *civilians* increased with the increased distance of the territory from the Reich. In Germany proper, that authority was virtually nonexistent; in the newly in-

1. The table is based on the following affidavits: Affidavit by von Brauchitsch, November 7, 1945, PS-3703. Affidavit by Warlimont, October 12, 1946, NOKW-121. Affidavit by Warlimont, October 31, 1946, NOKW-168. Affidavit by Jodl, September 26, 1946, NOKW-65. Affidavit by Bürkner, January 22, 1946, Office of U. S. Chief of Counsel for Prosecution of Axis Criminality, *Nazi Conspiracy and Aggression* (Washington, D.C., 1946–48), VIII, 647–53. Affidavit by Keitel, June 15, 1945, Keitel-25. Affidavit by Wilhelm Krichbaum, June 7, 1948, NOKW-3460.

In 1944 *Amt Ausland-Abwehr* was abolished. Two remnants of the office (*Amt Ausland,* under Bürkner, and *Amt Frontaufklärung und Truppenabwehr,* under Süsskind-Schwendi) were subordinated to the WFSt under Jodl. Affidavit by Warlimont, October 12, 1946, NOKW-121. The Wi Rü gave way to a *Wehrwirtschaftsstab* under Becker. Affidavit by Keitel, March 29, 1946, Keitel-11.

The *Generalquartiermeister's* Office was divided into several sections, including a military government section (GenQu 4) which was placed outside of the GenstdH. Affidavit by Keitel, June 15, 1945, Keitel-25.

On unit level (army groups and below), the staff was organized as follows:

Chief of staff of the unit
Ia Operations
Ib Supply
(The designation Ib was used in army groups and divisions. Supply officers on army level were called *Oberquartiermeister* (OQu); on corps level, *Quartiermeister* (Qu). See Army Manual 90: *Supply of the Field Army,* 1938, NOKW-2708.)
Ic Intelligence
Id Training
IIa Personnel (officers)
IIb Personnel (enlisted men)
III Legal
IVa Finance
IVb Medical
IVc Veterinary
IVd Chaplains
IV Wi Economic
V Motor transport
VI Indoctrination
VII Military government

Only officers in I sections were "general staff" officers.

Table 34 / *The Military Machine of Destruction*

Commander-in-Chief of the Armed Forces (*Oberster Befehlshaber der Wehrmacht*) Hitler

- *Chef*, OKW, Keitel
  - Operations (*Wehrmachtführungsstab*—WFSt), Jodl
    - Defense (*Landesverteidigung*—L), Warlimont
    - Propaganda (WPr), von Wedel
    - Signals (*Nachrichtenwesen*—WNW), Fellgiebel
  - Intelligence (*Amt Ausland-Abwehr*), Canaris (Chief of Staff: Oster)
    - *Ausland*, Buerkner
    - *Abwehr* I, Pieckenbrock (Hansen)
    - *Abwehr* II, Lahousen (von Freytag-Loringhoven)
    - *Abwehr* III, Bentivegny
    - Secret Field Police (GFP), Krichbaum
  - Economy-Armament Office (Wi Rü), Thomas
  - General Armed Forces Office (AWA), Reinecke
    - Prisoners of War, Breuer (von Graevenitz)
  - Armed Forces Sanitation (WSA), Handloser
  - Armed Forces Law, Lehmann

Commander-in-Chief of the Army (*Oberbefehlshaber des Heeres*—OBdH) von Brauchitsch (Hitler)—OKH

- Chief, General Staff of the Army
  - (*Chef*, GenStdH), Halder (Zeitzler, Guderian)
  - Quartermaster
  - General (GenQu), Wagner
  - Transport (HTr), Gercke
  - General for
  - Special Purposes, Eugen Müller
- Army Personnel, Schmundt
- Chief of Army Armament
  - and of the Replacement
  - Army (*Chef*, HRüst u.BdE), Fromm (Himmler)
  - General Army Office, Olbricht
  - Army Weapons Office, Loeb
  - Administration, Osterkamp

Commander-in-Chief of the Navy (*Oberbefehlshaber der Kriegsmarine*) Raeder (Doenitz)—OKM

- Chief of Naval Warfare (*Chef der Seekriegsleitung*) Schniewindt (Fricke)

Commander-in-Chief of the Air Force (*Oberbefehlshaber der Luftwaffe*) Göring—OKL

- Chief, General Staff of the Air Force Jeschonek (Korten)
- *Inspekteur* Milch

TABLE 35 / *The Territorial Organization of the Army*

AREA	REICH AND INCORPORATED AREAS	OCCUPIED TERRITORIES			NEWLY INVADED AREAS		
					Army Group Rear Areas	Army Rear Areas	Corps Areas
Types of territorial command	*Wehrkreisbefehlshaber**	*Wehrmachtbefehlshaber* (WB)	*Oberbefehlshaber* (OB)	*Militärbefehlshaber* (MB) *Befehlshaber* of specified area *Deutscher General* in specified area	*Befehlshaber rückwärtiges Heeresgebiet*	*Kommandeur rückwärtiges Armeegebiet* (Korück)	Corps Commander
Subordinated to	*Oberbefehlshader des Heeres/Befehlshaber des Ersatzheeres* ("Commander-in-Chief of the Army/the Commander of the Replacement Army": Fromm)	*Chef* OKW (Keitel)	*Oberbefehlshaber des Heeres* (Brauchitsch, succeeded by Hitler)	*Oberbefehlshaber des Heeres* or a territorial *Oberbefehlshaber* or an Army Group Commander	Army Group Commander	Army Commander	Army Commander

*The *Wehrkeisbefehlshaber* was the commander of an army district (designated by roman numeral). The WB, OB, or MB was the commander of a specified territory (such as the Ukraine, the Southeast, the *Generalgouvernement*). Sometimes a territorial command and a unit command (such as the OB Southeast and Commander of Army Group E) were united in the same person.

vaded areas it was nearly absolute. In the forward areas, therefore, an outside agency could operate only under a special arrangement with the Wehrmacht.

The only agency which was admitted to the forward areas during the Russian campaign was the Reich Security Main Office, the RSHA. It was the agency which, for the first time in modern history, was to conduct a massive killing operation. What sort of an organization was the RSHA?

The RSHA was a creation of Reinhard Heydrich. We have already seen Heydrich as a prominent figure in the *Einzelaktionen* of 1938 and in the concentration process within the German and Polish spheres. However, the Heydrich organization did not assume a pre-eminent place in the machinery of destruction until 1941. That year was crucial for the development of the entire destruction process, for it was during that period that Reinhard Heydrich laid the administrative foundations for the mobile killing operations and for the deportations to the killing centers.

The Heydrich organization reflected in its personnel composition a characteristic of German government as a whole: the RSHA, and its regional machinery, was an organization of party men and civil servants. The fusion of these two elements in the RSHA was so complete that almost every man could be sent into the field to carry out the most drastic Nazi plans with bureaucratic meticulousness and Prussian discipline. This personnel amalgamation in the RSHA was accomplished over a period of years in which Heydrich put his organization together piece by piece.

The building process began in the early days of the Nazi regime, when Himmler and his loyal follower Heydrich raided the Prussian Interior Ministry and took over its newly organized Secret State Police (*Geheime Staatspolizei*, or Gestapo). Göring was then Interior Minister and Daluege the chief of police:[2]

Prussian Ministry of Interior
(later Reich Interior Ministry)
Minister: Göring (followed by Frick)
|
Staatssekretar Grauert
|
Chief of Police Daluege
|
Chief of Gestapo [in succession]:
Diels, Hinkler, Diels, Himmler
(deputized by Heydrich)

Next, Heydrich (as Himmler's deputy) took over a special division in the office of the police president of Berlin: the *Landeskriminalpolizeiamt*, or Criminal Police (*Kripo*).[3] The Gestapo and the Criminal Police were subsequently detached from their parent organizations and joined together into the *Hauptamt Sicherheitspolizei* (Main Office Security Police). Heydrich had all key positions in this office:[4]

Chief of Security Police: Heydrich
  Administration and Law: Dr. Best
  Gestapo: Heydrich
  Kripo: Heydrich

The creation of the Security Police as an agency of the state was accompanied by the parallel formation of a party intelligence system, the so-called Security Service (*Sicherheitsdienst*, or SD). Heydrich now had *two* main offices: the *Hauptamt Sicherheits-*

2. Testimony by Gisevius, *Trial of the Major War Criminals*, XII, 168–73, 181. Gisevius was in the Gestapo in 1933. For significance of the Himmler-Heydrich expansion, see also chap. ix, pp. 555–56.

3. Heydrich, "Aufgaben und Aufbau der Sicherheitspolizei im Dritten Reich," in Hans Pfundtner (ed.), *Dr. Wilhelm Frick und sein Ministerium* (Munich, 1937), p. 152.

4. Dr. Ludwig Münz, *Führer durch die Behörden und Organisationen* (Berlin, 1939), p. 95. For budgetary purposes the new *Hauptamt* was put under the Interior Ministry.

polizei, which was a state organization, and the *Sicherheitshauptamt,* which was a party organization. On September 27, 1939, Himmler issued an order in pursuance of which the two main offices were amalgamated into the Reich Security Main Office (*Reichssicherheitshauptamt,* or RSHA).[5] (See Table 36.)

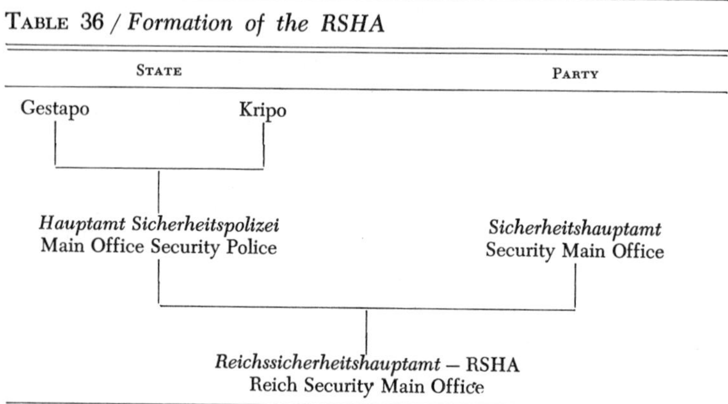

TABLE 36 / *Formation of the RSHA*

The organization of the RSHA is shown in abbreviated form in Table 37 (pp. 184–85).[6] Looking at this table, we may observe that the RSHA revealed in its structure the history of its organization. Thus the Security Police comprised Offices IV and V (Gestapo and *Kripo*), while the Security Service functioned in Offices III (Inland) and VI (Foreign).[7] Heydrich himself henceforth carried the title *Chef der Sicherheitspolizei und des SD,* abbreviated *Chef SP und SD.*

The RSHA disposed over a vast regional network, including *three* types of organization: one in the Reich and incorporated areas, another in occupied territories, a third in countries undergoing invasion.[8] This network is portrayed in Table 38.[9] It will be noted that outside the Reich the Security Police and SD were completely centralized, down to the local (or unit) level. For the moment, however, we shall be concerned only with the machinery which functioned in newly invaded areas: the so-called *Einsatzgruppen.* These *Einsatzgruppen* were the first mobile killing units.

The first reference to *Einsatzgruppen* operations is to be found in a "Barbarossa" directive, issued in the office of Warlimont (OKW/*Landesverteidigung*) and signed by Keitel. "Barbarossa" was the code word for the projected invasion of the USSR. By March, 1941, invasion plans were far advanced, and a great deal of the paper work had already been done. The March 13

5. Order by Himmler, September 27, 1939, L-361.

6. Organization chart of the RSHA, dating from 1941, L-185. Organization chart of the RSHA, October 1, 1943, L-219. Before the end of the war, Panzinger (IV-A) took over the *Kripo.* Organization chart of the Reich government in 1945, certified by Frick, PS-2905.

7. Office IV was designated "Search for and Combat against Enemies" (*Gegner-Erforschung und Bekämpfung*). Office V was concerned with "Combatting of Crime" (*Verbrechensbekämpfung*). Inland intelligence (Office III) styled itself "German Life Areas" (*Deutsche Lebensgebiete*).

8. Types two and three could sometimes be found in the same areas simultaneously.

9. Based on affidavits by Höttl and Ohlendorf, October 28, 1945, PS-2364.

directive was therefore only one paper among many, and it dealt with several subjects. The decisive paragraph did not even mention *Einsatzgruppen*. It was only a statement to the effect that the *Reichsführer-SS* (Himmler) would carry out in Russia special duties by order of the Führer. These duties had resulted from the clash of two opposing political systems. The *Reichsführer-SS* would bring his task to a final conclusion; he would act on his own responsibility. His operations would not be interfered with; details would be taken care of by agreement of the OKH with the *Reichsführer-SS*. The border of the USSR would be closed at the start of operations, except for the units employed by the *Reichsführer-SS* for the carrying-out of his special duties.[10] This directive made no mention at all of killings, and this omission is a characteristic which we shall find in most of the subsequent correspondence.

On April 4 the General Quartermaster of the Army, Generalmajor Wagner, sent a draft of a proposed Army-RSHA agreement to Heydrich. This draft outlined the terms under which the *Einsatzgruppen* could operate in Russia. The crucial sentence in the draft provided that "within the framework of their instructions and upon their own responsibility, the *Sonderkommandos* are entitled to carry out executive measures against the civilian population [*Die Sonderkommandos sind berechtigt, im Rahmen ihres Auftrages in eigener Verantwortung gegenüber der Zivilbevölkerung Exekutivmassnahmen zu treffen*]." The mobile units could move in army group rear areas and in army rear areas.

It was made clear that the *Einsatzgruppen* were to be administratively subordinated to the military command but that the RSHA was to retain functional control over them. The armies were to control the movements of the mobile units. The military was to furnish the *Einsatzgruppen* with quarters, gasoline, food rations, and, insofar as necessary, radio communications. On the other hand, the killing units were to receive "functional directives" (*fachliche Weisungen*) from the Chief of the Security Police and SD (Heydrich) in this way:

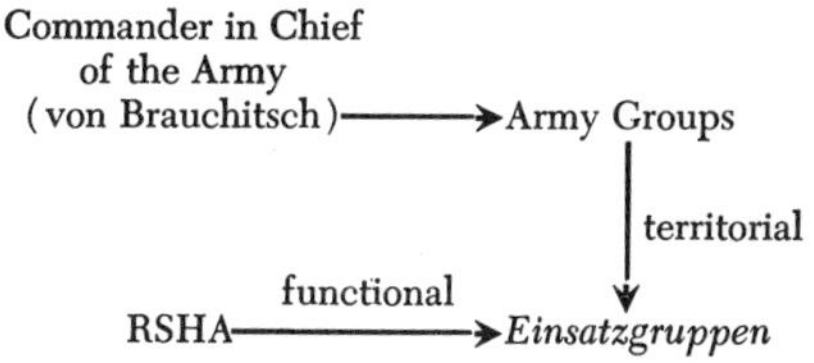

Commander in Chief of the Army (von Brauchitsch) ——→ Army Groups

Army Groups —territorial→ *Einsatzgruppen*

RSHA —functional→ *Einsatzgruppen*

The relations of the *Einsatzgruppen* with the army's Secret Field Police (*Geheime Feldpolizei* – GFP) were to be based on a strict separation of jurisdictions. Any matter affecting the security of the troops was to be handled exclusively by the Secret Field Police; however, the two services were to co-operate by prompt exchange of information, the *Einsatzgruppen* to report to the GFP on all matters of concern to it, and, conversely, the GFP to turn over to the *Einsatzgruppen* all information pertaining to their sphere of competence (*Aufgabenbereich*).[11]

The final negotiations between the army and the RSHA were carried out in May, 1941. At first the negotiators

10. Directive by OKW/L (signed Keitel), March 13, 1941, NOKW-2302. The use of mobile units (*Einsatzgruppen*) as such was not unprecedented. In September, 1938, a blueprint was already in existence for the commitment of two *Einsatzstäbe* in the event of a "total solution of the Czechoslovak problem" (occupation of Bohemia and Moravia). HStuf. Schellenberg to Oberführer Jost, September 13, 1938, USSR-509. The *Einsatzstäbe* consisted of Gestapo and SD men, a partial merger in the field which antedated the complete unification in Berlin. *Einsatzgruppen* were also used in Poland.

11. Text of draft, dated March 26, 1941, enclosed in letter by Wagner to Heydrich, April 4, 1941; copies to OKW/*Abwehr* (Canaris) and OKW/L (Warlimont), NOKW-256.

TABLE 37 / *Organization of the RSHA*

1941		1943	
Chief SP und SD	OGruf. Heydrich		OGruf. Dr. Kaltenbrunner
		Attache Group	Stubaf. Dr. Plötz
I. Personnel	Staf. Streckenbach	I Personnel & Organization	Bgf. Schulz
II. Organization and Law	Staf. Dr. Neckmann	II Administration & Finance	Staf. Prietzel
II A Organization and Law	Stubaf. ORR. Dr. Bilfinger		
II A 1 Organization	HStuf. RegAss. Dr. Schweder		
II A 2 Legislation	Stubaf. RR. Dr. Neifeind		
II A 3 Indemnification	Stubaf. RR. Suhr		
II A 4 Reich Defense	Stubaf. RR. Renken		
II A 5 Confiscations	Stubaf. RR. Richter		
II B Passports	Ministerialrat Krause	IV F	MinRat Krause
II C a Budget SP	Staf. MinRat Dr. Siegert		
II C b Budget SD	OStubaf. Bracke	II A Finance	OStubaf. ORR. Kreelow
II D Technical Matters	OStubaf. Rauff	II C	OStubaf. ORR. Hafke
III. SD-Inland	Staf. Ohlendorf		
III A Legal Practice	OStubaf. Dr. Gengenbach	Deputizing:	OStubaf. ORR. Neifeind
III B Ethnos (*Volkstum*)	Staf. Dr. Ehlich		
III C Culture	Stubaf. Dr. Spengler		
III D Economy	Stubaf. Seibert		
IV. Gestapo	Gruf. Müller		
Deputy for Border Police	Staf. Krichbaum		OStubaf. ORR. Huppenkothen
IV A Enemies	Ostubaf. ORR. Panzinger		
IV A 1 Communism	Stubaf. KD. Vogt		Stubaf. KD. Lindow
IV A 2 Sabotage	HStuf. KK. Kopkow		
IV A 3 Liberalism	Stubaf. KD. Litzenberg		
IV A 4 Assassinations	Stubaf. KD. Schulz		

TABLE 37 / *Organization of the RSHA (Continued)*

	IV B Sects	Stubaf. Hartl	Deputizing:	Stubaf. Roth
	IV B 1 Catholicism	Stubaf. RR. Roth		
	IV B 2 Protestantism	Stubaf. RR. Roth		Stubaf. RR. Hahnenbruch
	IV B 3 Freemasonry	vacant		OStubaf. Wandesleben
	IV B 4 Evacuations & Jews	OStubaf. Eichmann		
	IV C Card Files	OStubaf. ORR. Dr. Rang	Deputizing:	OStubaf. ORR. KR. Dr. Berndorf
	IV D Spheres of Influence	OStubaf. Dr. Weinmann		Staf. RD. Dr. Rang
	IV E Counterintelligence	Stubaf. RR. Schellenberg		OStubaf. ORR. Huppenkothen
	IV E 1 Treason	HStuf. KR. Lindow		Stubaf. ORR. Renken
V.	*Kripo*	Bgf. Nebe		
	V A Policy	Staf. ORR. KR. Werner		
	V B Crimes (*Einsatz*)	RR. KR. Galzow		Stubaf. ORR. KR. Lobbes
	V C Identification	ORR. KR. Berger		RR. KR. Schulze
	V D Criminal Institute	Stubaf. ORR. KR. Hesse		
VI.	SD-Foreign	Bgf. Jost		Obf. ORR. Schellenberg
	VI A General	Ostubaf. Filbert		Stubaf. RR. Herbert Müller
	VI B German-Italian sphere	vacant		OStubaf. Steimle
	VI C Russo-Japanese sphere	vacant		OStubaf. ORR. Dr. Graf
	VI D West	vacant		Stubaf. RR. Dr. Raeffgen
	VI E Investigation	Stubaf. Dr. Knochen		Stubaf. RR. Dr. Hammer
	VI F Technical Matters	OStubaf. Rauff		Stubaf. Dorner
			IV Wi Economy	HStuf. Dr. Krallert
			IV S Special	Stubaf. Skorzeny
VII.	Ideology	Staf. Dr. Six		OStubaf. Dr. Dittel
	VII B Evaluation	vacant	Deputizing:	Stubaf. Ehlerts
	Jews	vacant		HStuf. Ballensiefen

TABLE 38 / *The Regional Machinery of the RSHA*

REICH			OCCUPIED TERRITORIES	INVADED AREAS (MOBILE UNITS)
	Inspekteure SP und SD (IdS)		*Befehlshaber SP und SD* (BdS)	*Einsatzgruppen*
STAPO(leit)stellen (Gestapo Directorates in large cities, Gestapo Offices in small cities)	*KRIPO(leit)stellen* (*Kripo* directorates and offices)	*SD(leit)abschnitte* (SD Directorates and Sectors)	*Kommandeure SP und SD* (KdS)	*Einsatzkommandos*
Aussenstellen der STAPO (Field Offices of the Gestapo)	*Aussenstellen der KRIPO* (Field Offices of the *Kripo*)	*(Haupt)aussenstellen des SD* (Main Field Offices and Field Offices of the SD)	*Aussenstellen des SP und des SD* (Field Offices of the SP and SD)	*Sonderkommandos*

were Generalquartiermeister Wagner and Gestapo Chief Müller. The two could come to no final agreement. At the request of Wagner, Müller was therefore replaced by a subordinate, SS-Sturmbannführer Regierungsrat Schellenberg, then chief of IV E. Schellenberg, who was chosen because of his experience in matters of protocol, drew up the final terms. They differed from the earlier draft in only one important respect: the *Einsatzgruppen* were to be permitted to operate not only in army group rear areas and army rear areas but also in the corps areas right on the front line. This concession was of great importance to the *Einsatzgruppen,* for the Jews were to be caught as quickly as possible. They were to be given no warning and no chance to escape. The final version of the agreement was signed at the end of May by Heydrich for the RSHA and by Wagner for the OKH.[12] The partnership was established.

The next step – so far as the RSHA was concerned – was the formation of the *Einsatzgruppen.* Mobile units were not kept on hand; they had to be formed anew for each new invasion. Accordingly, orders were sent out to Security Police and SD men in the main office and regional branches to proceed to the Security Police training center at Pretsch and from there to the assembly point at Düben.

Altogether, four *Einsatzgruppen* were set up, each of battalion size. The operational units of the *Einsatzgruppen* were *Einsatzkommandos* and *Sonderkommandos,* of company size. Table 39 is a list of the officers who commanded *Einsatzgruppen* and *Kommandos.*[13]

Who were all these men? Where did they come from? Two of the initial *Einsatzgruppen* commanders were taken straight from the RSHA: Criminal Police Chief Nebe and Chief of SD-Inland Otto Ohlendorf. The story of Ohlendorf's assignment sheds a great deal of light on the attitude of the killers and, in a larger sense, upon the whole destruction process. Here, then, is a brief summary.

In 1941, Ohlendorf was a young man of thirty-four. He had studied at three universities (Leipzig, Göttingen, and Pavia); he held a doctor's degree in jurisprudence; and as a career man he had successfully worked himself up to a research directorship in the Institute for World Economy and Maritime Transport in Kiel. By 1938 he was also *Hauptgeschäftsführer* in the *Reichsgruppe Handel,* the German trade organization. While Ohlendorf had joined the party in 1925, the SS in 1926, and the SD in 1936, he regarded his party activities, and even his position as chief of SD-Inland, as a sideline of his career. Actually, he devoted only four years (1939-43) to full-time activity in the RSHA, for in 1943 he became a *Ministerialdirektor* and deputy to the *Staatssekretär* in the Economy Ministry.[14]

Now Heydrich was a man who did not like subordinates with divided loyalties. Ohlendorf was too independent. Heydrich wanted no one who functioned *ehrenamtlich* (i.e., in an honorary capacity). He was determined to teach Ohlendorf a lesson. The

12. Affidavit by Schellenberg, November 26, 1945, PS-3710. Statement by Ohlendorf, April 24, 1947, NO-2890. With reference to the task of the *Einsatzgruppen,* the final text was no more precise than the earlier one. However, it was generally understood that all Jews, Communist party functionaries, insane people, and a few others of undesirable categories were to be killed on the spot. A copy of the final text is not available, and our understanding of its terms derives mainly from the statements by Schellenberg and Ohlendorf.

13. Each *Einsatzgruppe* also had a staff consisting of officers who represented the RSHA offices, thus a Gestapo officer, a *Kripo* officer, etc.

14. Affidavit by Otto Ohlendorf, March 4, 1947, NO-2409.

"executive measures" to be taken in Russia were the kind of activity which required complete, undivided attention; thus it came about that the intellectual Otto Ohlendorf found himself in command of *Einsatzgruppe D*.[15]

TABLE 39 / *Officers of "Einsatzgruppen" and "Kommandos"**

Einsatzgruppe A		Stahlecker (Jost)
Sonderkommando	1*a*	Sandberger
Sonderkommando	1*b*	Ehrlinger
Einsatzkommando	2	Strauch
Einsatzkommando	3	Jäger
Einsatzgruppe B		Nebe (Naumann)
Sonderkommando	7*a*	Blume (Steimle, Rapp)
Sonderkommando	7*b*	Rausch (Ott, Raabe)
Sonderkommando	7*c*	Bock
Einsatzkommando	8	Bradfisch (Richter, Schindelm)
Einsatzkommando	9	Schäfer (Wiebens)
Vorkommando Moskau		Six (Nebe, Klingelhöfer, Buchardt)
Einsatzgruppe C		Rasch (Thomas)
Einsatzkommando	4*a*	Blobel (Weinmann, Steimle, Schmidt)
Einsatzkommando	4*b*	Herrmann (Fendler, Braune, Haensch)
Einsatzkommando	5	Schulz (Meier)
Einsatzkommando	6	Kröger (Mohr, Biberstein)
Einsatzgruppe D		Ohlendorf (Bierkamp)
Einsatzkommando	10*a*	Seetzen
Einsatzkommando	10*b*	Persterer
Einsatzkommando	11*a*	Zapp
Einsatzkommando	11*b*	B. Müller (W. Braune, P. Schulz)
Einsatzkommando	12	Nosske (Ministerialrat Müller)

*RSHA IV-A-1, Operational Report USSR No. 129, November 4, 1941, NO-3159. Affidavit by Eugen Steimle, December 14, 1945, NO-3842. Affidavit by Adolf Ott, April 29, 1947, NO-2992. Affidavit by Erwin Schulz, May 26, 1947, NO-3473. Affidavit by Karl Hennicke (SD-Inland Officer, *Einsatzgruppe C*), September 4, 1947, NO-4999. Affidavit by Heinz-Hermann Schubert (adjutant to Ohlendorf), December 7, 1945, NO-511. *Einsatzgruppen* commanders held the rank of *Brigadeführer* or *Gruppenführer;* that is, they were General officers. Leaders of *Kommandos* were *Sturmbannführer, Obersturmbannführer,* or *Standartenführer* (majors, lieutenant-colonels, or colonels).

A similar story, which is even more crass, can be told about Ernst Biberstein, who took over *Einsatzkommando* 6 in *Einsatzgruppe C* as a replacement in the summer of 1942. Biberstein was a somewhat older man, born in 1899. He had been a private in the First World War, and after his release from the army he devoted himself to theology. In 1924 he became a Protestant pastor; in 1933 he rose to *Kirchenprobst.* After eleven years as a minister, Biberstein entered the Church Ministry; in 1940 he was transferred to the RSHA. This transfer should not be too surprising, for the Church Ministry was an agency of the state, and, besides. Biberstein had joined the party in 1926 and the SS in 1936.

But Biberstein was still a man of the church. When he was shown around the offices of the RSHA, he developed some misgivings about his new surroundings. Heydrich thereupon sent him to Oppeln to take over the local Gestapo office. In that position Biberstein was already drawn into the destruction process, because he had to concern himself with the deportation of the Jews from the city of Oppeln to the killing centers in the East. In the spring of 1942, Heydrich was assassi-

15. Affidavit by Ohlendorf, July 14, 1946, SD(A)-44.

nated, and Biberstein, no longer protected by his personal understanding with the RSHA chief, was suddenly transferred to the field to conduct killings.[16]

Like Ohlendorf and Biberstein, the great majority of the officers of the *Einsatzgruppen* were professional men. As we look over their files, we discover among them a physician (Weinmann),[17] a professional opera singer (Klingelhöfer),[18] and a large number of lawyers. These men were in no sense hoodlums, delinquents, common criminals, or sex maniacs. Most were intellectuals. By and large, they were in their thirties, and undoubtedly they wanted a certain measure of power, fame, and success. However, there is no indication that any of them sought an assignment to a *Kommando*. All we know is that they brought to their new task all the skills and training which, as men of thought, they were capable of contributing. These men, in short, became efficient killers.

The total strength of the *Einsatzgruppen* was about 3000 men. Not all the personnel were drawn from the Security Police and SD. In fact, most of the enlisted personnel had to be borrowed – a whole battalion of Order Police was dispatched to the *Einsatzgruppen* from Berlin because the Security Police could not put so many people into the field.[19] In addition, the *Einsatzgruppen* received *Waffen-SS* men. Finally, they rounded out their strength in the field by adding indigenous units of Lithuanians, Estonians, Latvians, and Ukranians, as auxiliary police. The resulting personnel composition is indicated roughly in the following table showing a distribution of the members of *Einsatzgruppe A*:[20]

Waffen-SS	340
Motorcycle riders	172
Administration	18
Security Service (SD)	35
Criminal Police (*Kripo*)	41
State Police (*Stapo*)	89
Auxiliary Police	87
Order Police	133
Female employees	13
Interpreters	51
Teletype operators	3
Radio operators	8
Total	990

Einsatzgruppe A, incidentally, was the largest group. The smallest was *Einsatzgruppe D*, which had 400 to 500 men.[21]

While the *Einsatzgruppen* were being assembled, a plenary meeting took place early in June, in the OKW building in Berlin. It was attended by Canaris, Wagner, Heydrich, Schellenberg, and a large number of Ic (intelligence) officers. This was the last opportunity to plan for the close co-ordination of *Einsatzgruppen* and army activities.[22]

In the training center at Pretsch, the RSHA personnel chief addressed the *Einsatzgruppen* members. He told them where they were going and instructed them to proceed ruthlessly (*dass dort rücksichtslos durchgegriffen werden müsste*).[23]

16. Interrogation of Ernst Biberstein, June 29, 1947, NO-4997.
17. Affidavit by Eugen Steimle, December 14, 1945, NO-3842.
18. Affidavit by Waldemar Klingelhöfer, September 17, 1947, NO-5050.
19. Affidavit by Adolf von Bomhard (*Chef, Kommandoamt*, Order Police), July 13, 1946, SS(A)-82.
20. Report by *Einsatzgruppe A*, October 15, 1941, L-180.
21. Affidavit by Ohlendorf, November 5, 1945, PS-2620.
22. Affidavit by Schellenberg, November 20, 1945, PS-3710.
23. Affidavit by Wilhelm Förster, driver, *Einsatzgruppe D*, October 23, 1947, NO-5520.

At the beginning of June the four *Einsatzgruppen* assembled at Düben. After speeches by Heydrich and Streckenbach the mobile killing units moved into position. *Einsatzgruppe A* was assigned to Army Group North; *Einsatzgruppe B* was detailed to Army Group Center; *Einsatzgruppe C* moved into the sector of Army Group South; and *Einsatzgruppe D* was attached to the Eleventh Army, an independent army which operated in the extreme south. As the armies pushed over the first Soviet outposts, the *Einsatzgruppen* followed up, ready to strike.

2 / The First Sweep

When the *Einsatzgruppen* crossed the border into the USSR, five million Jews were living under the Soviet flag. A large majority of the Soviet Jews were concentrated in the western parts of the country; four million were living in territories which were later overrun by the German Army:

Buffer territories:[1]	
Baltic area	260,000
Polish territory	1,350,000
Bukovina and Bessarabia	300,000
	1,910,000
Old territories:[2]	
Ukraine (pre-1939 borders)	1,533,000
White Russie (pre-1939 borders)	375,000
RSFSR	
Crimea	50,000
Other areas seized by Germans	200,000
	ca. 2,160,000

About one and a half million Jews living in the affected territories fled before the Germans arrived.

1. Rough approximations of estimates by American Joint Distribution Committee, *Report* for 1939, pp. 31–38, and *Report* for 1940, pp. 19, 27.

2. Solomon M. Schwarz, *The Jews in the Soviet Union* (Syracuse, 1951), p. 15, citing 1939 census figures for Ukraine and White Russia. Figures for RSFSR areas are rough approximations based on 1926 census data in Peter-Heinz Seraphim, *Das Judentum im osteuropäischen Raum* (Essen, 1939), pp. 716–18.

Not only were the Jews concentrated in an area within reach of the German Army; they were concentrated there in the cities. The urbanization in the old USSR was 87 per cent.[3] In the buffer territories, it was over 90 per cent.[4]

City and Census Year	Jewish Population (Percentage of Total Population in Parentheses)
Odessa (1926)	153,200 (36.4)
Kiev (1926)	140,200 (27.3)
Moscow (1926)	131,200 (6.5)
Lvov (1931)	99,600 (31.9)
Leningrad (1926)	84,400 (5.3)
Dnepropetrovsk (1926)	83,900 (36.0)
Kharkov (1926)	81,100 (19.4)
Chisinau (1925)	80,000 (60.2)
Vilna (1931)	55,000 (28.2)
Minsk (1926)	53,700 (40.8)
Cernauti (1919)	43,700 (47.7)
Riga (1930)	43,500 (8.9)
Rostov (1926)	40,000 (13.2)
Bialystok (1931)	39,200 (43.0)
Gomel (1926)	37,700 (43.6)
Vitebsk (1926)	37,100 (37.6)
Kirovograd (1920)	31,800 (41.2)
Nikolaev (1923)	31,000 (28.5)
Kremenchug (1923)	29,400 (53.5)
Zhitomir (1923)	28,800 (42.2)
Berdichev (1923)	28,400 (65.1)
Kherson (1920)	27,600 (37.0)
Kaunas (1934)	27,200 (26.1)
Uman (1920)	25,300 (57.2)
Stanislav (1931)	24,800 (51.0)
Rovno (1931)	22,700 (56.0)
Poltava (1920)	21,800 (28.4)
Bobruisk (1923)	21,600 (39.7)
Brest Litovsk (1931)	21,400 (44.2)
Grodno (1931)	21,200 (43.0)
Pinsk (1931)	20,300 (63.6)
Vinnitsa (1923)	20,200 (39.2)
Botoshani (1925)	20,000 (58.5)
Tighina (1910)	20,000 (34.6)
Luck (1931)	17,400 (48.9)
Przemysl (1931)	17,300 (34.0)

Figures from Seraphim, *Das Judentum im osteuropäischen Raum*, pp. 716–18.

3. Schwarz, *The Jews in the Soviet Union*, p. 16.

4. Arthur Ruppin, *Soziologie der Juden* (Berlin, 1930), I, 348, 391, 398, 401. The following is a breakdown by city. With the exception of Moscow and Leningrad, only cities overrun by Germans are listed. Most figures upward revision to 1939.

Strategy

The geographic distribution of Soviet Jewry determined to a large extent the basic strategy of the mobile killing units. To reach as many cities as fast as possible, the *Einsatzgruppen* moved closely upon the heels of the advancing armies, trapping the large Jewish population centers before the victims had a chance to discover their fate. (It was for this reason that the RSHA had insisted upon the right to send its mobile units to the front lines.) In accordance with the agreement, units of *Einsatzgruppe A* entered the cities of Kaunas, Lepaya, Yelgava, Riga, Tartu, Tallin, and the larger suburbs of Leningrad with advance units of the army.[5] Three cars of *Einsatzgruppe C* followed the first tanks into Zhitomir.[6] *Kommando 4a* of the same *Einsatzgruppe* was in Kiev on September 19, the day that city fell.[7] Members of *Einsatzgruppe D* moved into Hotin while the Russians were still defending the town.[8] And so on.

Such front-line movements did entail some difficulties – occasionally the *Einsatzgruppen* found themselves in the middle of heavy fighting. *Einsatzkommando* 12, moving on the coastline east of Odessa to perform mass shootings of Jews, was surprised by a Soviet landing party of 2500 men and fled hurriedly under fire.[9] Sometimes, also, an army commander took advantage of the presence of the mobile killing units to order them to clear out an area infested by partisans or snipers.[10] Only in rare cases, however, did an army order direct the suspension of a killing operation because of the front-line situation.[11] On the whole, the *Einsatzgruppen* were limited in their operations only by their own size in relation to the ground they had to cover.

The *Einsatzgruppen* did *not* move as compact units. The *Kommandos* generally detached themselves from the group staffs and operated independently. Often the *Kommandos* themselves split up into advance detachments (*Vorkommandos*) which kept pace with the troops and platoon-size working parties (*Teilkommandos*) which penetrated into remote districts off the main roads.

As the *Einsatzgruppen* moved farther east, they encountered fewer and fewer Jews. The victims were thinning out for two reasons. The first was geographic distribution. By October-November, 1941, the largest concentrations of Jews had already been left behind; in the eastern Ukraine and beyond the White Russian areas around Smolensk, the Jewish communities were smaller and more widely dispersed. The second reason was the decreasing percentage of Jews who stayed behind. With increasing distance from the starting line, the Soviet evacuation of factory and agricultural workers gained momentum. Many Jews were evacuated and many others fled on their own. On September 12, 1941, *Einsatz-*

5. Report by *Einsatzgruppe A*, undated, L-180.

6. RSHA IV-A-1, Operational Report USSR No. 128 (55 copies), November 3, 1941, NO-3157.

7. RSHA IV-A-1, Operational Report USSR No. 97 (48 copies), September 28, 1941, NO-3145.

8. RSHA IV-A-1, Operational Report USSR No. 19 (32 copies), July 11, 1941, NO-2934.

9. 11th Army AO to 11th Army Ic, September 22, 1941, NOKW-1525.

10. 11th Army Ic/AO (Abwehr III), signed by Chief of Staff Wöhler, to *Einsatzgruppe D*, August 8, 1941, NOKW-3453. The struggle against partisans "is a job for the Security Police," Bgf. Stahlecker (*Einsatzgruppe A*) to Himmler, October 15, 1941, L-180.

11. War Diary, 17th Army/Operations, December 14, 1941, NOKW-3350. The order read: "Upon order of the chief of staff, Jewish Actions [*Judenaktionen*] in Artemovsk will be postponed, pending a clarification of the front-line situation." The commander of the 17th Army was Generaloberst Hermann Hoth. *Einsatzgruppe C* operated in the area.

gruppe C reported that "across the lines, rumors appear to have circulated among the Jews about the fate which they can expect from us [*Bei den Juden scheint sich auch jenseits der Front herumgesprochen zu haben, welches Schicksal sie bei uns erwartet*]." The *Einsatzgruppe* which operated in the central and eastern Ukrainian territories found that many Jewish communities were reduced by 70-90 per cent and some by 100 per cent.[12]

Such reports began to multiply in the fall. In Melitopol an original Jewish population of 11,000 had dwindled to 2000 before *Einsatzgruppe D* arrived.[13] Dnepropetrovsk had a prewar Jewish community of 100,000; about 30,000 remained.[14] In Chernigov, with a prewar Jewish population of 10,000, *Sonderkommando 4a* found only 309 Jews.[15] In Mariupol and Taganrog *Einsatzgruppe D* encountered no Jews at all.[16] On the road from Smolensk to Moscow *Einsatzgruppe B* reported that in many towns the Soviets had evacuated the entire Jewish population,[17] while in the frozen areas near Leningrad, *Einsatzgruppe A* caught only a few strayed Jewish victims.[18] These figures are not an accurate indication of the number of Jews who succeeded in getting away, for many of the victims fled only a short distance and—overtaken by the Germany Army—drifted back into the towns. Nevertheless, a comparison of the original number of Jewish inhabitants with the total number of dead[19] will show that upwards of 1,500,000 Jews did succeed in eluding the grasp of the mobile killing units.

The *Einsatzgruppen* had moved with such speed behind the advancing army that several hundred thousand Jews could be killed like sleeping flies. *Einsatzgruppe A* reported on October 15, 1941, that it had killed 125,000 Jews.[20] *Einsatzgruppe B* reported on November 14, 1941, an incomplete total of 45,000 victims.[21] *Einsatzgruppe C* reported on November 3, 1941, that it had shot 75,000 Jews.[22] *Einsatzgruppe D* reported on December 12, 1941, the killing of 55,000 people.[23]

Although over a million Jews had fled, and additional hundreds of thousands had been killed, it became apparent that many Jewish communities had hardly been touched. They had been bypassed in the hurried advance. To strike at these Jews while they were still stunned and helpless, a second wave of mobile killing units moved up quickly behind the *Einsatzgruppen*.

From Tilsit, in East Prussia, the local Gestapo sent a *Kommando* into Lithuania; these Gestapo men shot thousands of Jews on the other side of the Memel River.[24] In Krakow, the *Befehlshaber der Sicherheitspolizei und*

12. RSHA IV-A-1, Operational Report USSR No. 81 (48 copies), September 12, 1941, NO-3154.

13. *Ortskommandantur* I/853 Melitopol to Korück 533, October 13, 1941, NOKW-1632.

14. RSHA IV-A-1, Operational Report USSR No. 135 (60 copies), November 19, 1941, NO-2832.

15. *Ibid.*

16. RSHA IV-A-1, Operational Report USSR No. 136 (60 copies), November 21, 1941, NO-2822.

17. RSHA IV-A-1, Operational Report USSR No. 123 (50 copies), October 24, 1941, NO-3239. Schwarz, *The Jews in the Soviet Union*, pp. 220–22, states that there is no evidence of a Soviet evacuation plan for Jews in particular.

18. Bgf. Stahlecker to Himmler, October 15, 1941, L-180.

19. See pp. 190, 256.

20. Stahlecker to Himmler, October 15, 1941, L-180. In addition, about 5000 non-Jews had been killed.

21. RSHA IV-A-1, Operational Report USSR No. 133 (60 copies), November 14, 1941, NO-2825.

22. RSHA IV-A-1, Operational Report USSR No. 128 (55 copies), November 3, 1941, NO-3157. In addition, the *Einsatzgruppe* had shot 5000 non-Jews.

23. RSHA IV-A-1, Operational Report USSR No. 145 (65 copies), December 12, 1941, NO-2828.

des SD (BdS) of the *Generalgouvernement*, SS-Oberführer Schöngarth, organized three small *Kommandos.* In the middle of July these *Kommandos* moved into the eastern Polish areas and, with headquarters in Lvov, Brest Litovsk, and Bialystok, respectively, killed tens of thousands of Jews.[25] In addition to the Tilsit Gestapo and the *Generalgouvernement Kommandos,* improvised killing units were thrown into action by the Higher SS and Police Leaders. In the newly occupied Soviet territories Himmler had installed three of these regional commanders:[26]

HSSPf *Nord* (North):
OGruf. Prützmann (Jeckeln)
HSSPf *Mitte* (Center):
OGruf. von dem Bach-Zelewski
HSSPf *Süd* (South):
OGruf. Jeckeln (Prützmann)

Each Higher SS and Police Leader was in charge of a regiment of Order Police and some *Waffen-SS* units.[27] These forces helped out considerably.

In the northern sector the Higher SS and Police Leader (Prützmann), assisted by 21 men of *Einsatzkommando* 2 (*Einsatzgruppe A*), killed 10,600 people in Riga.[28] In the center the Order Police of Higher SS and Police Leader von dem Bach helped kill 2278 Jews in Minsk[29] and 3726 in Mogilev.[30] (The beneficiary of that co-operation was *Einsatzgruppe B.*) In the south Higher SS and Police Leader Jeckeln was especially active. When *Einsatzkommando 4a* (*Einsatzgruppe C*) moved into Kiev, two detachments of Order Police Regiment South helped kill over 33,000 Jews.[31] The role of the regiment in the Kiev massacre was so conspicuous that *Einsatzkommando 4a* felt obliged to report that, apart from the Kiev action, it had killed 14,000 Jews "without any outside help" (*ohne jede fremde Hilfe erledigt*).[32]

But Jeckeln did not confine himself to helping the *Einsatzgruppen.* His mobile killing units were responsible for some of the greatest massacres in the Ukraine. Thus when Feldmarschall Reichenau, commander of the Sixth Army, ordered the 1st SS Brigade to destroy remnants of the Soviet 124th Division, partisans, and "supporters of

24. RSHA IV-A-1, Operational Report USSR No. 19 (32 copies), July 11, 1941, NO-2934. RSHA IV-A-1, Operational Report USSR No. 26, July 18, 1941, NO-2941. The Stahlecker report to Himmler mentions that the Tilsit unit had killed 5500 persons. Stahlecker to Himmler, October 15, 1941, L-180.

25. Order by Commander, Rear Army Group Area South, Ic (signed von Roques), July 14, 1941, NOKW-2597. RSHA IV-A-1, Operational Report USSR No. 43 (47 copies), August 5, 1941, NO-2949. RSHA IV-A-1, Operational Report USSR No. 56 (48 copies), August 18, 1941, NO-2848. RSHA IV-A-1, Operational Report USSR No. 58, August 20, 1941, NO-2846. RSHA IV-A-1, Operational Report USSR No. 66, August 28, 1941, NO-2839. RSHA IV-A-1, Operational Report USSR No. 67, August 29, 1941, NO-2837. RSHA IV-A-1, Operational Report USSR No. 78 (48 copies), September 9, 1941, NO-2851. The above-cited reports, which do not cover all the operations of the three *Kommandos,* mention 17,887 victims.

26. RSHA IV-A-1, Operational Report USSR No. 129 (55 copies), November 4, 1941, NO-3159. RSHA IV-A-1, Operational Report USSR No. 141 (66 copies), December 3, 1941, NO-4425. RSHA IV-A-1, Operational Report USSR No. 149 (65 copies), December 22, 1941, NO-2833.

27. Report by Major Schmidt von Altenstadt, May 19, 1941, NOKW-486.

28. RSHA IV-A-1, Operational Report USSR No. 156, January 16, 1942, NO-3405. The action took place on November 30, 1941.

29. RSHA IV-A-1, Operational Report USSR No. 92, September 23, 1941, NO-3143. The army's *Feldgendarmerie* also participated in this action.

30. RSHA IV-A-1, Operational Report USSR No. 133 (60 copies), November 14, 1941, NO-2825.

31. RSHA IV-A-1, Operational Report USSR No. 101 (48 copies), October 2, 1941, NO-3137.

32. RSHA IV-A-1, Operational Report USSR No. 111 (50 copies), October 12, 1941, NO-3155. *Einsatzkommando 4a* had a total of 51,000 victims by that time.

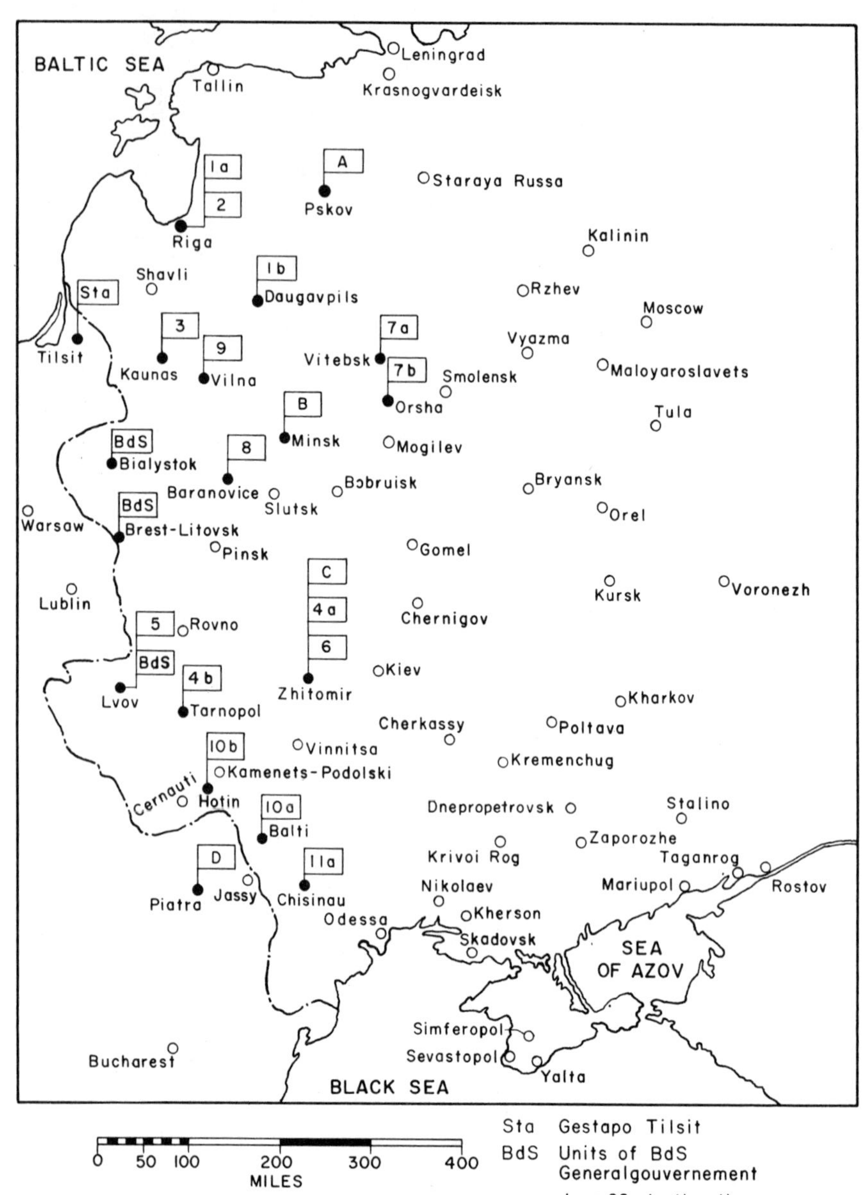

MAP 2
POSITIONS OF THE MOBILE KILLING UNITS
JULY 1941

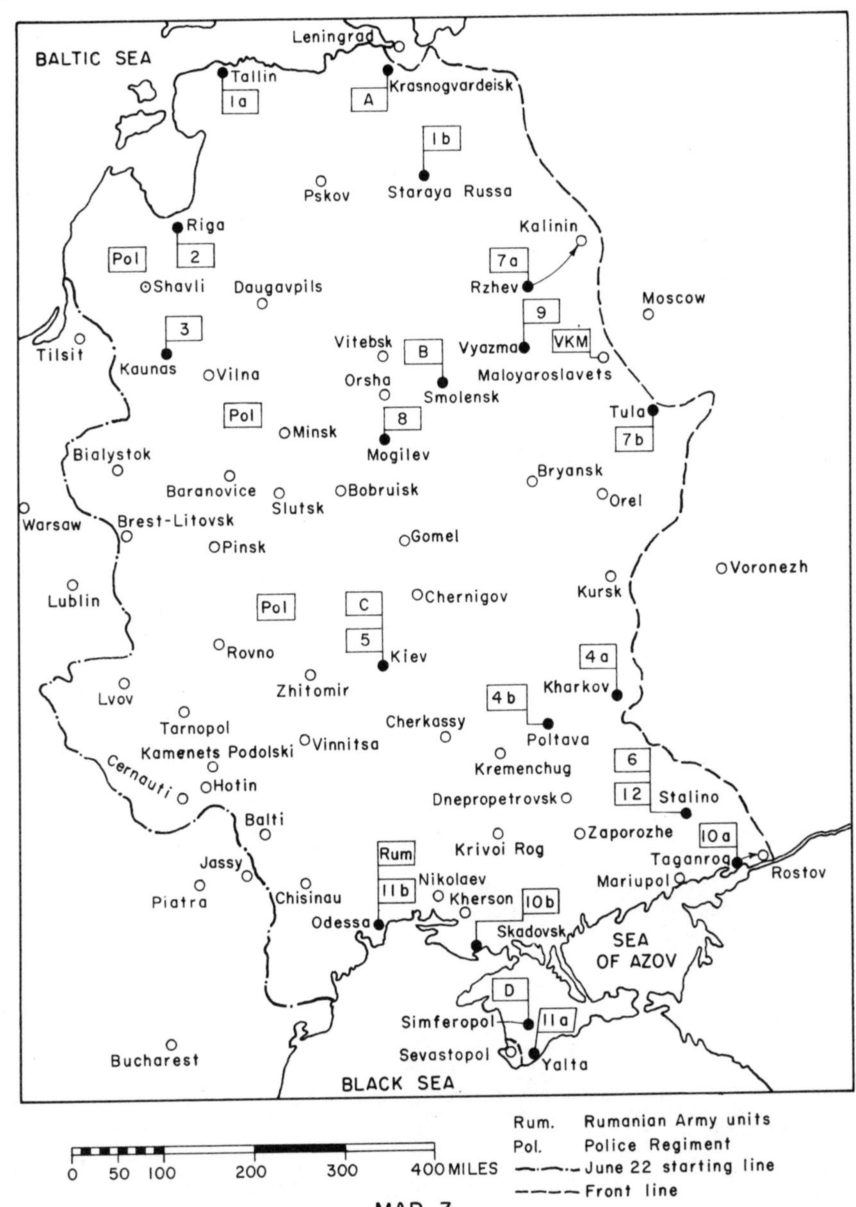

MAP 3
POSITIONS OF THE MOBILE KILLING UNITS
NOVEMBER 1941

the Bolshevik system" in his rear, Jeckeln led the brigade on a three-day rampage, killing 73 Red Army men, 165 Communist party functionaries, and 1658 Jews.[33] A few weeks later the same brigade shot 300 Jewish men and 139 Jewish women in Stara Konstantinov "as a reprisal measure for the unco-operative attitude of the Jews working for the *Wehrmacht*."[34]

Next Jeckeln struck at Kamenets Podolski, shooting there a total of 23,600 Jews.[35] Another action followed in Berdichev, where Jeckeln killed 1303 Jews, "among them 875 Jewesses over twelve years of age,"[36] still another in Dnepropetrovsk, where he slaughtered 10,000 Jews,[37] and still another in Rovno, where he massacred 15,000.[38] In connection with the Rovno massacre, *Einsatzgruppe C* reported that, whereas the action had been organized by the Higher SS and Police Leader and had been carried out by the Order Police, a detachment of *Einsatzkommando* 5 had participated to a significant extent in the shooting (*an der Durchführung massgeblich beteiligt*).[39]

While it is not possible to estimate the total number of Jews killed by the Higher SS and Police Leaders, we know that the figure runs into six digits. Thus, in the single month of August, the Higher SS and Police Leader South alone killed 44,125 persons, "mostly Jews."[40]

The mobile killing strategy was an attempt to trap the Jews in a wave of *Einsatzgruppen*, immediately followed up by a support wave of Gestapo men from Tilsit, *Einsatzkommandos* from the *Generalgouvernement*, and formations of the Higher SS and Police Leaders. Together, these units killed about five hundred thousand Jews in five months. (The locations of the mobile killing units in July and November, 1941, are indicated on the preceding maps.)[41]

Co-operation with the Mobile Killing Units

Movement was the basic problem of the mobile killing units during the first sweep. Once the killing units had arrived on a desired spot, however, they had to deal with a host of problems. The success of the operation, from that point on, depended on the attitudes of the military authorities, the native population, and the victims themselves.

The army co-operated with the *Einsatzgruppen* to an extent which far exceeded the minimum support functions guaranteed in the OKH-RSHA agreement. This co-operation was all the more remarkable because the Security Police had expected little more than grudging acquiescence in the killing operations. On July 6, 1941, *Einsatzkommando 4b* (*Einsatzgruppe C*) report from Tarnopol: "Armed forces surprisingly welcome hostility against Jews [*Wehrmacht erfreulich gute Einstellung gegen die Juden*]."[42] On Septem-

33. OGruf. Jeckeln to 6th Army, copies to Himmler, Army Group Rear Area South (General von Roques), Commander of 6th Army Rear Area (Generalleutnant von Puttkammer), and Chief of Order Police Daluege, August 1, 1941, NOKW-1165.

34. RSHA IV-A-1, Operational Report USSR No. 59 (48 copies), August 21, 1941, NO-2847.

35. RSHA IV-A-1, Operational Report USSR No. 80 (48 copies), September 11, 1941, NO-3154.

36. RSHA IV-A-1, Operational Report USSR No. 88 (48 copies), September 19, 1941, NO-3149.

37. RSHA IV-A-1, Operational Report USSR No. 135 (60 copies), November 19, 1941, NO-2832.

38. RSHA IV-A-1, Operational Report USSR No. 143 (65 copies), December 8, 1941, NO-2827. The action took place on Nov. 7/8, 1941.

39. *Ibid.*

40. RSHA IV-A-1, Operational Report USSR No. 94 (48 copies), September 25, 1941, NO-3146.

41. Locations are cited in almost every RSHA IV-A-1 operational report.

ber 8 *Einstazgruppe D* reported that relations with military authorities were "excellent" (*ausgezeichnet*).[43] The commander of *Einsatzgruppe A* (Brigadeführer Dr. Stahlecker) wrote to Himmler that his experiences with Army Group North were very good and that his relations with the Fourth Panzer Army under Generaloberst Höppner were "very close, yes, almost cordial [*sehr eng, ja fast herzlich*]."[44]

These testimonials were given to the army because it went out of its way to turn over Jews to the *Einsatzgruppen,* to request actions against Jews, to participate in killing operations, and to shoot Jewish hostages in "reprisal" for attacks on occupation forces. The generals had eased themselves into that pose of co-operation through the pretense that the Jewish population was a group of Bolshevist diehards who instigated, encouraged, and abetted the partisan war behind the German lines.[45] The army thus had to protect itself against the partisan menace by striking at its presumable source – the Jews.[46]

The first consequence of army "security" policy was the practice of handing over Jews to the *Einsatzgruppen* for shooting. In Minsk the army commander established a civilian internment camp for almost all the men in the city. Secret Field Police units and *Einsatzgruppe B* personnel together "combed out" the camp. Thousands of "Jews, criminals, functionaries, and Asiatics" were caught in the roundup.[47] In Zhitomir, General Reinhardt assisted *Einsatzgruppe C* in a "comb-out" (*Durchkämmung*) of the town.[48] Outside the cities several military units turned in stray Jews fleeing on the roads or in the woods.[49]

The second application of the theory that Jews were the instigators of the partisan war was army initiation of action against the Jews. In Kremenchug, the Seventeenth Army requested *Kommando 4b* to wipe out the Jews of the city because three cases of cable sabotage had occurred there.[50] In other towns army commanders did not even wait for sabotage occurrences, but requested anti-Jewish action as "pre-

42. RSHA IV-A-1, Operational Report USSR No. 14 (30 copies), July 6, 1941, NO-2940.

43. Ohlendorf via Stubaf. Gmeiner to 11th Army Ic/AO (received and initialed by Chief of Staff Wöhler), September 8, 1941, NOKW-3234.

44. Stahlecker to Himmler, October 15, 1941, L-180.

45. In line with that thinking, see letter by Gen. Eugen Müller (OKH Morale Chief) to commanders of Army Group Rear Areas, North, Center, and South, July 25, 1941, NOKW-182. Müller warned in that letter that the "carriers of the Jewish-Bolshevist system" were now starting an all-out partisan war in the German rear.

46. An illustration of army credulity is the ease with which the military was persuaded – without any evidence – that the great fire in Kiev had been started by the Jews. RSHA IV-A-1, Operational Report USSR No. 97 (48 copies), September 28, 1941, NO-3145. A subsequent *Einsatzgruppen* report disclosed that the fire had been set by a so-called annihilation battalion – a type of partisan unit employed by the Russians during the early days of the war in sabotage activities. RSHA IV-A-1, Operational Report USSR No. 127 (55 copies), October 31, 1941, N-4136.

47. RSHA IV-A-1, Operational Report USSR No. 21 (32 copies), July 13, 1941, NO-2937. RSHA IV-A-1, Operational Report USSR No. 73 (48 copies), September 4, 1941, NO-2844.

48. RSHA IV-A-1, Operational Report USSR No. 38 (48 copies), July 30, 1941, NO-2951.

49. For instance, the 99th Infantry Division of the 6th Army. See reports by 99th Division Ic, September 27 and 29, 1941, NOKW-1294. Also, 3rd Company of 683rd motorized *Feldgendarmerie* Battalion to *Feldkommandantur* 810, November 2, 1941, NOKW-1630. The *Feldgendarmerie* (not to be confused with the Secret Field Police) was the Army's military police. Many of its personnel had been drawn from the Order Police.

50. War diary, 17th Army Ic/AO, September 22, 1941, NOKW-2272. The commander of the 17th Army was General der Infantrie Heinrich von Stüplnagel.

cautionary" measures. Thus in the town of Kodyma an illiterate Ukranian woman who claimed to understand Yiddish was brought before a *Hauptmann* (Captain) Krämer, of Secret Field Police Group 647 with the XXX Corps. She revealed that she had overhead a Jewish plot to attack the army in the city. That same afternoon *Einsatzkommando* 10*a* in Olshanka was asked to send a detachment to Kodyma. The detachment, assisted by Secret Field Police men, then carried out the killings.[51] At Armyansk, in the Crimea, the local military commander simply sent the following report to his superior:

> For protection against the partisan nuisance and for the security of the troops in this area, it became absolutely necessary to render the fourteen local Jews and Jewesses harmless. Carried out on November 26, 1941.[52]

The third effect of the German theory of a "Jewish-Bolshevist" conspiracy was a policy of taking Jewish hostages and suspects in the occupied territories. The Seventeenth Army ordered that whenever sabotage or an attack on personnel could not be traced to the Ukrainian population, Jews and Communists (especially Jewish Komsomol members) were to be shot in reprisal.[53] The commander of the Southern Army Group Rear Area explained a similar order in the following terms:

> We must convey the impression that we are just. Whenever the perpetrator of an act of sabotage cannot be found, Ukrainians are not to be blamed. In such cases reprisals are therefore to be carried out only against Jews and Russians.[54]

Perhaps the most interesting order was issued by the Sixth Army Ia/OQu at Kharkov. The order provided that Jews and other hostages be placed in big buildings. It was suspected that some of these buildings were mined. Now that the supposed perpetrators were in the buildings, the military expected that reports of the location of the mines would soon be made to army engineers.[55] At least one unit carried its suspicion of the Jews so far as to order, in one breath, that all Red Army men in uniform or civilian clothes caught "loafing around," Jews, commissars, persons who carried a weapon, and those suspected of partisan activities were to be shot at once.[56]

It is difficult to estimate how many Jewish hostages or suspects fell victim to the German Army. *Einsatzgruppe A* reported that in White Russia alone, Army Group Center had shot 19,000 "partisans and criminals, that is, in the majority Jews," up to December, 1941.[57] The Jewish victims of army action were thus no insignificant group of people; the army was pitching in very seriously to help the Heydrich

51. XXX Corps Ic to 11th Army Ic, August 2, 1941, NOKW-650. *Sonderkommando* 10*a* (OStubaf. Seetzen) to *Einsatzgruppe D*, August 3, 1941, NOKW-586.

52. Ortskommandantur Armyansk to Korück 553/Qu in Simferopol, November 30, 1941, NOKW-1532.

53. 17th Army Ic/AO (signed by Stülpnagel) to corps commands, with copy to Commander of Southern Army Group Rear Area, July 30, 1941, NOKW-1693. The Komsomol was a Communist Party youth organization.

54. Order by Southern Army Group Rear Area/Section VII (signed by Gen. von Roques), August 16, 1941, NOKW-1691. For reports of "reprisal" shootings of Jews, see Proclamation by town commander of Kherson, August 28, 1941, NOKW-3436. Commander, Southern Army Group Rear Area Ic to Army Group South Ia/Ib, November 13, 1941, NOKW-1611. 202nd Replacement Brigade Ia to Commander, Southern Army Group Rear Area, November 13, 1941, NOKW-1611; There are many other such reports.

55. Order by 6th Army Ia/OQu, October 17, 1941, NOKW-184. The engineer chief in Kharkov was Oberst (Colonel) Herbert Selle, commander of the 677th Engineer Regiment.

56. Order by 52nd Infantry Division Ic, September 11, 1941, NOKW-1858.

57. Draft report by *Einsatzgruppe A*, winter 1941/42, PS-2273.

forces reduce the Jewish population of the East.

In all the examples cited so far, partisan activity was the explicit or implicit justification for the army's actions. Interestingly enough, however, there were instances after the start of operations when the military went out of its way to help the mobile killing units for no apparent reason save the desire to get things over with. The growth of this callousness in the face of mass death is illustrated by the following two stories.

In Dshanskoy, on the Crimean peninsula, the local mayor had established a concentration camp for Jews without notifying anyone. After a while, famine raged in the camp and epidemics threatened to break out. The military commander (*Ortskommandant*) approached *Einsatzgruppe D* with a request to kill the Jews; the Security Police turned down the request because it did not have enough personnel. After some haggling the army agreed to furnish its *Feldgendarmerie* for blocking the area off, so that a *Kommando* of the *Einsatzgruppe* could perform the killings.[58]

In Simferopol, the Crimean capital, the Eleventh Army simply decided that it wanted the shooting to be completed before Christmas. Accordingly, *Einsazgruppe D,* with the assistance of army personnel and with army trucks and gasoline, completed the shootings in time to permit the army to celebrate Christmas in a city without Jews.[59]

From an initial reluctance to participate in the destruction process, the generals had developed such an impatience for action that they were virtually pushing the *Einsatzgruppen* into killing operations. The German Army could hardly wait to see the Jews of Russia dead – no wonder that the commanders of the *Einsatzgruppen* were pleasantly surprised.

While most of the mobile killing units were operating in the territorial domain of the German Army, *Einsatzkommandos* of Groups *C* and *D* also moved into sectors of the Hungarian and Roumanian armies. A novel situation faced the Security Police in these sectors: the RSHA had made no agreements with the satellite commands; the German government had not even informed its allies of the special mission of the *Reichsführer SS.* New experiences were therefore in store for Himmler's men as they moved into areas held by alien authority.

References to the relations with the Hungarians are scarce, and whenever we find them, they do not show the Hungarians in a co-operative attitude. In Zhitomir, for instance, the Hungarian Army stopped an action by native police against the Jews.[60] Again, farther to the south, *Einsatzgruppe D* reported at the end of August that it had "cleared of Jews" a territory bordering on the Dniester from Hotin to Jampol, *except* for a small area occupied by Hungarian forces.[61] The Roumanian attitude, on the other hand, was quite different. Repeatedly, Roumanian forces on the march invaded Jewish quarters and killed Jews, and their actions took the form of atrocities rather than well-planned or well-reasoned killing operations. The German

58. Report by Major Teichmann (Korück 553/Ic), January 1, 1942, NOKW-1866.

59. Affidavit by Werner Braune (Commander, *Sonderkommando 11b*), July 8, 1947, NO-4234. Still another example of army co-operation is Zhitomir. See RSHA IV-A-1, Operational Report USSR No. 106 (48 copies), October 7, 1941, NO-3140. See also statement by Oberleutnant Erwin Bingel (undated) on Vinnitsa and Uman, NO-5301. Bingel was commander of the 4th Company, 783rd Landesschützen Battalion, 36th Division.

60. RSHA IV-A-1, Operational Report USSR No. 23, July 15, 1941, NO-4526. Control of the city passed subsequently into the hands of a German commander.

61. RSHA IV-A-1, Operational Report USSR No. 67 (48 copies), August 29, 1941, NO-2837.

witnesses of that Roumanian fury were slightly disturbed by what they saw and, at times, attempted to introduce discipline into the ranks of their ally.

Early in July *Sonderkommando* 10*a* of *Einsatzgruppe D* moved into the city of Balti. The *Sonderkommando* sent search parties into the Jewish quarter of the Roumanian-occupied city. "In one room," reported Obersturmbannführer Seetzen, "a patrol last evening discovered fifteen Jews, of different ages and both sexes, who had been shot by Roumanian soldiers. Some of the Jews were still alive; the patrol shot them to death for mercy's sake."[62] Another incident in the same town occurred on the evening of July 10: Roumanian Army authorities drove together four hundred Jews of all ages and both sexes in order to shoot them in retaliation for attacks on Roumanian soldiers. The commander of the 170th German Division in the area was taken aback by the spectacle. He requested that the shooting be limited to fifteen Jewish men.[63] By July 29 another report from Balti indicated that the Roumanians were shooting Jews en masse. "Roumanian police in Balti and surrounding area proceeding sharply against Jewish population. Number of shootings cannot be determined exactly." *Kommando* 10*a* pitched in by shooting the Jewish community leaders in the town.[64]

The *Einsatzgruppe* also had trouble with the Roumanians in Cernauti. In that city the Roumanians were busily shooting Ukranian intellectuals "in order to settle the Ukrainian problem in the North Bukovina once and for all." Among the victims the Security Police found many Ukrainian nationalists who had been potential collaborators in German service. *Kommando* 10*b* consequently had a dual reason for interfering. It requested the release of the pro-German nationalists (OUN men) in exchange for Communists and Jews.[65] The arrangement was successful. Two weeks later *Einsatzgruppe D* and Roumanian police were jointly shooting thousands of Jews.[66]

The occurrences at Balti and Cernauti were destined to be dwarfed by a blood bath which followed in the fall. On October 16, 1941, after a long siege, the Fourth Roumanian Army under General de Corp de Armata Jacobici captured the city of Odessa.[67] Shortly after the fall of the city a German military intelligence agent reported the following events:

> On the basis of a summons by the *Stadtkommandantur* all Jews must now report at the Central Prison of Odessa, which was already built during the czarist regime near the Jewish cemetery. This former imperial Russian and later Bolshevist GPU prison is today the concentration camp of Odessa Jewry. The former commander of the Jewish Ghetto in Kishinev, a Roumanian first lieutenant, now commands this concentration camp, which already houses eleven thousand people. For four days, according to the camp commander, the incarcerated Jews have received neither water nor food. Still in all, Jewish masses are streaming into this Jewish concentration camp time and again, without prodding by the Roumanians [*ohne Zutun der Rumä-*

62. *Sonderkommando* 10*a* (signed Seetzen) to *Einsatzgruppe D*, July 10, 1941, NO-2073.

63. RSHA IV-A-1, Operational Report USSR No. 25 (34 copies), July 17, 1941, NO-2939.

64. RSHA IV-A-1, Operational Report USSR No. 37 (45 copies), July 29, 1941, NO-2952.

65. RSHA IV-A-1, Operational Report USSR No. 22 (30 copies), July 14, 1941, NO-4135. The OUN was a pro-German organization of Ukrainians.

66. RSHA IV-A-1, Operational Report USSR No. 40 (45 copies), August 1, 1941, NO-2950. RSHA IV-A-1, Operational Report USSR No. 67 (48 copies), August 29, 1941, NO-2827.

67. OKW Communiques, October 16 and 17, published in the press.

nen], because in the city they no longer feel secure.[68]

On October 22, partisans blew up the Roumanian headquarters on Engel Street; several dozen officers and men were killed in the explosion. The Roumanian dictator, Marshal Antonescu, thereupon sent instructions to shoot 200 civilians for every dead officer, and 100 for every other rank.[69] The quotas were exceeded out of all bounds. During the night of October 22-23, 19,000 Jews were driven into the harbor area to be shot in a square enclosed by a wooden fence. The bodies were covered with gasoline and burned. After the completion of this action another 40,000 Jews were transported to the collective farm at Dalnic, outside the city, where they were shot down in anti-tank ditches. At Odessa the Roumanians had therefore killed nearly 60,000 Jews in the biggest massacre of the eastern operations. *Einsatzkommando* 11*b*, which was assigned to the city after its fall, was apparently no longer needed to teach the Roumanians anything.

Whereas the success of the mobile killing operations depended, in the first instance, upon the co-operation of the military leadership, much depended also on the attitude of the civilian population. How, precisely, would the Slavs react to the sudden annihilation of a people living in their midst? Would they hide the Jews or hand them over to German occupation authorities? Would they shoot at the killers or help in the killings? These were vital questions for *Einsatzgruppen* commanders and their subordinates.

In fact, the behavior of the population during the killing operations was characterized by a tendency toward passivity. That passivity was the product of conflicting emotions and opposing restraints. The Slavs had no particular liking for their Jewish neighbors, and they perhaps felt no overpowering urge to help the Jews in their hour of need. Insofar as there were such inclinations, they were effectively curbed by fear of reprisals from the Germans. At the same time, however, the Slavic population stood estranged and even aghast before the unfolding spectacle of the "final solution." There was on the whole no impelling desire to cooperate in a process of such utter ruthlessness; and the fact that the Soviet regime, fighting off the Germans a few hundred miles to the east, was still threatening to return, undoubtedly acted as a powerful restraint upon many a potential collaborator. The ultimate effect of this psychological constellation, was an escape into neutrality. The population did not want to take sides in the destruction process. If few were on the side of the Germans, fewer still were on the side of the Jews.

In all the *Einsatzgruppen* reports, we discover only one indication of a pro-Jewish act in the occupied lands. *Sonderkommando 4b* reported that it had shot the mayor of Kremenchug, Senitsa Vershovsky, because he had "tried to protect the Jews."[70] That incident appears to have been the only case of its kind. The counterpressure was evidently too great. Whoever attempted to aid the Jews acted alone and exposed himself as well as his family to the possibility of a death sentence from a German *Kommando*. There was no encouragement for a man with an awakened conscience. In Lithuania, Bishop Brizgys set an example for the entire population by forbidding the clergy to aid the Jews in any way.[71]

68. Report by confidential agent, code No. USSR 96, recorded in Bucharest, beginning of November, 1941, Wi/IC 4.2-a.

69. Eugene Levai, *The Black Book on the Martyrdom of Hungarian Jewry* (Zurich and Vienna, 1948), pp. 71–72 (based on statements by witnesses at trials of Roumanian war criminals, as reported in the Bucharest press).

70. RSHA IV-A-1, Operational Report USSR No. 156, Jan. 16, 1942, NO-3405.

Across the whole occupied territory Jews were turning to the Christian population for assistance – in vain. *Einsatzgruppe C* reported that many Jews who had fled from their homes were turning back from the countryside. "The population does not house them and does not feed them. They live in holes in the earth or pressed together [*zusammengepfercht*] in old huts."[72]

Sometimes the failure to help the Jews appears to have weighed on the consciences of the population. Thus in the northern sector, south of Leningrad, *Einsatzgruppe A* reported a subtle attempt by the local residents to justify their inactivity. The following anecdote was circulating in that sector: A group of Soviet prisoners of war was requested by its German captors to bury alive a number of Jewish fellow prisoners. The Russians refused. The German soldiers thereupon told the Jews to bury the Russians. The Jews, according to the anecdote, immediately grabbed the shovels.[73]

The refusal to help the Jews was only a little more tenacious than the reluctance to help the Germans. On July 19 *Einsatzgruppe B* in White Russia had already noted that the population was remarkably "apathetic" to the killing operations and that it would have to be asked to co-operate in the seizure of Communist functionaries and the Jewish intelligentsia.[74] From the Ukraine *Einsatzkommando* 6 of *Einsatzgruppe C* reported as follows:

> Almost nowhere can the population be persuaded to take active steps against the Jews. This may be explained by the fear of many people that the Red Army may return. Again and again this anxiety has been pointed out to us. Older people have remarked that they had already experienced in 1918 the sudden retreat of the Germans. In order to meet the fear psychosis, and in order to destroy the myth [*Bann*] which, in the eyes of many Ukrainians, places the Jew in the position of the wielder of political power [*Träger politischer Macht,*] *Einsatzkommando* 6 on several occasions marched Jews before their execution through the city. Also, care was taken to have Ukrainian militiamen watch the shooting of Jews.[75]

This "deflation" of the Jews in the public eye did not have the desired effects. After a few weeks, *Einsatzgruppe C* complained once more that the inhabitants did not betray the movements of hidden Jews. The Ukrainians were passive, benumbed by the "Bolshevist terror." Only the ethnic Germans in the area were busily working for the *Einsatzgruppe*.[76]

71. RSHA IV-A-1, Operational Report USSR No. 54, August 16, 1941, NO-2849.

72. RSHA IV-A-1, Operational Report USSR No. 94 (48 copies), September 25, 1941, NO-3146.

73. RSHA IV-A-1, Operational Report USSR No. 123 (50 copies), October 24, 1941, NO-3239.

74. RSHA IV-A-1, Operational Report USSR No. 27 (36 copies), July 19, 1941, NO-2942.

75. RSHA IV-A-1, Operational Report USSR No. 81 (48 copies), September 12, 1941, NO-3154.

76. RSHA IV-A-1, Operational Report USSR No. 127 (55 copies), October 31, 1941, NO-4136. The Poles in the Bialystok region were also reported to have engaged in "spontaneous denunciations" (*Erstattung von Anzeigen*). RSHA IV-A-1, Operational Report USSR No. 21 (32 copies), July 13, 1941, NO-2937.

From the Crimea *Einsatzgruppe D* reported: "The population of the Crimea is anti-Jewish and in some cases spontaneously brings Jews to *Kommandos* to be liquidated. The *starosts* [village elders] ask for permission to liquidate the Jews themselves." RSHA IV-A-1, Operational Report USSR No. 145 (65 copies), December 12, 1941, NO-2828. On Crimea, see also report by OStubaf. Seibert (*Einsatzgruppe D*) to 11th Army Ic, April 16, 1942, NOKW-628. During the Soviet reoccupation of the Crimean city of Feodosiya in the winter of 1941/42, collaborators were said to have been killed with pickaxes as they were asked:

Neutrality is a zero quantity which helps the stronger party in an unequal struggle. The Jews needed native help more than the Germans did. The *Einsatzgruppen,* however, not only had the advantage of a generally neutral population; they also managed to obtain – at least from certain segments of the local citizenry – two important forms of co-operation in the killing operations: pogroms and the help of auxiliary police in seizures and shootings.

What are pogroms? They are short, violent outbursts by a community against its Jewish population. Why did the *Einsatzgruppen* endeavor to start pogroms in the occupied areas? The reasons which prompted the killing units to activate anti-Jewish outbursts were partly administrative, partly psychological. The administrative principle was very simple: every Jew killed in a pogrom was one less burden for the *Einsatzgruppen.* A pogrom brought them, as they expressed it, that much closer to the "cleanup goal" *(Säuberungsziel).*[77] The psychological consideration was more interesting. The *Einsatzgruppen* wanted the population to take a part – and a major part at that – of the responsibility for the killing operations. "It was not less important, for future purposes," wrote Brigadeführer Dr. Stahlecker, "to establish as an unquestionable fact that the liberated population had resorted to the most severe measures against the Bolshevist and Jewish enemy, on its own initiative and without instructions from German authorities."[78] In short, the pogroms were to become a defensive weapon with which to confront an accuser, or an element of blackmail that could be used against the local population.

It may be noted in passing that *Einsatzgruppen* and military interests diverged on the matter of pogroms. The military government experts, like the civilian bureaucrats at home, dreaded any kind of uncontrollable violence. One rear (security) division, issuing a long directive for anti-Jewish measures, included also this sharply worded paragraph in its order: "Lynch justice against Jews and other terror measures are to be prevented by all means. The armed forces do not tolerate that one terror [the Soviet one] be relieved by another."[79] Most of the pogroms, therefore, took place in those areas which had not yet been placed into the firm grip of military government experts.

The *Einsatzgruppen* were most successful with "spontaneous" outbursts in the Baltic area, particularly in Lithuania. Yet even there Dr. Stahlecker observed: "To our surprise, it was not easy at first to set in motion an extensive pogrom against the Jews."[80] The Lithuanian pogroms grew out of a situation of violence in the capital city of Kaunas. As soon as war had broken out, anti-Communist fighting groups had gone into action against the Soviet rear guard. When an advanced detachment of *Einsatzkommando 1b* (*Einsatzgruppe A*) moved into Kaunas, the Lithuanian partisans were shooting it out with retreating Red Army men. The newly arrived Security Police approached the chief of the Lithuanian insurgents, Klimatis, and secretly persuaded him to turn his forces on the Jews. After several days of intensive pogroms Klimatis had accounted for 5000 dead: 3800 in Kaunas, 1200 in other towns.[81] Moving farther north,

"Why did you tolerate it that the Germans shot all the Jews?" AOK 11/IV Wi to WiStOst/Fü, February 1, 1942, Wi/ID 2.512.

77. Report by Bgf. Dr. Stahlecker (Chief of *Einsatzgruppe A*) (40 copies), October 15, 1941, L-180.

78. *Ibid.*

79. Directive by 454th Security Division/Ia to Ortskommandanturen in its area, September 8, 1941, NOKW-2628.

80. Stahlecker to Himmler, October 15, 1941, L-180.

Einsatzgruppe A organized a pogrom in Riga, Latvia. The *Einsatzgruppe* set up two pogrom units and let them loose in the city; 400 Jews were killed.[82] Both in Kaunas and in Riga, the *Einsatzgruppe* took photographs and made films of the "self-cleansing actions" (*Selbstreiningungsaktionen*) as evidence "for later times" of the severity of native treatment of the Jews.[83] With the disbanding of the anti-Communist partisans, the northern pogroms ended. No other outbursts took place in the Baltic states.[84]

In addition to Stahlecker's *Einsatzgruppe* in the North, *Einsatzgruppe C* had some success with pogroms in the South. The southern pogrom area was largely confined to Galicia, an area which was formerly Polish territory and which had a large Ukrainian population. The Galician capital of Lvov was the scene of a mass seizure by local inhabitants. In "reprisal" for the deportation of Ukrainians by the Soviets, 1000 members of the Jewish intelligentsia were driven together and handed over to the Security Police.[85] On July 5, 1941, about 70 Jews in Tarnopol were rounded up by Ukrainians when three mutilated German corpses were found in the local prison. The Jews were killed with dynamite (*mit geballter Ladung erledigt*). Another 20 Jews were killed by Ukrainians and German troops.[86]

In Kremenets 100-150 Ukrainians had been killed by the Soviets. When some of the exhumed corpses were found without skin, rumors circulated that the Ukrainians had been thrown into kettles full of boiling water. The Ukrainian population retaliated by seizing 130 Jews and beating them to death with clubs.[87] Although the Galician pogroms spread still further, to such places as Sambor[88] and Chortkov,[89] the Ukrainian violence as a whole did not come up to expectations. Only Tarnopol and Chortkov were scored as major successes.[90]

There are three observations which should be made about the pogroms. First, truly spontaneous pogroms, free from *Einsatzgruppen* influence, did not take place; all outbreaks were either organized or inspired by the *Einsatzgruppen*. Second, all pogroms were implemented within a short time after the arrival of the killing units; they were not self-perpetuating, nor could new ones be started after things had settled down. Third, most of the reported pogroms occurred in buffer territory, areas in which submerged hostility toward the Jews was apparently greatest and areas, also, in which the Soviet threat of a return could most easily be discounted, for the Communist government had been in power there for periods of less than two years.

We come now to a second and somewhat more efficient form of local co-operation: the help extended to the

81. Stahlecker to Himmler, October 15, 1941, L-180. RSHA IV-A-1, Operational Report USSR No. 8 (25 copies), June 30, 1941, NO-4543.

82. RSHA IV-A-1, Operational Report USSR No. 15 (30 copies), July 7, 1941, NO-2935. Stahlecker to Himmler, October 15, 1941. L-180.

83. Stahlecker to Himmler, October 15, 1941, L-180.

84. *Ibid.*

85. RSHA IV-A-1, Operational Report USSR No. 11 (25 copies), July 3, 1941, NO-4537. RSHA IV-A-1, Operational Report USSR No. 14 (30 copies), July 6, 1941, NO-2940.

86. RSHA IV-A-1, Operational Report USSR No. 14 (30 copies), July 6, 1941, NO-2940.

87. RSHA IV-A-1, Operational Report USSR No. 28 (36 copies), July 20, 1941, NO-2943.

88. RSHA IV-A-1, Operational Report USSR No. 24 (33 copies), July 16, 1941, NO-2938.

89. RSHA IV-A-1, Operational Report USSR No. 47 (47 copies), August 9, 1941, NO-2947.

90. *Ibid.*

Einsatzgruppen by auxiliary police. The importance of the auxiliaries should not be underestimated. Roundups by local inhabitants who spoke the local language resulted in higher percentages of Jewish dead. This fact is clearly indicated by the statistics of *Kommandos* which made use of local help. As in the case of the pogroms, the recruitment of auxiliaries was most successful in the Baltic and Ukrainian areas.

In the Baltic states the auxiliary police were organized very rapidly. The Lithuanian anti-Soviet partisans, who had been engaged in the pogroms, became the first manpower reservoir. Before disarming and disbanding the partisans, *Einsatzgruppe A* picked out "reliable" men and organized them into five police companies.[91] The men were put to work immediately in Kaunas.[92] By July 13, 150 Lithuanians were sent as reinforcements to Vilna. In that city the Lithuanians seized, held, and shot 500 Jews every day, around the clock.[93] In September a Lithuanian group attached to *Einsatzkommando* 3 swept through the districts of Raseinyai, Rokishkis, Sarasi, Perzai, and Prienai, killing all Jews found in this area.[94] (The total number of victims accounted for by *Einsatzkommando* 3 with Lithuanian help was 46,692 in less than three months.)[95]

In Latvia auxiliaries were similarly used by *Einsatzkommandos* 1*b* and 2.[96] Like the Lithuanians, the Latvians were able helpers. There was only one case of trouble: a Latvian *Kommando* was caught in Karsava by German Army men while stuffing its pockets with the belongings of dead Jews. The Latvian detachment in question had to be disbanded.[97] In the northernmost country, Estonia, the army had set up an indigenous auxiliary (*Selbstschutz*) which was taken over by *Sonderkommando* 1*a* of *Einsatzgruppe A* to do its entire dirty work of shooting a handful of Jews left behind after the Soviet retreat.[98]

In addition to the Baltic *Selbstschutz* used by *Einsatzgruppe A*, a Ukrainian militia (*Militz*) was operating in the areas of *Einsatzgruppen C* and *D*. The Ukrainian auxiliaries appeared on the scene in August, 1941,[99] and *Einsatzgruppe C* found itself compelled to make use of them because it was repeatedly diverted from its main task to fight the "partisan nuisance." Moving with speed, the *Einsatzgruppe* organized a network of local Ukrainian militias, making them partly self-financing by drawing upon Jewish money to pay their salaries.[100] The Ukrainians were used principally for dirty work – thus *Einsatzkommando* 4*a* went so far as to confine itself to the shooting of adults while commanding its Ukrainian helpers to shoot children.[101]

91. RSHA IV-A-1, Operational Report USSR No. 14 (30 copies), July 6, 1941, NO-2940.

92. *Ibid.* RSHA IV-A-1, Operational Report USSR No. 19 (32 copies), July 11, 1941, NO-2934.

93. RSHA IV-A-1, Operational Report USSR No. 21 (32 copies), July 13, 1941, NO-2937.

94. RSHA IV-A-1, Operational Report USSR No. 88 (48 copies), September 19, 1941, NO-3149.

95. *Ibid.*

96. RSHA IV-A-1, Operational Report USSR No. 24 (33 copies), July 16, 1941, NO-2938.

97. War diary, 281st Security Division, August 1, 1941, NOKW-2150.

98. RSHA IV-A-1, Operational Report USSR No. 111 (50 copies), October 12, 1941, NO-3155.

99. RSHA IV-A-1, Operational Report USSR No. 60 (48 copies), August 22, 1941, NO-2842. Report by *Sonderkommando* 11*a* (*Einsatzgruppe D*), covering August 22-September 10, 1941, NOKW-636.

100. RSHA IV-A-1, Operational Report USSR No. 80 (48 copies), September 11, 1941, NO-3154.

101. This action took place in Radomysl. RSHA IV-A-1, Operational Report USSR No. 88 (48 copies), September 19, 1941, NO-3149. For other reports of Ukrainian militia activity, see RSHA IV-A-1, Operational Re-

In the extreme south, on the Black Sea coast, *Einsatzgruppe D* discovered that the local ethnic Germans were eager volunteers during shootings. In that connection, a former chief of *Einsatzkommando* 6 (Biberstein) commented after the war: "We were actually frightened by the bloodthirstiness of these people [*Das hat uns direkt erschreckt, was die für eine Blutgier hatten*]."[102]

The *Einsatzgruppen* profited from the assistance of the military, and they made what use they could of local help. More important than the co-operation of the army and the attitude of the civilian population, however, was the role of the Jews in their own destruction. For when all was said and done, the members of the *Einsatzgruppen* were thousands. The Jews were millions.

When we consider that the Jews were not prepared to do battle with the Germans, we might well ask why they did not flee for their lives. We have mentioned repeatedly that many Jews had been evacuated and that many others fled on their own, but this fact must not obscure another, not less significant phenomenon: most Jews did not leave. They stayed. What prompted such a decision? What chained the victims to cities and towns which were already within marching reach of the approaching German Army? People do not voluntarily leave their homes for uncertain havens unless they are driven by an acute awareness of coming disaster. In the Jewish community that awareness was blunted and blocked by psychological obstacles.

The first obstacle to an apprehension of the situation was the prevailing conviction that bad things came from Russia and good things from Germany. The Jews were historically oriented away from Russia and toward Germany; not Russia but Germany had been their traditional place of refuge. During October and November, 1939, that conviction, among other things, drove thousands of Jews from Russian-occupied Poland to German-occupied Poland. The stream was not stopped until the Germans closed the border.[103] Similarly, one year later, at the time of Soviet mass deportations in the newly occupied territories, the Attaché Division of the OKH and *Amt Ausland-Abwehr* of the OKW received reports of widespread unrest among Ukrainians, Poles, and Jews alike. Almost everyone was waiting for the arrival of the German Army. When the army finally arrived, in the summer of 1941, old Jews in particular remembered that in the First World War the Germans had come as quasi-liberators. These Jews did not expect that now the Germans would come as persecutors and killers.

The following note was handed by a Jewish delegation of the little town of Kamenka in the Ukraine to a visiting German dignitary, Friedrich Theodor Prince zu Sayn und Wittgenstein, in the late summer of 1941:

> We, the old, established residents of the town of Kamenka, in the name of the Jewish population, welcome your arrival, Serene Highness and heir to your ancestors, in whose shadow the Jews, our ancestors and we, had lived in the greatest welfare. We wish you, too, long life and happiness. We hope that also in the future the Jewish population shall live on your estate in peace and quiet under your protection,

---

port USSR No. 106 (48 copies), October 7, 1941, NO-3140; Ortskommandantur Snigerevka to Korück 553 in Kherson, October 5, 1941, NOKW-1855; Ortskommandantur Kachovka to Korück 553, copy to *Feldkommandantur* 810, October 20, 1941, NOKW-1598.

102. Interrogation of Biberstein, June 29, 1947, NO-4997.

103. Office of the Chief of District (*Gouverneur*), Krakow (signed by Capt. Jordan) to Minister (*Gesandter*) von Wülisch, November 15, 1939, Wi/ID 1.210, Anlage 8.

> considering the sympathy which the Jewish population has always extended to your most distinguished family.[104]

The Prince was unmoved. The Jews, he said, were a "great evil" (*grosses Übel*) in Kamenka; and although he had no authority to impose any solutions (final or interim) upon his greeters, he instructed the local mayor to mark the Jews with a star and to employ them without pay in hard labor.[105]

Another factor which blunted Jewish alertness was the haze with which the Soviet press and radio had shrouded events across the border. The Jews of Russia were ignorant of the fate that had overtaken the Jews in Nazi Europe. Soviet information media, in pursuance of a policy of appeasement, had made it their business to keep silent about Nazi measures of destruction.[106] The consequences of that silence were disastrous.

A German intelligence official reported from White Russia on July 12, 1941, that

> the Jews are remarkably ill-informed [*auffallend schlecht unterrichtet*] about our attitude toward them. They do not know how Jews are treated in Germany, or for that matter in Warsaw, which after all is not so far away. Otherwise, their questions as to whether we in Germany make any distinctions between Jews and other citizens would be superfluous. Even if they do not think that under German administration they will have equal rights with the Russians, they believe, nevertheless, that we shall leave them in peace if they mind their own business and work diligently.[107]

104. Report by Georg Reichart, General Referent of *Geschäftsgruppe Ernährung* in the Office of the Four-Year Plan, November 15, 1941, enclosing travel report of Prince zu Sayn und Wittgenstein, August 28-September 1, 1941, Wi/ID .58.

105. Wittgenstein report, August 28-September 1, 1941, Wi/ID .58.

106. Schwarz, *The Jews in the Soviet Union*, p. 310.

We see, therefore, that a large number of Jews had stayed behind not merely because of the physical difficulties of flight but also, and perhaps primarily, because they had failed to grasp the danger of remaining in their homes. That means, of course, that precisely those Jews who did *not* flee were less aware of the disaster and less capable of dealing with it than those who did. The Jews who fell into German captivity were the vulnerable element of the Jewish community. They were the old people, the women, and the children. They were the people who at the decisive moment had failed to listen to Russian warnings and who were now ready to listen to German reassurances. The remaining Jews were, in short, physically and psychologically immobilized.

The mobile killing units soon grasped the Jewish weakness; they discovered quickly that one of their greatest problems, the seizure of the victims, had an easy solution. We have noted that in several places the *Einsatzgruppen* had enlisted the army's support in combing out prospective victims, and, so far as possible, *Einsatzgruppen* commanders had relied also upon the local population to discover Jewish residences and hide-outs. Now, however, the *Kommandos* had found their most efficient helpers: the Jews themselves. In order to draw together and assemble large numbers of Jews, the killers had only to "fool" the victims by means of simple ruses.

The first experiment with ruses was made in Vinnitsa, where a search for members of the Jewish intelligentsia had produced meager results. The commander of *Einsatzkommando 4b* called for "the most prominent rabbi in town" and told him to collect within

107. *Reichskommissar Ostland* to *Generalkommissar* White Russia, August 4, 1941, enclosing report by Sonderführer Schröter, Occ E 3a-2.

twenty-four hours the most intelligent Jews for "registration work." When the result still did not satisfy the *Einsatzkommando,* the commander sent the group back to town with instructions to bring more Jews. He repeated this stunt once more before deciding that he had a sufficient number of Jews to shoot.[108] In Kiev *Einsatzkommando 4a* followed the much simpler expedient of using wall posters to assemble the Jews for "resettlement."[109] Variations of the registration and resettlement legends were used repeatedly throughout the occupied territories.[110]

The psychological traps were effective not only for the seizure of Jews within the cities; the *Einsatzgruppen* actually managed to draw back large numbers of Jews who had already fled from the cities in anticipation of a disaster. We have seen that the Jews who had taken to the roads, the villages, and the fields had great difficulty in subsisting there because the German Army was picking up stray Jews and the population refused to shelter them. The *Einsatzgruppen* took advantage of this situation by instituting the simplest ruse of all: they did nothing. The inactivity of the Security Police was sufficient to dispel the rumors which had set the exodus in motion. Within a short time the Jews flocked into town. They were caught in the dragnet and killed.[111]

The Killing Operations and Their Repercussions

During the first sweep the mobile killing units reported approximately one hundred thousand victims a month, and by now we can understand how it was possible to seize so many people in the course of a mobile operation. A simple strategy, combined with a great deal of army assistance, native collaboration, and Jewish gullibility, had transformed the occupied Soviet cities into a series of natural traps. Now, however, we have to find out what happened after the Jews were caught; for, with the seizure of the victims, the administrative problems of the *Einsatzgruppen* were not entirely solved, while the psychological difficulties were only just beginning.

Depending upon the size of a Jewish community under attack, the strength of a killing party ranged from about four men to a full *Einsatzkommando,* supplemented by units of the Order Police or the army. (The Higer SS and Police Leaders could assign larger formations to an operation.) In almost every major action the victims outnumbered their captors 10 to 1, 20 to 1, or even 50 to 1; but the Jews could never turn their numbers into an ad-

108. RSHA IV-A-1, Operational Report USSR No. 47 (47 copies), August 9, 1941, NO-2947.

109. RSHA IV-A-1, Operational Report USSR No. 128 (55 copies), November 3, 1941, NO-3157. The relative success of the Kiev operation is difficult to gauge. Before the action started, *Einsatzgruppe C* expected to kill 50,000 Jews. RSHA IV-A-1, Operational Report USSR No. 97 (48 copies), September 28, 1941, NO-3145. After reporting 33,771 Jewish dead, *Einsatzgruppe C* claimed that only 5–6,000 Jews had been expected to respond. RSHA IV-A-1, Operational Report USSR No. 128, NO-3145. After the war *Einsatzkommando 4a* Commander Blobel declared that he had shot in Kiev no more than about 16,000 Jews. Affidavit by Paul Blobel, June 6, 1947, NO-3824.

110. For example, *Ortskommandantur* I/287 in Feodosiya to Korück 553, November 16, 1941, NOKW-1631. Also, report by Oberst Erwin Stolze, Deputy to Generalmajor Lahousen (OKW/Abwehr II), October 23, 1941, NOKW-3147. Stolze report verified in affidavit by Lahousen, March 17, 1948, NOKW-3230.

111. RSHA IV-A-1, Operational Report USSR No. 127 (55 copies), October 31, 1941, NO-4136. RSHA IV-A-1, Operational Report USSR No. 128 (55 copies), November 3, 1941, NO-3157. See also statement by Higher SS and Police Leader Center von dem Bach, in *Aufbau* (New York), September 6, 1946, p. 40.

vantage. The killers were well armed, they knew what to do, and they worked swiftly. The victims were unarmed, bewildered, and followed orders.

The Germans were able to work quickly and efficiently because the killing operation was standardized. In every city the same procedure was followed — with minor variations. The site of the shooting was usually outside of town, at a grave. Some of the graves were deepened anti-tank ditches or shell craters; others were specially dug.[112] The Jews were taken in batches (men first) from the collecting point to the ditch.[113] The killing site was supposed to be closed off to all outsiders; but this was not always possible, and, as we shall see, a lot of trouble resulted from that fact. Before their death the victims handed their valuables to the leader of the killing party. In the winter they removed their overcoats; in warmer weather they had to take off all outer garments and, in some cases, underwear as well.[114]

From this point on, the procedure varied somewhat. Some *Einsatzkommandos* lined up the victims in front of the ditch and shot them with submachine guns or other small arms in the back of the neck. The mortally wounded Jews toppled into their graves.[115] Some commanders disliked this method, which possibly reminded them of the Russian NKVD. Blobel, the commander of *Einsatzkommando 4a*, stated that he personally declined to use *Genickschussspezialisten* (specialists in shooting in the neck).[116] Ohlendorf, too, spurned the technique because he wanted to avoid "personal responsibility."[117] Blobel (*4a*), Ohlendorf (*D*), and Hänsch (*4b*) are known to have employed massed fire from a considerable distance.[118] There was, however, still another procedure which combined efficiency with the impersonal element. This system has been referred to as the "sardine method" (*Ölsardinenmanier*).[119] It was carried out as follows: The first batch had to lie down on the bottom of the grave. They were killed by cross-fire from above. The next batch had to lie down on top of the corpses, heads facing the feet of the dead. After five or six layers, the grave was closed.[120]

It is significant that the Jews allowed themselves to be shot without resistance — in all the reports of the *Einsatzgruppen* there are few references to "incidents."[121] The killing units never lost a man during a shooting operation. All their casualties were suffered during anti-partisan fighting, skirmishes on

112. Affidavit by Ohlendorf, November 5, 1945, PS-2620. Report by Hauptfeldwebel Sönnecken (received by Generalmajor Lahousen), October 24, 1941, PS-3047.

113. Statement by Oberleutnant Bingel (36th Division), undated, NO-5301. Affidavit by Wilhelm Förster (driver, *Einsatzgruppe B*), October 23, 1947, NO-5520.

114. Affidavit by Ohlendorf, November 5, 1945, PS-2620. Statement by Bingel, undated, NO-5301.

115. Interrogation of Ernst Biberstein (Commander, *Einsatzkommando* 6), June 29, 1947, NO-4997. Affidavit by Albert Hartl, October 9, 1947, NO-5384. Hartl (RSHA IV-B) watched shootings on an inspection trip.

116. Affidavit by Paul Blobel, June 6, 1947, NO-3824.

117. Affidavit by Ohlendorf, November 5, 1945, PS-2620.

118. Affidavit by Blobel, June 6, 1947, NO-3824. Affidavit by Ohlendorf, November 5, 1945, PS-2620. Statement by Walter Haensch, July 21, 1947, NO-4567.

119. The term was used by Generalmajor Lahousen (Chief, OKW/*Abwehr* II) after an inspection trip in the area of Army Group Center. See his report of November 1, 1941, NOKW-3146.

120. Affidavit by Alfred Metzner (civil employee who volunteered for shootings), September 18, 1947, NO-5558.

121. *Einsatzgruppe* A reported that, on the way to a killing site near Zagore, the Jews had attacked the guards. However, the Jews had quickly been brought under control. RSHA IV-A-1, Operational Report USSR No. 155, January 14, 1942, NO-3279.

the front, or as a result of sickness or accident. *Einsatzgruppe C* had to remark:

> Strange is the calmness with which the delinquents allow themselves to be shot, and that goes for non-Jews as well as Jews. Their fear of death appears to have been blunted by a kind of indifference [*Abstumpfung*] which has been created in the course of twenty years of Soviet rule.[122]

This comment was made in September, 1941. It turned out in later years that the non-Jewish "delinquents" could not be shot so easily after all, but the Jews remained paralyzed after their first brush with death and in spite of advance knowledge of their fate.

Although the Jews were being killed smoothly, the *Einsatzgruppen* commanders were worried about possible repercussions on the population, the army, and their own personnel. Repercussions are problems which arise or continue *after* the completion of an action. Like pebbles thrown into quiet ponds, these aftereffects caused ripples which travel far and wide from the scene of the event.

To minimize the shock of the shootings at their source, the *Einsatzgruppen* commanders, their deputies, and their adjutants frequently visited the killing sites. Ohlendorf tells us that he inspected shootings in order to be certain that they were military in character and "humane under the circumstances."[123] Ohlendorf's adjutant Schubert describes the reasons for the inspections more deliberately. Schubert supervised the killing operation in Simferopol, the capital of the Crimea. He watched the loading on trucks to make sure that the non-Jewish population was not disturbed. Furthermore, he kept an eye on the guards to prevent them from beating the victims. He worried about unauthorized traffic at the killing site and ordered that all outsiders be detoured. During the collection of valuables, he saw to it that the Order Police and *Waffen-SS* did not pocket anything. Finally, he convinced himself that the victims were shot humanely, "since, in the event of other killing methods, the psychic burden [*seelische Belastung*] would have been too great for the execution *Kommando*."[124] A former sergeant tells us of one more reason – an important one – for the inspections. When Ohlendorf arrived at the killing site of *Sonderkommando 10b* one time, he complained to the commander, Persterer, about the manner of burial. Ohlendorf ordered that the victims be covered a little better (*dass diese Leute besser zugeschaufelt werden*).[125]

In spite of the precautions taken by *Einsatzgruppen* commanders, the emergence of repercussions was inevitable. The inhabitants at first seemed to be unworried and carefree. Commanders reported that the population "understood" the shootings and judged them "positively."[126] In one town, Chmiolnik, the inhabitants were reported to have gone to church in order to thank God for their "deliverance" from Jewry.[127] However, the idyllic picture of a population completely at ease and even thankful for the elimination of the Jews soon began to fade away.

In February, 1942, Heydrich reported to the defense commissars in the army

122. RSHA IV-A-1, Operational Report USSR No. 81 (48 copies), September 12, 1941, NO-3154.

123. Affidavit by Ohlendorf, April 2, 1947, NO-2856.

124. Affidavit by Heinz Hermann Schubert, February 24, 1947, NO-3055.

125. Affidavit by Josef Guggenberger (*Hauptscharführer, Sonderkommando 10b*), September 9, 1947, NO-4959.

126. RSHA IV-A-1, Operational Report USSR No. 81 (48 copies), September 12, 1941, NO-3154.

127. RSHA IV-A-1, Operational Report USSR No. 86 (48 copies), September 17, 1941, NO-3151.

districts that the shootings were now being carried out in such a manner that the population hardly noticed them. The inhabitants, and even the surviving Jews, had frequently been left with the impression that the victims had only been resettled.[128] Already, the Security Police thought it wise to hide their killings, for it could no longer trust a population which was itself chafing under the increasing harshness of German rule and which was already fearful for its own security and safety.

A German eyewitness (in Borisov, White Russia) who knew Russian spoke to a number of local residents before the mass shooting of the Jews was to start in the town. His Russian landlord told him: "Let them perish; they did us a lot of harm!" But on the following morning the German heard comments like these: "Who ordered such a thing? How is it possible to kill 6500 Jews all at once? Now it is the turn of the Jews; when will it be ours? What have these poor Jews done? All they did was work! The really guilty ones are surely in safety!"[129]

The following report was sent by an army officer stationed in the Crimea to the Economy-Armament Office (OKW/Wi Rü) in Berlin:

> In the present situation of unrest the most nonsensical rumors – the bulk of which are started by partisans and agents – find willing ears. Thus, a few days ago, a rumor circulated that the Germans were intending to do away [*beseitigen*] with all men and women over fifty. The *Ortskommandantur* [in Simferopol] and other German offices were mobbed with questions about the veracity of the report. In view of the fact that the total "resettlement" of the Jewish population and the liquidation of an insane asylum with about 600 inmates cannot be hidden forever, such rumors are bound to gain in credibility among the inhabitants.[130]

Gradually, then, the local non-Jewish witnesses of the destruction process perceived the true nature of the German racial ladder. The lowest rung was already afire, and they were but one step above it.

The killing operations had repercussions not only for the population but also for the military. One of these consequences was an undercurrent of criticism in the army's ranks. On October 10, 1941, Feldmarschall Reichenau, commander of the Sixth Army, sent an order to the troops in which he exhorted them to be a little harsher in their treatment of partisans. He explained that this was not an ordinary war and recited all the dangers of the Jewish-Bolshevist system to German culture. "Therefore," he continued, "the soldier must have full understanding of the necessity for harsh but just countermeasures [*Sühne*] against Jewish subhumanity." These measures, Reichenau pointed out, had the added purpose of frustrating revolts behind the back of the fighting troops, for it had been proved again and again that the uprisings were always being instigated by Jews.[131] Hitler read this order and found that it was "excellent."[132] Feldmarschall von Rundstedt, commander of the Southern Army Group, sent copies to the Eleventh and Seventeenth Armies, as well as to the First Panzer Army, for distribution.[133] Von Manstein, the Eleventh Army commander, elaborated on the order, explaining that

128. RSHA IV-A-1 (signed Heydrich) to *Einsatzgruppen*, Higher SS and Police Leaders, and defense commissars in Army Districts II, VIII, XVII, XX, XXI, February 27, 1942, enclosing Activity Report No. 9 of the *Einsatzgruppen*, covering January 1942, PS-3876.

129. From a report by Hauptfeldwebel Sönnecken, received by Generalmajor Lahousen, October 24, 1941, PS-3047.

130. 11th Army/IV Wi (Oberstleutnant Oswald) via *Wirtschaftsstab Ost* to OKW/Wi Rü, March 31, 1942, Wi/ID 2.512.

131. Order by Feldmarschall Reichenau, October 10, 1941, D-411.

132. Order by Generalquartiermeister Wagner, October 28, 1941, D-411.

the Jew was the liaison man (*Mittelsmann*) between the Red Army on the front and the enemy in the rear.[134]

A second problem, more serious than lack of "understanding" of the killings, was soon discovered with dismay by unit commanders: Among the troops the shootings had become a sensation. Many times soldiers crowded around the killing sites and watched the show; moreover, the onlookers did not confine themselves to observation, but took pictures, wrote letters, and talked. With rapidity, the news spread in the occupied territories, and gradually it seeped into Germany.

To the army this was an embarrassing business. In Kiev a group of foreign journalists who had been invited to view the "Bolshevist destruction" of the city quickly looked up the representative of the civil administration with Army Group Center, Hauptmann Koch, and questioned him about the shootings. When Koch denied everything, the journalists told him that they had pretty exact information about these matters anyway.[135]

The army attempted to take various countermeasures. Initially, several officers blamed the *Einsatzgruppen* for performing the shootings where everybody could see them. One such protest was sent by the deputy commander of Army District IX in Kassel (Schirwindt) to Generaloberst Fromm, the Chief of the Replacement Army. In his protest the army district official dealt with the rumors about the "mass executions" in Russia. Schirwindt pointed out that he had considered these rumors to be vast exaggerations (*weit übertrieben*) until he had received the following report from a subordinate, Major Rösler, who had been an eyewitness.

Rösler commanded the 528th Infantry Regiment in Zhitomir. One day while he was sitting in his headquarters and minding his own business, he suddenly heard rifle volleys followed by pistol shots. Accompanied by two officers, he decided to find out what was happening (*dieser Erscheinung nachzugehen*). The three were not alone. From all directions, soldiers and civilians were running toward a railroad embankment. Rösler, too, climbed the embankment. What he saw there was "so brutally base that those who approached unprepared were shaken and nauseated [*ein Bild dessen grausame Abscheulichkeit auf den unvorbereitet Herantretenden erschütternd und abschreckend wirkte*]."

He was standing over a ditch with a mountain of earth on one side, and the wall of the ditch was splattered with blood. Policemen were standing around with bloodstained uniforms; soldiers were congregrating in groups (some of them in bathing shorts); and civilians were watching with wives and children. Rösler stepped closer and peeked into the grave. Among the corpses he saw an old man with a white beard and a cane on his arm. Since the man was still breathing, Rösler approached a policeman and asked him to kill the man "for good" (*endgültig zu töten*). The policeman replied in the manner of someone who does not need advice: "This one has already got something seven times into his —— he is going to perish by himself [*Dem habe ich schon 7 mal was in den —— gejagt, der krepiert schon von alleine*]." In conclusion, Rösler stated that he had already seen quite a few

133. Rundstedt to 11th Army, 17th Army, and 1st Panzer Army, and to Commander of Rear Army Group South, October 17, 1941, NOKW-309.

134. Order by von Manstein, November 20, 1941, PS-4064.

135. Report by Oberst Erwin Stolze (Deputy to Lahousen), October 23, 1941, NOKW-3147. The author of the report is identified in the Lahousen affidavit of March 17, 1948, NOKW-3230. For Koch's position, see his report of October 5, 1941, PS-53.

unpleasant things in his life but that mass slaughter in public, as if on an open-air stage, was something else again. It was against German customs, upbringing, etc.[136] Not once in his account did Rösler mention Jews.

Complaints in the field were not lacking either. A local battalion commander at Genicke protested (complete with sketch map) that a killing operation had been carried out near the city limit, that troops and civilians alike had become involuntary witnesses of the shooting, and that they had also heard the "whining" of the doomed. The SS officer in charge replied that he had done the job with only three men, that the nearest house was 500 to 800 yards from the spot, that military personnel had insisted on watching the operation, and that he could not have chased them away.[137]

As late as May 8, 1942, the military government officers of Rear Army Group Area South met in conference and resolved to persuade the killing units, in a nice way (*im Wege guten Einvernehmens*), to conduct their shootings "whenever possible" not during the day but at night – except, of course, for those "executions" which were necessary in order to "frighten" the population (*die aus Abschreckungsgründen notwendig sind*).[138]

However, in spite of the occasional attempts to regulate the location or even the time of the shootings, the army soon realized that it could not remove the killing sites from the reach of "involuntary" (let alone "voluntary") witnesses. The only other way to stop the entertainment (and the flow of rumors resulting from it) was to conduct an educational campaign among the soldiers. The army then tried that method also.

Even during the first weeks of the war, soldiers of the Eleventh Army watched Roumanian shootings at Balti.[139] Since the killers were Roumanians, the chief of staff of the Eleventh Army, Wöhler, allowed himself the use of some blunt language. Without making direct references to the incident, he wrote:

> In view of a special case, the following has to be pointed out explicitly.
>
> Because of the eastern European conception of human life, German soldiers may become witnesses of events (such as mass executions, the murder of civilians, Jews, and others) which they cannot prevent at this time but which violate German feelings of honor most deeply.
>
> To every normal person it is a matter of course that he does not take photographs of such disgusting excesses or report about them when he writes home. The distribution of photographs and the spreading of reports about such events will be regarded as a subversion of decency and discipline in the army and will be punished strictly. All pictures, negatives, and reports of such excesses are to be collected and are to be sent with a notation listing the name of the owner to the Ic/AO of the army.
>
> To gaze at such procedures curiously [*ein neugieriges Begaffen solcher Vorgänge*] is beneath the dignity of the German soldier.[140]

136. Deputy Commander of *Wehrkreis* IX (signed Schirwindt) to Chief of Replacement Army (Fromm), January 17, 1942, enclosing Rösler report, dated January 3, 1942, USSR-293(1).

137. See the following correspondence in document NOKW-3453: 11th Army Ic/AO (*Abwehr* II) to *Einsatzgruppe D*, copy to 22nd Infantry Division Ic, October 6, 1941; *Sonderkommando* 10*a*/*Teilkommando* (signed UStuf. Spiekermann) to *Sonderkommando* 10*a*, October 8, 1941; *Sonderkommando* 10*a* to *Einsatzgruppe D*, copy to Stubaf. Gmeiner (liaison officer of the *Einsatzgruppe* with the army), October 8, 1941; 3rd Battalion of 65th Regiment Ic (in 22nd Division) to regiment, October 12, 1941.

138. Summary of military government conference in Kremenchug (Oberkriegsverwaltungsrat Freiherr von Wrangel presiding), May 8, 1942, NOKW-3097.

139. Testimony by General Wöhler, Case No. 12, tr. pp. 5790, 5811–12, 5838–39.

Sensationalism and rumor-spreading did not exhaust the army's troubles; the operations of the mobile killing units had created another problem, even more far-reaching and disturbing in its implications. It happened that Jews were killed by military personnel who acted *without* orders or directives. Sometimes soldiers offered their help to the killing parties and joined in the shooting of the victims. Occasionally, troops participated in pogroms, and once in a while members of the German Army staged killing operations of their own. We have pointed out that the army had helped the mobile killing units a great deal. Why, then, was the military leadership concerned with these individual actions?

The army had several administrative reasons for anxiety. As a matter of status, the idea that soldiers were doing police work was not very appealing. Pogroms were the nightmare of military government experts, and unorganized killings on the roads and in occupied towns were dangerous, if only because of the possibility of mistakes or accidents. But in addition to these considerations, there was an over-all objection which was rooted in the whole psychology of the destruction process. The killing of the Jews was regarded as historical necessity. The soldier had to "understand" this. If for any reason he was instructed to help the SS and Police in their task, he was expected to obey orders. However, if he killed a Jew spontaneously, voluntarily, or without instruction, merely because he *wanted* to kill, then he had committed an abnormal act, worthy perhaps of an "eastern European" (such as a Roumanian) but dangerous to the discipline and prestige of the German Army. Herein lay the crucial difference between the man who "overcame" himself to kill and one who wantonly committed atrocities. The former was regarded as a good soldier and a true Nazi; the latter was a person without self-control who would be a danger to his community after his return home. This philosophy was reflected in all orders which attempted to deal with the problem of "excesses."

On August 2, 1941, the XXX Corps (in the Eleventh Army) distributed an order, down to companies, which read as follows:

> *Participation by soldiers in actions against Jews and Communists.*
>
> The fanatical will of members of the Communist Party and of the Jews, to stem the advance of the German Army at any price, has to be broken under all circumstances. In the interest of security in the Rear Army Area it is therefore necessary to take drastic measures [*dass scharf durchgegriffen wird*]. This is the task of the *Sonderkommandos.* Unfortunately, however, military personnel have participated in one such action [*in unerfreulicher Weise beteiligt*]. Therefore, I order for the future:
>
> Only those soldiers may take part in such actions as have specifically been ordered to do so. Furthermore, I forbid any member of this unit to participate as a spectator. Insofar as military personnel are detailed to these actions [*Aktionen*], they have to be commanded by an officer. The officer has to see to it that there are no unpleasant excesses by the troops [*dass jede uner-*

140. Order by Wöhler, July 22, 1941, NOKW-2523. An order by the *Quartiermeister* of the 6th Army similarly directed the confisation of photographs and specified, in addition, that complete co-operation was to be given to killing units in their efforts to keep spectators out. Order by 6th Army *Quartiermeister,* August 10, 1941, NOKW-1654. Somewhat later, on November 12, 1941, Heydrich forbade his own men to take pictures. "Official" photographs were to be sent undeveloped to the RSHA IV-A-1 as secret Reich matter (*Geheime Reichssache*). Heydrich also requested the Order Police commands to hunt up photographs which might have been circulating in their areas. Heydrich to *Befehlshaber* and *Kommandeure der Orpo,* April 16, 1942, USSR-297(1).

freuliche Auschreitung seitens der Truppe unterbleibt].[141]

An order by the commander of Rear Army Group Area South pointed out:

> The number of transgressions by military personnel against the civilian population is increasing. . . . It has also happened lately that soldiers and even officers independently undertook shootings of Jews, or that they participated in such shootings.[142]

After an explanation that "executive measures" were in the exclusive province of the SS and Police, the order continued:

> The army itself finishes on the spot [*erledigt auf der Stelle*] only those local inhabitants who have committed —or are suspected of having committed —hostile acts, and that is to be done only upon order of an officer. Moreover, collective measures [*Kollektivmassnahmem*] may be taken only if authorized by at least a battalion commander. Any kind of doubt about this question is inadmissible. Every unauthorized shooting of local inhabitants, including Jews, by individual soldiers, as well as every participation in executive measures of the SS and Police, is disobedience and therefore to be punished by disciplinary means, or — if necessary — by courts martial.

Clearly, the killing operations seriously affected the local inhabitants and the army. Among the population the operations produced a submerged, deep-seated anxiety. In the army they brought into the open an uncomfortably large number of soldiers who delighted in death as spectators or as perpetrators. The third group to be confronted with major psychological problems was the mobile killing personnel themselves. (In discussing the problem of the killers, we shall treat the officers and the enlisted men separately.)

The leaders of the *Einsatzgruppen* and *Einsatzkommandos* were bureaucrats — men who were accustomed to desk work. In the East it was their job to supervise and report about the operations. This was *not* mere desk work. We have already noted that "inspections" took the *Einsatzgruppen* leaders and their staffs to the killing sites. In *Einsatzgruppe C everybody* had to watch shootings; a staff member, Karl Hennicke, tells us that he had no choice about the matter:

> I myself attended executions only as a witness, in order not to lay myself open to charges of cowardice. . . . Dr. Rasch [*Einsatzgruppe* commander] insisted on principle that all officers and noncommissioned officers of the *Kommando* participate in the executions. It was impossible to stay away from them, lest one be called to account.[143]

The *Einsatzgruppe* officer had to "overcome" himself. He had to be in this business completely, not as a reporter but as a participant, not as a possible future accuser but as one who would have to share the fate of those who did this work. One of the officers who one day had been commanded to watch the shootings suffered the most horrible dreams (*Angstträume fürchterlichster Art*) during the following night.[144] Even the Higher SS and Police Leader Central Russia, Obergruppenführer von dem Bach-Zelewski, was

141. Order by XXX Corps/Ic, August 2, 1941, NOKW-2963. Generaloberst von Salmuth commanded the XXX Corps. Generaloberst von Schobert commanded the 11th Army. For similar directives, see also the following: Order by 6th Army/Qu, August 10, 1941, NOKW-1654; Army Group South Ic/AO (signed by von Rundstedt) to armies belonging to the army group, and to Army Group Read Area Command, September 24, 1941, NOKW-541.

142. Order by commander of Army Group Rear Area South (signed Major Geissler), September 1, 1941, NOKW-2594.

143. Affidavit by Karl Hennicke (SD-III officer in the staff of the *Einsatzgruppe*), September 4, 1947, NO-4999.

144. Report by Oberst Erwin Stolze, October 23, 1941, NO-3147.

brought into a hospital with serious stomach and intestinal ailments. He did not respond to treatment, and Himmler dispatched the top physician of the SS, Grawitz, to the bedside of his favorite general. Grawitz reported that von dem Bach was suffering from hallucinations in which he relived his experiences in the East, particularly the shooting of Jews.[145]

The leaders of the mobile killing units attempted to cope systematically with the psychological effects of the killing operations. Even while they directed the shooting, they began to repress as well as to justify their activities. The repressive mechanism is quite noticeable in the choice of language for reports of individual killing actions: the reporters were trying to avoid the use of direct expressions such as "to kill" or "murder"; instead, the commanders employed terms which tended either to justify the killings or to obscure them altogether. The following is a representative list:

hingerichtet: put to death, executed
exekutiert: executed
ausgemerzt: exterminated
liquidiert: liquidated
Liquidierungszahl: liquidation number
Liquidierung des Judentums: liquidation of Jewry
erledigt: finished [off]
Aktionen: actions
Sonderaktionen: special actions
Sonderbehandlung: special treatment
sonderbehandelt: specially treated
der Sonderbehandlung unterzogen: subjected to special treatment
Säuberung: cleansing
Grossäuberungsaktionen: major cleaning actions
Ausschaltung: elimination
Aussiedlung: resettlement
Vollzugstätigkeit: execution activity
Exekutivmassnahme: executive measure
entsprechend behandelt: treated appropriately
der Sondermassnahme zugeführt: conveyed to special measure
sicherheitspolizeiliche Massnahmen: security police measures
sicherheitspolizeilich durchgearbeitet: worked over in security police manner
Lösung der Judenfrage: solution of the Jewish question
Bereinigung der Judenfrage: cleaning up of the Jewish question
judenfrei gemacht: [area] made free of Jews

Next to terminology which was designed to convey the notion that the killing operations were only an ordinary bureaucratic process within the framework of police activity, we find, in logical but not psychological contradiction, that the commanders of the *Einsatzgruppen* constructed various justifications for the killings. The significance of these rationalizations will be readily apparent once we consider that the *Einsatzgruppen* did not have to give any reasons to Heydrich; they had to give reasons only to themselves. Generally speaking, we find in the reports one over-all justification for the killings: the Jewish danger. This fiction was used again and again, in many variations.

A *Kommando* of the BdS *Generalgouvernement* reported that it had killed 4500 Jews in Pinsk because a member of the local militia had been fired on by Jews and another militia man had been found dead.[146] In Balti the Jews were killed on the ground that they were guilty of "attacks" on German troops.[147] In Stara Konstantinov the 1st SS Brigade shot 439 Jews because the victims had shown an "unco-operative" attitude toward the Wehrmacht.[148] In Mogilev the Jews

145. Grawitz to Himmler, March 4, 1942, NO-600.

146. RSHA IV-A-1, Operational Report USSR No. 58, August 20, 1941, NO-2846.

147. RSHA IV-A-1, Operational Report USSR No. 37 (45 copies), July 29, 1941, NO-2952.

148. RSHA IV-A-1, Operational Report USSR No. 59, August 21, 1941, NO-2847.

were accused of attempting to sabotage their own "resettlement."[149] In Novo Ukrainka there were Jewish "encroachments" (*Übergriffe*).[150] In Kiev the Jews were suspected of having caused the great fire.[151] In Minsk about 2500 Jews were shot because they were spreading "rumors."[152] In the area of *Einsatzgruppe A* Jewish propaganda was the justification. "Since this Jewish propaganda activity was especially heavy in Lithuania," read the report, "the number of persons liquidated in this area by *Einsatzkommando* 3 has risen to 75,000."[153] The following reason was given for a killing operation in Ananiev: "Since the Jews of Ananiev had threatened the ethnic German residents with a blood bath just as soon as the German Army should withdraw, the Security Police conducted a roundup and, on August 28, 1941, shot about 300 Jews and Jewesses."[154] On one occasion *Einsatzgruppe B* substituted for rumor-spreading, propaganda, and threats the vague but all-inclusive accusation of a "spirit of opposition" (*Oppositionsgeist*).[155] At least one *Einsatzgruppe* invoked the danger theory without citing any Jewish resistance activity at all. When *Einsatzgruppe D* had killed all Jews in the Crimea, it merely enclosed in its summary report a learned article about the pervasive influence which Jewry had exercised on the peninsula before the war.[156]

These charges of dangerous Jewish attitudes and activities were sometimes supplemented with references to the hazard which Jews presented as carriers of sickness. The Jewish quarters in Nevel and Yanovichi were doomed because they were filled with epidemics.[157] In Vitebsk the threat of an epidemic (*höchste Seuchengefahr*) sufficed.[158] The following explanation was given for the shootings in Radomysl: Many Jews from surrounding areas had flocked into the city. This led to an overcrowding of Jewish apartments – on the average, fifteen persons lived in one room. Hygienic conditions had become intolerable. Every day several corpses of Jews had to be removed from these houses. Supplying food for Jewish adults as well as for Jewish children had become "impracticable." Consequently, there was an ever increasing danger of epidemics. To put an end to these conditions, *Sonderkommando 4a* finally shot 1700 Jews.[159]

It should be emphasized that psychological justifications were an essential part of the killing operations. If a proposed action could *not* be justified, it did not take place. Needless to say, the supply of reasons never ran out for anti-Jewish measures. However, just once, explanations did exhaust themselves with respect to the killings of insane people. *Einsatzgruppe A* had

149. RSHA IV-A-1, Operational Report USSR No. 124 (48 copies), October 25, 1941, NO-3160.

150. RSHA IV-A-1, Operational Report USSR No. 60 (48 copies), August 22, 1941, NO-2842.

151. RSHA IV-A-1, Operational Report USSR No. 97 (48 copies), September 28, 1941, NO-3145.

152. RSHA IV-A-1, Operational Report USSR No. 92, September 23, 1941, NO-3143.

153. RSHA IV-A-1, Operational Report USSR No. 94 (48 copies), September 25, 1941, NO-3146.

154. *Ortskommandantur Ananiev*/Staff of 836th *Landesschützen* Battalion to Korück 553 in Beresovka, September 3, 1941, NOKW-1702.

155. RSHA IV-A-1, Operational Report USSR No. 124 (48 copies), October 25, 1941, NO-3160.

156. OStubaf. Seibert (*Einsatzgruppe D*) to 11th Army Ic, April 16, 1942, NOKW-628.

157. RSHA IV-A-1, Operational Report USSR No. 92, September 23, 1941, NO-3143.

158. RSHA IV-A-1, Operational Report USSR No. 124 (48 copies), October 25, 1941, NO-3160.

159. RSHA IV-A-1, Operational Report USSR No. 88 (48 copies), September 19, 1941, (NO-3149). It was in this action that the children were shot by Ukrainian militia men.

killed 748 insane persons in Lithuania and northern Russia because these "lunatics" had no guards, nurses, or food. They were a "danger" to security. But when the army requested the *Einsatzgruppe* to "clean out" other institutions which were needed as billets, the *Einsatzgruppe* suddenly refused. No interest of the Security Police required such action; consequently, the army was told to do the dirty job itself.[160]

Like the leaders of the mobile killing units, the enlisted personnel had been recruited on a jurisdictional basis. While they had all had some ideological training, they had not volunteered to shoot Jews. Most of these men had drifted into the killing units simply because they were not fit for front-line duty (*nicht dienstverpflichtet*).[161] They were older men, not teen-agers. Many had already assumed the responsibility of caring for a family; they were not irresponsible adolescents.

It is hard to say what happened to these men as a result of the shootings. For many, undoubtedly, the task became just another job, to be done correctly and mechanically, i.e., the men made some sort of "adjustment" to the situation. However, every once in a while a man did have a nervous breakdown,[162] and in several units the use of alcohol became routine.[163] At the same time, indoctrination was continued, and occasionally commanders made speeches before major operations.[164]

Once Himmler himself visited Minsk. He asked *Einsatzgruppe B* Commander Nebe to shoot a batch of a hundred people, so that he could see what one of these "liquidations" really looked like. Nebe obliged. All except two of the victims were men. Himmler spotted in the group a youth of about twenty who had blue eyes and blond hair. Just before the firing was to begin, Himmler walked up to the doomed man and put a few questions to him.

> Are you a Jew?
> Yes.
> Are both of your parents Jews?
> Yes.
> Do you have any ancestors who were not Jews?
> No.
> Then I can't help you!

As the firing started, Himmler was even more nervous. During every volley he looked to the ground. When the two women could not die, Himmler yelled to the police sergeant not to torture them.

When the shooting was over, Himmler and a fellow spectator engaged in conversation. The other witness was Obergruppenführer von dem Bach-Zelewski, the same man who was later delivered to a hospital. Von dem Bach addressed Himmler:

> *Reichsführer*, those were only a hundred.
> What do you mean by that?
> Look at the eyes of the men in this *Kommando*, how deeply shaken they are! These men are finished [*fertig*] for the rest of their lives. What kind of followers are we training here? Either neurotics or savages!

Himmler was visibly moved and decided to make a speech to all who were assembled there. He pointed out that the *Einsatzgruppen* were called upon to fulfil a repulsive (*widerliche*) duty. He would not like it if Germans did such a thing gladly. But their conscience was in no way impaired, for they were soldiers who had to carry out every order unconditionally. He

160. Stahlecker to Himmler, October 15, 1941, L-180.

161. Affidavit by Ohlendorf, April 24, 1947, NO-2890.

162. Affidavit by Hauptscharführer Robert Barth (*Einsatzgruppe D*), September 12, 1947, NO-4992.

163. Report by Generalmajor Lahousen, November 1, 1941, NOKW-3146.

164. Affidavit by Barth, September 12, 1947, NO-4992.

alone had responsibility before God and Hitler for everything that was happening. They had undoubtedly noticed that he hated this bloody business (*dass ihm das blutige Handwerk zuwider wäre*) and that he had been aroused to the depth of his soul. But he too was obeying the highest law by doing his duty, and he was acting from a deep understanding of the necessity for this operation.

Himmler told the men to look at nature. There was combat everywhere, not only among men but also in the world of animals and plants. Whoever was too tired to fight must go under (*zugrunde gehen*). The most primitive man says that the horse is good and the bedbug is bad, or wheat is good and the thistle is bad. The human being consequently designates what is useful to him as good and what is harmful as bad. Didn't bedbugs and rats have a life purpose also? Yes, but this has never meant that man could not defend himself against vermin.

After the speech Himmler, Nebe, von dem Bach, and the chief of Himmler's Personal Staff, Wolff, inspected an insane asylum. Himmler ordered Nebe to end the suffering of these people as soon as possible. At the same time Himmler asked Nebe "to turn over in his mind" various other killing methods more humane than shooting. Nebe asked for permission to try out dynamite on the mentally sick people. Von dem Bach and Wolff protested that the sick people after all were not guinea pigs, but Himmler decided in favor of the attempt. Much later, Nebe confided to von dem Bach that the dynamite had been tried on the inmates with woeful results.[165]

At last, however, the RSHA technical unit (II-D) went to work in order to devise a different killing method, and the result of that experimentation was the gas van.[166] The vans were delivered to the *Einsatzgruppen* for use against women and children.[167] Soon, problems developed also with the vans. The apparatus produced suffocation, and the bodies, with distorted faces and covered with excrement, had to be unloaded by the men. To spare the SS personnel from nausea, the gas officer pleaded with II-D to let Jews do this work.[168] Still the vans remained unpopular with men and commanders alike.[169] The commander of *Einsatzgruppe B,* Brigadeführer Naumann (Nebe's successor), sent his vans to *Einsatzgruppen C* and *D* without using them at all.[170] The vans may therefore be regarded as a late and not very successful development in the course of the mobile killing operations. They are of interest chiefly because they got another chance in Serbia and Poland, where they were used with more success.

Alcohol, speeches, and gas vans did not eliminate the psychological problems caused by the killing operations. Nevertheless, the operations continued. There was no breakdown of the administrative process — to the contrary, the *Einsatzgruppen* were burdened with additional tasks, one of which will be discussed below.

3 / The Killing of the Prisoners of War

On July 16, 1941, barely four weeks after the opening of the eastern campaign, Heydrich concluded an agree-

165. The story of the Himmler visit, as told by von dem Bach, was printed in *Aufbau* (New York), August 23, 1946, pp. 1–2.

166. UStuf. Dr. Becker (gas officer for *Einsatzgruppen C* and *D*) to OStubaf. Rauff (Chief, RSHA II-D), May 16, 1942, PS-501.

167. Affidavit by Ohlendorf, November 5, 1945, PS-2620.

168. Becker to Rauff, May 16, 1942, PS-501.

169. Testimony by Ohlendorf, *Trial of the Major War Criminals,* IV, 332, 334.

170. Affidavit by Naumann, June 27, 1947, NO-4150.

ment with the chief of the General Armed Forces Office (*Allgemeines Wehrmachtsamt*), General Reinecke.[1] The agreement established a new partnership between the RSHA and the army, this time for the purpose of killing Jewish prisoners of war.[2] The central administrators of that undertaking are listed in Table 40.[3]

revolutionaries," Red Army political officers, "fanatical" Communists, and "all Jews."[4] Since Soviet prisoners of war were already pouring through the transit camps into the *Generalgouvernement* and the Reich, Heydrich had to set up screening teams in the newly occupied territories, in Poland, and in Germany. The plan of operations consequently called for a three-pronged search, shown in Table 41. The bulk of the work was to be done by the *Einsatzgruppen* because the Gestapo offices at home were already understaffed.[5]

Table 40 / *Central Administrators for Killing Prisoners of War*

	RSHA	Army	
		Directly Concerned	Interested
	OGruf. Heydrich	General Reinecke	Admiral Canaris (deputized by Generalmajor Lahousen)
RSHA IV	Gruf. Müller	Chief of PW Camps Oberst Breyer (succeeded by Generalmajor von Graevenitz)	
RSHA IV-A	Obf. Panzinger		
RSHA IV-A-1	Stubaf. Vogt (succeeded by Stubaf. Lindow)		
RSHA IV-A-1-c	HStuf. Königshaus		

The text of the agreement provided that the Wehrmacht was to "free itself" from all Soviet prisoners of war who were carriers of Bolshevism. The RSHA and the army agreed also that the situation required "special measures" which were to be carried out in a spirit free from bureaucratic controls. On the next day, Heydrich alerted his regional machinery to prepare for the selection (*Aussonderung*) of all "professional

While the screening teams were in the process of formation, military authorities began to segregate and exploit their Jewish prisoners. The Second Army ordered that Jewish prisoners and "Asiatics" be retained by the army for labor before their transport to Dulags in the Army Group Rear Area.[6] The XXIX Corps (Sixth Army) at Kiev or-

1. See OKW organization chart on p. 179 (Table 34).
2. Operational Order No. 8 (signed Heydrich) (530 copies), July 17, 1941, NO-3414.
3. Affidavit by Kurt Lindow (RSHA IV-A-1), September 30, 1945, PS-2545. Affidavit by Lindow, July 29, 1947, NO-5481. Affidavit by Lahousen, April 17, 1947, NO-2894.
4. Operational Order No. 8, July 17, 1941, NO-3414.
5. Operational Order No. 8, July 17, 1941, NO-3414.

dered that Jews from Dulags in the area be employed in dangerous mine-clearing operations.[7] At Uman, Jewish prisoners had to give up their coats and boots.[8] In Dulag 160, at Chorol, the Jewish prisoners were marked with a star; since the Chorol camp had no latrines, the marked men had to pick up the dirt with their hands and drop it into barrels.[9] In Army District XX (Danzig) one impatient Stalag commander ordered his own men to kill Communist and Jewish prisoners at once. Three hundred were shot.[10]

The screening teams entered the prisoner-of-war camps without difficulty, since camp commanders were notified in advance by their superiors.[11] One of these notifications will suffice to point once more to the choice of language in documents. "During the examination of prisoners," said this particular directive, "the SD is to be allowed to participate in order to sift out given appropriate elements [*Bei der Sichtung der Gefangenen ist der SD zu*

TABLE 41 / *The Regional Organization of the PW Killings*

SCREENING TEAMS	SS-LIAISON	CAMPS
Einsatzgruppen		Army Prisoner Collecting Points (*Armeegefangenen-sammelstellen*) and Transit Camps (*Durchgangslager* – Dulag) in newly occupied territories
BdS Krakow	Kriminalkommissar Raschwitz (succeeded by Stubaf. Liska) attached to General-leutnant Hergott, Commander of GG camps	*Generalgouvernement* camps
Gestapo Offices in Reich	Kriminalrat Schiffer (succeeded by Kriminalkommissar Walter) attached to Generalmajor von Hindenburg, Commander of PW camps in East Prussia	Permanent PW camps (*Stammlager* – Stalag) in Reich

6. Second Army OQu/Qu 2 to Commander of Rear Army Area, Corps Commands, Army Ic, Army IVa, and Army IVb (54 copies), August 5, 1941, NOKW-2145.

7. XXIX Corps Ia/Ic to Divisions in Corps, September 22, 1941, NOKW-1323. The corps commander was General der Infantrie Obstfelder.

8. Statement by Oberleutnant Bingel (783rd *Landesschützen* Battalion, 36th Division), undated, NO-5031.

9. Affidavit by Henrik Schaechter, October 21, 1947, NO-5510. Affiant, a Jewish Red Army man captured at Kharkov, did not step forward during the selection.

10. Affidavit by Generalleutnant von Österreich, December 28, 1945, USSR-151. The shooting had been ordered by one of his subordinates, Oberstleutant Dulnig, commander of Stalag XX-C. One SS unit did not even bother to deliver its Jewish prisoners to the rear. The Jews were shot on the spot. OStubaf. Zschoppe, Deputy Commander of 8th SS Infantry Reg. (mot.), to XVII Corps, August 20, 1941, NOKW-1350.

11. Affidavit by Oberst Hadrian Ried (PW Commander, Brest Litovsk), October 22, 1947, NO-5523.

beteiligen, um gegebenenfalls entsprechende Elemente auszusondern]."[12] The teams were relatively small, comprising one officer and four to six men.[13] The SS men had to rely, therefore, upon the preparatory work by the army, the co-operation of the counterintelligence officer (AO) in the Dulag or Stalag, and their own "ingenuity."[14]

On the whole, the army was co-operative. The commander at Borispol, for instance, invited *Sonderkommando 4a* to dispatch a screening team to his camp. In two separate actions the team shot 1109 Jewish prisoners. Among the victims were 78 wounded men who had been handed over by the camp physician.[15] Other reports were similarly matter-of-fact. *Einsatzgruppe A* reported on August 28 that it had screened prisoners of war on two occasions; the results were "satisfying" (*zufriedenstellend*).[16] From the prisoner-collecting point (*Armeegefangenensammelstelle*) of the Eleventh Army, Jewish soldiers were handed over every month, around the clock. A sample of the monthly prisoner-of-war reports from that army reads as follows:[17]

Died, shot	1,116
Turned over to SD	111

One *Einsatzgruppe* encountered a few complications. *Einsatzgruppe C* reported that in Vinnitsa the camp commander had initiated court martial proceedings against his deputy for having handed over 362 Jewish prisoners of war. At the same time the *Einsatzgruppe* was barred from the transit camps. However, these difficulties were ascribed to the fact that others had been delayed, and *Einsatzgruppe C* praised the commander of the Sixth Army, Feldmarschall von Reichenau, for his full co-operation with the Security Police.[18]

While the screening teams had few complaints about the army, not everybody in the army was happy about the screening operations, particularly about the way in which they were conducted. In the summer of 1941, shortly after the killing of prisoners of war had begun, a high-level conference took place under the chairmanship of General Hermann Reinecke.[19] The RSHA was represented by Gestapo Chief Müller; in addition, Reinecke's subordinate, the prisoner-of-war camps chief, Oberst Breyer, was present; another interested party, Admiral Canaris, was deputized by Oberst Lahousen. Canaris himself did not participate because he did not want to show "too negative an attitude" vis-a-vis the representative of the RSHA.

Reinecke opened the discussion with a few remarks to the effect that the campaign against the USSR was not a mere war between states and armies but a contest of ideologies, namely, National Socialism and Bolshevism. Since Bolshevism opposed National Socialism "to the death," Soviet pris-

12. Order by General von Roques (Commander, Southern Army Group Rear Area), August 24, 1941, NOKW-2595.

13. Operational Order No. 8, July 17, 1941, NO-3414.

14. Preliminary order by RSHA IV, June 28, 1941, PS-69.

15. RSHA IV-A-1, Operational Report USSR No. 132, November 12, 1941, NO-2830.

16. RSHA IV-A-1, Operational Report USSR No. 71 (48 copies), September 2, 1941, NO-2843.

17. 11th Army OQu/Qu 2 to Army Group South Ib, reports for January-September, 1942, NOKW-1284, NOKW-1286. The discrepancy between the two figures runs through most of these reports. It is explained by the fact that two million Soviet prisoners of war died in captivity from disease, hunger, and other causes. See OKW report covering period from June 22, 1941, to May 1, 1944, NOKW-2125.

18. RSHA IV-A-1, Operational Report USSR No. 128 (55 copies), November 3, 1941, NO-3157.

19. Affidavit by Erwin Lahousen, April 17, 1947, NO-2894.

oners could not expect the same treatment as the prisoners of the Western enemies. The harshness of the orders which had been issued was only a natural defense against Bolshevist subhumanity, in the sense that the carriers of Bolshevist thought—and thus also of the Bolshevist will to resist—were to be annihilated.

Oberst Lahousen then spoke up. He protested that the morale of the German Army was impaired because executions were carried out before the eyes of the troops. Second, the recruitment of agents from the ranks of the prisoners had become more difficult. Third, any surrender messages to the Red Army would now be unsuccessful, with the result that bloody German losses would increase to even greater heights.

Gestapo Chief Müller was aroused to defend his police. In the course of the "sharp argument" which ensued, Lahousen pointed out further that the "special treatment" meted out by the Security Police and SD was proceeding in accordance with very peculiar and arbitrary viewpoints *(nach ganz eigenartigen und willkürlichen Gesichtspunkten)*. For example, one *Einsatzgruppe* had confined itself to students, while another had used only race considerations. As a consequence of one selection, several hundred Moslems, probably Crimean Tatars, had been "conveyed to special treatment" (*der Sonderbehandlung zugeführt*) on the assumption that they were Jews. Müller acknowledged that mistakes had been made but insisted that the operation continue according to "world-philosophical criteria" (*weltanschauliche Grundsätze*). Reinecke concluded the discussion by pointing once more to the necessity for harshness, etc.

Lahousen tells us that he was motivated during the conference to help the prisoners, but whatever his motives may have been, the arguments he presented served only to increase the efficiency of the operations. Thus on September 12, 1941, Heydrich sent out another directive in which he cautioned the screening teams to be a little more careful. An engineer was not necessarily a Bolshevist. Moslems were not to be confused with Jews. Ukrainians, White Russians, Azerbaijanians, Armenians, Georgians, and Northern Caucasians were to be "treated according to directive" only if they were fanatical Bolshevists. Above all, the shootings were not to be carried out in the middle of camps. "It goes without saying," said Heydrich, "that executions must not be public. Spectators must not be allowed, on principle."[20]

As a result of all the discussions and directives, the screening teams appear to have improved their techniques considerably. So far as we know, they no longer shot Moslems en masse. In the Reich the shooting operation was transferred from the prisoner-of-war camps to concentration camps, where it could take place in complete privacy.[21] There were, in short, no longer any controversies over these questions between the army and the RSHA. This does *not* mean that all differences of opinion had ended; in fact, there were to be new disputes, only this time the viewpoints were almost reversed.

In November, 1941, Sturmbannführer Vogt of the RSHA sent a letter to the Gestapo office in Munich to notify that office that the Wehrmacht had complained of "superficial" examinations of Soviet prisoners of war in *Wehrkreis* VII. During one screening, for example, only 380 prisoners

20. Heydrich to *Einsatzgruppen*, Higher SS and Police Leaders, *Inspekteure der SP und des SD*, BdS in Krakow, BdS in Metz, BdS in Oslo, KdS in Krakow, KdS in Radom, KdS in Warsaw, KdS in Lublin, and State Police offices (*Staatspolizeileitstellen*) (250 copies), September 12, 1941, NO-3416.

21. See death lists of the Mauthausen concentration camp, May 10, 1942, PS-495.

had been selected from 4800.[22]

The Gestapo in Munich replied as follows: First, there had been 410 selections out of 3088 prisoners. The 410 men consisted of the following categories:

Communist party functionaries	3
Jews	25
Intellectuals	69
Fanatical Communists	146
Instigators, agitators, and thieves	85
Refugees	35
Incurables	47

The selection represented an average of 13 per cent. It was true that the Gestapo offices in Nuremberg and Regensburg had shown percentages of 15 and 17, but these offices had accepted many Russians who had been handed over by camp officers for small offenses against camp discipline. The Gestapo office in Munich only followed RSHA orders. If the figure was still too low, the army was to blame, because the counterintelligence officer (AO) had preferred to use Jews as interpreters and informers.[23]

Another example of changed army mentality is even more striking. During 1942 a number of conferences were held under the chairmanship of Generalmajor von Graevenitz, Oberst Breyer's successor as prisoner-of-war chief. The RSHA was usually represented by Oberführer Panzinger (IV-A) or by Sturmbannführer Lindow and Hauptsturmführer Königshaus. During one of these conferences Graevenitz and a number of other Wehrmacht officers, including doctors, requested Lindow and Königshaus to take over all Soviet prisoners of war who were suffering from some "incurable" disease, such as tuberculosis or syphilis, and to kill them in a concentration camp in the usual manner. The Gestapo men refused with indignation, pointing out that, after all, they could not be expected to act as hangmen for the Wehrmacht (*Die Staatspolizei sei nicht weiter der Henker der Wehrmacht*).[24]

Throughout occupied Russia, Poland, Germany, Alsace-Lorraine, and even Norway, wherever Soviet prisoners were sent, Heydrich's screening teams were at work.[25] After one year of operations, in July, 1942, Müller felt that he could order the withdrawal of screening teams from the Reich and confine further selections to the eastern territories. Needless to say (*selbstverständlich*), any requests by the army for additional searches in the Reich were to be complied with at once.[26]

On December 21, 1941, in Berlin, Müller revealed some figures to General Reinecke and representatives of several ministries: He reported that 22,000 Soviet prisoners (Jewish and non-Jewish) had been selected (*ausgesondert*) so far; approximately 16,000 had been killed.[27] No later figures are available, and the total number of Jewish victims is unknown.

4 / The Intermediary Stage

During the first sweep the *Einsatzgruppen* rolled for six hundred miles. Splitting up, the killing units covered

22. RSHA IV-A-1 (signed Stubaf. Vogt) to *Stapoleitstelle* Munich, attention Stubaf. Oberregierungsrat Dr. Isselhorst, November 11, 1941, R-178.

23. Report by *Stapoleitstelle* Munich (signed Scherner), November 15, 1941, R-178.

24. Affidavit by Kurt Lindow, July 29, 1947, NO-5481.

25. The territorial extent is indicated in the distribution list of the Heydrich order of September 12, 1941, NO-3416.

26. Müller to *Stapoleitstellen*, Higher SS and Police Leaders in Reich, BdS in Krakow, Liaison Officer Kriminalkommissar Walter in Königsberg, and Liaison Officer Stubaf. Liska in Lublin, July 31, 1942, NO-3422.

27. Ministerialrat Dr. Letsch (Labor Ministry) to Ministerialdirektor Dr. Mansfeld, Ministerialdirektor Dr. Beisiegel, Ministerialrat Dr. Timm, Oberregierungsrat Dr. Hoelk, ORR Meinecke, and Regierungsrat Dr. Fischer, December 22, 1941, NOKW-147.

the entire map of the occupied territory, and small detachments of five or six men combed through the prisoner-of-war camps. An administrative task of drastic proportions had been tackled successfully, but it was by no means solved. Of 4,000,000 Jews in the area of operations, about 1,500,000 had fled. Five hundred thousand had been killed, and at least 2,000,000 were still alive. To the *Einsatzgruppen* the masses of bypassed Jews presented themselves as a crushing burden.

When *Einsatzgruppe C* approached the Dnieper, it noted that rumors of killing operations had resulted in mass flights of Jews. Although the rumors were actually warnings which frustrated the basic strategy of the mobile killing operations, the *Einsatzgruppe* went on to say: "Therein may be viewed an indirect success of the work of the Security Police, for the movement [*Abschiebung*] of hundreds of thousands of Jews free of charge – reportedly most of them go beyond the Ural – represents a notable contribution of the solution of the Jewish question *in Europe*."[1] The mass departure of Jews had lightened the load of the mobile killing units, and the *Einsatzgruppen* welcomed this development.

All *Einsatzgruppen* commanders, with the possible exception of the relentless Dr. Stahlecker, realized that the Jews could not be killed in a single sweep. In one report there is even a note of despair over the Jewish refugees who were drifting back into the cities from which they had fled. The report was written by *Einsatzgruppe C*, which prided itself with the "extremely skilful organization" (*überaus geschickte Organisation*) of its trapping operation in Kiev. "Although 75,000 Jews have been liquidated in this manner so far," wrote *Einsatzgruppe C*, "today it is already clear that even with such tactics a final solution of the Jewish problem will not be possible." Whenever the *Einsatzgruppe* had left a town, it returned to find more Jews than had already been killed there.[2] On September 17, 1941, the same *Einsatzgruppe*, already struck by the immensity of its task, had gone so far as to suggest that the killing of the Jews would not solve the major problems of the Ukrainian area anyhow. This passage is unique in Nazi literature:

> Even if it were possible to shut out Jewry 100 per cent, we would not eliminate the center of political danger.
>
> The Bolshevist work is done by Jews, Russians, Georgians, Armenians, Poles, Latvians, Ukrainians; the Bolshevist apparatus is by no means identical with the Jewish population. Under such conditions we would miss the goal of political security if we replaced the main task of destroying the Communist machine with the relatively easier one of eliminating the Jews. . . .
>
> In the western and central Ukraine almost all urban workers, skilled mechanics, and traders are Jews. If we renounce the Jewish labor potential in full, we cannot rebuild Ukrainian industry and we cannot build up the urban administrative centers.
>
> There is only one way out – a method which has been familiar to the German administration in the *Generalgouvernement* for a long time: final solution of the Jewish question through complete labor utilization of the Jews.
>
> This would result in a gradual liquidation of Jewry – a development which would be in accord with the economic potentialities of the country.[3]

Not often have Nazis made such a clear separation between Jewry and Communism. But the demands of the killing operations, coupled with a realiza-

1. RSHA IV-A-1, Operational Report USSR No. 81 (48 copies), September 12, 1941, NO-3154, italics added.

2. RSHA IV-A-1, Operational Report USSR No. 128 (55 copies), November 3, 1941, NO-3157.

3. RSHA IV-A-1, Operational Report USSR No. 58 (48 copies), September 17, 1941, NO-3151.

tion that the vast Communist apparatus in the occupied areas continued to operate unhampered, opened the eyes and the minds of even the most indoctrinated Nazi elements.

The inadequacy of the first sweep necessitated an intermediary stage during which the first three steps of the destruction process – definition, expropriation, and concentration – were implemented with bureaucratic thoroughness. However, something happened to the usual order of procedure, for in the wake of the killings the bureaucrats thought first of ghettoization and only later of economic measures and definitions.

The initial concentrations were effected by the mobile units themselves. These ghettoizations were by-products of the killing operations, in the sense that the Security Police were forced to defer the complete annihilation of certain communities, either because they were too large to be wiped out in one blow or (as *Einsatzgruppe C* explained the situation) because "it could not be avoided, for reasons of a considerable skilled labor shortage, that Jewish workers who are needed for urgent reconstruction work, etc., be permitted to live temporarily [*wobei es sich nicht vermeiden liess, aus Gründen des erheblichen Facharbeitermangels jüdische Handwerker, die zur Vornahme dringender Instandsetzungsarbeiten usw. gebraucht werden, vorerst noch am Leben zu lassen*]."[4] Within a short time, therefore, the *Einsatzgruppen*, Higher SS and Police Leaders, and units of the BdS Krakow introduced marking and appointed Jewish councils.[5] These measures were sometimes supplemented by registration, a task performed by the newly organized councils.[6] With the help of registration lists the *Einsatzgruppen* put labor columns at the disposal of the army and the *Organisation Todt*.[7] In almost all large cities and many smaller ones, the mobile killing units wedged the Jewish population into closed districts. The Polish-type ghetto thus made its appearance in the occupied USSR.

One of the first ghettos was established in the Lithuanian capital of Kaunas. To obtain the maximum cooperation of the local Jewish community, Brigadeführer Stahlecker summoned a few prominent Jews and informed them that the entire Jewish population of the city would have to

4. RSHA IV-A-1, Operational Report USSR No. 135 (60 copies), November 19, 1941, NO-2832. Labor considerations prevailed also in the sector of *Einsatzgruppe B*. RSHA IV-A-1, Operational Report USSR No. 94 (48 copies), September 25, 1941, NO-3146. In the Ukraine *Einsatzgruppe C* discovered Jewish collective farms (*kolkhozy*). The *Einsatzgruppe* considered the Jewish *kolkhozy* workers to be unintelligent (*wenig intelligent*); therefore it "contented itself" with the shooting of the Jewish directors (who were replaced by Ukrainians). The remainder of the Jewish labor force on the farms was permitted to make a contribution to the harvest. RSHA IV-A-1, Operational Report USSR No. 81 (48 copies), September 12, 1941, NO-3154.

5. RSHA Summary Report No. 1, covering June 22-July 31, 1941, NO-2651. RSHA Summary Report No. 3 (80 copies), covering August 15-31, 1941, NO-2653. RSHA IV-A-1, Operational Report USSR No. 91, September 22, 1941, NO-3142, and other operational reports.

6. Report by *Sonderkommando* 11*a* (signed Stubaf. Zapp), covering August 18-31, 1941, NO-2066. Ohlendorf via Gmeiner to 11th Army Ic/AO, September 8, 1941, NOKW-3234.

7. RSHA IV-A-1, Operational Report USSR No. 43 (47 copies), August 5, 1941, NO-2949. RSHA Summary Report No. 3 (80 copies), covering August 15-31, 1941, NO-2653. Report by *Sonderkommando* 11*a* for August 18-31, 1941, NO-2066. Report by *Sonderkommando* 11*a* for August 22-September 10, 1941, NOKW-636. RSHA IV-A-1, Operational Report USSR No. 63 (48 copies), August 25, 1941, NO-4538. Ohlendorf via Gmeiner to 11th Army Ic/AO, September 8, 1941, NOKW-3234. RSHA IV-A-1, Operational Report USSR No. 107 (50 copies), October 8, 1941, NO-3139.

move into the Viliampol quarter, a district hemmed in by two rivers. When the Jewish representatives tried to plead with Stahlecker to desist from the action, he replied that the establishment of a ghetto was the only way to prevent new pogroms. The Jews thereupon agreed that a ghetto would afford the best protection against the Lithuanians and declared their readiness to co-operate with the Security Police. Stahlecker on his part assured them that, apart from a search of prisons which would involve "executions of a minor nature only," the Jews would henceforth be left in peace.[8]

When the civil administration took over part of the occupied territory in July and August, 1941, the mobile killing units had already completed a large part of the ghettoization process. *Einsatzgruppe A* prided itself that, upon transfer of jurisdiction, all Jewish communities (excepting only Vilna) had been incarcerated in ghettos.[9] However, the systematic concentration of the Jews was the task of the military and civilian authorities which exercised over-all governmental functions in the occupied territories. To understand what happened during the intermediary stage and the second sweep, which was to follow, we therefore need a rough outline of that administration.

Newly occupied areas were always placed under military government. In the beginning of this chapter we have seen the organization of the army in new territory: secured areas were held by *Befehlshaber* (that is, a *Wehrmachtbefehlshaber, Militärbefehlshaber,* or *Befehlshaber* of a specified region). Moving toward the front, a traveler would pass through the army group rear area, army rear area, and corps area. In occupied Russia the territorial organization of the army was extensive in its dimensions (see Table 42 and map on p. 229).[10]

On the map the "military area" refers to the territory of the three army groups (including army group rear areas, army rear areas, and corps areas). The secured territory, under the two *Wehrmachtbefehlshaber,* corresponded roughly to the areas marked "*Ostland*" and "Ukraine." These two areas were colonies governed by a colonial minister: *Reichsminister für die besetzten Ostgebiete* ("Reich Minister for the Eastern Occupied Territories") Alfred Rosenberg, whose office was in Berlin. His two colonial governors were called *Reichskommissare;* they had their headquarters in the East (Riga and Kaunas). The domain of a *Reichskommissar* was a *Reichskommissariat* (the *Reichskommissariat Ostland* and the *Reichskommissariat Ukraine*). Each *Reichskommissariat* was divided into general districts (*Generalbezirke*), and each *Generalbezirk* was divided into regions (*Kreisgebiete*). The chief of a *Generalbezirk* was a *Generalkommissar;* the chief of a *Kreisgebiet* was a *Gebietskommissar.*[11] Below is an abbreviated list showing the most important offices in the ministry, the two *Reichskommissariate,*

8. RSHA IV-A-1, Operational Report USSR No. 19 (32 copies), July 11, 1941, NO-2934. Stahlecker to Himmler, October 15, 1941, L-180.

9. RSHA IV-A-1, Operational Report USSR No. 94 (48 copies), September 25, 1941, NO-3146.

10. No single document has been used as a source for the table and the map. Many items have been drawn upon.

In this discussion, the term "military government" is intended to refer not solely to the work of the VII (military government) sections in the staffs but to all measures — whether ordered by the Ic/AO, the Ia, the VII, or any other officer — which affected the civilian population.

11. In White Russia there was a level between *Generalbezirk* and *Kreisgebiet*: the *Hauptgebiet,* which was governed by a *Hauptkommissar.* Major cities were governed by a *Stadtkommissar.* The *Stadtkommissar* was not subordinate, but equal in rank, to a *Gebietskommissar.*

Table 42 / *The Territorial Organization of the Army in the Occupied USSR*

Commanding Authority	*Chef* OKW	Army Group Commander	Army Commander	Corps Commander
Territorial Commander	*Wehrmachtbefehlshaber* (*Ostland* and Ukraine)	Army Group Rear Area Commander (North, Center, South)	Army Rear Area Commander (Korück)	
Lower Territorial Echelons	(Secured areas under civilian control: no military government functions)	*Sicherungsdivisionen* (security divisions) 2-3 per Army Group		
		Feldkommandanturen (district commands)	*Feldkommandanturen*	
		Ortskommandanturen (town commands)	*Ortskommandanturen*	

MAP 4
ADMINISTRATION OF THE OCCUPIED USSR

and the *Generalbezirke.*

Ministry for Eastern Occupied Territories (Berlin):[12]
Reichsminister, Dr. Alfred Rosenberg
Staatssekretär, Gauleiter Alfred Meyer
Chief, Political Division, Reichsamtsleiter Dr. Georg Leibbrandt
Deputy Chief, Political Division, Generalkonsul Dr. Bräutigam
Expert in Jewish Affairs, Amtsgerichtsrat Dr. Wetzel

Reichskommissariat Ostland:[13]
Reichskommissar, Gauleiter Hinrich Lohse
Chief, Political Division, RegRat Dr. Trampedach
Generalkommissar, Estonia, SA-OGruf. Litzmann
Generalkommissar, Latvia, Oberbürgermeister (Mayor) Staatsrat Dr. Drechsler
Generalkommissar, Lithuania, Reichsamtsleiter Dr. von Renteln
Generalkommissar, White Russia, Gauleiter Wilhelm Kube (succeeded by SS-Gruf. von Gottberg)

Reichskommissariat Ukraine:[14]
Reichskommissar, Gauleiter Erich Koch
Chief, Political Division, Regierungspräsident Dargel
Generalkommissar, Volhynia-Podolia, SA-OGruf. Schöne
Generalkommissar, Zhitomir, Regierungspräsident Klemm
Generalkommissar, Nikolaev, Oppermann (OGruf. in NSKK-Party Motor Corps)
Generalkommissar, Kiev, Gauamtsleiter Magunia (official in DAF–German Labor Front)
Generalkommissar, Dnepropetrovsk, Selzner (DAF)
Generalkommissar, Crimea-Tauria, Gauleiter Frauenfeld

As a brief glance at the list will indicate, most of the high officials in the Rosenberg apparatus were party men.[15] The machinery as a whole was rather small. In the Ukraine, for example, the entourage of Reichskommissar Koch, composed at its height of 800 Germans, was fixed in 1942 at 252.[16] At the same time, the office force of a *Generalkommissar* consisted of about 100 Germans, while the personnel of a *Gebietskommissar* numbered no more than about a half-dozen German bureaucrats.[17] In other words, the occupied territories were run by a handful of party men – not very efficiently but all the more ruthlessly.

Before we leave the administration of the occupied USSR, a word is due about the territories west of the two *Reichskommissariate* (see map). There were three such areas: the Bialystok district, Galicia, and the Roumanian territories. The Bialystok area became a quasi-incorporated district of the Reich. It was placed under the administration of Gauleiter Koch, the *Reichskommissar* of the Ukraine – not in his capacity as *Reichskommissar* but as an adjunct to his position as *Gauleiter* and *Oberpräsident* of the neighboring *Gau* and province of East Prussia.[18] Southeastern Poland (Galicia) became the fifth district of the *Generalgouvernement.*[19] Northern Bukovina

12. Memorandum by Rosenberg, April 29, 1941, PS-1024.

13. Lammers to Rosenberg, July 18, 1941, NG-1325. *Deutsche Zeitung im Ostland* (passim).

14. *Deutsche Ukraine Zeitung* (passim). The *Generalbezirke* Dnepropetrovsk and Crimea-Tauria (both east of the Dnieper river) were added in August, 1942. The Crimean *Generalbezirk* (seat, Melitopol) never included the Crimean peninsula, which remained under military control.

15. Originally, it was intended that the leadership of the Eastern Occupied Territories – the *Ostführerkorps,* as it was called – should have the following composition: Party men, 35 per cent; SS, SA, and party organizations, 20 per cent; agricultural and industrial experts and others, 45 per cent. See report by Dr. Hans-Joachim Kausch (journalist) June 26, 1943, Occ E 4-11.

16. Koch to Rosenberg, March 16, 1943, PS-192.

17. Report by Kausch, June 26, 1943, Occ E 4-11.

18. Decree (signed by Hitler, Keitel, and Lammers), July 17, 1941, NG-1280.

19. Dr. Max Freiherr von du Prel, *Das Generalgouvernement* (Würzburg, 1942), p. 363.

and Bessarabia reverted to Roumanian rule, whereas the area between the Dniester and the Bug became a new Roumanian territory.[20]

The fate of the Jews in the detached regions was henceforth linked to the fate of the Polish and Roumanian Jews to the west, and we shall therefore deal with these areas in the next chapter. The remainder of this chapter will be confined to the events which occurred in the military areas, the *Kommissariate,* and some of the eastern parts of the Bialystok district. That territory was the scene of the second wave of mobile killing operations.

The primary task of the military administration and of the Rosenberg machine was to prepare for the second sweep. First of all, this task was to be accomplished through the establishment of ghettos since, in its very nature, the ghetto prevented dispersal and crowded its victims into a defined area, thus facilitating future seizures. Reichskommissar Lohse of the *Ostland* explained the purpose of the ghetto in ponderous but explicit language. His basic ghettoization order states that[21]

> these provisional directives are designed only to assure minimum measures by the *Generalkommissare* and *Gebietskommissare* in those areas where — and so long as — further measures in the sense of the final solution of the Jewish question are not possible.

In short, the administration was to play a temporary role in an intermediary stage of the killing operations.

We do not have to go into detail about the concentration measures of the military and civilian authorities. In an avalanche of orders, the military provided for marking (in the form either of armbands or of patches worn in front and back), registration, *Judenräte,* ghettos, and ghetto police.[22] Interestingly enough, the army did not regard the establishment of ghettos as a task of great urgency. The ghettos were not to take precedence over genuinely military matters.[23]

The civil administration was more preoccupied with ghettoization; thus the "provisional directives" of Reichskommissar Lohse, and especially those of his subordinates, are a little more detailed than the military orders. In the directive of Generalkommissar von Renteln (Lithuania), for example, we find in addition to the regular instructions such points as these: All telephones and telephone lines were to be ripped out of the ghetto. All postal services to and from the ghetto were to be cut off. Whenever ghetto bridges had to be built over thoroughfares, the bridges were to be enclosed with barbed wire to prevent people from jumping down. With an eye to the future, von Renteln ordered that Jews be forbidden to tear down doors, window frames, floors, or houses for fuel.[24] A draft directive of the *Generalkommissar* in Latvia specified a pro-

20. See pp. 490, 493, 495.

21. Wetzel to Foreign Office, May 16, 1942, enclosing Lohse directive to *Generalkommissare* of August 19, 1941, NG-4815.

22. Order by Commander of Army Group Rear Area South (von Roques) (35 copies), July 21, 1941, NOKW-1601. Order by von Roques, August 28, 1941, NOKW-1586. Order by Commander of Army Group Rear Area North/VII (signed by Oberstleutnant Müller-Teusler) (about 65 copies), September 3, 1941, NOKW-2204. Order by 454th Security Division/Ia, September 8, 1941, NOKW-2628. Ortskommandantur in Dshanskoy (signed Hauptmann Weigand) to Commander of Area 553 (11th Army), November 10, 1941, NOKW-1582. 299th Inf. Division/Ic to XXIX Corps/Ic, November 29, 1941, NOKW-1517. Draft of Proclamation of XLII Corps/Ia, December 11, 1941, NOKW-1682. Order by 101st Light Inf. Division/Ic, May 24, 1942, NOKW-2699. Draft directive by 299th Division Ia/Ic, October 1, 1942, NOKW-3371.

23. Order by von Roques, August 28, 1941, NOKW-1586. Order by Rear Army Group Area North, September 3, 1941, NOKW-2204.

posed occupancy of four Jews per room and among other things prohibited smoking in the ghetto.[25]

While the directives of the civil administration were more elaborate than those of the military, they were not published in any proclamations or decrees. In an extraordinary attempt at secrecy, Lohse ordered his subordinates to "get by with oral instructions to the Jewish councils."[26]

Not only were the *Kommissare* very interested in ghetto administration; they also developed a feeling of proprietorship toward the Jewish districts. During the second sweep this feeling was to have administrative repercussions, but even during the intermediary stage it gave rise to difficulties.

On October 11, 1941, the *Generalkommissar* of Latvia, Dr. Drechsler, was sitting in his private apartment in Riga when a visitor arrived: Brigadeführer Dr. Stahlecker, chief of *Einsatzgruppe* A. Stahlecker informed his surprised host that, in accordance with a "wish" of the Führer, a "big concentration camp" was to be established near Riga for Reich and Protektorat Jews. Could Drechsler help out with necessary materials?[27]

Drechsler was now in a position similar to Regierungspräsident Uebelhoer, who had been fighting about the Lodz ghetto against the all-powerful Himmler. Like Uebelhoer, Drechsler was to be the recipient of tens of thousands of Jews who were sent from the Reich-Protektorat area to some form of destruction in the East. The late fall months of 1941 were a transition period during which deportations were already under way, but killing centers had not yet been established. The *Ostland* was looked over for possible sites while transports were shoved east. In fact, on October 21, 1941, Sturmbannführer Lange of the *Einsatzgruppe* telephoned Dr. Drechsler to report that the killing unit was planning to set up a camp for 25,000 Reich Jews about fourteen miles from Riga.[28]

By October 24, Reichskommissar Lohse was drawn into the picture. With Drechsler, Lohse complained to Lange that the *Einsatzgruppe* had contacted Drechsler not to *discuss* the matter but to *inform* him of developments. Lange repeated that higher orders were involved and that the first transport was due on November 10. Lohse replied that he was going to discuss the whole question in Berlin on October 25.[29]

By November 8, 1941, Lange sent a letter to Lohse, reporting that 50,000 Jews were on the move. Twenty-five thousand were due in Riga, 25,000 in Minsk. A camp was being built at Salaspils, near Riga.[30] Since the *Reichskommissar* was in Berlin, his political expert, Regierungsrat Trampedach, wrote to the capital to urge that the transports be stopped.[31] The chief of the ministry's Political Division, Dr. Leibbrandt, replied that there was no cause for worry since the Jews would be sent "farther east" anyway (that is, they would be killed).[32]

The Reich Jews began to arrive in November. Some were sent to the Salaspils camp to be worked to death in icy temperatures; the others were sent

24. Order by von Renteln, August 26, 1941, Occ E 3-19.

25. Draft directive signed by Bönner, undated, Occ E 3-20.

26. Lohse directive, August 18, 1941, NG-1815.

27. Drechsler to Lohse, October 20, 1941, Occ E 3-29.

28. Unsigned notation, October 21, 1941, Occ E 3-29.

29. Memorandum, office of the *Reichskommissar,* October 27, 1941, Occ E 3-30.

30. Stubaf. Lange to *Reichskommissar Ostland,* November 8, 1941, Occ E 3-31.

31. Trampedach to ministry, copy for Lohse at Hotel Adlon in Berlin, November 9, 1941, Occ E 3-32.

32. Leibbrandt to *Reichskommissar Ostland,* November 13, 1941, Occ E 3-32.

to the Riga ghetto, which had been divided in half to separate German from Latvian Jews. The new arrivals had a foreboding of what was going to happen to them when they entered the ghetto. The apartments were in a shambles, and some of the furnishings bore the traces of blood. The previous occupants were already dead.[33]

In the meantime, other transports also arrived in Minsk. The *Wehrmachtbefehlshaber Ostland* protested against the arrivals on purely military grounds: The German Jews, he pointed out, were far superior in intelligence to White Russian Jews; hence there was danger that the "pacification" of the area would be jeopardized. Furthermore, Army Group Center had requested that no trains be wasted on Jews. All railroad equipment was needed for the supply of military matériel.[34]

The protest of the *Wehrmachtbefehlshaber Ostland* was followed on December 16, 1941, by a letter from the *Generalkommissar* of White Russia, Gauleiter Kube. That letter was the first in a series of letters and protests by that official which were to shake at the foundations of the Nazi idea. It was addressed to Lohse personally (*Mein lieber Hinrich*).[35]

Kube pointed out that about 6000–7000 Jews had arrived in Minsk; where the other 17,000–18,000 had remained he did not know. Among the arrivals there were World War I veterans with the Iron Cross (both First and Second Class), invalided veterans, half-Aryans, yes, even one three-quarter Aryan. Kube had visited the ghetto and had convinced himself that among the Jewish newcomers, who were much cleaner than Russian Jews, there were also many skilled laborers who could produce about five times as much as Russian Jews. The new arrivals would freeze to death or starve to death in the next few weeks. There were no serums to protect them against twenty-two epidemics in the area.

Kube himself did not wish to issue any orders for the treatment of these Jews, although "certain formations" of the army and the police were already eyeing the personal possessions of these people. The SD had already taken away four hundred mattresses – without asking. "I am certainly hard and I am ready," continued Kube, "to help solve the Jewish question, but people who come from our cultural milieu are certainly something else than the native animalized hordes. Should the Lithuanians and the Latvians – who are disliked here, too, by the population– be charged with the slaughter? I could not do it. I ask you, consider the honor of our Reich and our party, and give clear instructions to take care of what is necessary in a form which is humane."

On January 5, 1942, the *Stadtkommissar* (city equivalent of *Gebietskommissar*) of Minsk, Gauamtsleiter Janetzke, going over the heads of Kube and Lohse, addressed a letter to Rosenberg personally. Janetzke had just been informed by the SS and Police that an additional 50,000 Jews were due from the Reich. In bitter language he pointed out that Minsk was a heap of rubble which still housed 100,000 inhabitants. In addition, there were 15,000–18,000 Russian Jews and 7000 Reich Jews. Any further arrival of transports would bring about a catastrophe.[36]

The Jewish expert in the ministry, Amtsgerichtsrat Wetzel, replied to the

33. Affidavit by Alfred Winter, October 15, 1947, NO-5448. Winter, a Jewish survivor, was a deportee.

34. *Wehrmachtbefehlshaber Ostland*/Ic to *Reichskommissar Ostland,* November 20, 1941, Occ E 3-34.

35. Kube to Lohse, December 16, 1941, Occ E 3-36.

36. Stadtkommissar Janetzke to Minister for Eastern Occupied Territories (Rosenberg), January 5, 1942, Occ E 3-37.

letter by addressing himself to Reichskommissar Lohse. Originally, wrote Wetzel, it had been intended to send 25,000 Jews to Minsk. Because of transport difficulties, the project could not be carried out. As for Janetzke, Wetzel requested that the *Stadtkommissar* be instructed to heed official channels in the future.[37]

Although the controversy was now over, Kube insisted on a last word. Writing to Lohse, he pointed out that had Janetzke used official channels, he not only would have been within his rights but would have done his duty.[38]

While the mobile killing units were interested only in concentrating the Jews so that the second sweep could be facilitated, the military and civilian administrations decided to exploit the situation while it lasted. Hence economic measures, both labor utilization and property confiscation, became an important aspect of the intermediary stage. Economic exploitation was *not* the exclusive task of the army groups and the Reich Ministry for Eastern Occupied Territories. We shall therefore have to look briefly at a few other agencies: the *Wirtschaftsinspektionen* ("economy inspectorates") and the *Rüstungsinspektionen* ("armament inspectorates").

Over-all economic control in the *military areas* was placed into Göring's hands. To carry out his task, the *Reichsmarschall* formed a policy staff, the *Wirtschaftsführungsstab Ost* ("Economy Leadership Staff East"). Göring himself headed the organization. The deputy was Staatssekretär Körner (Office of the Four-Year Plan). Other members included Staatssekretäre Backe and Neumann (also of the Office of the Four-Year Plan) and General Thomas, who was chief of the OKW/Wi Rü (Armed Forces High Command/Economy-Armament Office).[39] In the field, the policies of the *Wirtschaftsführungsstab Ost* were carried out by another staff, the *Wirtschaftsstab Ost* ("Economy Staff East"), headed by Generalleutnant Schubert.[40] The regional machinery of the *Wirtschaftsstab Ost* consisted of three *Wirtschaftsinspektionen* – one with each army group. Each inspectorate was subdivided territorially into *Wirtschaftskommandos* ("economy commands").

Originally it was intended that Göring have plenary economic control in the entire occupied territory (military areas and civilian *Reichskommissariate* alike);[41] that arrangement, however, hurt the sensibilities of the newly appointed Reichsminister Rosenberg. The functions of the economy inspectorates were therefore confined to the military areas, while the Rosenberg machinery was given a free hand to regulate general economic matters (finance, labor, agriculture) in the *Kommissariate*. Like all other regional potentates, however, Rosenberg had no control over war contracts placed in his territory. The continuous supervision of war production contracted for by the German Army, Navy, or Air Force was the function of the *Rüstungsinspektionen*, which belonged to General Thomas of the OKW/Wi Rü.[42]

Table 43 summarizes the basic economic jurisdictions in the East. From

37. Wetzel to *Reichskommissar*, January 16, 1942, Occ E 3-37.

38. Kube to Lohse, February 6, 1942, Occ E 3-37.

39. Von Lüdinghausen (Dresdner Bank) to Dr. Rasche (Dresdner Bank), July 20, 1941, NI-14475. Decree by Göring, July 30, 1941, Wi/ID .240.

40. Decree by Göring, July 30, 1941, Wi/ID .240.

41. Directive by OKH/GenQu (signed Wagner) (60 copies), May 16, 1941, NOKW-3335. Von Lüdinghausen to Dr. Rasche, July 20, 1941, NI-14475.

42. For precise functions of the armament inspectorates in the Rosenberg territories, see decree by Thomas, July 25, 1941, Wi/ID .240; decree by Göring, August 25, 1942, Wi/ID 2.205.

this chart it should now be apparent why the economy inspectorates in the military area dealt with *all* economic measures against Jews, whereas the armament inspectorates in the civilian area were concerned only with forced labor questions arising from war contracts.[43]

TABLE 43 / *Economic Jurisdictions in the East*

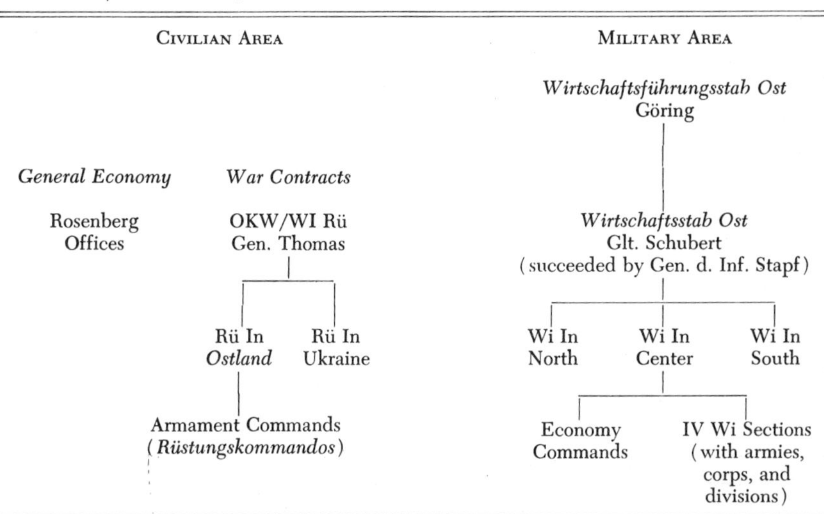

The economic measures against Jews comprised starvation, forced labor, and confiscations of property. So far as the German bureaucrats were concerned, the measure which gave rise to the *least* difficulty was the prescription of a starvation diet.

In the military area the *Wirtschaftsstab Ost* ordered that Jews receive half the rations allotted to people who did "no work worth mentioning." This meant that the Jews were entitled to no meat but that they could receive a maximum of two pounds of bread, two and a half pounds of potatoes, and one and a half ounces of fat per week.[44] Lohse's "provisional directives" provided that Jews would receive only whatever the rest of the population could do without, but in no case more than was sufficient for scanty nourishment.[45] The food rationing problem was thus easily solved – Jews simply did not have to eat. More difficult, however, was the question of labor utilization, for Jews did have to work.

To understand the role of Jewish labor in the newly occupied territories, we should examine in particular that early period of the occupation when the Germans first organized eastern production. The *Wirtschaftsstab Ost* planned to make maximum use of the productive capacity of the new areas,

43. In their internal organization, economy inspectorates were quite different from armament inspectorates. The economy inspectorates and commands were organized into sections dealing with economy, labor, agriculture, finance, etc. The armament inspectorates and commands were organized into a central section and three sections designated "Army," "Navy," and "Air Force."

44. Instructions by *Wirtschaftsstab Ost/Führung* Ia, November 4, 1941, PS-1189. The Jewish diet was the same as the allottment for children.

45. Lohse to *Generalkommissare* in *Ostland,* August 8, 1941, NG-4815.

but in the very beginning it hoped that this objective could be accomplished without the Jews. On July 16, 1941, Generalleutnant Schubert (chief of the *Wirtschaftsstab Ost*) reported in telegraphic style:

> With respect to the Jewish question important experience at Drohobycz, where [oil] refinery employed the leading Jews only during the first week, and runs today without any Jews [*ganz judenfrei*].[46]

No such pronouncements were made after July. In Przemysl-South, the IV Wi officer wrote the following report about his troubles in organizing war industries during the summer of 1941:

> Almost insoluble was the problem of finding expert managers. Almost all former owners are Jews. All enterprises had been taken over by the Soviet State. The Bolshevik commissars have disappeared. The Ukrainian trustee administrators, who were appointed upon the recommendation of the Ukrainian Committee, turned out to be incompetent, unreliable, and completely passive. Only a handful of Poles were useful. The real experts and real heads are Jews, mostly the former owners or engineers. Constantly, they stand as translators of the language or translators into action at the side of the Ukrainian straw man [*Immer stehen sie als sprachliche oder fachliche Dolmetscher neben dem ukrainischen Strohmann*]. They try their utmost and extract the very last ounce of production – until now almost without pay, but naturally in the hope of becoming indispensable. The assistance of Reich and ethnic Germans who offered their services as "trustees" had to be dispensed with because, without exception, they proved to be speculators or adventurers who pursued only selfish aims. Although they have already acquired plenty of enterprises in the *Generalgouvernement*, they are interested only in more booty.[47]

Reading these lines, one cannot escape from the conclusion that during the crucial organizing period the Jews had already become indispensable.

The reliance upon Jewish skills and Jewish brains was of course immediately recognized as a potential obstacle to the "final solution." On August 14, 1941, Göring himself declared that the Jews no longer had any business in German-dominated territories (*dass die Juden in den von Deutschland beherrschten Gebieten nichts mehr zu suchen hätten*). Wherever Jewish labor was needed, the Jews were to be grouped into work formations; insofar as they had not had an "opportunity" to "emigrate," they were to be incarcerated in "something like" prison camps, to be organized there into labor battalions. Any other type of employment was not to be permitted, save in exceptional cases during the beginning of the occupation.[48]

However, the implementation of that directive proved to be a difficult proposition. Expert mechanics can easily be employed as heavy laborers, but unskilled laborers cannot easily replace trained artisans. The attempt was made. In November, 1941, the Economy Inspectorate Center went so far as to order that Jewish skilled workers surrender their tools and report for work in labor columns.[49] To the north,

46. Chief of *Wirtschaftsstab Ost* (signed Schubert) to OKW/Wi Rü and other offices (90 copies), July 16, 1941, Wi/ID 0.10. The Drohobycz area (Galicia) was then under army control.

47. Report by *Feldkommandantur* Przemysl *Süd/Gruppe* IV Wi (signed Hauptmann Dr. Bode), August 29, 1941, Wi/ID 1.113.

48. Report by Nagel (OKW/Wi Rü liaison officer with the *Reichsmarschall*), August 14, 1941. Wi/ID 2.319.

49. Economy Inspectorate Center (signed Kapitän zur See Kotthaus), to *Wirtschaftsstab Ost*, Economy Inspectorates North and Center, Armament Inspectorate Ukraine, Army Group B, 2nd, 4th, and 9th Armies, Armament Command Minsk, and economy commands of the Economy Inspectorate Center, November 16, 1941, Wi/ID 2.124.

in Latvia, the forest administration of the *Generalkommissar* used "large contingents" of Jews to collect wood for heating.[50] To the south, in military territory, municipalities made use of labor columns for clearing away debris and reconstruction work.[51] But in the end the pressing need for irreplaceable Jewish skilled labor made itself felt everywhere.

The army needed Jewish workers in its repair shops and Jewish clerks in its offices.[52] The armament plants under "trusteeship" continued to be dependent upon Jewish labor.[53] In the Volhynian sector of the *Generalkommissariat* Volhynia-Podolia, the labor force in armament plants was 90 per cent Jewish throughout 1941 and 1942.[54] In the same area "intelligent Jews were in many cases the real factory managers."[55] Last but not least, the ghettos themselves employed a large labor force in workshops and administrative positions.[56] We can understand therefore that during the second sweep each captor of Jewish labor held on tightly to his gain.

Not much need be said about working conditions and wages. Labor columns returning to the Riga ghetto each night were received with rubber truncheons and fists.[57] In the Salaspils camp for Reich Jews, 900 men were buried in a single mass grave – i.e., about 60 per cent of the working force died.[58] With respect to wages, the Lohse directive provided that only subsistence money was to be paid. In White Russia wage scales for the *Slavic* population ranged from 0.5 ruble (child labor) to 2.5 rubles (foremen) per hour. The wage scale for Jews was 0.40 to 0.80 ruble.[59] This differential was not intended for the benefit of private firms, though; it was to be paid to the *Kommissariat*.[60] During the second sweep the civil administration, in particular, was also to have a financial reason for the retention of the Jewish labor supply.

The third economic measure against Jews was the confiscation of property. Unlike the Jews of the Reich-Protektorat area, or even the Jews of Poland, USSR Jewry could offer no major "objects" to German industrialists, bankers, and economy experts. In the USSR no private person owned enterprises, warehouses, real estate, or art collections. Such items were state property. The only prizes to be taken from Soviet Jews were their apartments, furniture, utensils, small amounts of cash, bits of jewelry, and large quantities of old clothes. In spite of the meagerness of this loot, there were jurisdictional disputes over possession of the Jewish be-

50. *Generalkommissar* Latvia/Division IIa to *Reichskommissar Ostland*/IIa, October 20, 1941, Occ E 3-27.

51. Order by Army Group Rear Area South (signed von Roques), July 21, 1941. NOKW-1601.

52. On September 12, 1941, Keitel prohibited the utilization of Jews in "preferential" jobs. Army Group Rear Area North/Ic to Army Group Rear Area North/VII, September 24, 1941, NOKW-1686.

53. For early recruitment, see report by Economy Command Riga to Economy Inspectorate North, July 21, 1941, PS-579 Riga was then still under military control.

54. Armament Command Luzk to Armament Inspectorate Ukraine, report for October 1-December 31, 1942, January 21, 1943, Wi/ID 1.101.

55. *Ibid.*

56. See chart of Statistical Office of the Vilna ghetto, June, 1942, Vilna Ghetto Collection, No. 286. According to this chart, Vilna had 7446 employed Jews, of whom 1401 worked for the ghetto.

57. Report by Soviet Extraordinary State Commission (signed by Burdentko, Nikolai, Trainin, and Lysenko), undated, USSR-41.

58. Affidavit by Alfred Winter (survivor), October 15, 1947, NO-5448.

59. Decree (signed Kube) of June 1, 1942, *Amtsblatt des Generalkommissars für Weissruthenien,* 1942, p. 105. One ruble = 0.10 reichsmark, according to official rate of exchange.

60. Decree (signed Kube) of August 18, 1942, *Amtsblatt des Generalkommissars in Minsk,* 1942, p. 166.

longings. In part, such disputes were an inevitable outgrowth of the chaotic state of affairs during the transition period; in part, they were a prelude to the struggle which was to follow, for the implication was clear that whoever owned the Jewish property also owned the Jews. There was a long list of "claimants" to the Jewish "estate."

One of the first collectors of Jewish property was invariably a killing unit.[61] As a rule, the mobile killing units generously handed out furniture and clothes to the native population, particularly to the ethnic Germans in the area.[62] A second claimant – of a very de facto character – was the civilian population, which helped itself to the abandoned Jewish apartments, often taking possession of them.[63] A third claimant appeared in the person of administrative officials of the military and the *Kommissariate* who needed offices, office furniture, and a variety of other things. On the front line the troops "requisitioned" things, although looting was of course prohibited.[64] What was left was subject to systematic confiscation by the economy inspectorates in the military areas and by the finance offices in the *Reichskommissariate*. The disposal of the Jewish property, like the requisition of Jewish labor, was consequently handled on a first come – first grab basis. Very few changes could be made in this scheme.

In the military area the *Wirtschaftsstab Ost*, armed with authority from the OKH, attempted to curb the looting by *Einsatzgruppen* and army units.[65] It was an uphill fight,[66] and the spoils were hardly worth it. In one report the Economy Inspectorate Center explained that by German standards the Jewish clothes and underwear could be classified only as "rags" (*Lumpen*).[67] On July 4, 1942, the Economy Inspec-

61. RSHA IV-A-1, Operational Report USSR No. 21 (32 copies), July 13, 1941, NO-2937. RSHA IV-A-1, Operational Report USSR No. 125 (50 copies), October 26, 1941, NO-3403. RSHA IV-A-1, Operational Report USSR No. 156, January 16, 1942, NO-3405.

62. RSHA IV-A-1, Operational Report USSR No. 103 (48 copies), October 4, 1941, NO-4489. In Zhitomir, *Einsatzgruppe C* handed 50,000-60,000 pounds of clothes and utensils to a representative of the NSV (National Socialist People's Welfare). RSHA IV-A-1, Operational Report USSR No. 106 (48 copies), October 7, 1941, NO-3140. *Einsatzgruppe D* delivered its loot to Reich finance offices – much to the chagrin of the 11th Army, which wanted the stuff for its own purposes. Ohlendorf to 11th Army, February 12, 1942, NOKW-631. In October, 1942, the Higher SS and Police Leader Center, Obergruppenführer von dem Bach, sent 10,000 pairs of children's socks and 2000 pairs of children's gloves to Himmler's Personal Staff for distribution to SS families. OStuf. Meine (Pers. St.) to Gruf. Hofmann (Chief, RuSHA), October 28, 1942, NO-2558. The Higher SS and Police Leader North, Jeckeln, presided over a huge warehouse in Riga. He spent hours sorting jewelry on his desk. Affidavit by Richard Dannler (SS mailman), September 19, 1947, NO-5124.

63. Report by 454th Security Division Ic, December 4, 1941, NOKW-2926. Also, report of looting in Kharkov: RSHA IV-A-1, Operational Report USSR No. 164 (65 copies), February 4, 1942, NO-3399.

64. Order by Commander, Rear Army Group Area South (signed von Roques), September 1, 1941, NOKW-2594. Ortskommandantur Nikolaev to Commander, Rear Army Area 553 (11th Army), September 25, 1941, NOKW-1729.

65. Order by *Wirtschaftsstab Ost/Führung* Ia, October 22, 1941, Wi/ID 0.82. The OKH order, investing the *Wirtschaftsstab Ost* with sole authority to conduct confiscations in the military area, was dated October 2, 1941.

66. Economy Inspectorate Center (signed Kapitän zur See Kotthaus), to *Wirtschaftsstab Ost*, November 6, 1941, Wi/ID 2.124. Report by Economy Inspectorate Center (signed Generalleutnant Weigand), November 22, 1941, Wi/ID 2.124. Report by Economy Inspectorate Center (signed Generalleutnant Weigand), December 22, 1941, Wi/ID 2.124. Report by Economy Inspectorate Center (signed Generalleutnant Weigand), April 4, 1942, Wi/ID 2.33. War diary, Economy Command in Klimovichi (signed Hauptmann Weckwerth) to Economy Inspectorate Center, December 31, 1941, Wi/ID 2.90.

torate reported that in the entire area of Army Group Center it had collected property amounting to 2,046,860 rubles (204,686 reichsmark, or about 80,000 dollars). A part of that property had been "relinquished" in favor of the suffering Russian communities in the area.[68]

The civilian administration approched its confiscation problem with stubbornness in the *Ostland* and with remarkable laxity in the Ukraine.

Reichskommissar Lohse of the *Ostland* made a determined attempt to stop confiscations by the mobile killing units, lay claim to property in the possession of the civilian population, and collect all "nonessentials" from the ghetto Jews. To establish his exclusive claim, Lohse declared in secret directive and public decree that he as *Reichskommissar* had sole jurisdiction in Jewish property matters.[69] But declarations are one thing, action another.

On September 8, 1941, the *Gebietskommissar* of Shavli, Latvia (Gewecke), complained to Lohse that he simply could not carry out a systematic seizure of Jewish property. A certain Hauptmann Stasys Senulis had appeared in his office that very day and had demanded in the name of Standartenführer Jäger (*Einsatzkommando* 3) that the local mayors hand over all the gold and silver which had been in Jewish possession.[70] On September 24, 1941, a file note in the office of the *Generalkommissar* in Kaunas recorded the fact that the SS had removed from Lithuanian banks 3,769,180 rubles in Jewish deposits and valuables.[71] On September 25, 1941, Lohse wrote to the Higher SS and Police Leader personally (Prützmann), pointing out that confiscations were in the exclusive province of the *Reichskommissar*. "I do not permit any sideswipes at Jewish property and expect to take all necessary measures to persuade your police officers to cease all self-empowered action."[72] But there was very little he could do. On November 15, 1941, Rosenberg and Himmler had a four-hour discussion; among the subjects aired were, in Himmler's words, the "fussiness of Reichskommissar Lohse" and the "ludicrous complaints of Generalkommissar Kube" about the "requisition of necessary items for the SS and Police" (*"Kleinlichkeit des Reichskommissars Lohse" und "lächerliche Beschwerden" des Generalkommissars Kube über "Sicherstellung des notwendigen Bedarfs für SS und Polizei"*).[73]

The second aspect of "exclusive jurisdiction" was the recovery of loot in the possession of the population. That was not much easier than taking things away from Himmler. A decree issued by Lohse on October 13, 1941, provided simply that whoever was holding Jewish property at the moment was to continue to "administer" it. Only extraordinary transactions required the permission of the *Reichskommissar*.[74] A year later Lohse ordered the registration of the property.[75] Many practical

67. Economy Inspectorate Center/Main Group Economy to *Wirtschaftsstab Ost*, July 1, 1942, Wi/ID 2.347.

68. Economy Inspectorate Center (signed Generalleutnant Weigand) to *Wirtschaftsstab Ost*, July 4, 1942, Wi/ID 2.70.

69. Temporary directive (signed Lohse), August 18, 1941, NG-4815. Decree (signed Lohse), October 13, 1941, *Verkündungsblatt des Reichskommissars für das Ostland*, 1941, p. 27.

70. Gewecke to Lohse, September 8, 1941, PS-3661.

71. Memorandum by *Generalkommissar* in Kaunas/Main Division II F, September 24, 1941, Occ E 3-24.

72. Lohse to Higher SS and Police Leader *Ostland* personally, September 25, 1941, Occ E 3-25.

73. Memorandum by Himmler, November 15, 1941, NO-5329.

74. Decree by *Reichskommissar Ostland*, October 13, 1941, *Verkündungsblatt des Reichskommissars für das Ostland*, 1941, p. 27.

difficulties developed in consequence of the registration order. On November 16, 1942, an article appeared in the German newspaper published in Riga under the title "Better One Registration Too Many" (*Besser eine Anmeldung zu viel*). The politely worded article pointed out that many Jewish belongings had been distributed by various agencies "at the time" (*seiner Zeit*) without receipt. On the other hand, many people had already reported these possessions at various places. Everyone was now asked to register his holdings, even if he had already done so.[76]

Whereas Lohse had his difficulties with the SS and Police and with the population, his confiscatory drive encountered no obstacles in the Jewish ghettos. In his "provisional directives" he ordered the registration of all Jewish property. The *Generalkommissare* were ordered to collect immediately all money, bankbooks, promissory notes, and valuables. Other items were to be collected systematically. The Jews were to retain only that portion of their household articles "required for a scanty subsistence" (*der der notdürftigen persönlichen Lebensführung dient*) and two rubles per person per day.[77]

In the Ukraine, Lohse's opposite number, Reichskommissar Koch, was far less ambitious in his efforts to collect Jewish belongings. On September 7, 1942, Koch received a directive, prepared in the East Ministry, to seize all Jewish and abandoned property. He was to use former Ukrainian officers and civil servants for the task. The Ukrainians were to seize the Jewish furniture in empty apartments, collect debts owed by the population to Jews, seize Jewish bank accounts, and pay Jewish debts. After some months, Koch replied that the implementation of this decree was a "political and organizational impossibility." He had already confiscated Jewish valuables, "particularly gold"; the remainder of the Jewish property consisted primarily of furnishings, part of which he was using in his offices and the rest of which he had burned. "To make lists now," he wrote, "to collect accounts in banks which in part no longer exist, to pay Jewish debts — that in my opinion is a presumption about my administration that cannot be justified in wartime. The suggestion, moreover, that I should use former Ukranian officers for such a purpose, I consider politically dangerous."[78]

The recovery of Jewish possessions from de facto owners thus made little headway. Lohse found that it was a most difficult administrative task; Koch did not even try.[79] So much, then, for the "confiscations."

During the intermediary stage the

75. Implementation decree (signed Lohse), October 14, 1942, in *Amtsblatt des Generalkommissars in Minsk,* 1942, pp. 246–248.

76. *Deutsche Zeitung im Ostland* (Riga), November 16, 1942, p. 5.

77. Lohse directive, August 18, 1941, NG-4815. For an example of a confiscatory measure on local level, see also order by police chief of Vilna ghetto, March 10, 1942, Vilna Ghetto Collection, No. 15.

78. Koch to Rosenberg personally, March 16, 1943, PS-192.

79. Interestingly enough, in the Roumanian-occupied territory of Transnistria, Germans were the de facto claimants and Roumanian authorities had to do the recovering. In the city of Odessa ethnic Germans had moved into Jewish apartments and had taken possession of the furnishings therein. The SS Welfare Agency for Ethnic Germans (*Volksdeutsche Mittelstelle* — VOMI) decided to protect these Germans. An agreement concluded in August, 1942, provided that, in view of the "fact" that during the Soviet regime many ethnic Germans had been forced to give up their apartments to Jews, the present German occupants should remain in possession. For the furniture they were to pay a "modest" amount to the Roumanian administration. Agreement signed by Governor Alexianu of Transnistria and Oberführer Horst Hoffmeyer of the VOMI, August 30, 1942, NO-5561.

missing steps of the destruction process were introduced one by one. To the SS and Police the concentration measures were most important, since they were to pave the way for the annihilation of the remaining Jews. Economic exploitation was of primary interest to the administration. In the field of labor, particularly, the SS and Police tolerated economic activities at first but fought hard against them during the second sweep. The third step, definition, was opposed by Himmler on principle. He could see no use in it to anybody.

The mobile killing units did not concern themselves with definitions. To the *Einsatzgruppen* it made little difference whether there were half-Jews or even quarter-Jews among their victims. Since the other half or other three-quarters were non-German, everybody who answered to the name "Jew" or was denounced as a Jew was killed as a Jew. However, there was a problem of categorizing a few ethnic groups who were suspect because they were believed to have Jewish characteristics. In the Vilna region, for instance, a small group of people who practiced the Jewish religion with some modifications but who claimed not to be Jews (backing up their claims with historical evidence from the time of the Czars) defied classification. These people were Karaims (also known as Karaites). They escaped death.[80] In the Crimea a tribe long separated from the main body of Jewry, the Krimchaks, did not answer to a call for "registration." It was decided that the Krimchaks were racially incontestable Jews (*rassisch einwandfreie Juden*).[81] They were seized and killed.[82]

While the mobile killing units were concerned only with broad categorizations of ethnic groups, the military and civilian offices in the occupied territories imported the Nuremberg definition (three Jewish grandparents, or two Jewish grandparents plus the Jewish religion or a Jewish marital partner) into regulations pertaining to marking, ghettoization, and so on.[83] The definitions, which could be found only in secret directives with limited distribution, aroused no protests from the SS and Police.

80. Dr. Steiniger, "Die Karaimen," *Deutsche Zeitung im Ostland* (Riga), November 15, 1942, p. 1. Also, correspondence in document Occ E 3b α-100.

81. *Orstkommandantur* Feodosia to Rear Army Area 553 (11th Army), November 16, 1941, NOKW-1631.

82. RSHA IV-A-1, Operational Report USSR No. 190 (65 copies), April 8, 1942, NO-3359. *Orstkommandantur* Kerch to Army Rear Area 553 (11th Army), July 15, 1942, NOKW-1709. *Ortskommandantur* Bachtshissaray to Army Rear Area 553 (11th Army), July 16, 1942, NOKW-1698. *Einsatzgruppe D* also killed the so-called Tati (mountain Jews from the Caucasus who had been resettled in the Crimea by the America Joint Distribution Committee). *Feldkommandantur* Eupatoria to Army Rear Area 553 (11th Army), March 16, 1942, NOKW-1851. Another group of victims were the Gypsies, not because it was thought that they were Jews but because they were regarded as a criminal element. RSHA IV-A-1, Operational Report USSR No. 150 (65 copies), January 2, 1942, NO-2834. RSHA IV-A-1, Operational Report USSR No. 178 (65 copies), March 9, 1942, NO-3241. RSHA IV-A-1, Operational Report USSR No. 184, March 23, 1942, NO-3235. RSHA IV-A-1, Operational Report USSR No. 195 (75 copies), April 24, 1942, NO-3277. After the systematic killing of Gypsies had begun, an order exempted all "non-migratory" Gypsies from destruction who could prove a two-year period of residence in the place where they were found. 218th Security Division to *Oberfeldkommandantur* 822, March 24, 1943, NOKW-2022. Other correspondence in document Occ E 3-61.

83. 454th Security Division Ia to *Ortskommandaturen* in its area, September 8, 1941, NOKW-2628. Lohse directive, August 18, 1941, NG-4815. The Lohse directive exempted half-Jews who had married Jewish partners *before* June 20, 1941, and who were *no longer* living with their partners on that date. The military definition specified no marriage cutoff date. Neither definition contained a cutoff date for Jewish religious adherence. Cf. original Nuremberg definition, p. 48.

In the beginning of 1942, however, the Ministry for Eastern Occupied Territories decided to issue a definition which was deemed more appropriate for the eastern area (that is, more stringent) than the Nuremberg decree. For this purpose, a conference was called on January 29, 1942, under the chairmanship of Generalkonsul Dr. Bräutigam (deputy chief, Political Division), and with a long list of participants, including Amtsgerichtsräte Wetzel and Weitnauer and Regierungsräte Lindemann and Beringer (all of the East Ministry); Ministerialrat Lösener, Jewish expert of the Interior Ministry and author of the original Nuremberg definition; Oberregierungsrat Reischauer of the Party Chancellery; Sturmbannführer Neifeind and Sturmbannführer Suhr (both RSHA officials); Legationssekretär Müller of the Foreign Office (*Abteilung Deutschland*); Korvettenkapitän Frey, representing the Canaris office (Armed Forces Intelligence); and a representative of the Justice Ministry, Pfeifle.

Over the objections of Ministerialrat Lösener, who preferred that his decree be applied in all territories under German control, the conferees decided upon a broader definition. Any person was to be considered as Jewish if he belonged to the Jewish religion or if he had a parent who belonged to the Jewish religion. For determination of adherence to the Jewish religion, the slightest positive indication was to be conclusive. A declaration that the father or mother was Jewish was to be entirely sufficient. In cases of doubt an "expert" race and heredity examination was to be ordered by the competent *Generalkommissar*.[84]

When Himmler heard about the definition-making, he wrote the following letter to the chief of the SS-Main Office, Obergruppenführer Berger:

> I request urgently that no ordinance be issued about the concept of "Jew." With all these foolish definitions we are only tying our hands. The occupied eastern territories will be cleared of Jews. The implementation of this very hard order has been placed on my shoulders by the Führer. No one can release me from this responsibility in any case. So I forbid all interference.[85]

No one could interfere with Himmler now, for the second sweep had begun, leaving in its wake the demolished ghettos of the occupied East.

5 / The Second Sweep

The first sweep was completed toward the end of 1941. It had a limited extension in newly occupied territories of the Crimea and the Caucasus during the spring and summer months of 1942. The second sweep, on the other hand, began in the Baltic area in the fall of 1941 and spread through the rest of the occupied territory during the following year. In short, while the first sweep was still proceeding in the South, the second sweep had already started in the North. At the pivotal point, in the center, the turn came around December, 1941.

The machinery employed in the second sweep was larger and more elaborate than that of the first. Himmler's forces were joined by army personnel in mobile and local operations which were designed for the complete annihilation of the remaining Soviet Jews.

In the ensuing operations the *Einsatzgruppen* played, proportionally, a smaller role than before. Organizationally, they were placed under the direction of the Higher SS and Police Leaders North, Center, and South, and gradually the *Einsatzgruppen* dissolved

84. Summary of interministerial conference (held on January 29, 1942), dated January 30, 1942, NG-5035.

85. Himmler to Berger, July 28, 1942, NO-626.

in the greatly expanded machinery of the SS and Police in Russia.[1]

The police regiments, on the other hand, were increased from three at the beginning of the war to ten at the end of 1942. Five regiments were on the front; the remainder, together with several independent battalions, were at the disposal of the Higher SS and Police Leaders in the rear.[2]

During the second sweep, mobile killing operations were also carried out by so-called anti-partisan formations (*Bandenkampfverbände*). The employment of these formations derived from one of Hitler's orders, issued in the late summer of 1942, for the centralization of anti-partisan fighting.[3] Pursuant to the order, anti-partisan operations *in the civilian areas* were to be organized by Himmler. In the military areas the same responsibility was to be exercised by the chief of the army's General Staff. Himmler appointed as his plenipotentiary Higher SS and Police Leader Center von dem Bach and gave him the title *Chef der Bandenkampfverbände* ("Chief of the Anti-Partisan Formations").[4] In his capacity as anti-partisan chief in the civilian areas, von dem Bach could draw upon army personnel (security divisions, units composed of indigenous collaborators, etc.), SS units, police regiments, and *Einsatzgruppen*, for as long as he needed them for any particular operation. These units became "anti-partisan formations" for the duration of such an assignment.[5] The device is of interest because in the guise of anti-partisan activity the units killed thousands of Jews in the woods and in the swamps.

The *Einsatzgruppen*, police regiments, and anti-partisan formations were supplemented and assisted by a large apparatus of relatively stationary personnel, which can be divided into three components also.

First, the stationary counterpart of the *Einsatzgruppen* was the machinery of the *Befehlshaber der Sicherheitspolizei und des SD* (BdS). This machinery was established in the areas of the Higher SS and Police Leaders North and South only. The chief of *Einsatzgruppe A* (Stahlecker, later Jost) was at the same time BdS in the *Ostland*, and the chief of *Einsatzgruppe C* (Thomas) was at the same time BdS Ukraine.[6]

The police regiments had their counterpart on a stationary level in the so-called *Einzeldienst* (single-man duty). The *Einzeldienst* was divided into city police (*Schutzpolizei*) and rural police (*Gendarmerie*). Both *Schutzpolizei* and *Gendarmerie* in the East were expanded enormously by the addition of native auxiliaries. (The statistics in Table 44 apply to the end of 1942.)[7]

1. RSHA Summary Report No. 6, June 5, 1942, NO-5187. A fourth Higher SS and Police Leader, Bgf. Korsemann, was installed in the Caucasus. *Einsatzgruppe D* operated in that area.

2. Oberst-Gruppenführer Daluege (Chief of the Order Police) to OGruf. Wolff (Chief of Himmler's Personal Staff), February 28, 1943, NO-2861.

3. Order by Hitler, September 6, 1942, NO-1666.

4. Von dem Bach recommended himself, as the most experienced Higher SS and Police Leader in the business, for the position. Von dem Bach to Himmler, September 5, 1942, NO-1661. The letter was written only a few months after von dem Bach had suffered his nervous breakdown. Grawitz to Himmler, March 4, 1942, NO-600. He had to wait for his title, *Chef der Bandenkampfverbände*, until 1943. Order by Himmler, June 21, 1943, NO-1621.

5. Affidavit by von dem Bach, January 21, 1947, NO-1906.

6. Below the level of BdS, the machinery branched out into the offices of the *Kommandeure der Sicherheitspolizei und des SD* (KdS). In the *Ostland* the chiefs of *Einsatzkommandos* became *Kommandeure*. However, this amalgamation did not take place in the Ukraine. RSHA Summary Report No. 6, June 5, 1942, NO-5187.

7. Daluege to Wolff, February 28, 1943, NO-2861.

TABLE 44 / *Size of Police Forces During the Second Sweep*

	SCHUTZ-POLIZEI	GENDAR-MERIE	TOTAL
Germans	5,860	9,093	14,953
Auxiliaries	23,411	214,694	238,105
Total	29,271	223,787	253,058

The third part of the local machinery was the network of military rear-echelon offices and their specialized personnel who roamed about the countrysides collecting information about hidden partisans and Jews: the Ic/AO offices, the *Feldgendarmerie* (military police), the *Geheime Feldpolizei* ("Secret Field Police," an intelligence branch), and the so-called *Partisanenjäger* ("partisan hunters," or anti-partisan patrols). The military intelligence machinery was formally incorporated into the killing apparatus by an agreement between Heydrich and Canaris for exchange of information in the field. The agreement provided specifically that "information and reports which might bring about executive activities are to be transmitted immediately to the competent office of the Security Police and SD."[8]

The killing machinery of the second sweep is summarized in Table 45, in which the terms "mobile" and "local" are primarily intended to convey a difference in the radius of operations.

In the military area the second sweep was comparatively brief. As we have noted, the density of the Jewish population decreased as the mobile killing units pushed east. The slowing of the advance enabled the units to work much more thoroughly. *Einsatzgruppe A* had little to do in the rear area of Army Group North. Accordingly, it shifted some of its *Kommandos* to the civilian areas of White Russia to work over terrain through which *Einsatzgruppe B* had passed hurriedly in the early months of the fall.[9] *Einsatzgruppe B* spent the winter in the Mogilev-Smolensk-Bryansk sector. Recoiling from the Soviet counteroffensive, the advance *Kommandos* pulled back, and in the course of the contraction the *Einsatzgruppe* systematically killed the surviving Jews in the rear areas of Army Group Center.[10] In the meantime, isolated Jews in the north and center, fleeing alone or in small groups, were hunted down relentlessly by the Secret Field Police, Russian collaborators in the German Army (*Russischer Ordnungsdienst*), an Estonian police battalion, and other units.[11]

TABLE 45 / *Killing Machinery of the Second Sweep*

ORGANIZATION	MOBILE	LOCAL
Security Police & SD	*Einsatzgruppen*	BdS and KdS offices
Order Police	Police regiments	*Einzeldienst*
Army	*Bandenkampfverbände*	Army rear echelons

8. Agreement between Wehrmacht and RSHA (signed by Canaris and Heydrich), March 1, 1942, in file note of Commander of Rear Army Group Area South Ic/AO, October 1, 1942, NOKW-3228.

9. Draft report by *Einsatzgruppe A*, winter 1941-42, PS-2273.

10. During the period March 6-30, 1942, the *Einsatzgruppe* killed 3358 Jews, as well as 375 other people, including 78 Gypsies. RSHA IV-A-1, Operational Report USSR No. 194 (75 copies), April 21, 1942, NO-3276.

11. Operational report by Secret Field Police Group 703 (signed Feldpolizeikommissar Gasch), June 24, 1942, NOKW-95. The unit operated in the Vyazma sector. 39th Estonian Police Battalion via 281st Security Division Ia to Higher SS and Police Leader North, August 28, 1942, NOKW-2513. Secret Field Police Group 722 to 207th Security Division Ic, etc., March 25, 1943, NOKW-

To the south, *Einsatzgruppen C* and *D* were engaged in heavier operations. In Dnepropetrovsk, 30,000 Jews at the time of the city's occupation were whittled down to 702 by February, 1942.[12] During March, 1942, several large cities east of the Dnieper, including Gorlovka, Makeevka, Artemovsk, and Stalino, were "cleared of Jews" (*judenfrei gemacht*).[13] In this area, too, the army tracked down escaping Jews. One security division actually encountered a Jewish partisan group (25 men) in the Novo Moskovsk-Pavlograd area.[14]

Einsatzgruppe D in the Crimea reported on February 18, 1942, that almost 10,000 Jews had now been killed in Simferopol – 300 more than had originally registered there.[15] This discovery was the signal for a systematic sweeping operation in the entire Crimea.[16] The drive was conducted with the help of local militia, a network of agents, and a continuous flow of denunciations from the population.[17] The army gave the drive every assistance. On December 15, 1941, Major Stephanus, anti-partisan expert of the Eleventh Army, had ordered the *Abwehr* and Secret Field Police to hand over escaped Jews to the *Einsatzgruppe*.[18] The local *Kommandanturen* and the *Gendarmerie* also joined in the operation.[19] By spring the Crimea no longer had any Jews, except for two groups in Soviet-held territory. *Einsatzgruppe D* caught them in July.[20]

The second sweep in the military areas was therefore carried out in a coordinated manner; the operations did not meet with any major obstacle, and they did not generate disputes. However, in the civilian territories the

2158. However, as late as July, 1943, the *Organisation Todt* was still employing 1615 Jews in the area of Army Group Center. Wi In Mitte to WiStOst, August 5, 1943, Wi/ID 2.59.

12. "Das Schicksal von Dnjepropetrowsk," *Krakauer Zeitung*, February 10, 1942, p. 4.

13. RSHA IV-A-1, Operational Report USSR No. 177 (65 copies), March 6, 1942, NO-3240. RSHA IV-A-1, Operational Report USSR No. 187, March 30, 1942, NO-3237. RSHA Summary Report No. 11 for March, 1942 (100 copies), PS-3876.

14. Report by 444th Security Division Ia, January 22, 1942, NOKW-2868. The Jewish partisans were referred to as *Judengruppe Dnjepropetrowsk*. For other reports of seizures by military, see Generalmajor Mierzinsky of *Feldkommandantur* 245/Ia to XLIV Corps/Qu, March 31, 1942, and other reports by same *Feldkommandantur*, in NOKW-767. The seizures took place in the Slavyansk-Kramatorskaya area. Also, *Feldkommandantur* 194 in Snovsk (signed Oberst Ritter von Würfel) to commander of Army Group Rear Area South/Ia, April 7, 1942, NOKW-2803.

15. RSHA IV-A-1, Operational Report USSR No. 170, February 18, 1942, NO-3339.

16. RSHA IV-A-1, Operational Report USSR No. 178 (65 copies), March 9, 1942, NO-3241. RSHA IV-A-1, Operational Report USSR No. 184, March 23, 1942, NO-3235.

17. RSHA IV-A-1, Operational Report USSR No. 190 (65 copies), April 8, 1942, NO-3359.

18. 11th Army Ic/Ia (signed Major Stephanus) to *Einsatzgruppe D*, Secret Field Police, and *Abwehr*, December 15, 1941, NOKW-502. Secret Field Police Group 647 to 11th Army Ic/AO, July 26, 1942, NOKW-848. Affidavit by Heinz Hermann Schubert, December 7, 1945, NO-4816.

19. Major Erxleben (*Feldgendarmerie*) to 11th Army OQu, February 2, 1942, NOKW-1283. *Ortskommandantur* Karasubar to Army Rear Area, February 14, 1942, NOKW-1688. Operational report by *Feldkommandantur* 810/*Feldgendarmerie* (signed Lt. Pallmann), March 3, 1942, NOKW-1689. *Feldkommandantur* 810 in Eupatoria to Rear Army Area, March 16, 1942, NOKW-1851. Report by *Sonderkommando* 10*b*, March 27, 1942, NOKW-635. *Feldgendarmerie* Battalion 683 to 11th Army OQu, April 2, 1942, NOKW-1285. *Feldkommandantur* 608 to Rear Army Area, April 28, 1942, NOKW-1870.

20. *Ortskommandantur* Kerch to Army Rear Area/Qu, July 15, 1942, NOKW-1709. Kerch is on the eastern end of the peninsula. *Ortskommandantur* Bakhtshissaray to Army Rear Area/Qu, July 16, 1942, NOKW-1698. Bakhtshissaray is on the road to Sevastopol. No documentary information is available about operations in Sevastopol itself. Possibly no Jews remained there when the German Army arrived.

second sweep did not progress so smoothly. The Jews in the *Kommissariate* were wiped out by stages. The preliminary stage began with sudden combings of the *Ostland.*

On September 11, 1941, the *Gebietskommissar* of Shavli (Latvia) sent a letter to Reichskommissar Lohse which contained a short preview of the problems posed by the onset of a new wave of killings. In Shavli *Einsatzgruppe A* had left behind a small detachment (*Restkommando*) under an SS sergeant. One day the commander of *Einsatzkommando* 2 (Standartenführer Jäger) dispatched a certain Obersturmführer Hamann to Shavli; Hamann looked up the sergeant and declared in an "extraordinary arrogant tone" that the Jewish situation in Shavli was a dirty mess (*ein Saustall*) and that all Jews in the city had to be "liquidated." Hamann then visited the *Gebietskommissar* and repeated "in a less arrogant tone" why he had come. When the Gebietskommissar explained that the Jews were needed as skilled laborers, Hamann declared curtly that such matters were none of his business and that the economy did not interest him at all.[21]

On October 30, 1941, Gebietskommissar Carl of Sluzk, White Russia, reported to Kube that the 11th Lithuanian Police Battalion had arrived in his city and had come suddenly in order to wipe out the Jewish community. He had pleaded with the battalion commander for a postponement, pointing out that the Jews were working as skilled laborers and specialists and that White Russian mechanics were, "so to speak, nonexistent." Certainly the skilled men would have to be sifted out. The battalion commander did not contradict him, and the interview ended upon a note of complete understanding. The police battalion then encircled the Jewish quarter and dragged out everybody. White Russians in the area tried desperately to get out. Factories and workshops stopped functioning. The *Gebietskommissar* hurried to the scene; he was shocked by what he saw. "There was no question of an action against the Jews anymore. It looked rather like a revolution." Shots were fired. Lithuanian police hit Jews with rifle butts and rubber truncheons. Shops were turned inside out. Peasant carts (*Panjewagen*) which had been ordered by the army to move ammunition stood abandoned with their horses in the streets. Outside the town the mass shootings were carried out hurriedly. Some of the Jews, wounded but not killed, worked themselves out of the graves. When the police battalion departed, Gebietskommissar Carl had a handful of Jewish workers left. In every shop there were a few survivors, some of them with bloody and bruised faces, their wives and children dead.[22]

When Kube received this report, he was incensed. He sent it on to Lohse, with a duplicate for Reichsminister Rosenberg. Adding a comment of his own, Kube pointed out that the burial of seriously wounded people who could work themselves out of their graves was such a disgusting business (*eine so bodenlose Schweinerei*) that it ought to be reported to Göring and to Hitler.[23]

In October, 1941, the *Reichskommissar* forbade the shooting of Jews in Lepaya (Latvia). The RSHA complained to the East Ministry, and Dr. Leibbrandt, chief of the ministry's Political Division, requested a report.[24] In the correspondence which followed, Regierungsrat Trampedach (Political Division, *Ostland*) explained that the "wild executions of Jews" in Lepaya

21. Gewecke to Lohse, September 11, 1941, Occ E 3-22.

22. Carl to Kube, October 30, 1941, PS-1104.

23. Kube to Lohse, November 1, 1941, PS-1104.

24. Leibbrandt to *Reichskommissar Ostland,* October 31, 1941, PS-3663.

had been forbidden because of the manner in which they had been carried out. Trampedach then inquired whether the letter from Dr. Leibbrandt was to be regarded as a directive to kill all Jews in the East, without regard to the economy.[25] The ministry's answer was that economic questions should *not* be considered in the solution of the Jewish problem. Any further disputes were to be settled on the local level.[26] This declaration ended the incipient struggle for the preservation of the Jewish labor force. The *Kommissare* were now resigned to its loss.

In the Ukraine the Armament Inspectorate looked forward to the massacres with some apprehension but declined to fight about the issue. On December 2, 1941, the Armament Inspector sent a report by an expert, Oberkriegsverwaltungsrat Professor Seraphim, to the chief of the Economy-Armament Office in the OKW (Thomas). The inspector took pains to point out that the report was personal and unofficial. He requested the receiving agency not to distribute it without the express permission of General Thomas.[27]

Seraphim wrote that, obviously, "the kind of solution of the Jewish problem applied in the Ukraine" was based on ideological theories, not on economic considerations. So far, 150,000 to 200,000 Jews had been "executed" in the *Reichskommissariat.* One result of this operation was that a considerable number of "superfluous eaters" had been eliminated. Undoubtedly, the dead had also been a hostile element "which hated us." On the other hand, the Jews had been "anxious" and "obliging" from the start. They had tried to avoid everything that might have displeased the German administration; they had played no significant part in sabotage; they had constituted no danger to the armed forces. Although driven only by fear, they had been producing goods in satisfactory quantities.

Moreover, the killing of the Jews could not be looked upon as an isolated phenomenon. The city population and farm laborers were already starving. "It must be realized," concluded Seraphim, "that in the Ukraine only the Ukrainians can produce economic values. If we shoot the Jews, let the prisoners of war perish, condemn considerable parts of the urban population to death by starvation, and lose also a part of the farming population by hunger during the next year, the question remains unanswered: Who in all the world is then supposed to produce something valuable here?" The answer to this rhetorical question was soon to be provided by Himmler's men.

The sweep through the *Ostland* in the fall of 1941 was only a warmup, but it settled a decisive issue. The Jews were at the disposal of the civil and military authorities only at the sufferance of the SS and Police. The killers had first claim.

The Jews, in the meantime, kept working. During the quiet months of the winter and spring of 1942 they began to adjust themselves to their hazardous existence. They tried to make themselves "indispensable."[28] The most important possession of any Jew in this period was a work certificate. None of the penalties which were threatened by the Jewish ghetto police for infractions of rules were as severe as the confiscation of a certificate,[29] since it was

25. *Reichskommissariat Ostland* to East Ministry, November 15, 1941, PS-3663.

26. Dr. Bräutigam (deputy of Leibbrandt) to *Reichskommisar Ostland,* December 18, 1941, PS-3663. For attempt at local compromise, see *Reichskommissar Ostland* IIa to Higher SS and Police Leader North, December, 1941, Occ E 3-33.

27. Armament Inspector Ukraine to General Thomas, enclosing Seraphim report, December 2, 1941, PS-3257.

28. *Hauptkommissar* Baranovice (ORR. Gentz) to Lohse, February 10, 1942, Occ E 3-38.

looked upon as a life insurance policy. Whoever lost it stared death in the face. Some certificate holders grew confident during the lull – in the Kamenets-Podolski district (Ukraine) one Jewish worker approached a *Gendarmerie* sergeant and pointed out: "You are not going to shoot us to death; we are specialists."[30]

The civil administration, however, utilized the time to brace itself for the coming sweep. The *Kommissare* prepared lists of irreplaceable Jewish workers and ordered that the vocational training of non-Jewish youths be stepped up.[31] In June, Regierungsrat Trampedach (Political Division, *Reichskommissariat Ostland*) wrote to Kube that in the opinion of the BdS (Jost) the economic value of the Jewish skilled worker was not great enough to justify the continuation of dangers arising from Jewish support of the partisan movement. Did Kube agree?[32] Kube replied that he agreed. At the same time, he instructed his *Gebietskommissare* to cooperate with the SS and Police in a review of the essential status of Jewish workers with the aim of eliminating (*auszusondern*) all those skilled laborers who under the "most stringent criteria" were not "absolutely" needed in the economy.[33] In the summer of 1942 the second sweep was in full force. The entire machinery of the SS and Police was mobilized for the task, and the *Ostland* and the Ukraine were covered with a wave of massacres.

Unlike the first sweep, which caught the Jews by surprise, the second wave was expected by everyone. It was no longer feasible to employ ruses. The ghetto-clearing operations were carried out in the open with ruthlessness and brutality. The actions were uncompromising in character and final in their effect. No one could remain alive.

In the bureaucracy the feverish pitch of the killers created a strange transformation. The *Gebietskommissare,* who had previously protested against the destruction of their labor force and against the methods of the SS and Police, now joined Himmler's men and, in some cases, outdid themselves to make their areas *judenfrei.* By November, 1942, the *Reichskommissar Ostland* was constrained to forbid the participation of members of the civilian administration in "executions of any kind."[34] Lohse was a little late. In town after town Jewish communities were disappearing in the frenzy of the killings.

The first step in a ghetto-clearing operation was the digging of graves. Usually, a Jewish labor detachment had to perform this work.[35] On the eve of an *Aktion* an uneasy air pervaded the Jewish quarter. Sometimes Jewish representatives approached German businessmen with requests to intercede.[36] Policemen were approached by Jewish girls who wanted to save their

29. Proclamation of the police chief in the Vilna ghetto, June 7, 1942, Vilna Ghetto Collection No. 17. Also, his order of March 10, 1942, Vilna Collection No. 15. For use of certificates to keep Jews at work during periodic shootings, see also Jewish Black Book Committee, *The Black Book,* pp. 321–23, 325.

30. Gendarmeriemeister Fritz Jacob to Obergruppenführer Rudolf Querner (personal letter), June 21, 1942, NO-5655.

31. *Hauptkommissar* Baranovice (ORR. Gentz) to Lohse, copy to Kube, February 10, 1942, Occ E 3-38. Memorandum by *Reichskommissariat Ostland*/IIb, November, 1941, Occ E 3-33.

32. Trampedach to Kube, June 15, 1942, Occ E 3-40.

33. Kube to *Reichskommissar Ostland,* July 10, 1942, enclosing directive of the same date, Occ E 3-40.

34. Order by *Reichskommissar Ostland,* November 11, 1942, NO-5437.

35. Affidavit by Alfred Metzner, October 15, 1947, NO-5530. Metzner, an employee of the *Generalkommissariat* Slonim (White Russia), personally killed hundreds of Jews.

36. Affidavit by Hermann Friedrich Graebe, November 10, 1945, PS-2992. Graebe was with a German firm in Sdolbunov, Ukraine.

lives. As a rule, the women were used during the night and killed in the morning.[37]

The actual operation would start with the encirclement of the ghetto by a police cordon. Most often, the operation was timed to begin at dawn,[38] but sometimes it was carried out at night, with searchlights focused on the ghetto and flares illuminating the countryside all around.[39] Small detachments of police, *Kommissariat* employees, and railroad men, armed with crowbars, rifles, hand grenades, axes, and picks, then moved into the Jewish quarter.[40]

The bulk of the Jews moved out immediately to the assembly point. Many, however, remained in their homes, doors locked, praying and consoling each other. Often they hid in cellars or lay flat between the earth and the wooden floors.[41] The raiding parties moved through the streets shouting, "Open the door, open the door!"[42] Breaking into the houses, the Germans threw hand grenades into the cellars, and some "especially sadistic persons" (*besonders sadistische Leute*) fired tracer bullets point-blank at the victims. During an operation in Slonim many houses were set afire, until the entire ghetto was a mass of flames. Some Jews who still survived in cellars and underground passages choked to death or were crushed under the collapsing buildings. Additional raiders then arrived with gasoline cans and burned the dead and wounded in the streets.[43]

Meanwhile, the Jews who had voluntarily left their homes were waiting at the assembly point. Sometimes they were forced to crouch on the ground to facilitate supervision.[44] Trucks then brought them in batches to the ditch, where they were unloaded with the help of rifles and whips. They had to take off their clothes and submit to searches. Then they were shot either in front of the ditch or in the ditch by the "sardine" method.

The mode of the shooting depended a great deal on the killers' sobriety. Most of them were drunk most of the time – only the "idealists" refrained from the use of alcohol. The Jews submitted without resistance and without protest. "It was amazing," a German witness relates, "how the Jews stepped into the graves, with only mutual condolences in order to strengthen their spirits and in order to ease the work of the execution commandos."[45] When the shooting took place in front of the ditch, the victims sometimes froze in terror. Just in front of them, Jews who had been shot were lying motionless. A few bodies were still twitching, blood running from their necks. The frozen Jews were shot as they stepped back from the edge of the grave, and other Jews quickly dragged them in.

At the shooting site, too, there were some "mean sadists." According to a former participant in these operations, a sadist was the type of man who would hurl his fist into the belly of a pregnant woman and throw her live into the grave.[46] Because of the killers' drunkenness many of the victims were left for a whole night, breathing and

37. Affidavit by Alfred Metzner, September 18, 1947, NO-5558.

38. Report by Hauptmann der Schutzpolizei Paier on operation in Pinsk, undated, probably November, 1942, USSR-119a.

39. Affidavit by Graebe, November 10, 1945, PS-2992.

40. Report by Paier, USSR-119a; and affidavits cited above.

41. Affidavit by Metzner, September 18, 1947, NO-5558.

42. Affidavit by Graebe, November 10, 1945, PS-2992.

43. Affidavit by Metzner, September 18, 1947, NO-5558.

44. Affidavit by Graebe, November 10, 1945, PS-2992.

45. Affidavit by Metzner, September 18, 1947, NO-5558.

46. *Ibid.*

bleeding. During an operation at Slonim some of these Jews dragged themselves, naked and covered with blood, as far as Baranovice. When panic threatened to break out among the inhabitants, native auxiliaries were dispatched at once to round up and kill these Jews.[47]

The *Gebietskommissar* of Slonim, Erren, used to call a meeting after every ghetto-clearing operation. The meeting was the occasion for a celebration, and those employees of the *Kommissariat* who had distinguished themselves were praised. Erren, who was perhaps more eager than most of his colleagues, acquired the title "Bloody *Gebietskommissar*."[48]

As the massive killing wave moved westward across the two *Reichskommissariate* and the Bialystok district, it became clear that *in the Ukraine* the operations would be over before the end of 1942. In the Volhynian-Podolian *Generalkommissariat* the armament industry gradually collapsed. Tens of thousands of Jewish workers in the plants of the western Ukraine were "withdrawn." Ghetto after ghetto was wiped out. In one report armament officials expressed the opinion that no one, not even skilled workers, would be saved; the very nature of these *Grossaktionen* precluded special arrangements. In Janow, for example, the entire ghetto with all its inhabitants had been burned to the ground (*das ganze Ghetto mit sämtlichen Insassen verbrannt*).[49] On October 27, 1942, Himmler himself ordered the destruction of the last major Ukrainian ghetto, Pinsk.[50]

In the western Ukraine, workshops that once produced *Panjewagen* (wooden carts), soap, candles, lumber, leather, and ropes for the German Army stood abandoned at the end of the year. There were no replacements. A report by the armament command in Luzk tabulated the damage: "The leather works in Dubno are closed. . . . In Kowel all *Panjewagen* workshops are paralyzed. . . . In the Kobryn works we have a single Aryan metals worker. . . . In Brest Litovsk the Jewish workshops now as before are empty [*nach wie vor leer*]."[51] The Jews of the Ukraine had been annihilated.[52]

A journalist traveling through the Ukraine in June, 1943, reported that he had seen only four Jews. He had interviewed a high official of the *Reichskommissariat* who had summed up the holocaust in these words: "Jews were exterminated like vermin [*Juden wurden wie die Wanzen vertilgt*]."[53]

At the end of 1942 the focus of attention shifted from the Ukraine to the *Ostland*. There, too, most of the Jews were already dead, but a sizable number (close to 100,000) were still alive. The killing of these remnants was a much more difficult process than the climactic waves of the second sweep could have led anyone to expect.

The *Ostland* remnant was divided into two groups, the forest Jews and the ghetto Jews (including camp inmates). The Jews in the forests and marshes

47. *Ibid.* There were similar occurrences at Sluzk and Terespol. Gebietskommissar Carl to Kube, October 30, 1941, PS-1104; affidavit by Franz Reichrath, October 14, 1947, NO-5439. Reichrath was a German eyewitness at Terespol.

48. Affidavit by Metzner, September 18, 1947, NO-5558.

49. Armament Command Luzk to Armament Inspectorate Ukraine, report for October 1–10, 1942, Wi/ID 1.97.

50. Himmler to OGruf. Prützmann, October 27, 1942, NO-2027.

51. Armament Command Luzk to Armament Inspectorate Ukraine, report for October 1-December 31, 1942, dated January 21, 1943, Wi/ID 1.101.

52. The figure of Jews killed in Bialystok, the Caucasus, and the Ukraine, from August through November, 1942, was 363,211. Himmler to Hitler, December 20, 1942, NO-511.

53. Report by Dr. Hans-Joachim Kausch, June 26, 1943, Occ E 14-11.

were a special problem because they were no longer under control. They had run away and were now in hiding. Consequently, they were more important than their numbers (in the thousands) would indicate. In the main, we may distinguish among the forest Jews three types of survivors: (1) individual Jews who were hiding out,[54] (2) Jews in the Soviet partisan movement,[55] and (3) Jews banded together in Jewish units.[56] The Jews still under control were living in the *Ostland* ghettos, as follows:[57]

Latvia	4,000
Lithuania	34,000
White Russia	30,000
	68,000

These ghettos became a problem because they, too, developed into focal points of resistance.

The drive against the forest Jews was launched early in 1942. During February and March of that year, the SS and Police Leader North (Jeckeln) struck against the partisans in a drive which became the precursor of later "anti-partisan" operations by von dem Bach. Each of these operations covered a specific area. As a rule, the smaller ghettos in the area were wiped out, and any fugitives encountered alone or with the partisans were shot. In the prototype *Aktion Sumpffieber* ("Action Marsh Fever"), carried out by Jeckeln in February-March, 389 "bandits" were killed in combat, 1274 persons were shot on suspicion, and 8350 Jews were mowed down on principle.[58]

Following the establishment of the anti-partisan command under von dem Bach, *Bandenkampfverbände* led by Brigadeführer von Gottberg were thrown into action in White Russia. On November 26, 1942, von Gottberg reported 1826 dead Jews, "not counting bandits, Jews, etc., burned in houses or dugouts." This was "Operation Nuremberg."[59] On December 21 von Gottberg reported another 2958 Jewish dead in "Operation Hamburg."[60] On

54. These Jews led a precarious existence. See M. Cherszstein, *Geopfertes Volk: Der Untergang des polnischen Judentums* (Stuttgart, 1946), pp. 26–40. Cherszstein is a survivor who hid in the woods.

55. First reports of Jewish movements to the partisans were received in the winter of 1941–42. *Wehrmachtbefehlshaber Ostland*/Propaganda Detachment (signed Oberleutnant Knoth) to commander of Army Group Rear Area North, undated report received February 8, 1942, NOKW-2155. For relations between Jews and non-Jews in partisan units, see Schwarz, *The Jews in the Soviet Union*, pp. 321–30.

56. OKH/Chief of Secret Field Police to army groups and armies in the East, July 31, 1942, NOKW-2535, p. 10. RR. Dr. Ludwig Ehrensleiter (deputizing for Gebietskommissar Erren of Slonim) to Kube, March 21, 1943, Occ E 3a-16. Reports by 69th Jäger Division (in Lithuania) to 3d Panzer Army, August 30–31, 1944, NOKW-2322. For relations between Jewish and Soviet units, see Tobias Bielski, "Brigade in Action," in Leo W. Schwarz (ed.), *The Root and the Bough* (New York, 1949), pp. 112–14.

57. RSHA Summary Report No. 7, June 12, 1942, NO-5158. RSHA Summary Report No. 8, June 19, 1942, NO-5157. *Generalkommissar* White Russia to East Ministry, November 23, 1942, Occ E 3-45. Estonia was *judenrein*. RSHA IV-A-1, Operational Report USSR No. 155, January 14, 1942, NO-3279. The ghetto figures do not include several thousand Jews in camps. When the camp Jews were transferred to the ghettos in 1943, the ghetto population in Latvia increased to almost 5000. KdS Latvia (Obf. Pifrader) to Lohse, August 1, 1943, Occ E 3bα-29. The ghetto population in Lithuania increased to over 40,000. Report by KdS Lithuania for April, 1943, Occ E 3bα-95; also, report by *Generalkommissar* Lithuania for April and May, 1943, Occ E 3bα-7. Later in 1943, hundreds of Jews were imported by the Kontinental Öl A. G. to augment its labor forces in the oil-bearing rock deposits of Estonia. See reports and correspondence of that company in Wi/I .32.

58. Report by Higher SS and Police Leader North, November 6, 1942, PS-1113.

59. Bgf. Gottberg to Gruf. Herff, November 26, 1942, NO-1732.

60. Gottberg to Herff, December 21, 1942, NO-1732. Also, RSHA Summary Report No. 38, January 22, 1943, NO-5156.

March 8, 1943, he reported 3300 dead Jews in "Operation Hornung."[61] In general, we may therefore conclude that this type of operation directed against the forest Jews was quite successful, although several thousand Jews in the woods were able to survive until the arrival of the Red Army.

In October, 1942, just before the end of the Ukrainian sweep and in conjunction with the anti-partisan operations, the stage was set for the destruction of the remaining *Ostland* ghettos, which held altogether about 68,000-75,000 Jews. On October 23, 1942, Dr. Leibbrandt, the chief of the Political Division in the East Ministry, sent the following letter to Generalkommissar Kube:

> I request a report about the Jewish situation in the *Generalbezirk* White Russia, especially about the extent to which Jews are still employed by German offices, whether as interpreters, mechanics, etc. I ask for a prompt reply because I intend to bring about a solution of the Jewish question as soon as possible.[62]

Kube replied, after a considerable delay, that in co-operation with the Security Police the possibilities of a further repression of Jewry (*die Möglichkeiten einer weiteren Zurückdrängung des Judentums*) were undergoing constant exploration and translation into action.[63]

As Kube had indicated, the reduction of the *Ostland* ghettos, with their remnants of the Jewish skilled labor force, was a slow, grinding process. In the course of that process two centers of resistance were emerging in the territory, one within the ghettos, the other in the person of Generalkommissar Kube himself.

Within the ghettos Jewish attempts to organize a resistance movement were largely abortive. In Riga and, to a lesser extent, in Kaunas, the Jewish police (*Ordnungsdienst*) began to practice with firearms. (However, in both places the police were caught before a shot was fired.)[64]

In the Vilna ghetto a Communist, Yitzhak Vitenberg, formed a resistance organization outside the framework of the Jewish police. According to an account pieced together from reports by survivors, the Germans demanded Vitenberg's surrender in July, 1943, under penalties of a fire attack on the ghetto. Vitenberg was holed up in the headquarters of his resistance organization and refused to budge. *Judenrat* chief Jacob Gens and his police commissioner, Sala Desler, thereupon summoned the masses and appealed to them to hand over Vitenberg to the Germans, lest the Gestapo "wipe out the ghetto in one blow with bombs, tanks, artillery, and all the fires of hell." The crowd "surged forward towards the defense headquarters like a wind-lashed tornado. They roared for the surrender of Vitenberg." Insults and stones began to fly. "There was no mistaking

61. Gottberg to Herff, March 8, 1943, NO-1732. RSHA Summary Report No. 46, March 19, 1943, NO-5164. See also report by Kube on "Operation *Kottbus*," June 1, 1943, R-135. This report does not specify Jewish dead, but Lohse, in reporting about the matter to Rosenberg, commented on the 9500 dead "bandits" and "suspects" as follows: "The fact that Jews receive special treatment requires no further discussion. However, it appears hardly believable that this is done in the way described in the report by the *Generalkommissar*. . . . What is Katyn against that?" Lohse to Rosenberg, June 18, 1943, R-135. Katyn is a reference to the German claim that the Soviets had massacred Polish officers in the Katyn forest.

62. Leibbrandt via Lohse to Kube, October 23, 1942, Occ E 3-45.

63. *Generalkommissar* White Russia to East Ministry, November 23, 1942, Occ E 3-45.

64. For account on Riga, see Jeanette Wolff in Eric H. Boehm (ed.), *We Survived* (New Haven, 1949), pp. 262–63. On Kaunas, see Samuel Gringauz, "The Ghetto as an Experiment of Jewish Social Organization," *Jewish Social Studies*, 1949, pp. 14–15, 19. Gringauz is a survivor.

the temper of the crowd. It was Vitenberg or bloodshed." Vitenberg proposed immediate resistance to his colleagues. He was overruled by a majority vote. Vitenberg was then surrendered by the Joint Defense Committee, including his own Communist comrades. His mutilated body was found on the next morning.[65]

After Vitenberg was killed by the Germans, the Jewish resistance organization fought a small and unsuccessful battle with invading German raiders during the closing days of the ghetto. One of the survivors of that engagement, Abraham Sutzkever, commented after the war: "Today we must confess the error of the staff decision which forced Vitenberg to offer himself as a sacrifice for the twenty thousand Jews. . . . We should have mobilized and fought."[66]

Generalkommissar Kube's post-climactic resistance was one of the strangest episodes in the history of the Nazi regime. His battle with the SS and Police was unique. Kube was an "old" Nazi who had once been purged (he had been a *Gauleiter*). As he had pointed out in a letter already cited in this chapter,[67] he was certainly a "hard" man, and he was ready to "help solve the Jewish question." But there were limits to his ruthlessness.

In 1943, Kube had a serious controversy with the commander of Security Police and SD (KdS) in White Russia, SS-Obersturmbannführer Strauch. On July 20, Strauch arrested seventy Jews employed by Kube and killed them. Kube called Strauch immediately and accused him of chicanery. If Jews were killed in his office but Jews working for the Wehrmacht were left alone, said Kube, this was a personal insult. Somewhat dumbfounded, Strauch replied that he "could not understand how German men could quarrel because of a few Jews." His record of the conversation went on:

> I was again and again faced with the fact that my men and I were reproached for barbarism and sadism, whereas I did nothing but fulfil my duty. Even the fact that expert physicians had removed in a proper way the gold fillings from the teeth of Jews who had been designated for special treatment was made the topic of conversation. Kube asserted that this method of our procedure was unworthy of a German man and of the Germany of Kant and Goethe. It was our fault that the reputation of Germany was being ruined in the whole world. It was also true, he said, that my men literally satisfied their sexual lust during these executions. I protested energetically against that statement and emphasized that it was regrettable that we, in addition to having to perform this nasty job, were also made the target of mudslinging.[68]

Five days later Strauch sent a letter to Obergruppenführer von dem Bach, in which he recommended Kube's dismissal. In a long list of particulars, Strauch pointed out that Kube had for a long time favored the Jews, especially the Reich Jews. So far as the Russian Jews were concerned, Kube could quiet his conscience because most of them were "partisan helpers," but he could not distinguish between Germans and German Jews. He had insisted that the Jews had art. He had expressed his liking for Offenbach and Mendelssohn. When Strauch had disagreed, Kube had claimed that young Nazis did not know anything about such things. Repeatedly, Kube had shown his feelings openly. He had called a policeman who

65. Joseph Tenenbaum, *Underground* (New York, 1952), pp. 349–50, 352–54.

66. Abraham Sutzkever, "Never Say This Is the Last Road," in Schwarz, *The Root and the Bough*, pp. 66–92; quotation from p. 90.

67. See p. 233.

68. File memorandum by Strauch, July 20, 1943, NO-4317. On teeth extractions, see report by prison warden Guenther to Kube, May 31, 1943, R-135.

had shot a Jew a "swine." Once, when a Jew had dashed into a burning garage to save the *Generalkommissar's* expensive car, Kube had shaken hands with the man and had thanked him personally. When the *Judenrat* in Minsk had been ordered to prepare 5000 Jews for "resettlement," Kube had actually warned the Jews. He had also protested violently that fifteen Jewish men and women who had been shot had been led, covered with blood, through the streets of Minsk. Thus Kube had sought to pin on the SS the label of sadism.[69]

While the recommendation by Strauch (technically a subordinate of the *Generalkommissar*) that Kube be dismissed was not carried out, Rosenberg decided to dispatch Staatssekretär Meyer to Minsk in order to give Kube a "serious warning."[70] On September 24, 1943, the German press reported that Kube had been murdered "by Bolshevist agents of Moscow"[71] (he was killed by a woman employed in his household). Himmler thought that Kube's death was a "blessing" for Germany. So far as Himmler was concerned, the *Generalkommissar* had been heading for a concentration camp anyway, for his Jewish policy had "bordered on treason."[72]

A few months before Kube died, Himmler had decided to liquidate the entire ghetto system. The ghettos were to be turned into concentration camps.[73] His decision appears to have been prompted, at least in part, by reports that Jews were employed in confidential positions and that, in Kaltenbrunner's words, the personal relations between Reich Germans and Jewish women had "exceeded those limits which for world-philosophical [*weltanschaulichen*] and race-political reasons should have been observed most stringently."[74] The East Ministry acquiesced to Himmler's decision.[75]

The changeover to concentration camp administration was carried out in Latvia without disturbance.[76] In Lithuania the surrender of jurisdiction to the SS and Police was accompanied by large-scale killing operations: in Kaunas, several thousand Jews were shot and the remainder distributed in ten labor camps; in the Vilna ghetto, the SS and Police encountered "certain difficulties" (Jewish resistance) and consequently cleared the ghetto, with its 20,000 inmates, "totally."[77] In White Russia two concentrations of Jews remained at Lida and Minsk; the Minsk Jews were ordered to Poland.[78] Thus, by the end of 1943, *Ostland* Jewry had shrunk to some tens of thousands who could look forward to evacuation or death. They were now concentration camp inmates, wholly within the jurisdiction of the SS and Police. But they

69. Strauch to von dem Bach, July 25, 1943, NO-2262. After the war, in Nuremberg, von dem Bach called Strauch "the most nauseating man I have met in my life [*den übelsten Menschen, dem ich meinem Leben begegnet bin*]." Von dem Bach in *Aufbau* (New York), September 6, 1946.

70. Berger (chief of SS-Main Office) to Brandt (Himmler's Personal Staff), August 18, 1943, NO-4315.

71. "Gauleiter Kube Ermordet," *Deutsche Ukraine-Zeitung*, September 24, 1943, p. 1.

72. Von dem Bach in *Aufbau* (New York) September 6, 1946, p. 40.

73. Himmler to Higher SS and Police Leader North and Chief of WVHA (Pohl), June 21, 1943, NO-2403.

74. Kaltenbrunner (Heydrich's successor as chief of RSHA) to SS main offices, August 13, 1943, NO-1247.

75. Memorandum by ORR. Hermann, August 20, 1943, on interministerial conference of July 13, 1943, NO-1831.

76. KdS Latvia (Obf. Pifrader) to Lohse, August 1, 1943, Occ E 3bβ-29.

77. Report by *Generalkommissar* Lithuania (von Renteln) for August-September, 1943, November 16, 1943, Occ E 3α-14.

78. Rudolf Brandt (Himmler's Personal Staff) to Berger, July 1943, NO-3304. See also: Summary of East Ministry conference, July 14, 1943, Wi/ID 2.705. Summary of WiStOst conference, September 13/14, 1943, Wi/ID .43.

were still the subject of some controversy.

As late as May 10, 1944, Ministerialdirektor Allwörden of the East Ministry addressed a letter to Obergruppenführer Pohl of the SS Economic-Administrative Main Office (WVHA) in which he said that the Rosenberg Ministry recognized the exclusive jurisdiction of the SS in Jewish matters. He also granted that the administration of the camps and the work activity in the camps would remain in the hands of the SS. But he "insisted" upon the continued payment of wage differentials to the Finance Office of the *Reichskommissar*. The Rosenberg ministry simply could not "resign" itself to this loss.[79]

This correspondence preceded the breakup of the Baltic camps by only a few months. From August, 1944, to January, 1945, several thousand Jews were transported to concentration camps in the Reich. Many thousands of Baltic camp inmates were shot on the spot, just before the arrival of the Red Army.[80]

During the final days of the second sweep the SS and Police was beset by a problem which weighed more and more heavily on its mind. The SS (and also the civil administration) was worried about the secrecy of the vast operation which was now coming to an end. Although photography control in the German ranks was now complete, Hungarian and Slovak officers had taken pictures of a number of "executions." The photographs were presumed to have reached America. This was considered especially "embarrassing" *(peinlich)*,[81] but nothing could be done about the matter. Even greater fears of discovery were generated as a result of the Red Army's steady westward advance. The occupied territories were full of mass graves, and Himmler was determined to leave no graves.

In June, 1942, Himmler ordered the commander of *Sonderkommando 4a*, Standartenführer Paul Blobel, "to erase the traces of *Einsatzgruppen* executions in the East."[82] Blobel formed a special *Kommando* with the code designation 1005. The *Kommando* had the task of digging up graves and burning bodies. Blobel traveled all over the occupied territories, looking for graves and conferring with Security Police officials. Once he took a visitor from the RSHA (Hartl) for a ride and, like a guide showing historical places to a tourist, pointed to the mass graves near Kiev where his own men had killed 34,000 Jews.[83] From the beginning, however, Blobel encountered difficulties in his job. The BdS Ukraine (Thomas) was apathetic about the entire project. There was a shortage of gasoline. The members of the *Kommandos* found valuables in the graves and neglected to comply with the rules for handing them in. (Some of the men were later tried in Vienna for stealing Reich property.) When the Russians overran the occupied territories, Blobel had fulfilled only part of his task.[84]

The SS and Police thus left behind many mass graves but few living Jews. The total number killed in this gigantic operation can now be tabulated as follows:[85]

79. Von Allwörden to Pohl, May 10, 1944, NO-2074. Also, Dr. Lange (East Ministry) to Finance Minister von Krosigk, July 24, 1944, NO-2075.

80. Tenenbaum, *Underground*, pp. 362–63.

81. Report by Dr. Hans-Joachim Kausch, June 26, 1943, Occ E 4-11.

82. Affidavit by Blobel, June 18, 1947, NO-3947.

83. Affidavit by Albert Hartl, October 9, 1947, NO-5384.

84. Affidavit by Blobel, June 18, 1947, NO-3947. Reference to the Vienna trial is made in an affidavit by a former defendant, Wilhelm Gustav Tempel, February 18, 1947, NO-5123. For descriptions of the work of the *Kommando*, see; affidavit by Szloma Gol (Jewish survivor), August 9, 1946, D-964; and affidavit by Adolf Ruebe (former *Kriminalsekretär* with KdS White Russia), October 23, 1947, NO-5498.

"Ostland" and Army Group Rear Areas North and Center:

An *Einsatzgruppe A* draft report (winter 1941/42) listed the following figures of Jews killed:

Estonia	2,000
Latvia	70,000
Lithuania	136,421
White Russia	41,000

Einsatzgruppe B reported, on November 14, 1941, an incomplete tabulation of 45,467 shootings. Kube reported, on July 31, 1942, the killing of 65,000 Jews during the preceding two months of operations.

Ukraine, Bialystok, Army Group Rear Area South, and Rear Area Eleventh Army:

Einsatzgruppe C reported that two of its *Kommandos* (4*a* and 5) had killed 95,000 people up to the beginning of December, 1941. *Einsatzgruppe D* reported, on April 8, 1942, a total of 92,000 dead. Himmler reported to Hitler on December 20, 1942, the following numbers of Jews shot in the Ukraine, South Russia, and Bialystok:

August, 1942	31,246
September, 1942	165,282
October, 1942	95,735
November, 1942	70,948
Total	363,211

These partial figures, none of which overlap, account for 900,000 dead Jews. Other fragmentary reports, most of which we have cited in this chapter, and which deal with the operations of the Higher SS and Police Leaders, the BdS Krakow, the German and Roumanian Armies, the *Bandenkampfverbände,* and SS and Police killings not covered by the figures cited above, account for an additional 250,000 Jewish dead.· The resultant figure (1,150,000) still does not cover the entire area of the mobile killing operations for all periods. When we supply an estimate for the gaps in our sources, the total number of Jews killed in this venture rises to 1,400,000.

85. *Ostland,* and Army Group Rear Areas North and Center; *Einsatzgruppe A* draft report (undated), PS-2273. RSHA IV-A-1, Operational Report USSR No. 133 (60 copies), November 14, 1941, NO-2875. Kube to Lohse, July 31, 1942, PS-3428.

Ukraine, Bialystok, Army Group Rear Area South, and Rear Area 11th Army: RSHA IV-A-1, Operational Report USSR No. 156, January 16, 1942, NO-3405. RSHA IV-A-1, Operational Report USSR No. 190 (65 copies), April 8, 1942, NO-3359. Himmler to Hitler, December 20, 1942, NO-511.

VIII / *Deportations*

The mobile killing operations in Russia were a prelude to far greater destructive measures in the remainder of Axis Europe. Shortly after the *Einsatzgruppen* crossed the June 22, 1941, line into the USSR, Hitler ordered the commencement of the "final solution of the Jewish question" on the entire European continent. The history of the "final solution" is not easy to reconstruct. We are dealing not with a sudden decision but with the emergence of an idea.

The idea of killing the Jews had its shrouded beginnings in the far-distant past. There is a hint of killing in Martin Luther's long speech against the Jews. Luther likened the Jews to the obstinate Egyptian Pharaoh of the Old Testament: "Moses," said Luther, "could improve Pharaoh neither with plagues nor with miracles, neither with threats nor with prayers; he had to let him drown in the sea."[1] In the nineteenth century the suggestion of total destruction emerged, in more precise and definite form, in a speech which Deputy Ahlwardt made to the Reichstag. Ahlwardt said that the Jews were, like Thugs, a criminal sect that had to be "exterminated."[2] Finally, in 1939, Adolf Hitler uttered a threat of total annihilation in language which was far more explicit than that of his predecessors. This is what he said in his speech of January, 1939:[3]

> And one other thing I wish to say on this day which perhaps is memorable not only for us Germans: In my life I have often been a prophet, and most of the time I have been laughed at. During the period of my struggle for power, it was in the first instance the Jewish people that received with laughter my prophecies that some day I would take over the leadership of the state and thereby of the whole people, and that I would among other things solve also the Jewish problem. I believe that in the meantime that hyenous laughter of the Jews of Germany has been smothered in their throats. Today I want to be a prophet once more: If international-finance Jewry inside and outside of Europe should succeed once more in plunging nations into another world war, the consequence will not be the Bolshevization of the earth and thereby the victory of Jewry, but the annihilation [*Vernichtung*] of the Jewish race in Europe.

These remarks by Hitler have much more significance than the suggestions and hints of earlier German writers and speakers. In the first place, the idea of killing the Jews had now matured. As a plan for administrative action, the idea was not yet obvious or even feasible; but as a thought of something that could happen, it was already ingrained in German minds. In the second place, Hitler was not only a propagandist but also the head of a state; he disposed not only over words and phrases but also over an administrative apparatus; he had power not only to speak but also to act. Third, Hitler was a man who had a tremendous urge – one could almost say a compulsion – to carry out his threats. He "prophesied." With words he committed himself to action.

In spite of the explicit threat, however, Hitler did not order the annihilation of the Jews immediately upon the outbreak of the war. Even Hitler shrank

1. Martin Luther, *Von der Jueden und Iren Luegen* (Wittenberg, 1543), p. Aiii2.

2. Reichstag, *Stenographische Berichte*, March 6, 1895, p. 1297.

3. Hitler speech, January 30, 1939, German press.

from so drastic a step. Even Hitler hesitated before the "final solution." Even Hitler had to be convinced that there was no other choice.

From 1938 to 1940, Hitler made extraordinary and unusual attempts to bring about a vast emigration scheme. The biggest expulsion project, the Madagascar plan, was under consideration just one year before the inauguration of the killing phase. The Jews were not killed before the emigration policy was literally exhausted.

Let us examine these emigration plans more closely. Characteristically, the first forced emigration schemes were worked out in 1938, after the Germans had acquired Austria. We have to remember that, when Hitler came to power, Germany had about 515,000 Jews. After five years, emigration and the death rate had brought that number down to 350,000; however, in March, 1938, when the Germans took Austria, 190,000 Jews were added to the 350,000, bringing the total to approximately 540,000 – that is, 25,000 more than the original number.[4] Obviously, this was not progress. Some extraordinary measures had to be taken.

Thus we find that, especially toward the end of 1938, Schacht, Wohlthat, and a number of other officials were conferring with the Western democracies on ways and means of facilitating Jewish emigration.[5] In October, 1938, the Foreign Office took a look at the statistics on the Jewish population and discovered that about 10 per cent of all Jews under German jurisdiction were Polish nationals. However, the Polish government was not anxious to recover its citizens. On October 6, Polish authorities issued a decree which provided that holders of Polish passports abroad would be denied entry into Poland after October 29, unless such passports were stamped by an examiner.

The German Foreign Office reacted instantly.[6] By the end of October thousands of Polish Jews were arriving in sealed trains at the Polish frontier town of Zbonszyn. The Poles barred the way. The trains were now sitting in "no man's land" between German and Polish cordons. Soon the Germans discovered that they had made a ghastly miscalculation. From the other direction, Polish trains filled with Jews of German nationality were moving toward the German frontier.

On October 29 the chief of the Foreign Office's Political Division, Wörmann, wrote a memorandum in which he expressed the view that conditions on the frontier were "untenable." The Foreign Office had not calculated on reprisals. "What will happen now?" asked Wörmann. The administrative chief of the Security Police, Best, proposed that the Polish Jews be withdrawn to concentration camps. Wörmann thought that this solution might be too risky. Finally the problem was solved by compromise: the Poles admitted about 7000 Jews; the Germans had to take in some of their own nationals; and the remainder of the evacuees went home.[7] During the discussions for the settlement of the problem, Staatssekretär Weizsäcker of the Foreign Office tried to prevail upon Polish Ambassador Lipski to take back the 40,000-50,000 Polish Jews in the Reich. Lipski contended that the figure was "exaggerated" and then stated that Weizsäcker was demanding of Poland an "enormous sacrifice."[8]

While Poland refused to accept Jews

4. Emigration statistics in Hans Lamm, "Entwicklung des Deutschen Judentums" (1951; mimeographed), p. 223.

5. See pp. 96–97.

6. Gauss (Foreign Office Legal Division) to German Mission in Poland, October 26, 1938, NG-2014.

7. Memorandum by Wörmann, October 29, 1938, NG-2012. Klemt (foreign political office of the party) to Staatssekretär Weizsäcker of the Foreign Office, January 24, 1939, NG-2589.

of its own nationality, some of the Western countries were liberally admitting Jews of German nationality. But even in the West the admission of poor Jews, who had no money, was considered a very painful duty. In December, 1938, Ribbentrop had a discussion on Jewish emigration with the foreign minister of the country of traditional asylum, France. This is Ribbentrop's record of his talk with French Foreign Minister Georges Bonnet:

> 1. The Jewish Question: After I had told M. Bonnet that I could not discuss this question officially with him, he said that he only wanted to tell me privately how great an interest was being taken in France in a solution of the Jewish problem. To my question as to what France's interest might be, M. Bonnet said that in the first place they did not want to receive any more Jews from Germany and whether we could not take some sort of measures to keep them from coming to France, and in the second place France had to ship 10,000 Jews somewhere else. They were actually thinking of Madagascar for this.
>
> I replied to M. Bonnet that we all wanted to get rid of our Jews but that the difficulties lay in the fact that no country wished to receive them. . . .[9]

The attitude displayed by Polish Ambassador Lipski and French Foreign Minister Bonnet prompted Hitler to make the following remark in his speech of January, 1939: "It is a shameful example to observe today how the entire democratic world dissolves in tears of pity but then, in spite of its obvious duty to help, closes its heart to the poor, tortured Jewish people."[10] This was not an idle accusation; it was an attempt to drag the Allied powers into the destruction process as passive but willing accomplices. It is significant that much later, when the killing phase was already under way and when its extent had become known in England and America, Goebbels remarked in connection with the Western protests: "At bottom, however, I believe both the English and the Americans are happy that we are exterminating the Jewish riffraff."[11]

As if to strengthen its case, the German bureaucracy continued in 1939 to exhaust the emigration policy. This time, however, the primary effort was internal. Many bureaucratic encumbrances had impeded the emigration process: every prospective emigrant had to acquire more than a dozen official papers, certifying his health, good conduct, property, tax payments, emigration opportunities, etc. Very soon the overburdened offices were jammed and "stagnation" set in. The congestion hit Vienna first. To remedy the situation, Reichskommissar Bürckel (the official in charge of the "reunification of Austria with the Reich") set up, on August 26, 1938, a Central Office for Jewish Emigration (*Zentralstelle für die jüdische Auswanderung*). Each agency which had some certifying to do sent representatives to the central office in the Vienna Rothschild Palace. The Jews could now be processed on an assembly-line basis.[12]

The Bürckel solution was soon adopted in the rest of the Reich. On January 24, 1939, Göring ordered the creation of a Reich Central Office for

8. Weizsäcker to Ribbentrop, Legal Division, Political Division, Minister Aschmann, Section Germany, November 8, 1938, NG-2010.

9. Ribbentrop to Hitler, December 9, 1938, "Documents on German Foreign Policy 1918-1945," Series D. Vol. IV, *The Aftermath of Munich, 1938–1939* (Washington, 1951), pp. 481–82.

10. Hitler speech, January 30, 1939, German press.

11. Louis P. Lochner (ed.), *The Goebbels Diaries* (Garden City, N.Y., 1948), entry for December 13, 1942, p. 241.

12. For history of the Vienna Central Office, see *Krakauer Zeitung*, December 15, 1939.

Jewish Emigration (*Reichszentrale für die jüdische Auswanderung*).[13] The Chief of the *Reichszentrale* was none other than Reinhard Heydrich; the *Geschäftsführer* or deputy taking care of the actual administrative details was the then Standartenführer Oberregierungsrat Müller, later chief of the Gestapo.[14] Other members of the *Reichszentrale* were Ministerialdirektor Wohlthat (Office of the Four-Year Plan) and representatives of the Interior Ministry, the Finance Ministry, and the Foreign Office.[15]

Under the *Reichszentrale,* three *Zentralstellen* were expediting the emigration process: the central offices in Vienna, Berlin, and Prague. Although each of the central offices was, like the *Reichszentrale* itself, an interministerial committee, the direction was always in the hands of the local Gestapo chief.

From the very beginning the central offices worked in close co-ordination with the Jewish communities. Some of the financial deals which facilitated the emigration of poor Jews were the product of this co-operation. When the war broke out, the central offices did not disband; the association with the Jewish communities was continued, though it became more and more one-sided. As we have seen, the central offices acquired control of the entire Jewish community organization in the Reich-Protektorat area.[16] This control was disastrous for the Jews, for later on the Central Offices for Jewish Emigration became, without change of designation, central offices for Jewish deportation. However, that transformation was very gradual. For at least a year after the outbreak of war the bureaucracy was still thinking in terms of emigration only.

In fact, the very first reaction to the victories in Poland and in France was to punish these countries for their attitude toward Jewish emigration by sending there some of the Jews who had previously been kept out. In the beginning of 1940, 6000 Jews were sent from Vienna, Prague, Moravska Ostrava, and Stettin to the *Generalgouvernement.*[17] In October, 1940, two *Gauleiter* in western Germany, Wagner and Bürckel, secured the co-operation of the Gestapo in the deportation of 6500 Jews to unoccupied France.[18] But by far the most ambitious project of 1940 was the Madagascar plan.

Until 1940, emigration plans had been confined to a consideration of the resettlement of thousands or – as in the case of the Schacht plan – 150,000 Jews. The Madagascar project was designed to take care of millions of Jews. The authors of the plan wanted to empty the Reich-Protektorat area and all of occupied Poland of their Jewish population. The whole idea was thought up in Section III of *Abteilung Deutschland* of the Foreign Office; indeed, *Abteilung Deutschland* was to concern itself a great deal with Jewish matters. The plan was transmitted to a friendly neighboring agency: Heydrich's Reich Security Main Office. Heydrich was enthusiastic about the idea.[19]

The reason for Heydrich's enthusiasm becomes quite clear the moment we

13. Göring to Interior Ministry, January 24, 1939, NG-5764.

14. Heydrich to Ribbentrop, January 30, 1939, NG-5764.

15. Göring to Interior Ministry, January 24, 1939, NG-5764. Heydrich to Ribbentrop, January 30, 1939, NG-5764. Foreign Office to Heydrich, February 10, 1939, NG-5764.

16. See pp. 122–25.

17. See p. 138.

18. Unidentified report, *Abteilung Deutschland* of the Foreign Office, October 30, 1940, NG-4933. Rademacher to Luther, October 31, 1940, NG-4934. Rademacher to Luther, November 21, 1940, NG-4934. Sonnleithner to Weizsäcker, November 22, 1940, NG-4934.

19. Memorandum by Luther (chief, *Abteilung Deutschland*), August 21, 1942, NG-2586-J.

look at this plan. Briefly, the African island of Madagascar was to be ceded by France to Germany in a peace treaty. The German Navy was to have its pick of bases on the island, and the remainder of Madagascar was to be placed under the jurisdiction of a police governor responsible directly to Heinrich Himmler. The area of the police governor was to become a Jewish reservation. The resettlement of the Jews was to be financed through the utilization of Jewish property which was left behind.

This plan, explained *Abteilung Deutschland* was greatly preferable to the establishment of a Jewish community in Palestine. In the first place, Palestine belonged to the Christian and Moslem worlds; and second, if the Jews were kept in Madagascar, they could be held as hostages to insure the good conduct of their "racial comrades" in America.[20] Heydrich did not need these arguments. For him it was enough that practically the whole island was to be governed by the SS and Police. But the Madagascar plan did not materialize. It hinged on the conclusion of a peace treaty with France, and such a treaty depended on an end of hostilities with England. With no end to the hostilities there was no peace treaty, and with no peace treaty there was no Madagascar.

The Madagascar plan was the last major effort to "solve the Jewish problem" by emigration. Many hopes and expectations had been pinned on this plan by offices of the Security Police, the Foreign Office, and the *Generalgouvernement*. When the project collapsed, the entire machinery of destruction was permeated with a feeling of uncertainty. No one could take the decisive step on his own, for this decision could be made only by one man: Adolf Hitler.

On March 13, 1941, Feldmarschall Keitel signed a directive for the operation of Himmler's special units in Russia.[21] With this directive the killing phase was starting to emerge in plans for operations in the still-unoccupied territories of the USSR. On March 25, 1941, Frank revealed to his close associates that Hitler had promised him "that the *Generalgouvernement,* in recognition of its accomplishments, would become the first territory to be free of Jews."[22] This promise no longer had reference to the Madagascar project; it referred to the fateful "prophecy" which Hitler had uttered before the war.

Then, during the spring of 1941, the bureaucracy was discussing an exceedingly complex legal measure: a declaration that all Reich Jews were stateless or, alternatively, "protectees" (*Schutzbefohlene*). The Interior Ministry desired the measure in order to remove the "awkward" fact that harsh action was taken against people who were still viewed, at least in the outside world, as Reich nationals. Because of the legal complexities of the issue it was decided to submit the question to Hitler.[23]

On June 7, 1941, the Chief of the Reich Chancellery, Lammers, addressed two identical letters to the Interior and Justice Ministries, in which he wrote simply that Hitler considered the measure to be unnecessary. Lammers then

20. Memorandum signed by Rademacher of *Abteilung Deutschland,* July 3, 1940, NG-2586-B. Rademacher to Dannecker (Security Police), August 5, 1940, NG-5764. Memorandum by Rademacher, August 12, 1940, NG-2586-B. Rademacher was a chief architect of the Madagascar plan.

21. Directive by OKW/L (signed Keitel), March 13, 1941, NOKW-2302.

22. Summary of *Generalgouvernement* conference, March 25, 1941, Frank diary, PS-2233.

23. Staatssekretär Pfundtner (Interior Ministry) to Reichskabinettsrat Ficker (Reich Chancellery), April 8, 1941, NG-299. See also earlier correspondence: Circular letter by Stuckart, December 18, 1940, NG-2610; summary of interministerial conference, January 15, 1941, NG-306.

addressed a third letter to his opposite number in the party, Bormann. In that letter Lammers repeated the message with an explanation. "For your own confidential information," he wrote, "may I add the following: the Führer has rejected the legislation proposed by the Reich Interior Minister primarily because he is of the opinion that after the war there would not be any Jews left in Germany anyhow [*dass es nach dem Kriege in Deutschland ohnedies keine Juden mehr geben werde*] and that therefore it is not necessary to issue a regulation now which would be difficult to enforce, which would tie up personnel, and which would still not bring about a solution in principle."[24]

Toward the end of the spring of 1941, officials in France were still approached with applications from Jews who were trying to emigrate. On May 20, 1941, a Gestapo official from the RSHA, Walter Schellenberg, informed the military commander in France that the emigration of Jews from his area was to be prevented because transport facilities were limited and because the "final solution of the Jewish question" was now in sight.[25] On June 24, 1941, Heydrich wrote to Foreign Minister Ribbentrop that the whole problem of approximately three and a half million Jews in the areas under German control could no longer be solved by emigration; a "territorial" final solution would be necessary.[26]

On July 31, 1941, six weeks after the invasion of the USSR had started, the order was given. It was signed not by Hitler but by Göring, and the recipient of the order was Heydrich. Its text is as follows:

> Complementing the task that was assigned to you on 24 January 1939, which dealt with carrying out emigration and evacuation, a solution of the Jewish problem as advantageous as possible, I hereby charge you with making all necessary preparation with regard to organizational and financial matters for bringing about a complete solution of the Jewish question in the German sphere of influence in Europe.
>
> Wherever other governmental agencies are involved, they are to co-operate with you.
>
> I request, furthermore, that you send me before long an over-all plan concerning the organizational, factual, and material measures necessary for the accomplishment of the desired solution of the Jewish question.[27]

The order of July 31 marks a turning point in anti-Jewish history. With the dispatch of that order, the centuries-old policy of expulsion was terminated and a new policy of annihilation was inaugurated. As such, the cryptic Göring letter has had an importance which far transcends the brief span of the German destruction process.

In substance, Göring had given Heydrich the sweeping authority to organize the "final solution." Heydrich had now grasped the reigns of the destruction process in his hands. His *Einsatzgruppen* were conducting the killing operations in the East; his Gestapo machinery was preparing for the deportations in the West. The power of organizing the deportations now fell to the RSHA expert on Jewish affairs, then a little-known major (later lieutenant-colonel) of the SS, Adolf Eichmann. The small section which Eichmann headed was IV-B-4. In the RSHA hierarchy, it was placed as follows:

24. Lammers to Bormann, June 7, 1941, NG-1123.

25. Schellenberg to Gen. Otto von Stülpnagel, BdS France, and Foreign Office *Abteilung Deutschland*/III, May 20, 1941, NG-3104.

26. Memorandum by Luther (Chief, *Abteilung Deutschland* of the Foreign Office), August 21, 1942, NG-2586-J.

27. Göring to Heydrich, July 31, 1941, PS-710.

Chief, RSHA: OGruf. Heydrich [later Kaltenbrunner]
  Chief, IV (Gestapo): Gruf. Müller
    Chief, IV-B (Sects): Stubaf. Hartl [later vacant]
      Chief, IV-B-4 (Jews): OStubaf. Eichmann
        Deputy: Stubaf. Günther

To carry out his task, Eichmann used the *Zentralstellen* and Gestapo offices in the Reich-Protektorat area, and experts in Jewish affairs in the occupied territories. Occasionally, Eichmann himself left Berlin to expedite matters.[28]

The RSHA machine went into action immediately. Heydrich was a man of decision who liked to act first and hold conferences afterwards. In September, 1941, Eichmann was consequently sent to Lodz to pave the way for the dumping of 20,000 Jews in that ghetto.[29] At the same time Heydrich prepared transports of Jews for dispatch to Riga and Minsk.[30]

Before long, however, Heydrich was beset by difficulties. He could not deport all the Reich Jews before dealing with such knotty problems as intermarriage, the Jews in the armament industry, and the foreign Jews. He could not even move in the occupied areas and Axis satellite states. Göring had specified in his order that Heydrich was to act in co-operation with other agencies which had jurisdiction in these matters. Heydrich now had to make use of that order. On November 29, 1941, he sent invitations to a number of *Staatssekretäre* and chiefs of SS main offices for a "final solution" conference. In his invitation, Heydrich said that "considering the extraordinary importance which has to be conceded to these questions, and in the interest of achieving the same viewpoint by all central agencies concerned with the remaining work in connection with this final solution, I suggest that these problems be discussed in a conference, especially since the Jews have been evacuated in continuous transports from the Reich territory, including the Protektorat of Bohemia and Moravia, to the East, ever since October 15, 1941."[31]

The reception of the Heydrich invitation was quite interesting. Heydrich had spoken only of a "final solution." He had not defined it and he had not mentioned killings. The meaning of the "final solution" had to be surmised. The recipients of the letter knew that the Jews were to be deported, but they were not told what was to be done to the deportees; that was something they had to figure out for themselves. The situation created an intense interest.

In the *Generalgouvernement* the news of the "final solution" conference was the thought, if not the topic, of the day. Frank was so impatient that he sent Staatssekretär Bühler to Berlin, to sound out Heydrich. In personal conversation with the RSHA Chief, Bühler found out everything there was to know.[32] The Reich Chancellery, too, was the scene of excited expectation. Even before the

28. For Eichmann's background and career, see his SS personnel record, NO-2259. Eichmann came to Office IV from the SD. In 1938 he had served in the Vienna *Zentralstelle*. His age in 1941 was 35.

29. See pp. 142–44.

30. See pp. 232–34.

31. Heydrich to Generalgouverneur Frank, Staatssekretäre Meyer, Stuckart, Schlegelberger, Gutterer, and Neumann, SS-OGruf. Krüger, SS-Gruf. Hofmann (Race and Resettlement Office), SS-Gruf. Greifelt, SS-Obf. Klopfer (Party Chancellery), and Ministerialdirektor Kritzinger (Reich Chancellery), November 21, 1941, PS-709. The Foreign Office received a separate invitation (see memorandum by *Abteilung Deutschland*, December 8, 1941, NG-2586-F.

32. Testimony by Bühler, *Trial of the Major War Criminals*, XII, 68–69. Bühler's testimony is incomplete and misleading with respect to the vital issue: how much he was told. That Bühler had definitely been informed that the Jews were to be "liquidated" was revealed by Frank in his speech to the main division chiefs in the *Generalgouverne-*

Heydrich letter was received, Lammers — who was one of the best-informed bureaucrats in the capital — had alerted his chancellery with an order that "if invitations to a meeting were sent out" by the RSHA, one of the chancellery officials was to attend as a "listening post."[33] In the Foreign Office, *Abteilung Deutschland* received the news of the conference with enthusiastic endorsement. The experts of the division immediately drew up a memorandum entitled "Requests and Ideas of the Foreign Office in Connection with the Intended Final Solution of the Jewish Question in Europe." The memorandum was a kind of priority deportation schedule, indicating which countries were to be cleared of Jews first.[34]

The conference was originally scheduled for December 9, 1941, but it was postponed, at the last minute, until January 20, 1942, at noon, "followed by luncheon."[35] On that day the conference was held in the offices of the RSHA, *Am Grossen Wannsee* No. 50/58. The following officials were present:[36]

SS-Obergruppenführer Heydrich, Chairman (RSHA)
Gauleiter Dr. Meyer (East Ministry)
Reichsamtsleiter Dr. Leibbrandt (East Ministry)
Staatssekretär Dr. Stuckart (Interior Ministry)
Staatssekretär Neumann (Office of Four-Year Plan)
Staatssekretär Dr. Freisler (Justice Ministry)
Staatssekretär Dr. Bühler (*Generalgouvernement*)
Unterstaatssekretär Luther (Foreign Office)
SS-Oberführer Klopfer (Party Chancellery)
Ministerialdirektor Kritzinger (Reich Chancellery)
SS-Obergruppenführer Hofmann (RuSHA)
SS-Gruppenführer Müller (RSHA IV)
SS-Obersturmbannführer Eichmann (RSHA IV-B-4)
SS-Oberführer Dr. Schöngarth (BdS *Generalgouvernement*)
SS-Sturmbannführer Dr. Lange (KdS Latvia — deputizing for BdS *Ostland*)

Heydrich opened the conference by announcing that he was the plenipotentiary for the preparation of the "final solution of the Jewish question" in Europe; his office was responsible for the central direction of the "final solution" regardless of boundaries. Heydrich then reviewed the emigration policy and cited statistics on emigrated Jews. Instead of emigration, he continued, the Führer had now given his sanction *(Genehmigung)* to the evacuation of the Jews to the East as a further "solution possibility" *(Lösungsmöglichkeit)*. The RSHA chief then drew out a chart which indicated the Jewish communities to be evacuated. (The list included even the English Jews.)

Next, Heydrich explained what was to happen to the evacuees: they were to be organized into huge labor columns. In the course of this labor utili-

---

ment conference of December 16, 1941, Frank diary, PS-2233. The Frank speech is recorded verbatim.

33. Testimony by Lammers, *Trial of the Major War Criminals,* XI, 50–53. As a *Reichsminister,* Lammers could not attend a conference of *Staatssekretäre* or *Ministerialdirektoren.* That was a matter of protocol. The Lammers testimony, like that of Bühler, must be read with caution. Lammers feigned ignorance and forgetfulness. Actually, he had excellent sources of information and a keen, analytical mind. For challenge by the prosecution, see his testimony on pp. 112–16.

34. Memorandum by *Abteilung Deutschland* submitted to Unterstaatssekretär Martin Luther (chief of the division), December 8, 1941, NG-2586-F.

35. Heydrich to Hofmann, January 8, 1942, PS-709.

36. Summary of the "final solution" conference of January 20, 1942 (30 copies), NG-2586-E.

zation a majority would undoubtedly "fall away through natural decline [*wobei zweifellos ein Grossteil durch natürliche Verminderung ausfallen wird*]." The survivors *(Restbestand)* of this "natural selection" process – representing the tenacious hard core of Jewry – would have to be "treated accordingly" (*wird entsprechend behandelt werden müssen*), since these Jews had been shown in the light of history to be the dangerous Jews, the people who could rebuild Jewish life. Heydrich did not elaborate on the phrase "treated accordingly," although we know from the language of the *Einsatzgruppen* reports that he meant killing.

Practically, Heydrich continued, the implementation of the "final solution" would proceed from west to east. That procedure seemed necessary to him because of the housing shortage. Next he touched on the subject of differential treatment of special classes of Jews. The old Jews, Heydrich announced, were to be sent to a ghetto for old people *(Altersghetto)* at Theresienstadt in the Protektorat. The Jews who had distinguished themselves on the German side in World War I also were to be sent to Theresienstadt. In that manner, he concluded, all interventions in behalf of individuals would be shut out automatically.

Unterstaatssekretär Luther, speaking for the Foreign Office, then made a few comments. Luther felt that the "deeply penetrating treatment of this problem [*tiefgehende Behandlung dieses Problems*]" would create difficulties in some countries, notably Denmark and Norway. He urged that evacuations in such areas be postponed. On the other hand, he foresaw no difficulties in the Balkans and in western Europe.

Following the Luther remarks, the conferees got into an involved discussion of the treatment of the *Mischlinge* and of Jews in mixed marriages. Although this problem affected victims only in the Reich, the *Staatssekretäre* spent about half the conference time in discussion of the issue.

Finally Staatssekretär Bühler urged that the "final solution" be organized immediately in the *Generalgouvernement.* He explained that in Poland the transport problem was negligible and that not many Jews were working there. The majority, he said, were incapable of work.

At the conclusion of the conference, the participants talked about "the various types of solution possibilities" *(die verschiedenen Arten der Lösungsmöglichkeiten)*. In the course of these concluding remarks, Staatssekretäre Meyer and Bühler urged that certain preparatory measures be started immediately in the occupied eastern territories and the *Generalgouvernement.*

After the meeting was concluded, thirty copies of the conference record were circulated in the ministries and SS main offices. Gradually, the news of the "final solution" seeped into the ranks of the bureaucracy. The knowledge did not come to all officials all at once. How much a man knew depended on his proximity to the destructive operations and on his insight into the nature of the destruction process. During the early months of 1942 one point was not yet clear: the character of the "appropriate treatment" – the details, in other words, of the killing methods. This problem was not solved until spring, when gas-chamber camps were established in Poland. There was consequently a gap in time between the beginning of the deportations and the actual construction of facilities for killing the Jews.

This lag is important. Administratively, it resulted in the overcrowding of some of the eastern ghettos. Psychologically, it lent itself to the creation of a myth. When the bureaucrats had to deal with deportation matters, they kept referring to a Jewish "migration."

In official correspondence the Jews were still "wandering." They were "evacuated" *(evakuiert)* and "resettled" *(umgesiedelt, ausgesiedelt)*. They "wandered off" *(wanderten ab)* and "disappeared" *(verschwanden)*. These terms were not the product of naívete; they were convenient tools of psychological repression.

On the very highest level the full burden of knowledge revealed itself in the written word. Hitler, Göring, Himmler, and Goebbels had a complete view of the destruction process; they knew the details of the mobile killing operations in Russia, and they saw the whole scheme of the deportations in the rest of Europe. For these men, it was difficult to resort to pretense. When Goebbels found out that the SS and Police Leader in Lublin, Globocnik, was constructing killing centers, he wrote: "Not much will remain of the Jews. . . . A judgment is being visited upon the Jews [which is] barbaric. . . . The prophecy which the Führer made about them for having brought on a new world war is beginning to come true in a most terrible manner."[37]

Göring spoke of burned bridges and of a position "from which there is no escape."[38] Himmler and also Goebbels explained that the "final solution" was a task that could not have been postponed because in world history there was only one Adolf Hitler and because the war had presented to the German leadership a unique opportunity for "solving the problem." Later generations would have neither the strength nor the opportunity to finish with the Jews.[39]

Hitler himself addressed the German people and the world once more. This is what he said on September 30, 1942:

> In my Reichstag speech of September 1, 1939, I have spoken of two things: first, that now that the war has been forced upon us, no array of weapons and no passage of time will bring us to defeat, and second, that if Jewry should plot another world war in order to exterminate the Aryan peoples of Europe, it would not be the Aryan peoples which would be exterminated, but Jewry. . . .
>
> At one time, the Jews of Germany laughed about my prophecies. I do not know whether they are still laughing or whether they have already lost all desire to laugh. But right now I can only repeat: they will stop laughing everywhere, and I shall be right also in that prophecy.[40]

1 / The Reich-Protektorat Area

At first glance, the term "deportations" implies only a series of transports moving with their captive passengers from home territory to an outlying destination. However, the deportations were not a mere matter of seizure and transport. Transportation was the central core of the operation — we might say its essential component. But before the transports were assembled, and after they were gone, important obstacles had to be overcome and major consequences dealt with. A community cannot be deported simply by loading it on trains. We know by now that, to start with, the victims must be defined, their property disposed of, and their movements restricted.

In areas outside the Reich and Poland these preliminary measures had to be implemented before anything else could be done. But even a concentrated community is still tied, in countless social and economic relationships, to its domi-

37. Lochner, *The Goebbels Diaries*, entry for March 27, 1942, pp. 147–48.

38. *Ibid.*, entry for March 2, 1943, p. 266.

39. Himmler speech, June 21, 1944, NG-4977. *Goebbels*, entries for March 27, 1942, and March 20, 1943, pp. 147–48, 314.

40. Hitler speech, September 30, 1942, German press.

nant neighbors. The Jews had to be pried loose from their homes. And that was no simple task. The more "essential" a Jew appeared to be in the economy, the more extensive his social or family connections with non-Jews, the more medals and wounds he had to show for service in the army, the deeper his roots in the social and economic structure of his mother country, that much greater was the difficulty with which he was torn out of his surroundings.

These difficulties increased tremendously beyond the German and Polish frontiers. When the Germans were no longer on home ground, they had to employ foreign machinery in the separation process, and they had to deal with foreign conceptions of the difficulties and consequences of the operation. Only after all the preparatory problems were solved could transports begin to roll. But with the dispatch of the trains the bureaucratic task was still not done, for the departing Jews were leaving a gap that had to be filled. Lost production had to be replaced; empty apartments had to be let; abandoned properties had to be confiscated; and – after the destination of the transports could no longer be hidden – the psychological repercussions on the minds of the population had to be smoothed and eliminated. We can see, then, that the deportations were a huge undertaking, in which three phases are always discernible: uprooting, transporting, and filling the gap. No other step of the destruction process was so costly and so staggeringly complex.

The deportations could not be started everywhere at once; rather, they had to be a series of area-clearing operations. That is to say, the operations had to be staggered. First one country was tackled, then another, then a third, and so on. The reason for this procedure was threefold: in the first place, each territory posed special problems; second, there was a shortage of transport; and third, the capacity of the killing centers was limited. The deportations were started in the Reich-Protektorat area before they began anywhere else. The Reich itself was to have priority because the German people were to be the first to "benefit" from the "final solution."

The Uprooting Process

Even in the Reich-Protektorat area the deportations could not be conducted smoothly. Before long the Heydrich machine was intruding upon many jurisdictions. Many prospective deportees were in controversial categories; that is, the deportation of these people was considered at one time or another to be disadvantageous to the Reich. Such categories included the *Mischlinge* and Jews in mixed marriages, prominent Jews, old Jews, war veterans, foreign Jews, and Jews in the armament industry. Other categories posed custody problems and required special arrangements, namely, the Jews in insane asylums, concentration camps, and prisons. In short, the RSHA had to negotiate on the very highest level with many agencies, before deporting the Reich-Protektorat Jews.

With a view to shortening the negotiations, Heydrich had invited all interested agencies to the "final solution" conference which was held on January 20, 1942. He had hoped to dispose of all his problems at once, but that was not possible. Of the controversial categories the conferees tackled only one issue: the 125,000 *Mischlinge* and 28,000 Jews in intermarriages who were living in the Reich-Protektorat area.[41]

41. For explanation of statistics, see pp. 268, 273. The definition of the term "Jew" was extended to Austria and the Protektorat by decree: decree of May 20, 1938, RGBl I, 594. Protektorat decree of June 21, 1939, *Verordnungsblatt des Reichsprotektors*, 1939, p. 45.

SPECIAL PROBLEM I: "MISCHLINGE" AND JEWS IN MIXED MARRIAGE. – The *Mischlinge* were the recurring problem children of the German bureaucracy. An original invention of Staatssekretär Stuckart and Ministerialrat Lösener, the *Mischlinge* comprised all half-Jews who did not belong to the Jewish religion and were not married to a Jewish person (the so-called *Mischlinge* of the first degree) and all quarter-Jews (*Mischlinge* of the second degree). The *Mischlinge* were neither black nor white, neither Jews nor Germans.

Discriminations against the *Mischling* group were comparatively slight. As non-Aryans, they were barred, as a matter of principle, from the civil service and "analogously" (*sinngemäss*) from the legal profession. They could not be editors, and they were excluded from the Reich Chamber of Culture. Under the Farm Inheritance Law (*Erbhofgesetz*) *Mischlinge* could not inherit a farm. They could not belong to the party, the SS, the SA, the *Stamm-HJ* (Hitler Youth elite), and all the other party formations. In the army they could not rise to non-commissioned or commissioned ranks. A *Mischling* of the first degree could not be a guardian of a German child (or, for that matter, of a *Mischling* child of the second degree), and tax reductions were not extended to parents of *Mischling* children.

In other matters, however, the *Mischling* was treated like a German. He did not wear the star, was not restricted in his business activities, and was even permitted membership in such non-political party organizations as the NSV (Welfare League) and DAF (German Labor Front).[42] Moreover, the "liberalization" procedure had enabled many *Mischlinge* to remain civil servants and to become officers.

In 1939 there were 64,000 *Mischlinge* of the first degree and 43,000 *Mischlinge* of the second degree in the Old Reich, Austria, and the Sudeten area.[43] The civil servants strove for the complete absorption of the *Mischlinge* of the second degree into the German community. Marriages between *Mischlinge* of the second degree and Germans were permitted without special consent; marriages with Jews were strictly prohibited.

On the other hand, the *Mischlinge* of the first degree posed difficulties, and towards the end of 1941, party circles began to equate these *Mischlinge* with the Jews again. The "final solution" was now at hand, and no solution could really be "final" unless the *Mischling* problem was also "solved."

On October 13, 1941, the chief of the Reich Chancellery, Lammers, and the chief of the party's Race-Political Office, Gross, had a conversation about the *Mischlinge*, the first major conversation on this topic during the deportation phase. Lammers declared himself willing to support the sterilization of all *Mischlinge* of the first degree in order to prevent the birth of future *Mischlinge*.[44] In addition, he proposed

42. Restrictions against *Mischlinge* are enumerated by Wilhelm Stuckart in his *Rassenpflege* (5th ed.; Leipzig, 1944), pp. 21, 26, 34, 40, 41; and in *Die Judenfrage* (*Vertrauliche Beilage*), April 25, 1941, pp. 22–24.

43. "Die Juden und jüdischen Mischlinge," *Wirtschaft und Statistik*, XX, 84. Affidavit by Lösener, October 17, 1947, NG-2982. The census figure of the *Mischlinge* of the first degree is 72,738. However, the figure includes *all* half-Jews, because the census takers, for administrative reasons, simplified the questionnaire. The true number of *Mischlinge* is given by Lösener in his affidavit.

We have no figures on the number of *Mischlinge* in the Protektorat. Judging from the statistics on intermarriages (p. 275), the number could have been as high as 30,000 in 1939. The bureaucrats in Berlin never discussed the problem of the Czech-Jewish *Mischlinge*, but their fate hinged on the treatment of the *Mischlinge* in the Reich.

44. The *child* of a *Mischling* of the first degree could have any status, from full Jew to full German, depending upon his grand-

strict controls for the prevention of the marriage of a *Mischling* of the second degree with another *Mischling* of the second degree.[45] Lammers argued that if *Mischlinge* of the second degree were allowed to marry only Germans, the Jewish characteristics would disappear completely in accordance with Mendelian laws. Gross thought about the proposition and made a counter-proposal: Why not do the opposite and, instead of diffusing Jewish traits in the German population, allow *Mischlinge* of the second degree to marry only other *Mischlinge* of the second degree? From such combinations, he said, there would emerge now and again persons possessing an accumulation of Jewish characteristics. Those persons, in turn, "might succumb to some form of extermination."[46]

One implication of this "scientific" discussion now came to the fore. The *Mischlinge* were unfinished business. The party wanted to subject them to the "final solution." The civil service still did not want to kill these people, but the representatives of the ministries were ready to propose compromise measures with the aim of allowing the *Mischlinge* to die out.[47]

During the conference of January 20 the *Mischling* issue was raised again. Under the heading of "Solution of the Mixed Marriage and *Mischling* Questions," the conferees considered the following proposal: *Mischlinge* of the first degree were to be equated with Jews. Exceptions:

1. *Mischlinge* of the first degree, married to Germans, who had children classified as *Mischlinge* of the second degree, and
2. *Mischlinge* of the first degree who, by reason of services rendered to the German people, had been accorded liberation permits. All liberations were to be reviewed, however, to establish that they had been granted because of the *Mischling's* own merits and not those of his parents or spouse.

Mischlinge of the second degree were to be treated as Germans, but a *Mischling* of the second degree *who was not married to a German* was to be treated as a Jew:

1. If he was a descendant of a "bastard marriage" (*Bastardehe*), that is, a marriage between *Mischlinge*,[48] or
2. If he looked like a Jew (*Rassisch besonders ungünstiges Erscheinungsbild des Mischling 2. Grades das ihn schon äusserlich zu den Juden rechnet*), or
3. If particularly unfavorable reports by the police or political offices indi-

parentage. In most cases, of course, the offspring of a first-degree *Mischling* was a *Mischling* of the second degree.

45. Such marriages were already prohibited.

46. Amtsgerichtsrat Dr. Wetzel (East Ministry and Race-Political Office) to Amtsgerichtsrat Dr. Weitnauer and Oberregierungsrat Dr. Labs, January 5, 1942, enclosing summary of Lammers-Gross discussion, NG-978.

47. Hitler himself did not think that the *Mischlinge* could be absorbed. Experience had shown, he said, that after a diffusion of four, five, or even six generations, "full Jews would Mendel out after all." He could name several examples of that phenomenon (e.g., President Roosevelt). The explanation: The Jewish people simply were tougher (*Das jüdische Volkstum sei eben zäher*). Henry Picker, *Hitler's Tischgespräche im Führerhauptquartier 1941–1942* (Bonn, 1951), entries for May 10, 1942, and July 1, 1942, pp. 303, 313. The *Tischgespräche* are a summary by Picker of remarks made by Hitler at the dinner table. From all indications, Hitler did *not* follow up his remarks with an order for action, one way or the other. Very likely, he was not asked for a decision.

48. Most marriages between *Mischlinge* of the first degree and *Mischlinge* of the second degree produced Jews who were classified as one-quarter Jews (*Mischlinge* of the second degree). This classification was the result of the circumstance that usually such an offspring had only one Jewish grandparent. If two *Mischlinge* of the second degree married, their offspring was a *Mischling* of the second degree only if he had a Jewish grandparent, that is, only if one of the half-Jewish grandparents belonged to the Jewish religion.

cated that the *Mischling* of the second degree "behaved" and "felt" like a Jew.

Faced with the drastic implications of the new categorization, the conferees considered the possibility that *Mischlinge* who were candidates for deportation should be given an opportunity to remain in the Reich if they submitted to sterilization. Gruppenführer Hofmann, chief of the Race and Resettlement Main Office, suggested that preparations would have to be made for performing sterilizations on a large scale "because the *mischling*, facing the choice of evacuation or sterilization, would prefer sterilization."

Staatssekretär Stuckart of the Interior Ministry then voiced his opinion that the proposed "solution possibility" was much too complex for administrative reasons. He had a much simpler solution for the whole *Mischling* issue, a solution moreover, which would take into account the "biological facts:" compulsory sterilization.[49]

The issue was now narrowed down, but it was far from solved. On March 6, 1942, a second "final solution" conference was convened for the purpose of dealing with the *Mischlinge* and the mixed marriages. This time the chairman was Adolf Eichmann. The participants were personages of correspondingly lower rank — a circumstance that did not facilitate decision-making. The East Ministry was represented by its expert on Jewish affairs, Amtsgerichtsrat Dr. Wetzel; the Interior Ministry had dispatched Regierungsrat Dr. Feldscher; the Office of the Four-Year Plan had sent Amtsgerichtsrat Liegener and an attorney, Pegler; the Justice Ministry's delegate was Oberlandesgerichtsrat Massfelder; the *Generalgouvernement* emissary was Dr. Kammerl; the Foreign Office representative was the draftsman of the Madagascar plan, Legationsrat Rademacher. The Party Chancellery was expertly represented by Oberregierungsräte Reischauer and Aucker, the Reich Chancellery by Oberregierungsrat Dr. Boley, and the SS Race and Resettlement Main Office by Hauptsturmführer Preusch and Obersturmführer Dr. Grohmann.

One other agency, not previously represented in "final solution" matters, had sent emissaries to the conference. That was the Propaganda Ministry. Goebbels had received a copy of the protocol of the January 20 conference, and his interest was immediately aroused by the "large number of exceedingly delicate questions" raised in that conference.[50] In matters of "delicacy" the Propaganda Ministry naturally had jurisdiction. Accordingly, two propaganda experts were dispatched to the second conference, Oberregierungsräte Carstersen and Dr. Schmidt-Burgh.

The conferees immediately began a discussion of the Stuckart proposal for compulsory sterilization. Everyone agreed that a "biological solution" would call for the sterilization of all *Mischlinge*. But how could such a measure be decreed? One could not very well give publicity to it. Someone suggested a provision to authorize a particular office "to regulate the living conditions of *Mischlinge*." That suggestion was rejected. Then someone else pointed out that sterilization for 70,000 *Mischlinge* of the first degree would entail medical treatment equiva-

49. Summary of "final solution" conference of January 20, 1942, NG-2586-G. See also report by Rademacher, July 11, 1942, NG-2586-I. Rademacher did not take part in the conference, but he seems to have received information about the proceedings from sources other than the conference summary cited above. According to Lösener, sterilization had first been suggested by Reichsärzteführer Wagner in 1935 and was proposed by Stuckart during the "final solution" conference only after he had been told by his colleague Staatssekretär Dr. Conti that the measure was impractical. Testimony by Lösener, Case No. 11, tr. p. 7653.

50. Lochner, *Goebbels Diaries,* entry for March 7, 1942, p. 116.

lent to 700,000 hospital days. Third, it was noted that after their sterilization the *Mischlinge* would still be *Mischlinge;* none of the administrative restrictions upon *Mischlinge* would thereby be removed. There would still be the problem of *Mischlinge* in sports, *Mischlinge* in the economy, *Mischlinge* as members of organizations, *Mischlinge* in the armed forces, *Mischlinge* as attorneys, *Mischlinge* as guardians, etc., etc.

It was consequently agreed that, should the Führer for political reasons still order their sterilization, the *Mischlinge* would have to be removed from the German community somehow. Since Staatssekretär Stuckart had objected to their deportation across the border, the *Mischlinge* might be concentrated in some sort of ghetto near the border. The representatives of the Party Chancellery then reiterated that in their opinion a sifting of the *Mischlinge,* in accordance with the criteria suggested during the conference of January 20, was the simplest solution as well as the *only* one which would assure the disappearance of this "third race." The small number of *Mischlinge* who would remain in the Reich after the sifting could always be sterilized; after such sterilization they could be freed from all restrictions and live out their lives in peace.

This "solution" appealed to the conferees so much that they decided to submit it to higher authority for decision, but since this would have been an affront to Staatssekretär Stuckart, the conferees also decided to submit the proposal for compulsory sterilization.[51]

In short, the issue was no nearer to a solution now than before. Instead of being thrashed out in conference, it was now perpetuated in correspondence. On March 16, 1942, Staatssekretär Stuckart addressed a long letter to his fellow *Staatssekretäre* as well as to Heydrich and Hofmann. Stuckart prefaced his letter with the remark that in considering this question it was hardly necessary to stress "that the interests of the German people must be the sole criterion to be applied."

Stuckart then went on to say that, while deportation of the *Mischlinge* would appear to be a conspicuously simple solution, it had certain fatal defects which were hardly in line with the interests of the German nation. In the first place, Stuckart wished to remind his colleagues that a sifting of part-Jews had already taken place. In the Nuremberg definition those half-Jews who inclined to Judaism by reason of their religion or marriage had already been relegated to the Jews. The other half-Jews, the *Mischlinge* of the first degree, had been integrated de facto into the German community. They were working and they were fighting. Many of them had been "liberated" by the Führer and had been given the status of Germans. Moreover, many persons classified as Jews under the Nuremberg definition had been elevated to the status of *Mischling* of the first degree. It would be incompatible with the authority inherent in a decision by the Führer if these persons were now rebranded as Jews by general ruling. But if the "liberated" Jews could not be touched, it would be nonsensical and illogical to deport real *Mischlinge* of the first degree, that is, half-Jews who had received the more favorable status to begin with.

Next Stuckart pointed out that each *Mischling* had a large number of German relatives. The psychological and political repercussions on the home front would therefore be beyond calculation. Even if all these objections were to be disregarded, Stuckart con-

51. Summary of "final solution" conference of March 6, 1942 (20 copies), NG-2586-H. Rademacher via Unterstaatssekretäre Luther, Gaus, and Wörmann to Staatssekretär Weizsäcker, July 11, 1942, NG-2586-I.

tinued, there was one argument which in his opinion was decisive. "It is the fact," he said, "that deporting the half-Jews would mean abandoning that half of their blood which is German." Taking all these considerations into account, he preferred the half-Jews to become extinct within the Reich by a natural process. Although one should then have to wait thirty or forty years, he, Stuckart, was prepared to resign himself to this "setback." The alternatives to sterilization would be "an enormous number of applications for exemptions . . . considerable transport difficulties . . . the burdensome necessity of taking the half-Jews away from their work," etc.[52]

Upon the heels of the Stuckart letter the acting Justice Minister, Staatssekretär Schlegelberger, wrote a letter of his own. Schlegelberger proposed that the *Mischlinge* of the second degree be equated with Germans, without exceptions and without restrictions. With respect to the *Mischlinge* of the first degree, Schlegelberger supported sterilization. He took care to point out that those *Mischlinge* who were already too old to have children would not have to be sterilized; neither, he said, would they have to be deported. No useful purpose would be served by either procedure. Furthermore, Schlegelberger thought that *Mischlinge* of the first degree who were married to Germans and who had children classified as *Mischlinge* of the second degree should also be left alone. Since the offspring, as a three-quarter German, had to be accepted as an equal member of the German national community – "and this must be aimed at," he said, "if the solution of the Jewish problem is really meant to be final" – one could not very well burden such a person with the knowledge that one of his parents had been subjected to "measures for protection of the national community."[53]

The Schlegelberger letter was the first insinuation of a status quo. Both deportation and sterilization became increasingly infeasible as party and ministerial offices heaped argument after argument upon each other. In fact, matters rested until September, 1942, when new rumors began to circulate in the Interior Ministry that the RSHA was preparing for the deportation of the *Mischlinge* of the first degree.

At this point, Ministerialrat Lösener sat down to write a letter to save his *Mischlinge*. When he wrote it, he was near desperation. Lösener had written (or helped to write) twenty-seven anti-Jewish decrees;[54] probably none of them had made him as proud as the one which defined the Jews. In the abortive East Ministry conference on definitions, he had vainly urged that the Nuremberg principle be adopted in the East "for the sake of uniformity."[55] Now all the *Mischlinge* in the Reich-Protektorat area were threatened with deportation.

Lösener wrote his letter around September 10, 1942, and addressed it to Himmler. He repeated all the arguments which Stuckart had enumerated. He wrote that Hitler had granted the status of *Mischling* of the first degree to 340 Jews, that there were many *Mischlinge* who had already become

52. Stuckart to Klopfer, Freisler, Heydrich, Neumann, Luther, Meyer, and Hofmann, March 16, 1942, NG-2586-I. Interestingly enough, Hitler had desired the removal of *Mischlinge* of the first degree from active military service lest they should later be in a position to refer to an "expenditure of blood and life for Führer and Reich." NSDAP/Party Chancellery to Reich Minister for Eastern Occupied Territories, March 2, 1942, Wi/ID .358.

53. Schlegelberger to Klopfer, Stuckart, Heydrich, Neumann, Luther, Meyer, and Hofmann, April 8, 1942, NG-2586-I.

54. Affidavit by Lösener, February 24, 1948, NG-1944-A.

55. Summary of East Ministry conference of January 29, 1942, NG-5035.

Germans, and that 260 more had been promised German status. Lösener admitted that sterilization was not feasible during the war. After all, he consoled Himmler, "one cannot rectify errors and sins committed during the last 200 years in one day." But after the war the sterilizations could be carried out easily. Since the census figure of 72,000 *Mischlinge* also included half-Jews who were Jews by legal definition, the true number of *Mischlinge* of the first degree was only 64,000; and since a large number of the true *Mischlinge* were already past childbearing age, the number of sterilizations would not have to exceed 39,000. Again Lösener stressed that the *Mischlinge* of the first degree were loyal people and that they were severely restricted anyhow. Finally, he urged that the whole matter be submitted to Hitler for a decision.[56]

On October 27, 1942, the third "final solution" conference was convened. This time the roll of participants was as follows:

- SS-OStubaf. Eichmann, presiding (RSHA IV-B-4)
- SS-Stubaf. Günther (RSHA IV-B-4)
- Regierungsrat Hunsche (RSHA IV-B-4)
- SS-OStubaf. ORR. Dr. Bilfinger (RSHA II-A)
- SS-Stubaf. RR. Neifeind (RSHA II-A-2)
- SS-Stubaf. Dr. Gengenbach (RSHA III-A)
- Amtsgerichtsrat Dr. Wetzel (East Ministry)
- Regierungsrat Dr. Feldscher (Interior Ministry)
- Amtsgerichtsrat Liegener (Four-Year Plan)
- Oberlandesgerichtsrat Massfelder (Justice Ministry)
- Landesoberverwaltungsrat Weirauch (*Generalgouvernement*)
- Gesandtschaftsrat Dr. Klingenfuss (Foreign Office)
- Reichsamtsleiter Kap (Party Chancellery)
- Regierungsrat Randies (Party Chancellery)
- Oberregierungsrat Dr. Boley (Reich Chancellery)
- SS-HStuf. Preusch (RuSHA)
- SS-OStuf. Harders (RuSHA)
- Oberregierungsrat Schmidt-Burgh (Propaganda Ministry)
- Bereichsleiter Lendschner (Race-Political Office)
- SS-Stubaf. Dr. Stier (Staff Main Office)

At the outset of the conference the participants were told that "owing to new knowledge gained in the field of sterilization," the reproductive *Mischlinge* of the first degree could be sterilized during the war. The conferees agreed upon a sterilization program to be implemented "without further ado." Sterilization was to be strictly voluntary, i.e., a service rendered by the person "for graciously allowing him to remain in Reich territory." A sterilized *Mischling* could live out his life in peace, subject only to the few restrictions in effect against *Mischlinge*. The *Mischlinge* of the second degree, without exception, were to be treated as Germans, but they too were to remain subject to *Mischling* restrictions.[57]

The pendulum had now swung the other way. However, the report of "new knowledge" in the field of sterilization was strictly a false alarm. Under the patronage of the SS and Police, sterilization experiments were conducted on Jews in the killing center of Auschwitz, and from time to time the experimenters sent in reports to the effect that a technique for large-scale sterilizations was about to be "perfected." Actually, the doctors never succeeded.[58] The upshot of their failure was that, after all the discussion and controversy, the *Mischlinge* were neither deported nor sterilized.[59]

56. Affidavit by Lösener, October 17, 1947, with enclosure containing his letter to Himmler, written in September, 1942, NG-2982.

57. Summary of conference of October 27, 1942, NG-2586-M.

58. See pp. 604–7.

59. An exception were the *Mischlinge* of the first degree in concentration camps.

To be sure, the anti-*Mischling* restrictions were somewhat intensified. For example, in the fall of 1942 the Education Ministry issued some elaborate regulations for the admission of *Mischlinge* to schools.[60] As late as September, 1944, Hitler ruled that *Mischlinge* of the first degree who were serving in the bureaucracy were no longer entitled to service medals and honors.[61] Moreover, *Mischlinge* were afflicted with a fatal vulnerability whenever they did or said something improper. A *Mischling* of the first degree had to be careful lest some overzealous party office report him as behaving "like a full Jew." Such a charge could cost him his life.[62] But, apart from these restrictions and suspicions, the *Mischlinge* were left alone.

The *Mischling* controversy illustrates as no other issue does bureaucracy's tremendous urge to make the "final solution" really final. The *Mischlinge* had not been bothered very much, but the mere fact that they existed was disturbing; they were living proof of a task unfinished, for they were carriers of "Jewish blood" and Jewish characteristics in the German community. This type of penetration into the German nation was something the German bureaucracy could not cope with, and the *Mischlinge* survived.

Closely allied to the *Mischling* issue was the problem of Jews in mixed marriages. The fate of these Jews was linked to that of the *Mischlinge* of the first degree because most Jews in mixed marriages were the parents of such *Mischlinge*. We may recall that during the concentration process Göring had issued instructions which provided that the following Jews in mixed marriage were to be considered privileged:

> 1. The Jewish husband of a German wife, provided the couple had one or more children classified as *Mischlinge* of the first degree
> 2. The Jewish wife of a German husband, provided that the children were classified as *Mischlinge* of the first degree, or that the couple was childless

However, even in the "star" decree of September 1, 1941, the concept of privileged mixed marriage was broadened so as to include Jews married to *Mischlinge* of the second degree. Furthermore, the privilege was also extended to those Jews whose marriage had already been terminated by divorce or death, provided that they were the parent of a *Mischling* child; and that privilege was upheld even in those cases in which the only *Mischling* child had been killed in action.[63] At the time

---

Himmler deported the *Mischlinge* to killing centers. See p. 296n.

60. *Mischlinge* of the first degree were no longer admitted to secondary schools and colleges. They were permitted to remain in class only if they had completed a substantial part of their education or if they were receiving training in trades or professions. *Mischlinge* of the second degree could continue in their studies, but their admission to secondary and higher schools was permitted only if there was no "overcrowding." Regulations by Education Ministry, August 20, 1942, and October 12, 1942, in *Die Judenfrage (Vertrauliche Beilage)*, March 1, 1943, pp. 17–19.

61. Staatsminister Dr. Meissner to Higher Reich Authorities, September 4, 1944, NG-1754.

62. A *Mischling* of the first degree, Oskar Beck, who owned a radio repair shop and sometimes removed radios to his home, was suspected of listening to foreign broadcasts and of behaving like a "full Jew." Party/*Gau* Vienna/*Kreis* II/*Ortsgruppe Rembrandtstrasse* 2 – the *Ortsgruppenleiter* to State Police, Vienna, April 5, 1943, NG-381. Shortly after the issuance of the report, Beck was condemned to death for remarking to a German woman who had volunteered for labor service that she was prolonging the war. He was thus guilty of *Wehrkraftzersetzung* or "undermining the war effort." Judgment by *Volksgerichtshof*/4th Senate (signed by Volksgerichtsrat Müller and Landgerichtsdirektor Mittendorf), September 21, 1943, NG-381.

63. Decree of September 1, 1941, RGBl I, 547. See also food instructions by Staats-

of the deportations privileged status was consequently enjoyed in all cases by:

1. The Jewish parent of a *Mischling* child, regardless of the continuation of the marriage, and even if the only *Mischling* child had been killed in action
2. The childless Jewish wife in a mixed marriage for the duration of the marriage

Not privileged were:

1. The Jewish parent whose half-Jewish children were classified as Jews
2. The childless Jewish husband in a mixed marriage (unless his only Mischling child had been killed in action)

Statistically, the picture looked like this:[64]

Total Intermarriages, December 31, 1942	
Old Reich	16,760
Austria	4,803
Protektorate	6,211
	27,774

Total Intermarriages, April 1, 1943 (Old Reich only)	
Privileged	12,117
Unprivileged	4,551
	16,668

In short, there was a tendency to exempt increasing numbers of Jews in mixed marriage from the application of anti-Jewish measures. When Heydrich attempted to deport all these Jews, he was bucking a trend.

During the conference of January 20, 1942, everyone had caught the "final solution" spirit. Without considering the matter in great detail, the conferees decided that all Jews in mixed marriages were to be deported. Jews were after all not *Mischlinge,* and, as of January 20, the fate of the *Mischlinge* themselves was in doubt. But while the bureaucrats were in a hurry, they were vaguely aware of certain difficulties in connection with the mixed marriages. Without distinguishing between privileged and unprivileged status, the conferees agreed that a decision would have to be made in each individual case whether the Jewish partner (*der jüdische Teil*) was to be "evacuated" or whether, in view of the possible repercussions "of such a measure" upon German relatives, he should be "transferred" to the "Old People's Ghetto" at Theresienstadt. Before the end of the conference, however, Staatssekretär Stuckart raised an interesting question. He pointed out that before the Jews in mixed marriages could be deported, there would have to be a law which would say, in effect, "these marriages are dissolved."[65]

Here, then, was the germ of a new controversy – only this time the line of argument did not run between the party and the ministries; it cut right across the hierarchies. The Stuckart proposal was certainly in the interest of the SS and Police. Not much imagination was required to realize what would happen to the secrecy of the entire killing operation if thousands of Germans, separated from their Jewish spouses only by the latter's deportation and aiming to take over the Jewish partner's property (or even to contract a new marriage), would crowd the courts with applications for the death certificate of the Jewish spouse. Clearly, such a procedure would be embarrassing. Only a divorce instituted *prior* to the deportation could avoid these complications. Even if the Jewish victims were deported only to Theresienstadt, their physical separation from their German spouses (presumably for

sekretär Riecke, September 18, 1942, NG-452.

64. Report by SS-Statistician Korherr, April 19, 1943, NO-5193.

65. Summary of conference of January 20, 1942, NG-2586-G.

life) could only be expected to lead to legal difficulties – hence the need for a compulsory divorce procedure. Nevertheless, the Stuckart proposal invoked opposition.

The oppositional front involved two strange allies: the Justice Ministry and the Propaganda Ministry. The judiciary was hurt because the contemplated divorce procedure ignored the courts. The propaganda experts deplored the lack of "delicacy" in the automatic divorce method.

When the second "final solution" conference was convened on March 6, 1942, the representatives of the Propaganda Ministry presented the case against the Stuckart method. First, they pointed to the likelihood of interference by the Vatican. The Catholic Church did not like divorces, let alone divorces by decree. Next, the propaganda men explained that the proposed measure failed to take into account the many sidedness of individual cases. Finally, they voiced the opinion that even the simplest divorce procedure would involve the courts, since the German spouses would go to court anyhow.

The conferees decided upon a compromise method. It was agreed that the German spouse would be permitted to apply for a divorce on his own and that the courts would grant such applications automatically. (Usual grounds for divorce: improper behavior by one partner or a three-year separation.) The conferees realized, however, that such a simplification of divorce procedure would not be enough. How many Germans would take advantage of it? In ordinary times a divorce was a divorce. In these circumstances it was a death sentence. Without mentioning this consideration out loud, the experts decided that if the German partner failed to take advantage of his opportunity within a given time, the public prosecutor would be directed to file a petition for divorce. The courts were to grant a divorce decree in all such cases; the judiciary was to have no discretion.

For the Justice Ministry this was a bitter pill, but the conferees did not stop even at this point. Since the fate of the *Mischlinge* was still in doubt, it was decided to include in the automatic divorce procedure (with few exceptions) marriages between *Mischlinge* of the first degree and Germans. There were thousands of such marriages, and they were not even "mixed" under existing regulations. To add insult to injury, the conferees decided that in all these cases, if the Chief of the Security Police and SD decided that one of the partners in a marriage was a Jew or a *Mischling* of the first degree, the determination was to be binding on the courts.[66]

Staatssekretär Schlegelberger of the Justice Ministry had hardly been notified of these decisions when he dispatched a letter to Lammers. "According to the report of my advisors," he wrote, "decisions seem to be under way which I am constrained to consider absolutely impossible, for the most part."[67] On April 8, 1942, Schlegelberger set forth his objections in great detail, and it is interesting to note how far the *Staatssekretär* was willing to go in order to frustrate the assault upon his jurisdiction. He insisted that no divorce be granted unless requested by the German partner. He rejected the automatic divorce procedure via the public prosecutor on the ground that emotional ties between the Jewish and German partners would not be severed thereby. In complete disregard for the police point of view, Schlegelberger insisted that compulsory divorces were superfluous in any case, "since the couples will be separated anyway by the deportation of the Jewish partner."

66. Summary of conference of March 6, 1942, NG-2586-H.

67. Schlegelberger to Lammers, March 12, 1942, PS-4055.

Finally, he suggested that those Jews who were scheduled to be transferred to Theresienstadt could be joined there by their German spouses.[68]

In spite of the strong opposition by Schlegelberger, who would rather have shipped the German wife of a Jewish husband to the old people's ghetto at Theresienstadt than permit a compulsory divorce, the third "final solution" conference, which was held on October 27, 1942, reaffirmed the decisions of the second conference.[69]

In anticipation of the decree, the RSHA made preparations for the deportation of Jews in mixed marriages. In March, 1943, the Gestapo, with growing impatience, picked up a handful of Jews who had enjoyed privileged status and deported them. Although the deportations occurred in Goebbels' own *Gau,* Berlin, the Propaganda Minister refused to become "sentimental" about the matter.[70] Probably no other mixed marriages were broken up by deportation, because in the end the contemplated divorce procedure could not be instituted. In its deadlock the bureaucracy had submitted the question to Hitler for a final decision, and the Führer had refused to consider it.[71]

The *Mischlinge* and the Jews in mixed marriages were the only candidates for deportation who escaped the fate which Heydrich had chosen for them. The *Mischlinge* were saved because they were more German than Jewish; the Jews in mixed marriage were finally made exempt because in the last analysis it was felt that their deportation might jeopardize the whole destruction process. It simply did not pay to sacrifice the secrecy of the whole operation for the sake of deporting 28,000 Jews, some of whom were so old that they would probably die naturally before the operation was over.

68. Schlegelberger to Klopfer, Stuckart, Heydrich, Neumann, Luther, Meyer, and Hofmann, April 8, 1942, NG-2586-I.

69. Summary of conference of October 27. 1942, NG-2586-M.

70. Lochner, *Goebbels Diaries*, entry for March 11, 1943, p. 294.

71. Summary of conversation between Lammers and Bormann, October 6, 1943, NG 1068.

Special Problem II: The Theresienstadt Jews. – During the first "final solution" conference of January 20, 1942, Heydrich announced without further ado that all Reich Jews over the age of sixty-five would be sent to an old people's ghetto to be allowed to die a natural death. To the old Jews he added a second group, the Jewish war veterans who were severely disabled (*schwerkriegsbeschädigt*) or who had received the Iron Cross First Class or better.[72] Later on, a small third category was made eligible for Theresienstadt: prominent Jews whose disappearance in a killing center might have resulted in inquiries from abroad.

We may ask why Heydrich created a ghetto especially for the old people and the invalided and decorated war veterans. It goes without saying that the consideration that old people do not live very long was very much on his mind, but in itself this consideration was not decisive. After all, he had to create a special ghetto city to accommodate these Jews, whose number he estimated at fully 30 per cent of the total Jewish population in the Reich, or 85,000 out of 280,000. Furthermore, the consideration of life expectancy did not apply to the veterans, most of whom were in their late forties or early fifties. The answer to the riddle was supplied by Heydrich himself: he wanted to avoid "interventions." This raises an interesting question. Why did he expect "interventions" for old people and war veterans but not for women and children? The answer to that question lies in the whole structure of

72. Summary of conference of January 20, 1942, NG-2586-G.

rationalizations and justifications which the bureaucracy had created as a means of dealing with its conscience.

The standard explanation for the deportations was that the Jews were a danger in the Reich and that therefore they had to be "evacuated" to the East, where they were performing hard labor such as road-building. The old people did not quite fit into the picture. They were no danger and they could build no roads – in fact, many were living in homes for the aged. Therefore, Heydrich created the "old-age ghetto" of Theresienstadt as a "reservation" for "old and sick Jews who could not stand the strains of resettlement."[73] In this manner Heydrich not only perpetuated the "resettlement" legend but actually strengthened it. Even so, the "transfers of residence to Theresienstadt" (*Wohnsitzverlegung nach Theresienstadt*), as these deportations were euphemistically called,[74] did not remove all difficulties. Every once in a while someone would inquire whether, for example, an eighty-seven year-old Jew had to be deported, or whether some other octogenarian could not be left alone.[75] During the deportations of old people from Berlin, Goebbels noted in his diary: "Unfortunately, there have been a number of regrettable scenes at a Jewish home for the aged, where a large number of people gathered and even took sides with the Jews."[76]

Like the old people, the Jewish war veterans presented a psychological problem. The war veterans had an argument which was so powerful that it did not have to be made at all: they had fought for Germany. Every German understood that argument. No one, not even the most Nazified SS-man, cared to face a Jew who was a war invalid or who had received high decorations. One of the charges by Obersturmbannführer Strauch against Generalkommissar Kube grew out of an episode in Minsk where Kube had stopped a policeman who was beating a Jew and had shouted at the German whether perhaps he had an Iron Cross like the Jew whom he was beating. Strauch, in reporting the matter, noted with an air of relief: "Fortunately, the policeman could reply with a 'yes.'"

Moreover, the Jewish war veterans had not only an argument but also a protector, the German Army. This is not to say that the German Army actually protected any Jews, but it did take an interest in the fate of its former soldiers. We may ask why the army, which was co-operating so "cordially" with the *Einsatzgruppen* in Russia, adopted a different policy at home. The answer is simple. A German does not take a uniform lightly. Those who had worn the German uniform, especially if they had been wounded or decorated in it, were entitled to a little respect. If they were Jews, they were entitled at least to a little consideration. Hence we find that in 1933 the first regulations for the dismissal of Jewish civil servants already contained exemptions for war veterans. When a few Jewish veterans were among the deportees transported from Vienna to Poland early in 1941, the army requested that "officers of proven merit" and those with 50 per cent disabilities be exempted from the action and permitted to live out their lives on German soil. Their deportation, the army argued, would not be in conformity with respect for the German Wehrmacht.

Relying upon their "argument" and

73. Testimony by Staatssekretär Bühler of the *Generalgouvernement, Trial of the Major War Criminals*, XII, 69. Bühler did not believe in this fairy tale himself.

74. *Polizeipräsident* of Frankfurt to Oberbürgermeister Krebs, October 9, 1942, G-113.

75. Staatssekretär Weizsäcker to Vortragender Legationsrat Wagner, April 10, 1943, NG-3525. Wagner to Weizsäcker, April 15, 1943, NG-3525.

76. Lochner, *Goebbels Diaries*, entry for March 6, 1943, p. 276.

the sympathetic interest of the Wehrmacht, the Jewish war veterans of Austria and Germany organized into two distinct pressure groups. In Vienna there was the *Verband Jüdischer Kriegsopfer Wien* ("Organization of Jewish War Invalids in Vienna"), under the direction of Siegfried Kolisch. It was one of the few organizations which remained outside the framework of the *Kultusgemeinde.* In Berlin the former *Reichsbund Jüdischer Frontsoldaten* ("Reich Society of Jewish Front-Line Soldiers") was maintained as the Kriegsopfer (war invalids) section in the welfare division of the *Reichsvereinigung;* that is, it became part of the central machinery of Dr. Leo Baeck, but without losing its special interest. The *Kriegsopfer* section was under the direction of Dr. Ernst Rosenthal.

When the "star" decree was published in September, 1941, the war veterans looked in vain for a regulation exempting them from wearing the burdensome identification. The Vienna *Verband Jüdischer Kriegsopfer* wrote a letter of inquiry to the *Kriegsopfer* section in Berlin. but the reply was negative.[77] However, at the end of September, just four weeks after the issuance of the star decree, Director Kolisch announced in a meeting of *Kriegsopfer* officials that the Gestapo man in charge of Jewish matters in Vienna, Obersturmführer Brunner, had ordered a statistical recapitulation of all Jewish war veterans in Austria. The same order had already been given in Prague and Berlin. Hopefully, one of the *Kriegsopfer* officials, Fürth, brought out that 2071 had already been listed. Besides, Fürth suggested, one could add the widows of specially decorated men, and veterans who had quit the *Verband.*[78]

Two weeks later the director of the "emigration" division of the Vienna *Kultusgemeinde,* Rabbi Benjamin Murmelstein, told Kolisch that he had made an "agreement" (*Vereinbarung*) with the Nazi Central Office for Jewish Emigration (the *Zentralstelle*) with respect to the compilation of "removal lists for the resettlement action" (*Enthebungslisten für die Umsiedlungsaktion*). The list contained six categories who were *not* to be removed:

1. Members of the Jewish administrative machinery, with their parents, brothers, and sisters
2. Persons who had already made arrangements for emigration to South America
3. Inmates of homes for the aged
4. Blind persons, total invalids, and the very sick
5. Persons in forced labor
6. War invalids and highly decorated war veterans

Murmelstein invited Kolisch to submit a *Kriegsopfer* list, keeping these criteria in mind.[79]

It should be noted that the "agreed" stipulations had a significance which was not quite understood by the Jewish leadership. The old people and war veterans were exempted for the moment because the Theresienstadt ghetto was not yet in existence; and the division of the war veterans into invalids and highly decorated men, on the one hand, and ordinary ex-soldiers, on the other, was undertaken by the RSHA in

77. *Reichsvereinigung der Juden in Deutschland/Abteilung Fürsorge – Kriegsopfer* (signed Dr. Ernst Israel Rosenthal) to *Verband Jüdischer Kriegsopfer* Wien, October 13, 1941, Occ E 6a-10. Hitler himself is said to have ruled out an exemption on the ground that "these pigs" had "stolen" their decorations. Ulrich von Hassel, *Vom Andern Deutschland* (Zurich, 1946), entry for November 1, 1941, p. 236.

78. Minutes of *Kriegsopfer* conference, under chairmanship of Kolisch, with Diamant, Fürst, Kris, Hnilitschek, Sachs, Schatzberger, Weihs, Schornstein, Schapira, and Miss Schapira participating, September 30, 1941, Occ E6a-18.

79. Memorandum by Kolisch, October 13/14, 1941, Occ E 6a-10.

order to please the army. Altogether, the list was not an agreement at all but a piece of paper drawn up in the Gestapo to secure the co-operation of the Jewish community machinery in organizing the first transports to the East.

Nevertheless, Kolisch expressed to Murmelstein his disappointment that an "agreement so pregnant with consequences" (*weitgehende Vereinbarung*) could have been concluded without prior consultations with the *Kriegsopfer Verband.* Kolisch found that points 1 and 6 as such were "favorable" (*günstig*); however, the "agreement" did not cover the very first transport, which was to leave on October 15, 1941. For this reason alone, Kolisch had to reserve the right to submit to the *Obersturmführer* his own list. Murmelstein countered that such a procedure was impossible. Kolisch answered hotly, "This means I should sacrifice the war invalids." Thereupon Murmelstein proposed that Kolisch petition for a few single individuals in "asking-for-mercy form" (*Rachmonesform*). The two men parted angrily.[80]

On October 15, 1941, Murmelstein telephoned the *Verband* that the war veterans who were to report for deportation had been made exempt at the last moment;[81] but on the very next day a German Army officer, Hauptmann Dr. Licht, called Kolisch in order to inquire whether three Jewish veterans, Colonel Grossmann and Cavalry Captains Wollisch and Eisler, had been included in the "resettlement transport." Kolisch's answer was as follows: "I am not entitled to give out any information without permission of my superior office [Gestapo]. At the same time, I am announcing [*Ich gebe gleichzeitig bekannt*] that the *Verband* has ordered its members not to make requests to any Aryan office [*dass es ihnen verboten ist arische Stellen in Anspruch zu nehmen*]." Kolisch then noted in his memorandum that only Eisler was a member of his organization. The closing line of his notation reads: "I shall report this telephone call to the Central Office for Jewish Emigration [Gestapo]."[82]

After the establishment of the Theresienstadt ghetto in the spring of 1942, the deportations of war veterans started in earnest. However, not all of the war veterans went to Theresienstadt. Only the privileged were eligible for transport to the old people's ghetto; the remainder were deported to camps, to be killed. When the spring deportations started, the chief of the Vienna *Verband,* Kolisch, was absent. The deputy chief of the *Verband,* Fürth, was approached one day by the direc or of the Vienna Jewish community, Dr. Josef Löwenherz. Löwenherz demanded from Fürth four lists: war veterans with 50 per cent (or more) disability, highly decorated officers, highly decorated enlisted men, and all other members of the *Verband.* When Fürth inquired why Löwenherz wanted the lists, the Jewish leader "answered evasively." Fürth then made the disastrous mistake of giving Löwenherz the lists.

On June 9, 1942, the *Verband* officials met in conference. The meeting was somber. Fürth announced that of 2500 members 1100 had been "evacuated." He concluded that within two months the *Verband* would no longer exist. Another conference participant, Schapira, cited statistics, indicating that among those members who were still in Vienna, 200 were severely disabled and another 200 had high decorations. The conferees then considered "rescue" schemes. One wanted a petition for the concentration of war veterans in or near

80. Memorandum by Kolisch, October 16, 1941, Occ E 6a-10.

81. Memorandum by Fürth, October 15, 1941, Occ E 6a-10.

82. Memorandum by Kolisch, October 16, 1941, Occ E 6a-16.

Vienna or, alternatively, a closed transport to a "favorable" destination. Another thought the best procedure would be an "agreement" with the Gestapo with respect to "high-ranking officers." Fürth, who had handed over the fatal lists to Löwenherz, remarked: "I am of the opinion that whoever wears the star around here will have to disappear from here [*von hier weg müssen wird*]."

Kolisch then began to speak. He thought that all the proposals discussed so far were sheer "insanity." His colleagues were about to "destroy everything." If they wanted to do that, he had no objection, but one thing he had to stress: every exemption granted to a veteran was "mercy" by the Central Office for Jewish Emigration (Gestapo). The Jewish community organization was nothing but an institution for the implementation of orders by the central office (*Die Kultusgemeinde ist nichts anderes als eine Institution zur Erfüllung sämtlicher Aufträge der Zentralstelle*). "There is certainly a reason," he continued, "when lists of war invalids and decorated front-line soldiers are demanded of us."

Fürth, who by now understood the reason only too well, proposed that the Gestapo be petitioned for a uniform transport of all war veterans. "I see black," he said, "and I speak from sensibility and experience when I say that we shall be glad if in a month we are still here as today." At this point Kolisch spoke openly about the lists which Fürth had given to Löwenherz, and when Fürth defended himself by stating in effect that Löwenherz had tricked him, one of the participants, Halpern, agreed with Fürth. "One can see," said Halpern, "that the Jewish community is only a messenger of the Gestapo." Löwenherz, he said, deserved to be punished.[83]

Whereas Fürth had correctly seen "black," the end did not come within a month. On August 4, 1942, the *Kriegsopfer* leaders had occasion to meet again. On the agenda was "the reduction of employees by the *Kultusgemeinde*." The Jewish community had to hand over some of its own employees to the Gestapo for deportation, since many Jews had already been deported and there was no longer any need for a large Jewish organization. Among the *Kultusgemeinde* employees who were threatened with dismissal were many members of the veterans' organization. The leaders of the *Verband* were now meeting in order to find a way of protecting its members. Hauptmann Kolisch pointed out that the Jewish community "naturally" would not show the reduction list to him; he proposed, therefore, that the *Verband* hand in a list of "worthy" veterans to the Central Office for Jewish Emigration. Debating this proposal, some of the *Verband* leaders suggested that it might be better to appeal to the Jewish community. Fürth thought that the *Verband* should hand to the *Kultusgemeinde* a list in which veterans would be divided into three groups differing in degree of "worthiness." Halpern preferred to request the *Kultusgemeinde* that "in a case of equal qualifications of two employees, the war invalid receive preference." Kolisch then remarked, "I don't want to fight a war with the Jewish community."[84]

On August 7, 1942, the conferees met again to resume the discussion. Schatzberger proposed that a single undifferentiated list be handed to the

83. Minutes of *Kriegsopfer* conference under chairmanship of Kolisch, and with participation of Fürth, Halpern, Hnilitschek, Kris, Sachs, Schapira, Schatzberger, and Schornstein, June 9, 1942, Occ E 6a-18.

84. Minutes of *Kriegsopfer* conference held on August 4, 1942, under chairmanship of Kolisch, with Diamant, Fürth, Halpern, Hnilitschek, Sachs, Dr. Schapira, Schatzberger, and Schornstein participating, August 5, 1942, Occ E 6a-10.

community. Fürth "agreed" but felt that the "military qualifications" would have to be noted. The *Kultusgemeinde* would then dismiss "less qualified" members. If the community did not agree, the same list could then be handed to the *Hauptsturmführer* (Brunner of the Gestapo). Schapira put in: "I am fundamentally of the opinion that we cannot afford to fight a war against the *Kultusgemeinde*. It is senseless to enter into conflicts during these final hours [*Schlussdrama*] of the Jews in Vienna. The reduction will be carried out, whether we like it or not; the *Zentralstelle* has ordered a fixed number of reductions, and the *Kultusgemeinde* is sending out dismissal notices on the fifteenth of this month." The conferees decided to negotiate with the *Kultusgemeinde*.

Only one question remained: What if the *Kultusgemeinde* was hostile? Should requests then be made to the central office? Schatzberger remarked: "The Hauptsturmführer will think, 'These are Jews and those are Jews. Let them fight among themselves; I don't care.' Eventually he will drop us in this matter." Kolisch answered, "In that case it is time to dissolve the *Verband*."[85]

Shortly after this "battle" with the *Kultusgemeinde* the veterans apparently dissolved. The last item in the files of the *Verband* is an undated order which reads in part: "Every day, beginning Friday, August 14, 1942, a hundred people are to be called, also Saturday and Sunday. The seizures [*Erfassungen*] are to be carried out by Diamant, Schornstein, Sachs, Neumann."[86]

Thus the deportation of the war veterans ran its course. The less "worthy" or less "qualified" veterans who were *not* 50 per cent disabled or who did *not* have an Iron Cross first class or its Austrian equivalent were sent to killing centers like all other Jews. The "worthy" and "qualified" veterans were sent to Theresienstadt as a concession to the Wehrmacht and to a vague feeling of German honor. As we have seen, the rather delicate job of dividing the veterans into the two groups was done by the Jewish machinery itself. The Gestapo official, Brunner, could not personally undertake to question thousands of Jewish veterans about their wounds and decorations; he had to have the co-operation of the Jews themselves for that.

How did he get this co-operation? Let us recapitulate. First, he made an "agreement" with Murmelstein which had the sole function of lulling the Jews into a sense of false safety. Brunner could not deport all Viennese Jews during the first "resettlement" action; therefore he decided to promise immunity for six categories if the Jewish machinery would assist him in the deportation of the other Jews. Carelessly, because of the lack of time, he ordered that the agreement should not cover the first transport, which included three former Jewish officers. The army lost no time in telephoning the *Verband* about these three men. Kolisch was too frightened to answer because he had been instructed by the Gestapo to deal with only the Gestapo. Thus he lost a unique opportunity for enlisting the Wehrmacht's aid.

During the second stage of the game the Gestapo dispatched the Jewish community leader, Löwenherz, to the *Verband* officer, Fürth, to obtain the necessary lists. Fürth did not ask himself: Why does this man want such lists? He did not see in Löwenherz the "messenger of the Gestapo"; he still saw in him the venerated and distinguished leader of the Vienna Jews.

85. Minutes of *Kriegsopfer* conference held on August 7, 1942, dated August 8, 1942, Occ E 6a-10.

86. File memorandum of *Verband*, undated, Occ E 6a-18.

Thus the Heydrich method of taking over the Jewish leadership rather than changing it paid off handsomely. Löwenherz got the lists.

In the third (and last recorded) stage the Gestapo dropped pretenses and demanded that the *Kultusgemeinde* dismiss a certain number of its employees. The Jews were now fighting among themselves, while the Gestapo could lean back and watch. This was of course the oldest weapon of political warfare: *divide et impera.*

We have said much about Theresienstadt and perhaps have aroused some curiosity about this ghetto. It was indeed a peculiar institution. Its creation was the last major anti-Jewish measure by Reinhard Heydrich (he was assassinated shortly thereafter), who used his position as *Reichsprotektor,* that is, chief representative of the Reich in the Protektorat, to order the complete dissolution of the small city of Theresienstadt, its evacuation by the resident Czech population, and the creation there of a "Jewish settlement" (*Judensiedlung*) or – as it was known in the Reich – an old people's ghetto (*Altersghetto*).[87]

Theresienstadt had its own SS command, headed (in succession) by Hauptsturmführer Dr. Siegfried Seidl, Hauptsturmführer Anton Burger, and Hauptsturmführer Karl Rahm, all Eichmann's men and all Austrians.[88] Under the direction of the SS there was a Jewish elder (in succession), Jakub Edelstein, Dr. Paul Epstein, and Rabbi Dr. Murmelstein.[89] We have already met Rabbi Murmelstein in Vienna, where he headed the "emigration" division of the *Kultusgemeinde.* In Theresienstadt he wanted to realize his ambition to become a modern Josephus Flavius.[90]

A total of 139,654 Jews were sent to Theresienstadt. The breakdown, by place of origin, was as follows:[91]

Protektorat	73,608
Old Reich	42,832
Austria	15,254
Holland	4,897
Slovakia	1,447
Denmark	466
Unaccounted for	1,150
Total	139,654

Only 17,320 Jews were still in Theresienstadt in May, 1945. The statistics of the reductions are as follows:[92]

Total arrived	139,654
Deported	–86,934
Died in the ghetto	–33,419
Unaccounted for	–1,981
Remained	17,320

That was the meaning of a "favored transport." To be sure, for the Protektorat Jews Theresienstadt was only a stopover on the way to the killing center of Auschwitz, but – as the stark figures conclusively show – even the "privileged" Reich Jews could not survive in this ghetto for long.

Heydrich's successor, Gruppenführer Kaltenbrunner, had little understanding for psychological matters. To him, Theresienstadt was a nuisance. In January, 1943, he transferred (with Hitler's permission) 5000 Jews *under* the age of sixty from Theresienstadt to Auschwitz. After the deportation of these Jews, in February, 1943, he counted 46,735 Jews in the ghetto. Taking a closer look at his statistics, he discovered that 25,375 of the Theresienstadt Jews could not work; he also found that 21,005 Jews were over sixty – a fairly close correlation.

87. Decree (signed Heydrich), February 16, 1942, *Verordnungsblatt des Reichsprotektors in Böhmen und Mähren,* 1942, p. 38.

88. Zdenek Lederer, *Ghetto Theresienstadt* (London, 1953), pp. 74–75, 90.

89. *Ibid.,* pp. 41–43, 149–50, 166–67.

90. *Ibid.,* pp. 166–67.

91. *Ibid.,* p. 249.

92. *Ibid.,* pp. 247–48.

Kaltenbrunner therefore urged Himmler to permit the "loosening up" (*Auflockerung*) of the group over sixty. These Jews, he explained, were carriers of epidemics. Besides, they tied up a large number of younger Jews who could be employed in "more useful work" (*einen zweckmässigeren Arbeitseinsatz*). Therefore, Kaltenbrunner asked Himmler to approve "for the moment" (*zunächst*) of the removal of just 5000 Jews over sixty. He assured Himmler that care would be taken – as in the case of previous transports – to seize only those Jews "who enjoy no special relations or connections with anybody and who possess no high decorations of any sort."[93]

All arguments notwithstanding, Himmler sent the following reply through his personal secretary, Obersturmbannführer Rudolf Brandt: "The *Reichsführer-SS* does not wish the transport of Jews from Theresienstadt because such transport would disturb the tendency to permit the Jews in the old people's ghetto of Theresienstadt to live and die there in peace."[94]

This tendency was, of course, vital to the preservation of the "resettlement" legend, and that alone explains Himmler's anxiety for the old Jews in Theresienstadt. Significantly, when the deportations came to a close, Himmler decided to empty Theresienstadt of most of its inmates. From September to October, 1944, continuous transports left for the killing center of Auschwitz with 18,400 Jews. Practically the whole *Judenrat* of Theresienstadt was among the victims. On the eve of this deportation (September 27, 1944), the last Jewish elder, Rabbi Murmelstein, took office; he served alone until the liberation. With him, only a few thousand privileged Jews were still privileged at the end.[95]

Special Problem III: The Deferred Jews. – In the order of privileged status, the *Mischlinge* and Jews in mixed marriages occupied top place; they were the only candidates for deportation who stayed at home. Next came the Theresienstadt deportees: old people, 50 per cent disabled or highly decorated war veterans, and a handful of "prominent" persons. In third place were three groups of people whose deportation to killing centers was subject only to delays: the Jews in essential labor, foreign Jews, and members of Jewish administrative machinery.

By 1941 tens of thousands of Jews had become embedded in the armament industry. With the onset of the deportations the efficiency of all the plants which were employing Jews was suddenly in jeopardy. The firm managers were acutely conscious of the turmoil which would inevitably beset them with a departure of their Jews. Here is a telegram dispatched by one of these firms to the army on October 14, 1941:

> As a matter of common knowledge, there is now proceeding a new deportation of Jews which affects our Jewish workers who have been arduously trained to become specialists. They have been broken in as electro-welders and zinc-plating experts, and their removal would entail a reduction of production, perhaps by a third. We are therefore telegraphing you in this matter.
>
> According to the opinion of the local armament command, the procedure is such that the OKH, through the *Reichsführung SS*, has to issue a general order [*Ukas*] for our people to the *Zentralstelle für jüdische Auswanderung*, Vien-

93. Kaltenbrunner to Himmler, February, 1943, Himmler Files, Folder No. 126. January-February statistics from the same letter.

94. Brandt to Kaltenbrunner, February 16, 1943, Himmler Files, Folder No. 126.

95. Lederer, *Ghetto Theresienstadt,* pp. 43, 149–50, 166–67, 248. See also an account of Theresienstadt life by Dr. Hugo Nothmann (survivor) in Lamm, "Entwicklung des deutschen Judentums im Dritten Reich," pp. 309–23.

na IV, Prinz Eugen St. 22. We would be grateful if, aside from a lot of good advice, a positive contribution would be made for the preservation of our productive capacity, in that you obtain through the OKH a proper directive.

Parenthetically, we should like to observe that these Jewish workers are the most capable and industrious of all, because they are after all the only ones who risk something if their output is not satisfactory, and they are actually achieving such records that one could almost compare the productivity of a Jew with that of two Aryan specialists.

For the rest, we can only repeat with emphasis that we do not after all need these iron casks for ourselves but that the Wehrmacht needs them, so that it is the business of these agencies to repress such – in our opinion not quite purposeful – ordinances.

Please let us know as soon as possible whether you are meeting with any success, because, on the one hand, the matter is urgent, and, on the other hand, the unrest among the Jewish workers is naturally considerable, since the deportation to Poland without any means of subsistence is more or less equivalent to a quick and certain doom and, under such auspices, their productivity must naturally decline measurably [*da die Verschickung nach Polen ohne jegliche Subsistenzmittel mehr oder minder den raschen und sicheren Untergang bedeutet und unter solchen Auspizien die Arbeitsleistung natürlich merklich nachlassen muss.*][96]

From Berlin, too, the Wehrmacht was receiving word of impending disturbances in the labor situation. The capital was employing 10,474 Jews in the metal industry alone. In all of Berlin's industries a total of 18,700 Jewish workers were involved.[97]

On October 23, 1941, representatives of the OKW/Wi Rü met with Lösener and Eichmann to save the Jewish labor forces. Lösener and Eichmann assured the officers that no Jews employed in groups would be deported without the consent of the competent armament inspectorate and labor office.[98] During the conference of January 20, 1942, Staatssekretär Neumann, as representative of the Office of the Four-Year Plan and spokesman for Hermann Göring himself, requested Heydrich by way of confirmation not to deport Jews who held critical jobs in war industry. Heydrich agreed.[99] The situation seemed to be under control; the armament Jews were saved, and so were their families.[100]

The task of protecting the working Jews from seizure by the Gestapo was now entrusted to the regional labor offices and the regional economy offices (*Landesarbeitsämter* and *Landeswirtschaftsämter*).[101] Most of the regional economy offices probably transferred their powers to the Chambers of Industry and Commerce.[102] The regional

96. OKH/*Chef* HRüst. u. BdE (Replacement Army)/Wa Amt (Weapons Office) to OKW/Wi Rü – Rü V, October 22, 1941, enclosing letter by Brunner Verzinkerei/Brüder Boblick (Vienna) to Dr. G. von Hirschfeld (Berlin W62), October 14, 1941, Wi/ID .415.

97. Rü In III/Z to OKW/Wi Rü, October 14, 1941, Wi/ID .415.

98. Memorandum by OKW/Wi Rü IVc, October 23, 1941, Wi/ID .415. OKW/Wi Rü IVc (signed Fikentscher-Emden) to armament inspectorates and commands in Reich, Prague, and GG, October 25, 1941, Wi/ID .415.

99. Rademacher via Luther, Gaus, and Wörmann to Weizsäcker, July 11, 1942, NG-2586-I.

100. OKW/Wi Rü IVc to armament inspectorates, October 25, 1941, Wi/ID .415. Lochner, *Goebbels Diaries*, entry for May 11, 1942, p. 211.

101. Labor Ministry (signed Dr. Beisiegel) to presidents of regional labor offices, December 19, 1941, L-61. Labor Ministry (signed Dr. Timm) to presidents of regional labor offices, March 27, 1942, L-61. Regional Economy Office in Koblenz (signed Gmeinder) to Chambers of Commerce in district, March 4, 1942, L-61.

102. Instructions by Gmeinder, March 4, 1942, L-61.

machinery had an absolute veto in deportations of Jewish workers – thus the Chambers of Commerce and Industry in the Koblenz district were specifically told that their decisions were "binding" on the police.[103] However, the field offices had been given the veto only for Jews employed in *groups*. Since the labor decree of October 31, 1941,[104] had provided that Jews were to be employed only in this manner, it was believed that all Jews were covered. This was a mistake. The decree of October 31, 1941, had not been implemented fully, and the Gestapo went from place to place to pick up all Jews who were employed not in groups but as individuals. Göring had to step in again and order that *all* Jews in war industries be exempt from deportation.[105]

The deferment of the working Jews did not last very long. Economic considerations, after all, were not to be considered in the "final solution of the Jewish problem." In the fall of 1942 Hitler himself ordered that the Jews be removed from the armament industry.[106] But the problem of *replacing* the Jews in the plants was not solved until the Reich Security Main Office hit upon an idea.

In the *Generalgouvernement* the Lublin district – which once was to have become a Jewish reservation – was now designated as a colony for the settlement of ethnic Germans. All Poles in the district were to be removed. The "criminal and asocial" Polish "elements" were to be transported to concentration camps, while the remaining Poles – insofar as they were suitable for labor – were to be brought to the Reich as replacements for the Jewish labor force. The Reich Security Main Office submitted this plan to the official who had over-all responsibility for labor recruitment and the labor supply: the Plenipotentiary for Labor Commitment in the Office of the Four-Year Plan, Gauleiter Sauckel. Armed with the RSHA proposal, which seemed reasonable to him, Sauckel ordered the regional labor offices to prepare for a shuttle system of deportations: Jews out, Poles in. Jews performing menial work could be deported as soon as their Polish replacements arrived; skilled Jewish workers could be deported as soon as the Polish laborers familiarized themselves with the work.[107]

As a consequence of this order tens of thousands of Jews were deported to killing centers in 1943.[108] However, when the Poles arrived to "familiarize" themselves with the work, the *Gauleiter* of Berlin, Goebbels, became worried lest the "Semitic intellectuals" combine with the foreign workers to produce a revolt. He was determined to prevent any "concubinage" between the Berlin Jews and the imported laborers and thus could not wait for the end of the deportations. "When Berlin is free of Jews," he wrote, "I shall have completed one of my greatest political achievements."[109]

The labor replacement theory, ad-

103. *Ibid.*

104. RGBl I, 681.

105. Labor Ministry (signed Dr. Timm) to presidents of regional labor offices, March 27, 1942, L-61. Economy office in Wiesbaden (signed Dr. Schneider) to Chambers of Commerce in district, copies to regional economy offices in Koblenz and Saarbrücken, April 11, 1942, L-61.

106. Testimony by Speer, *Trial of the Major War Criminals*, XVI, 519. According to Speer, many Jews were then employed in the electrical industry (AEG and Siemens). Speer and Labor Plenipotentiary Sauckel attended the conference during which Hitler gave the order.

107. Sauckel to regional labor offices, November 26, 1942, L-61. The RSHA plan is summarized in the Sauckel directive.

108. See letter by Sauckel to the regional labor offices, inquiring how they were getting along without their Jews, March 26, 1943, L-156.

109. Lochner, *Goebbels Diaries*, entries for March 9, 1943, and April 19, 1943, pp. 288, 290, 335.

vocated by the RSHA, had one basic defect: the Reich had an *absolute* labor shortage. If all available foreign laborers, prisoners of war, and concentration camp inmates had been added to the Jewish labor force, the labor gap could still not have been filled. It is true that the labor supply increased with German conquests in the West and East, but it is also true that with the great industrial expansion of the 1940's the demand for labor increased faster than the supply. If Jews were "replaced" in one plant, the only result was that another plant which needed laborers to expand production went short.

It is therefore not surprising that industrial firms clamored for increasing allocations of skilled workers and heavy laborers. The clamor began in 1940 and grew more insistant in 1941 and 1942. The industrialists and construction bosses were not particular about the nationality or type of worker they got: "volunteer" foreign worker, prisoner of war, concentration camp inmate, anyone at all who could perform skilled or heavy labor at starvation wages was welcome. But there is one phenomenon that, more than any other, illustrates the luxury of deporting Jewish workers. As the labor shortage grew, the industrialists were asking not only for replacements but, more specifically, for Jewish replacements. The number of such requests is significant.

In November, 1940, the Army High Command requested the Labor Ministry to import 1800 Jews for railway construction work in the *Reichsbahn* directorates of Oppeln, Breslau, and Lublin.[110]

On March 14, 1941, the Labor Ministry sent a circular to the regional labor offices advertising the availability of 73,123 Warthegau Jews for labor in the Reich, or approximately 3500 Jews per regional office. The ministry emphasized that requisitions for labor were already pending: for example, the Siemens-Schuckert Works had requested 1200 workers for its plants in Brandenburg and central Germany.[111] On April 7, 1941, the circular was canceled. Hitler had decided against the importation of Polish Jews into the Reich.[112]

In March, 1941, the *Reichswerke A. G. für Erzbergbau und Eisenhütten* (Göring's own works) mapped out a production program which called for the utilization of 2000 Jewish camp inmates as well as other workers.[113] Nothing happened. But the *Reichswerke* did not forget. On September 29, 1942, the Göring company sent a letter to the Speer ministry (Oberstleutnant von Nikolai) requesting the allocation of the camp labor in pursuance of an agreement which Generaldirektor Pleiger of the Göring Works had concluded with Himmler. A copy of this letter was sent to the SS Economic-Administrative Main Office/Office Group D (WVHA-D) – the agency which administered concentration camps.[114] On October 2, 1942, the concentration camp agency replied that Himmler had agreed to the utilization of camp inmates but that "Jews are not to be employed."[115]

In September, 1942, the Speer machinery went into action. The Speer ministry, which was in charge of armaments, operated through so-called industrial rings and main committees.

110. OKH to Letsch (Labor Ministry), November 26, 1940, NG-1589.

111. Dr. Letsch to regional labor offices, March 14, 1941, NG-363.

112. Staatssekretär Syrup to regional labor offices, April 7, 1941, NG-363.

113. Summary of meeting in Reichswerke A. G. (signed Rheinländer), March 13, 1941, NI-4285.

114. Reichswerke to von Nikolai, copy to WVHA-D, September 29, 1942, NI-14435.

115. Chief of WVHA-D II (Maurer) to *Reichswerke A. G. für Erzbergbau und Eisenhütten,* October 2, 1942, NI-14435.

Both rings and committees were staffed by industrial engineers. The rings were concerned with products (such as ball bearings) used in a number of different enterprises; the committees dealt with a finished product, for instance, shells.[116] During the middle of September, 1942, just before preparations were made to deport the Reich Jews for forced labor, the *Hauptausschuss Munition* (Main Committee Munitions, under Prof. Dr. Albert Wolff) sent questionnaires to all major munitions industries to find out which enterprises could "receive Jews" (*mit Juden belegt werden können*) and which plants could establish concentration camps for Jewish workers.[117] The Main Committee Munitions was soon joined in this survey by the Main Committee Weapons (*Hauptausschuss Waffen*),[118] but the project was doomed to failure. The Gestapo protested that it was absolutely inadmissible to shove German Jews to the east only to import foreign Jews from the west.[119]

Yet a very peculiar thing happened. After all the rejections, a few agencies that did not ask many questions went ahead on their own and brought Jewish workers into the Reich. We do not know very much about these movements, for there seems to be a scarcity of correspondence in the matter. But we do have some figures. SS-Statistician Korherr reported early in 1943 that as many as 18,435 Soviet Jews had been imported for various work projects in East Prussia. At the same time, an *Organisation Schmelt* had mobilized not fewer than 50,570 Jews for labor in Silesian camps.[120]

The big armaments enterprise Krupp A. G. was one of the firms which profited from these importations. In September, 1942, Krupp was planning the construction of a new plant at Markstädt, near Breslau. The plant was to produce naval artillery. Krupp discovered that the *Organisation Todt* (Speer's construction agency) was employing many Jews in projects near Markstädt. With the "complete approval" of Vizeadmiral Fanger, Krupp suggested that these Jews stay on to build the naval factory.[121] In 1944 the eastern Krupp plant was still employing thousands of these Jews.[122]

The fact that East Prussia and Silesia were eastern border provinces undoubtedly accounts for the fact that they benefited to such an extent from imported Jewish labor. But the importa-

116. For description of the Speer Ministry apparatus, see Franz L. Neumann, *Behemoth* (2nd ed.; New York, 1944), pp. 590–94.

117. Special Committee Munitions V (*Sonderausschuss M V*), signed Scheuer, to Direktor Dr. Erich Müller, artillery construction, Krupp, September 12, 1942, NI-5856. For organization chart of Krupp, see affidavit by Erich Müller, February 5, 1947, NI-5917.

118. Main committee weapons to Krupp, September 29, 1942, NI-5856. Krupp wanted Jewish labor: Krupp to Special Committee Munitions V, September 18, 1942, NI-5859. Krupp (signed by personnel chief Ihn) to Plenipotentiary for Labor (attention Landrat Beck), September 18, 1942, NI-5860. Krupp to Special Committee Munitions V, September 22, 1942, NI-5857. Krupp to Main Committee Weapons (attention Direktor Notz), October 5, 1942, NI-5855.

119. Memorandum by Kahlert, Chief Main Division Special Questions and Labor Allocation in Reich Association Iron (*Hauptabteilungsleiter Spezialwesen und Arbeitseinsatz, Reichsvereinigung Eisen*), September 23, 1942, NI-1626.

120. Report by Korherr, April 19, 1943, NO-5193. A certain Albrecht Schmelt was *Regierungspräsident* in Oppeln, Silesia. Kienast, *Der Grossdeutsche Reichstag*, p. 369.

121. Memorandum by Dr. Erich Müller (chief of artillery construction, Krupp) on discussion with Admiral Schmundt, Vizeadmiral Fanger, and Konteradmiral Rhein, September 9, 1942, NI-15505.

122. Krupp directorate to Reich Association Iron/Construction Division (*Reichsvereinigung Eisen/Abteilung Neubauten*), February 2, 1944, NI-12342. Krupp/technical bureau (signed Rosenbaum) to Krupp armament and machine sales (Eberhardt), March 14, 1944, NI-8989. Krupp Berthawerk A. G./Markstädt Plant to chief of Krupp steel plants, Prof. Dr. Houdremont, April 13, 1944, NI-12338.

tions did not stop in 1942, nor were they ultimately confined to the two border areas. Late in 1944 and early in 1945 many thousands of Jews were brought into the Reich from Hungary, the Polish labor camps, and the liquidated killing center of Auschwitz. Of course these Jews were hauled in during the liquidation phase of the destruction process, and they were confined to camps. But it is significant nevertheless that the machinery of destruction which wiped out the Jews of many lands was never able to make the Reich itself entirely *judenfrei*.

Another deferred group comprised the foreign Jews. In May, 1939, the Jews of non-German nationality in the Reich area numbered 39,466. At first glance, this figure, amounting to almost 12 per cent of the total Jewish population, seems rather large; however, 16,024 of these Jews were stateless. The actual number of foreign Jews was therefore only 23,442. But not all foreign Jews were considered foreign for deportation purposes. A Jew was a foreign subject only if he was protected by a foreign power—therefore, all Jews who possessed the nationality of an occupied country were stateless in German eyes. An occupied state simply could not protect anybody.

Jews who had immigrated from the Bohemian-Moravian provinces of Czechoslovakia were first to be affected; there were 1732. Next came the big block of Polish and Danzig Jews, numbering 15,249. The occupied countries of the West, including Norway, France, Belgium, Luxembourg, and the Netherlands, were represented by a total of 280 Jews. The number of Soviet, Estonian, Latvian, Lithuanian, and Greek Jews was 515. In addition, about 100 Yugoslav Jews (those who were not citizens of the new Croat state) were also considered stateless.

In short, the 23,442 foreign Jews dwindled, upon closer examination, to about 5600 who belonged to enemy states, neutral states, and Germany's allies. The Foreign Office made no attempt to deport the handful of British and American Jews (together with British dominions and Latin American countries only 386) because it wanted to exchange those Jews for Germans.[123] The "problem" was therefore confined to the 5200 Jews who belonged to neutral states and Germany's allies, or whose nationality was doubtful:[124]

Hungary	1,746
Roumania	1,100
Doubtful category	988
Slovakia	659
Turkey	253
Italy	118
Croatia	ca. 100
Switzerland	97
Bulgaria	30
Sweden	17
Spain	17
Portugal	6
Finland	2

Long before the deportations started, the Foreign Office took the view that no measures should be taken against foreign Jews without its consent.[125] This was an obvious precaution because the Foreign Office was the agency that had to answer to a foreign government for any discriminatory action. During the conference of January 20, 1942, Luther insisted that no foreign Jews be

123. Memorandum by Albrecht (Foreign Office Legal Division), February 4, 1943, NG-2586-N.

124. All statistics are taken from "Die Juden und jüdischen Mischlinge im Deutschen Reich," *Wirtschaft und Statistik*, 1940, pp. 84-87. The figures are census data, correct on May 17, 1939. Undoubtedly the numbers were smaller in 1942, but we would have to make an upward adjustment to include the foreign Jews in the Protektorat.

125. Wörmann to Dieckhoff, Luther, Albrecht, Wiehl, Freytag, Heinburg, and von Grundherr, March 1, 1941, NG-1515.

deported without Foreign Office clearance.[126] His demand covered foreign Jews in the Reich and Jews in foreign countries.

Of course the latter group was far more important than the former. There were only a few thousand foreign-protected Jews in the Reich and Reich-occupied territories, whereas there were millions of Jews in territories controlled by Germany's allies. However, there was an important administrative connection between the two groups. The Foreign Office soon discovered that if, for example, Slovakia agreed to the deportation of its few hundred Jews in the Reich and occupied territories, Slovakia would soon agree to the deportation also of tens of thousands of Jews living in Slovakia itself. The foreign Jews in the Reich were consequently used as a wedge. Once a foreign government had forsaken its Jews abroad, it was easier to induce it to give up its Jews at home.

We will see the full story of the Foreign Office's negotiations with Germany's Axis partners in subsequent sections of this chapter, for these negotiations were concerned only incidentally with the foreign Jews in the Reich and primarily with the Jews in foreign countries. Here it is enough to give a brief outline of the Foreign Office's operations.

The first countries to be approached were Slovakia, Croatia, and Roumania. The governments of these three states submitted to the German demand without much ado. (Roumania subsequently decided to protect a few of its Jews.)[127] Next came the Bulgarian and Italian governments. The Bulgarians had no objection, but the Italian government held out until its very collapse in September, 1943.[128] The Hungarian government was approached again and again, but like Italy refused to give up its Jews. The Italian and Hungarian governments consequently had to be treated like the neutral states.

The Foreign Office did *not,* of course, insist upon the deportation of the Jews in neutral countries, so there was little point in insisting upon the deportation of the handful of Jews with neutral nationalities in Germany. However, Germany had to become *judenfrei.* The neutral governments, together with Italy and Hungary, were therefore presented with an ultimatum that unless they withdrew their Jews within a specified time, these Jews would be included in general anti-Jewish measures. The limits were not heeded, though, and as a result the deportation expert of the RSHA, Eichmann, became very impatient.

On July 5, 1943, Eichmann reminded his opposite number in the Foreign Office, von Thadden, that the repatriation deadlines had already been passed. "We do not consider it worthwhile," he wrote, "to wait any longer or to meet these governments halfway. According to the present status of the final solution, there are now in the Reich area only those Jews who are partners in a Jewish-German mixed marriage and a few Jews of foreign nationality." In order to arrive at a "final solution" in this matter also, Eichmann requested von Thadden to fix one more deadline, August 3, 1943. Eichmann then listed the countries involved: Italy, Switzerland, Spain, Portugal, Denmark, Sweden, Finland, Hungary, Roumania, and Turkey. "In closing," Eichmann wrote, "we ask that you put aside any possible scruples in the interest of finally solving the Jewish problem, since in this matter the Reich has met the foreign governments half-

126. Memorandum by Luther, August 21, 1942, NG-2586-J.

127. Memorandum by Luther, August 21, 1942, NG-2586-J.

128. Luther via Wiehl to Wörmann, Weizsäcker, and Ribbentrop, September 19, 1942, NG-5123.

way in the most generous manner."[129]

Von Thadden agreed with his colleague Eichmann but extended the deadline to October, 1943. Only the Italian Jews, whose government had in the meantime surrendered to the Allies, were subject to deportation at once.[130] The Turks requested a further postponement, thus incurring the displeasure of the Foreign Office, which pointed to its repeated "extraordinary concessions." In the end the Foreign Office agreed to a final deadline of December 31, 1943, while the impatient Eichmann was demanding "general treatment" of all foreign Jews.[131]

So much for the Jews of foreign nationality. The third deferred group was hardly a problem at all. They were the members of the Jewish administrative machine and their families.

In the very beginning of the deportations the employees of the *Reichsvereinigung* and the *Kultusgemeinden* enjoyed exemption. As a matter of fact, the official Jews occupied first place in the exempt list "agreed" upon between Obersturmführer Brunner and Rabbi Murmelstein in Vienna,[132] but this deferment lasted only as long as the cooperation of the Jewish machinery was required in the deportations. As we shall see when we examine the deportation methods more closely, the Jewish self-destructive machinery was an essential component of the deportation apparatus. The Jewish officials were burdened with quite a few important tasks: the business of compiling lists, securing certain personal properties of the deportees, keeping track of vacant apartments, supplying police forces (*Ordner*) to help seize Jews and get them on trains, and handing over to the Gestapo the Jewish community assets (which, by the way, financed the deportations).

In short, these Jews were at least, for a while, quite essential, but as time passed, the "reduction of personnel" in the Jewish community agencies took its course.[133] The Jewish police were increasingly staffed with Jews in mixed marriages, that is, persons who were exempt anyhow.[134] Gradually, the very top strata of the Jewish administrative machine were engulfed in the deportations.

The first transports of Jewish officials and employees were organized in the late spring of 1942.[135] At that time, Goebbels decided to retain five hundred leading Jews (*führende Juden*) as hostages to assure the proper behavior (*anständiges Verhalten*) of the many thousands of Jewish precision workers in Berlin.[136] In a sense they were peculiar "hostages," for — regardless of the behavior of the Jewish workers — these "leading Jews" were subject to deportation sooner or later. Indeed, after the "replacement" of Jewish labor in the Reich was initiated, another transport of community officials left Berlin on November 29, 1942.[137]

129. Eichmann to von Thadden, July 5, 1943, NG-2652-E. Denmark, though occupied, was respected as a neutral state until the fall of 1943. Finland, an Axis partner, was the only European ally that was never pressured into deporting its Jews. Finland had a democratic form of government and only about 2000 Jews.

130. Von Thadden to German missions abroad, September 23, 1943, NG-2652-M.

131. Memorandum by Legationsrat Wagner, October 29, 1943, NG-2652-K. Eichmann to von Thadden, November 15, 1943, NG-2652-L.

132. See p. 279.

133. See pp. 281–82.

134. Werner Hellmann (survivor) in Lamm, "Entwicklung des deutschen Judentums," p. 132.

135. Norbert Wollheim, in Lamm's "Entwicklung des deutschen Judentums," lists fate of all major officials of the *Reichsvereinigung*, pp. 127–29.

136. Office of Gesandter Krümmer (Foreign Office) to Weizsäcker and Luther, May 27, 1942, NG-4816.

137. Dr. Alfred Karger in *Aufbau* (New York), October 3, 1952, p. 11.

The Jewish "Führer" in Berlin, as one of Eichmann's people called Rabbi Leo Baeck, was picked up in his home on January 27, 1943, at 5:45 A.M. Baeck, an early riser, was already awake, but he asked for an hour to put his things in order. During that hour he wrote a letter to his daughter in London (via Lisbon) and made out postal money orders for his gas and electric bills. He traveled to Theresienstadt in a railway compartment by himself. (Incidentally, Baeck, an old man, was the only member of the *Reichsvereinigung* who was still alive after 1945.)[138]

In Vienna the Jewish deportation chief Murmelstein was himself deported to Theresienstadt, where he survived as the last "Jewish elder" of the ghetto. The chief of the Vienna Jewish community, Löwenherz, who according to the Eichmann man was a "nice fellow" (*ein braver Kerl*), stayed in Vienna until the very end as the head of a skeleton Jewish community organization which took care of a few thousand Jews in mixed marriages.[139]

SPECIAL PROBLEM IV: THE INCARCERATED JEWS. – So far, we have discussed three broad deportation groups: the only truly exempt group, comprising the *Mischlinge* and the Jews in mixed marriages; the Theresienstadt Jews, including the old people, badly invalided and highly decorated war veterans, and prominent persons; and the deferred group, which consisted mostly of Jews who wound up in killing centers after suitable delays – the Jews in war industry, the foreign Jews, and the official Jews. A fourth group was also included at the beginning of this chapter – the incarcerated Jews. That was the category which comprised Jews in institutions: insane Jews, imprisoned Jews, and Jews in concentration camps. In order to deport these persons the Reich Security Main Office had to make special arrangements with the agencies which had jurisdiction over them.

The institutions for the mentally ill were under the control of the Health Division of the Interior Ministry. During the concentration process Staatssekretär Dr. Conti of the Interior Ministry ordered the mental institutions to report to him all incarcerated Jews.[140] In 1940 the Jewish insane were separated from the German insane,[141] and the Jews were concentrated in an institution of their own, at Bendorf-Sayn.[142] In the spring of 1942 the first transport of Jewish "imbeciles" (*Vollidioten*) arrived in the Lublin district for gassing in one of the killing centers.[143] By November, 1942, Bendorf-Sayn was closed.[144] The insane problem thus appears to have been disposed of.

The transfer of the imprisoned Jews, who were in the custody of the Justice

138. See account by Baeck in Eric H. Boehm (ed.), *We Survived* (New Haven, 1949), p. 290. The Eichmann man who called Baeck the Jewish "Führer" was Hauptsturmführer Wisliceny. See Levai, *Black Book on the Martyrdom of Hungarian Jewry*, p. 123. Baeck was sixty-nine at the time of his deportation. The only other *Reichsvereinigung* survivor, Moritz Henschel, died soon after his liberation. Baeck died in 1956.

139. Dr. Rezso Kasztner (Kästner), *Der Bericht des jüdischen Rettungskomitees aus Budapest 1942–1945*, pp. 154–55, 178.

140. Dr. Leonardo Conti to *Heil- und Pflegeanstalten* (insane asylums), October 24, 1939, NO-825.

141. Hermann Pfannmüller (Director of Bavarian Asylum at Eglfing-Haar) to Bavarian Ministry of Interior/Health Division, September 20, 1940, NO-1310.

142. Pfannmüller to *Gemeinnützige Kranken-Transport-GmbH.*, May 2, 1941, NO-1140. Circular decree of Interior Ministry, November 10, 1942 (*Ministerialblatt, 1942*, p. 2150); also in *Die Judenfrage* (*Vertrauliche Beilage*), March 1, 1943, pp. 17–19.

143. *Generalgouvernement* Main Division Propaganda, consolidated weekly reports from the district propaganda divisions, report by Lublin division, April 18, 1942, Occ E 2-2.

144. Circular decree of Interior Ministry, November 10, 1942, *Ministerialblatt*, 1942, p. 2150.

Ministry, was a more difficult affair. Although the imprisoned Jews were comparatively few, the judiciary's reluctance to surrender them was great. The reason for that reluctance was not so much a sense of justice or compassion as an administrative consideration. The transfer of the Jews was bound up with the transfer of other inmates, and the relinquishment of judicial power over Jews was connected with the diminution of judicial power as a whole. The SS and Police used the Jews as a wedge to weaken the judiciary and, ultimately, to engulf it. In a completely totalitarian state the police organization alone dispenses justice.

The judiciary foresaw this development and tried to forestall it. Characteristically, the Justice Ministry's forestalling attempts were based on the notion that the judiciary too could make its contribution to the destruction of the Jews. The Justice Ministry's conception of a contribution was not merely the enforcement of anti-Jewish discriminatory measures. It goes without saying that a German court did not inquire into the constitutionality of a measure, but enforced whatever decree bore the signature of a government authority. The judiciary wanted to do more than that. It wanted to add anti-Jewish discriminations of its own; it wanted to make life miserable for a Jew in court, either by reading an anti-Jewish intent into a decree that did not have it, by aggravating the scope of a decree when the language of its provisions justified no aggravations, or by changing the procedure in such way as to make it more difficult for a Jew to win a case, or by adding to the punishment so as to make a Jew pay a stiffer fine, serve a longer sentence, or even die.

It should be noted that most judicial discriminations were not centrally directed. On the whole, each judge made his own "contribution" to the extent of his eagerness to reveal himself as a true Nazi. Some justices, such as Rothaug in the Katzenberger "race pollution" case, were bent upon "achieving a death sentence against a Jew at any price."[145] As Rothaug explained after the war, "many of our judgments were National Socialist."[146]

The statistics on criminality in the Old Reich for 1942 reveal that whereas the ratio of convicted Germans to acquitted Germans was 14 : 1 (417,001 to 29,305), the ratio of convicted Jews to acquitted Jews was 20 : 1 (1508 to 74). Of the 1508 Jews convicted by the courts, 208 were sentenced to death. Since not a single Jew was convicted of murder, we must be highly suspicious of these death sentences.[147] Moreover, it is quite clear that in civil suits, also, Jews were subjected to discriminations. Although we have no statistics, a few of the cases already discussed in this book indicate a decided Jewish disadvantage in civil proceedings.

On the other hand, there were justices who could not bring themselves to subject the law to "artificial construction." We have noted the case of the coffee coupons.[148] There was also the Luftgas case. In October, 1941, a special court in Katowice (Upper Silesia, incorporated Polish territory) sentenced a seventy-four-year-old Jew, Markus Luftgas, to imprisonment for two and a half years on the ground that he had hoarded 65,000 eggs. Hitler heard of the judgment and informed Acting Justice Minister Schlegelberger, through Staatsminister Meissner, that

145. Affidavit by Dr. Georg Engert (prosecutor in Katzenberger case), January 18, 1947, NG-649.

146. Affidavit by Oswald Rothaug, January 2, 1947, NG-533.

147. Data from Justice Ministry (signed Grau) to *Präsident Reichsgericht, Präsident Volksgerichtshof, Oberlandesgerichtspräsidenten, Oberreichsanwälte beim Reichsgericht und Volksgerichtshof*, and *Generalstaatsanwälte*, April 4, 1944, NG-787.

148. See pp. 102–3.

he wanted Luftgas killed. Schlegelberger thereupon handed Luftgas to the SS for execution.[149] To the bureaucracy, court decisions such as those rendered in the coffee coupons and Luftgas cases pointed to the need for central direction, but the Justice Ministry's first inclination was to encourage rather than to direct the judges to be harsh in their treatment of Jewish defendants.

In May, 1941, Staatssekretär Schlegelberger suggested an interministerial decree to deprive Jews of the right of appeal by directing the judicial machinery to carry out any sentence pronounced against a Jew without delay. Characteristically, Schlegelberger suggested also that Jews be prohibited from charging a German judge with partiality. Third, he proposed *leniency* for Jews who committed acts against their own people, as, "for example, in the case of a Jewess who submitted to an abortion."[150] Needless to say, this last proposal was not intended as a favor to the Jews; it meant merely that Jews were to be free to injure themselves.

That same type of "generosity" was later extended to Jews in health protection matters, when the Interior Ministry, in agreement with the Party Chancellery, ruled that Jews, and *Mischlinge* of the first degree who wanted to marry Jews, were no longer required to show the customary certificates of health before marriage.[151] In any case, the Schlegelberger proposals were not implemented in 1941. (Schlegelberger had intended to attach them to a decree that was not issued: the draft ordinance to deprive the Jews of their German nationality.) But they were not entirely forgotten.

When "final solution" measures were initiated in Germany, in the fall of 1941, the Justice Ministry was thrown into some confusion. The judiciary wanted to jump on the bandwagon. But how?, On November 21, 1941, one of the Justice Ministry's experts, Ministerialdirigent Lutterloh, wrote to Staatssekretär Schlegelberger about the whole dilemma. "In view of the present position of the Jews," he said, "discussions are taking place here to determine whether the Jews are to be deprived of the right to sue and whether special regulations should be made about their representation in the courts." The decisive question, said Lutterloh, was whether the Jews were going to be shoved out right away. So far, he pointed out, only 7000 out of 77,000 Berlin Jews had been "shoved out" (*abgeschoben*). The Jews in war industry and mixed marriages had been "deferred" (*zurückgestellt*). On the other hand, all Jewish lawyers in Berlin, the so-called *Konsulenten*, had received "travel orders" (*Abreisebefehle*). In other words, he concluded, something had to be done.[152]

During the period of uncertainty, however, nothing happened. Perhaps Schlegelberger was too busy with the Jews in mixed marriages. When things had quieted down somewhat, the *Präsident* of the *Volksgerichtshof* ("people's court"), Dr. Freisler, circulated a draft decree by the Justice Ministry which resurrected the original Schlegelberger proposal that Jews be barred from making appeals in criminal cases. The draft decree contained also a wholly unnecessary provision to the effect that Jews were to be deprived of the right to appeal to the courts for a decision against sentences inflicted by the police.[153] The

149. Correspondence in Document NG-287.

150. Schlegelberger to Interior Ministry, May 8, 1941, NG-1123.

151. Circular decree by Interior Ministry, March 25, 1942, *Ministerialblatt*, 1942, p. 605, reprinted in *Die Judenfrage* (*Vertrauliche Beilage*), April 15, 1942, p. 29.

152. Ministerialdirigent Lutterloh to Oberregierungsrat Dr. Gramm with request to inform the *Staatssekretär*, November 21, 1941, NG-839.

153. Freisler to Interior and Propaganda Ministries, Foreign Office, Party Chancellery,

Interior Ministry proposed that appeals in administrative cases should also be abolished, and that the effect of the decree should be extended to the Protektorat and the incorporated eastern (Polish) territories.[154]

Schlegelberger replied that he had no objections to these changes and added that Jews should be deprived of the right to take oaths, though they should continue to be held responsible for their statements.[155] The Party Chancellery requested that Jews lose the right to institute civil suits and that they forego the right to challenge a judge on grounds of partiality.[156] (Neither of the party's suggestions was original.) On September 25, 1942, an interministerial conference was held for the purpose of incorporating all the proposals in a new draft, which also contained the provision that at the death of a Jew his fortune was to escheat to the Reich.[157] By that time the draft was obsolete.

At the end of August, 1942, Acting Justice Minister Schlegelberger retired because of old age, and a new Justice Minister, Thierack, took over. Thierack started his regime by making some extraordinary concessions to the SS and Police. On September 18, 1942, Thierack and his new Staatssekretär Rothenberger met with Himmler, SS-Gruppenführer Streckenbach (chief of personnel in the RSHA), and SS-Obersturmbannführer Bender (SS legal expert) to conclude an agreement. The two sides agreed that all Jews who had received sentences of more than three years were to be handed over to the SS and Police and that, in future, all punishable offenses of Jews were to be dealt with by Heinrich Himmler.[158]

In a fit of generosity the Justice Ministry subsequently decided – on its own – to surrender all Jews who were serving sentences of more than six months.[159] The second part of the Himmler-Thierack agreement, which altogether deprived the courts of criminal jurisdiction over Jews, could not be carried out until a decree was published (on July 1, 1943), in pursuance of which criminal actions by Jews were to be "punished" by the police.[160] In the meantime, the Justice Ministry handed all newly convicted Jews over to the Gestapo on an assembly-line basis.[161]

It should be noted that the Himmler-Thierack agreement dealt not only with Jews but also with Gypsies, Poles, Russian, Ukrainians, Czechs, and even "asocial" Germans. It was a far-reaching breach in the existing system of criminal law. Thierack explained his move in the following letter to Bormann:

> With a view to freeing the German people of Poles, Russians, Jews, and Gypsies, and with a view to making the eastern territories which have been incorporated into the Reich available for settlement by German nationals, I intend to turn over criminal jurisdiction over Poles, Russians, Jews, and Gypsies to the *Reichsführer-SS*. In doing so, I stand on the principle that the administration of justice can make only a

---

Reichsführer-SS, and *Reichsprotektor* in Prague, August 3, 1942, NG-151.

154. Interior Ministry to Justice Ministry, August 13, 1942, NG-151.

155. Schlegelberger to Propaganda Ministry, August 13, 1942, NG-151.

156. Bormann to Justice Ministry, September 9, 1942, NG-151.

157. Frick to Party Chancellery, Ministries of Justice, Propaganda, and Finance, and Foreign Office, September 29, 1942, NG-151.

158. Memorandum by Thierack, September 18, 1942, PS-654. The agreement covered the Greater Reich area.

159. Directive by Dr. Eichler (Office of the Justice Minister), April 1, 1943, PS-701.

160. RGBl I, 372. Order by Himmler, July 3, 1943, *Ministerialblatt,* p. 1085.

161. Affidavit by Senatspräsident Robert Hecker, March 17, 1947, NG-1008. Hecker was in charge of transferring Jews to the police; he worked in Division V of the Justice Ministry.

small contribution to the extermination of these peoples.[162]

The third group of Jews subjected to a custodial transfer were the inmates of the concentration camps. In the 1930's tens of thousands of Jews had been arrested in *Einzelaktionen* and thrown into one of Himmler's camps for an indefinite period of time; most of them were released for emigration, but a group of about 2000 were still languishing in the camps long after the war had broken out.[163] Now, in the fall of 1942, Himmler decided to make his German concentration camps *judenfrei.* The Jews involved were to be shipped to the killing centers of Auschwitz and Lublin.[164] The transfers involved no change of jurisdiction because the concentration camps in the Reich and the killing centers in Poland were under the same management. However, the killing center was quite different in character from an ordinary concentration camp, as the victims were soon to discover.[165]

So far, we have discussed the problems faced by the Gestapo in deporting various categories of people: the exempt Jews, the Theresienstadt Jews, the deferred Jews, and the incarcerated Jews. Needless to say, there was also a very large amorphous category which posed no problems at all. Nobody (with the possible exception of an official in the Justice Ministry) was worried about the *Konsulenten,* or lawyers, and no one was worried about the many thousands of other people who fell into no problem category and who could therefore be shipped off without further ado. But, as always in history, only the "problems" attract attention, and so we have devoted most of our space to what may well have been only a minority of the victims.

Seizure and Transport

In the Reich-Protektorat area the biggest hurdle in the operation was overcome with the conclusion of negotiations for the deportation of the various troublesome categories of Jews. With the completion of the preliminary step, the major problem was solved. However, two matters remained to be taken care of. One was the actual seizure and transport of the Jews — that was probably the easiest part of the operation. The other matter was the more burdensome and wearisome process of confiscating the Jewish estate.

There were virtually no seizure difficulties such as those encountered in the occupied USSR. In Germany the Gestapo was after all in home territory. Tens of thousands of Gestapo men were available for the operations, and only a few hundred thousand Jews had to be deported. Only in the big cities, like Berlin and Vienna, were the Gesta-

162. Thierack to Bormann, October 13, 1942, NG-558. During a half-year period, the Justice Ministry delivered to the concentration camp chief Pohl 12,658 prison inmates of various nationalities. The prisoners were intended for forced labor projects of the SS. They died, however, like flies. By April 1, 1943, 5935 were dead. Draft letter by Pohl to Thierack, April, 1943, NO-1285.

163. Statistics in Korherr report, March 27, 1943, NO-5194.

164. Müller (Chief, RSHA IV) to all *Staatspolizeileitstellen,* BdS and KdS offices, and *Beauftragte des Chefs der Sicherheitspolizei,* November 5, 1942, NO-2522. Characteristically, the order stipulated that *Mischlinge* of the first degree were to be included in the transfers. These were the only *Mischlinge* killed in the destruction process. The transfer of Jewish women inmates had already been ordered in September. OStubaf. Dr. Berndorff (RSHA IV-C-2) to *Stapoleitstellen,* etc., October 2, 1942, NO-2524.

165. The Reich camps wanted 1600 Polish and Ukrainian labor replacements from Auschwitz. There were no replacements. WVHA D-II (concentration camp labor allocation) to commander of Auschwitz, October 5, 1942, *Dokumenty i Materialy,* I, 73–74; Auschwitz Command/III A to WVHA D-II, October 10, 1942, *Ibid.*

po forces stretched thin. Accordingly, the *Zentralstellen* started to make use of *Ordner*, or Jewish police, which helped in the seizures and in the guarding of the Jews at the collecting points (*Sammelstellen*). The Gestapo demand for orderlies was undoubtedly the most critical challenge to the Jewish leadership, for in addition to all the tasks which the Jewish apparatus had already performed, such as the confiscation of Jewish properties and the compilations of deportation lists, the Jewish community was now expected to do the ultimate. Jews had to seize Jews, in order to lighten the Gestapo's load and guarantee the smooth success of this operation. Rabbi Leo Baeck, the Jewish leader in Berlin, explained his fatal decision to employ Jewish police in the following words:

> I made it a principle to accept no appointments from the Nazis and to do nothing which might help them. But later, when the question arose whether Jewish orderlies should help pick up Jews for deportation, I took the position that it would be better for them to do it, because they could at least be more gentle and helpful than the Gestapo and make the ordeal easier. It was scarcely in our power to oppose the order effectively.[166]

The victims themselves did not resist, either. The criminality statistics for the deportation year 1942 indicate the conviction of only one Jew for "resistance to the state" (*Widerstand gegen die Staatsgewalt*).[167] However, the deportations were not always smooth, because the Jews were sometimes aware of what was going to happen; and then they tried to elude seizure for at least a brief period.

It seems that during the roundup of the factory-employed Jews in Berlin a few "short-sighted" industrialists "warned the Jews in time." The expression "warned" comes from the Goebbels diary. It is not clear whether he meant that the industrialists actually tried to save the Jews; possibly he tried to convey that, with typical Prussian meticulousness, the German plant managers had inadvertently tipped off the Jews by handing out dismissal notices, telling them not to report for work on the next day, or something of the sort. At any rate, Goebbels complained that "we therefore failed to lay our hands on about 4000. They are now wandering about Berlin without homes, are not registered with the police and are naturally quite a public danger. I ordered the police, Wehrmacht, and the Party to do everything possible to round these Jews up as quickly as possible."[168]

Only a few hundred Jews in the entire Reich actually succeeded in hiding for any length of time. In Jewish parlance, they were known as *U-Boote* (submarines or U-boats).[169] To be a "U-boat" a man had to have money, steady nerves, unusual presence of mind, and extraordinary social ability. Not many persons possess these qualities.[170]

The hidden Jews received a little assistance from a few Germans; the Vienna Jews were helped by a Jewish relief committee in Budapest.[171] Most of the time, however, the "immersed" (*untergetauchten*) Jews had to rely upon themselves. Hunted by the Ges-

166. Leo Baeck in Boehm, *We Survived*, p. 288.

167. Circular by Justice Ministry, April 4, 1944, NG-787.

168. Lochner, *Goebbels Diaries*, entry for March 11, 1943, p. 294.

169. Kasztner, *Der Bericht des jüdischen Rettungskomitees aus Budapest 1942–1945*, pp. 7–8.

170. See the account by Werner Hellmann in Lamm, "Entwicklung des deutschen Judentums," pp. 324-29. Hellmann saved not only himself but also his girl friend – probably a unique achievement.

171. Kasztner, *Bericht des jüdischen Rettungskomitees*, pp. 7–8.

tapo and professional Jewish informers employed by the Gestapo, dodging the entire network of party offices and Nazi vigilantes, living in ruins and passing themselves off as bombed-out people, the "U-boats" scurried to and fro, waiting for their liberation. Slim as their chances might have been, they still faced better odds than the deportees who arrived at the killing centers.

The actual transport of the Jews was not handled by the Gestapo. The Reich Security Main Office only made arrangements with the German railways (*Deutsche Reichsbahn*) to set up so-and-so many trains in such-and-such cities for these-and-those destinations. As a rule the deportation trains consisted of freight cars, specially sealed to prevent escapes.[172] About 1000 Jews were loaded on each train.[173] For the *Reichsbahn* the allocation of these trains was a significant contribution. Almost all transports were heading east, in precisely the same direction taken by soldiers and supplies moving to the eastern front. Moreover, the first fifty transports, scheduled for the period November 1 – December 4, 1941,[174] were dispatched at the very time when the German Army, near Moscow, was making its last offensive before the winter crisis – apparently military considerations also were not to be considered in the "final solution of the Jewish problem."

The Reich Security Main Office had no personnel to guard the trains. As in the case of the mobile killing operations in Russia, Heydrich had to approach the Order Police for help; and, in pursuance of an arrangement between the two main offices, the Order Police furnished one officer and twelve men to guard each train.[175] As we shall see, the RSHA relied on the railways and on the Order Police, not only in the Reich-Protektorat area but also in the occupied territories. In fact, the Order Police came to regard the guarding of "special trains" (*Sonderzüge*) as one of its regular functions.[176]

One of the more interesting aspects of the transport problem was its financing. Apparently the *Reichsbahn* and the Order Police did not cover the expenses incurred from their respective budgets; the Reich Security Main Office paid for the costs of the deportations, including the food supplied by the local authorities (trips on the *Sonderzüge* were very long), the trains allotted by the *Reichsbahn*, and the personnel lent by the Order Police. Very possibly, the payments were designed to assure all-around co-operation.

However, the RSHA did not actually furnish the funds from its own money, either. Instead, the Gestapo used its very close association with the Jewish community machinery to confiscate the money which the *Reichsvereinigung* had collected from the Jews in the form of special taxes. This money was now expended for the deportations. In short, this was an example of self-financing; the Jews paid for their own transport to the killing centers. There

172. This information comes from numerous survivors' accounts.

173. Order by Daluege, October 24, 1941, PS-3921.

174. Order by Daluege, October 24, 1941, PS-3921.

175. *Inspekteur der Ordnungspolizei* Vienna to *Polizeipräsident* Vienna/*Kommando der Schutzpolizei* ("Protective Police"), October 27, 1941, enclosing order by Chief of Order Police Daluege to *Inspekteure* and *Befehlshaber* (IdO and BdO) in Berlin, Hamburg, Hannover, Münster, Kassel, Nuremberg, Stuttgart, Munich, Vienna, Breslau, Prague, and Riga, with copies to Higher SS and Police Leaders in Berlin, Hamburg, Braunschweig, Düsseldorf, Kassel, Munich, Stuttgart, Vienna, Breslau, Prague, and Riga, and to *Polizeipräsident* in Berlin and Chief of Security Police (Heydrich), October 24, 1941, PS-3921.

176. *Reichsführer-SS* (by Daluege), *Vorschrift für die Führung und Verwendung der Polizeitruppe* (Lübeck, 1943), p. 4.

was only one snag in the arrangement: the bureaucrats in the Finance Ministry felt that if any confiscating was to be done, they were to do it.[177] The result was a jurisdictional dispute which was not resolved until the Finance Ministry agreed to Himmler's exclusive use of these particular funds.[178]

The destination points of the first transports were Riga and Minsk in the *Ostland* and the Lodz ghetto in the Warthegau. The Riga and Minsk Jews were subsequently shot by the mobile killing units. The deportees in Lodz shared the fate of the Polish Jews in that ghetto; that is, they were deported to the killing centers of Kulmhof and Auschwitz. In 1942 and 1943, transports were directed to Theresienstadt or directly to a killing center. The major receiving point for the Reich Jews was the huge death camp at Auschwitz in the Upper Silesian *Gau* (incorporated Polish territory).

The deportation statistics for the Reich-Protektorat area are complete only to December 31, 1942; the figures are given in Table 46.[179]

TABLE 46 / *Deportation Statistics for Reich-Protektorat Area*

	"EVAKUIERT" (DEPORTED)	REMAINING ON JANUARY 1, 1943	ELIGIBLE FOR DEPORTATION	IN MIXED MARRIAGE
Old Reich	100,516	51,327	34,567	16,760
Austria	47,555	8,102	3,299	4,803
Protektorat	69,677	15,550	9,339	6,211
Total	217,748	74,979	47,205	27,774

Although the statistics for 1943 and 1944 are not complete, we may assume that almost all the 47,205 remaining eligible Jews (not living in mixed marriage) were deported.[180]

With the gradual disappearance of more than a quarter-million Jews in the mysterious "East," a wave of rumors drifted back to Germany. The rumors were connected and combined with earlier reports of mobile killing operations in Russia, and as the flow seeped into every town and every social quarter, the Gestapo felt itself surrounded by whispers.

Above the murmur one man prepared to raise his voice in protest. On the eve of the deportations, a sixty-six-year-old Catholic priest, Dompropst Bernard Lichtenberg of St. Hedwig's Cathedral in Berlin, dared to pray openly for the Jews, including those who were baptized and those who were unbaptized. Following a denunciation, he was arrested. In the course of a search of his apartment the police found notes for an undelivered sermon in which the priest was going to ask the congregation to disbelieve the official claim that the Jews wanted to kill all Germandom. Held in custody, he insisted that he wanted to join the Jews in the East to pray for them there. He was placed on trial before a special court and given a sentence of two years.

177. Memorandum by Ministerialrat Maedel, December 14, 1942, NG-4583.

178. Schlüter (Finance Ministry) to Himmler, March 17, 1943, NG-4583.

179. Report by Korherr, April 19, 1943, NO-5193. The Old Reich statistics include the Sudeten *Gau*. The deported column includes the transport of 6,500 Jews to France (1940), probably includes earlier transports to Poland. Koerherr might or might not have included the Jews in insane asylums, prisons, and concentration camps.

180. Nearly 20,000 Jews were deported from the Old Reich alone during the first three months of 1943. Korherr reported that the 51,327 Old Reich Jews had dwindled to 31,910 by April 1, 1943. Proportional reductions were probably effected in Austria and the Protektorat. See report by Korherr, April 19, 1943, NO-5193.

Upon his release on October 23, 1943, he was picked up by the Gestapo to be brought to Dachau; too sick to travel, he died on the way in a hospital at Hof.[181] Thus a solitary figure had made his singular gesture. In the buzz of the rumor mongers and sensation seekers, Bernard Lichtenberg fought almost alone.

To be sure, Lichtenberg was not the only one to be arrested. Every once in a while a careless man made a careless remark to the wrong person. The house painter Louis Birk, of Wiesbaden, could not do his work without a great deal of talk with *Hausfrauen* in whose apartments he was working. The charges assert that "from dark wells he scooped rumors about an unfavorable turn of the war" and spread them to his employers. With respect to the Jewish question, he remarked that all the remaining Jews in Germany would soon be poisoned with gas. Furthermore, he assured the housewives that the party leaders were all blacklisted and that they would some day be forced to reconstruct the Jewish synagogues. Louis Birk was executed.[182]

By and large, only a handful of rumor-carriers could be caught, and the Party Chancellery therefore decided to combat the rumor wave by issuing an official explanation of the deportations. The Jews, said the party, were being sent "to the East" (*nach dem Osten*) in order to be employed there in work camps. Some of the Jews were being sent "farther East" (*weiter nach dem Osten*). The old Jews and decorated Jews were being resettled in Theresienstadt. "It lies in the nature of things," the party circular concluded, "that these partially very difficult problems can be solved in the interest of the permanent security of our people only with ruthless hardness (*rücksichtsloser Härte*)."[183] End of explanation. Obviously the rumors continued, unabated.

Confiscations

In the bureaucracy one thing at least was certain: the Jews were not expected back in Germany. In 1942, certainly by 1943, most of them were dead. The dead Jews left behind them a legacy which was to occupy the bureaucrats for months and years: personal property, apartments, Jewish community property, blocked accounts, goods in customs houses, sequestered securities, firms and real estate still under trusteeship, credits and debts, pensions, insurance, and inheritance problems. All these odds and ends, unliquidated expropriations and unfinished business, were now dropped into the laps of the Finance Ministry's experts.

In order to proceed properly the Finance Ministry needed a law, that is, a decreed principle that all property left behind by the deported Jews would fall to the Reich. Up to the end of 1941 the principal excuse for confiscating Jewish property was the allegation that Jews were "enemies of

181. Legationsrat Dr. Haidlen (Foreign Office/Political Division – Section III – Vatican) via Ministerialdirigent Erdmannsdorff and Unterstaatssekretär Wörmann to Weizsäcker, November 11, 1941, NG-4447. Günter Weisenborn, *Der Lautlose Aufstand* (Hamburg, 1953), pp. 52–55. It is of interest to note that the police waited almost two months before they took him into custody. Since Lichtenberg was in charge of converted Jews, one is apt to speculate that the Gestapo was prone to extend to him a limited bureaucratic courtesy. The delay was terminated when two female university students denounced the priest.

182. Indictment of Louis Birk, signed by *Oberreichsanwalt beim Volksgerichtshof* (prosecutor at people's court), Lantz, April 29, 1943, NG-926. Judgment of People's Court/6th Senate, signed by Presiding Judge Hartmann, July 13, 1943, NG-926. Prosecutor to Justice Ministry, September 14, 1943, NG-926.

183. Party Chancellery, *Vertrauliche Informationen* (for *Gau* and *Kreis* offices only), October 9, 1942, PL-49.

the state"; in other words, the bureaucracy availed itself of decrees which covered the confiscation of property belonging to Communists and similar opponents of the Reich. In fact, there were instances when Jews were forced to sign papers stating that they were Communists and that, therefore, their property was subject to confiscation.

For many reasons this procedure was not quite satisfactory, but the most important reason was that each Jew had to be declared a *Staatsfeind* ("enemy"), and the property of each Jew had to be confiscated under a separate order. The Finance Ministry wanted a general order, an automatic "forfeiture" of all such properties to the Reich.[184] Hardly less important was the need to regulate the rights of German claimants and debtors. To what extent were German creditors to be paid from confiscated property? How much was to be given to German heirs? How much could the Reich collect from German debtors?

All these problems were dealt with in the 11th Ordinance to the Reich Citizenship Law, which was decreed on November 25, 1941.[185] This decree formulated the principle that a Jew "who takes up his residence abroad" could not be a Reich national and that the property of such a Jew fell to the Reich. The provision with respect to German creditors was that the Reich would assume Jewish liabilities only to the extent of the sales value of the confiscated property, and only when such payments were not contrary to national sentiment. Non-Jews who had been supported by deported Jews were entitled to some compensation, but again not in excess of the sales value of the confiscated property. The compensation could consist of a single cash payment or the return of confiscated objects.

Undoubtedly, that stipulation had been drafted with a view to paying off German relatives of deported Jews. In effect, it was a provision to take care of the German heirs, although the term "heirs" of course was not used. In view of the subsequent exemption of the Jews in mixed marriages, the application of the dependants' clause was in any case limited. If private German claims upon Jewish property received some consideration in the law, Jewish claims against private German interests could not be treated with less attention. The bureaucracy did not want to sacrifice these claims since such a disposition would have benefited only the German debtors who had neglected to make payments, and one of the cardinal principles of the destruction process was that only the Reich was to profit from the destruction of the Jews. Accordingly, the ordinance directed debtors to the estate, and possessors of property belonging to deported Jews, to declare such debts within six months. Elaborate hardship clauses followed this provision. The designated central authority for the entire question of claims was the *Oberfinanzpräsident* in Berlin-Brandenburg. In the Protektorat the same function was performed by the property office of the *Reichsprotektor*.[186]

The Eleventh Ordinance then established for the first time the principle of the outright confiscation of Jewish property: all that the Jews possessed was to be taken away, and nothing was to be given in return, since the victims no longer needed anything. There were

184. Summary of interministerial conference under chairmanship of Ministerialdirigent Hering of the Interior Ministry, and with representatives from the Foreign Office, Justice Ministry, Finance Ministry, East Ministry, *Reichskommissar* for the Strengthening of Germandom, RSHA, Deputy of the Führer, and Foreign Organization of the party participating, January 15, 1941, NG-300.

185. RGBl I, 722.

186. See decree on loss of Protektorat nationality, November 2, 1942, RGBl I, 637.

only two exceptions to that rule: The deportees were permitted to take along some personal possessions and money. (That provision was necessary in order to give substance to the "resettlement" legend. The personal items, incidentally, were collected to the last hairpin in the killing centers.) The other exception was the property of Jews in mixed marriages. That property could not be touched, and the bureaucracy chafed about the situation to the very end.

The principle of outright confiscation was supplemented, as usual, by the rule that only the Reich was to profit from anti-Jewish measures. We know from the history of the expropriations in the 1930's how long it took to establish that principle, but even in 1941 it was not yet firmly rooted in bureaucratic practice. Properly interpreted and strictly enforced, the rule should have insured that the confiscated assets would be administered – like taxes – only for the benefit of the Reich, and not for the benefit of any of its agencies, let alone its employees. However, as we shall see – and as we have already seen in the case of the Jewish community funds – that aspect of the principle was difficult to observe. Now, let us have a closer look at how the Reich went about collecting its loot.

Comparatively speaking, the simplest problem was probably posed by the pensions and insurance policies. In 1939 the Minister of Postal Affairs had urged the revocation of pensions on the ground that the Jews were going to be incarcerated in protective custody, security arrest, "or the like" anyway.[187] However, pensions did remain in effect for officials who had served in the bureaucracy for at least ten years or who had been soldiers on the front line during the First World War. Now the pensions were indeed superfluous. They were consequently stopped as soon as the Jewish pensioners were on their way.[188] In the matter of *private* pensions the regulation was just a bit more complicated; these pensions were subject to *confiscation* because "waiver by the Reich of pension claims would benefit not the general welfare but a private institution." Still, the private companies were permitted to make a lump-sum settlement.[189]

Like the public pensions, insurance payments flowing from the Reich were cut off.[190] An interesting problem, concerning which we have no documentation, was the matter of private life insurance. If a Jew and his family were deported to the "East," the simple result in most cases was that both the principal and the beneficiaries were dead. Under the rule of "all profits to the Reich" the Finance Ministry should have had good ground to collect the insurance, but in order to do so, it would have had to disclose the facts. Such disclosure would have been "awkward." We may assume therefore that the life insurance companies got away with the profits.

Without any serious difficulty the bureaucracy proceeded to confiscate goods of emigrated Jews in customs houses[191] and securities deposited and blocked under the decree of December 3, 1938.[192] Bank accounts belonging to emigrated Jews had been transformed

187. Ohnesorge to Frick, November 30, 1939, NG-358.

188. Schlüter (Finance Ministry) to *Oberfinanzpräsidenten,* April 29, 1942, NG-5313.

189. *Ibid.* If the pension claim arose from the employment of a Jewish manager, lump-sum payment was fixed, on principle, by an arbitrator of the Reich Administrative Court; *Ibid.* For regulation of pensions, see also the decree of the Ministry of Labor, January 24, 1942, *Reichsarbeitsblatt,* Pt. II, p. 90.

190. Labor Ministry (signed Dr. Zschimmer) to Reich Insurance Office, December 20, 1941, *Reichsarbeitsblatt,* Pt. II, p. 15.

191. Notation by Ministerialdirektor Wucher (Finance Ministry/Customs Division), July 8, 1941, NG-4906.

192. Affidavit by Amtsrat Parpatt, January 23, 1948, NG-4625.

into blocked accounts under the currency law,[193] and since the deported Jews were also "emigrating," their accounts too were blocked under the law. Now, *all* blocked accounts were confiscated.[194]

When the deportations began, a few Jewish enterprises and quite a few parcels of Jewish real estate were still under trusteeship. These properties were automatically confiscated.[195] In view of the large number of real estate items now in the hands of the Reich, the Aryanization expert of the Dresdner Bank, Dr. Rasche, suggested that the bank give the Finance Ministry a hand in the disposal of the property. (Rasche, it may be remembered, had once proposed collecting taxes for the Finance Ministry. His plan for the "mobilization of the confiscated Jewish real estate" consequently need not be startling.) He estimated that the properties were worth one billion reichsmark, and he contemplated with pleasure the huge profit which awaited the Dresdner Bank in commissions.[196]

On March 12, 1942, Ministerialrat Mädel, expert on Jewish confiscated property in the Finance Ministry, met with three representatives of the Dresdner Bank, Deutsche Bank, and Commerzbank. During this meeting the enthusiasm of the banks must have waned. Mädel explained that under the 11th Ordinance the Reich was responsible for Jewish debts up to the sales value of the property, and the Jewish real estate had been mortgaged to the "roof antenna." Furthermore, there was a danger that if the banks participated in the realization of the property, emigrated Jews might institute lawsuits against bank branches in neutral countries.[197]

During the following months the Finance Ministry went ahead on its own. By May, 1943, the sales had proceeded so far that the *Staatssekretär* of the ministry ordered further disposals stopped. The remainder of the real estate was to be set aside for war veterans.[198]

A special problem was posed by the Jewish community property. The Finance Ministry could not get its hands on this property because the community (a legal concept) did not emigrate. Needless to say, the *Reichsvereinigung* and the other organizations of the community were under the complete control of the Gestapo. To the SS and Police, this relationship was an open invitation to move in. The SS society *Lebensborn* was charged with the care of young mothers and children of "good blood," and *Lebensborn* was forever on the lookout for buildings, particularly hospitals, sanatoriums, convalescent homes, and similar *Objekte*. That was precisely the type of real estate owned by the *Reichsvereinigung* and the other *Gemeinden*. Since the *Reichsvereinigung* was an "institution of the Security Police" (*Einrichtung der Sicherheitspolizei*), the *Lebensborn* representatives did not ask many questions. An official simply wrote a letter to Obersturmbannführer Eichmann to ask him "to instruct the *Reichsvereinigung der Juden in*

193. Law of December 12, 1938, RGBl I, 1734.

194. Circular decree by Economy Ministry, July 10, 1943, in *Reichswirtschaftsministerium's Devisengesetz, Durchführungsverordnungen und Richtlinien für die Devisenbewirtschaftung*, 1944.

195. Circular decree by Economy Ministry, December 15, 1941, in *Ministerialblatt des Reichswirtschaftsministers*, December 24, 1941; also in *Die Judenfrage* (*Vertrauliche Beilage*), January 20, 1942, p. 6.

196. Busch to Dr. Leese (Dresdner Bank internal correspondence), March 16, 1942, NI-15651.

197. Dr. Leese to Direktor Andre (Dresdner Bank correspondence), March 17, 1942, NI-6774.

198. Dr. R. Wölfel (Secretariat of Dr. Rasche) to Dr. Erich Rajakowitsch (Gestapo legal expert), May 22, 1943, NI-4252.

Deutschland to transfer the sanatorium [or whatever else it might be] to *Lebensborn* e.V., Munich 2, Herzog Max Strasse 3-7."[199]

The biggest part of the confiscatory operation was the seizure and disposal of the apartments and furniture left behind by the deportees. During the conference of January 20, 1942, Heydrich had given the apartment shortage as the main reason for extending priority in the deportations to the Reich-Protektorat area; the apartment allocation which followed in the wake of the deportations is therefore not without interest.

The first apartment regulation was confined to Berlin and Munich, the capital of the Reich and the capital of the "movement." The choice of these two cities was not accidental. In prohibiting a landlord from renting a vacant Jewish apartment without official approval, the experts were in fact reserving space for the bureaucrats of the ministries who resided in Berlin, and for bureaucrats of party offices, which, for the most part, were located in Munich. Incidentally, the decree was issued only in June, 1942; the landlords were consequently directed that, in the event that they had already rented a Jewish apartment without permission, the next vacant apartment, whether Jewish or non-Jewish, was to be subject to bureaucratic control.[200]

On the very day of the publication of the ordinance, the General Plenipotentiary for Reich Administration, a co-ordinating office headed by Frick and run by Stuckart, demanded an extension of the regulation to the entire Reich area, with the provision that bombed-out persons and families with many children would have priority in the allocations.[201] Finance Minister von Krosigk did not agree – he only wanted to take care of the civil servants. Moreover, von Krosigk felt that not even the huge postal service, the railway administration, and the armed forces should be included in the priorities, for he thought that these agencies were already taking care of their own needs.[202] After another letter from the plenipotentiary, the Finance Ministry agreed to a compromise regulation,[203] which was confined to apartments in houses confiscated by the Reich. Insofar as a Jewish apartment in such a house had not already been earmarked for a civil servant, the landlord was obliged to submit the name of the prospective tenant to the competent *Oberbürgermeister* or *Landrat;* and if within ten days no other tenant was designated, the lease could be concluded.[204]

Whereas apartment allocation was handled in a sluggish fashion, the distribution of the personal belongings in the apartments had to be planned for quickly. The first move was an order, transmitted through the *Reichsvereinigung* and *Kultusgemeinden* by the "supervising agency" (*Aufsichtsbehörde,* the title given to the Gestapo by the Jewish bureaucracy), which prohibited

199. HStuf. Dr. Tesch (Lebensborn) via *SS-Oberabschnitt Süd* to Eichmann, September 30, 1942, NG-3199. Gruf. Kaul to Obf. Dr. Ebner, October 2, 1942, NG-3201. For list of properties acquired by Lebensborn, see affidavit by Max Sollmann (*Lebensborn Vorstand*), June 27, 1947, NO-4269.

200. Decree of June 12, 1942, RGB1 I, 392. For apartment scramble in the Foreign Office, see Rademacher to Foreign Office Personnel Division, August 1, 1940, NG-2879. Also, von Erdmannsdorff to Personnel Division, March 21, 1942, NG-2895.

201. Finance Ministry memorandum, January 16, 1943, NG-5784.

202. Von Krosigk to Stuckart, September 23, 1942, NG-5337.

203. Finance Ministry memorandum, January 16, 1943, NG-5784.

204. Instructions by Finance Ministry to *Oberfinanzpräsidenten* (except Prague), undated, NG-5784. Apartment allocation in the Protektorat was controlled by the Order Police, which facilitated occupancy of apartments by bombed-out Germans. Report by Order Police *Einsatzstab* II (signed Major Jurk), September 3, 1943, NO-2043.

the Jews from selling or disposing of their personal belongings in any way.

The order had to be drafted carefully, lest it read like a death sentence, because no Jew who asked himself "what for?" could fail to arrive at the right answer. The measure was too blunt. It affected every Jew except those who lived in a privileged mixed marriage, and it came just after the first transports had left. The *Reichsvereinigung* therefore added the following purposely misleading introduction: "In connection with the fact that, lately, considerable transactions in Jewish properties have taken place without any good reason, the supervising agency has decided to avoid disturbances in an orderly market by ordering that Jews of German nationality and stateless Jews in the sense of paragragh 5 of the First Ordinance to the Reich Citizenship Law" were forbidden to dispose of their property.[205]

Next, the *Gestapoleitstellen* and *Gestapostellen* distributed printed questionnaires on which the Jews had to list items of their possessions. The checklists were collected and handed over to the finance offices.[206] All property except 100 reichsmark and about a hundred pounds of luggage, which each Jew was permitted to carry along for his "resettlement" in the "East," was to be confiscated.[207] Of course, it was intended that all the things, whether left behind or taken along, should eventually find their way into the Reich Treasury.[208]

As soon as an apartment was vacated, the Gestapo men deposited the keys with the janitor, and the Finance officials took over. The Finance Ministry directive for the disposal of the contents of the apartments is quite interesting. It stated that before any items could be disposed of, articles useful to the Finance administration – particularly desks, bookcases, carpets, armchairs, pictures, typewriters, but also musical instruments and even linen of better quality – was to be set aside for internal consumption. Articles of lesser value were to be sold to the NSV (a party welfare organization) or to junk dealers. If precious metals (jewelry) and stamp collections were found, they were to be sent to the Municipal Pawnshop of Berlin (*Pfandleihanstalt*). Securities were to be delivered to the Reich Treasury (*Hauptkasse*). Cases in doubt were to be reported to the expert on Jewish affairs in the Finance Ministry, Ministerialrat Dr. Mädel.[209]

Apparently quite a few items had not been anticipated in the directive, for a few months afterwards additional instructions had to be sent to the *Oberfinanzpräsidenten* to take care of some of the diverse objects found in Jewish apartments; thus "Jewish writings and other cultural and artistic creations of Jewish endeavor" were to be handed over to a Rosenberg agency, the Einsatzstab Rosenberg, for scientific studies. Phonographs and records were to be delivered to the Propaganda Ministry/*Ministeramt* (Regierungsinspektor Staiger). Sewing machines were to be sold to the Lodz ghetto administration, which needed them for the production of uniforms, while printing machinery

205. Announcement by the *Reichsvereinigung, Die Judenfrage (Vertrauliche Beilage)*, December 24, 1941, p. 85.

206. RSHA (signed Bilfinger) to *Staatspolizeileitstellen* and *Staatspolizeistellen*, December 9, 1941, NG-5325. Finance Ministry (signed Schlüter) to *Oberfinanzpräsidenten*, November 4, 1941, NG-5784.

207. Schlüter directive, November 4, 1941, NG-5784.

208. Not everything, of course, was collected by the Reich. There is evidence coming to us from survivors that Gestapo men on roundup duty helped themselves to a bit of cash and jewelry and that Order Police detachments detailed to guard the "special trains" carried out similar "confiscations."

209. Schlüter to *Oberfinanzpräsidenten*, November 4, 1941, NG-4905.

was to be shipped to the president of the Reich Press Chamber.[210]

The idyllic setup which enabled the Finance Ministry to take sole charge of the distribution of Jewish furnishings — and, incidentally, to reserve for itself the pick of the loot — did not last very long. The first agency to break the Finance Ministry's monopoly was the Gestapo. The Reich Security Main Office did not have to wait until the Finance Ministry threw a few crumbs to the Gestapo offices; the Gestapo could "secure" property *before* the Jews were deported. Items thus secured were out of the Finance Ministry's reach, since they were confiscated through the *Reichsvereinigung* and the *Kultusgemeinden*. In the beginning the Gestapo confined itself to the appropriation of typewriters, adding machines, bicycles, cameras, film projectors, and binoculars. The Gestapo alleged that it needed these things for the proper furnishings of its new offices in incorporated and occupied territories.[211]

As the Gestapo confiscations increased in scope, their repercussions were felt in a sister agency: the *Stabshauptamt* of the *Reichskommissar* for the Strengthening of Germandom. The *Stabshauptamt* was engaged in buying all sorts of useful household articles and clothes for its ethnic Germans; the things were, of course, Jewish property. The *Stabshauptamt* acquired the goods from the Economy Group Retail Trade/Purpose Community Consumers Goods Trade (*Wirtschaftsgruppe Einzelhandel / Zweckgemeinschaft Gebrauchwarenhandel*), which in turn bought the articles from the Finance Ministry.

One day the *Stabshauptamt* noticed that the flow of goods had thinned to a trickle. When it complained to the economy group about the "qualitatively and quantitatively meager supply of underwear resulting from the latest evacuations," the economy group traced the decline to the fact that "in a sense" the goods had been "skimmed" before they were sold. To "clarify" this "impossible" situation, the *Stabshauptamt* representative went straight to the *Stapoleitstelle* in Berlin, where he talked to the official who handled deportations, Prüfer. The Gestapo man explained that he had indeed drawn on the supplies and that he had even taken aluminum pots from Belgian and French supplies, because these things were needed in Theresienstadt. The Jews had to have a pot from which to eat (*einen Essnapf*). The *Stabshauptamt* representative thereupon complained about the matter to the Higher SS and Police Leader in Berlin.[212]

While the Gestapo was "skimming" the supply even before the Finance Ministry had a chance to confiscate the loot, a frontal assault was launched upon the Finance Ministry's dwindling stocks of furnishings by the East Ministry and the party's *Gau* administrations. The East Ministry required some good furniture for its new offices in occupied Russia; the *Gau* administrations could use almost anything for their bombed-out and other deserving constituents. The result of these demands was a new arrangement which allowed the East Ministry to work with the Finance Ministry in the disposal of the furniture. The object of this collaboration was the equipping of Rosen-

210. Schlüter to *Oberfinanzpräsidenten* (except Prague), March 31, 1942, NG-5340.

211. Finance Ministry (signed Groth) to *Oberfinanzpräsidenten* (except Prague), August 31, 1942, NG-5312. See also questionnaire issued by *Israelitische Kultusgemeinde* in Vienna, December, 1941, Occ E 6a-10, and confiscatory orders pertaining to clothes and electrical instruments in *Jüdisches Nachrichtenblatt* (Berlin), June 9, 1942, and June 19, 1942, respectively.

212. Labes (*Stabshauptamt*) to Regierungsrat Dr. Reichert (*Stabshauptamt*), August 31, 1942, NO-2700.

berg's eastern offices. Anything not needed by the East Ministry was sold to the various *Gauleiter;* to handle that new business, the *Gauleiter* appointed "plenipotentiaries for the disposal of Jew-furniture."

However, the Rosenberg-von Krosigk partnership did not endure. In March, 1943, the East Ministry charged the *Oberfinanzpräsidenten* with "stiffness" (*Unbeweglichkeit*) and announced that henceforth its people would handle the furniture disposal by themselves. The East officials also claimed the proceeds from the sale of furniture for their own budget. A bit stunned, the Finance Ministry asked for an explanation.[213] We do not know the outcome of the quarrel. In any case, not much was left for that amorphous and all-encompassing beneficiary, the Reich.

One problem remained to be solved: the property of the Jews in mixed marriages. Somehow it irked the bureaucracy that the Jews in mixed marriages were permitted not only to live but also to keep their personal belongings. It was difficult, however, to confiscate anything while both husband and wife were still living, because couples usually share their personal belongings. The only thing that could be done was to issue a regulation to cover the property of Jews who died in the Reich. That regulation was the 13th Ordinance to the Reich Citizenship Law, dated July 1, 1943; it provided that the property of a Jew was to be confiscated after his death. The ordinance also stipulated that, at the discretion of the Reich, the heirs could be granted a lump sum or some of the articles of the estate.[214]

213. Finance Ministry memorandum, March 26, 1943, NG-5542. For "*Gau* plenipotentiaries for the disposal of Jew-furniture" (*Judenmöbeln*), see *Gau* Cologne-Aachen/Penipotentiary Kreisleiter Eichler to Oberfinanzpräsident Dr. Kühne in Cologne, January 8, 1943, NG-5543.

214. RGBl I, 372.

The 13th Ordinance was inadequate in two respects: First, it put all Jews in mixed marriages on notice. Nothing prevented them from transferring all their earthly possessions to the German partner during their lifetime. In that case the Reich was cheated. Another contingency not covered by the ordinance was the possibility that the German spouse died first, leaving all the property to the Jewish partner. To the SS and Police this was an intolerable situation. In the beginning of 1944 the Interior Ministry (then headed by Himmler) therefore requested the Justice Ministry to issue a new regulation which would (1) prohibit, during the lifetime of the Jewish owner, the sale and acquisition of Jewish property that would be subject to confiscation if he should die; and (2) prohibit Jews from inheriting the property of non-Jewish relatives.[215]

The inheritance problem had been tackled before. Under paragraph 48, section 2, of the inheritance law of 1938[216] the courts had been empowered to declare null and void any will which ran counter to the "healthy people's instinct" (*gesundes Volksempfinden*). The Justice Ministry in September, 1941, issused an authoritative interpretation of this provision, in pursuance of which all German wills in favor of Jews were invalidated.[217] Under general principles of law, however, a person can inherit property in *two* ways: as a named beneficiary if there is a will, or as a legal heir if there is no will. That is to say, if there is no will, the law makes provision for surviving relatives, who become "legal heirs." The wills in favor of Jews were already voided, but the law had not

215. Affidavit by Ministerialdirektor Altstötter, chief of Justice Ministry's Division VI, December 12, 1947, NG-4015.

216. RGBl I, 973.

217. General instructions by Justice Ministry, September 24, 1941, *Deutsche Justiz,* 1941, p. 958.

been changed; a Jew could still be a legal heir. He therefore had a certain minimum protection, and that was the "inheritance gap."

The Justice Ministry's inheritance expert, Ministerialdirigent Dr. Hesse, pondered the problem and then tried to induce the Interior Ministry to withdraw its proposals for an amendment to the thirteenth ordinance. (This, it must be remembered, was 1944.) But the Interior Ministry had to have peace of mind. Accordingly, on September 1, 1944, the Ministry issued a decree, without the participation of the Justice officials, to settle the inheritance problem once and for all.

2 / Poland

When the *Generalgouvernement* administration received an invitation to attend the first "final solution" conference in Berlin, Frank immediately dispatched his deputy Bühler to Heydrich with instructions to find out more details. Bühler returned with the inside information. Shortly afterward (December 16, 1941) Generalgouverneur Frank, Health Präsident Dr. Walbaum, Labor Präsident Dr. Frauendorfer, Security Police and SD Commander Schöngarth, Gouverneur Kundt of Radom, and Amtschef Dr. Hummel of Warsaw met in Krakow in conference. Frank did not speak about the topic which weighed on his mind. Instead, he opened the meeting with a minor matter: measures against Jews who were slipping out of ghettos. It was agreed that they had to be punished with death. Such Jews were a health hazard, for they carried yellow fever to the Polish population. Dr. Hummel said that the Warsaw administration was grateful to the commander of the Order Police (BdO) for having issued an order in pursuance of which all Jews encountered on country roads were to be shot on sight. The special courts, however, were working too slowly. So far, only forty-five Jews had been condemned to death and only eight sentences had been carried out. Something would have to be done to simplify the procedure. The discussion continued in this vein for a while. Then, suddenly, Frank changed the subject.

"I want to say to you quite openly," he began, "that we shall have to finish with the Jews, one way or another. The Führer once spoke these words: 'If united Jewry should succeed once more in releasing another world war, the peoples who have been hounded into this war will not be the only ones to shed their blood, because the Jew of Europe, too, will then have found his end.' I know that many measures now taken in the Reich are criticized. Consciously, repeated attempts are being made to speak about harshness and brutality. Morale reports indicate that quite plainly. Before I continue to speak, let me therefore ask you to agree with me upon the following principle: we want to have mercy only for the German people, otherwise for no one in the whole world. The others had no mercy for us."

Frank then pointed out that if Jewry survived the war, victory would be in vain. He was therefore approaching the problem from only one point of view: the Jews had to disappear. They had to go. For that reason he had begun negotiations in Berlin to shove the Jews east. In January a big conference was to be held in the Reich Security Main Office; Staatssekretär Bühler was to attend for the *Generalgouvernement*. "Certainly," said Frank, "a major migration is about to start. But what is to happen to the Jews? Do you think they will actually be resettled in *Ostland* villages? We were told in Berlin: Why all this trouble [*Scherereien*]? We can't use them in the *Ostland* either; liquidate them yourselves! Gentlemen, I must ask you to arm yourself against all feelings of sympathy. We have to annihilate the Jews wherever we find them and wherever it is at all possible."

This task, said Frank, would have to be carried out with methods quite different from those which Dr. Hummel had just mentioned. Judges and courts could not be made responsible for such an undertaking, and ordinary conceptions could not be applied to such gigantic and singular events. "At any rate, we will have to find a way which will lead to the goal, and I have my thoughts about that." Frank continued, as though he were almost on the defensive: "The Jews are for us also very parasitical eaters. We have in the *Generalgouvernement* an estimated 2,500,000 [a gross overestimate], maybe—together with *Mischlinge* and all that hangs on, 3,500,000 Jews. We can't shoot these 3,500,000 Jews, we can't poison them, but will be able to take some kind of action which will lead to an annihilation success, and I am referring to the measures to be discussed in the Reich. The *Generalgouvernement* will have to become just as *judenfrei* as the Reich. Where and how this is going to happen is a task for the agencies which we will have to create and establish here, and I am going to tell you how they will work when the time comes."[1]

When the conference was adjourned, its participants were aware that a new phase of the destruction process had been inaugurated in Poland; they knew now that the Jews were to be killed. Still, an air of haze and unreality had pervaded the conference room. What precisely was meant by such phrases as "we can't use them in the *Ostland*," "liquidate them yourselves," "we can't shoot these 3,500,000 Jews," "we can't poison them," "a task for the agencies which we will have to create and establish here"? Obviously, they were only hints. No one knew that at that very moment experts from the RSHA, the Führer Chancellery, and the Inspectorate for Concentration Camps were peering at maps and examining the Polish terrain for places to establish killing installations. Poland was to become the headquarters of the killing centers. Poland was the "East."

Preparations

The administrative officials in Poland found out about these things only by degrees. In the meantime, however, the bureaucrats lost no time in making preparations. All offices were on the alert, and everyone was in a hurry. Everyone, from top to bottom, was eager to clear the ghettos. In Berlin, Staatssekretär Bühler spoke up at the "final solution" conference of January 20, 1942, to demand that the deportations in the *Generalgouvernement* get under way as soon as possible.[2] To the west of the *Generalgouvernement,* in the neighboring Wartheland, Reichsstatthalter Greiser secured Heydrich's agreement for an immediate *Aktion* encompassing the "special treatment" of 100,000 Jews in the *Gau* area.[3] For that purpose, Greiser and the SS and Police in the *Gau* established a killing center at Kulmhof, in the middle of the Wartheland. Kulmhof served a large part of Greiser's needs. (Incidentally, the camp was the first killing center to go into operation.)

Locally, the civil offices, police, and railways planned together the details of the deportations. What the planners had to be concerned with most was the sheer magnitude of the operation. Accounting for at least a half-million ghetto dead, the number of Jews in the deportation area remained about 2,200,000, including 1,600,000 in the *General-*

1. Summary of conference of December 16, 1941, including verbatim remarks by Frank, Frank diary, PS-2233.

2. Summary of conference of January 20, 1942, NG-2586-G.

3. The agreement is mentioned in Greiser's letter to Himmler, May 1, 1942, NO-246.

gouvernement, 400,000 in the incorporated territories, and up to 200,000 in the western parts of the Bialystok district. To the civil offices these figures meant that the entire structure of urban population was to be altered. With the disappearance of the ghettos important changes in housing accommodations, the food supply, and the productive capacity were to be expected. In the *Generalgouvernement* the office which was most immediately concerned with these problems was the Population and Welfare Division (*Abteilung Bevölkerungswesen und Fürsorge*) of the Interior Main Division. A directive by Staatssekretär Bühler, dated December 16, 1941, consequently empowered the Population and Welfare Division to approve or veto every "resettlement" which affected more than fifty persons.[4]

The actual ghetto-clearing operations were conducted by the SS and Police. The police forces were facing a formidable task. Although figures for the Security Police and SD are not available, we know that the total network of the RSHA comprised fewer than 70,000 men;[5] the Polish sector could therefore have held no more than a few thousand. The Order Police complement was somewhat stronger. We may estimate its strength in the *Generalgouvernement* at 25,000-30,000 Germans and auxiliaries.[6] In Bialystok the Order Police had 2400 men,[7] while in Lodz a police battalion of 600 men was detailed to ghetto duty.[8] However, the Order Police too were stretched thin. By 1942 they were involved in *three Aktionen*: the deportation of the Jews, the seizure of the Polish harvest (*Ernteerfassung*), and the seizure of Polish workers for labor in the Reich (*Arbeitererfassung*). No wonder that the SS and Police needed help.

Help came in the first instance from the Jews themselves. The *Jüdische Ordnungsdienst,* as the Jewish police in the ghettos were called, furnished thousands of men for seizure operations. In the Warsaw ghetto alone the Jewish police numbered approximately 2500;[9] in Lodz they were about 1200 men strong;[10] the Lvov ghetto had an *Ordnungsdienst* of 500 men;[11] and so on. The SS and Police drew also upon outside assistance. Latvian units were imported from the *Ostland;*[12] *Waffen-SS* units were pressed into service, for example in the Sosnowiec area of Upper Silesia, where the personnel of an SS cavalry school were employed in the roundup;[13] the *Ghettoverwaltung*

4. *Generalgouvernement*/Main Division Interior/Division of Population and Welfare to Lublin District/Interior Division/Subdivision Population and Welfare, February 10, 1942, *Dokumenty i Materialy,* II, 4. We have no record of any vetoes.

5. Affidavit by Schellenberg, November 21, 1945, PS-3033.

6. According to BdO Glt. Becker, the figures at the end of 1942 totalled 10,190 Germans and 16,337 non-Germans. *Generalgouvernement* police conference of January 25, 1943, Frank presiding, Frank diary, PS-2233. Roughly at the same time, the chief of the Order Police listed 15,186 Germans and 14,297 Poles. Oberst-Gruppenführer Daluege to "Wölffchen" (Obergruppenführer Wolff, chief of Himmler's Personal Staff), February 28, 1943, NO-2861. The discrepancies may be due to the inclusion or omission of various auxiliary units.

7. Daluege to Wolff, February 28, 1943, NO-2861.

8. *Polizeipräsident* in Lodz to *Ghettoverwaltung,* February 3, 1942, *Dokumenty i Materialy,* III, 219.

9. Berg, *Warsaw Ghetto,* p. 187.

10. Bendet Hershkovitch, "The Ghetto in Litzmannstadt (Lodz)," *YIVO Annual of Jewish Social Science,* V (1950), 89.

11. *Krakauer Zeitung,* November 15, 1941, p. 5.

12. Tadeusz Bor-Komorowski, *The Secret Army* (London, 1950), p. 99.

13. *Polizeipräsident* in Sosnowiec to *Regierungspräsident* in Katowice, August 1, 1943, *Dokumenty i Materialy* II, 60. *Polizeipräsident* in Sosnowiec via IdO in Breslau to Himmler, August 14, 1943, *ibid.,* p. 71. IdO in Breslau to *Polizeipräsident* in Sosnowiec, August 25, 1943, *ibid.,* p. 70.

in Lodz furnished about 60 of its employees for seizure operations throughout the Warthegau;[14] and the army lent its units for roundups of escaped Jews in the *Generalgouvernement.*[15] Help was not lacking in the ghetto-clearing operations.

While general administration offices were concerned with the destruction of the ghettos, and the SS and Police were involved in the roundups, the German railways had to deal with the transport of the Jews. As we have seen, the responsibility for railway administration in the incorporated areas rested in the *Reichsbahn* itself. Railway transport in the *Generalgouvernement* was in the hands of the Gedob, or *Generaldirektion der Ostbahn,* under Präsident Gerteis.

The *Ostbahn* should receive our special attention for two reasons: First, there is a geographic factor. We need only glance at a map to realize that the *Ostbahn* lay astride the principal routes of communication from Germany to the Russian front; yet this railway network managed to carry about 2,000,000 Polish Jews to their deaths in 1942 and 1943. Second, the *Ostbahn* is of interest to us also because of its personnel composition. We have already seen its enormous personnel expansion after 1939,[16] an expansion which consisted primarily of an addition of Polish personnel. It is true that the German railway administration endeavoured never to place a Pole above a German, and that it was contrary to German policy to employ Poles as locomotive drivers altogether.[17]

We know, however, that later on, German supervision stretched thin, and all-Polish trains prowled along the minor routes.[18] It is therefore doubtful whether the Polish railway workers could have escaped a significant role in the destruction of the Jews.

The deportations started first in the Warthegau, where the killing center at Kulmhof was already operating in December, 1941. In February Jews were already moving in the *Generalgouvernement.* At that time there were still no killing centers in the area, but that circumstance did not stop the deportation agencies. The Jews were simply shifted to overcrowded ghettos near the proposed killing sites. In the midst of winter some of these "resettlers" arrived in their temporary quarters "naked and barefoot," starving and freezing.[19]

In the spring of 1942, killing centers were set up, one by one, by "specialists" from Berlin. At Malkinia, on the Bug, the death camp of Treblinka was built up as a receiving center for Jews from the Warsaw and Bialystok districts. Three killing centers were then established in the Lublin district: Sobibor, Belzec, and Lublin (Maydanek). These camps received deportees not only from Lublin but also from Krakow, Radom, Galicia, and even the Reich-Protektorat area, Slovakia, and Holland. In the incorporated territory of Upper Silesia the giant killing center at Auschwitz (Oswiecim) accepted Jews from the Warthegau, Upper Silesia, Krakow, and the other *Generalgouvernement* districts, as well as all countries of Europe from which Jews were deported. There were, in short, six killing centers: Kulmhof and Auschwitz in the incorporated

14. *Ghettoverwaltung* (signed Ribbe) to municipal health office in Lodz, September 21, 1942, *Dokumenty i Materialy* III, 232.

15. See p. 344.

16. See pp. 133–34.

17. Transport Ministry to chief of transport in OKH, January 5, 1940, H 12/101.2.

18. Internal correspondence, office of chief of transport in OKH, December 4, 1940, H 12/102.

19. *Generalgouvernement*/Interior/Population and Welfare to Lublin/Interior/Population and Welfare, February 10, 1942, enclosing memorandum by Jewish welfare organization, *Jüdische Soziale Selbsthilfe,* dated February 8, 1942, *Dokumenty i Materialy* II, 4–6.

territories; Treblinka, Sobibor, Belzec, and Lublin in the *Generalgouvernement* (see map on p. 573). With the establishment of these camps a vast movement began which did not end until Polish Jewry had virtually ceased to exist.

The Conduct of the Deportations

In the Reich-Protektorat area, considerable difficulties were caused by privileged or semi-privileged categories of Jews. No such encumbrances hindered the deportations in Poland. There was no *Mischling* problem, no mixed-marriage problem, no old-Jews problem, no war-veterans problem. There were only a handful of foreign Jews in Poland, some of whom were pulled out of the ghettos at the very last minute and some of whom were shipped to killing centers by mistake. Only one major difficulty arose in connection with any particular group of Jews, and that problem did not become acute until the end of 1942: the labor shortage. Arrangements had to be made to keep a few skilled laborers alive a little longer. We shall discuss these arrangements, which were concluded at the close rather than at the beginning of the deportations, under the heading of "economic consequences."[20]

With the onset of the ghetto-clearing operations the policemen and their helpers had to face a novel problem – physical revulsion. The ghetto invaders became covered with filth, sewage, and vermin. In the words of the *Ghettoverwaltung*, the work was "nauseous in the extreme" (*im äussersten Grade ekeleregend*).[21] In the Galician ghettos the police were confronted by vast epidemics. In the ghetto of Rawa-Ruska, the Jewish population had concealed its sick in holes, in the hope of saving them from deportation; before the Rawa-Ruska *Aktion* was over, the SS and Police had dragged 3000 sick and dying Jews out of their hiding places.[22] We have no over-all figures for German losses incurred by reason of the epidemics, but in Galicia alone SS and Police Leader Katzmann reported that one of his men had died of spotted fever and that another 120 had fallen ill with the disease.[23]

The dirty work was not done when the Jews were removed. After a ghetto was cleared of Jews, the police and municipal officials had to re-enter the Jewish quarter and clean it up; and, although Poles and Jews could be used for some of the dirtiest labor, the job was still far from pleasant. A large ghetto could be emptied in two or three days, but the cleanup operation required weeks or even months. Thus the Lublin ghetto was disbanded and its inhabitants deported April 17–20, 1942,[24] but the clean-up action (*Säuberungsaktion*) was still in progress two months later.

The operation was carried out in stages. First, a demolition *Kommando* entered the ghetto and blew up all uninhabitable buildings. Next came the salvage crew (*die Lumpensammelkolonne*), which collected all sorts of junk left behind by the deportees. This detachment was followed by a clearing *Kommando* (*die Aufräumungskolonne*) which had to do the hardest work, the cleaning of the latrines. In some latrines the feces were piled up to a height of three feet. The *Aufräumungskolonne* had to use hoses to clean up the mess. The fourth crew consisted of carpenters and glass workers who

20. See p. 332.

21. Ribbe (*Ghettoverwaltung*) to *Reichsstatthalter* Warthegau/*Landesernährungsamt* (regional food office)/Division A in Poznan, July 15, 1942, *Dokumenty i Materialy* III, 230–31.

22. Gruf. Katzmann (SS and Police Leader in Galicia) to OGruf. Krüger, June 30, 1943, L-18.

23. *Ibid.*

24. *Krakauer Zeitung*, June 24, 1942, p. 5.

sealed heremetically all doors and windows in order to enable the gas column (*Vergasungskolonne*) to kill all vermin in the apartments. Finally, the cleanup column (*Reinmachungskolonne*) was called up to remove the dead rats, mice, flies, and bugs, and to tidy up the place.[25]

Still, the dilapidation in the ghettos was a comparatively minor annoyance in the total picture, and the bureaucrats were not much concerned with it. Their primary worry was the progress of the deportations, the rate at which Jewry was disappearing. The top men were interested only in speed. As early as June 18, 1942, Staatssekretär Dr. Bühler asked Higher SS and Police Leader Krüger when he would get through. Krüger replied that in August he would be able to "survey" the situation.[26]

Krüger was a bit cautious because just then he was experiencing his first *Transportsperre*, a complete shut-down of traffic in deportation trains. The *Transportsperre* was instituted only for two weeks, and Krüger managed even during the closed period to wangle a few trains from Präsident Gerteis of the *Ostbahn*. Moreover, after the lifting of the restrictions, Krüger expected to resume the deportations with redoubled effort.[27] Then in July another hitch occurred when the railway line to the killing center of Sobibor, on the Bug, broke down and had to be repaired. The SS and Police had hoped to deport several hundred thousand Jews to Sobibor.

On July 16, 1942, Obergruppenführer Wolff, chief of Himmler's Personal Staff, telephoned Staatssekretär Dr. Ganzenmüller of the Transport Ministry for help. Ganzenmüller looked into the situation and found that the matter had already been settled locally. Three hundred thousand Warsaw ghetto Jews had been diverted from Sobibor to Treblinka. Beginning on July 22, 1942, a daily train stuffed with not fewer than 5000 Jews per run was to leave Warsaw for Treblinka, while twice weekly another train carrying 5000 Jews was to run from Przemysl to Belzec.[28] When Wolff received this news, he wrote the following letter of thanks:

> Dear Party Member Ganzenmüller:
>
> For your letter of July 28, 1942, I thank you — also in the name of the *Reichsführer-SS* — sincerely [*herzlich*]. With particular joy [*mit besonderer Freude*] I noted your assurance that for two weeks now a train has been carrying, every day, 5000 members of the chosen people to Treblinka, so that we are now in a position to carry through this population movement [*Bevölkerungsbewegung*] at an accelerated tempo. I, for my part, have con-

25. *Krakauer Zeitung*, June 24, 1942, p. 5. That even the cleaned-up quarters were unfit places for human habitation was clearly indicated by Frank in a letter to Hitler. The *Generalgouverneur* complained that his rival, the *Reichsführer-SS*, had brought ethnic German resettlers into the Lublin district. To make room for the ethnic Germans, Polish workers had been shoved off to Germany and their families had been sent into "empty Jew-ghettos." In their new homes the Poles were apparently suffering and dying under many of the same privations that had once plagued Jewry. Frank to Hitler, June 19, 1943, PS-437.

In Radom, room had to be found for many Polish workers employed by an expanding German industry. In August, 1943, the chief of the local armament command, together with the local housing expert and a representative of Steyr-Daimler-Puch A. G., surveyed the situation in the empty ghetto. The three officials concluded unanimously that the former Jewish quarter had been looted, dilapidated, and damaged to such an extent as to be beyond repair. War diary, Armament Command Radom, August 24, 1943, Wi/ID 1.37.

26. Summary of police conference, June 18, 1942, Frank diary, PS-2233.

27. *Ibid.*

28. Dr. Ing. Ganzenmüller (*Staatssekretär* in the Transport Ministry and deputy *Generaldirektor* of the *Deutsche Reichsbahn*) to OGruf. Wolff, July 28, 1942, NO-2207.

> tacted the participating agencies to assure the implementation of the process without friction. I thank you again for your efforts in this matter and, at the same time, I would be grateful if you would give to these things your continued personal attention.
>
> With best regards and
>
> Heil Hitler!
>
> Your devoted
>
> *W.*[29]

At the end of 1942, when the deportations were already two-thirds over, the SS and Police offices were confronted by another breakdown. Urgently, Krüger wrote to Himmler:

> SS and Police Leaders today report unanimously that by reason of *Transportsperre* every possibility of transport for Jewish resettlement is cut off from December 15, 1942, to January 15, 1943. Because of this measure, our master plan for Jewish resettlement is severely jeopardized.
>
> Obediently request that you negotiate with central offices of Armed Forces High Command and Transport Ministry for allocation of at least three pairs of trains for this urgent task [*dass mindestens 3 Zugpaare für die vordringliche Aufgabe zur Verfügung stehen*].[30]

Apparently the negotiations were not very successful this time, for on January 20, 1943, Himmler wrote to Ganzenmüller for more trains. The *Reichsführer* pointed out that he knew under what strain the railway network was operating but that the allocation of the trains was, in the last analysis, in Ganzenmüller's own interest. The Jews, said Himmler, were responsible for all the railway sabotage in the *Generalgouvernement,* the Bialystok district, and the occupied eastern territories. Hence, the sooner the Jews were "cleared out," the better for the railways. While writing about the eastern Jews, Himmler also took occasion to remind Ganzenmüller that unless trains were made available for the Jews of the western occupied areas, sabotage would break out there, too.[31]

While the shortage of transport was a particularly pressing problem in the planning of the whole operation, a host of complications was to arise after the organizational problems were solved. These complications developed like shock waves from a single point of impact: the discovery by outsiders of the true nature of the "resettlements."

If concealment was difficult within the German-Czech area, it was doubly difficult in Poland. The Reich-Protektorat area had no killing centers, and most Reich transports were moving out to the east. Poland, on the other hand, was the home of all six killing centers, and Polish transports were moving in short hauls of not more than two hundred miles in all directions. Many eyes fixed on those transports and followed them to their destinations. The deputy chief of the Polish Home Army (London-directed underground force), General Tadeusz Bor-Komorowski, reports that in the spring of 1942 he had complete information about the Kulmhof (Chelmno) killing center in the Warthegau. When the Germans cleared the Lublin ghetto, the Polish underground traced the transports to Belzec. The underground command could not find out what was going on inside Belzec, but, estimating that 130,000 Jews had been shoved into the camp, the Poles concluded that it "was not big enough to accommodate such a large number of people." In July, 1942, the Home Army collected reports from railroad workers that several hundred thousand Jews had disappeared in Treblinka without a trace. At that point there was no doubt anymore about the fate of the Jews.[32]

29. Wolff to Ganzenmüller, August 13, 1942, NO-2207.

30. Krüger to Himmler, December 5, 1942, Himmler Files, Folder No. 94.

31. Himmler to Ganzenmüller, January 20, 1943, NO-2405.

What the Home Army had found out through careful investigation ordinary people had suspected without much proof. The population drew its conclusions quickly and spread them as rumors throughout the occupied Polish territory. By late summer of 1942 almost every inhabitant of Poland, whether outside or inside a ghetto, had some inkling of what was going on. In the end even children knew the purpose of the deportations. When, during the summer of 1944 in the Lodz ghetto, the children of an orphanage were piled on trucks, they cried, *"Mir viln nisht shtarbn!* [We don't want to die!]"[33]

What was the over-all reaction of the Jews in the face of certain death? Did Jewry prepare for armed resistance? The district propaganda divisions in the *Generalgouvernement* watched the reactions of the Jewish population minutely. Here are three sample reports from the propaganda division in Lublin. On April 18, 1942, the Lublin division reported that Jews in the Hrubieszow area had approached the Catholic Church with requests for baptisms.[34] On September 26, 1942, the division reported:

> Among the Jews of Cholm there is a rumor that, henceforth, the extermination [*Ausrottung*] of Jewry will be carried out by sterilization. Although this method would be more humane than the current one, it would lead to the ultimate extermination of Jewry nevertheless. The Jews think they will just have to accept this fact. [*Die Juden müssten sich mit dieser Tatsache eben abfinden*].[35]

On November 28, 1942, the Lublin division reported the following incident:

> A seventeen-year-old Jewess reported to the director of the harvest-gathering troop, Majdan-Sopocki, in the Zamosc area, and requested to be shot, since her parents had already been shot. She referred to an alleged Führer order in accordance with which all Jews have to be done away with before the end of the year. Since the Jewess was an escapee, she was handed over to the competent offices for further treatment [*zur weiteren Veranlassung übergeben*].[36]

With a few powerful strokes of the pen, the Lublin propaganda division had charted the trend of the Jewish reaction: a feeble conversion attempt in April, a sterilization rumor in September, and the offer of a seventeen-year-old girl to give up her life in November. Without a doubt, the Jews were not preparing for armed resistance. They were preparing for automatic compliance with German orders.

The Jewish leadership in the Polish ghettos stood at the helm of the compliance movement, and ghetto chiefs were the implementors of the surrender. Always they delivered up some Jews to save the other Jews. Having "stabilized" the situation, the ghetto administration would bisect the remaining community. And so on. Moses Merin, president of the Central Council of Elders for Eastern Upper Silesia, presided over such a shrinking process. On the eve of the first deportations, Merin

32. Bor-Komorowski, *The Secret Army*, pp. 97–99.

33. Solomon F. Bloom, "Dictator of the Lodz Ghetto," *Commentary*, 1949, p. 120.

34. *Generalgouvernement* / Main Division Propaganda, consolidated weekly reports from district propaganda divisions for April, 1942, report by Lublin division, April 18, 1942, Occ E 2-2.

35. Consolidated reports for September, 1942, reported by Lublin division, September 26, 1942, Occ E 2-2.

36. Consolidated reports, report by Lublin division, November 28, 1942, Occ E 2-2. With respect to the reference to an "alleged" Führer order, see the letter from Himmler to Krüger, of July 19, 1942: "I order that the resettlement of the entire Jewish population in the *Generalgouvernement* be carried out and finished by December 31, 1942." NO-5574.

made his first decision. "I will not be afraid," he said, to "sacrifice 50,000 of our community in order to save the other 50,000." During the summer of 1942 the other 50,000 Jews were lined up in a mass review, from which half were sent to Auschwitz. Merin commented after that deportation: "I feel like a captain whose ship was about to sink and who succeeded in bringing it safe to port by casting overboard a great part of his precious cargo." By 1943 there were only a few survivors. Merin addressed them in the following words: "I stand in a cage before a hungry and angry tiger. I stuff his mouth with meat, the flesh of my brothers and sisters, to keep him in his cage lest he break loose and tear us all to bits. . . . "[37]

Throughout Poland the great bulk of the Jews presented themselves voluntarily at the collecting points and boarded the trains for transport to killing centers. Like blood gushing out of an open wound, the exodus from the ghettos quickly drained the Polish Jewish community of its centuries-old life.

Now, however, we must remember that in an operation of such dimensions not everybody could be deported so smoothly. As the circle of Jewish survivors shrank, the awareness of death increased, and the psychological burden of complying with German "evacuation" orders became heavier and heavier. Therefore we discover that toward the end of the operations increasing numbers of Jews hesitated to move out, that still others fled from the ghettos or jumped from trains to find refuge in the woods, and that in the Warsaw ghetto a few of the surviving Jews rallied in a last-minute stand against the Germans.

The Germans reacted to the recalcitrant Jews with utmost brutality. Howling raiders descended upon the ghettos with hatchets and bayonets. In the Warthegau the police were sent into such actions in a half-drunken stupor. Every Gestapo man assigned to ghetto-clearing duty received daily an extra ration of a little over one-half pint of brandy.[38] The *Ghettoverwaltung* in Lodz demanded a brandy allocation for its employees also, on the ground that employment without such brandy was "irresponsible."[39] In Galicia the Jews were particularly aware of their fate because they had already witnessed the mobile killing operations in 1941. In the words of the SS and Police report, they "tried every means in order to dodge evacuation." They concealed themselves "in every imaginable corner, in pipes, chimneys, even in sewers." They "built barricades in passages of catacombs, in cellars enlarged to dugouts, in underground holes, in cunningly contrived hiding places in attics and sheds, within furniture, etc."[40] The Germans in Galicia proceeded without restraint.

Again and again reports were sent to Krakow and Berlin about the "indescribable" methods of the SS and Police in Galicia. The deportations aroused excitement in the entire district. Once a Polish policeman told of his experiences freely to an ethnic German woman who then wrote anonymously to Berlin. Her letter reached the *Reichskanzlei*. The Polish policeman, she wrote, had asked her whether she was not finally ashamed of being an ethnic German. He had finally become acquainted with German culture. During the dissolution of the ghettos children had been

37. Philip Friedman, "Two 'Saviors' who Failed – Moses Merin of Sosnowiec and Jacob Gens of Vilna," *Commentary*, December, 1958, pp. 481–83.

38. Biebow (*Ghettoverwaltung*) to *Reichsnährstand/Reichsbeauftragter für das Trinkbrandweingewerbe* ("Agricultural Association/Plenipotentiary for the Brandy Trade"), June 25, 1942, *Dokumenty i Materialy* III, 228.

39. *Ibid.*

40. Katzmann to Krüger, June 30, 1943, L-18.

thrown on the floor and their heads trampled with boots. Many Jews whose bones had been broken by rifle butts were thrown into graves and covered with calcium flour. When the calcium began to boil in the blood, one could still hear the crying of the wounded.[41]

During the second half of 1942, reports were also received about Jews who scattered into the woods during the "evacuations." Again the greatest activity seems to have occurred in Galicia. In October, 1942, the propaganda division of Lvov reported:

> The resettlement of the Jews, which in part takes on forms that are no longer worthy of a *Kulturvolk*, actually provokes comparison of the Gestapo with the GPU. The transport trains are said to be in such bad condition that it is impossible to prevent breakouts by Jews. As a consequence there is wild shooting, and there are regular manhunts at the transit stations. Furthermore, it is reported that corpses of shot Jews are lying around for days in the streets. Although the German and also the non-German population are convinced of the necessity of a liquidation of all Jews, it would be appropriate to carry out this liquidation in a manner which would create less sensation and less disgust [*auf eine weniger Aufsehen und Anstoss erregenden Art durchzuführen*].[42]

The escapes from the ghettos and transports also took place in other districts. On December 7, 1942, Gouverneur Zörner of the Lublin district complained in a *Generalgouvernement* conference that in the past few weeks the *Judenaktion* had become somewhat disorganized *(überstürzt)*, with the result that a large number of Jews had escaped from the ghettos and had joined the Polish "bandits."[43] Before long, several thousand Jews were hiding in the woods, joining the partisans, and – sometimes, banded together in units of their own – shooting it out with German *Gendarmerie* units. We have reports of such clashes in all five districts of the *Generalgouvernement*.[44] In the district of Galicia the fleeing Jews were able to buy or acquire rifles and pistols from Italian troops who had fought in Russia and who were now going home. As a result the SS and Police in Galicia lost eight dead and twelve wounded in its attempts to seize Jews in bunkers and forests. It appears that the Galician Jews also attempted to fight back with a primitive biological warfare weapon, for the police found several vials filled with lice which carried spotted fever.[45]

The largest single clash between Jews and Germans occurred in the ghetto of Warsaw. Let us say at once that, for

41. Anonymous letter via Frank to Hitler, received and stamped by the Reich Chancellery on March 25, 1943, NG-1903.

42. *Generalgouvernement* / Main Division Propaganda, consolidated weekly reports from district propaganda divisions for October, 1942, report by Galician division, October 26, 1942, Occ E 2-2.

43. Summary of *Generalgouvernement* conference, December 7, 1942, Frank, Bühler, Böpple, Siebert, Fischer, Wächter, Zörner, Kundt, Wendler, and Oberlandesgerichtsrat Dr. Weh participating, Frank diary, PS-2233. An escape from a death train is described by a survivor, Aaron Carmi, "The Journey to 'Eretz Israel,'" *Extermination and Resistance* (Israel: Kibbutz Lahomei Haghettaot, 1958), I, 87–101.

44. *Generalgouvernement*/Main Division Propaganda, consolidated weekly reports from district propaganda divisions for November, 1942, report by Lublin division, November 7, 1942, and report by Radom division, November 14, 1942, Occ E 2-2. OGruf. Krüger to Gruf. Knoblauch, chief of personnel and training in *SS-Führungshauptamt* (military main office), January 8, 1943, NO-2044. *Generalgouvernement*/Main Division Propaganda, consolidated weekly reports from district propaganda divisions for January, 1943, report by Warsaw division, January 9, 1943, Occ E 2-2. Summary of remarks by Gouverneur Zörner in *Generalgouvernement* conference, January 25, 1943, Frank diary, PS-2233.

45. Katzmann (SS and Police Leader, Galicia) to Krüger, June 30, 1943, L-18. With casualties from accidents and the fever, Katzmann's total losses were 11 dead, 117 wounded and ill.

the further development of the destruction process, this armed encounter was without consequence. In Jewish history, however, the battle is literally a revolution, for after two thousand years of a policy of submission the wheel had been turned and once again Jews were using force.

As we might expect, the Jewish resistance movement did *not* emerge from the *Judenrat,* because that organization was composed of precisely those elements of the community that had staked everything on a course of complete cooperation with the German administration. To mobilize the Jews of the ghetto against the Germans, it was necessary to create a new hierarchy which was strong enough to challenge the council successfully in a bid for control over the Jewish community. The nucleus of such an illegal organization was formed from the political parties that had been represented in the prewar Jewish community machinery. These parties, which had managed to survive in the ghetto by looking out after their members – each party protecting and assisting its own people so far as possible – now banded together into a resistance bloc.

Not all parties veered to a resistance policy with the same speed. The movement began in two extreme camps which had no contact with each other: the Moscow-dominated Communists (PPR) and the self-reliant nationalists (Revisionist Party). From there the idea spread to the Zionist youth groups *(Hechalutz),* the socialist trade unionists *(Bund)* and the Labor Zionists *(Poale Zion Left).* Ultimately the movement embraced all major parties save one: the Orthodox Party *(Agudah).* By that time, however, 85 per cent of the ghetto Jews were already dead.[46]

In the early days of 1942, when the ghetto community was still intact, the resistance movement was confined to verbal action only. Secret talks were initiated and secret pamphlets distributed. That was all. When crisis struck, therefore, the resistance Jews were still without a single gun.

On July 20, 1942, the *Judenrat* was presented with an order to prepare for the "resettlement" *(Aussiedlung)* of "non-productive elements," beginning on July 22, the day for which transport to the Treblinka killing center had been arranged with the *Ostbahn.* The people affected by the order were to report voluntarily at the *Umschlagplatz* ("collecting point") at the corner of Stawki and Djika Streets, near the railway siding and the waiting freight cars (see map on p. 325). The quota was 10,000 a day. (The Germans had transport facilities for only 5000.) The deportations were to be limited to 60,000 nonproductive persons.[47] Exempt were all Jews employed in enterprises or registered for employment and fit for work, plus their wives and children; Jewish bureaucrats and their wives and children; Jewish policemen and their wives and children; Jewish hospital and sanitary personnel with wives and children; and all Jews who were patients in hos-

46. For growth of the resistance movement, see, in general, Philip Friedman (ed.), *Martyrs and Fighters* (New York, 1954), pp. 193–218, and Joseph Tenenbaum, *Underground* (New York, 1952), p. 82 ff. A brief word about some of the political groupings: The Jewish Communists had no party of their own. They belonged to the Polish Workers [Communist] Party: the *Polska Partija Robotnicza* (PPR). The Jewish nationalists had seceded from the Zionist Organization to form the Revisionist Party (later, in Israel, *Heruth*). The military arm of the Revisionists was called the *Irgun Zwai Leumi* ("National Military Organization"). The *Hechalutz* consisted of the youth groups of various Zionist parties. The *Bund* was the party of the Jewish trade unionists. Socialist in leaning, it was both anti-Communist and anti-Zionist. It maintained contact with the Polish Socialist Party (PPS – not to be confused with the PPR).

47. Bernard Goldstein, *The Stars Bear Witness* (New York, 1949), pp. 106–9, particularly p. 109.

pitals and were not fit for removal.[48]

As soon as the order was posted, a mad rush started for working cards. Many forgings took place, and in the whole ghetto everyone from top to bottom was frantic. On the evening of July 23, 1942, the chairman of the *Judenrat*, Adam Czerniakow, committed suicide. His place was taken by another engineer, Marek Lichtenbaum.[49]

While the impotent machinery of the *Judenrat* responded mechanically to German command, feverish activity began in the Jewish party organizations. Committees were established, meetings were held, co-ordinating bodies were set up. On the afternoon of July 23, the very day of Czerniakow's suicide, about sixteen representatives of all major parties except the Revisionists (who were not invited) met to discuss the crucial question of immediate resistance. From the fragmentary postwar accounts of that conference it is not altogether clear how the conferees divided on that question. All accounts agree, however, that the advocates of resistance were voted down. The consensus was that the Germans would deport perhaps 60,000 people but not all 380,000 Jews in the ghetto. It was felt that by resistance the ghetto's doom would be hastened and that, for the acts of a few, the multitude would be punished.[50]

At the end of July or the beginning of August another conference took place, this one outside the ghetto. The Polish commanders of the London-directed underground forces, the *Armia Krajowa*, met under the chairmanship of General Stefan Rowecki to discuss the question whether the underground could remain passive in the face of the destruction of the Warsaw ghetto. Several commanders expressed doubts about the advisability of active intervention. The argument ran: "If America and Great Britain with powerful armies and air forces behind them and equipped with all the means of modern warfare, are not able to stop this crime and have to look on impotently while the Germans perpetrate every

48. Text of order in Marie Syrkin, *Blessed Is the Match – The Story of Jewish Resistance* (Philadelphia, 1947), p. 209.

49. Republic of Poland, Ministry of External Affairs, *The Mass Extermination of Jews in German Occupied Poland* (London, 1943), pp. 7–8. Goldstein, *The Stars Bear Witness*, pp. 114–15.

50. A list of the conference participants was sent to London in a report from the remnant Jewish underground in March, 1944. Excerpts from the report in English reproduced by Friedman, *Martyrs*, p. 199. The absence of a Revisionist representative may be explained by the Communist version of the conference. According to that version, the Communist leader, Jozef Lewartowski-Finkelstein, initiated the conference by inviting all "activists" (apparently including even a member of the *Judenrat* and an orthodox rabbi), but not the Revisionists, who have often been described by the Communists as bourgeois-nationalistic Jewish fascists. See M. Edin, "The 'PPR' and Ghetto Resistance," *Jewish Life*, April, 1951, pp. 12–15. (*Jewish Life* is a Communist monthly published in the United States.)

On the division of opinion in the conference, we know with certainty only that the Communists and the *Hechalutz* ("Zionist Youth Group") were for immediate resistance, while *Judenrat* member I. Szyper and Rabbi Zishie Friedman were against it. Szyper, a historian, apparently recited instances from Jewish history when the Jews had gained more by not fighting than by fighting. Rabbi Friedman cautioned the Jews not "to raise our hands" against the Germans, lest disaster be visited upon hundreds of thousands of Jews. I. Cukierman (*Hechalutz* leader) in Friedman, *Martyrs*, pp. 193–95.

The position of the Socialists (*Bund*) at the conference is not quite clear. According to the postwar accounts of two prominent *Bund* leaders, the *Bund*, through its representative Maurycy Orzech, urged the participants to resist. Goldstein, *The Stars Bear Witness*, pp. 108–12; Marek Edelman, *The Ghetto Fights* (New York, 1946), p. 18. However, *Hechalutz* leader Cukierman and the Communists in *Jewish Life* report that Orzech urged resistance subject to the condition that the Poles fight too.

kind of horror in the occupied countries, how can be hope to stop them?" However, General Rowecki, the commander of the Home Army, had a different opinion. He feared that after the Jews the Poles would be destroyed. He therefore felt that helping the Jews was a measure of self-protection.

The Polish underground thereupon contacted the Ghetto. The answer of the Jewish leaders was that perhaps 60,000 Jews would be deported, but that it was "inconceivable that the Germans would destroy the lot." The Jews had one request, which the Polish Home Army was glad to fulfill. They handed to the Poles an appeal "addressed to the civilized world and to the Allied nations in particular." The Jewish leadership demanded that the German people be threatened with reprisals. The appeal was immediately transmitted to London, but the BBC maintained complete radio silence.[51] As we shall have occasion to find out later, the Jews did not have many friends in London or, for that matter, in Washington.

In the meantime the pace of the "evacuations" increased rather than lessened. Fifty-nine thousand persons were "evacuated" by July 31.[52] The "non-productive" elements were going fast, and the SS was not stopping. Worried proprietors of the German ghetto firms, together with armament officials and representatives of the *Transferstelle,* moved quickly to save their working force. They had no time to lose.[53] The *Aktion* was growing by leaps and bounds.

On or about August 12 the children of the orphanage were marched away. Before the end of the month the entire southern section (see map) was virtually cleared. For a brief period in mid-August the Germans stopped in order to empty the small ghettos in the district; then the raiders returned to Warsaw. Each Jewish policeman was told to bring seven people for deportation each day or face "resettlement" himself. Now every policeman brought whomever he could catch – friends, relatives, and even members of his immediate family. By September 5 about 120,000-130,000 Jews remained. On that day all Jews were called out to the *Umschlagplatz* for a giant selection.[54]

When the *Aktion* was over, the population of the Warsaw ghetto had been reduced from 380,000 to 70,000; a total of 310,322 had been deported.[55] The size of the ghetto had also been reduced,.and the principal inhabited section was now confined to the northeast corner. However, factories were still

51. Bor-Komorowski, *The Secret Army,* pp. 99–100. The failure of the BBC to broadcast the threats is confirmed by Goldstein, *The Stars Bear Witness,* p. 170.

52. Office of the *Gouverneur* of Warsaw to *Staatssekretär* of the *Generalgouvernement,* report for June and July, 1942, dated August 15, 1942, Occ E 2-3.

53. The principal ghetto firms were Többens, Schultz, Wilhelm Döring, and Transavia. An agreement concluded with the SS and Police on August 26, 1942, provided that 21,000 workers in ghetto enterprises be retained. Többens and Schultz got 8000 each in this deal. War diary Armament Command Warsaw, reports for July, August, and September, 1942 (signed Oberst Freter), Wi/ID 1.91.

54. Goldstein, *The Stars Bear Witness,* pp. 124–45. The Jewish police themselves were caught in the final action; about 2000 policemen were among the victims. Berg, *Warsaw Ghetto,* p. 187. A "combing-out" (*Auskämmeaktion*) of the factories took place on September 2, and again on September 6/7. Object of these selections was the reduction of the working force to the agreed 21,000. War diary Armament Command Warsaw, report for September, 1942, Wi/ID 1.91. Jewish policemen in the factories were subjected to a "combout" on September 11; *ibid.*

55. Bgf. Stroop to Krüger, May 16, 1943, PS-1061. Only half the remaining Jews were registered; the other half were in hiding. See also *Gouverneur* of Warsaw district to *Staatssekretär, Generalgouvernement,* report for October and November, 1942, dated December 10, 1942, Occ E 2-3.

in existence on Leszno, Karmelicka, Twarda, Prosta and a few outlying streets (see map, p. 325). The rest of the ghetto was empty.[56]

Many questions were asked in the ghetto upon the conclusion of the operation – thus the self-interrogation by the historian Emmanuel Ringelblum, recorded in mid-October: "Why didn't we resist when they began to resettle 300,000 Jews from Warsaw? Why did we allow ourselves to be led like sheep to the slaughter? Why did everything come so easy to the enemy? Why didn't the hangmen suffer a single casualty? Why could 50 SS men (some people say even fewer), with the help of a division of some 200 Ukrainian guards and an equal number of Letts, carry out the operation so smoothly?"[57] And again: "The resettlement should never have been permitted. We ought to have run out into the street, have set fire to everything in sight, have torn down the walls, and escaped to the Other Side. The Germans would have taken their revenge. It would have cost tens of thousands of lives, but not 300,000."[58]

The fall of 1942 was the time when the Jewish political parties finally banded together and decided to resist further deportations with force. To accomplish this aim, the parties built a complex organization to co-ordinate their activities (see Table 47).[59] This organization was built from the bottom up. First, the Jewish National Committee (ZKN) was formed to bring together the Zionist groups and the Communist PPR.[60] A co-ordinating committee (KK) was then established to bring the Bundists and the merged Zionists and Communists under the same roof. This political amalgamation was accomplished by October 20, 1942.

At the same time, the building of the fighting forces also proceeded from the bottom to the top. Each party set up platoon-size "battle groups" of its own;[61] thus there were battle groups composed of Bundists, *Hashomer Hatzair* battle groups, Communist battle groups, and so on.[62] On October 20, 1942, these units, twenty-two in all, were placed under the command of the military arm of the KK: the Jewish Fighting Organization (ZOB). The ghetto Jews therefore fought in party formations under a centralized command. The commander of the ZOB was a *Hashomer Hatzair* leader, Mordechai Anielewicz. What is most remarkable about Anielewicz is that he was twenty-four years old. The doors to command positions in the Jewish community leadership are usually not open to young men who offer only their ability.[63]

Two major parties remained outside the framework of the new resistance organization, the nationalist Jews of the Revisionist Party and the orthodox Jews of the *Agudah*.[64] The Revisionists had a military force of their own; the *Irgun Zwai Leumi*, which maintained three battle groups.[65] The *Agudah* had no fighting forces at all.

56. Berg, *Warsaw Ghetto*, p. 188.

57. Emmanuel Ringelblum, *Notes from the Warsaw Ghetto* (New York, 1958), entry for October 15, 1942, p. 310.

58. *Ibid.*, November entry, p. 326.

59. The information in this table is taken in its entirety from a report sent by survivors of the ZOB from Warsaw to London in March, 1944. English excerpts from that report in Friedman, *Martyrs*, pp. 201–3.

60. The Zionist groups: *Dror, Hashomer Hatzair, Akiba, Gordonia, Poale Zion Left, Poale Zion Z.S.*, and *Hanoar Hazioni*.

61. A battle group had approximately sixty men and women. Stroop to Krüger, May 16, 1943, PS-1061.

62. In the table are indicated the number of battle groups contributed by each party.

63. On Anielewicz, see Tenenbaum, *Underground*, pp. 121–22, 127–29.

64. Underground Report A of the *Bund*, received in New York on June 22, 1943, in Edelman, *The Ghetto Fights*, p. 46.

65. David Wdowinski, "The History of the Revolt," *The Answer* (Revisionist publication in U.S.), June, 1946, pp. 18, 24. Wdowinski

The first blow of the resistance movement was struck at Jewish collaborators of the *Judenrat* machinery. On August 21, 1942, when the deportations were at their peak, one Israel Kanal fired the first shot in the struggle; the bullet felled the Jewish police chief, Jozef Szerynski.[66] His successor, Jacob Laikin, was also shot. Assassins' bullets struck down policemen, informers, and collaborators, including the chief of the economic division of the *Judenrat*, Israel First.[67] Under the steady fire of the Jewish underground the *Judenrat*, under chairman Ing. Marek Lichtenbaum, gradually atrophied and ultimately lost its power.[68]

TABLE 47 / *The Organization of the Jewish Resistance in the Warsaw Ghetto*

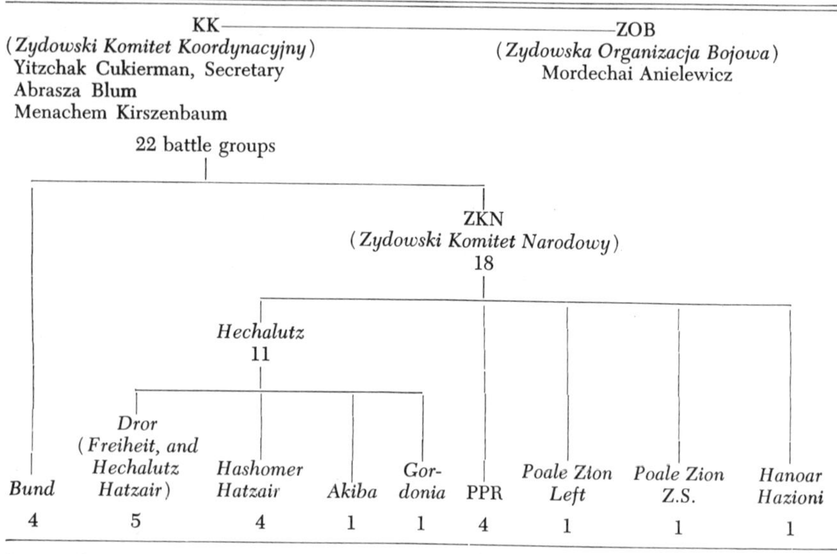

Defense measures were now rushed to completion. While pretending to build air raid shelters, the Jews constructed several hundred dugouts which partially connected with the sewer system. (In the privately built hiding places social stratification was not affected even during these last hours, for the well-to-do Jews enjoyed considerably more luxurious dugouts than the poor.) A propaganda campaign was launched by means of posters, handbills, and word of mouth, impressing upon the Jews that in case of trouble they were to stay in their dugouts, come what might. At the same time negotiations were conducted with General Rola-Zymierski's Communist People's Guard and with General Rowecki's London-directed Home Army in order to procure arms for the battle groups. According to a post-war Communist account, the People's Guard

was head of the Warsaw ghetto Revisionists and the *Irgun*. The tactical command of the *Irgun* was in the hands of Paul Frenkel.

66. ZOB report in Friedman, *Martyrs*, pp. 196-97. According to this report two shots fatally wounded the police chief. According to other accounts, Szerynski later took his own life.

67. Goldstein, *The Stars Bear Witness*, pp. 178–79. Jonas Turkow (survivor) in Friedman, *Martyrs*, p. 84.

68. During the revolt Lichtenbaum and his assistants were shot by SS men "after a sort scuffle." Bulletin No. 7 of the KK, April 29, 1943, in Friedman, *Martyrs*, pp. 242–43.

supplied the Jews with twenty-five rifles, "the last" in its "arsenal."[69] The Home Army's contribution consisted of "a supply of revolvers, rifles, some machine guns and about a thousand hand-grenades, as well as explosives for the production of mines."[70] In addition, several hundred pistols were acquired by purchase from the Polish population.[71] Thus prepared, the Jews waited for the blow.

In the meantime, the Germans made plans of their own. In January, Himmler visited Warsaw. There he got the information that about 40,000 Jews were still in the ghetto. (Actually, the number was about 70,000.) He decided that there were too many and ordered that 8000 be deported at once; from the remainder he wanted to save about 16,000 for forced labor camps.[72] To Oberst Freter of the Armament Command in Warsaw he remarked that Keitel had agreed to this plan.[73]

The January push came quite suddenly and caught the ghetto defenders by surprise. Sixty-five hundred Jews were snatched away. In the ensuing fracas one German police captain was severely wounded in the abdomen.[74]

After this encounter Himmler ordered the total dissolution of the ghetto. The emptied Jewish quarter was to be torn down completely. No Poles were to be permitted to settle there, for Himmler did not want Warsaw to grow back to its former size.[75]

The German SS and Police Leader in Warsaw, Oberführer von Sammern-Frankenegg, expected some difficulties in the operation and therefore concentrated his own forces and secured some assistance from the army's *Oberfeldkommandantur* in Warsaw. He made his preparations thoroughly and, on the first day of the *Aktion*, handed over his command to his successor, Brigadeführer Stroop.

On the eve of the Warsaw ghetto battle the opposing sides faced each other in the strength shown in Table 48.

At three o'clock in the morning on April 19, 1943, the ghetto was surrounded, and three hours later the *Waffen-SS* entered the ghetto at Zamenhof Street (map, p. 325). The invaders were met by concentrated fire, and incendiary bottles put the tank out of action. The SS men withdrew with casualties. Later in the morning, raiding parties again entered the ghetto, and this time they proceeded systematically from house to house. By afternoon they encountered machine-gun fire. Since it became apparent that the ghetto could not be cleared in one sweep, the Germans withdrew again at night to resume operations in the morning.

On April 20 and 21 slow progress was made. The Jews held the factories, and it was decided, after some negotiations with the managers and the army, to destroy the buildings with artillery and explosives. By April 22 several sections of the ghetto were afire, and

69. S. Zachariash, "The Ghetto Was Not Alone," *Jewish Life*, April, 1951, pp. 10–12.

70. Bor-Komorowski, *The Secret Army*, pp. 104–5. A Jewish observer, Dr. Isaac I. Schwarzbart, has described the totality of Polish help as "negligible, insignificant." Schwarzbart, *The Story of the Warsaw Ghetto Uprising* (New York: World Jewish Congress, 1953), p. 6. The author was a deputy in the Polish legislature in exile during the war.

71. The price of these weapons was extraordinarily high: 10–15,000 zloty were demanded for a pistol; 20–25,000 zloty for a rifle. The chief purchaser of black-market arms was the ZOB, but a few weapons were privately bought. See survivors' accounts in Friedman, *Martyrs*, pp. 207–14.

72. Himmler to Krüger, copies to RSHA, Pohl, and Wolff, January, 1943, NO-1882.

73. Freter to Rüstungsinspekteur Schindler, January 12, 1943, Wi/ID 1.46.

74. Goldstein, *The Stars Bear Witness*, pp. 176–77. Stroop to Krüger, May 16, 1943, PS-1061. *Generalgouvernement*/Main Division Propaganda, consolidated weekly reports from district propaganda divisions, report by Warsaw Division, January 18, 1943, Occ E 2-2.

75. Himmler to Krüger, February 1, 1943, NO-2514. Himmler to Krüger, February 13, 1943, NO-2494.

TABLE 48 / *Comparative Strength of Opposing Forces in Warsaw Ghetto*

JEWS*

Jewish War Organization (*Zydowska Organizacja Bojowa* – ZOB)
Commander: Mordechai Anielewicz
Manpower: Twenty-two platoon-size "battle groups," composed of men and women between 18 and 25, territorially divided and commanded as follows: Central District (Israel Kanal), nine battle groups; Többens-Schultz area (Eliezer Geler), eight battle groups; Brushmakers' area (Marek Edelman), five battle groups
Not operating under the ZOB:
Irgun Zwai Leumi, under the command of Paul Frenkel, with three battle groups
A few Poles who were inside the ghetto and Polish partisans (Communists and nationalists) who carried out diversionary attacks outside the ghetto
Total armed strength: about 1500
Total equipment:
Two or three light machine guns; about a hundred rifles and carbines (give or take a few dozen); a few hundred revolvers and pistols of all types, including German Lugers and Polish Vis pistols; a few thousand hand grenades (Polish and homemade), homemade incendiary bottles (Molotov cocktails), a few pressure mines and explosive contraptions (*Höllenmaschinen*); gas masks, German steel helmets, and German uniforms
Objective: to hold out as long as possible

GERMANS†

Commander: Oberführer von Sammern-Frankenegg; relieved at 8 A.M. on April 19, 1943, by Brigadeführer Stroop
Manpower:
Waffen-SS men (with three or four weeks of basic training only):
SS-Armored Grenadier Training and Replacement Battalion No. 3, Warsaw
SS-Cavalry Training and Replacement Battalion, Warsaw
Order Police (including veterans of the eastern front):
1st and 2d Battalions of the 22d Police Regiment
Technical Police (*Technische Nothilfe*)
Polish police
Polish fire brigade
Security Police (small detachments)
Army:
One light anti-aircraft battery
One howitzer crew
Two engineer platoons
A medical unit
Collaborators (Ukrainians): one battalion from Trawniki camp
Total Strength: ca. 2000-3000
Equipment:‡
One captured French tank and two heavy armored cars; three light (2 cm.) anti-aircraft guns; one medium (105 mm.) howitzer; flame throwers, heavy and light machine guns, submachine guns, rifles, and pistols; grenades, smoke candles, and large amounts of explosive charges
Objective: to clear the ghetto in three days

*ZOB report in Friedman, *Martyrs*, pp. 201-3. Wdowinski in *The Answer*, June, 1946, pp. 18-19, 24. Tenenbaum, *Underground*, p. 96. Stroop to Krüger, May 16, 1943, PS-1061.

†Stroop to Krüger, May 16, 1943, PS-1061.

‡A howitzer is a short-barreled artillery piece, designed for close-range destructive power. Ordinarily, a Panzer-Grenadier battalion was equipped with nine 37-mm. anti-tank guns, three 75-mm. anti-tank guns, and four 75-mm. howitzers. No mention is made of such weapons in the Stroop report, and it is conceivable that the training unit did not have them. The Stroop report similarly fails to mention mortars. The absence of mortars is strange, but it is possible that they were not used.

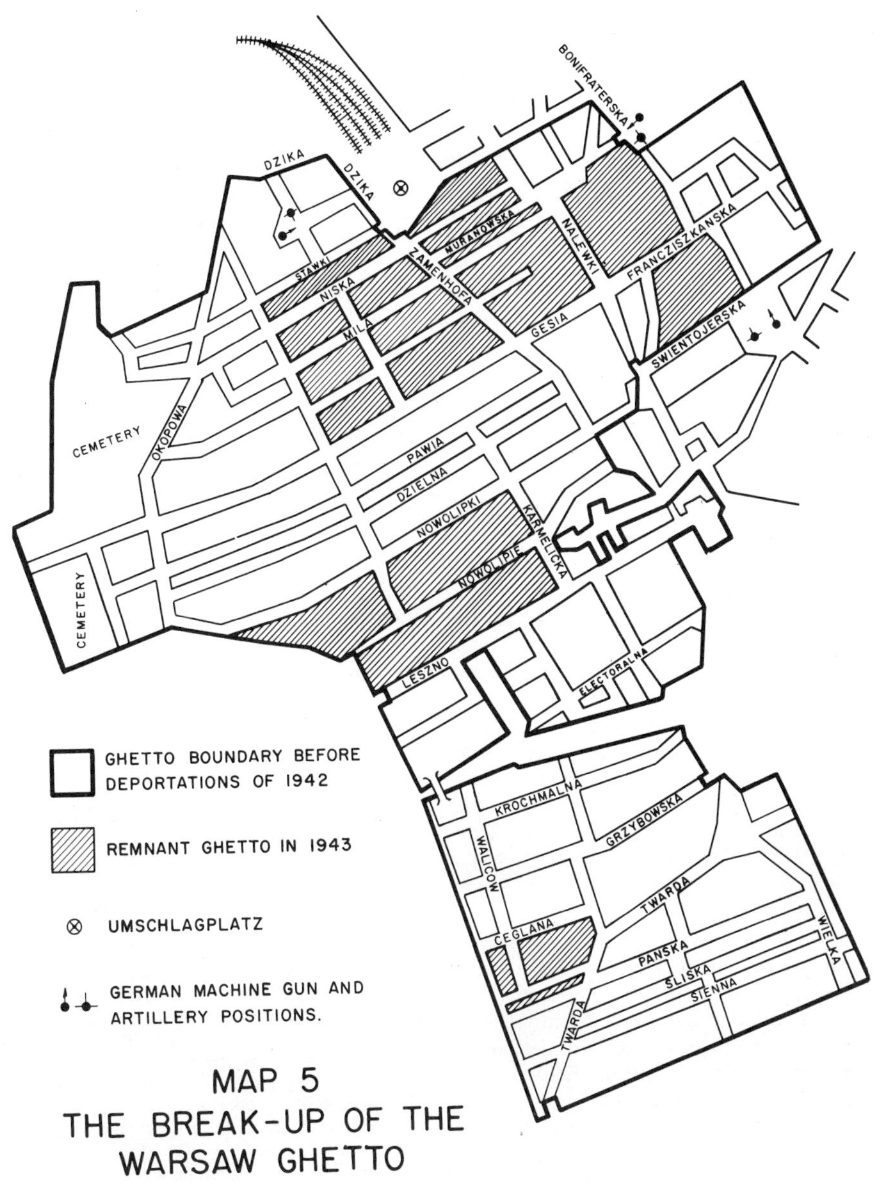

MAP 5
THE BREAK-UP OF THE WARSAW GHETTO

Jews jumped from the upper stories of the burning buildings after having thrown mattresses and upholstered articles into the street. The raiders attempted to drown Jews moving around in the sewers, but the Jews managed to block off the flooded passages.

After April 22, Jews were caught and killed in increasing numbers. Sewers and dugouts were blown up one by one. Captured Jews reported to the Germans that the inmates of the dugouts "became insane from the heat, the smoke, and the explosions." A few of the Jewish prisoners were forced to reveal hiding places and centers of resistance.

The Jews now tried to slip out of the ghetto through the sewer system; the army engineers countered this move by blowing up the manholes. Smoke candles were lowered into the underground passages, and Jews who mistook the candles for poison gas came up for air. In May the ghetto was a sea of flames. Only a few parties of Jews were still above ground in the burning buildings, and in their dugouts they were buried in debris and suffocated. Corpses were observed floating in the sewers. One desperate Jewish unit, emerging from a sewer, seized a truck and staged a successful getaway. The Jews were thinning out rapidly.

On May 8 the Jewish commander, Mordechai Anielewicz, was killed. The Germans now sent night patrols into the ghetto, and the remaining Jewish dugouts were systematically destroyed. By May 15 the shooting became sporadic. The Jews had been overwhelmed. At 8:15 P.M. on May 16 the German commander, Stroop, blew up the great Tlomacki Synagogue, in the "Aryan" section of the city, as a signal that the Warsaw ghetto battle was over.

Several thousand Jews had been buried in the debris, and 56,065 had surrendered. Seven thousand of the captured Jews were shot; another 7000 were transported to the death camp at Treblinka; another 15,000 were shipped to the concentration camp and killing center at Lublin; the remainder were sent to labor camps. Nine rifles, fifty-nine pistols, several hundred grenades, explosives, and mines were captured. The rest of the Jewish equipment had been destroyed. The losses to the Germans and their collaborators consisted of sixteen dead and eighty-five wounded.

It is possible that in the final tabulation a few casualties were omitted and that additional losses were inflicted upon the Germans after the official end of the fighting; however, there is no doubt that in the main the Stroop report, with all its statistics, is accurate. It must be remembered that the Jews did not have enough weapons to equip a modern infantry company. It must also be remembered, that Stroop's report was secret and that he listed the name of every casualty at the beginning of his account, as if to emphasize his losses.[76]

After the armed resistance of the

76. The Stroop report (PS-1061) is called "The Warsaw Ghetto Is No More." It was addressed to Krüger. The document contains a final summary as well as daily battle reports and photographs. When Generaloberst Jodl (OKW/WFSt) was shown the Stroop report after the war, he commented: "The dirty arrogant SS swine! Imagine writing a 75 page boastful report on a little murder expedition, when a major campaign fought by soldiers against a well-armed enemy takes only a few pages!" G. M. Gilbert, *Nuremberg Diary* (New York, 1947), p. 69. To this report, however, we owe the most detailed account of the battle, including the role of the army in the "expedition."

For Jewish accounts, see primarily Marek Edelman, *The Ghetto Fights.* Edelman commanded the Brushmakers area. Our summary is taken from the Stroop report. The name of the Jewish commander, Anielewicz, comes from Jewish sources. The figure of 15,000 Jews transported to the Lublin camp is taken from the affidavit by OStuf. Friedrich Wilhelm Ruppert (Chief, Technical Division, Lublin camp administration), August 6, 1945, NO-1903.

Jews was broken, two tasks had to be completed. In accordance with Himmler's wish the entire ghetto was to be razed, and every dugout, cellar, and sewer was to be filled in. After the conclusion of this work the whole area was to be covered with earth and a large park was to be planted in the former ghetto.[77] Thus, in the summer of 1943, Oswald Pohl, the chief of the SS Economic-Administrative Main Office, established a concentration camp in the ruins,[78] and Brigadeführer Dr. Ing. Kammler, chief of the construction division of the economic-administrative main office, was put in charge of the demolition work. Contracts were let with three construction firms. The *Ostbahn* laid 12 miles of narrow-gauge railway track to haul away debris. Twenty-five hundred concentration camp inmates and 1000 Polish workers labored for more than a year, clearing the 445 acres of demolished buildings and breaking down the 3,400,000 cubic yards of wall. The work was interrupted in July, 1944, before the park could be planted. For the incomplete job Himmler presented to Finance Minister von Krosigk a bill for 150,000,000 reichsmark.[79]

More difficult but a little less expensive than the rubble clearance work was the task of rounding up 5000-6000 Jews who had escaped from the ghetto before and during the battle and who were now hiding in various parts of the district.[80] The Poles appear to have aided the Germans in this roundup only "in a handful of cases" *(in einzelnen Fällen)*.[81] However, Polish gangs were roaming the city, seeking out Jewish hiding places and forcing the victims to pay high sums of money or face denunciation. We have no exact statistics on how many Jews were left when the Red Army arrived in January 1945. In the city itself it seems that only 200 survived.[82]

After the conclusion of the Warsaw ghetto fighting, only a few major ghettos were still in existence, particularly Lvov in the Galician district, the Bialystok ghetto, and the Warthegau ghetto of Lodz. When Brigadeführer Katzmann, the Galician SS and Police Leader, moved into what was left of the Lvov ghetto in June, 1943, he discovered that the 20,000 Jews in the ghetto had begun to build dugouts and bunkers on the Warsaw pattern. "In order to avoid losses on our side," Katzmann reported, "we had to act brutally from the beginning." Blowing up and burning down houses, Katzmann dragged 3000 corpses out of the hiding places.[83]

In Bialystok, too, the Jews contemplated some form of resistance. A "militant anti-fascist bloc" was formed in the ghetto, and when the Germans struck on August 15, 1943, there was scattered fighting for about twenty-four hours.[84]

The Lodz ghetto followed the cycle

77. Himmler to Pohl and Kaltenbrunner, June 11, 1943, NO-2496.

78. Pohl to Himmler, July 23, 1943, NO-2516.

79. Pohl to Himmler, October 29, 1943, NO-2503. Pohl to Himmler, February 13, 1944, NO-2517. Pohl to Himmler, April 20, 1944, NO-2505. Pohl to Himmler, June 10, 1944, NO-2504. Kammler to Staf. Rudolf Brandt (Himmler's personal secretary), July 29, 1944, NO-2515. Von Krosigk to Economic-Administrative Main Office, June 15, 1944, NG-5561. Memorandum by Gossel (Finance Ministry), July, 1944, NG-5561. Lörner (Economic-Administrative Main Office) to Finance Ministry, August 25, 1944, NG-5561. The project was interrupted when the Russians approached the east bank of the Vistula at Warsaw.

80. Report by Armament Command Warsaw for October 1-December 31, 1943, Wi/ID 1.43.

81. Report by Armament Command Warsaw for January 1-March 31, 1944, Wi/ID 1.74.

82. Goldstein, *The Stars Bear Witness*, pp. 207–95. Goldstein hid in Warsaw.

83. Katzmann to Krüger, June 30, 1943, L-18.

84. Tenenbaum, *Underground*, pp. 231–46.

of Warsaw and Lvov: partial reduction of the population, employment in war labor of those able to work, followed by total dissolution. During the first half of 1942, 55,000 Lodz Jews were transported to the killing center of Kulmhof; 102,516 Jews remained.[85] Apparently that number was still too great; in the late summer of 1942 all "sick and sickly" Jews were "resettled" to Kulmhof. After these two shattering experiences the Jewish community was soothed with the following poster, signed by the chief of the *Ghettoverwaltung*, Biebow:

> REOPENING
> of all factories and workshops
> as of Monday, September 14, 1942
>
> Since the resettlement has been concluded yesterday, ALL FACTORIES WILL RESUME FULL OPERATION on Monday, September 14, 1942.
>
> Every foreman, worker, and employee had better report for work as usual, if he desires to protect himself against the greatest conceivable unpleasantness [*denkbar grössten Unannehmlichkeiten*]. Every recognized [registered] laborer will now be asked to fulfil his task with utmost diligence, and to do his utmost to make up for production lost during the rest period [*Ruhepause*].
>
> I am going to institute the strictest controls for the enforcement of this order.
>
> *Ghettoverwaltung*
> BIEBOW[86]

The Jews worked. A twelve-hour day was instituted. On their prison diet, which cost 30 pfennige a day, they labored on in the hope of surviving to the end. Although 4658 Jews died from hunger and disease between September 12, 1942, and March 31, 1943, the workers struggled desperately and hung on, through all of 1943 and most of 1944,[87] but their hopes were in vain. In August, 1944, announcements were posted in the ghetto under the heading of *Verlagerung des Ghettos* ("transshipment of the ghetto"). The 60,000 surviving Lodz Jews were ordered to present themselves for *Verlagerung* on penalty of death.[88]

This time the Jews knew where Biebow wanted to send them, and as a result, something like a sitdown strike ensued in workshops I and II. These Jews had held out for so long that now, with the end of the war in sight, they were not willing to go to their deaths voluntarily. The Germans decided to proceed with propaganda warfare. On August 7, 1944, at 4:45 P.M., the Jewish workers were called together for a speech. After a few introductory remarks by the *Präsident* of the *Ältestenrat,* Chaim Rumkowski, Amtsleiter Biebow of the *Ghettoverwaltung* began to speak. Biebow was a very fluent speaker, but his words had the desired effect.

"Workers of the ghetto," he began, "I have already spoken to you various times, and I hope that what I have said until now you have always taken to heart. The situation in Litzmannstadt [Lodz] has again changed, and I mean from today noon. There is a total evacuation of women and children on the German side. That means that all ethnic Germans have to leave this place. Whoever thinks that the ghetto is not going to be dissolved totally is making a tremendous mistake. To the last man, everyone has to be out of here and will be out of here. Some will think it is better to be the last to go. In the vicinity of Litzmannstadt bombs have already fallen, and if they had fallen

85. Lodz Ghetto Collection No. 58, pp. 19, 22.

86. Order by Biebow, September 12, 1942, *Dokumenty i Materialy,* III, 236.

87. Statistics from report by Biebow to Oberbürgermeister Ventzki, April 19, 1943, *Dokumenty i Materialy,* III, 245–48.

88. Announcement No. 418, signed Oberbürgermeister of Lodz, August 4, 1944, *Dokumenty i Materialy,* III, 269. Announcement No. 422, signed Biebow and Rumkowski, August 7, 1944, *Dokumenty i Materialy,* III, 270.

in the ghetto, not one stone would have remained on another."

It would be insanity, Biebow continued, if workshop areas I and II refused to go along. For four and one-half years, they – the *Ghettoverwaltung* and the Jews – had worked together. Biebow had always tried to do his best. He still wanted to do his best – namely, "to save your lives by moving this ghetto." Right now, Germany was fighting with her last ounce of strength. Thousands of German workers were going to the front. These workers would have to be replaced. Siemens and Schuckert needed workers; Union needed workers; the Czestochowa munitions plants needed workers. In Czestochowa everybody was "very satisfied with the Jews, and the Gestapo is very satisfied with their output. After all, you want to live and eat, and that you will have. After all, I am not going to stand here like a silly boy, make speeches, and nobody comes. If you insist upon measures of force, well then, there will be dead and wounded." The trip, said Biebow, was going to take ten to sixteen hours. Food had already been loaded on the trains. Everybody could take along forty pounds of luggage. Everyone was to hold on to his pots, pans and utensils, because in Germany such things were given only to bombed-out people. So, common sense. If not, and then force were used, Biebow could not help anymore.[89]

The Jewish workers of workshop areas I and II changed their minds. They surrendered. By the end of August the ghetto was empty except for a small clean-up *Kommando*.[90] The victims were shipped not to Germany, to work in plants, but to the killing center in Auschwitz, to be gassed to death.[91]

Why did the striking Jewish workers of Lodz surrender to Biebow's appeal? For the Jews of Poland resistance was not merely a matter of digging fortifications and procuring arms; resistance required in the first instance a shake-up of the entire institutional structure of the community and a reversal of ancient thought processes. The ghetto inmates of Lodz were not capable of breaking with a historical pattern under which they had survived destruction for two thousand years. That was why the flight into fantasy, the false hopes, the voice of Biebow, were more assuring to them than the new and untried path into violent, desperate self-defense. Only the ghetto of Warsaw had produced the complete turn from compliance to resistance, and that turn was accomplished, after the loss of more than 300,000 Jews, under the leadership of a twenty-four-year-old commander. It came too late to change the fundamental Jewish reaction pattern; it was too feeble to interfere with German plans.

The Germans did not suffer much from Jewish resistance; however, the breakdown of secrecy resulted in disturbances, not only in the Jewish community but also in the local population and, ultimately, among the Germans themselves. These repercussions were in some respects more serious than the reactions of the Jews. In speaking of the *local* inhabitants, we must remember that there were essentially *two* populations: the Ukrainians in Galicia and the Poles. The reactions of these two groups were not the same.

The Ukrainians were involved in the

89. Speech by Amtsleiter Biebow, August 7, 1944, *Dokumenty i Materialy*, III, 267–68.

90. Proclamation No. 428 by Gestapo, August 22, 1944, *Dokumenty i Materialy*, III, 271–72. Proclamation No. 429 by Gestapo, August 23, 1944, *ibid.*, pp. 273–74. *Ghettoverwaltung* to *Oberbürgermeister* of Lodz/Treasury, October 17, 1944, *ibid.*, p. 274.

91. Economic-Administrative Main Office (WVHA) – D IV (signed Stubaf. Burger) to WVHA-B (Gruf. Lörner), August 15, 1944, NO-399.

fate of Polish Jewry as perpetrators. The SS and Police employed Ukrainian units in ghetto-clearing operations, not only in the Galician district but also in such places as the Warsaw ghetto[92] and the Lublin ghetto.[93] The Ukrainians have never been considered pro-Jewish (the Ukraine had been the scene of intermittent pogroms and oppressions for three hundred years); on the other hand, these people had no stomach for the long-range systematic German destruction process. Short violence followed by confession and absolution is one thing; organized killing is quite another.

In September, 1943, a French collaborator, going under the name of Dr. Frederic, had a discussion with Monsignor Szepticki, metropolitan of the Greek Catholic Church in Lvov. The metropolitan accused the Germans of inhuman action against the Jews: in Lvov alone they had killed 100,000, and in the Ukraine, millions; he had heard the confession of a young man who had personally slain 75 persons in one night at Lvov. Dr. Frederic replied that according to his information the Ukrainians had certainly taken part in these massacres but that, in view of the execution of 18,000 persons in and near Lvov by the Soviets, such participation was only natural. Furthermore, almost all members of the NKVD had been Jews, which should explain the hatred of the population. Moreover, wasn't Jewry a deadly danger to Christendom, and hadn't the Jews avowed the destruction of Christianity? The metropolitan agreed, but repeated that the annihilation of the Jews was an impermissible action.[94]

While the Greek Catholic metropolitan in Lvov was troubled by the fact that the Germans were drawing the Ukrainians into the destruction process as partners, the Poles began to fear that they would soon be joining the Jews as victims. We have already noted that General Rowecki considered this possibility when he decided to assist the Warsaw ghetto Jews.[95] The same consideration was also expressed in pamphlets circulated in the Warsaw district in August, 1942, calling upon the Poles to help the persecuted Jews. The theme of these pamphlets was that only dumb people and idiots, who could not understand that after the Jews the Poles would get the same treatment, would be happy about the Jewish fate.[96]

The Polish leadership (to say nothing of the Polish people) did not know that the Germans actually were toying with the idea of getting rid of the Poles. No one knew, for example, that on May 1, 1942, Gauleiter Greiser had proposed to Himmler the "special treatment" of some 35,000 tubercular Poles in his *Gau* as a sanitary measure for the protection of the ethnic Germans in the incorporated territory.[97] Even without this knowledge the anxiety was

92. See names of Trawniki camp trainees in Stroop report, May 16, 1943, PS-1061.

93. *Generalgouvernement*/Main Division Propaganda, consolidated weekly reports from district propaganda divisions for March, 1942, report by Lublin division, March 21, 1942, Occ E 2-2.

94. Memorandum by Dr. Frederic, September 19, 1943, Document CXLVa 60, Centre de Documentation Juive Contemporaine, Paris; courtesy of Dr. John Armstrong. Thoughts similar to those which troubled the metropolitan were expressed by Sapieha, Prince-Archbishop of Krakow, in a letter to Generalgouverneur Frank: "I shall not enlarge upon so dreadful a fact as the employment of the inebriated youth of the Labor Service [*Polnischer Baudienst*] for the extermination of the Jews. . . ." Sapieha to Frank, November 8, 1942, quoted by L. Poliakov in "The Vatican and the 'Jewish Question'," *Commentary*, November, 1950, p. 442.

95. See pp. 319–20.

96. *Generalgouvernement*/Main Division Propaganda, consolidated weekly reports from district propaganda divisions for August, 1942, report by Warsaw division, August 8, 1942, Occ E 2-2. Authorship of the pamphlet was not identified.

real, not only in informed underground circles but in every workers' section of every Polish city. Their fear came to the surface in October, 1942, in the Lublin district, as the result of a bizarre misunderstanding.

The SS and Police (i.e., Himmler) had decided to make Lublin a German city and to make the Lublin district a German district.[98] On October 1, 1942, the police carried out a *razzia* in the northern section of the city of Lublin. All inhabitants of the section were called out and assembled in one place. All work certificates were checked, and all Poles – male or female – who could not prove that they were employed were carted away to a camp, while their children under fifteen were sent to an orphanage.

Immediately, rumors swept the city like wildfire. Many Poles stopped in the streets and said: "Weren't we right that the resettlement across the Bug was going to come? It has come, earlier than we supposed. Punctually on October 1, 1942, in the morning it has come!" The Poles were convinced that this *Aktion* was the same as the "resettlement" of the Jews. In Lublin the belief was strong that the Jewish "resettlers" had been killed and that the fat from their corpses had been used in the manufacture of soap. Now pedestrians in Lublin were saying that it was the turn of the Poles to be used – just like the Jews – for soap production.[99]

When the first Polish deportees from Lublin arrived at the labor camp at Lubertow, the rumors were fanned still further, and the belief was formed that all Poles in the *Generalgouvernement* would be shipped across the Bug. Heaping rumor upon rumor, the Polish residents of Lublin also voiced the opinion that a few privileged Poles would be offered Reich citizenship in preference to "resettlement," and a number of Lublin inhabitants were already discussing the acceptance of such citizenship as an escape from death. That, we must remember, was when the Germans were actually only resettling, not killing, the Poles.[100] It took a long time before the Poles were quieted down.[101]

Last but not least, the breakdown of secrecy had repercussions on the Germans themselves. In Poland, particularly, the Germans were jittery and afraid. They feared reprisals and retribution. On October 3, 1942, the Propaganda Division in Radom reported a disturbing incident which had resulted from the dispatch of a postcard. The Germans were publishing a paper in Poland for the local German population, the *Krakauer Zeitung*. The chief of the Radom branch of the paper had received from Lvov a postcard which began, in German: "I don't know German. You can translate everything from the Polish into German." The postcard then continued in Polish:

97. Greiser to Himmler, May 1, 1942, NO-246. The proposal was vetoed. See Greiser to Himmler, November 21, 1942, NO-249.

98. For the effects of this policy on the *Generalgouvernement,* see Frank to Hitler, May 23, 1943, NO-2202; also, Frank to Hitler, June 19, 1943, PS-437.

99. *Generalgouvernement*/Main Division Propaganda, consolidated weekly reports from district propaganda divisions for October, 1942, report by Lublin division, October 3, 1942, Occ E 2-2.

100. *Generalgouvernement*/Main Division Propaganda, consolidated weekly reports from district propaganda divisions, report by Lublin division, October 24, 1942, Occ E 2-2.

101. See Krüger's remarks in *Generalgouvernement* police conference of January 25, 1943, Frank diary, PS-2233. Long after the Lublin affair, in April, 1944, Archbishop Sapieha advised Generalgouverneur Frank to convince the Poles in newspaper propaganda that they would not be treated "worse" than the Jews. Summary of conference between Frank, Staatssekretär Dr. Boepple, Präs. Dr. von Craushaar, Archbishop Sapieha, and Prelate Domasik, April 5, 1944, Frank diary, PS-2233.

> You old whore and you old son of a whore, Richard [In the German translation: *Alte Hurenmetze und du alter Hurenbock Richard*]. A child has been born to you. May your child suffer throughout his life, as we Jews have suffered because of you. I wish you that from the bottom of my heart.

This anonymous postcard actually disturbed its recipient and worried the propaganda experts. The Propaganda Division feared that it was the beginning of a flood of postcards, and the card was transmitted to the Security Police for tracing.[102]

In September, 1942, a German Army officer in Lublin told a German judge that in the United States reprisals against Germans had started because of the treatment of the Jews in the *Generalgouvernement*. A large number of Germans, according to this officer, had already been shot in America.[103]

The jittery feeling reached the very top of the German administrative apparatus in Poland: On August 24, 1942, forty-eight officials of the *Generalgouvernement* met in conference to discuss some problems in connection with anti-Jewish and anti-Polish measures. After a presentation by agricultural chief Naumann, Frank was particularly candid in referring to a "sentence of hunger death" against 1,200,000 Jews. At the end of the meeting Staatssekretär Dr. Boepple pointed out that he had the attendance list and that, if any rumors should reach the public, he would trace them to their source.[104] Again, during the conference of January 25, 1943, after a lot of talk about anti-Jewish measures, Generalgouverneur Frank remarked: "We want to remember that we are, all of us assembled here, on Mr. Roosevelt's war-criminals list. I have the honor of occupying first place on that list. We are therefore, so to speak, accomplices in a world-historical sense."[105]

The following story is told by the KdS (Commander of Security Police) in the Lublin district, Johannes Hermann Müller. He had once attended a conference under the chairmanship of the Lublin SS and Police Leader, Odilo Globocnik. The SS and Police Leader was thinking just then about the transport of Polish children from Lublin to Warsaw and the death by freezing of many of these children. Globocnik turned to Sturmbannführer Höfle (one of his trusted assistants) and told him that he had a three-year-old niece; Globocnik could no longer look at the little one without thinking about the others. Höfle did not know what to reply and "looked at Globocnik like an idiot." In the spring of 1943 Höfle's two children, twins who were only a few months old, died of diphtheria. At the cemetery Höfle suddenly went wild and shouted: "That is the punishment of heaven for all my misdeeds!"[106] It is perhaps not accidental that the Germans, who were particularly brutal in their treatment of Jewish children, were now most afraid for their own.

Economic Consequences

The relentless manner in which the deportations were brought to their completion is most clearly recognizable in their economic consequences. The economic results may be divided into

102. *Generalgouvernement*/Main Division Propaganda, consolidated weekly reports from district propaganda divisions for October, 1942, report by Radom division, October 3, 1942, Occ E 2-2.

103. *Generalgouvernement*/Main Division Propaganda, consolidated weekly reports from district propaganda divisions for September, 1942, report by Lublin division, September 5, 1942, Occ E 2-2.

104. *Generalgouvernement* conference of August 24, 1942, Frank diary, PS-2233.

105. *Generalgouvernement* police conference of January 25, 1943, Frank diary, PS-2233.

106. Interrogation of Müller, November 5, 1947, Occ E 2-134.

losses and gains: losses incurred primarily in the sacrifice of productive Jewish manpower and gains resulting from a saving of food and the collection of some personal belongings (mostly *Lumpen,* or rags). There is no doubt that in the balance the deportations in Poland were very costly.

When the ghettos began to be emptied out in 1942, the army representatives in Poland, who were most anxious to keep production going, were caught in a squeeze. Gauleiter Sauckel, the Plenipotentiary for Labor Allocation, was just launching his *Ostarbeiter* recruitment drive; that is, he was shipping Polish and Ukrainian workers to the Reich. To replace the Poles the army was counting on the increased employment of Jews. Whereas until 1942, Jews had been utilized only in construction projects and ghetto workshops, the present situation required that they be employed also in war industry, including aircraft plants, munitions works, the steel industry, etc.[107] This replacement program was just getting under way when the SS and Police swept into the ghettos and deported Jews by the hundreds of thousands. The army was now in the impossible position of trying to replace the departing Poles with the vanishing Jews, and to make up for the dead Jews with unavailable Poles. (Some of the Poles, incidentally, were replacing deported Jewish workers in Germany.)

Three armament inspectorates were involved in the attempt to conserve the Jewish labor supply: the Armament Inspectorate XXI in the Wartheland, Armament Inspectorate VIIIb in Upper Silesia, and the Armament Inspectorate in the *Generalgouvernement.*

In the Wartheland the efforts of the armament officials were directed toward the conservation of the Lodz ghetto, an attempt which met with many ups and downs and which was, on the whole, successful beyond expectations, since the ghetto was not destroyed until August, 1944.[108]

In Upper Silesia thousands of Jews were employed in the construction of war plants. They seemed to have made themselves so indispensable that even Obergruppenführer Schmauser, Higher SS and Police Leader of Upper Silesia, wrote to Himmler in April, 1942, that replacements for 6500 Jews then employed in major construction projects (*Grossbauten*) would hardly be available.[109]

The main deportations in Upper Silesia did not come until August, 1943, but from all indications in the documents it appears that no Jews, however indispensable, survived on their jobs. The representative of the *Reichskommissar* for the strengthening of Germandom in Katowice (a Himmler man) reported that a Jewish construction unit (*Judenbautruppe*) of 500 that had built homes for German resettlers had been completely withdawn.[110] Armament in-

107. As late as November 22, 1941, the armament inspectorate in the *Generalgouvernement* had directed that, in the interest of security, no ghetto labor be employed in secret war work. Report by inspectorate to OKW/Wi Rü/Rü III A, covering July 1, 1940, to December 31, 1941, dated May 7, 1942, p. 153, Wi/ID 1.2. By April, 1942, however, the first Jews were sent to a war plant: the aircraft works in Mielec (Krakow District). War diary, Armament Command Krakow, containing report for October 1-December 31, 1942, Wi/ID 1.148. Shortly thereafter, Jews were detailed to other plants in the district, including the steel works Stawola-Wola and the aircraft-motor works at "Reichshof" (Rzeszow). War diary, Armament Command Krakow, August 3–9, 1942, August 17–23, 1942, and September 7–13, 1942, Wi/ID 1.145.

108. See conference summary of Armament Commission XXI, November 30, 1943, Wi/ID 1.26. Also, Defense Economy Officer (*Wehrwirtschaftsoffizier*) of Army District XXI to OKW/Defense Economy Staff (*Wehrwirtschaftsstab*), March 6, 1944, Wi/ID 1.13.

109. OGruf. und General der Polizei Schmauser via chief of the Order Police (attention Hauptmann der Schutzpolizei Goebel) to Himmler, April 20, 1942, NO-1386.

spectorate VIIIb in Katowice reported at the same time the sudden loss of 700 Jews employed in the Adolf Hitler *Panzer* (construction) program of the Iron Works Trzynietz and A. G. Ferrum/Works Laurahütte. In addition, 130 Jews in the company camp of the Ernst Erbe firm of Warthenau had been withdrawn during the night of August 24–25, 1943, without notice.[111]

In the *Generalgouvernement* the labor situation was most serious, and it is there that we find the biggest struggle over a remnant of some tens of thousands of Jewish skilled workers. Many interests participated in the struggle. The year 1942 was a time when the civil administration, the *Ostbahn*, private firms under contract to the military commander or the armament inspectorate, as well as the SS itself, were all making use of Jewish labor in various business ventures. Foremost among the offices attempting to check the flow of irreplaceable Jewish workers into the killing centers were the military commander, General Gienanth, and the armament inspector, Generalleutnant Schindler.

The first move in the labor preservation drive was made in July, 1942, when Generalleutnant Schindler came to a hurried understanding with the Higher SS and Police Leader, Kruger, in pursuance of which Jewish workers in armament enterprises were to be held in plant barracks and SS labor camps for the sake of production.[112] On July 19, 1942, Himmler accepted the agreement, but he made it very clear that no further concessions would be made: "I order that the resettlement of the entire Jewish population in the *Generalgouvernement* be carried out and completed by December 31, 1942. As of December 31, 1942, no persons of Jewish descent must remain in the *Generalgouvernement* unless they are living in camps at Warsaw, Krakow, Czestochowa, Radom, or Lublin. All other undertakings which employ Jewish labor have to be finished by that time or, if completion is not possible, have to be transferred to one of the camps."

These measures, Himmler continued, were necessay for the new order in Europe, as well as for the "security and cleanliness" of the German Reich and its spheres of interest. Every violation of this regulation would endanger peace and order and would create in Europe "the germ of a resistance movement and a moral and physical center of pestilence."[113]

The military offices soon found out that Himmler's concessions were even more restrictive than they appeared to be in the agreed stipulations. The generals discovered that their understanding with Krüger covered only a part of the armament industry, the so-called *Rüstungsbetriebe*, or "armament plants" under contract with the armament inspectorate. Apparently the agreement did not cover those armament enterprises which were filling orders placed directly by agencies in the Reich or the myriads of small repair shops and finishing plants which were under contract with the military commander (*Wehrkreisbefehlshaber im Generalgouvernement*).

On September 18, 1942, Wehrkreisbefehlshaber von Gienanth reported to the Armed Forces High Command/Operations Staff that urgent contracts with priority designations "winter" were falling by the wayside in the "resettlement" action of the police. Von Gienanth estimated that at the moment

110. *Stabshauptamt/Stabsführer* in Katowice (signed OStubaf. Brehm) to Schmauser, August 21, 1943, NO-3083.

111. War diary, Armament Inspectorate VIIIb in Katowice, August 27, 1943, Wi/ID 1.224.

112. See Krüger to Himmler (copy to SS and Police Leader of Krakow, Obf. Scherner), July 7, 1942, Himmler Files, Folder No. 94.

113. Himmler to Krüger, July 19, 1942, NO-5574.

the labor situation in the *Generalgouvnement* was as shown in Table 49. The replacement of the 200,000 *unskilled* Jewish workers might have been possible, were it not for the urgent requirement of 140,000 Polish workers by the Plenipotentiary for Labor Allocation. Under the circumstances von Gienanth asked the OKW for its assistance in negotiating for a slower reduction (*Zug um Zug*) of the Jewish workers. "The criterion should be," he wrote, "to shut out the Jews as fast as possible without endangering the war work."[114]

TABLE 49 / *Labor Forces in the Generalgouvernement, September, 1942*

	TOTAL WORKERS	JEWS ONLY	JEWISH SKILLED LABOR ONLY
All enterprises	1,000,000	300,000	100,000
Firms producing military shoes, uniforms, etc.	22,700	22,000	16,500

When Himmler received a copy of this letter, he replied to it as follows: There was a difference between "so-called armament enterprises" which consisted mainly of tailor shops, carpenters' workshops, and shoe shops, and the "real" armament enterprises, such as weapons plants. As for the "so-called" war work, Himmler was prepared to confiscate the shops. "The Wehrmacht should give its orders to us, and we shall guarantee the continuation of deliveries of the desired uniforms. However, if anyone thinks he can confront us here with alleged armament interests, whereas in reality he only wants to protect the Jews and their business, he will be dealt with mercilessly."

In the "real" armament enterprises, Himmler continued, the Jews would have to be segregated in work halls. In the weeding-out process the work halls could then be consolidated into factory camps, which in turn would give way to a few big Jewish concentration camp enterprises, preferably in the eastern portions of the *Generalgouvernement (tunlichst im Osten dest Generalgouvernements).* "However, there too, the Jews should – in accordance with the Führer's wish – disappear some day [*Jedoch auch dort sollen eines Tages dem Wunsche des Führer's entsprechend die Juden verschwinden*]."[115]

Himmler was now actually proposing that the SS itself go into business and handle all the "so-called" armament production, principally the manufacture of uniforms. In the heavy or "real" armament enterprises the SS proposed to be in charge of the labor supply. That control was to be assured through the establishment of labor camps. Needless to say, all wages were to be paid not to the laborers but to the SS; the profit motive shone very clearly through Himmler's proposal.

The army accepted Himmler's conditions word for word.[116] On October

114. *Wehrkreisbefehlshaber im Generalgouvernement* (signed von Gienanth) to OKW/WFSt (Jodl), September 18, 1942, Himmler Files, Folder No. 126. The number of Jews then working for the direct needs of the armed forces was approximately 50,000. Report by Armament Inspectorate *Generalgouvernement* for July–September. 1942, Wi/ID 1.131.

115. Himmler to Pohl, Krüger, the RSHA, Wolff; copies to Generalquartiermeister Wagner and Oberstleutnant Tippelskirch, October 9, 1942, NO-1611.

116. OKW/WFSt/Qu II to *Wehrkreisbefehlshaber im GG*/OQu (Forster), October 10, 1942, passed on by Forster to *Oberfeldkommandanturen* in Lvov, Kielce, Lublin, Krakow, Warsaw, *Luftgaukommandos* II and III, armament inspectorate, and offices of the

14 and 15, 1942, Oberst Forster, the *Oberquartiermeister* of the military commander in the *Generalgouvernement*, met with Higher SS and Police Leader Krüger to iron out a few points. This time the military found the SS much more receptive to production problems. The new agreement covered all firms operating under contract with the army (that is, the armament inspectorate *or* the *Wehrkreisbefehlshaber*). The keynote of the arrangement was the *organized* reduction of the Jewish labor force, to be undertaken only after mutual consultation; the key phrase of the understanding was "no disturbance of production." The SS was to be paid for camp labor at the daily rate of 5 zloty per man and 4 zloty per woman, from which the firms were to deduct a maximum of 1.60 zloty for maintenance[117] (5 zloty equaled 1 dollar; 1.60 zloty were 20 cents).

The October agreement was a last-minute arrangement to save a Jewish labor force for military needs. No provision had been made for firms in civilian endeavors, for the *Ostbahn*, or for the civil administration. By the tens of thousands, Jews were withdrawn from projects and plants which were outside the scope of the written stipulations. The unblunted effects of the deportations were consequently felt everywhere except in a narrowly defined armament industry, and even in that industry the Jews were to disappear eventually.[118] On December 9, 1942, Generalgouverneur Frank said in conference:

> Not unimportant labor reserves have been taken from us when we lost our old trustworthy Jews [*altbewährten Judenschaften*]. It is clear that the labor situation is made more difficult when, in the middle of the war effort, the order is given to prepare all Jews for annihilation. The responsibility for this order does not lie with the offices of the *Generalgouvernement*. The directive for the annihilation of the Jews comes from higher sources. We can only deal with the consequences of this situation, and we can tell the agencies of the Reich that the taking away of the Jews has led to tremendous difficulties in the labor field. Just the other day I could prove to Staatssekretär Ganzenmüller, who complained that a large construction project in the *Generalgouvernement* has come to a standstill, that that would not have happened if the many thousands of Jews who were employed there had not been taken away. Now the order provides that the armament Jews also are to be taken away. I hope that this order, if not already voided, will be revoked, because then the situation will be even worse.[119]

Wehrkreisbefehlshaber, October 11, 1942, NOKW-134.

117. Forster to IVa, IVb, 02, and liaison officer of military commander to *Generalgouverneur*, October 14, 1942, NOKW-134. *Wehrkreisbefehlshaber/Chef Generalstab* to *Oberfeldkommandanturen* and offices of *Wehrkreisbefehlshaber*, copies to liaison officer and armament inspectorate, October 15, 1942, NOKW-134. A detailed agreement, naming the firms involved, was concluded by armament command in Galicia with the local SS and Police Leader. Bgf. Hofmann (Galicia) to armament command in Lvov, October 23, 1942, in report by Katzmann (Hofmann's successor) to Krüger, June 30, 1943, L-18. Galician firms not protected by inscription in that agreement were deprived of their workers "pretty ruthlessly" (*ziemlich rücksichtslos*). Armament Command Lvov (signed Sternagel) to OKW/Rü Ic, July 8, 1943, Wi/ID 1.73.

118. This was the understanding of armament officials. See report by Armament Inspectorate *Generalgouvernement* for July-September, 1942, Wi/ID 1.131. During October, 1942, the expectation was that the arrangement would last only to the beginning of 1943. See summary of first conference of the *Generalgouvernement* Armament Commission, October 24, 1942, Wi/ID 1.155. (The armament commission was composed of top officials of the armament inspectorate and civil administration.) In fact, the arrangement was to last until 1944.

119. Remarks by Frank in *Generalgouvernement* conference of December 9, 1942,

The Jews, on their part, sensed what the new arrangement had in store for them. There was no hope for anyone who could not work. Only the best and strongest workers, "the Maccabees," as Krüger called them,[120] had a chance to live; all others had to die. There was not even room in the SS-army agreement for dependants. Survival had become synonymous with work. The Jews were grasping labor certificates as a drowning man grasps a straw. How deeply this labor-survival psychology had penetrated into the Jewish community is illustrated by a small incident observed by a Pole. When, in 1943, an SS officer (Sturmbannführer Reinecke) seized a three-year-old Jewish girl in order to deport her to a killing center, she pleaded for her life by showing him her hands and explaining that she could work. In vain.[121]

The Himmler program called for the deportation of all non-productive Jews in the *Generalgouvernement* by the end of 1942. Because of administrative difficulties Himmler was behind schedule, but even so, two-thirds of all the Jews in the Polish deportation area had been transported to killing centers by December 31, 1942. On that date the number of deportees was 1,496,283, including 1,274,166 *Generalgouvernement* Jews and 222,117 Jews from the incorporated territories and Bialystok.[122] Fewer than 700,000 remained to be deported on the target day, and the fate of those Jews was already decided. In the Galician district the deportations were in high gear;[123] in the Warsaw ghetto the bulk of the remaining Jews had only a few months to live; while in Lodz, Bialystok, Krakow, Radom, and such other ghettos as were still in existence, the survivors were cut down relentlessly. From the remnant ghettos of the *Generalgouvernement*, particularly Warsaw, Lvov, Radom, and Krakow, the SS and Police drew the strongest and best-trained workers to build up an industrial forced labor reservoir that was to last for about two years.

Jewish laborers were dispatched from the ghettos to SS labor camps (*SS Arbeitslager*) and to company camps (*Firmenlager*). The SS camps housed two SS-owned enterprises, a Galician project of the *Ostbahn* and some armament firms. In addition the SS supplied workers from ghettos and SS camps to companies that maintained their own installations (see Table 50).[124] *All* Jews who had left the ghettos were labor prisoners of the SS. Insofar as these Jews were not employed by the SS itself, the employers had to pay wages to the SS and Police at the agreed rates of 5 zloty per man and 4 zloty per woman, minus 1.60 zloty for food. While the SS thus maintained its clutch on all laboring Jews in the *Generalgouvernement*, there was a significant difference between the type of hold exercised by the SS on the Jews in its own camps and the somewhat more remote control which it enjoyed in company compounds. The SS labor camps, namely, were subjected to a constant consolidation and weeding-out process from which the company camps remained largely immune.

The SS camps were originally under the jurisdiction of the SS and Police Leaders, but starting in October, 1943, and continuing in 1944, a series of

---

Frank diary, PS-2233.

120. See Krüger's remarks in conference of May 31, 1943, Frank diary, PS-2233.

121. Affidavit by Jerzy Skotnicki, August 26, 1947, NO-5257. The incident occurred at or near Sandomierz, in the Radom district.

122. Based on statistics in Korherr report, April 19, 1943, NO-5193.

123. There were 254,989 Jews deported by November 10, 1942; a total of 434,329 by June 27, 1943. Katzmann to Krüger, June 30, 1943, L-18.

124. Statistics on bottom line of table represent maximum labor utilization. They are taken from sources to be cited below.

transfers took place, in the course of which the camps were taken over by the SS Economic-Administrative Main Office (WVHA), i.e., the agency which controlled the concentration camps. A heretofore undisputed territorial and functional control of the camps by the SS and Police Leaders was now reduced to a purely territorial (disciplinary) jurisdiction. The new master was the WVHA. The following is a list of the principal labor camps with an indication of their new functional direction.[125]

Satellites of WVHA Lublin camp:
- Trawniki
- Poniatowa
- Old Airport, Lublin
- SS-Company DAW, Lublin
- Blizyn
- Radom
- Budzyn

Independent WVHA camps:
- Krakow-Placzow
- Lvov (Janov Street)

TABLE 50 / *The Flow of Ghetto Labor*

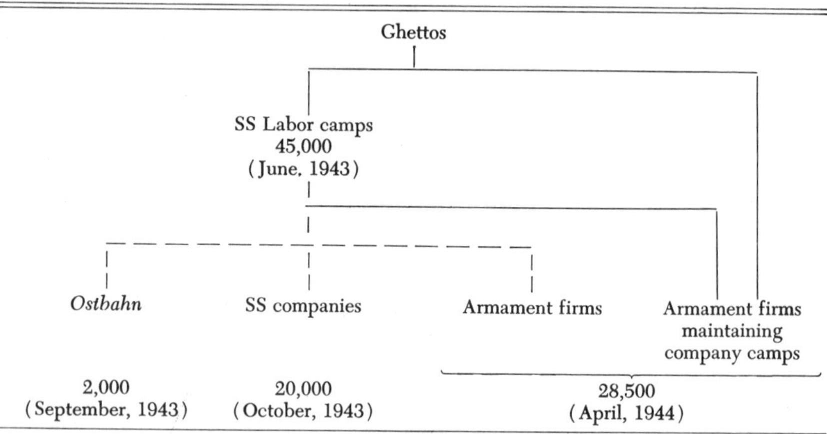

These changes were not without significance, for on November 3, 1943, immediately after the first transfer arrangements, the Lublin camp administration started mass withdrawals of Jews from its labor camps and proceeded to shoot as many as 17,000 workers in a single operation.[126] A number of enterprises that had depended on SS camp labor thereupon "lost the ground under their feet."[127] What kind of business establishments were operating in the SS labor camps? What, in particular, were the SS enterprises?

The SS industries in the *Generalgouvernement* were organized in a typical fashion, and their short life is an ironic postscript to the history of Polish Jewry under the Nazis, for in these enterprises Himmler himself attempted at the last moment to slow down the deportations – to hold up the works, as it were – and to make some profits.

Originally, SS enterprises had been

125. Memorandum by Obergruppenführer Pohl (Chief of WVHA), September 7, 1943, NO-599. Globocnik to Himmler, January 18, 1944, NO-57. Memorandum by HStuf. Opperbeck (WVHA-W IV), January 13, 1944, NO-1036. Obf. Baier (WVHA-W) to Opperbeck (WVHA-W IV), January 19, 1944, NO-1036.

126. Affidavit by Friedrich Wilhelm Ruppert (Lublin camp administration), August 6, 1945, NO-1903.

127. Report by Dr. Horn (WVHA official, SS company Osti), March 13, 1944, NO-2187.

set up in the concentration camps with a view to exploiting the cheap inmate labor supply. Now that the end phase of the Polish deportations had arrived, one of the SS firms, the Deutsche Ausrüstungswerke (DAW), emerged from the concentration camps and stretched out its arms for a share of the surviving Jewish labor force. But the SS enterpreneurs faced one major difficulty: they had no capital. The DAW solved that problem in typical SS manner. One of the "so-called" armament firms in the Galician district, Schwarz and Company, which was exclusively engaged in the production of uniforms and which employed 2000 Jewish slave laborers, fitted the needs of the DAW nicely. The SS moved swiftly. In July, 1943, the management of Schwarz and Company was arrested "because of serious irregularities," and the entire firm, with laborers and machines, was swallowed by the DAW.[128]

A more ambitious project than the acquisition of Schwarz and Company was the SS plan to take over all the machines located in the ghettos. On December 1, 1942, Himmler wrote to the chief of the Economic-Administrative Main Office, Pohl, that he had just had a look at the machinery and equipment in the Warsaw ghetto. These machines, according to Himmler, were worth "hundreds of millions," and such a uniquely high value was "not to be lost to the Reich." Pohl was instructed to cart away the machines as quickly as possible.[129] The Economic-Administrative chief immediately sent three experts to Warsaw to take inventory of the machines and raw materials in the ghetto; then he informed Himmler that preparations for their removal had been made.[130] On the very next day Himmler wrote that he agreed with this arrangement "wholeheartedly" (*sehr einverstanden*). "Believe only," he said, "that it is necessary that you get written permission from the Economy Ministry to transfer the machines to our industries."[131] The machines in question were for the most part private property.

In January, 1943, Himmler was in Warsaw again. He summoned Oberst Freter, the chief of the armament command in Warsaw, to tell him that he was astonished *(erstaunt)* that so many Jews were still in Warsaw. In Himmler's opinion, it was necessary that the German businessmen who owned enterprises in the ghetto, particularly the biggest one, Walter C. Toebbens, be inducted into the army just as soon as possible and sent to the front line *(tunlichst eingezogen und an die Front gebracht werde)*. He ordered the RSHA to examine Toebbens' books "with a microscope." "If I am not mistaken," he said, "a man who had no property three years ago has become a well-to-do man here, if not a millionaire, and only because we, the state, have driven cheap Jewish labor into his arms."[132]

That, in short, was Himmler's way of getting hold of the necessary machinery and labor. Actually, he failed — not because of Toebbens, to be sure, but because of Jewish resistance and the resulting destruction of property. As the SS and Police Leader in Lublin, Gruppenführer Globocnik, put it in a rare Nazi understatement: "A major loss has occurred only in Warsaw, where, owing to a misunderstanding of the situation, the windup was carried out incorrectly."[133]

128. Armament Command Lvov (signed Sternagel) to Armament Inspectorate/Ic, July 8, 1943, Wi/ID 1.73.

129. Himmler to Pohl, December 1, 1942, Himmler Files, Folder No. 188.

130. Pohl to Himmler, December 4, 1942, *ibid.*

131. Himmler to Pohl, December 5, 1942, *ibid.*

132. Himmler to Krüger, copies to RSHA, Pohl, and Wolff, January, 1943, No-1882.

133. Globocnik to Himmler, January 18, 1944, NO-57.

Nevertheless, the SS went ahead, and on March 12, 1943, it formed a brand new company, the Ostindustrie GbmM (Osti), within the framework of the WVHA. The Osti was a peculiar company. It was established with an initial capital investment of only 100,000 reichsmark. The Vorstand consisted of the chief of the WVHA, Pohl, and the chief of *Amtsgruppe B* of the WVHA, Gruppenführer Lörner; the Aufsichtsrat contained the following membership: Pohl, Krüger, Lörner, and the Warsaw SS and Police Leader von Sammern-Frankenegg. Krüger and von Sammern subsequently withdrew, and the representative of the WVHA in the *Generalgouvernement,* SS - Economist Schellin, was elected in their stead. The managers of the company were the SS and Police Leader in Lublin, Odilo Globocnik, and the WVHA accountant, Dr. Max Horn.[134]

Although most of the Warsaw ghetto machinery was destroyed, the company started operations in the summer of 1943 with odds and ends recovered from the Warsaw and Bialystok ghettos, and with exceedingly primitive tools. Thus, in the brush factory, 600 Jewish workers who had only one or two dozen hammers had to use pieces of iron and stones. Even so, 396,000 brushes were produced from May to October, 1943.[135] The Osti enterprises grew until they employed, at their height, the following numbers of people:[136]

Peat works in Dorohucza	1,000
Brush Factory in Lublin	1,800
Equipment works in Radom (textiles)	4,000
Iron foundry in Lublin	1,500
Fur manufacturing works in Trawniki	6,000
	14,300

In the fall of 1943 the Ostindustrie combine failed. Its failure was due to the usual reason: no profits. However, the coup de grace was given to the Osti by the SS itself. In accordance with Himmler's wish to "consolidate" the camps, the Osti, which had been operating mostly in camps under Globocnik's jurisdiction, became at the end of October, 1943, the guest of the somewhat less hospitable administration of the Lublin concentration camp, which was then absorbing the labor camps located in the Lublin and Radom districts. Hardly two weeks had passed under the new arrangement when, on November 3, 1943, the Osti suddenly found itself without a labor force.[137] Thousands of Osti Jews were being shot in the Lublin killing center.[138] This is how the Osti had the ground cut from under its feet.[139]

The sudden end of the SS business venture should not be too surprising, for in the words of one of the Osti managers, Dr. Horn, the economic task of the Ostindustrie met with "negation" and "lack of understanding" even in SS circles. When, for example, one of the Osti representatives reported to the SS and Police Leader in Warsaw (we do not know whether it was von Sammern-Frankenegg or Stroop), he remarked: "Ostindustrie! I only have to hear 'industry' to become nauseated! [*Ostindustrie! Wenn ich schon 'Industrie' höre, wird mir übel!*]"[140]

134. Report by UStuf. Fischer, March, 1944, NO-1271.

135. Report by Dr. Horn, March 13, 1944, NO-2187.

136. Report by UStuf. Fischer, March, 1944, NO-1271.

137. Globocnik to Himmler, January 18, 1944, NO-57.

138. Affidavit by Friedrich Wilhelm Ruppert (chief, technical division, Lublin camp administration), August 6, 1945, NO-1903.

139. The DAW plant in Lvov lost all its workers at the same time. War diary, Armament Inspectorate *Generalgouvernement*/Administrative Division, November 19–26, 1943, Wi/ID 1.93. The DAW Lvov works, however, were rehabilitated with new workers allocated by the WVHA. Memorandum by WVHA-W IV, January 13, 1944, NO-1036; WVHA-W (Obf. Baier) to WVHA-W IV, January 19, 1944, NO-1036.

140. Report by Horn, March 13, 1944, NO-2187.

The Ostindustrie people still did not give up. In January, 1944, Dr. Horn went to Lodz, where he discovered that the profits shown by the *Ghettoverwaltung* were actually "disguised losses." He had a solution to the problem: transfer of the Lodz Jews to the Osti.[141] However, once again the SS failed (Greiser demanded payment of 18-20 million reichsmark for his ghetto enterprises),[142] and so the liquidation of the Ostindustrie proceeded upon its course. Its assets were taken over by one of the more permanent SS enterprises, the aforementioned Deutsche Ausrüstungswerke (DAW), operated by section W IV of the WVHA.[143]

The SS companies Osti and DAW at no time employed more than about 20,000 Jewish laborers; on the whole, therefore, the SS industries were no great success. But Himmler had still another source of profit: under his agreement with the army all Jews in the *Generalgouvernement* were labor prisoners of the SS, for sale at daily rates. Here too Himmler's expectations were not wholly fulfilled. Table 51 contains the statistics of Jewish workers employed by the armament industry in the *Generalgouvernement* from January, 1943, to May, 1944:[144]

TABLE 51 / *Labor Forces in the Armament Industry*

	JEWS ONLY	TOTAL WORKERS
January, 1943	15,091	105,632
April, 1943	15,538	112,499
July, 1943	21,643	123,588
October, 1943	22,444	130,808
January, 1944	26,296	140,057
April, 1944	28,537	179,244
May, 1944	27,439	172,781

These employment figures, which represent the armament industry's utilization of Jews in SS labor camps and company camps were somewhat smaller than those that Himmler and Globocnik had hoped to realize.[145] In the SS labor camps several thousand Jews were idle. In June, 1943, Globocnik complained to Himmler that in the big Trawniki camp the SS industries and private firms employed 90 per cent of the available labor force; in camp Poniatowa employment was only 60 per cent. Globocnik accused the Wehrmacht of "stuffing" the Lodz ghetto with contracts only in order to prevent a "resettlement" there, and he accused the business organizations of boycotting his own labor for "profit" reasons.[146]

To be sure, the employment of Jewish labor had its advantages. There was a critical labor shortage and skilled Jewish workers were made available at very low rates. On the other hand, it

141. Dr. Horn to Pohl, copies to Obf. Baier and HStuf. Dr. Volk, January 24, 1944, NO-519.

142. Memorandum by Volk, February 9, 1944, NO-519.

143. WVHA-W to W IV, January 19, 1944, NO-1036. The DAW inherited the Osti plants at Radom and Blizyn. Eight thousand workers were employed there in July, 1944. Memorandum by HStuf. Sommer (deputy chief, WVHA-D II), July 31, 1944, NO-4181. The DAW also operated a small plant at Lublin and the former Schwarz factory in Lvov (together, 3000 workers). These two enterprises were liquidated in July, 1944. WVHA-W IV/Krakow office (signed Oberscharführer Dorndorf) to WVHA-W IV, October 25, 1944, NO-3765.

144. Draft report by Army District Command *Generalgouvernement*/Armament Economy officer to OKW/Field Economy Office, July 7, 1944, Wi/ID 1.246. The Army District Command (*Wehrkreiskommando*) was a new designation for the military commander; the armament economy officer (*Wehrwirtschaftsoffizier*) took the place of the armament inspectorate; the Field Economy Office of the OKW (*Feldwirtschaftsamt*) was the successor of the Economy Armament Office (Wi Rü). Jews had been employed in the armament industry since April, 1942.

145. The success was even smaller when it is considered that some of the DAW plants were classified as armament works.

146. Globocnik to OStubaf. Brandt (Himmler's secretary), June 21, 1943, NO-485.

was hazardous to depend upon labor that could be withdrawn by the SS without a moment's notice – hence there probably was an attempt to keep the percentage of Jews in the total labor force within bounds.[147]

The principal beneficiaries of Jewish labor were large firms engaged in heavy industry. The following is a list of some of the more important enterprises with Jewish labor forces:[148]

Stahlwerke Braunschweig/Werk Stawola Wola
Stahlwerke, Starachowice
Ostrowiecer Hochöfen
Ludwigshütte
Kabelwerk, Krakow
Warthewerk
Luftwaffenbetrieb Vereinigte Ostwerke GmbH, Mielec
Heinkel Flugzeugwerk, Budzyn (under construction)
Flugzeugmotorenwerk Reichshof (Rzeszów)
Steyr-Daimler-Puch AG, Radom
Hasag, Kamienna
Pulverfabrik, Pionki (with plants also at Kielce and Czestochowa)
Delta Flugzeughallen- und Barackenbau GmbH, Muszyna and Zakopane
Karpathen-Öl, Drohobycz
Walter C. Toebbens, Poniatowa
Schultz & Co., Trawniki

All except three of the above-listed firms maintained their own company camps. The three enterprises in SS camps were Heinkel Budzyn, Toebbens Poniatowa, and Schultz Trawniki. Toebbens and Schultz were in a shaky position. Himmler did not like them. They had been forced to move into the SS labor camps after the Warsaw ghetto battle in order to retain a labor supply,[149] and the new arrangement did not last very long. On November 5, 1943, the armament inspectorate noted in its diary that the two firms had suffered an "unexpected and complete withdrawal" of their Jewish workers.[150] The Lublin camp administration had massacred, together with the workers of the Osti and DAW, the entire labor force of Toebbens and Schultz.[151]

The enterprises which maintained their own installations for Jewish workers enjoyed, on the whole, a little more stability. They were not so vulnerable to "sudden withdrawals" of their Jewish labor; they were left alone. There was, however, an exception in this picture—Galicia. In Galicia the SS and Police displayed an "overenthusiasm" (*Übereifer*), whereas the interventions of the armament command were only very cautious *(Intervention des Rüstungskommandos nur sehr behutsam)*.[152] By August, 1943, all but two Galician armament firms, the SS company DAW and Karpathen-Öl, had lost their Jewish

147. See statistics above. On November 2, 1943, Schindler and Krüger agreed that 10,000 Jewish workers would be transferred from SS labor camps to armament firms. Globocnik to Himmler, January 18, 1944, NO-57; war diary, Armament Inspectorate GG/Central Division, November 4, 1943, Wi/ID, 1.93. On the very next day mass shootings began in the Lublin camp. Only 4000 Jews from the Krakow-Placzow camp (not part of the Lublin complex) could be delivered. War diary, Armament Inspectorate *Generalgouvernement*/Central Division, November 18, 1943 Wi/ID 1.93; war diary, Armament Command Radom/Central Group, November 18, 1943, Wi/ID 1.30.

148. From war diaries of the armament inspectorate and armament commands, 1942–44, in the following document folders: Wi/ID 1.15, Wi/ID 1.17, Wi/ID 1.21, Wi/ID 1.30, Wi/ID 1.46, Wi/ID 1.93, Wi/ID 1.121, Wi/ID 1.145, Wi/ID 1.148, Wi/ID 1.152.

149. Report by Armament Command Warsaw for January–March, 1943, Wi/ID 1.46.

150. War diary, Armament Inspectorate *Generalgouvernement*/Central Division, November 5, 1943, Wi/ID 1.93. Report by Armament Command Warsaw for October 1-December 31, 1943, Wi/ID 1.43.

151. The Heinkel works in the SS labor camp Budzyn received notice in March, 1944, that its workers were to be withdrawn by the end of the following month. War diary, Armament Command Krakow, March 20–26, 1944, Wi/ID 1.21.

152. Armament command in Lvov via inspectorate in Krakow to OKW/Wi Rü, January 5, 1943, Wi/ID 1.75.

labor.[153] One additional firm, Metrawatt A. G., was permitted to keep twelve absolutely irreplaceable watchmakers. The twelve men were transferred to the Lvov SS labor camp, where they continued to work for Metrawatt until November 19, 1943, when the inexorable fate of Polish Jewry caught up with them.[154]

The Jews in the arms industry tried to hold on. They had lost their families; they were starving; and they did not know each night what the morning would bring. Still they were efficient and reliable workers. Those "whose strength was ebbing" were "resettled" and "replaced";[155] the others continued to labor. To Reichsminister Seyss-Inquart, Frank's former deputy, this submissiveness never ceased to be a source of wonder. "I could not imagine," he said, "that Jews capable of labor were working while their relatives were being destroyed. I believed that in that case one could expect nothing else than that every Jew would attack a German and strangle him."[156] But Jews do not react to such disasters by strangling their opponents. There was no armed resistance; there was little sabotage.[157] Only the number of escapes is significant. The company plants were weakly guarded by Galician Ukrainians which the armament inspectorate and the SS had organized into a *Werkschutz,* and by army-recruited collaborators imported from the occupied USSR – units of the so-called *Osttruppen.* At least a few hundred Jews took advantage of this police shortage to make their getaway before the final breakup of the camps.[158]

The end came for several thousand armament Jews in the summer of 1944. In July of that year the Red Army, in a lightning offensive, engulfed the Galician and Lublin districts, occupied the Przemysl region in the Krakow district, and smashed thirteen miles across the Vistula River into the Radom district. In the face of this advance the DAW plans in Lvov and Lublin were hurriedly evacuated.[159] On July 20, 1944,

153. Armament Command in Lvov to OKW/Wi Rü/Ic, October 7, 1943, Wi/ID 1.60. For complete list of Galician firms, see Katzmann to Krüger, June 30, 1943, L-18.

154. Armament Command Lvov to Wi Rü/Ic, October 7, 1943, Wi/ID 1.60. Armament Command Lvov to Wi Rü/Ic, January 7, 1944, Wi/ID 1.62. Drohobycz Oil still had 2000 Jewish workers in March, 1944, when the commander of Security Police *Generalgouvernement,* Bierkamp, approached the Armament Inspectorate to discuss their "evacuation" (*Abtransport*). War diary, Armament Inspectorate *Generalgouvernement*/Central Division, March 24, 1944, Wi/ID 1.92. For withdrawal of Jewish workers from Krakow firms, see war diary, Armament Command Krakow/Central Group, August 30–September 5, 1943, Wi/ID 1.121, and war diary, Armament Command Krakow/Group Army, August 30-September 5, 1943, Wi/ID 1.121.

155. Report by Armament Command Krakow on conditions at Heinkel construction in Budzyn, April 12, 1943, Wi/ID 1.17. Stawola Wola Works/Counterintelligence Plenipotentiary Schulte-Mimberg to Industry Plenipotentiary Major Schmolz, February 25, 1943, NG-5694.

156. Testimony by Seyss-Inquart, *Trial of the Major War Criminals,* XVI, 3.

157. At Starachowice *Ostbahn* freight cars were sabotaged. War diary, Armament Command Radom/Central Group, October 15, 1943, Wi/ID 1.30. At Stawola Wola two Jews were shot because of "mutiny." Schulte-Mimberg to Major Schmolz, December 28, 1942, NG-5692. The Jews at the Pionki ammunition plant, however, were specially cited for their reliability. Report by Propaganda Division Radom, February 13, 1943, Occ E 2-2.

158. For escapes at Stawola Wola, see monthly reports from Schulte-Mimberg to Major Schmolz, July, 1942–March, 1943, NG-5687 through NG-5695. Also, report by Armament Inspectorate *Generalgouvernement* for April–June, 1943, July 24, 1943, Wi/ID 1.45. A Tartar guard of twenty-one men (*Osttruppen*) deserted from one of the camps, Judenlager C "Hasag" Kamienna. War diary, Armament Command Radom/Central Group April 15, 1944, and May 5, 1944, Wi/ID 1.4.

159. WVHA-W IV (Krakow office) to Chief of WVHA-W IV in Berlin, October 25, 1944, NO-3765.

BdS Oberführer Bierkamp issued a circular order that inmates of prisons and Jews in armament enterprises were to be evacuated before the arrival of the Red Army. In the event of sudden developments making transport impossible, the victims were to be killed on the spot and their bodies disposed of by "burning, blowing up of buildings, etc."[160]

In the Radom district the SS and Police Leader (Böttcher) ordered the removal of all Jews east of the line Pionki-Radom-Kielce as soon as transport became available.[161] Although the Russian spearhead had come to rest some miles east of that line, the evacuation fever reached much farther into the hinterland, as thousands of Jews were withdrawn from Steyr-Daimler-Puch, "Hasag," and Pionki.[162] In the Krakow district a nervous SS and Police Leader, together with the SS-Economist (representative of the WVHA) and the armament command, decided to cut the Jewish labor force in the armament plants by 70 per cent.[163] This move, too, was premature, because the Russian offensive was not resumed until January 12, 1945, but in the meantime transports with thousands of Jews were moving to the killing center of Auschwitz, while the army hunted down escaped Jews to turn them over to the SS or to shoot them outright.[164]

Hitler's wish was thus fulfilled. Even in the SS enterprises and even in munitions-producing armament plants, the Jews had to "disappear," and indeed few lived to see the light of day.

That was the price paid for the "final solution" in Poland. What about the profits? There is not very much we can put on the other side of the balance sheet – the principal gains consisted of food savings and the confiscation of personal property abandoned by the deported Jews.

As early as August, 1942, the *Präsident* of the food and agriculture division of the *Generalgouvernement*, Naumann, made plans for the curtailment of food allocations to Jews. These plans were part of a major food reduction program which also affected the Poles. Its goal was the increase of food shipments to the Reich. Naumann pointed out in conference that he had simply cut all food allocations to 1,200,000 Jews then undergoing deportation and that he had reserved food for only 300,000 Jews who were then employed in the economy. This disclosure is of interest primarily because Naumann was anticipating rather than following the deportation measures. In Frank's works, the non-working population still in the ghettos was being condemned to a "hunger death" *(Hungertod)*.[165]

160. KdS Radom district to SP and SD commander in Tomaschow (HStuf. Thiel), July 21, 1944, enclosing order by BdS, dated July 20, 1944, L-53. Before his assignment to the *Generalgouvernement*, Bierkamp headed *Einsatzgruppe D* in Russia.

161. War diary, Armament Command Radom/Central Group (signed Major Oherr), July 24, 1944, Wi/ID 1.64.

162. Armament Inspectorate *Generalgouvernement* to Armament Command Radom, July 23, 1944, Wi/ID 1.146. War diary, Armament Command Radom/Central Group (signed Major Oherr), July 23/24, 1944, Wi/ID 1.64. War diary, Armament Command Radom, July 26-August 22, 1944, Wi/ID 1.64. Generalleutnant Schindler (armament inspectorate) to Army Group Center/chief of staff (Krebs), August 21, 1944, NOKW-2846. "Hasag" Kamienna retained 1000 Jewish workers under the "full responsibility" of the plant manager. War diary, Armament Command Radom, July 29, 1944, Wi/ID 1.64.

163. War diary, Armament Command Krakow, August 7–13, 1944, Wi/ID 1.141.

164. Auschwitz is specifically mentioned as the destination of 1800 Jews withdrawn from Steyr-Daimler-Puch. War diary, Armament Command Radom/Central Group (signed Major Oherr), July 23, 1944, Wi/ID 1.64. On army activities, see war diary, 9th Army/Ia, October 28 and October 31, 1944, NOKW-2636. The commander of this army was General der Panzertruppen Freiherr von Lüttwitz.

165. Verbatim remarks by Naumann and

It is impossible to estimate how much food the Germans were able to save as a result – or in anticipation – of the deportations. Table 52 indicates food deliveries from the *Generalgouvernement* to the Reich and shows food savings, though, of course, we must remember to ascribe a part of these totals to reduced allocations for Poles.[166]

TABLE 52 / *Food Deliveries from "Generalgouvernement" to Reich*

	1940/41	1941/42	1942/43
Wheat	nothing	53,000 t.	630,000 t.
Potatoes	121,000 t.	134,000 t.	520,000 t.
Sugar	4,500 t.	4,465 t.	28,666 t.
Cattle	7,510 t.	21,498 t.	55,000 t.
Fats	800 t.	900 t.	7,500 t.

As for the rags, furnishings, and other things left behind by the ghetto Jews, we have no quantitative record at all. We know only that the empty ghettos were subjected to looting by the local population. As in the case of the East, the police employed in the ghetto-clearing operations helped themselves too.[167] The remaining properties were the subject of considerable controversy between Himmler, who issued a confiscatory decree on his own, and Generalgouverneur Frank, who did not recognize the decree.[168] It appears that for once Frank won his point, for he took over the depots in which the abandoned Jewish property was kept.[169] However, this victory was achieved only after Himmler had removed machines,[170] confiscated some choice real estate,[171] and collected debts owed by Poles to Jews in the amount of 11,000,000 zloty – a sum which, incidentally, helped balance the books of the Ostindustrie at its liquidation.[172]

The Polish Jews were annihilated in a process in which economic factors were truly secondary. A Nazi expert on the East, Peter-Heinz Seraphim, described eastern Jewry as "the greatest concentration of Jews anywhere, the spiritual center of orthodox Jewry, and above all the inexhaustible reservoir from which the Jewish migrations were fed and which, again and again, had released smaller and larger groups of Jews to be soaked into other countries."[173] That great concentration, spiritual center, and inexhaustible reservoir of Jewry was now destroyed – reduced to a few straggling survivors of labor camps and killing centers.

3 / THE SEMICIRCULAR ARC

The destruction process was to reach its maximum potentialities not only functionally, in its step-by-step development, but also territorially, in its country-by-country spread. We have seen

Frank in conference of August 24, 1942, Frank diary, PS-2233.

166. Report by Staatssekretär Bühler, October 26, 1943, Frank diary, PS-2233.

167. Biebow to *Gauleitung* Wartheland/*Kreisleitung* Welungen, October 5, 1942, *Dokumenty i Materialy*, II, 147–48. Proclamation by Mayor A. Wasilewski of Biala Podlaska (Lublin district), threatening death penalty for looting of the ghetto, September 28, 1942, *ibid.*, p. 57.

168. Remarks by Frank in *Generalgouvernement* conference of January 26, 1943, Frank diary, PS-2233.

169. Agreement between Staatssekretär Bühler and Higher SS and Police Leader Koppe, February 21, 1944, reported in circular of *Generalgouvernement* Main Division Economy, PS-2819, *Trial of the Major War Criminals*, XII, 100.

170. These machines were transferred to the Osti. Report by Dr. Horn, March 13, 1944, NO-2187.

171. Obf. von Sammern-Frankenegg to Prof. Teitge (Main Division Health), urging transfer of Jewish hospital Zofioska to Lebensborn, since the Jewish patients "did not exist anymore [*nicht mehr vorhanden sind*]," February, 1943, NO-1412.

172. Globocnik to Himmler, January 18, 1944, NO-57.

173. Peter-Heinz Seraphim, *Das Judentum im osteuropäischen Raum* (Essen, 1938), p. 10.

how the "final solution" was carried out in the Reich itself and how it was then applied against the center of gravity of the European Jewish community: Polish Jewry. The destruction of the Jews was not to be confined to the Reich and Poland; it was to be implemented in all European areas under German domination. Heydrich had been instructed to organize the deportations in the entire "German sphere of influence in Europe."[1] And that is precisely what he did.

Before long the German machinery of destruction covered a vast semicircular arc, extending counterclockwise from Norway to Roumania (see map). For our purposes, we may divide this arc into three broad sections: the North (comprising Denmark and Norway), which had fewer than 10,000 Jewish inhabitants; the West (including the Low Countries, France, and Italy), with a Jewish population of 600,000; and the Balkan area, with a Jewish community of 1,600,000. In the center of that huge semicircle, the death camp of Auschwitz received the special transports converging with their victims from north, west, and south.[2]

The geographic widening of the "final solution" was the most complex administrative operation of the destruction process. Unlike the Reich-Protektorat area, in which the Germans were at home, and unlike Poland and Russia, which were regarded as a kind of private reserve, suitable for German colonization and settlement, the semicircular arc was more nearly a German power sphere, a "sphere of influence." In the occupied East no central authority of non-German character was allowed to exist.[3] In the great semicircle the Germans gave orders to puppet agencies and presented demands to satellite governments. The Poles and Russians had no right to a national existence; they were regarded as subhumans and work slaves, destined perhaps to disappear some day. On the other hand, the northern, western, and southern Europeans were allies, or at least potential allies. The Poles and Russians did not have to be consulted about anything; the puppet and satellite authorities in the great semicircle were at least heard, and sometimes their sensibilities had to be taken into account. In short, we are going to deal

1. Göring to Heydrich, July 31, 1941, PS-710.

2. By reason of the German domination of France and Italy, the first stages of the destruction process reached also some half-million Jews in Morocco, Algeria, Tunisia, Libya, Lebanon, and Syria. The German influence was felt even in the Far East, where about 35,000 Jews were living under Japanese rule. The African areas will be discussed in this chapter. Little, however, is known about the Japanese sphere.

As late as 1938 and 1939, Japanese dignitaries made pro-Jewish speeches in Harbin, Manchuria. The speakers were General Higuchi and Prof. Kotsuchi. The latter spoke to a Jewish audience in Hebrew. See *Hauptstelle Ferner Osten* (a party office) to Kanzlei Rosenberg, April 6, 1939, G-231. After 1941 two military personalities, Admiral Terajima and General Nobutaka Shioten, spearheaded an anti-Jewish propaganda movement in Japan. *Die Judenfrage,* July 1, 1942, p. 144; October 1, 1942, pp. 202–5.

Sixteen thousand Jewish refugees from the Reich in Shanghai were subjected to registration and ghettoization measures. The Shanghai ghetto (February, 1943, to August, 1945) was as elaborate as its European counterparts. For a history of the ghetto, see the following materials: *Die Judenfrage,* October 15, 1941, p. 211; May 1, 1943, p. 154. *Aufbau* (New York), April 1, 1955, p. 14A, and May 13, 1955, p. 6. Dr. Felix Gruenberger (Jewish psychiatrist in Shanghai ghetto), "The Jewish Refugees in Shanghai," *Jewish Social Studies,* October, 1950, pp. 329–48. Shanghai Ghetto Collection, YIVO Institute for Jewish Research, New York. Legationsrat Braun (Foreign Office/Pol VIII) to Inland II, August 29, 1944, NG-3002. Staf. Zindel (RSHA/Attache Group) to Foreign Office/Inland II B, November 1, 1944, NG-3002. We shall deal no more with the Far Eastern area.

3. The Protektorat had central Czech ministries.

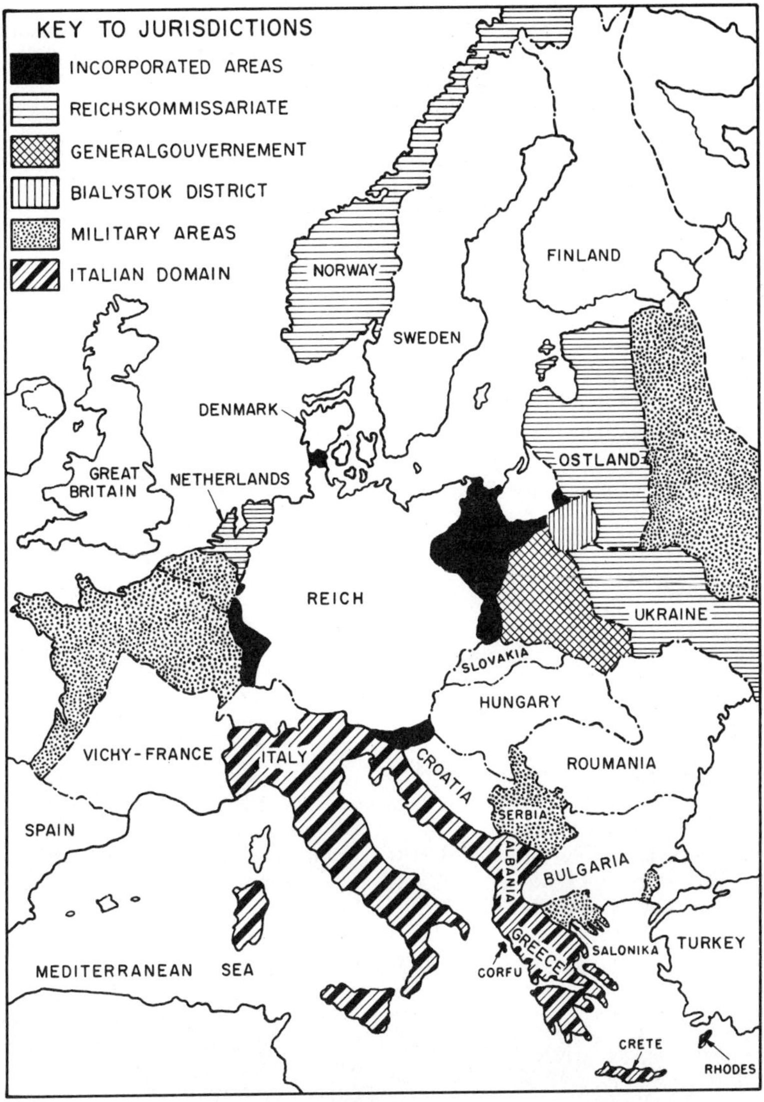

KEY TO JURISDICTIONS
INCORPORATED AREAS
REICHSKOMMISSARIATE
GENERALGOUVERNEMENT
BIALYSTOK DISTRICT
MILITARY AREAS
ITALIAN DOMAIN
NORWAY
SWEDEN
FINLAND
DENMARK
GREAT BRITAIN
NETHERLANDS
OSTLAND
REICH
UKRAINE
SLOVAKIA
HUNGARY
VICHY-FRANCE
ITALY
CROATIA
ROUMANIA
SERBIA
SPAIN
ALBANIA
BULGARIA
GREECE
SALONIKA
TURKEY
CORFU
MEDITERRANEAN SEA
CRETE
RHODES

MAP 6

AXIS EUROPE IN MID-1942

0 100 200 300 400 500
MILES

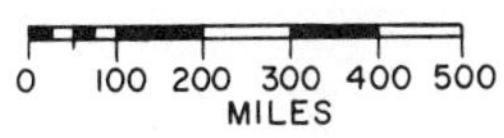

here with an area in which the Germans were masters, but not absolute masters, powerful but not all-powerful.

German authority in the semicircular arc was exercised by civil administrators in tightly controlled territory, by military governors in other occupied areas, and by the Foreign Office in the more loosely controlled satellite regions. Let us consider each in turn.

Civil administration was established in incorporated territories (shaded black on the map) and in Holland and Norway (horizontal lines). Each incorporated area was ruled by its neighboring *Gauleiter*, as follows:[4]

The French areas:
  Alsace to Gauleiter Robert Wagner of Baden
  Lorraine to Gauleiter Bürckel of Saarpfalz
Luxembourg to Gauleiter Simon of Koblenz-Trier
The northern Yugoslav areas:
  Oberkrain to Gauleiter Dr. Rainer of Kärnten
  Untersteiermark to Gauleiter Dr. Uiberreither of Steiermark

The non-incorporated areas under civil administration, Norway and the Netherlands, were each placed under a *Reichskommissar* responsible directly to Hitler: Terboven in Oslo and Seyss-Inquart in The Hague. Norway had a complete puppet government headed by Vidkun Quisling; the Netherlands retained only the Dutch administrative network headed by the top civil servants (secretaries general).[5] Neither occupied Norway nor occupied Holland was permitted any diplomatic relations with other countries.[6] The two states were cut off, isolated under their *Reichskommissare*.

The German armed forces controlled important areas in the West and in the Balkans (dotted on the map). Control in these regions meant not merely the presence of occupation forces but also the exercise of *territoriale Befugnisse und die vollziehende Gewalt* – "territorial jurisdiction and functional power."[7]

In western Europe the German Army maintained two territorial commands exercising functional power: one command was called "Belgium and Northern France"; the other was "France."[8] In Belgium, just as in Holland, there was a central administration headed by the highest Belgian civil servants. In occupied France the Vichy government maintained a complete bureaucratic apparatus which was responsible to Vichy, subject to overriding orders, directives, and requests by the German military administration. In 1942 unoccupied France was occupied; however, the territory just west of Italy was held by Italian troops, and the final integration of all of France under German rule thus did not occur until the Italian collapse in September, 1943.

On the Balkan peninsula three areas were originally under military rule: Serbia, "Saloniki-Aegaeis," and South Greece (the latter a few enclaves in the Athens-Piraeus area, plus part of the

4. For purposes of party administration, the new areas were merged with the old *Gaue*. Thus Alsace was joined with Baden, Untersteiermark with Steiermark, Oberkrain with Kärnten; Lorraine and the Saarpfalz became the *Gau* Westmark; Luxembourg and Koblenz-Trier became the *Gau* Moselland. State offices, however, were not merged. In the new areas each *Gauleiter* had the title *Chef der Zivilverwaltung* ("Chief of Civil Administration" – CdZ). Stuckart and Schiedmair, *Neues Staatsrecht* (Leipzig, 1944), II, 82–87. The Belgian area of Eupen-Malmedy and Moresnet was simply incorporated into the *Regierungsbezirk* Aachen of the *Rheinprovinz* in Prussia; *ibid.*, pp. 77–78.

5. The ministers were in London.

6. Stuckart, *Neues Staatsrecht*, II, 123–25, 126–27.

7. The German troops in Norway, Denmark, and Holland were merely occupation forces.

8. The map shows the border between the two commands, *not* the border between the two states.

island of Euboea). When Italy weakened as a German ally, the Southeast Command took over "Fortress Crete," and at the time of Italy's collapse, in September, 1943, an additional expansion took place. The areas of "Saloniki-Aegaeis" and South Greece were merged into a single region called "Greece," which included all previously Italian areas on the Greek mainland. To the north, the Southeast Command acquired Montenegro and Albania; west of the Greek mainland German military control was extended to the island of Corfu; in the eastern Aegean, the Dodecanese Islands (Italian since 1912, now renamed *Ost-Aegaeis)* became part of this military organization. Within the framework of the German Southeast Command we find also three puppet governments: one in Belgrade, Serbia; one in Tirana, Albania; and one in Athens, Greece.

The most important agency in the semicircular arc was the German Foreign Office. To the Foreign Office's jurisdiction fell all areas in the arc which are unshaded on the map. Foreign Office influence was especially strong in Slovakia and Croatia, satellites par excellence; both states were German creations – in fact, creations of the Foreign Office. Two other countries under the mercy of the Foreign Office were Vichy France and Denmark; their reason for submission was overwhelming German military power. Three countries were reduced to satellite status because they had thrown in their lots with Germany for purposes of territorial aggrandizement: Bulgaria, Roumania, and Hungary. (A glance at the map will indicate the peculiar borders which these three countries enjoyed under the Nazi regime.) Finally, there was one more country which sank from full-fledged partner to minor satellite in a period of some four years: Italy. In the early years of German-Italian relations the Foreign Office had to be cautious in Italy; in the end it could afford to be dictatorial there. Incidentally, we should note that at the height of its power Italy held considerable territory in the Mediterranean area: the Dodecanese Islands, Albania (acquired in 1939), "New Albania," Montenegro, part of the Dalmatian coast and western Slovenia (1941), most of the Greek mainland and some of its islands (1941), and the French region adjacent to Italy for some forty miles inland (occupied in 1942).

The influence of the Foreign Office was not confined to the satellite areas; Ribbentrop's ministry had quite a bit to say in the military territories as well. Generally speaking, Foreign Offices have always looked askance at military efforts to rule territory. The diplomats are always ready to help out with advice and counsel in an army-ruled area, and they are eager to contribute their adroitness and skill to the conduct of military government – the object of all this concern is, in most cases, an eventual transfer of jurisdiction. While the German Foreign Office did not wrest any territory from the army, the trend was nevertheless discernible. Ribbentrop's men were busy in the southeast, handing out advice and participating in decisions, while in the west the course of German-French relations was dictated in no small measure by the German Embassy in Paris. Even in civilian areas – where, of course, no open Foreign Office competition could be tolerated – representatives of the Foreign Office *(Vertreter des Auswärtigen Amts,* abbreviated VAA) reported in detail about every event transpiring before their observing eyes. No wonder, then, that some Foreign Office officials regarded the entire semicircular arc as a kind of Foreign Office area. In Jewish matters, that was almost true.

Who were the Foreign Office officials charged with the implementation of the "final solution" in the satellite areas?

Table 53 is an abbreviated chart showing the Foreign Office apparatus in 1940 and 1943.[9] As we can see from the chart, the division most concerned with Jewish affairs was *Abteilung Deutschland* (Germany) and its successor, Inland II.[10] The peculiar designation *Deutschland* stemmed from the days of the Weimar Republic, when the office was a liaison agency to the Reichstag.[11] After 1933 there was no longer a functioning Reichstag, but administrative agencies die hard. Still titled *Deutschland,* we find our office in 1936 as a *Referat* under the chief of protocol. There it dealt with such minor and miscellaneous matters as maps, buildings, surveys, and so on.

In 1938 *Referat Deutschland* was taken over by one Martin Luther. Unlike his predecessors and associates, Luther was not a civil servant. He was a party man – more specifically, he was a protege of the new Foreign Minister, Ribbentrop. Under Luther, *Referat Deutschland* was raised to a division. It began to concern itself with party matters, and by 1940 it had also acquired jurisdiction in Jewish affairs.

Luther's division was located not on the Wilhelmstrasse in the main Foreign Office building but in the Rauchstrasse, quite a few blocks away. Physical isolation, as any administrator knows, is conducive to independence, and there is some evidence that Luther took advantage of his separate address.[12] However, he always asked the Political Division to countersign *all* – not merely his important – instructions.[13] Thus, before a deportation directive was dispatched to a Foreign Office mission in a foreign country, the paper was sent to the proper desk in the Political Division (e.g., Pol. IV) from where it was sent to the deputy director of the division and to the division chief.[14] Luther wanted his colleagues to share in the responsibility for the frightful decisions he made.

In 1943 Luther developed delusions of grandeur: he wanted to replace his old boss, Ribbentrop. In a letter to Himmler, Luther revealed confidentially that Ribbentrop was insane. Himmler backed Ribbentrop. Luther spent the rest of his career in a concentration camp, and his division was broken up.[15] Horst Wagner, Luther's successor in Jewish matters, carried on the work relentlessly.

If Luther was a party man and a driving force in the deportations, most of his subordinates were party men also. Does this mean that the "final solution" in the satellite areas was a party affair? No, not exactly. The Foreign Office was not a party club. The chief of the Political Division, Dr. Ernst

9. Organization chart of the Foreign Office, dated August, 1940, and September, 1943, NG-35.

10. Except where indicated otherwise, the description of *Abteilung Deutschland* has been taken from Paul Seabury's comprehensive work, *The Wilhelmstrasse: A Study of German Diplomats under the Nazi Regime* (Berkeley, 1954), pp. 71–74, 107–8, 131–33.

11. Testimony by Staatssekretär Weizsäcker, Case No. 11, tr. p. 8571.

12. Luther was reluctant to inform Weizsäcker of things that were going on or of action he was taking. See Luther-Weizsäcker correspondence of September, 1941, on Jewish star decree in document Weizsäcker 488. Luther's reluctance to part with information also affected Ribbentrop. See Luther memorandum of August 21, 1942, NG-2586-J; also, Ribbentrop's admonition to Luther not to undertake independent action in letter by von Rintelen to Luther, August 25, 1942, NG-2586-K.

13. Affidavit by Dr. Karl Klingenfuss, November 7, 1947, NG-3569. Klingenfuss was a subordinate of Rademacher (D III).

14. Affidavit by Dr. Kurt Heinrich Franz Heinburg, September 5, 1947, NG-2570. Heinburg was chief of Pol. IV (Italy and the Balkans).

15. According to Seabury, who made an exhaustive study of Luther's career, the division chief survived his incarceration but died shortly after the war. Seabury, *The Wilhelmstrasse,* pp. 131–33.

TABLE 53 / *Foreign Office Machinery in 1940, 1943*

AUGUST, 1940	SEPTEMBER, 1943
Foreign Minister:	
[von Neurath] Ribbentrop	Ribbentrop
Office of the Foreign Minister (*Büro* RAM):	
Dr. Paul Otto Schmidt	Dr. Schmidt
Dr. Erich Kordt	Dr. von Sonnleithner
Dr. von Sonnleithner	Dr. Burns
Dr. Burns	Dr. Johann Georg Lohmann
	Bergmann
	Hilger
Staatssekretäre:	
In charge:	
[von Bülow, von Mackensen] von Weizsäcker	Steengracht von Moyland
For special purposes:	
Keppler	Keppler
Foreign organization of the party:	
Bohle	Bohle
Minister for special purposes:	Ambassadors for special purposes:
Dr. Ritter	Dr. Ritter
	von Rintelen
	Gaus
	Hewel
Personnel: Kriebel	Schröder
Protocol: von Dörnberg	von Dörnberg
Special tasks: Wagner	
	Inland I (party): Frenzel
Germany: Luther	
Party: Luther	Inland II (SS & Police): Wagner
Deputy: Kramarz	II A (Jews): von Thadden
II (SS & Police): Likus	II B (RSHA, Order Police, police attaches): Geiger
Deputy: Picot	
III (Jews): [Dr. Schumburg] Rademacher	
Political: Wörmann	Hencke
Deputy: Ritter	von Erdmannsdorff
Second Deputy: von Rintelen	Special Ambassador: Dr. Prüfer
	Special Minister: Dr. von Hentig
	I (England): Dr. Weber
II (England, France, Belgium, Netherlands, Switzerland): Dr. Schlitte	II (France, Belgium, Netherlands, Switzerland): von Bargen
	III (Spain, Portugal): Dr. Heberlein
III (Spain, Portugal, Vatican): Dr. Haidlen	XV (Vatican): Dr. Hoffmann

(*Continued on page 352*)

Table 53 / *Foreign Office Machinery in 1940, 1943 (Continued)*

August, 1940	September, 1943
IV (Italy,	IV (Italy): Dr. Mey
Bulgaria, Greece, Yugoslavia, Albania, Roumania, Slovakia, Hungary): Dr. Heinburg	IV b (Bulgaria, Greece, Croatia, Serbia, Montenegro, Albania, Roumania, Slovakia, Hungary, Protektorat): Feine
V (Poland, Russia): Dr. Schliep	von Tippelskirch
VI (Scandinavia): von Grundherr	von Grundherr
VII (Near East): Dr. Melchers	Dr. Melchers
VIII (Far East): Dr. Kroll	Dr. Braun
IX (United States, Latin America): Freytag	Reinebeck
Political Economy: Wiehl	
Deputy: Dr. Clodius	
Legal: Dr. Gaus	Dr. Albrecht
Deputy: Dr. Albrecht	Dr. Sethe
I (International Law): Dr. Conrad Rödiger	Dr. Conrad Rödiger
V (Passports): Gustav Rödiger	(Passport functions transferred to RSHA)
Cultural: Dr. von Twardowski	Dr. Six
Press: Dr. Paul Schmidt	Dr. Paul Schmidt

Wörmann, was an old civil servant;[16] his deputy, Otto von Erdmannsdorff, was a civil servant;[17] and the chief of Pol. IV (Balkan desk), who was described by Wörmann as one of his experts in Jewish matters, was not even a nominal member of the party.[18] In *Abteilung Deutschland* itself, the chief of the Jewish *Referat*, Rademacher, was a civil servant.[19] Luther's successor, the chief of Inland II, appears to have started out in the Protocol Division.[20] His *Referent* in Jewish affairs, von Thadden, "was a man from the Foreign Office who knew his job."[21] In charge of all divisions, powerful Staatssekretär von Weizsäcker had come to the Foreign Office from the navy, in which he

16. Affidavit by Wörmann, May 27, 1947, NG-1639. Wörmann joined the party in 1937.

17. Affidavit by von Erdmannsdorff, November 21, 1947, NG-3650. Von Erdmannsdorff joined the party in 1937.

18. Interrogation of Wörmann by Kempner, June 9, 1947, NG-4158. Affidavit by Heinburg, September 5, 1947, NG-2570.

19. Seabury, *The Wilhelmstrasse*, p. 108.

20. Organization chart of the Foreign Office, August, 1940, NG-35.

21. Testimony by Staatssekretär von Steengracht, *Trial of the Major War Criminals*, X, 133. Von Thadden was an assessor in Pol. V before the war. Organization chart of the Foreign Office, June 1, 1938, Dept. of State, *Documents on German Foreign Policy 1918–1945*, Ser. D, II, 1031-40.

had served as an attaché.[22] In the Foreign Office as in the RSHA, party zealots and bureaucratic efficiency experts had joined hands.

The Foreign Office's involvement in the deportation of the Jews resulted in a close association between the diplomats and the SS and Police, and that co-operation was particularly strong in the field. Table 54, a chart of Foreign Office missions and consulates, also shows the representatives of the Eichmann *Referat* (RSHA IV-B-4) who either were attached to Foreign Office embassies and legations (as in Paris, Croatia, Slovakia, Bulgaria, and Roumania) or who worked in close co-operation with Foreign Office representatives (as in Salonika, Athens, and Hungary).[23]

TABLE 54 / *Representatives in the Foreign Office Area*

Foreign Office Representatives		Eichmann Representatives
Minister, Denmark	[von Renthe-Fink] Best*	
VAA, Holland	[Kühn] Bene	Zoepf
VAA, Belgium	von Bargen	
Ambassador, Paris	Abetz	Dannecker Röthke
Consul General, Monaco	Hellenthal	
Representative, Tunisia	Rahn	
Ambassador, Italy	[von Mackensen] Rahn	
Ambassador, Vatican (1943–45)	von Weizsäcker	
Minister, Serbia	Benzler	
Consul, Salonika	Schönberg	Wisliceny Brunner
Special Plenipotentiary, Southeast (Athens, 1944)	Neubacher	Burger
Minister, Croatia	Kasche	Abromeit
Minister, Slovakia	[von Killinger] Ludin	Wisliceny Brunner
Minister, Bulgaria	Beckerle	Dannecker
Minister, Roumania	[Fabrizius] von Killinger	Richter
Minister, Hungary	[v. Erdmannsdorff, v. Jagow] Veesenmayer	Eichmann Krumey Hunsche Wisliceny Dannecker Abromeit Novak Seidl

*Best, Rahn, Benzler, and Veesenmayer also had the title of "General Plenipotentiary" (*Generalbevollmächtigter*). Our list does not include traveling emissaries.

The Foreign Office's representatives in the Balkans (Kasche, Ludin, Beckerle, von Killinger) were former SA men, that is, brown shirts.[24] The

22. Affidavit by Ernst von Weizsäcker, November 21, 1947, NG-3708. Von Weizsäcker was *Leitender Staatssekretär* (*Staatssekretär* in charge), as distinguished from Keppler and Bohle, who were *Staatssekretäre* charged with special tasks. Von Weizsäcker became *Staatssekretär* in 1938. At the same time, he joined the party and became an honorary *SS-Oberführer*.

23. Names of Foreign Office officials are taken from several documents and newspapers. Most of the RSHA men were listed by Wisliceny in his affidavit of November 29, 1945, *Conspiracy and Aggression*, VIII, 606–21.

24. Seabury, *The Wilhelmstrasse*, p. 127.

SA had once included the SS in its ranks, but in 1934 Himmler broke away, killed many SA leaders, imprisoned others, and in general reduced his parent organization to impotence. Needless to say, not much love was lost between the SA and SS after 1934, but this animosity did not have much effect upon SA-SS co-operation in the four Balkan countries – except perhaps in Roumania, where the friction between the minister, von Killinger, and the Eichmann representative, Hauptsturmführer Richter, developed into an open quarrel.

The substantive task of the Foreign Office in the satellite states was, first of all, the introduction of those preliminary steps (definition, expropriations, and concentration), without which no large-scale deportations could be commenced with any chance of success. So far as possible, the introductory measures in the satellites were to be patterned after their prototypes in the Reich. This was particularly true in the case of definitions, for the Foreign Office interpreted any deviation from the Nuremberg principle as an attempt to save thousands of Jews.

When, finally, a Jewish community was "ripe" for deportation, the Foreign Office diplomats shifted into second gear. As an entering wedge, the foreign government was asked to forego protection of its Jewish citizens in the Reich. With the achievement of this "harmless" concession, the critical moment had arrived. The satellite country was now asked to agree to the "resettlement" of its Jews in the "East." To reduce the possibility of objections and resistance, the Foreign Office did not make claims upon the property of the deportees. (However, arrangements were made to "resettle" the Jews with their personal belongings, and this baggage was later collected by the Reich in the killing centers.) In addition, the Foreign Office would sometimes demand from a satellite government payments to reimburse Germany for the cost of the deportations. Behind this demand was the reasoning that the removal of the Jews was a favor rendered by Germany to her allies, who could then derive lasting benefits from remaining forever *judenfrei.*

At one time the international lawyers in the Foreign Office also considered the possibility of confiscating the property of refugees from the Reich who were residing in the satellite states. This idea, however, was given up in a conference held on July 30, 1942. It was decided to press the "territorial principle": the property of all Jews in a foreign country would fall to that country; the property of all Jews in the Reich would fall to the Reich.[25]

Transport, the final step in the operation, was no longer in the hands of the Foreign Office. Transportation schedules were worked out for the entire European deportation area by Hauptsturmführer Franz Novak of Eichmann's office and Ministerialrat Stange of the *Deutsche Reichsbahn.*[26]

Sweeping over Europe, in north, west, and south an army of specialists was now at work attempting to root out all vestiges of Continental Jewry. To be sure, the German machinery of destruction was not quite so successful in these areas as in the Reich itself

25. Gesandtschaftsrat Klingenfuss (a Rademacher subordinate in D III) to Ministerialrat von Normann (Office of the Four-Year Plan), Ministerialrat Lösener (Interior Ministry), Oberregierungsrat Bangert (Justice Ministry), and Oberregierungsrat Dr. von Coelln (Economy Ministry), July 31, 1942, NG-424.

26. Affidavit by Wisliceny, November 25, 1945, *Conspiracy and Aggression,* VIII, 606–21. In the military areas transport was under the jurisdiction of the OKH/*Chef des Transportwesens,* Gen. Gercke. The western sector was handled in Paris by the *Eisenbahntransportabteilung* (ETRA) West under Glt. Kohl; the southeast fell to the ETRA *Südost* in Vienna under Obst. von Ludwiger.

and the territories to its east. However, the enormous difficulties that had to be overcome in the semicircular arc mattered little to the prime mover of this vast operation, Heinrich Himmler. As the *Reichsführer* wrote (April 9, 1943) to the chief of his Security Police:

> To me the most important thing, now as before, is that there be shipped off to the East, in Jews, all that is humanly possible. In the short monthly reports of the Security Police I want to be informed only of what was shipped off during the monthly interval and what was still left, in Jews, at the end of the month.[27]

The North

Compared to the events which transpired in Poland, the destruction process in northern Europe was microcosmic. The three northern countries within the German sphere, Norway, Denmark, and Finland, contained only about 10,000 Jews. That figure was no accident. For centuries Lutheran Scandinavia had not liked the Jews, and very few had been allowed to settle there. However, the few who had been permitted to come were given complete equality of treatment by about 1870.[28] Henceforth, the Jews were not merely undergoing emancipation; they were being absorbed into the Scandinavian way of life, and that was a process from which the North was reluctant to retreat even under Nazi pressure.

The Germans knew their problem in this region: they would have to make strenuous efforts to achieve meager results. It is therefore understandable that Unterstaatssekretär Luther should have suggested in the conference of January 20, 1942, a postponement of action in the northern domain.[29] Still, a postponement is only a delay. The German bureaucracy could not look on forever while Jews were living peacefully within its reach. No matter how big the cost, no matter how small the yield, the Germans had to strike. They struck first in subjugated Norway; then they engulfed the occupied state of Denmark. The destruction process never did reach remote and independent Finland.

NORWAY. – In 1939 about 2000 Jews were living undisturbed in Norway. A half-Jew, Hambro, had risen to leadership of the Conservative Party and to the post of chief Norwegian delegate to the League of Nations. Hambro's position, and the position of all Jews in the country, was resented only by a small and unimportant political group, the nationalistic, pro-Nazi, and anti-Semitic "National Meeting" Party, which had 15,000 members and was headed by a former General Staff officer and Minister of War, Vidkun Quisling.[30]

When Norway was occupied in a lightning invasion in the spring of 1940, Quisling became the head of the new Norwegian government. He was, of course, no absolute ruler; above him stood his German masters: Reichskommissar Terboven, in charge of all German offices in the country; Generaloberst von Falkenhorst, commander of the German armed forces in the area; and Obergruppenführer Rediess of the SS and Police. Below him Quisling faced his own unruly Norwegian people, whose rebellious elements were rumbling even in his party.

To understand what happened in

27. Himmler to Kaltenbrunner, April 9, 1943, NO-5197.

28. Hugo Valentin, "The History of the Jews in Sweden," in Hermann Bary (ed.), *European Jewish Yearbook* (Frankfurt and Paris, 1953/54), pp. 290–94.

29. Summary of the "final solution" conference of January 20, 1942, NG-2586-E.

30. Memorandum by Rosenberg on discussion with Quisling in Berlin, December, 1939, C-64.

Norway, one has to glance at a map and observe the position of neutral Sweden, paralleling the Norwegian peninsula along a thousand-mile frontier. The Swedes could not remain indifferent to the fate of Norwegian Jewry — the Norwegian Jews were, after all, Scandinavians. When the roundups began in Norway, Sweden opened her frontier to the victims and offered them refuge.

The document-stamping and preparatory measures were not started in Norway until the beginning of 1942. On October 25–26, 1942, all Jewish men over sixteen were suddenly arrested. (Jews in mixed marriages were exempted in Oslo.)[31] The seizure of men only was a Nazi trick, practiced also in Holland and France, to disguise the deportation roundups as a forced labor drive. However, the trick was not entirely successful in Norway. The rumor network within the Norwegian population carried the news to all corners of the country; many Jews went into hiding; and on the two Sundays of November 15 and 22, 1942, special services were held for the arrested Jews in the Lutheran churches of Sweden. On November 17 the Quisling government issued a decree directing all Jews to register,[32] and on November 25–26 police forces seized the women and children.[33] A ship was already in harbor. Zero hour had arrived.

On December 17, 1942, the Swedish Minister in Berlin, Richert, declared his government's readiness to accept the Norwegian Jews who were about to be deported. Staatssekretär Weizsäcker replied that he would not even enter into a conversation on this subject.[34] In Oslo the Swedish Consulate General made strenuous attempts to renaturalize Jews who had formerly been Swedish citizens. To the great annoyance of the Germans, these attempts were carried to the point of inviting some of the arrested Jews, whose connections with Sweden were somewhat tenuous, to apply for Swedish nationality. When the Germans protested against that interference, a Swedish consular official admitted being in possession of an official directive to extend to the "poor Jews who, after all, are only human beings" his helping hand.[35]

As the first victims were loaded on the boat, excitement ran high throughout the Norwegian peninsula. The population was disturbed, and some of Quisling's own men resigned from their party positions in protest. The Germans, however, continued upon their course. By the end of the year 532 Jews had been shipped to Auschwitz; by March 31, 1943, the figure had risen to 690;[36] by 1944 it was 770.[37]

Nevertheless, the German drive had not been altogether successful. Many prospective victims had been smuggled in small parties across the long border into hospitable Sweden. By the end of the war 930 Jews had found sanctuary there,[38] and a few more had survived

31. Hugo Valentin, "Rescue and Relief Activities in Behalf of Jewish Victims of Nazism in Scandinavia," *YIVO Annual of Jewish Social Science*, III (1953), 232. Trial of OStubaf. ORR. Gerhard Friedrich Ernst Flesch (KdS Trondheim), U.N. War Crimes Commission, *Law Reports of Trials of War Criminals*, VI, 112–13.

32. *Reichskommissar* for the Occupied Norwegian Territories (Terboven) to Foreign Office, February 18, 1943, NG-5217.

33. Valentin in *YIVO Annual*, III, 232. The strength of the German Order Police in Norway was 3300. Norwegian police forces totaled 3960. Daluege to Wolff, February 28, 1943, NO-2861.

34. Memorandum by Weizsäcker, December 17, 1942, NG-2461. Also, Weizsäcker to Albrecht (Legal Division) on Richert's attempt to save five families who had or had formerly possessed Swedish nationality, December 17, 1942, NG-3516.

35. Terboven to Foreign Office, February 18, 1943, NG-5217.

36. Korherr report, April 19, 1943, NO-5193.

37. Valentin in *YIVO Annual*, III, 232.

38. *Ibid.*, p. 234.

in hiding.

In the Oslo area a group of 64 Jews in mixed marriages were "quartered" in a camp (*lagermässig untergebracht*); in the fall of 1944 the Swedish Consulate in Oslo approached the BdS (Fehlis) with a request to permit the passage of these Jews to Sweden. The matter was referred to Eichmann's deputy in the RSHA, Sturmbannführer Günther, who advised rejection of the Swedish offer.[39] Von Thadden of the Foreign Office's Inland II concurred.[40] Ribbentrop too wanted the 64 Jews to remain in Norway.[41] However, in March, 1945, they were allowed to leave for Sweden.[42]

So far as property disposal was concerned, Reichskommissar Terboven, casting his eye on the possessions of the 300 Jewish refugees in Norway, proposed to the Finance Ministry that he issue an ordinance for the confiscation of these possessions in favor of the Reich. The Finance experts in Berlin agreed to the confiscations and to the retention of the proceeds by the *Reichskommissar's* office, but they thought the whole move too petty to require the consent of the Finance Minister himself.[43]

All in all, the diminutive character of the operation did not escape the attention of the perpetrators. Some hundreds of Jews had been sent to Auschwitz to be gassed. How could the killing of this handful be justified? That could be done only by exploring in some way the Jewish "influence" in the country. In 1943 a Ministerialrat Huhnhäuser of the Education Ministry, endowed with a grant of 2000 reichsmark from the SS organization *Ahnenerbe,* went to Norway to study Jewish migrations and intermarriages there. His researches in libraries, archives, and church-registration offices aroused the ire of SS colleagues in the Race and Resettlement Main Office, who protested that uniformly planned research into Jewish genealogy was hampered by separate projects like these.[44]

39. Günther to von Thadden, October 2, 1944, NG-5217.

40. *Gruppe* Inland II via Hencke and Steengracht to Ribbentrop, October 11, 1944, NG-5217.

41. Brenner (*Büro* RAM) via Steengracht to Wagner, October 27, 1944, NG-5217.

42. Valentin in *YIVO Annual,* III, 234.

43. Finance Ministry memorandum, prepared by Dr. Delbrück and initialed by the Ministerialräte Kallenbach, Dr. Mädel, and Beyhan, April 2, 1942, NG-4039.

DENMARK. – On the day on which the German Army invaded Norway, it also occupied, without resistance, the kingdom of Denmark. For their lack of resistance and also for their "racial" qualities, the Danes were awarded a degree of autonomy which was unusual for a region under German occupation. They were allowed a Danish government, headed by Prime Minister Scavenius, complete with a Parliament, a Foreign Office, and even an army. The German agencies in Denmark were limited in their functions. The *Befehlshaber der deutschen Truppen in Dänemark,* General der Infantrie von Hanneken, was a troop commander, not a military governor. The German envoy in Copenhagen, Gesandter von Renthe-Fink, was a diplomat, not a *Reichskommissar.* Any interference in Danish internal affairs, particularly Jewish affairs, was considered out of the question.

Nevertheless, the German bureaucrats could not sit still while 6500 Jews were living freely in a country dominated by German arms. From time to time, therefore, the two Foreign Office officials most concerned with Danish and Jewish matters, respectively – the chief of the Scandinavian *Referat* in the Political Division, von Grundherr, and his colleague in *Abteilung Deutschland,*

44. Stubaf. Osiander to Chief of RuSHA OGruf. Hildebrandt, June 3, 1943, NO-4039.

the Jewish expert Rademacher – prodded the minister in Copenhagen, von Renthe-Fink, to remind the Danish government of the Jewish problem.[45] However, there was little that von Renthe-Fink could do. His only suggestion was that Jewish firms in Denmark no longer receive allocations of coal and fuel from Germany.[46]

In November, 1942, von Renthe-Fink was replaced by a more forceful personality: Ministerialdirigent Dr. Werner Best, formerly chief of the administrative office in the Main Office Security Police, now minister and plenipotentiary in Denmark. But even Best had few suggestions. He reported that Prime Minister Scavenius had threatened to resign with his entire cabinet if the Germans raised a demand for the introduction of anti-Jewish measures. Under the circumstances, Best could propose only the following: (1) the systematic removal of Jews from public life by reporting them individually to the Danish government as intolerable for further co-operation, (2) the systematic removal of Jews from commerce through a stipulation in all orders by German firms that no business would be done with Danish companies owned or partially owned by Jews, and (3) arrests of individual Jews for political or criminal activities.[47] Ribbentrop liked the proposals and scribbled on them his *Ja*.[48]

However, Best was not quite satisfied with his own suggestions. He surveyed the situation with a view to discovering further possibilities for action, and in the course of his survey he found that the Danish Jews actually had little influence in the country. There were no Jews in Parliament. Only 31 Jews served in public administration, most of them in positions of little importance. Thirty-five Jews were lawyers, 21 were artists, 14 were editors, though none were editors-in-chief. A total of 345 Jews were in business, but here too the Jews played no important role. The armament officials in Denmark found that only 6 out of 700 firms which had armament contracts could be considered Jewish under the German definition of a Jewish enterprise. Two of these firms had already completed their orders, and one had been "Aryanized" by the resignation of a Jewish member of the *Verwaltungsrat.*

That was the sum total of Jewish influence in Denmark. Was it worthwhile to step on the Danish government to take action against these Jews? Best thought that there was a possibility of taking some action at least against the Jewish refugees in the country. They numbered 845 men, 458 women, and 48 children, or 1351 in all. But these Jews had been deprived of their German nationality by the 11th Ordinance to the Reich Citizenship Law; they were therefore stateless and under Danish protection. If only that ordinance could be revoked, Best reasoned, the Reich could take hold of these Jews without stepping on Danish sovereignty.[49] That proposal, however, seemed much too complicated in Berlin,[50] and so the Jews in Denmark were still undisturbed when, in August, 1943, the situation radically changed.

What happened in Denmark in the late summer and early fall of 1943 is of great interest to us, not because of the physical extent of the operation, which was small, but because of an extraordinary obstacle which arose in the path of the German destructive ma-

45. Luther to Weizsäcker, January 15, 1942, NG-3931.

46. Luther to legation in Copenhagen, October, 1942, NG-5121.

47. Luther to Ribbentrop, January 28, 1943, NG-5121

48. *Ibid.* Sonnleithner via Weizsäcker to Luther, February 1, 1943, NG-5121.

49. Best to Foreign Office, April 24, 1943, NG-5121.

50. Memorandum by von Thadden, undated, NG-5121.

chine: an unco-operative Danish administration and a local population unanimous in its resolve to save its Jews.

For some time during 1943 the situation in Denmark had been deteriorating. Restlessness had increased, and sabotage had grown to disturb the war effort. In August, 1943, Best was called to the *Führerhauptquartier,* where Hitler himself demanded to know what was going on. Hitler ordered Best to declare a state of military emergency in Denmark, a decision which meant that Best would temporarily have to hand over the reins to the military commander. When Best returned to Copenhagen on August 27, 1943, "pale and shaken" by the rebuff he had received, he found that General der Infantrie von Hannecken and members of the legation staff were already discussing the imposition of a state of emergency and the internment of the Danish Army.[51] Two days later, with the Danish Army in dissolution, the Scavenius government resigned and left the direction of its ministries in the hands of permanent civil servants. The emergency had begun.

On August 31 the director of the Danish Foreign Ministry, Nils Svenningsen, who was now chief spokesman of the Danish administration, was sitting in his office when a representative of the Jewish community organization telephoned that community records containing the names and addresses of all Jews had just been seized by the Germans. Svenningsen immediately went to see Dr. Best, but the German plenipotentiary replied that he did not know anything at all about the seizures.[52] On September 17 confirmation of the document confiscations came from the German Legation. The confiscations were described, however, as a "very small action" (*eine recht kleine Aktion*), a routine search for proof of anti-German activity; they had nothing to do with the "Jewish question."[53]

The Jews were still worried. On September 25 the chairman of the Jewish community organization, C. B. Henriques, accompanied by the deputy chairman, Lachmann, visited Svenningsen in his office and voiced the fear that the Germans might raise the Jewish question now. Svenningsen repeated what the Germans had told him. The Jews wanted to know what would be the attitude of the Danish department chiefs in the event that the Germans started an *Aktion* anyhow. Svenningsen answered that the Danish officials would under no circumstances co-operate with the German administration, and that they would protest as strongly as possible against any unilateral German move. Lachmann then inquired whether the Jews might not be "expatriated." Svenningsen replied that an attempted flight to Sweden might provoke the Germans into action. He advised against the move.[54] These explanations apparently quieted the Jewish leaders, but in the meantime the Germans were planning their *Aktion.*

On September 8, Best sent a telegram to Berlin, suggesting that advantage be taken of the present emergency to deport the Jews. For this purpose he needed police, soldiers, and ships.[55] This was the kind of proposal Berlin wanted to hear; on the very next day Best was reinstated with full powers as plenipotentiary.[56] He was now

51. Summary of testimony by Präsident Paul Ernst Kanstein (Legation, Copenhagen), April 29, 1947, NG-5208. Summary of testimony by von Hannecken, December 10, 1947, NG-5208.

52. Memorandum by Svenningsen, August 31, 1943, NG-5208.

53. Memorandum by Svenningsen on conversation with Director Dr. Stalmann, September 17/18, 1943, NG-5208.

54. Memorandum by Svenningsen, September 25, 1943, NG-5208.

55. Best to Foreign Office, September 8, 1943, NG-5121.

dictator of Denmark. On September 18, Hitler decided that the Danish Jews would be deported;[57] at the same time Ribbentrop requested Best to submit data on his plans and needs for the coming operation.[58]

The men in direct charge of the undertaking were the newly installed Higher SS and Police Leader, Gruppenführer Pancke, and his BdS, Standartenführer Dr. Mildner.[59] The Standartenführer faced a major difficulty from the start: he had no forces of his own and could not count upon Danish help. His only recourse, therefore, was to ask for the assignment of German police and army units. Since no police battalions were stationed in Denmark, formations of the Order Police had to be sent into Copenhagen from the Reich.[60] To augment the strength of these forces, Mildner wanted to borrow also the army's Secret Field Police and Field *Gendarmerie*, but the military commander refused to transfer his men to the BdS.[61] Plenipotentiary Dr. Best then requested General von Hannecken to issue a decree requiring the Jews to report at Wehrmacht offices for "work." Again von Hannecken refused. This refusal meant that, instead of catching the Jews by ordering them to present themselves at assembly points, the police would have to institute a door-to-door search.[62]

On September 23 von Hannecken wrote to Berlin to request postponement of the deportations to a period *after* the conclusion of the state of emergency – he did not wish the emergency to be used as an excuse for anti-Jewish action. "The implementation of the Jewish deportations during the military state of emergency," he wrote, "impairs the prestige of the Wehrmacht in foreign countries."[63] Generaloberst Jodl did not take to this suggestion kindly. Reading the report, he wrote on it the following words: "Nonsense. These are matters of state necessity [*Geschwätz. Es geht um staatliche Notwendigkeiten*]."[64] Rebuffed, von Hannecken agreed to a minimum co-operation. He promised the dispatch of a fifty-man detachment to cordon off the harbor area as a precaution against disturbances during the loading. This measure, he reasoned, involved the army not in "arrests" but only in the maintenance of law and order.[65]

On September 28, 1943, Best reported that the deportations would be carried out in one night, October 1-2.[66] Also on September 28 a German shipping expert in Copenhagen, G. F. Duckwitz, decided to reveal the German plan to a prominent Danish acquaintance, Hans Hedtoft (later Prime Minister of Denmark). Hedtoft lost no time in notifying his friends of the news, and he himself set out to warn Henriques, the president of the Jewish community. After requesting to speak to the president in private, Hedtoft informed Henriques of the impend-

56. Summary of testimony by Kanstein, April 29, 1947, NG-5208.

57. Sonnleithner via Steengracht to Hencke, September 18, 1943, NG-5121.

58. Sonnleithner via Steengracht to Hencke, September 8, 1943, NG-5121.

59. See affidavit by Dr. Rudolf Mildner, November 16, 1945, PS-2375.

60. OKW/WFSt/Qu 2 (N), signed by Jodl, to Foreign Office, att. Ambassador Ritter, and General von Hannecken, copies to *Reichsführer-SS/SS-Kommandostab* at Hochwald, and Chief of the Replacement Army (Fromm), September 22, 1943, UK-56.

61. Ritter to Best, September 19, 1943, NG-5105. Best to Foreign Office, September 29, 1943, NG-5105. Ribbentrop to Best, September 29, 1943, NG-5105.

62. Best to Foreign Office, October 2, 1943, NG-3921.

63. *Befehlshaber Dänemark* Abt. Ia/Qu to OKW/WFSt (Jodl), September 23, 1943, NOKW-356.

64. Remarks initialed by Jodl, on report by von Hannecken, NOKW-356.

65. Summary of testimony by von Hannecken, December 10, 1947, NG-5208.

66. Best to Foreign Office, September 28, 1943, NG-5121.

ing deportation in all its details. When the Dane had finished, the Jewish leader spoke only two words. "You're lying." It took a long time before Hedtoft could convince Henriques of the truth. The president repeated despairingly that he just could not understand how it could be true; after all, he had just returned from a visit to Svenningsen, who had assured him that nothing could happen. At last, however, Henriques was convinced. On the following morning, September 29, when the Jewish congregation met in synagogues on the occasion of the Jewish New Year, the news was communicated to the entire community.[67]

At the very moment when the Jewish leaders warned the community to scatter, they informed Svenningsen that they were absolutely certain of the advent of the deportations. Svenningsen called together the top civil servants and, following a conference of the department chiefs, looked up the German plenipotentiary, Dr. Werner Best. Svenningsen began the conversation with Best by pointing out that ordinarily it was proper to ignore rumors; the rumors of the impending deportations, however, were so persistent and so detailed that they could no longer be ignored. Best had to understand that the consequences of this action were not predictable. Excitement was running high throughout the country, for the question was of tremendous importance to the population as a whole and to the civil servants and the leaders of the Danish administration in particular. Best replied cautiously by asking a few questions: What precisely was being said? What were the rumors based on? Where did they originate? Svenningsen told Best what the rumors said: Deportations to Poland. Only full Jews. Ships in harbor.

Then Svenningsen reminded Best that almost a month before the Germans had raided the Jewish community headquarters on Nybrogade and Ny Kongensgade, where they had seized the address lists. Everything, therefore, pointed to a completed deportation plan. Best reiterated that he had no plans. He did not know anything about ships. Svenningsen then asked the plenipotentiary whether he was prepared to deny the truth of the rumors. Well, replied Best, it was rather difficult to explain that something was *not* going to happen, but if Svenningsen insisted, he would ask Berlin whether he could issue a denial.[68]

In Berlin, in the meantime (October 1), the Swedish Minister, Richert, offered in behalf of his government to accept the Danish Jews about to be deported. Staatssekretär Steengracht replied that he knew nothing about an intended operation against the Jews.[69] That same night, the roundups began.

Svenningsen, with a letter of the King and a decision of the Danish Supreme Court in his pocket, attempted to see Best again. The German plenipotentiary, however, was indisposed, and Svenningsen handed the documents to Best's deputy, Minister Barandon. Shortly thereafter the Danish chief prosecutor, Hoff, received notice from the legation that the roundups were under way. Hoff was requested to inform the Danish police of the action, "in order to avoid clashes between the police and German agencies participating in the arrests."

Svenningsen now tried to reach Best by phone but found that the telephone lines had been cut. Shortly after midnight he at last succeeded in seeing

67. Account based on the foreword by Hans Hedtoft, in Aage Bertelsen, *October '43* (New York, 1954), pp. 17–19.

68. Memorandum by Svenningsen, September 30, 1943, NG-5208.

69. Memorandum by Steengracht, with copies to Hencke and von Grundherr, October 1, 1943, NG-4093.

the plenipotentiary. Best confirmed everything but explained that Jews capable of labor would be employed and that the older and unemployable deportees would be sent to Theresienstadt in Bohemia, "where the Jews were enjoying self-government and where they were living under decent conditions" (*wo die Juden Selbstverwaltung genössen und unter anständigen Verhältnissen lebten*). Best then told the Danish official some good news: the imprisoned Danish soldiers would be released; only officers would remain under detention. During the following morning Präsident Kanstein of the legation telephoned Svenningsen and promised him that the seizures would cease. At the same time he requested that the Danish bureaucracy establish a trusteeship administration over the empty Jewish apartments.[70]

Throughout the night German police armed with address lists moved from door to door to arrest Jews. Because the policemen had to be careful to avoid clashes with Danish police forces, they were under orders to seize only those Jews who voluntarily opened their doors in response to ringing or knocking.[71] In the morning it was clear that less than 10 per cent of the Danish Jews had been apprehended. Only 477 Jews were shipped to Theresienstadt.[72] The drive was a failure.[73]

But the Jews were still not out of danger. Almost the entire community, about 6000 in all, was hidden in Copenhagen and its vicinity, and they could not remain in hiding forever. On October 4 the Swedish Minister in Berlin, stressing public opinion in his country, requested the German Foreign Office to grant exit permits for Jewish children. Staatssekretär Steengracht brushed off the request and, in a memorandum written on the same day, criticized the "Bolshevik" attitude of the Swedish press which had given so much publicity to the operation;[74] but the Swedes did not give up that easily. In Copenhagen the Swedish envoy, Gustav von Dardel, promised Danish officials that sanctuary would be given to all Jews who could be ferried across to Sweden.[75] That assurance was the signal for one of the strangest rescue operations in history.

The organizers of the expedition were private people who simply made themselves available for the task at a moment's notice. They were doctors, schoolteachers, students, businessmen, taxi drivers, housewives. None were professionals in a business like this. They faced considerable problems: To reach Sweden, the Jews had to cross the Sund, a stretch of water five to fifteen miles in width. The organizers had to mobilize the Danish fishing fleet to ferry the Jews to the opposite shore; they had to see to it that the fishermen were paid; they had to make sure that the Jews were moved undetected to the beaches and loaded safely on the vessels. That was no mean trick.

70. Memorandum by Svenningsen, October 2, 1943, NG-5208.

71. Best to Foreign Office, October 5, 1943, NG-3920.

72. Judgment of Danish court in trial of Best *et al.*, September 20, 1948, NG-5887. According to statistics kept by the Jewish Council in Theresienstadt, only 466 Danish Jews arrived there. Lederer, *Ghetto Theresienstadt*, p. 249. Various sources place the number of Danish deportees who died in Theresienstadt at around forty or fifty. Representatives of the Danish Red Cross and International Red Cross were permitted to visit the deportees in the ghetto. Affidavit by Dr. Eberhard von Thadden, June 21, 1946, Ribbentrop-319.

73. See Hencke to Copenhagen Legation, October 4, 1943, NG-3920. Also, Best to Foreign Office, October 5, 1943, NG-3920. Understandably, Best heaped all the blame upon the military.

74. Steengracht to von Sonnleithner, October 4, 1943, NG-4093.

75. Bertelsen, *October '43*, p. 73. The author, a Danish schoolteacher, was one of the rescue organizers.

The financial problem was solved in a unique manner. On the average, the one-way trip cost 500 kroner ($100) per person; theoretically, the Jews were to pay for their own passage. However, the Danish Jews were not particularly well-to-do, and many did not have the required cash. The deficit had to be made up somehow. Danish state funds and Jewish community reserves could not be used because of German surveillance. It was therefore necessary to rely heavily upon contributions by Danes.

In the words of one of the organizers, Aage Bertelsen, "the entire economy of the assistance to the Jews could be based on nothing but a personal relationship of trust. Money was paid and received without the giving of any receipts at all, to say nothing of any kind of account-keeping."[76] Bertelsen sent a Pastor Krohn to a lumber merchant, Johannes Fog, to borrow some money. "Mr. Bertelsen? Who is he?" inquired the merchant, while he handed over 2000 kroner with a promise of 10,000 more. When Pastor Krohn turned to go, Fog shouted after him, "Tell him I'll make it 20,000." Within ten days, this merchant had lent almost 150,000 kroner to the undertaking.[77]

The financial problem was not the only one to be solved. The organizers required many additional forms of assistance, and help came from every quarter. The Danish police shielded the operators by warning them of danger; individuals helped sell Jewish belongings; taxi drivers transported the Jews to the ports; house and apartment owners offered the victims shelter; Pastor Krohn handed out *blank* baptismal certificates; druggists supplied free stimulants to keep people awake; etc., etc.[78]

Throughout October, transports left the Copenhagen area almost daily. Not a single ship was sunk. There were mishaps. Some of the organizers were arrested, a few were subjected to a rifle fusillade, and one – Heiteren, son of a supreme court attorney – was killed by German bullets when a loading party was discovered.[79] When the operation was over, 5919 full Jews, 1301 part Jews, and 686 non-Jews who were married to Jews had been ferried across.[80] Danish Jewry was safe in Sweden.

One of the ironies of the Danish operation was a little propaganda announcement issued by Best on October 2, 1943. In this announcement he underscored the necessity for the deportations by pointing out that the Jews had "morally and materially abetted" the Danish sabotage movement. The Danish population, for whom this proclamation was intended, was not taken in by the propaganda – but the German Foreign Office was. The Foreign Office bureaucrats wired for additional facts on Jewish espionage and sabotage. On October 18, Best was forced to report that there really was no Jewish sabotage, that ever since the occupation had started the Jews had "restrained themselves very much," that the announcement had been made only in order to justify the deportations (*um des Zweckes Willen*) and that it was not based on any concrete proof (*ohne dass konkrete Unterlagen hierfür vorlagen*).[81]

The West

German influence was extended westward and south, from Holland to Italy, as a consequence of the lightning war of May and June, 1940. In the course of that campaign the Low Countries and a large part of France were delivered into the German power sphere as occupied territories, while Italy was

76. Bertelsen, *October '43*, p. 60.
77. *Ibid.*, p. 64 ff.
78. *Ibid.*, pp. 147–48, 64, 138, 84 ff., 168.
79. Bertelsen, *October '43*, pp. 168, 172.
80. Valentin in *YIVO Annual*, III, 239.
81. Best to Foreign Office, October 18, 1943, NG-5092.

brought into the German fold as an ally. Ultimately, all of France was engulfed, and Italy too was to be little more than an occupied area.

As we proceed counterclockwise through the western regions, we may observe the progress of this consolidation. From the outset the German hold was strongest on the Netherlands, whose central administration – devoid of ministers – was completely subjected to the dictates of a *Reichskommissar*. Belgium, like Holland, had a central administration without any political direction save that which was supplied by a German military governor. In France the armistice marked the establishment of a satellite regime which enjoyed diplomatic relations with the outside world and maintained armed forces in unoccupied portions of the metropolitan area and in possessions overseas. The French jurisdiction, however, was subject to the overriding orders of a German military government in the occupied territory and to German diplomatic and military pressure in the unoccupied zone. Late in 1942 the free zone too was occupied. Now Italy alone remained fully independent in policy and action, and after the Italian downfall of 1943, German power became paramount there too.

In general, the extent of Jewish vulnerability in a western territory varied with the degree of German control that was exercised therein. Thus we find that the Jews of the Netherlands were living in the greatest jeopardy, whereas the Jews of Italy were for the longest time in the safest position. These geographic differences in vulnerability may be viewed in the percentages of survivors: the lowest undoubtedly in Holland, the highest most probably in Italy. To some extent, the vulnerability pattern was reflected also in a downward flight of Jews from Holland to Belgium, from Belgium and Luxembourg to northern France, from northern France to southern France, and – within the southern French area – from German-controlled provinces to regions dominated by the Italians.

Within each country of the western arc there was also a difference in the vulnerability of old Jewish residents and more recent arrivals. The western areas had old established, wholly assimilated, and completely integrated Jewish populations which had resided in their homes for centuries. But the western states were host also to a fairly large number of newly arrived, unassimilated, and frequently stateless Jewish immigrants who had been admitted from Poland and Germany in the period between the two wars. These immigrants (whose numbers approached roughly 25 per cent of the total Jewish population) were more vulnerable to anti-Jewish action than the established segment. The new Jews tended to be siphoned off in the first deportation transports.

Many factors contributed to this situation. The refugees were poor; they were alone; they were conspicuous. Above all, they had too little protection. The indigenous western authorities were somehow prone to defend and protect their recently admitted Jewish charges with less fervor and less determination than they expended for their old, well established, and thoroughly absorbed Jewish communities. Once, in fact, Jewish immigrants were sacrificed in an attempt to save the long-assimilated Jews.

We find, therefore, that the operations in the West were marked by variations in destructive effect. The Germans could count on maximum damage only where power and might were all their own. Where help was needed from indigenous sources, native Jews became immune. In the total operational picture the persistence of these variations spelled out something less than complete success; nevertheless, the Germans managed in the course of that operation to inflict upon the western Jewish communities frightful wounds in size and depth.

The Netherlands. — In the Netherlands the Jews were destroyed with a thoroughness comparable to the relentless uprooting process which had struck the Jews in the Reich itself. The Dutch destruction process was built upon two solid foundations. One was the peculiar geographic position of the Jews in Holland. The Netherlands were bounded on the east by the Reich, on the south by occupied Belgium, and on the west and north by the open sea. Holland itself is a flat country, and, apart from marshlands in the coastal regions, there are no woods or other hiding places. The Jewish community of some 140,000 people lived densely in a few large cities. It was as though the Dutch Jews had already been placed in a natural trap.

One other factor, perhaps more important than the geographic one, contributed from the outset to the Jewish catastrophe. The office of the *Reichskommissar* was an agency not merely invested with absolute power but prepared to exercise its power with utter ruthlessness and efficiency. Several Austrian personalities stood at the helm of that destructive machine: Reichskommissar Seyss-Inquart; his director for economic affairs, Fischböck; and his director for security, Higher SS and Police Leader Brigadeführer (later Obergruppenführer) Rauter. Propaganda Minister Goebbels had already said in admiration of the Austrians that their Habsburg training had endowed them with special abilities in the treatment of subject peoples.[82]

The *Reichskommissar* lost little time in beginning the destruction process in Holland. As Seyss-Inquart stated himself, he acted not upon instructions from Berlin but upon his own initiative.[83] As a jurist, he was perhaps not wholly without scruples in proceeding toward a headlong clash with the international law, but he reasoned that the armistice that had been concluded with Holland did not apply to Germany's eternal enemy, the Jews. "The Jews for us," he said, "are not Dutchmen. They are those enemies with whom we can come neither to an armistice nor to a peace."[84]

By October 22, 1940, Seyss-Inquart had a definition of the term "Jew" which followed in every respect the Nuremberg principle.[85] The only change was in the date from which half-Jews had to be free from adherence to the Jewish religion or marriage to a Jewish partner in order to be excluded from the ranks of the Jewish victims. In the Reich the cut-off date was September 16, 1935 (that is, the day before the publication of the Nuremberg decree); in Holland that date was May 9, 1940 (the day preceding the commencement of the western campaign). All in all, then, the definition decree was an orthodox measure.

Again, the economic destruction process in the Netherlands followed almost in its entirety the German pattern; we need therefore say nothing about the dismissals from office and jobs and about the curtailments of Jewish activities in the professions. Only the field of Aryanizations revealed peculiarities unlike those we have noted in the Reich, but even here we are on familiar ground, for the Aryanization problems in Holland were not unlike those of the Protektorat. Both Holland and the Protektorat were areas in which Ger-

82. Lochner, *Goebbels Diaries*, entry for September 8, 1943, p. 426.

83. Testimony by Seyss-Inquart, *Trial of the Major War Criminals*, XV, 666.

84. Seyss-Inquart, "Four Years in Holland," 1944, PS-3430.

85. *Verordungsblatt für die besetzten niederländischen Gebiete*, 1940, p. 33.

man enterprises were interested in Jewish property not only for its own sake but also as a lever to be used against native industrial concentrations. Moreover, the Netherlands and Bohemia-Moravia both were places in which German firms, spearheaded by banks, could indulge in their acquisition game, relatively free from official guidance and bureaucratic interference. Finally, the Dutch and Czech transactions both were characterized—at least in some major cases—by the same novel settlement features, notably the granting of exit permits. Let us examine the Aryanizations in Holland in a little more detail.

The Jewish capital investment in the Netherlands, i.e., all the Jewish property except household items and clothes, was not inconsiderable. Nearly 21,000 enterprises in Holland were classified as Jewish,[86] or, to put it another way, about half the total Jewish population derived an income from investments or managerial activities. However, only negligible portions of the Jewish capital investment represented holdings in Holland's major industrial concerns, and there is no evidence that Jews exercised any influence in combines such as Unilever, Shell, or Phillips.[87] Financial institutions also were largely non-Jewish. Of twenty-five leading banks in Holland, only three appear to have been in Jewish hands.[88] About 40 per cent of the Jewish investment was concentrated in real estate, and the bulk was spread out in a myriad of distributive concerns, both wholesale and retail, topped by four big department stores.[89] Still, the Germans were interested in every Jewish firm, in every Jewish stock, in every Jewish option, and in every Jewish claim, for one could never tell when a minority Jewish holding in an enterprise or in a market could be combined with a minority German share to produce control.[90]

Holland was a wide-open market, and within a few months it was overrun by a phalanx of German businessmen in search of opportunities for capital penetration. Among the enterprises with representatives in the Netherlands were Siemens; Brown, Boverie et Cie; Schering A. G.; Rheinmetall-Borsig A. G.; Vereinigte Papierfabriken, Nuremberg; Reiwinkel K. G., Berlin; and a host of others.[91] To bring together buyers and sellers, German banks moved into Holland and established branches there. The most important financial institution in the Dutch Aryanization

86. Armament Inspectorate Niederlande/Z/WS to OKW/Wi Rü, March 11, 1941, Wi/IA 5.12. *Die Judenfrage,* May 15, 1942, p. 101.

87. Von Jagwitz (Economy Ministry) to Ministerialdirektoren Wiehl (Foreign Office), Gramsch (Four-Year Plan), Berger (Finance Ministry), Dr. Merkel (Food and Agriculture Ministry), RR Dr. Diesselberg (Party Chancellery), Reichsbankdirektor Wilhelm (Reichsbank), Amtsleiter Schwarz (AO), MinRat von Boekh (*Generalkommissariat* Finance and Economy, Holland), Reichsbankdirektor Bühler (Trustee, Nied. Bank), KVC Schlumprecht (MB Belg-NFr), October 7, 1941, enclosing report of interministerial conference of September 23, 1941, on capital penetration in Holland and Belgium, NI-10698.

88. Warburg & Co.; Lippman, Rosenthal, & Co.; and Hugo Kaufmanns Bank. Report by Wohlthat (Four-Year Plan), December 9, 1940, EC-465.

89. Report by Dutch government, October 16,1945, PS-1726. *Die Judenfrage,* May 15, 1942, p. 101. The four major retail establishments were Bijenkorf; Gebr. Gerzon; N. V. Hirsch & Co.; and Maison de Bonneterie. Report of interministerial conference, September 23, 1941, NI-10698.

90. Aryanizations accounted for about one-half of all capital penetrations (*Kapitalverflechtungen*) in Holland. Affidavit by Dr. Robert Hobirk (Dresdner Bank capital-interlacing expert), November 12, 1947, NI-13647. The largest outright acquisitions, moreover, involved purchases of Jewish, rather than Dutch, concerns. Rademacher to Luther, November 22, 1941, NI-8853.

91. Rinn (Dresdner Bank director in charge of Securities Division) to Rasche, March 13, 1942, NI-8863. Affidavit by Dr. Robert Hobirk, October 2, 1947, NI-13743.

business was the Dresdner Bank; its subsidiary in the Netherlands was the Handelstrust West.[92]

After a few months of unhampered "voluntary Aryanizations" the *Reichskommissar* stepped in to lay the foundation for a bureaucratic regulation of the Aryanization process. The function of the *Reichskommissar* was indeed a difficult one: in a broad sense, he had to safeguard the German interest vis-à-vis the Jews and the Dutch. Thus the marking and registration of enterprises tended to frustrate Jewish camouflage; the provision for official approval of transactions was a device for eliminating the interested Dutch concerns; the appointment (wherever necessary) of trustees responsible to the state could hurry the process along; and the compulsory deposit of Jewish securities assured to the German investor an opportunity to penetrate into a variety of Dutch enterprises.

At the same time, however, the *Reichskommissar* had to preserve also a more narrow interest, for he had to protect the claims of the state vis-à-vis those of the German business sector. In the last analysis the Jewish sellers were acting as agents of the state, for the less they received for their property, the less could be confiscated from them in the end. In attempting thus to use the regulatory mechanism not only to help German business but also to supervise its activities, the *Reichskommissar* faced an almost impossible task; for, while the German businessmen were quite ready to accept official assistance, they were far less happy to submit to official control.

On October 22, 1940, the first decree was issued.[93] It provided for the registration of enterprises and the approval of transactions. For the enforcement of these measures the *Reichskommissar* created a new agency, the *Wirtschaftsprüfstelle.* This agency, which was headed by a Foreign Office bureaucrat, Konsul Kühn,[94] was soon in difficulty. It goes without saying that in making its decisions to approve the price and the purchaser in proposed transactions, the *Wirtschaftsprüfstelle* had to take into account the "preparatory work" done by the banks. But that was not all. A second agency was set up, with very similar functions. That office was the *Generalkommissariat* for Finance and Economic Questions. It was headed by a triumvirate consisting of Dr. Mojert (Deutsche Bank), Dr. Ansmann (Dresdner Bank), and Dr. Holz (*Reichskreditgesellschaft*).[95] The functions of the *Generalkommissariat* comprised the approval of all transactions exceeding 100,000 guilders in value and the disposal of all Jewish securities.[96] As one German observer noted, the two agencies were engaged in a certain amount of "duplication" (*Nebeneinanderarbeiten*).[97] To put it a little more plainly, the businessmen had actually succeeded in neutralizing the power of the *Wirtschaftsprüfstelle* by building their own agency right into the office of the *Reichskommissar.*

A Jewish enterprise in Holland was

92. Rienecker (Handelstrust West) to Dr. Rasche (Dresdner Bank), December 9, 1940, NI-13416. Organization plan of Handelstrust West (signed Stockburger), March 28, 1941, NI-8864. The Dresdner Bank itself was also a purchaser of Jewish securities. See Vorstand meeting, June 11, 1942, NI-14841.

93. *Verordnungsblatt für die besetzten niederländischen Gebiete,* 1940, p. 33.

94. Memorandum by Dellschow (Handelstrust West), October 23, 1940, NI-13415. Rienecker to Dr. Rasche, Bardroff, Dr. Hobirk, Dellschow, Dr. Entzian (all of Dresdner Bank), March 5, 1941, NI-8866. Note by Dellschow, March 17, 1941, NI-13418.

95. Rienecker to Rasche and other Dresdner Bank officials, March 5, 1941, NI-8866.

96. Affidavit by Dr. Robert Hobirk, November 12, 1947, NI-13647. Handelstrust West to *Generalkommissariat,* attention Dr. Pfeffer, March 16, 1942, NI-8929. 100,000 guilders = RM 132,000 = $53,000.

97. File note, Handelstrust West, April 2, 1941, NI-13398.

exposed—just as in the Reich—to one of three fates: liquidation, "voluntary Aryanization," or Aryanization in pursuance of trusteeship administration. As a matter of general policy, small firms were to be "bled white" through an interruption of their merchandise supply.[98] The effect of this bleeding could be the death of the enterprise: its liquidation. Liquidation was the fate of about 10,000 Jewish firms in Holland.[99] Companies which were classified as Jewish only because of the presence of a minority of Jews on the board or in the management were encouraged to remove the "Jewish influence" by means of "self-Aryanization." "Self-Aryanization" occurred in the case of 8000 companies.[100] The remaining firms – a hard core of about 3000 Jewish enterprises whose productive capacity was suitable for acquisition by German interests – were the subject of scrutiny for the possible installation of trustees.

A trustee was, of course, empowered to act with complete freedom from the owners. He could sell the enterprise to a buyer, subject only to the permission of the two competing agencies which had jurisdiction in approving transactions: the *Wirtschaftsprüfstelle* and the *Generalkommissariat*. And who controlled the trustees? A clue to that situation may be found in a report of the Handelstrust West to its parent institution, the Dresdner Bank. According to that report the Handelstrust West advised clients who were interested in Jewish firms to submit names of prospective trustees, complete with recommendations from the party and competent Chamber of Commerce, to the *Wirtschaftsprüfstelle* of Konsul Kühn.[101]

98. Armament Inspectorate Niederlande/Z/WS to OKW/Wi Rü, February 11, 1941, Wi/IA 5.12.

99. Report by Dutch government, October 16, 1945, PS-1726.

100. *Die Judenfrage,* May 15, 1942, p. 101.

In other words, the initial choice of a trustee was in the hands of the very people to whom he was going to sell the property. Here again we are reminded strongly of the procedure which had evolved in the Reich and the Protektorat.[102]

The last stage of the Aryanization process, the deposit of securities, was ordered in August, 1941. The depository was a liquidated Jewish bank which had been taken over by the *Reichskommissar*, Lippmann-Rosenthal; however, the agency which controlled the disposal of the securities was the aforementioned bank-oriented *Generalkommissariat*. To obtain a parcel of papers for a client, the interested bank had only to request an official in the *Kommissariat* to direct Lippmann-Rosenthal to free the securities for sale.[103]

Statistics are lacking to determine precisely how much the German investors profited from pocketing the difference between purchase price and actual value. We may assume that the amount was in the hundreds of millions of guilders.[104]

101. Handelstrust West to Dresdner Bank/syndicate division, March 22, 1941, NI-10617.

102. The German investors in Holland were serviced also by the *Niederländische Aktiengesellschaft für die Abwicklung von Unternehmungen* (NAGU). The NAGU had been established by three accounting firms (including the Treuhandvereinigung A. G., which was owned by directors of the Dresdner Bank). Affidavit by Dr. Hans Pilder (Vorstand, Dresdner Bank), October 2, 1947, NI-13738; Handelstrust West N. V. (Signed Knobloch and Dellschow) to Dresdner Bank/*Auslandssekretariat* S, March 29, 1941, NI-13758.

103. Dutch banks participated in this business; however, the Dresdner Bank subsidiary, Handelstrust West, got the lion's share. File note, Handelstrust West, undated, NI-13754; affidavit by Dr. Walter von Karger (German manager of Lippmann-Rosenthal), September 24, 1947, NI-13904. The Dresdner Bank itself purchased Jewish securities. Vorstand meeting, Dresdner Bank, August 11, 1941, NI-14798.

Let it be said at once, however, that in Holland the Jews had few opportunities to spend their money before the machinery of destruction closed in on them. In August, 1941, all Jewish assets, including bank deposits, cash, claims, securities, and valuables, were blocked with a view to their ultimate confiscation. A maximum of only 250 guilders a month was made available to a Jewish owner for his private use.[105] With the exception, then, of the very small Jewish proprietors who were concerned with receiving enough compensation to avert privation, the owners were not materially affected by the amount that they were paid, for that amount was basically an indication only of how *Reichskommissar* and purchaser divided the Jewish loot.

We must not conclude, however, that the destruction process in Holland obliterated all differences between the rich and the poor, for there were moments when the well-to-do did have at least a better chance to save themselves and—in some cases—a part of their wealth. For example, at the very beginning of the occupation, when Germany was still looking forward to the conclusion of peace treaties with the Western countries, emigration, even with some allocations of foreign currency, was not altogether impossible.[106] During this early phase of the Aryanizations the owner of one of the major retail establishments, Reveillon, was able to obtain sympathetic consideration for his request to emigrate with some foreign currency.[107] That case was not the only one.

Three refugees from Germany, Dr. Lippman Bloch, Dr. Albert Bloch, and Karl Ginsberg, owners of the Nord Europeesche Erts- en Pyriet Maatschappij N. V. (NEEP), a trading company in ores and minerals at Amsterdam, managed to leave Holland in 1940 without relinquishing their hold on the enterprise. The two Blochs were able to accomplish this feat because they were nationals of Liechtenstein, a principality which may be found on a good map between Switzerland and Austria. Throughout the occupation the enterprise was run by a Dutch director and two agents (*Prokuristen*), one of whom was the Swiss consul. (Switzerland handles Liechtenstein's foreign affairs.) Moreover, the company was able to pay salaries to its Jewish employees who were in hiding. The only loss sustained by the owners during the occupation period was the relinquishment, under pressure of the Handelstrust West, of the company's share in a Greek mining establishment. The share was bought for a token payment by

104. The *Reichskommissariat* ultimately confiscated 400,000,000 guilders from the Jews. Testimony by Seyss-Inquart, *Trial of the Major War Criminals,* XVI, 65–66. The few individual transactions at our disposal reveal not only that the Jews contracted to sell their property for less than it was worth but that often long-term payment features reduced still further the effective compensation. Thus, if a business worth 100,000 guilders was sold for 50,000 guilders with the proviso that payment be made in ten equal yearly installments, no more than perhaps 10,000 guilders (or one-tenth of value) may ultimately have been collected. One guilder = RM 1.327 = $0.53.

105. The agency in charge of blocking was Lippman-Rosenthal. Affidavit by Dr. Walter von Karger, September 24, 1947, NI-13904.

106. Memorandum by Stiller (Dresdner Bank), February 13, 1941, NI-9915. Memorandum by Knobloch (Handelstrust West), May 5, 1941, NI-13771. BdS Niederlande to *Generalkommissariat* for Finance and Economy, December 14, 1942, NI-13768. Handelstrust West to Kammergerichtsrat Dr. Schröder (*Reichskommissar*/Enemy Property Division), July 21, 1942, NI-13770.

107. Dellschow (Handelstrust West) to Dr. Rasche, Dr. Entzian, and Kühnen (all of Dresdner Bank), December 21, 1940, NI-13748. Reiwinkel K. G. – Das Haus für Geschenke (purchaser) to von Richter (Dresdner Bank), October 9, 1941, NI-3948. The ultimate fate of the Reveillon owner is not indicated.

Krupp.[108]

Again, the Gerzon family, which owned Gebr. Gerzon Modemagazijnen N. V., Amsterdam, one of the largest department stores in Holland, concluded a contract with Helmut Horten, owner of the Warenhaus Helmut Horten K. G., Duisburg, for the sale of their enterprise in exchange for $100,000 and exit permits. (The $100,000 represented about 10 per cent of real value.) The exit permits, it seems, did not materialize in full, for at least one of the directors spent the remainder of the occupation period in a concentration camp.[109]

In 1941, when prospects of peace settlements were beginning to fade, emigration became more difficult. The Jews were now fortunate if they could escape *without* any funds at all.[110] In the summer of 1941 discussions were held about a project that one Dresdner Bank official called the "ransoming of Dutch Jews against payment of a penance in Swiss francs" (*Auslösung holländischer Juden gegen Zahlung einer Busse in Schweiz. Francs*).[111] In other words, instead of receiving part of their proceeds in foreign exchange, prospective emigrants now had to add to the German haul by drawing upon whatever accounts or credit they possessed in neutral countries. Initially, the amount of the "penance" was fixed at 20,000 Swiss francs per family;[112] later the requirement was raised to 50,000 francs, and, with the advent of the deportations, to 100,000.[113] On October 28, 1942, the Handelstrust West informed a client that "the amount of a hundred thousand Swiss francs which you mentioned will certainly not be sufficient for the departure of the entire family."[114] Survival had become expensive in Holland. As the holocaust came closer, only a handful of Jews could afford to buy their lives.

108. Statement by Karl Ernst Panofsky (postwar *Generaldirektor* of the company), November 6, 1947, NI-12694. Statement by Beelaerts van Blockland (Dutch director during the occupation), November 6, 1947, NI-12694. Handelstrust West N. V. (signed Knobloch and Dellschow) to directorate of the NEEP, October 29, 1941, NI-12695. Affidavit by Blockland, February 9, 1948, NI-14879.

109. Affidavit by Arthur Marx (member of the Gerzon family), September 24, 1947, NI-13751. Summary of discussion between Marx, Worst, Horten, Dr. Hobirk, and Bardroff, October 10, 1941, NI-13773. Handelstrust West to Dr. Schröder, July 21, 1942, NI-13770.

110. Keesing of the Rothschild interests attempted to secure the emigration from Holland of ten family members in exchange for a sales contract calling for payment in 180 monthly installments (15 years). Memorandum by Stiller (Dresdner Bank), February 3, 1941, NI-9915; Keesing correspondence with Handelstrust West in NI-9916.

111. Entzian to Stiller, August 8, 1941, NI-9914.

112. Dresdner Bank to Economy Ministry, attention RR Meck, August 5, 1941, NI-8928. Entzian to Stiller, August 8, 1941, NI-9914.

113. RSHA to Himmler, November 24, 1942, NO-2408.

114. Handelstrust West N. V. to D. J. I. van den Oever, October 28, 1942, NI-14818. Up to November, 1942, only 8 permits involving 36 Jews had been granted by the RSHA. The payments for these authorizations totaled 1,290,000 Swiss francs, plus certain additional concessions. RSHA to Himmler, November 24, 1942, NO-2408. The money was apparently retained by the SS and Police for their own purposes. An attempt was made to broaden the scheme. Thus it was proposed that Swiss banks advance 5,000,000 francs to bail out 500 Jews, repayment of the loan to be guaranteed by the Dutch government in exile. The British indignantly refused to entertain the proposal. British Foreign Office/Press Division/Special Service for Political News/PXII, *Bulletin,* November 25, 1942, NG-3379. Gruppenführer Berger of the SS-Main Office, who needed 30,000,000 Hungarian pengö for recruitment of *Waffen-SS* men in Hungary, wanted to introduce the Dutch method to Slovakia. Thus Slovak Jews who had pengö would be able to buy their freedom for suitable amounts. RSHA to Himmler, November 24, 1942, NO-2408. These ransoming schemes spread later from Slovakia to Hungary. They were not very successful because of British opposition.

The Aryanization process had affected the entire Jewish community. The rich were made poor, the shopkeepers were brought down to a subsistence level, and thousands of Jewish laborers who had lost their jobs were taken over by the *Werkverruiming*, an agency of the Dutch Welfare Ministry, to work – segregated – in industrial plants or outdoor projects.[115]

While the German economic apparatus in Holland gradually impoverished the Jews, the machinery of the SS and Police was preparing for the total re-

The first step to ensnare the Jews in a tight network of identification and movement controls was a decree signed by Seyss-Inquart on January 10, 1941, which provided for the registration of the victims.[117] The decree contained an interesting feature, although it remained without decisive significance: not only Jews were obliged to register, but also all those persons who had so much as one Jewish grandparent. The total registration figures showed that there were 140,000 Jews and 20,000 Mischlinge.[118]

Table 55 / *Deportation Machinery of the SS and Police in Holland*

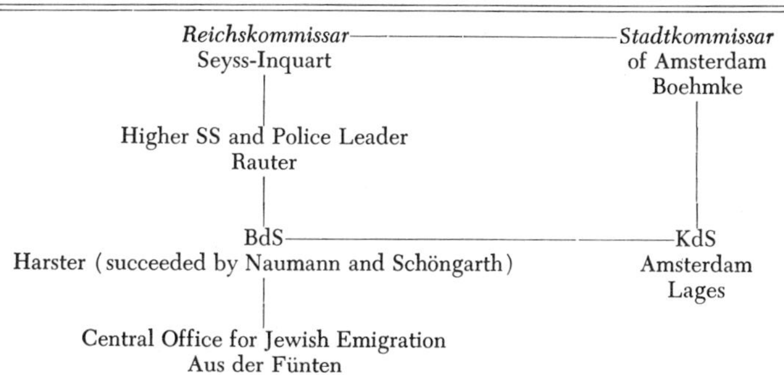

moval of the Jews to killing centers in the East. The officials who were chiefly responsible for that stage of the operations are listed in Table 55. We have already met two of these personalities before. Brigadeführer Erich Naumann, who took command of Security and SD forces in Holland in September, 1943, had previously been a killer of tens of thousands of Jews as commander of *Einsatzgruppe B* in Russia; his successor, Schöngarth, came to Holland in June, 1944, after rich experiences as BdS in the *Generalgouvernement*.[116]

In the office of the police president of The Hague, a genealogical division (*Genealogische Afdesling* – GA) maintained a pink card file of all the *Mischling* registrations.[119] The man in

115. Report by Dutch government, October 16, 1945, PS-1726. Higher SS and Police Leader Rauter to Himmler, September 24, 1942, *Nederland in Oorlogstijd*, March, 1949, p. 7.

116. Boehmke had functions not only in Amsterdam. He was Seyss-Inquart's deputy for deportations in all of Holland. Testimony by Seyss-Inquart, *Trial of the Major War Criminals*, XVI, 3.

117. *Verordnungsblatt für die besetzten Niederländische Gebiete*, 1941, Part 2, p. 19. The enforcement of the measure was in the hands of the Dutch Secretary General for the Interior, Frederiks. On Dutch secretaries general, see testimony by Heinz Max Hirschfeld (Secretary General for Economy and Agriculture), *Trial of the Major War Criminals*, XVI, 210–11.

118. Report by Dutch government, October 16, 1945, PS-1726.

119. OStubaf. Ispert to Rauter, copies to Stubaf. Aust and Stubaf. Osiander of the RuSHA, February 25, 1944, NO-4038. Report

charge of the file, the Dutch SS-Untersturmführer ten Cate, was certain that the 20,000 *Mischling* registrants represented only a fraction of all the people in Holland who had foreign or mixed "blood." He wanted to establish a card index of 300,000 records of such people, and complained that already two Dutch SS men with Jewish names had been killed in action and that their names were being read with the names of Aryan heroes at official celebrations.[120] Untersturmführer ten Cate, who set out to "seize" in his files "the totality of *Mischling* blood" (*sämtliches Mischlingsblut*) in Holland, pursued his task until September, 1944, when he suddenly deserted the SS and his cards.[121]

The German administration's second step followed closely upon the heels of the registration order. In February, 1941, the Jews were placed under the direction of a council, the *Joodsche Raad*. Two chairmen stood at the helm of the council: a merchant, A. Ascher, and a professor, D. Cohen.[122] The usual far-reaching powers were vested in the Jewish leaders: the *Joodsche Raad* maintained community registers; it disposed over a police force; and in January, 1943, the individual deposits, from which a maximum of 250 guilders had hitherto been paid to the Jewish owners, were transformed into a collective account from which payments were made only to the council. A sum of 600,000 guilders was handed over to the council that month; lesser amounts followed thereafter.[123] During the deportations that accumulation of power in the council was to reveal itself in all its importance.

At the time of the council's formation a series of incidents in Amsterdam tested the Germans' ability to crush all opposition to the unfolding destruction process in Holland. On a February day in 1941, military formations of the Dutch Nazi Party (NSB), "in extension of training exercises," swarmed over the city into the Jewish quarter.[124] In Seyss-Inquart's words, "synagogues were also burned. Apparently, someone ambitiously tried to imitate the 8th November, 1938."[125] The Dutch Nazis, however, had a rougher time of it in Amsterdam than their German party colleagues had experienced during the *Einzelaktionen* in the Reich. The NSB raiders were attacked by Dutch workers and "hordes of youthful Jews who were equipped with all sorts of weapons." Dutch Nazi stores were smashed, and a uniformed Dutchman was "literally trampled by a band of thirty Jews" to the point that he could not be identified upon his delivery at a hospital. He died from his wounds.

The Germans now struck back. Six of the defenders were killed and many more wounded; the Jewish section was cordoned off; and the Dutch inhabitants of the quarter were evacuated.[126] The new Jewish council under Ascher and Cohen hurriedly called upon all Jews to surrender their weapons.[127] The ghetto was born.

If the Germans thought that every-

---

by UStuf. Dr. Grotefend (Dutch SS-man in charge of *Ahnentafeln*, or ancestral charts), August 23, 1944, NO-3807.

120. Ten Cate to OStubaf. Osiander (RuSHA), December 25, 1941, NO-3643.

121. Report by OStuf. Neumann-Reppert, September 20, 1944, NO-4033.

122. Report by Dutch government, October 16, 1945, PS-1726. *Die Judenfrage*, March 10, 1941, p. 43.

123. Affidavit by Dr. Walter von Karger (German manager, Lippmann-Rosenthal), September 24, 1947, NI-13904.

124. Armament Inspectorate Niederlande/Z/WS to OKW/Wi Rü, March 11, 1941, Wi/IA 5.12.

125. Testimony by Seyss-Inquart, *Trial of the Major War Criminals*, XV, 667.

126. Armament Inspectorate Niederlande/Z/WS to OKW/Wi Rü, March 11, 1941, Wi/IA 5.12.

127. *Die Judenfrage*, March 10, 1941, p. 43.

thing was now under control, they were mistaken. A German Security Police detachment, patrolling in the Jewish quarter, entered an apartment on Van Wonstreet and surprised a group of people there in a "secret meeting." The policemen were attacked with bullets and acid. Higher SS and Police Leader Rauter thereupon proclaimed that, in reprisal for the assault, 400 Jews in the age group 20–35 had been sent to a German concentration camp.[128] The deportation of these Jews resulted in a series of unforseen repercussions.

On February 25, 1941, a wave of strikes began to paralyze transport and industry in the provinces of North Holland and Utrecht. The trolleys stopped in Amsterdam, utilities went dead, shipyards were deserted, and the Focker Works, the Hollandschen Draad- en Kabelfabrik, and the Staatsbedrijf in Hemburg stopped operations. In Hilversum, where the Germans had arrested ten prominent physicians as hostages, 2000 workers struck at the Philips plant. All together 18,300 workers had walked out of the armament industries alone.

On the second day of the strike German Order Police clashed with crowds in the streets as Dutchmen hurled "insults" at the German Wehrmacht. Intercepted leaflets revealed that the population's antagonism over the deportation of the 400 Jews was linked to a fear that the Dutch shipyard workers would forcibly be transported for labor to the Reich.

The commander of the German armed forces in Holland, General der Flieger Christiansen, now stepped into the picture. Martial law – with threats of the death penalty – was established in the two northern provinces, as the General ordered the strikers back to work and forbade all gatherings and meetings. Within three days the strike was broken. To penalize the Dutch population for its behavior, fines were imposed on three cities: 15,000,000 guilders on Amsterdam; 2,500,000 guilders on Hilversum; 500,000 guilders on Zaandam. The money was collected in the form of a special income tax from people whose incomes exceeded 10,000 guilders a year.[129]

In the meantime, a total of 430 Amsterdam Jews (to be followed by 230 more in June) had arrived in the Reich. The ultimate destination of these Jews was the concentration camp of Mauthausen. There they were detailed to the stone quarries to carry heavy boulders up a long steep slope. The "work" took its toll. Men began to drop from exhaustion, and after a while the Jews joined bands and jumped down, splattering the quarry with bones, brains, and blood.[130]

The Mauthausen command, following the old concentration camp routine, sent death notices to the survivors in Holland. This was a mistake. The notices were collected by the Jewish Council and transmitted to the Swedish government, which according to the customs of war was entrusted with the protection of Dutch citizens in the Reich and of German nationals in the Dutch colonies. The Swedish Minister in Berlin, Richert, protesting to the Foreign Office legal expert, Albrecht, pointed to the fact that the deaths were occurring on certain days each time and that all the victims were "rather young men." He therefore wanted to visit the camp in fulfilment of Sweden's func-

128. Proclamation by Rauter, February 25, 1941, NG-2285.

129. Armament Inspectorate Niederlande/Z/WS to OKW/Wi Rü, March 11, 1941, Wi/IA 5.12. Also, memoranda by Unterstaatssekretär Wörmann (Foreign Office Political Division), February 25 and 26, 1941, NG-2805.

130. Eugen Kogon, *Der SS-Staat* (3d ed.; Frankfurt, 1949), pp. 209–10. Kogon, a German journalist, was an inmate of Buchenwald.

tion as a protective power.[131]

Albrecht could not flatly refuse the Swedish request, for the Jews in question were Dutch nationals on German soil, but he managed to forestall the unwelcome visit. His colleague Luther meanwhile wrote to Gestapo Chief Müller to request that the SS be a little more careful in the future.[132] A lengthy chain of complications had thus been brought on by those Dutch Nazis who on February 9, 1941, decided to have some fun in the Jewish quarter.

The concentration process was now continued with systematic deliberation. With the addition of a *J* to the identification cards of Jews in July, 1941, the Rauter machinery began to tighten the screws. Travel restrictions were imposed in September and October, to be followed by a partial clearing of the provinces and the completion within Amsterdam of three ghetto sections which housed about half of Holland's Jews. After May, 1942, the Jews also had to wear the star.[133] Once again the Germans noted signs of opposition, but the character of the resistance now had changed. Although several days had been allowed for putting on the star, the Jews began to wear the yellow mark on the first day. Dutch inhabitants openly showed their sympathy for the victims by wearing yellow flowers on their coat lapels, and in Rotterdam signs were plastered on walls to remind the Dutchman to show his respect if he should see a Jew with a star on the street.[134]

The population remained quiet, however, and anti-Jewish restrictions followed one another in more rapid succession. A curfew was instituted to keep the Jews off the streets between 8 P.M. and 6 A.M.; shopping was allowed only between 3 P.M. and 5 P.M.; public conveyances could no longer be used without special permission; telephoning was henceforth prohibited; and Jews were forbidden to enter the homes of non-Jews.[135] The Jewish community was now immobile, helplessly awaiting its fate.

On June 22, 1942, the deportation chief of the RSHA, Eichmann, informed the Jewish affairs expert in the Foreign Office, Rademacher, that arrangements had been concluded with the railways for the deportation of 100,000 Jews from the Netherlands, Belgium, and occupied France to Auschwitz. The Dutch quota was 40,000.[136]

The Eichmann letter was a more or less routine communication in which the Foreign Office was asked to "kindly take note" of the SS operation. Eichmann had received no protests from any quarter, and so he added: "I assume that there are no objections against these measures on the part of the Foreign Office, either." Indeed, the Foreign Office had no objections "in principle" to the planned deportations; for certain "pychological" reasons, however, the diplomats desired that the first transports be composed of stateless Jews. "There are," said Division Germany, "nearly 25,000 of these Jews in the Netherlands alone."[137]

131. Memorandum by Dr. Albrecht, October 31, 1941, NG-2710.

132. Luther to Müller, November 5, 1941, NG-3700. The Mauthausen Jews are said to have died to the last man. Kogon, *Der SS-Staat*, p. 210.

133. Report by Dutch government, October 16, 1945, PS-1726.

134. Armament Inspectorate Niederlande/Z/WS to OKW/Wi Rü, May 13, 1942, Wi/IA 5.20.

135. Report by Dutch government, October 16, 1945, PS-1726.

136. Eichmann to Rademacher, June 22, 1942, NG-183.

137. Foreign Office note (initialed by Luther) to RSHA IV-B-4, attention Eichmann (undated, presumably July, 1942), NG-183. The "stateless" Jews were mainly refugees from the Reich. There were few Jews with foreign nationalities in Holland; the largest group consisted of 193 Hungarians. Foreign

Apparently the echoes of the strike in Amsterdam and the interventions of the Swedish Minister in Berlin were still ringing in Foreign Office ears, although the proposed solution was only a device and hardly a practical one at that, for it would have been difficult to conduct selective seizures. Thus, on July 17, 1942, the Foreign Office representative in Holland, Bene, transmitted to Berlin a proposal that the *Reichskommissar* divest all Jews of their nationality as a means of preventing all future Swedish interventions.[138] The proposal was kicked around a bit in the legal, political, and Luther divisions. The principal difficulty was that in the eyes of neutral states the *Reichskommissar* could not deprive people of Dutch nationality; only a Dutch government could do that.

After a while the diplomats' thinking was reduced to a single idea which can be summarized in the words of the Foreign Office legal expert, Albrecht: "Should it be unavoidable to place the Dutch Jews outside Holland, it would be expedient if the police would not allow any information to leak out with regard to their whereabouts, especially in possible cases of death."[139] Rademacher of Division Germany agreed. He thought that the Protective Power had no jurisdiction in the eastern territories anyway, but added by way of reinforcement: "In principle, no information whatsoever will be given to the outside world by the police." There would then be no visits to camps, "etc."[140]

The effectiveness of the Foreign Office remedy was quickly confirmed from the field. As the first two trains left Holland with Jewish deportees, there were no "incidents."[141] The legend was spreading among Jews that the deportations were a true "resettlement." "In Jewish circles the opinion is widespread," wrote Bene, "that the Jews who are fit for labor service are being deported to prepare the necessary quarters for the Jews in the East."[142]

The Dutch population was generally uneasy. Its morale, observed an armament officer, was strained by "the confiscation of bicycles, the evacuation of the Jews to the labor camps of the East, and the continued arrests of hostages;"[143] but no word of protest was received from the Dutch Secretary General of the Interior.[144] There were interventions only by the Protestant and Catholic Churches. To placate the clergy, the converted Jews and Jews in mixed marriages were exempted from deportation for the moment.[145] (There were at least 1500 converts[146] and perhaps ten times as many Jews in mixed marriages.[147])

Aside from that rather substantial category of deferments, there were a few other privileged classes which followed closely the pattern established in the Reich. The armament inspectorate exacted from the Central Office for Jewish Emigration an agreement for the preservation of a few thousand ab-

Office Representative in Holland (Bene) to Foreign Office, July 3, 1942, NG-23.

138. Bene to Foreign Office, July 17, 1942, NG-2634.

139. Albrecht to Weizsäcker, July 31, 1942, NG-2633.

140. Memorandum by Rademacher, August 10, 1942, NG-2632.

141. Bene to Foreign Office, July 17, 1942, NG-84.

142. Bene to Foreign Office, July 31, 1942, NG-2631.

143. Report by Armament Inspectorate Niederlande, July 31, 1941, Wi/IA 5.8.

144. Bene to Foreign Office, July 31, 1942, NG-2631.

145. Bene to Foreign Office, July 17, 1942, NG-84. Bene to Foreign Office, July 31, 1942, NG-2631.

146. Bene to Foreign Office, July 17, 1942, NG-84.

147. In the official German correspondence the estimates of mixed marriages ran as high as 20,000 and 22,000. Rauter to Himmler, September 24, 1942, *Nederland en Oorlogstijd*, March, 1949, p. 7; Bene to Foreign Office, August 31, 1942, NG-2631.

solutely essential Jewish workers.[148] Ultimately, about 3500 armament Jews and 1200 diamond cutters were placed on the exempt lists.[149] Deferred were also a handful of foreign Jews, a few special cases, and a fairly large number of Jewish administrative personnel in the community machinery. But the deportations were in full swing. The Rauter machine was over the hump.

On September 10, 1942, Rauter revealed to Himmler some of his detailed plans. The classification of the mixed marriages, munitions workers, diamond cutters, and so on, was expected to be completed by October 15. By that time, too, Rauter hoped to have two big transit camps running. One, Westerbork, at Assen, had originally been established by Dutch authorities for Jewish refugees. It was already receiving Jewish deportees. The second camp, Vught, was under construction at 's Hertogenbosch. The two camps were to have a combined capacity of 40,000 Jews and were to serve as assembly points for masses of Jews seized in sudden paralyzing raids. "I am harnessing up everything that exercises police or assistant police functions," said Rauter, "and anything anywhere that looks as if it belongs legally or illegally to Jewry will be put into these camps after October 15, 1942."[150]

On September 24, 1942, Rauter sent another "progress report" to Himmler. "Until now," he wrote, "we have set in motion – together with the Jews shoved off for penal reasons to Mauthausen – altogether 20,000 Jews to Auschwitz. In all of Holland some 120,000 Jews are being readied for departure, although this includes the mixed Jews [*Mischjuden*], who after all will remain here for a while. In Holland there are approximately 20,000 mixed marriages. With the agreement of the *Reichskommissar*, however, I am going to shove off also all Jewish parts of the mixed marriages, insofar as these marriages have produced no children. There will be about 6000 cases in that category, so that ca. 14,000 Jews in mixed marriages will stay here for the moment."

Rauter then continued: "In the Netherlands there is a so-called *Werkverruiming* – a labor service of the Dutch Welfare Ministry – which sends Jews for labor to closed enterprises and camps. We have not touched these *Werkverruiming* camps so far, in order to let the Jews take refuge there. In the *Werkverruiming* camps there are ca. 7000. We hope to have 8000 Jews there by October. These 8000 Jews have ca. 22,000 dependents in the entire country. On October 1 the *Werkverruiming* camps will be occupied by me with one lightning blow, and on the same day the relatives outside will be arrested and taken to the two big Jewish camps newly erected at Westerbork near Assen and Vught near 's Hertogenbosch."

Having thus accounted for 55,000 Jews, Rauter had a vision of uprooting the remaining victims in one vast manhunt: "Every Jew found anywhere in Holland will be put into those big camps." Aryans who undertook to help Jews across the border or to hide them in the country would have their property seized, and the perpetrators would be taken to a concentration camp. Nothing was now going to stand in the way of success.[151] Himmler read that report with approval; he wrote on the

148. War diary, Armament Inspectorate Niederlande, June 24, 1942, Wi/IA 5.10. Also, war diary of the inspectorate, April 20, 1942, and July 14, 1942, Wi/IA 5.8. The armament inspector of the Netherlands was Vizeadmiral Reimer.

149. Bene to Foreign Office, August 31, 1942, NG-2631.

150. Rauter to Himmler, September 10, 1942, NO-2256.

151. Rauter to Himmler, September 24, 1942, *Nederland in Oorlogstijd*, March, 1949, p. 7.

paper, *Sehr gut.* As yet, however, all the obstacles had not been overcome. The deportations were not completed in 1942 or even in 1943.[152] It took two years to finish the job, but in the end few Jews were left alive.

Because of the prolongation of the operation, the two transit camps, Westerbork and Vught, became regular institutions of the destructive machinery in Holland. Within each camp the SS and Police set up a Jewish *Kampleiding*, or camp directorate, complete with Jewish policemen and other administrative personnel. External security was provided, in view of the police shortage, by forces of the Dutch SS Guard Battalion Northwest, a group of volunteers who had agreed to tours of duty within the country.[153] Gruppenführer Jüttner, the chief of the SS Operational Main Office (the military headquarters of the SS), was, incidentally, not quite happy with that arrangement. "Through the task given to these men," he wrote, "to guard Jews and criminals, the idealism and readiness for unrestricted performance of duty will not be furthered in the *Waffen-SS*."[154] Nevertheless, for want of German manpower, the Dutchmen continued to be exposed to this strain upon their idealism.[155]

Relentlessly the Rauter machinery drew its victims into the transit camps and death. The exempt categories dissolved in this process. Converted Jews were among the first to be seized.[156] The Jews in mixed marriages, too, were unable to retain their immunity. There are no figures of deported Jewish partners of intermarriages, but we can form a picture of the situation by subtracting the number of survivors from the original estimate of more than 20,000 – by February, 1944, only 8610 intermarried Jews were still living in their homes. These Jews were accorded complete exemption from anti-Jewish measures, to the point of permission to dispose of the star, if they could prove their sterility. A total of 2256 Jews had submitted such proof; hundreds of them had acquired it by subjecting themselves to an operation.[157]

The armament Jews followed in the path of "indispensable" Jews everywhere. In November, 1942, the armament industry lost hundreds of its fur and textile workers;[158] on December 3, 1942, Himmler ordered that the diamond cutters be brought to Vught to work under the supervision of the SS. The new enterprise was appropriately placed under the direction of the WVHA-WI (the Earth and Stone Works). The diamond workers were deported en masse in March, 1944, and while the Dutch diamond industry in Amsterdam closed under the eyes of the Germans on May 18, 1944, there was some talk in the WVHA of saving

152. Deportations from Holland totaled 38,571 by December 31, 1942. The figure rose to 52,403 by March 31, 1943. Report by Korherr, April 19, 1943, NO-5193.

153. Rauter to Himmler, September 10, 1942, NO-2256.

154. Jüttner to Himmler, May 27, 1943, NO-8024.

155. From January, 1943, the WVHA listed "Herzogenbusch" on its camp roster. See directive by Liebehenschel (WVHA-D), January 22, 1943, NO-1526. Westerbork, near Assen, remained under Rauter's jurisdiction. The commander of Herzogenbusch was Stubaf. Hüttig. The Westerbork commander was OStuf. Gemecke.

156. Bene to Foreign Office, November 16, 1942, NG-2631.

157. Bene to Foreign Office, February 9, 1944, NG-2631. Seyss-Inquart testified after the war that these Jews would not have been deported in any case. The Christian churches had protested against the sterilizations, but in Seyss-Inquart's view "no compulsion" had been exerted upon the victims. Testimony by Seyss-Inquart, *Trial of the Major War Criminals*, XVI, 45. It appears that sterility of the Christian partner was not an acceptable ground for releasing restrictions. It was the Jewish partner who had to be sterile.

158. Report by Armament Inspectorate Niederlande for November, 1942, Wi/IA 5.1.

150 or 200 Jewish specialists for a diamond workshop in Bergen-Belsen.[159] Some of these specialists survived to the end.[160]

We have seen that in Poland Jewish laborers often lost their families before the end of their own deferment, and the same appears to have been true in Holland. During the late spring of 1943 the Germans decided to ship out of the Vught camp two transports consisting of the children and wives of working men. According to the proclamation issued by the Jewish camp directorate – the *Kampleiding* – on June 5, 1943, children from the age of less than one to sixteen were to be accompanied by their mothers to a "special children's camp."[161] That "special children's camp" was Sobibor, a pure killing center in which all but a handful of people were gassed upon arrival.

The spring and summer months of 1943 were the period of the last large-scale roundups in Holland. From March to May the Germans attempted to clear the small towns and countryside. The Foreign Office representative, Bene, observing the progress of the operation, noted that 1302 Jews had reported voluntarily at Vught. "With the aid of the Jewish Council," wrote Bene, "the deportations from the provinces proceeded without a hitch."[162] On June 20, 1943, Jewish camp police from Westerbork were detailed to help Security and Order Police forces in a round up of 5550 Jews in South Amsterdam. The hour had now arrived for some of the Jewish collaborators. Members of the *Joodsche Raad* were among the deportees. Bene reported that at the sight of this deportation many Jews, including particularly refugees from the Reich, "did not conceal their heartfelt joy."[163]

As the deportation machinery broke up the last major concentrations of Jews, the drive against Jews in hiding was intensified. Large numbers had sought refuge in concealment, but the number of those who were caught was also considerable. We can form an idea of the odds faced by these people when we examine the statistics of Jews reported in hiding at specified periods during the occupation.[164]

September 11, 1942:	25,000
March 20, 1943:	10,000–15,000
June 25, 1943:	20,000
February 11, 1944:	11,000
At time of liberation:	7,000

Nevertheless, the concealed Jews were better off than the victims who had surrendered voluntarily or who had been seized in the great police roundups. Not only did the hidden Jews have a better chance to escape deportation altogether, but they could increase their chances for survival by deferring their arrest. These chances had arisen because in its last stages the deportation program included also some "favored" transports.

On August 19, 1943, BdS Brigadeführer Harster requested Seyss-Inquart's permission to "resettle" to Theresienstadt three classes of Jews:

159. WVHA-WI (OStubaf. Mummenthey) to WVHA-W (Obf. Baier), June 8, 1944, NO-1278.

160. Report by Dutch government, October 16, 1945, PS-1726.

161. Proclamation by *De Kampleiding* of Vught, June 5, 1943, *Nederland in Oorlogstijd*, January 25, 1947, p. 87. The order provided that in the case of non-working fathers, both parents could go along.

162. Bene to Foreign Office, May 3, 1943, NG-2631.

163. Bene to Foreign Office, June 25, 1943, NG-2631. The two co-chairmen of the council, Ascher and Cohen, survived. Fritz Rothgiesser, "Befehl ist Befehl," *Aufbau* (New York), August 5, 1949, pp. 1–2.

164. Reports by Bene to Foreign Office, bearing dates cited above, NG-2631. Report by Dutch government, October 16, 1945, PS-1726. A large percentage of the Jews who had survived in hiding were children. They were to pose a special problem after the war. See Israel Cohen, *Contemporary Jewry* (London, 1950), pp. 263–64.

those with First World War decorations, those who had performed services for Germany in peacetime, and those who already had relatives in the Protektorat ghetto.[165] In all, 4897 Jews were brought to Theresienstadt from Holland in 1943 and 1944.[166] Early in 1944 another thousand Jews were scheduled to be transported to the newly established concentration camp of Bergen-Belsen in anticipation of their possible exchange for Germans from British-controlled areas.[167] In the course of that year, as the railways under bombing found it more and more difficult to transport the Jews across Germany to far-distant Auschwitz and as the labor shortage in the industries of the Reich grew ever more desperate, the final deportation trains unloaded their passengers in Bergen-Belsen and other concentration camps. When the operation was over, some 115,000 Jews had been deported from Holland and fewer than 20,000 were left.[168]

165. Bgf. Harster to Seyss-Inquart, August 19, 1943, *Nederland in Oorlogstijd*, January 25, 1947, p. 88.

166. Lederer, *Ghetto Theresienstadt*, p. 249. Actually, most of these Jews did *not* survive. About half were shipped from Theresienstadt to Auschwitz during the *Aktion* of September-October, 1944.

167. Bene to Foreign Office, February 9, 1944, NG-2631.

168. Bene to Foreign Office, February 9, 1944, NG-2631. Dutch government report, October 16, 1945, PS-1726. Gerald Reitlinger, *The Final Solution* (New York, 1953), pp. 337–41. About 100,000 deportees were sent to the killing centers at Auschwitz and Sobibor, and 15,000 more to Theresienstadt, Bergen-Belsen, and various concentration camps in the Reich. Other reductions of the Jewish population in Holland took place through emigration and flight (4000), aggravated deaths and suicides (2000), and an excess of normal deaths over births (perhaps another 2000). The remaining group comprised chiefly the Jews in mixed marriages (8000) and Jews in hiding (7000). There were also some special cases, including a few hundred Portuguese Jews, persons pursuing legal remedies to determine their non-Jewish descent, etc.

Even while the SS and Police were sluicing their victims through Westerbork and Vught, the civilian machinery closed in behind the deportees to confiscate their property. The abandoned Jewish belongings comprised mainly papers and valuables in banks and apartment furnishings in homes. Two agencies were employed in Holland for the purpose of seizing these assets: Lippmann-Rosenthal and the Einsatzstab Rosenberg.

We have already noted that the liquidated Jewish bank Lippmann-Rosenthal had been designated as the official depository of Jewish papers and valuables. The Lippmann - Rosenthal machinery was now set into motion to digest the loot. Some of the Jewish investments were turned into cash: securities were sold, claims were called in, and insurance policies were redeemed as soon as possible. Special regulations applied to the disposal of valuables. In the case of jewelry the most valuable items were delivered to Göring (attention: Oberstleutnant Veltjens); other valuable jewelry was offered to the highest bidders in the Reich. Cheap jewelry was to be handed over to Oberregierungsrat Dr. Heinemann for Göring's Christmas *Aktion.* Jewelry with metal value only was to be melted down.

Similar directives were issued with respect to art objects. The most valuable items were to be offered to Staatssekretäre Mühlmann and Posse; second priority was to be given to the *Reichsführer-SS*, Himmler; moderately valuable art objects were to be sold to the German art trade; cheap paintings were to be made available for the Christmas *Aktion;* and "degenerate art" was to be sold, with the consent of the Economy Ministry, in Switzerland. Pictures of Jews and pictures by Jews posed a special problem whose solution appears to have been deferred.

Stamp collections were to be delivered to the Reichspost, and coins were to go to the Reichsbank.[169] Jewish cash deposits and the proceeds from all sales were transferred to a special agency of the *Reichskommissar,* the *Vermögens- und Rentenanstalt.*[170] According to postwar testimony by Seyss-Inquart, the amounts accumulating in the *Vermögensanstalt* ultimately reached 400,000,000 guilders.[171]

The second part of the confiscatory operation — the seizure of furniture in empty apartments — was carried out by the East Minister and party ideological chief Alfred Rosenberg. We may recall that Rosenberg performed a somewhat similar function in the Reich, where he laid claim to Jewish furniture in order to equip his offices in Russia and sold the surplus to the *Gauleitungen* for bombed-out people at home. In the West, Rosenberg invoked his position as *Reichsleiter* for ideology to get his hands on all "ownerless" Jewish cultural property (*Kulturgut*), a jurisdiction which was soon expanded to embrace furniture in France, Belgium, and Holland.

The seizures in the occupied areas were entrusted to a special agency, the Einsatzstab Rosenberg. We have no statistics of the Einsatzstab's operations in Holland;[172] all we know is that the great bulk of the furniture was made available to bombed-out persons in the Reich on a "permanent loan" basis.[173] Many of the empty Jewish homes, incidentally, were ripped apart and carried off piece by piece by a starving Dutch population during the winter of 1944/45.[174]

While the Einsatzstab Rosenberg carted away Jewish furnishings, it did not neglect its original "cultural" mission to collect, among other things, private libraries for the "Hohe Schule," the Party's ideological university. The Einsatzstab seized libraries from rabbinical seminaries and also such choice items as the library of the Spinoza Society, which contained "extremely valuable works of great importance for the exploration of the Spinoza problem," and the Rosenthaliana, a collection which had been donated to the City of Amsterdam and which was examined carefully for the light it could shed on Cromwell's attitude toward the Jews and "possibly even on the Jewish influence on the development of the secret service."[175]

The confiscations of Jewish property in Holland were as thorough as the killings of its owners. In no occupied territory of the great semicircle from Norway to Roumania did the Germans manage, in one form or another, to collect so much Jewish wealth. That phenomenon is explained, of course, by the fact that in most of the areas under Axis domination the Germans had to make property concessions to indige-

169. *Generalkommissar* for Finance and Economy/Personal *Referent* (signed Dr. Holz) to Lippmann-Rosenthal & Co., att. Dr. von Karger, October 16, 1942, enclosing Seyss-Inquart directive of same date, NI-13772.

170. Affidavit by von Karger, September 24, 1947, NI-13904.

171. Seyss-Inquart deducted from that account the sum of 14,000,000 guilders to cover the cost of constructing the Vught camp. Testimony by Seyss-Inquart, *Trial of the Major War Criminals,* XVI, 65-66. According to the official exchange rate, 400,000,000 guilders = RM 530,800,000 = $212,320,000.

172. See draft report by Dienststelle Westen of the Einsatzstab on furniture *Aktion,* end of 1944 or beginning of 1945, L-188. Also, memorandum by Dellschow (Handelstrust West), July 31, 1943, NI-14822.

173. Rosenberg to Hitler, October 3, 1942, PS-41. Lippmann-Rosenthal, which claimed the proceeds from the sale of the furniture, never received any payments. Affidavit by von Karger, September 24, 1947, NI-13904.

174. Reitlinger, *The Final Solution,* pp. 341–42.

175. Hohe Schule report, undated, PS-171. Report by Working Group Netherlands of Einsatzstab Rosenberg, undated, PS-176. Rosenberg had authority to seize all libraries and archives in Holland. Keitel to von Brauchitsch and Befehlshaber Netherlands, July 9, 1940, PS-137.

nous authorities for the purpose of obtaining all possible co-operation in the deportations. In Holland such concessions were not necessary. Every three out of four Jews who inhabited the Netherlands at the beginning of the occupation were dead at its end.

We have already seen that to begin with, the geographic situation of Holland and the nature of the German administration which had been installed there were odds that favored the destructive work. Extraordinary efforts on the part of the Jews and Dutch would have been required to change these odds. We know that the Jews were incapable of concerted counteraction.

Jewish survival efforts in Holland were essentially a product of individual initiative for private benefit. The pattern was set with the individual deals for emigration conducted by well-to-do Jews at the beginning of the occupation. That method was continued with appeals for exemption or deferment on grounds ranging from indispensability to sterility. As a last resort, a desperate Jewish family could hope to save itself only by hiding. Those who could not help themselves were seized by Rauter's police or delivered to the Germans by the *Joodsche Raad.* This was a pattern which in its very nature spelled doom for the vast majority.

What about the Dutch? What kind of factor was the Dutch population in the destructive arena? When the Germans attacked Holland in May, 1940, the Dutch reacted by fighting openly for a few days, to settle back for five years to a mixture of bureaucratic collaboration and underground sabotage. Much the same thing happened on a somewhat smaller scale in relation to the Jews. We may recall that once, on the occasion of the Mauthausen deportation in February, 1941, the Dutch had signified their feelings toward their Jewish neighbors with an unmistakable general strike; but when the strikers were overwhelmed, there were no further demonstrations. There was, in fact, a great deal of administrative co-operation, from the participation of Dutch banks in the disposal of securities to the registration work by the Dutch civil service and the police role of the Dutch SS. Considerable as this collaboration may have been, it was matched at least in part by the attempt to sabotage the destructive process through massive concealments of thousands of Jews in cloisters, orphanages, and homes. Few Jews survived in Holland, but those few were saved as a result of the most strenuous efforts, for Holland was the one territory of the occupied West in which the Jews did not have an even chance to live.

LUXEMBOURG. – Wedged in between the Reich, Belgium, and France, there lay a small country which was quickly overrun in the lightning campaign of 1940 – Luxembourg. The duchy became a quasi-incorporated territory under the jurisdiction of Gauleiter Gustav Simon of the neighboring *Gau* of Koblenz-Trier.[176] Simon had the title of *Chef der Zivilverwaltung* ("Chief of Civil Administration") in the new territory. There was thus no automatic application of Reich statutes in Luxembourg, but Simon lost little time in catching up with the mother country.

The prewar Jewish population of Luxembourg had been approximately 3000,[177] but most of the Luxembourg Jews fled to Belgium and France during the initial period of invasion and occupation. Gauleiter Simon moved against the remaining ones with swiftness and dispatch. Drafts of ordinances with definitions, expropriatory provisions, and concentration measures were

176. Order by Hitler, August 2, 1940, NOKW-3474.

177. American Joint Distribution Committee, *Report for 1939*, p. 30.

submitted to Hitler for his approval within a matter of weeks.[178] The economic part of that program was carried out expeditiously. We have a rather candid account of it in the German publication *Die Judenfrage.*

On September 5, 1940, barely one month after he took office, Simon issued his decree for the expropriation of Jewish property. The administration of that ordinance was entrusted to Gauinspektor Ackermann, "who had previously carried out with great success the Aryanizations in the *Gau* Moselland [Koblenz-Trier] and who brought to his new task a large measure of experience." The Jewish population was now counted, and its property was catalogued.

The expropriators discovered that there were 335 Jewish enterprises in Luxembourg; only 75 of them were judged worthy of Aryanization. Trustees appointed for the management of these firms were drawn exclusively from the ranks of "Luxembourg ethnic Germans." The liquidated enterprises were in "overcrowded" branches and were therefore struck off the list with the approval of the director of the local Chamber of Industry and Commerce.

In Luxembourg the Jews also owned 380 farms. These properties were immediately leased to new managers. Another 394 acres of uncultivated Jewish land was going to be offered to neighboring "Luxembourg ethnic German" peasants for sale.

The furniture which had been left behind by the fugitive Jews was placed at the disposal of the administration, including the *Zivilverwaltung,* the *Reichsbahn,* the Reichspost, the Hitler Youth, and other agencies. A small portion of the furniture was sold to "local Germans."[179]

Within a year (by summer of 1941) Gauleiter Simon was ahead of the Reich in the implementation of his anti-Jewish measures. He had instituted a number of prohibitions affecting freedom of movement, and his Jews were forced to wear yellow armbands on their left sleeves.[180] Some hundreds of Jews were assigned to forced labor projects within and near Luxembourg, and a special transit camp, the SS-Sonderlager Hinzert, was readied for its victims.[181]

In the fall of 1941 Simon contributed a contingent of more than 500 Jews to the first eastern transports. We know where these Jews went. They were brought to the Lodz ghetto, from where they were sent on to the killing center of Chelmno.[182] Simon still had on his hands a few hundred old and sickly Jews. There is reason to believe that he planned to send them to Berndorf-Sayn, central collecting point for the Jewish institutionalized insane, who were moved out from there to Poland to be killed.[183]

BELGIUM. — As we turn from civilian-controlled Holland and Luxembourg

178. Frick to Lammers, August 31, 1940, NG-2297. Reich Chancellery memorandum, September 6, 1940, NG-2297.

179. "Verwaltung und Verwendung des Judenvermögens in Luxemburg," *Die Judenfrage,* May 31, 1941, p. 97.

180. *Die Judenfrage,* September 10, 1941, p. 167. In respect of marking, Simon anticipated every jurisdiction in the deportation area, save only Poland.

181. Hinzert was under the direct jurisdiction of the Inspectorate for Concentration Camps (later the WVHA). Inspectorate distribution list, October 13, 1941, NO-1536. The Hinzert Commander was OStuf. Sporrenberg. Pohl via SS-Personnel Main Office to Himmler, July 28, 1942, NO-1994.

182. Lodz Ghetto Collection, No. 58, pp. 11, 19.

183. As late as September, 1942, however, a barracks camp for Jews was under construction in the town of Ulflingen. War diary, Rü Kdo Metz/*Aussenstelle* Luxemburg (signed Major Knorth), August 31 and September 9, 1942, Wi/IA 6.3. Not stated is the geographic origin of the Jews for whom the camp was intended.

to the military areas of Belgium and France, we come into contact with a different kind of German administration. The military governments differed from their civilian neighbors both in purpose and in character. The Netherlands and Luxembourg were "Germanic" areas; they were therefore made into a "protectorate" *(Schutzstaat)* and a quasi-incorporated territory, respectively.[184] That status was intended to be final. Belgium and France, on the other hand, were "Romanic" regions. Apart from the annexed provinces (Malmédy-Eupen in Belgium, Alsace-Lorraine in France), these countries were not destined to become administrative units in a Greater German Reich. They were to be placed in a separate, though subordinate, position by a victorious Germany at the end of the war. The occupation of Belgium and France was therefore meant to be temporary. The entire German administrative apparatus in these states was provisional in its aim, and the officers in charge of that apparatus were emergency wartime overlords.

In the light of the over-all purpose of that occupation, the German generals in Belgium and France were prone to regard their mission as one which comprised mainly the furtherance of military security and economic exploitation. To these generals the destruction of the Jews was bound to present itself as a secondary task. There is even some evidence that during the planning stage preceding the commencement of the western campaign the military had hoped to avoid an entanglement in Jewish matters altogether. Thus a directive by the *Oberquartiermeister* of the Sixth Army, dated February 22, 1940, stated significantly:

> An unrolling [*ein Aufrollen*] of the *racial question* is to be avoided because annexation intentions could be inferred therefrom. The sole circumstance that an inhabitant is a Jew must not serve as the basis for special measures directed against him.[185]

The generals in the West were not eager to proceed against the Jewish minority because they already had their hands full with the "ordinary" functions of a military government. However, they do not appear to have been motivated by any humanitarian consideration; their reluctant reception of a special assignment which intruded upon the basic tasks of occupation is not to be confused with a desire to preserve the Jewish community from utter destruction. The German Army was not the protector of the Jews, and it was capable, under pressure, of solving its secondary problems also.

In Belgium the Jewish population on the eve of the German invasion was roughly 90,000 strong. The peacetime distribution of that population was such that almost all the Jews were living in four major Belgian cities (about 50,000 in Antwerp, 30,000 in Brussels, a few thousand each in Liége and Charleroi).[186] The great majority of the Jews in Belgium were immigrants and newcomers who did not possess Belgian nationality. About 30,000 were refugees from the Reich.[187]

As German forces began to cross the border, mass flights into France reduced the prewar figures to fractions. One Jew in every three sought sanctuary in the South. The newly created German military government looked for

184. Stuckart, *Neues Staatsrecht,* II, 121, 84.

185. Directive by 6th Army/OQu/Qu 2 (signed by Oberquartiermeister Pamberg) for "Administration and Pacification of the Occupied Areas of Holland and Belgium," February 22, 1940, NOKW-1515.

186. Postwar report by Belgian government, UK-76. U.S. Army Service Manual M 361-2A, *Civil Affairs Handbook Belgium* (prepared by Office of Strategic Services), May 16, 1944, p. 37.

187. American Joint Distribution Committee, *Report for 1939,* p. 30.

a way to lighten its burdens still more, and before long the generals shoved another 8000 Jews (mainly refugees from the Reich) into neighboring France.[188] Toward the end of 1940 only about 52,000 Jews were still in the country, and fewer than 10 per cent were citizens of the Belgian state.[189] The German administration in Brussels could now begin.

The chief personalities on the Belgian scene were the Military Commander, von Falkenhausen; the Chief of his Administrative Staff, Reeder; the Higher SS and Police Leader, Jungclaus; the Foreign Office representative, von Bargen; and a number of German businessmen.[190] Within five months from the start of the occupation the work of these men was reflected in the first anti-Jewish measures in Belgium. In October, 1940, the *Militärbefehlshaber* issued two decrees which ran the whole gamut of the preliminary steps of the destruction process. The concept of "Jew" was defined; Jewish lawyers and civil servants were ousted from their positions; Jewish enterprises and stocks were subjected to registration; and all transactions were made subject to official approval. Finally, the Jewish population was also ordered to register for future surveillance.

Unlike the Dutch Jews, the Jews of Belgium did not have much wealth. A report of the *Militärbefehlshaber* for October, 1940, mentions that "the influence of Jewry upon economic life in Belgium has been rather slight. Apart from the diamond industry in the Antwerp area, Jewish participation in the Belgian economy is hardly worth mentioning."[191] Notwithstanding the trifling amounts of prospective loot, the German business sector evidenced considerable interest in the Belgian Aryanization market. In pursuance of an order by the *Militärbefehlshaber,* three German commercial banks were established in Belgium: the Continentalbank, the Hansabank, and the Westbank.[192] They had hardly been organized for business when a number of customers appeared on their lists as parties interested in "useful hints": the Schultheiss Brauerei, Krupp, Siemens, the Allgemeine Elektrizitätsgesellschaft (AEG), Brown Boverie, and Deutsche Asbest Zement A. G.[193]

The over-all campaign of capital penetration in Holland and Belgium was subject, in fundamental policy questions, to the approval of the Foreign Trade Division of the Economy

188. Interior Ministry (signed Jacobi) to Foreign Office (att. St.S. Weizsäcker), November 19, 1940, enclosing report by military commander in Belgium and Northern France for October, 1940, NG-2380.

189. The total of 52,000 is based on a registration figure of 42,000, to which the Germans added 10,000 to account for unregistered children. Von Bargen (representative of the Foreign Office in Brussels) to Foreign Office, November 11, 1942, NG-5219; *Donauzeitung* (Belgrade), August 9, 1942, p. 2. Two northern French *départements* were attached to the *Militärbefehlshaber* in Brussels. The Jewish inhabitants of these *départements* had been evacuated or had fled before the Germans arrived.

190. The office of the *Militärbefehlshaber* was divided into two staffs, a *Verwaltungsstab* headed by Reeder and a *Kommandostab* which was concerned with purely military matters. Regionally, the military administration branched out into *Feld-* and *Ortskommandanturen.* For details, see *Civil Affairs Handbook Belgium,* pp. 15–19.

191. Report by *Militärbefehlshaber* for October, 1940, NG-2380.

192. Continentale Bank/*Abwicklungsstelle* Reich to *Devisenstelle Frankfurt,* January 31, 1945, NI-10229. Statement by Paul-Georges Janmart (Belgian employee of the Continentalbank), March 22, 1947, NI-13940. The Continentalbank was a Dresdner Bank subsidiary.

193. Fritz Andre (Dresdner Bank) to Direktor Overbeck (future manager of the Continentale Bank in Brussels), August 15, 1940, NI-13827. For a typical operation of the Continentale Bank, see Overbeck to Georg Stiller (Sekretariat Dr. Rasche of the Dresdner Bank), July 21, 1941, enclosing report on attempt to acquire Grands Moulins de Bruxelles and other firms, NI-13831.

Ministry.[194] In September, 1941, after about a year of Aryanization in Belgium, the army made an unsuccessful attempt to secure a part of the Jewish business for its soldiers. Upon the occasion of a capital penetration conference in the Economy Ministry, the representative of the *Militärbefehlshaber* in Belgium, Kriegsverwaltungsrat Dr. Pichier, suggested that 300 un-Aryanized wholesale and retail enterprises in his territory, with a yield of about 10,000 reichsmark a year, be reserved for German war veterans. Dr. Pichier's proposal was rejected decisively. It was pointed out that the war was still in progress, that trustee administration would have to be instituted until the veterans came back, and that such business enterprises – in which personal contacts between proprietors and customers were so important – were not suitable for trustee administration. It was therefore advisable, concluded the conferees, that these Aryanizations be conducted by German businessmen who were well provided with capital and who could withstand a Belgian boycott.[195] There is no evidence that Kriegsverwaltungsrat Pichier made any further attempt to benefit the soldiers in the Aryanization campaign.

By the end of 1942, the Aryanizations in Belgium were largely completed. Table 56, which was prepared in the *Militärbefehlshaber's* office, indicates how many enterprises in each branch were "de-Jewed" *(entjudet* i.e., transferred), liquidated, or "floating" *(in Schwebe* i.e., awaiting disposition) on December 31, 1942.[196] The value of sequestered Jewish assets *(überwachtes Judenvermögen)* in reichsmark is indicated in Table 57.[197]

TABLE 56 / *Belgian Aryanizations and Liquidations*

	TOTAL	PERCENTAGE	TRANSFERRED	LIQUIDATED	AWAITING DISPOSITION
Textile trade	1,220	15.8	22	1,161	37
Clothing industry	965	12.5	50	876	39
Commercial agents	685	8.9	23	599	63
Diamond industry	675	8.7	13	647	15
Leather industry	520	6.7	8	494	18
Diamond trade	500	6.5	14	469	17
Leather trade	453	5.9	20	399	34
Food products trade	383	4.9	12	361	10
Metal industry	163	2.1	56	87	20
Metal products trade	156	2.0	26	111	19
Chemicals	142	1.8	65	39	38
Nursing	137	1.8	5	124	8
Real estate	122	1.6	9	0	113
Miscellaneous	1,608	20.8	265	1,021	322
Total	7,729	100.0	588	6,388	753

194. Directive by the Economy Ministry, May 28, 1940, NG-55. The Foreign Trade Division was under Unterstaatssekretär von Jagwitz. The Western countries were detailed to Ministerialdirigent Dr. Schlotterer. The *Referat* "capital-interlacing" in Schlotterer's section was headed by Dr. Gerhard Saager. Affidavit by Saager, December 16, 1947, NI-13775.

195. Summary of Economy Ministry conference under chairmanship of Ministerialrat Schultze-Schlutius (deputizing for USt.S. von Jagwitz), September 23, 1941, NI-10699.

196. Report by *Militärbefehlshaber* on economic exploitation, April 1, 1943, Wi/IA 4.60. At the same time, the status of 652 Jewish enterprises in the two northern French *départements* was as follows: transferred, 33; liquidated, 207; awaiting disposition, 412. *Ibid.*

197. Economic report by *Militärbefehlshaber,* April 1, 1943, Wi/IA 4.60.

We should hasten to add that the banks were slow in reporting Jewish accounts; therefore the amount of cash in the banks — swelled by the proceeds from the sale of nearly six hundred enterprises — was much greater than the six million reichsmark indicated in the *Militärbefehlshaber's* report. Nevertheless, the total deposit ultimately accumulated in Belgium must have fallen far short of the half-billion figure which was surpassed in Holland. The Belgian Jews had comparatively little cash to begin with; the six hundred or so Aryanizations probably did not bring in vast sums; and the sale of securities and real estate posed very special difficulties to the German military administration.

During a conference in the Finance Ministry in December, 1942, Kriegsverwaltungsrat Pichier revealed some of the administration's efforts to get rid of real estate, diamonds, and other items. The Belgian public, he said, had exhibited an "aversion" *(Abneigung)* to the acquisition of Jewish real property from the *Militärbefehlshaber*. For that reason many real estate parcels had been exempted from confiscation. Their sale was accomplished by a state institution, the Brussels Trusteeship Corporation, which appeared in such cases as trustee for the Jewish owner. The proceeds were then confiscated. So far, however, the *Militärbefehlshaber* had not solved still another difficulty in the disposal of real estate: prices had been frozen, and the official price ceilings were only 40 per cent of current value. To alleviate that price retardation, the Trusteeship Corporation hoped to increase the mortgages on the Jewish houses to the greatest possible extent. Creditors were available in sufficiently large numbers, and the borrowed money could be confiscated at once.

Another item calling for caution in disposal was the stock of diamonds from liquidated shops in the Antwerp area. A small amount, reported Dr. Pichier, had been sold for foreign currency in southern France. Not much progress had been made as yet with the disposal of furniture. The Trusteeship Corporation was moving into the Jewish apartments as soon as they became empty. Nevertheless, some of the furniture had to be sold to pay back rent, and some of it was wanted by the Wehrmacht finance officer for the troops. Valuable furnishings would be sold in the Reich. Art objects were being handed over to Red Cross Oberfeldführer von Behr, Director of the Einsatzstab Rosenberg in Paris. Gold and jewelry was melted down.

During the opening of safes, the military administration also had found securities in considerable quantity. An attempt was being made, reported Dr. Pichier, to collect large parcels of shares in order to secure "already the later influence of the Reich."[198] However, the

TABLE 57 / *Value of Sequestered Jewish Assets*

	END OF 1941	END OF 1942
Cash in banks	none	6,150,000
Securities and papers	80,000,000	70,650,000
Real estate parcels (2814)	36,000,000	50,000,000
Total	116,000,000	126,800,000

198. Summary of Finance Ministry conference with participation of MinRat Dr. Mädel and several *Kriegsverwaltungsräte* from the west, December 11/12, 1942, NG-5369. The Finance Ministry was the ultimate booking agency for assets confiscated in favor of the Reich. Not mentioned in this conference was, among other things, an item of 1000 women's furs which had been "made available" from liquidated Jewish firms for the OKW. War

disposal of the unneeded securities in the Belgian market was to run headlong into a major obstacle. The president of the Brussels Stock Exchange, van Dessel, refused to accept the papers in the absence of the Jewish owners. Under the direction of the *Devisenschutzkommando West,* the agency in charge of securities and other papers in Belgium, France, and Holland, the shares were then stamped "property of the German Reich," to be sold on the exchange or auctioned off to the highest bidder by the three German banks in the country.[199] That was how the Germans attempted to loot what they could in Belgium.

When the *Militärbefehlshaber* in October, 1940, laid the foundations for the economic destruction process, he instituted at the same time the first concentration measure: the registration of the Jews. Within the following year attempts were made to establish a Jewish council, but it seems that at the beginning of the invasion all the Jewish leaders except two prominent rabbis had left the country. One of these rabbis (Dr. Salomon Ullmann, who was head of Jewish chaplains in the Belgian Army) was chosen by the Jews, after consultation with Belgian secretaries general and Cardinal van Roey, as *Grand Rabbi de Belgique.* He was to head a committee which was transformed on November 25, 1941, into the *Association des Juifs en Belgique,* the Belgian *Judenrat.* All Jews were subjected to direction from this organization, and local committees were created in Brussels, Antwerp, Liége, and Charleroi.[200]

In October, 1941, the *Militärbefehlshaber* also instituted a curfew and ordered the restriction of all Jewish residences to the same four cities. As usual, the reason assigned for these measures was the allegation that Jews "still dared to engage in black market activities."[201]

In May, 1942, the Jews were marked with a star, and thousands of men between the ages of 16 and 60, as well as women from 16 to 40, were rounded up for forced labor in projects of the *Organisation Todt* at Audinghem and other areas.[202] During the following month Belgium received her quota for the first deportations: a modest 10,000.[203] A transit camp was thereupon set up for the prospective deportees at Malines.[204]

On February 9, 1942, Foreign Office representative von Bargen reported that Militärverwaltungschef Reeder was conferring with Himmler about the proposed deportations. There were, said von Bargen, a number of difficulties in the path of the German administration. The Belgians had no "understanding" *(Verständnis)* of the Jewish question; the Jews themselves were exhibiting "unrest" *(Unruhe);* and the Germans were suffering from a shortage of police forces. The seizures were therefore going to be directed first against the Polish, Czech, Russian, and "other" *(sonstige)* Jews.[205]

diary, *Rü In Belgien,* May 19, 1942, Wi/IA 4.69.

199. Memorandum by Count Philip Orssich (Continentale Bank), undated, probably 1944, NI-5776. For statistics of transactions involving also securities transmitted to Belgium by Lippmann-Rosenthal in Holland and Bank der Deutschen Arbeit in Luxembourg, see Chief Inspector of Registry Office, Brussels (signed Hopchet) to Commissar with Audit General, Brussels (Jans), March 22, 1947, NI-7358.

200. *Civil Affairs Handbook Belgium,* pp. 38–39.

201. *Die Judenfrage,* October 15, 1941, p. 208.

202. Final report by the *Militärbefehlshaber* on wage policy and labor utilization, undated, after September, 1944, pp. 78–79, 254–55, Wi/IA .24. *Civil Affairs Handbook Belgium,* p. 40.

203. Eichmann to Rademacher, June 22, 1942, NG-183.

204. Report by Belgian government, undated, UK-76.

By the middle of September the initial quota had been filled; already, however, von Bargen had observed large-scale evasions. The Jews were hiding out with Belgian families. Many prospective victims had Belgian identification cards, and still others were fleeing to occupied and unoccupied France.[206]

On the day on which this pessimistic report was sent to Berlin, an SS deportation expert, Obersturmführer Asche, called the members of the Jewish Association into his office and informed them that in punishment for their passive resistance all the Jews would be evacuated from Belgium. Rabbi Ullmann and four of his associates were then sent for a few days to the concentration camp of Breendonck, presumably so that they might think about the possible consequences of their intransigence.[207]

On November 11, 1942, von Bargen reported that the deportation figure had now reached 15,000 men, women, and children, among them a few Belgian citizens who had dared to remove the Jewish star from their clothes. Von Bargen went on to describe the increasing difficulties faced by the machinery of destruction in the roundups. In the beginning, he said, prospective deportees had been served with a "report-for-work order" *(Arbeitseinsatzbefehl)* via the Jewish Association. After a while, however, the intended victims had been dissuaded from obeying the order by rumors about the "butchering of the Jews, etc." *(Abschlachten der Juden, usw.)*. The last transports therefore had to be filled by means of *razzias* and *Einzelaktionen*.[208]

Shortly after this report was received in Berlin, Unterstaatssekretär Luther of the Foreign Office requested von Bargen to ask the Militärbefehlshaber to deport the Jews of Belgian nationality too. Only complete deportation, said Luther, could put an end to the "unrest"; the Jews could in any case no longer be surprised, and "sooner or later" everything had to happen anyway.[209]

The military administration appears to have tried its best. As the operations moved into 1943, a transport of 1500 to 1600 Jews was filled every two or three months.[210] The decreasing flow of deportees is traceable, of course, to the renewal of flights into France, the concealment of many thousands in Belgian homes and institutions, and the existence of a privileged class, which included the Jews of certain foreign and doubtful nationalities and the intermarried Jews. So far as the Jews in intermarriage were concerned, we may observe again the precarious nature of their immunity. There is a report, dated May 27, 1944, about one of these intermarried Jews, a refugee who was a wounded war veteran and who held the Iron Cross Second Class. "The idea," said the report, "of submitting to a voluntary sterilization is not repugnant to S."[211]

Belgium was overrun by the Allies in September, 1944. Up to then, the German agencies in Belgium had man-

205. Von Bargen to Foreign Office, July 9, 1942, NG-5209. The armament inspector, Generalmajor Franssen, reported at this time a "strong rush" of Jewish workers into industry. *Rü In Belgien* to OKW/Wi Rü, August 1, 1942, Wi/IA 4.64.

206. Von Bargen to Foreign Office, September 24, 1942, NG-5219. Flights reported also in *Donauzeitung* (Belgrade), August 9, 1942, p. 2.

207. *Civil Affairs Handbook Belgium*, p. 40. Rabbi Ullmann was replaced upon his release by Marcel Blum, *ibid.*

208. Von Bargen to Foreign Office, November 11, 1942, NG-5219.

209. Luther to von Bargen, December 4, 1942, NG-5219.

210. Report by Belgian government, undated, UK-76.

211. Office of Gruf. Jungclaus/SS-Führer in Race and Resettlement Matters (signed Stubaf. Aust) to RuSHA/Genealogical Records Office (Ahnentafelamt), May 27, 1944, NO-1494.

aged to deliver about 25,000 Jews to their fate.[212]

FRANCE. — In France the anti-Jewish destruction process was a product of the Franco-German armistice. To the French authorities which in Vichy picked up the strands of government in June, 1940, the defeat was decisive; the war was irrevocably lost. From 1940 to 1944, then, the unequal relationship between victor and vanquished manifested itself in a stream of German demands which could not easily be opposed. The destruction of the Jews in France was such a German demand.

In its reactions to German pressure the Vichy government tried to confine the destruction process to certain limits. These limits were set forth first of all with a view to arresting the destructive development as a whole. The French authorities sought to avoid drastic action. They recoiled from the idea of adopting measures which were unprecedented in history. When German pressure was intensified in 1942, the Vichy government fell back upon a second line of defense — the foreign Jews and immigrants were abandoned, and an effort was made to protect the native Jews. To no small extent that Vichy strategy met with success. By giving up a part, most of the whole was saved.

The Vichy regime's ability to bargain with the Germans over the fate of the Jews rested upon a simple fact: the Germans needed French help. In no territory that we have covered so far was German dependence upon native administration so great as in France. To the French bureaucracy fell the burden of performing a large part of the destructive work, and the roster of Frenchmen in controlling positions of the machinery of destruction is impressively long. Here is an abbreviated table of the Vichy machine:

Chief of State: Pétain
Vice-President (to April, 1942): Laval (Darlan)
Chief of Government (from April, 1942): Laval
  Commissar for Jewish Affairs (from June, 1942): Darquier de Pellepoix
Delegate for Occupied Zone: La Laurencie (de Brinon)
Foreign Affairs: Laval (Flandin, Darlan, Laval)
Interior: Peyrouton (Darlan, Pucheu)
  Commissar for Jewish Affairs (to June, 1942): Vallat
Justice: Alibert (Barthelémy)
Finance: Bouthillier (Cathala)
Industry: Pucheu (Bichelonne)
  Service du Controle: Fournier
Labor: Lagardelle (Bichelonne, Déat)
Armed Forces: Darlan
  War: Huntziger (Brideux)
Chief of Police: Bousquet
  Delegate for Occupied Zone: Leguay
  Paris Prefect and Chief of Camps: François
  Jewish Card Index, Paris: Tulard
  Anti-Jewish Police: Schweblin

Even a superficial examination of the prominent names on the list will indicate at once that the Vichy regime had a conservative base. Starting with Marshal Pétain, the government contained a number of military personalities, and it was on the whole strongly Catholic. In some respects it was perhaps more than a faint reflection of the anti-Dreyfus coalition of the previous century, and there were moments when the regime forgot itself and hit the Jews more strongly than German coercion could have compelled.[213]

As we look over our table a little more closely, we may observe in it also a few administrative innovations. The first of these was the institution of delegates. Each ministry at Vichy main-

212. Statistics of deportations from Malines camp in report by Belgian government, undated, UK-76. For partial totals, see also Korherr report, April 19, 1943, NO-5193.

213. For a general description of the Vichy regime, see Paul Farmer, *Vichy — Political Dilemma* (New York, 1955).

tained a special delegate in Paris through whom it controlled its regional machinery in occupied territory – thus the delegate of the French police in occupied France was Leguay. The delegates of all the ministries in Paris were subordinated to a general delegate. At first this was General La Laurencie; later, Ambassador de Brinon.

Another peculiarity of the Vichy regime was the installment of commissars for the handling of special problems, such as captive soldiers or French laborers in Germany. One of these commissars was in charge of Jewish affairs. The initial one, Xavier Vallat, was placed under the Interior Minister; his successor, Darquier de Pellepoix, served directly under the Chief of Government, Laval. We should note, incidentally, that several other officials were exclusively concerned with the Jews – for example, the chief of the Aryanization agency (the *Service du Controle),* Fournier; the chief of the Jewish card index in the Paris prefecture of police, Tulard; and the chief of the Anti-Jewish Police, Schweblin. Indeed, the French outdid the Germans in developing administrative specialization in matters of destruction.

As a consequence of the armistice, most of France was covered by a German occupation regime made up of the following territorial jurisdictions: (1) the provinces of Alsace-Lorraine, which were ruled as quasi-incorporated areas by Gauleiter Robert Wagner and Gauleiter Bürckel, respectively; (2) the *Oberfeldkommandantur* in Lille, under Generalleutnant Niehoff, which was subordinated to the *Militärbefehlshaber* in Belgium; and (3) the main occupation area under the *Militärbefehlshaber in Frankreich.* Below is an abbreviated picture of the *Militärbefehlshaber's* office:

Militärgouverneur in Paris: Gen. von Bockelberg (June-October, 1940)
Militärbefehlshaber: Gen. Otto von Stülpnagel (October, 1940- February, 1942), Gen. Heinrich von Stülpnagel (February, 1942-July, 1944)
ETRA (Railway Office): Glt. Kohl
Administrative Staff: Dr. Schmidt (Dr. Michel)
Administration: Dr. Best
Economy: Dr. Michel
Chief, Paris District: Staatsrat Turner (Glt. Schaumburg)
Stadtkommissar, Paris: Ministerialrat Rademacher

The office of the *Militärbefehlshaber* was a skeleton organization which made use of the French bureaucracy in occupied territory for the enforcement of German policy. The administrative center for the formulation of occupation directives was the administrative staff; the head of that office, Dr. Schmidt, was a former Württemberg Minister of the Interior and Economy. Below him we may note the presence of Ministerialdirigent Dr. Best, who had also handled administrative matters for Heydrich's prewar Security Main Office and who was to become still later the German plenipotentiary in Denmark. His colleague Ministerialdirektor Dr. Michel, who was entrusted with the direction of economic affairs in France, hailed from the Economy Ministry.

Regionally, the military government was made up of five *Militärverwaltungsbezirke* ("military administration districts"): A, B, C, Bordeaux, and Paris. The *Militärbezirkschef* of Paris was Staatsrat Turner; his successor, Generalleutnant von Schaumburg, had the title *Kommandant in Gross-Paris.* Below the level of the military district the regional network spread out into *Feldkommandanturen* and *Kreiskommandanturen;* the former controlled the French *départements,* the latter supervised the *arondissements.* In the big cities the Germans had also established *Stadtkommissare.* One is listed above: the *Stadtkommissar* of Paris, Ministerialrat Rademacher.[214]

Within a short time after the establishment of the *Militärbefehlshaber's* office in France, two other German agencies made their appearance in the occupied territory. These agencies were to outflank and crowd out the *Militärbefehlshaber* to no small extent.

In June, 1940, the name of Gesandter Abetz turned up in official army correspondence.[215] Abetz was the Foreign Office designate for its newly established post in Paris, and his appointment rested on an oral agreement between Keitel and Ribbentrop. In Keitel's words, Abetz was "attached to the staff of the military governor." However, when Keitel uttered this formulation to Weizsäcker, hoping perhaps to receive some confirmation of that interpretation of the agreement, the Foreign Office *Staatssekretär* remained silent. As Weizsäcker reported the conversation to Ribbentrop: "This topic I did not care to discuss [*Auf dieses Thema liess ich mich nicht ein*]."[216]

On August 3, Ribbentrop sent to Keitel a long list of powers which Abetz, newly elevated to the rank of ambassador, would henceforth exercise in France. In the concluding paragraph of that letter, Ribbentrop wrote: "The Führer has expressly ordered herewith that only Ambassador Abetz is responsible for the treatment of all political questions in occupied and unoccupied France. Insofar as his task should involve military interests, Ambassador Abetz will act only with the agreement of the *Militärbefehlshaber* in France."[217] That directive sounded hardly as though Abetz was an assistant to General von Stülpnagel; it seemed, rather, that the *Militärbefehlshaber* had been attached to the ambassador.

Abetz, however, had a very small staff. Its most important members were: deputy Schleier; Zeitschel and Achenbach in charge of Jewish affairs; von Krug in the Vichy office; and Rahn in Tunisia.[218] Just as the *Militärbefehlshaber* was dependent on the French administration for the enforcement of his decrees, so Abetz had to rely on the *Militärbefehlshaber's* office for the implementation of his policy. That was not a situation conducive to a complete harmony of purposes. Nevertheless, the arrangement did work, as the Jews were to discover in a short time.

The second agency which intruded upon the *Militärbefehlshaber's* jurisdiction was of course the SS and Police. The Himmler men began attaching themselves to Abetz, and they ended up by dominating, in Jewish matters at least, a large part of the scene. The SS men arrived in France in a slow procession – experts first, the Higher SS and Police Leader last. The following table is a very abbreviated outline of the SS organization in France; the Jewish experts are listed in the order of their arrival.

- Higher SS and Police Leader: Bgf. Oberg
  - BdS: (Thomas) Staf. Knochen
    - Deputies: OStubaf. Lischka, Stubaf. Hagen
    - Jewish Experts: HStuf. Dannecker, OStuf. Röthke, UStuf. Ahnert, HStuf. Brunner

By now the names of some of these

214. Rademacher supervised the administration of the entire Seine prefecture, which comprised Paris and suburban areas. *Pariser Zeitung*, January 15, 1941, p. 4. For general description of German administration in France, see *Krakauer Zeitung*, November 3/4, 1940.

215. Keitel to von Bockelberg, June 30, 1940, RF-1301.

216. Weizsäcker to Ribbentrop, July 22, 1940, NG-1719.

217. Ribbentrop to Keitel, August 3, 1940, PS-3614.

218. Abetz spoke French, was considered a lenient Francophile. Schleier was a former *Landesgruppenleiter* in France. Rahn, a Foreign Office trouble shooter, served briefly in Paris as well as in Tunisia.

personalities should be familiar. Oberg had been an SS and Police Leader in Galicia; Thomas was moved from France to the Ukraine, where he was to command *Einsatzgruppe C;* Brunner came from Greece. In France as elsewhere, the conduct of the anti-Jewish destruction process was to rest in expert hands.

The object of all this machinery was the destruction of the largest Jewish community in the western arc. At the end of 1939 the Jewish population of France had reached a total of about 270,000. More than 200,000 Jews were living in Paris alone. However, with the onset of the German invasion in May, 1940, a number of changes were introduced into this picture. The first one came when more than 40,000 Jews streamed into France from Holland, Belgium, and Luxembourg. The second upset occurred when more than 50,000 Jews abandoned the cities of northern France and Paris for safer places to the south. The third upheaval began when the German administrators of Alsace-Lorraine decided upon a complete removal of their Jews.

In a maneuver reminiscent of the expulsions in Poland, the Jews of the incorporated provinces were moved to the unoccupied zone. The movements started suddenly, on July 16, 1940, when the Jews of Colmar (in Alsace) were rounded up and shoved across the demarcation line.[219] During the following months, quiet prevailed. By October, 1940, however, local administrative pressure had been built up to such a point that General von Stülpnagel, as chief of the German Armistice Commission, met with General Huntziger, French Minister of War and chief of the French Armistice Commission, to conclude an agreement which provided for the deportation of all Jews of French nationality from Alsace-Lorraine to unoccupied France.[220] Twenty-two thousand Jews were involved in these movements from Alsace alone.[221] The victims were piled on trucks, driven across, and dumped out at night on a deserted country road in Vichy France.[222]

The Alsace-Lorraine deportations, incidentally, had a by-product which was mentioned before. The chiefs of civil administration, Wagner of Alsace and Bürckel of Lorraine, had decided – in a very broad interpretation of the Stülpnagel-Huntzinger agreement – to deport not only the French Jews from the occupied provinces but also the German Jews from the home *Gaue.* Thus about 6300 Jews from Baden and 1150 Jews from Saarpfalz were also dumped in unoccupied France.[223]

As a consequence of all these population shifts, a new situation had arisen in which the center of gravity had been moved a considerable distance to the south. The occupied zone was left with 165,000 Jews (in Paris alone, 148,000); the unoccupied zone now had about 145,000, or almost half the total.[224]

219. Trial of Robert Wagner, *Law Reports of Trials of War Criminals,* III, 34.

220. Report on deportations received by Interior Ministry, October 30, 1940, NG-4933.

221. Trial of Wagner, *Law Reports,* III, 34. Most of the Alsace Jews lived in Strasbourg and Mulhouse. Few Jews lived in Lorraine. The Alsace expulsions of 1940 affected 105,000 people, including Jews, Gypsies, criminals, "asocials," insane people, Frenchmen, and Francophiles. Other categories, including all the remaining Jews, were to be added in 1942. Summary of expulsion conference held on August 4, 1942, R-114; memorandum by OStubaf. Hardens (RuSHA/*Rasseamt*), September 28, 1942, NO-1499.

222. Jacob Kaplan (Acting Grand Rabbi of France), "French Jewry under the Occupation," *American Jewish Year Book 5706,* 1945, p. 73.

223. Report to Interior Ministry, October 30, 1940, NG-4933. Memorandum by Division Germany, October 31, 1940, NG-4934. Hencke (German Armistice Commission) to Foreign Office, November 19, 1940, NG-4934. Von Sonnleithner to Weizsäcker, November 22, 1940, NG-4934.

224. Statistics on occupied zone in letter by

In Paris, Ambassador Abetz was satisfied with this situation. He proposed that a re-entry of Jews into the occupied zone be prohibited.[225] (Abetz, like Frank, was thinking of Madagascar.[226]) The demarcation line, however, proved to be a two-sided barrier: it was an obstacle not only for Jewish refugees who in the beginning might conceivably have wished to return but also for the German occupation authorities who later sought to extend the "final solution" to the unoccupied zone.

No country in Europe posed such complexities in the mere territorial implementation of anti-Jewish measures as did France. The Vichy French legislation covered occupied as well as unoccupied territory;[227] the German regime was restricted to the occupied area. As a result, the Jews of the occupied zone were suffering under a double oppression – French and German – while the unoccupied Jews were exposed only to the regulations of the Vichy regime. In 1942 the demarcation line collapsed, and French and German measures alike were enforced in all of France.

In 1940 the Vichy authorities enacted a few anti-Jewish decrees which revealed in barest outline the beginnings of a destruction process: the Jews were defined in accordance with the Nuremberg principle; dismissals from government service went into effect; and at the time of the expulsions of the Baden-Saarpflaz Jews, in October, 1940, the Vichy government foreshadowed its policy of separating the new Jews from the old by enacting a law in pursuance of which foreign Jews could be interned.

Dismayed by these Vichy outbursts, Jewish leaders dispatched letters of bewilderment to Marshal Pétain. It seemed to the Jews that the marshal must have made some kind of mistake. In one of the letters, Grand Rabbi Weill explained to the French Chief of State that "studies of anthropology have proved beyond a doubt that there is no such thing as a Jewish race."[228] Why, then, all these decrees?

The Stülpnagel machine, on its part, was ready to fill out the French framework of destruction with heavy measures in the economic sphere. On September 27, 1940, General von Stülpnagel signed a decree which contained a definition and a provision for the registration of Jews. On October 18, 1940, he followed with the definition and registration of Jewish enterprises; that decree provided also for the voidance of transactions and the appointment of trustees. The content of these measures was of course not new, but their implementation was novel.

For the first time in German experience a foreign authority had to be employed for the administrative paper work. The initial task of the French bureaucracy was the enforcement of the registration provisions of the German decrees. In the entire occupied zone the prefects of the *départements* and the subprefects of the *arrondissements* were now mobilized for the registrations. The information received was to be collated on lists, to be prepared in four copies; one copy was to be submitted to the Vichy Undersecretary for Industrial Production and Labor; an-

Dannecker to Zeitschel, October 20, 1941, NG-3264. To the total should be added several thousand Jewish prisoners of war.

225. Memorandum by Best, August 19, 1940, Centre de Documentation Juive Contemporaine, *La persecution des juifs en France*, 1947, p. 48. Abetz to Foreign Office, August 20, 1940, NG-2433.

226. Hitler told Abetz on August 3, 1940, of the plan to remove all Jews from Europe. Affidavit by Abetz, May 30, 1947, NG-1893; memorandum by Luther, August 21, 1942, NG-2586-J.

227. In some cases French laws were extended also to North Africa, a complication to be dealt with later.

228. Kaplan, *American Jewish Year Book*, 1945, p. 89.

other copy went to the Undersecretary for Finance; two copies were to be handed over to the German command.[229]

On November 1, 1940, the economic chief of the *Militärbefehlshaber's* administrative staff, Dr. Michel, informed the regional offices of the military government that the German administration in occupied France was making use of the French authorities because it was not large enough to tackle the Aryanization problem alone. To assure control over the French apparatus, the prefects had been ordered to submit two copies of the lists to the Germans. One of these copies was to be kept in the competent *Militärverwaltungsbezirk;* the other was to be retained by the local *Feldkommandantur.* The German commanders were to make spot checks on their French collaborators and, independently of the lists, information was to be gathered and collected on enterprises under preponderant Jewish influence or affected by undercover arrangements, etc.

In principle, said Dr. Michel, the French were to appoint their own trustees. "It will be endeavored," he explained, "to replace the Jews by Frenchmen in order to let the French population, too, benefit from the elimination of the Jews and to avoid the impression that the Germans want nothing but to get the Jewish positions for themselves." However, exceptions were to be made in all cases "where important German interests" were at stake.[230]

A few days after the issuance of this directive von Stülpnagel informed the *Militärbezirkschefs* that the Commander-in-Chief of the Army, Generalfeldmarschall von Brauchitsch, had ordered the immediate Aryanization of all Jewish enterprises in the occupied territory. The prefects were now called upon to nominate trustees for appointment by the *Distriktchefs.* The installment and work of the trustees was subject to certain principles, the chief among which was speed.

Von Stülpnagel ruled that enterprises with only minor Jewish participation were to be given an opportunity to eliminate their Jewish character by effecting the necessary sale of stocks or ouster of key personnel. Such enterprises needed no trusteeship at all.

Firms which, by reason of their predominant Jewish influence, had to be placed under trustees could be disposed of in three ways. The first of these was the voluntary sale of the firm by its Jewish owners; this method was preferred, provided that it entailed no "loss of time." Trustees in such cases had to insure only that the *buyers* were free from Jewish influence. Suspicious agreements could of course be voided by the *Militärbefehlshaber.* If the owners refused to sell, the trustee, with the prior approval of the *Militärbefehlshaber,* could conclude the transaction. If a sale was not possible because of a lack of demand, the trustee, after securing the authorization of the *Militärbefehlshaber,* could proceed with a liquidation. To make sure that the disposal of the Jewish enterprises was handled with a sense of immediacy, the trustees were instructed to make a report on the progress of the sales negotiations within four weeks after their appointment.[231]

Within a matter of months the trusteeship apparatus was built up into a formidable machine; however, it had

229. The Delegate General of the French government for the occupied territories (signed La Laurencie) to all prefects in the occupied zone, October, 1940, NOKW-1237.

230. *Militärbefehlshaber*/Adm. Staff/Economy (signed Dr. Michel) to *Militärbezirkschefs* A, B, C, Paris, and Bordeaux, and all *Feldkommandanturen,* November 1, 1940, NOKW-1237.

231. *Militärbefehlshaber*/Adm.. Staff/Economy (signed Stülpnagel) to chiefs of military districts, November 12, 1940, NOKW-1237.

come into being in a somewhat decentralized manner. The French government, with its long tradition of administrative centralization, decided to do something about this situation; accordingly, the Vichy regime established within the Ministry of Industrial Production and Labor a special *Service du Controle,* which was headed by a former governor of the Bank of France, president Fournier. The *Service du Controle* dealt centrally with trusteeship nominations; it briefed the trustees and ruled on the legality of transactions. In the German *Verwaltungsstab* Dr. Michel immediately recognized that the new agency would lighten the load of the Germans without depriving them of their ultimate veto. He therefore instructed his regional machinery to make use of this apparatus, which the French had created in a spirit of "collaboration," for the accomplishment of the Aryanization process.[232]

To be sure, the willingness of the Germans to avail themselves of French collaboration had its limits. The French prefects and their superiors in Vichy were not to concern themselves with nominations for trustee appointments in Jewish-owned *industrial* plants. Factories were to be handled by the *Militärbefehlshaber* through his own channels.[233] The object of that important reservation of course, was to retain an opportunity for German business interests to acquire Jewish industrial enterprises.[234]

Two major difficulties arose during the administration of the Aryanization program. One was caused by the failure of the legal draftsmen to make a distinction between French Jews and foreign Jews. Needless to say, that failure was intentional: a German agency could not very well admit that the protections afforded by elementary rules of international law applied also to Jews. However, the experts in Paris decided to issue unpublished instructions to field offices exempting American Jews from the requirement (in the decree of September 27) of marking their stores with a Jewish star.[235]

That unpublicized exemption was apparently not very effectual, for in December the United States complained of vandalism committed against establishments owned by American citizens.[236] When the protest was brought to Ribbentrop's attention, he declared that no exemptions should have been accorded to American Jews in the first place, and, pointing to the fact that protests of friendly nations such as Spain and Hungary had been rejected, he ordered that no reply be made to the U.S. note.[237] Ribbentrop's obstinacy worried Staatsminister Dr. Schmidt in Paris and the Foreign Office's American expert, Freytag, in Berlin. Both feared anti-German repercussions in America.[238] But Ribbentrop refused

232. Michel to *Militärverwaltungsbezirke* and *Feldkommandanturen,* January 28, 1941, NOKW-1270.

233. *Militärbefehlshaber*/Adm. Staff/Economy (signed Stülpnagel) to French Ministry for Industrial Production and Labor, December 9, 1940, NOKW-1237.

234. In that connection, see, for example, the documents on efforts by Krupp to acquire by means of a "lease" the Rothschild-owned Austin automobile works at Liancourt: Affidavit by Alfried Krupp, June 30, 1947, NI-10332; Ing. Walter Stein (director general of Krupp SA in France) to Schürmann, November 8, 1943, NI-7013; Stein to Direktor Schröder, November 25, 1943, NI-7012.

235. Schleier (Paris) to Schwarzmann (office of Ribbentrop), October 9, 1940, NG-4893.

236. Luther to Embassy in Paris, December 18, 1940, NG-4893.

237. Notation by Rademacher, December 19, 1940, NG-4893. Luther to embassy in Paris, December 23, 1940, NG-4893.

238. Schmidt (chief of administrative staff in *Militärbefehlshaber's* office) to Staatssekretär Weizsäcker of Foreign Office, February 22, 1941, NG-1527. Freytag (Pol. IX) via Erdmannsdorff to Wörmann, February 27, 1941, NG-4406.

to give in. The exemption of the U.S. Jews had to be canceled.[239]

More serious in its immediate import than the foreign repercussions was the attitude of the French themselves. On January 28, 1941, economy expert Dr. Michel of the *Militärbefehlshaber's* administrative staff warned the regional command offices that a propaganda campaign designed to deter potential buyers and to undermine the trustees had been launched in French business circles. "In particular," he wrote, "attempts are being made to raise doubts as to whether the contracts concluded by the trustees will be legally valid after the end of the occupation."

Dr. Michel believed that this propaganda could be countered with the following array of arguments: (1) The *Militärbefehlshaber's* authority to issue laws derived from international law and the armistice agreement. (2) Suitable provisions in the peace treaty would insure against subsequent nullification. (3) The contracts were legally so complex as to make subsequent voidance difficult in any case. (4) The French government was collaborating in the Aryanizations; hence, the sales were based, in a manner of speaking, upon French law also. For the rest, Dr. Michel thought it best that the Jews themselves sell their firms. Such participation, he said, would "ease the mind of the French purchaser."[240]

Dr. Michel's arguments were not potent enough to overcome the French reluctance to acquire Jewish property. After twenty-one months of Aryanizations in the occupied zone (and a year of such operations in the unoccupied territory), the German press published statistics revealing the state of affairs in the Aryanization business (see Table 58).[241]

Table 58 / *The Progress of Aryanizations by August, 1942*

	Occupied Zone	Paris	Provinces	Unoccupied Zone
Under trusteeship	31,699	24,914	6,785	1,500
Sold	4,000	3,000	1,000	
Liquidated	2,800	1,700	900	
Trusteeship pending	2,000			
Status undetermined	600			

In brief, only 21 per cent of the Jewish enterprises under trusteeship in the occupied zone had been disposed of through sale or liquidation by August, 1942. Although the operation was not over, its progress continued to creep along. By October, 1943, 11,000 cases (or about one-third of the total) had been "finished" in the occupied zone; another 4000 were completed in the Vichy area. The cautious French purchasers were forming an association of "owners of former Jewish enterprises";[242] evidently these Frenchmen

239. *Militärbefehlshaber* / Administrative Staff/Administration to *Bezirkschefs* A, B, C, and Bordeaux, *Kommandant Gross-Paris, Feld-* and *Kreiskommandanturen,* April, 1941, NOKW-1270.

240. *Militärbefehlshaber*/Adm. Staff/Economy (signed Dr. Michel) to *Militärverwaltungsbezirke* and *Feldkommandanturen,* January 28, 1941, NOKW-1270.

241. *Deutsche Ukraine Zeitung* (Luck), August 4, 1942, p. 4; August 11, 1942, p. 4. *Donauzeitung* (Belgrade), August 28, 1942, p. 5. Insurance companies, utilities, and the French state itself were reported to have participated significantly in the purchase of Jewish property. The 2000 enterprises which had not yet been placed under trusteeship were described as "insignificant" (*allerdings bedeutungslos*). The Aryanizations had been extended to the unoccupied territory by the French law of July 22, 1941.

242. *Donauzeitung* (Belgrade), October 20,

were worried about trouble. Dr. Michel, however, was not troubled by their worries – his thinking was confined to the statistics on the sales. When in the summer of 1944, at a time when Allied forces were already fighting on French soil, speculators were pressing for last-minute acquisitions, he expressed his satisfaction that the "de-Jewing of the French economy" was proceeding without change.[243]

Under the impact of the dismissals and Aryanizations, increasingly heavy burdens fell upon the network of Jewish organizations in France. The most important of these institutions was the *Consistoire Central des Israelits de France.* Until 1940 the *Consistoire Central* was headed by Baron Edouard de Rothschild, the powerful industrialist whom we have already met in negotiations with the Dresdner Bank. Baron Edouard fled to the United States during the invasion, and his place was taken by Jacques Helbronner, who ruled until October, 1943, when he was arrested and replaced by Leon Meiss.[244] Under Helbronner, in the winter of 1940/41, the Jewish organizations consolidated their resources for the purpose of helping the impoverished Jews, and the product of these consolidations was the Jewish Co-ordinating Committee. The committee soon had much to do.

On May 28, 1941, the *Militärbefehlshaber* ruled for the occupied zone that Jews were no longer permitted to dispose over their funds (in amounts exceeding normal transactions) without the consent of the *Service du Controle.* On July 1, 1941, the SS adviser in the embassy, Obersturmführer Dannecker, reported that with the help of Abetz, Schleier, and Zeitschel he had persuaded the *Militärbefehlshaber* to deal with no Jewish organization save the co-ordinating committee. At the same time an agreement had been made with the French welfare system (the *Bureau de Secours National*) to deprive all Jews of French relief assistance.[245] On July 22, 1941, the French Aryanization law was enacted, with a clause which provided for the automatic blocking of the proceeds collected by the trustees in the disposal of Jewish enterprises. A portion of the blocked money was to be retained to defray administrative costs; the remainder was to be used for needy Jews.

The Jewish leadership was now faced with a difficult question. Should use be made of the blocked accounts accumulating from the sale of Jewish firms to help the poor and starving community? The capitalists of the consistory and the rabbis functioning under its direction decided against such a utilization of the funds on the ground that it "would have constituted a new stage in the spoliation of Jewish wealth." Accordingly, the Jewish leaders launched an intensive fund-raising campaign under the title "Fund of the Grand Rabbi of France." At the same time the French Jews enlisted the aid of the American Jewish Joint Distribution Committee, which promised to match the amount collected.[246]

On November 29, 1941, the Vichy regime forced the Jews into a new constriction by decreeing that all Jewish organizations were to be dissolved and their property turned over to a

1943, p. 8; January 14, 1944, p. 1.

243. Report by *Militärbefehlshaber Frankreich*/MVZ Group 3 (signed chief of military administration Dr. Michel) for July 22-29, 1944, on administration and economy, July 30, 1944, Wi/I .288. Report by Michel, August 6, 1944, Wi/I .288.

244. Kaplan, *American Jewish Year Book,* 1945, pp. 71–72, 75, 93, 109.

245. Unsigned report by an OStuf. (believed to be Dannecker), July 1, 1941, RF-1207. Notwithstanding the "agreement," the bureau continued to give some help to Jews in distress. *Die Judenfrage,* November 15, 1942, p. 249.

246. Kaplan, *American Jewish Year Book,* 1945, pp. 78, 96.

new council, the *Union Generale des Israelites de France* (UGIF). The UGIF was the *Judenrat* of France. It was headed by Raymond-Raoul Lambert.[247]

The newly constituted UGIF entered into operation under a series of blows. On December 10 the entry into the war of the United States cut off French Jewry from its only major source of outside help.[248] One week later a fatal obstacle was placed into the path of the fund-raising drive: the Germans had decided to do some fund-raising of their own. On December 14, 1941, the *Militärbefehlshaber* made use of a pretext based on the assassination of a German officer to impose upon Paris Jewry a billion-franc "fine." On December 17 he charged the UGIF with the task of collecting the money. All decisions of the *Union Generale* in pursuance of that German directive were to be backed by the French administration in accordance with the enforcement provisions of the tax statutes of France.[249]

The Jewish leadership was now in a corner. The fund drive collapsed in the wake of the "fine." The *Union Generale* was faced with the clear necessity of dipping into the reservoir of the blocked accounts to help the poor Jews. The chiefs of the community, however, were determined to confine the withdrawals to a minimum. In 1943, at a time when the first Jews were inducted into forced labor, the Jewish leaders obtained from the French authorities a decree authorizing the UGIF to impose a monthly head tax on every Jewish adult. The tax amounted to 120 francs in the occupied territory and 320 francs in the Vichy zone; its yield was supplemented by withdrawals from the blocked funds in the amount of 80,000,000 francs.[250] At the end of 1943 the blocked accounts amounted to 485,000,000 francs.[251]

During the creation of centralized Jewish machinery with compulsory powers, a parallel process took place in the French administration. Early in March, 1941, Ambassador Abetz requested the number-two man in Vichy, Admiral Darlan, to establish a central office for Jews in France.[252] Darlan now had the job of convincing the reluctant Pétain to accede to this step. Pétain finally agreed.[253] On March 29, 1941, a commissariat for Jewish affairs was consequently set up in Vichy with an old anti-Semite, Xavier Vallat, as commissar. His functions were twofold: he was to oversee the work of the trustees and the Jewish organizations, and to propose new anti-Jewish legislation. From that second function flowed increasingly tight economic restrictions, which culminated in the Vichy Aryanization and funds-control law of July 22.

To the Jewish leadership these developments were something unbelievable, a nightmare which did not make sense. On July 31, 1941, Grand Rabbi Weill's deputy, Jacob Kaplan, addressed a letter to Xavier Vallat which was designed to convince the Frenchman once and for all of the error of his ways. Kaplan pointed out that for a pagan or an atheist to defame Judaism

247. Kaplan, *American Jewish Year Book*, 1945, pp. 78, 93–96. Within the *Union Generale* the old organizations continued to function. However, only the cover organization had compulsive powers and legal responsibilities.

248. Later the Joint Distribution Committee was able to conduct covert operations from Geneva.

249. One billion francs = 50 million reichsmark = $20 million.

250. Kaplan, *American Jewish Year Book*, 1945, pp. 78–79, 95–96. *Donauzeitung* (Belgrade), June 13/14, 1943, p. 2.

251. *Donauzeitung* (Belgrade), January 14, 1944, p. 1.

252. Abetz to Foreign Office, March 6, 1941, NG-2442.

253. Abetz to Foreign Office, April 3, 1941, NG-2432.

was not strange and not illogical. "But," asked Kaplan, "on the part of a Christian, does not such an attitude appear spiritually illogical as well as ungrateful?" Kaplan then answered his own question. The Jewish religion, he said, was the mother of the Christian religion; the Ten Commandments were the moral and religious charter of civilized humanity; Jesus Christ and all his apostles were Jews. Therefore, Kaplan concluded triumphantly, did Vallat not realize that when he attacked the Jews he was assailing at the same time the founders of Christianity? Kaplan then inserted a number of quotations from Pascal, Bossuet, Fénelon, Montesquieu, Rousseau, Chateaubriand, Guizot, Renan, Leon Bloy, Ignatius de Loyola, Pope Pius XI, Lacordaire, and de Sasy.

Having nailed this point, Kaplan went on to discuss the Jewish military record in World War I, quoting statistics and tributes. While Kaplan had no figures for World War II, he assured Vallat that "when the final story is written, it will reveal that the Jews have done their duty like all other French citizens." The letter concluded with the statement that, in view of this overwhelming proof, Vallat no doubt would see the light and realize that the day would come when reason would prevail once more and anti-Semitism would lose out.

On August 5, 1941, Vallat replied through his *Chef de Cabinet*, Jarnieu. The letter read as follows:

> Dear Rabbi:
>
> I have the honor to acknowledge receipt of your letter of July 31, in which you quoted to me a certain number of texts which are of course quite well known. They would not have been refuted in any French legislation if there had not been, during the last few years, an invasion of our territory by a host of Jews having no ties with our civilization.

Having dealt with that argument, Jarnieu tackled the second:

> I do not intend to refute in detail a certain number of your arguments, in particular the statistics you give of the Jews who have entered the armed forces and died for France. That is a matter which deserves too much respect to become the object of a controversy.

Not quite satisfied with the trend of that answer, Jarnieu closed abruptly:

> Let me simply point out that in the government's attitude there is no anti-Semitism, simply the application of reasons of state.

Finished, he added the greeting:

> Please be assured, Rabbi, of my genuine regard,
>
> JARNIEU[254]

Jarnieu's letter revealed that the anti-Jewish persecution had generated within the French bureaucracy a certain uneasiness as well as defensiveness. In August, 1941, the French administrators had to ask themselves how far, as Christians, they could proceed against the Jews, and that question had to be faced in the very top strata of the Vichy regime. Only two days after Jarnieu dispatched his reply to Kaplan, Marshal Pétain himself sent an inquiry to the French Ambassador at the Holy See, Léon Bérard, to ascertain the Vatican's attitude toward the anti-Jewish laws.

The ambassador replied with a detailed exposition of the writings of Saint Thomas Aquinas, who had long ago recommended that Jews be barred from government activity and limited in the exercise of their professions. Regulations for special dress, said Bérard, were also not new to the Catholic Church. In the light of that traditional policy, an "authorized person at the Vatican" had assured the ambassador

254. Text of correspondence in Kaplan, *American Jewish Year Book*, 1945, pp. 113–17.

that "they have no intention of quarreling with us over the Jewish statute." The Vatican had expressed only the desire that no provisions be enacted relating to [inter]marriage and that precepts of justice and charity be observed in the liquidation of business establishments.[255] Clearly, the French government had not yet committed any "sins," but it was close to having reached the limits of "permissible" action.

Almost from the beginning of the occupation, the Vichy regime sensed that under increasing German pressure it would have to shift to a second line of defense. If the destruction process could not be halted at a certain point, efforts would have to be made to deflect the full force of the attack from the old-established, assimilated Jews to the newly arrived immigrants and refugees. On April 6, 1941, the newly appointed anti-Jewish commissar, Xavier Vallat, declared before members of the press that there was no such thing as a "standard solution" of the Jewish question in France. So far as the Jews of North Africa were concerned, there was no Jewish problem at all. "We must also," said Vallat, "take into account the old Jewish families, mostly of Alsatian origin, who appear to be assimilated." Another exceptional group was composed of the front-line soldiers of 1914-18 and 1940. The eastern Jews, however, "who in the last few years have flooded France," Vallat concluded without realizing the full import of his words, "will in all likelihood be shoved off again."[256]

The Jewish front-line soldiers were privileged to some extent in every European Axis state. Unlike the Reich veterans, who sought every privilege they could get, the Jewish veterans of the French Army felt disposed to declare their solidarity with the rest of Jewry. On August 11, 1941, a delegation of eighteen veterans, headed by General André Boris, former inspector General of Artillery and a member of the *Consistoire Central*, handed Xavier Vallat a statement which brought home the point that the anti-Jewish legislation was "valid only insofar as we are legally forced to comply with it and does not signify any agreement on our part." Having stated their general attitude as forcefully as they could, the veterans continued their protest with the words: "Would the General Commissar for Jewish Affairs consider subversive a statement . . . in the following terms: We solemnly declare that we renounce any exceptional benefits we may derive from our status as ex-servicemen."[257]

The problem of the Jewish veterans was not confined to their treatment in France itself, since there was still a contingent of several thousand Jewish soldiers in German captivity. No records are available of any French interventions in behalf of these soldiers. To be sure, the German regulations against Jewish prisoners of war from the western armies were in no way comparable to the drastic measures which were applied to the Jewish prisoners from the Red Army. The only western Jewish prisons subject to shooting were the emigrants from the Reich, who were shot immediately upon ascertainment of their identity at the army prisoner collecting points (*Armeegefangenensammelstellen*), that is, prior to the transfer of the prisoners to the permanent Stalags.[258] The former Reich

255. Excerpts from report by Ambassador Berard to Marshal Pétain in Leon Poliakov, *Harvest of Hate* (Syracuse, 1954), pp. 299–301.

256. *Die Judenfrage*, May 5, 1941, pp. 70–71.

257. Kaplan, *American Jewish Year Book*, 1945, pp. 91–92.

258. Directive by Army Group B, as transmitted by 4th Army Ic/AO Abw I (signed by Chief of Staff Gen. d. Inf. Brenecke) to

Jews who were caught in this procedure were beyond help, but the main body of Jewish prisoners enjoyed relative immunity. Enlisted men in the Stalags and officers in the Oflags were to be separated from other French prisoners, and Jewish enlisted personnel were to be assigned to special work parties; however, there was to be no marking of the Jews.[259] Undoubtedly, the fear of reprisals restrained the German generals in their operations against the Jewish prisoners of war.

During his interview with the press on April 6, 1941, Vallat had also mentioned that he could see no Jewish problem in Africa. This statement is wholly in conformity with what we would expect, for German influence as well as interest in Africa was comparatively remote. So far as the Germans were concerned, the African Jews could have been left alone. But they were not. The Catholic-military hierarchy in Vichy took its own measures against these people.

One of the first Vichy measures in Africa was the abolition of the so-called Cremieux Decree, under which the Jews of Algeria had enjoyed since 1870 the status of French citizens. Next the Algerian Jews were hit by a number of provisions in French laws which had been enacted for the metropolitan area, but which were applied to Algeria as well, because that territory was an "integral" portion of France. Under these provisions, dismissals were effected in the civil service, limitations were placed on professional activity, and Aryanizations were introduced into business. Finally, a number of measures in Algeria and the neighboring "protectorates" of Morocco and Tunisia were prepared by the resident French military men who ruled North Africa during the early forties:

Delegate General Africa, Gen. Maxime Weygand
- Resident General Moroccan "Protectorate," Gen. Nougès (200,000 Jews)
- Governor General Algeria, Adm. Abrial (120,000 Jews)
- Resident General Tunisian "Protectorate," Adm. Esteva (80,000 Jews)

Under the leadership of General Weygand little Jewish commissariats were established in Algeria and Morocco. Most of the discriminations in effect in Algeria were now enforced through "decrees" of the Sultan in Morocco; in addition, the Sultan forbade his Jews such activities as moneylending, while the Resident General of Morocco, General Nougès, was busy with plans for the establishment of compulsory ghettos and concentration camps up to the very moment when Allied forces invaded his domain.[260]

divisions, June 18, 1940, NOKW-1483. The commander of Army Group B was von Bock, while the 4th Army was commanded by von Kluge. No records are available of the number of shootings, and it is likely that none were carried out after the conclusion of the French campaign. In 1944 a directive of the OKW/*Chef* Kgf., which had jurisdiction only over permanent camps in the rear, provided merely that the bodies of Jewish prisoners who had been deprived of German nationality by the 11th ordinance to the Reich Citizenship Law were to be buried without military honors. OKW/*Chef Kriegsgefangenenwesen, Befehlssammlung* No. 48 (signed Meurer), December 15, 1944, OKW-1984.

259. OKW/*Chef* Kgf., *Sammelmitteilungen* No. 1 (signed Obstl. Breyer), June 16, 1941, OKW-1984. *Befehlssammlung* No. 11 (signed von Graevenitz), March 11, 1942, OKW-1984. *Befehlssammlung* No. 48 (signed Meurer), December 15, 1944, OKW-1984. A Red Cross delegation reported in March, 1941, that it had seen about 50 Jewish prisoners in Stalag XIa with the large indelible inscription *Jud* on their French uniforms. International Red Cross report (signed Dr. Marti and Dr. Descoedres), March 16, 1941, NG-2386. The report may have contributed to the prohibition.

260. See, in general, *Donauzeitung* (Belgrade), August 17, 1941, p. 2; and *Die Judenfrage,* September 10, 1941, p. 168; February 15, 1942, p. 37; April 15, 1942, p. 76; May 15, 1942, p. 101; October 15, 1942, p. 223.

The application of dismissals and Aryanizations to Tunisia led to difficulties with the Italians, who insisted upon the protection of 5000 *Italian* Jews in the territory. Ambassador Abetz now found himself in the peculiar position of defending the French before General Gelich of the Italian armistice commission. Abetz wanted to know what sort of impression was created when France was persecuting and Italy protecting the Jews; he asserted that in Tunisia Italian Jews controlled almost all commercial activities and tried to talk Gelich into a scheme which would allow Italian Aryans to take over the property of Italian Jews.[261] The Italian government refused to assent to any such scheme.[262] We shall come back to Tunisia to describe what happened there when German troops landed in the Protectorate in November, 1942; let us now return to the destruction process in France itself.

The most important remark by Vallat at the press conference following his appointment as commissar concerned the Jewish immigrants who had "flooded" France between the two wars and who were now to be "shoved off" again. Here was the wedge which became the starting point of the "final solution" in France. At the time when Vallat took office, the general policy toward the foreign and stateless Jews had already been fixed. Under the law of October 4, 1940, these Jews were subject to internment, and the French government lost little time in implementing that law.

The 7500 Reich Jews who had been dumped in unoccupied France from Baden and the Saarpfalz were promptly interned at a camp in Gurs. According to a report by Rabbi Kaplan, these Jews "lived in crowded barracks, sleeping on the ground, devoured by vermin, suffering from hunger and cold in a damp muddy region. During the one winter of 1940–1941, they suffered 800 deaths."[263] By 1941 the Vichy government had established in southern France a network of camps: Gurs, Rivesaltes, Noé, Récébédon, La Vernet, and Les Milles.[264] Besides the Baden-Saarpfalz Jews, the camps contained recent arrivals from the Reich-Austria-Protektorat-Polish area, as well as an assortment of "stateless" Jews of all kinds. The total number of inmates was 20,000.[265]

In Paris the German administration watched these developments with approving acceptance; they saw in the French measure a basis for similar action in the occupied territory.[266] Under the direction of SS-Obersturmführer Dannecker, the Jewish expert detailed to the embassy, the Paris prefecture of police compiled a card index in which every Jew was listed (1) alphabetically, (2) according to street address, (3) by profession, and (4) in accordance with the crucial criterion of nationality.[267]

The list was first put to use in May, 1941, with a roundup of Polish Jews, and again in August with a seizure of Jews who were involved in "Communist de Gaullist misdeeds and assassination attempts against members of the Wehrmacht" (i.e., intellectuals.)[268] The victims of these raids were men only, and they were placed in three camps.

261. Abetz to Foreign Office, July 4, 1942, NG-133.

262. Weizsäcker to Luther, political and legal divisions, September 2, 1942, enclosing note from Italian Ambassador Alfieri of the same date, NG-54.

263. Kaplan, *American Jewish Year Book*, 1945, p. 84.

264. *Ibid.*

265. Schleier (embassy in Paris) to Foreign Office, September 11, 1942, NG-5109.

266. Summary of conference attended by Abetz, Dannecker, Achenbach, and Zeitschel, February 28, 1941, NG-4895.

267. Dannecker to RSHA IV-B, February 22, 1942, NG-2070.

268. Kaplan, *American Jewish Year Book*, 1945, pp. 82–83. Schleier to Foreign Office, October 30, 1941, NG-3264.

After considerable delay it was discovered that the arrest figures totaled 7443, distributed as follows:

Drancy,	4,331
Pithiviers,	1,560
Beaune la Rolande,	1,552

According to nationality, the breakdown looked like this:[269]

Poles	3,649
Frenchmen	1,602
"Emigrants"	368
Turks	271
Miscellaneous nationalities	564
Nationality undetermined	624

The arrests of some of the foreign Jews led to protests from foreign consuls in Paris. The *Militärbefehlshaber's* office and the SS were agreed that the release of individual Jews would create "precedents" which of course were undesirable, and the German bureaucrats thought that the French law was quite sufficient to cover all the arrests.[270]

Staatssekretär Weizsäcker of the Foreign Office believed, however, that it was dangerous to detain Jews of the various American nationalities. He wanted these Jews released, lest reprisals be launched against Germans in America, in which case "we would get the worst of it."[271] Ribbentrop, whose mind was well atuned to reprisal thinking, immediately put on the memorandum his *Ja*. The Paris Embassy followed suit, though somewhat reluctantly. When, some months later, the Foreign Office was prodded by a Chilean protest to request the release of one Norbert Goldflus, the embassy's Dr. Zeitschel replied that Goldflus was a Jew, that this status had not been altered by his baptism in Vienna twenty-two years before, that his citizenship was French, and that his marriage to a "Chilean woman of high society" was really beside the point. Nevertheless, the embassy was going to do everything in its power to effect the man's release, although the recent frequency of such requests was not making a "good impression" on the SS.[272]

Since the internment camps were run by French personnel, a slight problem also developed in matters of administration. The *Deutsche Ukraine Zeitung* in Luck one day featured an article entitled "Merry Concentration Camp" (*Fröhliches Konzentrationslager*). The camp was Beaune la Rolande. It seemed that the management of the camp was in the hands of a retired French captain who granted passes to inmates against payments of certain sums of money. The inmate roll had thus declined by 384. The "corruption" of the French personnel had also revealed itself in the successful attempts of relatives and friends of the Jews to smuggle food to the prisoners. Surely, said the *Ukraine Zeitung*, the Jews had no cause to be dissatisfied in such a concentration camp.[273]

The circumstance that the arrested victims were heads of families developed into still another problem: A French informant of the German *Rüstungskontrollinspektion* (the Armament Control Inspectorate in the unoccupied zone) offered the opinion that the arrest of the men without their women and children had been a mistake. These women, said the French informant, were now wandering around in the streets of Paris, arousing the sympathy of "unknowing Frenchmen." Other Jews, he said, were disappearing in Paris and the provinces under false

269. All statistics from Dannecker to Zeitschel, October 20, 1941, NG-3264.

270. Schleier to Foreign Office, October 30, 1941, NG-3264.

271. Memorandum by Weizsäcker, November 1, 1941, NG-3264.

272. Zeitschel to Foreign Office, April 30, 1942, NG-5348.

273. *Deutsche Ukraine Zeitung* (Luck), March 28, 1942, p. 5.

names.[274]

A tense and unstable situation was thus developing with respect to the arrested Jews in the occupied zone toward the end of 1941, when a slight incident in Paris was seized upon to set into motion a more drastic phase of the operations. A Luftwaffe major was slightly wounded by a would-be assassin. For the *Militärbefehlshaber* that unsuccessful attempt was an opportunity for unleashing a few blows. On December 5, 1941, von Stülpnagel proposed to the *Generalquartiermeister* the enactment of three measures. First, he wanted to shoot a hundred hostages. Second, he desired to collect the aforementioned billion-franc "fine." Third, he requested approval for the deportation of a thousand Jews to the East.[275] Hitler approved all three measures.[276]

On December 12 about 750 Jews were arrested in Paris and taken, with 300 others from the internment camp at Drancy, to Compiegne.[277] Two days later von Stülpnagel published his order. The French Delegate General in the occupied territory, Ambassador de Brinon, protested immediately against the shooting of the hundred "Jews, Communists, and anarchists" as hostages. His note failed to bring up the billion-franc "fine," and it did not even mention the proposed deportation of the thousand Jews.[278] The timing of the deportations, however, was ill-chosen. The OKH informed the *Militärbefehlshaber* that December and January were overcrowded months for the military transport command; the Jews would have to wait until February or March.[279]

During the waiting period, the chief of the French "social revolutionary" movement, Eugene Deloncle, decided to blow up a few Paris synagogues. In the ensuing demolitions a number of Wehrmacht members were hurt, and as a result, the *Militärbefehlshaber* angrily requested the withdrawal of the newly installed BdS Dr. Knochen. The embassy now had to step in to protect this "politically experienced" man who was going to be needed so much in the coming operations, and von Stülpnagel agreed to accept an apology.[280] Mollified, the *Militärbefehlshaber* a few days later issued an ordinance imposing a curfew on the Jews.

By March 9, 1942, the transport problem was solved, and Eichmann wrote to his opposite number in the Foreign Office, Legationsrat Rademacher, to inquire whether the diplomats had any objections to the deportations.[281] Neither Luther in Berlin nor Schleier in Paris could think of any objections.[282]

Eichmann's Paris representative, in the meantime, thought that things were going a little too slowly. At a conference held in Eichmann's chambers on March 4, Hauptsturmführer Dannecker suggested that it would be necessary to propose to the French government "something really positive, like the deportation of several thousand Jews" *(etwas wirklich Positives, wie etwa den*

274. *Rüstungskontrollinspektion*/Z (signed Glt. Stud) to *Waffenstillstandskommission*/Rü in Wiesbaden, December 4, 1941, enclosing special report by Sonderführer (Z) Rohden, Wi/IA 3.74.

275. Von Stülpnagel to OKH/GenQu, December 5, 1941, NG-3571.

276. GenQu to Ambassador Ritter (Foreign Office), December 12, 1941, NG-3571.

277. Kaplan, *American Jewish Year Book*, 1945, pp. 82–83.

278. Memorandum by Welck on telephone conversation with Legationsrat Strack, containing text of French protest, December 16, 1941, NG-5126.

279. MB *Frankreich*/Adm. Staff/Adm. (signed Best), to representative of RSHA in Paris, January 6, 1942, R-967.

280. Paris Embassy to Ambassador Ritter in the Foreign Office, February 2, 1942, NG-119.

281. Eichmann to Rademacher, March 9, 1942, NG-4954.

282. Luther to Paris Embassy, March 10, 1942, NG-4954. Schleier to Foreign Office, March 13, 1942, NG-4954.

Abschub mehrerer tausend Juden). Eichmann thought that, subject to Heydrich's approval, some preliminary negotiations could be instituted with the French for the deportation of about 5000 Jews to the East.

Eichmann had in mind Jewish men, not over 55 years of age, who were capable of work (in short, the arrested Jews in the internment camps). The negotiations with the French, he believed, would also have to include the subject of the "service charge" which the Germans were to collect for removing the Jews, but to determine the amount of the charge, one would first have to gain a picture of the total Jewish wealth in the country. These and other details, he said, would have to be settled in the next few months.[283]

On March 11, Eichmann decided to get the Foreign Office's permission to deport the 5000 Jews to Auschwitz, along with the 1000 whose deportation was already scheduled.[284] This request also went from hand to hand and was approved by Rademacher, Luther, Schleier, Weizsäcker, and Wörmann.[285]

The deportation fever now increased in the ranks of the German bureaucracy in Paris. On March 18, 1942, an embassy official commented that the appointment of a Higher SS and Police Leader in France (Oberg) would have "an especially favorable effect on the final solution" in the country.[286] On May 5, 1942, Heydrich himself arrived in Paris. In a talk with the French police chief, Bousquet, he announced that there was now sufficient transport to remove the stateless Jews interned at Drancy in the occupied zone. Nonchalantly, the French police chief asked Heydrich whether he could not also remove the stateless Jews who had already been interned for a year and a half in the unoccupied zone. Heydrich replied that it was all a matter of transport.[287] In the meantime, therefore, the deportations had to be confined to the Jews in the camps of the *occupied* zone. A total of 5138 victims were removed from these camps to Auschwitz.[288]

Encouraged by these developments, the bureaucrats began to make preparations for concentrations and deportations on a major scale. By the middle of May the *Militärbefehlshaber's* office was hard at work on a decree compelling every Jew who had reached the age of six to wear a Jewish star with the inscription *Juif*.[289] Although the decree was to apply to French and foreign Jews alike, the treatment of some of the foreign nationalities had to be handled with caution. After consultations with the Foreign Office, the following nationalities were determined to be safe targets for the measure: Reich, Polish, Dutch, Belgian, French, Croat, Slovakian, and Roumanian.[290]

The decree was issued on May 29 and went into effect on June 7. Difficulties in its enforcement made themselves felt immediately. Some of the Jews decided not to wear the star. Others wore it in the wrong way. Still others wore several stars instead of one. Some Jews provided their star with additional inscriptions. And, finally, a number of non-Jews took to wearing the star or something that looked like it. Angrily, the Germans arrested some of the Jewish offenders and their French supporters to intern them in one of the camps.[291]

283. HStuf. Dannecker to OStubaf. Dr. Knochen and Stubaf. Lischka, March 10, 1942, RF-1216.

284. Eichmann to Rademacher, March 11, 1942, NG-4954.

285. Correspondence in NG-4954.

286. Embassy memorandum, March 18, 1942, NG-4881.

287. Schleier to Foreign Office, September 11, 1942, NG-5109.

288. *Ibid.*

289. Abetz to Foreign Office, May 15, 1942, NG-2455.

290. Zeitschel to MB von Stülpnagel and Higher SS and Police Leader Oberg, May 22, 1942, NG-3668.

In Berlin the machine ground on. On June 11, Eichmann called together his experts from The Hague, Brussels, and Paris to discuss further measures. The experts were considering statistics to be used in negotiations with the Railway Transport Division (ETRA Paris, Generalleutnant Kohl) and the French authorities. The figure for France was an initial 100,000. The deportees were to consist of men and women in the age group 16–40, and a sum of 700 reichsmark per person was mentioned as the transportation fee to be charged the French state. The first train was to roll on July 13.[292]

Within a matter of days a major obstacle loomed on the horizon: Generalleutnant Kohl could not furnish the transport. The buildup of the spring offensive had resulted in the sudden transfer from the occupied zone to the Reich of 37,000 freight cars, 800 passenger cars, and 1000 locomotives. The need for this equipment was so urgent that the trains had to be moved out empty. The remaining rolling stock was hardly sufficient to transport Gauleiter Sauckel's 350,000 French laborers to the Reich. The news was communicated to Hauptsturmführer Dannecker on June 16, 1942.[293]

The SS men were still undeterred. On June 26, 1942, Dannecker drew up a set of rules *(Richtlinien)* for the deportation of the French Jews. He fixed the age limits from 16 to 45 and decided that the deportations could embrace Jews of French nationality as well as those "stateless" Jews who were not effectively protected by a foreign power. Next, he prepared a list of things which the victims were to take along: two pairs of socks, two shirts, two pairs of underdrawers, a towel, a cup, a spoon, etc. For the guidance of the transport command, he itemized the qualities of food to be stocked in the supply car of each train. Since the trains were to be made up of freight cars, he directed that each car be provided with a pail. Finally, he dealt with the question of guards, who were to be furnished by the army's *Feldgendarmerie* in the strength of one officer and forty men per train to the Reich border.[294]

By the end of June, Dannecker had some idea of the number of transports that could be wangled from the Wehrmacht. As a start, he could get a train every other day – enough to transport 15,000 Jews a month. The grand strategy could now be laid out for all of France. The 100,000 Jews to be deported in the first sweep were to be drawn in two groups of 50,000 each from the occupied and unoccupied zones. The implementation of the plan in the occupied zone was expected to proceed without friction *(reibungslos und klar)*. The operation in the occupied area was to start in the provincial cities. The first transport was to leave Bordeaux on July 13, 1942. The following transports were scheduled to leave at two-day intervals: Bordeaux again, Angers, Rouen, Châlons sur Marne-Nancy, and Orléans. The deportation machine was then to descend on Paris.[295] The Parisian quota was 22,000 Jews, who were to be seized in each *arrondissement* in proportion to the distribution of the Jews within the city.[296]

Now that the transport difficulty was partially overcome, the SS men in Paris

291. Announcement in *Pariser Zeitung*, June 26, 1942, p. 4.

292. HStuf. Dannecker to Staf. Dr. Knochen and OStubaf. Lischka, June 15, 1942, RF-1217.

293. Dannecker to RSHA IV-B-4, June 16, 1942, RF-1218.

294. Directive by Dannecker, June 26, 1942, RF-1221.

295. Memorandum signed by Eichmann and Dannecker, July 1, 1942, RF-1223. Dannecker to Knochen and Lischka, July 1, 1942, RF-1222.

296. Memorandum by Dannecker, July 4, 1942, RF-1224.

were confronted by still another shortage: police. In all of occupied France the German Order Police had only three battalions with 3000 men in all. (How weak these forces were in relation to their task may be glimpsed in the fact that little Holland had more than 5000 men.[297]) Clearly, the Order Police could not be enlisted to help. For the relatively small operation of guarding the trains the RSHA had secured the assistance of the *Feldgendarmerie,* but for the major undertaking of conducting the seizures the SS men had to draw upon the French police. In the occupied zone the French police force was 47,000 strong.[298] The Frenchmen were needed particularly in Paris, a city of nearly 3,000,000 people that had more than 140,000 Jews.

To secure the complete support of the French police, BdS Standartenführer Knochen stepped into the office of Chief of the French Government Pierre Laval and informed him that the German government had decided to deport every Jewish man, woman, and child living in France. No distinction was going to be made between Jews of French nationality and others. The prefect of police in Paris had already been notified by the German authorities of their decision in this matter. Laval thereupon interceded with Higher SS and Police Leader Oberg to save the situation.

Oberg made a compromise proposal. If the French police would co-operate in the operation, the seizures would be confined for the moment to stateless Jews. "The trains are ready," explained the SS-man. "They have to be filled at any price. The Jewish problem has no frontiers for us. The police must help us or we shall do the arresting without any distinction between French Jews and others." Oberg then offered the assurance that the Jews were being sent to Poland, where a "Jewish state" would be set up for them.

Laval now had to make a "rapid decision." He decided to save the French nationals and involve the police in the roundup. Writing his memoirs in the death house after the liberation, Laval defended his decision in the following words: "I did all I could, considering the fact that my first duty was to my fellow-countrymen of Jewish extraction whose interests I could not sacrifice. The right of asylum was not respected in this case. How could it have been otherwise in a country which was occupied by the German Army? How could the Jews have been better protected in a country where the Gestapo ran riot?"[299]

The compromise which brought temporary immunity to all Jews of French nationality had an upsetting effect on the German deportation strategy. For example, a transport scheduled to leave Bordeaux on July 15 had to be canceled because only 150 stateless Jews could be found in the city. The cancellation caused particular annoyance to Obersturmbannführer Eichmann; calling his expert Röthke from Berlin, he demanded an explanation for this fiasco. The RSHA had conducted lengthy negotiations with the Reich Transport Minister to obtain the cars, and now Paris canceled a train. Such a thing had never happened to him before. He could not even report it to Gestapo Chief Müller, lest the blame fall on his own shoulders. Disgusted, Eichmann uttered the threat that he might even drop France as an evacuation land.[300]

If Laval had made a dent in the German plan by saving the French Jews, he

297. Daluege to Wolff, February 28, 1943, NO-2861.

298. *Ibid.*

299. Quotation and account of meetings with Knochen and Oberg from Pierre Laval, *Diary* (New York, 1948), pp. 97–99.

300. Memorandum by Röthke on long-distance telephone conversation with Eichmann, July 15, 1942, RF-1226. Eichmann had called at 7 P.M. on July 14.

made up for the loss in part by throwing in the children of the stateless victims. The question of the Jewish children remaining behind in the occupied territory did not "interest" him.[301] The Germans and their helpers among the French police could now proceed with the seizure of men, women, and children alike.

On the eve of the Paris roundup, a "working committee" met for the first time to discuss the "technical" details of the operation. The committee consisted of Dannecker and the following Frenchmen: the anti-Jewish commissar, Darquier de Pellepoix; the deputy of the French police chief in the occupied zone, Leguay; the director of the transit camps, François; the director of the Street Police, Hannequin; the director of the Jewish register in the Paris prefecture of police, Tulard; a representative of the prefect of the Seine *département*, Director Garier; the director of the Anti-Jewish Police, Schweblin; the *Chef de Cabinet* of the anti-Jewish commissariat, Gallieu; and a staff officer of the Street Police, Guidot.[302]

As the raids struck the French capital, 12,884 stateless Jews were rounded up by the French police.[303] Men without family were sent directly to Drancy; families were routed through the race track (the Velodrome d'Hiver) to Pithiviers and Beaune la Rolande. At these camps the children were separated from their parents, who were moved rapidly to the evacuation center at Drancy. The children were to follow.[304]

The German plan for the initial deportation of 100,000 Jews had called for 50,000 from each zone, and the two operations were to be implemented simultaneously. Thus, on June 27, Hauptsturmführer Dannecker mentioned in a conversation with Legationsrat Zeitschel that he would need 50,000 Jews from the Vichy zone "as soon as possible." Zeitschel communicated the matter immediately to Ambassador Abetz and Gesandtschaftsrat Rahn.[305] The diplomats and SS men now joined forces to apply the necessary pressure *(Druckarbeit)* upon Laval.

Not much pressure was needed. Laval declared himself ready to hand over the foreign Jews from the unoccupied zone and proposed that the Germans also "take along" the children under sixteen.[306] The Germans were elated. They were also surprised. After one meeting a German negotiator, Gesandtschaftsrat Rahn, could not help remarking to Laval that the whole business was just a little unsavory. Irritated, Laval jumped at Rahn: "Well, what am I to do? I offered these foreign Jews to the Allies, but they didn't take them off my hands."[307]

On August 13, 1942, the delegate of the French police in the occupied zone, Leguay, declared in a conference with Dannecker that the first transport with Jews from the occupied zone would cross the demarcation line on August 17, 1942. The transports from southern France were to be routed to Drancy, where they were to be "mixed" with the Jewish children from Pithiviers and Beaune la Rolande in the proportion of 500–700 adults per 300–500 children. At the same time Leguay assured the German representative that renewed

301. Dannecker to RSHA IV-B-4, July 6, 1942, Centre de Documentation Juive Contemporaine, *La persecution des Juifs en France*, p. 128.

302. Dannecker to Lischka, Knochen, and Oberg, July 8, 1942, *ibid.*, p. 144.

303. Schleier to Foreign Office, September 11, 1942, NG-5109.

304. Kaplan, *American Jewish Year Book*, 1945, pp. 82–84.

305. Zeitschel to Knochen, June 27, 1942, RF-1220.

306. Dannecker to RSHA IV-B-4, July 6, 1942, Centre de Documentation Juive Contemporaine, *La persecution des Juifs en France*, p. 128.

307. Testimony by Rudof Rahn, Case No. 11, tr. pp. 17581–83.

roundups had been launched in the unoccupied zone in order to fill the German quota. The German negotiators listened carefully and bluntly warned Leguay that it was a question of a "permanent *Aktion*" which eventually would have to include the Jews of French nationality.[308]

The Vichy authorities understood. By September 1 they had handed over 5000 Jews, and during the same interval another 7100 were arrested in the unoccupied zone.[309] A low point had been reached in the ability of the Pétain-Laval regime to withstand German pressure. But counter-pressures were already building up.

In the southern city of Toulouse the archbishop instructed the clergy of his diocese to protest from their pulpits against the deportation of the Jews. When Laval heard of these instructions, he called a representative of the Nuncio, Monsignor Rocco, and requested him to call to the attention of the Pope and Cardinal State Secretary Maglione the French government's determination not to permit interferences of this type in the internal affairs of the state of France. Laval then warned Rocco that in the event of any attempt on the part of the clergy to shield deportable Jews in churches and cloisters, he would not hesitate to drag out the Jews with French police. In conclusion, Laval expressed his surprise that the Church was so adamant in its attitude; after all, he said with reference to the "yellow hat," anti-Jewish measures were not exactly new to the Church.[310]

Laval implemented his threat. In the Lyon diocese a number of priests were arrested for reading protest declarations to the congregations and for harboring Jewish children on the church grounds.[311] Among the arrested men was the Jesuit Elder Chaillet, the "right hand" of Archbishop Gerlier of Lyon. Chaillet was accused of hiding eighty Jewish children.[312]

While Laval was fighting off the Church, counter-pressure was being applied to him from still other quarters – the United States and Switzerland. Diplomatic relations between the United States and Vichy France persisted through the summer months of 1942, but the relationship was already strained when in August, 1942, the Americans watched the preparations of the Vichy regime to return the Jewish refugees to the German Reich. When the delegate of the American Friends Service Committee protested against the impending deportations, he was told by Laval "that these foreign Jews had always been a problem in France and that the French Government was glad that a change in the German attitude towards them gave France an opportunity to get rid of them." Laval asked the Quaker delegate why the United States did not take these Jews and concluded with "a rather bitter general discussion of the Jewish problem."[313]

The American chargé d'affaires in Vichy then approached the Chief of the French Government to obtain a few exit permits for threatened Jewish victims. During these discussions the American diplomat expressed the attitude of the United States toward the deportations, stressing the contention that "the world, and the people of

308. Summary of German-French police conference, August 13, 1942, RF-1234.

309. Schleier to Foreign Office, September 11, 1942, NG-5109.

310. Abetz to Foreign Office, August 28, 1942, reporting conversation of August 27 with Laval, NG-4578.

311. Bergen (German Ambassador at the Vatican) to Foreign Office, September 14, 1942, NG-4578.

312. Abetz to Foreign Office, September 2, 1942, NG-5127.

313. Thompson (Second Secretary of Legation in Switzerland, temporarily in France) to Secretary of State Hull, August 7, 1942, *Foreign Relations of the United States 1942* (Washington, D.C., 1960), I (general, etc.), 463–64.

France, would some day pass judgment on Laval for this callous act."[314] At the same time, U. S. Secretary of State Hull told French Ambassador Henry Haye in Washington what the American government thought of Vichy's decision to deport the Jewish refugees.[315]

The government of Switzerland, casting its eyes upon the developments in neighboring France, had a momentary vision of a mass invasion of refugees. As frightened Jews from southern France and prospective Wehrmacht draftees from Alsace-Lorraine began to drift across the border, the federal authorities sent back a few of the Jewish arrivals on the ground that the Jews did not qualify for "political" asylum. Faced with considerable criticism of this action, the chief of the Federal Justice and Police Department declared that "we cannot turn our country into a sponge for Europe and take in for example 80 or 90 per cent of the Jewish refugees."[316]

While Swiss police were engaged in tightening the frontier, the Swiss Minister in Vichy, Walter Stucki, acting as the delegate of the International Red Cross Committee for France, stepped into the office of Pétain and, pounding the table, delivered his protest to the old French marshall. Pétain is said to have "deplored" the situation, adding that it was a matter of "internal concern"; Stucki is reported to have replied that he disagreed and that, under the deportation measures, children were being taken from institutions where they had been cared for by Swiss charity.[317]

The Germans, in the meantime, were not wholly satisfied with the pace of the deportations in France. During an RSHA conference of Jewish experts in Berlin on August 28, 1942, the remark was dropped that other countries were ahead of France in final solution matters and that the French sector would have to catch up.[318] A few days later Untersturmführer Ahnert sent Oberg a compilation of figures which revealed that, up to September 2, deportations had totaled 18,000 Jews from the occupied zone and 9000 from the unoccupied area – 27,000 in all. Although operations were to be stepped up in September, said Ahnert, the Germans faced an obvious difficulty in the French insistence upon a distinction between French and foreign Jews. It would therefore be necessary to effect at least a French revocation of naturalizations granted to Jews after 1933.[319]

During the following few weeks BdS Knochen talked to French Police Chief Bousquet and to Premier Laval about the possible concentration of the Jews of French nationality. The talks were unsuccessful. Pétain was opposed to the deportation of French Jews, and the Vichy bureaucracy was reluctant to act in contravention to Pétain's wish. Higher SS and Police Leader Oberg then informed Himmler of the situation. Himmler, backing down, agreed that for the time being no Jews of French nationality were to be deported. All

314. President Roosevelt to Representative Celler (U.S. Congress), October 21, 1942, in Emanuel Celler, *You Never Leave Brooklyn* (New York, 1953), pp. 90–92.

315. Abetz to Foreign Office, September 18, 1942, reporting conversation between Sauckel and Laval, NG-2306.

316. Harrison (U.S. Minister in Switzerland) to Hull, September 5, 1942, *Foreign Relations 1942,* I, 469–70.

317. Harrison to Hull, September 26, 1942, *ibid.*, p. 472. See also the conversations carried on by French Protestant Pastor Boegner with Bousquet, Darlan, and Laval, in Alexander Werth, *France 1940–1955* (New York, 1956), pp. 61–62.

318. Röthke to Knochen and Lischka, September 1, 1942, RF-1228.

319. Ahnert via Hagen to Oberg, September 3, 1942, RF-1227. The figure of 18,000 for the occupied zone includes the deportation of the 5000 Jews who had been rounded up in 1941. Schleier to Foreign Office, September 11, 1942, NG-5109.

efforts were now to be concentrated on another front: the deportation of those foreign Jews who were protected only by Axis states – the Italian Jews, the Hungarian Jews, and the 3000 Roumanian Jews in France.[320]

Again the Germans were checked. The negotiations with the Roumanians and Hungarians turned out to be a slippery affair. The Roumanians would agree to relinquish their Jews, only to turn around and withdraw their consent. When pressured, the Roumanian negotiators would agree, subject to prior co-operation by the Hungarians, while the Hungarians insisted that the Roumanians move first. In part at least, this reluctance was due to the Italians, who refused to move at all. The German Foreign Office did all in its power to persuade the Italians to co-operate. From the pen of Unterstaatssekretär Luther flowed letter after letter on the need to do something about the Italians,[321] but Germany's principal Axis partner remained absolutely firm.

In Paris the Italian Consul General, Dr. Gustavo Orlandini, exacted from Obersturmführer Röthke an agreement that no Italian subject in France would be touched by the Germans without prior Italian consent. In considering such consent, the Italian consuls were going to be guided by the Italian "racial laws" and the higher directives received from Rome.[322] And in Rome even the highest circles had no sympathy with the killing of the Jews.

The increasing difficulties encountered with the attempted deportations of Jews holding French or Axis nationalities were reflected in a decreasing number of transports leaving France for the East. Instead of "catching up" with the rest of Europe, the French sector appeared to fall further and further behind. Then, one day in the beginning of November, an event in North Africa shook up the equilibrium. Allied troops had started landings in Morocco and Algiers. The Germans, in a lightning countermove, occupied Vichy France and the Protectorate of Tunisia. The demarcation line had disappeared.

A large new area was now under German control, but newly acquired opportunities were matched by a host of fresh obstacles and barriers. The first of these was the geographic factor; if the SS and Police had been stretched thin in the old occupied zone, there were now tens of thousands of additional square miles to cover. Another obstacle presented itself in the form of the Italian opposition, for if Italian influence was felt in Paris, it was felt much more strongly east of the Rhone and in Tunisia. A third difficulty was perhaps the most important: it was Vichy's realization that Germany had lost the war.

In Tunisia the German sphere of activity was most restricted. For one thing, the geographic position of the area was forbidding. The Germans knew that in the event of an Allied breakthrough they would not be able to evacuate the fighting army from there. How, then, could they have shipped out the Jews? Besides, Tunisia was Africa, and the "final solution" by its very definition was applicable only to the European continent. These considerations, however, were not going to stop the German bureaucrats from inflicting upon the Tunisian Jews a

320. Knochen to RSHA IV-B-4, September 25, 1942, NG-1971.

321. Luther to Weizsäcker, July 24, 1942, NG-5094. Luther to Weizsäcker and Wörmann, September 17, 1942, NG-5093. Luther via Weizsäcker to Ribbentrop, October 22, 1942, NG-4960. Only about 500 Italian Jews were living in the occupied zone, "but this," said Luther, "does not detract from the importance of the question." Luther to Ribbentrop, October 22, 1942, NG-4960.

322. Orlandini to Röthke, August 4, 1942, in Leon Poliakov (ed.), *La condition des Juifs en France sous l'occupation italienne* (Paris, 1946), p. 149.

certain amount of suffering. The bureaucrats were determined to start as quickly as possible, and they proceeded as far as they could.

Tunisia was a military area, and the German forces there were under the command of the *Oberbefehlshaber Süd*, Generalfeldmarschall Kesselring in Rome. The first local commander was General Nehring. During the first month (to December 9, 1942) the setup was thus a simple one. By December 10, German forces in Tunisia had been built up to a point that permitted the establishment of the Fifth Panzer Army, commanded by von Arnim. This army was joined by another one retreating into Tunisia from Libya, the Panzer Army Africa under Rommel. By February 23, 1943, the two armies were placed under an army group, and this organization remained to the end:

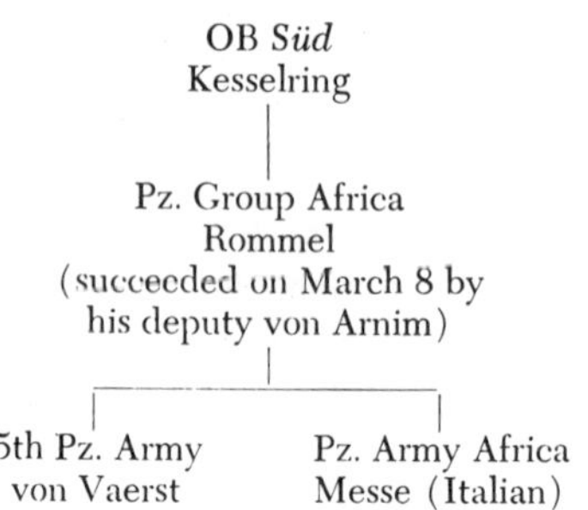

Although the generals were in control of the situation, they were not alone. The Foreign Office was represented by one of its trouble shooters, Minister Rahn; the SS and Police had sent down an *Einsatzkommando;* the French still had their Resident General, Admiral Esteva; and the Tunisians still had their Bey.

As soon as the German Army was established in Tunisia, the *Einsatzkommando* arrested the Jewish community leaders. The arrest had hardly been made when an order was received from the *Oberbefehlshaber Süd*, Generalfeldmarschall Kesselring, to mobilize Jewish labor for fortification work. The local commander, General der Panzertruppen Nehring, now conferred with Minister Rahn, French Resident General Esteva, and the SS men to find a way of implementing the order. It was decided that the Jewish community leaders would have to be freed in order to organize the labor service; to kill two birds with one stone, it was also decided to levy from the Jewish community a 20,000,000-franc "fine" as a condition for the release.[323] Since, according to the official report, "international Jewry" was responsible for the Anglo-American attack on North Africa, the money was handed over to a mixed Arab-Italian-French committee for immediate assistance to bombed-out people.[324] The released Jewish leaders were then made responsible, upon penalty of death, for the creation of the labor service.

The order, issued by Nehring on December 6, 1942, specified that the Jewish leaders were to select the manpower and that the Jewish communities were to furnish equipment and food for the men. The labor columns were to be detailed to the German commanders in Bizerte, Tunis-North, and Tunis-South for work on the main defense line (*Hauptkampflinie*).[325] Italian Jews had to be excepted upon protest of the Italian Consul General.[326]

The Germans in Tunisia were not able to proceed beyond the forced labor system. The Wehrmacht Propa-

323. Rudolf Rahn, *Ruheloses Leben* (Düsseldorf, 1949), pp. 203–4. Testimony by Rahn, Case No. 11, tr. pp. 17578–79.

324. Rahn to Foreign Office, December 22, 1942, NG-2676. 20,000,000 francs = RM 1,000,000 = $400,000.

325. Order by Nehring, forwarded to Rahn, December 6, 1942, NG-2271. Rahn to Foreign Office, December 6, 1942, NG-2099. Nehring was a former Africa Corps commander.

326. OKH/Chef GenSt (signed Pomser) to Rahn, with copy for 5th Pz. Army/Ia, December 9, 1942, NG-2360. Rahn to Foreign Office, December 9, 1942, NG-3150.

ganda Office of the OKW wanted the propaganda platoon in Tunisia to foment pogroms and the looting of Jewish stores, but Minister Rahn took a dim view of these instructions. He thought them unenforcible until such time as German troops stood "at least" at the Algerian border.[327]

On the island of Djerba, off the eastern coast of Tunisia, the Germans managed to present to the Jews a parting gift. Some 4500 Jews were living in two ancient ghettos there. A major in charge of the *Kommandantur* on the island is said to have approached the chief rabbi of the principal ghetto, the Hara Khebira, and demanded the delivery within two hours of 50 kilograms of gold under threat of bombardment by two German planes. The major departed with 47 kilograms, leaving the community impoverished.[328]

The Tunisian expedition was at an end. The 80,000 Jews were left there, benumbed by the German cyclone which had touched them.

While in Africa the Germans were confined to looting and labor exploitation, they hoped to accomplish something more in the newly occupied regions of metropolitan France. The Higher SS and Police Leader, Brigadeführer Oberg, sent his *Einsatzkommandos* south. On the river Rhone he discovered an obstacle: a large area east of that river was occupied by Italian troops. Acting under the assumption that the Italian forces were under German command, Oberg asked Generalfeldmarschall von Rundstedt, the *Oberbefehlshaber West*, to "pave the way" with the Italians for his *Einsatzkommandos*. Rundstedt, however, had no jurisdiction in the matter. The Italian divisions were under the command of the Italian Fourth Army, stationed in Turin.[329] In the new Italian occupation zone the Jews were to enjoy complete sanctuary, and as the Germans turned toward the Pyrenees, Spain too became a place of refuge for some Jews.[330]

The Germans now attempted to bring down as many police forces as could be scraped up on a moment's notice. The 3000 men of the Order Police stretched out from the Belgian frontier to the Mediterranean were reinforced by a police regiment under Colonel Griese, and by January, 1943, another 2000 men with heavy weapons were on their way.[331]

Pressure was then exerted upon the chief of the French police, Bousquet, for his full co-operation. Bousquet appeared to agree. "The French police," reported Himmler, "are prepared to collect the Jews within the prefectures, from which we could then transport them to the East."[332] As if to show its good faith in the matter, the Vichy regime "of its own accord" forbade Jewish travel in the newly occupied zone and ordered identity and food ration cards to be stamped with the *J*. The German Embassy, however, was afraid that without Italian co-operation east of the Rhone River the Jews would simply wander off from the German to

327. Rahn to Foreign Office, December 22, 1942, NG-2676. Testimony by Rahn, Case No. 11, tr. pp. 17583–84. The SS and Police in Paris contacted the embassy with a similar request that a clandestine radio station, under control of the embassy, broadcast in Arab dialects to North Africa with a view to inciting natives to riot against the Jews and American occupation authorities. Schleier to Foreign Office, November 24, 1942, NG-57.

328. Mane Katz (Paris painter), "Bei den Juden von Djerba," *Aufbau* (New York), September 3, 1954, p. 9.

329. Oberg to Himmler, November 16, 1942, NO-3085.

330. Abetz to von Krug in Vichy, November 14, 1942, NG-3192. Schleier to embassy's Vichy branch, November 20, 1942, NG-3192. The small state of Andorra, wedged in the Pyrenees, was reported to be filled with Jewish refugees. *Die Judenfrage*, April 15, 1943, p. 136.

331. Daluege to Wolff, February 28, 1943, NO-2861.

332. Himmler to Ribbentrop, January, 1943, NO-1893.

the Italian occupation zone.[333] From the end of 1942 to the summer of 1943, therefore, the Germans attempted to secure the collaboration of their Axis partner. They failed.

On December 4, 1942, the *Comando Supremo* in Rome had assured the German military attaché that all Jews in the newly occupied Italian zone would be interned.[334] The French prefects, in possession of their own orders to round up the Jews, attempted to proceed. Within a matter of weeks the Vichy authorities were confronted by a solid wall of opposition on the part of the Fourth Italian Army, the Italian Armistice Commission, and the Italian Foreign Office itself. French Police Chief Bousquet now turned around and handed to the Germans a written note of the Italian government of December 20, 1942; it protested the decree of the French prefect in the Maritime Alps concerning the Jews' internment.[335] The controversy was thereupon transferred to the German Embassy in Rome for an airing with the Italian Foreign Minister, Count Ciano.

On January 16, 1943, Ambassador Mackensen explained to Ciano the German "viewpoint" on the question of the treatment of the Jews in the occupied West. Ciano listened carefully and remarked that he personally could understand the German viewpoint and that he shared it basically; however, the implementation of these measures touched a great many other agencies and would raise various questions. In view of these complications, Ciano suggested that the matter could be discussed at some other time, on a lower level.[336] The issue was to be brought up again – but on the highest level.

The occasion for the new German move was a report received from the French *Intendant de Police* at Lyon, on February 20, 1943, about his attempt to implement a Vichy order for the arrest of 200-300 Jews in the regional prefecture of Lyon. The Jews were to be brought to an internment camp in order to be transported from there to Auschwitz "for labor." The Italian general in Grenoble protested against the order and demanded the release of the Jews. The police *intendant* was forced to comply. When Standartenführer Knochen saw this report, he wrote to Gestapo Chief Müller: "I want to point out again that the French government, which approaches the solution of the Jewish question unwillingly enough, is actually strengthened in this attitude by the measures of the Italian administration." The Italian area was already "flooded" with Jews, and rumors had been received of Italian intentions to permit not only illegal departures to Switzerland but emigration to Italy itself.[337]

On February 25, 1943, Ribbentrop himself produced the *intendant's* report in a conference with Mussolini. The Italian leader remarked that he was aware of the "radical" German position in the Jewish question. Ribbentrop replied that the Jews had to be evacuated. Now he realized that in "military circles" – German as well as Italian – the Jewish problem was not fully appreciated. That was the only explanation he could offer for the *Comando Supremo's* cancellation of the French or-

333. Schleier to Foreign Office, January 15, 1943, NG-3453. Staf. Knochen via Stülpnagel to Gfm. von Rundstedt, February 3, 1943, NG-2268.

334. OKW/WFSt/Qu via RSHA to OGruf. Wolff and Ambassador Ritter, December 4, 1942, NO-1118.

335. Schleier to Foreign Office, January 23, 1943, NG-4959. Knochen via Stülpnagel to Rundstedt, February 3, 1943, NG-2268.

336. Mackensen to Foreign Office, January 16, 1943, NG-5459.

337. Knochen to Müller, February 22, 1943, in Poliakov, *La condition des Juifs en France sous l'occupation italienne,* pp. 150–52. Note by Bergmann (Foreign Office), February 24, 1943, NG-4956.

der in the Italian zone. At this point Mussolini broke in to contest the accuracy of the report. He attempted to trace it to the "French tactics of causing dissension between Germany and Italy." The Jews, thought Mussolini, had been concentrated in the Italian area, but the Foreign Minister was right in saying that military people did not understand these things. The military had a special education and mentality of their own. Ribbentrop then came back to the "Jewish danger," asserting that the retention of 100,000 Jews in the area was equivalent to the introduction there of 100,000 secret service agents.[338]

One week after this discussion another incident occurred. After an attack on two German officers in Paris, the French police were requested to make available 2000 Jews for a "penance" transport to the East. The French *gendarmerie* arrested its Jews in various towns, including Grenoble and Annecy in the Italian zone. In the Grenoble area the Italian Army promptly "blockaded" the hundred arrested Jews to prevent their departure; at Annecy Italian troops surrounded the French *gendarmerie* barracks and forced the release of the Jews who were held captive there.[339]

On March 18, 1943, Ambassador von Mackensen approached Mussolini with the new evidence of Italian interference. Mussolini thanked him for the documents and pointed out that, if his generals had made difficulties, it had happened because their "mode of thinking" prevented them from comprehending the scope of all these measures. This was to be taken not as an expression of bad intentions but simply as the "logical consequence of their mode of thinking." To remove the possibility of any further difficulties, the chief of the *Comando Supremo,* Colonel General Ambrosio, would receive orders not to allow any interference with the French police.[340]

During the next twenty-four hours Mussolini instituted what seemed at first glance to be major changes in the Italian occupied zone. He transferred jurisdiction in Jewish matters from the Italian Army to the Interior Ministry in Rome. The ministry established a Commissariat for Jewish Questions in Nice and appointed as commissar a police inspector with general rank: Lospinoso. Italian *gendarmerie* detailed to his command were constituted into a *Polizia Raziale* – racial police.

Lospinoso's task was the removal of all Jews from the coastal area to the interior. There, in easily guarded towns, the Jews were to be assigned to *residenza forzatta* ("forced residence"). The "dangerous" elements among the Jews were to be incarcerated in a concentration camp at Sospello. However, when Ambassador von Mackensen inquired at the Italian Foreign Office what would happen to all these Jews after they were concentrated, "that is, whether it was intended to ship them off," the Italian official, Bastianini, replied that "this was not being considered at present."[341]

Bastianini's remark was an indication

338. Summary of Mussolini-Ribbentrop conference, held on February 25, 1943, in the presence of Bastianini, Alfieri, and von Mackensen, February 27, 1943, D-734.

339. Rademacher and Bergmann to Pol. II, March 3, 1943, NG-5087.

340. Report by von Mackensen, undated, NG-2242.

341. Report by von Mackensen on conference of March 20, 1943, with Bastianini, NG-2242. Also: Italian liaison officer with OB West (Div. Gen. Marazzani) to Stubaf. Hagen, March 19, 1943, in Poliakov, *La condition des Juifs en France sous l'occupation italienne,* p. 154. OStuf. Moritz (*Einsatzkommando* Marseille) to OStuf. Röthke, May 26, 1943, *ibid.,* p. 156. Stubaf. Muehler of Ekdo. Marseille to BdS IV-B, July 10, 1943, *ibid.,* p. 161.

of the manner in which the Italians were going to proceed in the matter. Early in April, Lospinoso detailed a Lieutenant Malfatti of the Italian Embassy in Paris to discuss some problems with BdS Knochen. Standartenführer Knochen refused to deal with Malfatti; indignantly, he wrote to Müller of the Gestapo that he had declined "to enter into a discussion about this – after all – quite important problem with a first lieutenant [*dieses immerhin wichtige Problem mit einem Oberleutnant zu erörtern*]."[342]

In May the Germans were disconcerted by a report that Lospinoso's chief assistant was a half-Jew. The assistant, Donati, was a man who during World War I had served as a liaison officer between the French and Italian armies and who was later the manager of the Franco-Italian Bank in Paris. "Donati," reported Obersturmführer Röthke, "is possibly even a full Jew" (*möglicherweise sogar ein Volljude*) and "maintains excellent relations with Italian officers."[343]

Subsequent discoveries made the Germans more and more uneasy. The elusive Lospinoso did not wish to confer with the Germans. Upon one occasion in July the chief of the *Einsatzkommando* in Marseille, Stubaf. Mühler, had to content himself with an interview of Luceri Tommaso, Vice-Questor of the Race Police, who promptly declared that in Jewish questions he was powerless to make any decisions. The Race Police, said Tommaso, had registered 22,000 Jews in the coastal area of the Italian zone; these Jews were now on their way to forced residences in Megève, St. Gervain, Castellane, and other places. To Mühler these towns sounded like "famous resorts." The Italians, he concluded, were not serious; they revealed their pro-Jewish attitude "quite openly." Thus the French police had been forced again and again to release Jews who had already been arrested, and so on.[344]

To the Security Police in Paris the chief villain in this situation seemed to be the "Jew" Donati. Accordingly, a plan was laid for kidnapping Donati from Nice to Marseille, but the plot did not succeed because the German agents, who were under instructions to proceed with "the utmost care," could not grab their victim before he flew to Rome on a business trip.[345]

The Germans were completely stymied in the Italian occupation zone, and thousands of Jews found complete sanctuary there until the day of the Italian collapse. In the rest of France the continued German dependence upon the French police assured to the French Jews, both native-born and naturalized, a measure of immunity. Even among the stateless and foreign Jews there were privileged categories.

The Germans did whatever they could to cut down these protected groups. For instance, on March 19 Office IV-B of the BdS transmitted to the police prefecture of Paris a request to deport from a list of 720 Jewish fur workers those whose nationality made them eligible for arrest. In that same communication the Security Police demanded the seizure of foreign Jews employed by the UGIF.[346] During this period of scraping the bottom of the barrel, the Foreign Office bureaucrats in Paris and Vichy did not hesitate to attempt the deportation of a seventy-five-year-old Jew, Edward Leyba, who was a native of Dutch Curaçao and

342. Knochen to Müller, April 8, 1943, *ibid.*, p. 155.

343. OStuf. Moritz (Marseille) to Röthke, May 26, 1943, *ibid.*, p. 156. Röthke to Knochen, May 27, 1943, *ibid.*, p. 160.

344. Mühler to BdS IV-B, July 10, 1943, *ibid.*, p. 161.

345. Röthke to RSHA IV-B-4, September 26, 1943, *ibid.*, pp. 163-65.

346. BdS *Frankreich* IV-B to police prefecture of Paris, March 19, 1943, Occ 17.

who was now the chargé d'affaires of Paraguay. Only fear for the safety of "Germandom in Paraguay" restrained the German Foreign Office from violating the law of diplomatic immunity by "shoving" this man "off" or "rendering" him "harmless."[347]

The occupation of Vichy France had not been a true breakthrough since the increased opportunities for pressure had been offset by new obstacles. There had been no "catching up" in France. Instead, the German Security Police in Paris had fallen further and further behind. The statistics of deportations reveal the full extent of the situation in France compared to the state of affairs in the much smaller Netherlands to the north. By December 31, 1942, 41,911 Jews had been deported from France, and 38,511 from the Netherlands. Three months later, the figures were 49,906 and 52,343, respectively.[348]

On June 18, 1943, Standartenführer Knochen presented himself to Marshal Pétain's private physician and confidante, Dr. Ménétrel, and complained that the French government was hindering the implementation of the evacuations. Knochen said he was under the impression that the marshal "did not agree" with the solution of the Jewish problem. Ménétrel replied that the marshal wished a solution in the form that Jews of the younger generation would be deprived of every opportunity to serve in important posts in France. One had to understand that, at his age, the marshal naturally preferred a "humane" solution to a "radical" one. He would not therefore like to throw out all the Jews from their jobs in order to let them perish from hunger (*um sie evtl. vor Hunger krepieren zu lassen*). Ménétrel added "privately" that on his part he "admired" the German resolution to carry out the "final uprooting of Jewry."[349]

In August, 1943, the Germans made a last attempt to negotiate with the French for a widening of the operations against the Jews. The principal topic on the agenda was the cancellation of naturalizations granted to Jews after 1927. On August 14, Hauptsturmführer Geissler and Obersturmführer Röthke, two experts from the office of the BdS, met with Laval in Vichy to discuss the issue. The law had already been drawn up and a draft of it signed by Laval, but now the French Premier claimed that he did not know what he had been signing, that he had not dreamed that the Germans were planning to arrest the denaturalized Jews en masse, that a law of such gravity would have to have the consent of the Council of Ministers, that Marshal Pétain would have to approve it, that in the last analysis nothing could be done so long as there was opposition from the Italians, and that even without the Italians the law after its promulgation would have to be held in abeyance for three months to give individual Jews a chance to appeal.

When the German negotiators heard these arguments, they concluded that the French government "no longer wished to follow" them in the Jewish question. With unmistakable clarity Laval had told them that he was neither "anti-Semitic" nor "pro-Semitic." The Germans had enough insight to understand that remark. "It is no longer possible," they concluded, "to count on any large-scale help from the French police for the arrest of the Jews, unless, a few days or weeks from now, the military situation in Germany changes radically in our favor."[350]

347. Schleier to Foreign Office, January 31, 1943, NG-3377.

348. Report by Korherr, April 19, 1943, NO-5193. The Korherr report specifies "occupied France." However, a figure of 49,000 is given for all of France in a report by Röthke, dated March 6, 1943, RF-1230.

349. Memorandum by Stubaf. Hagen, June 21, 1943, Occ 21.

350. Röthke to Knochen, August 15, 1943,

The military situation did not exactly change in Germany's favor. At the beginning of September Italy surrendered to the Allies, and the Germans were left as the undisputed though overextended masters of all France. Within a matter of days the Security Police swept over the zone vacated by the Italians. Thousands of Jews were caught at Nice. Several hundred families who had taken refuge in Monaco left their sanctuary in fear of a German invasion. Many of these victims walked to their undoing as they tried to reach the frontiers of Switzerland or Spain.[351]

Notwithstanding the temporary flareup of activity in the former Italian zone, the German machinery of destruction in France was forced to slow down by an emergence of formidable barriers. Because of the increasing French reluctance to co-operate in arrests and seizures, the German police were gradually forced to rely upon their own resources. Raids were staged on arbitrary targets without much regard for the nature of the victims. One of these raids was described in some detail by the KdS in Lyon. In the early morning hours of April 6, 1944, Security Police in the Lyon sector had forced their way into the children's home in Izieu-Ain and had moved out with fifty-one persons, including five women and forty-one children between the ages of three and thirteen. Cash or other valuables, according to the report, could not be secured.[352]

While the Germans thus stepped into the open, the Jews, with the aid of French organizations, began to submerge. The prospective victims went into hiding by the tens of thousands, and, wherever possible, they moved across the borders.[353] The growing tendency of the Jews not to move blindly to their death is illustrated by an incident reported by a sergeant of the Order Police who guarded a transport to Auschwitz. At Leroville, reported the policeman, nineteen Jews had jumped off the train during the night. By way of self-defense, he pointed out that these Jews were the same ones who had previously tried to tunnel their way out of the Drancy transit camp. Those men, the report continued, should have been entrained without their clothes. The date of the report was December 3, 1943.[354]

The increasing recalcitrance of the French administration and the organized submersion by masses of Jews finally resulted in a German decision to employ all the available forces of the Security Police for an all-out drive against the remaining Jews. This final phase of the French deportations was inaugurated with an order signed by the BdS, Standartenführer Knochen, and his assistant, Hauptsturmführer Brunner, on April 14, 1944, a little more than four months before the Germans lost France. The order directed the seizure of all Jews of French nationality, save only those who were living in mixed marriages. The targets of the raids were to be children's homes,

---

in Poliakov, *Harvest of Hate*, pp. 178–81, fn. Also, Pierre Laval, *Diary*, p. 96.

351. Between the Security Police and the Foreign Office, a long correspondence ensued about the advisability of conducting seizures within Monaco: Von Thadden to Hencke, September 21, 1943, NG-4978. Steengracht to Consulate General in Monaco, September 23, 1943, NG-4978. Von Thadden to Eichmann, October 25, 1943, NG-4978. German Consul General in Monte Carlo (signed Hellenthal) to Foreign Office, July 14, 1944, NG-4964.

352. KdS Lyon IV-B (signed OStuf. Barbie) to BdS Paris IV-B, April 6, 1944, RF-1235.

353. Marie Syrkin, *Blessed is the Match* (Philadelphia, 1947), pp. 294–95, 301. Kaplan, *American Jewish Year Book*, 1945, pp. 97–98. *Einsatzkommando* Marseille (signed Stubaf. Mühler) to BdS IV-B, November 18, 1943, Occ 20.

354. Meister der Schupo Friedrich Köhnlein (5./Pl. Wachbatl. V) to OStuf. Röthke, December 3, 1943, Occ 19.

prisons, labor camps, and, in residential areas, city blocks and whole villages. Significantly, the order cautioned the police raiders not to advertise their arrival in prisons and camps under French control, lest the French release or transfer the inmates before the Germans could get there.

The Jews in mixed marriages were to take the place of deportable Jews in camps of the *Organisation Todt.* To get at the Jews in hiding, rewards were to be paid to Frenchmen who revealed hideouts or brought in victims. The amount of the reward was to be higher in the city than in the country. Payments were to be made, after seizure, from the effects of the arrested Jews. The guarding of the people who were rounded up and their transport to Drancy was to be accomplished with special care, for in the past most transports arriving at the transit camp had lost one or two Jews on the way. To prevent escapes, Knochen and Brunner recommended that the Jews be tied to each other with a long rope.[355]

Statistics are not available to indicate how successful the last drive turned out to be. Nearly a quarter of a million Jews were still living in France when the order was issued, and perhaps a hundred thousand were located in Paris alone. However, with the onset of the Allied invasion on June 6, 1944, the operations of the French underground multiplied the tasks of the police to such an extent that, quite apart from other difficulties such as forced labor recruitment and disruption of transport, not much could be done in those last few weeks.

On July 25, in fact, Reichsstatthalter Mutschmann of Saxony wrote a very interesting letter to Himmler, in which he referred to a press report to the effect that Jews had turned up in portions of Normandy occupied by the American and British armies. Mutschmann expressed his "astonishment" (*bin tatsächlich erschrocken darüber*) that there could still be Jews in France after all the years of German occupation. These Jews, continued the *Reichsstatthalter,* should have been removed a long time ago. So long as a single Jew was still living in Europe, said Mutschmann in his letter to Himmler, partisans, criminals, and saboteurs would always have leaders in the back of the German front.[356] The embarrassed Himmler could only reply that the total removal of the Jews from France was "extremely difficult" because of the "very strained relations" (*sehr misslichen Verhältnisse*) with the *Wehrmachtbefehlshaber* there. However, continued Himmler in the same paragraph, in Hungary, the SS was having much more success and was still continuing the operation.[357]

In Holland the Germans had deported more than three-fourths of all the Jews; in France the percentages were exactly reversed. Stalled in their efforts to effect a total deportation of the French Jews, the Germans threw themselves on the property of the community. In that area the German administration was a little more successful, for while many Jews were able to hide themselves they could not also hide their property. In brief, the confiscatory operation may be divided into three parts. It began with a hunt for art treasures, expanded into a seizure of furniture, and ended with a sequestration of liquid funds.

The collection of art may be traced to an order issued as early as June, 1940, by Hitler.[358] Art collection was in

355. Order by Knochen and Brunner, April 14, 1944, NO-1411.

356. Mutschmann to Himmler, July 25, 1944, NO-2779.

357. Himmler to Mutschmann, July 31, 1944, NO-2778.

358. Keitel to Gen.d.Art. Bockelberg, June 30, 1940, RF-1301.

fact one of the original tasks of Ambassador Abetz.[359] The embassy staff, in co-operation with the *Devisenschutzkommando* and the Einsatzstab Rosenberg, was conducting searches for art objects left behind by wealthy Jews who had fled the country.[360] In the course of these operations some choice objects turned up – to the discomfiture of Staatssekretär Weizsäcker – as decorations in the offices of the Paris Embassy.[361] Of the treasures which went to the Reich, some of the finest items were picked by Göring and Hitler for their personal collections.[362] On the other end of the scale, unwanted items were to be disposed of by the Finance Ministry, which had "experience" in such matters.[363] The bulk of the loot was kept in storage, to be catalogued and studied by Rosenberg's experts.[364]

As we have already observed in connection with the property confiscations in Holland, the Einsatzstab Rosenberg moved from art collecting into the furniture business. All apartments which had been vacated by departed and deported Jews were to be cleaned out with "the least possible fuss" (*möglichst wenig Aufsehen*) by the Einsatzstab Rosenberg.[365] The final report of the western office of the Einsatzstab reveals that 71,619 Jewish apartments had been seized, 38,000 of them in Paris. To crate all this furniture for shipment to Germany, the office drew upon Paris shippers, who made available daily up to 150 vans and 1200 to 1500 French workers. However, "sabotage" on the part of the French personnel was so great that the Einsatzstab hit upon the idea of employing 700 Jews for the sorting, packing, and loading operations. To prevent sabotage by French, Belgian, and Dutch railway workers, the Einsatzstab induced the *Reichsbahn* to supply German personnel. A total of 29,436 carloads was moved out in 735 freight trains for distribution to the following recipients:[366]

Cities and *Gaue*	18,665
Depots	8,191
Reichsbahn	1,576
SS divisions	577
Police	231
Reichspost	196
Total	29,436

At the end of 1942 the *Militärbefehlshaber* inaugurated the final phase of the confiscations. Having already raked in a billion-franc fine, he decreed the confiscation by the Reich of the property of all those stateless Jews whose

359. Weizsäcker to Ribbentrop, July 22, 1940, NG-1719. Ribbentrop to Keitel, August 3, 1940, PS-3614. Abetz to von Brauchitsch, August 16, 1940, NG-90.

360. Abetz to Major Hartmann of the *Devisenschutzkommando*, September 10, 1940, NG-2849. Memorandum by Galleiske (*Devisenschutzkommando*), March 19, 1941, NG-4091. Zeitschel to BdS and OStuf. Dannecker, June 20, 1941, NG-2851. Zeitschel to Gesandter Schleier, July 29, 1941, NG-2855. Schleier to Foreign Office, April 26, 1943, NG-3452. Report by Einsatzstab Rosenberg (signed Bereichsleiter Scholz) on art seizures, July, 1944, PS-1015-B.

361. Schleier to Foreign Office, July 31, 1942, NG-2970. Weizsäcker to Ministerialdirektor Schröder (Foreign Office personnel division), October 1, 1942, NG-2971.

362. Dr. Bunjes (Einsatzstab Rosenberg) to Staatsrat Turner (military district, Paris), February, 1941, PS-2523. Rosenberg to Hitler, March 20, 1941, PS-14. Göring to Rosenberg, May 30, 1942, PS-1015-I. Rosenberg to Hitler, April 16, 1943, PS-15.

363. Mayer to Patzer, March 26, 1941, NG-4063.

364. Report by Scholz, July, 1944, PS-1015-B.

365. Schleier to Foreign Office, copy via Strack to Abetz, January 30, 1942, NG-5018. Schleier to Foreign Office, February 6, 1942, NG-3444. Schleier to Foreign Office, February 10, 1942, NG-3444. Luther via Rintelen to Ribbentrop, May 19, 1942, NG-5018. Von Russenheim (Reich Chancellery) to Foreign Office, June 16, 1942, NG-5018. The chief of the Einsatzstab was Gerhart Utikal. See affidavit by Utikal, August 27, 1947, NO-5178.

366. Final report of *Dienststelle West* of Einsatzstab Rosenberg, undated, L-188.

last nationality had been German.[367] On September 15, 1943, he extended the decree to the property of "former" Polish and Protektorat Jews. Thus were the French to be punished for their lack of co-operation in the closing stages of the deportations.

ITALY. – As we move from France to Italy, we can observe for the first time the development of a destruction process in a country which was one of Germany's allies. The anti-Jewish regime in the Italian realm was established without German participation; in fact, the status of the Jews in Italy was a subject which could not easily be touched in German-Italian negotiations throughout the duration of the Axis partnership.

The first Italian measures were as thorough in appearance as any which had been drafted by German hands, but the Italian government failed to follow up its decrees and, frequently, even to enforce them. In certain basic respects the Italian approach to anti-Jewish persecutions was similar to the Italian attitude towards the war: the Italians wanted to keep up with their powerful German ally; they strove, above all, to be taken seriously, like the Germans. As Foreign Minister Ciano once put it, "The Germans have loved us without respecting us."[368] But in the end the Italians did not match the Germans in expenditure of ferocity and the shedding of blood. Quite unlike the German Nazis, the Italian Fascists committed themselves in words without fulfilling themselves in deeds, for in their hearts the Italians had no use for the Germans and the German way of life. "We have respected them," said Ciano, "without loving them."[369]

In a more narrow sense, there is another reason why the Italian operation against the Jews never quite got off the ground: Not only was the Fascist government no ideal persecutor, but the Italian Jews were not its ideal victims. That is not to say that the Italians were wholly incapable of hurting subject peoples; there were incidents, too serious to be overlooked, against Yugoslavs, Greeks, and African inhabitants. Nor must we conclude that the Jews in Italy were more able to take care of themselves than Jews elsewhere. The Italian Jews turned out to be as vulnerable to *German* attack as Jews were everywhere in Axis Europe. But the relationship between Jews and Italians had progressed to a point which made Italian persecutions of Jews psychologically as well as administratively difficult. The Jews had rapidly and thoroughly been absorbed into Italian life. From the abolition of the papal ghetto in Rome in 1870 to the first anti-Jewish laws by the Fascist government in 1938, the integration of Jewry in Italy had been greater than almost anywhere else in the world.

The acceptance of the Italian Jews is reflected to some extent in statistics. Thus we find that conversions affected approximately 10 per cent of the Jewish population[370] and that in a city like

367. Decree of December 2, 1942, *Verordnungsblatt des Militärbefehlshabers in Frankreich*, 1942, p. 451. From the billion-franc fine, the sum of 50,000,000 francs was made available at this time to the French government for the support of families whose breadwinners were working in Germany. Schleier to Foreign Office, December 9, 1942, NG-3335. Nothing appears to have been charged to the French state for the transport of the Jews. However, the French railway system, in which 400,000 French employes were serving under 10,000 German supervisors, bore a heavy part of the burden. On the role of the French railway men, see in general the memorandum by OB West Ic/AO, August 8, 1943, NOKW-2627.

368. Galeazzo Ciano, *Ciano's Hidden Diary 1937–1938* (New York, 1953), entry for November 17, 1938, p. 195.

369. *Ibid.*

370. The converted Jews numbered **5000**. Institute of Jewish Affairs, *Hitler's Ten-Year War on the Jews*, 1943, p. 294.

Trieste about 50 per cent of all the married Jews had Christian spouses.[371] Significant also was the occupational distribution, which in 1910 already looked like this:[372]

41.5 per cent in trade and commerce
23.0 per cent in professions, civil service, and military service
8.1 per cent in agriculture

Jews were unusually active not only as officers in the armed forces but also as public servants in the highest positions of government. The Institute of Jewish Affairs provides us with an enumeration of Jews who in the brief history of modern Italy had held the offices of Prime Minister, Foreign Minister, War Minister, Finance Minister, Labor Minister, Justice Minister, and Minister of Education.[373] These, then, were the people who became the victims of a sudden hostile outburst in 1938. How did that happen?

In Ciano's so-called *Hidden Diary* (1937-38), there has been preserved for us an inside story of the evolution of the Italian anti-Jewish laws. On December 3, 1937, just when the Italians began to feel a strong breeze from the north, Ciano made the following entry in his diary:[374]

> The Jews are flooding me with insulting anonymous letters, accusing me of having promised Hitler to persecute them. It is not true. The Germans have never mentioned this subject to us. Nor do I believe that we ought to unleash an anti-Semitic campaign in Italy. The problem doesn't exist here. There are not many Jews and, with some exceptions, there is no harm in them. . . .

A few weeks later Ciano refused to lend his support to an anti-Jewish campaign to Giovanni Preziosi, renegade priest and editor of the anti-Semitic periodical *La Vita Italiana*.[375] On February 6, 1938, Ciano remarked, in a talk with his father-in-law, Duce Benito Mussolini, that he favored " a solution which will not raise a problem which fortunately does not exist here." Mussolini agreed. "He will pour water on the flames," wrote Ciano, "though not enough to suppress the thing altogether."[376] A few days later the Duce was already pouring so much water as to declare himself in *Informazione Diplomatica* No. 14 in favor of a Jewish state. Ciano thought that this was going too far.[377]

On June 3, 1938, Mussolini was in turn angry with Roberto Farinacci, a member of the Fascist Grand Council and leader of the anti-Semitic movement in Italy, for having himself a Jewish secretary, Jole Foa. This was the kind of thing, wrote Ciano, "which foreigners see as proof of a lack of seriousness in many Italians."[378]

Some time later in July, Pope Pius XI made a speech "violently critical" of racism. The Pope's remarks were received with something less than good humor by the Fascist leadership, to whom racism implied not a mere assertion of power vis-a-vis Jewry but, much more importantly, a feeling of superiority over the recently conquered African populations of the empire. Upon hearing of the papal criticism, Foreign Minister Ciano called the nuncio, Borgongini-Duca, to express his displeasure. Ciano pointed out that the Duce regarded the racial question as fundamental. It was the lack of racial preparedness which had caused the Am-

371. In 1927, Trieste had 255 mixed marriages per 100 Jewish marriages. Arthur Ruppin, *Soziologie der Juden* (Berlin, 1930), I, 213.

372. *Ibid.*, p. 348.

373. *Hitler's Ten-Year War*, p. 286.

374. *Ciano's Hidden Diary*, p. 40.

375. *Ibid.*, entry for December 29, 1937, p. 52.

376. *Ibid.*, entry for February 6, 1938, p. 71.

377. *Ibid.*, entry for February 18, 1938, p. 75.

378. *Ibid.*, entry for June 3, 1938, p. 93.

hara insurrection in Ethiopia. Ciano's entry continues: "I spoke quite plainly to Borgongini, explaining the premises and aims of our racial policy. He seemed pretty convinced, and I may add that he showed himself personally very anti-Semitic. He will confer with the Holy Father tomorrow."[379] Mussolini himself was worked up about the Catholic offensive and in a state of agitation gave his son-in-law Ciano an order for the first anti-Jewish measure in Italy. He ordered all Jews to be struck off the diplomatic list.[380]

In September, 1938, the Interior Ministry, under the direction of the Duce, was working on an anti-Jewish charter. In the months from September to November the Fascist Grand Council met several times to discuss the law.[381] At the council meeting of October 6, Marshals Italo Balbo and Emilio de Bono, as well as president of the Senate Federzoni, spoke in favor of the Jews; however, the Education Minister, Giuseppe Bottai, opposed any mitigation of the anti-Jewish measure. "They will hate us," he said, "because we have driven them out. They will despise us if we let them in again." Between speeches the Duce turned to his son-in-law and remarked, "The discriminatory measures mean nothing." The important thing, he thought, was to raise the problem and then to allow anti-Semitism to develop "of its own accord."[382] At a subsequent meeting Lieutenant General Achille Starace, as Secretary General of the Fascist Party, proposed the unconditional expulsion of all Jews from the party. Mussolini rejected this proposal without ado.

By the middle of November the anti-Jewish provisions were ready. They contained a curious mixture of all the influences at work on the Italian scene: "racialism," anti-foreignism, clericalism, and bureaucratic paternalism. The definition of the term "Jew" was drawn up in such a way that everyone was affected (*a*) if both of his parents belonged to the Jewish religion, or (*b*) if one parent belonged to the Jewish religion and the other was a foreigner, or (*c*) if the mother was Jewish by religion and the father unknown, or (*d*) if one parent was Jewish and the other Italian, provided, however, that on October 1, 1938, the offspring belonged to the Jewish religion, or was a member of the Jewish community, or "in some other way participated in some Jewish undertaking."

The anti-Jewish decrees then went on to exclude the Jews from membership in the armed forces, the civil service, and the party, and from ownership or management of armament firms or enterprises of any other sort which employed at least a hundred Italians. Jews were also forbidden to own real estate in excess of 20,000 lira and agricultural property valued over 5000 lira. However, war veterans, old Fascists, etc., their children, grandchildren, parents, and grandparents, were not affected by the restrictions on enterprises and immobile property.

In a later decree, dated June 29, 1939, the professionals (including doctors, lawyers, auditors, engineers, architects, etc.) were restricted "except in cases of proven necessity and urgency" to serving Jews. Once again, however, exceptions were made for war veterans, old Fascists, etc.

In the field of social concentration the Italian legislation was very detailed. The formation of marriages between Jews and Italians was forbidden except on the point of death or to legitimize an offspring.[383] The employment

379. *Ibid.*, entry for July 30, 1938, p. 141.
380. *Ibid.*, entry for August 8, 1938, p. 141.
381. *Ibid.*, entries for September 1 and 4, October 6 and 26, November 6 and 10, pp. 149–51, 174, 184, 190, 192.
382. *Ibid.*, entry for October 6, 1938, p. 174.

383. The Pope's suggestion that an exception be made also for converted Jews was

of non-Jewish household help was barred. The adoption or care by Jews of non-Jewish children was forbidden, and provision was made for depriving a Jewish parent of his Christian child if proof was adduced that the child did not obtain an education consonant with Christian principles or national aims. The basic law and the decrees which followed provided for expulsions from schools, revocation of name changes, and registration in the civil lists.

Finally, the law of November 17 ordered the nullification of all naturalizations obtained by Jews after January 1, 1919, and stipulated that all foreign as well as denaturalized Jews – except those who were over sixty-five or living in mixed marriage – were to leave Italy and its possessions by March 12, 1939.[384]

When the drafting of the first two laws was finished, Benito Mussolini had a discussion with the man who had to sign his name to all the anti-Jewish decrees, King Victor Emmanuel. Three times during the conversation the King remarked that he felt an "infinite pity for the Jews." He cited cases of persecution, among them that of General Pugliese, "an old man of eighty, loaded with medals and wounds, who had been deprived of his housekeeper." Annoyed, the Duce pointed out that there were "20,000 spineless people" in Italy who were moved by the fate of the Jews. The King replied that he was one of them.[385]

It is perhaps unnecessary to stress that the Italian anti-Jewish code was not altogether mild. Its victims must have felt that code severely, precisely because in the past they had found in their country such complete acceptance. The provisions against employment by the state and possession of farms, for example, had an import more serious than that of similar decrees elsewhere, because in Italy a comparatively large number of Jews had found a livelihood as government workers and farmers. To be sure, the Italian laws allowed for many exceptions, and the implementation of the legislation as a whole was both slow and lax. There is perhaps no better illustration of the total effect of the Italian laws than the figures on Jewish emigrations given in Table 59.[386]

TABLE 59 / *Jewish Emigrations from Italy*

	EMIGRATED BY OCTOBER 15, 1941	JEWISH POPULATION AT END OF 1941
Citizens	5,966	39,444
Foreigners	1,338	3,674
Total	7,304	43,118

Of the foreign Jews, most of whom had been obliged to leave, only about 27 per cent had gone by 1941, but of the native Jews, who did not have to go, 13 per cent had left as well.

The remaining foreign Jews were not to have an easy time. By May, 1942, about a thousand of them had been interned in camps at Salerno and Cosenza as well as in a women's camp at

rejected. *Ibid.*, entry for November 6, 1938, p. 190.

384. For full texts of the decrees of November 17, 1938/XVII No. 1728 (basic law); November 15, 1938/XVII No. 1779 (schools); December 22, 1938/XVII No. 2111 (military pensions); June 29, 1939/XVII No. 1054 (professions); July 13, 1939/XVII No. 1055 (name changes); see the *Gazetta Ufficiale*, 1938 and 1939. Complete German translations in *Die Judenfrage* (*Vertrauliche Beilage*), October 15, 1942, pp. 78–80; December 1, 1942, pp. 91–92; December 15, 1942, pp. 94–96; March 1, 1943, p. 20. For summary and explanations, see also Emilio Canevari, "Die Juden in Italien," *Die Judenfrage*, October 1, 1940, pp. 143–46. On administration of expropriated agricultural property, see Rademacher to Luther, November 14, 1940, NG-3934.

385. *Ciano's Hidden Diary*, entry for November 28, 1938, p. 199.

386. *Die Judenfrage*, March 15, 1942, p. 56.

Chieti.[387] In the late summer of 1942, Jews of Italian nationality were called up for labor in Rome, Bologna, Milan, and the African colony of Tripoli.[388] The Jews of Rome were forced to wash the retaining wall of the Tiber River; for the Jews of Milan a work camp was erected in the city. Near the Tripolitanian town of Giado, between 2000 and 3000 Jews were incarcerated in a desert camp, and when the British arrived at Giado early in 1943, they found that a typhus epidemic was raging there.[389] According to Jewish sources, 318 of the Giado Jews had died.[390]

From the German viewpoint, however, all these measures were extremely inadequate. A large segment of the Italian Jews was almost wholly unaffected by anti-Jewish action. The pace of the destruction process since the first laws had been issued in 1938 and 1939 was much too slow to suggest that the Italians would ever arrive under their own power at the critical point at which deportations would become a feasible proposition. In Italy there was as yet no total deprivation of Jewish property and no foolproof regulation of Jewish residence and movements. Still, the Germans were reluctant to interfere. Italy was still Germany's principal ally, and the Germans did not forget that fact.

On September 24, 1942, Ribbentrop called Luther on the telephone to issue instructions about the deportation strategy in various countries of Europe. With respect to Italy, however, Luther was to undertake nothing. That question was to be reserved for a personal discussion between the Führer and the Duce or between the Foreign Minister and Count Ciano.[391]

By January, 1943, the SS was exhibiting signs of impatience. Jews were being deported all over Europe, but Italian Jews in German-controlled areas continued to be immune. Their immunity made them more and more conspicuous. By January 13, 1943, Ribbentrop therefore instructed Ambassador Mackensen to inform Foreign Minister Ciano that in German eyes Jews of Italian nationality were also Jews. In German-controlled territories, at least, the Germans wanted complete freedom of action after March 31, 1943.[392]

In February Ribbentrop asked, in preparation for a visit to Rome, about the wishes of the SS in the Jewish question. Himmler replied immediately that he would like the Italians to cease sabotaging the measures of the RSHA in areas under German occupation. In Italy itself he wanted measures parallel to those in force in Germany.[393] The wishes of the SS were not destined to be quickly fulfilled. The Italians were not approachable in matters of destruction.

In May, 1943, Dr. Zeitschel of the Paris Embassy wrote a letter to his friend Dr. Knochen, who was the BdS in France, in which he set down his impressions of what he had observed during a visit to Rome. The German Embassy in Rome, he wrote, had for years been in possession of instructions from Berlin in no case to undertake anything that could cloud the friendly relations between Italy and Germany.

387. *Ibid.*, May 1, 1942, p. 92.

388. *Ibid.*, August 1, 1942, p. 172; September 15, 1942, p. 197; October 15, 1942, p. 223; September 1, 1942, p. 183.

389. Maj. Gen. Lord Rennel of Rodd, *British Military Administration of Occupied Territories in Africa during the Years 1941–1947* (London, 1948), p. 272.

390. *Hitler's Ten-Year War*, pp. 294–95.

391. Luther to Weizsäcker, September 24, 1942, NG-1517.

392. Ribbentrop to Embassy in Rome, January 13, 1943, NG-4961. Bergmann to Embassy in Rome, February 18, 1943, NG-4958. Rademacher to Foreign Office representative in Brussels, February 27, 1943, NG-4955.

393. Minister Bergmann to office of Ribbentrop, February 24, 1943, NG-4956.

It therefore appeared utterly hopeless, he continued, that the German Embassy in Rome would ever grasp so hot an iron as the Jewish question in Italy. The Italian government, on its part, was "not interested" in the Jewish question. As the RSHA representative in Rome, Obersturmbannführer Dr. Dollmann, had told Zeitschel, the Italian armed forces were "still shot through with full Jews and countless half-Jews" (*noch mit Volljuden and zahllosen Halbjuden durchsetzt*). From the Fascist party itself action could be expected only under direct instructions from the Duce.[394]

But on July 25, 1943, the Duce was overthrown, and three days later the Fascist party was dissolved. As yet the new government of Marshal Badoglio made no other move. The war was still on, and the anti-Jewish laws were still in force.[395] Then, suddenly the Badoglio government surrendered to the Allies. The Germans reacted with lightning speed. The Italian forces were disarmed, and Italy became an occupied country.

During September, 1943, and the period which followed, a horde of German bureaucrats moved into Italy in order to direct its affairs. From the multitude of German agencies which were then in existence on the Italian peninsula, we select the three which appear to have had decisive functions in the attempt to destroy the Italian Jews:

The German General Plenipotentiary and Ambassador: Rahn
- Police Attaché (RSHA): OStubaf. Kappler

The German Plenipotentiary General and Higher SS and Police Leader: OGruf. Wolff
- Chief of Military Administration: Gruf. Wächter

Oberbefehlshaber Süd and commander of Army Group C: Gfm. Kesselring
- Commander, Fourteenth Army: Gen. von Mackensen
- Commander, Rome: Gen. Stahel (Mälzer)

Italy thus had a civilian German overlord, the Foreign Office trouble shooter, Minister (later Ambassador) Rahn, whom we last saw in Tunisia. Then there was a military governor who also fulfilled the functions of Higher SS and Police Leader; this was the chief of Himmler's Personal Staff, Wolff. Incidentally, his chief of military administration, Wächter, came from Poland, where he had served as *Gouverneur* of Galicia. Finally, there was a commander of armed forces, Generalfeldmarschall Kesselring.

This, of course, was not all. In areas that before the conclusion of World War I had been Austro-Hungarian, the Germans installed two special overlords who had the title *Der Oberste Kommissar*. One such *Kommissar* was the *Gauleiter* of Tyrol, Hofer; his added area was southern Tyrol. The other was the *Gauleiter* of Carinthia, Rainer, who acquired the operations zone *Adriatisches Küstenland*, with the important city of Trieste. Under Rainer, Himmler had established a special Higher SS and Police Leader, none other than Odilo Globocnik, late of Lublin, now back in his home town.

The new machinery went to work immediately. Characteristically, the Germans did not wait for the re-establishment of a shadow government under Benito Mussolini. Just as, previously, the Italians had been too powerful to be approached, they were now too weak to be consulted. On September 25, 1943, the RSHA sent a circular to all its branches at home and abroad, specifying that "in agreement with the

394. Dr. Carltheo Zeitschel to BdS in France, May 24, 1943, in Poliakov, *La condition des Juifs en France sous l'occupation italienne*, pp. 157–58.

395. "Judengesetze in Italien noch in Kraft," *Donauzeitung* (Belgrade), August 7, 1943, p. 1.

Foreign Office" all Jews of listed nationalities could now be included in deportation measures. Italy headed the list. The circular continued: "The necessary measures will be carried out with regard to (*a*) Jews of Italian nationality at once. . . ."[396]

The operations in Italy itself started in Rome and gradually shifted north. The Italian capital had a Jewish community of perhaps 8000 people. The chief of the *Giunta* of the Rome community was Ugo Foa; the chief rabbi was Israel Zolli. The only account of what transpired within the Jewish leadership in the city comes from Zolli, one of the strangest figures of European Jewry during the days of the great catastrophe.[397]

When the Germans entered Rome, Zolli immediately went into hiding. He wanted to close the temple and urged everybody else to hide. Zolli was convinced that the Church with its monasteries and convents would offer refuge to the Jews; he believed that the Jews could never be traced through their old addresses, for he thought that the files in the Interior Ministry and the city hall were neither up-to-date nor complete. He feared only that the accurate Jewish community files might fall into German hands, and he therefore urged that they be destroyed. According to Zolli, none of these recommendations were carried out; on the contrary, President Foa ordered the head usher of the temple, Romeo Bondi, to deliver the address lists to the Fascist authorities upon demand.[398]

While Zolli was in hiding, the German police attaché, Obersturmbannführer Kappler, in an outburst of preliminary activity demanded from the Jewish community 50 kilograms of gold and threatened as a penalty for nondelivery the taking of 300 hostages. (Fifty kilograms of gold represent $56,264 in American currency.) Although there were 8000 Jews in the city, so many well-to-do members of the community were already in hiding that the amount could not be raised in full. When word of the dilemma reached Zolli, he left his hiding place to negotiate with Bernardino Nogana, head of the Vatican Treasury, for a loan in the amount of 15 kilograms of gold ($16,879). The loan, which had the approval of the Pope, was to be granted upon receipt of a simple guarantee signed by Zolli and the president of the Jewish community in Rome. Zolli then sent his daughter to transmit the terms to Foa and, as he recounts, to offer himself as a hostage.[399] The gold was apparently delivered to Kappler in the German Embassy, just before the big guns were opened on the Jewish community in the city.[400]

With the Germans everything had so far proceeded according to plan, but the Jewish leaders faced with a sense of frustration their ancient blueprints for survival. Rabbi Zolli in his hideout remained convinced that everything would have worked out for the best if only President Foa had listened to his

396. Von Thadden to missions abroad, October 12, 1943, enclosing RSHA circular dated September 23, 1943, NG-2652-H.

397. Eugenio (Israel) Zolli, *Before the Dawn* (New York, 1954).

398. *Ibid.*, pp. 140–55. In the Rome police Maresciallo Mario di Marco was especially busy with the preparation of false identity cards for Jews. His superior, Angelo de Fiore, who was in charge of the registration lists, flatly refused to hand them over to the Germans. Interview of di Marco in *Aufbau* (New York), September 5, 1952, p. 11.

399. *Ibid.*, pp. 159–61. Also, declaration by Giorgio Fiorentino, *ibid.*, pp. 206–7. Fiorentino, who hid the Zolli family during the occupation, accompanied the rabbi on his mission to the Vatican.

400. Declaration by Prof. Elena Sonnino-Finzi (daughter of the chief rabbi of Genoa), July 2, 1944, *ibid.*, p. 209. Testimony by Albrecht von Kessel (member of the German Embassy staff at the Vatican from 1943 to 1945), Case No. 11, tr. p. 9518.

advice. What the president thought of the rabbi is revealed in the following letter dispatched by Foa to Zolli on July 4, 1944, one month after Rome's liberation.

> Illustrious Sir:
>
> I have attentively read the typewritten memorandum dated the 31st of September [*sic*] that you have sent me. I have the duty nevertheless, for the sake of the facts, to clarify a few affirmations concerning me which are not exact.
>
> 1. You have made no request for a conversation with the President of the Union and me, to present a project of yours intended to ward off the danger menacing our co-religionists on the part of the Germans.
>
> 2. No note with your signature was given me on September 28th, in which you said that you had assured to the Community a loan of fifteen kilograms of gold. On that day I only had from your daughter a very general promise of eventual help in presence of third parties who will be able to confirm this.
>
> 3. Neither by voice nor in writing did you declare to me your readiness to offer yourself as hostage. Furthermore, all your conduct gives the lie to such an affirmation.
>
> I received from you only one note during the German Occupation. That was in February 1944 and in that note was mentioned exclusively a request for money. So much for the truth.
>
> Best regards,
> the President
> UGO FOA[401]

Zolli, by the way, came out of hiding and resumed his post in the temple of Rome after the liberation. While conducting the high holiday services there in the fall of 1944, he saw a vision of Christ. On February 13, 1945, he was baptized a Christian.[402]

The crisis came in October, 1943. Although the Jews of Rome were the only people threatened with immediate destruction, the operation which was now to transpire did not affect them alone, for Rome was also the city of the Catholic Church, and whatever happened there could not fail to concern the Pope himself. The Germans in Rome were aware of this situation, and they were not exactly enthusiastic about the prospect of a major clash with the Church. On October 6, Consul Moellhausen addressed a letter to Ribbentrop personally, to tell him that Obersturmbannführer Kappler had received an order from Berlin to arrest the 8000 Jews of Rome and to transport them to northern Italy, "where they are supposed to be liquidated" *(wo sie liquidiert werden sollen)*. General Stahel had declared his intention to allow the implementation of this *Aktion* only if he had the agreement of the German Foreign Minister. "Personally, I am of the opinion," concluded Moellhausen "that it would be better business [*dass es besseres Geschäft wäre*] to mobilize Jews for defense construction just as in Tunis, and will propose this together with Kappler to Generalfeldmarschall Kesselring. Please send instructions."[403] The answer from Berlin stated that on the basis of an order by Hitler, the Jews of Rome were to be brought to the Austrian concentration camp Mauthausen as hostages. Rahn and Moellhausen were not to interfere with this matter under any circumstances *(sich auf keinen Fall in diese Angelegenheit einzumischen)*.[404]

On October 16, 1943, Bishop Hudal, rector of the German church in Rome, sent a last-minute appeal to General Stahel:[405]

401. Zolli, *Before the Dawn*, p. 203.
402. *Ibid.*, pp. 182–84.

403. Konsul Moellhausen (Rome) to Ribbentrop personally, October 6, 1943, NG-5027.

404. Von Sonnleithner to Bureau of the Foreign Minister, October 9, 1943, NG-5027. Von Thadden to Moellhausen, October 9, 1943, NG-5027.

405. Gumpert to Foreign Office, enclosing message from Hudal, October 16, 1943, NG-5027.

> I have just been informed by a high Vatican office in the immediate circle of the Holy Father that the arrests of Jews of Italian nationality have begun this morning. In the interest of the good relations which have existed until now between the Vatican and the high German military command – which in the first instance is to be credited to the political insight and greatness of heart of Your Excellency and which will some day go down in the history of Rome – I would be very grateful if you would give an order to stop these arrests in Rome and its vicinity right away; I fear that otherwise the Pope will have to make an open stand, which will serve the anti-German propaganda as a weapon against us.

The *Aktion* could no longer be stopped. It began during the night of October 15/16 and was finished in less than twenty-four hours. For its implementation General Stahel made available to Obersturmbannführer Kappler Company 5 of the 15th Police Regiment, Company 3 of the 20th Police Regiment, and Company 11 of the 12th Police Regiment. Since Company 5 of the 15th Police Regiment had been performing guard duties for General Stahel, he detailed a unit of the 2nd Parachute-Pursuit Regiment to relieve the policemen in their regular assignment. During the *Aktion* there were no "incidents." All together, 1259 people were seized in the roundup. After the release of some half-Jews and Jews in mixed marriages, a total of 1007 were shipped off, on October 18, 1943, to the killing center of Auschwitz.[406]

From the statistics in the official German correspondence we may readily conclude that nearly 7000 Jews – seven out of eight – had been able to hide during the *Aktion*. Although there are no figures on Jews sheltered by the Vatican, the Church had undoubtedly done its part.[407] The Germans, however, were relieved that their greatest fear had not been realized, for to them the elusion of a few thousand victims was not nearly so important as a fact which was to have tremendous significance for the bureaucracy, not only then but in years to come: the silence of the Pope.

One day after the completion of the roundup, the German Ambassador at the Vatican and former Staatssekretär of the Foreign Office, Weizsäcker, reported to Berlin that the College of Cardinals was particularly shocked because the event had, so to speak, transpired under the windows of the Pope. *(Die Kurie ist besonders betroffen, da sich der Vorgang sozusagen unter den Fenstern des Papstes abgespielt hat.)* The reaction, said Weizsäcker, might have been muffled if the Jews had been kept in Italy for forced labor. Now anti-German circles in Rome were putting pressure on the Pope to step out of his reserve. "It is said," reported Weizsäcker, "that bishops in French cities where similar things happened [*wo ähnliches vorkam*] had taken a clear stand"; the Pope, as head of the Church and Bishop of Rome, could not

406. War diary, German commander in Rome (Gen. Stahel), October 16, 1943, October 17, 1943, and October 18, 1943, NO-315. The figure of 1007 is taken from the report by Kappler to OGruf. Wolff, October 18, 1943, NO-2427. The arrival of the Rome Jews in Auschwitz on October 22, 1943, was noted by a Jewish doctor there, Otto Wolken. See Filip Friedman, *This was Oswiecim* (London. 1946), pp. 24–25.

407. A high estimate of the number of Jews protected by the Pope himself was given to the International Refugee Organization by Father Killion, Official Observer for the Holy See, who "recalled that before the inception of the IRO, His Holiness Pius XII gave asylum within the Vatican City to 3000 people who were not of his own faith during the occupation of Rome by an enemy power." IRO/General Council, 2d Session, Summary Record of 25th Meeting held at Geneva, April 4, 1949, GC/SR/25. The Jewish researcher Leon Poliakov estimates the number at a few dozen. "The Vatican and the 'Jewish Question,'" *Commentary*, November, 1950, pp. 439–49.

very well do less. Already, said Weizsäcker, comparisons were being made between the present pontiff and the "much more temperamental Pius XI."[408]

The pressure, however, was unsuccessful. "The Pope," wrote Weizsäcker on October 28, "although reportedly beseeched by various sides, has not allowed himself to be drawn into any demonstrative statement against the deportation of the Jews of Rome. Even though he has to calculate that this attitude will be held against him by our opponents and taken advantage of by Protestant circles in Anglo-Saxon countries for propagandistic purposes against Catholicism, he has also in this touchy matter done everything in order not to burden relations with the German government and German agencies in Rome." The *Osservatore Romano* (pro-Vatican newspaper in Rome) had printed a communique about the "benevolent activity of the Pope" *(über die Liebestätigkeit des Papstes)*, but this statement was so "richly embroidered and unclear" *(reichlich gewunden und unklar)* that very few people would be able to read into it a special reference to the Jewish question. The whole affair could therefore be looked upon as "liquidated."[409]

One more incident was to occur during the remaining months of the German occupation of Rome. On March 23, 1944, a bomb exploded in the midst of a German police company marching through Rosella Street. Thirty-three men were killed. That same evening an order was transmitted from Hitler to Kesselring to "kill ten Italians for every German." A second order during the night specified that Kesselring charge the SD with the shootings. Both orders were passed down to General von Mackensen, commander of the Fourteenth Army, and to General Maelzer, then military commander of Rome. The final recipient of the instructions was Kappler. Since the Führer's orders had included a provision for "immediate" executions, Kappler had to carry out his task in twenty-four hours.

The military desired that, so far as possible, only persons under sentence of death be included among the victims. Kappler, however, did not have a sufficient number of condemned men at his disposal. He therefore drew up a list of persons who for various reasons he deemed "worthy of death." The shootings were carried out on March 24, 1944, in the Ardeatine Cave. When the job was done, army engineers blew up the cave entrance. Kappler had shot 335 people (five more than he had to) because there had been some mistake in the counting. Among the victims were 57 Jews.[410]

From Rome the operation was shifted to the northern Italian area, which held perhaps 35,000 Jews. Here, too, the vast majority of the prospective deportees eluded the grasp of the Germans.

The dispersal of the Jews into hiding places began with the onset of the German occupation. In Florence the prominent American art critic Bernard Berenson (himself in hiding) noted that the newly installed Fascist prefect was warning the Jews as soon as he took office to leave their homes and move into concealment. Berenson observed ten or twelve Jews hiding in a single villa near Siena. "One great landed proprietor, brother and cousin of officers high in the army and navy," wrote Berenson, "has been flitting from hole to hole, and at last has decided to take shelter in a small apartment of a friend in the heart of Florence on the Arno."[411]

The flight of the Jews from their

408. Weizsäcker to Foreign Office, October 17, 1943, NG-5027.

409. Weizsäcker to Foreign Office, October 28, 1943, NG-5027.

410. Trial of Generals von Mackensen and Maelzer, and trial of Albert Kesselring, *Law Reports of Trials of War Criminals*, VIII, 1–2, 9–10, 13.

homes and apartments was thus well under way when, on December 1, 1943, the radio broadcast an announcement of a new Italian law, in pursuance of which all Jews were to be sent to concentration camps and their belongings confiscated as enemy property.[412]

In a sense the new Fascist law was a warning as well as a threat. The movement into hiding was now intensified. The Italians were shocked; the Jews were filled with panic. In Florence, Berenson heard that the prefect was "beside himself" and was threatening to resign. Now that the hunt was on, wrote Berenson from his hideout, "even a Dominican of Hebrew origin had to flee his monastery for fear of arrest, and found his way here." In another incident a parish priest was seized for harboring a Jew. Elia Cardinal da Costa of Florence himself intervened in this case, declaring himself to be the culprit and requesting to be jailed in place of the priest.[413]

In Berlin the chief of the Foreign Office's Inland II, Wagner, surveyed the situation with a cautious mixture of hopefulness and anxiety. The RSHA had just notified him that the seizure of the Jews in Italy had failed to achieve any success worthy of mention *(zu keinem nennenswerten Ergebnis geführt)* because the Italian delays had enabled a majority of the Jews to find hiding places in small villages, etc. The available forces of the SS and Police were not sufficient for a thorough search of all Italian communities. Now that the Fascist government had issued a law for the transfer of all the Jews to concentration camps, however, Inland II, in agreement with the RSHA, proposed "that Ambassador Rahn be instructed to convey to the Fascist government the happiness [*Freude* – crossed out in the draft and 'satisfaction' (*Genugtuung*) substituted] of the Reich government" with the new Italian decree. It was advisable also, thought Wagner, to inform the Italian government of the necessity for a rapid construction of concentration camps in northern Italy and of the Reich's willingness to supply the Italians with "experienced advisers" (*erfahrene Berater*) for this purpose. Wagner believed that in such fashion the *Einsatzkommando* in Italy could be "built into" the Italian government, so that the entire Fascist apparatus could be mobilized to implement the anti-Jewish measures.

The RSHA, continued Wagner, had also proposed that a demand be made to the Italians for the subsequent surrender of the Jews to German agencies, for shipment to the East. Inland II, however, was of the opinion that such a request had better be delayed. The experts of Inland II thought that the concentration would proceed with less friction if the transfers to the camps appeared to constitute a "final solution" rather than a "preparatory measure in the evacuation to the eastern territories." The RSHA, added Wagner, would have no objection to this tactical procedure.[414]

Botschaftsrat Hilger replied in behalf of the Foreign Minister that Ribbentrop was in agreement with these proposals. "His agreement," wrote Hilger, "applies to the content of the instructions to Ambassador Rahn discussed in paragraph 2 of the proposal, as well as to the recommendation in the concluding paragraph of the proposal of Group

411. Bernard Berenson, *Rumor and Reflection* (New York, 1952), p. 143.

412. "Konzentrationslager für Juden–keine Ausnahmen mehr," *Donauzeitung* (Belgrade), December 2, 1943, p. 2. The new law was instituted by the Duce, after a Fascist Party manifesto issued at Verona had branded the Jews as "enemy foreigners." *Ibid.*, December 10, 1943, p. 2.

413. Berenson, *Rumor and Reflection*, pp. 163, 218.

414. Group Inland II (signed Wagner) via Hencke to Ribbentrop, December 4, 1943, NG-5026.

Inland to delay for the moment the request for the removal of the Jews to the eastern territories."[415]

While the German experts implemented their plan to lull the Jews and their Italian protectors into a false sense of security, the Security Police and their Fascist helpers slowly concentrated the victims in camps, and Italian bureaucrats busied themselves with the confiscation of the abandoned property.[416] In the spring of 1944 the Germans sprang the trap. From April to October of that year, transports arrived with Italian Jews from assembly points at Trieste, Carpi, and Bolzano at the killing center of Auschwitz.[417] Although we have no accurate figures for these deportations, the number must be reckoned in the thousands. In Italy, too, the German destructive machine had left its mark.

The Balkans

Within the German sphere of influence the largest concentration of Jews was in the Balkans. About 1,600,000 Jews lived in the southeastern portion of Europe. The deportations there were accomplished with least difficulty in the military-controlled areas of Serbia and Greece. The Jews of Serbia and Greece were annihilated.

Croatia and Slovakia, the two satellites which owed their very existence to Germany, presented to the Germans one major obstacle: the institution of "honorary Aryans" *(Ehrenarier)*, "protective letters" *(Schutzbriefe)*, and other devices for the exemption of influential, indispensable, or baptized Jews. The reason for these exemptions is to be found in the fact that both Croatia and Slovakia were Balkan countries, somewhat backward and rigorously Catholic.

In Bulgaria, Roumania, and Hungary the Germans encountered considerable difficulties. These three countries were in the German camp because of their opportunism, and all three pursued a policy of maximum gain and minimum loss. They had no understanding for the German all-or-nothing principle. They realized – sooner than Germany did – who was winning the war, and they tried to make arrangements accordingly. That opportunism was of the utmost importance for the development of the destruction process in the three countries.

The Roumanians, Bulgarians, and Hungarians did not share the German conception of the "Jewish problem"; they regarded the Jews primarily as a strategic commodity to be traded for political gain. The governments in Bucharest, Sofia, and Budapest knew that Germany wanted to destroy European Jewry, but they also believed that the Allies wanted to preserve the Jews. Hence, when Germany was on the ascent, handing out territory to her Axis associates, anti-Jewish measures were enacted as a concession to the Germans. When Germany was losing and the necessity for some contact with the Allies became apparent, anti-Jewish measures were opposed as a concession to the Allies.

It is therefore understandable that in all three countries the destruction process was cut off just as soon as the tide had unmistakably turned. The Germans found that at a certain point they were completely stymied in Roumania and Bulgaria. Ultimately, these two countries slipped away from the Axis

415. Hilger via Steengracht and Hencke to Group Inland II, December 9, 1943, NG-5026.

416. Steengracht to von Papen (Turkey), July 29, 1944, NG-4993. In Florence 500 Jews had been seized out of 1600, and property amounting to 600 million lira (RM 7,520,000, or $3,150,000) was sequestered there. *Deutsche Zeitung* (Budapest), May 16, 1944, p. 3; *Donauzeitung* (Belgrade), May 17, 1944, p. 2; June 23, 1944, p. 2.

417. See partial data compiled by Wolken, in Friedman, *This was Oswiecim*, pp. 24–25.

fold and joined the Allies as co-belligerents against Germany. Hungary too attempted to make the switch but it did not succeed. In a daring and desperate maneuver the Germans moved into Hungary. Germany's unhappy ally was kept in the fight, and, as late as the spring of 1944, the bulk of Hungarian Jewry was destroyed.

Military Area "Southeast." – The Serbian-Greek section of the Balkans was, next to the military occupation zone in Russia and the military governments in the West, the third largest German Army stronghold in Axis Europe. The planning and design of the anti-Jewish operations in this area followed the pattern of the West, although the conditions in the Balkans more closely resembled the situation in the Russian East. In fact, so close was the resemblance of circumstances that in Serbia the operation began to look more and more like a replica of the mobile killings in the occupied USSR.

The military organization "Southeast" was established in Serbia and Greece after the smashing of Yugoslav-Greek resistance in the short Balkan campaign of April, 1941. Table 60 indicates the changes in the southeast command from 1941 to 1944.[418] Until August 26, 1943, military government, i.e., power over civilians (*die vollziehende Gewalt*), and troop command, or power over military units in the area, were concentrated in one person, first List, then Löhr. That same "personal union," or concentration of two offices in one man, applied also to the lower territorial commanders. However, from August to December, 1943, military government and troop command were gradually separated.

At the end of that separation process, power over civilians was exercised by Felber (who was responsible, in military government matters only, to Keitel), while Generalfeldmarschall von Weichs was confined to the command of troops. Von Weichs thus had no military government powers except in new territories wrested from the Italians as a consequence of Italy's collapse on September 8, 1943. Actually, when things settled down, most of the new territories too were placed – in civilian matters only – under the *Militärbefehlshaber Südost,* Felber. The newly occupied Greek mainland was transferred from Löhr's Army Group E (actually an army and not an army group) to General Felber on October 30, 1943; six weeks later, on December 12, 1943, Montenegro and Albania, heretofore under Rendulic's Second Panzer Army, were similarly subordinated to Felber.

So far as the military correspondence indicates, von Weichs retained military government control only over the island strongholds: Corfu, Crete, and the east Aegean group of Rhodes, Cos, Leros. The islands remained under army group command because of their exposed position. In its entirety the southeast seemed never to have been permanently conquered.

Serbia. – Although the Serbian area was under German occupation for almost four years, we shall be interested only in the Serbia of 1941 and 1942, for by the middle of 1942 the destruction process there was over except for the liquidation of some Jewish property. The machinery of destruction which carried out that cataclysmic operation may be divided into five offices.

1. The keystone in the administrative structure was the military commander in Serbia: (in succession) Schröder, Danckelmann, Böhme, Bader.

418. Böhme to U.S. Prosecution, Nuremberg, February 3, 1947, NOKW-743. Statement by Speidel, February 10, 1947, NOKW-742. Report by OB *Südost*/Ia, January 1, 1943, NOKW-832. Order by OB *Südost* (signed Förtsch), October 30, 1943, NOKW-1010. Order by Keitel, December 12, 1943, NOKW-1471.

Table 60 / *German Military Government Southeast*

	1941—Aug., 1942	Aug.-Dec., 1942	Jan.-Aug., 1943	Aug., 1943-44	
				Hitler	
					Chef OKW: Keitel
	Wehrmachtbefehlshaber Südost (12th Army) List	OB *Südost* Löhr	OB *Südost* (Army Group E) Löhr	*Oberbefehlshaber Südost* (Army Group F) von Weichs	*Militärbefehlshaber Südost* Felber
	Oberbefehlshaber Südost Kuntze			Army Group E Löhr	2d Panzer Army Rendulic
Serbia:	Schröder, Danckelmann, Böhme, Bader Bader	Bader	Bader		Felber
Salonika-Aegean:	von Krenzki	von Krenzki	Studnitz, Haarde } *Greece*	Speidel — Oct., 1943 —	Speidel
South Greece:	Felmy	Felmy, Speidel	Speidel } *Greece*		
Croatia:			Lüters		Glaise-Horstenau
Crete:			Bräuer	Bräuer	
Montenegro:				Keiper Dec., 1943 —	Keiper
Albania:				von Geib Dec., 1943 —	von Geib
East Aegean:				Kleemann	
Corfu:				Jäger	

The first two of these commanders were called *Befehlshaber in Serbien*. In the fall of 1941 General der Gebirgstruppen Franz Böhme, a former chief of the Austrian General Staff, took over the command. He now had the title "Plenipotentiary Commanding General in Serbia" *(Bevollmächtigter Kommandierender General in Serbien)*. In reading documents it is important to keep this title in mind, because there was also a "Commanding General in Serbia" (without the "Plenipotentiary"). That was General Bader. When Böhme left at the end of the year, Bader became the highest territorial officer in Serbia, but he did not inherit Böhme's title. In diagram form, the command structure under Böhme was as follows:

Böhme ⟶ Chief of Staff: Pemsel
Chief of Administrative Staff (military government): Turner
↓
Bader ⟶ Chief of Staff: Geitner

Two divisions, the 113th and 342d, were placed directly under Böhme; the other units were commanded by Bader. Staatsrat Turner, an old civil servant whom we have already met in France, remained, incidentally, as chief of the administrative staff after Böhme's departure. He played a crucial role in the destruction of the Serbian Jews.

2. Economic matters, particularly Aryanizations, were handled by a special office outside the military hierarchy and responsible to Göring: the General Plenipotentiary for the Economy in Serbia (Dr. Franz Neuhausen).

3. A watchful eye on general political developments was kept by the Foreign Office plenipotentiary, Minister Benzler.

4. Political security was of course a function of the SS and Police. Like many newly invaded territories, Serbia first had an *Einsatzgruppe* of the RSHA, commanded by Standartenführer Dr. Fuchs. In January, 1942, a Higher SS and Police Leader (Meyszner) was installed in Serbia. Under him, a Commander of Security Police and SD (Ostubaf. Dr. Schäfer) took the place of *Einsatzgruppe* Commander Fuchs. The Order Police in Serbia consisted of Germans (ca. 3400) and the Serbian State Guard *(Serbische Staatswache*, ca. 20,000).[419]

5. Finally, Serbia also had, after August, 1941, a puppet regime headed by the former Yugoslav Minister of War, General Milan Nedic.

The destruction process descended upon the Jews of Serbia with immediate force. On May 30, 1941, the military administration issued a definition of the Jews (Lösener principle), ordered the removal of Jews from public service and the professions, provided for registration of Jewish property, introduced forced labor, forbade the Serb population to hide Jews (*Beherbergungsverbot*) and ordered the Jewish population to wear the star.[420] In other words, the first three steps of the destruction process had been introduced in a single day. Of course the confiscation of Jewish property was a somewhat lengthy procedure.

Compulsory Aryanization was decreed on July 22, 1941. The General Plenipotentiary for the Economy, Dr. Neuhausen, slowly went about his business of providing for the transfer of Jewish enterprises to "Aryan" interests. The "Aryan" interests in this case were preponderantly, if not ex-

419. Daluege to Wolff, February 28, 1943, NO-2861.

420. In the town of Grossbetscherek (Petrovgrad) an SS unit (not identified) and the local military commander anticipated things. Barely two weeks after the occupation of the town the local "well-to-do" Jews had to pay a "fine" of 20 million dinars (1 million reichsmark) and the entire Jewish community (2000) was ordered to wear a star and move into a ghetto. Hauptmann Rentsch (Commander, *Ortskommandantur* I/823) to *Militärbefehlshaber Serbien*, April 23, 1941, NOKW-1110.

clusively, German. For instance, the sixteen trustees (*kommissarische Leiter*) listed in the *Donauzeitung* of Belgrade from July, 1941, to March, 1942, do not include one with a Yugoslav name. The ethnic Germans were definitely in the saddle again.

The proceeds from the sale of the Jewish firms, and ultimately also of the Jewish furniture that was left behind, was of course confiscated. Serbs who had any kind of Jewish property in their possession were ordered to register such assets. Credits and debts, too, were to be registered. Officially, the beneficiary of the confiscated assets was the "Serb state" – the puppet regime of General Nedic.[421] However, the "Serb state" did not actually receive all these funds because the Germans withheld money to cover claims for war damages, etc.

While the bookkeeping could barely be finished before the occupation ended in 1944, the owners of the property were dealt with much more quickly. In Serbia there was less delay in the killing operation than almost anywhere else, for here the German machine of destruction worked with a particularly dedicated zeal and feverish endeavor to "solve the Jewish problem."

In Russia the German Army had been very nervous about the partisans, and that same scourge struck the Germans in Serbia. The Serbs dislike foreign domination in practically any form, and German-occupied Serbia was consequently the scene of continuous partisan warfare. As in the case of Russia, so also in Serbia the German Army reacted to the rebellious outbreaks by shooting hostages, especially Jewish hostages.

In the beginning the shootings were carried out on a relatively small scale. For instance, 10 Communists and 3 Jews were shot on July 5, 1941, after packages containing explosives had been discovered on a public square just before a mass meeting of ethnic Germans was to get under way;[422] 122 Communists and "Jewish intellectuals" (mostly the latter) were shot on July 28, on the ground that someone had attempted to set a German vehicle afire;[423] and so on. During the late summer of 1941, however, two camps were set up, one in Belgrade, the other in Sabac. At the same time, systematic roundups of Jewish men were set in motion in the entire Serb territory.[424] Apparently the military was already beginning to think in terms of large-scale shootings of Jews.

These measures attracted attention in the Foreign Office. At the beginning of September a traveling envoy from Berlin joined Foreign Office Plenipotentiary Benzler in Belgrade; the traveler was Edmund Veesenmayer, a party member, businessman, and Foreign Office trouble shooter.[425] On September 8, 1941, Veesenmayer and Benzler sent a joint dispatch to the Foreign Office, pointing out that, again and again, Jews had participated in sabotage and terroristic acts. Accordingly, Veesenmayer and Benzler proposed that 8000 Jewish men be removed from Serbia, perhaps in barges moving downstream on the Danube to the delta

421. *Donauzeitung* (Belgrade), August 30, 1942, p. 3.

422. *Befehlshaber in Serbien/Kommandostab* Ia (signed Heimann) to *Wehrmachtbefehlshaber Südost* (12th Army), July 5, 1941, NOKW-1057. War diary, commanding general and *Befehlshaber in Serbien* Ia, July 5, 1941, NOKW-902.

423. *Befehlshaber in Serbien* Ic to *Wehrmachtbefehlshaber Südost* (12th Army), July 27, 1941, NOKW-1057. Benzler to Foreign Office, July 28, 1941, NG-111. *Donauzeitung* (Belgrade), July 29, 1941, p. 3.

424. *Befehlshaber in Serbien* Ia to *Wehrmachtbefehlshaber Südost* (12th Army), September 17, 1941, NOKW-1057.

425. On Veesenmayer career, see his affidavit of May 27, 1947, NG-1628. At the time of his arrival in Serbia he was thirty-four years old.

of the river in Roumania.[426]

Two days later the two diplomats sent an even more urgent message to Berlin:

> Quick and Draconic settlement of Serbian Jewish question is most urgent and appropriate necessity. Request authorization from the Foreign Minister to put maximum pressure on *Militärbefehlshaber* Serbia. No opposition is to be expected from the Serb [puppet] government. . . .[427]

Foreign Minister Ribbentrop was not enthusiastic about the plan. He indicated that one could not dump Serbian Jews on Roumanian soil without Roumania's consent.[428] Undeterred by the lack of higher approval, Benzler sent another message to Berlin, explaining that the Sabac camp, then holding 1200 Jews, was practically on the firing line and that the Jews had to be deported.[429]

Upon receipt of that communication *Abteilung Deutschland's* expert in Jewish affairs, Rademacher, consulted Sturmbannführer Baetz (RSHA IV-D-4), who dealt with Gestapo matters in occupied territories, about the feasibility of the proposal. Baetz pointed out that deportations were out of the question; not even the Reich Jews could be deported yet. Rademacher then turned to Adolf Eichmann for advice. The RSHA's expert on Jewish affairs had a remedy: "Eichmann proposes shooting."[430] The idea appealed to Rademacher very much, and on September 13 he wrote Luther that there was really no necessity for deporting the 1200 Jews in the Sabac camp. The shooting of "a large number" of hostages would solve the problem just as well.[431]

On September 28, 1941, however, another message was received from Serbia. Benzler now explained that General Böhme, the plenipotentiary commanding general, wanted to deport all 8000 Jewish men in Serbia. Böhme could not place 8000 people into camps; besides, the general had heard that deportations had successfully been carried out in other countries, such as the Protektorat.[432] The tone of that letter aroused *Abteilung Deutschland's* Luther. Addressing Staatssekretär Weizsäcker, he wrote on October 2, 1941:

> It is my opinion that the military commander is responsible for the immediate elimination of those 8000 Jews. In other territories [Russia] other military commanders have taken care of considerably greater numbers of Jews without even mentioning it.

Luther then proposed having a discussion with Heydrich (then *Reichsprotektor* in Prague, but expected to visit Berlin momentarily) for the purpose of clearing up the question.[433] But on that very day, October 2, 1941, things were already happening in Serbia.

At the town of Topola a truck convoy of Company 2, 521st Signal Battalion, was ambushed by partisans. Twenty-one men were killed immediately; another died later. Two days afterwards, General Böhme instructed the 342d Division and the 449th Signal Battalion to shoot 2100 inmates of the Sabac and Belgrade camps.[434] The ice was broken.

426. Veesenmayer and Benzler to Foreign Office, September 8, 1941, NG-3354.

427. Veesenmayer and Benzler to Foreign Office, September 10, 1941, NG-3354.

428. Sonnleithner via Wörmann to Weizsäcker, September 10, 1941, NG-3354. Luther to Benzler, September 11, 1941, NG-3354.

429. Benzler to Foreign Office, September 12, 1941, NG-3354.

430. Notation by Rademacher on Benzler report, NG-3354.

431. Rademacher to Luther, September 13, 1941, NG-3354.

432. Benzler to Rademacher, September 28, 1941, NG-3354.

433. Luther to Weizsäcker, October 2, 1941, NG-3354. Also, Luther to Rademacher, October 3, 1941, NG-5224.

434. Böhme to Chief of Military Administration, 342d Infantry Division, 449th Signal Battalion, October 4, 1941, NOKW-192. *Wehrmachtbefehlshaber Südost* Ic/AO to

The shootings started on October 9. To make sure that the victims were Jews and Gypsies only, a detachment of the *Einsatzgruppe* in Serbia screened the inmates and prepared them for killing. This was an odd reversal of functions – in Russian camps the Wehrmacht had done the screening and the *Einsatzgruppen* the shooting. Now, however, the Army had to do the "dirty work."[435]

On October 10 Böhme decided to go all the way. He ordered the "sudden" (*schlagartige*) arrest of all Communists and suspected Communists, "all Jews" (*sämtliche Juden*), and a "certain number" of "nationalistically and democratically inclined inhabitants." The arrested victims were to be shot according to the following key: for every *dead* German soldier or ethnic German, a hundred hostages; for every *wounded* German soldier or ethnic German, fifty hostages. (This was the key Böhme had applied to the Topola ambush.) Limiting the role of the SS in the killings, Böhme specified that "the shootings are to be carried out by the troops. If possible, the executions are to be performed by the unit which suffered the losses."[436] Straight revenge on the Jews. At first there was some doubt whether the hostage order also applied to women, but that question was clarified in the negative. Only men were to be shot.[437]

The army was now fully involved in the destruction process. Having introduced the first steps into Serbia, the military was about to carry out the last steps also. The divisions were mobilized for the *schlagartige Aktion,* the sudden and quick roundup of the Jewish male population. *Feldkommandanturen, Kreiskommandanturen,* the police, and the Serb mayors were pressed into service.[438]

Staatsrat Turner, the chief of civil administration under Böhme, explained to the field commands the necessity for the *Aktion.* "Basically," he wrote, "one must remember that Jews and Gypsies quite generally are an element of insecurity and thereby a danger to public order and peace. It is the Jewish intellect which has brought on this war, and which must be annihilated. The Gypsy," continued Turner, "cannot, by reason of his inner and outer makeup [*Konstruktion*], be a useful member of an international society [*Völkergemeinschaft*]."[439]

Attending to the more immediate problems of the operation, Böhme issued "special instructions for the implementation of shootings" (*Einzelanordnungen für Durchführung von Erschiessungen*). These instructions equal in detail any orders the *Einsatzgruppen* ever got. The shooting detachments were to be officer-led; the shootings were to be carried out with rifles from a distance of eight to ten yards; there was a provision for simultaneous aiming at head and chest. "To avoid unnecessary touching of corpses,"

OKW / *Wehrmachtführungsstab* / *Abteilung Landesverteidigung* (Warlimont), October 9, 1941, NOKW-251. RSHA IV-A-1, Operational Report USSR No. 120, October 21, 1941, NO-3402. Reports from the *Einsatzgruppe* in Serbia were sandwiched into the reports from the *Einsatzgruppen* in Russia.

435. RSHA IV-A-1, Operational Report USSR No. 108, October 9, 1941, NO-3156. RSHA IV-A-1, Operational Report USSR No. 119, October 20, 1941, NO-3404.

436. Order by Plenipotentiary Commanding General in Serbia/Chief of Military Administration (signed Böhme), October 10, 1941, NOKW-557.

437. Glt. Max Pemsel (Böhme's chief of staff) to Gfm. List, October 19, 1941, NOKW-197. Staatsrat Turner to all *Feldkommandanturen* and *Kreiskommandanturen* in Serbia (20 copies), October 26, 1941, NOKW-802.

438. Affidavit by Glt. Friedrich Stahl (Commander, 714th Division), June 12, 1947, NOKW-1714.

439. Turner to *Feld-* and *Kreiskommandanturen* (20 copies), October 26, 1941, NOKW-802.

Böhme ordered that the candidates for shooting stand at the edge of the grave. In mass shootings, he said, it would be appropriate to have the hostages kneel facing the grave. Each *Kommando* was to be accompanied by a military doctor, who was to give the order for any mercy shots. Clothes and shoes were to be handed over to the local military officer, and under no circumstances were personal effects to be handed out to the population.[440]

The army's experience with the shootings was similar to that of the *Einsatzgruppen* in Russia. We have a report on such an operation by a company commander, Oberleutnant Walther, whose unit (Company 9 of the 433d Regiment) was engaged in extensive killings at the Belgrade camp. When Company 9 removed hostages from the camp enclosure, the wives of the Jews were assembled outside, "crying and howling" (*die heulten und schrien, als wir abfuhren*). Baggage and valuables of the victims were collected and delivered by truck to the NSV (*Volkswohlfahrt* – Welfare Agency). At the killing site three light machine guns and twelve riflemen were posted as security. "The digging of ditches takes a long time," observed Walther, "while the shooting itself is very quick (100 men, 40 minutes)."

Walther then noted some differences in the behavior of Jews and Gypsies. "The shooting of Jews is easier than the shooting of Gypsies," he said. "One has to admit that the Jews are very composed when they go to their death [*sehr gefasst in den Tod gehen*] – they stand still – while the Gypsies cry out, howl, and move constantly, even when they are already standing on the shooting ground. Some of them even jumped into the ditch before the volley and pretended to be dead."

As for the effects of the shootings upon his own men, Walther had this to say: "In the beginning my men were not impressed [*nicht beeindruckt*]. However, on the second day it became obvious that one or another did not have the nerve to carry out shootings over a lengthy period of time. It is my personal impression that during the shooting one does not have psychological blocks [*seelische Hemmungen*]. They set in, however, if after several days one reflects about it on evenings, alone [*Diese stellen sich jedoch ein, wenn man nach Tagen abends in Ruhe darüber nachdenkt*]."[441]

As the shootings took their course, the military administration was not unaware of a basic contradiction: the insurgents were Serbs and Croats; the hostages were Jews and Gypsies. This awareness was revealed in a private letter from Staatsrat Turner to the Higher SS and Police Leader in Danzig, Gruppenführer Hildebrandt; the letter was written on October 17, 1941. Turner thanked Hildebrandt for a birthday present, a little book, "which will be a welcome diversion in the eternal monotony [*in dem ewigen Einerlei*] of my present job."

Having gotten over the introduction, Turner wrote: "That the devil is loose here you probably know [*Dass hier der Teufel los ist, weisst Du ja wohl*]." There was murder, sabotage, etc. Five weeks before, Turner had put 600 men to the wall, then 2000, more recently 1000; "and in between [*zwischendurch*] I had 2000 Jews and Gypsies shot dur-

440. Böhme to LXV Corps, 704th Division, 764th Division, October 25, 1941, NOKW-907.

441. 734th Inf. Regiment to 704th Division, November 4, 1941, enclosing report by Oblt. Walther (Commander, 9th Company, 433d Regiment), dated November 1, 1941, NOKW-905. See also affidavit by a Yugoslav eyewitness, Milorad-Mica Jelesic, February 25, 1945, J-29. Affiant, a peasant who was employed to collect valuables at a shooting, observed Jews and Gypsies bound to stakes. He reports also that the Germans took many photographs of the event.

ing the last eight days in accordance with the quota 1:100 for bestially murdered German soldiers, and another 2200, again almost exclusively Jews, will be shot in the next eight days. This is not a pretty business [*Eine schöne Arbeit ist das nicht*]. At any rate, it has to be, if only to make clear to these people what it means to even attack a German soldier, and, for the rest, the Jewish question solves itself most quickly this way.

"Actually," Turner continued, "it is false, if one has to be precise about it [*wenn man es genau nimmt*], that for murdered Germans – on whose account the ratio 1:100 should really be borne by Serbs – 100 Jews are shot instead; but the Jews we had in the camps – after all, they too are Serb nationals, and besides, they have to disappear. At any rate, I don't have to accuse myself that on my part there has been any lack of necessary ruthless action [*Rücksichtslosigkeit des Durchgreifens*] for the preservation of German prestige and the protection of members of the German Wehrmacht."[442]

In Berlin, Staatssekretär Weizsäcker of the Foreign Office was troubled by still another question: Hadn't the German Minister, Benzler, pushed things a little too much? Were shootings any business of the Foreign Office? In a carefully worded note to *Abteilung Deutschland,* Weizsäcker pointed out that Benzler had to concern himself with the transport of Jews *from* Serbia *to* other countries. "On the other hand, said Weizsäcker, "it is beyond Benzler's and the Foreign Office's task to take an active part in decisions on how the competent military and interior jurisdictions should overcome the Jewish question within the Serbian frontiers." The agencies involved were receiving their instructions from places other than the Foreign Office. Weizsäcker had told Minister Benzler this very fact that day, and he thought it appropriate to repeat the rebuke in writing.[443]

This time, however, Luther took Benzler under his wing. After all, it was Benzler who had urged deportation, and it was Luther who had rammed down the "territorial solution." Luther therefore replied, that in view of Ribbentrop's decision to submit the question of the 8000 Jews to a discussion with Heydrich (now no longer necessary), Benzler was acting in accordance with Ribbentrop's wishes when he intervened "in this certainly rather delicate matter."[444]

The reason for Weizsäcker's annoyance and for Luther's reference to the "delicacy" of the matter was of course the fact that the publicized shootings had evoked protests from neutral countries. Weizsäcker was the recipient of these protests. In 1941, at any rate, most countries were still under the impression that the shooting of hostages was contrary to international law, and the Foreign Office was consequently deluged with representations from such states as Mexico and Haiti.

On December 5 the papal representative was about to make a protest. In Weizsäcker' words: "The nuncio today groped around to the well-known subject of hostages, in order to determine whether a discussion between him and me about the question of shooting

442. Turner to Hildebrandt, October 17, 1941, NO-5810. Reports on the German prestige were, incidentally, collected by the OKW/*Ausland-Abwehr.* Thus, one informant who was a lawyer and board member of various German firms wrote in after a trip to Hungary that "the shootings of the Jews in Belgrade were reported to me by three different Hungarians, in part with little friendly commentary [*Die Judenerschiessungen in Belgrad wurden mir von 3 verschiedenen Ungarn berichtet, teils mit wenig freundlichen Kommentar*]." Report by Amt *Ausland-Abwehr,* December 13, 1941, Wi/IF 2.24.

443. Weizsäcker to *Abteilung Deutschland,* November 22, 1941, NG-3354.

444. Luther to Weizsäcker, December 12, 1941, NG-3354.

hostages — of late in Serbia — would be fruitful [*erspriesslich*]. I replied to the nuncio that, among all foreign governments which have concerned themselves with this question, the Vatican had conducted itself most cleverly [*am Klügsten*], in that it took the hint I had furtively extended to Papal Counselor Colli upon a social occasion. If the Vatican should nevertheless feel constrained to return to this subject, I would be obliged to give to the nuncio the same answer that Mexico, Haiti, and other governments had received already. The nuncio saw this point completely and pointed out that he had not really touched this topic and that he had no desire to touch it."[445]

While the German Army was completing the shooting of 4000-5000 men,[446] there remained a problem of killing about 15,000 women and children,[447] for "it was contrary to the viewpoint [*Auffassung*] of the German soldier and civil servant to take women as hostages," unless the women were actually wives or relatives of insurgents fighting in the mountains.[448] The Jewish women and children consequently had to be "evacuated."

At the end of October Minister Benzler, Staatsrat Turner, and Standartenführer Fuchs — joined by the Foreign Office's Jewish expert, Rademacher — were considering various methods of quietly removing the women and children. The bureaucrats planned a ghetto in the city of Belgrade, but Staatsrat Turner, who did not like ghettos, urged the quick removal of the Jews to a transit camp on a Danubian island at Mitrovica, not far from the Serbian capital.[449] When the proposed Danubian island turned out to be under water, the choice fell upon Semlin (Zemun), a town (opposite Belgrade) orginally under the jurisdiction of the *Befehlshaber* in Serbia but now transferred to Croatia. The Croat government graciously gave its permission for the construction of a camp in Semlin.[450]

On November 3, 1941, Turner instructed the *Feld-* and *Kreiskommandanturen* to start counting the Jewish women and children in all Serbian towns.[451] Preparations were completed in December.[452] Troop units began to move the families of the dead hostages to Semlin, where Commander of Security Police and SD (BdS) Schäfer waited for his victims. There is no indication that any transports moved out to Poland; Semlin was the end of the line. As the Jews arrived, they were accommodated in the camp. From time to time a batch of women and children were loaded on a special vehicle which drove off into the woods. The vehicle was a gas van.[453]

Slowly but methodically the gas van

445. Weizsäcker to Wörmann, von Erdmannsdorff, and Legationsrat Haidlen, December 5, 1941, NG-4519.

446. Not 8000, as had originally been planned — see memorandum by Rademacher, October 25, 1941, NG-4894.

447. Rademacher noted an estimate of 20,000 Jews and 1500 Gypsies. Memorandum by Rademacher, October 25, 1941, NG-4894. However, a later report by the *Oberbefehlshaber Südost*/Ia mentioned 16,000 Jews and Gypsies. OB *Südost*/Ia to WB *Südost*/Ic, December 5, 1941, NOKW-1150. The OB *Südost* was General der Pioniere Kuntze. The *Donauzeitung* (Belgrade), July 3, 1943, p. 3, gave a figure of 15,000 Jews "according to last reports" (*nach letzten Angaben*).

448. Turner to *Feld-* and *Kreiskommandanturen,* October 26, 1941, NOKW-802.

449. Memorandum by Rademacher, October 25, 1941, NG-3354.

450. Rademacher to Luther, December 8, 1941, NG-3354.

451. Turner to *Feld-* and *Kreiskommandanturen* (20 copies), November 3, 1941, NOKW-801.

452. *Oberbefehlshaber Südost*/Ia to *Wehrmachtbefehlshaber Südost* (12th Army)/Ic, December 5, 1941, NOKW-1150.

453. OStubaf. Schäfer to Stubaf. Pradel (RSHA II-D-3-a; Technical Office/Security Police Motor Vehicles *Referat*), June 9, 1942, PS-501. See also Gerald Reitlinger, *The Final Solution* (New York, 1953), pp. 362–64.

did its work. In March, 1942, the Jewish population of the Semlin camp fluctuated between 5000 and 6000;[454] in April the number dropped to 2974;[455] and in June Dr. Schäfer reported that apart from Jews in mixed marriages there was no longer any Jewish problem in Serbia (*keine Judenfrage mehr*).[456] At the same time he returned to Berlin the gas van, which was to see further service in White Russia.[457]

When in August, 1942, Generaloberst Löhr took over as *Oberbefehlshaber Südost,* Staatsrat Turner jotted down a few notes for a personal report to his new chief. In that report Turner itemized all the achievements of the previous administration. With considerable satisfaction he wrote down a unique accomplishment: "Serbia only country in which *Jewish question and Gypsy question solved* [Serbien einziges Land in dem *Judenfrage und Zigeunerfrage gelöst*]."[458]

454. Bader to *Wehrmachtbefehlshaber Südost,* copies to General Plenipotentiary for the Economy, Plenipotentiary of the Foreign Office, Higher SS and Police Leader, *Abwehrstelle* (Counter Intelligence Office) Belgrade, Ia, Qu, Ic, Adm., War diary, March 10, 1942, NOKW-1221. Bader to WB *Südost* (same distribution), March 20, 1942, NOKW-1221. Bader to WB *Südost* (same distribution), March 31, 1942, NOKW-1221.

455. *Kommandierender General* and *Befehlshaber Serbien*/Chief of Staff (signed Oberst Kewisch) to WB *Südost,* April 20, 1942, April-1444. *Kommandierender General* and *Befehlshaber Serbien*/Chief of Staff (signed Obstlt. Kogard) to WB *Südost, Kampfgruppe* (Combat Group) General Bader, Plenipotentiary Foreign Office, General Plenipotentiary Economy, Higher SS and Police Leader, German Liaison Staff with 2d Italian Army, Counter Intelligence Office Belgrade, German Liaison Officer with Bulgarian Occupation Corps, Adm. Staff, Ia, OQu, Ic, War diary, April 30, 1942, NOKW-1444.

456. Report by Hauptmann Leeb (OB *Südost*/Id), June, 1942, NOKW-926.

457. Schäfer to Pradel, June 9, 1942, PS-501. Rauff (Chief, RSHA II-D) to BdS *Ostland,* June 22, 1942, PS-501.

458. Note by Turner for personal report to Löhr, August 29, 1942, NOKW-1486.

Greece. — When Greece was overrun in 1941, it was carved into three sections. The northeastern territory (Thrace), which held between 5000 and 6000 Jews, was incorporated into Bulgaria. (We shall discuss the fate of these Jews when we get to the Bulgarians.) The remainder of the country was divided into Italian and German areas, and a puppet government, seated in Athens, functioned in both Italian and German zones. The Italian area was much larger than the German, for the Italians, after all, had been the first to attack Greece, and the Germans had come in only after the Italian invaders had been pushed by the Greek Army almost 50 miles into Albania.

However, while the Italians held most of the Greek territory, the Germans had acquired most of the Greek Jews. About 13,000 Jews lived in the Italian zone, but the number of Jewish inhabitants in German-dominated Macedonia and eastern Thrace (Salonika-Aegean) was over 55,000. The prewar Jewish population of the city of Salonika alone was 53,000. That was geographic fate.[459]

Although most of the Greek Jews were in German hands, the Germans for a long time undertook no action; in fact, the operations in nearby Serbia had been over for about nine months before deportations were started in Greece. Many factors were probably responsible for this delay: the distance from Salonika to Auschwitz, the scarcity of SS and Police personnel, and a desire to co-ordinate measures with the Italians. At least, so far as the Italians were concerned, German efforts in Greece were as fruitless as they had been everywhere else.

On July 13, 1942, the German commander in Salonika-Aegean (General-

459. Based upon statistics compiled by Josef Nehama in Michael Molho (ed.), *In Memoriam — Hommage aux victimes juives des Nazi en Grèce* (Salonika, 1948), II, 164.

leutnant von Krenzki) struck the first blow at the Greek *Judenmetropole* ("Jewish metropolis"). On that day, at 8 A.M., 6000 to 7000 Jewish men between the ages of 18 and 48 were lined up in huge blocks on "Liberty Square" in Salonika to be registered for forced labor.[460] The "fit" Jews were sent to work in the malaria-infested swamps, where many a victim perished from sickness and starvation.[461]

As the forced labor system was put into effect, the Salonika Jews began to emigrate to the Italian zone.[462] The Germans sought to check this flow by inviting the Italian administration to co-operate in the joint introduction of a Jewish star. The Italians refused any such co-operation.[463]

At the beginning of 1943 the Germans knew that the Italians could not be counted upon; the deportations would have to be confined to the German zone. Early in February two RSHA emissaries, Hauptsturmführer Wisliceny and Hauptsturmführer Alois Brunner moved into Salonika to carry out the operation.[464] As soon as the two men arrived, they went into conference with Generalkonsul Schönberg of the Foreign Office, Kriegsverwaltungsrat Merten (representing the *Befehlshaber* Salonika-Aegean, then Generalleutnant Haarde), and Kriminalkommissar Paschleben, the local commander of Security Police and SD. There were no special problems. Merten demanded only the temporary retention of 3000 Jews for railway construction by the *Organisation Todt*, on the understanding that these Jews would be released for deportation before the completion of the *Aktion*.[465] The operation could begin.

The uprooting and deportation process in Salonika was accomplished with unprecedented rapidity in the space of a few months. Three men were instrumental in bringing the *Aktion* to such a speedy conclusion: Kriegsverwaltungsrat Merten, Hauptsturmführer Wisliceny, and Chief Rabbi Koretz. The hierarchical relationship between these three officials is indicated in Table 61.[466]

TABLE 61 / *Deportation Machinery in Salonika*

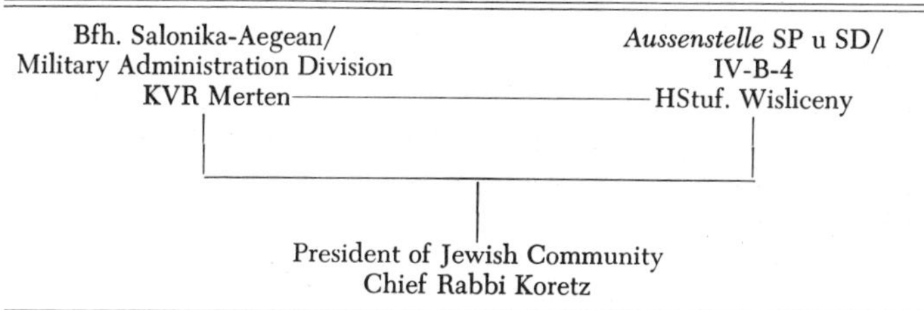

Dr. Merten was in charge of all civilian affairs in the district. He had over-

460. *Donauzeitung* (Belgrade), July 14, 1942, p. 3. Photograph in *Donauzeitung* of July 26, 1942, p. 3.

461. Cecil Roth, "The Last Days of Jewish Salonica," *Commentary*, July, 1950, pp. 50–51. The author, a historian, interviewed survivors and examined the community records after the war.

462. Luther via Weizsäcker to Ribbentrop, October 22, 1942, NG-4960.

463. *Ibid.*

464. Testimony by Wisliceny, *Trial of the Major War Criminals*, IV, 363.

465. Affidavit by Wisliceny, November 29, 1945, *Conspiracy and Aggression*, VIII, 606–21.

466. The *Befehlshaber* was then Gen. Haarde. The chief of the *Aussenstelle* was Paschleben. During the middle of March, Wisliceny became independent of Paschleben by assuming the direction of a *Sonderkommando für Judenangelegenheiten* in Salonika.

all responsibility for what was happening to civilians in his area, and he never relinquished that responsibility. In fact, many of the orders received by the Jewish community came from Dr. Merten himself. All other orders were issued by Hauptsturmführer Wisliceny in pursuance of an express authorization by the *Kriegsverwaltungsrat*.[467]

Wisliceny was, of course, an expert in Jewish matters. His sole task was to see to it that all Jews were deported as quickly as possible. To fulfill that assignment, he made maximum use of the Jewish community leadership. The Jewish leader, Chief Rabbi Dr. Koretz, was an Eastern Jew with a Western education; the Salonika Jews had chosen him as their spokesman because they felt that a German-speaking emissary would be most effective in dealing with the German overlords. In Koretz the Jews actually had a leader who believed in "unquestioning compliance."[468] He was an ideal tool for the German bureaucrats.

The Salonika operation was launched almost hastily by Kriegsverwaltungsrat Merten with an order to the Jewish community dated February 6, 1943.[469] The directive contained two operative provisions: (1) All Jews, excepting only the possessors of foreign passports, were to be marked; similarly, Jewish stores were to be identified by means of shields bearing Greek and German inscriptions. (2) All Jews – again excepting the foreign Jews – were to move into a ghetto. Both orders were to be carried out by February 25, 1943.

Within the next few days implementation directives rained down upon the Jewish community. On February 12, Wisliceny communicated to Rabbi Koretz a definition in accordance with which a person was a Jew if he had three or four Jewish grandparents, or if he had two Jewish grandparents and (*a*) belonged to the Jewish religion on April 1, 1941 (that is, just prior to the German invasion of Greece), or (*b*) was the offspring of an extramarital relationship and was born after that date.[470] In the same letter to Koretz the methodical Wisliceny also described the Jewish star, its size, material, etc. He directed the Jewish community to hand out with each star an identification card; the cards were to be numbered consecutively, and the number on each card was to be inscribed on the yellow cloth star to be worn by the card-holder. Wisliceny ordered that every Jew who had reached the age of five wear the Jewish star and that in the case of mixed marriages the Jewish partner be marked. "Petitions for exemptions from the identification," wrote the all-powerful Wisliceny, "are useless."[471] In a subsequent directive, Wisliceny defined the term "Jewish enterprise," ordered Jewish doctors and lawyers to mount stars on their offices, and required Jewish tenants to identify their apartments.[472]

Even while the Jewish community was turning out 100,000 stars at top speed,[473] orders were received to move into a ghetto. The Salonika ghetto was

467. Bfh. Salonika-Aegean/Mil Adm. (signed Merten) to Jewish community in Salonika, February 6, 1943, in Molho, *In Memoriam*, I, 135.

468. Roth, "Salonica," p. 51.

469. Merten to Jewish community, February 6, 1943, Molho, *In Memoriam*, I, 135.

470. There was a minor omission in the definition. Apparently a little careless, Wisliceny had left out Christian half-Jews married to Jews.

471. Wisliceny to Koretz, February 12, 1943, Molho, *In Memoriam*, I, 136–37. Wisliceny's last pronouncement notwithstanding, petitions were not entirely useless. See, for example, the certificate signed by Merten and dated March 30, 1943, exempting the Greek Jew Morris Raphael from wearing the star because he was married to a non-Jewish Frenchwoman with whom he "possessed four children." Molho, *In Memoriam*, I, 37.

472. Wisliceny to Koretz, February 17, 1943, Molho, *In Memoriam*, I, 140.

473. Apparently two stars per person. Roth, "Salonica," p. 52.

to be divided into several non-contiguous sections, completely severed from one another.[474] Jews were forbidden to leave their quarters; the use of trolley-cars, buses, and taxis was prohibited; public telephones were closed to Jews, and all private phones had to be surrendered to the Greek telephone company, accompanied by payment of all outstanding bills.[475]

The division into ghetto sections was part of a definite plan. The poorest Jews were sent into the Baron de Hirsch quarter near the railway station. This particular section was fenced in, and at the three entrances signs were mounted forbidding passage in German, Greek, and Ladino.[476] The Baron de Hirsch Jews were to be the first to go, and the emptied quarter was then to be filled with victims from the other ghetto sections. In short, the Salonika Jews were to be deported, section by section, via the Baron de Hirsch houses, which were to serve as a funnel leading to the death transports.

On February 13, Merten invested Koretz with authority over all Jews in the German *Befehlshaber* area, both inside and outside the city, in order to facilitate a "uniform solution" of the Jewish question in the entire district.[477] Shortly thereafter Merten called Koretz for an audience. The German officer explained to the rabbi that the Jewish population had no cause for worry; the Baron de Hirsch ghetto would have to be emptied because a large number of Communists in that section were threatening the safety of the occupation army, but these Jews would not be harmed. The emigrants would take up life anew in the Polish city of Krakow, where the local Jewish community would welcome them with open arms.[478]

Koretz returned to the ghetto and informed the victims of their forthcoming trip to Poland. He assured them that they would find new homes there, that the Jewish community in Krakow would receive them with open arms, that each man would find employment in the Polish city, etc., etc. It was a disquieting explanation, but the Jews made their preparations. Polish paper money was distributed, the permitted items were packed, and the deportees were marched off to the trains.[479]

Within hours the Germans struck again. The ghetto section in the Aghia Paraskevi district was surrounded, and its inhabitants were driven to the Baron de Hirsch quarter. Again the rabbi was summoned to German headquarters. This time he was told that all the common sections were infested with Communists but that the middle classes living in the center of the city had nothing to fear. Once more, feverish preparations gripped the Baron de Hirsch quarter. Family possessions were packed, plans were made, and young couples concluded hasty marriages to face life together in the East.[480] When the Aghia Paraskevi Jews were deported, the Germans seized the middle class.

Restlessness was now increasing in the Jewish community. During the night of March 18-19 a physician, Dr. Cuenca, made his getaway. On March 21 a special messenger brought Rabbi Koretz a note from Merten;[481] the

474. *Ibid.*, p. 53.

475. Merten to Jewish community, February 13, 1943, Molho, *In Memoriam*, I, 138. Doctors and Jewish community officials were allowed to retain their vehicles.

476. Roth, "Salonica," p. 53. Ladino, a Spanish dialect mixed with Hebrew, was spoken by Greek Jews in Salonika.

477. Merten to Koretz, February 13, 1943, Molho, *In Memoriam*, I, 139.

478. Albert Menasche, *Birkenau* (New York, 1947), p. 12. Menasche, a Jewish doctor who resided in Salonika, is a survivor.

479. Roth, "Salonica," p. 53.

480. *Ibid.* Menasche, *Birkenau*, p. 13.

481. Merten to Jewish community, March 21, 1943, Molho, *In Memoriam*, I, 144.

Kriegsverwaltungsrat announced that twenty-five hostages would be seized, to be shot upon the slightest indication of any further Jewish "opposition" (*Zuwiderhandlung*). Henceforth Jews were permitted to be in the streets only between 10 A.M. and 4 P.M., and anyone caught in the open outside these hours would be shot on sight by German and Greek police. The Jewish police (*Ordner*) and the foreign Jews alone, he specified, were exempted from this provision.

The end was now approaching for the privileged Jews, the professionals and the Jewish community leaders themselves. But the Germans did not cease their attempts to keep the populace quiet. At the end of May a transport was given to understand that its destination was Theresienstadt. The news caused a big commotion, as zloty were hurriedly exchanged for reichsmark.[482] The Jewish community organization was kept busy; it was made responsible for the seizure of all movable assets left behind by the "resettled Jews" (*ausgesiedelte Juden*),[483] and on March 29, Wisliceny sent to the Chief Rabbi a complete table of reorganization for the Jewish community, with a note requesting Koretz to submit by April 1 a statement of personnel needs and a work program for the future.[484] The new table of organization was, incidentally, as follows:

Koretz
Advisory Committee
Central Secretariat
Finance Division
Records Division (to keep records of the "population movement")
Division for Resettlement and Commission for Labor Allocation in Camp "Baron Hirsch"
Division for Health and Cemeteries
Division for Public Kitchens and Supplies
Jewish Police (*Ordner*) Division
Division for Cash and Valuables (to be headed by Koretz personally)

Within a few months that entire organization was swept away and deported.[485]

From the middle of March through May, Wehrmacht trains carrying 2000 to 2500 Jews rolled almost daily from Salonika via Belgrade to Auschwitz.[486] When the game was over, about 46,000 Salonika Jews had been deported.[487]

482. Menasche, *Birkenau*, pp. 15–17. The author was on this transport. It arrived, of course, in Auschwitz.

483. Merten to Koretz, March 13, 1943, Molho, *In Memoriam*, I, 142. Wisliceny to Koretz, March 15, 1943, *ibid.*, p. 143.

484. Wisliceny to Koretz, March 29, 1943, *ibid.*, p. 145.

485. Koretz, it seems, did not go to Auschwitz. He was shipped to the Bergen-Belsen camp instead, but he did not survive there. Roth, "Salonica," p. 55.

486. Testimony by Wisliceny, *Trial of the Major War Criminals*, IV, 365. Wagner to German Consul in Sofia, April 30, 1943, NG-4924. Affidavit by Heinburg (Foreign Office/Pol. IV), September 5, 1947, NG-2570. Report by Korherr, April 19, 1943, NO-5193. A final transport left in August. Roth, "Salonica," p. 54.

487. The breakdown is as follows:

City of Salonika	43,850
Towns in vicinity of Salonika	1,132
East-Aegean area (facing Turkish border)	1,002
Total	45,984

Compiled from a detailed town-by-town deportation chart prepared by Josef Nehama in Molho, *In Memoriam*, II, 164. The figures are based on Jewish Community statistics. About 45,000 of these Jews went to Auschwitz. Executive Office of the President/War Refugee Board, "The Extermination Camps of Auschwitz and Birkenau," November, 1944, mimeographed, declarations by escaped Slovak Jews, p. 17. Also, Olga Lengyel, *Five Chimneys: The Story of Auschwitz* (Chicago and New York, 1947), p. 70. Only a few hundred privileged and foreign Jews (discussed below) were shipped to Bergen-Belsen. Roth, "Salonica," p. 55. Wisliceny mentions as many as 55,000 deportees. See his affidavit of November 29, 1945, *Conspiracy and Aggression*, VIII, 606–21. According to the Nehama table referred to above, no more

Short disposition was made of the property of the deported Jews. The cash sum of 280,000,000 drachmas (ca. RM 3,500,000, or $1,500,000) was turned over to the military administration;[488] the empty Jewish apartments were transferred to the Greek puppet governor of Macedonia;[489] and the abandoned Jewish stores were magnanimously handed over to the Macedonian governor, to be run under "trusteeship" by the Agrarian Bank of Salonika in behalf of the Greek state.[490]

Rarely had a major operation been carried out so smoothly. Still, the Germans were not spared a few headaches. This time the difficulties were caused by two foreign representatives, one the Italian Consul General in Salonika, the other the Spanish chargé d'affaires in Athens. Through the efforts of these men the fate of the Salonika Jews was altered for at least two special groups.

In February the RSHA dispatched to the Foreign Office a note complaining that Italian Consul General Castrucci was handing out Italian naturalization papers to Greek Jews in Salonika. The Foreign Office was requested to intercede with the Italian government for the purpose of stopping that development immediately and effecting a revocation of the naturalizations.[491] In April news was received that the Italian Consul General was protecting 281 Jews whose Italian citizenship was uncontested, plus 48 more who had lost their Italian nationality and to whom he now wanted to restore citizenship. Wagner of Inland II immediately instructed the German Consul General (Schönberg) to decline the Italian request. Castrucci, however, did not give up. With a "pointed hint" to "special Italian rights in the Greek sphere" he repeated his request, and Wagner thereupon decided to exempt the 48 contested Jews "for the moment." Appealing for support, he wrote to Unterstaatssekretär Hencke of the Political Division and Staatssekretär Steengracht himself, to secure their approval for the deportation of these Jews. Hencke and Steengracht scribbled "agreed" *(einverstanden)* on the memorandum.[492] The Italian Consul General, in the meantime, was taking some measures of his own: he put uncontested and contested Italian citizens on an Italian troop train and smuggled them to the Italian zone of Greece.[493]

The Jewish community in Salonika also had about 600 Jews who were Spanish citizens. When the deportations started, the RSHA intercepted messages from the Spanish chargé d'affaires in Athens (Eduard Gasset) to the Spanish Foreign Ministry in Madrid which revealed that Gasset, with the aid and abetment of the chief of the Political Division of the Spanish Foreign Office (Doussinague), was trying very hard to save the Spanish Jews. It seemed that on April 1, 1943, the Spanish government had opened a branch of the Falange (Franco's sole political party) in Athens. The branch

---

than about 55,000 Jews resided in the Salonika-East Aegean area in 1940. There was a slight decline of population between 1940 and 1943, due to excess of deaths over births. In addition, several thousand Jews had escaped to the Italian zone or had remained in hiding at Salonika.

488. Testimony by Wisliceny, *Trial of the Major War Criminals,* IV, 363.

489. *Donauzeitung* (Belgrade), June 22, 1943, p. 3.

490. Merten to Governor of Macedonia/Office for Jewish Property in Salonika, June 15, 1943, Molho, *In Memoriam,* II, 179.

491. Bergmann (Bureau of the Foreign Minister) and Wörmann to embassy in Rome, February 15, 1943, NG-4957. Castrucci's name is mentioned only by Molho, *In Memoriam,* I, 124.

492. Wagner via Hencke to Steengracht, April 29, 1943, NG-5052.

493. Von Thadden to embassy in Rome, April 30, 1943, NG-5053. The Italian Jews were actually withdrawn in small batches. Memorandum by Erdmannsdorff, June 10, 1943, NG-5207.

was directed by the counselor of the Spanish Legation, Eugen Palssewsky, and was financed by "rich Jews."[494]

The German Foreign Office thereupon tried to pressure the Spanish government into withdrawing its 600 Jews to Spain. In making that proposal, the Foreign Office struck a telling blow, for the Spaniards did not want to accept such a large number of Jews. From Madrid, Gasset was instructed that his government would be willing to receive at most about 50 Jews. In Berlin a member of the Spanish Embassy orally informed Inland II that Madrid would much rather transfer these 600 Jews to German jurisdiction, if only "one could be sure that they would not be liquidated" *(wenn man sicher wäre dass sie nicht liquidiert würden).* Inland II then proposed as an interim solution the transport of the Jews to some camp in the Reich. Eichmann was requested for that purpose to treat the Spanish Jews in a manner that would not – in the event of their later emigration – lead to "undesired atrocity propaganda."[495]

During the subsequent months the Germans and Spaniards continued to haggle about the Jews. The Spanish government was given "two or three" months to make up its mind.[496] On December 22, 1943, the secretary of the Spanish Embassy in Berlin, Diez, requested that all Spanish Jews be "treated as Spanish citizens and be permitted to emigrate freely, for they were after all neutrals and no enemies of Germany." Von Thadden replied that "every Jew was an enemy of Germany, even if by chance he had a Spanish passport." Free emigration from Salonika was out of the question, but as an extraordinary concession a collective transport might be organized.[497] The final outcome of these negotiations was the transfer of the Spanish Salonika Jews to a very favored "residence camp" in Germany, Bergen-Belsen.[498] Three hundred and sixty-five of these Jews reached Spain at the end of the war.[499]

While the Foreign Office had its hands full with foreign Jews in Salonika, it did not forget the Greek Jews in the Italian area. Before the deportations started in the German zone, Ambassador von Mackensen in Rome and Minister Altenburg in Berlin attempted in vain to persuade the Italian government to deport the 13,000 Jews in its jurisdiction.[500] On March 13, 1943, von Mackensen reported to the Foreign Office that the Italian government had decided to intern its Jews either on the Ionian Islands or in Italy.[501] Ribbentrop was skeptical. He wanted to know whether the SS was satisfied with this measure and, if so, whether the Italians actually planned to carry it out. "If that should not be the case," thought Ribbentrop, "we on our part would have to take new steps."[502] Obersturmbannführer Eichmann pointed out unequivocally that the measure was "unsatisfactory" and that experience had shown the necessity for serious doubt of the "sincerity of implementation" on the part of the Italians. The Foreign Office's Jewish expert, Rademacher,

494. Obf. Schellenberg (RSHA-VI) to Konsul Geiger (Inland II-B), June 22, 1943, NG-5352.

495. Von Thadden to Eichmann, July 24, 1943, NG-5050.

496. Wagner to consulate in Salonika, July 26, 1943, NG-5050.

497. Memorandum by von Thadden, December 22, 1943, NG-5262.

498. Von Thadden to von Erdmannsdorff, January 11, 1944, NG-5332.

499. Nehemiah Robinson, "Die Juden in Franco-Spanien," *Aufbau* (New York), September 11, 1953, p. 3.

500. Report by Minister Bergmann, February 24, 1943, NG-4956.

501. Von Mackensen to Foreign Office, March 13, 1943, NG-5051.

502. Von Sonnleithner (Bureau of the Foreign Minister) via Weizsäcker to Minister Bergmann, March 16, 1943, NG-5051.

agreed with that evaluation completely.[503]

On May 7, 1943, the new Inland II chief, Horst Wagner, wrote a memorandum in which he voiced the opinion that the Italians could not be persuaded to agree to the deportation of their Jews to the East. Under the circumstances Wagner thought it advisable that the RSHA at least make sure that the Italians carry out what promises they made. The Italians, he said, were now beginning to make excuses – such as lack of transportation facilities – for going back on their word. If the Jews could not be removed right away, Wagner continued, the Italians should at least be prevailed upon to impress the Jews into forced labor, such as road construction, fortification work, and railway improvement projects.[504]

Following the circulation of this memorandum in the Foreign Office, Wagner repeated his proposal in the form of draft instructions to the embassy in Rome. The Italians he reiterated, should be pressed to carry out "the deportation of the Jews to the Ionian Islands or to Italy"; in the meantime, use of the Jews in labor battalions for work on fortifications and railways would result in great savings of occupation costs, etc.[505] Before these instructions were dispatched to Rome, the new Staatssekretär, Steengracht von Moyland, made a significant change in their meaning: in the sentence "deportation of the Jews to the Ionian Islands or to Italy," he crossed out the words "to the Ionian Islands or to Italy," leaving only "deportation of the Jews."[506] Steengracht still had not given up hope.

503. Bergmann via Weizsäcker to Ribbentrop, March 17, 1943, NG-5051.

504. Wagner via Hencke to Steengracht, May 7, 1943, NG-5048.

505. Wagner to Rome Embassy, June 4, 1943, NG-5048.

506. *Ibid.* Bielfeld to Wagner, May 13, 1943, NG-5048.

At the end of July, Mussolini was succeeded by Marshal Badoglio, and by September 8, 1943, Italy had ceased to be an Axis partner. The German Army now turned on its former ally. In the entire Mediterranean area Italian garrisons were overwhelmed and disarmed. All of Greece, together with Albania, Montenegro, and the Dodecanese Islands, came under German domination. Some 16,000 Jews were living in these areas.

The new territory of Greece was important enough for the assignment of a special plenipotentiary of the Foreign Office, Minister Neubacher, and the appointment of a Higher SS and Police Leader, Gruppenführer Walter Schimana. The entire Greek civil apparatus, the Albanian puppet government, and the Italian civil administration in the Dodecanese *(Ost-Aegaeis)* – which was responsible to the new Fascist regime in northern Italy – were now placed under the direction of the expanded military organization in the southeast. The new military overlord in Greece was Generaloberst Löhr (under Weichs). In October, 1943, he transferred civil affairs to the *Militärbefehlshaber* in Greece, Speidel (under Felber). However, Löhr's Army Group E did not thereby pass from the scene; he retained complete control in the islands. The *Admiral Aegaeis* was responsible for the shipping which carried the island Jews to the mainland, and, on the mainland itself, the division and corps commanders continued to regard it as a matter of course that every move against Jewry was brought to their attention.[507]

On October 3, 1943, Higher SS and Police Leader Schimana ordered all Jews to register. In Athens the Jewish community organization was entrusted

507. On that point, see XXII Mountain Corps/Ic (signed by Corps Commander Lanz) to Army Group E/Chief of Staff, November 8, 1943, NOKW-1915.

with the supervision of the registration; in the rest of the country the local Greek officials were designated for this task. It appears that registrations did not come up to expectation – in Athens, for example, the number of registrants was 1200. Schimana, evidently not well informed, had expected 8000. (There were 3500 Jews in the city.) To "punish" the Jews for their failure to register, the *Militärbefehlshaber* in Greece (General der Flieger Speidel), in agreement with the Foreign Office Plenipotentiary Neubacher, confiscated the Jewish property and transferred it to the Greek state.[508]

The Jews were rather spread out on the Greek mainland, and for that reason it was necessary to mobilize trucks and guards in preparation for the roundup.[509] In March, 1944, the RSHA was ready to order the sudden *(schlagartige)* arrest of all Jews (except those in mixed marriages); the seizures were to be completed in three days, from March 23 to March 25.[510] We can form some idea about the precision work that was involved in this operation from a report about the removal of the Jews from the town of Ioannina.

The Ioannina operation was carried out by Order Police Major Hafranek with his own men, Greek police, Army *Feldgendarmerie* (Military Police), Secret Field Police (Counterintelligence), and soldiers stationed in the area. At 3 A.M. Hafranek surrounded the ghetto; at 5 A.M. the chairman of the Jewish community was informed that within three hours all Jews were to assemble at designated points for "evacuation." Each family was allowed 100 pounds of luggage. Greek police and members of the Jewish council passed on the announcement to the ghetto residents. Strong detachments of Order Police patrolled the streets. There was "no incident" (*kein Zwischenfall*).

At 10 A.M. 1725 Jews were moved out to Trikkala. About a hundred were retained to clean up. All furnishings and food in the vacated apartments were handed over to Greek offices for distribution to the Greek population – the purpose of this generosity was to combat hostile propaganda by the insurgent EAM organization (pro-Communist). From the EDES (nationalist anti-Communist), said the report, one could hear only "full approval" (*volle Zustimmung*).[511]

When the German Army had first moved into the Italian zone of Greece, the Jewish population of the prefecture of Ioannina had been estimated at about 2000;[512] six months later, more than 90 per cent of these people were caught in the Ioannina ghetto. To be sure, that kind of performance could not be repeated with the same success at all the mainland points, but the March raids did result in the deportation of about 5400 Jews.[513]

The roundups spread from the mainland of Greece to neighboring Albania. In April, 1944, the commanding general in Albania reported that SS Division

508. *Militärbefehlshaber* Greece/Mil. Adm. to *Militärbefehlshaber Südost* (Felber), December 18, 1943, NOKW-692.

509. War diary, Army Group E, March 15, 1944, NOKW-923.

510. *Militärbefehlshaber* Greece/Mil. Adm. Ic/Ia (signed Speidel) to *Militärbefehlshaber Südost* Ia, Ic, and chief of mil. adm., copies to Army Group E and Higher SS and Police Leader, April 14, 1944, NOKW-2520.

511. Report by noncommissioned officer Bergmayer (Secret Field Police Group 621 with XXII Mountain Corps), March 27, 1944, NOKW-1915. The history of the Greek underground movements ELAS-EAM and EDES is quite complex. By the spring of 1944, the former was Moscow-oriented; the latter was poised to fight the EAM and later on did.

512. Memorandum by Major Brandner (1st Mountain Division), September 13, 1943, NOKW-1104.

513. Nehama in Molho, *In Memoriam,* II, 164. In the Volos-Trikkala-Larissa area, as well as in Athens and the Peloponnesus, the seizures were less than 50 per cent successful.

Skanderbeg (Albanian collaborators) had arrested 300 Jews in Pristina ("new" Albania, in Yugoslav territory, near the frontier of the domain of the *Befehlshaber* in Serbia).[514] Between May 28 and July 5, 1944, the SS division rounded up another 510 "Jews, Communists, partisans, and suspicious persons" in the Albanian area. From that group, 249 were deported.[515]

The removal of the island Jews was more complicated than the mainland deportations. Approximately 2000 Jews lived on the Ionian island of Corfu, close to 300 on Zante, a little over 300 on Crete, and around 2200 on the east Aegean island of Rhodes. All these islands were under the complete control of Army Group E (Generaloberst Löhr).

On April 25, 1944, the intelligence officer on Corfu reported that the Jews on his island had been registered *(karteimässig erfasst)* and that from his point of view there was no fundamental objection (*keine grundsätzliche Bedenken)* to the removal of these Jews.[516] These impressions were confirmed by the corps intelligence officer who had visited Corfu on April 23 and 24. He thought that the deportation of the Jews would ease the food situation, and he requested the army group to "bring about implementation measures" by contacting the Security Police and SD.[517] On May 12 the Order Police in Athens approached the army group with a request for ships to transport the Corfu Jews to Patras and the Crete Jews to Piraeus. Army Group E/Operations approved of the request, on the condition that the tactical situation would not be jeopardized by the diversion of transport.[518]

Two days later the commander of Corfu, Oberst Jäger, sent a long memorandum to the XXII Mountain Corps. Jäger reported, first, that the *Admiral Aegaeis* had been requested to dispatch the ships. On the day before (May 13) a Himmler representative, Obersturmführer von Manowsky, had arrived on the island; he had left as soon as he had arrived. Jäger then came to the main point. He was uncomfortable about the whole undertaking. In fact, he found seven good reasons why the Jews should *not* be removed from Corfu. He thought that the "Badoglio Italians" (demobilized Italian soldiers) should be taken off the island first, since they were "far more dangerous than the Jews, about whom, incidentally, there has never been a complaint." The Jews had already been warned, and he feared that they would hide in the mountains. There was danger also that the Jews might bribe the Greek police. The *Aktion* could not be carried out quickly enough. Passive resistance by Greek sailors was a distinct possibility.

Next Jäger mentioned a most important consideration: Under an Allied-Nazi arrangement, Red Cross ships were permitted to enter Greek harbors with food in order to combat widening starvation among the Greeks. There was now such a Red Cross ship in the harbor of Corfu, where the visitors could observe everything and see to it that plenty of "atrocity propaganda" was spread about this matter. Finally, Jäger reminded the XXII Mountain

514. *Militärbefehlshaber Südost* (signed Chief of Staff von Geitner) to Army Group F, copies to OKH/Gen Qu, OKW/WFSt, 2d Panzer Army, German Plenipotentiary General in Albania, German Plenipotentiary General in Croatia, Luftwaffe Commander in Croatia, V SS Mountain Corps, April 16, 1944, NOKW-668.

515. Report by XXI Mountain Corps (signed Chief of Staff von Klocke), July 13, 1944, NOKW-838.

516. Oberleutnant König (Ic – *Aussenstelle Korfu*) to Corps Group Ioannina Ic, April 25, 1944, NOKW-1916.

517. Corps Group Ioannina Ic to Army Group E Ic/AO, April 28, 1944, NOKW-1985.

518. War diary, Army Group E Ia, May 12, 1944, NOKW-885.

Corps that Corfu was an exposed area (*militärisches Vorfeld*). For all these reasons he urged an indefinite postponement of the *Aktion*. Then he added in stenographic language: "Only if sudden *(schlagartige)* action possible, otherwise disadvantages."[519]

Corps headquarters took these objections seriously and sent them to Army Group E.[520] However, on May 15 Obersturmführer Burger (Theresienstadt) arrived on Corfu. The deportations could not be stopped any more; the machinery of destruction was in motion. On May 24 a fleet of six ships came in; on May 26, in expectation of the arrival of Security Police personnel, the island commander ordered the printing of posters calling upon the Jews to assemble. On May 28, with no Security Police in sight, the *Admiral Aegaeis* withdrew the ships — empty.

The next day Obersturmführer Burger finally brought in a company of *Feldgendarmerie* and Secret Field Police dispatched from Ioannina, and the island commander immediately set aside an old fortress to accommodate the Jews. On May 30, Kapitän zur See Magnus arrived. He announced that another fleet was on the way and promised to use the ships for the "evacuation" in spite of the expenditure of another 2600 gallons of gasoline.[521] By June 11 the *Aktion* was "rolling" *(im Rollen)*.[522] On June 17 the Security Police could report that 1795 Corfu Jews had been seized and transported from the island; their property was given to the Greek governor of Corfu for distribution to the islanders.[523]

More than one hundred miles south of Corfu, 270 Jews slipped off the Ionian island of Zante and escaped by sea to Italy. From Crete, however, the Germans deported some 260 Jews according to plan.[524]

On the east Aegean islands the Commander of the 999th Division *(Sturmdivision Rhodos)*, Generalleutnant Ulrich Kleemann, was in charge; he reported directly to Generaloberst Löhr, commander of Army Group E. The east Aegean islands were exposed territory. In September, 1943, barely two weeks after the Italian collapse, British forces had landed on Samos, Leros, and Cos; but the British could not hold the islands. Kleemann counterattacked and within two months overwhelmed the three British garrisons, one by one. He then turned his attention to the Jews.

In June, 1944, two SS officers arrived by plane on Rhodes to hold discussions with Kleemann.[525] On July 13 Kleemann issued an order designating the city of Rhodes and the towns of Trianda, Cremasto, and Villanovo as collecting points for the Jews. The entire Jewish population of Rhodes had to be in those towns by July 17 at noon.[526]

The order had its repercussions, not only among the Jews but also among the troops. On July 16, Kleemann was therefore forced to issue another order in which he stated that the Jewish question on Rhodes had apparently given rise to "doubts" *(Zweifeln)*. A soldier,

519. Jäger to XXII Mountain Corps, May 14, 1944, NOKW-1915.

520. XXII Mountain Corps/Ic to Army Group E, May 18, 1944, NOKW-1915.

521. Memorandum by Oberst Jäger (Commander, 1017th Infantry Regiment and Island Commander, Corfu) and Kapitän zur See Magnus (Naval Commander, Western Greece), June 1, 1944, NOKW-1915.

522. Jäger to XXII Mountain Corps, June 11, 1944, NOKW-1997.

523. BdS Greece/*Aussenstelle Janina* IV-B to XXII Mountain Corps/Ic and *Feldkommandantur* 1032/Ic, June 17, 1944, NOKW-1915.

524. Nehama in Molho, *In Memoriam*, II, 68–69, 72–74, 164.

525. Affidavit by Erwin Lenz (artillery man, *Sturmdivision Rhodos*), May 10, 1947, NOKW-1715.

526. Order by Kleemann, July 13, 1944, NOKW-1802.

Kleeman pointed out, could not possibly judge this matter from a soldier's narrow point of view; in the interest of the measures now started, the Jewish question on Rhodes and its solution was no longer to be made the topic of daily conversation among the troops.[527]

A soldier who on the day of the deportation went to the city of Rhodes to have his teeth fixed, noticed about 1200 men, women, and children standing with faces to the wall in the blistering heat. Greek and Turkish civilians who wanted to hand food and drink to the deportees were kept away. (There was a food shortage on Rhodes also.) The visiting soldier noticed that the victims had very little baggage. He started to gossip with the German soldiers standing guard and was told that the Jews did not need any baggage since they would not, after all, live very long.[528]

Thus, by July, 1944, the "final solution" was no longer a secret even on Rhodes, more than 1000 miles from Auschwitz as the crow flies. One month later, on August 17, 1944, the Rhodes Jews arrived at their destination.[529] When the British occupied the island in May, 1945, only a handful of Jews waited for their liberators in Rhodes City.[530]

All in all, more than 60,000 Jews had been deported from Greece, Albania, and Rhodes. Perhaps 12,000 remained.

527. Kleemann to subordinate units, July 16, 1944, NOKW-1801.

528. Affidavit by eyewitness Lenz, May 10, 1947, NOKW-1715.

529. See list of transports compiled by Dr. Otto Wolken (Jewish Auschwitz inmate) in Friedman, *This was Oswiecim,* p. 25.

530. Major General Lord Rennell of Rodd, *British Military Administration of Occupied Territories in Africa During the Years 1941–1947,* (London: H. M. Stationery Office, 1948), p. 513. While the Germans waited for the surrender, they fought for the spoils with local Italian officials. See *Kreiskommandantur Rhodos* to *Sturmdivision Rhodos* Ic, September 3, 1944, NOKW-1795.

Satellites Par Excellence. – During the German march across Europe, some territories were occupied and others were allotted to Axis allies. Two areas were in a special category. Germany did not wish to incorporate them, but they were not to be absorbed by her partners. Hence, these regions became countries themselves. The new entities – states by default and satellites par excellence – were Croatia and Slovakia.

Croatia. – Although the State of Croatia was a German creation, its establishment was not planned very far in advance. In fact, it was a rush job. On March 25, 1941, Yugoslavia followed in the footsteps of some of her neighbors and joined the Axis. Two days later a new government in Belgrade repudiated the agreement, and that same day Hitler decided to destroy Yugoslavia.[531] Military operations against the Yugoslavs began on April 6; by April 10 the German Army had occupied the Croat city of Zagreb. One day later the German Foreign Office trouble shooter Veesenmayer was in the city, discussing with Croat leaders an "exact plan for the assumption of power."[532] By April 16 there was a Croat government. Its most important personalities were:[533]

Chief of State: Dr. Ante Pavelic
Prime Minister: Dr. Pavelic (succeeded on September 4, 1943, by Nikola Mandic)
Foreign Minister: Dr. Pavelic (Lorkovic, Dudak)
Commander, Armed Forces: Gen. Slavko Kvaternik
Interior Minister: Dr. Artukovic (Nikic, Lorkovic, Frkovic)
Justice Minister: Dr. Puk (Artukovic)
Economy Minister: Dr. Dudak (Toth)

531. Summary of Führer conference, March 27, 1941, PS-1746.

532. Vessenmayer to Ribbentrop, April 11, 1941, NG-5875.

533. *Krakauer Zeitung,* April 18, 1941, p. 2. *Donauzeitung* (Belgrade), passim.

Finance Minister: Koshak
Minister of Mines: Ing. Frkovic
Minister of Transport: Beshlegic
Director of Public Security: Eugen Kvaternik (son of Gen. Kvaternik; succeeded by Jurcic)

At the time of its creation the new Croat state had very uncertain boundaries. To the north the Germans annexed a good chunk of Slovenia, stopping only a few miles from Zagreb. To the west the Italians annexed Ljubljana, most of the Dalmatian coast, and a few Adriatic islands. To the east the German commander in Serbia held the town of Semlin (Zemun), while in the northeast the Hungarians annexed the basin between the Danube and the Tisza. The Croat state itself was under occupation. Most of the country was host to the German Army, but in the southeastern part Italian units had taken up residence.

In spite of these unsettled conditions the Croat government lost no time in proceeding against its 30,000 Jewish inhabitants. On April 30, 1941, the three-week-old Croat state issued its first anti-Jewish law, a definition of the term "Jew." As one might expect, the Croat authorities dutifully followed, and even improved upon, the original Lösener definition (see Table 62).[534]

TABLE 62 / *German and Croat Definitions of "Jew"*

German	Croat
(1) A person who had at least three Jewish grandparents.	(1) A person who had at least three Jewish grandparents.
(2) A person who had two Jewish grandparents and who	(2) A person who had two Jewish grandparents and who
(*a*) belonged to the Jewish community on September 15, 1935, or joined it on a subsequent date, or	(*a*) belonged to the Jewish community on April 10, 1941, or joined it on a subsequent date, or
(*b*) was married to a three-quarter or full Jew on September 15, 1935, or married one on a subsequent date, or	(*b*) was married to a Jewish person on April 30, 1940, or married a Jewish or half-Jewish person on a subsequent date, or
(*c*) was the offspring of an extramarital relationship with a three-quarter or full Jew, and was born out of wedlock after July 31, 1936.	(*c*) was the offspring of an extramarital relationship with a Jew, and was born after January 31, 1942, or
	(*d*) was classified as a Jew by decision of the Croat Interior Minister acting upon a recommendation of a "race-political" commission, or
	(*e*) was born outside of Croatia of parents not resident in Croatia.
	(3) Any child of an unmarried Jewish mother.
	(4) Any person (including one-quarter Jews and full Aryans) entering into marriage with a Jew after April 30, 1941.

We need only recall the problems to which the original German definition gave rise to realize that the Croat definition, with all its improvements, was drafted by expert hands. However, the Croat decree-law contained an important excepting clause empowering the Chief of State to grant to all non-Aryans who had made worthwhile contributions to the Croat cause before April 10, 1941, the full rights of

534. *Die Judenfrage,* March 1, 1943, pp. 74–75.

Aryans.[535] As every so often, the tightly shut front door concealed the wide-open back entrance.[536]

In a very short time the Croat government also proceeded to enact all those measures which German bureaucrats had toiled over for eight years: the prohibition of intermarriage, of employing female Aryan servants under forty-five, of raising the Croat flag; the revocation of name changes adopted since December 1, 1918; the marking of Jewish stores and persons; the registration of property; the removals from the bureaucracy and the professions; the termination of business activities; and transfer of enterprises.[537]

The impoverishing process spread with great rapidity. By the end of August, 1941, after only four months of Croat government, most Jewish enterprises worth less than 200,000 kuna (RM 10,000 or $2,500) had been "Aryanized."[538] By mid-October, 1941, the Jews had been drawn out of the cities and sent to labor camps. Out of a population of 30,000 (only 25,000 in the German zone of occupation), 6000 Jews were employed in the salt mines at Karlovac and Yudovo,[539] and several hundred Jews were working in the torture camp of Yasenovac.[540] By summer of 1942 the Croat Jews were "ripe" for deportation. A representative of the RSHA, Hauptsturmführer Abromeit, joined German Minister Kasche in the Croat capital.[541] Thousands of Jews were trekking to the Italian-occupied zone of Croatia[542] and to the Hungarian-annexed Yugoslav Backa[543] to find refuge. But already the German Foreign Office was moving ahead with clock-like precision.

Some time at the end of 1941 or beginning of 1942 the Croat government was asked to express its disinterest in the fate of a few dozen Croat Jews residing in the Reich. This request was always put into the form of a courteous question: Did the Croat government plan to recall its Jews, or did it agree to their deportation?[544] The Croat government expressed "its gratitude for the gesture of the German government," but indicated that "it would appreciate the deportation of its Jews to the East."[545]

That reply doomed not only the handful of Croat Jews in Germany but almost all of Jewry in Croatia itself, for when consent has been given to the death of even one victim, the threshold has been crossed and the decisive involvement has begun. The killer of one person is no less a murderer than the killer of thousands, and, conversely, the mass killer is no more accountable than he who has killed only once. The experts of the RSHA and the German Foreign Office knew that principle better than anyone; therefore they always started a foreign campaign by applying pressure for the deportation of those few Jews who were already in the Reich.

535. *Ibid.*

536. The number of honorary Aryans increased steadily from month to month. RSHA IV-E-3 (signed Schellenberg) to Himmler, September, 1942, Himmler Files, Folder No. 120.

537. *Die Judenfrage,* March 1, 1943, pp. 74–75.

538. *Donauzeitung* (Belgrade), August 23, 1941, p. 3.

539. *Die Judenfrage,* October 15, 1941, p. 209.

540. *Deutsche Ukraine-Zeitung,* (Luck), February 22, 1942, p. 5. See also documents and photographs in Izdanje Saveza Jevrejskih Opstina fur Jugoslavije, *Zlocnini Fasistickih Okupatora i Njihovih Pomagaca Protiv Jevreja u Jugoslaviji* (Belgrade, 1952).

541. Affidavit by Wisliceny, November 25, 1945, *Conspiracy and Aggression,* VIII, 606–21.

542. *Ibid.*

543. *Deutsche Ukraine-Zeitung* (Luck), January 28, 1942, p. 8.

544. Rademacher via Luther to Weizsäcker, October 28, 1941, NG-182. Memorandum by Luther, August 21, 1942, NG-2586-J.

545. *Ibid.*

The relinquishment of those Jews by the Croat government required no administrative buildup and no bureaucratic action save a word of consent. Thus the initiation into the killing phase was brought about with ease, almost imperceptibly. The second request affected a much larger group of people, but it was already routine. The Croat government agreed – and the Germans had free rein.[546]

There was, however, one complication: nearly 5000 Jews were living in the Italian-occupied zone. So far, not even the Croat laws enacted in the German-dominated capital of Zagreb could be implemented in the Italian area. The Italian commander in Mostar, for instance, had promised equal treatment to all inhabitants, and he had even refused to evict Jewish tenants to make room for the German *Organisation Todt.* When asked for an explanation, he declared that anti-Jewish measures were "incompatible with the honor of the Italian Army."[547] The Foreign Office experts were now encountering the same problem in Croatia that we have already observed in southern France and Greece. In Croatia, too, the Foreign Office tried to goad the Italians into action, and in Croatia, too, the Foreign Office failed.

The German Minister in Zagreb, Kasche, advised that the deportation machinery start collecting Jews in the Italian zone without asking any questions. "We should take a chance," he said, "and see whether any complications would arise in the course of the operation."[548] Vortragende Legationsrat von Sonnleithner (Bureau Ribbentrop) and Staatssekretär Weizsäcker thought that perhaps the German Ambassador in Rome, von Mackensen, should be heard first.[549] On August 20, 1942, Kasche wrote to the Foreign Office that the key man in the Italian zone was the Italian commander, General Roatta. This was the man whose collaboration was required, and therefore it was necessary to convince the Rome government to issue the proper directives to him.[550] But Ribbentrop decided *not* to interfere in Rome. In his view, the deportation of the Jews from the Italian zone was "a matter concerning the Croat government"; hence, he thought that the Croat government was the proper authority to carry on negotiations with the Italians.[551]

Apparently the Croat government did not do much negotiating, for on September 24, 1942, on the eve of a Führer-Duce meeting, Minister Kasche was instructed to draw up a memorandum for possible presentation by Hitler to Mussolini. The memorandum was to deal with two subjects: the Jews and the supply of bauxite from Mostar. Suggested Ambassador Ritter: "The correct diplomatic language is to be adopted so as not to offend Italy and the Duce."[552]

The available documents unfortunately do not indicate what transpired during the Hitler-Mussolini conference, although we do know that negotiations between the Croats and Italians continued in October and November. The trend of these discussions shows a remarkable resemblance to the course of the Greek negotiations: The Italians first offered to take the Jews to Italy.[553]

546. *Ibid.*
547. *Ibid.*
548. *Ibid.*
549. Handwritten notation by Weizsäcker, undated, NG-3560. Lohmann (Bureau Ribbentrop) via Weizsäcker to Luther, August 8, 1942, NG-3560.

550. Kasche to Foreign Office, August 20, 1942, NG-2368.

551. Rintelen to Luther, August 25, 1942, NG-2586-K.

552. Note by Ritter, copy to Kasche, September 24, 1942, NG-3165.

553. Kasche to Foreign Office, October 20, 1942, NG-2814. Klingenfuss (D III) to German Embassy in Rome, October 24, 1942, NG-2366. Kasche to Foreign Office, November 10, 1942, NG-2814.

Next the negotiators considered the possible removal of the victims to the island of Lopud, off the Dalmatian coast.[554] Finally the Italian government promised to concentrate the Jews on the spot; however, it declined to permit Croat confiscations of Jewish property and, more important, refused a German request for Jewish "labor battalions."[555] The German Foreign Office was therefore blocked in its efforts to deport the Jews from the Italian-controlled part of Croatia. As in the case of Greece, the deportations were begun in the German zone, without Italian participation.

At the beginning of August, 1942, the Croat government published its version of the 11th Ordinance to the Reich Citizenship Law: all Jews leaving the country were to lose their Croat nationality in order that they might also lose their personal property. Again there was an improvement over the original German decree: any dependents left behind by the deported persons were to lose their nationality, too.[556] On October 9, 1942, Finance Minister Koshak agreed to pay to the German Government 30 reichsmark for each deported Jew – payment by the Croat people to the German people for the German contribution to the "final solution of the Jewish problem" in Croatia. The details of payment were worked out by Kasche and Foreign Minister Lorkovic.[557]

Our statistics of deported Croatian Jews are incomplete. Up to the end of 1942 the number was only 4927,[558] but Jews were deported in small batches during 1943 and 1944. In March, 1943, the representative of the *Reichsbahn* in Zagreb agreed to furnish cars, to be hooked to regularly scheduled trains, for the deportation of about 2000 Jews via Austria to Auschwitz.[559] On the occasion of these deportations another vain attempt was made to induce the Italians to co-operate in their zone.[560] In July, 1943, Inland II Chief Wagner urged Kasche to do his utmost to deport some 800 Jewish women and children who still remained in Croat concentration camps.[561] In September the Italian zone disappeared – not, however, before a large number of the Jews in the area had disappeared too.[562]

In April, 1944, Kasche and the police attaché, Obersturmbannführer Helm, sent their final report to Berlin. The Jewish question in Croatia, said Kasche, had been solved, but for three general exceptions: the Jews recognized as honorary Aryans, Jews in mixed marriages, and *Mischlinge*. Police Attaché Helm added that the problem of honorary Aryans was admittedly unsolved; some of them were still holding office. One Jew, Alexander Klein, had even been dispatched by Ustasha headquarters – that is, the headquarters of the Croat counterpart of the German SS – as a procurement official to Hungary and Italy. With respect to the mixed marriages and *Mischlinge*, Helm re-

554. Kasche to Foreign Office, November 20, 1942, NG-2345.

555. *Ibid.*

556. *Donauzeitung* (Belgrade), August 13, 1942, p. 3.

557. Kasche to Foreign Office, October 14, 1942, NG-2367.

558. Report by Korherr, April 19, 1943, NO-5193.

559. Kasche to Foreign Office, March 3, 1943, NG-2348.

560. Wagner to legation in Zagreb, April 10, 1943, NG-2347.

561. Wagner and von Thadden to Kasche and police attaché in Zagreb, July 15, 1943, NG-2413.

562. Many had apparently found sanctuary at Fiume, Italy, where they survived until the end of the war. The Jewish property in the Croat areas wrested from the Italians became the subject of German-Croat quarrels. See German Plenipotentiary General in Croatia/Ia to XV Mountain Corps, December 6, 1943, enclosing report by Vladimir Jonic (Ustasha commissar and representative of the Croat civil administration in Dalmatia) of November 8, 1943, NOKW-1419.

marked that quite a few Croat leaders had strong family ties with Jews (some Cabinet members had Jewish wives). Furthermore, Helm pointed out, that question had not been solved in the Reich either. Nevertheless, he promised to make every effort to secure a "review" of every privileged case.[563] Neither Kasche nor Helm mentioned that many Jews had found refuge among Marshal Tito's partisans, who at that time had already liberated a considerable portion of Yugoslav territory.[564]

Slovakia. – The Germans created two satellites in Europe: one was Croatia; the other was Slovakia. It may be recalled that, beginning with the Munich agreement in the fall of 1938, the Czechoslovak state was subjected to dismemberment. The Germans occupied the Sudetenland in the west of the country; the Hungarians marched into the southern portions of Slovakia; and the Poles acquired a small area at Teschen-Bohumin. At the end of 1938 the crippled remainder of Czechoslovakia therefore consisted of Bohemia-Moravia, the bulk of Slovakia, and the major part of the Carpatho-Ukraine. Even in October, 1938, the German Foreign Office was drawing up plans for the final division of Czechoslovak territory. The Germans decided to acquire Bohemia-Moravia for themselves (that is how the "Protektorat" was born). The Hungarians were permitted to annex the Carpatho-Ukraine. Only Slovakia remained to be disposed of. The Germans did not want to incorporate it outright, nor did they wish to transfer it to the Hungarians – who were ready to take over anything. As a consequence, Slovakia was to become an "independent" state, a satellite.[565]

Without waiting for the final breakup of Czechoslovakia, the Germans encouraged the formation of an "autonomous" Slovak government in Bratislava. In the winter of 1938–1939, while the Slovak state was in its prenatal stage, Göring held a conference with the deputy prime minister of the autonomous government, Dr. Durkansky. The Slovak representative promised that in Slovakia the Jews would be treated in the same way as in Germany.[566] On the eve of the destruction of Czechoslovakia (March 11, 1939) the German Foreign Office trouble shooter Veesenmayer cabled from Bratislava that things were going well and that he had "all Jews in hand" (*alle Juden in der Hand*).[567] A few days later Slovakia was "independent."

The Slovaks were now called upon to pay their debts to the Germans, and one of these debts was "the solution of the Jewish problem." The Slovak government officials who were to concern themselves most intimately with the "Jewish question" are listed below:[568]

President: Dr. Josef Tiso
Prime Minister: Tuka (succeeded in 1944 by Stephan Tiso)
Foreign Minister: Dr. Durkansky (after 1940, Tuka)

563. Kasche to Foreign Office, April 22, 1944, enclosing report by Helm, dated April 18, 1944, NG-2349.

564. Affidavit by Wisliceny, November 25, 1945, *Conspiracy and Aggression,* VIII, 606–21. Report by XV Mountain Corps Ic, December 2, 1943, on 4th Partisan Brigade, which contained a detachment of 160 Jews led by a Captain Aaron Kabiljo (Captain, Yugoslav Army) of Sarajevo, NOKW-1375.

565. Wörmann via Weizsäcker to Ribbentrop, October 5, 1938, NG-3056.

566. Summary of Göring-Durkansky discussion, undated, PS-2801. On the German side, Seyss-Inquart and the chief of the ethnic Germans in Slovakia, Karmasin, participated in the conference. Durkansky was accompanied by Sano Mach, later Slovak Interior Minister.

567. Seyss-Inquart to Minister Schmidt (Foreign Office), March 11, 1939, NG-5135.

568. For a description of the Slovak government, see Jozef Lettrich, *History of Modern Slovakia* (New York, 1955).

Interior Minister: Sano Mach
Jewish expert: Dr. Vasek
Central Economy Office: Moravek (chairman)

The Central Economy Office was an interesting institution. It was set up in August, 1940, for the exclusive purpose of enforcing anti-Jewish measures; its powers were *not* confined to economic matters. The Economy Office could deal with any matter placed into its sphere of competence by the Cabinet: expropriations, labor certificates, direction of the Jewish community organization, etc. In a sense, the Economy Office was almost a Ministry of Jewish Affairs. (We have already seen such an organization in France, and we shall find similar agencies in other countries as well.) But the Interior Minister, Sano Mach, was more powerful than the Economy officials; his jurisdiction comprised definition problems, the forced labor camps, concentration, and deportation. Since Mach was also commander of the Hlinka Guard (the Slovak counterpart of the SS), he combined in his offices the powers which in Germany were exercised by Frick and Himmler. In Slovakia, then, Jewry was caught between two swords, Moravek and Mach. The Jews were struck alternately by one, then the other.

Staying in the background but always present was the German Legation in Bratislava. The legation, of course, supplied the initiative. From the beginning of Slovak "independence" to December, 1940, the mission was headed by the aristocratic SA man von Killinger; he was succeeded by a non-aristocratic SA man: Hans Elard Ludin. On August 1, 1940, von Killinger requested the services of an "advisor on Jewish questions."[569] The advisor, Hauptsturmführer Dieter Wisliceny of the RSHA, arrived in Slovakia on September 1, 1940,[570] and with the arrival of Wisliceny, the machinery of destruction in Slovakia was complete.

From all this it might be expected that the Slovak bureaucracy, under German direction, worked quickly and efficiently in the German manner, but that was not quite so. The Slovak government was not a German machine, nor was it entirely a German tool. It was subject to several outside influences, and although these influences were weaker than the German, they were not without effect.

To begin with, Slovakia had a strong Catholic Church, and that strength was expressed not merely in the number of Catholic followers in the country but in the Church's ability to guard and preserve its interests. The Church displayed its ability sooner than expected. On April 18, 1939, the month-old Slovak state enacted its first anti-Jewish decree: a definition of the Jews. When a German writer examined this definition, he observed – in the manner of a master who is looking over the first product turned out by his apprentice – that the measure had a "basic defect" (*grundliegenden Fehler*): it embraced only those persons who were Jews by religion, plus those "recent" converts to Christianity who had acquired their new faith since October 30, 1918 – a very mild formulation by German standards.[571] Nor was the influence of the Catholic Church confined to definition problems. The Church was to make itself felt again and again, but that intervention was perhaps not accidental in a country so Catholic that even its pro-Nazi President, Dr. Josef Tiso, was a Catholic priest.

569. Von Killinger to Luther, August 1, 1940, NG-4399.

570. Affidavit by Wisliceny, October 7, 1940, NG-2867. Von Killinger to Himmler, January 9, 1941, Himmler Files, Folder No. 8.

571. *Donauzeitung* (Belgrade), December 10, 1941, p. 3. The Slovak law had a close resemblance to the early Hungarian definition, which was also a compromise between Nazi and Church interests. See pp. 512, 513.

A slight influence was exercised in Slovakia by Italy. The Italians were far away from Slovakia, and there was not even a boundary between the two countries; yet the fact that Italy did little to harm its Jews and, above all, the Italian refusals to heed German requests for deportations did not escape attention in Bratislava. When the Slovaks hesitated to take prompt action, the SS men in Berlin were quick to smell an Italian influence at work.[572]

It is curious that so long as the Slovak government labored under its early definition, not much happened in Slovakia. Perhaps for that very reason, the Germans and their loyal collaborator, Slovak Interior Minister Sano Mach, did not tire in their efforts to introduce the Lösener principle into the satellite state. When they finally succeeded in changing the law, in September, 1941, they scored a "breakthrough," not merely in the matter of the definition but also in the expropriatory sphere and in the concentration process.

The new definition was adopted as part of the Jewry-code (*Judenkodex*) of September, 1941, so called because it contained not fewer than three hundred anti-Jewish paragraphs. Table 63 is a comparative chart of the original German and new Slovak definitions.[573] With the new definition came the expropriations.

TABLE 63 / *German and New Slovak Definitions of "Jew"*

German	Slovak
(1) A person who had at least three Jewish grandparents.	(1) A person who had at least three Jewish grandparents.
(2) A person who had two Jewish grandparents and who	(2) A person who had two Jewish grandparents and who
(*a*) belonged to the Jewish community on September 15, 1935, or joined it on a subsequent date, or	(*a*) belonged to the Jewish community on April 20, 1939, or joined it on a subsequent date, or
(*b*) was married to a three-quarter or full Jew on September 15, 1935, or married one on a subsequent date, or	(*b*) entered into marriage with a Jewish person after April 20, 1939, or
(*c*) was the offspring of an extramarital relationship with a three-quarter or full Jew, and was born out of wedlock after July 31, 1936.	(*c*) was the offspring of an unwed Jewish mother and was born after February 20, 1940, or was the offspring of an unwed non-Jewish mother and proven Jewish father, and was born after February 20, 1940, or
	(*d*) was the offspring of a mixed marriage concluded after April 20, 1939.
	(3) A person who had one Jewish grandparent and who belonged to the Jewish religion on April 20, 1939, or joined it on a subsequent date.

Slovakia was a small country with a population of 2,500,000. The total number of Jews counted in the census of December 15, 1940, was 88,951.[574] About 12,300 Jews owned "enterprises" (that is, they were shopkeepers); another 22,000 were private employees; a few thousand were government employees and professionals.

In Germany, we may recall, the expropriatory measures started with the

572. Gruf. Berger (Chief, SS-Main Office) to Himmler, April 9, 1942, NO-3069.

573. *Krakauer Zeitung*, September 19, 1941, p. 3.

574. *Wirtschaft und Statistik*, XXI (June 2, 1941), 244.

dismissal of civil servants. In Slovakia the Jews in government service were not dismissed until a general tightening-up took place in September, 1941,[575] and even this regulation allowed for exceptions. Some Jews remained in the employ of the government, though at reduced salaries.[576] The professionals, too, were largely undisturbed until September, 1941, and they too were not entirely barred from the exercise of their functions.[577]

The "entrepreneurs" were subjected to a long Aryanization process which lasted for approximately three years, from 1939 to the beginning of 1942. We have noted repeatedly that the Aryanizations contributed to a concentration within industry, and Slovakia was no exception. By January, 1942, 9950 enterprises had been entirely liquidated, 2100 had been transferred, while a few "complicated" cases awaited disposition.[578]

Just like the German Finance Ministry, the Slovak government wanted to share in the profit-making. Accordingly, in September, 1941, the Jews were ordered to register their property in order that the government might find out how much the Jews owned. In Germany all Jews owning assets of more than 5000 reichsmark had to make a report; in Slovakia the amount was fixed at 5000 crowns, that is, 430 reichsmark or less than 200 dollars. In 1941, 52,000 Slovak Jews owned property worth 200 dollars or more, and the total amount registered, after deduction of debts, was 3,164,000,000 crowns, or 272,000,000 reichsmark, or a little over 100,000,000 dollars at official rates of exchange.[579]

More than one-fourth of the Jewish assets (861 million crowns) were invested in real estate. The Slovak government decided to confiscate this Jewish immobile property.[580] Needless to say, the real estate was not a cash acquisition; the houses and grounds had to be rented or sold to yield funds to the treasury. The Slovak government was hoping to sell the great bulk of the housing for the dual purpose of raising money and reducing inflation. By the fall of 1943, however, that program had hardly gotten started.[581] Apparently real estate was as difficult an item to dispose of in Slovakia as it proved to be in the Western areas and in the Reich itself.[582]

Like the Germans, the Slovaks were also interested in valuables and other movables. In December, 1941, the Bratislava police started to collect Jewish-owned typewriters and adding machines.[583] Next the Hlinka Guard undertook a "fur action" to relieve the suffering of Slovak troops fighting in the Russian winter.[584] Finally the Central Economy Office "discovered" that the Jews had bought large quantities of clothes and other textiles; accordingly, the Jews were ordered to surrender the

575. *Donauzeitung* (Belgrade), September 11, 1941, p. 3.

576. *Ibid.*, September 26, 1941, p. 3.

577. *Die Judenfrage*, December 10, 1941, pp. 231–32.

578. On Slovak Aryanization history, see *Krakauer Zeitung*, September 4, 1940, page *Wirtschafts-Kurier;* October 18, 1941, p. 7. *Donauzeitung* (Belgrade), September 11, 1941, p. 3; September 26, 1941, p. 4; October 21, 1941, p. 3; December 10, 1941, p. 3; January 25, 1942, p. 3. *Deutsche Ukraine-Zeitung* (Luck), January 27, 1942, p. 8.

579. *Donauzeitung* (Belgrade), December 10, 1941, p. 3.

580. *Ibid.*, October 11, 1941, p. 3; December 10, 1941, p. 3; January 25, 1942, p. 3. *Deutsche Ukraine-Zeitung* (Luck), January 27, 1942, p. 8.

581. Report by the German general with the Slovak Defense Ministry/Group Armament Economy, November 20, 1943, Wi/IF .2.

582. This was true even though the Slovakian mortgages were probably lower. The principal cause of the difficulty was in all likelihood psychological. Mobile property could be hidden in the event of a return of the former owners; houses could not.

583. *Donauzeitung* (Belgrade), December 18, 1941, p. 4.

584. *Ibid.*, January 17, 1942, p. 3.

"hoarded goods."[585]

Although the collection of these items foreshadowed a considerable reduction in the haul of personal belongings in the killing centers, the Germans did not interfere with the *Aktion*. Only when the Slovak Consul General in Prague decided to extend the collection of furs and clothes to Slovak Jews residing in the Protektorat did *Abteilung Deutschland* of the Foreign Office become alarmed. Nevertheless, Luther felt inclined not to interrupt the Slovak drive, provided that Reich Jews in Slovakia were not required to make deliveries, for in the latter case Slovak confiscations in the Protektorat were "naturally out of the question."[586]

The Slovak government was not satisfied with the confiscation of property, real and movable. Like other governments, the Slovaks needed some cash, and the Jews had registered assets valued at some 3,164,000,000 crowns. These assets were now subjected to a property tax, fixed at the traditional 20 per cent and payable in five installments. The expected intake was 600 to 700 million crowns, and 650 million crowns (that is, 56 million reichsmark) were actually collected by the Jewish community organization and delivered to the Slovak Finance Ministry.[587] The Germans knew that amount, and they kept it in mind.

While Slovakia had about 12,300 Jewish shopkeepers, it had 22,000 Jewish employees. The Central Economy Office undertook the task of reviewing the status of all these employees in order to bring about the gradual elimination of the unessential workers. By October, 1941, the number of Jews still holding work permits was stabilized at about 3500; the maximum permissible monthly wage was fixed at 1500 crowns (129 reichsmark or 52 dollars).[588] Their low pay notwithstanding, the 3500 Jews who remained in the free economy were privileged in several respects: they were not subject to forced labor in a camp, and they were for a long time exempted from concentration and deportation measures. A destruction process is a step-by-step procedure, and it is usually impossible to enforce step 4 before having implemented steps 1, 2, and 3. The Germans knew that and watched the privileged Jews with a wary eye.

The forced labor camps came into existence in the fall of 1941, when most Jews were already out of work. The camp network was run by a government commissar in the Interior Ministry who supervised the camp commanders; the Jewish community organization stood by as an "auxiliary organ."[589]

Interior Ministry-
Government Commissar → Jewish Central Organization
Bratislava-
Central Chancellery for
Labor Camps

Interior Ministry-Government Commissar ↓ Camp Commissar and
Commander of
Camp Hlinka Guard

Jewish Central Organization Bratislava-Central Chancellery for Labor Camps ↓ Jewish Camp Council

Camp Commissar and Commander of Camp Hlinka Guard → Jewish Camp Council

585. *Ibid.*, March 7, 1942, p. 3.

586. Luther and Rademacher to Representative of the Foreign Office in Prague (Gerlach), February 5, 1942, NG-4555.

587. *Donauzeitung* (Belgrade), September 11, 1941, p. 3; September 16, 1941, p. 3; August 15, 1942, p. 3.

588. *Krakauer Zeitung*, October 18, 1941, p. 7. *Donauzeitung* (Belgrade), October 21, 1941, p. 3.

589. Slovak government report, June 30, 1943, Occ E 7b-8.

There were three camps (Sered, Novaky, and Vyhne) and eight satellite labor centers for heavy workers. A parallel labor organization was maintained by the Defense Ministry; however, unlike the labor camps, which contained entire families, the Defense Ministry employed only young men who would otherwise have been subject to military service. (It is interesting to note that the forced labor system was not disbanded with the advent of the deportations. About 3500 Jews remained in the camps in 1943, and the number of inmates was still growing when the Defense Ministry transferred its laborers to the Interior Ministry in a consolidation move.)[590]

The Slovak government was also tardy in the enforcement of concentration. One of the first important ghettoization measures was the creation of a central Jewish organization (*Judenzentrale*), to which all Jews were subject.[591] We have already seen some of the important functions of the *Judenzentrale* in the expropriation process; it collected the property tax and helped administer the labor camps. The functions of the Jewish machinery in the concentrations and deportations were even more important. In fact, one of the first tasks of the *Zentrale* was the issuance of identity cards to all Jews.[592]

The second major step in the concentration field consisted of identification measures. The marking of the Jews started locally in eastern Slovakia,[593] but there was no extension of this regulation to the rest of the country until the appearance of the Jewry Code in September, 1941. Even the code was not all-inclusive, for it exempted the Jews who were working in the free economy and those Jews (with families) who remained in government employ. Only on March 9, 1942 – when the Jewish star was extended in diameter from two and a half inches to four inches – were the Jewish workers and the families of government employees (but not the government employees themselves) forced to wear that identification.[594]

The code of September, 1941, provided for the marking not only of persons but also of letters. The Jewish star had to be affixed to every letter sent by a Jew. The police were empowered to open such letters and to destroy them – a measure which not even the German bureaucrats had thought of in the Reich. In addition, the code provided for various regulations already traditional in Germany but new in Slovakia. For the first time, intermarriages were prohibited; Jews were limited to travel in third-class railway compartments; they were not permitted to drive cars; etc. Most important, however, was the provision empowering the Central Economy Office to assign new residences to Jews.[595] By October that power had already been put into effect.

In October, 1941, the Jews were to be expelled from Bratislava. The Slovak capital had a Jewish population of about 15,000, but only 10,000 Jews were subject to expulsion. The remaining 5000, comprising holders of work permits, government employees, entrepreneurs, and professionals (with their families), were permitted to stay. All others were scheduled for departure to provincial towns, labor camps, and labor centers.

To accomplish the smooth implementation of the resettlement – incidentally a real resettlement rather than a "resettlement" – the Jewish community

590. *Ibid.*

591. *Krakauer Zeitung*, October 2, 1940, p. 2. *Die Judenfrage*, February 20, 1941, pp. 28–29.

592. *Ibid.*

593. *Donauzeitung* (Belgrade), August 30, 1941, p. 3.

594. *Ibid.*, March 7, 1942, p. 3.

595. *Krakauer Zeitung*, September 19, 1941, p. 3.

organization had to create a new division for the processing of questionnaires required of all Bratislava Jews. The questionnaires were then handed to the statistical division of the *Zentrale,* and from there to a special *Referat* for rechecking. Finally, the administrative division of the *Zentrale* designated the new residence of the victim and handed him over to the police. The last step of the procedure involved the dispatch of *Ordner* of the *Judenzentrale* to the apartments of the prospective expellees. There the Jewish *Ordner* divided the furnishings into two categories: personal things that could be taken along and belongings that had to be left behind to be confiscated by the state.[596]

On Tuesday, October 28, 1941, the first transport of 238 Jews left Bratislava, and during the next three months approximately half the capital's Jews were ejected.[597]

All these events were watched closely in Berlin. When the concentration process in Slovakia reached its height, the RSHA began to make inquiries in the Foreign Office with a view to deporting the Slovak Jews in the Reich. The Foreign Office expert on Jewish affairs, Legationsrat Rademacher, took a look at the situation and decided that in view of the harsh measures taken by Slovakia itself, the RSHA request could be granted. He proposed that Slovakia be subjected to a courtesy inquiry.[598] His proposal was endorsed by Staatssekretär Weizsäcker, Unterstaatssekretär Wörmann of the Political Division, and the director of the Legal Division. The first move could now be made.

Shortly afterward, the German Legation in Bratislava (Hans Elard Ludin) reported that the Slovak government had consented to the deportation of its Jews from the Reich; the Slovaks were reserving only the right to confiscate the victims' property. Himmler could now have asked for the deportation of all the Jews in Slovakia, but he did not. Instead, he instructed the RSHA to request that the Foreign Office ask the Slovak government to make available "20,000 young, strong Slovak Jews" for deportation to the "East" – a master stroke that helped establish the "resettlement" legend in Slovakia. The Foreign Office must have had identical thoughts, for it lost no time in drafting new instructions to its legation in Bratislava.

Again the papers were passed from desk to desk, this time to be signed and cosigned by Weizsäcker, Luther, Wörmann, and Heinburg. When the Slovak government expressed its "pleased concurrence" with the deportation of the "20,000 young, strong Jews," Himmler proposed – without waiting for the deportation of these victims – that Slovakia be made free of Jews. Instructions were now drafted for a third time, and Slovakia agreed once more.[599]

The deportation agreement contained two special provisions: one a concession to the Slovaks, the other an exaction by the Germans. The concession was a stipulation to the effect that no internal difficulties were to be permitted to arise from the deportations; that is, no measures were to be taken that would antagonize the churches to such an extent as to threaten Slovakia's internal stability. The exaction consisted of a bill presented by the Reich to the Slovak government for the cost incurred by Germany in deporting the Jews. That bill was not less than 500 reichsmark per head, or 45 million reichsmark if all 90,000 Slovak Jews were to be deported. (We may recall that the total amount collected by the

596. *Die Judenfrage,* December 10, 1941, pp. 231–32.

597. *Donauzeitung* (Belgrade), November 2, 1941, p. 4. *Deutsche Ukraine-Zeitung* (Luck), January 27, 1942, p. 8.

598. Rademacher via Luther to Weizsäcker, October 28, 1941, NG-182.

599. Memorandum by Luther, August 21, 1942, NG-2586-J.

Slovak government in its tax upon the registered Jewish assets was only 56 million marks. In other words, the Germans were claiming up to 80 per cent of the Slovak government's Jewish tax haul.) Nevertheless, and to the surprise of the Germans themselves, the Slovak authorities also agreed to that demand "without any German pressure."[600] Only later were the Germans to discover that the combination of a payment provision with a church concession was poor diplomacy, for now the Slovaks had been told in effect that they could save money by exempting baptized Jews.

The deportations did not catch the Jews by surprise. Some weeks before the movement started, they were put on notice by preparatory measures, official speeches, and rumors. At the beginning of March the Jewish star worn by prospective deportees was increased in size; at the same time the Jews were prohibited to change their residence.[601] The purpose of these measures was clear, for the identical regulations had preceded the deportations going on within the Reich itself. Also just about then, Interior Minister Mach, addressing a Slovak *Gauleiter* convention in the town of Trencín, declared that the Slovak people had become impatient in the matter of solving the Jewish problem but that it would be solved very definitively now.[602] By the middle of March there were rumors that the deportations were imminent.[603] On March 26, 1942, they began.[604]

What did the Jews do in the face of the catastrophe? The great majority waited helplessly. A small minority – growing steadily – sought refuge in the woods, in Hungary, and with the churches. In the woods of Homenau, in eastern Slovakia, the deportation machinery suffered what was probably its only casualty: the Slovak *Gendarmerie* man Andreas Pazicky was shot and killed while searching for hidden Jews.[605] The flight into Hungary proceeded in steady trickles until at the end of the year about 7000 Jews – nearly one-tenth of Slovak Jewry – had found refuge in that country.[606] Many Jews who did not hide in the woods and who did not flee to Hungary sought protection at home by becoming Christians. We have no statistics from which to calculate the exact number of conversions during the deportation phase, but it is certain that the figure was in the thousands.[607]

Although the dominant church in Slovakia was the Catholic hierarchry, newspaper reports indicate that the lion's share of the conversions fell to the Protestant and Greek Orthodox Churches.[608] Why was that? Did the

600. *Ibid.*

601. *Donauzeitung* (Belgrade), March 7, 1942, p. 3.

602. *Ibid.*

603. *Ibid.*, March 21, 1942, p. 3.

604. *Ibid.*, May 21, 1942, p. 3.

605. *Ibid.*, April 17, 1942, p. 3. *Die Judenfrage*, May 15, 1942, p. 102.

606. *Donauzeitung* (Belgrade), May 1, 1942, p. 3. Moravek of the Central Economy Office reported that 5000 had fled by mid-May. *Ibid.*, May 21, 1942, p. 3. Dr. Vasek (Jewish expert, Slovak Interior Ministry) reported 7000 across the border in November. *Ibid.*, November 3, 1942, p. 3. Zionist officials in Budapest counted 6000–8000 refugees at the end of 1943. Kasztner, *Der Bericht des jüdischen Rettungskomittees aus Budapest 1942–1945*, p. 9. Kastner was associate president of the Zionist Organization in Hungary.

607. Vasek put the number of Christian Jews, converted after 1939 and not deported by November, 1942, at 6000. *Donauzeitung* (Belgrade), November 3, 1942, p. 3. Veesenmayer estimated the total number of converted Jews in Slovakia at the end of 1943 at 10,000. Memorandum by Veesenmayer, December 22, 1943, NG-4651. A somewhat earlier estimate in the *Donauzeitung* (Belgrade), May 18, 1943, p. 3, put the number at 15,000. None of these sources disclose how many Jews had been converted before 1939, and how many Christian Jews were deported during 1942.

Jews prefer the Protestant and Greek Orthodox religions to the Catholic faith? Hardly, for the Jews were primarily concerned with protection, and such protection could best be rendered by the Catholic Church. The Jews were not interested in theology just then. But therein, precisely, lay the reason for the imbalance of conversions – the Catholic Church was *not* primarily interested in the saving of lives; it wanted to save souls. Of course the Church protected its converts. The priesthood was angry when the state presumed to nullify the sacred baptism and turn Christians into Jews. But for exactly that reason the Catholic Church did not bestow baptism lightly. The applicant had to be "sincere." If it took a catastrophe to make him "see the light," well then, all right, he could be admitted. However, if he was suspected of merely wanting to save his life, perhaps to revert to Judaism after the end of the war, he was turned away. When the wave of deportations overtook the Jewish community in Slovakia, there was little time for religious instruction, preparation, and meditation. That is why the less rigid Protestant and Orthodox Churches converted a disproportionately large number of Jews.

Why did the Jews bother to become Christians? What protection could be offered to them by the churches? The Slovak code of 1941 had defined the term "Jew" in terms of the Lösener principle, and the religion of the victim was not controlling in that definition; what was decisive was the religion of his grandparents. Indeed, the new converts were deported to Auschwitz and Lublin with the rest of Jewry to die there as Christians, but still the conversions did not halt. The Jews were clinging to a straw, although right and left and all around "new Christians" were drowning. Truly, these desperate conversions were held in check only because all hope for protection by the church was so forlorn and beoause the Catholic Church in particular was so reluctant to grant to the Jews even this forlorn hope.

Nevertheless, the conversions alarmed the Slovak government. On March 26, 1942, the day on which the deportations started, Interior Minister Mach spoke on the air. The Slovak public, he declared, was not influenced by the whining of the Jews who on this day wanted to arouse pity, although they were in no danger save that of work. No one could save the Jews from this labor commitment, not even those clergymen who were now conferring baptism on the Jews. The Jewish question in Slovakia, concluded Mach, would be solved humanely, without doing violence to Christian principles.[609]

From the ethnic German organ, the *Grenzbote*, criticism was more vociferous. The baptisms were termed a blasphemy, and the churchmen who engaged in them were accused of having monetary motives.[610] Two Calvinist pastors, Puspas and Sedivy, were subsequently arrested, and Sedivy was accused of having performed not fewer than 717 baptisms.[611]

In the meantime, what did the churches do to protect the *old* converts who had already been Christians before the onset of the deportations? The churches were not sitting idly by, for on May 15, 1942, something happened: the Slovak Parliament issued a deportation law. In its main outlines the law was not extraordinary – it was a measure for the confiscation of abandoned Jewish property, in other words, the

608. *Donauzeitung* (Belgrade), September 1, 1942, p. 3; June 20, 1943, p. 3.

609. *Donauzeitung* (Belgrade), March 27, 1942, p. 3.

610. *Ibid.*, March 21, 1942, p. 3; April 17, 1942, p. 3.

611. *Ibid.*, March 27, 1942, p. 3; August 30, p. 3.

counterpart of the 11th Ordinance to the Reich Citizenship Law. However, the Slovak measure had a provision which came almost as a shock to the Germans: a new definition of the term "Jew." This revision was a little late, for 30,000 Jews had already been shipped away.[612] Nevertheless, it had an immediate effect upon the progressing operation – for 60,000 Jews were still in the country. The law provided that henceforth a Jew was any person who belonged to the Jewish religion, or who had been converted after March 14, 1939.[613]

It should be noted that the third definition strongly resembled and in its leniency even exceeded the first. The law still did not exempt *all* converted Jews, but it did exempt all Jews converted before the founding of the Slovak state, and that formulation was far more palatable to the churches than the decree of September, 1941.

Moreover, the law contained a number of other exemptions which were numerically even more important. To begin with, the exemptions conferred on the Christian Jews were extended automatically to their family members, including wife (or husband), children, *and* parents. In addition, the law exempted from deportation so-called essential categories – professionals, labor certificate holders, and the remaining entrepreneurs. These people were allowed to stay, along with their wives and children. Finally, the law exempted all Jews in mixed marriages.[614]

It seemed as though the Slovak authorities were not merely giving in to church pressure but responding to it with enthusiasm. One is almost inclined to think that the Slovaks did not have a strong stomach for these deportations. The clerical position, plus the fact that for each exempted Jew the government was saving 500 marks, had given the Slovaks sufficient impetus for action.

The Germans themselves did not know at first how many Jews were exempted by the deportation law, and the machinery of destruction plodded ahead until, at the end of June, it slowed down and almost ground to a halt. On June 26, Prime Minister Tuka, German envoy Ludin, and his expert in Jewish affairs Hauptsturmführer Wisliceny met in conference. Most of the talking was done by Wisliceny, who summarized the state of the deportations to date. A total of 52,000 Jews had been deported; 35,000 (the number was actually closer to 30,000) remained. Many of the remaining Jews were in possession of "protective letters" (*Schutzbriefe*) certifying that the bearer was essential to the economy. Those letters, Wisliceny pointed out, would have to undergo a review before he could proceed any further. The review was to be accomplished by inviting the Slovak employer to testify about the expendability of his Jewish workers. Wisliceny then praised the Jewish Division of the Slovak Interior Ministry (Division 14), which, he said, worked very well, apart from its director (Dr. Vasek). The Slovak Transport Ministry had also been very co-operative.

Prime Minister Tuka put in that in a cabinet meeting on the day before, the government had decided that every ministry which had issued protective letters to Jews was to notify the Interior Ministry of the persons involved, so that the ministry could undertake a "revision." Tuka then wanted to know what was wrong with the director of the Jewish Division of the Interior Ministry (Dr. Vasek), whom Wisliceny had refused to praise.

612. *Ibid.*, May 21, 1942, p. 3. The figure, comprising deportations from March 26 to May 15, was given by Moravek.

613. *Die Judenfrage*, June 1, 1942, pp. 108–9.

614. *Ibid.*

Wisliceny replied that while Moravek (the chief of the Economy Office) was "clean and adamant" (*sauber und kompromisslos*), Dr. Vasek was a compromiser who had made agreements with everybody so that his hands were tied. Vasek, in Wisliceny's opinion, would be unable to carry out the revision of the protective letters.[615] On this sour note the meeting ended.

That same day Ludin wrote to the Foreign Office that 35,000 Jews had received special legitimation, that the deportations were unpopular, and that British counter-propaganda had started in Slovakia. Nevertheless, the letter continued, Tuka was willing to press on and had in fact asked Ludin to arrange for strong diplomatic pressure to be put on the Slovak government.[616]

The strange request by a Prime Minister for pressure on his own government can be understood only in terms of the satellite mentality. A satellite official does not like to talk back to his master. He therefore says, in effect: "I would like to do it, but my colleagues are opposed. Put pressure on them." Of course as soon as the pressure is exerted on someone else, the game starts all over again. In any case, the German Foreign Office decided to supply the requested pressure. A note was drafted which stated that the Slovak decision to exempt 35,000 Jews from deportation was making a "very bad impression" in Germany, particularly in view of previous Slovak cooperation. However, that draft was judged to be too harsh. The words "very bad impression" were crossed out; instead, the Foreign Office said that the exclusion of the 35,000 Jews came as a "surprise" to the Germans.[617]

615. Summary of Slovak deportation conference held on June 26, 1942, dated June 30, 1942, NG-4553.

616. Ludin to Foreign Office, June 26, 1942, NG-4407.

617. Weizsäcker to Ludin, June 30, 1942, NG-4407.

And, in a way, a surprise it was.

The Germans did not make very much progress after the end of June. According to SS-Statistician Korherr, the total number of deportees at the end of the year was 56,691; by March 31, 1943, the figure had risen to 57,545.[618] After accounting for about 7000 escapees, the number of Jews remaining in Slovakia was a little over 25,000.[619]

The German diplomats never ceased to apply pressure. They even tried to make a concession. Coming back to the 500 reichsmark per capita payment, the German Foreign Office adopted a benevolent attitude. Perhaps, it was reasoned, if the Slovaks could make a little more money, the Germans would get a few more Jews.

During the negotiations pertaining to Slovak Jewish property in Germany and German Jewish property in Slovakia, the Foreign Office (in accordance with established procedure) proposed the adoption of the "territorial principle." The Slovaks were suspicious. They thought that they might lose in the swap. The Germans thereupon suggested that the territorial principle might be agreeable to the Slovaks if the per capita payment for the deported Jews were reduced from 500 to 300 marks. That difference, it was argued, would certainly more than cover any discrepancy in the values of the abandoned properties.

618. Report by Korherr, April 19, 1943, NO-5193.

619. Dr. Vasek gave somewhat different figures to the press in November, 1942. He said that 62,444 had been deported, ca. 20,000 remained. *Donauzeitung* (Belgrade), November 3, 1942, p. 3. However, other press reports put the number of deportees at 56,000 to 57,000. *Ibid.*, July 18, 1942, p. 3; *Deutsche Ukraine-Zeitung* (Luck), July 19, 1942, p. 2. Veesenmayer, at the end of 1943, estimated the number of Jews remaining in Slovakia at 26,000–28,000, including 10,000 converts. Memorandum by Veesenmayer, December 22, 1943, NG-4651.

Incidentally, the Foreign Office also thought that the Slovaks already knew the price paid by other governments for the "final solution." For example, the Croats were making a per capita payment of only 30 reichsmark. The Foreign Office consequently felt that the reduction was eminently justified and reasonable, but at this point the negotiations were sabotaged by the Economy Ministry. The Economy people pointed out that Germany already owed Slovakia 280,000,000 marks and therefore could not afford to "renounce" any foreign currency claim (*auf keine Devisen verzichten*).[620] Luther asked the Trade-Political Division to intervene, and we do not know whether the Economy Ministry ultimately changed its mind.

One thing seems certain. The Germans in their foreign relations found nothing so difficult as the making of concessions. One other point is also definite. The promise – or the prospect – of a 200 mark reduction in the per capita payments was no longer an inducement to the Slovak government, for now the Germans encountered an obstacle that they had not faced before: the destruction of the "resettlement" myth.

It is unclear how much the Slovak government knew at the beginning of the deportations. If the Slovaks knew anything, they played a game of make-believe. For instance, something very interesting happened on April 18, 1942, when Prime Minister Tuka requested Ludin to conclude a treaty with Slovakia in which Germany would guarantee *not* to return evacuated Jews and which would also provide for a German renunciation of all claims upon Jewish property in Slovakia (except, of course, claims upon the 500-mark payment).[621]

At first glance this proposal seems purely an economic matter – an attempt by the Slovak Prime Minister to remove all legal obstacles to the confiscation of the abandoned Jewish property. But upon closer examination the proposal turns out to have had also a psychological function, for with such an agreement in hand Tuka could always claim later that, naturally, he had assumed the Jews were only subjected to a resettlement; why else should he have exacted a guarantee against their return? Now, it may be argued that this is far-fetched reasoning, that such deductions stem from the assumption that in April, 1942, Tuka already saw himself as a defendant in a court, answering for war crimes. Nevertheless, that assumption is not unreasonable. Tuka must have weighed the chances of a German victory, and it is doubtful that he considered them better than fifty-fifty. We have already seen the same kind of weighing and the same kind of reasoning taking place in other countries. Moreover, such precautions must be expected from a man who had already faced a court when in 1928 he was sentenced to fifteen years' imprisonment for espionage and treason.

By the way, the German Minister was taken aback by Tuka's request for a written treaty. In such matters, Ludin pointed out, the Reich did not conclude treaties, although he was prepared to request permission to extend to Tuka the desired assurances in the form of a verbal note.[622]

Some time after the deportations had started, the Vatican stepped in. As is well known, the Catholic Church has an efficient intelligence apparatus, and in 1942 that apparatus was put to work. Two notes were handed to Tuka. In these notes, the Vatican explained that

620. Luther via Trade-Political Division to Weizsäcker, January 29, 1943, NG-5108.

621. Ludin to Foreign Office, April 18, 1942, NG-4404.

622. *Ibid.*

it was not correct to suppose that the Jews were being sent to the *Generalgouvernement* for labor service; the truth was that they were being annihilated there.[623]

There is more evidence that news of the killing centers trickled into Slovakia, not only into government circles but to the public as well. In July, 1942, a group of 700 ethnic German "asocials" were "resettled" from Slovakia. As the "asocials" were about to leave, a rumor began to circulate that the "resettlers" would be "boiled into soap" (*zur Seife verkocht werden*).[624] That rumor referred to the popular belief that the Germans in the killing centers were turning human fat into soap cakes. (We may recall that in October, 1942, an identical rumor was spread in the *Generalgouvernement* district of Lublin.[625] Probably the rumor originated there.[626])

The Germans were not unprepared for reports and rumors that the Slovak Jews were dead, and to combat these revelations, the Germans spread false reports of their own. In great detail the German stories pictured a tolerable life of Slovakian Jewry in exile. The Jews were said to have rabbis, doctors, and officials. The converted Jews had priests. There was warm water, and a children's kitchen. There were meat, milk, and vegetables in sufficient supply. The ghettos were equipped with stores. There was even a Jewish coffee house. The Slovak Jews were supporting themselves by their labor. Their chief justice, Moszek Merin, was receiving a monthly salary. Etc., etc.[627]

To reinforce this mirage of a resettled community, the camp command in Auschwitz and the Eichmann *Referat* of the RSHA had devised a bizarre scheme. When the deportees arrived at the killing center, they were encouraged to write postcards to friends and acquaintances at home. These cards were stockpiled, and long after the deportees were dead, their little notes were sent in small batches to the addressees. In that way the impression was created that the community was still alive and writing.[628]

However, the feeling of uneasiness about the fate of the deported Jews could not be dispelled. One of the hardest tasks of a propagandist is to destroy rumors and to allay doubts, and in this case the task was even harder because the Slovak bishops put pressure on Tuka. The Prime Minister, on his part, put pressure on the German Legation in Bratislava. He wanted a mixed commission to inspect one of the camps to which the Jews had been sent. The legation passed on the request to the Jewish expert of the Foreign Office, von Thadden, and, helpless, the *Legationsrat* transferred the burden to Eichmann. This was Eichmann's reply, dated June 2, 1943:

> With reference to the proposal put forward by Prime Minister Dr. Tuka to the German Minister in Bratislava to send a mixed Slovakian commission to one of the Jewish camps in the occupied territories, I wish to state that an inspection of this kind has already been undertaken recently, on the part of Slovakia, by Fiala, the chief editor of the periodical *Der Grenzbote* [ethnic German newspaper].
>
> With regard to the description of

623. Affidavit by Hans Gmelin, June 15, 1948, NG-5921. Affiant was a member of the German Legation in Bratislava.

624. Karmasin (chief of ethnic Germans in Slovakia) to Himmler, July 29, 1942, NO-1660.

625. See p. 331.

626. See pp. 623–24. The first Slovak transports were sent not only to Auschwitz but also to Lublin. Affidavit by Wisliceny, November 29, 1945, *Conspiracy and Aggression*, VIII, 606–21.

627. *Donauzeitung* (Belgrade), November 21, 1942, p. 3.

628. This trick was used as late as 1944 with Hungarian Jews. See Lengyel, *Five Chimneys – The Story of Auschwitz*, p. 30.

conditions in Jewish camps requested by Prime Minister Dr. Tuka, attention should be drawn to the comprehensive series of articles by this editor which have appeared with numerous photographs, etc., in the periodicals *Der Grenzbote, Slovak, Slovenská Politika, Gardiste, Magyar Hirlap,* and the *Pariser Zeitung. . . .*

For the rest, to counteract the fantastic rumors circulating in Slovakia about the fate of the evacuated Jews, attention should be drawn to the postal communications of these Jews with Slovakia, which are forwarded directly through the adviser on Jewish affairs with the German Legation in Bratislava [Wisliceny] and which, incidentally, amounted to more than 1000 letters and postcards for February–March this year. Concerning the information apparently desired by Prime Minister Dr. Tuka about the conditions in Jewish camps, no objections would be raised by this office against any possible scrutinizing of the correspondence before it is forwarded to the addressees.[629]

A few weeks after this not very reassuring answer to Tuka's doubts, the Germans turned on the pressure again. In Bratislava a Foreign Office spokesman, Minister Schmidt (evidently the press Schmidt, not the interpreter), "discussed" the "Jewish question" with the press in the following terms: "The Jewish question is no question of humanity and no question of religion, but a question of political hygiene. Jewry is to be combatted wherever it is found, because it is a political infectant, the ferment of the disintegration and death of every national organism. . . ."[630]

In the beginning of July, 1943, Ribbentrop decided not to put any "official" pressure on President Tiso of Slovakia. On the other hand, the Foreign Minister had no objection to an "unofficial" attempt to influence the Slovak President into speeding the "cleanup" (*Bereinigung*) of the Jewish question. In German Foreign Office parlance, the principal difference between "official" and "unofficial" pressure was that the former was written, whereas the latter was oral; obviously the "unofficial" method afforded greater opportunity for maneuverability. Also, the "unofficial" emissary had to be a specialist in verbalistics. The specialist appointed – or rather self-appointed – for this mission was Edmund Veesenmayer.[631] The Slovak leaders did not give in. They no longer had the protection of ignorance, and they knew the war was lost.

In December, Veesenmayer went to Bratislava again. Standing in Ludin's waiting room, he demanded from Wisliceny a statistical report. Scanning the figures, he told Wisliceny that he had a Führer order to pay a visit to the Slovak President. This time, Veesenmayer said, he would talk with Tiso "bluntly" (*Fraktur reden*).[632]

At the conclusion of the Veesenmayer-Tiso "discussion," the Slovak President agreed to place in concentration camps the remaining 16,000–18,000 *unconverted* Jews; no exemptions were to be granted in this operation, which was to be completed by April 1, 1944. The baptized Jews were not mentioned. (Tiso was a priest.) However, the Christian Jews were dealt with in a subsequent conversation between Veesenmayer and the Prime Minister, Dr. Tuka. In that discussion it was agreed that the 10,000 or so baptized Jews would also be concentrated – in a camp of their own.[633]

Slowly the Slovak administration

629. Eichmann to von Thadden, June 2, 1943, Document Steengracht 64.

630. *Donauzeitung* (Belgrade), July 3, 1943, p. 3.

631. Vessenmayer to von Sonnleithner, July 3, 1943, NG-4749. Sonnleithner via Wagner to Steengracht, July 5, 1943, NG-4749. Wagner to Ludin, July 21, 1943, NG-4749.

632. Affidavit by Wisliceny, June 11, 1947, NG-1823.

633. Memorandum by Veesenmayer, December 22, 1943, NG-4651.

started to make its preparations. In January, 1944, all Bratislava Jews were ordered to register with the police;[634] in February new movements of Jews to Hungary were observed by Slovak and Hungarian police authorities.[635] But, by April 1, 1944, the Jews had not been concentrated. The Slovaks were plainly hesitant.

In June, when deportations were already in progress in Hungary, Veesenmayer (then the German Minister in Budapest) wanted to meet Ludin, the minister in Bratislava, for joint planning of the removal of Hungarian and remaining Slovak Jews.[636] The meeting did not take place because Ludin had made it conditional on the presence of his indispensable assistant in Jewish affairs, Wisliceny, who was then in Budapest being just as indispensable to Eichmann.[637]

The Slovak Jews now had another reprieve, but the fate of the refugees in Hungary was sealed. The Germans and the Hungarians exerted pressure on the Slovak government to relinquish protection of its Jews in Hungary. The Slovaks declared that they were interested in the repatriation of a few Jews but "disinterested" in the fate of the refugees, particularly the "orphaned children who had recently crossed the Hungarian border illegally."[638]

As the summer months rolled by, the Red Army came closer and closer to Slovakia's eastern frontier. At the end of August a revolt broke out in Slovakia, and within forty-eight hours the Slovak government descended from a puppet regime to a shadow. The Germans took over complete control.

A new personality had now arrived: SS-Obergruppenführer Gottlob Berger, chief of the SS-Main Office, chief of the *Führungsstab-Politik* in the Ministry for Eastern Occupied Territories, chief of prisoner of war camps of the Wehrmacht, and now, in addition, *Wehrmachtbefehlshaber* in Slovakia. Berger stayed in Slovakia for a period of only four weeks, but his four-week stay was decisive.[639] Together with Berger, another SS officer had arrived in Bratislava: Obersturmbannführer Vitezka, Commander of Security Police and SD, Slovakia, and chief of *Einsatzgruppe H*.[640] Vitezka's *Sonderkommandos* pushed forward into the new combat zone, while in the rear they rounded up all Jews. Assisting Vitezka was an old hand in deportation matters: Hauptsturmführer Brunner (Salonika and France).[641]

In desperation the Jewish leaders in Bratislava turned to the Germans with a ransom scheme; they proposed that their brethren overseas pay money in foreign currency in exchange for the safety of the remaining community. The Germans turned down the proposal. For years the Foreign Office and the SS had preached to allies and satellites that the deportation of the Jews was a necessity, that if the Jews were not deported there would be unrest, trouble, and revolt. Now there *was* a revolt. The SS needed foreign currency very much, but Himmler needed even more a confirmation of his untested theory. Berger had reported to Himmler that the Jews had partici-

634. *Donauzeitung* (Belgrade), January 28, 1944, p. 3.

635. *Ibid.*, February 6, 1944, p. 3.

636. Altenburg to Veesenmayer, June 14, 1944, NG-2829. Altenburg to Ludin, June 16, 1944, NG-2261. Von Thadden to Personnel Division, July 5, 1944, NG-2261.

637. Affidavit by Wisliceny, June 11, 1947, NG-1823.

638. Veesenmayer (in Budapest) to Foreign Office, June 13, 1944, NG-2563. Only a few hundred refugee Jews survived in Hungary. Affidavit by Dr. Rudolf Kastner, September 13, 1945, PS-2605.

639. Affidavit by Hans Gmelin (Legation, Bratislava), June 15, 1948, NO-5921.

640. *Ibid.*

641. Affidavit by Wisliceny, November 29, 1945, *Conspiracy and Aggression*, VIII, 606–21.

pated decisively in the revolt. That was enough confirmation for the *Reichsführer-SS*, who never doubted the word of his old confidant.[642] For the sake of historical accuracy, it should be noted that the "outside" Jews in Switzerland — who were in ignorance of Himmler's adamant attitude — failed to come through with an offer of money. We shall deal with that phenomenon in a subsequent chapter.[643]

In the meantime the new Slovak Prime Minister, Tiso (no relation to the President), became worried about the German moves. On October 4, 1944, he told Ludin that some weeks before he had agreed to the concentration of the Jews within Slovak territory; now, however, he had heard that the Germans, without even notifying the Slovak government, were about to transport the Jews from the country. Undoubtedly, such a move would result in diplomatic difficulties, since protests could be expected from the Vatican and also from Switzerland. (By "Switzerland" Tiso actually meant the Western Allies.) Ludin replied that the "Jewish question" would not have to be "solved radically in any case" (*auf alle Fälle radikal gelöst werden müsse*). In the event of foreign protests Tiso was to point out that the Reich demanded from Slovakia a radical solution. "In that eventuality," said Ludin, "we shall be ready to accept responsibility for the anti-Jewish measures undertaken here."[644] Ribbentrop and Hitler thought that Ludin's explanation was very good.[645]

About six hundred appeals on behalf of individual Jews poured into the German Legation from Slovak authorities and private persons. All interventions were in vain. Vitezka would not consider them. He had orders, he said, to send everybody who was "suspicious" or who "sympathized" with the rebels to the concentration camp of Sered.[646]

Approximately 13,000–14,000 Jews were caught in the roundup; the majority were transported to the killing center of Auschwitz. After the killing installations were dismantled in the great death camp, a few thousand of the victims were sent to the "residence camp" of Bergen-Belsen and the "Old People's Ghetto" of Theresienstadt.[647] A few thousand Jews were able to hide. And that was the end of the deportations in Slovakia.

THE OPPORTUNISTIC SATELLITES. — We can always learn something about the destruction process in an Axis country by examining its attitude towards the war. Somehow the fate of the Jews in a German satellite state was always linked to the extent of war enthusiasm in that state. The implementation of the destructive program and the prosecution of the war show close parallels, primarily because both the Jews and the war were a measure of a satellite's desire and ability to withstand German demands. In no country was this fact more evident than in Bulgaria.

Bulgaria. — The Bulgarians were part ally, part satellite. Unlike Slovakia or

642. Affidavit by Kurt Becher, March 1, 1948, NO-4548. Becher was a *Standartenführer* who had jurisdiction in ransom matters. Also, affidavit by Dr. Rudolf Kastner (executive vice president of Jewish Relief Committee in Budapest), August 4, 1947, NO-4824.

643. See pp. 727–28.

644. Ludin to Foreign Office, October 4, 1944, NG-5100.

645. Reinebeck (Bureau of the Foreign Minister) via Steengracht and Hencke to Wagner, October 10, 1944, NG-5100.

646. Affidavit by Gmelin, June 15, 1948, NO-5921.

647. Affidavit by Kastner, September 13, 1945, PS-2605. Kasztner, *Bericht des jüdischen Rettungskomittees*, p. 99. The BdS reported 9653 Jews and 172 Gypsies arrested by December 9, 1944; 8975 Jews had been deported by that date. Report by BdS-IVc, December 9, 1944, in Lettrich, *Slovakia*, pp. 308–9.

Croatia, Bulgaria did not *owe* its existence to Germany; it was in the German camp solely for opportunistic reasons. As a result of two lost contests, the Second Balkan War and the First World War, Bulgaria had territorial grievances against all its neighbors.

Under German patronage Bulgarian hopes for redress were realized to a far greater extent than any optimist in Sofia could reasonably have expected. In September, 1940, Bulgaria received southern Dobrudja from Roumania; in March, 1941, the German Army was admitted to Bulgaria, and during the following month the country acquired Macedonia from Yugoslavia and Thrace from Greece. The Bulgarian domain now extended to Lake Ohrid (on the Albanian frontier) in the west and to the Aegean Sea in the south.

It is interesting to observe what the Bulgarians did after they had made these gains. There were, of course, Bulgarian occupation troops in Macedonia and Thrace; however, the Bulgarians were very careful to limit their military contributions to the territorial confines of "Greater Bulgaria." No Bulgarian armed forces were dispatched to fight on fronts outside the country, and no expeditionary forces were sent to Russia. When Germany opened its eastern campaign, Bulgaria did not even declare war on the "Bolshevik enemy." In the West, too, the Bulgarians were reluctant to acquire unnecessary foes. Declarations of war against the Western powers were postponed as long as possible – that is, until the United States became a belligerent.

The United States, incidentally, took its time in replying to the Balkan declarations of war. When on June 2, 1942, President Roosevelt recommended to the Congress that it recognize a state of war between the United States and the Balkan states, he said:

> The Governments of Bulgaria, Hungary, and Roumania have declared war against the United States. I realize that the three Governments took this action not upon their own initiative or in response to the wishes of their peoples, but as the instruments of Hitler.[648]

That was the kind of realization Bulgaria was eager to foster, for, above all, the Bulgarians wanted to play it safe. They were unwilling to be involved in anything irrevocably. It was vital to them that the back door be open and the escape route be clear. They wanted, in short, to play the game in such a way that there was chance of gain but no risk of loss. And when the Axis powers were finally defeated, the Bulgarians emerged from their adventure without Greek Thrace and Yugoslav Macedonia – but with southern Dobrudja.[649]

The Bulgarian refusal to become a full-fledged Axis partner in war was mirrored in a similar reluctance to take irrevocable measures against the Jews. In the occupied territories of Macedonia and Thrace, where Bulgaria was, so to speak, really at war, the Jews were delivered into German hands for deportation to killing centers; in Old Bulgaria, on the other hand, the destruction process was developed through definition, expropriation, and concentration, only to be broken off before the deportation stage. It was as though the degree of involvement had already been predetermined. The operation was brought to a halt as if stopped by an invisible sign which said, "So far and no farther."

Old Bulgaria had about 50,000

648. Department of State *Bulletin*, June 6, 1942, pp. 509-10.

649. Under the peace terms Bulgaria did have to pay $25,000,000 to Yugoslavia and $45,000,000 to Greece as reparations. However, Bulgaria had done some looting in the occupied territories. Also, it is true that Bulgaria became a Communist satellite, but that is a fate which in eastern Europe overtook victors and vanquished alike.

Jews,[650] and approximately 15,000 more were added to the Bulgarian power sphere in the newly won territories of Macedonia and Thrace. During the war an American Jewish organization compiled a book called *Hitler's Ten-Year War on the Jews;*"[651] the writers of that book lamented the fate of the European Jewish communities by reciting the notable contributions by great Jews in Germany, France, Italy, etc. When the editors came to the Bulgarian section, they found nothing special to say about the Bulgarian Jewish community, and so they noted somewhat apologetically that the Bulgarian Jews had no "spectacular" achievements.[652]

Indeed, the Bulgarian Jews were not "essential." They were not "indispensable." They were not especially talented or particularly well off. They attracted neither extraordinary sympathy nor exceptional hostility. There was no need to preserve them and no reason to destroy them. The Bulgarian Jews were a pawn in the hands of an opportunistic power: they were like a surplus commodity, to be traded for political advantage. The Reich could not completely destroy the Bulgarian Jews because it could not offer sufficient gain to the cautious Bulgarian rulers.

On the German side, the chief protagonists who helped decide the fate of Bulgarian Jewry were: Minister Beckerle; the Jewish Adviser, Dannecker, and the Police Attaché, Hoffmann. Beckerle, like the other German emissaries in the Balkans, was an SA man. His relations with the SS, however, were quite good. In fact, Beckerle was police president of Frankfurt when the Foreign Office snatched him from the Himmler hierarchy and appointed him Minister to Bulgaria.[653] Dannecker did not come to Bulgaria until January, 1943; as we have already learned, he was in France until then. The other SS-man, Hoffman, represented the Attaché Group of the RSHA in Bulgaria.[654]

The Bulgarian government's principal personalities in Jewish affairs were the following:[655]

King: Boris
Prime Minister: Filov (Bojilov)
Foreign Minister: Popov (Kirov)
Interior Minister: Gabrowski (Christov)
Justice Minister: Partov
Jewish Commissar (from 1942): Belev (Stomonjakov)

As an Axis country, Bulgaria had a few peculiarities. There was a Parliament in Sofia (the *Sobranje*) which actually passed laws. Unlike the Slovakian Parliament (which also passed laws), it was not entirely a rubber-stamp body, for it was the scene of discussion, debate, protest, and even amendment of policy. We shall see some of these amendments in the anti-Jewish legislation. A second factor of some importance in the Bulgarian political arena was the King. The Bulgarian King (or *Czar*) was respected for his shrewdness even by Hitler.[656] Boris displayed some of that shrewdness in Jewish matters.

One of the most important personali-

650. Census of 1934: 48,565.

651. Institute of Jewish Affairs.

652. *Ibid.*, p. 113.

653. See memorandum by Weizsäcker, April 5, 1941, NG-2064. Beckerle's predecessor was Richthofen.

654. A police attaché was the counterpart of a military attaché. A Himmler invention, police attachés were dispatched to some embassies and legations, in pursuance of an agreement between Himmler and Ribbentrop. Himmler to main offices and Higher SS and Police Leaders, May 23, 1942, enclosing Himmler-Ribbentrop agreement of August 8, 1941, and supplementary agreement between Weizsäcker and Heydrich of August 28, 1941, NO-763.

655. Names taken from German documents and newspapers.

656. Picker *Hitler's Tischgespräche im Führerhauptquartier 1941–1942,* entry for April 2, 1942, p. 223.

ties on our list was Commissar Belev, whose office was established in August, 1942. Whereas King Boris was above the Cabinet, Belev was below it. Belev did not have unlimited authority in his sphere. He had to have authorization in law. Sometimes the law provided that he could take no action in a particular matter without the consent of the Cabinet, and once in a while the consent of the Cabinet was frustrated by action of the King. The Bulgarian machinery was thus precision-designed for delaying and procrastinating tactics, a fact that the Germans did not discover immediately.

The first anti-Jewish law passed its first reading in Parliament in November, 1940, as "representatives and ministers accused each other of having taken money from the Jews."[657] The law was enacted on January 21, 1941, at a time when the Bulgarian regime was moving closer into the arms of the Germans – the period after the acquisition of southern Dobrudja, but before the occupation of Macedonia and Thrace. In scope, the law was wide. It contained provisions for the definition, expropriation, and concentration of the Jews. In its effect, it was not exactly a mild law, for the Bulgarians did not start out with mildness. Restraint was applied only afterwards, when the prospects of a German victory began to fade. But, of course, the law was not written by the Germans. The Bulgarian authorship can be seen in the definition, which differed considerably from the Lösener version.

In the Bulgarian law a person with three or more Jewish grandparents was *not* considered a Jew if he had been married in a Christian rite to a Bulgarian by September 1, 1940, and if in addition he had been baptized at the time of the publication of the law (January 21, 1941). The Bulgarian law also specified that a person with two Jewish grandparents was not to be considered Jewish, even if married to a Jewish person, if he had been baptized by September 1, 1940. However, the law allowed for the possibility of classifying a quarter-Jewish person as a Jew if his half-Jewish parent had not been baptized before the marriage ceremony, or if he himself was not raised with the Christian faith as his first religion.[658] In short, the Bulgarian definition was somewhat milder than the German in its total effect but sharper in some of its provisions. The Germans, for example, exempted some persons because they did not belong to the Jewish religion; the Bulgarians freed some of their part-Jews only if they belonged to the Christian religion. That is an important distinction, for it reveals fundamentally different modes of thinking.[659]

One other divergence from German practice may be noted: The Bulgarians, like the Slovaks and Croats, had privileged Jews – war volunteers, all veterans with certain decorations, war invalids, and war orphans. This group numbered about a thousand without dependants, or, if families are included,

657. Foreign Mail Census Office (*Auslandsbriefprüfstelle*) Vienna (signed by Obstlt. Gross) to OKW/Wi Rü, attention Oblt. Beyer, and Economy Ministry, attention MinRat Schultze-Schlutius, December 19, 1940, enclosing letter from Petraschka in Sofia to Jordan Tassef in Berlin, November 30, 1940, Wi/Ic 5.19. Also, report on "Bulgarian Press Circles" received by *Reichsstelle für Aussenhandel* in Sofia on November 18, 1940, Wi/IC 5.35.

658. *Donauzeitung* (Belgrade), June 24, 1942, p. 3.

659. Characteristically, intercepted mail from Sofia revealed that a "conversion epidemic" was rampant in the capital. *Auslandsbriefprüfstelle* Vienna to *Zentralauswertestelle*, February 18, 1941, Wi/IC 5.35. In 1942 the definition was made sharper in that half-Jews were henceforth to be treated like three-quarter Jews. The basic emphasis on the Christian religion, however, remained. *Donauzeitung* (Belgrade), August 28–30, 1942.

a little less than a tenth of the Jewish community.[660]

In the expropriatory sphere the law provided for the summary dismissal of Jewish civil servants and the introduction of the *numerus clausus* among the self-employed — that is, a reduction of Jewish participation in the professions and enterprises to the proportion of Jews in the population. Jews were 1 per cent of the population; hence, the basic *numerus clausus* was also 1 per cent.

What was the effect of that quota? The answer appears to be simple. Since Bulgaria was predominantly agricultural, while the Jewish community was almost entirely urban, the application of the *numerus clausus* could mean almost total expropriation. Actually, however, the *numerus clausus* was later modified so as to be based on Jewish population in individual cities, a very important change.[661]

What was the position of the privileged category in the reduction process? The law specified that privileged Jews were to have preference "in competition with" unprivileged Jews. That formulation was interpreted by the Interior Ministry as a directive to include to the greatest possible extent privileged Jews among the surviving Jewish professionals and businessmen; however, the supreme administrative tribunal ruled that privileged Jews were not to be included in the *numerus clausus* at all.[662] That decision — which, by the way, would have been inconceivable in a German court — was another important modification.

The final statistics were consequently as follows:[663]

	Professions	Business Enterprises
Before the law	521	4,272
Admitted by *numerus clausus*	76	498
Privileged	71	263
Total remaining	149 [*sic*]	761

In spite of the modifications, therefore, a considerable reduction had been effected. What happened to the enterprises which were not permitted to continue? Were they confiscated? The answer is no. They were subjected to forced sale, or, as it would be known in the Reich, compulsory Aryanization.

We need not go into detail about the many implementation decrees which put additional restrictions on the Jews in the economic sphere. Jews were barred from certain business activities altogether; the size of Jewish enterprises was limited to a certain capital; so-called mixed enterprises (Jewish-Bulgarian) were dissolved; and so on.[664] Finally, the accumulated Jewish cash which accrued from the compulsory sales was confiscated by the government in quite the same way as the German Finance Ministry collected the money from the Jewish entrepreneurs in the Reich. The Bulgarian measure was not called a fine, however; it was simply a property tax, and it netted a total of 575 million leva (RM 17.5 million, or $7 million).[665]

The Bulgarian Jews were not rich; they were primarily workers. It is therefore not surprising that simultaneously with the expropriation of Jewish property there was an exploitation of Jewish labor. At first Jews served with Bulgarians in the regular labor service maintained by the military establish-

660. *Ibid.*, June 24, 1942, p. 3.

661. *Ibid.*, July 25, 1941, p. 3.

662. *Ibid.*, June 24, 1942, p. 3.

663. *Ibid.;* also, February 20, 1942, p. 3. The discrepancy of 2 in the figure of 149 is unexplained.

664. *Ibid.*, December 16, 1941, p. 3; February 4, 1942, p. 4; February 15, 1942, p. 4; June 24, 1942, p. 3; August 13, 1942, p. 3; August 28–30, 1942.

665. *Ibid.*, August 20, 1941, p. 4; September 5, 1941, p. 3; November 21, 1941, p. 3; June 24, 1942, p. 3.

ment. The Jews wore Bulgarian uniforms and did the same work as Bulgarians.

The German Labor Service (*Reichsarbeitsdienst*) protested against this state of affairs and refused co-operation with the Bulgarian Labor Service in any function so long as Jews were receiving such favorable treatment. German Minister Beckerle informed Bulgarian Foreign Minister Popov of this protest, and the Bulgarian agreed to do his best. The Jews were to be separated from the Bulgarian Labor Service; they were to be divested of the uniform and mobilized for "especially heavy labor" (*verschärft zu besonders schweren Arbeiten herangezogen*).[666] By August, 1941, there was a special Jewish labor service.[667] The Jews wore no uniform; instead, they had to wear a star – the first instance of marking in Bulgaria.[668]

Initially, the Jewish labor draft affected all Jews between the ages of 21 and 31;[669] later it was extended to men between the ages of 31 and 47.[670] Numerically, it expanded from about 3300 in June, 1942, to about 10,000 in the spring of 1943.[671] Like everywhere else in Europe, the Jews in forced labor were building roads and railroads for the Axis.[672]

The first concentration measures in Bulgaria may be traced to the law of January 21, 1941, which prohibited, among other things, intermarriages between Jews and Bulgarians. In fact, it was to this provision that the law owed its title, "Law for the Protection of the Nation" (the counterpart of the "Law for the Protection of German Blood and Honor"). But the law of January 21, 1941, also contained some more important stipulations, notably the prohibition to travel without police permit and a clause permitting the Cabinet, acting upon petition of the Interior Minister, to assign to Jews new addresses in specified towns and villages.[673]

At first these two provisions were not operative at all. The police granted travel permits to Jews as a matter of course. By spring of 1942, however, these permits were withheld.[674] The assignment of new addresses, which effectively could become operative only after the enforcement of travel prohibitions, was a potentially very dangerous measure, for in its very nature it could be merged with deportations. We have already seen how the Slovak expulsions of Jews from Bratislava to provincial towns and camps led to further deportations from those points to Poland. In Bulgaria this potentiality was even greater, for, while only one-sixth of Slovak Jewry lived in Bratislava, more than half of Bulgarian Jewry lived in Sofia.

However, in the hands of the Bulgarians this measure ultimately became a weapon of delay and procrastination, a justification for frustrating the deportations altogether. The Germans, in the meantime, were completely unaware of the possibility that the Bulgarians would not follow Germany to the end of the road.

On November 26, 1941, Bulgarian Foreign Minister Popov had a discussion with Ribbentrop, in the course of which Popov mentioned that the Bulgarian government was encountering certain difficulties in the enforcement

666. Beckerle to Foreign Office, July 31, 1941, NG-3251.
667. *Krakauer Zeitung*, August 22, 1941, p. 4.
668. *Donauzeitung* (Belgrade), May 13, 1942, p. 3.
669. *Ibid.*
670. *Die Judenfrage*, July 15, 1942, p. 151.
671. *Donauzeitung* (Belgrade), May 19, 1942, p. 3. *Die Judenfrage*, June 1, 1942, p. 113; July 15, 1942, p. 151. *Donauzeitung* (Belgrade), May 28, 1943, p. 3.
672. *Die Judenfrage*, July 15, 1942, p. 151. *Donauzeitung* (Belgrade), May 28, 1943.
673. *Ibid.*, June 24, 1942, p. 3.
674. *Ibid.*

of its anti-Jewish legislation. In particular, a large number of countries – including Hungary, Roumania, and Spain – were protesting against the inclusion of some of their citizens in the application of these laws. Popov suggested that this was undoubtedly one of those questions which all European countries should settle on a common basis.[675]

The experts in *Abteilung Deutschland* were very enthusiastic when they read the Popov proposal, since they assumed that the Bulgarian Foreign Minister had asked Germany's help in aquiring a free hand over foreign Jews in Bulgaria.[676] Indeed, the experts went to work right away and emerged with the "territorial principle" of property disposal.[677]

Ribbentrop himself assured the Bulgarian Foreign Minister "that at the end of the war all Jews would have to leave Europe [*dass am Ende des Krieges sämtliche Juden Europa würden verlassen müssen*]." "That was an unalterable decision of the Führer [*Dies sei ein unabänderlicher Entschluss des Führers*]." Hence there was no need to listen to foreign protests. The Germans, at any rate, were not listening to protests anymore, not even protests from the United States.[678]

The statement that "at the end of the war" all Jews would have to leave Europe was a reference to the resettlement legend in its most elaborate form: the Jews were to be deported to Poland as an "intermediary measure." In Poland the deportees were working in hard labor projects and were waiting until, at the end of the war, they could be shoved out of Europe, etc. By stating that this plan was an "unalterable decision of the Führer," Ribbentrop was, in effect, telling the Bulgarians that he anticipated no arguments and no difficulties and that, when the time came, the Bulgarians were naturally expected to hand over their Jews to the Reich for safekeeping, just as other European countries were doing.

However, the time had not yet come. The German killing centers were not yet in operation, and Bulgaria was not sufficiently advanced in its anti-Jewish measures to qualify as a deportation country. The measure for which the Germans were instinctively waiting was the concentration of the Jews, the assignment of new addresses. In June, 1942, there were signs that a move was in the offing: A Bulgarian newspaper complained that Sofia had a housing shortage and suggested that an alleviation might be achieved by the removal of the Jews.[679] Later that month Interior Minister Gabrowski requested authorization to eject the Jews from the capital and other Bulgarian towns.[680]

In Berlin, Luther promptly sent instructions (approved by Ribbentrop, Weizsäcker, Wörmann, Wörmann's subordinates, and the Trade-Political Division) requesting Beckerle to inquire in Sofia how the Bulgarians would feel about deportations. Beckerle was not to conclude any agreements or set any dates; he was merely to find out the Bulgarian attitude in the matter. The German Minister made the inquiry and reported that the Bulgarians were prepared to agree to deportations.[681] On July 6–7 there was an exchange of notes

675. Summary of discussion between Ribbentrop and Popov held on November 26, 1941, in Berlin, November 27, 1941, NG-3667.

676. See memorandum prepared by *Abteilung Deutschland* for Weizsäcker and Ribbentrop, December 1, 1941, NG-4667.

677. See p. 354.

678. Summary of Ribbentrop-Popov discussion, November 27, 1941, NG-3667.

679. *Donauzeitung* (Belgrade), June 3, 1942, p. 3.

680. *Deutsche Ukraine-Zeitung* (Luck), June 27, 1942, p. 2.

681. Memorandum by Luther, August 21, 1942, NG-2586-J. Luther's instructions were sent on June 19. There is no date for the Bulgarian acquiescence.

in pursuance of which Bulgarian Jews in the Reich were to be treated like Reich Jews and German Jews in Bulgaria were to be treated like Bulgarian Jews.[682] The main blow was now close at hand, but the Germans were still waiting.

In August, 1942, the Bulgarians took several steps forward: The definition was tightened. The Office of the Commissar for Jewish Questions was formed. Blocked funds in the banks were transferred to a "Jewish community fund." (The object of this fund was to help the poor Jews and the Jews in forced labor and, most important, to finance resettlements.) All unemployed Jews in Sofia were ordered to leave the city by September 1. Apartment restrictions were announced for the remaining Jews: for a family of two – one room; for a family of three or four – two rooms; for a family of five or six – three rooms; for a family of more than six – four rooms. At the same time the Jewish star, already worn by the Jews in forced labor, was introduced for the entire population. In fact, in the matter of the star the Bulgarians seemed to be going on a binge. Everything conceivably Jewish had to be marked: apartments, stores, business correspondence, bills, and even merchandise.[683]

In Germany these developments were watched closely. As soon as the marking regulations had come out, Müller ordered his Gestapo offices to subject Bulgarian Jews in the Reich to marking and movement restrictions.[684] At the same time the RSHA approached the Foreign Office with a request to go into action; the legation had already sounded out the Bulgarians and reported that Sofia was ready "to come to an agreement with us."[685]

On September 11, 1942, Luther consequently dispatched a cautious report to Weizsäcker and Ribbentrop. First he mentioned an incident that he considered disturbing: The Central Jewish Consistory of Bulgaria had transmitted birthday greetings to the young Crown Prince, and the Czar had thereupon sent a telegram to Josef Geron, chairman of the consistory, thanking him and Bulgarian Jewry sincerely for the regards and best wishes. However, continued Luther, the anti-Jewish policy in Bulgaria had made notable progress.

Luther then summarized all the recent Bulgarian measures, including the expulsion orders affecting the Jews of Sofia. "These resettlement plans," wrote Luther, "have occasioned the Reich Security Main Office here to bring up the question whether the Reich should not – in view of the previously announced attitude of the Bulgarian government – interpose itself at this point and offer its services in the resettlement actions [*sich jetzt einschalten und seine Dienste bei der Aussiedlungsaktion anbieten soll*]." Accordingly, Luther requested Weizsäcker's and Ribbentrop's decision "whether Minister Beckerle may bring up before the Bulgarian Foreign Minister, in properly cautious form, the question of the resettlement of the Bulgarian Jews."

Luther thought that the Bulgarians would now accept a German offer to take over the Jews *(zur Übernahme der Juden)* with pleasure. Ribbentrop, on the other hand, did not think that the

682. Rintelen to Luther, August 25, 1942, NG-2586-K. Memorandum by Klingenfuss, November 19, 1942, NG-3746.

683. *Donauzeitung* (Belgrade), August 27–30, 1942; September 2, 1942, p. 3; September 5, 1942, p. 3; September 9, 1942, p. 3. *Die Judenfrage*, October 1, 1942, pp. 209–10.

684. Müller to state police offices, central offices for Jewish emigration in Vienna and Prague, commanders of Security Police and SD in Prague, Metz, Strassbourg, Velde, Marburg, and *Einsatzkommando* Luxembourg, September 4, 1942, NG-3715.

685. Memorandum by Luther, August 21, 1942, NG-2586-J.

time was ripe, and so he scribbled two words on Luther's report: *noch warten* ("wait some more").[686] Two weeks later Ribbentrop changed his mind and gave the go-ahead signal,[687] but these two weeks made a difference.

While Berlin waited, Sofia took its time. The expulsions proceeded at a leisurely pace, and the marking ran into difficulties. On November 9, 1942, the RSHA's foreign intelligence chief, Schellenberg, sent a report on Bulgarian anti-Jewish developments to Luther. The report already revealed evidence of deliberate procrastination. The Bulgarian government, said the RSHA, had come to the conclusion that with the latest anti-Jewish ordinances the "point of toleration" (*das Mass des Erträglichen*) had already been exceeded.

This attitude was revealed in a number of ways. On September 27, for example, about 350 Jews assembled in the courtyard of the Interior Ministry to deliver a petition for the extension of expulsion deadlines. Interior Minister Gabrowski stepped into the courtyard and, "to the amazement of all his officials and employees watching from the windows, delivered a half-hour speech to calm the Jews." On top of that, he said that "the worst was already over" and personally accepted the Jewish petition. The next day Gabrowski directed the press to cease discussion of the Jewish question, basing his order on the ground that the Jewish question had already been regulated and that the people were satisfied with these measures against the Jews. In addition, Gabrowski "hinted" repeatedly to Jewish Commissar Belev that the Cabinet and the Czar wished an alleviation of anti-Jewish activities. In accordance with that alleviation policy, Gabrowski had refused to sign an ordinance introducing certain movement restrictions in the capital.

Bulgarian procrastination, continued the RSHA report, was particularly noticeable in the matter of marking. The Bulgarian government had originally introduced a Jewish star, "albeit a little one" (*einen "allerdings nur kleinen" Judenstern*). As of the moment, however, very few Jews were wearing the star. The opening salvo against the star had been fired by the "Anglophile" Metropolitan Stephan of Sofia, who on September 27 had delivered a sermon pointing out that God had already punished the Jews "for having nailed Christ to the cross" by driving them from place to place and allowing them no country of their own. God had thereby determined the Jewish fate, and men had no right to torture the Jews and to persecute them. This applied especially to Jews who had accepted Christianity. The metropolitan had then succeeded in freeing all baptized Jews from wearing the star. Prime Minister Filov on his own had liberated the Jews in mixed marriage; thereupon, on September 30, Justice Minister Partov demanded that the wearing of the star should not be obligatory and that all expulsions should be halted.

By the beginning of October about a fifth of Bulgarian Jewry was wearing the emblem, and at that point the Bulgarian government halted star production by cutting off the electricity supply from the plant that was producing the badges. This measure was justified on the ground of the power shortage. Many Jews who had already been wearing the star took it off again, while others wore it in an "arrogant" manner, pinned next to a patriotic symbol such as a picture of the Czar or the Queen.

686. Luther via Weizsäcker to Ribbentrop, September 11, 1942, NG-2582. Von Sonnleithner via Weizsäcker to Luther September 15, 1942, NG-2582. Luther to Rademacher, September 15, 1942, NG-2582.

687. Luther to Weizsäcker, Wörmann, von Erdmannsdorff, Pol. I, Pol. IV, D II, D III, Legal and Trade Political divisions, September 24, 1942, NG-1517.

The RSHA experts thought that a partial explanation of these developments was to be found in the actions of some foreign powers – including Italy, Hungary, Roumania, Vichy France, and Spain – who were putting "pressure" on the Bulgarian government. Italy in particular had handed four or five protest notes to the Bulgarian Foreign Ministry. Popov had collected all these notes and had handed them to Commissar Belev to convey to the commissar which way the wind was blowing.[688]

A few days after receiving this report from the RSHA, *Abteilung Deutschland* had a first-hand opportunity to observe that something had gone wrong. On November 18 the Bulgarian Legation Secretary inquired about the treatment of foreign Jews in the Reich. Legationsrat Klingenfuss pointed out that this question had already been settled by exchange of notes in July, but the Bulgarian replied that he had never heard about any exchange of notes.[689]

There remained, however, one approachable spot in the Bulgarian picture: the occupied territories of Macedonia and Thrace. On June 10, 1942, a Bulgarian ordinance which regulated the acquisition of citizenship in the new territories had gone into effect. That ordinance was specifically inapplicable to Jews. According to "informed sources" the omission meant that the Jews would not stay long in those provinces.[690]

In January, 1943, an Eichmann representative, Hauptsturmführer Dannecker, arrived in Bulgaria from France and was attached to the German police attaché in the legation. Dannecker's mission was to deport as many Jews as possible, starting with the Jews in the occupied territories. The Bulgarian Interior Minister now declared himself willing to deport 14,000 Jews from Macedonia and Thrace. Commissar Belev, "a convinced anti-Semite," then proposed adding 6000 "leading Jews" of Old Bulgaria *(die jüdische Führungsschicht)*. Gabrowski also approved of this plan, and the Cabinet concurred with Gabrowski's decision. On February 22, 1943, Hauptsturmführer Dannecker could therefore conclude a written agreement with Commissar Belev, which provided for the deportation of 8000 Jews from Macedonia, 6000 from Thrace, and 6000 from Old Bulgaria -- a total of 20,000.

The agreement also contained detailed provisions for luggage, confiscation of property, the exemption of Jews in mixed marriages, and so on. The German side demanded that Bulgaria pay 250 reichsmark for each deported Jew, but the Bulgarians considered this price a little too high, and the matter was amiably dropped. On March 2, 1943, the Bulgarian Cabinet approved the allocation of transports and at the same time drafted a law providing for the loss of nationality by deportees crossing the border. The nationality law was approved by the *Sobranje* but not published in the official gazette. During the next few days 11,343 Jews from the occupied territories were deported: 7122 Macedonian Jews left the town of Skopje by rail; 4221 Thrace Jews were deported from the port of Lom by ship.

Commissar Belev now ordered the internment of the "influential" Jews from the towns of Plovdiv, Kyustendil, Russe, and Varna. But opposition was growing fast. A delegation from Kyustendil headed by the vice president of the *Sobranje*, Peshev, intervened with the Ministry of Interior. Peshev, supported by forty deputies, then introduced in the *Sobranje* a resolution of censure accusing the government of atrocities al-

688. Schellenberg to Luther, November 9, 1942, NG-5351.

689. Memorandum by Klingenfuss, November 19, 1942, NG-3746.

690. *Donauzeitung* (Belgrade), June 11, 1942, p. 3.

leged to have occurred during the deportations. Peshev was voted down and lost his office; however, his intervention was followed by another one described only as a "hint from the highest quarter" – presumably from the Czar – to stop all planned deportations from Old Bulgaria. "Prominent" Jews who had already been interned were thereupon set free again.[691]

In concluding his report about the deportations, Police Attaché Hoffman explained that, considering the fact that nothing at all had yet been accomplished in "Italy, Hungary, Spain, etc.," the Bulgarians had done quite well. Furthermore, a "Jewish problem" in the form in which it had existed in Germany was actually unknown in Bulgaria. The deportation of 11,343 Jews was consequently quite "satisfactory" (*zufriedenstellend.*) Based on the agreed total of 20,000, this meant an achievement of 56 per cent – quite a normal "reduction" in a Balkan country.[692]

Ribbentrop, however, was by no means satisfied with such reductions. When King Boris visited Berlin in the beginning of April, the German Foreign Minister had a chance to express his displeasure. Boris explained that he had given the order confining the evacuations to Macedonia and Thrace and that he intended to deport "only a small number of Bolshevik-Communist elements" from Old Bulgaria because he needed the rest of the Jews for road construction. Ribbentrop replied that "in our view the only correct solution of the Jewish problem was the most radical solution" *(dass nach unserer Auffassung in der Judenfrage die radikalste Lösung die allein richtige sei).*[693]

Under the application of new pressure from the German Legation in Sofia, Commissar Belev, a man with divided loyalties, prepared two alternate plans: one provided for the deportation of all Jews to Poland; the other allowed for the complete evacuation of the Sofia Jews to the country. The two plans were submitted to Boris, who naturally chose the latter.[694] The new expulsion order was published on May 25.[695]

For the Germans there was not much to be done any more. But the RSHA pressured the Foreign Office to pressure Beckerle into pressuring the Bulgarian government. On June 7, Beckerle replied: "I would like to assure you that we here are doing everything in our power to arrive in a suitable manner at a final liquidation of the Jewish question." Unfortunately, Beckerle continued, direct pressure just didn't work. The Bulgarians had been living with peoples like the Armenians, Greeks, and Gypsies for so long that they simply could not appreciate the Jewish problem.[696]

Police Attaché Hoffmann was more optimistic. He reported that the expulsion of all but 2000–3000 privileged Jews from Sofia was now nearing its completion. The expelled Jews were quartered with Jewish families in the

691. Hoffmann (police attaché in Sofia) to RSHA/Attaché Group, April 5, 1943, NG-4144. The Hoffmann report was marked "seen: Beckerle." Memorandum by Wagner, April 3, 1943, NG-4180. The above account is based on both reports. There are minor discrepancies in the statistics. Hoffmann mentions 11,343 deportees, including 7122 Macedonian and 4221 Thrace Jews. Wagner lists 11,459, including 7240 from Macedonia and 4219 from Thrace. Korherr reported a total of 11,364 deportees. Korherr to Himmler, April 19, 1943, NO-5193.

692. Hoffmann to Attaché Group, April 5, 1943, NG-4144.

693. Ribbentrop to Beckerle, April 4, 1943, NG-62.

694. Hoffmann to Attaché Group, June 7, 1943, NG-2357.

695. *Donauzeitung* (Belgrade), May 26, 1943, p. 3; May 28, 1943, p. 3; June 1, 1943, p. 3.

696. Beckerle to Foreign Office, June 7, 1943, NG-2357.

country and in schools. The schools, he reasoned, would have to be reopened in the fall; hence there would still be an opportunity for deporting the Bulgarian Jews.[697]

On June 24, Beckerle reported that the expulsions had been completed with the removal of 20,000 Jews from Sofia. He repeated that pressure at this point would not work, but he associated himself with the view of his police attaché that the stoppage of the "final solution operation" (*Endlösungsaktion*) was only temporary, that the Jews would make such a nuisance of themselves in the country as to furnish before long the "precipitating factor for a further development in our sense."[698]

However, the summer ended without any change in Bulgarian policy, and on August 31, 1943, the chief of Inland II, Wagner (Luther's successor), himself wrote the finish to the Bulgarian *Aktion*. Addressing himself to Kaltenbrunner, Wagner wrote that again and again the RSHA had approached the Foreign Office with requests for putting pressure on the Bulgarians. The RSHA had pointed out that with each passing week "a radical solution would become more difficult." The RSHA had also told the Foreign Office that the dispersal of the Jews in the entire country was unwise (*bedenklich*) from the viewpoint of counterespionage and that in the event of Allied landings in the Balkans these Jews would be positively dangerous.

The Foreign Office, Wagner continued, had thereupon asked Minister Beckerle to explore the matter further, but the envoy had gained the distinct impression that every German "offer" (*Antrag*), no matter how strongly put, would be rejected by the Bulgarians. Wagner then explained the true reason for the Bulgarian refusal to deport the Jews: the Bulgarians were afraid of the enemy powers. There was in Bulgaria an "insane fear of air raids." Just as the Bulgarians did not publish the fact that Bulgarian pursuit planes had participated in the shooting down of American bombers during the attack on Ploesti, just as all anti-Bolshevik propaganda was prohibited in Bulgaria (particularly propaganda directed against the person of Stalin), so the Bulgarian government was not inclined "to permit a continuation in the Jewish question."

Wagner concluded that only one factor could influence the Bulgarian decision, and that was a "new activation of the German war effort" (*eine neue Aktivierung der deutschen Kriegsführung*). Doubtless the Bulgarians had also been influenced by the attitude of the Roumanians and Hungarians, for Bulgaria, naturally, did not wish to stand out as an anti-Jewish power. But these influences too would fall away once German successes stood "in the foreground again." Meanwhile, Wagner could do no more than ask Kaltenbrunner for additional materials about the danger and noxiousness of Jewry in Bulgaria.[699]

For twelve months the Bulgarian Jews remained subject to all the discriminations and persecutions of the disrupted destruction process.[700] Then on August 30, 1944, one year after Wagner had written his letter and on the eve of the Soviet invasion of Bulgaria, the morning newspapers in Sofia displayed in prominent headlines the Cabinet's decision to revoke all of the anti-Jewish laws.[701]

697. Hoffmann to Attaché Group, June 7, 1943, NG-2357.

698. Beckerle to RSHA/Attaché Group, June 24, 1943, NG-2753.

699. Wagner to Kaltenbrunner, August 31, 1943, NG-3302.

700. *Donauzeitung* (Belgrade), October 8, 1943, p. 3; October 13, 1943, p. 3; October 27, 1943, p. 3; November 9, 1943, p. 3; December 3, 1943, p. 3; December 14, 1943, p. 3; December 16, 1943, p. 3.

701. *Ibid.*, August 31, 1944, p. 3.

Roumania. – Like the Bulgarians, the Roumanians joined the Axis for opportunistic reasons. Unlike Bulgaria, however, Roumania became an ally of Germany only after the loss of considerable territory: northern Bukovina and Bessarabia to the USSR, northern Transylvania to Hungary, and southern Dobrudja to Bulgaria. These territorial losses came like hammer blows in a period of two months.[702] Roumania now had enemies east and west; Russia and Germany were responsible for her losses. The Roumanians joined the Axis and reconquered the eastern provinces; when the fortunes of war turned and Bukovina and Bessarabia were irretrievably lost, the Roumanians, moving with the tide, joined the Russians and recovered Transylvania.

However, there was something in Roumanian action which was more than mere opportunism – an overpowering need to hurl oneself with all one's might at some enemy target. That factor was responsible for the circumstance that the Roumanians made more than a token contribution in their war against the USSR. Measured in sheer numbers, Roumania was Germany's most important ally in the East. The Roumanian armies fought without restraint and bled heavily in such places as Odessa and Stalingrad. And it is interesting to note that when the Roumanians changed sides, they displayed that same ferocity in battles against the Germans and Hungarians.

In Jewish matters, too, the Roumanian attitude was partly opportunistic and partly something more. There were times, for example, when the Germans complained that the Roumanians were exasperatingly slow. At one time, Eichmann even wanted to withdraw his expert in Jewish matters from Bucharest, on the ground that the Roumanians did not follow the expert's advice. But there also were instances when the Germans actually had to step in to restrain and slow down the pace of Roumanian measures. At such times the Roumanians were moving too fast for the German bureaucracy. Not hasty measures but thorough ones were required by the Germans.

If the Roumanians overstepped the bounds of opportunism in the speed of their action, they virtually forgot all motives of profit in the extent of their measures. What is significant in the case of the Roumanians is not only how fast they were going but also how far.

In Old Roumania (that is, the Roumania without the lost provinces) the Jews were hardly ever concentrated, and, although deportations from Old Roumania to Auschwitz were actually planned, the Roumanian government abruptly changed its mind and virtually stopped the destruction process in its tracks.

East of the Prut River, on the other hand, the picture was quite different. In Bukovina and Bessarabia, which were recovered from Russia in 1941, the Roumanians took the most drastic action. In these provinces the Roumanian authorities did not follow the usual pattern of concentrating the Jews and handing them over to the Germans; instead, the Bukovina and Bessarabia Jews were transported to what we might call the Roumanian "East" – the territory of "Transnistria" (in the Soviet Ukraine), which was under Roumanian occupation. In that territory the Roumanians maintained true killing centers. Besides Germany itself, Roumania was thus the only country which implemented all the steps of the destruction process, from definitions to killings.[703]

Characteristics of group activity and

702. Bukovina and Bessarabia were lost on June 28, 1940; Transylvania on August 30, 1940; Dobrudia on September 12, 1940.

703. As we have seen, the Roumanians also were significantly involved in the mobile killing operations. See pp. 199–201.

individual behavior are not always alike, but in the case of Roumania there were pronounced similarities. Unlike the Germans, who did not ordinarily practice their official behavior patterns in private life, the Roumanians were a fairly consistent lot. Opportunism was practiced in Roumania not only on a national basis but also in personal relations. Roumania was a corrupt country. It was the only Axis state in which officials as high as minister and mayor of the capital city had to be dismissed for "dark" transactions with expropriated Jewish property.[704]

The search for personal gain in Roumania was so intensive that it must have enabled many Jews to buy relief from persecution. The institution of bribery was, in fact, so well established that it was diverted for the benefit of the state: the Roumanian government permitted Jews to *purchase* exemptions from such anti-Jewish measures as forced labor and travel restrictions. However, what was true of personal opportunism in Roumania was true also of personal involvement in killings. Repeatedly the Roumanians threw themselves into *Aktionen.* Witnesses and survivors testifying to the manner in which the Roumanians conducted their killing operations speak of scenes unduplicated in Axis Europe. Even in German reports there are criticisms of these operations, and in some cases – as we have already seen – the Germans stepped in to halt killings that seemed offensive even to so hardened an establishment as the German Army.

In examining the Roumanian bureaucratic apparatus, one is therefore left with the impression of an unreliable machine that did not properly respond to command and that acted in unpredictable ways, sometimes balking, sometimes running away with itself. That spurting action, unplanned and uneven, sporadic and erratic, was the product of an opportunism which was mixed with destructiveness, a lethargy periodically interrupted by outbursts of violence. The product of that mixture was a record of anti-Jewish actions which is decidedly unique.[705]

The Roumania of 1939 had the third-largest Jewish community in Europe – the figure was approximately 800,000.[706] The provinces ceded to Russia in June, 1940, contained about 300,000 Jews;[707] the Jewish population in ceded Transylvania was in the neighborhood of 150,000.[708] The remaining Jews in

704. The dismissed officials were the mayor of Bucharest, Modreanu; his deputy, Dohary; and the Colonization Minister, General Zwiedeneck, who, incidentally, was ethnic German. German Legation in Bucharest/Military Attaché (signed Spalcke) to OKH/Attaché Division, December 12, 1941, Wi/IC 4.66, p. 274.

705. A three-volume work about the destruction of the Jews in Roumania has been published in the Roumanian language. See Matatias Carp, *Cartea Neagra – Suferintele Evreilor din Romania 1940–1944* (Bucharest, 1946–48). Copies, marked vol. I, II*a*, and III, are available in the YIVO Institute for Jewish Research in New York City. Vol. I deals with Roumanian measures to the end of 1940. Vol. II*a* is devoted to the Iasi pogrom. Vol. III is an account of the Transnistria camps. A volume II, presumably covering events in Old Roumania from 1941 to 1944, is not available and may not have been written. The available volumes are based upon Roumanian documents and survivors' accounts. Because of the language difficulty, little use has been made of the work of Matatias Carp in this chapter. It is to be hoped, however, that specialists will not fail to examine closely that voluminous study.

706. During the census of 1930 the count was 756,930. Some Jewish estimates place the number for 1939 as high as 850,000. Probably these estimates are too high.

707. The 1930 census figure was 307,340, including 92,492 in Bukovina and 204,858 in Bessarabia. From 1930 to 1940, the population probably increased to 330,000. However, southern Bukovina was not transferred to Russia; hence the 1940 total for the transferred provinces must have been about 300,000.

708. The 1930 census figure was 138,917. An official Roumanian estimate for January 1, 1940, was 148,573. These figures apply to

Old Roumania consequently numbered about 350,000.[709] In each of these regions the Jews suffered a different fate: the Jews of Old Roumania survived, on the whole; those in Transylvania were engulfed in the Hungarian deportations; while in the eastern provinces – lost in 1940 but recovered in 1941 – the Jews were subjected to the brunt of the Roumanian destruction process.

At the time when the first anti-Jewish measures were launched, Roumania had hardly emerged from an earlier system of ghettoization. The emancipation of the Jews had been a recent occurrence in most of Europe, but it was particularly recent in Roumania. Most Jews had acquired Roumanian citizenship after the end of World War I, in pursuance of a minority treaty concluded by Roumania with the Allied Powers – part of the price that Roumania had to pay for its new-won territories. There was considerable sentiment in Roumania against payment of that price, and in the 1930's the rise of the pro-Nazi and anti-Jewish Iron Guard cast a shadow on Jewish security in the country. When in December, 1937, Roumania acquired its first pro-Nazi regime under Prime Minister Octavian Goga, about 120,000 Jews lost their citizenship.[710]

The Goga regime fell, Iron Guard "legionnaires" were arrested by the thousands, and Iron Guard leaders were massacred while "trying to escape," but the Jews were not entirely forgotten. Under Goga's successors Jewish engineers were excluded from the railways,[711] the quota system was introduced into the labor force in industry,[712] and dismissals were begun in the government service.[713] These measures, incidentally, applied only to "Jews," that is, persons who belonged to the Jewish religion.

After Roumania's frontiers in the East crumbled under a Russian ultimatum, the government of Prime Minister Gigurtu decided to move one step closer to the Germans and to take a big stride forward in the destruction of the Jews. On August 8, 1940, two laws were proclaimed which already contained the seeds of administrative continuity, and which for that reason may be said to have inaugurated the destruction process in Roumania. For the first time the Roumanian government adopted a definition that included, besides Jews by religion, some baptized Jews, such as the baptized children of unbaptized Jewish parents, and the baptized wives of Christian husbands, in the case of women whose baptism did not predate by more than one year

the ceded portion of Transylvania only. Kingdom of Roumania/Ministry of Foreign Affairs, *Memorandum on Transylvania* (Bucharest, 1946), pp. 9, 37–38.

709. The Jews in the Bulgarian-occupied Dobrudja numbered only about 1000. The figure of 350,000 which is arrived at by subtraction, poses a difficulty in that a census of Jewish population on April 6, 1941, yielded a figure of only 302,092. *Wirtschaft und Statistik*, October 2, 1941, p. 392. This result cannot be reconciled with the 1930 census unless we presume an absolute decline during the years 1930–40. Such a decline is very unlikely. (See Roumanian estimate for Transylvania, above). It is quite possible that, like other measures, the Roumanian census was not very efficient. To make matters even more confusing, a census taken in the summer of 1942 yielded only 272,409 Jews. While we may conceivably explain a reduction of nearly 30,000 Jews (or, at any rate, 20,000) from 1941 to 1942, we cannot account for the fact that in the 1942 census the Bucharest and Iasi figures are higher than in the 1941 census. In the case of Bucharest, the figures are 91,268 (1941 census) and 97,868 (1942 census). In the case of Iasi, there was an increase from 32,942 in 1941 (just before the great pogrom) to 34,000 in 1942. Figures of 1942 count in *Donauzeitung* (Belgrade), August 8, 1942, p. 3.

710. *Die Judenfrage*, May 21, 1938, p. 10; December 22, 1938, pp. 1–2.

711. *Ibid.*, July 14, 1938, p. 5.

712. *Ibid.*, February 26, 1940, p. 20.

713. *Krakauer Zeitung*, June 29, 1940; August 3, 1940, p. 1.

the formation of King Carol's Unity Party.

In the economic sphere, Jews were dismissed from the army and from the civil service; they lost their jobs as editors and company board members; they were restricted in the right to practice law and other professions; they lost their liquor licenses; they were prohibited from acquiring real estate, industrial enterprises in the provinces, and so on. Two ghettoization measures were also included in the laws of August 8 – the prohibition of intermarriage and the revocation of name changes.

Nevertheless, the effect of all those provisions upon the Jews was not necessarily decisive. The laws set up three Jewish categories. The most privileged were Jews who had possessed Roumanian citizenship before December 30, 1918, and their descendants, as well as Jews who had been front-line soldiers in World War I and their descendants – about 10,000 people all together. Only a part of the discriminations applied to that group. The next category comprised Jews who were residents (but not citizens) of Old Roumania before December 30, 1918; and the least favored category – which was subjected to all restrictions – consisted of the Jews in the provinces annexed after World War I, and immigrants.[714] On the whole, therefore, the Gigurtu government's measures were still very mild by German standards. But the Gigurtu administration did not last very long.

At the beginning of September, 1940, as Hungarian troops were marching into Transylvania, Roumania acquired a new government which was to last for four years. At the head of that government was a man who called himself the Chief of State: General (later Marshal) Ion Antonescu. His Cabinet was called the "regime of the legionnaires" because never before had Iron Guard leaders held so many positions of power: the Vice Premier was the Iron Guard commander himself, Horia Sima; the Foreign Minister was Iron Guardist Count Michael Sturdza; the Interior Ministry was in the hands of another "legionnaire," General Petrovicescu; the Labor Minister was the Iron Guard commander of Bucharest, Jasinchi.[715] In spite of the makup of this regime, the center of power was soon revealed to be in other hands.

The Jews reacted to the new government with apprehension. In the fall of 1940 thousands of them left Roumanian ports in unseaworthy ships bound for Palestine. Some of the ships sank on their way with hundreds of passengers; hundreds of other emigrants were threatened with deportation when they arrived in the British-ruled Jewish homeland.[716] However, during the brief period of legionnaire participation in the government, only two measures were enacted: a decree dated October 5, 1940, for the state's expropriation of Jewish agricultural property, and a decree dated November 16, 1940, which provided for the gradual dismissal of Jews employed in private commerce and industry. Both measures were implemented by a newly formed Central Office of "Roumanianization" in the Labor Ministry.[717] The use in this connection of the Term "Roumanianization" in preference to a phrase like "Aryanization" is not with-

714. *Ibid.*, August 3, 1940, p. 1; August 10, 1940, p. 2. *Die Judenfrage*, September 15, 1940, pp. 126–28.

715. *Krakauer Zeitung*, September 17, 1940, p. 2.

716. Ira A. Hirschmann, *Lifeline to a Promised Land* (New York, 1946), pp. 11–13. The author was the representative of the U.S. War Refugee Board in Turkey.

717. *Donauzeitung* (Belgrade), February 3, 1942, p. 3; June 14, 1942, p. 3. The same office was later employed in the administration of expropriated Jewish real estate. *Die Judenfrage*, April 25, 1941, pp. 57–58.

out significance; "Aryanizations" could hardly have been aimed at anyone but Jews, but the office of "Roumanianization" directed its activities against Armenians and Greeks as well.[718]

All in all, the two fall measures did little more than round out the basic Gigurtu decree. The Roumanians never got around to issuing a law for the compulsory transfer of commercial and industrial enterprises (as distinguished from state expropriations of agricultural and real property). There was a secret regulation by the Finance Ministry, partially blocking credits due to Jewish suppliers,[719] and the Iron Guard did attempt to push the progress of voluntary Aryanizations. However, German observers watched these transactions with skepticism – apparently the new owners had neither capital nor business acumen. "Wise men raise a warning finger and shake their heads," commented one German writer. In particular, he noted that the ethnic German community had not gotten an even break. But these things he concluded amiably, were the inevitable attributes of a "revolution."[720]

In the meantime the Iron Guard "revolution" was still unfinished business. For one thing, the Iron Guard was only a minority in the Cabinet; for another, the Chief of State was not an Iron Guardist but an army general. On January 20 the Iron Guard launched a revolution to overthrow General Antonescu, and for three days there was street fighting in Bucharest. The putsch was crushed, but before it was over it had been widened into a pogrom.

Iron Guardists had stormed into the Jewish quarter, burning down synagogues, demolishing stores, and devastating private apartments. For miles around the city the Guardists had left traces of their revolution. On January 24, travelers on the Bucharest-Ploesti road discovered at Baneasa over a hundred Jewish bodies without clothes. Gold teeth had been knocked out of the mouths of the dead. (Gypsies were believed to have been the looters.) On the road to Giurgiu passers-by stumbled upon another eighty bodies of Jewish slain. In the city itself the German military attaché was busy collecting casualty reports. "In the Bucharest morgue," he wrote, "one can see hundreds of corpses, but they are mostly Jews [*doch handelt es sich meistens um Juden*]." Jewish sources report that the victims had not merely been killed; they had been butchered. In the morgue bodies were so cut up that they no longer resembled anything human, and in the municipal slaughterhouse bodies were observed hanging like carcasses of cattle. A witness saw a girl of five hanging by her feet like a calf, her entire body smeared with blood. On January 27 the Jewish community organization had identified 630 of the dead; another 400 were missing.[721]

Two weeks after the putsch Iron

718. *Donauzeitung* (Belgrade), February 3, 1942, p. 3.

719. For details, see *Auslandsbriefprüfstelle* Vienna to OKW/Abw III (N), attention Obstlt. Jacobsen, November 22, 1940, Wi/IC 4.66.

720. Michael Maier, "Beginnende Neuordnung in Rumänien," *Volk im Osten* (Bucharest), January, 1941, p. 37. The ethnic German complaints with regard to Roumanian discrimination in the distribution of Jewish property continued well into 1942. See report by VOMI to Himmler's aide Rudi Brandt, August 3, 1942, Himmler Files, Folder No. 8.

721. H/MA *Auslandsdienst* Report No. 185/41, January 27, 1941, Wi/IC 4.2-b. Reports on slaughterhouse in Institute of Jewish Affairs, *The Jews in Nazi Europe* (New York, 1941), p. 11. Also, U.S. Minister in Roumania (Franklin Mott Gunther) to U.S. Secretary of State Hull, January 30, 1941, *Foreign Relations of the United States, 1941*, II (Europe) (Washington, 1959), 860. Published reports in the press listed only 118 Jews killed and 26 wounded, 118 Roumanians killed and 228 wounded. *Krakauer Zeitung*, February 6, 1941, p. 2.

Guard leader Horia Sima blamed the Jews for his defeat. He complained to Himmler that Antonescu was really a friend of the British; then he added: "Lacking political sense, General Antonescu did not realize that he was simply used as an instrument by the Jews and Masons."[722] But Himmler did not interfere, for with every passing day Antonescu was moving closer to the German side. His regime was strong and unshakable. In a matter of months it was to become a fearful instrument of war and destruction.

The chief personalities of the stabilized Antonescu regime were:[723]

Chief of State: Marshal Ion Antonescu
President ad interim of the Council of Ministers: Mihai Antonescu
Minister of Defense ad interim: Gen. Hano Pantazi
- Chief of the Great General Staff: Gen. I. Steflea
- Chief of the Army Staff: Gen. Tataranu

Economy: Marinescu
Transport: Busila
Interior: Gen. Dumitru Popescu
- Undersecretary for Police and Public Security (in succession): Gen. Ion Popescu, Gen. Constantin Vasiliu

General Commissar for Jewish Questions: Radu Lecca
Territorial chiefs in provinces conquered during 1941:
- Governor, Bukovina (in succession): Gen, Alexandru Riosanu, Gen. Corneliu Calotescu, Gen. Cornel Dragalina
- Governor, Bessarabia: Gen. Constantin Voiculescu
- Governor, Transnistria (in succession): Georghe Alexianu, Gen. Gheorghe Potopeanu

It may be noted that the new government had two Antonescus, the marshal and Mihai. A telling description of these two men appeared in a secret report by a German journalist, Dr. Hans-Joachim Kausch, who took a trip to Roumania in 1943. Kausch wrote:

> In many quarters we have been told that Marshall Antonescu has syphilis, a disease that is notoriously as common among Roumanian cavalry officers as in Germany the cold [*der Schnupfen*], but which attacks the marshal very heavily every few months and manifests itself in serious disturbances of his vision. The most important political figure in Roumania at the moment is his deputy, Mihai Antonescu, who controls, practically speaking, the entire administrative apparatus and who is on very good terms with the King and the Queen Mother. He concerns himself, to the point of detail, with every political development; and, while he agrees to the defensive battle against the Soviet danger, he remains – with respect to the conflict with the Western powers – an Anglophile.[724]

Paralleling the Roumanian government but staying in the background was the German organization in Roumania. We might mention three of its officials here: Minister von Killinger; chief of the German army mission, Generalmajor Hauffe; and the Jewish adviser in the legation, Hauptsturmführer Richter. Von Killinger dealt with the two Antonescus, primarily with Mihai. Hauffe was the German liaison officer to the Roumanian Army,

722. Sima to Himmler, February 6, 1941, NO-488.

723. From lists in *Donauzeitung*, documents, and Carp, *Cartea Neagra*, III, 17–21. The portfolio of Defense Minister belonged formally to Marshal Antonescu himself. The "Great General Staff" (*Marele Stat Major*), later transformed into the "Great Headquarters" (*Marele Cartier General*), was the Roumanian OKW. The Roumanian Army Chief of Staff (*Statul Major al Armatei*) occupied a position similar to Chief of the General Staff in the German Army. Radu Lecca, the General Commissar for Jewish Questions, handled concentration and deportation matters. Economic measures, including the "Roumanianization" of the labor force, transfer of enterprises, and expropriation of real property, were regulated by the Undersecretary for "Roumanianization" in the Labor Ministry.

724. Report by Kausch, June 26, 1943, Occ E 4-11.

and his position was a powerful one. Richter was Lecca's opposite number.

Not very much happened during the first few months of 1941. Only one important law was enacted: the decree of March 27, 1941, for the state's expropriation of Jewish real estate. The Jews were to be paid for their houses in negotiable bonds. Like the agricultural property, the real estate was entrusted to the Roumanianization Office. In its provisions on applicability the decree retained the basic design of the Gigurtu legislation. The definition was a little wider, the privileged category a little narrower, but the approach was the same.[725]

The position of Jewish business at this time remained virtually unchanged. Censored private correspondence in Vienna revealed that Jewish enterprises frequently could be bought only for dollars, pounds, or Swiss francs. Moreover, the Roumanians had trouble in managing their newly acquired enterprises.[726]

The slow pace of the Roumanian machine of destruction was changed suddenly into rapid action in June, 1941. It is significant that the events of the second half of 1941 and the first half of 1942 took place under a militaristic regime that only a few months before had rid itself of those elements (the Iron Guard) which – like the Slovak Hlinka Guard, the Croatian Ustasha, and the German SS – were the principal proponents and prime movers of anti-Jewish activity. Apparently the presence of uniformed ideologists is not necessary for the accomplishment of very drastic action. The mainsprings of such action do not lie in the mere agitation of party formations. The impetus comes from deeper wells in the national character.

The immediate precipitatory event for the new holocaust was the war against Russia. On the eve of the outbreak of war the Interior Ministry ordered the removal of Jews from the frontier areas as a "precautionary" measure against "sabotage and espionage." That is to say, Jews were to be transported in a *westerly* direction within Old Roumania, from frontier districts to the interior of the country. In that highly charged atmosphere, on the night of June 25, 1941 (three days after the outbreak of war), a rumor circulated through Iaşi that Soviet parachutists had landed near the city. The army ordered an immediate search of Jewish homes.

At this point some deserters who were hiding in Iaşi, and who believed that the search was designed to effect their arrest, fired on the troops. The report then spread that the Jews were firing upon the soldiers, and a massacre ensued.[727] The Iaşi pogrom, carried out by Roumanian soldiers, dwarfed the Bucharest outburst of the Iron Guard. At least 4000 Jews died in Iaşi.[728] At the end of June several freight trains, carrying thousands of Jews, were dispatched from the frontier zones to the interior. The cattle cars were padlocked, and the trains moved for days around the countryside. There are said to be mass graves containing the bodies of thousands of Jews who died on those trains of suffocation and starvation, and who were dropped by the

725. *Die Judenfrage*, April 25, 1941, pp. 57–58.

726. Reports by *Auslandsbriefprüfstelle* Vienna, April 1, 1941, April 30, 1941, Wi/IC 4.2-b.

727. Levai, *Black Book on the Martyrdom of Hungarian Jewry*, p. 68. While the bulk of that book is devoted to Hungary, pages 58–73 deal with Roumania.

728. Von Killinger to Foreign Office, September 1, 1941, NG-4962. Some Jewish estimates run as high as 8000 dead. See Carp, *Cartea Neagra*, Vol. II A. The entire volume (complete with photographs) is devoted to the pogrom. See also the account of the Italian eyewitness Curzio Malaparte, *Kaputt* New York, 1946), pp. 122–24, 126–29, 137–43, 165–74.

wayside.[729] But these occurrences in Old Roumania were mere foreshadowing of things to come.

As we have already seen, northern Bukovina and Bessarabia were territory of *Einsatzgruppe D,* which, together with Roumanian Army units, conducted mobile killing operations in such cities and towns as Cernauti, Balti, Chisinau, and others.[730] The *Einsatzgruppe* was also responsible for the establishment of ghettos and the introduction of marking – measures that had not been taken in Old Roumania. The first major ghetto was set up at Chisinau on August 4, 1941;[731] another ghetto was formed three days later at Tighina.[732] At that very time, in the first week of August, something happened that caught even the Germans by surprise.

A glance at a map will indicate that there are three rivers flowing parallel in the area of these operations: from west to east, the Prut, the Dniester, and the Bug. West of the Prut was Old Roumania. Between the Prut and the Dniester lay the Bessarabian province. Between the Dniester and the Bug was a territory which had always belonged to Russia and which later became Roumanian-occupied Transnistria. East of the Bug lay an area which was later constituted into the *Generalkommissariat* Nikolaev of the *Reichskommissariat* Ukraine.

During the first week of August the Roumanians, acting upon local initiative, prepared to shove Bessarabian Jews across the Dniester into what was then still a German military area and a German sphere of interest (*deutsches Interessengebiet*). The object of these movements was clarified immediately: the Roumanians wanted to utilize the services of *Einsatzgruppe D* in the killing of these Jews.

As soon as the Eleventh Army observed the concentration of Jews on the west bank of the Dniester, an order was given to block traffic across the river.[733] But the Roumanians already had driven thousands of Jews into the military area. At Mogilev-Podolsk, *Sonderkommando* 10*b* of *Einsatzgruppe D* collected 12,000–15,000 Jews and prepared to drive them back into Bessarabia. However, on the other side of the bridge, Roumanian soldiers blocked the way, and a Roumanian colonel declared that if the Jews were driven on the bridge, he would open fire. The Germans thereupon detoured the column and moved it across on another bridge.[734] But the stream of Jews continued like a flood through a broken dike. Again and again the *Einsatzkommando* turned back Jews, and again and again more Jews came across. In the process of shoving back and forth, thousands of Jews died on the roadsides from exhaustion and bullet wounds.[735] Already, the Germans suspected the Roumanians of planning to play this game until the Jews remained lying in the ditches. Actually, the Roumanians had even bigger plans.

On August 5, 1941, the police chief of Bucharest, General Palangeanu, ordered all Jews of military age to report for work.[736] A few days later a report reached Berlin that Marshal An-

729. Levai, *Martyrdom,* pp. 68–69. Carp, *Cartea Neagra,* Vol. II A (particularly photographs). Malaparte, *Kaputt,* pp. 165–74.

730. See pp. 191, 194, 199–200.

731. Ohlendorf to 11th Army Ic/AO, August 4, 1941, enclosing report by Stubaf. Zapp (Skdo. 11*a*) to Ohlendorf, dated August 4, 1941, NOKW-3233.

732. RSHA IV-A-1, Operational Report USSR No. 45 (47 copies), August 7, 1941, NO-2948.

733. Order by Wöhler (chief of staff, 11th Army), August 3, 1941, NOKW-2302.

734. Affidavit by Felix Rühl (staff officer, *Sonderkommando* 10*b*), May 26, 1947, NO-4149.

735. RSHA IV-A-1, Operational Report USSR No. 64 (48 copies), August 26, 1941, NO-2840. RSHA IV-A-1, Operational Report USSR No. 67 (48 copies), August 29, 1941, NO-2837.

tonescu had directed that 60,000 Jews be transported from Old Roumania to Bessarabia for "road construction."[737] The Germans were now truly alarmed. They began to see a specter of more than a half-million Jews driven across the Dniester into the rear of the thinly stretched *Einsatzgruppe D*, which was already overburdened with the staggering task of killing the southern Ukrainian Jews. The six hundred men of the *Einsatzgruppe* would be swamped with Jews, front and rear.

The Germans moved quickly. Less than a week after the labor mobilization order the German Legation advised Deputy Premier Mihai Antonescu "to proceed with the elimination of the Jewish element only in a systematic and slow manner." The younger Antonescu replied that he had already recommended a revocation of the order, since the marshal had obviously "overestimated" the number of Jews capable of work, anyhow. The police prefects had accordingly been told to stop the measure.[738]

Shortly after this intervention the chief of the German army mission in Roumania, Generalmajor Hauffe, took steps to prevent the movement of Jews into the area of *Einsatzgruppe D*. To give the *Einsatzgruppe* a breathing spell, he fixed a line beyond which the Jews were not to be moved for the duration of the war against Russia. (The end was expected shortly.) Since the area between the Dniester and the Bug (Transnistria) was to be transferred to Roumanian control and since the *Einsatzgruppe* was already crossing the Bug, Hauffe abandoned the Dniester and held on to the Bug. On August 30, 1941, Hauffe and the Roumanian Army chief of staff, General Tataranu, signed an agreement in the town hall of the Bessarabian town of Tighina. The agreement provided that no Jews were to be driven across the Bug "at present." To make sure that the Jews would remain in Transnistria until "the end of operations," Hauffe also specified that the Jews would have to be placed in concentration camps.[739]

Marshal Antonescu did not wait for the end of operations; he had to have his Jews killed now. Since the Germans could not do the job for him, he did it himself. On October 17, 1941, the following note was written by an official in the legation (probably Hauptsturmführer Richter):

> According to information received today from Generaldirektor Lecca, 110,000 Jews are being evacuated from the Bukovina and Bessarabia into two forests in the Bug river area. So far as he could learn, this *Aktion* is based upon an order issued by Marshal Antonescu. Purpose of the action is the liquidation of these Jews [*Sinn der Aktion sei die Liquidierung dieser Juden*].[740]

A vast movement now started across the Dniester. Unlike the August expulsions, which were based on local initiative and which claimed as victims primarily those who were unable to buy themselves free, the fall deportations took on an organized character. There was now a quota which had to be met, and while there appears to have been no rule for the inclusion of

736. *Krakauer Zeitung*, August 5, 1941, p. 2. *Donauzeitung* (Belgrade), August 6, 1941, p. 4; August 7, 1941, p. 3.

737. Rademacher to Reichsbahnoberinspektor Hoppe and Ministerialdirektor Wohlthat (Four-Year Plan), August 12, 1941, NG-3104.

738. *Ibid.* Incidentally, the Roumanian government just then was negotiating with the Jewish community organization for a 2.5 billion-lei loan. Report by German military intelligence agent, Code Ru No. 62, Wi/IC 4.2-a, pp. 211–16.

739. Bräutigam (deputy chief, Political Division, East Ministry) to Foreign Office, March, 1942, enclosing Hauffe-Tataranu agreement signed at Tighina (Bessarabia) on August 30, 1941, PS-3319.

740. File memorandum by a HStuf. (probably Richter), October 17, 1941, PS-3319.

certain Jews and the exclusion of others, the total number of exemptions was limited by the need to seize 110,000 victims.[741]

Exemptions in Bukovina were granted particularly to those Jews who, by reason of their industrial or commercial activity, were essential to the economy. It is not unlikely that bribery played an important role in the determination of indispensability. The number of Jews who gained dispensation in Bukovina was probably in the tens of thousands; the ghetto of Cernauti itself had 16,000 inmates in the summer of 1942.[742]

In the purely agrarian province of Bessarabia only a baptismal certificate offered any salvation. Since the Roumanians in that province appear to have had no other definition than religious adherence, the converted Jews had a chance of exemption. It is therefore understandable that baptism became a widespread practice during those months even in so orthodox a community as Bessarabian Jewry. According to the *Donauzeitung*, not fewer than 40,000 Jews (one in every five) accepted conversion to escape deportation. Although this figure stands unverified, no other categories of Jews are mentioned among the tens of thousands who remained in the ghetto of Chisinau.[743] All the others, said Bessarabia Governor Voiculescu, were "exterminated" (*ausgemerzt*).[744]

The Transnistria influx – including the early arrivals, the fall deportees, and those who followed in 1942 – reached a total volume of 185,000.[745] All but 10,000 of these victims – who were deported, in the rush of things, from the Old Roumanian region of Dorohoi – came from northern Bukovina and Bessarabia. This means that the great bulk of the Jews of these two provinces were sent to Transnistria. To the best of our calculations, only about 75,000 could have remained behind.[746]

As the masses of Jews from the eastern provinces were driven across the Dniester, echoes of the deportations were picked up in Bucharest. Jewish pamphlets circulated during the Odessa victory parade in the capital charged that "our girls from Bessarabia are hauled to houses of prostitution on the eastern front."[747] The German military attaché in Bucharest reported that one of his agents, who had mingled with countless uniformed Roumanians on furlough from the front, had discovered that every one of these Roumanian officers was loaded down with rings, furs, silk, and other valuables taken from thousands of Jewish deportees.[748]

When the Transnistria deportations

741. According to a memorandum prepared by the Subsecretariat for State Police in the Interior Ministry, the statistics of the fall deportations were as follows:

Bessarabia	55,867
Bukovina	43,793
Dorohoi region	10,368
Total	110,028

Roumanian text in Carp, *Cartea Neagra,* III, 447–51. The Dorohoi region, which was in Old Roumania, was included by "mistake."

742. *Donauzeitung* (Belgrade), July 3, 1943, p. 3; August 8, 1942, p. 3.

743. *Ibid.*, June 9, 1942, p. 3; August 1, 1942, p. 3; August 8, 1942, p. 3.

744. *Ibid.*, November 13, 1941, p. 3.

745. *Ibid.*, August 8, 1942, p. 3.

746. It is assumed that the original population of the ceded provinces was 300,000. Allowance must be made for roughly 50,000 Jews removed by Soviet authorities before the invasion or shot by mobile killing units during the campaign. Of the remaining 250,000 Jews, 175,000 were deported. This leaves approximately 75,000.

747. German translation of the pamphlet in enclosure to letter by a German businessman, December, 1941, Wi/IC 4.66, pp. 278–85. The fate of these girls is confirmed by the Italian war correspondent Curzio Malaparte. See his *Kaputt,* pp. 288–300.

748. German Embassy in Bucharest/Military Attaché (signed Spalcke) to OKH/Attaché Division, December 2, 1941, Wi/IC 4.66, pp. 255–56.

neared their climax in October, 1941, the president of the Jewish community, Fildermann, addressed a petition to Marshal Antonescu. Fildermann was an experienced petitioner; only a few years before he had protested in the League of Nations against Roumania's violations of the minority treaty, and now he was petitioning for the lives of hundreds of thousands. His letter is not available, but we have some excerpts from a document which is perhaps even more significant: Antonescu's reply.

"You speak of tragedy," said the marshal, "and appeal for the Jews. I understand your pain, but you should have understood, in time, the pain of the entire Roumanian nation." The Roumanians, said Antonescu, had paid with their blood for the hatred of Fildermann's Jews. In Odessa the Jews had "goaded" the Soviet troops into unnecessarily prolonged resistance, "merely in order to inflict casualities upon us." In the Bukovina and Bessarabia the Jews had received the Red Army with flowers, and during the "Communist terror" they had denounced Roumanians, thus causing sorrow in many Roumanian families. But when the Roumanian Army returned, it was not received with flowers. "Why," asked Antonescu, "did the Jews set their houses on fire before abandoning them? Why have we found Jewish children of fourteen and fifteen who had hand grenades in their pockets?" Tirelessly, the marshal recited atrocity after atrocity. Then he concluded with the words, "Have mercy, rather, for the mothers who have lost their sons, and do not pity those who have done this evil."[749]

Marshal Antonescu did not enjoy that sure-footedness of action which characterized Hitler. The German Führer did not have to answer petitions, for none were addressed to him. The German Jews did not "protest." Fildermann petitioned, and he received a reply. In that reply Marshal Antonescu had found it necessary to give reasons for his actions and had even concluded with a rhetorical appeal for Fildermann's approval. Still, Marshal Antonescu was the only man besides Hitler who placed upon himself the burden of an order to commence a full-fledged killing operation. Two years later, as we shall see, that order frightened him.

Transnistria was a Jewish disaster. The 185,000 victims who were deported to that territory were concentrated in camps. So far as we can determine, the camps were under the command of army officers (captains or majors),[750] who were in turn responsible to the local prefects (army colonels).[751] Although the prefects reported to the governor of Transnistria, Professor Alexianu, we must conclude from the actual occurrences in the camps that the spirit in which the Antonescu order was carried out was left to the discretion of the prefects and, perhaps, the individual camp commanders.

All camps seemed to have had one characteristic in common: there was no regular food distribution. To obtain food, the Jews had to sell everything they had. According to survivors' accounts collected by the writer Eugene Levai, the inmates of the Pecsara camp had sold all their clothes and were running around naked. "Parentless children were roaming about the district in a state of semi-starvation."[752] In several camps the Jews were eating grass. "Potato peelings were a veritable delicacy." In the Vertujen camp the

749. *Donauzeitung* (Belgrade), October 28, 1941, p. 3.

750. Matatias Carp lists the commanders of the Vapniarka camp (in succession): Major I. Murgescu, Captain Sever Baradescu, Captain Christodor Popescu. See his *Cartea Neagra*, III, 21.

751. Carp, *Cartea Neagra,* III, 17–21.

752. Levai, *Martyrdom*, p. 68.

arriving Jews were told: "You have come in on two feet, and if you do not end your lives here, you will be allowed to leave on four feet only." In that camp the Jews were fed on a diet of cattle food that apparently resulted in paralysis. Levai writes that when the trial of war criminals opened in Bucharest after the war, a number of witnesses, including the Jewish ballerina Rebecca Marcus, "were indeed able to walk on all fours only."[753]

In the Golta prefecture Colonel Modest Isopescu ran three camps (Bogdanovka, Dumanovka, and Akmecetka) on the same starvation principle. The most deadly of these camps – which turned out to be Roumania's greatest killing center – was Bogdanovka. In Bogdanovka a camp bakery sold fresh bread for gold at the rate of one loaf for five gold rubles. When the gold gave out, Colonel Isopescu ordered the commencement of mass shootings. Between December 21 and 23, 1941, Jews were driven into four stables, where the killings took place. When the stables were filled with corpses, they were set on fire.

The Jews who could not be accommodated in the stables were marched in groups of between eighty and one hundred persons to a precipice overhanging the Bug river, about two miles from Bogdanovka. "There, they were stripped of all their belongings and their ring-fingers were chopped off, if the rings could not easily be removed. Even their gold teeth were forcibly extracted. After that, standing stark naked in a temperature of 40 degrees below zero, they were shot. The corpses fell over the precipice into the river." These shootings continued for several days, until December 30. At the end of the operation 48,000 Jews had been massacred.

About 200 selected survivors were detailed to burn the bodies that remained on top of the precipice. For two months corpses were burned at the Bug River, and at the end of that operation 150 of the 200 survivors were shot.[754] According to Levai, Colonel Isopescu extended his killing operations to two other camps in his prefecture: Dumanovka, where 18,000 Jews were shot, and Akmecetka, where 5000 were killed.[755] It appears, therefore, that in the Golta prefecture alone more than 70,000 Jews were massacred in mass shootings.

In the meantime, the starvation policy created acute problems in other prefectures as well. Levai quotes a Roumanian newspaper (the *Frontal Plugarilov,* June 15, 1945) to the effect that 23,000 Jews died in the Vertujen camp.[756] The Germans were beginning to worry about vast epidemics, and even to the Roumanians the situation appeared untenable. The prefects now had a choice: they could follow Isopescu's lead and shoot their Jews, or they could retreat and make life livable for the camp inmates. So far as we know, there was no disposition to repeat the Golta experiment in other prefectures, but the time for retreat had not yet come, either. Under the circumstances a compromise "solution" emerged: the Jews were to be squeezed out of Transnistria. There was only one direction in which they could be squeezed; that was the eastern route, across the Bug River into the *Reichskommissariat* Ukraine.

The Germans, however, were not prepared to receive the Transnistria Jews; the German bureaucrats did not want epidemic-ridden masses of people in the Ukraine. As Roumanian restlessness increased on the west bank of the Bug, the Germans remembered the

753. *Ibid.*, pp. 67–68, 73.

754. *Ibid.*, pp. 72–73.

755. *Ibid.*, p. 73. Levai took the statistics from the indictment against Isopescu and others before the Roumanian People's Court.

756. *Ibid.*

agreement which Generals Hauffe and Tataranu had concluded at Tighina on August 30, 1941. The relevant provision of that accord read as follows:

> Deportation of Jews across the Bug is not possible at present. They must therefore be collected in concentration camps and set to work, until a deportation to the east is possible after the end of operations.[757]

To the Germans, this provision was clear, simple, and categorical: there were to be no Bug deportations until after the end of military operations in Russia. But the Roumanians evidently were not disturbed by that stipulation. Conceivably, they read the treaty as a temporary arrangement made obsolete by the prolongation of the war. Conceivably, they did not read the agreement at all. In any case, the dispute was not headed for an arbitral tribunal; it was to be settled, in the Axis manner, by the shoving method.

At the beginning of February, 1942, the Ministry for Eastern Occupied Territories informed the German Foreign Office that the Roumanians had suddenly deported 10,000 Jews across the Bug in the Vosnesensk area and that another 60,000 were expected to follow. The ministry asked the Foreign Office to urge the Roumanian government to refrain from these deportations because of the danger of typhus epidemics.[758] As the situation grew tense, three experts in Berlin put their heads together and drew out the Tighina agreement. They were Amtsgerichtsrat Wetzel of the East Ministry, Legationsrat Rademacher of the Foreign Office, and Obersturmbannführer Eichmann of the RSHA.[759] Eichmann was ambivalent in his attitude toward the Roumanians; he could not bring himself to condemn them for calling upon the Germans to kill some Jews, but he felt that they were doing it in a disorderly manner. The Roumanian deportations, he wrote to the Foreign Office, "are approved as a matter of principle," but they were undesirable at the present time because of their "planless and premature" character.[760]

In Bucharest, Vice Premier Mihai Antonescu called in Governor Alexianu to report on the matter.[761] By that time the crisis was beginning to pass. The *Generalkommissar* in Nikolaev reported that the movement of Jews across the border had stopped. Those who were already across were shipped back to the Transnistrian port of Odessa.[762] As the flow of Jews across the Bug was stemmed, the Foreign Office received a report that the receding masses of Jews were being subjected to renewed killing operations. "About 28,000 Jews were taken to German villages in Transnistria," wrote a Foreign Office official. "Meanwhile, they have been liquidated."[763] Whatever the mysterious reference to the ethnic German villages may mean, these shootings were not the beginning of a new operation; they were the end phase of the old. From now on the Roumanians were retreating.

By May, 1942, about two-thirds of the Transnistria Jews were dead. We do not know, and may never know, the exact number – it was certainly more than a hundred thousand. The remaining third of the deportees were put on ice; their fate was decided no longer by officials in Transnistria but by events in Old Roumania.

757. Bräutigam to Foreign Office, March, 1942, enclosing Tighina agreement, PS-3319.

758. Luther via Weizsäcker to Ribbentrop, February 11, 1942, NG-4817.

759. Bräutigam to Foreign Office, March, 1942, PS-3319.

760. Eichmann to Foreign Office, April 14, 1942, NG-4817.

761. Rademacher to East Ministry and Eichmann, May 12, 1942, NG-4817.

762. Bräutigam to Foreign Office, May 19, 1942, NG-4817.

763. Note by Triska, May 16, 1942, NG-4817.

In Old Roumania, in the meantime, the climax of events had not yet arrived. Developments in the Old Roumanian areas lagged behind the swift deportation-killing operations in the eastern provinces. At the time when the first Bessarabian Jews were being driven across the Dniester, the destruction process in Old Roumania had proceeded no further than the partial "Roumanianization" of employees, the confiscation of agricultural and real estate properties, the prohibition of intermarriage, and the revocation of name changes. For a brief moment it seemed that Marshal Antonescu would skip a few steps and crowd the Old Roumanian Jews, with those of the eastern provinces, across the Dniester; but, as we have seen, the German Legation intervened, and the plan was canceled. The Germans now put pressure on the Roumanian government to make a more methodical approach to the "solution of the Jewish question." Accordingly, during the fall of 1941 and the following winter, the Roumanian authorities attempted to tighten their preliminary measures against the Jewish community. The tightening process was carried out, first of all, in the economic sector.

As usual, the expropriations were conducted in two forms, the confiscation of property and the conscription of labor. In the fall a clothing drive was launched. It yielded 1,583,000 items, mainly for use by the freezing Roumanian Army in the East.[764] At the same time the confiscation of Jewish community property was instituted,[765] and simultaneously, a forced loan of 2 billion lei was imposed on the Jews.[766] (Two billion lei were the equivalent of 33,400,000 reichsmark, or less than 14,000,000 dollars.) That was not an extraordinary sum. However, the Roumanian Jews had to remain in business.

Jewish manufacturers and distributors were filling an essential position in the Roumanian economy, which was working full-blast for the German war machine. A German businessman in Roumania, himself the owner of a lumber plant with 3000 workers, complained bitterly that the Jews were largely responsible for an inflation which had tripled prices within a period of two years. The German military procurement agencies were bearing the brunt of that inflation, while the Roumanian government was complacently profiting from it to the extent of a 2.5 to 3 billion lei increase in the sales tax intake – enough to finance the entire Roumanian war effort.[767] The Germans made an attempt to expel the Jews from the Roumanian economy by means of trade agreements, but the attempt remained largely unsuccessful.[768] There were as yet no sufficient resources, either in capital or in know-how, for a complete replacement of the Jews.

Jewish indispensability was evident in the nature of the forced labor system, for there was a direct relationship between the mobilization of forced labor and the extent to which the Jews were permitted to continue in their old jobs, businesses, or professional activities. Labor service was not made compulsory for essential workers and capitalist Jews. At the end of 1941 more than half the Jewish employees were still essential.[769] The moneyed Jews were privileged until their money gave out, for they *bought* their exemp-

764. *Donauzeitung* (Belgrade), October 24, 1941, p. 4; July 18, 1942, p. 3.

765. *Ibid.*, November 27, 1941, p. 4.

766. *Ibid.*, July 18, 1942, p. 3.

767. Letter by a German businessman (signature cut out with scissors from original document), December, 1941, Wi/IC 4.66, pp. 278–85. Sales tax receipts appear to have been counted monthly.

768. See the memorandum by the *Wehrwirtschaftsoffizier Rümanien/Abteilung Rohstoff*, on the Fabrica de Cauciuc in Braşov, March 16, 1943, Wi/IC 4.51, Anlage 17.

tion by making payment to the state — a somewhat novel and characteristically Roumanian regulation.[770] Only the poor Jews, who had no jobs and no money, were forced into the labor service. They were employed in various projects, such as road-building (by the Transport Ministry), the construction of workers' homes (Labor Ministry), and snow-shoveling.[771] There is no indication of the financial profit from the labor service, and it is not impossible that the state profited more from the collection of exemption payments than from the actual labor performed.

We can see now that the Roumanians never completed the expropriation stage. They made even less progress in the field of concentration. Only one important ghettoization measure was taken in Old Roumania: the creation of a *Judenzentrale*, a sort of *Reichsvereinigung*. In December, 1941, the troublesome president of the federation of Jewish community organizations, Fildermann, was removed from his post, and his federation was dissolved. In its stead, a *Judenzentrale* was organized and placed under the direction of a puppet, Dr. Gingold (or possibly Ghingold), a man who took orders without protest or petition from the Roumanian Commissar for Jewish Affairs, Radu Lecca.[772] Significantly, the jurisdiction of the new *Zentrale* was not confined to full Jews and Jews by religion. All persons who had at least one Jewish grandparent were forced to register with the *Zentrale* by February 20, 1942.[773] The Nuremberg principle had thus broken through, but only partially, for it was not applied to the earlier expropriation measures.

The concentration process did not progress beyond the reorganization of Jewish machinery and the registration of the prospective deportation candidates. The elaborate system of movement restrictions and marking which we have seen in the Reich was never introduced in Old Roumania, although there was a regulation which required *all* inhabitants to obtain a police permit for travel on the state railways. In September, 1942, after the deportation crisis had already passed, Jewish travelers were not given a permit unless they paid 1000 lei (16.7 reichsmark — 6 dollars) per travel day.[774] That was of course not so much a concentration decree as a revenue measure, a diversion of bribe money to the state.

In spite of these rather incomplete preparatory measures, the Germans began to exert pressure upon Roumania for the deportation of its Jews to Poland. The Germans could not afford to wait indefinitely; they had to take advantage of the Roumanian government's readiness to take the most drastic measures against the Jews. In a destruction process, as in a military operation, it is sometimes necessary to seize a favorable moment to attack, even though the buildup phase may still be incomplete.

Accordingly, in November, 1941, when Roumanian operations in Transnistria were at their height, the German Legation in Bucharest requested the Roumanian government to express its

769. The statistics were as follows:

November 16, 1940 (Start of "Roumanianization"), 28,225
December 31, 1941, 16,972
December 31, 1942, 6,506

Figure for 1941 from *Donauzeitung* (Belgrade), June 4, 1942, p. 3. Figures for 1940 and 1942 from Cl. Usatiu-Udrea, "Der Abwehrkampf des rumänischen Volkes gegen das Judentum," *Volk im Osten* (Bucharest), May–June, 1943, p. 38.

770. *Donauzeitung* (Belgrade), March 11, 1942. *Die Judenfrage*, March 15, 1942.

771. *Ibid.*

772. *Donauzeitung* (Belgrade), December 30, 1941, p. 3; February 3, 1942, p. 3; August 8, 1942, p. 3. *Die Judenfrage*, March 15, 1942.

773. *Donauzeitung* (Belgrade), February 15, 1942, p. 3.

774. *Ibid.*, September 15, 1942, p. 3.

disinterest in the fate of the Roumanian Jews in the Reich. Although the number of Jews involved was far from negligible,[775] the Roumanians gave their consent immediately and without reservation.[776] The Germans assumed that the Roumanian approval automatically covered the Roumanian Jews who were living outside the Reich itself, in the Protektorat and other German-occupied territories.[777] However, this assumption proved to be incorrect, and as a result, interventions and protests were launched by various Roumanian consulates and the Roumanian Legation in Berlin.

In fact, the deportations of Roumanian nationals from the Reich and the occupied territories had reached a snag. On July 18, 1942, the First Secretary of the Roumanian Legation in Berlin, Valeanu, pointed out that the Hungarian Jews were not affected by the deportations and that — as a matter of prestige — Roumania could not very well consent to worse treatment of its Jews. Furthermore, Valeanu claimed, Roumania had no agreement with the Reich; hence the legation was powerless to give permission for the removal of these people. Taken aback, the German expert Klingenfuss of *Abteilung Deutschland* replied that the Jewish problem required a "European solution," and if the Roumanian Legation lacked directives, it could inform its government of the issues involved.[778] Finally, on August 17, 1942, Luther reported that the question had been ironed out in discussions with the Secretary General of the Roumanian Foreign Office, Davidescu. The Jews in controversy could now be deported.[779]

The Germans could not immediately follow up their initial success of November, 1941 (when they secured for the first time an agreement for the deportation of Roumanian Jews in the Reich), by pressing for the deportation of all Jews from Roumania. In November, 1941, there were as yet no killing centers. Installations for mass killings were not set up in Polish camps until 1942, and these installations were for the most part not in operation until the spring of 1942. Thus there was an unavoidable delay of some months at a time when the Roumanians were most amenable to German pressure. During this interval a few Jews tried to make a getaway.

On December 16, 1941, a broken-down vessel, the "SS Struma" of Panamanian registry, arrived at Istanbul, Turkey, with 769 Roumanian Jews aboard. The ship could not go any farther. It was totally unseaworthy. The passengers, however, could not be debarked, for they had entry permits neither to Turkey nor to Palestine. On February 24, 1942, the Turkish government ordered the ship to move out; when it did not proceed, a tug towed the vessel out of the harbor and cut it loose five miles from shore. A few minutes later, the "SS Struma" broke apart. One man and one woman swam to shore, 767 drowned.[780] There were no exit restrictions in Roumania; yet the Roumanian Jews were as securely trapped as were the Jews in the Reich.[781]

775. More than 1000 were counted in the Reich census of 1939.

776. Von Killinger to Foreign Office, November 13, 1941, NG-3990.

777. The number of Jews in the occupied territories was quite large; 3000 Roumanian Jews were counted in France alone. Staf. Knochen to RSHA IV-B-4, September 25, 1942, NG-1971.

778. Memorandum by Klingenfuss, July 21, 1942, on conversation with Valeanu held on July 18, NG-2355.

779. Luther via Wörmann and Weizsäcker to Ribbentrop, August 17, 1942, NG-3558. Klingenfuss to Eichmann, August 20, 1942, NG-2198.

780. Ira A. Hirschmann, *Lifeline to a Promised Land* (New York, 1946), pp. 3–8.

781. When the Turkish Minister in Bucharest suggested to the American Minister there

On July 26, 1942, the Eichmann *Referat* of the RSHA reported that its representative in Bucharest, Hauptsturmführer Richter, had scored a complete breakthrough. "Political and technical preparations for a solution of the Jewish question in Roumania," reported Eichmann, "have been completed by the representative of the Reich Security Main Office to such an extent that the evacuation transports will be able to roll in a short time. It is planned to remove the Jews of Roumania in a series of transports beginning approximately September 10, 1942, to the district of Lublin, where the employable segment will be allocated for labor utilization, while the remainder will be subjected to special treatment."

Provision had been made to insure that the Roumanian Jews would lose their nationality upon crossing the border. Negotiations with the *Reichsbahn* with respect to train schedules were already far advanced, and Hauptsturmführer Richter was in possession of a personal letter from Mihai Antonescu that confirmed all arrangements. Accordingly, Eichmann now requested permission "to carry out the shoving-out work in the planned manner [*Ich bitte um Genehmigung, die Abschiebungsarbeiten in der vorgetragenen Form durchführen zu können*]."[782]

Luther wrote to the chief of the Gestapo, Gruppenführer Müller, that "in principle" the Foreign Office had "no objection" (*keine Bedenken*) to the deportation of the Roumanian Jews to the "East." However, Luther felt that there were still some doubts about the circle of deportable people and the "attitude of the Roumanian government" to the whole question. Pending the clarification of these matters, he requested the RSHA to undertake no action.[783] At the same time Luther requested the legation in Bucharest to "clarify, fundamentally, the question of the transportation of the Jews from Roumania." Furthermore, he wanted to know whether a much-postponed visit to Berlin by the Roumanian commissar for Jewish affairs, Radu Lecca, would now take place.[784]

On August 17, 1942, Luther informed Wörmann, Weizsäcker, and Ribbentrop that Mihai Antonescu and Marshal Antonescu had now given their consent to the deportation of the Jews and had agreed that transports would begin to move out from the districts of Arad, Timisoara, and Turda. Roumanian "*Ministerialdirektor*" Lecca wished to come to Berlin to discuss the details with the Foreign Office and the RSHA.[785] A few days later Luther wrote to the legation in Bucharest that Lecca was definitely coming to the German capital.[786]

Lecca visited Berlin sometime during the week of August 20–27. It seems that in *Abteilung Deutschland* his visit was regarded as a mere formality. The two Antonescus had, after all, already voiced their agreement, and Lecca was not considered an important Roumanian personage. In Berlin, Lecca therefore received the brushoff treatment. That was a mistake. When he returned to Roumania on or about August 27,

---

that some 300,000 Roumanian Jews be transported via Turkey to Palestine, the European Division of the U.S. Department of State reacted with considerable antipathy to the idea. See memorandum by Cavendish W. Cannon of the division, November 12, 1941. *Foreign Relations, 1941,* II, 875–76.

782. Rintelen to Luther, August 19, 1942, enclosing Eichmann report of July 26, 1942, NG-3985.

783. Luther to Müller, August 11, 1942, NG-2354.

784. Luther to legation in Bucharest, August 11, 1942, NG-2354.

785. Luther via Wörmann and Weizsäcker to Ribbentrop, August 17, 1942, NG-3558.

786. Luther and Klingenfuss to legation in Bucharest, probably August 20, 1942, NG-2198.

the German diplomats were already aware that things had gone wrong. The Foreign Office promptly dispatched a letter to the legation in Bucharest, blaming Minister von Killinger for his failure to properly conduct the preliminary negotiations and accusing him of leaving this important matter to Hauptsturmführer Richter. We do not have the text of the Foreign Office letter, but we may infer its contents from the reply sent by von Killinger to Berlin on August 28.[787]

He could not understand, von Killinger wrote, how the Foreign Office could assume that he left it exclusively to an SS leader to settle such important questions. Referring to the letter Mihai Antonescu had handed to Richter, von Killinger noted: "Herr Mihai Antonescu may write letters to whomever he wants; that does not concern me in the slightest." It was a matter of course, he said, that his SS consultant should have done the "preliminary work" under his "orders." Then, coming to the most important point, he stated, "There can be no question of a conclusion of the negotiations." When Lecca had come back to Bucharest, he had complained of severe insults in Berlin. Luther had not received him, and during a conversation between Lecca and Rademacher, the latter had been called away, "purposely, as it seemed."

Under the circumstances, von Killinger had immediately handed a note to the Roumanian government, in which he had announced that preliminary negotiations had been concluded, and in which he had asked the Roumanian government for its opinion on all outstanding questions. Apparently, however, this note had not repaired the damage. "If such important personages as Ministerialdirektor Lecca come to Berlin," he wrote, "I ask that they should not be put off in such a way that the good relationship between Germany and Roumania could be affected." Von Killinger then added a few remarks about the "gentlemen of the SS" (*Herren der SS*) and particularly "Herr Eichmann," who, he said, had not found it necessary to contact the Foreign Office. "Besides," he continued, "I would like to remark that all matters which I report to *Abteilung Deutschland* get into the hands of the SD in the shortest possible time."

On September 7 von Killinger wrote a second letter in which he regretted that the Foreign Minister had not learned of his "counter-arguments" in the matter.[788] To this letter Foreign Office Personnel Chief Schröder added the notation: "Herr Von Killinger does not *want* to understand at the present moment."[789]

The German attempt had failed, and the Jews remained where they were.[790] The Roumanian reversal was not partial but complete. Could trivialities like Minister von Killinger's relations with the *Herren der SS* (von Killinger was an SA man) and the subsequent snobbish reception of a Roumanian "*Ministerialdirektor*" have had an effect upon a decision to deliver more than 300,000 Jews to their deaths? The answer is that ordinarily trivialities do not matter, but even a slight incident can be decisive in a situation that is already in delicate balance. By August, 1942, the Roumanians were no longer at the peak of their enthusiasm;

787. Von Killinger to Foreign Office, August 28, 1942, NG-2195.

788. Von Killinger to Foreign Office, September 7, 1942, NG-2195.

789. Notation by Schröder, September 13, 1943, NG-2195.

790. The presence of Jews in Timisoara and Arad is indicated quite clearly in a letter by Landesgruppenleiter Ludwig Kohlhammer to party representatives in Timisoara, Arad, Sibiu, Brasov, Galati, Brăila, and Chernauti, on employment of Jews by German firms, dated August 5, 1943, PS-3319. The *Landesgruppenleiter* was the party's *Auslandsorganisation* chief in Roumania. His jurisdiction extended only to Reich citizens.

they had just about exhausted their exuberance and were in turn exhausted by it. The Roumanian receptivity to German demands for destructive action was at an end.

The Germans at first refused to accept the fact that the Roumanian reversal was final. That refusal to acknowledge defeat is evident in von Killinger's statement of August 28 that "there can be no question of a conclusion of the negotiations." As late as September 24, Luther made a short oral report to Ribbentrop "about the current evacuation of Jews from Slovakia, Croatia, Roumania, and the occupied territories [*über die im Gange befindliche Judenevakuierung aus der Slovakei, Kroatien, Rumänien und den besetzten Gebieten*]"[791] – an unparallelled piece of deception within the German diplomatic hierarchy.[792]

The finality of the Roumanian reversal was not immediately apparent because the frustration of the deportations was not accompanied by an immediate cancellation of all the preparatory measures that had been taken up to the summer of 1942. The Jewish community was still suffocating in the grip of the interrupted destruction process, and that grip was not relaxed. There was even a small deportation across the Dniester in September, 1942, when the Roumanians, searching the building of the former Soviet Legation in Bucharest, discovered lists of persons who for one reason or another had applied for permits to enter Bessarabia and Bukovina during the Soviet occupation of these provinces in 1940–41. On the basis of these lists 700 Jews were arrested in the capital and deported to Transnistria.[793]

791. Luther to Weizsäcker, copies to Wörmann, von Erdmannsdorff, Pol. I, Pol. IV, Legal and Trade-Political Divisions, D II and D III, September 24, 1942, NG-1517.

792. See also a discussion about Roumania in Budapest, between Wisliceny and a Hungarian official, October 6, 1942, pp. 522–23.

More serious even than this episodic deportation was the continued "Roumanianization" of the employee force;[794] the continued induction of forced labor;[795] the continued confiscations of real estate, agricultural properties,[796] and Jewish community buildings;[797] the new regulations making possible the termination of leases for apartments;[798] and the brand new imposition of a four-billion-lei property tax which had to be paid by about 40,000 Jews.[799] The tax amounted to about 67 million reichsmark, or about 27 million dollars. Coming, as it did in 1943, to an impoverished community, it was a sizable burden. The deposed Jewish leader, Fildermann, considered it advisable to make another protest in which he pointed out that the amount was too high. He was thereupon deported to Transnistria.[800]

Notwithstanding this continuation and even intensification of the expropriatory process, the Roumanian decision to stop short of a "final solution" became more rigid every month. The attitude of the Roumanians was perhaps not so evident in the pace of their public anti-Jewish measures, but the reversal was all the more obvious in the Roumanian government's unpublicized moves.

On December 12, 1942, von Killinger

793. *Donauzeitung* (Belgrade), September 13, 1942, p. 3.

794. *Ibid.*, October 9, 1942, p. 3; November 27, 1942, p. 3; January 8, 1943, p. 3; July 7, 1943, p. 3.

795. *Ibid.*, September 20, 1942, p. 3; October 13, 1943, p. 3; February 2, 1944, p. 3; March 12, 1944, p. 3.

796. *Ibid.*, January 28, 1943, p. 3; February 6, 1944, p. 3.

797. *Ibid.*, May 7, 1943, p. 3; September 14, 1943, p. 3.

798. *Ibid.*, May 7, 1943, p. 3.

799. *Die Judenfrage*, June 15, 1943, p. 205. *Donauzeitung* (Belgrade), June 27, 1943, p. 3; July 29, 1943, p. 3.

800. *Ibid.*, May 29, 1943, p. 3. *Die Judenfrage*, June 15, 1943, p. 205.

reported to the Foreign Office that Lecca had told him of a plan by Marshal Antonescu to allow 75,000 to 80,000 Jews to emigrate to Palestine, in return for a payment by the Jews to the Roumanian state of 200,000 lei (that is, RM 3340 or $1336) for each emigrant. Von Killinger added that, in his opinion, Antonescu wanted to collect 16 billion lei (RM 267,000,000 or $107,000,000) and at the same time get rid of a large number of Jews "in a comfortable manner." Tiredly, the German envoy concluded his message with the words: "I am in no position to judge from here as to whether it would be advisable to oppose this plan."[801] Unterstaatssekretär Luther and one of his experts, Geheimrat Klingenfuss, replied that the Foreign Office refused to believe in the seriousness of the project but that it had to be prevented, by all means. Then they outlined a series of arguments for von Killinger's use, namely, that the 80,000 Jews were enemies of the Axis, that the action would be construed as showing a lack of unity in the Axis, and so on.[802]

The feeling of alarm in *Abteilung Deutschland* was somewhat premature, for, although the Jews could now buy their way out, any possibility of mass emigration was frustrated by two major obstacles: the lack of shipping and the lack of a destination. Neither Axis nor Allied shipping was available for the transport of the Jews; only small, unseaworthy ships of neutral registry could be used, and passage even in such vessels was a difficult proposition because of their great cost and the German unwillingness to grant them safe conduct. But even if the vessels could be procured and their departure secured, they had no place to go. Entry restrictions into neutral countries, Allied states, and Palestine were very tight. The fate of the "SS Struma" was still a vivid memory.

Briefly, the Jews tried to overcome the shipping shortage by using the overland route across Bulgaria. They attempted to pry open the doors to Palestine by restricting the emigration to children, who could not be turned away so easily for lack of proper entry permits. To a very limited extent this solution worked. On March 11, 1943, Rademacher and Consul Pausch dispatched a communication to von Killinger in which they stated that 72 Jewish children had arrived in Athlit, Palestine, from Hungary, through Roumania, Bulgaria, and Turkey; that these were apparently a part of the 270 Jewish children from Hungary and Roumania mentioned in the British House of Commons as having arrived in Palestine; and that von Killinger was to do everything possible to prevent any further emigration or transhipment of Jews to Palestine.[803] A similar letter was sent by Rademacher to the German Consulate in Sofia.[804]

Apparently, however, the Foreign Office was not entirely successful, for on May 13, 1943, the exiled Grand Mufti of Jerusalem, Amin el Husseini, who had thrown in his lot with the Axis, wrote to the Foreign Office that 4000 Jewish children accompanied by 500 adults had recently reached Palestine, and for that reason he asked the German Foreign Minister "to do his utmost" (*das Äusserste zu tun*) to prevent further emigrations from Bulgaria, Roumania, and Hungary.[805] The Germans now did their utmost. When, two weeks later, von Killinger reported that a representative of the International

801. Von Killinger to Foreign Office, December 12, 1942, NG-3986.

802. Luther and Klingenfuss to von Killinger, January 3, 1943, NG-2200.

803. Rademacher and Pausch to von Killinger, March 11, 1943, NG-2184.

804. Rademacher to consulate in Sofia, March 12, 1943, NG-1782.

805. Amin el Husseini via Ambassador Prüfer to Ribbentrop, May 13, 1943, G-182.

Red Cross had approached Marshal Antonescu with a request to permit the emigration of the Jews in Red Cross ships,[806] the German Foreign Office applied the brakes by refusing safe conduct and proclaiming that Palestine was an Arab country.[807] There was much additional correspondence about Red Cross ships and about children, but nothing came of it.[808]

While the Foreign Office was fighting off Roumanian emigration schemes, the SS and Police hierarchy decided to pull up its stakes in Roumania. After a particularly pessimistic report by Gestapo Chief Müller in January, 1943, Himmler decided that the situation was hopeless. In Roumania, he wrote, nothing could be done anymore *(gar nichts zu machen).* He therefore suggested that the Jewish expert in Bucharest be withdrawn. Nothing, said Himmler, was going to happen there anyway, and if the expert remained, the only thing that could happen "is that we are going to be accused of something."[809] Himmler's estimation of the situation was correct. The erstwhile Roumanian collaborators were gradually turning away, and the years 1943 and 1944 revealed developments even more significant than Marshal Antonescu's willingness to sell the Old Roumanian Jews to the Allies. These developments began in Transnistria.

The Jews in Transnistria were still camp prisoners, but a slight improvement in their situation resulted from Marshal Antonescu's acceptance of a Jewish offer to send clothes, medicines, and money to the victims. The money had to be changed into the local Transnistria currency *(Reichskreditkassenscheine)* at a two-thirds loss, but the transmission of these funds was of as much importance to the Jews as to the Roumanian profiteers.[810]

Toward the end of 1943 the relaxation of the Transnistria camp regime gave way to its gradual dissolution. The immediate cause of that total reversal was the Red Army's massive crossing of the Dnieper River, the Soviet recapture of Kiev and Dnepropetrovsk, and the sweeping Russian advance toward the Bug. In Bucharest, Marshal Antonescu and some of his colleagues met to discuss the evacuation of Transnistria. Nervously, the marshal explored the possibilities of returning the imprisoned Jews to Old Roumania, for he was now afraid that the Germans, in their retreat across Transnistria, might kill these victims.

That fear is significant enough, but even more remarkable is the fact that the marshal could no longer recall why so many Jews had died in Transnistria. He was disturbed and ill at ease because he had so many dead Jews on his hands; however, he seems to have forgotten who was responsible for these deaths. His searching remarks appear to have been an attempt to find a culprit who had perpetrated this dirty trick upon him, but he did not discover that culprit in himself. Verbatim excerpts from this historic conference have survived. A copy was sent to the General Commissar for Jewish Questions, who immediately passed on the manuscript, with his comments, to the Germans. Besides Marshal Antonescu, the Undersecretary for Security in the Interior Ministry, General Vasiliu, and the Governor of Bukovina, General Dragalina, participated in the discussion. The conference opened with an estimation

806. Von Thadden via Political and Legal Divisions and Staassekretär Steengracht to Ribbentrop, June 1, 1943, NG-3987.

807. *Ibid.,* and correspondence in document NG-5049.

808. Correspondence in documents NG-5049, NG-4786, NG-5138, NG-1794, and NG-2236.

809. Himmler to Müller (copy to Wolff), January 20, 1943, Himmler Files, Folder No. 8. The files do not contain Müller's report, which was dated January 14.

810. Levai, *Martyrdom,* p. 67.

of the number of Transnistria survivors, a troublesome statistical problem with which the Roumanians were obviously unable to cope.[811]

Marshal Antonescu: I am now switching to the Jewish question. According to the latest statistics we have now in Transnistria a little over 50,000 Jews. [Notation by Lecca: "There are 80,000."]

General Vasiliu: Add to that 10,000 from Dorohoi, makes 60,000.

Antonescu: I think there are 70,000–80,000. But if there are only so many, that means they are dying off too fast.

Vasiliu: There was some mistake. We have talked with Colonel Radulescu, who has carried out a census. There are now exactly 61,000. [Notation by Lecca: "Inaccurate."]

Antonescu: These Jews of Transnistria are grouped in Vapniarka [a camp].

Vasiliu: From Vapniarka they were moved to Grosulovo, that lies near Tiraspol.

Antonescu: That means they are saved!

Vasiliu: In Vapniarka there are many Communists, 435 Jews from Târgu-Jiu.

Antonescu: Anyone who is a Communist Jew I don't bring into the country.

Vasiliu: The rest stayed where they were.

Antonescu: Also those from the Tiraspol camp do not get into the country if they are Communists.

Vasiliu: We have still another camp in Slivina, near Oceacov. These are criminals who have been accused fifteen times or more, convicts, etc.

Antonescu: I am interested neither in the Communists nor in the criminals. I am talking about the other Jews, [for instance] those whom we forcibly removed from Dorohoi.

Vasiliu: They [the Jews] have decided in a regular conference who is to have priority in the evacuations. They want to start with the orphans, who number about 5000.

Antonescu: We want to establish a big sanatorium in Vijnita. There was a major Jewish center there that was dissolved long ago. There too we will bring a lot of Jews. Regarding the Jews who are in danger of being murdered by the Germans, you have to take measures and warn the Germans that I don't tolerate this matter, because in the last analysis I will have a bad reputation for these terrible murders. Instead of letting this happen, we will take them away from there and bring them into this area. There they will be organized securely in a camp, so that we can fill up Bukovina again. They should be organized for labor service there. We will pay them. Until they are organized, however, they will be supplied by the Jewish community. I have just talked with Mr. Lecca, and I told him he should call those from the Jewish community – he says he has already collected 160 million lei [2,672,000 reichsmark, or slightly over 1,000,000 dollars] – in order that clothing and foodstuffs become available. At the same time, the foreign countries should be informed, so that foodstuffs may be sent from there too – just like the shipments to the American prisoners of war – from Switzerland, and clothing, because I will not take anything from supplies allocated for the Roumanian soldier, worker, and civil servant to clothe the Jews. I have sympathy also with the Jews, but more so with the Roumanians. They will therefore be supplied from their own resources. We contribute nothing. They already have 160 million. If misfortune strikes and we have to withdraw from Vijnita, then they stay there. From Vijnita I take no further step into the interior of the country.

Vasiliu: All of them do not have room there.

Antonescu: Thirty to thirty-five thousand used to live there.

Vasiliu: In the city were 5000. It is a little town. We bring them only to cities from which they came, in the Bukovina and Bessarabia.

Antonescu: How?

Vasiliu: They have to return to the places from which they went.

Antonescu: Not only those who came from Old Roumania?

811. Barabeanu to Lecca, November 25, 1943, enclosing minutes of Transnistria conference held on November 17, 1943, in German translation in the files of the Bucharest Legation, Occ E 5a-5.

VASILIU: In addition to those. But the majority are from Bukovina and Bessarabia.

ANTONESCU: And one brings them back to their places of origin?

VASILIU: To other places we can't bring them, because we have no room.

ANTONESCU: Let's bring them to Vijnita. Under what conditions? I also told Lecca he should send them supplies. Orazean told me he will put railway coaches at their disposal in order to bring them there.

[There appears to be a gap at this point.]

ANTONESCU: I was told those in Golta [prefecture] were murdered.

VASILIU: It is not true, Marshal.

ANTONESCU: In any case the Germans should be warned that I don't tolerate such murders.

VASILIU: The Germans took only a few columns of Jews and drove them across the Bug.

ANTONESCU: Please tell the German Secret Service that I don't tolerate it that they are murdered.

VASILIU: Do you want to send all 60,000 Jews to Vijnita?

ANTONESCU: It is not possible, since all of them do not have room there. Those in the villages stay put until the front line is stabilized.

VASILIU: The Mogilev district, which has 39,000 Jews, must be relieved; then comes Balta with 10,000. Tulcin and Jampol no less.

ANTONESCU: Relieve Mogilev and bring the Jews to Vijnita.

VASILIU: Those who came from Dorohoi will return there.

ANTONESCU: Those from Old Roumania, who have been removed by mistake, will be brought back to their homes.

VASILIU: Dorohoi was regarded as a part of the Bukovina.

GENERAL DRAGALINA: In Dorohoi all Jewish stores are closed.

ANTONESCU: Now you are not going to give them permission any more to open their stores. In Vijnita, they will trade among themselves.

VASILIU: The Jews from Mogilev then will come to Vijnita; the others will stay put. We will only select the intellectuals and skilled workers [from the other Jewish groups].

DRAGALINA: It is to be observed that the Jews in Bukovina are attempting to travel surreptitiously to Bucharest. First they request a travel permit for 30 days; then they demand an extension of this permit. I hinder them as much as possible.

ANTONESCU: You should hinder them completely.

VASILIU: We have checked all permits, and we sent them back immediately upon expiration.

ANTONESCU: But how do they travel? I thought they should not travel at all.

DRAGALINA: They have to have operations, doctors.

ANTONESCU: Yes, if one sends them into a camp, right away they need doctors and dentists. Mr. Tatarescu now has the hernia; when he did what he did nothing was wrong with him. Gentlemen, we have settled the mode of evacuation for all categories. This chapter is now finished.

We know nothing about the extent to which the somewhat hazy evacuation plans of the Transnistria conference were actually carried out. All we know is that there was a movement of Jews from Transnistria to Bukovina and Bessarabia, and then farther back into Old Roumania.[812]

Marshal Antonescu's fear that the Germans would renew operations against the Jews during the retreat was not without foundation. At the beginning of May, 1944, marking was introduced for the first time in the Old Roumanian province of Moldavia, which adjoined Bessarabia.[813] The German commander in that sector, General Wöhler, was very annoyed when he

812. Sometime in February or March, 1944, the Roumanian Minister in Ankara, Alexander Cretsianu, assured the representative of the U.S. War Refugee Board, Ira A. Hirschmann, that the Transnistria camps would be disbanded. The number of Jewish survivors mentioned in these talks was only 48,000. See Hirschmann, *Lifeline to a Promised Land*, pp. 46–58.

813. *Donauzeitung* (Belgrade), May 9, 1944, p. 3.

discovered that so many Jews were still around. The town of Iasi, he said, should have been evacuated, but that was impossible because the Jews had made large payments of a special tax. In another Moldavian town, Bârlad, Wöhler reported that Jews had tried to buy clothes and food from his men. "I ordered arrest of these creatures," he wrote. Then, concluding, he said: "Jews must disappear" [*Zusammenfassung: Juden müssen verschwinden*].[814] A few weeks later Wöhler organized a forced labor system for the Moldavian Jews – the German Army's parting gift to the Jews of Roumania.[815]

In those closing days of Roumania's war effort on Germany's side, an interesting conference was held in Bucharest, under the chairmanship of Mihai Antonescu, on the subject of Jewish emigration, particularly the emigration of children repatriated from Transnistria. The record of that conference, dictated by Mihai Antonescu, is even more remarkable than the minutes of the Transnistria conference in its distortion of past events; the record reads almost as though it had been prepared for postwar consumption. When Radu Lecca, a participant in the discussion, handed over a copy to the German Legation, he remarked that alleged statements by Mihai Antonescu, Radu Lecca, and three other participants (Interior Minister Popescu, Undersecretary Vasiliu, and Marine Undersecretary Sova) had not been made at all but had simply been invented by the Roumanian Vice Premier.[816] Whether the distortion of past history had in fact occurred during the conference, or whether it was created as an afterthought in a false summary, the record of that discussion remains a true indicator of how Mihai Antonescu and perhaps also his colleagues felt about the events that had taken place under their direction for the past four years.

Mihai Antonescu, according to his own summary, opened the talks by pointing out that even in 1940 a decision had been made not to impede any Jewish emigration. Von Killinger's and Richter's demands to place the Roumanian anti-Jewish regime under German control had been rejected. The Office of the Commissar for Jewish Questions (Lecca) had never been a public office. When Ribbentrop in 1943 had attempted to curtail emigrations by referring to the Arabs, the Roumanians had replied that Roumania had the same right to be spared from the Jews as the Arabs. The British government's inquiry whether the Roumanian government permitted emigration was answered "positively." Only transport difficulties had frustrated a mass emigration. Roumania naturally could not allocate its own ships, which were needed for national defense; consequently, it was left to the Jews to organize their own emigration. But very few ships had come to Constanza. The foreign maritime companies which had sent these ships had collected "fantastic sums" from the Jews and had also exercised a bad influence on Roumanian offices. Marshal Antonescu had consequently held up the ships in Constanza to check abuses.

General Vasiliu observed that no obstacles had been placed in the way of Jewish emigration. The Roumanian

814. *Armeegruppe* Wöhler/Ia (signed Wöhler) to Army Group South Ukraine, May 31, 1944, NOKW-3422. An *Armeegruppe* was an improvised army organized in the field; the Wöhler in question is the same general who, three years before, had complained about Roumanian atrocities. See p. 213.

815. *Armeegruppe* Wöhler OQu/Qu 2 to Corps Group Mieth, Corps Kircher, XVII Corps, XL Corps, XLIX Mountain Corps, Army Rear Area, Army Engineers commander, copy to Ia, July 15, 1944, NOKW-3118.

816. Von Killinger to Foreign Office, July 17, 1944, enclosing summary by Mihai Antonescu dated July 15, 1944, NG-2704. The conference had been held on June 9, 1944.

government had merely collected 40,000 lei per person (RM 668 or $267), a very low tax in view of the exemptions from military duty and labor service. In addition, the companies had to pay a profits tax to the state.

General Sova, the Marine Undersecretary, pointed out that Roumanian ships could actually carry Jewish emigrants. Radu Lecca put in that, since the sinking of the "SS Struma," the Great Headquarters of the Armed Forces had prohibited transport in Roumanian ships, but that prohibition did not apply to foreign ships. The Jews, said Lecca, had paid 600 dollars (U.S. currency) for passage on a Bulgarian or Turkish ship. But Lecca, too, agreed that there was no reason for preventing the use of Roumanian vessels. The emigration, he said, could be organized by the Jewish leader Zissu (Roumanian representative of the Jewish Agency for Palestine).

Interior Minister Popescu also saw no reason why the Roumanian ships now lying at anchor in Constanza could not be used for the transport of the Jews, particularly children from Transnistria and refugees from Hungary. Any excess capacity could be used for emigrants chosen jointly by Mr. Zissu and Mr. Lecca. Everyone happily agreed with this solution.[817]

No, the Roumanian bureaucrats had never really done anything to the Jews, and now they even offered their own ships for the emigration of the survivors. However, that project never came to fruition, for soon afterwards the Red Army broke into Old Roumania, and on August 24, 1944, Roumania surrendered.

Hungary. – As the German destruction process covered Axis Europe, one Jewish community after another was swept away. In country after country the Jews were caught by the machinery of destruction and died, helpless, in its grasp. By 1944 only one important area was still untouched by deportations, only one community still intact. The area was Hungary, and 750,000 Jews had survived within its borders.

When the Hungarian Jews looked at a map of Axis Europe at the beginning of 1944, they could see that all around them Jewish communities had been attacked and destroyed. The cataclysmic German destruction process had struck the Jews as far east as Russia, as far north as Norway, as far west as France, as far south as Greece. Conversely, when a German official looked at his map in Berlin, he could see that everywhere "the Jewish problem" had been "solved," except in one relatively small area: Hungary. And when he looked at Hungary, he could see the largest concentration of Jews who still survived in the German sphere of influence. Truly, the Hungarian Jews were living on an island. But the island was not surrounded by water; it was a land-island enclosed and protected only by a political boundary. The Jews depended on that boundary for their survival, and the Germans had to break the barrier down. In March, 1944, the Hungarian frontiers began to crumble. The Germans overran the country, and catastrophe overtook the Jews.[818]

817. Mihai Antonescu reported the results of the conference in summary form to Zissu. See his letter to Zissu, June 17, 1944, NG-2704.

818. A comprehensive book has been written about the destruction of the Hungarian Jews. See Eugene Levai, *Black Book on the Martyrdom of Hungarian Jewry* (Zurich and Vienna, 1948). Levai has used three types of source materials: (1) survivors' accounts, (2) Hungarian legal gazettes and newspapers, and (3) a few particularly valuable documents from the archives of the Hungarian Foreign Office, the Jewish Council in Budapest, and the Catholic Church in Hungary. His emphasis is upon Hungarian action and upon the response of the Jewish leadership. Here we shall draw upon the German documents that were not available to Levai. Through these documents we shall discover

We have seen all the deportations in Europe; we have seen how, one by one, the Jewish communities were crushed. What, then, was so unusual in the fate of Hungarian Jewry? There is only one circumstance which distinguishes the Hungarian case from all others, only one factor which requires explanation: in Hungary the Jews *had* survived until the middle of 1944. They were killed in Hitler's final year of power, in an Axis world that was already going down to defeat. In none of the countries with which we have dealt so far was the "final solution" started so late. Hungary was the only country in which the perpetrators knew that the war was lost when they started their operation. The Hungarian Jews were almost the only Jews who had full warning and full knowledge of what was to come while their community was still unharmed. Finally, the Hungarian mass deportations are remarkable also because they could not be concealed from the outside; they were carried out openly in full view of the whole world. These are facts which we cannot take lightly. These are circumstances which must be explained. For, the success of these operations, in the twilight of the Axis, should tell us much about the Germans, who began the venture, about the Hungarians, who were drawn into it, about the Jews, who suffered it, and about the outside powers, who stood by and watched it come to pass.

What accounts for this development? Why was Hungarian Jewry doomed to ultimate destruction? Again we must look to a satellite relationship – the German-Hungarian partnership – for our principal clues.

The Hungarians were opportunists who joined the German camp in order to gain territory. There was in Hungary a strong desire to expand in three directions: north (Czechoslovakia), east (Roumania), and south (Yugoslavia). With Germany's help that threefold expansion was accomplished in less than three years; however, once the Hungarians had committed themselves to action on the German side, they found that there was no easy escape from the fatal entanglement. Hungary was too close to Germany, too indispensable to the German war effort, to be able simply to surrender to the other side.

Thus in 1943, and increasingly in 1944, the Hungarians were subjected to German threats. The Hungarian government was unable to reply to these threats with the language of force. The country was fettered in its striking capacity by its smallness and location, by its traditions and outlook. The Regent of Hungary, Admiral Horthy, was a man in his seventies. The backbone of the Hungarian regime was a class of old-established and long-decayed generals and landowners. These men could not, ultimately, withstand German pressure; they swayed and faltered under German demands. From the beginning of 1938 to the end of 1944 the wavering reaction of the Hungarian leadership was reflected in a succession of Prime Ministers who were alternately pro-German personalities and reluctant collaborators (see Table 64).

It should be noted that the wavering reaction of the Hungarians was not confined to the preliminary period preceding the "final solution"; this reaction continued to the very end. In fact, if we examine these personalities in the order in which they served, we discover in their succession another interesting pattern: as time went on, the pro-German Prime Ministers were increasingly pro-German, and the reluctant collaborators were more and more reluctant. The contrast widened with every change. This development was

---

how the Germans introduced the destruction process into Hungary and how the operation looked from Berlin.

not accidental; it reflected an increasing divergence of German and Hungarian interests. Germany fought for all or nothing; Hungary had more limited aims. The Germans wanted to make history; the Hungarians wanted only to annex territory. The Germans wanted to fight to the end; the Hungarians wanted to quit when the end was in sight. The pro-German Prime Ministers, appointed under German pressure, served the increasing German need to hold Hungary in line. The reluctant collaborators, who were appointed when the Germans were not looking, served the increasing Hungarian desire to escape from the whirlpool of total defeat. In the final tally German pressure triumphed.

TABLE 64 / *The Hungarian Prime Ministers*

	BEFORE GERMAN INTERVENTION:	
Preliminary phase	to March, 1939	Imredy (pro-German)
	March, 1939, to April, 1941	Teleki (reluctant collaborator)
	April, 1941, to March, 1942	Bardossy (pro-German)
	March, 1942, to March, 1944	Kallay (reluctant collaborator)
	AFTER GERMAN INTERVENTION:	
"Final solution"	March, 1944, to August, 1944	Sztojay (pro-German)
	August, 1944, to October, 1944	Lakatos (reluctant collaborator)
	October, 1944, to end	Szalasi (pro-German)

As Prime Ministers changed, the fate of Hungarian Jewry changed also. There was a close correlation between the succession of Hungarian rulers and the pacing of anti-Jewish action. The moderate Prime Ministers slowed down and arrested the catastrophe; the extremists hurried it along. The destruction process in Hungary was therefore an erratic development in which periods of near-tranquility alternated with outbursts of destructive activity. The Jews, in their ordeal, passed through cycles of hope and disappointment, relief and shock. No Jewish community in Europe was subjected, to such an extent and for so long a time, to the hot-and-cold treatment. The Jews of Hungary felt in the fullest measure, and to the very end, the effects of the wavering Hungarian reaction to overwhelming German force.

The destruction of the Hungarian Jews began as a voluntary Hungarian venture, and the first Hungarian measures were enacted without much German prodding and without any German help. The earliest law was drafted in 1938, when Hungary approached the Reich for help in the realization of Hungarian plans against Czechoslovakia.[819] The second law was presented to Ribbentrop in 1939, at a moment when the Budapest government was pleading with the German Foreign Office for its support in the liberation of Hungarian minorities in Roumania and Yugoslavia.[820] A third sequence of measures was taken when Hungary joined Germany in the war against Russia.

If we look at these early decrees, which span the period of Imredy, Teleki, and Bardossy, we see little in them that set Hungary apart from its neighbors. Imredy started the destruction process; Teleki allowed himself to be dragged along; Bardossy was moving more rapidly toward a "final" goal.

819. See Ribbentrop to Keitel, March 4, 1948, PS-2786.

820. Summary of discussion, held on April 29, 1939, by Ribbentrop, Prime Minister Teleki, and Foreign Minister Czaky, prepared by von Erdmannsdorff on April 30, 1939, D-737. The law was actually brought up as a bargaining point in this discussion.

From the German viewpoint the Hungarians in those days were coming up to expectation. Little in that early history gave hint of the later convulsions on the Hungarian scene.

Like everyone else, the Hungarians started with a definition. They wrote their first definition of the term "Jew" into their first anti-Jewish law. That definition was changed slightly in the second law. (Both laws, incidentally, were the product of the Imredy regime, although the law of 1939, drawn up in the closing days of the Imredy government, was promulgated under Teleki.) The third definition, which was written in 1941, represents a radical departure from the earlier formulations. It was an attempt to approach and in some respects even to surpass the Nuremberg principle. Table 65 shows the three definitions, together with the standard German one, for comparison.[821]

A closer look at these Hungarian definitions will reveal that they were the products of a struggle between pro-Nazi elements and the Catholic Church. If we compare the first two laws, we may note that the changes in the law of 1939 represented a partial victory, and thus also a partial defeat, for both sides. Under the law of 1938, for example, a person who had been converted at the age of twelve in the year 1900 was considered a non-Jew. Under the law of 1939 that same person was reclassified as a Jew. Clearly, such a change was a victory for the pro-Nazis and a defeat for the Church. Now, however, let us take the case of a young man born as a Christian in 1920, of Jewish parents who were themselves converted when he was born and whose ancestors had been residents of Hungary for a century. This man was a Jew under the law of 1938 but a non-Jew under the law of 1939. Here, then, was a defeat for the pro-Nazis and a victory for the Church. But was this Church victory permanent? Not at all, for if we pass on to the law of 1941 we observe that the same young man was classified as a Jew again.

The definition of 1941 was adopted after an open controversy in the upper house of Parliament. The Hungarian upper house was a peculiar body; it had 254 members, including a delegation of Habsburg royalty, a delegation of nobles, representatives appointed by Regent Horthy, representatives of public corporations, and members who held important positions in public life, among them 34 representatives of the Church. By 1941 the Jewish community representatives (a public corporation) were no longer present, but among the other members there were still eleven persons of Jewish descent, including eight baptized ones.[822] This was consequently a unique struggle. The Church waged its battle as an integral component of the lawmaking apparatus, while eleven lawmakers were directly affected by the outcome of the argument. (The Jews, incidentally, continued to sit in the upper house after the argument was lost, for the Hungarians were slow in the dismissal process.)

When the law of 1941 was adopted, the Church suffered a bad defeat. Of all the definitions in Europe this Hungarian one was probably the widest in scope; it reached out furthest in its application to persons who did not adhere to the Jewish faith. In Germany, for example, a half-Jew who did not belong to the Jewish religion and was married to a quarter-Jewish person was

821. *Die Judenfrage,* July 14, 1938, p. 5. Israel Cohen, "The Jews in Hungary," *Contemporary Review* (London), CLVI (November, 1939), 571–79. Veesenmayer to Foreign Office, April 7, 1944, enclosing texts of Hungarian laws in German translation, including par. 9 Law Article XV, 1941, which contains the third definition, Occ E 6b-2.

822. *Donauzeitung* (Belgrade), August 9, 1941, p. 3.

TABLE 65 / *Hungarian and German Definitions of "Jew"*

LAW OF 1938	LAW OF 1939	LAW OF 1941	GERMAN LAW
Jews by religion.	Jews by religion.	A person with three or more Jewish grandparents.	A person with three or more Jewish grandparents.
A person who left the Jewish community or was converted after July 31, 1919.	Any convert who became a Christian on or after his seventh birthday.	A person with two Jewish grandparents who was himself born as a Jew, or one of whose parents was not baptized at time of marriage, or who was married to a person with as much as one Jewish grandparent.	A person with two Jewish grandparents who himself belonged to the Jewish religion on September 15, 1935, or later, or who was married to a person Jewish by definition on September 15, 1935, or later.
A person born of Jewish parents after July 31, 1919, regardless of his own religion.	Any other convert (including even those who became Christian before their seventh birthday) provided that he had a Jewish parent who was not converted before January 1, 1939, or who did not come from a family resident in Hungary since 1849.	The child of a Jewish mother and an unknown father.	The child of a Jewish mother and an unknown father, only in certain cases.
		The child of a half-Jewish mother and an unknown father, if at time of birth either mother or child was not baptized.	A person who was the offspring of a forbidden intermarriage or extramarital relationship.
		A person with a single Jewish grandparent, provided that the half-Jewish parent was Jewish by definition, and provided further that the offspring was born after the law entered into force.	

not considered a Jew; in Hungary, under the law of 1941, a half-Jew in the same position was considered a Jew.

The all-embracing character of the new Hungarian definition is perhaps most discernible when we look at its effects in statistics. In 1941 about 725,000 persons in Hungary belonged to the Jewish religion.[823] At the same time an estimated 787,000 persons were affected by the law. Sixty-two thousand people were consequently non-Jews by religion and Jews by definition.[824] If we assume that the share of each church in these 62,000 victims was di-

823. Veesenmayer (German Minister in Hungary) to Ambassador Ritter, June 8, 1944, enclosing 1941 census statistics, NG-5620. *Donauzeitung* (Belgrade), August 15, 1944, p. 3, also citing census statistics. Veesenmayer's figure is 724,307; the *Donauzeitung* lists 725,007. The discrepancy is unexplained.

824. *Donauzeitung* (Belgrade), August 15, 1944, p. 3. The number of persons who had at least one Jewish grandparent but were not covered by the definition was estimated at 15,000. (Hungary had no *Mischlinge*.) *Ibid.*

rectly proportional to its share in the total Christian population, we may calculate further that the law applied to roughly 43,000 Catholics, 12,000 Calvinists, 3000 Lutherans, and 3000 miscellaneous Christians.[825] Unquestionably, many of these Christians had already been classified as Jews under the law of 1938 or the law of 1939, but the definition of 1941 was still a blow to the churches. Especially after their partial success in 1939, they had expected nothing like this.

In the scale of history, however, the primary importance of the church struggle of 1938–41 does not lie in its outcome. To be sure, the fate of tens of thousands of victims is not to be waved aside, but more significant even than the settlement of this controversy was the controversy itself. In waging the struggle for the baptized Jews in the first place, the church had implicitly declined to take up the struggle for Jewry as a whole. In insisting that the definition exclude Christians, the church in effect had stated the condition upon which it would accept a definition that set aside a group of people for destruction. And this decision was only a prelude to what was to come; for as we shall see, when the Hungarian destruction process came to its climax in 1944, the church was to battle even more fiercely for its Christian Jews and even less ardently for the Jews who were not in its fold.

The Hungarians completed only the first step of the destruction process under their own power. Far slower progress was made in the implementation of the subsequent steps. The expropriatory operations began at the same time as the first definition, but they took far longer to mature. There was a reason for this slowness.

The Jews of Hungary, unlike the Jews of most other countries, were not merely a middle class; they were to a large extent the *only* middle class, the backbone of all professional and commercial activity in the country. In the 1930's, more than half the private doctors were Jews, nearly half the lawyers were Jews, more than a third of the trading population was Jewish, and nearly a third of the journalists were Jews.[826] The Jews were truly indispensable to a normal economic life. The Hungarians therefore approached the expropriation problem cautiously; the method they adopted was the quota regulation – that is, the specification that in various fields of economic endeavor the Jewish participation was not to exceed certain maximum percentages fixed by law. However, war veterans and their families were initially exempted from the quotas. A sense of national honor dictated that veterans were not to be forced to compete for economic survival in the ensuing reduction process. (The quotas, as they were laid down by the Imredy regime in the laws of 1938 and 1939, are summarized briefly in Table 66.[827])

If the percentages in Table 66 appear to be large in relation to the numerical strength of Hungarian Jewry (approximately 5 per cent of the total population), it must be stressed that the effectiveness of a quota system is to be measured not in the number of

825. According to the 1941 census, reported by Veesenmayer in NG-5620, there were 9,775,310 Catholics, 2,785,782 Calvinists, and 729,289 Lutherans. Other non-Jewish religions and persons belonging to no religion totaled 665,059. The total population (other than Jews by religion) was thus 13,955,440. The entire population of Hungary was 14,679,747. We do not have actual statistics of the Christian and nondenominational Jews. If such statistics should in future be unearthed – as they well might – it would be interesting to note whether the division of these 62,000 victims among the various denominations actually corresponded to the relative numerical strength of the churches.

826. Cohen, "The Jews in Hungary," pp. 571–79.

827. *Ibid.*

people which that quota accommodates but rather in the numbers of victims it excludes. If we consider the statistics of the Jewish economic position in Hungary during the 1930's, it becomes clear that the Hungarian lawmakers envisaged reductions in Jewish business and employment of at least 50 per cent.[828]

TABLE 66 / *The Jewish Quotas in Hungary*

FIELD	JEWISH SHARE UNDER THE LAW OF 1938	JEWISH SHARE UNDER THE LAW OF 1939
Trading licenses		6 per cent
Licenses for sale of state monopoly products		Complete withdrawal within 5 years
Public contracts		20 per cent (after 1943, automatic reduction to 6 per cent)
Agricultural property		Compulsory Aryanization authorized without time limit
Professions	20 per cent	6 per cent (total exclusion of civil servants, journalists, managers of entertainment establishments)
University students		6 per cent
Private employees in industrial, commercial, and banking firms	20 per cent of labor force in individual firms (5-year goal)	12 per cent of labor force in individual firms (immediate goal)

Moreover, the quotas were in all cases maximum limits. Nothing in the law prevented the Hungarian administration from employing its licensing procedures for the purpose of restricting Jewish activities still further or of pushing the Jews out of certain lines of business altogether. The only difficulty was the practical necessity of replacing Jews with Hungarians, and that was in many cases an insurmountable obstacle.

In January, 1941, *Amt Ausland-Abwehr* of the OKW received a report from a "reliable" executive of a German export firm who had just completed a trip to Hungary. The executive (a *Prokurist)* was in the textile business, and he was acutely interested in changes taking place in the Hungarian textile sector. He concluded quickly that there was no comparison between the Aryanizations in Germany and those which were now transpiring in Hungary. For the implementation of Aryanizations, he said, the Hungarians lacked two prerequisites: capital and brains. The upper class had an aversion to all participation in business activity. For example, one prominent Hungarian had confided that in his circles he was looked upon as having "strayed" because he was now occupying himself as a wholesaler in textiles.

About 1500 new textile licenses had been handed out to Aryans. Those who were worthy of credit and trust in this group were believed to number 30 or

828. The reductions became even more stringent when non-invalided and non-decorated war veterans (originally exempt) were placed under the quota system in 1939, and when persons classified as non-Jews in 1938 and 1939 were reclassified as Jews in 1941.

40, while reliable sources had it that the names of over 100 women of ill repute were represented on the new textile trading licenses (*"während, wie ich von ernst zu nehmender Seite hörte, die Namen von über hundert übelberüchtigter Frauen auf den neuen Textilgewerbescheinen vertreten seien"*). The Jewish businessmen, in the meantime, were experiencing increasing difficulties in the procurement of import authorizations. As a result, the German suppliers were beginning to resign themselves to a partial loss of the Hungarian market. "No German exporter," the *Prokurist* wrote flatly, "can be expected to take up connections with the questionable Aryan firms described above."[829]

So far as the Germans were concerned, the Aryanizations in Hungary were a hopeless proposition. Still in all, the Hungarian authorities slowly managed to make some inroads into Jewish economic life. The Jews were being hurt, and in some branches of commerce they were being ousted entirely. Thus the complete cessation of Jewish business activity in the following lines was reported by May, 1942, and January, 1943, respectively:[830]

May, 1942	*January, 1943*
Cattle trading	Textile rag trade
Potato export	Fats and hogs trade
Wholesale sugar	Eggs and milk trade
Fruit export	Trade in church articles
Wholesale gasoline	Restaurants
Wholesale fodder	Cement trade
Wholesale coal	Onion and wine trade
Wholesale leather	Export of hay and straw
Wholesale milk	

Curiously enough, German exporters and importers do not appear to have contributed much to this development. The Germans needed Hungarian currency, and they could not very well afford simply to stop shipments to Jewish customers.[831] The boycott of Jewish suppliers in Hungary could be entertained to an even lesser degree because the Jewish armament industry within Hungary was far from negligible in its volume and importance. The nature of German dependence upon Jewish producers may be glimpsed in the following excerpt from a report which the German Economy Officer in Hungary sent to the OKW on January 15, 1944:

> The Jewish firm Tungstram A. G., in the course of negotiations conducted with it, has declined to accept further Wehrmacht orders for pipes. It based its refusal on the need for exporting its products to the foreign neutral market.[832]

While the Aryanizations were floundering in industry, they proceeded with a little more ease in agriculture. The Hungarians were more interested in land, and the Jews were less involved in it. Only about 4 or 5 per cent of the land was in Jewish hands when the law of 1939 authorized the government to order the sale of Jewish agricultural properties. From 1939 through 1942 the

829. *Abwehr-Nebenstelle* Cologne to OKW/*Ausland-Abwehr*/Abw Abt. I (I Wi), January 20, 1941, enclosing report by a *Prokurist* of a "known Rhenish textile firm, reliable," Wi/IF 2.24.

830. *Donauzeitung* (Belgrade), May 23, 1942, p. 3; November 20, 1942, p. 3; January 6, 1943, p. 3.

831. When the Germans halted shipments in 1941, Italian and Swiss suppliers moved into the gap. *Auslandsbriefprüfstelle* Vienna to *Zentralauswertestelle*/Major Dr. Huth, November 4, 1941, Wi/IF 2.24. There was also a problem in that Hungarian firms could make the purchases for the Jews. Hans Vermehren Import-Fabrikation-Export (Berlin) to OKW/WWi, December 18, 1941, Wi/IF 2.24. *Donauzeitung* (Belgrade), June 22, 1943, p. 3. As late as April, 1943, German exports to Jewish firms in Hungary were apparently still going strong. German Economy Officer in Hungary to OKW/WSt Wi/*Ausland* (draft), May 17, 1943, Wi/IF 2.13.

832. German Economy Officer (WO) in Hungary to OKW/WSt *Ausland,* January 15, 1944, Wi/IF .2.

turnover of land had reached the following proportions:[833]

	Total in 1939	*Sold by 1942*
Forests	373,000 acres	213,000
Farmland	914,000 acres	299,000
	1,287,000 acres	512,000

Forest land went to the state, farmland to private interests. The 299,000 acres of farm property were broken down as follows:[834]

Held in trust for veterans: 89,000 acres
"Free sale": 85,000 acres
Small holders: 85,000 acres
Land fund: 27,000 acres
Christian heirs of Jewish possessors: 13,000 acres

In October, 1942, the administration was planning the distribution of another 276,000 acres of farmland according to the following key: parcels up to 5 acres (a total of 27,000 acres) were available to anyone; those from 5 to 107 acres (139,000 acres) were allotted to veterans; and those over 107 acres (90,000 acres) went to big landowners.[835] Evidently the Hungarian upper class, which looked down somewhat on matters of business, did not display an equal aversion to the acquisition of land. The agricultural expropriations in Hungary were not exactly a land reform.

As the Jews found themselves exposed to increasing economic restrictions, they made preparations to retrench. In the ensuing accommodation process, the Jews were attempting to accomplish a large-scale occupational shift. The following figures, showing Jewish enrollments in the commercial and trade schools of Budapest, are a partial indication of what was happening:[836]

	1936	*1942*
Commercial schools	454	17
Trade schools	614	2,379

However, the occupational shift did not fill the ever widening gap between the available Jewish manpower and the remaining opportunities for gainful employment. That gap was finally closed by a government measure: forced labor.

The basis for the Hungarian forced labor system was a provision of the mobilization law in accordance with which Jews were liable to be drafted into the army for "auxiliary service" as distinguished from "armed service."[837] Large-scale inductions began after Hungary's entry into the war, under *Honved* (War) Minister Bartha and his chief of staff, Colonel General Werth. At first the maximum draft age was 25; in April, 1943, the age limit was raised to 37;[838] in April, 1944, it was pushed up to 48;[839] and in October of that year, to 60.[840] According to Jewish sources, the number of men serving in the labor forces was 130,000. At its peak, the auxiliary contained 80,000 laborers; it brought death to 30,000 or 40,000.[841]

833. German Economy Officer in Hungary to OKW/WSt *Ausland,* December 14, 1943, citing figures presented by Prime Minister Kallay to Parliament, Wi/IF .2. The report does not make clear whether totals for 1939 and 1942 include annexed territories. The Hungarian *Joch* was converted here into acres at the rate of 1 *Joch* = 1.067 acres.

834. *Ibid.*

835. *Donauzeitung* (Belgrade), October 18, 1942, p. 3. For other statistics, see same newspaper, December 30, 1941, p. 3; March 1, 1942, p. 3; April 2, 1942, p. 6; May 24, 1942, p. 3; September 10, 1942, p. 3; February 14, 1943, p. 3.

836. *Ibid.*, October 31, 1942, p. 3.

837. *Die Judenfrage,* March 15, 1942, p. 58. *Donauzeitung* (Belgrade), June 11, 1942, p. 3; June 28, 1942, p. 3; July 16, 1942, p. 3; March 11, 1943, p. 3.

838. *Ibid.*, April 3, 1943, p. 3.

839. Veesenmayer (German Minister in Hungary) via Ambassador Ritter to Ribbentrop, April 14, 1944, NG-5626.

840. *Donauzeitung* (Graz), October 24, 1944, p. 3.

841. Testimony by Dr. Rudolf Kastner

The Jewish labor service men were employed within the framework of the army engineers, in construction projects, mine-clearing operations, and miscellaneous dirty work. Thousands of Jews were sent to the front, where they served in the strength of one battalion per Hungarian division.[842] Many additional battalions were dispersed behind the lines and within Hungary.

The concentration of such a large labor force in Hungarian hands could not, of course, fail to attract attention in Berlin. The growing labor shortage in Germany and Germany's occupied territories furthered this interest to an acute degree. From early 1943 to the beginning of 1945 one man in particular attempted to integrate the Hungarian Army's Jewish labor service into his industrial machine. This man was the Reich Minister of Armaments and chief of the *Organisation Todt*, Albert Speer. Some very important developments during the "final solution" phase of the Hungarian destruction process are traceable to his efforts. In 1943, however, Speer made only one request: his *Organisation Todt* needed workers for the Serbian copper mines at Bor.[843] Since all Jews had been killed in Serbia during the previous year and no other labor was available in the territory, Speer (with Himmler's consent) approached the Foreign Office with a request for 10,000 Hungarian Jews.[844] The negotiations were moderately successful; the Hungarians agreed to deliver 3000 Jews in exchange for 100 tons of unrefined copper per month.[845] In September, 1944, as many as 6000 Jews were reported there.[846]

While a strong exploitative movement developed in the Speer sector, a killer reaction made itself felt on the eastern front. Some Germans became uneasy at the sight of thousands of Jews in Hungarian uniform, moving about unmolested and virtually rubbing shoulders with German units. When the great retreat began in the winter of 1942–43, that uneasiness came to the fore. The Russians attacked the Hungarians at Voronezh and hurled them back toward Kursk. On the vast plain between the Don and Donets Rivers, Hungarian, Italian, Roumanian, and German armies retreated in panic and confusion.

From Kursk a German agricultural

(associate president, Zionist Organization of Hungary), Case No. 11, tr. pp. 3640–43. Some 15,000 Jews were captured by the Russians. *Report by the Anglo-American Committee of Enquiry regarding the problems of European Jewry and Palestine* (London, 1946), Cmd. 6808, p. 59.

842. Functionally, the position of these Jews was equivalent to the Russian auxiliaries (*Hilfswillige* or *Hiwis*) in the German Army. Noteworthy, however, is the fact that the Second Hungarian Army in Russia maintained a highly skilled technical company (analogous to the technical battalions in the German armies) for repairs and demolitions of public utilities, which in its personnel composition was 75 per cent Jewish. Oberst von Oheimb (German Economy Staff with Second Hungarian Army) to *Wirtschaftsstab Ost*, January, 1943, Wi/I .217.

843. The copper mines belonged to a French concern, the Compagnie des Mines de Bor. See advertisement, *Donauzeitung* (Belgrade), November 15, 1941, p. 9.

844. Bergmann (Office of the Foreign Minister) via Trade-Political Division, Wörmann, and Weizsäcker to Office of Foreign Minister, February 23, 1943, NG-5629.

845. German economy officer in Hungary to OKW/WSt. *Ausland*, June 15, 1943, and July 15, 1943, Wi/IF 2.13.

846. *Oberbefehlshaber Südost* / Chief of General Staff (signed General der Gebirgstruppen Winter) to OKW/WFSt/OP (H) (Generalmajor Horst Buttlar-Brandenfels), September 10, 1944, NOKW-981. The *Oberbefehlshaber Südost* was Gfm. von Weichs. The Bor camp was liquidated a few days later. Some 2000 Jews were marched out. At Cservenka (under Hungarian jurisdiction) they were shot by SS men. See the story of a survivor who crawled out of a death pit, "The Memoirs of Zalman Teichman" (ed. Nathan Eck), *Yad Washem Studies* (Jerusalem, Israel, 1958), II, 255–94.

expert with the Economy Inspectorate reported that the Hungarians had in part released Jewish construction battalions who, with pieces of German uniforms, were moving "like marauders" through the countryside under the slogan: the Hungarians are beaten, the Germans too; now we and the Russians are masters of the situation.[847]

In Budapest, Colonel Keri, first adjutant of the War Minister, looked up the German military attaché and informed him that the army was planning to draft all Jewish men up to the age of thirty-seven. The Hungarians, he said, would have liked very much to detail to the German security divisions (*Sicherungsdivisionen*) in the Ukraine twelve construction battalions made up of Jewish labor companies. Budapest, however, had a few reservations (*gewisse Bedenken*) because of the exceptionally bad treatment German offices had accorded to Jewish companies during the withdrawal (*Rückmarsch*) from the Don; it had also happened that "in the general confusion of the retreat" (*in den allgemeinen Trubel des Rückzuges*) and in the course of partisan operations, the Germans, in particular the SD, had shot members of the Jewish companies. It would therefore be "difficult" (*schwierig*) to detail Jewish labor companies to the Ukraine. However, the "difficulties" (*Schwierigkeiten*) would be removed by an assurance from the military attaché that "nothing evil" (*nichts Böses*) would be done to the Jews. The German was evasive. He could not deny the Hungarian assertions, for he knew from reports by German liaison officers in the Hungarian High Command that there was at least a "possibility" that Jews had been shot by Germans.[848]

The German attitude towards the Jewish labor service men revealed itself again and again in a series of small incidents. It seems that the Germans had a little difficulty in restraining themselves in the presence of these people. From Krakow, for example, the Foreign Office representative in the *Generalgouvernement* reported that a Hungarian Jewish construction battalion was quartered at Stanislawow, Galicia. The Jews had first been in civilian clothes but were now wearing Hungarian uniforms. There was a suspicion, said the Foreign Office man, that members of the construction battalion included Galician Jews who had escaped to Hungary in 1941. The following had happened to a German police sergeant: a Jew had walked up to him and had declared in Yiddish-German jargon, "Sergeant, I am a Jew, and you can't do anything to me because I am a Hungarian soldier."[849]

Another episode involving the labor service men was reported early in March, 1944, when members of the Propaganda Office attached to the *Generalkommissar* Volhynia - Podolia had to retreat from the seat of their activity at Brest Litovsk. Moving southward toward Stanislawow, the propagandists ducked through several towns where Ukrainians were about to slaughter the local Polish population (*die an Ort ansässigen Polen abzuschlachten*). While this slaughter was going on, the German officials observed that Jews belonging to the Hungarian Army and acting explicitly upon orders by Hungarian officers had the "nerve" (*erdreisten sich*) to "steal everything within reach, from pots and pans to cattle." Looking in vain for

847. Sonderführer Bertram to Economy Inspectorate Don-Donets, February 2, 1943, Wi/ID 2.206.

848 Legation in Budapest/Military Attaché to OKH/GenStdH/Attaché Division, April 5, 1943, NG-5636.

849. Von Thadden to RSHA/Gruf. Müller, January 6, 1944, enclosing report by VAA GG (signed Klötzel), November 23, 1943, NG-3522.

Wehrmacht units to put an end to this requisitioning, the propagandists finally took matters into their own hands and "successfully stopped the Jewish mob" (*dem jüdischen Raubgesindel erfolgreich entgegengetreten*).[850]

It appears as though the very existence of the Jewish labor service men offended the German onlookers; that was true especially because many of these men were outside of Hungary and thus particularly noticeable. But if the labor service men attracted attention because they were the sole Jews in a territory that had once had many Jewish residents, so Hungarian Jewry as a whole became more and more conspicuous in a European continent that was rapidly being drained of its Jewish population.

The history of the "final solution" in Hungary is a long one. It had its beginnings in 1941 and early 1942, while the country was ruled by pro-German Prime Minister Bardossy. During that period it seemed that Hungary would emerge as the first Axis satellite to become "Jew-free." Two major incidents occurred under the Bardossy regime, the deportation of the "Eastern Jews" from the Carpatho-Ukraine and the killing of the Yugoslav Jews at Novi Sad.

In August, 1941, the Bardossy government suddenly began a roundup of 12,000 Jews who had emigrated to Hungary from Galicia many years before, and who had not acquired Hungarian citizenship, with a view to shoving them into the teeth of the German mobile killing units operating in the newly overrun Soviet territories.[851] Jews in the Carpatho-Ukraine, which the Hungarians took from the Czechs in 1939, were particularly affected because the anti-Jewish law of 1939 had denied naturalization to those Jews if they could not prove that their ancestors had resided there since 1867.[852] The Germans were unprepared for the Hungarian push. The situation of the killing units near the Hungarian frontier, however, was unlike the position of *Einsatzgruppe D*, which operated in front of the Roumanians. The Roumanian Jews, it will be recalled, were pushed back – not so the Hungarian deportees.

On August 25, 1941, officers of the German Army and representatives of the newly formed East Ministry met in the office of the *Generalquartiermeister*-OKH. The summary of that conference indicates that the participants briefly considered the problem created by the sudden appearance of Hungarian Jews in the new territories. "Near Kamenets Podolski," the conference record states, "the Hungarians have pushed about 11,000 Jews over the border. In the negotiations up to the present it has not been possible to arrive at any measure for the return of these Jews. The Higher SS and Police Leader [SS-Obergruppenführer Jeckeln] hopes, however, to have completed the liquidation of these Jews by September 1, 1941."[853] Three days later *Einsatztrupp* Tarnopol (a unit of the BdS Krakow) reported that it had turned back 1000 Jews who had been shoved

850. *Generalkommissar* Volhynia-Podolia/Propaganda Office (Signed Maertius) to Propaganda Ministry/Eastern Division, March 31, 1944, Occ E 4-2. Excerpts of the Maertius report were sent by the eastern division of the Propaganda Ministry to the OKW on April 14, 1944, Occ E 4-2.

851. *Krakauer Zeitung*, August 5, 1941, p. 2. *Donauzeitung* (Belgrade), August 5, 1941, p. 3; August 15, 1941, p. 3.

852. Cohen, "The Jews in Hungary," p. 578.

853. Summary of conference held on August 25, 1941, in OKH/Qu on transfer of jurisdiction in the Ukraine, August 27, 1941, PS-197. The chairman was Major Altenstadt. Other participants were Ministerialdirigent Dr. Dankwarts, Oberst von Krosigk, Regierungspräsident Dargs, Obberregierungsrat Dr. Labs, Hauptmann Dr. Bräutigam, and Major Wagner.

across the Dniester by the 10th Hungarian Pursuit Battalion.[854] The situation was under control.

A second outburst of major proportions occurred in January, 1942, when the Hungarian commander in occupied Yugoslavia, General Feketehalmi-Zeisler, went on a rampage and shot several thousand Jews and Serbs in the town of Novi Sad.[855] This massacre had a curious aftermath. Following the Moscow declaration on war criminals in 1943, a scared Hungarian government indicted the general and two of his accomplices for the killing of 6000 Serbs and 4000 Jews. Feketehalmi-Zeisler and his helpers escaped before the trial to Germany, seeking refuge there under the protection of the Gestapo.[856] When the Hungarians wanted their men back, Hitler himself decided to give them sanctuary, as an example to all Europe of his readiness to stand by those who took action against the Jews.[857]

The enthusiastic Bardossy regime, which was responsible for the organization of the labor companies, the deportation of the Eastern Jews, and the killing of the victims in Novi Sad, came to an end in March, 1942. For the next two years, from March, 1942, to March, 1944, Hungary was ruled by a reluctant collaborator, Prime Minister Kallay. The Kallay government thus spanned the period during which Germany was attempting to organize deportations to the "East" from all parts of Europe. Naturally, the Germans wanted to include Hungary in this scheme also; Kallay was therefore the first Hungarian Prime Minister to be asked to deport the Hungarian Jews. He gave way by inches and in small ways. He widened the expropriatory process and extended the labor companies, but he refused to deport a single Jew. For the entire two years of his reign he resisted German pressure. When finally he was deposed, the dam which had held up the German flood was broken.

The negotiations started in August, 1942. On August 11 the Hungarian Minister in Berlin, Sztojay, protested to Unterstaatssekretär Dr. Martin Luther of *Abteilung Deutschland* that Jews of Hungarian nationality were being marked with the Jewish star in France, while Roumanian Jews were not affected. Sztojay added that the transmission of this protest was very distasteful to him. He had always considered himself an anti-Semite of the first rank (*ein Vorkämpfer des Antisemitismus*). Luther replied that the acceptance of this protest was indeed an unpleasant task for him too because, as Sztojay was aware, the Führer had ordered the speedy solution of the Jewish problem in Europe. Slovakia and Croatia had already agreed to the evacuation of their Jews, and even the French government was contemplating the introduction of anti-Jewish measures in its territory (unoccupied area).

Luther expressed special surprise that Hungary had based its protest on the fact that Roumanian Jews in France did not have to wear the Jewish star, while a few days before the Roumanian government had protested on the ground that Hungarian Jews had been exempted. No progress could be achieved in that manner. Sztojay then requested that German agencies in Brussels refrain from confiscating the property of Hungarian Jews. His government intended to take this property for its own purposes. Luther promised that the matter would be

854. RSHA IV-A-1, Operational Report USSR No. 66 (48 copies), August 28, 1941, NO-2839.

855. Affidavit by Dr. Rudolf Kastner, September 13, 1945, PS-2605.

856. Werkmeister (German Legation in Budapest) to Foreign Office, January 16, 1944, NG-2594.

857. Hewel to Ribbentrop, January 19, 1944, NG-2594.

settled in a satisfactory way, and that present measures were designed only to safeguard the property.[858]

On September 24, 1942, Ribbentrop ordered the Foreign Office to press for evacuations in Bulgaria, Denmark, and Hungary.[859] Eight days later, on October 2, Luther had another conversation with Sztojay. Luther began the discussion by demanding that Hungary allow its Jews in German-occupied areas to be deported by December 31, 1942. The Hungarian Minister inquired whether Italian Jews would receive the same treatment. When Luther answered in the affirmative, Sztojay replied that his government would probably consent to the evacuation of Hungarian Jews from the occupied territories; Hungary naturally did not intend to lag behind other states. Luther thereupon promised that the property of the Jews involved would be placed under trusteeship administration and that Hungary would be able to participate in the disposal of the property.

Next Luther pressed for the deportation of Hungarian Jews from the Reich. He proposed the same deadline (December 31, 1942) but added that the property should fall to the Reich, in accordance with the "territorial principle." Again the Hungarian envoy wanted to know whether the same arrangements were being made for Italian Jews. When Luther assured him that Italian Jews would get the same treatment, Sztojay remarked that his government laid great stress on the most-favored-nation principle.

Finally the German *Unterstaatssekretär* mentioned the Jews in Hungary. He demanded that Hungary introduce legislation aimed at eliminating all Jews from economic life, that the Jews be marked and that they be evacuated to the East. For the third time the Hungarian Minister asked whether the same measures would be taken in Italy, and once more Luther answered in the affirmative. Sztojay thereupon stated that Prime Minister Kallay was disturbed by certain rumors (which he, Sztojay, naturally did not believe) with regard to the treatment of Jews in the East, and that Kallay would not want to be accused of having exposed the Hungarian Jews to misery (or worse) after their evacuation. In answer to this observation, Luther said that the Hungarian Jews, like all evacuated Jews, would first be used in road construction and would later be settled in a Jewish reserve.[860]

A few days after this "pressure conference" another sort of discussion took place in Budapest. The SS advisor in the German Legation in Bratislava, Hauptsturmführer Wisliceny, had come to the Hungarian capital for a "private visit." On October 6, 1942, he had lunch at the Gulf Club with the personal secretary to Prime Minister Kallay, a Baron "von Fay." The Hungarian interested himself especially in "the solution of the Jewish problem in Slovakia." Wisliceny told him quite briefly and "without going into detail" how the "Jewish problem" in Slovakia was being solved.

Von Fay then wanted to know what Wisliceny thought about the Jewish problem in Hungary, and the SS-man replied cautiously that he knew of the Jewish problem in Hungary only through "literary sources." The Hungarian thereupon launched into a lengthy description of his country's anti-Jewish measures, criticizing them as insufficient but explaining that a "resettlement" could be carried out only

858. Memorandum by Luther, August 11, 1942, NG-5085.

859. Luther to Weizsäcker, September 24, 1942, PS-3688.

860. Memorandum by Luther, October 6, 1942, NG-5086. The Kallay government did not ratify Sztojay's tentative concessions in the matter of Hungarian Jews in German territories.

in stages. In that connection, the baron asked whether the Roumanian Jews were being resettled yet. Wisliceny answered that, according to his knowledge, appropriate preparations were being made there.

Suddenly, Fay asked whether Hungary, too, could be included in the course of a general "resettlement" program. The Hungarians, he explained, wanted to deport, first of all 100,000 Jews from the Carpatho-Ukraine and Transylvania. As a second step, the Hungarian plains would have to be cleared and, finally, Budapest. Wisliceny, somewhat flabbergasted, said that he was in Hungary only for a private visit and that he could not give a reply to such a question. He did not know, he said, whether "reception possibilities" for Hungarian Jews existed in the eastern territories. Two days after this discussion Wisliceny sent a report to Ludin, who after some further delay forwarded the memorandum to Berlin.[861]

Even before the receipt of the report in the Foreign Office, the pressure in Berlin was intensified. On October 14, 1942, Staatssekretär Weizsäcker stepped into the picture; speaking to Sztojay, the *Staatssekretär* quoted Ribbentrop to the effect that the Jews were spreading panic in Hungary.[862] On October 20, when the Hungarian Minister was about to make a routine visit to Budapest, Weizsäcker requested Sztojay to bring on his return trip the Hungarian government's reply to the German proposals about the Jewish question.[863]

However, the expected reply did not come. The Germans had not been speaking to the Hungarian government; they had addressed themselves to a few Hungarian anti-Semitic fanatics who had listened sympathetically to every German demand but who did not have the power to bring these demands to fruition. The true position of the Kallay government was revealed clearly enough a few weeks later, when a deputy in the Hungarian Parliament, Count Serenyi, demanded that the Jews be incarcerated in labor camps and ghettos. To this demand the Prime Minister replied in writing that "the incarceration of Jews in labor camps and ghettos cannot be carried out within the existing framework of legal norms."[864]

The Germans did not give up. Every avenue of approach was explored, and every sympathetic visitor was received. On December 11, 1942, the chief of the SS-Main Office, Berger, reported that Archduke Albrecht von Habsburg had arrived from Hungary in Berlin hoping to meet all important personalities from Hitler down. Berger could not avoid meeting the Archduke. Albrecht had complained that the Hungarian government was not taking earnest action against the Jews and that the labor service was only a show, and he had suggested that Hitler exert pressure on Horthy and the Hungarian Prime Minister. Berger passed on the recommendation to his chief, Himmler.[865] In March, 1943, a member of the Kallay Cabinet, Lukacs, arrived in Berlin for talks with Bormann. The Foreign Office seized the opportunity to request Bormann to call the Hungar-

861. Ludin (Bratislava) to Foreign Office, October 17, 1942, enclosing report by Wisliceny, dated October 8, 1942, NG-4586. The report was seen by Luther, Rademacher, and Hofrat Jüngling, all of *Abteilung Deutschland*. The Germans made no attempt to spell Hungarian names correctly, and we shall not make any attempt here to correct the German spellings. The "von Fay" mentioned by Wisliceny may have been Baron Vay.

862. Memorandum by Weizsäcker, October 14, 1942, NG-5085.

863. Memorandum by Weizsäcker, October 20, 1942, NG-5727.

864. *Donauzeitung* (Belgrade), December 8, 1942, p. 3.

865. Berger to Himmler, December 11, 1942, NO-1117.

ian visitor's attention to the three standard German wishes: (1) exclusion of the Hungarian Jews from economic life, (2) marking with the star, and (3) evacuation to the East.[866]

During the following month, on April 17, 1943, the whole question was reopened on the highest level, by Hitler and Ribbentrop, in a conversation with the Hungarian Regent, Admiral Horthy. The three men were conferring alone, attended only by the official interpreter Schmidt, in Klessheim Castle. (The meeting has since become known as the Klessheim conference.) Hitler began the discussion by remarking that the English were suffering greater losses than the Germans during the raids upon German cities, because fliers were key personnel and also the best type of human material. Furthermore, severe German measures had put a stop to all crimes during blackouts. Horthy remarked that energetic measures had been taken also in Hungary but that, oddly enough, crimes of this nature were continuing. Hitler said that this was the work of asocial elements. He went on to describe the German rationing system and claimed that the black market had disappeared. Horthy put in that he could not master the black market, and Hitler answered that the Jews were at fault.

When Horthy asked what he should do with the Jews, now that he had removed the base of their economic existence – he could not, after all, kill them all – Ribbentrop declared that the Jews either had to be annihilated (*vernichtet*) or placed in concentration camps. Another alternative did not exist. Upon Horthy's rejoinder that Germany had an easier job in that respect, since she did not possess so many Jews, Hitler recited statistics to prove how strong the Jewish influence in the Reich had been. Horthy replied that all this was news to him, and Hitler thereupon began to make a speech about two cities: Nuremberg and Fürth. The former city stood in all its glory; it had not had so many Jews. The latter town had decayed; it had held too many Jews. Wherever the Jews were left to themselves, they brought brutal misery and depravity. They were pure parasites. In Poland this situation had been cleared up thoroughly. If the Jews there did not wish to work, they were shot; if they could not work, they had to rot away (*verkommen*). They had to be treated like tubercular bacilli that threatened a healthy body. That was not so cruel when one kept in mind that even innocent creatures like hares and deer had to be killed in order to prevent damage. Why should the beasts (*Bestien*) who wanted to bring in Bolshevism be treated any better? Nations which could not defend themselves against the Jews had to perish – the best example of that was the decline of once so proud a people as the Persians, who now had to continue their miserable existence as Armenians.[867]

With Hitler's words still ringing in Horthy's ears, the Germans waited anxiously for a favorable reply. The chief of the SS-Main Office, Gottlob Berger, was skeptical. The Hungarians, he wrote to Himmler, would not consent to the "liquidation" of the Jews

866. Bergmann (Office of the Foreign Minister) via Weizsäcker to Ribbentrop, March 5, 1943, NG-5628. Bergmann to Bormann, March 9, 1943, NG-5628.

867. Summary of Klessheim conference held on April 17, 1943, signed by Schmidt, April 18, 1943, D-736. In testimony before the international military tribunal, Ribbentrop claimed that he had never made a remark to the effect that the Jews had to be annihilated, and that Schmidt had had the habit of writing summaries of discussions several days after they were held. Testimony by Ribbentrop, *Trial of the Major War Criminals*, X, 409–10. The summary of the Klessheim conference was written one day after it had taken place.

during the war. To the contrary, he said, the Kallay government, in an effort to ingratiate itself with the "Anglo-Americans," would give to the Jews the best possible treatment.[868] Ribbentrop too thought that the Klessheim conference had not quite succeeded, and he therefore decided to give the follow-up treatment to the Hungarian Minister, Sztojay.

The envoy was not hard to convince. On April 23, 1943, he wrote a letter to Kallay which was almost pleading in its tone. Several times, Sztojay wrote, he had reported that the Reich considered itself "engaged in a life and death struggle" with the Jews and that the *Reichskanzler* had "decided to rid Europe of Jews." Hitler had decreed that by the summer of 1943 all Jews of Germany and German-occupied countries had to be removed to the East. Most Axis governments were already co-operating in this task. "In my report No. 23/pol. 1943 I mentioned that competent German quarters had told me bluntly and without ado that the Jewish question was, so to speak, the only obstacle to intimate Hungaro-German relations." Several German interventions had already taken place. This time the German Foreign Minister himself had discussed the Jewish question with Sztojay in a talk "lasting till long after midnight." Ribbentrop had complained that the Hungarian government was not passing any new anti-Jewish laws and that the existing ones had been allowed to fall into "a certain stagnation." This could not go on because the Jews were undermining the morale of the people, etc.

Furthermore, Ribbentrop had mentioned "that according to reliable information, our former Minister in London, M. Barcza, had not long ago been received in audience by His Holiness the Pope." On that occasion M. Barcza had declared that Hungary did not wage war or fight against the Anglo-Saxon powers. In support of this thesis and to stress Hungary's position in this question, "he is said to have declared – allegedly on Government orders – that Hungary offers safe asylum not only to its own Jews, but, moreover, to 70,000 Jews who have sought refuge here." Sztojay could only say that, knowing the "mentality" of leading German circles, this question had better be solved speedily, in a manner that would exclude the possibility of further German interventions.[869]

Sztojay's letter did not fail to produce a disturbing effect in the Hungarian capital, for on May 21, 1943, the Hungarian envoy mentioned to Luther's successor, Wagner, that Kallay was now ready "to consider seriously the implementation of decisive anti-Jewish measures." However, the Hungarian Prime Minister was insisting that the Jews have an "opportunity to exist" (*Existenzmöglichkeiten*). Kallay, reported the Hungarian envoy, was anxious and worried because the Führer and Ribbentrop, in "misconstruing" his intentions, had come to mistrust him (*dass er in Verkennung seiner Absichten bei dem Führer und RAM in einem sehr schlechten Ruf gekommen wäre*).[870]

There was, however, no misconstruing of intentions in Berlin, and even if there were, Kallay removed the last vestige of doubt about his stand in a public speech which was delivered at the end of May. A German newspaper, with that gesture of automatic praise so characteristic of a totalitarian press, printed his remarks verbatim and titled them "The Great Speech of Kallay [*Die Grosse Rede von Kallays*]." This is what he said:

> In Hungary live more Jews than in all of western Europe. . . . It is self-explanatory that we must attempt to

868. Berger to Himmler, April 19, 1943, NO-628.

869. Full text of the letter in Levai, *Martyrdom,* pp. 33–36.

solve this problem; hence the necessity for temporary measures and an appropriate regulation. The final solution [*endgültige Lösung*], however, can be none other than the complete resettlement [*restlose Aussiedlung*] of Jewry. But I cannot bring myself [*Ich kann mich aber nicht dazu hergeben*] to keep this problem on the agenda so long as the basic prerequisite of the solution, namely, the answer to the question [*die Beantwortung der Frage*] where the Jews are to be resettled [*wohin die Juden auszusiedeln sind*] is not given. Hungary will never deviate from those precepts of humanity which, in the course of its history, it has always maintained in racial and religious questions.[871]

In the shrouded terminology of the Axis world a man could not have said "no" more clearly than Kallay had done in this speech. In fact, the speech marked the close of the diplomatic struggle over the Hungarian Jews. The talking phase of the German pressure campaign was over, and from now on the Kallay regime was to be faced with altogether different challenges.

The Germans were already convinced that the Hungarian refusal to co-operate in the "Jewish question" was based not solely on a humanitarian consideration. They perceived in that refusal the sign of a Hungarian desire to make peace with the Allies. Confirmation of that belief came to Berlin almost daily in the reports about the lagging Hungarian war effort at home, the sparing use of Hungarian divisions on the front, and even the furtive attempts to contact the Western Allies in Turkey. The Germans were therefore beginning to think that Hungary would be lost and the German frontier opened to an Allied advance unless the Kallay regime were overthrown. The thought was quickly translated into action.

870. Wagner to Steengracht von Moyland, May 21, 1943, NG-5637.

871. *Donauzeitung* (Belgrade), June 1, 1943, p. 3.

Shortly after the Klessheim conference, the Foreign Office trouble shooter Veesenmayer, whom we have already met in Serbia and Slovakia, arrived in Budapest in order to reconnoiter the situation.[872] He came for a second visit at the end of the year, this time to make contact with anti-Kallay forces.[873] When Horthy became aware of Veesenmayer's activities, he vowed never to grant him an entry visa again.[874] But the German machine kept grinding. At the beginning of March, 1944, the Reich Security Main Office felt that the time had come for intervention. Busily the Security Police people drew up lists of acceptable Hungarian Cabinet members, and carefully they weighed the alternative methods of overturning the Kallay regime.[875]

On March 15, Horthy was called to Klessheim Castle on the pretext of discussing with Hitler the withdrawal of the long-suffering and ill-equipped Hungarian divisions from the Russian front. At Klessheim a surprise awaited him. Bluntly, Hitler gave him the choice between a German military occupation and a German-approved government. Horthy chose the latter course.[876] Arriving in Budapest on March 19, Horthy experienced another surprise: a special sleeping car had been attached to his train, and the car had carried the new German Minister to Hungary, the honorary SS-*Standartenführer*, Dr. Edmund Veesenmayer.[877]

872. See report by Veesenmayer to Himmler, April 30, 1943, NG-2192.

873. Affidavit by Dr. Karl Werkmeister (*Legationsrat* in Budapest Legation during 1943), September 23, 1947, NG-2969.

874. *Ibid.* The German Minister in Hungary, Jagow, was not happy about Veesenmayer's presence, either.

875. RSHA memorandum, distributed to Kaltenbrunner, Höttl, Urban, Krallert, and Weneck, March, 1944, D-679.

876. Testimony by Horthy, Case No. 11, tr. pp. 2703–4.

877. Affidavit by Werkmeister, September 23, 1947, NG-2969.

Immediately upon his return Horthy informed the Crown Council of what had happened. He told them of what Hitler had demanded and then added bitterly: "Hitler also objected to the fact that Hungary has not yet introduced the steps necessary to settle the Jewish question. We are accused, therefore, of the crime of not having carried out Hitler's wishes, and I am charged with not having permitted the Jews to be massacred."[878] Following that report, the outgoing Kallay sought refuge in the Turkish Legation, and Horthy began to negotiate with Veesenmayer about the appointment of a new Prime Minister. Veesenmayer proposed Imredy, and Horthy nominated the Hungarian Minister in Berlin, Sztojay. The choice fell upon the latter. During the next few days, Veesenmayer and Sztojay drew up a list of Cabinet ministers. The list was approved by Horthy.[879]

The new Hungarian government took office on March 22, 1944. It included the following important officials:[880]

Prime Minister and Foreign Minister: Döme Sztojay
Economy: Imredy
War: Csatay
Finance: Remenyi-Schneller
Agriculture and Supply: Jurcsek
Justice: Antal
Trade: Kunder
Industry: Szasz
Interior: Jarosz
State Secretary in charge of political (Jewish) matters: Endre
State Secretary in charge of *Gendarmerie*: Baky
Gendarmerie officer in charge of deportations: Lt. Col. Ferenczy

878. Quoted from the minutes of the Crown Council meeting of March 19, 1944, by Levai, *Martyrdom*, p. 78.

879. Testimony by Horthy, Case No. 11, tr. pp. 2707–8, 2724–25.

880. *Deutsche Zeitung* (Budapest), March 23, 1944, p. 1. Affidavit by Staf. Kurt Becher, February 7, 1946, NG-2972. Affidavit by Kastner, September 18, 1945, PS-2605. The Economy Minister, Imredy, was appointed subsequently.

The new Hungarian government was not merely created by the Germans; it was to be responsible to its German masters for every step it took. On March 19, 1944, an army of German policy makers, supervisors, co-ordinators, and advisers swarmed into the country. These officials – representatives of the Foreign Office, the SS and Police, the army, the Pursuit Planes Staff, and private industry – directed Hungarian affairs from a multitude of offices in the Hungarian capital and in the provinces. Foremost among the offices of this shadow government was the German Legation.

The man in charge of the diplomatic mission – who also claimed to be the supreme co-ordinator of all German agencies within Hungary – was Minister and General Plenipotentiary Veesenmayer. The chargé d'affaires (his second in command) was Vortragende Legationsrat Feine; the legation's economic expert was Dr. Boden. The foreign Jews in the country were handled by Legationsrat Hezinger (after the end of May by Legationsrat Grell); the expert on Hungarian legislation (particularly anti-Jewish legislation) was von Adamovic, a man of limited use because he suffered from arthritis and sciatica. There were also three propaganda men: Triska, Brunhoff (press), and Ballensiefen (Anti-Jewish Institute). Finally, the legation had a liaison official, Consul Rekowsky.[881] To summarize:

881. The composition of the mission is described in a letter by von Thadden to Wagner, May, 1944, NG-2980. Also, von Thadden to Wagner, June 8, 1944, NG-2952. On Veesenmayer's appointment as minister and plenipotentiary, see Steengracht to East Ministry, March 20, 1944, enclosing appointment order by Hitler, March 19, 1944, NG-1543. The order also defined the (theoretical) relationship between Veesenmayer and other agencies in Hungary. On Veesenmayer's background,

Veesenmayer
Feine
Economy: Boden
Foreign Jews: Hezinger (Grell)
Propaganda:
  Triska
  Brunhoff
  Ballensiefen
Consul Rekowsky

Next to the legation, and perhaps even more important than the diplomats, was the SS and Police. This organization made its debut in Hungary on March 19, and so many SS and Police agencies were represented in the country that it was found necessary to appoint a Higher SS and Police Leader.

The *Sondereinsatzkommando,* formed shortly before March 19 in Mauthausen, the concentration camp, was the most formidable component of the machinery of destruction in Hungary. Here, under the command of Eichmann himself, the top deportation specialists of the RSHA had been concentrated into a single, devastatingly hard-hitting unit. These men had hardly arrived, and the German regime in Hungary had hardly been established, when the destruction process was set into motion with a speed and efficiency which displayed the accumulated experience of several years of European-wide deportations.

TABLE 67 / *The Himmler Organization in Hungary*

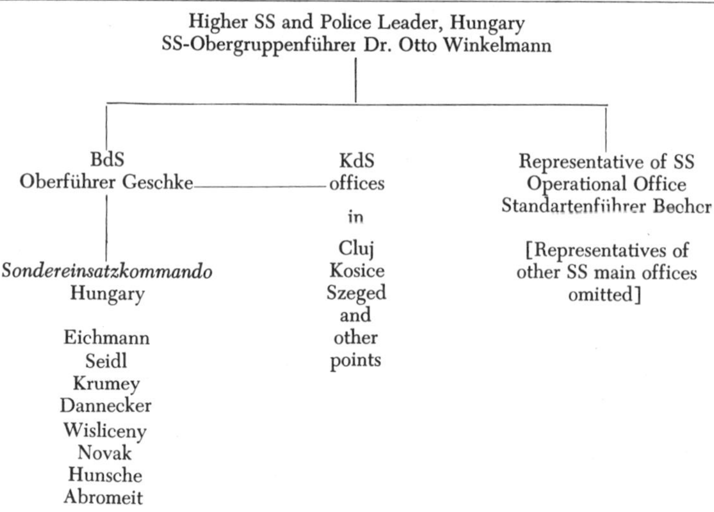

Schematically, the Himmler organization in Hungary is represented in Table 67.[882]

In two lightning moves the Germans maneuvered the Jewish community leadership into absolute submission and mobilized the Hungarian government for instantaneous destructive action.

education, and career, see his SS personnel record, NG-3004. On Adolf Hezinger's role, see his affidavit of January 16, 1948, NG-4457.

882. Affidavit by Kurt Becher, February 7, 1946, NG-2972. Affidavit by Kastner, September 18, 1945, PS-2605. Affidavit by Wisliceny, November 29, 1945, *Conspiracy and Aggression,* VIII 606–21. Affidavit by Wisliceny, June 11, 1947, NG-1823.

To win the co-operation of the Jewish leaders, Eichmann had to dispel the doubts of a group of men who knew exactly what they could expect. In the words of Dr. Rudolf Kastner, former associate president of the Zionist Organization in Hungary:

> In Budapest we had a unique opportunity to follow the fate of European Jewry. We had seen how they had been disappearing one after the other from the map of Europe. At the moment of the occupation of Hungary, the number of dead Jews amounted to over five million. We knew very well about the work of the *Einsatzgruppen*. We knew more than it was necessary about Auschwitz. . . . We had, as early as 1942, a complete picture of what had been happening in the East with the Jews deported to Auschwitz and the other extermination camps.[883]

This "complete picture" now had to be dispelled completely. The Eichmann *Sondereinsatzkommando* succeeded in doing precisely that.[884]

During the evening of March 19 the Jewish community leaders were ordered to appear for a conference with the *Sondereinsatzkommando* at 10 A.M. of the next day. The Jews arrived at the appointed hour and, after being allowed to cool their heels for a few hours, were received by a small delegation of SS men. The Germans were courteous. The president of the Jewish community, Dr. Samuel Stern, was addressed as *Herr Hofrat*. When Krumey noticed that the Jews had suitcases, he smiled and said: "No one is going to be arrested." The Jews were then informed that they would have to form a *Judenrat*. For the rest, the Germans wanted only a list itemizing the real estate owned by the Jewish community. With a reminder to stay in town the Jews were dismissed.

On the following day the Jews were ordered to hand in some blankets and mattresses. The Jewish leaders were then addressed by Wisliceny, who told them, "Everything goes on as usual [*Alles geht weiter wie bisher*]." During the next few days there were more German requests for blankets, typewriters, mirrors, women's lingerie, eau de cologne, original Watteau landscapes, etc. Once Hauptsturmführer Novak (Eichmann's transportation expert) declared soulfully that it was his dream to possess a piano; he had hardly uttered this wish when no less than eight pianos were presented to him. This brought the laughing reply, "But gentlemen, I don't want to open a piano store; I only want to play the piano [*Meine Herren, ich will ja kein Klaviergeschäft eröffnen, ich will nur Klavier spielen*]."

Eichmann himself expressed an interest in Jewish culture. He wanted to inspect the Jewish Museum and the Jewish Library. Then on March 31 Eichmann invited the members of the Jewish council to attend a conference in the Hotel Majestic. During that meeting Eichmann performed one of the greatest shows of his career. In the words of the historian Levai, "he virtually hypnotized the Jewish Council and through that body, the whole of Hungarian Jewry."

Eichmann began his speech by giving the assembled Jews the bad news. First, he said, the Jewish labor battalions would have to be increased; however, he assured his listeners that the Jewish workers would be treated well and that they might even be permitted to return home at night. Second, a *Judenrat* would have to be formed with jurisdiction over all Jews in Hungary. The *Judenrat* would have to act as a channel for German orders, as a central financing and taxation agency, and as a central depository of

883. Testimony by Kastner, Case No. 11, tr. pp. 3620–22.

884. The following pages are based on Levai's excellent account in *Martyrdom*, pp. 79–98.

information concerning Hungarian Jews. Third, the *Judenrat* would have to publish a newspaper which would contain all the German orders. The paper was to be self-financing and even profitable. At this point a representative of the Orthodox Jews inquired whether his group could publish a separate paper. Eichmann rejected the request. Fourth, the *Judenrat* would have to comply with all German requisition orders; the requisitioned articles, however, would be either returned or paid for.

So much, said Eichmann, for the German requests. He had nothing further to add except that the Jews had nothing to fear unless they refused to co-operate. No one would be shot for co-operating. No one was to try to mislead him because in such matters he had much experience. The present measures were all temporary. After the war the Germans would be *gutmütig* again; in the meantime he would not tolerate any molestation of Jews, and he wished to have any incidents reported to him.

The Jews were relieved. Now they knew what they had to do. Falling all over each other, they began to draw up plans for their *Judenrat*. Heated debates raged, and memoranda were written in great quantities. Finally the Jewish effort was crowned with success: the *Judenrat* was approved by Eichmann. Immediately the new council sent a letter to the presidents of the various Jewish communities in the provinces, calling upon them to obey all instructions emanating from Budapest.

At the same time the council addressed a manifesto to the Jewish population to maintain discipline and obey orders: "On receiving orders from the Central Council it is the duty of every person to report at the place and time indicated. The Central Jewish Council has been granted the right of absolute disposal over all Jewish spiritual and material wealth and over all Jewish manpower. You, women and girls, men and boys, are all the executors of the instructions issued by the Central Council. You must realize that every decision, however momentous it may be, is the outcome of official intervention, and that the life of every individual and the existence of the community as a whole depend on such instructions being fully observed. May God guide you and give you strength to attend faithfully to your duty!"

The impossible had been achieved: the Jewish community leadership was a pawn in German hands. Now there remained only the conversion of the Hungarian government into a tool of the German machinery of destruction, and that task was easy. The Hungarian co-operation was secured by means of an agreement concluded by Veesenmayer and Sztojay, in the presence of Winkelmann and Eichmann, during the deliberations preceding the formation of the Cabinet.[885] The Hungarians could then be told to proceed with the necessary anti-Jewish legislation. On March 29 the new Cabinet, meeting under the chairmanship of Sztojay, discussed the legislation in a marathon session that lasted – with but one interruption – from 11 A.M. to 10 P.M.[886]

At the end of the month the new State Secretary in the Interior Ministry who handled Jewish affairs, Endre, declared with a satisfied air that the new Hungarian anti-Semitism was "no imitation" *(Der ungarische Antisemitismus keine Nachahmung)*.[887] Just to make sure that the Hungarian laws would not become too original, however, Veesenmayer installed an RSHA man in

885. Affidavit by Kastner, September 13, 1945, PS-2605.

886. *Deutsche Zeitung* (Budapest), March 31, 1944, p. 1. A shorter meeting followed on March 31, between 10 A.M. and 2 P.M. *Ibid.*, April 1, 1944, p. 3.

887. *Ibid.*

Endre's office to advise the Hungarians "in steady personal contacts" *(in dauernder persönlicher Fühlungsnahme)* on the drafting and implementation of ordinances.[888]

The legislation was issued with what Veesenmayer described as "an unusual rapidity under local conditions" *(mit einer für hiesige Verhältnisse ungewöhnlichen Schnelligkeit)*.[889] The impoverization process so arduously begun in the 1930's was now completed with a few giant strides. The Hungarians dismissed or struck from the registers the remaining Jewish journalists, civil servants, notaries, patent lawyers, accountants, lawyers, even seventeen musicians of the Budapest Royal Opera House.[890]

Significantly, the March-April decrees contained no provisions against doctors. Although the Interior Ministry would have wished very much to restrict the practice of Jewish doctors to Jewish patients, a "practical implementation" of that principle was not possible so long as 4000 of Greater Hungary's 13,000 doctors were Jews.[891] Accordingly, the Hungarian government decided to make use of its Jewish doctors as long as it could. That their withdrawal in the deportations was felt acutely is indicated by the appointment of a commissar for the more efficient utilization of the doctor supply, in June, 1944.[892]

Next the Hungarians turned their attention to the Jewish stores. Following the usual pattern, a decree was published which required the Jews to register their property. Trading with registered assets was prohibited, and all but normal transactions concluded after March 22, 1944, were declared null and void.[893] Barely a week after the issuance of the registration ordinance the Ministry of Trade ordered the Jews to close their stores, offices, and warehouses. Out of a total of 110,000 establishments in Hungary, 40,000 were reported to be Jewish. Most of these stores were to stay closed; only a few were to reopen under trustees appointed by the local mayors, after consultation with the local Chambers of Industry and Commerce.[894]

In Budapest, with 30,000 stores in all, the closing of 18,000 Jewish establishments caused "considerable disturbances" *(empfindliche Störungen)*.[895] Nevertheless, the Hungarians plodded on. Perishable goods in the closed stores had to be sold immediately to non-Jewish enterprises;[896] non-perishable items were sold by government commissions in co-operation with the appropriate trade associations to non-Jewish merchants.[897] (These sales, incidentally, took place at a time when most of the Jewish owners were already dead.)

Having closed the Jewish stores, the Hungarian government also closed the Jewish bank accounts.[898] Then, stretch-

888. Veesenmayer to Foreign Office, April 22, 1944, NG-5725.

889. Veesenmayer to Foreign Office, April 7, 1944, enclosing texts of first Hungarians decrees, Occ E 6b-2.

890. *Ibid.* For statistics, see: Veesenmayer to Foreign Office, March 31, 1944, NG-5528. *Deutsche Zeitung* (Budapest), April 1, 1944, p. 3; April 2, 1944, p. 3; April 25, 1944, p. 6; May 6, 1944, p. 4. *Donauzeitung* (Belgrade), April 1, 1944, p. 3; April 2, 1944, p. 3; April 9/10, 1944, p. 3.

891. Interview of State Secretary Endre, *Deutsche Zeitung* (Budapest), April 18, 1944, p. 4.

892. *Donauzeitung* (Belgrade), June 11, 1944, p. 3; June 14, 1944, p. 3.

893. *Deutsche Zeitung* (Budapest), April 16, 1944, p. 3.

894. *Ibid.*, April 22, 1944, p. 3. *Donauzeitung* (Belgrade), April 25, 1944, p. 3; April 28, 1944, p. 4.

895. Economy officer in Hungary (Korvettenkapitän Krantsdorfer) to OKW/*Feldwirtschaftsamt*, May 14, 1944, Wi/IF .2.

896. *Deutsche Zeitung* (Budapest), April 23, 1944, p. 6.

897. *Ibid.*, June 22, 1944, p. 4; July 6, 1944, p. 3; September 30, 1944, p. 5.

898. *Donauzeitung* (Belgrade), April 28,

ing out their hands to take some personal property from the Jews, the Hungarians confiscated automobiles, radios, books, art objects, and old clothes, without distinction.[899] Finally the Food and Agriculture Ministry moved to complete the agricultural expropriations, a measure which left "without any actual management" (*ohne eigentliche Führung*) over 600,000 acres of land which had been owned or operated by Jews.[900] As if in retaliation, the Food Ministry issued instructions to deprive the Jews of all butter, eggs, paprika, rice, and poppy seeds; to restrict the Jewish meat supply to a few weekly ounces of beef or horsemeat; and to reduce the allocated quantities of sugar, fat, and milk. Special shopping hours in Budapest were added later.[901]

While the Hungarians fell all over themselves capturing and consuming the Jewish loot, the German invaders quickly snatched from under their very noses a choice morsel of Jewish property: At the very beginning of the coup, around March 19, Himmler dispatched to Hungary a representative of the SS Operational Main Office (that is, the military headquarters of the SS) with a special mission. The representative, Obersturmbannführer (later Standartenführer) Kurt Becher, was to secure for the SS the largest munition enterprise in Hungary, the Jewish-controlled Manfred Weiss Works.[902]

Secretly, without even informing the Veesenmayer legation, Becher entered into negotiations with the Jewish owners. The SS-man wanted to get hold of the enterprise before the Hungarians had an opportunity to frustrate the plan; the Jews wanted to leave the country before it was too late to leave. That was the basis of the bargain.

The Weiss-Chorin family, which owned the concern, was composed of prominent Jews who had intermarried extensively with Christians. The "Aryan" members of the family held 55 per cent of the stocks, and these "Aryan" stocks – which were believed to be unaffected by Hungarian restrictions on the transfer of Jewish property – were handed over to Becher, to be held by the SS under a "trusteeship" for a period of twenty-five years. In return for these stocks, the SS permitted forty-eight members of the family, including "roughly thirty-six Jews and twelve Aryans," to emigrate to Portugal, retaining, however, nine other family members as hostages to insure the good behavior of the emigrated Jews. In addition the SS agreed to make available to the emigrants 3 million reichsmark in foreign currency as partial payment for "lost profits."[903]

After the conclusion of these arrangements Himmler had to break the news to Veesenmayer so that the envoy could inform the Hungarians of the deal. Himmler's explanation, as transmitted to Veesenmayer through the legation's Consul Rekowsky, was somewhat as follows: The SS, said Himmler, had been committed unconditionally during this war. That was why he had decided to acquire an industrial concern which would assure to his SS men a dependable supply of the finest weapons for the remainder of the war and which would provide the basis for equipping the *Waffen-SS* to the greatest possible

1944, p. 4. *Deutsche Zeitung* (Budapest), May 6, 1944, p. 4.

899. Veesenmayer to Foreign Office, April 11, 1944, Occ E 6b-2. Veesenmayer to Foreign Office, June 8, 1944, NG-5620. *Deutsche Zeitung* (Budapest), April 12, 1944, p. 4; June 16, 1944, p. 4. *Donauzeitung* (Belgrade), May 3, 1944, p. 3; May 19, 1944, p. 3; June 7, 1944, p. 3.

900. German Economy Officer in Hungary to OKW/*Feldwirtschaftsamt/Ausland*, May 14, 1944, Wi/IF .2.

901. *Deutsche Zeitung* (Budapest), April 23, 1944, p. 7; June 7, 1944, p. 4.

902. Affidavit by Becher, February 7, 1946, NG-2972.

903. *Ibid.* Also, undated memorandum (presumably from SS files), NO-1254.

extent during the peaceful reconstruction effort *(Friedensaufbauarbeit)* to follow. In short, the SS was to become self-sufficient. For this purpose he had taken over Hungary's most important industrial concern under a trusteeship arrangement that was to last for twenty-five years. Binding contracts had already been signed, and a majority of the stocks were already in his hands.

When Consul Rekowsky returned to Budapest with this explanation, Veesenmayer wrote a letter to Ribbentrop personally, pointing out that Himmler's transaction could jeopardize everything that had so far been accomplished in Hungary.[904] Nevertheless, Veesenmayer dispatched his assistant, Rekowsky, and his economic expert, Dr. Boden, to Becher in order to smooth things over with the Hungarians. The three men concluded an agreement with Hungarian Economy Minister Imredy. The agreement did not cover all outstanding questions, but it validated the deal in principle.[905] With the completion of negotiations Himmler appointed four men to the new *Aufsichtsrat*: the industrialist and honorary Brigadeführer Freiherr von Schröder; the chief of the SS Operational Main Office, Obergruppenführer Juettner; the chief of the SS Economic-Administrative Main Office, Obergruppenführer Pohl; and the air force's Generalfeldmarschall Milch.[906]

904. Vessenmayer to Ribbentrop personally, May 26, 1944, NG-2770.

905. Affidavit by Becher, February 7, 1946, NG-2972.

906. Identical letters of appointment by Himmler to Schröder, Juettner, Pohl, and Milch, August 16, 1944, NO-601. Himmler to Schröder, August 16, 1944, NI-44. Schröder to Himmler, August 23, 1944, NI-45. Staf. Rudolf Brandt (Personal Staff, *Reichsführer-SS*) to Dr. Schmidt-Rohr (a curious inquirer), September 25, 1944, NO-595. Apparently Himmler had toyed with the idea of also appointing Staatssekretär Pleiger to the *Aufsichtsrat,* but Pohl objected strenuously to sharing the prize with a Göring man. Pohl to Himmler, June 15, 1944, NO-603.

While the SS sank its teeth into the richest prize of the Hungarian destruction process, the Hungarian administration continued to grind out anti-Jewish decrees. Almost nothing had been done before March 19, 1944, to effect a physical separation of Jews and Christians. The Bardossy regime had taken the first step in the concentration process when, as a by-product of the definition law, it prohibited marriages and extramarital intercourse between Jews and non-Jews.[907] At the end of March, 1944, the Sztojay government continued where the Bardossy administration had left off: on March 29 the employment of non-Jews in Jewish households was prohibited.[908] Then within a month the Jews were subjected to a central Jewish council, the Jewish star, movement restrictions, and finally ghettoization in designated apartments, city districts, and cities.

We have already seen how, in the very first days of the new regime the Eichmann *Sondereinsatzkommando* had managed to transform the existing Jewish community machinery into an organization which transmitted German orders to the Jewish population. (The Central Council, incidentally, was issuing orders for some weeks before the Hungarians got around to legalizing it.[909])

The star decree – a measure which the Germans had long waited for – was issued on March 29. Marking was not altogether new in Hungary; the Jewish labor companies had at times been set off with a yellow armband,[910] and even in 1941, Jewish students in the

907. Vessenmayer to Foreign Office, April 7, 1944, enclosing text of par. 9 of Law Article XV 1941, Occ E 6b-2.

908. Veesenmayer to Foreign Office, April 7, 1944, enclosing Ordinance No. 1200/1944 ME (signed Sztojay) of March 29, 1944, Occ E 6b-2.

909. Levai, *Martyrdom,* p. 130.

910. *Die Judenfrage,* March 15, 1942, p. 58.

Technical College of Budapest had made a "voluntary" agreement with "Aryan" students to wear special insignia.[911] Now, however, a decree had been passed which provided that all Jews above the age of six had to wear a Jewish star on a yellow patch of cloth measuring four by six inches. The only people freed from the application of the decree were World I veterans who were 75 per cent disabled or who had received one golden or two large silver medals (equivalent of U.S. Distinguished Service Cross or Silver Star with cluster), in the case of enlisted men, or the corresponding decorations, in the case of officers.[912]

The star decree hit the Catholic Church with tremendous impact. It was now apparent that tens of thousands of Christians, including even members of the clergy, would soon appear in the streets wearing a Jewish symbol. This was too much for the Church to take silently. Immediately upon publication of the decree on March 31, Justin Cardinal Seredi, Prince Primate of Hungary, sat down to write a letter to Sztojay in which he threatened to forbid his clergymen to wear the Jewish star.[913] Sztojay backed down. On April 4, one day before the Jews were to sew the patch on their clothes, an ordinance was issued which exempted members of the Christian clergy; the wives, widows, and children of exempted veterans; widows and orphans of *soldiers* (not labor service men) of the *Second* World War; Jews in mixed marriages; the Jewish widow of a Christian (provided that she belonged to the Christian religion and did not have Jewish children); and foreign Jews.[914]

Cardinal Seredi now moved to protect the rest of his Christian Jews. On April 23, 1944, he handed Sztojay a note in which he demanded that regulations concerning persons of the Jewish faith should not be applied to Christians. He considered it particularly offensive that people of the Christian faith should be represented on the same council with those of the Jewish faith. "It is not right," he said, "that Jews should have a particular power over Catholic priests or monks, or over Christians in general." Next he demanded that "Christians should no longer be obliged to wear the Star of David" because "the exhibition of this sign by Christians is tantamount to apostasy." Finally, Seredi requested that Catholic priests, aged people, and the infirm have the right to employ non-Jewish domestics and that the property of intermarried families remain untouched.[915]

This time, however, the Cardinal did not succeed. It was clear that an exemption from wearing the star would result in an exemption from deportation, and Sztojay knew full well that the Germans would not relinquish tens of thousands of their victims without an argument. Sztojay accordingly turned down Seredi's request, and the Church was beaten. Interestingly enough, a rumor reached the German Consul in Kosice (Kassa) to the effect that the Cardinal, as a last resort, had petitioned that permission be given to the Catholic Jews to exchange their Stars of David for white crosses.[916]

911. *Donauzeitung* (Belgrade), November 22, 1941, p. 3.

912. Veesenmayer to Foreign Office, April 7, 1944, enclosing Ordinance No. 1240/1944 ME (signed Sztojay), March 29, 1944, Occ E 6b-2.

913. Levai, quoting excerpts from the Seredi letter, in *Martyrdom,* p. 92.

914. Veesenmayer to Foreign Office, April 7, 1944, enclosing Ordinance No. 1450/1944 ME (signed Sztojay), April 4, 1944, Occ E 6b-2.

915. The Seredi letter is quoted in full by Levai, *Martyrdom,* pp. 118–20.

916. Affidavit by Hans Josef Count Matuschka (German Consul in Kosice), August 26, 1947, NG-2440.

Within days of the issuance of the star decree the Jewish community was restricted in its movements. In one of its first "official" acts the newly formed *Judenrat* prohibited Jews to leave or enter Budapest without its consent.[917] A few days later the civil defense–evacuation commissioner of the Hungarian capital ruled that no person who had to wear the star could henceforth leave the city,[918] and on April 7 the Hungarian government prohibited all Jewish travel without official permission by city police or rural *Gendarmerie*.[919] Jews who made application for permission to travel had to pay a fee of 10 pengö (RM 6 or $2.40) and, in the event that such permission was granted, a further fee of 20 pengö.[920] City after city then imposed a curfew which barred the Jews from the streets at night.[921] In conjunction with these movement restrictions the Hungarian Post Office confiscated all telephones in Jewish possession.[922]

The last stage of the concentration process – the physical isolation of the Jews – began with a massive wave of arrests. The Eichmann *Sondereinsatzkommando*, in co-operation with the machinery of the BdS and the Hungarian police, seized all Jews moving without permission in and out of Budapest, plus a large number of Jews who were believed to be particularly dangerous.[923] The arrest figures reached 3364 on March 31 and 8142 on April 28.[924] Many of these Jews were slated to be among the first victims in the deportations.

The over-all concentration of the Jews was effected on the basis of areas: the entire Hungarian territory was divided into five zones and the city of Budapest. In each zone a rapid ghettoization was to be followed by immediate deportation; the roundup and transport was to proceed from zone to zone, in consecutive operations, according to the schedule shown in Table 68.[925]

TABLE 68 / *Concentration Schedule*

Area		Start of Systematic Concentration	End of Deportation
Zone I	Carpathians	April 16	June 7
Zone II	Transylvania	May 4	June 7
Zone III	North of Budapest from Kosice to Reich frontier	June 7	June 17
Zone IV	East of Danube without Budapest	June 17	June 30
Zone V	West of Danube without Budapest	June 29	July 9
Budapest		early July	end of July

917. *Donauzeitung* (Belgrade), April 2, 1944, p. 3; April 16, 1944, p. 3.

918. *Deutsche Zeitung* (Budapest), April 5, 1944, p. 1.

919. The same decree contained restrictions on the use of trolleycars and withheld the right to drive automobiles from all Jews except doctors. Veesenmayer to Foreign Office, April 11, 1944, enclosing Ordinance No. 1270/1944 ME, April 7, 1944, Occ E 6b-2.

920. *Deutsche Zeitung* (Budapest), April 30, 1944, p. 4.

921. *Donauzeitung* (Belgrade), April 16, 1944, p. 3; May 9, 1944, p. 3; June 30, 1944, p. 3.

922. *Deutsche Zeitung* (Budapest), March 30, 1944, p. 2. *Donauzeitung* (Belgrade), March 31, 1944, p. 3. The use of public telephones was not restricted until August, 1944. *Ibid.*, August 12, 1944, p. 3.

923. Affidavit by Kastner, September 13, 1945, PS-2605. 22d Jäger Division to XXII Mountain Corps, April 7, 1944, NOKW-1995. Veesenmayer to Ritter, May 10, 1944, NG-5601. Veesenmayer to Ritter, May 20, 1944, NG-5605.

924. Veesenmayer to Foreign Office, March 31, 1944, NG-5527. Veesenmayer to Foreign Office, April 28, 1944, NG-5595.

925. Veesenmayer to Foreign Office, April 23, 1944, NG-2233. Veesenmayer to Foreign

The order of the zones was determined by three considerations. The first of these was the approach of the Red Army, which threatened to enter Hungary through the Carpathian Mountains.[926] The second consideration was the belief that Hungarian co-operation could most easily be secured in the deportation of those Jews who had most recently been subjected to the Hungarian flag and who were therefore least identified with the Hungarian nation. In that connection, we may recall that in 1943 the private secretary to Prime Minister Kallay had advised Hauptsturmführer Wisliceny to start the operation in the new territories (Zones I and II), continue in the old provinces (Zones III to V), and finish in the capital. The third reason for proceeding from the outer perimeter to the center was based on the premise that the Jews would have to be fooled as long as possible. While the Jews from the Carpatho-Ukraine and Transylvania were being removed, the Jews in Old Hungary could be assured that radical measures were being directed only at the non-Magyarized element of the Jewish population, and that the well-established Hungarian Jews would have nothing to worry about.[927] In this sense the German plan was a most literal application of the rule "divide and conquer."

Ways and means of implementing the concentration plan were worked out by the *Sondereinsatzkommando* Eichmann and the Hungarian Interior Ministry at the beginning of April,[928] and for the individual zones during periodic conferences thereafter. The roundup was to be carried out by Hungarian police and *Gendarmerie;* Eichmann's men were to stay in the background and act as advisers.[929] In principle, all Jews living in towns of less than 10,000 inhabitants were to be transferred to larger cities and to camps. For this part of the operation the *Sondereinsatzkommando* needed a sociographic map, which it requested from the Jewish Council.

When the map was not produced by April 23, the Jews were summoned to a meeting. Wisliceny, Novak, and Hunsche sat around a table while the Jews were forced to stand. Wisliceny announced that no Jews would remain in towns of less than 10,000, then demanded angrily why the map had not been prepared. Criticizing the council for its slowness, he pointed in contrast to President Löwenherz of the Vienna community, who was "a fine fellow" (*ein braver Kerl*). Löwenherz was still in Vienna. On the other hand, Wisliceny knew full well what he had to do with Jewish leaders who would not obey—they would be sent to Dachau, like the "Jewish Führer" in Berlin.[930]

Frightened and dismayed, the Jewish Council now watched the unfolding of the ghettoization process. Trains were moving out of the small towns and dumping Jews in improvised

Office, May 4, 1944, NG-2262. Von Thadden to Wagner, May 25, 1944, NG-2980. Veesenmayer to Foreign Office, June 10, 1944, NG-2237. Veesenmayer to Foreign Office, June 13, 1944, NG-5619. Veesenmayer to Foreign Office, June 30, 1944, NG-2263. Veesenmayer to Foreign Office, July 11, 1944, NG-5615.

926. *Die Lage* (confidential circular of the party propaganda office and the Propaganda Ministry), August 23, 1944, D-908.

927. An announcement to that effect was actually circulated through the Jewish machinery. Report by von Thadden, May 26, 1944, NG-2190.

928. See text of instructions by Hungarian Interior Ministry to Royal Police and *Gendarmerie,* April 7, 1944, in Levai, *Martyrdom,* pp. 111–13.

929. Directive by Hungarian Interior Ministry, April 7, 1944, in Levai, *Martyrdom,* pp. 111–13. Testimony by Horthy, Case No. 11, tr. p. 2735. Affidavit by Kastner, September 18, 1945, PS-2605.

930. Levai, *Martyrdom,* p. 123. Baeck, the Jewish "Führer" in Berlin, who had obeyed instructions to the hilt, was sent to Theresienstadt. See p. 292.

camps. In the large cities the Jews were shoved into makeshift ghettos. At Oradea, Szeged, and Sighet ghettos were established in city sections. At Cluj, Uzhorod, and Kosice the Jews were pushed into brick factories. At Baia-Mare, Târgu-Mureş, and Dej the victims were concentrated under the open sky.[931] Whereas a few essential workers and (in some cities) also the indispensable doctors were exempted from the roundup, the masses of men, women, children, Christian Jews, and foreign Jews were packed indiscriminately behind barbed wire.[932] A lone official from the German Legation, Legationsrat Hezinger (later Grell), circulated through the camps and ghettos to pull out the foreign Jews.[933] The Hungarian authorities, in the meantime, reduced the food rations of the incarcerated victims to a daily allocation of one-fifth of a pound of bread and two cups of soup, for these Jews were not expected to remain in Hungary very long.[934]

When the roundup in the provinces neared its completion, the compression of the Jewish population began in the capital also. Budapest, however, was to have no ghetto; the Hungarians were afraid that the establishment of a closed Jewish district would invite Allied retaliatory air raids upon the non-Jewish sections of the city. To preclude such a result, State Secretary Endre decided to crowd the Jews into apartment houses located near factories, railway stations, and other potential targets of "terror bombers."[935]

The German propaganda experts were not entirely happy with this Hungarian maneuver, which was almost an experiment to test the theory of world Jewish rule. If the raids were actually organized by world Jewry, presumably the Hungarian capital would henceforth be spared; if, on the other hand, allied Jewry were powerless, the Budapest Jews would be bombed. On May 4, 1944, the Reich propaganda office in Munich consequently advised the newspapers that the transfer of Budapest Jews to areas threatened by bombing attacks was "for the moment not worth mentioning in the German press."[936] The apprehensions of the propaganda experts were well founded; at the end of June, in two consecutive raids, Allied bombers demolished eleven Jewish apartment houses, killing 116 Jews and wounding 342.[937]

The Hungarians now proceeded with the housing relocations in earnest, determined that the Jews of Budapest should suffer "their share" of the "Anglo-American terror."[938] At the beginning of July a total of 2639 houses containing 33,294 apartments with 70,197 rooms were set aside for the

931. Affidavit by Kastner, September 18, 1945, PS-2605. Affidavit by Hans Josef Count Matuschka (German Consul, Kosice), August 26, 1947, NG-2440. *Donauzeitung* (Belgrade), May 21, 1944, p. 3.

932. On essential workers, see order of Hungarian Interior Ministry, in Levai, *Martyrdom,* pp. 111–13. On doctor exemptions, see: Veesenmayer to Ritter, May 6, 1944, NG-5600. *Donauzeitung* (Belgrade), May 21, 1944, p. 3.

933. Veesenmayer to Foreign Office, May 4, 1944, NG-2262. Report by von Thadden, May 26, 1944, NG-2190. Affidavit by Adolf Hezinger, January 16, 1948, NG-4457. The concentration and deportation of Slovak Jews in Hungary was protested by the Slovak Legation in Budapest. The Slovaks, however, expressed their disinterest in Jews who had illegally crossed the Hungarian frontier, "especially orphans" (*namentlich elternlose Kinder*). Veesenmayer to Foreign Office, June 13, 1944, NG-2583.

934. Affidavit by Kastner, September 18, 1945, PS-2605.

935. Explanation by Endre in *Deutsche Zeitung* (Budapest), April 18, 1944, p. 4.

936. Confidential instructions (*Vertrauliche Informationen*) by Reich propaganda office (a party agency), May 4, 1944, NG-3413.

937. *Donauzeitung* (Belgrade), June 30, 1944, p. 3.

938. Declaration by mayor of Budapest (Dr. Doroghi-Farkas) in *Donauzeitung* (Belgrade), June 18, 1944, p. 3.

Jewish population.[939] What these statistics meant may be glimpsed in Table 69.[940] Some 19,000 Jewish apartments were won for bombed-out and overcrowded Hungarians. The Jewish apartment density was to reach about 3 per room. In principle, an ordinary Jewish family was entitled to only one room, although doctors, lawyers, and engineers were permitted to apply for two rooms. All Jewish apartments were to be marked with a twelve-inch Jewish star.[941]

Table 69 / *Apartment Density in Budapest*

	Population	Apartments August, 1941	Apartments July, 1944
Total	1,000,000	270,000	270,000
Jewish	200,000	52,300	33,294

Throughout the Hungarian domain the concentration process was so devised that in each zone the roundup was to be followed by immediate deportations. There was to be no waiting until the last Jews in Budapest were assigned to their special house. The deportations were to begin in the first two zones before the ghettoization in the third zone got under way, and the Jews were to be shipped out of the third zone before the seizures in the fourth zone began. The ghettos of the fourth zone were to be emptied before the round-up in the fifth zone was to start, and the Jews of the fifth zone were to be deported before the Jews of Budapest were ready. This type of operation required immediate preparations for transport.

On April 20, Veesenmayer wrote to the Foreign Office that he was experiencing the greatest difficulties in the procurement of freight cars.[942] A week later, on April 27 and 28, two special trains loaded with 4000 Jewish men and women left the internment camp of Kistarcsa, bound for the killing center of Auschwitz.[943] These were advance transports. The arrivals were forced to write encouraging cards to relatives with datelines from "Waldsee." The notes were brought by an SS courier to Budapest, to be distributed there by the Jewish Council.[944] Now no time was lost. On May 4–5 a *Reichsbahn* conference, attended by representatives of the Hungarian and Slovak railways and delegates from the Eichmann *Sondereinsatzkommando* and Hungarian *Gendarmerie,* was held in Vienna. It was decided to begin the dispatch to Auschwitz of four daily transports, holding 3000 Jews each, in the middle of May.[945] On the very day of that conference the roundup in Zone I was completed with the concentration of some 200,000 Jews in ten ghettos and camps.[946] Zero hour was approaching.

On this, the eve of the deportations, some of the participants in the destruction process felt clearly and deeply its meaning and implications. In the town of Dej two regional officials, the *Obergespan* and *Vizegespan* of the *Komitat Szolnok-Doboka,* went on sick leave.

939. *Donauzeitung* (Belgrade), July 11, 1944, p. 3.

940. 1941 statistics from *Donauzeitung* (Belgrade), August 23, 1941, p. 4.

941. *Ibid.,* June 18, 1944, p. 3.

942. Veesenmayer to Foreign Office, April 20, 1944, NG-5546.

943. Veesenmayer to Foreign Office, April 27, 1944, NG-5535.

944. Affidavit by Kastner, September 18, 1945, PS-2605.

945. Von Thadden to legation in Bratislava, May 2, 1944, NG-5565. Veesenmayer to Foreign Office, May 4, 1944, NG-2262.

946. Veesenmayer to Foreign Office, May 4, 1944, NG-2262. Zone I included the Carpatho-Ukraine with some contiguous areas stretching into former Roumanian territory.

The two men, Count Bela Bethlen and Dr. Janos Schilling, did not "approve of" the *Judenaktion* that was in progress in their district. Count Bethlen declared that he did not want to become a mass murderer and that he would rather resign (*Graf Bethlen hat erklärt dass er nicht zum Massenmörder werden wolle und lieber zurücktrete*).[947] The Catholic Church, too, began to understand that it was facing one of its greatest challenges, and it protested — within the bounds set by its 2000-year history.

There were, strictly speaking, two centers of Catholic influence in Hungary: the papal nuncio, Angelo Rotta, and the Prince Primate, Cardinal Seredi. The nuncio took the first step. On May 15, the day on which the deportations started in Zone I, the Vatican representative handed the following note to the Hungarian Foreign Office:

> The Hungarian Government is prepared to deport 100,000 persons. . . . The whole world knows what deportation means in practice.
>
> The Apostolic Nuntiature considers it to be its duty to protest against such measures. Not from a false sense of compassion, but on behalf of thousands of Christians, it once again appeals to the Hungarian Government not to continue this war against the Jews beyond the limits prescribed by the laws of nature and the commandments of God and to avoid any proceedings against which the Holy See and the conscience of the whole Christian world would be compelled to protest.[948]

While this protest was delivered to the Sztojay regime, the Cardinal remained silent. He was tiring of the fight. The challenge, however, had not passed. On May 27 and again on June 17, Bishop Apor of Györ urged the Cardinal to issue a public declaration, lest the "flock" equate silence with acquiescence. Stung, Seredi replied to the second letter in these words: "I also have a conscience and I am aware of my responsibility. That is why, for the duration of the discussion [with the government] I did not want to do what your Excellency urges, or carry out the actions I have prepared myself. I am now going to act, but expect no result from this step either."[949]

A few days later a pastoral letter was drafted by Seredi, his deputy vicar John Drakos, "who tempered the stronger expressions," and a number of archbishops and bishops who suggested minor changes. In its final form, signed by Justinianus Seredi and dated June 29, 1944, the document was over three pages long. The letter began with a discussion of such subjects as wages, fixed working hours, insurance, and the bombardment of Hungarian towns, including "the disablement of innocent children by means of explosive toys scattered by aeroplanes." One passage was devoted to the Jews. It read in part as follows:

> We do not deny that a number of Jews have executed a wickedly destructive influence on the Hungarian economic, social, and moral life. It is also a fact that the others have not protested against the actions of their co-religionists in this respect. We do not doubt that the Jewish question ought to be settled in a lawful and just way. Consequently we raise no objections to steps being taken, so far as the financial system of the State is concerned. Neither do we protest against the objectionable influence being eliminated; on the contrary, we would like to see it vanish. However, we would be neglecting our moral and episcopal duties were we not to guard against justice suffering damage and against our Hungarian fellow-citizens and our Catholic faithful being wronged

947. Veesenmayer to Ritter, May 8, 1944, enclosing report by Higher SS and Police Leader Winkelmann, NG-5510.

948. Text in Levai, *Martyrdom,* p. 197.

949. Seredi to Apor, June 20, 1944, quoted in Levai, *Martyrdom,* p. 207.

merely on account of their origin. . . .

We were unable to achieve what we most desired, namely that the unlawful limitations of civil rights and especially the deportations are stopped. However, as we relied upon the Christianity and the humanity of the members of the Government, we had not given up all hope, in spite of the meager results obtained up to now. For this reason we issued no proclamation to you, but restrained ourselves, in the meantime taking all steps to achieve our purpose. . . . We see now, however, with great consternation, that despite our efforts all our negotiations on the most important points have up to now proved almost ineffective. Therefore we solemnly refuse all responsibility for the consequences. . . . Pray and work for all our Hungarian fellow-citizens and especially for our Catholic brethren, our Catholic Church and our beloved Hungary.[950]

Since the letter was dispatched through the Hungarian postal censorship, only seven hundred copies were received by pastors to be read during the Sunday service. Sunday was July 1, the day after the fourth zone had been cleared of Jews. On July 6, at a time when the fifth zone was worked over by Hungarian *Gendarmerie,* Cardinal Seredi and Justice Minister Antal met to discuss the Church's complaints. Antal promised that the deportations of Christian Jews would henceforth cease, and during the next day (a Saturday) Seredi gave instructions that the pastoral letter be suppressed. There was considerable wrangling about the publication of a substitute letter, but no more letters were published.[951]

The Cardinal had had enough. But still the Church was not let alone; it was now plagued by new challenges. During the middle of July the chief of the Nazi-like Arrow Cross Party in Veszprém demanded that the Franciscans conduct a Mass to thank God for the removal of the Jews. The bishop, declaring that many Christians were among the deported victims, denounced the project, but the pressure from the Arrow Cross men increased. Finally the Church compromised by conducting the service without the *Te Deum.*[952]

Another threat developed from the desire by the Jews of Budapest to acquire the protection of the Church through baptism. Conversions were not exactly new in Hungary; since 1941 the Hungarian Catholic Cross Society had been conducting two-month courses (two lectures per week) for prospective Christians.[953] During a single week following the Seredi-Antal conference, however, more Jews applied for baptism than had sought Christianity in the preceding fifteen years.[954]

Laughing at the dilemma facing the clergy, State Secretary Baky of the Interior Ministry ordered police to guard the Jews standing in line in front of the churches, lest the public order be disturbed.[955] Shortly afterward the Vicar of Budapest issued two orders: one required a three-month preparatory course for the receipt of baptism;[956] the other demanded a release certificate signed by a rabbi.[957]

While the Church was confronted with a battle for moral survival, the Jews were facing a threat to sheer phys-

950. Text of complete letter with discussion of its history in Levai, *Martyrdom,* pp. 207–10.

951. *Ibid.,* pp. 211–12.

952. Veesenmayer to Ritter, July 20, 1944, NG-5613.

953. Veesenmayer to Ritter, May 20, 1944, NG-5604.

954. Declaration by a representative of the archbishhop vicar in *Deutsche Zeitung* (Budapest), July 14, 1944, p. 4.

955. *Deutsche Zeitung* (Budapest), July 14, 1944, p. 2.

956. *Ibid.,* July 27, 1944, p. 3.

957. *Ibid.,* July 30, 1944, p. 8. The Evangelical and Unitarian Churches followed suit in barring quick conversions. *Ibid.,* August 5, 1944, p. 3; August 15, 1944, p. 3.

ical existence. In the ghettos, however, there was still hope. On May 6, 1944, Veesenmayer reported to Ambassador Ritter that among the Jews in Târgu-Mures (Transylvania), who had suddenly been hurled into a ghetto at 5 A.M. on May 3, excitement ran high. The Jews were still hoping for a "temporary concentration" (*zeitlich begrenzte Unterbringung*) and a "favorable solution" (*günstige Lösung*).[958] In the ghetto of Oradea 20,000 inmates were subjected to systematic questioning by the Hungarian *Gendarmerie* because of a suspicion that the Jews, probably in the hope of an early return to their homes, had hidden valuables with Christian families in the city.[959]

To be sure, there were indications also of some apprehension within the Jewish community. A sizable number of Jews, acting individually were attempting in various ways to evade the coming blow. Thus a Budapest newspaper, the *Magyar Szo,* complained that many people had recently advertised the loss of personal and family documents. These persons, said the paper, were Hungarians who had sold their birth certificates to Jews.[960] On April 30, Vessenmayer reported that many Jews were trying to take refuge in the labor companies and suggested that many who were not subject to induction might have bribed their way in.[961]

In Zones I, II, and III a number of Jews were attempting to flee to Slovakia and Roumania.[962] The movement to Slovakia apparently was large enough to induce Veesenmayer to urge the Foreign Office that preventive measures be taken by deporting the remaining Slovakian Jews.[963] In the ghettos of Mukachevo, Oradea, and Tizabogdany, Jews walled themselves in and hid in earth holes. The Hungarian *Gendarmerie* was still discovering these hiding places long after the ghettos had been evacuated.[964]

Yet on the whole the Jews were unable to extricate themselves from the net. This is how an SS observer on the scene, Sturmbannführer Höttl, described the victims' reaction:

> Without resistance and in submission, they marched by the hundreds in long columns to railway stations and piled into the trains. Only very few gendarmes were supervising the operation; it would have been easy to flee. In the Carpatho-Ukraine, which contained numerically the strongest Jewish settlements, the forbidding mountains and forests offered an opportunity for prolonged hiding. But only few removed themselves in this way from their doom.[965]

In Budapest the Central Jewish Council (or Union of Hungarian Jews, as it came to be called) found itself at the crossroads. The Jewish leaders felt that they had to do something, but even petitioning had become difficult for them. On May 3 the council wrote to Interior Minister Jarosz:

958. Veesenmayer to Ritter, May 6, 1944, NG-5600.

959. *Deutsche Zeitung* (Budapest), June 1, 1944, p. 6.

960. *Donauzeitung* (Belgrade), May 9, 1944, p. 3.

961. Veesenmayer to Ritter, April 30, 1944, NG-5597.

962. Veesenmayer to Ritter, May 2, 1944, NG-5598. Veesenmayer to Ritter; May 8, 1944, NG-5510. Veesenmayer to Ritter, June 17, 1944, NG-5567. Veesenmayer to Foreign Office, July 11, 1944, NG-5586.

963. Veesenmayer to Foreign Office, June 14, 1944, NG-5533. Altenburg to Veesenmayer, June 14, 1944, NG-2829. Altenburg to Ludin, June 16, 1944, NG-2261.

964. Veesenmayer to Ritter, July 20, 1944, NG-5613.

965. Walter Hagen (pseud. for Höttl), *Die Geheime Front* (Zurich, 1950), p. 39. The extent to which hidden Jews were denounced by the Hungarian population is not quite clear. See Altenburg to Veesenmayer, May 17, 1944, NG-2425. Also, Veesenmayer to Ritter, May 20, 1944, NG-5604.

> We emphatically declare that we do not seek this audience to lodge complaints about the merit of the measures adopted, but merely ask that they be carried out in a humane spirit.[966]

On May 12, 1944, the council sent the following communication to Jarosz:

> On the 9th inst. the Jews living in Heves were transported a distance of 80 kilometers to the abandoned mining settlement of Bagölyk near Egerseki. . . . We would take the liberty of mentioning that the town of Heves has, according to the 1941 census, a population of 10,597.[967]

From the middle of May to the middle of June the council watched the removal of the Jews from Zones I, II, and III. On June 23 the council finally dispatched a letter to Horthy which rang with a note of despair. "In the twelfth hour of our tragic fate we appeal to you in the name of humanity to influence the Royal Hungarian Government to cease immediately the deportation of hundreds of thousands of innocent people." The letter branded as "false" the explanations offered to the Jews that the deportations were dictated by military necessity and that the deportees would be engaged in forced labor. The Jews, said the council, were being sent on a "fatal journey from which they will never return." The letter concluded with a detailed breakdown of deportation statistics and a plea that the Jews be allowed to use their strength and their labor "for the sake of defending our country and in the interest of production."[968]

The masses of Jewish deportees, numb, fantasy-ridden, and filled with illusions, reacted with mechanical cooperation to every German command. The Jewish council, hoping against hope for a postponement of the inevitable, woke up too late to act. Hungarian Jewry's last chance thus depended on a group of men who were awake from the start and who were disposed to undertake action. Such a group did exist in Hungary when the Germans broke in, but its plans for action depended on outside help.

In January, 1943, a number of Zionists (mainly Transylvanians) had formed an assistance and rescue committee (*Vaadat Ezra v' Hazalah*) for the purpose of helping Jews escaping to Hungary from Slovakia, Poland, and the Reich-Protektorat area. The chief personalities of the committee were the following:[969]

President: Dr. Otto Komoly
Executive vice president: Dr. Rudolf Kastner
Finance: Samuel Springmann
Tijul (underground rescue of Jews from Poland): Joel Brand

The division of work between the president and the executive vice president was such that Komoly represented the committee in negotiations with the Hungarian government, whereas Kastner handled the Germans.[970] By the end of 1943 the committee had come to the conclusion that the rescue and relief work would soon have to give way to the far greater task of dealing with the German threat in Hungary. To the committee the fulfilment of this task presented itself in three alternate forms, which were tried concurrently.

The first plan called for the creation of a resistance organization. The committee members did not think that they could create such an organization themselves; therefore they called upon the Jewish Agency in Palestine for help. This move was initiated before 1943.[971]

966. Levai, *Martyrdom*, p. 134.
967. *Ibid.*, p. 135.
968. Full text of letter, *ibid.*, pp. 192–96.

969. Kasztner, *Der Bericht des jüdischen Rettungskomittees aus Budapest 1942–1945*, p. 7. A copy of this scarce report is located in the Library of Congress.
970. *Ibid.*, pp. xii, 20. Otto Komoly did not survive.

The Jewish Agency, after lengthy negotiations with the British, managed to secure British consent for the dispatch of a few parachutists to Europe; however, the agreement provided that the parachutists were to carry out military missions before they were to concern themselves with Jewish matters. These terms were "strictly honored."[972]

Three parachutists were dropped in Croatia on April 14, 1944, and crossed the Hungarian border on June 13. Under continuous observation by the SS and the Hungarian General Staff, the three were seized in Budapest, and Veesenmayer reported the arrest on July 8, 1944, the day before Zone V was completely cleared of Jews.[973] That was the extent of resistance activity in Hungary.

Another scheme was developed in May, 1944, when a Slovak railway official furnished to the Jewish relief committee in Bratislava information about the number and the direction of the special trains which were scheduled to carry the Hungarian Jews to Auschwitz. The Bratislava committee promptly transmitted the details to the committee in Budapest.[974] In the Hungarian capital the Jewish leaders recognized that a systematic bombing by Allied planes of two or three railway junctions on the Kosice-Presov-Silina-Bohumin line could upset the entire deportation program and conceivably save hundreds of thousands of lives. Upon request of the Budapest relief committee, the Bratislava Jews telegraphed to Switzerland a request for the bombing of these railway junctions. From the Allies, however, there was no response.[975]

The third effort of the relief committee was based on a direct approach to the Germans. At the beginning of April, the vice president in charge of German negotiations, Dr. Rudolf Kastner, and his colleague, the rescue expert Joel Brand, established contact with Hauptsturmführer Wisliceny of the *Sondereinsatzkommando* Eichmann. There are two versions of the ensuing discussions.

According to Kastner, the SS man promised that, for 6.5 million pengö (ca. RM 4,000,000 or $1,600,000 at the official rate of exchange), 600 Jews would be permitted to leave for Palestine. The committee immediately turned to the central council for financial help, and after weeks of canvassing, the council managed to collect 5 million pengö from rich Jews. The committee itself added the missing million and a half. The Germans then raised the number of prospective emigrants by a thousand.[976]

Eichmann stated in his memoirs that Kastner "agreed to keep the Jews from resisting deportation – and even keep order in the camps – if I would close my eyes and let a few hundred or a few thousand young Jews emigrate illegally to Palestine. It was a good bargain."[977]

Whatever the price may have been, the Jewish leadership now had to select from the 750,000 doomed Hungarian Jews 1600 who were to live. Their first reaction was to select only children. Wisliceny, however, vetoed this plan on the ground that the Hungarians would notice a children's transport. The Jews thereupon proceeded to compile a list of ten categories: Orthodox Jews, Zionists, prominent Jews (*Prominente*), orphans, refugees, Revisionists, etc. One category consisted of "paying persons." The geographic distribution was a bit

971. *Ibid.*, pp. 15, 70–73.

972. On Palestine end of the negotiations and the assignment of the parachutists, see Syrkin, *Blessed Is the Match*, pp. 18–35.

973. Veesenmayer to Ritter, July 8, 1944, NG-5616.

974. Affidavit by Kastner, September 13, 1945, PS-2605.

975. Kasztner, *Bericht*, pp. vi–vii.

976. *Ibid.*, pp. 24–27, 58, 63.

977. *Life*, December 5, 1960, p. 146.

lopsided: 388 persons, including Kastner's father-in-law, came from the Transylvanian city of Cluj. "Eichmann knew," reports Kastner, "that we had a special interest in Cluj" (*dass Klausenburg uns besonders nahestand*). The transport left, at the height of the deportations, for Bergen-Belsen. In the fall of 1944 some of the rescued Jews arrived in Switzerland.[978]

On May 8, one week before the deportations were to start, Eichmann called Kastner's colleague Joel Brand to discuss a new proposition. Eichmann acted upon Himmler's direct orders and – as usual – without the knowledge of the German Legation. He proposed a scheme whereby the lives of the Hungarian Jews could be saved for a price, to be paid in goods. The following quantities were mentioned: 200 tons of tea, 200 tons of coffee, 2,000,000 cases of soap, 10,000 trucks for the *Waffen*-SS to be used on the eastern front, and unspecified quantities of tungsten and other war materials. The SS would be most interested in the trucks. To procure these items, Brand was to leave for Istanbul, Turkey, to contact the Western Allies. The Jews, in the meantime, would be sent to Auschwitz to be gassed until such time as a favorable reply was received.[979]

On May 17, two days after the first transports had left Hungary, Brand (accompanied by a Jew, Grosz, who had once worked for the Canaris office) moved out of Budapest for Vienna, and from there the two men proceeded to Istanbul. Caught by British agents, Brand and Grosz were transported to Cairo, to be held in solitary confinement for several months by Deputy Minister of State Lord Moyne.

In Budapest the Jewish leadership waited in vain for some Allied counteroffer that might induce the Germans to stop the gassings. The relief committee did not expect the Allies to deliver actual war matériel to the German war machine; they hoped only for a verbal maneuver – a gesture, a promise – that would bring about protracted negotiations while the Jewish deportees in Auschwitz would stay "on ice" waiting for the arrival of the Red Army. But week after week passed, and there was no acceptance, no reply, no stir. Only silence. In Auschwitz death enveloped Hungarian Jewry.[980]

The relief committee in Budapest was now thrown back upon its own resources. From the Allies it had received no backing; from world Jewry it had received no help. There was in Budapest particular recrimination for those outside Jews who had not done their utmost. "They were outside," said Kastner, "we were inside. They were not immediately affected, we were the victims. They moralized, we feared death. They had sympathy for us and believed themselves to be powerless; we wanted to live and believed rescue *had* to be possible."[981]

The Germans, too, somehow believed that the ransom idea was not yet dead. In holding on to that idea, the Germans reasoned that the Allies – who after all were fighting this war for the Jews – would not fail to rescue them in their hour of crisis. But behind this thought there was another consideration: the Germans were convinced that the Allies were really afraid of Com-

978. Kasztner, *Bericht,* pp. 41, 43–44, 46, 56, 90. Wagner via Hencke and Steengracht to Ribbentrop, September 29, 1944, NG-2994. Wagner to Ribbentrop, November 11, 1944, NG-2994.

979. Affidavit by Kastner, September 13, 1945, PS-2605. Kasztner, *Bericht,* pp. 33, 36–37. Executive Director, War Refugee Board (William O'Dwyer), *Final Summary Report* (Washington, D.C., 1945), pp. 39–40. Veesenmayer via Ritter to Ribbentrop, July 22, 1944, NG-2994.

980. Kasztner, *Bericht,* pp. 36–38. Ira Hirschman (special agent of the War Refugee Board), *Journey to a Promised Land* (New York, 1945), pp. 109–27.

981. Kasztner, *Bericht,* pp. 88–89.

munist Russia and that at the last moment they would not be averse to making a deal with the Reich for the purpose of stopping the Red tide. That is why the SS and Police awaited with great interest the Western reaction to the proposal that 10,000 trucks be delivered for exclusive use on the eastern front. The Germans did not know, of course, that the Allies took far more seriously their alliance with Soviet Russia than the fate of Hungarian Jewry. In the meantime, however, the SS waited, and during the waiting period Himmler was susceptible to all sorts of financial discussions.[982]

On June 7, 1944, the mayor of Vienna, the Honorary SS-Brigadeführer Blaschke, requested Kaltenbrunner to assign Hungarian Jews to labor-starved factories in the Viennese area.[983] At that very time the finance experts of the relief committee figured out that goods valued at 4 or 5 million Swiss francs (about 2.5 million reichsmark, or 1 million dollars) could still be mobilized in Hungary. That sum was immediately offered to the *Sondereinsatzkommando*. On June 14, Eichmann declared himself ready to transport up to 30,000 Jews to the Vienna area. For 5 million Swiss francs he was prepared to make a start, and the remaining Jews (to a maximum of 30,000) were to be shipped to Austria just as soon as additional sums rolled in. The committee now promised to deliver everything it possibly could. The Kastner report does not make entirely clear how much was delivered to the *Kommando*. About 15 tons of coffee ("a little rancid") could be placed at the disposal of the Germans at once; 65,000 reichsmark were paid out in cash; and 30 Swiss tractors were promised, although the tractors never left Switzerland. Again, the Jewish sources make no mention of "keeping order in the camps." Only Eichmann does. The deal, at any rate, covered six transports with 17,500 or 18,000 Jews.[984]

The committee now had the awful task of selecting the Jews to be saved. Lists were made in Budapest and in the provinces. The lists were altered, enlarged, cut down. There were original lists and replacement lists. In the end, accident also played a part. An SS-man – whether by mistake or as a "little joke" – switched two trains. A transport from Györ, and with it the rabbi of the Györ community, Dr. Emil Roth was delivered to Auschwitz. Instead of the Györ train, another which had been scheduled to go to Auschwitz arrived in Vienna.[985]

The 18,000 Hungarian Jews in Austria were laid "on ice." They remained under the jurisdiction of the *Sondereinsatzkommando* Hungary, which dispatched Obersturmbannführer Krumey to head its new branch (*Aussenstelle*) in Vienna. The Jews lived there under a strict regime: they wore stars, were allowed to have no money, were not permitted to shop or to smoke, and were forced to work in industry for no wage. A thousand of the Jews died; a few were sent to Bergen-Belsen, a few to Auschwitz.[986]

Eichmann, though the chief negotiator, performed his task with a sense of

982. When, during the second half of July, the London radio broadcast an indignant reply to the ransom offer, Legationsrat Grell in the Budapest Legation conjectured that the Allies were still willing to enter into the transaction and that the report from London denying such an intention was camouflage designed to fool the Russians. Veesenmayer via Ritter to Ribbentrop, July 22, 1944, NG-2994.

983. Kaltenbrunner to Blaschke, June 30, 1944, PS-3803.

984. Kasztner, *Bericht*, p. 50. Eichmann's Story, *Life*, December 5, 1960, p. 146. Wisliceny mentions a figure of 9,000. See his affidavit, November 29, 1945, *Conspiracy and Aggression*, VII, 606–21.

985. Kasztner, *Bericht*, pp. 48–55, 76, 151–52.

986. *Ibid.*, pp. 151–52.

frustration. At heart, he preferred dead Jews to live ones, and once his attitude was said to have become so overbearing that Himmler told him that he – Himmler – had created the Reich Security Main Office and that if it were Himmler's pleasure, Eichmann would have to become a nursemaid to the Jews.[987]

The committee, in the meantime, had little reason to rejoice. Considering the impotence of Hungarian Jewry and the lack of all outside support, its success was remarkable. Considering, on the other hand, that the task before the committee was the disruption of the killing operations, the success was also very limited. When one must save lives, failure means death. Hundreds of thousands of Jews were now going through a nightmare on their way to be killed.

As the empty freight cars rolled into railway stations at the various cities of departure, the Hungarian *Gendarmerie* moved to complete the concentration by emptying the hospitals and institutions, dumping the sick, the newborn babies, the blind and the deaf, the mental cases and prison inmates, into the ghettos.[988] The *Gendarmerie* subjected the deportees to thorough bodily searches, anxious lest all the valuables fall into German hands at Auschwitz. At the station seventy victims were piled into a cattle car with a bucket of water, and the car was sealed.[989] From Kosice the trains had to leave at night, for the railway yard in the brick factory where the Jews had been kept was connected with the main line by a track which bisected one of the city's main streets. The population, however, often heard the crying of women and children who could not stand the suffocating heat in the cars.[990]

Under Hungarian guard the trains, forty-five cars to a transport, wound their way to the Slovak frontier.[991] There German guards (presumably Order Police) took over the transports from the Hungarian *Gendarmerie*.[992] While the trains were passing through the Slovakian countryside, the Slovak intelligence service reported a disturbing incident: On May 24 the German guards had entered three trains at the railway station of Kysak and, under threat of shooting, had taken from the Jews money and valuables. The Germans then had gone to the station restaurant to eat and to get drunk. When the train pulled out of Kysak, the Jews threw out jewelry, rings, and money – the latter mostly torn to shreads – which railway workers and children picked up on the embankment. The news of this incident had spread like wildfire.[993]

In Budapest the relief committee petitioned to the *Sondereinsatzkommando* for some alleviation of the suffering endured by the deportees. Kastner pointed out to Hauptsturmführer Hunsche that hundreds of Jews were dying on the way for lack of food and water, and Hunsche promised to look after the matter. A few days later he told Kastner: "Will you finally stop bothering me with your horror stories? I have investigated. Here are the reports: There are at most fifty to sixty

987. Affidavit by Becher, February 7, 1946, NG-2972.

988. Affidavit by Kastner, September 13, 1945, PS-2605.

989. The figure of 70 may be calculated from a report by Veesenmayer to Foreign Office, June 13, 1944, NG-5619.

990. Affidavit by Hans Josef Count Matuschka (German Consul in Kosice), August 26, 1947, NG-2440.

991. Train length specified in Veesenmayer report to Foreign Office, June 13, 1944, NG-5619. An average train carried 3150.

992. In a few cases the Hungarians seem to have accompanied the transports all the way to Auschwitz. Lengyel, *Five Chimneys*, pp 114–15. The author was deported from Cluj.

993. Ludin (German Minister in Slovakia) to Foreign Office., June 15, 1944, NG-5569.

persons per transport who die on the way."[994]

For Hunsche and Eichmann the deaths in the freight cars were a minor administrative detail not worth bothering about. The SS men were interested only in the total picture; they looked at the holocaust with statistical eyes and calculated that soon it would be finished. From Zones I and II an average of 12,000 people were being deported daily.[995] On the single day of June 1 nearly 20,000 Jews were deported.[996] The provinces were rapidly being emptied, and at the beginning of July the ring was already closing around Budapest. Table 70 shows the results for Zones I through V.[997]

TABLE 70 / *The Statistics of Deportations from Hungary*

ZONE	DATE OF COMPLETION	NUMBER DEPORTED
I and II	June 7	289,357
III	June 17	50,805
IV	June 30	41,499
V	July 9	55,741
All five zones	July 9	437,402

At the end of June, when the first four zones were almost emptied out, Veesenmayer requested Hungarian Supply Minister Jurczek to send food shipments to the Reich, corresponding to the amount which the deported Jews would have consumed. The Hungarian agreed to the demand.[998] The Germans were now ready for the finish.

The evacuation of the 20,000 Jews of Budapest was planned for July. In a single day the Jews of the capital were to be transferred to an island above the city. All bus and streetcar traffic was to be halted. The *Sondereinsatzkommando*, strong units of Hungarian *Gendarmerie* from the provinces, and all Budapest mailmen and chimney sweeps were to be employed in the roundup.[999] The Foreign Office was a little uneasy about the operation – Budapest was too much in the limelight, too often the center of world attention. In Berlin, Minister Dr. Schmidt (Foreign Office, press division) pointed out to Staatssekretär Steengracht that the drive against the Budapest Jews would result in "atrocity propaganda" abroad. Schmidt therefore thought it advisable to discover explosives in Jewish clubs and synagogues, to unearth Jewish sabotage, plots, attacks on the police, illegal currency transactions, etc.[1000]

On June 6, the day of the Allied landings in France, von Thadden suggested that the Budapest *Aktion* be so timed as to be drowned out by the invasion news.[1001] Veesenmayer, however, did not see the need for special precautions, since he did not think that the world would be shocked, anyhow.[1002] But Veesenmayer *was* worried that the repeated press reports about concentrations and evacuations would lead to a "disturbance of the Jewish

994. Kasztner, *Bericht*, p. 47.

995. Veesenmayer to Foreign Office, June 13, 1944, NG-5619.

996. Veesenmayer to Ritter, June 1, 1944, NG-5622. Veesenmayer to Ritter, June 2, 1944, NG-5621.

997. Statistics for Zones I and II reported by Veesenmayer to Foreign Office, June 13, 1944, NG-5619. Statistics for Zones III and IV reported by Veesenmayer to Foreign Office, June 30, 1944, NG-2263. Statistics for Zone V reported by Veesenmayer to Foreign Office, July 11, 1944, NG-5615. It is almost certain that the 18,000 Jews shipped to Austria are included in the totals. The early Kistarcsa transports, however (see p. 538), are not included.

998. Veesenmayer to Foreign Office, June 25, 1944, NG-5571. Altenburg to Veesenmayer, June 28, 1944, NG-5571.

999. Report by von Thadden, May 26, 1944, NG-2190.

1000. Schmidt to Steengracht, May 27, 1944, NG-2424.

1001. Von Thadden to Wagner, June 6, 1944, NG-2260.

1002. Veesenmayer to Foreign Office, June 8, 1944, NG-2260.

element," and he wanted his Jews to remain quiet.[1003] On June 30, Veesenmayer intimated that something had gone wrong. Horthy was restless and had objected to the deportations. The Budapest drive would therefore have to be postponed for a while.[1004] At just about that time Hungarian *Gendarmerie* began to arrive in the capital on the pretext of attending a festival. Horthy ordered the removal of the gendarmes.[1005]

On the evening of July 4, Veesenmayer had a two-hour discussion with the Hungarian Regent. Horthy started to talk about Sztojay and indicated that he was not quite satisfied with the Prime Minister. He then characterized Imredy as a party politician. For the two State Secretaries of the Interior Ministry, Endre and Baky, Horthy reserved his sharpest criticism. The Regent described Endre as not quite normal and added "confidentially" that two of Endre's uncles had died in an insane asylum. Nothing, said Horthy, could be expected from Baky, for Baky was a flag that would blow with the political wind; today he was with us, tomorrow he might be with the Bolshevists.

With regard to the Jewish question, Horthy mentioned that daily he was being bombarded with telegrams from all sides, from the Vatican and the King of Sweden, from Switzerland and the Red Cross. He – Horthy – was certainly no friend of the Jews, but for political reasons he had to intervene in behalf of the Christian Jews, the Jewish doctors, the Jewish labor companies, and the essential Jewish war workers. Horthy then lapsed into memories of past glories and also mentioned the possibility of resignation. Veesenmayer replied that the evacuation of the Jews was absolutely necessary for the conduct of the war. Furthermore, it was precisely Horthy's name which since the First World War had been associated with the battle against Jewry and Bolshevism, and now the Germans were doing nothing else than to bring this picture of Horthy to its complete realization.[1006]

Horthy's uneasiness was to some extent a reflection of interventions by neutral states in behalf of surviving Hungarian Jews. The neutral countries, particularly Switzerland and Sweden, were now presenting specific demands. Negotiations were initiated for the purpose of enabling thousands of Jews to emigrate, and protective foreign passports were issued to individual Budapest Jews to shield them from the application of destructive measures. It was clear that through these neutral channels the British Foreign Office and the American War Refugee Board were applying pressure. The Sztojay government, no longer so sure of itself, wanted to give in. Veesenmayer, on his part, thought that the protection of a few thousand Jews was a small price to pay for the mass evacuation of Budapest Jewry. Even Wagner of Inland II felt that the Hungarian argument pointing to possible American reprisals against persons of Hungarian descent in the United States was "weighty" (*schwerwiegend*).[1007] But Ribbentrop did not agree.

On the evening of July 5, one day after the talk with Horthy, Veesenmayer showed Sztojay a telegram from Ribbentrop warning the Hungarians that it was "not opportune" to go into various offers from abroad to help the Budapest Jews. Shaken by the tele-

1003. Veesenmayer to Foreign Office, June 8, 1944, NG-5568.

1004. Veesenmayer to Foreign Office, June 30, 1944, NG-5576.

1005. Testimony by Horthy, Case No. 11, tr. p. 2713.

1006. Veesenmayer via Ritter to Ribbentrop, July 6, 1944, NG-5684.

1007. Wagner via Hencke and Steengracht to Ribbentrop, July 6, 1944, NG-2236.

gram, Sztojay, urged a reversal of this German view for the following reasons: First, said the Hungarian Prime Minister, nothing was happening to the Jews in Roumania. Second, nothing was happening to them in Slovakia. Third, the arrival of the Jewish millionaires (Manfred Weiss family) in Lisbon had caused a "sensation" about anti-Jewish measures here. If the Reich could permit the emigration of Jews, why not Hungary? Fourth, the Hungarian government was "deluged" with telegrams from the King of Sweden and the Pope. The nuncio was calling "several times" a day. The Turkish, Swiss, and Spanish governments had also intervened. All this did not include the protestations of influential Hungarians.

Fifth, the Hungarian Prime Minister brought up his strongest point. In strict confidence Sztojay read to Veesenmayer three secret teletype messages sent by the U.S. and British missions in Bern to their governments and deciphered by Hungarian counterintelligence. They contained a "detailed description" of the fate of the deported Jews. They mentioned that one and a half million Jews (*sic*) had been killed before the Hungarian action was started. The messages then suggested the bombing and destruction of destination points and railroad lines, "target bombing of all collaborating Hungarian and German agencies – with exact and correct street and house numbers in Budapest" – and finally "world-wide propaganda with detailed descriptions of the state of affairs." In another teletype message seventy Hungarian and German personalities who were said to constitute the main culprits were mentioned by name.

Sztojay hastily added that this threat left him personally cold, because in the case of an Axis victory he did not consider the matter interesting, and in the other case he had concluded his life anyway; however, Veesenmayer gained the impression that the Hungarian Prime Minister was very impressed with the intercepted messages. Later Veesenmayer heard that they had been submitted to the Ministerial Council, where they also had produced their "due effect."[1008]

History plays strangely with its participants. The Jewish relief committee in Budapest had sent these requests to Bern to be transmitted through diplomatic channels to the Allied capitals, where no action was taken upon them. But fate had intervened. The Hungarians in their eagerness had intercepted the messages and had thereupon frightened themselves to death.

On July 6, Veesenmayer was informed by Sztojay that the Regent had ordered the deportations stopped.[1009] Three days later the Hungarian Interior Minister, Jarosz, told Veesenmayer that he was worried that SS units might be introduced into Budapest to carry out the *Judenaktion*. In this connection, Jarosz mentioned that he had completed the deportations in Zone V and the Budapest suburbs in violation of the Regent's directives. Jarosz also was willing to empty Budapest against Horthy's wishes, but to avoid difficulties he would have to remove the Jews to the provinces first. Once this bluff was successful, the second lap of the journey would be easy. Veesenmayer listened to this plan with delight and immediately promised his assistance. Writing to Ribbentrop, he asked the Foreign Minister to see to it that no SS men were sent into the capital, because the legation had "all political strings tightly in hand" (*alle politischen Drähte fest in der Hand*).[1010]

Within a matter of days, however, the strings were slipping rapidly from

1008. Veesenmayer via Ritter to Ribbentrop, July 6, 1944, NG-5523.

1009. *Ibid.*

1010. Veesenmayer via Ritter to Ribbentrop, July 9, 1944, NG-5532.

Veesenmayer's controlling palm. In a lightning move Horthy dismissed State Secretaries Endre and Baky and issued warrants for the arrest of the two men. Veesenmayer protested immediately, menacingly pointing to the possible consequences of the action. Horthy retreated, reinstating the officials, but not without complaining that his personal influence had apparently declined to zero and that he could not even effect the removal of two State Secretaries. Repeating that he was swamped with messages about the Jews, he said that he had written a personal letter about the Jewish question to Hitler.[1011]

Meanwhile, Eichmann fretted outside of Budapest. Moving swiftly, he deported 1700 Jews from the internment camp of Kistarcsa, which was located some seventeen miles from the capital. Horthy learned of the transport and gave orders that the train be stopped before it reached the frontier. Intercepted at Ratvang, the Jews were shipped back to Kistarcsa.[1012] A few days later the persevering Eichmann called the Jewish Council to his office and, while the Jewish leaders were detained, successfully emptied out the internment camps of Kistarcza and Szarva.[1013]

On July 16, Ribbentrop decided to break the stalemate. He instructed Veesenmayer to deliver to Horthy an ultimatum which expressed in blunt terms the German attitude toward the Sztojay government and the German terms with respect to the Budapest Jews.[1014] The warning began:

> With utmost surprise the Führer learned from the report of the *Reichsverweser* [Horthy], transmitted by the Reich plenipotentiary [Veesenmayer], that he intends to recall the present Sztojay government. . . . With still greater surprise the Führer learned from the report of the Reich plenipotentiary that the *Reichsverweser* issued warrants for the arrest of individual ministers and State Secretaries of the Sztojay government who recently took measures against Jews.

Pointing out that any such move would result in total military occupation of Hungary, the ultimatum continued:

> The Führer expects that the measures against the Budapest Jews will now be taken without any further delay by the Hungarian government, with those exceptions which were allowed to the Hungarian government by the German government, on principle, upon suggestion of Minister Veesenmayer [the protected Jews]. However, no delay of any kind in the execution of the general measures against Jews must take place due to these exceptions; otherwise the Führer would be compelled to withdraw his consent to these exceptions.

After delivering this note to Horthy, Veesenmayer remarked that two additional armored units would soon be sent into Hungary.[1015]

The warning was not successful. Already Russian troops were pouring into neighboring Galicia, and the entire southern front was in retreat. Interior Minister Jarosz and his two State Secretaries lost their posts. On July 27 the Sztojay government, still in office but no longer enthusiastic, declared its readiness to transfer the Budapest Jews to camps within Hungarian territory.[1016] On August 2, Higher SS and Police Leader Winkelmann sent a note to Veesenmayer in which he voiced the opinion that a more reliable government had to be formed in Hungary at

1011. Veesenmayer to Foreign Office, July 13, 1944, NG-5577. Ribbentrop to Veesenmayer, July 16, 1944, NG-2739.

1012. Testimony by Horthy, Case No. 11, tr. p. 2713.

1013. Testimony by Kastner, Case No. 11, tr. p. 3626.

1014. Ribbentrop to Veesenmayer, July 16, 1944, NG-2739.

1015. Memorandum by Altenburg, July 21, 1944, NG-2739.

1016. Affidavit by Kastner, September 13, 1945, PS-2605.

once.[1017] Once again the Germans set up lists of candidates. But Veesenmayer did not form a new government. Horthy did.

During August 23–24 an event occurred in Roumania which shook the German position in Hungary to its roots. The Soviet Army had broken through the German-Roumanian lines in Bessarabia and Moldavia. On August 23, King Mihai informed the Germans that he had to conclude an armistice and that they had three days to remove their army from the country. One hour after the receipt of this ultimatum German bombers attacked the royal palace in Bucharest, and the consequences for the Reich were disastrous. Within a few weeks twenty-six German divisions were hacked to pieces by the inrushing Soviets and their new Roumanian allies. The German Legation personnel were trapped, and their chief, von Killinger, committed suicide.[1018] It was during the Roumanian turnabout, on August 25, that Horthy installed a new Prime Minister: General Geza Lakatos.[1019] Once more Hungary was ruled by a reluctant collaborator.

The government of General Lakatos was, in fact, unwilling to co-operate with the Reich in any matter whatsoever. When Lakatos was shown the agreement concluded by Sztojay to remove the Budapest Jews to the provinces, he pleaded that there was no transportation, that there were no guards, and that there were no camps.[1020] Encouraged by the German inability to strike back, he instructed his minister in Berlin to demand "a free hand in the Jewish question."[1021] Lakatos then asserted Hungarian sovereignty by requesting the Germans to remove the Eichmann *Sondereinsatzkommando*.[1022] The *Kommando* was disbanded at the end of September,[1023] but one of its leading personalities, Wisliceny, remained behind just in case. The presence of Wisliceny so disturbed the Jewish Council that it sent a deputation to the Hungarian *Gendarmerie* officer Ferenczy with a request to remove the Budapest Jews to labor camps in the country as a means of forestalling any deportations to Auschwitz.[1024] Lakatos in the meantime sought with a few token measures to show exactly where he stood. Thus, the curfew was relaxed,[1025] and Jewish stores were permitted to reopen, provided that one of the managers was a non-Jew.[1026]

The Germans knew what these developments meant. The legation and the SS and Police watched closely every move of the Hungarian Government. They observed the secret flight of high-ranking Hungarian Army officers to undisclosed destinations. It was clear that the Lakatos regime had been appointed for only one purpose: to conclude an armistice with the Allies. It was also

1017. Veesenmayer to Foreign Office, enclosing note by Winkelmann, August 3, 1944, NG-2973.

1018. Rudolf Rahn, *Ruheloses Leben* (Düsseldorf, 1949), pp. 268, 262. Kingdom of Roumania, Ministry of Foreign Affairs, *Memorandum on the Military and Economic Contribution of Roumania to the War against Germany and Hungary* (Bucharest, 1946).

1019. Affidavit by Lakatos, June 10, 1947, NG-1848.

1020. *Ibid.* Veesenmayer to Foreign Office, October 10, 1944, NG-4985.

1021. Hoffmann (Hungarian Minister in Berlin) to Hennyey (Hungarian Foreign Minister), September 22, 1944, NG-2604.

1022. Affidavit by Kastner, September 13, 1945, PS-2605.

1023. Feine to Veesenmayer, September 29, 1944, NG-4985.

1024. Grell to Veesenmayer, September 30, 1944, NG-4985.

1025. *Deutsche Zeitung* (Budapest), September 22, 1944, p. 3.

1026. *Ibid.*, September 30, 1944, p. 5. Significantly, the reversal began in the last days of the Sztojay regime, when an ordinance was passed to confer exemptions from the effect of anti-Jewish decrees upon individual Jews who had made outstanding contributions in the field of science, art, and the economy. *Ibid.*, August 23, 1944, p. 4.

clear that this aim was being pursued by Horthy himself.

At the beginning of October the Red Army broke into southern Hungary, taking Hódmezövásárhely and Szeged. The spearhead of the Soviet Second Ukraine Army was now only a hundred miles from the capital. On October 14 the Germans sent into Budapest the 24th Panzer Division with forty Tiger tanks. The division's assignment, however, was not to reinforce the sagging frontline but to overthrow Horthy and Lakatos. With the division three well-known personalities arrived to take charge: the anti-partisan chief, Obergruppenführer von dem Bach-Zelewsky; the Foreign Office provocateur, Ambassador Dr. Rudolf Rahn; and the RSHA man in charge of special tasks, Obersturmbannführer Skorzeny.

On the morning of October 15, Skorzeny succeeded in luring Horthy's son to a surrounded building; Horthy Jr. was quickly wrapped in blankets, thrown on a truck, and brought to an airport to be flown to the Mauthausen concentration camp. That same day, while the Hungarian radio was preparing to broadcast an armistice appeal, Veesenmayer told the Regent that upon the least sign of "treason" his son would be shot. The old Horthy broke under the strain. "Horthy cried like a little child, held Rahn's hand, promised to annul everything, ran to the telephone – without calling anyone however – and in general appeared to be totally deranged." During the next morning (October 16), under the guns of the Tiger tanks, Horthy and Lakatos surrendered.[1027]

The new Hungarian Führer, who combined the offices of Regent and Prime Minister, was the Arrow Cross leader, Szalasi. This man was no aristocrat. Once a major, he had been dishonorably discharged and in civilian life had served a prison sentence for three years.[1028] To be sure, the Szalasi regime had not been chosen for its respectability; Szalasi had been installed because in October, 1944, he was the only pro-Nazi candidate in Hungary. For the Jews the coup could have only one consequence: they now had to go through another nightmare. New ordeals were in the making.

When the Szalasi government came into power, the killing center of Auschwitz was approaching its liquidation stage. At the same time, new scarcities of labor made themselves felt on a vast scale. Across the border in the Reich, the construction chief of the SS Economic-Administrative Main Office, Gruppenführer Kammler, was building large underground plants for the assembly of pursuit planes and V-2 weapons. Kammler needed laborers, tens of thousands of slave laborers; and now that German control was once more established in Hungary, the underground chambers were to be fed with Budapest Jews. There was only one obstacle: the transportation system had broken down. Trains could no longer be dispatched, and the Jews had to be marched out on foot.

On October 18, Veesenmayer and the new Hungarian Interior Minister, Vajna Gabor, came to the following agreement: A total of 50,000 Jews, men as well as women, were to be moved to the Reich. All other Jews capable of work were to be concentrated in four labor camps. For the remaining Jews a ghetto was to be created on the periphery of the city or in the outskirts. In his report to the Foreign Office Veesenmayer added confidentially that Eichmann intended to press for another 50,-

1027. For the complete story of the putsch, see: Winkelmann to Himmler, October 25, 1944, NG-2540. Testimony by Ernst Kienast (*Hauptsturmführer* on Winkelmann's staff), Case No. 11, tr. p. 7153. Rahn, *Ruheloses Leben*, pp. 265–71.

1028. Testimony by Horthy, Case No. 11, tr. p. 2715.

000 Jews later.[1029] Eichmann could not rest until all the Hungarian Jews were in their graves. From Ribbentrop there was no objection. The German victory in Hungary had to be exploited without restraint, and the Hungarians now had to "proceed with utmost severity against the Jews" *(auf das allerschärfste gegen die Juden vorgehen.)*[1030]

On the morning of October 20 the Hungarian police knocked on the doors marked with the star and seized all men from 16 to 60 who were fit for labor, whether converted or unconverted, protected or unprotected. By nightfall 22,000 had been rounded up.[1031] During the next few days the drive was extended to women between 16 and 40, and by October 26 the forced labor reservoir had grown to 25,000 men and 10,000 women.[1032]

At the end of the month the treks began. Without food, the slave laborers walked over a hundred miles in snow, rain, and sleet to Austria. Riding in the opposite direction toward Budapest, the chief of the SS Operational Main Office, Obergruppenführer Jüttner, spotted the long column of Jews driven on by Hungarian soldiers. Most of the trekers, so far as he could see, were women. As the car made its way past the marching people, Jüttner noticed exhausted men and women in the ditches.[1033] On November 13, Veesenmayer reported that 27,000 Jews of "both sexes" had been marched off. He was counting on 40,000 additional Jews in "daily rates" of 2000 to 4000; the remaining Budapest Jews – about 120,000 in all – were to be concentrated in a ghetto. In an ominous tone Veesenmayer added that the "ultimate disposition" of these Jews depended upon the availability of transport facilities.[1034]

The treks did not continue much longer, since Szalasi had become uneasy. On November 21 he canceled all further foot marches because of the death rate of the Jewish women. The SS man in charge of Jewish labor on the Danube, Obersturmbannführer Höse consoled Veesenmayer by informing him that he could not use women anyway; he could employ only men fit for the heavy subterranean work. In his message to the Foreign Office Veesenmayer concluded that 30,000 marchers had been sent out so far and that it would hardly be possible to reach the figure of 50,000.[1035]

Now there remained in the Hungarian capital about 160,000 Jews, who were shoved into a ghetto within range of Russian artillery. As this movement got under way, some tens of thousands of Jews were still holding on to "protective passports." The passports offered very little protection. The Szalasi government refused to recognize their validity,[1036] and the Germans backed Szalasi. Thus, when the Portuguese Minister in Berlin interceded in behalf of his "protectees," Staatssekretär Steengracht replied that he could not accept the intercessions because the

1029. Veesenmayer to Foreign Office, October 18, 1944, NG-5570.

1030. Ribbentrop to Veesenmayer, October 20, 1944, NG-4986.

1031. Veesenmayer to Foreign Office, October 20, 1944, NG-5570.

1032. Veesenmayer to Foreign Office, October 26, 1944, NG-5570.

1033. Affidavit by Jüttner, May 3, 1948, NG-5216.

1034. Veesenmayer to Foreign Office, November 13, 1944, NG-5570.

1035. Veesenmayer to Foreign Office, November 21, 1944, NG-4987. The SS, however, did not stop trying. In December the Hungarian Interior Minister, Vajna Gabor, had conferences with Himmler, Berger, and Kaltenbrunner about further removals of Budapest Jews by rail. Transport difficulties frustrated these plans. Affidavit by Vajna Gabor, August 28, 1945, NO-1874. On employment of Jews in west Hungarian fortifications project, see Army Group South/Wi (signed Zörner) to OKW/*Feldwirtschaftsamt*, January 10, 1945, Wi/I .226.

1036. Declaration by Gabor reported in *Donauzeitung* (Graz), October 21, 1944, p. 3.

Hungarian government was "sovereign" and "any intervention on our part in Hungarian affairs was out of the question."[1037] Twenty thousand passports had been handed by the papal nuncio to the baptized Jews; these Jews, said Veesenmayer in his report, could mark their houses in the ghetto with a cross instead of the Star of David.[1038]

Many Jews in Budapest now had authorization to emigrate. In this connection, it is interesting to note that the Szalasi regime was more amenable to foreign pressure than was the Reich. This can be seen in the following statistics of exit permits authorized by the Reich and by Hungary, respectively:[1039]

	Reich	*Hungary*
To Palestine	7,000	8,800
To Sweden	400	4,500
To Spain	3	300
To Portugal	9	700

The Reich list was of course the one which had originally been promised to Sztojay. It goes without saying that an exit authorization, like a protective passport, no longer meant anything, for the Jews had nowhere to go. The neutral states were slow in actually admitting Jews, and the Soviet Army was fast surrounding the Hungarian capital.

From November, 1944, to February, 1945, the Budapest Jews were at the mercy of Szalasi's Arrow Cross men. All Jewish property except religious articles, graves, family photographs, furniture, and utensils, plus food and fuel to last fourteen days, was declared the property of the state.[1040] The Jews were huddled in their ghetto, starving, shivering, dying under bombardment. Uniformed Arrow Cross men seized Jews in the streets and threw them from bridges into the icy Danube River.[1041] Between 10,000 and 20,000 Jewish bodies piled up in houses, in the streets, and in the river during these winter months. The Jews of Budapest were going through their last ordeal. On February 13 the surrounded German-Hungarian garrison surrendered to the Russians.[1042]

1037. Memorandum by Steengracht, November 16, 1944, NG-4988.

1038. Veesenmayer to Foreign Office, November 21, 1944, NG-4987.

1039. Veesenmayer to Foreign Office, November 18, 1944, NG-4987.

1040. *Donauzeitung* (Graz), November 5, 1944, p. 3.

1041. Affidavit by Wilhelm Höttl (OStubaf. RSHA, in Hungary), April 24, 1947, NG-2317.

1042. For a complete story of the Budapest Jews under the Szalasi regime, see Levai, *Martyrdom*, pp. 335–421, and photographs.

IX / *Killing Center Operations*

1 / Origins of the Killing Centers

The most secret operations of the destruction process were carried out in six camps located in Poland in an area stretching from the incorporated areas to the Bug. These camps were the collecting points for thousands of transports converging from all directions with Jewish deportees. In three years the incoming traffic reached a total of close to three million Jews. As the transports turned back empty, their passengers disappeared inside.

The killing centers worked quickly and efficiently: a man would step off a train in the morning, and in the evening his corpse was burned and his clothes packed away for shipment to Germany. Such an operation was the product of a great deal of planning, for the death camp was an intricate mechanism in which a whole army of specialists played their parts. Viewed superficially, this smoothly functioning apparatus is deceptively simple, but upon closer examination the operations of the killing center resemble in several respects the complex mass-production methods of a modern plant. It will therefore be necessary to explore, step by step, what made possible the final result.

The most striking fact about the killing center operations is that, unlike the earlier phases of the destruction process, they were unprecedented. Never before in history had people been killed on an "assembly line" basis.[1] The killing center, as we shall observe it, has no prototype, no administrative ancestor. This is explained by the fact that it was a composite institution which consisted of two parts, the camp proper and the killing installations in the camp. Each of these two parts has its own administrative history. Neither was entirely novel. As separate establishments, both the concentration camp and the gas chamber had been in existence for some time. The great innovation was effected when the two devices were fused. We should therefore begin our examination of the death camp by learning something about its two basic components and how they were put together.

The German concentration camp was born and grew amid violent disputes and struggles between Nazi factions. Even in the earliest days of the Nazi regime the importance of the concentration camp was fully recognized; whoever gained possession of this weapon would wield a great deal of power.

In Prussia Interior Minister (and later Prime Minister) Göring made his bid: he decided to round up the Communists. This was not an incarceration of convicted criminals but an arrest of a potentially dangerous group. "The prisons were not available for this purpose";[2] hence Göring established concentration camps, which he put under the control of his Gestapo (then, Ministerialrat Diels).

Almost simultaneously, rival camps appeared on the scene. One was set up at Stettin by Gauleiter Karpfenstein; another was established at Breslau by SA leader Heines; a third was erected near Berlin by SA leader Ernst. Göring moved with all his might against these "unauthorized camps." Karpfenstein lost his post; Ernst lost his life.

But a more powerful competitor

1. The phrase was used by a camp doctor, Friedrich Entress, in his affidavit of April 14, 1947, NO-2368.

2. Testimony by Göring, *Trial of the Major War Criminals*, IX, 257.

emerged. In Munich the police president, Himmler, organized his own Gestapo, and near the town of Dachau he set up a concentration camp which he placed under the command of SS-Oberführer Eicke.[3] Soon Himmler's Gestapo covered the non-Prussian *Länder,* and in the spring of 1934 Himmler obtained through Hitler's graces the Prussian Gestapo (becoming its "deputy chief"). Along with Göring's Gestapo, Himmler captured the Prussian concentration camps; henceforth, all camps were under his control.[4]

Eicke, the first Dachau commander, now became the Inspector for Concentration Camps; his *Totenkopfverbände* ("Death Head Units") became the guards. Thus the camps were severed from the Gestapo, which retained in the administration of each camp only one foothold: the political division, with jurisdiction over executions and releases. After the outbreak of war Eicke and most of his *Totenkopfverbände* moved into the field (he was killed in Russia), and his deputy, the later Brigadeführer Glücks, took over the inspectorate.

Eicke's departure marks the midpoint in the development of the concentration camps. Up to the outbreak of war the camps held three types of prisoners:[5]

1. Political prisoners:
   a. Communists (systematic roundup)
   b. Active Social Democrats
   c. Jehovah's Witnesses
   d. Clergymen who made undesirable speeches or otherwise manifested opposition
   e. People who made remarks against the regime and were sent to camps as an example to others
   f. Purged Nazis, especially SA men
2. So-called asocials, consisting primarily of habitual criminals and sex offenders
3. Jews sent to camps in *Einzelaktionen*

After 1939 the camps were flooded with millions of people, including Jewish deportees, Poles, Soviet prisoners of war, members of the French resistance movements, and so on.

The inspectorate could not keep up with this influx; therefore, from 1940 on the Higher SS and Police Leaders established camps of their own. We have already noted in previous chapters the transit camps in the West and the labor camps in Poland. During the last stage of the destruction process, the Higher SS and Police Leaders also put up killing centers.

At this point an office stepped in to centralize and unify the concentration camp network: the SS Economic-Administrative Main Office, the organization of Obergruppenführer Oswald Pohl. In a process which took several years Pohl finally emerged as the dominant power in the camp apparatus. His organization incorporated the inspectorate and enveloped almost completely the camps of the Higher SS and Police Leaders.

As the name "Economic-Administrative Main Office" implies, Pohl entered into the concentration camp picture from an oblique angle. He was not a camp commander, nor was he a Higher SS and Police Leader. In World War I he had been a naval paymaster and in the early days of the SS had served in the *Verwaltungsamt* ("Administrative Office") of the SS-Main Office. (The *Verwaltungsamt* dealt with financial and administrative questions for the SS.) On February 1, 1934, Pohl took

3. See orders by Eicke, October 1, 1933, PS-778.

4. Camps for foreign laborers and prisoner of war camps were outside of Himmler's sphere. However, in October, 1944, Himmler took over the PW camps in the rear.

5. By October, 1943, 110,000 German prisoners, including 40,000 "political criminals" and 70,000 "asocials," had been sent to the concentration camps. Himmler speech before *Militärbefehlshaber,* October 14, 1943, L-70.

over the *Verwaltungsamt*, and by 1936 he had expanded its activities. It was now concerned also with construction matters, including the construction of SS installations in concentration camps. The *Verwaltungsamt* was therefore reorganized to become the *Amt Haushalt und Bauten* ("Budget and Construction Office") – the first major step toward over-all control.

In 1940 Pohl broke loose from the SS-Main Office and established his own main office: The *Hauptamt Haushalt und Bauten*. At the same time he set up a chain of SS enterprises in labor and concentration camps. This business venture could not be placed under the *Hauptamt Haushalt und Bauten*, which was nominally a state agency financed entirely with Reich funds; therefore Pohl organized another main office, the *Hauptamt Verwaltung und Wirtschaft* (VWHA) or Main Office Administration and Economy. This was Pohl's second step. The double organization, which was analogous to Heydrich's apparatus before the merger of the *Hauptamt Sicherheitspolizei* (Gestapo and *Kripo*) and the *Sicherheitshauptamt* (SD) into the RSHA, is shown in Table 71.[6]

On February 1, 1942, Pohl followed Heydrich's example and combined his two main offices into a single organization: the SS Economic-Administrative Main Office, or *Wirtschafts-Verwaltungshauptamt* (WVHA).

One month after this consolidation Pohl took his third major step. To insure better labor utilization in the camps and to make possible the unhampered growth of his SS enterprises, he swallowed the inspectorate. The WVHA was now fully engaged in the concentration camp business. Table 72 shows how the *Hauptamt Haushalt und Bauten* (I and II) became *Amtsgruppen A, B,* and *C;* how the inspectorate was transformed into *Amtsgruppe D;* and how the VWHA (III) emerged as *Amtsgruppe W.*[7]

With the inspectorate's incorporation into the Pohl machine the administration of the concentration camps acquired an economic accent. The exploitation of the inmate labor supply, which had motivated Pohl to undertake this consolidation, now became the very reason for the existence of concentration camps. This factor brought into the killing center operations the same dilemma which we have already observed in the mobile killing operations and the deportations: the need for labor vs. the "final solution." This time the dilemma was entirely an intra-SS affair. (The growth of the Pohl organization from 1929 to March, 1942, is summarized in Table 73).

The consolidation process did not stop with the incorporation of the inspectorate, for Pohl also bit into the camps of the Higher SS and Police Leaders. He annexed some camps outright;[8] he controlled others by installing regional officials responsible to the WVHA, the SS-economists (SS-*Wirtschafter*);[9] and he invaded the killing centers in the *Generalgouvernement* by acquiring control over the entire camp confiscation machinery in the territory.[10] Concentration camps had become the principal factor in the power structure of Pohl. He in turn had emerged as the dominant figure in the sea of concentration camps.

6. Organization charts of *Hauptamt Haushalt und Bauten* and *Hauptamt Verwaltung und Wirtschaft*, 1941, in NO-620. The early history of the Pohl organization is based on his affidavit of March 18, 1947, NO-2574.

7. Organization charts in NO-52 and NO-111.

8. See pp. 337–38.

9. Order by Pohl, July 23, 1942, NO-2128. Pohl to Himmler, July 27, 1942, NO-2128. SS-economists were installed in Riga, Mogilev, Kiev, Krakow, Belgrade, and Oslo, later in Hungary also.

10. See p. 611.

Table 71 / *Organization of the "Haushalt und Bauten" and VWHA*

Pohl		
Haushalt und Bauten		*Verwaltung und Wirtschaft*
Office I Budget Obf. Lörner	Office II Construction Gruf. Pohl	Office III Administration and Economy (SS enterprises) Gruf. Pohl
I-1 Salaries OStubaf. Prietzel	II-A *Waffen-SS* HStuf. Sesemann	III-A Staf. Dr. Salpeter
		III-A/1 German Earth and Stone Works (*Deutsche Erd-und Steinwerke* – DEST) Stubaf. Mummenthey
I-2 Legal HStuf. Fricke	II-B Special Tasks UStuf. Geber	III-B Obf. Möckel
I-3 Uniforms and Clothes Stubaf. Weggel	II-C Concentration Camps and Police HStuf. List	III-C OStubaf. Maurer
		III-C/3 German Equipment Works (*Deutsche Ausrüstungswerke* – DAW) HStuf. Niemann
I-4 Lodgings OStubaf. Köberlein	II-D HStuf. Dr. Flir	III-D Stubaf. Vogel
I-5 Allocation of Inmate Labor HStuf. Burböck	II-E Personnel	III-S Special Tasks Stubaf. Klein
I-6 Food HStuf. Fichtinger		
I-H Personnel UStuf. Lange		
I-K Transportation UStuf. Leitner		

TABLE 72 / *Organization of the WVHA*

Chief, WVHA		OGruf. Pohl
Deputy		(Bgf. Frank) Gruf. Georg Lörner
Chief, *Amtsgruppe* A	Troop administration	(Frank) Bgf. Fanslau
Amt A-I	Budget	Obf. Hans Lörner
Amt A-II	Finance	(OStubaf. Eckert) HStuf. Melmer
Amt A-III	Law	Obf. Salpeter
Amt A-IV	Auditing	Staf. Vogt
Amt A-V	Personnel	Bgf. Fanslau
Chief, *Amtsgruppe* B	Troop economy	Gruf. Georg Lörner
Deputy		(Staf. Prietzel) Obf. Tschentscher
Food inspector, *Waffen-SS*		Staf. Prof. Schenk
Amt B-I	Food (not including concentration camps)	Obf. Tschentscher
Amt B-II	Clothes (including inmates)	OStubaf. Lechler
Amt B-III	Lodgings	Staf. Köberlein
(*Amt* B-IV: transferred to B-II, March 3, 1942)	Raw materials	OStubaf. Weggel
Amt B-V	Transport and weapons	Staf. Scheide
Chief, *Amtsgruppe* C	Construction	Gruf. Dr. Ing. Kammler
Deputy		(Stubaf. Basching) OStubaf. Schleif
Amt C-I	General construction Matters (including concentration camps)	OStubaf. Rall
Amt C-II	Special construction	OStubaf. Kiefer
Amt C-III	Technical	Stubaf. Flote
Amt C-IV	Artistic	Stubaf. Schneider
Amt C-V	Central inspection	(Lenzer) OStubaf. Noell
Amt C-VI	Financial	Staf. Eirenschmalz
Chief, *Amtsgruppe* D	Concentration camps	Bgf. Glücks
Deputy		OStubaf. Liebehenschel
Amt D-I	Central office	(Liebehenschel) OStubaf. Höss
Amt D-II	Labor allocation	Staf. Maurer
Amt D-III	Sanitation	Staf. Dr. Lolling
Amt D-IV	Administration	(Kaindl) Stubaf. Burger
Chief, *Amtsgruppe* W	Economic enterprises	OGruf. Pohl
German Economic Enterprises, Inc.		
First manager		OGruf. Pohl
Second manager		Gruf. Lörner Obf. Baier

(*Continued on page 560*)

Table 72 / *Organization of the WVHA (Continued)*

Chief, W-Staff		
Amt W-I	German Earth and Stone Works (DEST) – Reich	OStubaf. Mummenthey
Amt W-II	DEST – East	Stubaf. Dr. Bobermin
Amt W-III	Food enterprises	HStuf. Rabeneck
Amt W-IV	Wood products (including DAW)	(HStuf. Dr. May) HStuf. Opperbeck
Amt W-V	Agricultural	OStubaf. Vogel
Amt W-VI	Textiles and leather	OStubaf. Lechler
Amt W-VII	Books and pictures (including Nordland Publishing Company and Deutscher Bilderdienst)	Stubaf. Mischke
Amt W-VIII	Special tasks (monuments, etc.)	Obf. Dr. Salpeter

Table 73 / *Pohl Organization, 1929–42*

	Pohl	
Year	Reich Budget	Party Budget, Profits, Loans, etc.
1929		SS-*Hauptamt* (*Verwaltungsamt*)
1936	SS-*Hauptamt* (*Amt Haushalt und Bauten*)	
1940	Inspectorate; *Hauptamt Haushalt und Bauten*	*Hauptamt Verwaltung und Wirtschaft*
March, 1942	WVHA (A, B, C, D,	and W)

While Pohl tightened his hold over the camps, the camps absorbed ever larger number of inmates. The following figures indicate the growth of the increasingly important army of slaves in concentration camp enclosures:

September, 1939: 21,400[11]
April 19, 1943: over 160,000[12]
August 1, 1944: 524,286[13]

The compilations do not include the camps of the Higher SS and Police Leaders, nor do they show the millions of deaths.

To keep up with the influx of victims, the camp network had to be extended.

11. Pohl to Himmler, April 30, 1942, R-129.

12. Pohl to OStubaf. Brandt, April 19, 1942, Himmler Files, Folder No. 67.

13. WVHA-D IV (signed Stubaf. Burger) to WVHA-B (Gruf. Lörner), August 15, 1944, NO-399.

In 1939 there were 6 relatively small camps.[14] In 1944 Pohl sent Himmler a map which showed 20 full-fledged concentration camps (*Konzentrationslager* – KL) and 165 satellite labor camps grouped in clusters around the big KL's. (Again the camps of the Higher SS and Police Leaders were not included.)[15] Himmler received the report with great satisfaction, remarking that "just such examples show how our business has grown" [*Gerade an solchen Beispielen kann man sehen, wie unsere Dinge gewachsen sind*].[16] Pohl's empire was thus characterized by a threefold growth: the jurisdictional expansion, the increase in the number of camp slaves, and the extension of the camp network.

The six killing centers appeared in 1941–42, at a time of the greatest multiplication and expansion of concentration camp facilities. This is a fact of great importance, for it insured that the construction and operation of the killing centers could proceed smoothly and unobtrusively. Let us now trace the history of these special camps.

The death camps operated with gas. There were three types of gassing installations, for the administrative evolution of the gas method had proceeded in three different channels. One development took place in the Technical *Referat* of the RSHA. This office produced the gas van. We have already observed the use of the van in two places, Russia and Serbia. In both of these territories the vans were auxiliary devices used for the killing of women and children only, but there was to be one more application. In 1941, Gauleiter Greiser of the Wartheland obtained Himmler's permission to kill 100,000 Jews in his *Gau*.[17] Three vans were thereupon brought into the woods of Chelmno, the area was closed off, and the first killing center came into being.[18]

The construction of another type of gassing apparatus was pursued in the Führer Chancellery, Hitler's personal office. After the outbreak of war, Hitler signed an order (predated September 1, 1939) empowering the chief of the Führer Chancellery, Reichsleiter Bouhler, and his own personal physician, Dr. Brandt, "to widen the authority of individual doctors with a view to enabling them, after the most critical examination in the realm of human knowledge, to administer to incurably sick persons a mercy death."[19] Actually this order was intended for and applied to incurably insane persons only.[20] The administrative implementation of the plan, which became known as the "euthanasia program," was in the hands of Bouhler's Führer Chancellery. The man who was actually in charge of the operation was a subordinate of Bouhler, Reichsamtsleiter Brack. The *Reichsamtsleiter* obtained the services of one Kriminalkommissar Wirth, chief of the Criminal Police office in Stuttgart and an expert in tracking down criminals, for the technical side of the project. Wirth constructed carbon monoxide gas chambers, a device which overwhelmed its victims without their apprehension and which caused them no pain.[21]

14. Pohl to Himmler, April 30, 1942, R-129.
15. Pohl to Himmler, April 5, 1944, NO-20.
16. Himmler to Pohl, April 22, 1944, NO-20.
17. Greiser to Himmler, May 1, 1942, NO-246.
18. Judge Wladyslaw Bednarz (Lodz), "Extermination Camp at Chelmno," in Central Commission for Investigation of German Crimes in Poland, *German Crimes in Poland* (Warsaw, 1946), pp. 107–17.
19. Order by Hitler, September 1, 1939, PS-630.
20. Affidavit by Dr. Konrad Morgen, July 19, 1946, SS(A)-67. Affiant was an SS officer whose assignment was the investigation of SS corruption. From this vantage point he gained insight into the killing phase of the destruction process.
21. Affidavit by Morgen, July 19, 1946,

In the summer of 1941 "the final solution of the Jewish question" was officially inaugurated. Himmler consulted with the Chief Physician of the SS, Reichsarzt SS und Polizei Gruppenführer Dr. Grawitz, upon the best way to undertake the mass-killing operation. Grawitz advised the use of gas chambers.[22]

At this point the SS and the Führer Chancellery got together. In October, 1941, three officials in Berlin – Brack, Eichmann, and Amtsgerichtsrat Wetzel of the East Ministry – were considering the introduction of gassing apparatus in the *Ostland*. Brack offered to send his chemical expert, Dr. Kallmeyer, to Riga for an inspection of sites. Wetzel was in complete agreement. "As affairs now stand," wrote Wetzel, "there are no objections to doing away with those Jews who are not able to work, with the Brack remedy."[23] However, the problem of finding suitable sites was not so simple. It will be recalled that in October and November, 1941, transports from the Reich began rolling into Lodz and the *Ostland*. Sixty thousand Jews were to be quartered in the Lodz ghetto "over the winter," to be transported farther to the "East" in the spring;[24] fifty thousand were to be brought to the *Ostland* to be housed in barracks near Riga and in the ruins of the ghetto of Minsk.[25] As Heydrich shoved his transports into Lodz, Riga, and Minsk, over strenuous objections by local officials, the movement tapered off, and before the onset of winter it was abandoned. The location of the proposed killing centers was shifted to the *Generalgouvernement*,[26] and in the spring of 1942 Brack ordered Kriminalkommissar Wirth to report to Gruppenführer Globocnik in Lublin.[27]

As the Wirth *Kommando* prepared to leave for its new post, it was put under an oath of silence by Himmler personally. Having received the oath, Himmler told the *Kommando* that he expected them to be "superhuman-inhuman" (*er mute ihnen Übermenschlich-Unmenschliches zu*).[28] Wirth and his crew immediately and under primitive conditions began to construct chambers into which they piped carbon monoxide from diesel motors.[29] The administrative channels under which this operation had been set up are shown in Table 74.[30]

While the Wirth *Kommando* was setting up shop in the Lublin district, transports with Jewish deportees from Krakow, the Reich, and the Protektorat began to arrive in the Hrubieszów-Zamosc area. There were no camps in that vicinity, and the Jews were crammed into already overcrowded ghettos. The director of the Population and Relief Subdivision of the Interior Division in the Office of the Lublin *Gouverneur* (Türk), was directed by the *Generalgouvernement* Interior Main Di-

SS(A)-67. The psychologist Leo Alexander has called the "euthanasia" stations established in pursuance of this program "killing centers." In this book Alexander's term is used as a designation for the camps in which the gassing of the Jews took place.

22. Affidavit by Morgen, July 13, 1946, SS(A)-65.

23. Draft memorandum by Wetzel for Lohse and Rosenberg, undated, probably end of October, 1941, NO-365.

24. Himmler to Greiser, copies to Heydrich and Koppe, September 18, 1941, Himmler Files, Folder No. 94.

25. Stubaf. Lange to *Reichskommissar Ostland,* November 18, 1941, Occ E 3-31.

26. When Generalgouverneur Frank was in Berlin (middle of December, 1941), he was told that "nothing could be done with the Jews in the *Ostland*." Frank in GG conference, December 16, 1941, Frank diary, PS-2233.

27. Brack to Himmler, June 23, 1942, NO-205.

28. Affidavit by Morgen, July 19, 1946, SS(A)-67.

29. Affidavit by OStuf. Kurt Gerstein, April 26, 1945, PS-1553.

30. Interrogation of H. G. W. Wied (SS corruption expert), July 21, 1945, G-215.

vision (Siebert) to assist Globocnik in making room for the Jews who were pouring into the district. Türk went to the expert in Jewish matters with the SS and Police Leader, a Hauptsturmführer Höfle. The *Hauptsturmführer* made a few remarkable statements: A camp would be built at Belzec. Where on the Deblin-Trawniki railway line could 60,000 Jews be dumped? He was ready to receive 4 to 5 transports of 1000 Jews daily at Belzec. "The Jews would cross the border and would never return to the *Generalgouvernement*."[31]

While Higher SS and Police Leader Koppe in the Wartheland was running Kulmhof with his gas vans and Globocnik was establishing his network of killing centers in the *Generalgouvernement,* a third development came into fruition in the incorporated territory of Upper Silesia. This project was built up by a man who had come up in the concentration camp world. He was an early Nazi who had been imprisoned, before Hitler came to power, with a top Nazi: Bormann. During the thirties he held several posts in Dachau and Sachsenhausen until (in 1940) he took over a camp of his own. The new camp was located in Upper Silesia.

TABLE 74

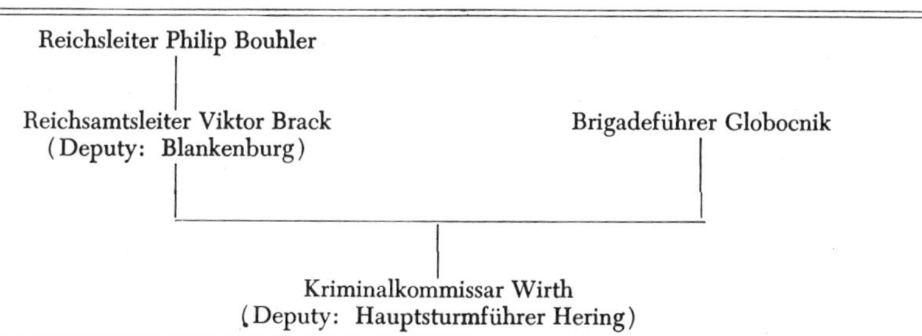

What seemed to be a bewildering mess to a local official was actually a frantic effort to establish killing installations in the area. In June, 1942, Brack wrote to Himmler that Globocnik had requested further personnel. On this occasion Globocnik had given a reason for his hurry: he was afraid to get "stuck."[32] The whole operation seemed, particularly to its closest participants, like a unique opportunity that could not be missed – European Jewry could be annihilated only once. Before long, four killing centers were established in the *Generalgouvernement*: Belzec, Sobibor, and Treblinka on the Bug river, and Lublin (Maydanek) near the city of that name.

Originally no great destiny had been intended for this place. The camp was encircled by stagnant fish ponds which permeated the compound with dampness, mist, and mud.[33] The German Army quartered a company of its construction troops there, and the Inspectorate for Concentration Camps, making a survey of the area, decided that after certain "sanitary and construction" measures it could use the camp as a quarantine center.[34] A few months later the new commander approached the German land acquisition agency in the area, the *Bodenamt Schlesien,* to

31. Memorandum by Türk, March 17, 1942, *Dokumenty i Materialy,* II, 32–33.

32. Brack to Himmler, June 23, 1942, NO-205.

33. Judge Jan Sehn (Krakow), "Extermination Camp at Oswiecim," in *German Crimes in Poland,* pp. 27–29.

34. Obf. Glücks to Himmler, copies to Pohl and Heydrich, February 21, 1940, NO-34.

confiscate the necessary grounds.[35] Another concentration camp was born. Its commander was Rudolf Höss. Its name was Auschwitz.

In the summer of 1941 Höss was summoned to report (over the head of his chief Glücks) to Himmler for personal orders. During the interview – which was to leave its mark upon the fate of Jews from all the deportation countries of Europe – Himmler told Höss that the Führer had given the order for the "final solution" of the Jewish question. He, the *Reichsführer-SS*, had chosen Auschwitz because its location at Katowice in Upper Silesia afforded easy access by rail and also because the extensive site offered space for measures ensuring isolation. For the details Himmler directed Höss to talk to Eichmann. Having placed that burden upon the shoulders of Höss, Himmler had only this to add: "We, the SS must carry out this order. If it is not carried out now, then the Jews will later on destroy the German people."[36] During the following weeks Eichmann came to Auschwitz and discussed with Höss the necessary "details."[37] Höss moved slowly but methodically; bit by bit, he built his camp into the largest death center the world had ever seen.

To begin with, the camp grounds were expanded. A considerable area in the vicinity was declared to be a "sphere of influence" (*Interessengebiet*). All people in this area were evicted, so as not to be in the way of the "state-political" tasks of the camp. It was planned to establish a *Gutsbezirk der Waffen-SS*, a district *owned* by the SS.[38] In line with these plans, which took a long time to materialize, Pohl wrote to the Finance Ministry in November, 1942, that the *Reichsführer-SS* wished to enlarge the area of Auschwitz to 4640 hectares (17.9 square miles) and that Himmler desired this area to be Reich (SS) property.[39]

On November 3 and December 17–18 two conferences were held under the chairmanship of Oberfinanzpräsident Dr. Casdorf of the Finance Ministry with the participation of the following officials:

Ministerialrat Dr. Gossel (Finance Ministry)
Regierungsrat Keller (Finance Ministry)
Amtsrat Pape (Finance Ministry)
Ministerialrat Hoffmann (Interior Ministry)
Oberregierungsrat Menke (Interior Ministry)
Brigadeführer Frank (WVHA-A)
Dr. Ast
Dr. Evert (Main Trusteeship Office East)
Schutz (Main Trusteeship Office East)

The reason for the presence of so many officials of various agencies was the complicated nature of the land-transfer process: transfer to Reich ownership of private Polish agricultural and urban property, of land which belonged to the Polish state (then regarded as the former Polish state), of municipal property, of ecclesiastical property, and, last but not least, of property belonging to Germans in the affected area. It was decided that the various agencies would transfer their jurisdictions to the Land Office of the commissioner for the Strengthening of Germandom (Himmler).[40] But even

35. Bodenamt Schlesien in Katowice (signed Kusche) to Director, *Zentralbodenamt beim RF-SS/RKfdFdV* (Gruf. Freiherr von Holzschuher), May 22, 1940, PS-1352.
36. Testimony by Höss, *Trial of the Major War Criminals,* XI, 398.
37. *Ibid.,* p. 399.
38. Bgf. Lörner to Finance Ministry, October 1, 1941, NG-5545.
39. Pohl to Finance Ministry, November 7, 1942, PS-1643.
40. Records of conferences in PS-1643. Full power signed by Casdorf in agreement with the chief of the Main Trusteeship Office East (Winkler), January 12, 1943, PS-1643. Hoffmann to *Regierungspräsident* in Katowice, January 22, 1943, PS-1643.

Himmler must have had a few difficulties, for on May 31, 1942, the aim of a Reich-owned district (*Gutsbezirk*) not yet having been accomplished, the *Oberpräsident* of Upper Silesia (Bracht) issued a decree establishing the administrative district (*Amtsbezirk*) of Auschwitz.[41]

In the meantime, Höss went ahead with the construction of killing installations, which were to contain two major improvements. The first of these was compactness. Höss built his installations as combination units, each of which contained an anteroom, a gas chamber, and an oven for body disposal. Second, he decided after visiting Treblinka that the carbon monoxide method was not very "efficient."[42] Accordingly, he introduced in his camp a different type of gas: quick-working hydrogen cyanide (prussic acid — commercial name, Zyklon B). Unlike carbon monoxide, however, this gas was *not* produced on the spot; and a major administrative effort, stretching out over a period of years, was required to solve some of the complicated problems arising during the erection of the special combination units and the establishment of a dependable gas supply.

The construction program was directed centrally by *Amtsgruppe C* (the Construction Office) of the WVHA, under Gruppenführer Dr. Ing. Kammler. Locally, the *Amtsgruppe* set up a branch: the *Zentralbauleitung der Waffen-SS und Polizei Auschwitz,* under Hauptsturmführer (later Sturmbannführer) Bischoff. At the end of 1941 the *Zentralbauleitung* began the construction of a special camp on the moor of Brzezinka (Birkenau).[43]

The first chambers were not built-in combination units but makeshift affairs. Two old peasant houses were remodeled; the windows were filled in, the interior walls removed, and a special airtight door constructed. These were the first gas chambers. A barracks nearby served as a dressing room for the deportees entering the gas chambers.[44] The installations were put into operation in the summer of 1942. Himmler, Gauleiter of Upper Silesia Bracht, and local Higher SS and Police Leader Schmauser were present at the first test. Himmler had nothing to criticize, but neither did he enter into any conversation.[45]

The two gas chambers were only provisional, and plans were laid out for the construction of the combination units, each of them complete with a gas chamber, anteroom, and oven. To carry out this project the *Zentralbauleitung* in Auschwitz engaged the help of two companies: the SS company *Deutsche Ausrüstungswerke* (DAW) to make the doors and windows, and the firm Topf and Sons, Erfurt, oven builders. The Topf concern, which specialized in the construction of cremation furnaces, had done such work in concentration camps before.[46]

Originally it had been intended to build two furnaces; however, on February 27, 1942, Oberführer Kammler arrived in Auschwitz and decided to erect five of them. The money for the extra ovens was simply taken off

41. Order by Bracht establishing *Amtsbezirk* of Auschwitz (with detailed description of the area), May 31, 1943, PS-1643. For "controversial" southern border, see Stabshauptamt correspondence, October 12, 1943, NG-932.

42. Affidavit by Höss, April 5, 1946, PS-3868.

43. Sehn, "Oswiecim," p. 31.

44. Affidavit by Friedrich Entress, April 14, 1947, NO-2368.

45. Affidavit by Höss, January 11, 1947, NO-4498-B.

46. Topf had built the crematorium in Buchenwald, where the mortality rate in 1940 had become very high. See *Hauptamt Haushalt und Bauten/Neubauleitung* Buchenwald: construction report and estimate, January 10, 1940, NO-4401.

another building project.[47] The five furnaces were designated I, II, III, IV, and V. One of the crematoriums remained single; two were built as units, each containing a huge underground gas chamber called *Leichenkeller* (corpse cellar) complete with an electric elevator for hauling up the bodies. The other two were also built as units, but with surface gas chambers called *Badeanstalten* (bath houses).[48] The *Leichenkeller* were very large (250 square yards), and 2000 persons could be packed into each of them. The *Badenstalten* were somewhat smaller.[49] The hydrogen cyanide, solidified in pellets, was shaken into the *Leichenkeller* through shafts, into the *Badeanstalten* through side walls. In the gas chamber the material immediately passed into the gaseous state. Thus an altogether more efficient system, guaranteeing much more rapid processing than in the other camps, had been devised in Auschwitz.

However, the construction of these elaborate installations required much more time than the building of the *Generalgouvernement* killing centers, and it is therefore not surprising that a certain hurry was in evidence. On January 13, 1943, the *Zentralbauleitung* in Auschwitz complained to the *Deutsche Ausrüstungswerke* that the doors for Crematorium I, "which is urgently needed for the implementation of the special measures" (*welches zur Durchführung der Sondermassnahmen dringend benötigt wird*) were not yet finished. By way of emphasis the *Zentralbauleitung* reminded the DAW that some time ago it had transferred its own workshops to the SS company.[50] On March 31 a note was sent about a door that was to have a peephole, with a reminder that this order was "especially urgent."[51]

In the meantime (January 29, 1943) the *Zentralbauleitung* reported to Kammler that after the commitment of all available manpower and in spite of tremendous difficulties, including freezing weather, Crematorium II was finished except for a few "minor construction details" (*bauliche Kleinigkeiten*). The *Leichenkeller* could not be used yet because transportation difficulties had prevented Topf from delivering the air-conditioning system, but the oven had been tried out, and it worked. The whole unit was due to be completed on February 20, 1943.[52]

While the Auschwitz management was struggling with the completion of the four combination units, the chief of WVHA-D (Glücks) made an inspection tour of concentration camps and noticed that "special buildings" (crematoriums) were not situated in particularly favorable locations. He wished that in future such "special constructions" would be put in a place where it would not be possible for "all kinds of people" to "gaze" at them.[53] Thinking this over, Höss ordered that a "green belt" of trees be planted around Crematoriums I and II.[54] The construction was finished.

47. HStuf. Bischoff to WVHA-C III (Stubaf. Wirtz), March 30, 1942, NO-4472.

48. *Zentralbauleitung* Auschwitz to DAW Auschwitz, January 23, 1943, NO-4462. Topf und Söhne, Erfurt, to *Zentralbauleitung* Auschwitz, February 12, 1943, in report of Soviet Extraordinary State Commission on Auschwitz, May 6, 1945, USSR-8. Memorandum by *Zentralbauleitung* Auschwitz, August 21, 1942, in report of Soviet Commission, USSR-8. Sehn, "Oswiecim," pp. 84–85.

49. Sehn, "Oswiecim," pp. 84–85.

50. *Zentralbauleitung* Auschwitz to DAW Auschwitz, January 13, 1943, NO-4466.

51. *Zentralbauleitung* to DAW, March 31, 1943, NO-4465.

52. *Zentralbauleitung* to Kammler, January 29, 1943, NO-4473.

53. Chief, WVHA-D (signed by Deputy OStubaf. Liebehenschel) to commanders of Sachsenhausen, Dachau, Neuengamme, and Auschwitz, June 15, 1943, NO-1242.

54. *Zentralbauleitung* to *Leiter der Landwirtschaftlichen Betriebe* (Stubaf. Caesar), November 6, 1943, NO-4463.

With the erection of the cremation units Höss had solved half his task. The procurement of the gas was the other half of the problem. Hydrogen cyanide, or Zyklon B, was a powerful lethal agent – a deadly dose was 1 milligram per kilogram of body weight. Packed in containers, the Zyklon was put to use simply by opening the canister and pouring the pellets into the chamber; the solid material would then sublimate. The Zyklon had only one drawback: within three months it deteriorated in the container and thus could not be stockpiled.[55] Now Auschwitz was a receiving station, always on call. Whenever trains arrived, whether during the day or the night, the machine went into motion, shunting the victims through the assembly line into the gas chambers. Consequently, it was necessary to have a dependable gas supply.

The SS did not manufacture Zyklon, so the gas had to be procured from private firms. The enterprises which furnished it were part of the chemical industry, specialists in the "combating of vermin" (*Schädlingsbekämpfung*) by means of poison gases. Zyklon was one of eight products manufactured by these firms,[56] which undertook large-scale fumigations of buildings, barracks, and ships; disinfected clothes in specially constructed gas chambers (*Entlausungsanlagen*); and deloused human beings – protected by gas masks.[57] In short, this industry used very powerful gases to exterminate rodents and insects in enclosed spaces; that it should now have become involved in an operation to kill off Jews by the hundreds of thousands is not mere accident. In German propaganda Jews had frequently been portrayed as insects. Frank and Himmler had stated repeatedly that the Jews were parasites who had to be exterminated like vermin, and with the introduction of Zyklon into Auschwitz that thought had been translated into reality.

How was the gas supply maintained? To answer this question, we must examine the organization of the extermination industry a little more closely. Basically, we must differentiate here between three structural components: the share-holding channels (ownership), the production and sales organization, and the allocation apparatus. The company which developed the gas method of combating vermin was the Deutsche Gesellschaft für Schädlingsbekämpfung mbH (German Vermin-Combating Corporation), abbreviated DEGESCH.[58] The firm was owned by three corporations and itself controlled two retailers (see Table 75).[59]

The capital investment figures shown in the table are no indication of the volume of business and profits. The DEGESCH profit in 1942 was 760,368 reichsmark. From its HELI holdings alone, the DEGESCH received 76,500 reichsmark; from TESTA, 36,500 reichsmark. In 1943, after the TESTA shares were sold, the DEGESCH made 580,-999 reichsmark, of which 102,000 reichsmark were netted from the HELI in-

55. Characteristics of Zyklon described in undated report by Health Institute of Protektorat: "Directive for Utilization of Zyklon for Extermination of Vermin" (*Ungeziefervertilgung*), NI-9912.

56. Lectures by Dr. Gerhard Peters and Heinrich Sossenheimer (gas experts), February 27, 1942, NI-9098.

57. *Ibid.*

58. For the interesting history of that corporation, see lectures by Peters and Sossenheimer (both DEGESCH officials), February 27, 1942, NI-9098.

59. Contract between DEGESCH, DEGUSSA, IG, and Goldschmidt, 1936/37, NI-6363. Affidavits by Paul H. Haeni (prosecution staff) based on analysis of documents, July 27, 1947, and October 28, 1947, NI-9150 and NI-12073. The Zyklon B Case, *Law Reports of Trials of War Criminals,* I (London, 1947), 94. The *Verwaltungsausschuss* (administrative committee) of the DEGESCH had the powers of an *Aufsichtsrat* (board of directors).

vestment.[60] Every year from 1938 through 1943, excepting only 1940 and 1941 the I. G. Farben received a DEGESCH dividend of 85,000 reichsmark (200 per cent). In 1940 and 1941 the I. G. made a profit of 42,500 reichsmark (100 per cent).[61] The reasons for these tremendous profits were threefold: a comparatively low overhead (DEGESCH had less than fifty employees), ever increasing demands of the war economy,[62] and, most important, a monopoly.

The Zyklon was produced by two companies: the Dessauer Werke and the Kaliwerke at Kolín. An I. G. Farben plant (at Uerdingen) produced the stabilizer for the Zyklon.[63] Distribution of the gas was controlled by DEGESCH, which in 1929 divided the world market with an American corporation, Cyanamid.[64] However, DEGESCH did not sell Zyklon directly to users; two other firms handled the retailing, HELI and TESTA. The territory of these two corporations was divided by

TABLE 75 / *Share Holdings in the Extermination Industry*

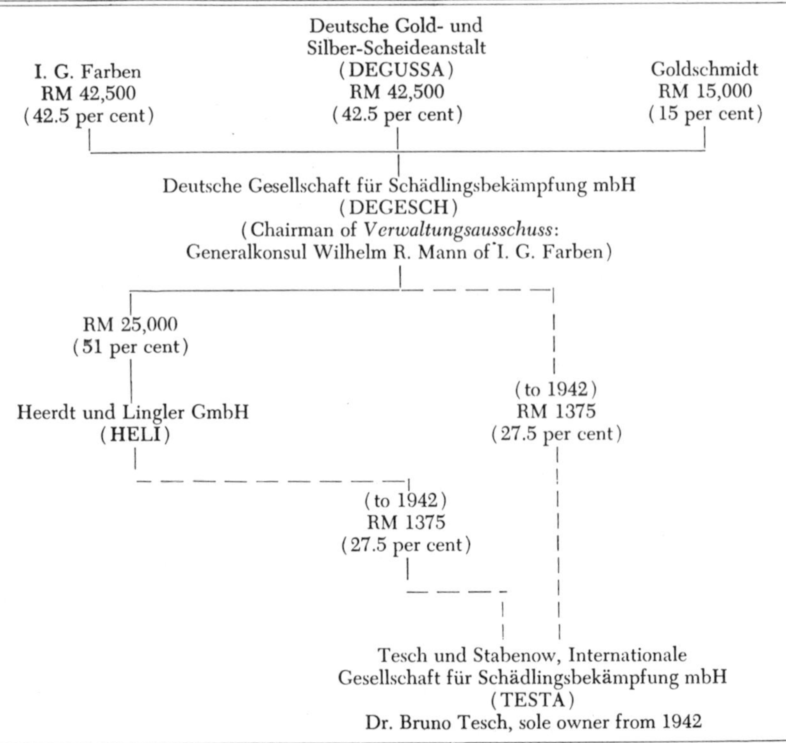

60. Affidavit by Haeni, July 29, 1947, NI-9150.

61. Hearings before subcommittee of committee on military affairs, U.S. Senate, 79th Congress, 1st Session, Exhibits 31–40, NI-9774.

62. For statistics of sales and construction of gas chambers, see DEGESCH business reports for 1942 and 1944, NI-9093.

63. Affidavit by Karl Amend (DEGESCH *Prokurist*), November 3, 1947, NI-12217.

64. Lectures by Peters and Sossenheimer, February 27, 1942, NI-9098.

a line drawn from Cuxhaven through Öbisfelde to Plauen. The area northeast of that line, including Auschwitz, belonged to Tesch und Stabenow.[65] (Schematically, the production and marketing of Zyklon is presented in Table 76.)

and upon submission of such evidence certain quantities are allocated to him. In other words, the territorial monopoly tells him where he has to buy, and the allocation system determines how much he can get.

The central allocation authority was

TABLE 76 / *Production and Marketing of Zyklon*

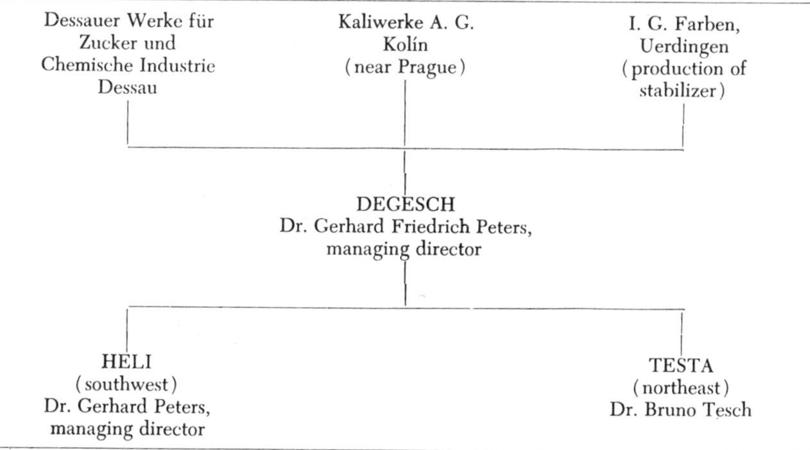

The territorial division between HELI and TESTA gave to HELI mostly private customers and to TESTA mainly the governmental sector, including the Wehrmacht and the SS. On the whole, neither firm sought to invade the territory of the other, but on occasion Dr. Tesch supplied Dachau via Berlin.[66]

We have dealt so far with two aspects of extermination industry: the investment and profit channels (Table 75), and the buying and selling mechanism (Table 76). There remains the allocation system. In a war, one cannot simply buy and sell. Each user has to show why he needs the supplies,

a committee in the Speer ministry. The committee divided the supply among export, private firms, and the armed forces. The Armed Forces Main Sanitation Depot fixed the needs of the Wehrmacht and the SS,[67] and the *Waffen-SS* Central Sanitation Depot was in turn responsible for allocations to SS offices and concentration camps.[68] The working of this apparatus is illustrated in Table 77, which indicates distributions of Zyklon B to various users.[69]

65. Contract between DEGESCH and TESTA, June 27, 1942, NI-11393. TESTA bought Zyklon from DEGESCH at RM 5.28 per kg.

66. Affidavit by Peters, October 16, 1947, NI-9113.

67. *Ibid.*

68. Testimony by Joachim Mrugowski, Case No. 1, tr. pp. 5403–4.

69. Affidavit by Peters, October 16, 1947, NI-9113. Figures given by Peters do not entirely agree with sales figures in DEGESCH business report for 1944, April 23, 1946, NI-9093. The Auschwitz figures are for 1942 and 1943 (*not* 1943 and 1944) and refer to actual deliveries. Affidavit by Alfred Zaun (TESTA bookkeeper), October 18, 1947, NI-11937.

The amounts required by Auschwitz were not large, but they were noticeable. Almost the whole Auschwitz supply was needed for the gassing of people; very little was used for fumigation.[70] The camp administration itself did not buy the gas. The purchaser was Obersturmführer Gerstein, Chief Disinfection Officer in the Office of the Hygienic Chief of the *Waffen-SS* (Mrugowski).[71] As a rule, all orders passed through the hands of TESTA, DEGESCH, and Dessau. From the Dessau Works, which produced the gas, shipments were sent directly to Auschwitz Extermination and Fumigation Division (*Abteilung Entwesung und Entseuchung*).[72]

Notification generally came from *Amtsgruppe D*, which authorized the Auschwitz administration to dispatch a truck to Dessau "to pick up materials for the Jewish resettlement" (*Abholung von Materialien für die Judenumsiedlung*).[73] Deliveries to SS installations for fumigation purposes were made every six months or so, but Auschwitz required a shipment every six weeks, because Zyklon deteriorated easily and

TABLE 77 / *Distribution of Zyklon B*

Reich Ministry for Armaments and War Production/
Special Committee Chemical Products/
Working Committee Space-Fumigation and Counter-Epidemics
Composition of working committee: Dr. Gerhard Peters (DEGESCH), chairman; Generalarzt Prof. Dr. Rose (Robert Koch Institute); Obermedizinalrat Dr. Christiaensen (Interior Ministry); a representative of Generalarzt Dr. Schreiber (OKW) – generally Dr. Finger or Dr. Wieser

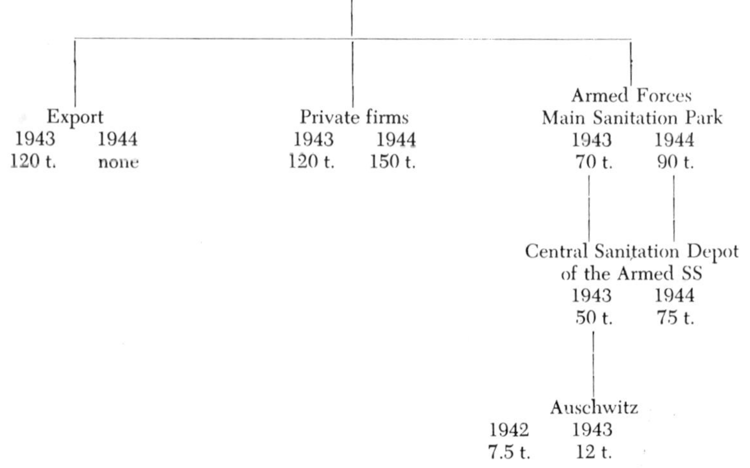

70. Testimony of Dr. Charles Sigismund Bendel (Jewish survivor) at Trial of Bruno Tesch, tr. pp. 28–31, NI-11953. Heinrich Schuster, former Austrian intelligence agent imprisoned in Auschwitz, estimated the annual consumption of Zyklon for fumigations of barracks and freight cars at 1700 kg. Affidavit by Schuster, October 13, 1947, NI-11862.

71. Gerstein account of DEGESCH, NI-7278. Affidavit by Höss, May 17, 1946, NI-34.

72. Dessau to DEGESCH, April 11, 1944, NI-9913. The man in charge of gas storage in Auschwitz was OSchaf. Klehr. Affidavit by Perry Broad (SS-man), December 14, 1945, NI-11397.

73. Liebehenschel to Auschwitz, October 2, 1942, NO-2362.

a supply had to be on hand at all times. To discerning eyes that frequency was noticeable too.[74]

The delivery system worked dependably until March, 1944, when the Dessau Zyklon plant was bombed and heavily damaged.[75] The sudden curtailment of the supply came at a time when the SS was making preparations to send 750,000 Jews to Auschwitz – then the only killing center still in existence. A crisis developed. On April 5, 1944, a Mrugowski representative wrote to DEGESCH requesting immediate shipment of 5 tons of Zyklon B without odor ingredient; the shipment had already been approved by the Armed Forces Main Sanitation Park and was "urgently needed" (*dringendst benötigt*) by the *Waffen-SS*.[76] A week later Dr. Evers of Armed Forces Sanitation himself ordered about 2800 kg. and had them shipped to Auschwitz. TESTA hurriedly inquired who was to be billed.[77] A DEGESCH official became worried that the production of Zyklon without odor ingredient would endanger the firm's monopoly.[78] The High Command of the Navy protested that it urgently needed Zyklon for the fumigation of ships.[79]

The SS in the meantime began to be concerned over the possibility that it had received the Zyklon too early. On May 24 the disinfection officer, Obersturmführer Gerstein, wrote a letter to Dr. Peters inquiring how long the shipment would last. When would it deteriorate? So far, it had not been used at all. "On the other hand, under certain circumstances large quantities – that is to say, actually the entire quantity – might have to be used all at once" (*Andererseits werden erhebliche Mengen – d.h. eigentlich die ganzen verwahrten Mengen–unter Umständen plötzlich benötigt.*)[80]

The SS did not have to wait too long. By end of May transports were rolling into Auschwitz, and on August 6 the *Referat für Schädlingsbekämpfung der Waffen-SS und Polizei in Auschwitz* ("Anti-vermin Office of the SS and Police in Auschwitz") asked for more Zyklon.[81] The supply was kept up to the very end. The SS did not run out of gas.

We have seen how the gas-killing method evolved through three separate channels, each more advanced than the previous one: first the carbon monoxide gas vans, then the carbon monoxide gas chambers, and finally the hydrogen cyanide (or Zyklon) combination units. The advantages of Zyklon as a lethal gas became known. Even while Höss was still building his gas chambers in 1942, a distinguished visitor from Lublin, Brigadeführer Globocnik, visited Auschwitz in order to learn of the new method.[82] The Höss discovery posed an immediate threat to his *Generalgouvernement* rival, Kriminalkommissar Wirth.

This rivalry came to a head one day in August, 1942, when Eichmann's deputy, Günther, and the chief disinfection officer, Kurt Gerstein, arrived in Belzec. They had about 200 pounds of Zyklon with them and were about

74. Interrogation of Höss, May 14, 1946, NI-36.

75. DEGESCH business report for 1944, April 23, 1946, NI-9093.

76. Bremenburg to Peters, April 5, 1944, NI-9909.

77. Dessau to DEGESCH, April 11, 1944, NI-9913. TESTA to DEGESCH, April 11, 1944, NI-9096. DEGESCH to TESTA, April 13, 1944, NI-9096.

78. Dr. Heinrich to Amend, June 21, 1944, NI-12110.

79. OKM (signed Dr. Klebe) to DEGESCH, August 16, 1944, NI-10185.

80. Gerstein to Peters, May 24, 1944, NI-9908.

81. Communication from Auschwitz to DEGESCH, enclosed in letter from DEGESCH to TESTA for booking, August 14, 1944, NI-9095.

82. Interrogation of Höss, May 14, 1946, NI-36.

to convert the carbon monoxide chambers to the hydrogen cyanide method. The unwelcome guests stayed to watch a gassing which took an especially long time (over three hours) because the diesel engine had failed. To Wirth's great embarrassment and mortification, Gerstein timed the operation with a stop watch. Facing the greatest crisis of his career, Wirth dropped his pride and asked Gerstein "not to propose any other type of gas chamber in Berlin." Gerstein obliged, ordering the Zyklon to be buried on the pretext that it had spoiled.[83]

Höss and Wirth were henceforth enemies. The Auschwitz commander – even after the war – spoke proudly of his "improvements."[84] Conversely, Wirth looked down on Höss as a latecomer and called him his "untalented pupil."[85] Thus there had arisen a class of "founders" and "originators" in mass death devices, and among these architects of the killing centers there was fierce competition and rivalry.

Let us pause now to review the essential facts about the six camps (see Table 78).

TABLE 78 / *Characteristics of the Death Camps*

CAMP	LOCATION	JURISDICTION	TYPE OF KILLING OPERATION	NUMBER OF JEWS KILLED
Kulmhof	Wartheland	Higher SS and Police Leader (Koppe)	gas vans (CO)	over a hundred thousand
Belzec	Lublin district	SS and Police Leader (Globocnik)	gas chambers (CO)	hundreds of thousands
Sobibor	Lublin district	SS and Police Leader (Globocnik)	gas chambers (CO)	hundreds of thousands
Lublin	Lublin district	WVHA	gas chamber (CO) shooting	tens of thousands
Treblinka	Warsaw district	SS and Police Leader	gas chambers (CO)	hundreds of thousands
Auschwitz	Upper Silesia	WVHA	gas chambers (HCN)	one million

2 / ORGANIZATION, PERSONNEL, AND MAINTENANCE

The establishment of the killing centers was accomplished by introducing into the ordinary concentration camp a special apparatus for the gassing of people. Administratively, we must therefore look at the killing centers as concentration camps with a special task. The two WVHA centers, Auschwitz and Lublin, actually had been concentration camps before the gassing machinery was added to them. They retained large numbers of Jewish inmates for labor purposes, and they also had many non-Jewish prisoners who were not subject to gassing. Hence Auschwitz and Lublin followed the elaborate pattern of camp administration in the Reich most closely.

The four camps of the Higher SS and Police Leaders were more exclusively death camps. They were built

83. Statement by Gerstein, April 26, 1945, PS-1553.

84. Affidavit by Höss, April 5, 1946, PS-3841.

85. Affidavit by Dr. Konrad Morgen, July 19, 1946, SS(A)-67.

MAP 7

THE KILLING CENTERS

as killing centers and had no non-Jewish inmates. Except for very minor industrial activity in Treblinka and Sobibor, they were not linked with war production. Krüger's and Koppe's camps were therefore simpler in structure. They had to concern themselves only with the confiscations of personal belongings brought into the compounds by the deportees and with the maintenance of an efficient killing procedure. We may therefore regard these four camps – and especially Belzec and Kulmhof – as the most "advanced" killing centers, for these institutions recognized no other purpose than the rapid and thorough destruction of their victims. These, then, are the differences between the six killing centers which should be kept in mind (see Table 79).

TABLE 79

CAMP	GASSING DEVICES	INDUSTRIAL ACTIVITY	NON-JEWISH INMATES
Kulmhof	X		
Belzec	X		
Sobibor	X	X	
Treblinka	X	X	
Lublin	X	X	X
Auschwitz	X	X	X

The three most important officials in the standard prewar concentration camp in Germany were the commander, who had over-all responsibility for the camp; the *Schutzhaftlagerführer*, who was charged with inmate control, and a chief of administration, who attended to financial matters, procurement, etc. In Dachau, Buchenwald, and Sachsenhausen, the camp commander was a *Standartenführer* (colonel), the *Schutzhaftlagerführer* an *Obersturmbannführer* (lieutenant colonel), and the administrative chief a *Sturmbannführer* (major). Besides these top officials, there was a deputy *Schutzhaftlagerführer*, an adjutant, a camp engineer, a camp doctor, etc.[1] This basic hierarchy could also be found in the Lublin and Auschwitz camps.

The Lublin organization was as follows:[2]

Commander (in succession):
- Opitz
- Staf. Koch
- OStubaf. Koegel
- Stubaf. Florstedt
- OStubaf. Weiss
- OStubaf. Liebehenschel

Schutzhaftlagerführer (in succession):
- HStuf. Hackmann
- HStuf. Wimmer
- OStuf. Thurmann

Administration (in succession):
- HStuf. Worster
- HStuf. Michel

Commander of guard forces (in succession):
- OStuf. Borrell
- Stubaf. Langleist
- HStuf. Melzer

Similarly, Auschwitz was organized in the following way:[3]

Commander: OStubaf. Höss
Administration: (Burger) OStubaf. Möckel
Zentralbauleitung: Stubaf. Bischoff
Guards: Stubaf. Hartjenstein
Chief physician: HStuf. Wirtz
Political division: UStuf. Grabner
Rapportführer (inmate count): OSchaf. Palitsch
Crematoriums: OSchaf. Moll

In November, 1943, Höss was temporarily replaced by Obersturmbannführer Liebehenschel and the camp was simultaneously broken into three parts (see Table 80). Auschwitz I was the *Stammlager* (old camp); Auschwitz II, in the Birkenau Woods was the killing center; Auschwitz III, also called Monowitz, was the industrial

1. Budget for *Waffen-SS* and concentration camps for fiscal year 1939 (signed Oberführer Frank), July 17, 1939, NG-4456.

2. Mainly from an affidavit by Friedrich Wilhelm Ruppert (chief of technical division at Lublin), August 6, 1945, NO-1903.

3. Unsigned chart, undated, NO-1966.

camp. Liebehenschel (with his headquarters) remained in over-all control and had to be consulted by the commanders of Auschwitz II and III in all important questions; but they in turn had direct access to *Amtsgruppe D*, and the guard forces were placed under their direct command.[4]

So much for camp organization; let us now consider what type of people manned the concentration camps, what qualifications and characteristics were required for camp duty. At the outset we should make a distinction between the administrative officials and the guard forces, for these two groups posed separate problems.[5]

TABLE 80 / *The Organization of Auschwitz, November, 1943*

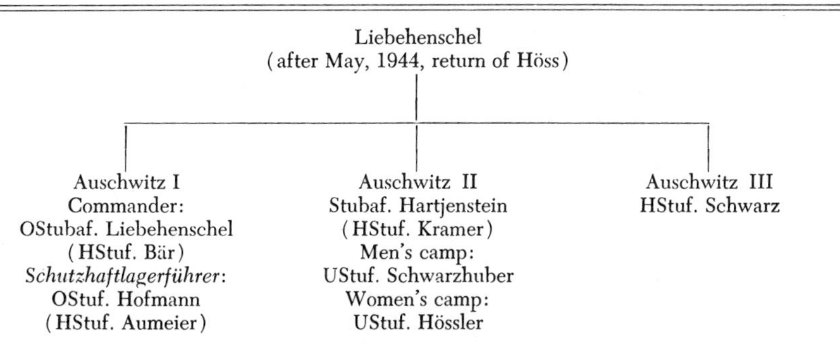

The core of the administrative force consisted of a few hundred officers and men who had served in concentration camps before the outbreak of war.[6] This core contained a number of old SS men whose outlook upon life was completely identified with SS ideology and who were capable of carrying out any task assigned to them by their *Reichsführer*-SS. Such a man – to cite the most prominent example—was Höss.

Born in 1900, Höss had had a modestly good education (six Gymnasium classes). He was brought up in a very strict Catholic home, and his father intended him to become a priest. "I had to pray and go to church endlessly, do penance over the slightest misdeed." During the First World War he volunteered for service at the age of fifteen and fought with the Turkish Sixth Army at Bagdad, at Kut-el-Amara, and in Palestine. Wounded three times and a victim of malaria, he received the Iron Cross Second Class and the Iron Crescent. From 1919 to 1921 he fought in Free Corps in the Baltic area, Silesia, and the Ruhr. While French occupation forces were in the Ruhr, a German terrorist, Leo Schlageter, was betrayed to the French by a schoolteacher, Walter Kadow. Höss murdered the schoolteacher. In consequence of this act, he was sentenced to ten years in prison (serving five).

Already somewhat distinguished, he joined the SS in 1933 without any rank. From 1934 on he served in concentration camps, rising in the hierarchy until he became commander of Auschwitz

4. Orders by Liebehenschel, November 11 and 22, 1943, *Dokumenty i Materialy*, I, 76–77.

5. The ratio between administrators and guards in Auschwitz was approximately 1:6 (500 to 3000). Affidavit by Höss, March 20, 1946, D-749-B.

6. The total administrative force, listed in the budget of the *Waffen-SS* and concentration camps for fiscal year 1939 was 953, including 62 officers, 791 enlisted men, and 100 women. Budget, signed by Obf. Frank, July 17, 1939, NG-4456.

and an Obersturmbannführer. SS-Gruppenführer von Herff found him to be soldierly, a good commander, a good farmer, quiet and simple, practical and sure of himself. In Herff's words, "He does not push himself forward but lets his actions speak for him." Compared to the intellectuals in the *Einsatzgruppen* and the paymasters in the WVHA, the man was almost made for his job. In one respect he had become a bit more bourgeois: while commanding an enterprise in which a million people were killed, Höss did not personally commit another murder.[7]

Höss was the ideal SS-man, ideally suited for his work, but he was by no means typical of *all* camp officials. The hard core of men like Höss was supplemented by a good many officials from the WVHA and its depots and by other personnel with administrative backgrounds. These reinforcements were not exactly camp enthusiasts. Many took their assignments indifferently and even apathetically. When Möckel, an experienced WVHA official, was ordered to take over the administration office in Auschwitz, he declared that he did not like to go to a concentration camp and "especially not to Auschwitz"; however, Brigadeführer Fanslau, the WVHA personnel chief, sent him to Auschwitz anyway.[8] The administrative personnel of the concentration camps was consequently a mixture of old-type SS men identified with the "movement" and a number of bureaucrats specialized in finance and general administration.

Let us now consider the guard forces. Up to 1939 the guard personnel were drawn from the *Totenkopfstandarten* – Death Head Regiments, as they were called. After the outbreak of war the departure of these "elite" units to the front and the expansion of the camp network necessitated the assignment of about 15,000 new men. The continuation of the war and the uninterrupted growth of the camps resulted in further turnovers, in the course of which the guard forces began to look more and more like second-rate SS troops.[9]

Thus we find that an Auschwitz company commander, Untersturmführer Hans Mehrbach, owed his position to the fact that he was suffering from paralysis of the heart muscles;[10] that, at the end of 1941, ethnic Germans (*Volksdeutsche*) made their appearance in Auschwitz;[11] and that, in

7. The account of Höss' life is based on his personnel record, NO-2142, and his affidavit of March 14, 1946, NO-1210. The quoted statement about his youth is from C. M. Gilbert, *Nuremberg Diary* (New York, 1947), p. 269.

8. Affidavit by Karl Möckel, July 21, 1947, NO-4514.

9. The statistics indicating *Waffen*-SS men in the WVHA camps are as follows:

	Number of Personnel in: All WVHA Camps	Auschwitz alone
May, 1940		ca 65[a]
March, 1942	ca 15,000[b]	1,800[c]
1943	25-30,000[d]	
December, 1943		ca 3,500[e]
April, 1945	30-35,000[f]	
Cumulative March, 1942 – April, 1945	ca 45,000[g]	
Cumulative May, 1940 – January, 1945		ca 7,000[h]

a. Affidavit by Höss, March 20, 1946, D-749-B.

b. Affidavit by August Harbaum (Stubaf., Chief of WVHA A-V-4), March 19, 1946, D-750.

c. Auschwitz administration (HStuf. Wagner) to WVHA D-IV, March 25, 1942, NO-2146.

d. Affidavit by Pohl, March 19, 1947, NO-2571.

e. Affidavit by Höss, March 20, 1946, D-749-B.

f. Affidavit by Harbaum, March 19, 1946, D-750.

g. *Ibid.* Cumulative figures include rotations.

h. Affidavit by Höss, March 20, 1946, D-749-B.

10. Affidavit by Hans Mehrbach, February 24, 1942, NO-2192.

1942, Ukrainian guards filled Treblinka, Belzec, and Sobibor.[12] We may therefore look upon the guard forces as a residuum assigned to dirty work while the better units of the *Waffen-SS* were selected for the more enobling task of shedding their blood on the battlefield.

The concentration camps exerted a certain influence upon the guards and administrators, an effect which was produced by the enormous distance between SS-man and inmate. Because of this distance many members of the camp personnel lost their perspective and fell into patterns of behavior which could no longer be reconciled with conduct desired or prescribed by Nazi policy. The immediate danger of such lapses in conduct was their threat to the over-all efficiency of the concentration camp, but beyond this narrow consideration there were fears, far wider in scope, which we shall presently consider.

The personnel problem arose in two different forms — sadism and corruption. The former was posed primarily by the guards, the latter chiefly by the old officials of the camps.

With regard to sadism, it must be kept in mind that the bureaucracy was not so much concerned with the suffering of the victims as with the contamination of the perpetrators. Thus the SS paid no attention whatsoever to the host of indirect tortures which it had built into the camp routine: hunger, exposure to freezing weather, overwork, filth, and utter lack of privacy. All this suffering was a consequence of the very nature of SS camp maintenance and operations. It was simply no problem.

Beyond these built-in tortures there was a category of pain which was administered for the achievement of specific aims: punishment for infractions of discipline, medical experiments on live human beings, and above all the gassing of the Jewish victims. These operations and the suffering they caused were considered necessary. They were therefore subjected only to an over-all control mechanism which, as we shall see, consisted of directives and procedures designed to hold to a minimum the possibilities of individual action by participating SS personnel. In short, the perpetration of that suffering had to be impersonal.

A third category of torture was a little more problematical. Many times, for instance, inmates had to perform exhausting calisthenics for a guard or had to pick up a cap or some other object while an SS man playfully shot them with a bullet from his rifle. This kind of exercise was called *Sport machen* ("to make sport"). Essentially it was regarded as a way in which the guards relieved their boredom, and while not exactly encouraged in official directives, little was done to stop that practice.

The whole problem of sadism was therefore narrowed down to a special kind of activity: the so-called excesses. In general, an "excess" involved a massive orgy or a sexual aberration. Among survivors certain persons acquired a reputation for such sadistic behavior. An example might be Irma Grese, a woman guard in Auschwitz who sought out well-formed Jewish women and cut their breasts open with a whip. Her victims were then brought to a woman inmate doctor who performed a painful operation on them while Irma Grese watched, cheeks flushed, swaying rythmically and foaming at the mouth.[13] So far as we know,

11. *Ergänzungsamt der Waffen-SS/Dienststelle SS Oberabschnitt Donau* (signed OStuf. Dietz) to *SS-Hauptamt/Ergänzungsamt,* October 22, 1941, NO-3372.

12. For Treblinka, see Judge Lukaszkiewicz (Siedlce), "Extermination Camp at Treblinka," in *German Crimes in Poland,* p. 97. For Belzec, see statement by OStuf. Kurt Gerstein, April 26, 1945, PS-1553. For Sobibor, see Joseph Tenenbaum, *Underground* (New York, 1952), pp 261–64.

the camp administration never interfered with Grese's doings.

Another Auschwitz personality, Oberscharführer Moll, who was in charge of the crematoriums there, is mentioned quite often in survivors' literature. Among other things, Moll is said to have selected from a newly arrived transport twenty of the most beautiful women. He stood them up in a row, stark naked, and practiced shooting at them; some of the women were hit in several places before they died.[14]

Although Auschwitz was to become the subject of a special Nazi investigation, these particular incidents appear to have been overlooked. There was no concerted effort to curb sadism. Such an effort would have been difficult in any case. The only prescribed remedy would have rendered the offending guards into "asocials" (sex criminals). However, the problem was recognized. For one thing, the camp administration established a number of brothels.[15] Another measure was to charge inmates instead of guards with the performance of disciplinary action, including the beating of prisoners. That substitution (to be discussed in connection with the inmate hierarchy) had far-reaching effects on the inmates. As a last resort, there was the possibility of getting rid of personnel who were overdoing things, but that remedy seems to have been applied only very rarely. On one occasion when SS men and German political prisoners tossed ninety Jewish women from a third-floor window into a courtyard below, the SS men were transferred to another post.[16]

Sadism, then, was regarded – insofar as it was conceived of at all – as a menace to the health of the 50,000 guards who circulated through the camps. The other problem, corruption, was seen as a threat to the entire Nazi system. Here was a practice which was taken much more seriously and which called for much stronger and concerted countermeasures. As early as 1941 Nebe's corruption specialists (RSHA-V) and an SS and Police Court began to pay attention to this vital issue.

The corruption investigations were an extremely touchy matter because they came to the core of a dilemma which was very acute, particularly among the old Nazis. A man could not be an idealist and at the same time stuff his pockets, make love to Jewish women, or engage in drunken orgies. That was why Himmler, who regarded the SS as an organization sanctified by its mission to safeguard the future of the German nation for hundreds of years, could not tolerate such "lapses" by his SS men. The corruption officers therefore had a very firm basis upon which to proceed, but they had to be careful lest someone be implicated who had too much power.

In 1941 SS and Police Court XXII in Kassel started an investigation directed against Koch, the Buchenwald commander. The proceedings failed, and Pohl congratulated Koch in writing. In this letter, which was to become notorious in SS circles, Pohl said in effect that he would step in shieldingly "whenever an unemployed lawyer should stretch out his hangman's hands

13. Gisela Perl, *I Was a Doctor in Auschwitz* (New York, 1948), pp. 61–62.

14. Philip Friedman, *This Was Oswiecim* (London, 1946), p. 69.

15. Ukrainian guards could secure the services of Polish women for two reichsmark (one mark to be paid to the prostitute, the other to be deposited into a special account). Glücks to camp commanders, December 15, 1943, NO-1545. The brothel did not, of course, close off the outlets for sadistic behavior. But in competition with these outlets it could possibly arrest and prevent the growth of the abnormal impulse into a dominant and lasting pattern in the individual's life.

16. Ella Lingens-Reiner, *Prisoners of Fear* (London, 1948), p. 40. The author was a German woman prisoner in Auschwitz.

again to grasp the white body of Koch" (*wenn wieder einmal ein arbeitsloser Jurist seine Henkershände nach dem weissen Körper Koch's ausstrecken wolle.*)[17] But the court did not let loose. After Koch had taken over the killing center of Lublin, two corruption officers from the RSHA (Hauptsturmführer Dr. Morgen and Kriminalkommissar Hauptsturmführer Wied) trailed him to the *Generalgouvernement*.[18] On August 20, 1942, he toppled from his post.[19]

While Koch was being held for trial, the investigation started in earnest. In Buchenwald a Hauptscharführer Koehler was arrested as a material witness. A few days after his arrest he was found dead in his cell, apparently poisoned. The investigating official, Dr. Morgen, was furious. Suspecting the camp doctor (Dr. Hoven) of the murder, Morgen ordered that samples of the chemical found in the dead man's stomach be administered to four Soviet prisoners of war. The four men died in the presence of several witnesses, including Morgen, corruption officer Wehner, and Hoven's colleague Dr. Schuler (alias Ding). Armed with this proof, Morgen arrested Hoven.[20] Koch himself could not escape from the net – he was tried, sentenced to death, and executed.[21]

The vise also closed upon Koch's immediate subordinate, the Lublin Schutzhaftlagerführer Hackmann. Condemned to death, Hackmann was later put into a punishment unit.[22]

Having bitten into the Lublin camp, the corruption officers suffered a reverse: they discovered that all potential Jewish witnesses there had been killed. Deciding to investigate this matter also, the SS and Police court was confronted with the mass murder of all the remaining Jewish inmates at Lublin.[23]

Resistance increased in other camps, too, as the old guard fought for its life. Thus in Sachsenhausen the corruption commission was "thrown out bodily" (*gewaltsam herausgesetzt*).[24]

SS and Police Court XXII in Kassel now constituted itself into the "SS and Police Court for Special Purposes." Preparations were made to capture the greatest prize of all: Obersturmbannführer Höss of Auschwitz. A special commission (chief, Hauptsturmführer Drescher) was installed in the camp, and an informer in the person of Hauptscharführer Gerhard Palitsch gave information about Höss. The commander, he said, was responsible for the pregnancy of an inmate, Eleonore Hodys, born in 1903 in Vienna. After considerable difficulties, corruption officers interrogated Hodys.[25] But the Auschwitz campaign was doomed to failure. The suction mechanism of the camp began to work. Open threats

17. Affidavit by Dr. Werner Paulmann, July 11, 1946, SS-64. Paulmann was Second Judge and later chief of the SS and Police court in Kassel.

18. Affidavit by Paulmann, July 11, 1946, SS-64. Interrogation of Wied, July 21, 1945, G-215.

19. Pohl to chief of SS Personnel Main Office (OGruf. Schmitt), July 28, 1942, NO-1994. OStubaf. Brandt to Pohl, August 23, 1942, NO-1994. Transfer order by Fanslau, sending Koegel to take Koch's place as commander of Lublin, August 24, 1942, NO-4334. At the same time the commander of Flossenbürg, OStubaf. Künstler, was removed from his post because of "feasts and drunkenness," and the commander of Dachau, OStubaf. Piorkowski, was removed for more serious offenses to stand trial. Brandt to Pohl, August 23, 1942, NO-1994.

20. Testimony by Eugen Kogon, Case No. 1, tr. pp. 1183–84.

21. Affidavit by Paulmann, July 11, 1946, SS-64.

22. Affidavit by Dr. Erwin Schuler, July 20, 1945, NO-258.

23. Affidavit by Paulmann, July 11, 1946, SS-64.

24. *Ibid.*

25. Affidavit by Gerhard Wiebeck, February 28, 1947, NO-2330. Wiebeck, a subordinate of Morgen, questioned the woman in October, 1944.

were sent to the SS and Police court.[26] In the camp itself, Hauptscharführer Palitsch was discovered with a Jewish woman and thrown into a coal bunker.[27] Höss had won.

The savage attack by the SS and Police court had claimed its victims, but the camp structure as a whole withstood the attack, protected by the almighty hand of Pohl, who stood ready to shield and defend his commanders in their hour of crisis.

Let us now shift attention from the camp personnel to the inmates. The first question which should logically be asked is: How did it happen that a killing center had any inmates at all? Why should anybody have been left alive? Jews were left alive mainly for three reasons: temporary congestion of the killing installations (gas chambers and crematoriums), camp construction and maintenance, and labor for industrial purposes. Persons remaining in barracks because of temporary overcrowding in the gas chambers or the ovens were no administrative problem at all. They were not registered; they were not given numbers. In most cases they were not given clothes or food. Administratively speaking, they were already written off, already dead. Camp maintenance did not require many inmates; in the pure killing centers and in those which had little industrial activity (Kulmhof, Belzec, Sobibor, and Treblinka) there were relatively few work parties. Only two camps had a large inmate population: the WVHA camps, Auschwitz and Lublin. These, then, were the only camps which posed a maintenance problem: the provision of shelter, food, and medical care for the prisoners.

Maintenance planning was characterized by a lack of concern for life itself. It is significant that "accounting for the life of an inmate" (even a German inmate) was defined as a complete and accurate report of his death (name, birth date, nationality, etc.).[28] When a Jew died, no special report had to be made; a death list sufficed.[29] Whether an individual Jew lived or died did not matter at all.

There had to be a sufficient number of inmates to take care of work requirements, and if the supply was too big, the SS weeded out the Jewish inmate population by sending the excess number to the gas chamber. The inmate count was therefore subject to great fluctuation. Depending on the arrival of new transports or a selection of victims to be put to death, the camp population could be doubled or halved within a matter of weeks or even days.[30]

Obviously, expenditures of money for the upkeep of inmates were extremely low. Living quarters were

26. "*Von Auschwitz wurde dem Gericht ganz offen gedroht.*" Affidavit by Paulmann, July 11, 1946, SS-64.

27. Sehn, "Oswiecim," p. 82.

28. Glücks to camp commanders, November 21, 1942, NO-1543.

29. *Ibid.* WVHA D-I-1 (signed Liebehenschel) to camp commanders, July 15, 1943, NO-1246. Memorandum by Höss (WVHA-I), undated, NO-1553.

30. KL Auschwitz/administration (HStuf. Wagner) reported to WVHA D-IV on March 25, 1942, that it expected an inmate increase from 11,000 to 27,000 in the next few days; NO-2146. On October 17, 1944, the women's camp in Auschwitz II had 29,925 inmates. On November 25, 1944, the number was 14,271. *Frauen-Lager* KL Au II/Abt. IIIa (Birkenau) strength reports, October 18 and November 26, 1944, *Dokumenty i Materialy,* I, 118.

Auschwitz as a whole had 11,000 inmates in March, 1942, 140,000 inmates in December, 1943, 67,000 inmates in April, 1944. Wagner to WVHA-D-IV, March 25, 1942, NO-2146. Affidavit by Höss, March 14, 1946, NO-1210. Pohl to Himmler, April 5, 1944, NO-21. Lublin dropped from 20,000–25,000 in September, 1942, to 6000 in December, 1943. Affidavit by Ruppert, August 6, 1945, NO-1903. Interrogation of Wied, July 21, 1945, G-215.

about as primitive as could be imagined. Lublin, for example, in the fall of 1942 had five blocks with a total of twenty-two barracks. The barracks were partially unfinished. Some had no windows. Others had cardboard roofs. None had water. Provisional latrines (fill-in type) spread odors throughout the habitat.[31] During an Auschwitz construction conference on June 16, 1944 (Pohl, Maurer, Höss, Bischoff, Bär, and Wirths participating, among others), the "completion" (*Ausbau*) of barracks in Camp II was still a subject of discussion. In this connection, it was pointed out that the installation of washing and toilet facilities was necessary only in every third or fourth barrack.[32]

The overcrowding in the barracks was a constant plague for the inmates; there was simply no limit to the number of people who could be put into a hut. Inmates slept without blankets or pillows on so-called *Pritschen*, wooden planks joined together. On October 4, 1944, the administrative division of Auschwitz II wrote to the central administration for 230 new *Pritschen*. Instead of having been used by five inmates, as regulations prescribed, each of the *Pritschen* had held up to fifteen inmates. Because of this weight the upper layer of the *Pritschen* had broken apart, and all the inmates had fallen on top of the people lying on the middle layer. The second layer had thereupon collapsed, and everybody had crashed through the lowest layer.[33] The result was a twisted mass of bodies and splinters.

In the matter of clothes the situation was even worse. Jews arriving in camps were deprived of all their belongings, including their clothes. Up to the beginning of 1943, prisoners' clothing was issued to all inmates. Estimates of requirements were sent by *Amtsgruppe D* to *Amt B*-II, which had to bargain with the civilian sector (Speer and Economy Ministry) for allocations.[34] As shortages increased, the supply of prisoners' clothing was choked off. On February 26, 1943, it was therefore ordered that inmates were to get ordinary clothes (properly marked), with remaining supplies of the striped variety to be given only to work parties moving about outside the camp compounds.[35] Since any clothes which could be dignified by the word were generally picked out for distribution to needy Germans – a complicated confiscation process to be described later – the Jewish inmates usually received only rags. Such things as toilet articles, handkerchiefs, and paper (including toilet paper) were not issued at all. During 1944, conditions were such that many thousands of people had to go around without any clothes whatsoever.[36]

The third plague was the lack of food. The administrative basis for food allocation in the camps was the ration system worked out by the Food and Agriculture Ministry, complete with discriminatory rations for Jews.[37] Each camp administration obtained the supplies from the food depots of the *Waf-*

31. Affidavit by Ruppert, August 6, 1945, NO-1903.

32. Summary of Auschwitz conference, June 17, 1944, NO-2359. In Auschwitz II, at that time, up to 32,000 women shared a single latrine barracks. Perl, *I was a Doctor in Auschwitz*, pp. 32–33.

33. *Kommandantur* KL Au II/*Verw.* to *Zentralverw.* Au, October 4, 1944, *Dokumenty i Materialy*, I, 95–96.

34. Affidavit by Georg Lörner, December 1, 1945, NO-54.

35. Liebehenschel to camp commanders, WVHA D-II, and WVHA D-III, February 26, 1943, NO-1530.

36. Hungarian Jewish women in Auschwitz were particularly affected. Friedman, *Oswiecim*, pp. 67–68.

37. Inspectorate to camp commanders, October 13, 1941, NO-1536. Decree by Food Ministry (signed Dr. Moritz), August 6, 1944, NG-455.

fen-SS (Standartenführer Tschentscher) and in the open market.[38] What happened to the food after it got into the camp was the administration's own business. The basic diet of Jewish inmates was watery turnip soup drunk from pots;[39] it was supplemented by an evening meal of sawdust bread with some margarine, "smelly marmalade," or "putrid sausage."[40] Between the two meals inmates attempted to lap a few drops of polluted water from a faucet in a wash barrack.[41]

The living conditions in the killing centers produced sickness and epidemics – dysentery, typhus, and skin diseases of all kinds. Sanitation measures were almost nil. The Auschwitz grounds were not suitable for canalization; hence fill-in latrines were the only facilities available. Water was not purified. Soap and articles for cleansing were very scarce. Rats ran loose in the barracks. Only occasionally was a block fumigated with Zyklon. Hospitals were barracks, and inmate doctors worked with few medicines and few instruments. When the sickrooms became overcrowded, the SS doctor made an inspection and dispatched the worst cases to the gas chamber.[42]

The prisoners tried to survive, and they worked out a few compensatory mechanisms. Food was stolen and traded in the black market.[43] Inmate doctors worked frantically and tirelessly, but the tide of death was too great. Up to the end of 1942, Lublin had received 26,258 *registered* Jewish inmates. A total of 4568 had been released: 14,348 had died. Auschwitz had obtained 5849 *registered* Jewish inmates up to the same date; 4436 had died.[44] In July, 1943, Auschwitz was short of inmates for its industrial requirements, and a commission was sent to Lublin to take some prisoners from there. Out of 3800 people set aside for Auschwitz a preliminary check revealed only 30 per cent fit for work. The Auschwitz commission was so indignant that the Lublin administration scraped up everyone whom it could call fit for work "with a good conscience"; after a second examination a Lublin doctor, Untersturmführer Dr. Rindfleisch, admitted that Lublin inmates could not really be classified as employable.[45] Fifteen hundred inmates were finally chosen. When they arrived, five women were already dead, forty-nine

38. Affidavit by Wilhelm Max Burger, May 14, 1947, NO-3255. Burger was administrative chief of Auschwitz before Möckel.

39. The soup was the midday meal. "There were pieces of wood, potato peeling and unrecognizable substances swimming in it." Perl, *I Was a Doctor in Auschwitz,* pp. 38–41. The soup meal was issued in cans which weighed about 120 pounds. They had only two handles and no cover. Before it was distributed in the pots, the scalding brew had to be carried under the blows of SS men from the kitchen to the block. Report by a De Gaullist, August 20, 1946, NO-1960.

40. Perl, *I Was a Doctor in Auschwitz,* p. 36.

41. *Ibid.*, p. 32. For an expert discussion of the medical aspects of nutrition in the camps, see Dr. Elie A. Cohen, *Human Behavior in the Concentration Camp* (New York, 1953), pp. 51–58. The author is a survivor of Auschwitz.

42. On diseases and sick treatment, see Cohen, *Human Behavior in the Concentration Camp,* pp. 58–81.

43. A few Auschwitz black market prices were as follows:

One cigarette	RM	6–7
1 lb of bread	RM	150
1 lb of margarin	RM	100
1 lb of butter	RM	200
1 lb of fat	RM	280–320
1 lb of meat	RM	400–480

Report by a De Gaullist, August 20, 1946, NO-1960. Most often there was only barter trade. An old man in Auschwitz traded a sack of diamonds he had smuggled in for three raw potatoes which he ate at once. Perl, *I Was a Doctor in Auschwitz,* pp. 114–15. Women sometimes lent their bodies to German or Polish political prisoners in order to eat. *Ibid.*, pp. 76, 78–79.

44. Report by Korherr, March 27, 1943, NO-5194.

45. Report by an Auschwitz *UStuf.*, July 6, 1943, *Dokumenty i Materialy,* I, 138–40.

were dying, and most others had skin eruptions or were suffering from "exhaustion" (*Körperschwäche*).[46] Whatever other talents the camp officials may have had, keeping prisoners alive was not one of them – even if on rare occasions that became necessary.

For the SS, a far more serious task than maintaining inmates was the problem of keeping them under control. To have an iron grip on the inmate population, the camp administration expended a great deal of money and effort. The three elements of inmate control were guards, contraptions, and internal controls. We shall examine these measures in reverse order, for the most important means by which inmates were held in check were internal controls.

The Germans proceeded from the fundamental assumption that an individual prisoner would not resist. He would obey an order even if it were against his interests. When confronted with a choice between action and inertia, he would be paralyzed; he would reason that nothing is ever certain, not even death in Auschwitz.[47] The primary danger of resistance was consequently not the reasoning power of the individual – for he was helpless in spite of it and because of it – but the establishment of an organization which would pit against the concentration camp a compulsive mechanism of its own. Internal controls sought to prevent the formation of any such resistance movement. Camp commanders were ordered to watch developments in their camps at all times, lest one day they be surprised by "major unpleasant events."[48] The commanders were to keep track of things by making use of inmate spies,[49] and inmate resistance was frustrated further by the institution of an inmate bureaucracy and inmate privileges.

The distribution of power and privilege among the inmates was determined in the first instance by the racial hierarchy. Even in a concentration camp a German was still a German; a Pole was a Pole; a Jew, a Jew. This stratification could not be broken by the inmates; the racial hierarchy was as rigid as any bureaucratic hierarchy had ever been. No combining, no delegation of power, no mutiny, was possible here.

The inmate bureaucracy was divided into two parts: one in charge of quarters, the other in charge of work parties. In quarters, the hierarchy was *Lagerältester* (highest in camp), *Blockältester* (in charge of block), and *Stubendienst* (in charge of barrack). In work parties, it was *Oberkapo, Kapo,* and *Vorarbeiter.* In Auschwitz and Lublin the top echelons of the inmate bureaucracy were filled by German prisoners;[50] consequently, there was an inmate leadership, but it was responsible, and responsive, to camp command.

Not only were German prisoners in the most important positions of the inmate bureaucracy; they also enjoyed the most extensive privileges within the framework of concentration camp life, such as the right to receive packages, supplementary food rations, less overcrowding in barracks, and bed linen in camp hospitals.[51] Far less privileged and much worse off were Poles, Czechs, and other Slavs.[52] On the bottom were the Jews. Between the Jew-

46. *Standortarzt* (camp doctor) Auschwitz to *Kommandantur* Auschwitz, July 8, 1943, *Dokumenty i Materialy*, I, 138–40.

47. See Cohen, *Human Behavior in the Concentration Camp,* pp. 115–210.

48. Glücks to camp commanders, March 31, 1944, NO-1554.

49. *Ibid.*

50. Sehn, "Oswiecim," pp. 38–39. Irene Schwarz in Leo W. Schwarz (ed.), *The Root and the Bough* (New York and Toronto, 1949), pp. 193–96. Affidavit by Ruppert, August 6, 1945, NO-1903.

51. Lingens-Reiner, *Prisoners of Fear,* pp. 52, 56, 100.

52. *Ibid.*, pp. 44, 49.

ish and the German inmates there was an unbridgeable gulf: the Germans were entitled to live – they had at least a minimum of privileges to make a fight for life; the Jews were doomed. It is characteristic that the Jews in Auschwitz were hoping that an air raid might destroy the killing installations,[53] while the Germans were consoled by the thought "that the Allied airmen knew and avoided the camp."[54]

Perhaps the extreme example of the crushing force that separated Germans from Jews is this incident told by Dr. Ella Lingens-Reiner, who had been sent to Auschwitz because she had hidden some Jews in her apartment in Vienna (*Judenbegünstigung*). In Auschwitz she took under her protection a young Jewish woman from Prague, Gretl Stutz. One day Stutz was brought into the hospital hut with typhus, one patient among seven hundred. As Dr. Lingens-Reiner gave her an injection, a voice protested from the German corner: "Of course, you give something to the Jewess, and let us Germans die like dogs. You're a nice example of a German prisoner!" Thereupon she did not visit her friend again. Gretl Stutz was transferred to another ward and after a few days she succumbed, deserted, to her sickness.[55]

Another internal control measure was marking. In the concentration camp, too, the Jewish inmate had to wear the six-pointed Star of David. In addition, his registration number was tattooed on his arm.[56] Still another precaution was taken in the form of daily roll calls which sometimes lasted hours. The roll calls kept track of all prisoners and prevented hiding within the camp. The prisoners were not dismissed until everyone was accounted for, dead or alive.[57] As a last means the Germans also resorted to reprisal, usually a public hanging. They thus sought to frustrate the formation of an internal resistance movement by a system of spies, inmate bureaucracies, inmate privileges, marking, roll calls, and reprisals. However, preventive measures did not stop with these devices.

In February, 1943, Himmler became worried that air raids on the concentration camps might occasion mass breaks. To prevent any such occurrence he ordered that each camp be divided into blocks, 4000 inmates per block, each block to be fenced in with barbed wire. Every camp was to be surrounded by a high wall, and barbed wire was to be strung on *both* sides of the wall. The interior passageway between wire and wall was to be patrolled by dogs; the outer passageway was to be mined, just in case a bomb tore a hole in the wall. In the vicinity of the camp, dogs trained to tear a man apart (*zerreissen*) were to roam at night.[58] All these elaborate contraptions were set up pursuant to Himmler's wishes. Searchlights were mounted on poles of the wire fence, and the interior wire was electrically charged. Inmates who tired of life had only to lean on this wire to end their misery.

The third element of inmate control was the guard force. In spite of all internal measures and the construction of contraptions, there had to be an armed body of men to deal with the eventuality of "major unpleasant events." However, these camps, in which more than 3,000,000 people were killed, were – all other devices notwithstanding – rather thinly guarded. All in

53. Olga Lengyel, *Five Chimneys* (Chicago and New York, 1947), pp. 123, 155–56. The author was a Jewish woman doctor in Auschwitz.

54. Lingens-Reiner, *Prisoners of Fear,* p. 36.

55. *Ibid.*, pp. 83–84.

56. Lengyel, *Five Chimneys,* p. 106. Cohen, *Human Behavior in the Concentration Camp,* pp. 26–28.

57. Lengyel, *Five Chimneys,* pp. 37–40.

58. Himmler to Pohl and Glücks, February 8, 1943, Himmler Files, Folder No. 67.

all, about 6000–7000 men may have manned the killing centers at any one time; about 10,000–12,000 if rotation is taken into account. Auschwitz had about 3000 guards;[59] Lublin had a battalion;[60] Treblinka may have had about 700 men, including Ukrainians;[61] Kulmhof was run by a *Sonderkommando* of 150 to 180 men.[62] Little is known about the guard forces of Belzec and Sobibor, except that they numbered in the hundreds and that, again, they were mostly Ukrainian. In the WVHA camps the guards were equipped with small arms, including machine guns mounted on observation towers.[63] At night they trained searchlights on the camp grounds. Getting these guards – even though their number was small for the size of the task – was no easy problem. Curiously enough, an even bigger obstacle proved to be the acquisition of their armament.

Since the guard forces were not exactly first-class units, the SS men in charge of weapons supply did not consider it necessary to furnish them with first-class arms. The distribution of weapons and munitions in the entire *Waffen-SS* was handled by the *SS-Führungshauptamt,* the main office concerned with purely military matters. In the WVHA, *Amt B*-V, under Standartenführer Scheide, handled weapons and munitions for the WVHA camps. Whenever the WVHA had requests for weapons, Scheide submitted the requests to the *Führungshauptamt;* very often, however, he was turned down or was offered Italian rifles without ammunition, etc.

All in all, *Amtsgruppe D* obtained only about 15,000 rifles and 30 machine guns for all its camps. This was of course not enough, so it made use of its business connections to procure weapons independently. Companies making use of camp labor, particularly the Steyr armaments firm, were approachable in such matters. Scheide protested to Glücks against this gunrunning (*Waffenschieberei*), whereupon Glücks replied that he would take his weapons wherever he could get them. In the matter of trucks, the situation was the same: the trucks were usually obtained when firms made available the necessary transport to get laborers, then somehow forgot to ask for the return of the trucks.[64]

Thus by hook and crook the guards and the weapons and the transport were assembled. But Pohl was still worried. There were many doomed people in the camps. In a report to Himmler dated April 5, 1944, Pohl outlined the preparations he had made for the eventuality of a mass break from Auschwitz.

The number of Auschwitz inmates was then 67,000; from that total he deducted 18,000 sick inmates and 15,000 in work parties who could be "done away with" (*abgesetzt*) "so that practically one has to count 34,000 inmates." At that time, he had 2950 guards. From the Higher SS and Police Leader in the area, Obergruppenführer Schmauser, he procured another police company of 130 men as a standby force. At the start of a mass break, a defense line in the interior of the camp would be manned by all the guards; in addition, Schmauser had made an agreement with the commander of the VIII Corps, General der Kavallerie von Koch-Ersach, in pursuance of which

59. Pohl to Himmler, April 5, 1944, NO-21.

60. *Schutzmannschaftsbataillon* 252 to July, 1943. Krüger to Himmler, copy to SS and Police Leader Krakow (Obf. Scherner), July 7, 1943, Himmler Files, Folder No. 94.

61. Yankel Wiernik, "Uprising in Treblinka," in Schwarz, *The Root and the Bough,* pp. 119–21.

62. Bednarz, "Chelmno," in *German Crimes in Poland,* p. 117.

63. Pohl to Himmler, April 5, 1944, NO-21.

64. Affidavit by Rudolf Hermann Karl Scheide, January 16, 1947, NO-1568.

the Wehrmacht was to man an outer defense line. Furthermore, the air force had promised to furnish 1000 men if the breakout did not coincide with an air raid. Finally, the *Kripo-Leitstelle* in Katowice was prepared to undertake a major search (*Grossfahndung*) for the capture of anyone who got through.[65]

There was no mass break from Auschwitz. Only a few inmates managed to run the triple gauntlet of informers, wires, and guards, and most of them were brought back. Sometimes the corpse of an escaped prisoner was propped up on a chair with a sign reading, "Here I am."[66] Only a handful made good their escape.

In two of the smaller camps, Treblinka and Sobibor, the unexpected happened. Unlike Auschwitz, which had a very large inmate population, Treblinka kept only a few work parties (all Jews) for maintenance and other purposes. The inmate-guard ratio in Auschwitz during 1943–44 ranged from about 20:1 to 35:1. In Treblinka the inmate-guard ratio was about 1:1 (700 inmates to 700 guards). Nevertheless, Treblinka had a breakout. Precisely because they were only 700 men, these inmates could not reason that they would get through the war alive; within the square-mile compound there was no possibility of hiding, no possibility of eluding one's fate. After a while every inmate realized this.

The breakout plan was very simple. A locksmith made a duplicate key to the arsenal, and a former captain of the Polish Army, Dr. Julian Chorazyski, worked out the escape plan. He was killed just before the coup was to take place, but his place was taken by a new inmate, the physician Dr. Leichert, also a former officer. On August 2, 1943, 20 hand grenades, 20 rifles, and several revolvers were secretly removed from the arsenal. At 3:45 P.M. the guards were rushed. Of 700 men in the camp, 150 to 200 got out. The escapees were hunted down one by one. About 12 survived.[67]

The Sobibor revolt by about 150 inmates was an almost exact duplication of the Treblinka break. The date of the battle was October 14, 1943. The Germans lost an *Untersturmführer* in the fighting.[68]

3 / Labor Utilization

The primary reason for keeping up an inmate population was labor utilization, although the use of Jews for construction projects, maintenance, or industry was merely an intermediary step to be followed by killing. As in the case of the mobile killing operations in the East, the Jews were to be granted only a respite, or, in the ponderous words of Pohl, "Employable Jews who are migrating to the East will have to interrupt their journey and work in war industry [*Die für die Ostwanderung bestimmten arbeitsfähigen Juden werden also ihre Reise unterbrechen und Rüstungsarbeiten leisten müssen*]."[1]

Unlike the respite granted to the Jews in the occupied eastern territories, the postponement of killings in the camps was occasioned and desired entirely by the SS. Those among the

65. Pohl to Himmler, April 5, 1944, NO-21.

66. Report based on account of two Slovak Jews who made their way from Auschwitz to Switzerland, in War Refugee Board, "The Extermination Camps of Auschwitz and Birkenau" (Washington, D.C., 1944; mimeographed), pp. 5–6.

67. Samuel Rajzman, "Uprising in Treblinka," *Hearings before the House Committee on Foreign Affairs,* 79th Cong., 1st sess., on H.J. Res. 93 (punishment of war criminals), March 25–26, 1945, pp. 120–25. Yankel Wiernik in Schwarz, *The Root and the Bough,* pp. 119–21. Both Rajzman and Wiernik were in this break.

68. Tenenbaum, *Underground,* pp. 261–64. The author's account is based on two survivors' accounts.

1. Pohl to Himmler, September 16, 1942, NI-15392.

doomed Jews who were strong enough to do some work were to donate their remaining lives to the end that the SS might develop an industrial base and exercise economic power. "Major economic tasks will be faced by the concentration camps in the next few weeks," wrote Himmler to Glücks on January 25, 1942, as he requested him to prepare for the reception of "100,000 male Jews and up to 50,000 Jewesses."[2]

The one circumstance which enabled the SS to undertake any major tasks at all was its supply of labor at a time when that supply began to grow short in Europe. It is one of the ironies of the destruction process that the labor gap which the SS now proposed to fill had been created in the first place by the removal of a sizeable working force in the name of the "final solution of the Jewish question in Europe." In fact, the SS had a little trouble fulfilling its promise, for the camp officials were poor caretakers of the manpower in their custody. The newly arrived transports were handled in an extremely careless manner. At times of labor shortages in Auschwitz the camp doctor would often send almost an entire transport to the gas chamber. Such happenings infuriated the authorities in charge of camp labor allocation, WVHA D-II Chief Standartenführer Maurer and his assistant, Sommer. Two instances may be cited.

On January 27, 1943, Sommer informed Höss that 5000 Jews from Theresienstadt were being sent to Auschwitz; he requested that the prospective workers among them be selected "carefully" (*sorgfältig zu erfassen*) because they were needed by the construction department at Auschwitz and by the I. G. Farben Works there. After some delay Schwarz sent the following statistical reply: Out of 5022 Theresienstadt Jews, 4092 had been gassed (*gesondert untergebracht*). The men had been too "frail" (*gebrechlich*); the women were mostly children.[3]

On March 3, 1943, Maurer announced that transports of skilled Jewish workers were beginning to roll from Berlin. He reminded Höss that these workers had been employed in war industry; they were consequently employable in the camp. The I. G. Farben Company was to fill its needs from these transports. To make sure that the selections would be made more carefully this time, Maurer suggested that the trains be unloaded "not in the usual place" (at the crematory) but, more suitably (*zweckmässigerweise*), near the I. G. Farben plant.[4] Two days later Obersturmführer Schwarz made his reply, adopting a gruff tone. A total of 1750 Jews had arrived from Berlin; 632 were men, the rest women and children. The average age of men selected for work was between 50 and 60. Of the 1118 women and children, 918 had to be subjected to "special treatment" (*SB*). "If the transports from Berlin continue to have so many women and children as well as old Jews," he wrote, "I don't promise myself much in the matter of labor allocation." The following four transports did not fare much better (2398 killed, 1689 saved for industry).[5]

While the camp administration was woefully inefficient in making selections, it was, as already noted, even more lethargic and incapable in its task of keeping prisoners alive. The camp labor supply was like water in a barrel with a big hole in the bottom. Trans-

2. Himmler to Glücks, January 25, 1942, NO-500.

3. Sommer to *Kommandant* Auschwitz, January 27, 1943, *Dokumenty i Materiały*, I, 115–17. Schwarz to WVHA D-II, February 20, 1943, *ibid.*

4. Maurer to Höss, March 3, 1943, *ibid.*, p. 108.

5. Schwarz to WVHA D-II, March 5, 1943, *ibid.*, pp. 108–10, 117. Schwarz to WVHA D-II, March 8, 1943, *ibid.* Schwarz to WVHA-D, March 15, 1943, *ibid.*

ports had to come continuously. If the flow was stopped for any reason, the camp labor supply would run dangerously low, as it did in July, 1943, when the Auschwitz administration scurried to Lublin in order to borrow some inmates. But in spite of this system a labor supply was gradually built up.[6]

Not all inmates were available for industrial purposes. In the spring of 1943 the 160,000 prisoners of the WVHA camps were allocated as follows:[7]

For camp maintenance: 15 per cent
For industry: 63 per cent
Unable to work: 22 per cent

As a matter of fact, the percentages are misleading. They were given by Himmler to Speer. More accurately, the breakdown would look like this:

Camp maintenance: 15 per cent
WVHA-C (construction) }
WVHA-W (SS enterprises) } 63 per cent
Private employers }
Unable to work: 22 per cent

This gives us four different kinds of employers: the first three were SS employers, and only the fourth represented war industry, strictly speaking.

Economically and administratively, the four employer groups were not in identical positions. The camp administration did not have to apply for allocation and did not have to pay for labor. Kammler, the SS industries, and the private plants obtained labor by applying for it in Maurer's office (D-II). The camp administrators and Kammler did not have to pay for their workers. The SS industries and private firms made payments to the Reich (see Table 81).

TABLE 81 / *Camp Labor Administration*

	Allocation by Maurer	Payment for Inmates
Camp Administration		
Amtsgruppe C	X	
Amtsgruppe D	X	X
Private Industry	X	X

All employed inmates were organized in work parties (*Kommandos*) and were placed under the supervision of inmates (*Oberkapos, Kapos,* and *Vorarbeiter*). There were two types of maintenance *Kommandos* reflecting the dual purpose of the killing center: those engaged in ordinary maintenance tasks (kitchen personnel, sick bay attendants, latrine cleaners, electricians, plumbers, etc.) and those involved in the killing operations (the *Transportkommandos* which cleaned up the freight cars after unloading, the *Kommandos* in the *Effektenkammer* which sorted valuables, and, most important, the *Sonderkommandos* which worked in the crematories;[8] we will come back to the *Son-*

6. The following statistics are a compilation of WVHA camp reports showing registered arrivals and departures during the period of June to November, 1942. Since the totals were calculated by adding the figures furnished by the individual camps, inter-camp transfers show up in the arrivals *and* departures:

Arrivals totaled 136,780, including 109,861 new arrivals ("deliveries") and 26,919 transfers-in.

"Departures" were 112,434, broken down into 4711 discharges, 27,846 transfers-out, 70,610 deaths, and 9267 executions.

These figures show a net gain of 24,346 in six months. Alarmed, Glücks sent the statistics to the camp doctors, pointing out that "with such a large death rate the number of inmates can never be brought up to the figure ordered by the *Reichsführer-SS*," and directing the doctors to pay closer attention to food distribution and working conditions. WVHA D-III (signed Glücks) to camp commanders, December 28, 1942, PS-2171.

7. Himmler to Speer, June, 1943, Himmler Files, Folder No. 67. The percentages refer to March 31, 1943. In the beginning of 1945 (470,000 inmates), the percentages were approximately 9, 74, 17. Affidavit by Pohl, May 21, 1947, NO-2570.

8. For breakdowns with statistics, see report by KL Auschwitz II on labor allocation, May 11, 1944, *Dokumenty i Materialy,* I, 100–105. Also, Rajzman in *Hearings,* House Foreign Affairs Committee, 79th Cong., 1st

derkommandos a little later). Besides the camp itself, there were two other SS employers: *Amtsgruppe C* and the SS industries.

The chief of *Amtsgruppe C*, Kammler, was the builder of concentration camps and concentration camp installations. In Auschwitz alone, during 1942 and 1943, he used an average of about 8000 inmates per day.[9]

We have already spoken of the SS industries in connection with the labor camps set up by Himmler during the deportation of the Polish Jews; they were the ones that went in for the production of such items as brushes, baskets, and wooden shoes. The contribution to the war effort made by the SS plants in the concentration camps was of the same order. Because of its limited financial resources (capital investment, RM 32,000,000) the SS combine had to confine itself to production which did not require great capital outlay and which was suited to exploitation of slave labor. Table 82 is a brief outline of the SS industry network in the killing centers.[10]

The SS industries enjoyed excellent relations with the camp administrators and the SS and Police Leaders. In an atmosphere of co-operation and good will they grew to a respectable size. For example, Sturmbannführer Mummenthey (DEST) reported that the gravel works in Treblinka were doing well. The fact that Treblinka was not under the jurisdiction of *Amtsgruppe D* was no disadvantage.[11] The DAW in Lublin obtained a loan of 71,000 zloty from Brigadeführer Globocnik, and the camp commander (Koch) agreed to feed the DAW employees for the sum total of 0.30 reichsmark per person per day.[12] In Auschwitz the DAW received the patronizing attention of Höss. From

Table 82 / *SS Industry in the Killing Centers*

Office	Enterprise	Manager	Establishments
WVHA W-I	Earth and stones DEST	OStubaf. Mummenthey	Gravel works in Auschwitz and Treblinka (also granite works in Mauthausen, diamond-cutting in Herzogenbusch)
WVHA W-II	Cement	OStubaf. Bobermin	Cement works in Lublin
WVHA W-III	Food products	HStuf. Rabeneck	Auschwitz, Lublin
WVHA W-IV	Wood products DAW	HStuf. Opperbeck	Auschwitz, Lublin

sess., on H.J. Res. 93, March 25–26, 1945, pp. 120–25. *Kommandos* had different names in different camps. They were also organized somewhat differently in every camp.

9. Sehn, "Oswiecim," pp. 30–31.

10. Organization chart of SS industries, September 30, 1944, NO-2116. Wage chart of SS industries, April 1, 1944, NO-653. The granite works in Mauthausen utilized the 1000 Dutch Jews who were deported there in 1941, and Dutch Jews were also employed at Herzogenbusch. Most of the SS plants were in ordinary labor and concentration camps, not shown above.

11. Mummenthey to Pohl, June 28, 1943, NO-1031.

12. Report by HStuf. May (W-IV), June 11, 1942, NO-1216.

the *Bauleitung* it acquired two workshops and orders for doors and windows to be fitted into the gas chambers.[13] In such ways the SS enterprises were soon able to take on several thousand inmate laborers.

A special enterprise was ordered by Himmler for Sobibor. This camp was set aside for the disassembly of captured ammunition in order to salvage the metals and explosives. The enterprise was not incorporated into the WVHA industry network because it was designated to work for the *SS-Führungshauptamt* exclusively.[14]

The Jewish inmates working for their SS employers did not last long. The SS insisted on great tempo: potatoes had to be unloaded at a run;[15] wheelbarrows filled with gravel had to be pushed up steep slopes at a trot.[16] For those who could not keep up there was only quick death.

Unlike the SS, private firms moved into the concentration camps with large capital and made them a factor in war production. For a long time the SS attempted to lure industry into the camps. As early as 1935, I. G. Farben officials visited Dachau,[17] but the invitation did not turn out to be successful. While camp labor was certainly cheap (in the beginning the price was one reichsmark per inmate per day), its employment was coupled with drawbacks. To begin with, a plant had to be built within a camp (or the camp extended to cover the plant). There had to be enough labor in the camp to justify the construction of a work hall or building. Key labor and, to some extent, skilled labor had to be brought in by the firm. Even if all these requirements were met, the concentration camp routine was not attuned to promote labor efficiency, and for a long time Himmler was unable to find any clients. The SS obtained its first major customer only after the disadvantages of camp operation were outweighed by a few special inducements. The first company to move in on a big scale was I. G. Farben.

In dealing with the I. G., one must discard certain conventional notions about company management and operations. The I. G. was not a mere company; it was a bureaucratic empire and a major factor in the destructive machine. We have met it in connection with dismissals of employees and have seen it in action during the Aryanizations; now we shall follow it into a killing center. How did I. G. Farben direct its operations into Himmler's territory? To answer this question, we must say a few words about how it operated at all.

In the conventional scheme stockholders elected the Aufsichtsrat, which in turn elected the Vorstand, and these elective offices were the focal points of power.[18] In the I. G., the Aufsichtsrat and Vorstand were mere outer trappings; membership in these bodies without a position in a committee, a plant combination, or the central administration meant nothing. The nominal head of the company, Vorstand Chairman Hermann Schmitz, held no bureaucratic position. He appears to have been a rubber stamp. The Vorstand (84 members to 1937, 27 after 1937) was an unwieldy body with perfunctory activities. It accepted *all* policy recommendations presented for

13. *Ibid.*, and crematorium correspondence, p. 566.

14. Himmler to WVHA, *Führungshauptamt,* Higher SS and Police Leaders GG, *Ostland,* Ukraine, Russia Center, SS and Police Leader Lublin, and Chief of Anti-Partisan units, July 5, 1943, NO-482.

15. Sehn, "Oswiecim," p. 53.

16. War Refugee Board, "Auschwitz-Birkenau," Polish major's report, p. 12.

17. Affidavit by Höss, May 17, 1946, NI-34.

18. The chairman of the Aufsichtsrat and the Vorstand chairman may be compared to chairman of the board of directors and president, respectively.

its approval. The still larger and even more perfunctory Aufsichtsrat met three or four times a year to receive reports from the Vorstand.[19] We do not need to discuss the stockholders.

The organization of I. G. Farben was bewilderingly complex. To draw a simplified and abbreviated picture of that power structure, we can divide the hierarchy into three parts: the top echelon, the plants, and the central services.

The top echelon, or policy-making part of the organization, was *not* one office with one man at its head. In a Führer state, the I. G. had no Führer; instead, it had three separate centers of direction: The Krauch office, The TEA, and The KA. The first of these bodies was not even a part of the I. G. Krauch was a high I. G. Farben official until 1940 only; he then became General Plenipotentiary for Special Questions of Chemical Production in the Office of the Four-Year Plan – without relinquishing his I. G. Farben salary.[20] From his new office Krauch guided the *expansion* of the entire chemical industry.

The TEA (*Technischer Ausschuss,* or "technical committee"), headed by Dr. Fritz Ter Meer, concerned itself with *production*: scientific questions, raw material, production methods, plant expansion, and so on. The TEA was at the apex of a large number of commissions which dealt with individual problems:[21]

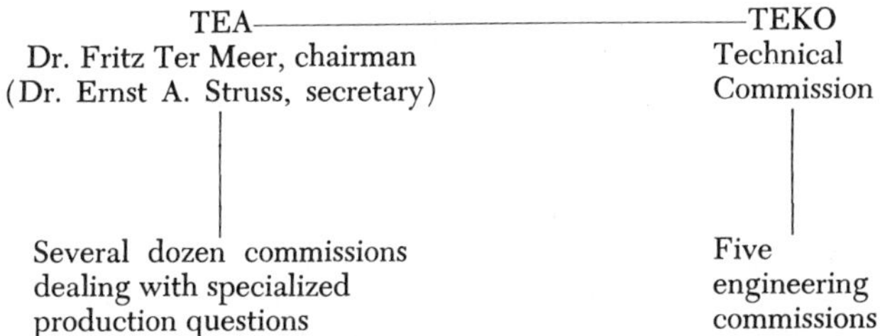

Third was the KA (*Kaufmännischer Ausschuss,* or "commercial committee"). This committee, under Dr. Georg von Schnitzler, dealt with *commercial* problems: marketing, sales, prices, taxes, etc. It was placed over the sales combines (see Table 83).[22]

The top policy-making echelon thus consisted of a triumvirate: Krauch (expansion), Ter Meer (production),

Table 83 / *KA Machinery*

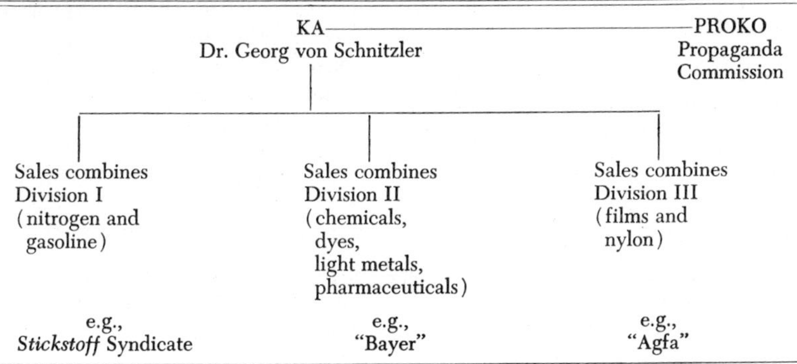

and Schnitzler (marketing and financial aspects).

The second part of the I. G. Farben machinery was its plant organization. We have said that the I. G. was a true industrial empire. It had more plants (fifty-six) than Pohl had concentration camps, and its production spanned the entire chemical field. The plants were arranged into three divisions (*Sparten*), according to production specialization, and into work combines (*Betriebsgemeinschaften*), grouped territorially. Table 84 shows the divisions, work combines, main plants, and a few of the other plants to which we shall have to refer.[23]

The third component of the I. G. consisted of the central service departments, divided into the Berlin and Frankfurt offices. "I. G. Berlin," headed by Dr. Max Ilgner, took care of such diverse but important matters as personnel, protocol, legal problems, press, export, and political economy.[24] Frankfurt was the headquarters of commercial services: the central bookkeeping and central insurance departments, the customer index, and so on.[25]

The I. G. hierarchy – committees, plants, and central administration – was a headless colossus, running like an autonomous machine which someone had once set into motion and which drove on relentlessly to keep producing and expanding. Significantly, the I. G.'s involvement in Auschwitz can be traced not to a desire to kill Jews or to work them to death but to a complicated manufacturing problem: the expansion of synthetic rubber ("Buna") production.

Before the war the I. G. built two Buna plants: Buna I at Schkopau in 1936, and Buna II at Hüls in 1938.[26] On November 2, 1940, I. G. Farben officials met with Unterstaatssekretär von Hannecken of the Economy Ministry and decided to step up the production of synthetic rubber.[27] Accordingly, it was decided to build Buna III at Ludwigshafen. The Ludwigshafen plant did not suffice to bring production to the required level, and the planners consequently considered two alternatives: expansion of the Hüls plant from 40,000 tons to 60,000 tons or construction of a new plant with a capacity of 25,000 tons. The new plant could be constructed in Norway or at Auschwitz.

From the beginning the Economy Ministry pushed the Auschwitz site. There was at that time great interest in making the incorporated territories a part of Germany, not only administratively but also economically and demographically. On December 11, 1940, an inducement was offered to that end: a decree which tendered tax exemptions to companies building plants in the incorporated areas.[28] On February 6, 1941, the final decisions

19. Affidavit by Dr. Fritz Ter Meer, April 29, 1947, NI-5184. Affidavit by Dr. August von Knierim, April 15, 1947, NI-6173. Ter Meer's position will be shown below; von Knierim was legal chief.

20. Interrogation of Dr. Ernst A. Struss, April 26, 1947, NI-11109.

21. Affidavit by Ter Meer, April 29, 1947, NI-5184.

22. Affidavit by Dr. Günther Frank-Fahle, June 10, 1947, NI-5169. Affiant was a member of the KA.

23. Affidavit by Dr. Ernst Struss, July 16, 1947, NI-10029. A complete chart is in the affidavit.

Up to 1940, Krauch headed Division I. Compare these divisions with the organization of the sales combines.

24. For chart, see affidavit by Ilgner, April 30, 1947, NI-6544.

25. Affidavit by Frank-Fahle, June 10, 1947, NI-5169.

26. Affidavit by Struss, July 6, 1947, NI-10029.

27. The goal was 150,000 tons. Memorandum by Ter Meer, February 10, 1941, NI-11112.

28. RGBl I, 1505.

TABLE 84 / *The Plant Organization of I. G. Farben*

Division I Dr. Christian Schneider nitrogen and gasoline		Division II Dr. Fritz Ter Meer chemicals, dyes, light metals, pharmaceuticals				Division III Dr. Fritz Gajewski films and nylon
Dr. Bütefisch	Work Combine Upper Rhine Dr. Wüster		Work Combine Main Dr. Lautenschläger	Work Combine Lower Rhine Dr. Kühne	Work Combine Central Germany Dr. Bürgin	
LEUNA[†] Dr. von Staden	OPPAU[†] Dr. Müller-Cunradi	LUDWIGSHAFEN[†] Dr. Wüster Deputy, Dr. Ambros	HÖCHST[†] Dr. Lautenschläger Deputy, Jahne	LEVERKUSEN[†] Dr. Haberland Deputy, Dr. Brüggemann	BITTERFELD[†] Dr. Bürgin	WOLFEN FILM[†] Dr. Gajewski Deputy, Dr. Kleine
AUSCHWITZ Dr. Dürrfeld Division I, Dr. Braus	HEYDEBRECK Dr. Sönsken	BUNA I (SCHKOPAU) Dr. Wulff		UERDINGEN Dr. Haberland		
		BUNA II (HÜLS) Dr. Hoffmann				
		BUNA III (LUDWIGSHAFEN) Niemann				
		BUNA IV (AUSCHWITZ) Dr. Dürrfeld Division II, Dr. Eisfeld				
		DYHERNFURTH Palm				

†Main plant.

were made. Three conferences were held on that day. In one conference Ministerialdirigent Mulert of the Economy Ministry vetoed Norway. In another conference Ministerialrat Römer promised, subject to the approval of the price commissar, that the saving of 60,000,000 reichsmark which could be made by expanding Buna II in preference to the construction of the new plant was partially going to be covered by maintaining rubber prices at their current high level. In the third conference Ter Meer and the deputy chief of the main plant at Ludwigshafen, Dr. civilian population to make room for the I. G. construction workers. Poles could remain if employable by the I. G. In addition, all available skilled labor in the Auschwitz camp was at the disposal of the new enterprise.[30]

On March 19 and April 24, 1941, the TEA decided upon the details of Auschwitz production. There were to be two plants: a synthetic rubber plant (Buna IV) and an acetic acid plant. The TEA suggestions were accepted by the Vorstand on April 25, 1941.[31] I. G. Auschwitz was on the map (see Table 85).

TABLE 85 / *The I. G. Auschwitz Administration*

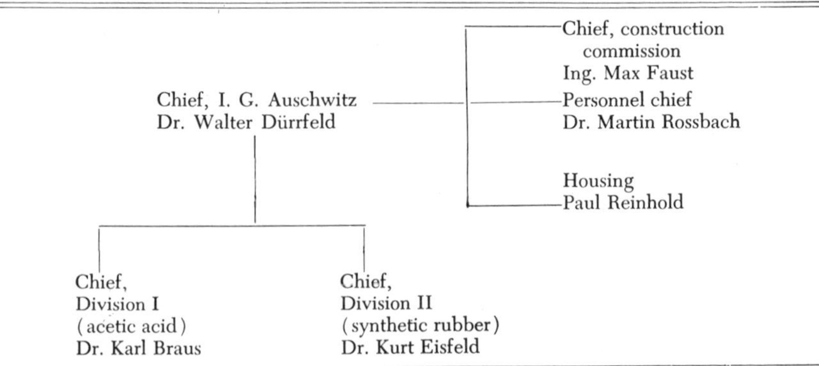

Otto Ambros, candidly talked over the advantages and disadvantages of Auschwitz with Krauch.

Ambros brought out the facts that Auschwitz had good water, coal, and lime supplies. Communications were also adequate. Disadvantages were the lack of skilled labor in the area and the disinclination of German workers to live there.[29] These remaining difficulties were soon removed. Krauch suggested to Göring that Himmler give a helping hand, and on February 26, 1941, Himmler ordered that the town of Auschwitz be cleared entirely of the

The investment in Auschwitz was initially over 500,000,000 reichsmark, ultimately over 700,000,000 reichsmark.[32] The central I. G. construction department at Ludwigshafen (Ing. Camill Santo) established a branch at Auschwitz (under Ing. Max Faust) analogous to the SS setup (Kammler-Bischoff).[33]

29. Memoranda by Ter Meer, summarizing all three conferences, February 10, 1941, NI-11111-3.

30. Göring to Labor Ministry, February 18, 1941, NG-1587. Krauch office (signed Wirth) to I. G. Farben, March 4, 1941, enclosing Himmler order of February 26, 1941, NI-11086.

31. Summary of 25th Vorstand meeting, April 25, 1941, NI-8078.

32. Interrogation of Struss, April 16, 1947, NI-11109.

33. Affidavit by Santo, November 21, 1947, Dürrfeld-882. Affidavit by Gustav Murr (Deputy of Faust), November 3, 1947, Dürr-

About 170 contractors were put to work.[34] The plant was put up; roads were built; barracks were constructed for the inmates; barbed wire was strung for "factory pacification" (*Fabrikeinfriedung*);[35] and after the town of Auschwitz was flooded with I. G. personnel, two company villages were built.[36] To make sure that I. G. Auschwitz would have all the necessary building materials, Krauch patronizingly ordered that Buna enjoy first priority (*Dringlichkeitsstufe I*) until completion.[37] Spreading out, I. G. Auschwitz acquired its coal base, the *Fürstengrube* and *Janinagrube*. Both mines were filled with Jewish inmates.[38]

From the start there was complete co-operation between the I. G. and the SS. The two organizations complemented each other in Auschwitz. While the I. G. built the barracks, the SS supplied the "furnishings" (bunks).[39] The SS provided the guards, and the I. G. added its *Werkschutz* ("factory police").[40] The I. G. requested punishments for inmates who violated its rules, and the SS administered the punishments.[41] The SS fed the inmates with a standard Auchwitz diet, and the I. G. added some "Buna soup" to insure work output.[42] Social relations were also friendly. Thus we find that every once in a while Höss would invite Dr. and Mrs. Dürrfeld or Dr. and Mrs. Eisfeld to his home near the camp.[43] But the I. G. involvement went even further than administrative co-operation and friendly social relations; the I. G. adopted in its factory the methods and the mentality of the SS.

Far from enjoying any protection because of their employment in Buna, the inmates were worked to death. Even during the construction stage the I. G. foremen adopted the SS "work tempo" – for instance, the unloading of cement at a trot.[44] One day in 1944 a large group of arriving inmates were greeted with a speech in which they were told that they were now in the concentration camp of the I. G. Farbenindustrie. They had come not in order to live there but to "perish in concrete." This welcoming speech referred, according to a survivor, to an I. G. Farben practice of throwing the corpses of inmates into ditches which had been dug for cables. Like the ancient children of Israel, these corpses were then covered as concrete was poured over them.[45]

---

feld-853. In 1942 the Speer ministry formed an *Amt für Rüstungsausbau* ("Office for Expansion of War Plants") which henceforth supervised a good part of the construction work. Affidavit by Murr, November 3, 1947, Dürrfeld-853.

34. Affidavit by Murr, November 3, 1947 Dürrfeld-853. Affidavit by Faust, December 11, 1947, Dürrfeld-961.

35. I. G. Auschwitz to Technical Commission (TEKO) requesting credits, November 28, 1942, and November 13, 1944, NI-9110.

36. On housing shortage, see report by Faust for August 17–23, 1941, NI-15254. The two company villages were at Dwory. Affidavit by Murr, November 3, 1947, Dürrfeld-853.

37. Körner and Steffler to Speer and Milch, June 27, 1943, NOKW-307.

38. Affidavit by Günther Falkenhahn (*Fürstengrube*), September 30, 1947, NI-12010. Memorandum by Braus, February 2, 1942, NI-12014. Report by I. G. Frankfurt/Bookkeeping, September 28, 1944, NI-12015. I. G. Auschwitz to Falkenhahn, Dürrfeld, Sobel (*Fürstengrube*), and Kröger (*Janinagrube*), July 28, 1943, NI-12019.

39. I. G. Auschwitz/*Hauptgruppe* 2 to Technical Commission (TEKO) requesting credits for barracks expansion, November 28, 1942, NI-9110. Affidavit by Rudolf Dämming (I. G. architect), June 17, 1948, Dürrfeld-102.

40. Interrogation of Dürrfeld, February 24, 1947, NI-11046, pp. 30–33.

41. For typical punishment reports, see NI-11000 to NI-11038, NI-11040 to NI-11045.

42. Affidavit by Faust, January 16, 1948, Dürrfeld-478.

43. Affidavit by Höss, May 17, 1946, NI-34.

44. Affidavit by Ervin Schulhof (ex-inmate), June 21, 1947, NI-7967.

How completely the SS mentality had taken hold even of I. G. Farben directors is illustrated by the following story. One day two Buna inmates, Dr. Raymond van den Straaten and Dr. Fritz Löhner-Beda, were going about their work when a party of visiting I. G. Farben dignitaries passed by. One of the directors pointed to Dr. Löhner-Beda and said to his SS companion, "This Jewish swine could work a little faster [*Diese Judensau könnte auch rascher arbeiten*]." Another director then chanced the remark, "If they can't work, let them perish in the gas chamber [*Wenn die nicht mehr arbeiten können, sollen sie in der Gaskammer verrecken*]." After the inspection was over, Dr. Löhner-Beda was pulled out of the work party and was beaten and kicked until, a dying man, he was left in the arms of his inmate friend, to end his life in I. G. Auschwitz.[46]

About 35,000 inmates passed through Buna. At least 25,000 died.[47] The life expectancy of a Jewish inmate at I. G. Auschwitz was three or four months;[48] in the outlying coal mines, it was about one month.[49] The I. G., like the SS, had forgotten how to keep its inmates alive.

The SS was in turn peculiarly influenced by its first customer. In the WVHA, imaginations were aroused, ambitions were fired, plans were made. Specifically, the WVHA had two things in mind: first the I. G. Farben camp (Auschwitz III) was to be expanded to accommodate more industry; next the SS began to think in terms of taking over whole sections of German industry and turning these plants into a giant network of concentration camps. On September 15, 1942, a major move was made toward the realization of these plans. Reichsminister Speer and three of his top men – Staatsrat Dr. Schieber (honorary *SS-Brigadeführer*), Dipl. Ing. Saur, Ministerialrat Steffen, and Ministerialrat Dr. Briese – met in conference with Pohl and Kammler. Two items were on the agenda: enlargement of the Auschwitz camp in consequence of the "eastern migration," and "taking over complete armament tasks of major proportions by the concentration camps."

There was no difficulty on the first point. Speer approved the acquisition of building materials (in the amount of 13,700,000 reichsmark) to construct 300 barracks with room for 132,000 inmates at Auschwitz. With regard to the second item, Pohl announced that henceforth the SS would not be concerned with "small stuff" (*Kleckerkram*) anymore. They were going to take over a plant only if they could fill it with 5000 or 10,000 or even 15,000 inmates. They agreed with

45. Affidavit by Dr. Nikolae Nyiszli, October 8, 1947, NI-11710. Affiant, a physician, was a survivor of Auschwitz III.

46. Affidavit by van den Straaten, July 18, 1947, NI-9109. Affiant does not identify the I. G. Farben officials who made the remarks but mentions that he saw five visitors: Dürrfeld, Ambros, Bütefisch, Krauch, and Ter Meer.

47. The 35,000 figure is given in an affidavit by Schulhof, June 21, 1947, NI-7967. The average number of inmates utilized by the I. G. was about 10,000, according to Höss. See his affidavit of May 17, 1946, NI-34. Ten thousand is the maximum figure according to Schulhof. In January, 1944, the number of inmates working in I. G. Auschwitz was 5300. Pohl to Kranefuss (deputy of Krauch), January 15, 1944, NO-1905. The records of the "hospital" in Auschwitz III show 15,684 entries between June 7, 1943, and June 19, 1944 (not counting 23 illegible entries). The entries cover 8244 persons, some having been delivered to the hut more than once. Eighty-three per cent of the sick inmates (about 6800) were Jews; 632 Jews died in the hospital hut; 1336 were sent to Birkenau (Auschwitz II) to be gassed. Affidavit by Karl Haeseler (analyst for the defense), April 7, 1948, Dürrfeld-1441.

48. Affidavit by Prof. Berthold Epstein, March 3, 1947, NI-5847. Affiant was a hospital orderly at Buna.

49. Affidavit by Dr. Erich Orlik, June 18, 1947, NI-7966. Affiant was an inmate doctor in the Janina mine.

Speer that such a plant could not be built *in* a concentration camp; as Speer had correctly pointed out, the plant had to lie on the "green grass." The SS men would therefore propose that certain establishments not working at full capacity because of the labor shortage be emptied out; the labor force in these plants would fill out other plants. The empty factories, however, would be surrounded with electric wire and filled with inmates, to be run as SS-armament plants (*SS-Rüstungsbetriebe*).

Of course, the WVHA did not have so many inmates at its disposal; the RSHA would therefore lend a helping hand by taking Jews out of the free economy and sending them into concentration camps. Speer agreed that one could use 50,000 Jews in short order. Saur could name the plants. Pohl did not trust Saur very much, and to make sure that the program would really get under way, he ordered his manpower expert, Obersturmbannführer Maurer (WVHA D-II), to move into the office of Speer's manpower expert, Staatsrat Schieber. That, thought Pohl, would do the trick.[50]

As a matter of fact, it did not quite do the trick. No plants were handed over. In December, 1942, Himmler wrote to Müller that only Auschwitz needed labor, and Müller was therefore instructed to send 15,000 Jews to Auschwitz during the next month.[51] In April of the following year came a blow from which the SS never recovered. It meant that Himmler could never establish the industrial empire which he had hoped to achieve with the use of doomed Jewry.

Speer had made an inspection trip to Mauthausen and had come to the conclusion that the SS was undertaking constructions which were "extravagant" (*grosszügig*). In a sharply written letter to Himmler – of the kind which the *Reichsführer* very seldom got – he pointed out that he needed tanks, mineral oil, and submarines very quickly. "Dear Comrade Himmler, as I see this development, you will not be able to get done with your plans this year, simply because you will never get the necessary building materials." Therefore, advised Speer, it would be necessary to proceed along totally different lines. From now on one would have to apply the principle of *Primitivbauweise* ("primitive construction"); that is, the inmates working with practically no tools and no expensive materials would have to accomplish the greatest possible results by labor alone. All allocations of materials for construction would have to be reviewed.[52]

This letter of course meant that Speer was backing out of point one of the agreement, with all that that implied for point two. Pohl was incensed. Writing to Himmler's personal *Referent,* Oberstrumbannführer Brandt, he voiced the opinion that Speer's letter was "actually a pretty strong piece" (*eigentlich ein recht starkes Stück*); but since he had forgotten the art of being astonished, he merely wished to point out that Speer had already given preliminary approval for the construction in the camps and certainly could have consulted Schieber about labor utilization. Finally Pohl came to the most vexing point. He had been accused by implication of treating inmates too mildly, of not driving out of them their last ounce of strength. Did Speer realize, he asked, how many deaths there were in the concentration camps? Did he realize the tremendous rise in mortality that "primitive methods" would occasion?[53] While Pohl

50. Report on conference by Pohl to Himmler, September 16, 1942, NI-15392.

51. Himmler to Müller, December 17, 1942, Himmler Files, Folder No. 67.

52. Speer to Himmler, April 5, 1943, Himmler Files, Folder No. 67.

53. Pohl to Brandt, April 19, 1943, Himmler Files, Folder No. 67.

was deeply mortified, Himmler was on the defensive too. Painstakingly he counted up the 2200 tons of steel which had been made available for Auschwitz, broke down the inmate labor supply in percentages to show that 67 per cent were working in armaments, and pointed out that the type of construction work going on now fully satisfied the label *Primitivbauweise*.[54]

Appeased, Speer replied in a more friendly letter that his ideas about primitive construction had already been recognized (*Verständnis entgegengebracht*) but in the next sentence confounded Himmler by pointing out a remaining difficulty: the inmates were dropping dead too fast, particularly in Auschwitz. Something would have to be done to remove at least the worst conditions.[55]

The SS was now pretty much restricted to Auschwitz. In this killing center, however, several big firms joined I. G. Farben. On March 5, 1943, the Krupp fuse plant in Essen was bombed out,[56] and by March 17, 1943, plans were laid to move the remaining machinery to Auschwitz. At the same time an enterprising Krupp official, Hölkeskamp, grabbed 500 Jewish workers from two Berlin firms, Krone-Presswerk and Graetz, who were promptly deported to Auschwitz and made available to Krupp through the courtesy of Obersturmbannführer Sommer of WVHA D-II.[57] By the time fuse production was to get under way[58] another firm, the "Union" Metallindustrie, which had had to retreat from the Ukraine, took over the plant.[59] Besides Krupp, the ubiquitous Hermann Göring Works (coal mines), Siemens-Schuckert, and a number of other firms drew upon the inmate resources of Auschwitz III, setting up satellite camps for miles around.[60] The average number of inmates used by these firms was about 40,000.[61]

With so many new patrons competing for Auschwitz labor, the SS did not forget its original customer. In 1943 Pohl, Glücks, Frank, and Maurer came to visit the Buna works and promised the I. G. Farben representatives that I. G. Auschwitz would enjoy priority over other firms in the allocation of inmates,[62] but early in 1944 the situation became tight. Pohl wrote to Krauch's deputy Kranefuss that he could not furnish any more inmates. After all, the chemical industry had already gotten more than its fair share.[63] Though the price of a skilled inmate had risen from about 1.5 reichsmark in 1941 to 5 reichsmark in 1944,[64] labor had become so scarce that a strict and complicated system of allocation had to be worked out. Each firm had to make its request in triplicate forms to the Speer ministry (Major von den Osten). The forms were checked with labor offices to prevent double requests for inmates and free labor, and, if everything was found to be in order, Sauckel would be consulted to determine whether the allocation was justi-

54. Himmler to Speer, June, 1943, Himmler Files, Folder No. 67.

55. Speer to Himmler, June 10, 1943, Himmler Files, Folder No. 67.

56. Affidavit by Erich Luthal (Krupp employee), September 24, 1947, NI-11674.

57. Memorandum by Hölkeskamp, March 17, 1943, NI-2911.

58. For specifications, see OKH/Chief of the Replacement Army/Wa Chef Ing Stab IVa to Friedrich Krupp A. G./Auschwitz Works, attention Dr. Jannsen, September 22, 1943, NI-10650.

59. Krupp memorandum (signed Müller), September 20, 1943, NI-12329. Armament Inspectorate VIIIb Katowice (signed Oberst Hüter), report for July–September, 1943, Wi/ID 1.224.

60. Affidavit by Höss, May 17, 1943, NI-34.

61. *Ibid.* The figure includes many non-Jews.

62. *Ibid.*

63. Pohl to Kranefuss, January 15, 1944, NO-1905.

64. Affidavit by Höss, March 12, 1947, NI-4434.

fied. Only after this test had been passed could the requests be sent on to Maurer.[65]

In the summer of 1944, when about 425,000 Jews arrived in Auschwitz from Hungary, the SS once again had hopes for big business. On March 1, Speer and Milch had formed the *Jägerstab* ("Pursuit Planes Staff"), a co-ordinating committee which had the job of building aircraft factories in huge bunkers. The following were some of the chief personalities:[66]

Speer, chairman
Milch, co-chairman
Saur, Speer's deputy
Dorsch (OT), in charge of construction
Schlemp, deputy of Dorsch
Kammler, special construction
Schmelter
(*Ministerialdirigent*, Central Division Labor Allocation, Speer ministry), labor procurement

For its building projects the *Jägerstab* needed about a quarter of a million construction workers.[67] The experts took one look at the labor supply and decided that Jews would have to be employed. On April 6 and 7, 1944, Saur talked about the problem to Hitler personally, with the result that Hitler consented as a last resort to the utilization of 100,000 Hungarian Jews who were shortly expected in Auschwitz.[68]

Before long, however, an old and familiar obstacle emerged: the Hungarian transports had relatively few young men, for the Hungarian Army had been drafting Jews into labor battalions that were being retained in Hungary. On May 24, 1944, Pohl wrote to Himmler that the first transports seemed to indicate that about half the physically capable arrivals were women. Could these women, asked Pohl, be employed in the construction program of the *Organisation Todt*?[69] The reply came quickly: "My dear Pohl! Of course, the Jewish women are to be employed. One will have to worry only about good nourishment. Here the important thing is a supply of raw vegetables. So don't forget to import plenty of garlic from Hungary."[70]

Speer's labor expert, Schmelter, did not find the situation so funny. "Until now," he said in the *Jägerstab* meeting of May 26, "two transports have arrived in the SS camp Auschwitz. What was offered for the pursuit plane constructions were children, women, and old men with whom very little can be done. If the next transports do not contain some men in the proper age group," he warned, "the whole *Aktion* will fall through."[71]

On June 9 Schmelter announced that he could get 10,000 to 20,000 "Hungarian Jewesses." Were there any takers? "Excellent!" he exclaimed, "what I experienced at Siemens once with the Jewesses doing electromechanical installations was unique."[72] There were,

65. Ministry for Armaments and War Production (Speer) to chairmen of armament commissions, directors of main committees, industrial rings and production committees, *Reichsvereinigung Eisen*, Sauckel, and WVHA, October 9, 1944, NI-638.

66. Affidavit by Fritz Schmelter, December 9, 1946, NOKW-372. Interrogation of Schmelter, November 15, 1946, NOKW-319. Affidavit by Xaver Dorsch, December 28, 1946, NOKW-447. Interrogation of Milch, October 14, 1946, NOKW-420. Interrogation of Milch, November 8, 1946, NOKW-421. Summary of Air Ministry conference, March 31, 1944, NOKW-417. Summary of *Jägerstab* meeting, March 24, 1944, NOKW-162.

67. Minutes of *Jägerstab* meeting, May 25, 1944, NOKW-349.

68. Summary by Saur of discussions with Hitler, April 9, 1944, R-124. Speer Ministry to *Jägerstab*, April 17, 1944, PS-1584-III. Interrogation of Albert Speer, October 18, 1945, PS-3720.

69. Pohl to Himmler, May 24, 1944, NO-30.

70. Himmler to Pohl, May 27, 1944, NO-30.

71. Minutes of *Jägerstab* meeting, May 26, 1944, NOKW-336.

72. Minutes of *Jägerstab* meeting, June 9, 1944, NG-1593.

however, very few takers, even for the reduced figure of 20,000, since the problems of guarding and quartering were almost insurmountable. The I. G., Himmler's most loyal customer, now turned him down.[73] Krupp picked out 520 Jewish women to perform heavy labor in its Essen plant, although a personnel expert had voiced the opinion that the victims were "fine soft-boned creatures" who were not suitable for the work.[74]

The meager result of the labor allocation program (only a few thousand Hungarian Jews were recruited from *Amtsgruppe D*) is explained also by another factor which had nothing to do with administrative efficiency: the problem was not only to get workers while the war was on but also to get rid of them in case the war was lost. In the summer of 1944, representatives of the Württemberger Metallwaren Fabrik asked Obergruppenführer Hofmann, Higher SS and Police Leader in Army District V, to intercede with Pohl for an allocation of Jewish labor. Seven hundred Jewish women from Hungary were thereupon sent to the plant. In March, 1945, the director of the Metallwaren Fabrik phoned Hofmann with an urgent plea to take the 700 women off his hands because American troops were closing in. Hofmann replied that it was none of his business and that he could do nothing.[75] The utilization of Jewish labor was expensive in more ways than one, and that is one of the reasons why the great bulk of the 1944 deportees were gassed in the Auschwitz killing center upon arrival.

4 / Medical Experiments

There was another and more sinister utilization of doomed Jews – the medical experiments. Numerically, the use of inmates for experiments did not approach the dimensions of industrial exploitation, but psychologically, the experiments pose a much more significant problem.

We must establish two broad categories of experiments: the first comprised medical research which is usual and normal except for the wilful utilization of unwilling subjects – *Versuchspersonen,* as they were called; the second was more complex and far-reaching because it was research conducted neither with ordinary methods nor with ordinary aims. Both classes of experiments were the product of a single administrative machine, the structure of which is shown in abbreviated form in Table 86.

An experiment was initiated when someone conceived of the possibility of using inmates to try out a serum, to test a hypothesis, or to solve some other problem. For instance, the chief of the Air Force Medical Service was interested in altitude experiments and the revival of half-frozen pilots shot down over the Atlantic.[1] Stabsarzt Dr. Dohmen of the Army Medical Service wanted to do research on jaundice; so far, he had injected healthy animals

73. Warnecke (I. G. Farben/Leverkusen) to Guenter (Reich office for economic construction), June 2, 1944, NI-8969. Summary of I. G. Leverkusen technical conference (Haberland presiding), July 10, 1944, NI-5765.

74. On Krupp employment, see: Affidavit by Adolf Trockel, September 24, 1947, NI-11676. Affidavit by Johannes Maria Dolhaine, September 18, 1947, NI-11675. Affidavit by Walter Hölkeskamp, September 15, 1947, NI-11679. Affidavit by Günther Hoppe, October 8, 1945, NI-5787. Affidavit by Hans Kupke, September 19, 1945, NI-6811. Interrogation of Dr. Wilhem Jäger, June 6, 1946, NI-5823. Memorandum by Wilshaus (Krupp Essen Werkschutz), August 28, 1944, NI-15364. Air raid report by Hoppe (camp commander, Jewish women's compound), December 12, 1944, NI-5785. Affidavit by Anneliese Trockel, May 28, 1947, NI-8947.

75. Affidavit by Otto Hofmann, November 30, 1945, NO-2412.

1. Hippke to Wolff, March 6, 1943, NO-262.

TABLE 86 / *The Medical Machine of Destruction**

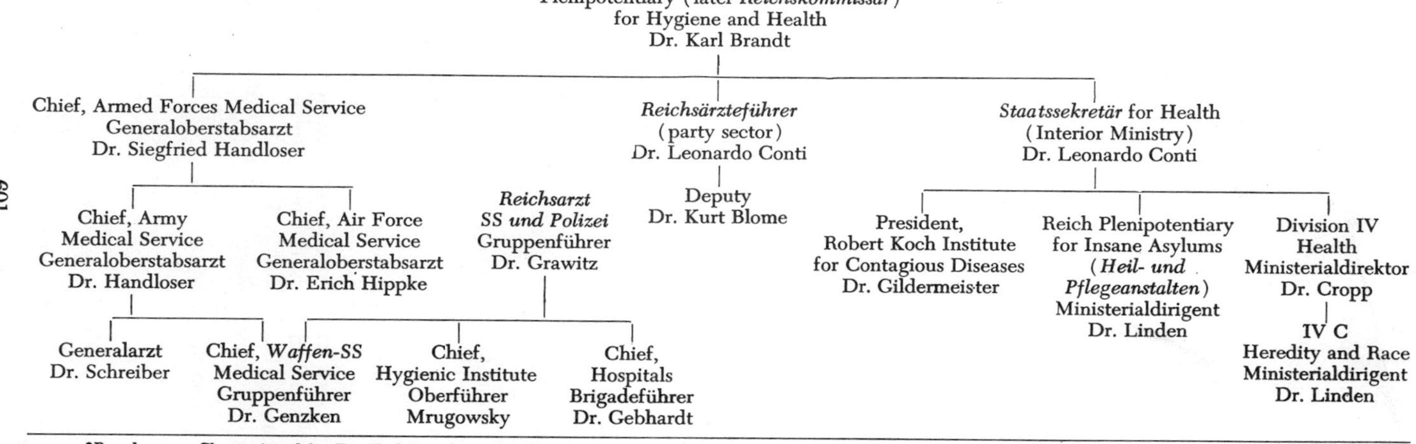

*Based upon: Chart, signed by Dr. Karl Brandt, undated, NO-645, and *Taschenbuch für Verwaltungsbeamte*, 1943, PS-3475.

with virus from jaundiced humans, but now he wanted to reverse the process and inject humans with virus from diseased animals.[2] The "Bayer" research laboratories of I. G. Farben wanted to test a preparation against typhus. The product existed in two forms, tablet and granulated, and it seemed that some patients were throwing up the tablets. The I. G. researchers approached a "friendly insane asylum" to make experiments, then found themselves in an embarrassing position because the insane inmates were unable to tell whether the preparation was less obnoxious in granulated than in tablet form. The I. G. thereupon remembered that one of its researchers was now an *Obersturmführer* in Auschwitz and asked him to help out.[3] However, most interested parties did not adopt the informal route which I. G. Farben had chosen in this case; they submitted their requests to Reichsarzt SS and Polizei Grawitz or to Himmler directly.

From the beginning Himmler personally took a great interest in these matters. Experiments fascinated him, and if he became convinced that the research was of "tremendous importance," he would go out of his way to facilitate the administrative arrangements. This patronizing interest prompted Himmler to order, in 1943, that no experiments were to be started without his express approval.[4] In 1944 the procedure became a bit more elaborate; henceforth, proposals were to be submitted to Grawitz, who was to transmit them to Himmler with attached advisory opinions by Gebhardt, Glücks, and Nebe.[5] Gebhardt's opinion was medical, while Glücks and Nebe advised on the important question of choosing the victims.

As a rule, doctors asked for permission to use "habitual criminals"[6] or inmates who had been "condemned to death."[7] This formulation was the result of the doctor's attempt to make a compromise with his conscience. A criminal, a man condemned to death – it was reasoned – was certainly not entitled to more favorable treatment than German soldiers risking their lives and dying of wounds, etc. However, in the consideration of the request the SS often added its own notion of criminality, with the consequence that the final choice fell upon "race-defiling Jewish habitual criminals" (*rassenschänderische Berufsverbrecher-Juden*) or perhaps "Jewish criminals of the Polish resistance movement who have been condemned to death."[8]

On one occasion the selection of victims became a subject of discussion from a "racial viewpoint." The experiment under consideration was the conversion of sea water to make it potable. Glücks proposed the utilization of Jews, Nebe countered with "asocial Gypsy *Mischlinge*" (Gypsy affairs were under Nebe's jurisdiction), while Grawitz for racial reasons suggested that Gypsies were not suitable for sea water experiments.[9]

Himmler was interested not only in the initiation of the experiments. He followed their progress, studied the findings, and occasionally suggested some improvements. Above all, he was

2. Grawitz to Himmler, June 1, 1943, NO-10.

3. "Bayer" Research Division II (signed König) to Dr. Mertens in the division, January 19, 1943, NI-12242. Dr. Weber and Dr. König to OStuf. Dr. Vetter in Auschwitz, January 27, 1943, NI-11417.

4. Pohl to OStubaf. Brandt, August 16, 1943, NO-1610.

5. Order by Himmler, May 15, 1944, NO-919.

6. Rascher to Himmler, May 15, 1941, PS-1602.

7. For instance, Dohmen. See Grawitz to Himmler, June 1, 1943, NO-10.

8. Himmler's authorization for the Dohmen experiments in his letter to Grawitz, with copy to Pohl, June 16, 1943, NO-11.

9. Grawitz to Himmler, June 28, 1944, NO-179.

the guardian angel of the doctors; he stood ready to assume "full responsibility" for their doings and to deal severely with their critics.

The SS and the participating doctors were ever watchful for undercurrents of disapproval in the medical profession. In May, 1943, Professor Handloser, chief medical officer of the Wehrmacht, called the fourth conference of consulting physicians to the armed forces. During the conference Gebhardt rose to introduce the featured speaker. The lecture was to deal with the transplantation of human bones, and the findings were based on actual experimentation (removal of bones from Polish women in Ravensbrück). "I carry," said Gebhardt, "the full human, surgical, and political responsibility for these experiments." The introduction finished, Dr. Fritz Ernst Fischer mounted the rostrum and with the help of charts explained the operations he had performed. His lecture was followed by a discussion. No criticism was raised.[10]

Once, during the Rascher experiments for the air force, an eruption did take place. Rascher, an air force *Stabsarzt* (captain), was a man who enjoyed Himmler's friendship and patronage. (Thus, on being informed that Rascher's mistress was pregnant for the second time, Himmler sent her fresh fruit to make sure that mother and child would be well.) Rascher's involvement began one day when he was attending an air force course which dealt with altitude problems and pilots' stamina. Upon the instructor's chance remark that no experiments had ever been carried out with human beings, Rascher conceived of the idea of using some "habitual criminals" for this purpose. He communicated his proposal to Himmler[11] and received the permission of Generaloberstabsarzt Hippke to perform the experiments.

After a while insinuations and criticisms by other air force doctors began to make the rounds. One man, Professor Holzlöhner, even made remarks about Himmler's person while visiting the experimental site at Dachau. Rascher made a strong complaint to Himmler, and the *Reichsführer-SS* replied that he, too, would classify people who rejected the use of human beings for experiments at a time when German soldiers were dying as traitors of the second and first degree (*Hoch- und Landesverräter*).[12] To Generalfeldmarschall Milch, Himmler wrote in the same vein, omitting references to treason but emphasizing that he would *not* be deterred by these "Christian" circles. Rascher, said Himmler, could be transferred to the SS, and the conscience problem would be solved. The air force would still have the benefit of all findings by Dr. Rascher.[13]

A few months later, Hippke wrote a letter to Wolff accepting the arrangement but taking the opportunity of correcting a few false impressions. First of all, nobody had objected to these experiments. Hippke had "immediately agreed" to them. The difficulty lay in another sphere: it was all a question of vanity. Everyone wanted to be the one to come out with new research discoveries. But if Rascher wished to create his own research institute in the *Waffen-SS*, Hippke would have no objection and would bid him good riddance.[14]

These were all doctors who made use of human guinea pigs. But some went

10. Affidavit by Fischer, November 21, 1945, *Conspiracy and Aggression*, VIII, 635–42.

11. Rascher to Himmler, May 15, 1941, PS-1602. In this letter Rascher thanked Himmler for the fruit.

12. Himmler to Rascher, October 24, 1942, PS-1609.

13. Himmler to Milch, November 13, 1942, PS-1617.

14. Hippke to Wolff, March 6, 1943, NO-262.

one step further, carrying out experiments which were no longer characterized by any desire to help patients. These experiments had an altogether different direction — they were identified with Nazi aims. In these activities, one may glimpse an attempt to widen the destruction process. The medical technicians who became involved in this research were not merely engaged in tinkering with inmates; they were trying to discover a means by which Germany could rule Europe forever.

One day in October, 1941, a retired Army doctor, Adolf Pokorny, sat down to write a letter to Himmler. To avoid the possibility that a subordinate might open the letter and read its contents, it was sent to Himmler by a messenger, Professor Höhn. In his letter Pokorny pointed out that he had read an article in a medical journal by a certain Dr. Madaus of the biological institute at Radebeul-Dresden. The article dealt with the effect of injecting the extract of a South American plant — *Caladium seguinum* — into mice and rats: the animals were sterilized. While reading this article, Pokorny had thought of the "tremendous importance" of this drug "in the present struggle of our people." It should be possible, continued Pokorny, to produce in short order a preparation which would lead to the sterilization of people without their knowledge. In this connection he dropped a hint that Germany had three million Soviet prisoners of war, and in conclusion he made a few urgent suggestions: Madaus to publish no more articles, the plant to be produced in hothouses, chemical analysis to determine whether an extract could be synthesized, and "immediate experiments on human beings."[15]

A few months later Himmler ordered Pohl to offer Dr. Madaus possibilities of doing research.[16] Himmler was actually quite impatient, and in September, 1942, Pohl, Lolling (medical chief, WVHA D-III), and Madaus agreed to transfer the work to the concentration camps.[17]

While these preparations were being made, someone else took note of the Madaus article: On August 24, 1942, the deputy *Gauleiter* of Lower Austria, SS-Oberführer Gerland, also addressed a letter to Himmler. Impressing upon Himmler the "tremendous importance" of the Madaus discovery, he requested that the *Gau* expert on racial questions, Dr. Fehringer, be permitted to conduct experiments — in collaboration with the Pharmacological Institute of the Medical Faculty of Vienna University — in a Gypsy camp at Lackenbach.[18] Himmler's reply (through Obersturmbannführer Brandt) was friendly. The matter was already under investigation, but there were difficulties because the plant was not available in sufficient quantity; if Dr. Fehringer had a supply at hand, the *Reichsführer-SS* would be very glad to hear about it.[19]

The obstacles proved insurmountable, and scientific reinforcements were called up. In November, 1942, Dr. Müller-Cunradi, director of the I. G. Farben laboratory at Ludwigshafen, sent one of his biochemists, Dr. Tauboeck, to the Madaus Institute. Tauboeck and Madaus had a discussion about the matter. The whole investigation had started when Madaus had read in the literature that a Brazilian tribe was using *Caladium seguinum* to sterilize its enemies. The natives accom-

15. Pokorny to Himmler, October, 1941, NO-35.

16. Himmler to Pohl, March 10, 1942, NO-36. Adjutant of Himmler (signed OStuf. Fischer) to RSHA IV-B-4, attention Stubaf. Günther, July 4, 1942, NO-50.

17. Pohl to Rudi Brandt, September 7, 1942, NO-41. Affidavit by Rudolf Brandt, October 19, 1946, NO-440.

18. Gerland to Himmler, August 24, 1942, NO-39.

19. Brandt to Gerland, August 29, 1942, NO-40.

plished the sterilization by shooting arrows at the enemy (that is, by intramuscular injection), and the victim was usually unaware of his fate. But Germany did not have the climate for growing this plant, and the feat could not be repeated.[20]

The Madaus method was not the only attempt to reconcile the short-range needs of the war with the long-range policy of destruction. The idea that after intensive labor utilization during the emergency subject peoples would be allowed to die a natural death, without a chance to replenish themselves, was a recurring thought in Nazi medical circles. Thus in May, 1941, Himmler became interested in "nonsurgical sterilization of inferior women." The author of this idea was Professor Carl Clauberg, chief physician of the women's clinic in Knappschaft Hospital and St. Hedwig Hospital at Königshütte, Upper Silesia. Clauberg proposed that an irritant be introduced into the uterus by means of a syringe. This procedure became known as the "Clauberg method."

Three doctors were lined up to assist Clauberg in making experiments (Standartenführer Prof. von Wolff, Berlin; Sturmbannführer Prof. Erhardt, Graz, University Women's Clinic; and Hauptsturmführer Dr. Günther F. K. Schultze, Greifswald, University Women's Clinic).[21] But there was one administrative obstacle. Himmler wanted Clauberg to work in the large women's concentration camp at Ravensbrück; Clauberg did not wish to move there with his cumbersome apparatus. And in spite of Grawitz' urgings that because of the "tremendous significance" of these experiments inmates should be made available at Königshütte,[22] all plans collapsed at this point.

One year later Clauberg had a "scientific discussion" with a Himmler man, Obersturmbannführer Arlt. In the course of the conversation Clauberg brought up his now vastly expanded plans for experiments. Arlt pointed out that in such matters Himmler was the right man. Clauberg thereupon wrote to Himmler requesting permission to set up his apparatus in Auschwitz and to perform experiments there with a view to perfecting mass sterilization methods for "unworthy women" (*fortpflanzungsunwürdige Frauen*) as well as producing fertility in "worthy women."[23] His letter produced results.

On July 7, 1942, Himmler, Gebhardt, Glücks, and Clauberg met in conference and decided to start experiments in Auschwitz. The aim of the experiments was, first of all, the discovery of means by which a victim could be sterilized without becoming aware of what was being done to her. The experiments were to be performed in "major dimensions" upon Jewish women in the camp. Secondly, it was agreed to call upon a foremost X-ray specialist, Professor Hohlfelder, to find out whether X-ray castration of men was feasible. In conclusion, Himmler warned all those present that these were most secret matters and that anyone drawn into the work had to be pledged to secrecy.[24]

Three days later Himmler's Secretary Brandt sent a letter to Clauberg

20. Affidavit by Dr. Karl Tauboeck, June 18, 1947, NO-3963. Apart from this difficulty, there were others. The effect of *Caladium seguinum* upon reproduction is the same as overdoses of nicotine, morphine, or just plain hunger. Apparently no one had informed Himmler that many of Madaus' rats had died from poisoning. Affidavit by Dr. Friedrich Jung, undated, Pokorny-30.

21. Grawitz to Himmler, May 30, 1941, NO-214.

22. Grawitz to Himmler, May 29, 1941, NO-1639.

23. Clauberg to Himmler, May 30, 1942, NO-211.

24. Memorandum by Brandt, July, 1942, NO-216. See also his memorandum dated July 11, 1942, NO-215.

with a few additional requirements and suggestions. Himmler wanted to know how fast 1000 Jewish women could be sterilized. "The Jewesses themselves should know nothing." The results of the experiments were to be checked by taking X-ray pictures and studying them for any changes. In one or the other case, Clauberg could also make a "practical test" such as locking a "Jewess and a Jew" into a room for a certain period of time and waiting for the effects.[25]

One more year passed while Clauberg worked busily in Block 10 of Auschwitz I, the experimental block. To "fool" the victims, he told the women before injecting the irritant fluid that they were undergoing artifical insemination.[26] Clauberg liked his work and wanted to show off. When Pohl visited Auschwitz one day, Clauberg approached the *Obergruppenführer* at dinner and invited him to witness a few experiments. Pohl declined.[27]

In June, 1943, Clauberg sent his first report to Himmler. The method was "almost perfected" (*so gut wie fertig ausgearbeitet*), although he still had to devise a few "improvements" (*Verfeinerungen*). At the moment it was effective in "usual" cases; furthermore, he could assure the *Reichsführer-SS* that the sterilization could be performed imperceptibly in the course of a normal gynecological examination. With ten assistants a doctor could sterilize 1000 women in one day.[28] (Clauberg did not specify how secrecy could be maintained in the mass sterilization procedure.)

While Clauberg went on to "perfect" his method, there was still a third attempt to work out a mass sterilization program: the X-ray experiments. As early as March, 1941, Himmler and the Führer Chancellery (Bouhler and Brack) had discussed sterilization problems, and in the course of these discussions Brack wrote a letter to Himmler in which he gave his expert opinion on the subject. This letter was quite amazing. It started as a sober account of the possibilities of X-rays in the field of sterilization and castration. Preliminary investigations by medical experts of the chancellery, wrote Brack, had indicated that small doses of X-rays achieved only temporary sterilization; large doses caused burns. Having come to this conclusion, Brack ignored it completely and continued with the following fantastic scheme: The persons to be "processed" (*die abzufertigen Personen*) would step up to a counter to be asked some questions or to fill out forms. Thus occupied, the unsuspecting candidate for sterilization would face the window for two or three minutes while the official sitting behind the counter would throw a switch which would release X-rays through two tubes pointing at the victim. With twenty such counters (cost: 20,000–30,000 marks apiece) 3000–4000 persons could be sterilized daily.[29]

The proposal was not immediately followed up, but Brack brought it up again, in June, 1942, in connection with the installation of the gassing apparatus in the *Generalgouvernement* camps. It seemed to Brack that among the 10 million Jews who were doomed to die, there were at least 2 or 3 million who

25. Brandt to Clauberg, copies to Pohl, OStubaf. Kögel (Ravensbrück), and Stubaf. Günther (RSHA IV-B-4), July 10, 1942, NO-213. Kögel and Günther received copies because Himmler was still attempting to persuade Clauberg to sterilize the "Jewesses" in Ravensbrück.

26. Affidavit by Jeanne Ingred Salomon, October 9, 1946, NO-810. Affiant, a survivor, was a victim of experimentation.

27. Affidavit by Pohl, July 14, 1946, NO-65.

28. Clauberg to Himmler, June 7, 1943, NO-212.

29. Brack to Himmler, March 28, 1941, NO-203. Brack testified after the war that this letter was *deliberate* nonsense. See his testimony in Case No. 1, tr. pp. 7484–93.

were needed desperately in the war effort. Of course they could be utilized only if they were sterilized. Since the usual surgical sterilization was too slow and expensive, he wished to remind Himmler that already a year before he had pointed out the advantages of X-rays. The fact that the victims would become aware of their sterilization after a few months was a trifling consideration at this stage of the game. In conclusion, Brack stated that his chief, Reichsleiter Bouhler, was ready to furnish all the necessary doctors and other personnel to carry out the program.[30] This time Himmler replied that he should like to have the X-ray method tried out in at least one camp in an experimental series.[31]

The experiments were carried out in Auschwitz by Dr. Horst Schumann, on women and men. As Schumann moved into Auschwitz, competition in the experimental blocks was shifted into high gear.[32] Schumann and Clauberg were joined by the chief camp doctor, Wirtz, who started his own experimental series, performing operations on girls aged seventeen and eighteen and on mothers in their thirities.[33] A Jewish inmate doctor from Germany, Dr. Samuel, was also impressed into the experiments.[34] Another camp doctor, Mengele, confined his studies to twins, for it was his ambition to multiply the German nation.[35] All these experiments, which consumed many hundreds of victims, led to nothing. Not one of the rivals succeeded. One day Brack's deputy, Blankenburg, admitted failure of the experiments conducted on men: the X-rays were less reliable and less speedy than operative castration.[36] In other words, it had taken three years to find out what was known in the beginning.

Although the sterilization experiments were infused with dilettantism and plain deception, they were a significant episode in European history. In the very conception of these explorations, the destruction process threatened to escape from its narrowly defined channel and to engulf everyone within reach who might be branded as "inferior." Already, the fate of *Mischlinge* of the first degree hung in the balance while the Interior Ministry waited for the perfection of mass sterilization techniques. In consequence of the failure of these experiments a development was arrested which had spelled in its dim outlines the doom of large sections of the population of Europe.

This, then, marks the difference between the ordinary experiments and the mass sterilization attempts. If in the course of an ordinary experiment a victim died, the doctor performing the experiment had transformed himself from a healer into a killer. The doctor who tampered with sterilization, however, rendered himself into an architect of mass destruction. And that was not yet the end. The Nazi hierarchy also promoted a few researchers who

30. Brack to Himmler, June 23, 1942, NO-205.

31. Himmler to Brack, copies to Pohl and Grawitz, August 11, 1942, NO-206. Also, acceptance of Himmler's offer by Brack's deputy Blankenburg, August 14, 1942, NO-207.

32. See Clauberg letter to OStubaf. Brandt, August 6, 1943, NO-210, in which Clauberg complained that in his absence one of his X-ray machines had been used by other gentlemen. Though he did not mind this procedure, he did need the second machine to perform his "positive" experiments (increase of fertility), etc.

33. Affidavit by Jeanne Salomon, October 9, 1946, NO-810.

34. Testimony by Adelaide de Jong, *Law Reports of Trials of War Criminals* (London, 1947), VII, 25. Witness, a Jewish survivor, was sterilized by Dr. Samuel.

35. Perl, *I Was a Doctor in Auschwitz*, pp. 125–27.

36. Blankenburg to Himmler, April 29, 1944, NO-208. Schumann actually produced X-ray cancer. Affidavit by Dr. Robert Levy (survivor), November 19, 1946, NO-884.

wanted to fortify the mass destructive aim with an unassailable scientific reason; in their search for such a reason these doctors regressed from medical discovery and, redirecting their steps into a dead end, destroyed their science.

How did this research emerge? We have pointed out from time to time how the extreme Nazis viewed the destruction process as a race struggle. To these Nazis the anti-Jewish measures were a defensive battle of the "Nordic racial substance" against the creeping onslought of an "inferior racial mixture." This rationalization had its difficulties. Many officials failed to see any intrinsic connection between physical characteristics and *Weltanschauung;* ideologists in the party and the SS were therefore hard put to prove their theory. It is not surprising that in their quest for substantiation they resorted to experiments. Let us look at two of them.

In the spring of 1942 an attempt was made to show that Gypsies had different blood than Germans had. Two doctors, Professor Werner Fischer and Stabsarzt (Captain) Dr. Hornbeck – both of whom had acquired experience while working on Negro prisoners of war – received permission to perform experiments on Gypsies in Sachsenhausen. Hornbeck dropped out because he was sent to the eastern front, and Fischer started out on forty Gypsies. At Himmler's request he promised to widen his research by exploring Jewish blood also.[37]

Another approach was tried by "Ahnenerbe," an organization formed by the SS in 1939 to investigate "the sphere, spirit, deed, and heritage of the Nordic Indo-Germanic race."[38] The president of the organization was Himmler; its business manager was Standartenführer Sievers; and one of its researchers was Hauptsturmführer Prof. Hirt, director of anatomy in the Reich University at Strasbourg.

At the beginning of 1942 Hirt lay in the clinic, his lungs bleeding and his blood circulation gravely impaired. From his sickbed he sent the following report to Himmler: All nations and races had been studied by examination of skull collections; only in the case of the Jews were there too few skulls to permit scientific conclusions. The war in the East offered an opportunity to correct this situation. "In the Jewish-Bolshevist commissars, who embody a repulsive but characteristic subhumanity, we have the possibility of obtaining a plastic source for study [*ein greifbar wissenschaftliches Dokument*] if we secure their skulls." The commissars, proposed Hirt, had best be handed over to the Field Police alive. A doctor would then take down vital statistics, kill the Jews, carefully remove the head, etc.[39] Brandt replied that Himmler was very interested in this project but that, first of all, Hirt's health had to be restored. Perhaps a little fresh fruit would help.[40]

After a few months Hirt recovered sufficiently to do his work. In view of the scarcity of "Jewish-Bolshevist commissars," Ahnenerbe declared itself ready to accept 150 Jews from Auschwitz.[41] An Ahnenerbe official, Hauptsturmführer Dr. Bruno Beger, was sent to the camp; 115 persons – including 79 Jewish men, 30 Jewish women, 4 central Asians, and 2 Poles – were quarantined, and arrangements were made with Eichmann to have them transferred to Natzweiler, where they

37. OStubaf. Brandt to Grawitz, June 9, 1942, NO-410. Grawitz to Himmler, July 20, 1942, NO-411.

38. See charter of the institute, signed by Himmler, January 1, 1939, NO-659.

39. Sievers to Stubaf. Dr. Brandt, February 9, 1942, enclosing report by Hirt, NO-85.

40. Brandt to Sievers, February 27, 1942, NO-90.

41. Sievers to Brandt, November 2, 1942, NO-86.

were gassed.[42] The bodies were brought to Strasbourg and preserved for race studies.[43] There, in the anatomical laboratory of the university, the utmost that German doctors were capable of ran its course.

Administratively, then, the medical experiments were only peripheral to the destruction process. Taking advantage of a huge supply of doomed human beings, the doctors appropriated a few thousand victims. Psychologically, the experiments pose a wider problem, bringing into focus the enormous extent of latent destructiveness in German society. In order to deal with these psychological implications, we have paid much attention to this subject, but now we must come back to the killing center operations in the midst of which the experiments went on.

5 / Confiscations

We come now to the remaining two killing center operations: the confiscation of property and the killings themselves. The utilization of inmates for labor and experiments was an interruption of the process, an introduction of intermediary procedures for economic and other extrinsic purposes. Only the expropriations and killings were organic in an administrative sense. They were the only two operations which were implemented in all six death camps and which embraced all but a few Jewish deportees.

The confiscation of personal belongings was a catchall affair. Everything the Jews had managed to keep, everything they had succeeded in hiding, was collected in the killing centers. Property which the satellite states had been forced to relinquish in order that the deportees could start life anew in the "East" now also fell into the bag. Everything was collected and turned into profit. But the salvage of that property was a precise, well-planned operation.

A preliminary step toward systematic salvage was taken in the spring of 1941. In April of that year the RSHA informed the inspectorate that returning to relatives and dependants the personal belongings taken from Jews in concentration camps was "out of the question." The property was subject to confiscation through the normal channels (that is, the *Regierungspräsidenten*).[1] This procedure, it must be remembered, applied to all camps before the start of mass deportations. After the establishment of the killing centers the collection, sorting, and distribution of the vast number of personal belongings became a major problem which could no longer be handled on an ad hoc basis; accordingly, special administrative machinery was set up for the purpose of carrying out these expropriations. Under the new arrangements collection was handled by the individual camps, but the inventory and disposal of the items became much more complicated.

Jurisdiction over sorting and distribution of the Kulmhof loot was centralized under an organization which was outside SS and Police control: the Ghetto Administration of Lodz. Kulmhof was strictly a local enterprise, set up by Gauleiter Greiser for the Jews in his *Gau*. As previously pointed out, Greiser conferred on the *Ghettoverwaltung* of Litzmannstadt (Lodz) the

42. OStubaf. Brandt to Eichmann, November 6, 1942, NO-116. Staf. Sievers to Eichmann, copies to HStuf. Beger, Prof. Hirt, and OStubaf. Brandt, June 21, 1943, NO-87. Affidavit by Dr. Leon Felix Boutbien, October 30, 1946, NO-532. Affidavit by Ferdinand Holl, November 3, 1946, NO-590. Boutbien and Holl were inmates of Natzweiler.

43. Staf. Sievers to Staf. Brandt, September 5, 1944, NO-88.

1. Liebehenschel to camp commanders, May 5, 1941, enclosing letter by RSHA II-A-5 (signed Dr. Nockmann) to inspectorate, dated April 3, 1941, NO-1235.

plenary power to confiscate the belongings of all Jews deported in the Wartheland.[2] This power extended not only to abandoned property in the ghettos but also to the belongings which the deportees took along to the Kulmhof camp. Amtsleiter Biebow of the *Ghettoverwaltung* therefore established a central inventory station at Pabianice (eight miles southeast of Lodz) which he placed under the direction of one of his *Abteilungsleiter,* Seifert, and which sorted all the belongings hauled from the abandoned Warthegau ghettos and the Kulmhof camp by a fleet of sixteen trucks.[3] The Kulmhof confiscations were consequently "receipts" flowing to the *Ghettoverwaltung.* With one exception (furs) the inventory and ultimate realization of the property was entirely in Biebow's domain.

In Auschwitz the administrative chief (Burger, later Möckel) took care not only of collection but also of sorting, inventory, and packing. For the distribution of the items, however, he was dependent on the directives of WVHA *Amtsgruppe A* (Gruppenführer Frank).

In the *Generalgouvernement* the SS and Police Leader of Lublin, Globocnik, ever mindful of new opportunities to stretch out his jurisdiction in Jewish matters, instructed his men to draw up a *Zentralkartei* ("central register") of all the properties collected in his camps. Sturmbannführer Wippern was put in charge of all the hardware (jewelry, foreign currency, etc.), and Hauptsturmführer Höfle, whom we have met in connection with the deportations and the establishment of Belzec, took over the sorting of clothes, shoes, and so on.[4] From all four camps, including Treblinka, properties were sent to the stock rooms in Lublin.[5] This whole operation became the last phase of *Aktion Reinhardt.*

Globocnik had hardly established his organization when pressure was put on the SS and Police Leader in Warsaw and on Globocnik himself to distribute some of the accumulating goods. On April 25, 1942, Gruppenführer Grawitz, the *Reichsarzt SS und Polizei,* sent a letter of inquiry to Oberführer Wigand, then SS and Police Leader in Warsaw. "It has come to my attention," wrote Grawitz, "that deposits of old gold of Jewish origin are kept by the SS and Police Leaders Warsaw and Lublin." He could use the gold for dental work.[6] Wigand replied by requesting Grawitz to obtain a Himmler directive, and a long correspondence ensued.[7] On August 12, 1942, Brandt informed Krüger that Himmler had vested Pohl with responsibility for the distribution *(Weiterleitung)* of all Jewish valuables to the "competent agencies" of the Reich.[8] In notifying Pohl of

2. Memorandum by Biebow, April 20, 1942, *Dokumenty i Materialy,* II, 118–19.

3. Seifert to Biebow, May 7, 1942, *Dokumenty i Materialy,* I, 25–26. *Oberbürgermeister Litzmannstadt* (signed Luchterhand) to *Landeswirtschaftsamt Posen,* attention Regierungsrat Gerlich, May 27, 1942, *Dokumenty i Materialy,* III, 233–34. Gerlich to *Ghettoverwaltung,* August 28, 1942, *Dokumenty i Materialy,* III, 235.

4. Globocnik to Wippern and Höfle, July 15, 1942, *Dokumenty i Materialy,* II, 183.

5. Affidavit by Georg Lörner, February 4, 1947, NO-1911. Von Sammern-Frankenegg to Himmler's Personal Staff, July 9, 1942, NO-3163.

6. Grawitz to Wigand, April 25, 1942, NO-3166.

7. Wigand to Grawitz, May 8, 1942, NO-3166. Grawitz to OStubaf. Brandt, May 16, 1942, NO-3166. OStubaf. Brandt to Wigand, May 23, 1942, NO-3165. Himmler's Personal Staff to SS and Police Leader Warsaw, July 3, 1942, NO-3164. Von Sammern-Frankenegg to Personal Staff, July 7, 1942, NO-3163. Von Sammern-Frankenegg to Personal Staff, July 9, 1942, informing Himmler that the gold had already been transferred to Globocnik, NO-3163.

8. Brandt to Higher SS and Police Leaders in eastern territories, August 12, 1942, NO-3192.

the order, Brandt pointed out that Himmler expected the Economy Ministry to accord to the SS "magnanimous treatment" *(grosszügige Behandlung)* of any requests for gold and silver.[9]

About this time (on August 11, 1942) Globocnik asked for permission to "pinch off" (*abzweigen*) 2,000,000 zloty from the "Jewish evacuation" *(Judenumsiedlung)* to finance schools for German resettlers in the district. This procedure, Globocnik explained, had already been applied in the matter of clothes.[10] Brandt wrote directly to Gruppenführer Greifelt, Staff Director of the *Reichskommissar* for the Strengthening of Germandom, telling him that Himmler wished Greifelt to finance the project himself. The money collected in the *Judenumsiedlung* would be delivered to the Reichsbank without deduction of even one penny. "In this manner, it will be much easier to get the required funds through normal channels from the Finance Ministry," concluded Brandt.[11]

We should note that the power to dispose of valuables as well as currency in all the *Generalgouvernement* camps was vested in Pohl. This power was to manifest itself in the form of fundamental directives from *Amtsgruppe A* of the WVHA to the Auschwitz administration and to Lublin.[12]

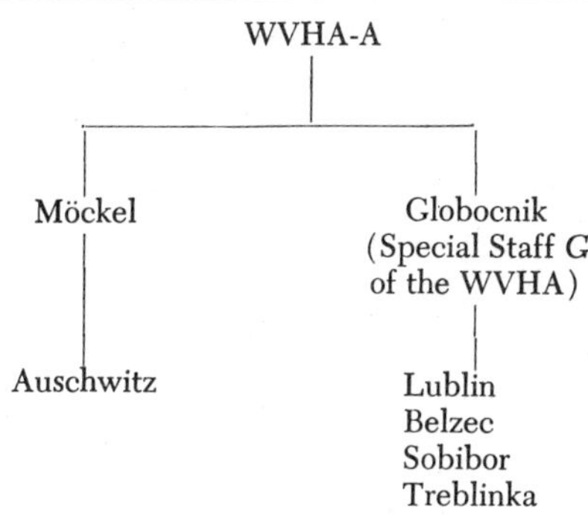

Kulmhof alone remained outside the apparatus:

Ghettoverwaltung Litzmannstadt

Camp Pabianice

Kulmhof

Let us examine how the system actually worked. We have said that the confiscations were a catchall operation, but they were more than that. They were a model of conservation. Everything was collected, and nothing was wasted.

How was it possible to be so thorough? The answer lies in the assembly line, a method which was foolproof. Inmate work parties picked up the luggage left in the freight cars of the transports and on the platform. Other inmate *Kommandos* collected clothes and valuables in the dressing rooms. Women's hair was cut off in the barber shops near the gas chambers. Gold teeth were extracted from the mouths of the corpses, and the human fat escaping from the burning bodies

9. Brandt to Pohl, August 12, 1942, NO-3192. Also, Brandt to Grawitz, August 14, 1942, NO-3191.

10. Bgf. Globocnik to Himmler, August 11, 1942, Himmler Files, Folder No. 94.

11. OStubaf. Brandt to Gruf. Greifelt, August 14, 1942, Himmler Files, Folder No. 94.

12. In spite of the centralization, requests for special distributions continued to be sent to Lublin. On September 19, 1942, the Gestapo chief in Vienna requested, on behalf of Kaltenbrunner, clothes for Germanized Poles and prisoners. Huber to SS and Police Leader Lublin – "Reinhardt," September 19, 1942, *Dokumenty i Materialy,* II, 190. In November SS and Police Court VI in Krakow asked for a gift (*Überlassung*) of carpets, glasses, civilian clothes, etc., from the "Jewish estate" (*Judennachlass*). SS and Police Court VI to SS *Standortverwaltung* Lublin, November 10, 1942, *Dokumenty i Materialy,* II, 192–93.

was poured back into the flames to speed the cremations. Thus the two organic processes of the death camp, confiscations and killings, were fused and synchronized into a single procedure which guaranteed the absolute success of both operations.

A corollary to the thoroughness of the collections was the care with which the inventory was conducted. Every item of foreign currency was counted; watches were sorted and valuable ones repaired; unusable clothes and rags were weighed. Receipts were passed back and forth, and everything was accounted for. All this was done in accordance with Himmler's wish for "painstaking exactness" (*die grösste Genauigkeit*). "We cannot be accurate enough."[13]

However, there was one problem which threatened to defeat the thoroughness of the confiscations and the "painstaking accuracy" of the inventory: German personnel were tempted to help themselves to some of the property. Something had to be done about that. Seifert, the *Ghettoverwaltung's* chief in Pabianice, requested that his men receive the same bonus of 15 reichsmark per day for "hazardous" duty that personnel in Kulmhof were receiving. Like the Kulmhof personnel, Seifert reasoned, his men were exposed to dangers of "infection" (*Infektionsgefahren*).[14] The police company in Pabianice was also given the opportunity to buy items they desired.[15] Globocnik considered the absence of major thefts a great achievement; at the conclusion of *Aktion Reinhardt* he reported to Himmler that only "the decency and honesty" of his men had guaranteed a complete delivery of the assets.[16]

However, the Auschwitz commander had considerably more trouble. On November 16, 1943, Liebehenschel issued an order in which he said that all the belongings of the inmates, whether clothes, valuables, food or other objects, were state property, and that the state alone could decide about their utilization. "Whoever touches state property," the order continued, "brands himself a a criminal and excludes himself automatically from the ranks of the SS".[17]

Perhaps the most interesting aspect of the confiscations was the distribution of the property. In the case of the *Ghettoverwaltung*, the problem was to sell, since the *Ghettoverwaltung* did not give anything away. (Furs were an exception; by order of Himmler they were sent to the SS clothing plant in Ravensbrück for ultimate wear by his *Waffen-SS*.[18]) For the rest, the *Ghettoverwaltung* could rely upon the Greiser directive and upon the fact that it was a Reich agency, attached to the *Oberbürgermeister* of Lodz for ordinary administrative purposes and responsible to the Main Trusteeship Office East in confiscation matters. This did not mean that any funds were passed upward; the *Ghettoverwaltung* ran a close balance sheet and could use all the money it received.

13. Himmler to Krüger and Pohl, January 15, 1943, NO-1257.

14. Seifert to Ribbe, May 29, 1942, *Dokumenty i Materialy*, I, 27. The *Ghettoverwaltung* granted only 6 reichsmark. Biebow to *Ghettoverwaltung* personnel office, June 20, 1942, *Dokumenty i Materialy*, II, 75.

15. Second Police Company (ghetto) to *Ghettoverwaltung*, July 27, 1942, *Dokumenty i Materialy*, II, 140–42.

16. Undated reports by Globocnik to Himmler, PS-4024.

17. Sehn, "Oswiecim," p. 43. According to ex-inmates, enormous quantities of jewelry, watches, and money were stolen by guards. Affidavit by Werner Krumpe, September 23, 1945, NO-1933.

18. Koppe to OStubaf. Brandt, August 28, 1942, NO-3190. The SS reserve hospital in Sieradz asked for a few items because the makeshift furnishings of the new hospital were a "catastrophe." Biebow to Meyer (division for administration of goods), September 7, 1942, *Dokumenty i Materialy*, II, 138.

What, then, was the attitude of Biebow's customers? Naturally, purchase of such items posed a few dilemmas. For example, in August, 1942, a relief organization in Poznan (the NSV) asked for 3000 suits, 1000 items of women's apparel, and some underwear and bedsheets. The stuff was urgently needed for resettlers. The NSV requested a low price offer.[19] A couple of months later the items were delivered, and the bill was sent to the NSV.[20] The deal was closed.

But on January 16, 1943, the *Ghettoverwaltung* received a complaint. The first shipment of 1500 suits had been sent in unopened crates to local offices of the relief organization; upon opening the cases, relief officials dicovered with dismay that the shipment in no way compared with samples viewed at Kulmhof. Many of the suits were not suits at all but unmatched coats and pants. Worse, a large part of the clothes were badly spotted with dirt and bloodstains (*Ein grosser Teil der Bekleidungsstücke ist stark befleckt und teilweise auch mit Schmutz und Blutflecken durchsetzt*). In Poznan, several hundred items still had the Jewish star attached to them. Since most of the workers unpacking the crates were Poles, there was danger that the resettlers would find out about the origin of the things, thereby plunging the Winter Relief into "discredit."[21]

The *Ghettoverwaltung* replied laconically six weeks later, acknowledging return of 2750 suits and 1000 dresses. The stains were not blood but rust; they could not be removed. Therefore a bill would be made out only for 250 suits and the underwear.[22] This reply brought forth another letter from Winter Relief stating that the welfare organization could not resign itself to the loss of the suits. If the rust spots could not be removed, then at least the Jewish stars should have been severed from the clothes.[23]

So much for the *Ghettoverwaltung's* business deals. The WVHA strategy was more complex. Himmler insisted that the property belonged to the Reich and that straight business deals with customers were out of the question, but this did not mean that the Jewish belongings could not be used in a way to further SS interests. First the WVHA gave away large quantities of "state property" to groups of people who regularly enjoyed SS generosity, namely, SS men (particularly wounded or decorated soldiers), families of SS men, and ethnic Germans. Second and more important was the use of deliveries to state agencies as levers to obtain "magnanimous treatment" from them. These WVHA tactics deserve to be described in more detail.

On September 7, 1942, Pohl wrote to Himmler that he intended to give a large number of women's coats, children's clothes, gloves, raincoats, stockings, etc., to the Race and Resettlement Main Office (RuSHA) for presentation as Christmas gifts to families of SS men. The items derived from the Dutch *Sonderaktion*.[24]

Barely two weeks later Brigadeführer August Frank, chief of WVHA-A, issued a basic allocation directive to Auschwitz and Lublin which turned the SS into a veritable Salvation Army and at the same time provided for consider-

19. *Gauleitung* Wartheland/*Amt für Volkswohlfahrt Posen/Organisation* to *Oberbürgermeister Litzmannstadt*, August 12, 1942, *Dokumenty i Materialy*, II, 156–57.

20. *Ghettoverwaltung* to *Gauleitung Wartheland*/NSV – *Kreis Litzmannstadtland*, November 28, 1942, *ibid.*, p. 166.

21. *Winterhilfswerk des Deutschen Volkes/Der Gaubeauftragte Wartheland* to *Ghettoverwaltung*, January 16, 1943, *ibid.*, pp. 168–70.

22. *Ghettoverwaltung* to *Gau Plenipotentiary Winterhilfswerk*, April 3, 1943, *ibid.*, p. 177.

23. *Gau Plenipotentiary* to *Ghettoverwaltung*, April 22, 1943, *ibid.*, pp. 179–80.

24. Pohl to Himmler, September 7, 1942, NO-1258.

able leverage against Economy Minister Funk. To make sure that everything was properly camouflaged, Frank ordered at the outset that the Jewish property be referred to henceforth as "goods originating from theft, receipt of stolen goods, and hoarded goods." The disposal was as follows:

a. Cash money in Reichsbank notes was to be delivered to the WVHA account in the Reichsbank.

b. Foreign currency, rare metals, jewelry, precious and semiprecious stones, pearls, gold from teeth, and scrap gold were to be delivered to the WVHA for transmission to the Reichsbank.

c. Watches, clocks, fountain pens, mechanical pencils, razors, pocketknives, scissors, flashlights, wallets, and purses were to be sent to WVHA repair shops to be delivered from there to post exchanges for sale to troops.

d. Men's underwear and clothing was to be handed over to the *Volksdeutsche Mittelstelle* (VOMI), the welfare organization for ethnic Germans.

e. Women's underwear and clothing was to be sold to the VOMI, except pure silk underwear (men's or women's), which was to be sent directly to the Economy Ministry.

f. Featherbeds, quilts, blankets, umbrellas, baby carriages, handbags, leather belts, shopping bags, pipes, sunglasses, mirrors, suitcases, and cloth were to be delivered to the VOMI, the question of payment to be decided later.

g. Linen (bedsheets, pillows, towels, tablecloths, etc.) was to be sold to the VOMI.

h. Spectacles and glasses without frames were to be delivered to the medical *Referat* (D-III).

i. Valuable furs were to be sent to the WVHA; ordinary furs were to be reported to *Referat* B-II and delivered to the SS clothing plant at Ravensbrück.

k. Low-value and useless items were to be delivered to the Economy Ministry for sale by weight.[25]

25. Frank to Chief, *Standortverwaltung* Lublin and Chief, Administration Auschwitz (6 copies), September 26, 1942, NO-724.

One item was not mentioned in the directive – human hair. The collection of hair had already been ordered on August 6, 1942; it was to be put to use in manufacturing felt footwear for U-boat personnel and *Reichsbahn* employees.[26]

Very briefly, the directives from the WVHA may be reduced to the following:

	Gifts through	Deliveries to state
Textiles	VOMI	Economy Ministry
Hardware	WVHA	Reichsbank

The gifts were distributions which did not flow through state agencies; the deliveries to the Economy Ministry and to the Reichsbank were used for the purpose of obtaining special benefits for the SS. Let us see how both aims were accomplished; first we shall look at the distribution of the soft items, then at the hardware.

Before distribution, clothes had to be searched for sewed-in valuables and, contrary to Kulmhof practice, the Jewish star had to be removed. This was a

26. Glücks to camp commanders, August 6, 1942, USSR-511. In connection with hair, two other items should be mentioned: blood and human fat. Dr. Perl states that she witnessed the bleeding of 700 young Jewish women in Auschwitz. Race theory had evidently been ignored in order to procure the plasma. The exaction of the blood was not carried out in modest quantities or with elementary safeguards; the women were lying on the ground, faint, "and deep rivers of blood were flowing around their bodies." Perl, *I Was a Doctor in Auschwitz*, pp. 73–75. Blood extractions from women are mentioned also by an inmate nurse. Deposition by Renée Erman (undated), in Raymond Phillips (ed.), *Trial of Josef Kramer* (*The Belsen Trial*) (London, 1949), pp. 661–62. The use of human fat for soap cannot be established as a fact from available documentary evidence and eyewitness reports. For origin of the soap-making rumor and its importance, see pp. 623–24.

strict order from Frank.[27] The best textile items were reserved for distribution to *Volksdeutsche*. According to a Himmler order of October 14, 1942, over 200,000 ethnic Germans in Trans-Dnistria, the Ukraine, and the *Generalgouvernement* were to be supplied with suits, dresses, coats, hats, blankets, underwear, and utensils. The items had to be delivered by Christmas.[28]

On February 6, 1943, Pohl reported on the textile *Aktion*. Apologetically, he pointed out that a very large percentage of the clothes in the Auschwitz and Lublin depots consisted of rags. The transportation of the gifts to the East was meeting with difficulties because the *Reichsbahn* had closed traffic to the Ukraine *(Transportsperre)*; however, the Economy Ministry was negotiating with the Transport Ministry for allocation of freight cars, since it was in the greatest interest of the economy to make maximum utilization of old clothes. Up to the time of the report the following quantities had been delivered:[29]

VOMI:	*Freight cars*
Men's clothes Women's clothes Children's clothes Underwear, etc	211
Economy Ministry:	
Men's clothes Women's clothes Women's silk underwear	34
Rags	400
Bed feathers	130
Women's hair (3 tons)	1
Other salvage	5
Total	781

In general, then, what was not good enough for the *Volksdeutsche* was sent to the Economy Ministry. (Silk was of course an exception; the war effort had a priority on silk material.) Shipments set aside for the ministry went to private firms to be worked over for one purpose or another.[30] For the contribution which the WVHA made to the conservation program by delivering the rags and old clothes, Pohl naturally demanded certain favors. Accordingly, he had a "nice conversation" (*freundliches Gespräch)* with Economy Minister Funk, in the course of which he requested priorities for textiles to be made into SS uniforms, "on account of the delivery of the old clothes of the dead Jews."[31]

While the great bulk of the textiles went to the VOMI and to the Economy Ministry, some of the clothes were distributed in the concentration camps for inmates. (Prisoners' uniforms, it may be recalled, had become scarce.) In the summer of 1943, shipments of clothes from Auschwitz and Lublin arrived at Dachau. Before handing them

27. Frank directive, September 26, 1942, NO-724.

28. Himmler to Pohl and VOMI Chief OGruf. Lorenz, copies to OGruf. Prützmann and Obf. Hofmeyer, October 14, 1942, NO-5395.

29. Pohl to Himmler, February 6, 1943, NO-1257. The figures represented a mere beginning. See later report by Globocnik stating that he alone had sent out 2900 freight cars with textile materials, while enough clothes to fill still another 1000 cars were still in stock. Globocnik to Himmler, undated, probably autumn 1943, PS-4024. The huge quantities of suits and dresses in the killing centers were supplemented by clothes and utensils accumulating in the transit camps. These camps were integrated in the distribution system. Affidavit by Dr. Konrad Morgen, October 5, 1947, NO-5440. Morgen saw clothing stores in Herzogenbusch, Holland. From this camp alone several freight cars were sent to the VOMI.

30. Affidavit by Georg Lörner (WVHA-B), February 4, 1947, NO-1911. A Strasbourg firm, Strassburg GmbH, applied to the Berlin officer of the Dresdner Bank for 200,000–300,000 reichsmark in credits. Upon investigation, it was discovered that the firm was handling bloodstained clothes (*blutdurchtränkt*) with holes in them. The credit was refused. Affidavit by Werner von Richter (Dresdner Bank, Berlin), May 3, 1948, NI-15646.

31. Affidavit by Pohl, July 15, 1946, PS-4045.

out to inmates, SS officers waded in the "mountains of clothes" looking for valuables and picking out the more attractive pieces of apparel.[32]

The clothes given to the inmates were of course "state property." A former woman inmate, Dr. Perl, tells of an incident in Auschwitz which affected a Jewish singer who, in conformity with common practice, had torn strips from her slip to use in lieu of unavailable handkerchiefs and tissues. One day a guard accosted her, jerked up her dress, and discovered that only the shoulder straps remained. "You revolutionary swine! You thief! Where is the camp chemise?"[33] he shouted at the woman, beating her unmercifully.

The same pattern which we have seen in the textile distribution – gifts and leverage – applied also to hardware. The biggest gift item in the durable goods category consisted of watches. On May 13, 1943, Frank could already make a report about the "realization of Jewish stolen goods" *(Verwertung des jüdischen Hehler- und Diebesgutes)* in which he mentioned receipt of 94,000 men's watches, 33,000 women's watches, 25,000 fountain pens, and other items. He had already sent 1500 watches to three SS divisions *(Leibstandarte Adolf Hitler, Das Reich,* and *Totenkopfdivision*) and proposed sending 1000 watches to each division in the *Waffen-SS,* plus 6000 watches to the U-boat command (a favored service arm). In addition, he was distributing scissors to the DAW, Lebensborn, camp doctors, and camp barbershops.[34]

Four months later Hildebrandt of the RuSHA put in a claim for "larger quantities" (*grössere Mengen*) of watches and fountain pens. He wanted to distribute gifts to wounded SS men during Christmas of 1943. "Many a wounded man," he said, "who does not own a watch or fountain pen will enjoy such a gift."[35] We need not go into the subsequent correspondence in the course of which such weighty decisions were made as to whether the SS and Police Division should get 500 or 700 watches, the delivery of 15,000 women's watches to ethnic Germans, the distribution of 3000 clocks (500 to concentration camps, 2500 to bombed-out Berliners), and the allocation of especially valuable watches for exceptionally brave soldiers of new divisions.[36]

Most the valuables, including money, jewelry, gold watches, and dental gold, were duly delivered at the Reichsbank. The Reichsbank was Germany's central bank; its president was Economy Minister Funk. There were two vice presidents: Emil Puhl, a long-time employee of the bank, and Kurt Lange, who hailed from the Economy Ministry and was the ministry's expert in monetary, stock, exchange, and insurance matters.[37] Below the vice presidents were the *Reichsbankdirektoren,* each in charge of some aspect of the bank's operation (i.e., securities, foreign exchange, etc.). Connected with or operating in conjunction with the Reichsbank were several other organizations:[38]

32. Affidavit by Karl Adam Roeder, February 20, 1947, NO-2122. Affiant was an inmate of Dachau.

33. Perl, *I Was a Doctor in Auschwitz,* pp. 101–2.

34. Gruf. Frank to Himmler, May 13, 1943, NO-2003.

35. OGruf. Hildebrandt to Himmler, August 18, 1943, NO-2752.

36. See the following correspondence: Gruf. Frank to OStubaf. Brandt, September 2, 1943, NO-2751. Pohl to Brandt, November 6, 1943, NO-2753. Brandt to Pohl, December 3, 1943, NO-2754. WVHA D-II to WVHA-A and Auschwitz administration, January 24, 1944, NO-4468. Pohl to Himmler, July 4, 1944, NO-2755. Pohl to Himmler, July 29, 1944, NO-2756. Himmler to Pohl, August 13, 1944, NO-2749.

37. The two vice presidents had the rank of *Staatssekretär.* Funk to Lammers, March 11, 1941, NI-14457.

The Golddiskontbank
The *Reichshauptkasse* (Treasury)
The *Reichsrechnungshof* (Auditing Office)
The *Preussische Staatsmünze* (Mint)
The Berlin *Pfandleihanstalt* (Pawnshop)

The disposal of the items to the Reichsbank rested on an agreement between Funk and Himmler which was concluded in the summer of 1942.[39] The matter was then discussed by Funk, Puhl, Pohl, and a number of other officials at lunch in the Reichsbank building.[40] The arrangement for the actual receipt of the items was worked out by Reichsbankrat Thoms of the Reichsbank Precious Metals Division and Brigadeführer Frank.[41] The deliveries were made by the chief of WVHA A-II (finance and payroll), Hauptsturmführer Melmer.[42] There were a total of seventy-six or seventy-seven shipments, each filling a truck.[43] Although Melmer wore civilian clothes by arrangement, he was accompanied by a few uniformed SS guards; hence the deliveries did not remain a secret very long.[44]

In the storerooms the articles were emptied on tables and sorted. About twenty-five to thirty people passed through these rooms every day.[45] The objects themselves were sometimes stamped "Auschwitz" and "Lublin," and the large quantity of dental gold was noticed.[46] When Pohl visited the Reichsbank, he was conducted to the premises by Puhl, who remarked, "Your things are here too [*Ihre Sachen sind auch darunter*]."[47]

The problem of what to do with the accumulating deliveries was brought up by Puhl one day in a *Reichsbankdirektoren* meeting. The vice president announced that the Reichsbank was going to realize the gold and jewelry of the SS. Reichsbankdirektor Wilhelm, chief of foreign currency and currency control, protested: "The Reichsbank is not a dealer in second-hand goods."[48] Wilhelm – no frien l of the SS – was consequently left out of the picture.[49]

The channeling of the property from the storerooms was finally as follows: Coin was retained by the Precious Metals Division (Thoms).[50] Stocks, bonds, and bankbooks were transferred to the Securities Division.[51] The gold teeth were sent to the Prussian State Mint for melting.[52] Jewelry was delivered to the Berlin Pawnshop, where it was handled by Amtsrat Wieser.[53] The proceeds

38. The following were members of the Aufsichtsrat of the Golddiskontbank: Vizepräsident Puhl, Reichsbankdirektor Wilhelm, Reichsbankdirektor Kretschmann, Ministerialdirigent Bayrhoffer (Finance Ministry), Staatssekretär Dr. Landfried (Economy Ministry). Affidavit by Karl Friedrich Wilhelm, January 23, 1948, NI-14462. The *Reichshauptkasse* ("Main Treasury") was attached to the Reichsbank; the Auditing Office and the Mint were agencies of the Finance Ministry. Chart by Frick, PS-2905. The Municipal Pawnshop of Berlin was under the city treasurer. Memorandum by Kropp (*Hauptkasse*), March 31, 1944, PS-3947.

39. Affidavit by Puhl, May 3, 1946, PS-3944.

40. Affidavit by Pohl, July 15, 1946, PS-4045. Affidavit by Wilhelm, January 23, 1948, NI-14462.

41. Statement by Thoms, May 8, 1946, PS-3951.

42. *Ibid.*

43. Testimony by Thoms, *Trial of the Major War Criminals,* XIII, 604–5, 615.

44. Statement by Thoms, May 8, 1946, PS-3951.

45. Testimony by Thoms, *Trial of the Major War Criminals,* XIII, 603.

46. Statement by Thoms, May 8, 1946, PS-3951.

47. Draft affidavit by Pohl, undated, NI-15307.

48. Affidavit by Wilhelm, January 23, 1948, NI-14462.

49. He speaks of his "generally known aversion for these people." *Ibid.*

50. Statement by Thoms, May 8, 1946, PS-3951.

51. *Ibid.*

52. Main Treasury (signed Thoms) to Prussian State Mint, December 24, 1944, NI-15534. Testimony by Thoms, *Trial of the Major War Criminals,* XIII, 612.

53. Pohl to Finance Ministry, July 24, 1944, NG-4096.

from disposal of the metals and papers were deposited in the Treasury; there they were credited to the Finance Ministry on a special account designated "Max Heiliger."[54] From time to time the account was drawn upon by the Finance Ministry's old expert in Jewish matters, Dr. Maedel, who booked the withdrawals in the budget (Chapter XVIII, title 7, paragraph 3).[55]

The realization of the Jewish valuables did not proceed as efficiently as the above procedure might seem to indicate. Principally, three obstacles had to be faced. In the first place, it was difficult to get rid of certain items. For example, the Securities Division was stuck with unendorsed papers which had been made payable to holders;[56] the pawnshop complained that most of the jewelry and watches it had received were of low value because they were old-fashioned or damaged in transit.[57]

Another difficulty was the lack of time. In the course of the processing a number of bottlenecks developed. Just before the German collapse 207 containers filled with gold, currency, and other valuables were sent to salt mines, where the entire shipment remained until discovered by American troops.[58]

The third limitation was, of course, the price the SS asked for its deliveries. Although not "one penny" was to be deducted, Wippern and Möckel were authorized to withhold sufficient amounts to defray expenses connected with the *Aktion* itself.[59] Gold was handed over subject to the condition that three kilograms be made available if needed by the SS for bribery or intelligence.[60] Most important of all, the Reichsbank and the Golddiskontbank had to establish a fund from which the SS could borrow money to finance its various activities. This loan, known as the Reinhardt fund, infused the SS industries with new life. The SS combine owed 6,831,279.54 reichsmark to the SS Savings Bank Association and 1,000,000 reichsmark to the German Red Cross; these debts could now be repaid. In addition, some money was plowed into capital expansion.[61] After the conclusion of these arrangements the disapproving Reichsbankdirektor Wilhelm took the occasion to "warn" Puhl against visiting the concentration camps in connection with the credits.[62]

This is the history of the camp confiscations – perhaps not the greatest looting operation in history but certainly the most thorough one. Its organizational scheme appears in Tables 87A and 87B.

6 / The Killing Operations

We turn now to the second part of the organic killing center operations – the death of three million Jews.

The success of the killing operations depended, in the first instance, upon the maintenance of secrecy. Unlike any

54. *Ibid.* Ministerialdirektor Gossel (Finance Ministry) to Reichsrechnungsdirektor (Chief Auditor) Patzer, September 7, 1944, NG-4094.

55. Patzer to Gossel, November 16, 1944, NG-4097.

56. Affidavit by Thoms, May 8, 1946, PS-3951.

57. *Pfandleihanstalt* to *Hauptkasse*, September 14, 1943, NI-13818.

58. Affidavit by Albert Thoms, May 26, 1948, NI-15533. Itemized account of the valuables, found in salt mine at Merkers, in report by F. J. Roberts, chief, claims section, foreign exchange depository of Office of American Military Government, January 30, 1947, NI-15647.

59. Pohl to main offices, Higher SS and Police Leaders, SS-economists, WVHA-B, WVHA-D, WVHA A-IV, Gruf. Sporrenberg (Globocnik's successor), Stubaf. Wippern, and OStubaf. Möckel, December 9, 1943, NO-4566.

60. Himmler to Staf. Baumert, June 25, 1944, NO-2208.

61. Memorandum by WVHA-W, May 26, 1943, NO-2190. DWB (SS industry network) to Gruf. Frank and HStuf. Melmer, June 7, 1943, NO-554.

62. Affidavit by Wilhelm, January 23, 1948, NI-14462.

other administrative task confronting the bureaucracy, secrecy was a continuous problem. Precautionary measures had to be taken before the victims arrived, while they went through the processing, and after they were dead. At no point could any disclosure be permitted; at no time could the camp management afford to be caught off guard. The killers had to conceal their work from every outsider; they had to mislead and fool the victims; and they had to erase all traces of the operation.

Concealment

We have already noted – or at least hinted at – a number of concealment measures. Thus the very speed and haste with which the deportation-killing process was carried out was prompted to no small extent by considerations of secrecy. When Viktor Brack of the Führer Chancellery wrote to Himmler about the necessity of speeding up the construction of the *Generalgouvernement* camps, he pointed out: "You yourself, *Reichsführer,* said to me some time ago that for reasons of concealment alone we have to work as quickly as possible."[1]

Another concealment measure was verbal camouflage. The most important – and possibly the most misleading – term used for the killing centers collectively was the "East." This phrase was employed again and again during the deportations. When reference to an individual death camp was necessary, the term used was *Arbeitslager* ("labor camp") or *Konzentrationslager* ("concentration camp"). Birkenau, the Auschwitz killing site, was called *Kriegsgefangenenlager* ("PW camp") in accordance with its originally intended purpose, later KL Au II (concentration camp Auschwitz II).[2] Sobibor was appropriately called *Durchgangslager* ("transit camp"). Since it was located near the Bug, on the border of the occupied eastern territories, the designation fitted into the myth of the "eastern migration." When Himmler proposed one day that the camp be designated a *Konzentrationslager,* Pohl opposed the change.[3]

The gas chamber and crematorium units in Auschwitz were known as *Spezialeinrichtungen* ("special installations"), *Badeanstalten* ("bath houses"), and *Leichenkeller* ("corpse cellars").[4] The diesel engine operated in Belzec was located in a shack called the "Heckenholt Foundation." (Unterscharführer Heckenholt was the operator of the diesel.)[5] The primary term for the killing operation itself was the same which had been employed for the killings in Russia – *Sonderbehandlung* ("special treatment"). In addition, there was some terminology more appropriate to the killing center operations, such as *durchgeschleusst* ("dragged through") or *gesondert untergebracht* ("separately quartered").

Next to verbal camouflage it was most important to close the mouths of the inner circle; hence all camp personnel, especially top personnel, were sworn to silence. Höss made such a promise to Himmler before he started his task. He observed complete secrecy, not speaking to any outsider about his work. Only once did he break his word: "At the end of 1942," relates Höss, "my wife's curiosity was aroused by remarks made by the *Gauleiter* of Upper Silesia, Bracht, regarding happenings in the camp. She asked me whether this was the truth, and I admitted that it was. That was the only

1. Obf. Brack to Himmler, June 23, 1942, NO-205.

2. Sehn, "Oswiecim," p. 32.

3. Himmler to Pohl, July 5, 1943, NO-482. Pohl to Himmler, July 15, 1943, NO-482.

4. Sehn, "Oswiecim," p. 32.

5. Affidavit by Gerstein, April 26, 1945, PS-1553.

TABLE 87A / *Administration of the Killing Center Loot: Soft Items*

Allocation	*Ghettoverwaltung* Lodz		WVHA-A			
Camps	Kulmhof		Auschwitz		*Generalgouvernement* camps	
Collection / Sorting / Distribution	*Ghettoverwaltung*/ Camp Pabianice Seifert		Camp administration (Burger) Möckel		Special Staff G (*Aktion Reinhardt*) Globocnik — Hauptsturmführer Höfle	
	NSV Wartheland	Ravensbrück	RuSHA	VOMI	Camps	Economy Ministry
	clothes	furs	clothes	clothes linens blankets	clothes	clothes hair
Intermediary channel						Firms
Final utilization	Ethnic German resettlers	*Waffen-SS*	Families of SS men	Ethnic Germans in *GG* and Russia	Inmates	Budget

TABLE 87B / *Administration of the Killing Center Loot: Hard Items*

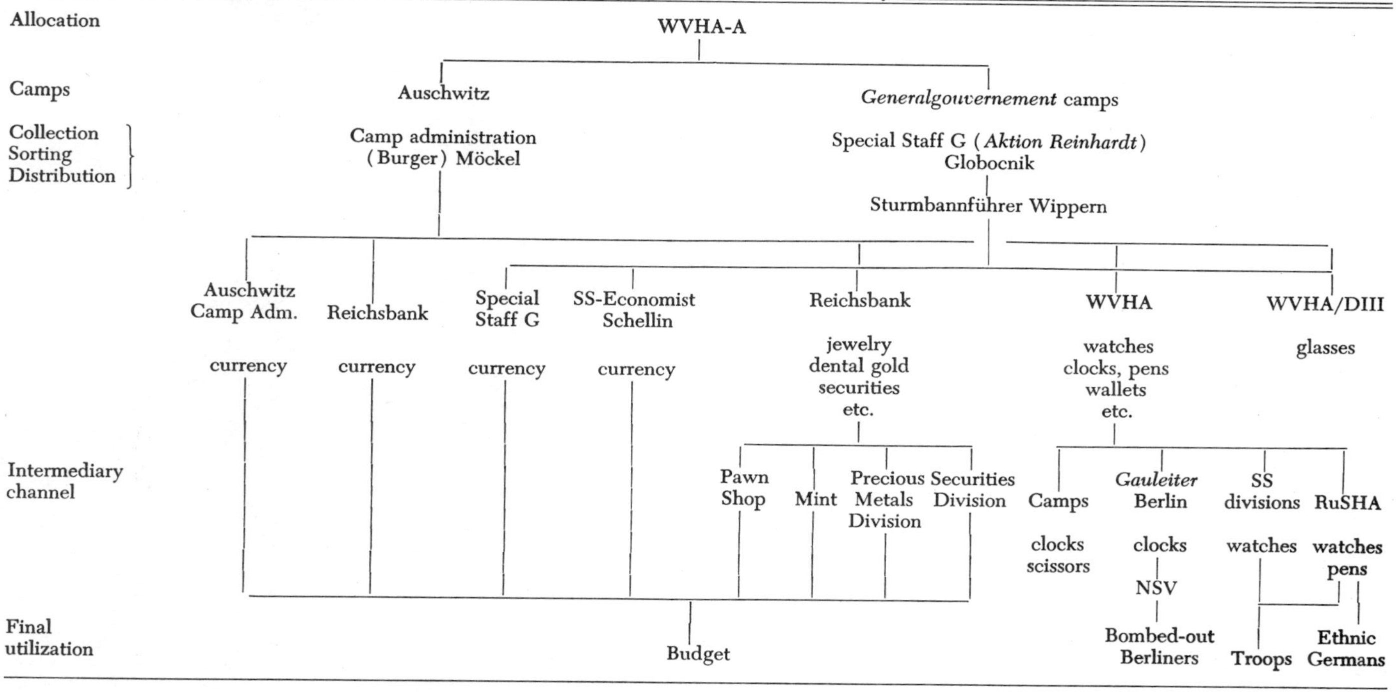

Allocation

WVHA-A

Camps

Auschwitz

Generalgouvernement camps

Collection
Sorting
Distribution

Camp administration
(Burger) Möckel

Special Staff G (*Aktion Reinhardt*)
Globocnik

Sturmbannführer Wippern

Auschwitz Camp Adm. — currency

Reichsbank — currency

Special Staff G — currency

SS-Economist Schellin — currency

Reichsbank — jewelry, dental gold, securities, etc.

WVHA — watches, clocks, pens, wallets, etc.

WVHA/DIII — glasses

Intermediary
channel

Pawn Shop

Mint

Precious Metals Division

Securities Division

Camps — clocks, scissors

Gauleiter Berlin — clocks — NSV

SS divisions — watches

RuSHA — watches, pens

Final
utilization

Budget

Bombed-out Berliners

Troops

Ethnic Germans

breach of the promise I had given to the *Reichsführer*."[6]

A Treblinka guard, Unterscharführer Hirtreiter, once spent a furlough with his girl friend, Frieda Jörg, in Germany. The girl knew of Hirtreiter's past experiences with "euthanasia" operations at the insane asylum of Hadamar; full of curiosity, she asked him, "What are you doing in Poland now? Bumping people off, eh? [*Was macht ihr denn in Polen? Gelt, ihr legt da Menschen um?*]" Hirtreiter did not reply.[7]

However, not all the participants could keep the burden of their knowledge to themselves. Instances are recorded which indicate that guards sometimes trumpeted out the news to newly arrived victims in the killing centers.[8] Again, when Obersturmführer Gerstein, the gas expert, completed his tour of the *Generalgouvernement* camps in the late summer of 1942, he spilled the whole secret on the Warsaw-Berlin express to a fellow passenger, Swedish diplomat Baron von Otter.[9] The baron reported the existence of the killing centers to Stockholm, but the Swedish government did not disseminate the information to the world.[10]

Closely related to the oath of silence was another precautionary measure, the control of visitors. Visitors were high officials of the Reich or of the party who arrived for "inspections." The concentration camp administration was especially touchy about such inspections. On November 3, 1943, Glücks ordered that visitors were not to be shown the brothels and the crematoriums; neither was there to be any talk about these installations.[11] In case anyone did happen to notice the smoking chimneys, he was given the standard explanation that the crematorium was burning corpses which resulted from epidemics.[12]

There were welcome visitors and unwelcome visitors. Following a visit by Justice Minister Thierack to Auschwitz on January 8, 1943, Höss sent him an album of photographs with a little note in which he expressed the hope that the Reichsminister would "enjoy them" (*in der Hoffnung, Ihnen damit gleichzeitig eine Freude bereitet zu haben*).[13] Unwelcome visitors were primarily unannounced visitors. Frank, the *Generalgouverneur* of Poland, was extremely anxious to get details about killing centers. Once, he got a report "that there was something going on near Belzec"; he went there the next day. Globocnik showed him how Jews were working on an enormous ditch. When Frank asked what would happen to the Jews, he got the standard answer: they would be sent farther east. Frank made another attempt. He expressed to

6. Testimony by Höss, *Trial of the Major War Criminals*, XI 396–411.

7. "Ein Wachmann von Treblinka," *Frankfurter Zeitung*, November 11, 1950, p. 3.

8. Julius Ganszer, a survivor, tells of his reception in Auschwitz after he had been given prison clothes, and after a number was tattooed on his arm. A guard said: "You are only numbers. A shot, and the number is gone. Don't try to escape; the only way to get out of here is by the chimney." Friedman, *Oswiecim*, p. 26. Identical experience by Dr. Bernard Lauber, Case No. 4, tr. pp. 282–97.

9. Statement by Gerstein, May 4, 1945, in *Vierteljahreshefte für Zeitgeschichte* (Stuttgart), April, 1953, p. 192.

10. Comment by Prof. Hans Rothfels, citing letter from Swedish Ministry of Foreign Affairs to Centre de Documentation Juive Contemporaine (Paris), November 10, 1949, *Vierteljahreshefte*, 1953, p. 181.

11. Glücks to camp commanders, November 10, 1943, NO-1541.

12. Affidavit by Wilhelm Steffler, January 28, 1948, NI-13953. Steffler was *Ministerialrat* in charge of raw materials in the Office of the Four-Year Plan. He visited Auschwitz with a party which included Krauch and Körner. Affidavit by Dr. Karl Rühmer, February 7, 1947, NO-1931. Rühmer, a *Stubaf.* in WVHA W-V, was a fishery expert.

13. Höss to Thierack, March 4, 1943, NG-645.

Himmler the wish to pay a visit to Lublin; Himmler urged him not to go there. Finally, Frank tried to spring a surprise visit to Auschwitz. His car was stopped and diverted with the explanation that there was an epidemic in the camp. Later Frank complained to Hitler about his frustrated visit. Hitler is said to have replied: "You can very well imagine that there are executions going on – of insurgents. Apart from that I do not know anything. Why don't you speak to Heinrich Himmler about it?" And so, Frank was back where he started.[14]

If the front door could be watched, there was a very wide back door, especially in Auschwitz. The great extent of industrial activity in this camp resulted in a constant stream of incoming and outgoing corporation officials, engineers, construction men, and other temporary personnel, all excellent carriers of gossip to the farthest corners of the Reich. An I. G. Farben official, Ernst A. Struss, traveling in January, 1942, in a railroad compartment from Heydebreck to Breslau just after he had paid a short visit to the camp, overheard a worker remarking in a loud voice that in Auschwitz large numbers of people were being burnt, that the cremations were being carried out in crematories and on stakes, and that the air in the I. G. Farben factory in Auschwitz was putrid with the smell of corpses. Struss jumped up and shouted, "These are lies; you should not spread such lies!" The man answered, "No, these are not lies; in Auschwitz there are 10,000 workers and all know it."[15] Similarly, in the central insurance department of I. G. Farben the killing installations at Auschwitz were the subject of animated discussion.[16]

The powerful rumor network did not reach German listeners alone. We have already had occasion to note that the news of the killing centers was carried to the populations of several countries in the form of a story that out of the fat of corpses the Germans were making soap. To this day the origin of the soap-making rumor has not been traced; the best clue is probably the postwar testimony of the SS investigator Dr. Konrad Morgen, who at one time was quite active in Poland. One of Morgen's subjects of special interest was Brigadeführer Dirlewanger. Now it must be stressed that Dirlewanger had nothing to do with the killing centers. He was the commander of a notorious unit of SS unreliables which in 1941 was stationed in the *Generalgouvernement*.[17] What did this man do? According to Morgen:

> Dirlewanger had arrested people illegally and arbitrarily, and as for his female prisoners – young Jewesses – he did the following against them: He called together a small circle of friends consisting of members of a Wehrmacht supply unit. Then he made so-called scientific experiments, which involved stripping the victims of their clothes. Then they [the victims] were given an injection of strychnine. Dirlewanger looked on, smoking a cigarette, as did his friends, and they saw how these girls were dying. Immediately after that the corpses were cut into small pieces, mixed with horsemeat, and boiled into soap.
>
> I would like to state here, emphatically, that here we were only concerned with a suspicion, although a very urgent one. We had witnesses' testimony concerning these incidents, and the Security Police in Lublin had made certain investigations. . . .[18]

14. Testimony by Frank, *Trial of the Major War Criminals,* XII, 17–19.

15. Affidavit by Ernst A. Struss, April 7, 1947, NI-6645.

16. Affidavit by Dr. Gustav Kuepper, June 10, 1947, NI-8919.

17. See p. 165n.

18. Testimony by Morgen, Case No. 11, tr. pp. 4075–76.

On July 29, 1942, the chief of the ethnic Germans in Slovakia, Karmasin, had written a letter to Himmler in which he described the "resettlement" of 700 "asocial" ethnic Germans. One of the difficulties, wrote Karmasin, was the spreading of the rumor (furthered by the clergy) that the "resettlers" would be "boiled into soap" (*dass die Aussiedler "zur Seife verkocht werden"*).[19] In October, 1942, the Propaganda Division in the Lublin district reported the rumor circulating in the city that now it was the turn of the Poles to be used, like the Jews, for "soap production" (*Die Polen kommen jetzt genau wie die Juden zur Seifenproduktion dran*).[20]

We are not concerned here with the question whether soap cakes of human fat were produced in the killing centers (the answer is probably not) or whether such cakes were produced at all. To us the importance of the soap rumor lies in its effectiveness as a carrier of information about the mass killings. In 1942 that rumor had already been recorded in two different places, Lublin and Bratislava. Such spacing indicates that the rumor had a powerful impact and a wide distribution.[21]

If the SS and Police could do little about the rumors, it could do nothing about the intellectual power of deduction and prediction. One may conceivably hide killing centers, but one cannot hide the disappearance of millions of people. We have already noted that in Poland the victims were frequently aware of their fate; this awareness was a function of the mere proximity of the Jews to the places of death. In Hungary, too, the Jews knew what would happen; for two and a half years they had watched the disappearance of the Jews in other parts of Europe. How, then, did the few thousand guards of the killing centers handle the millions of arrivals? How did the Germans manage to kill their victims?

The "Conveyer Belt"

The Jewish crowds which surged into the gas chambers were incapable of striking back. In two thousand years they had deliberately unlearned the art of revolt. They were helpless. It is true that in a moment of extreme despair long-forgotten and long-repressed powers of combat may be recalled, to be applied in a last-minute struggle for survival. But such extreme despair depends upon very precise knowledge, and the Jewish knowledge of the danger that faced them was not that precise. Undoubtedly, many incoming Jews had a premonition that they had arrived in a killing center. Reports,

19. Karmasin to Himmler, July 29, 1942, NO-1660.

20. GG Main Division Propaganda, consolidated weekly reports from district propaganda divisions, report by Lublin division, October 3, 1942, Occ E 2-2.

21. The soap rumor appears to have been also quite persistent. According to Friedman (*Oswiecim,* p. 64), the Polish population actually boycotted soap because of the belief that human ingredients had been used in its manufacture. A document by Prof. R. Spanner, director, Anatomical Institute of the Medical Academy, Danzig, February 15, 1944 (USSR-196), contains a prescription for soap-making from fat remains (*Seifenherstellung aus Fettresten*) with recommendations for the removal of odors. The document does not specify human fat. However, on May 5, 1945, the new (Polish) mayor of Danzig, Kotus-Jankowski, testified before a session of the National Council: "In the Danzig Institute of Hygiene we discovered a soap factory in which human bodies from the Stutthof Camp near Danzig were used. We found 350 bodies there, Poles and Soviet prisoners. We found a cauldron with the remains of boiled human flesh, a box of prepared human bones, and baskets of hands and feet and human skin, with the fat removed." Quoted by Friedman, *Oswiecim,* p. 64. The soap rumor was perpetuated even after the war. Cakes of soap, allegedly made with the fat of dead Jews, have been preserved in Israel and by the YIVO Institute in New York.

rumors, and logical deductions had accomplished that. But the victims did not know the details of the killing operation, the when and the how. They did not know what to expect from step to step.[22]

Resistance, in short, depends upon two factors: the disposition and readiness to think in terms of opposition, and the knowledge of the danger of compliance. The less disposition a people has to resist, the greater must be its precise knowledge of the threat with which it is confronted. The Jews needed all the details. They had few, if any.[23] The Germans exploited Jewish submissiveness and Jewish ignorance to the utmost. The killing operation was a masterful combination of physical layout and psychological technique. The camp officials covered every step, from the train platform to the gas chamber, with precise orders, and in that way the Germans took maximum advantage of the long-conditioned Jewish reaction pattern. In addition, they supplied misleading explanations. These deceptive measures calmed the Jews sufficiently so that they obeyed once more – and for the last time.

The procedure following arrival varied from camp to camp. At Kulmhof the deportees were brought to a large mill in the nearby village of Zawadki; they were then taken in small groups by truck to the waiting vans, where their clothes were collected and where they were gassed.[24]

In Belzec the process started at the platform. Instructions were given by loudspeaker to undress. The SS-man told the Jews that they would be marched into an inhalation chamber. "Breathe deeply," he said, "it strengthens the lungs."[25] This crude deception did its work. Even when doubts were raised in the minds of the victims, their nakedness benumbed any thought of resistance. The collection of clothes thus had the effect of facilitating the killing operation. From the platform the naked columns were marched a considerable distance to the gas chambers. Near the entrance, guards received the Jews with whips to facilitate the last step. Without counting, they drove men and women into the death chamber, crushing them like sardines in the enclosed space.[26]

What the outside-undressing method meant in the winter is told by a survivor of Treblinka.[27] At temperatures of 20 to 30 degrees below zero, mothers were forced to take off their children's clothes. The "bath" hoax did not work; Höss tells us that at Treblinka the victims almost always knew that they were about to die.[28] Some of them suffered nervous shock, crying and laughing alternately. Irritated guards made use of their whips. Babies who interfered with the shaving of their mother's hair were grabbed by the legs and smashed against the wall. Upon occasion the guard handed the bloody mess to the mother.[29]

22. A survivor who had been transported to Auschwitz from Holland reports: "I refused to . . . leave any room for the thought of the gassing of the Jews, of which I could surely not have pretended ignorance. As early as 1942 I had heard rumors about the gassing of the Polish Jews. . . . Nobody had ever heard, however, *when* these gassings took place, and it was definitely not known that people were gassed immediately upon arrival." Cohen, *Human Behavior in the Concentration Camp*, p. 119.

23. Note, for instance, the Treblinka revolt, which was carried out by people who were aware of everything.

24. Bednarz, "Chelmno," pp. 111–13.

25. Affidavit by Gerstein, April 26, 1945, PS-1553.

26. *Ibid.*

27. Samuel Rajzman in *Hearings*, House Foreign Affairs Committee, 79th Cong., 1st sess., on H.R. 93, March 22–26, 1945, pp. 121–25.

28. Affidavit by Höss, April 5, 1946, PS-3836.

In Auschwitz the process was more elaborate. On the platform camp doctors (i.e., König, Mengele, Thilo, Klein) were waiting to choose employable Jews for the industrial machine. The separation of those fit for work – which we shall call positive selection – was haphazard in nature; the victims were paraded in front of the doctor, who made spot decisions by pointing with the thumb. "Right" was Auschwitz (work); "left" was Birkenau.[30]

Those who were sent right augmented the Jewish inmate population and were detailed to forced labor and, occasionally, to medical experiments. For those who had to go left the first step was the loss of their luggage. Next the men and women were separated. Then the condemned Jews were led from the platform to the Birkenau area, still unaware of what was going on. Sometimes they passed the outdoor inmate symphony orchestra, conducted by the Jewish violinist Alma Rose – an Auschwitz specialty.[31] Most of the Birkenau arrivals saw great flames belching from the chimneys and smelled the strange, sickening odor of the "bakery" (crematoriums).[32] In the halls in front of the gas chamber, which had signs reading *Wasch- und Desinfektionsraum* ("Wash- and Disinfection room"), clothes and valuables were collected. Receipts were given for the clothes. Women had their hair cut off. Then, under the eyes of guards and Jewish work parties, the deportees were crowded into the gas chambers. Many believed that they were going to take a shower,[33] but those who hesitated were driven in with rods and whips.[34]

Once there was a major incident in front of an Auschwitz gas chamber. A transport which had come in from Belsen revolted. The incident occurred when two thirds of the arrivals had already been shoved into the gas chamber. The remainder of the transport, still in the dressing room, had become suspicious. When three or four SS men entered to hasten the undressing, fighting broke out. The light cables were torn down, the SS men were overpowered, one of them was stabbed, and all of them were deprived of their weapons. As the room was plunged into complete darkness, wild shooting started between the guard at the exit door and the prisoners inside. When Höss arrived at the scene, he ordered the doors to be shut. A half-hour passed. Then, accompanied by a guard, Höss stepped into the dressing room, carrying a flashlight and pushing the prisoners into one corner. From there they were taken out singly into another room and shot.[35]

In Auschwitz selections were carried out not only on the platform, in order to pick out deportees who would be able to work, but also within the camp, to eliminate inmates too sick or too weak to work any longer. We have called the first procedure a positive selection; let us call the second a negative one. The principal agents of both were the camp doctors. Jewish inmates were constantly living in dread of the negative selections.

The usual occasion for the choosing of victims was the roll call, where everybody was present;[36] another place was the hospital;[37] and sometimes selections were carried out block by block.[38] The victims tried every subterfuge to

29. Rajzman, House *Hearings* on H.R. 93, 1945, pp. 121–25.
30. Lengyel, *Five Chimneys*, p. 10. Testimony by Auerbach (Jewish survivor), Case No. 11, tr. pp. 2512–14. Sehn, "Oswiecim," pp. 41, 77–78.
31. Lengyel, *Five Chimneys*, p. 72. Lingens-Reiner, *Prisoners of Fear*, p. 145.
32. Lengyel, *Five Chimneys*, p. 22.
33. *Ibid.*, pp. 72, 74. Sehn, "Oswiecim," p. 85.
34. *Ibid.*
35. Affidavit by Höss, March 14, 1946, NO-1210.
36. Lengyel, *Five Chimneys*, p. 40. Perl, *I Was a Doctor in Auschwitz*, p. 103.

escape. They tried to hide. Occasionally they tried to argue. A nineteen-year-old girl asked the Auschwitz women's camp commander, Hössler, to excuse her. He replied: "You have lived long enough. Come, my child, come."[39] Driven with whips between cordons of *Kapos* and guards, the naked people who had been picked out were loaded on trucks and driven to the gas chamber or to a condemned block. Before Christmas, 1944, 2000 Jewish women were packed into Block 25, which had room for 500. They were kept there for ten days. Soup cauldrons were pushed through a gap in the door by the fire guard. At the end of ten days 700 were dead. The rest were gassed.[40]

The gassing was a short process in Auschwitz. As soon as the victims were trapped in the *Badeanstalt* or *Leichenkeller,* they recognized in a flash the whole pattern of the destruction process. The imitation shower facilities did not work.[41] Outside, a central switch was thrown to turn off the lights.[42] A Red Cross car drove up with the Zyklon,[43] and a masked SS-man lifted the glass shutter over the lattice, emptying one can after another into the gas chamber. Untersturmführer Grabner, political chief of the camp, stood ready with stop watch in hand.[44] As the first pellets sublimated on the floor of the chamber, the law of the jungle took over. To escape from the rapidly rising gas, the stronger knocked down the weaker, stepping on the prostrate victims in order to prolong their life by reaching the gas-free layers of air.[45] The agony lasted for about two minutes; then the shrieking subsided, the dying men slumping over. Within four minutes everybody in the gas chamber was dead.[46] The gas was now allowed to escape, and after about a half-hour the doors were opened.[47] The bodies were found in tower-like heaps, some in sitting or half-sitting position under the doors. The corpses were pink in color, with green spots. Some had foam on their lips; others bled through the nose.[48]

In the carbon monoxide camps the agony was prolonged. We have already mentioned the episode in Belzec.[49] With no room to move – for these chambers were very small – the victims had to stand for an hour, two hours, or even three hours. One of the visitors in Belzec, Professor Pfannenstiehl, wanted to know what was going on inside. He put his ear to the wall and listened. After a while he remarked, "Just like in a synagogue."[50] Not only was the gassing operation longer in the carbon monoxide chambers; apparently it also left a bigger

37. Lingens-Reiner, *Prisoners of Fear,* pp. 64–65, 82–83, 85. Perl, *I Was a Doctor in Auschwitz,* pp. 55, 94, 108–9.

38. Perl, *I Was a Doctor in Auschwitz,* pp. 128–30.

39. Testimony by Helene Klein in Phillips, *Trial of Josef Kramer,* pp. 127–30. Witness herself was given this answer by Hössler, but she managed to hide. A survivor, Dr. Bertold Epstein, once witnessed a selection of children in which the decisive criterion was height. The children marched up to a pole at the height of 4 feet and 3.18 inches. Those who did not make it were gassed. Friedman, *Oswiecim,* p. 72.

40. Lingens-Reiner, *Prisoners of Fear,* pp. 85–86.

41. Sehn, "Oswiecim," p. 85.

42. Affidavit by Dr. Nikolae Nyiszli (survivor), October 8, 1947, NI-11710.

43. *Ibid.* Affidavit by Dr. Charles Sigismund Bendel (survivor), October 21, 1945, NI-11390.

44. Affidavit by Perry Broad (SS-man working under Grabner), December 14, 1945, NI-11397.

45. Affidavit by Nyiszli, October 8, 1947, NI-11710.

46. Affidavit by Broad, December 14, 1945, NI-11397.

47. Affidavit by Höss, April 5, 1946, PS-3868.

48. Affidavit by Nyiszli, October 8, 1947, NI-11710. Sehn, "Oswiecim," pp. 85–87.

49. See pp. 571–72.

50. Affidavit by Gerstein, April 26, 1945, PS-1553.

mess. When the gas chamber doors were opened, "the bodies were thrown out blue, wet with sweat and urine, the legs covered with excrement and menstrual blood."[51]

The disposal of the bodies – a very nasty job – was left to Jewish work parties known as *Sonderkommandos.* Membership in these work parties was brief, indeed, since the *Sonderkommandos* were periodically gassed. The first task of the body-disposal squads was to haul out the corpses from the gas chambers; for this task they were sometimes equipped with special hook-tipped poles.[52] Then the *Kommandos* had to examine the corpses, lest some jewelry be hidden in them, and extract gold teeth from the mouths.[53] Only then could the corpses be destroyed. That was a special problem.

Erasure

There were three methods of body disposal: burial, cremation in ovens, and burning in open pits.

In the early days of the killing centers, corpses were buried in mass graves in the woods.[54] Burial had several disadvantages: The earth cover tended to collapse, and as a result, odors spread for miles around and more earth had to be piled on top of the graves.[55] Secondly, the increasing pace of gassings required more and more room for graves. But most important, mass graves left a trace of the killing operation. They could be discovered.

In August, 1942, Globocnik had a number of conversations about his killing centers with visiting officials from Berlin who proffered their advice to him. In one of these discussions Ministerialrat Dr. Herbert Linden, sterilization expert of the Interior Ministry, chanced to remark: "But Mr. Globocnik, do you consider it right and proper to bury all these corpses instead of burning them? After all, a future generation might not understand the whole thing." Globocnik allegedly replied: "Gentlemen, if ever a generation should arise so slack and soft-boned that it cannot understand the importance of our work, then of course our entire National Socialism will have been in vain. I am, on the contrary, of the opinion that bronze plaques should be erected with inscriptions to show that it was we who had the courage to carry out this great and necessary task."[56]

However, Himmler thought otherwise about these matters. It will be recalled that in June, 1942, Gestapo Chief Müller had ordered Standartenführer Blobel, commander of *Einsatzkommando* 4*a,* to destroy the mass graves in the eastern occupied territories.[57] Later that summer Blobel and his "*Kommando* 1005" moved into Kulmhof to investigate what could be done with the graves there. He constructed funeral pyres and primitive

51. *Ibid.*

52. Lengyel, *Five Chimneys,* p. 75.

53. Affidavit by Dr. Morgen, July 13, 1946, SS(A)-65. Affidavit by Krumme (political prisoner), September 23, 1945, NO-1933.

54. Sehn, "'Oswiecim," p. 87.

55. Accounts by Jakob Gutman and Ing. Tymon Karwowski (survivors of Belzec) in Chersztein (ed.), *Geopfertes Volk* (Stuttgart, 1946), pp. 91–92. Accounts by various survivors of Treblinka, *ibid.,* p. 92.

56. Statement by Gerstein, May 4, 1945, *Vierteljahreshefte für Zeitgeschichte* (Stuttgart), 1953, p. 189. Also affidavit by Gerstein, April 25, 1945, PS-1553. The affidavit, which was written by Gerstein in French, differs in some details from the German statement. According to both statement and affidavit, the above conversation was told to Gerstein by Globocnik shortly after it had taken place. In Gerstein's account Hitler was present when Linden made his proposal. The Führer allegedly approved of Globocnik's reply. Prof. Rothfels has established, however, that Hitler did not leave his headquarters at that time. *Vierteljahreshefte,* p. 189. The Hitler remark is therefore a piece of fiction, added either by Gerstein or by Globocnik.

57. Affidavit by Blobel, June 18, 1947, NO-3947.

ovens, and even tried explosives.[58] In addition to these devices, Kulmhof had something special: a bone-crushing machine (*Knochenmühle*).

On July 16, 1942, the deputy chief of the *Ghettoverwaltung*, Ribbe, sent a letter to "Eldest of the Jews" Rumkowski, requesting a canvass of the Lodz ghetto for a bone crusher, "whether manually operated or motor driven." He added openly, "The *Sonderkommando Kulmhof* is interested in this crusher."[59] The ghetto apparently had no such machine, for a few months later Biebow sent to the Lodz Gestapo the papers concerning the purchase of a mill from the firm Schriever and Company in Hamburg. Biebow asked the Gestapo to keep the sales record. "For certain reasons" he himself did not wish to keep it.[60] When Höss visited Kulmhof, Blobel promised the Auschwitz commander that he would send him a mill "for solid substances."[61] However, Höss preferred to destroy his bone material with hammers.[62]

By 1942–43, the liquidation of graves in all killing centers was in progress. Auschwitz transferred the corpses to the five new crematoriums, which could burn about 12,000 bodies a day.[63] In Belzec and Sobibor the corpses were burned in open pits. Gradually, Auschwitz too shifted to pits. By 1944 the transports exceeded the crematoriums' capacity. The Hungarian Jews were being gassed at the daily rate of 10,000 and over; the Lodz Jews were killed in a few batches, 20,000 a day.[64]

The Auschwitz SS-man in charge of body disposal, Oberscharführer Moll, was working full steam. He employed four Jewish *Sonderkommandos* in four shifts, a total force of between 1500 and 2000 men.[65] Eight pits were dug, each about four by sixty yards in size.[66] On the bottom of the pits the human fat was collected and poured back into the fire with buckets to hasten the cremations.[67] Survivors report that children were sometimes tossed alive into the inferno.[68] Thc rotten remains were cleaned up once in a while with flame throwers.[69] Although the corpses burned slowly during rain or misty weather,[70] the pits were found to be the cheapest and most efficient method of body disposal. In August, 1944, when over 20,000 corpses had to be burned on some days, the open pits broke the bottleneck.[71]

Thus, the capacity for destruction was approaching the point of being unlimited. Simple as this system was, it took years to work out in constant application of administrative techniques. It took millenia in the development of Western culture.

58. Affidavit by Höss, January 11, 1947, NO-4498-B. In the end Kulmhof appears to have acquired a crematorium. Jewish Black Book Committee, *The Black Book* (New York, 1946), p. 378.

59. Ribbe to Rumkowski, July 26, 1942, *Dokumenty i Materialy*, III, 279.

60. Biebow to Fuchs, March 1, 1943, *Dokumenty i Materialy*, III, 279.

61. Report by UStuf. Dejaco (Auschwitz administration) on trip to Kulmhof, September 17, 1942, NO-4467.

62. Affidavit by Höss, March 14, 1946, NO-1210.

63. Sehn, "Oswiecim," p, 87. Lengyel, *Five Chimneys*, pp. 68–69, figures the theoretical daily maximum capacity at 17,280.

64. Affidavit by Heinrich Schuster (political prisoner), October 13, 1947, NI-11862.

65. Lengyel, *Five Chimneys*, p. 74.

66. *Ibid.*, p. 69. Sehn, "Oswiecim," p. 88.

67. Affidavit by Höss, March 14, 1946, NO-1210.

68. Friedman, *Oswiecim*, p. 72. Perl, *I Was a Doctor in Auschwitz*, pp. 50, 91. Lengyel makes reference also to the burning of gassed Jews who were still breathing. Lengyel, *Five Chimneys*, p. 73.

69. Affidavit by Werner Krumme (political prisoner), September 23, 1945, NO-1933.

70. Five to six hours. Affidavit by Höss, March 14, 1946, NO-1210.

71. Sehn, "Oswiecim," p. 89.

7 / Liquidation of the Killing Centers and the End of the Destruction Process

Although the killing centers were employed almost constantly, their existence was comparatively short. The first camp to be liquidated was Kulmhof. The *Sonderkommando* of Higher SS and Police Leader Koppe (*Kommando Hauptsturmführer Bothmann*) ceased its work there at the end of March, 1943,[1] and went to Croatia. In February, 1944, Greiser proposed Bothmann's recall in order to "reduce" the Lodz ghetto,[2] but Kulmhof had only a brief revival – and that did not affect the Lodz Jews, who were gassed in Auschwitz. The camp was finally liquidated on January 17–18, 1945. The Jewish burial *Kommando* was shot, and the buildings were set afire.[3]

In the *Generalgouvernement* the Bug camps (Treblinka, Sobibor, and Belzec) were evacuated in the fall of 1943. The Wirth *Kommando*, which had constructed these camps, was ordered to destroy them without leaving a trace.[4] Having accomplished this task, Wirth and his men were transferred as a unit to the Istrian Peninsula (Italy) to defend roads against partisans. Wirth met his death there in the spring of 1944, a bullet in his back.[5]

Lublin was evacuated more hurriedly. At the end of July, 1944, a Red Army salient overtook the camp, and with it huge stores of *Aktion Reinhardt*.[6] The discoveries made by the Soviets in Lublin were immediately publicized in the world press, to the great consternation of Generalgouverneur Frank. The frightened Frank immediately accused Koppe, the former Higher SS and Police Leader in the Wartheland, who had replaced Krüger in the *Generalgouvernement*. "Now we know," Frank said, "you cannot deny that." Koppe replied that he knew absolutely nothing about these things and that apparently it was a matter between Heinrich Himmler and the camp authorities. "But already in 1941," said Frank, "I heard of such plans, and I spoke about them." Well then, the Higher SS and Police Leader replied, that was Frank's business, and he, Koppe, could not be expected to worry about it.[7]

During the latter part of 1944 only one camp was still operating at full capacity – Auschwitz. From May through October the reduction of most of the remaining Jewish population clusters was in progress. During this

1. *Ghettoverwaltung* Litzmannstadt to Gestapo Litzmannstadt, August 4, 1943, *Dokumenty i Materialy*, III, 281–82. Gestapo Litzmannstadt to *Oberbürgermeister* there, August 14, 1943, *ibid.*

2. Greiser to Pohl, February 14, 1944, NO-519.

3. Bednarz, "Chelmno," p. 121. Two Jews survived.

4. Affidavit by Dr. Konrad Morgen, July 19, 1946, SS(A)-67.

5. *Ibid.*

6. Eyewitness report by *Christian Science Monitor* correspondent Alexander Werth, September 1, 1944, reproduced in Jewish Black Book Committee, *The Black Book*, pp. 379–81. The *Reinhardt* pileup in Lublin had already been reported by Globocnik to Himmler at the end of 1943, PS-4024.

7. Testimony by Frank, *Trial of the Major War Criminals*, XII, 19. See also summary of discussion between Frank, Bühler, and Koppe, September 15, 1944, Frank diary, PS-2233. According to this conference summary, Frank remarked that the world press was defaming Germany on account of Maydanek (Lublin). Bühler put in that nothing was known about this matter in the administration of the *Generalgouvernement*, that these camps had been established by the Higher SS and Police Leader, had been under his jurisdiction, etc. Bühler regarded a discussion of this topic in a meeting of main division chiefs as "inopportune." Frank agreed and repeated that the responsibility for these camps belonged entirely to the Higher SS and Police Leader, etc. It is not quite clear whether Frank's testimony refers to this very discussion or whether the subject was brought up twice.

period about 600,000 Jews were brought into the killing center. In May, June, and July the Hungarian Jews were gassed; in August the Lodz Jews were killed; in September and October the Slovakian and Theresienstadt transports arrived. With Roumania and Bulgaria already out of reach, transport breaking down, Jewish laborers desperately needed in war industry, and the Jews in mixed marriages exempt, the destruction process was nearing its conclusion.

In August, 1944 – the end in sight – Eichmann had to report to Himmler the total number of Jews who had been killed (the death camps kept no statistics). Eichmann's figure was 6,000,000. He estimated that 4,000,000 of the victims had died in camps and that most of the remainder had been shot by mobile units. Although that total was most probably an overestimate, Himmler was dissatisfied with the report; he was sure that the number must have been greater. Accordingly, he told Eichmann that he would send to the RSHA a statistical expert who would work out the figures more exactly.[8] While the figures were added up again, the Auschwitz death machine ground to a halt. In November, 1944, Himmler decided that for all practical purposes the Jewish question had been solved. On the twenty-fifth of that month he ordered the dismantling of the killing installations.[9]

The I. G. Farben works had already made preparations for a departure. During the summer the front was stabilized at the Vistula. However, the Red Army was across the river at two points, Opatow and Baranow, and this was enough ground for Dr. Dürrfeld, the I. G. Auschwitz chief, to make his evacuation plans.[10]

Among the inmates there was restlessness. A resistance organization had finally been set up in Auschwitz. It had links with the resistance movement outside the camp, including the London Poles and the Communists. At the end of the summer the Auschwitz resistance was alerted to fight, but at the last moment the outside underground remanded the order. There was only one group which did not obey these counter-instructions: that was the Jewish *Sonderkommando,* which faced death.[11] On the afternoon of October 7, 1944, one of the crematoriums was blown up by the *Sonderkommando.* Overpowering a few SS men, the doomed men succeeded in scattering over the entire camp, but in the pursuit which followed they were shot one by one.[12] The camp counterintelligence system quickly traced the revolt to four women in the "Union" plant who had furnished the *Sonderkommando* with explosives to do the job. The women were publicly hanged by Camp Commander Hössler.[13]

What the Jews could not accomplish with their meager resources the camp administration was to undertake itself. The remaining crematories were cleaned out by Jewish work details. A girl survivor describes that while cleaning the ovens, she got bones and ashes in her hair, her mouth, and her nostrils. Another party had to clean out eight-

8. Affidavit by Dr. Wilhelm Höttl, November 26, 1945, PS-2738. Höttl, a *Sturmbannführer* in the RSHA-VI, got the story from Eichmann, who also gave him the 6,000,000 figure – though it was a Reich secret – because Höttl, as a historian, "would be interested" in it. Eichmann later scaled down the total to 5,000,000. Affidavit by Wisliceny, November 25, 1945, *Conspiracy and Aggression,* VIII, 606–21.

9. Affidavit by Kurt Becher, March 8, 1946, PS-3762.

10. Report by Dürrfeld, February 7, 1945, NI-11956.

11. Friedman, *Oswiecim,* pp. 76–77.

12. Lengyel, *Five Chimneys,* pp. 161–63. Sehn, "Oswiecim," p. 91.

13. Affidavit by Israel Mayer Mandelbaum (survivor), October 26, 1945, NI-8187.

een-inch deposits of fat in the chimneys.[14] In November, Crematoriums II and III were dismantled, and the buildings were blown up.[15]

But Auschwitz still existed, still held on to tens of thousands of inmates, and for two months the camp awaited the Soviet offensive. During November, Soviet reinforcements were observed moving into the Baranow bridgehead. On December 16, 1944, the U.S. Army Air Force discovered the camp and dropped a few bombs. One month later, on January 12, 1945, Soviet armored columns moved out of Baranow. The general offensive had begun. By January 16 the Soviets had reached the I. G. Farben calcium mines at Kressendorf, and on the evening of the same day Soviet planes attacked the camp. During the next day German officials scurried out of the city of Katowice. That same night the rumble of artillery fire was heard in Auschwitz itself. On January 19 the German self-defense units – the *Volkssturm* – melted away.

At 4 P.M. the camp administration marched out 58,000 inmates in freezing weather. The starving and emaciated prisoners were on their death march. About 6000, too ill to move, had been left behind. During the same evening the Red Air Force appeared again; this time huge fires were started, and there were dead and wounded. By January 20, I. G. Farben destroyed its records. The next day Soviet artillery was shelling Auschwitz I. The camp officials were on their way. The evacuated killing center was on the front line. From the Wehrmacht it had originally been acquired, and to the Wehrmacht it was now returned. Within a few days the camp was occupied by the Red Army.[16]

When the Soviets moved in, twenty-nine of thirty-five storerooms had been burned down. In six of the remaining ones, the liberators found part of the camp's legacy: 368,820 men's suits, 836,255 women's coats and dresses, 5525 pairs of women's shoes, 13,964 carpets, large quantities of children's clothes, toothbrushes, false teeth, pots and pans. In abandoned railway cars hundreds of thousands of additional items of apparel were discovered, and in the tannery the Soviet investigation commission found seven tons of hair.[17]

With the killing centers gone, tens of thousands of ex-Auschwitz inmates, Hungarian deportees, and surviving forced laborers from Polish camps were dumped into the German concentration camps. Between May, 1944, and March, 1945, over 20,000 Jews poured into Buchenwald alone.[18] The influx resulted in a new labor supply for war industry.[19] However, there was not enough room in the old-established concentration camps, and hence one camp was expanded to take in the overflow. This was Bergen-Belsen, at Celle, near Hannover in the northwestern part of Germany.

Bergen-Belsen was originally a Wehrmacht camp for wounded prisoners of war. In the fall of 1943 Pohl acquired half the grounds in order to set up an internment camp there. He needed a place from which foreign nationals could be repatriated – in the

14. Irene Schwarz (survivor) in Schwarz *The Root and the Bough*, pp. 193–96.

15. Sehn, "Oswiecim," p. 91

16. The timetable is taken from the report by Dürrfeld, February 7, 1945, NI-11956. Figures of evacuated and abandoned inmates in: Friedman, *Oswiecim*, pp. 78–79. Sehn, "Oswiecim," p. 92.

17. Undated report by Soviet Extraordinary State Commission on Auschwitz (Shvernik, Trainin, the Metropolitan Nikolai, Lyssenko, and Burdenko), USSR-8.

18. Compiled from Allied report, "The Numerical Expansion of the Concentration Camp Buchenwald During the Years 1937–1945," PS-2171.

19. Buchenwald labor statistics (apparently incomplete chart), February 24, 1945, NO-1974.

words of a Foreign Office official, a camp which would not give rise to "atrocity propaganda" (*Greuelpropaganda*).[20] While Bergen-Belsen thus started out as a model camp, it could not afford an inspection by a foreign government even in its early days. Instead of calling the camp an *Internierungslager*, a legal brain had therefore designated it as an *Aufenthaltslager*, which means a camp where people stay.[21]

Toward the end of 1944, Pohl took over the second half of the camp. This transfer was simple because the Wehrmacht prisoner of war chief by that time was Obergruppenführer Berger of the SS-Main Office.[22] Some of the old Auschwitz officials now moved into Bergen-Belsen: Hauptsturmführer Kramer, former Birkenau (Auschwitz II) commander, got the top post; Dr. Fritz Klein, an Auschwitz camp doctor, became chief camp doctor of Bergen-Belsen.[23] Kramer immediately introduced the Auschwitz routine, including the lengthy roll calls.[24]

In February and March the front lines began to disintegrate. A catastrophic reaction set in. More and more soldiers surrendered, major cities were given up, labor camps and concentration camps had to be evacuated. From east and west, transports with forced laborers and camp inmates were rolling inward. The commander of Mauthausen, near Linz (Austria), received orders to take in thousands of Jews who had been building the *Süd-Ostwall* ("southeast defense line"). These Jews were marched on foot, many of them without shoes, clad in rags and full of lice.[25] From the western sector other thousands were brought on foot and by rail to Bergen-Belsen. Some of the railway cars were shunted to side rails and abandoned to Allied bombers.[26]

In Bergen-Belsen itself the camp administration broke down. As tens of thousands of new inmates were dumped into the camp – in the single week of April 4–13, 1945, the number was 28,000 –[27] the food supply was shut off, roll calls were stopped, and the starving inmates were left to their own devices. Typhus and diarrhea raged unchecked, corpses rotted in barracks and on dung heaps. Rats attacked living inmates, and the dead ones were eaten by starving prisoners.[28]

In the meantime Himmler, who had long despaired of victory, made some of the biggest concessions of his life. He permitted several thousand inmates to go to Switzerland and Sweden. He allowed Red Cross trucks to distribute food to some of the camps.[29] Finally, he ordered that the evacuation of threatened concentration camps be stopped and that they be handed over to the Allies intact. The last order was overruled by Hitler, who was incensed

20. Von Thadden to Eichmann, July 24, 1943, NG-5050. The letter dealt with the Spanish Jews in Salonika who were later sent to Bergen-Belsen.

21. The term *Aufenthaltslager Bergen-Belsen* appears in the distribution list of a Liebehenschel order dated November 10, 1943, NO-1541.

22. The history of Bergen-Belsen is described in an affidavit by former Oberst Fritz Maurer, February 13, 1947, NO-1980.

23. Testimony by Kramer and Klein, *Law Reports of Trials of War Criminals*, II, 39–41.

24. Testimony by Anita Lasker (survivor), *ibid.*, pp. 21–22.

25. Affidavit by Hans Marsalek (political prisoner), April 8, 1946, PS-3870. Marsalek interrogated the Mauthausen commander, Franz Ziereis, before the latter's death from wounds, during the night of March 22/23, 1945.

26. Perl, *I Was a Doctor in Auschwitz*, p. 166.

27. Testimony by Kramer, *Law Reports of Trials of War Criminals*, II, 40.

28. Perl, *I Was a Doctor in Auschwitz*, pp. 166–67. The author was also in Bergen-Belsen.

29. Executive Director, War Refugee Board, *Final Report*, September 15, 1945, pp. 34, 40, 43, 45, 59.

by reports that liberated Buchenwald inmates were plundering Weimar.[30] On April 24, 1945, the General Secretary of the International Red Cross, Dr. Hans Bachmann, visited Kaltenbrunner in Innsbruck; the chief of the RSHA invited him to send foodstuffs to Jews and offered to liberate a few Jews who were Allied nationals. After the conference, at dinner, Kaltenbrunner directed the conversation to politics and attempted to give a lengthy explanation of the character of National Socialist *Weltanschauung*.[31]

By the end of April the front was dissolving. Prospective war criminals looked east and west and saw Allied armies coming from both directions. The end was staring them in the face. Some committed suicide. Some gave up. Some went into hiding. In Munich on April 30, 1945, as American troops were moving into the city, the former chief of *Amtsgruppe* A of the WVHA, August Frank, walked into the office of the police president and obtained a false identification card. He was caught anyway.[32] In Austria Odilo Globocnik was arrested; he committed suicide.[33]

From Oranienburg, the WVHA headquarters, a motorcade of SS officials and their families set out for Ravensbrück and from there to Flensburg; Obersturmbannführer Höss was among them. In Flensburg he sought out Himmler, who advised him to cross into Denmark as a Wehrmacht officer. Höss managed to get false papers from Kapitän zur See Luth — he was now Franz Lang, *Bootsmaat*. But not for long. He too was caught.[34]

Himmler himself wandered about Germany, a lone, hunted figure. He was recognized and arrested, whereupon he swallowed poison.

Eichmann realized that the war was lost when he gave Sturmbannführer Höttl, the historian, a compilation of "final solution" statistics.[35] In February, 1945, Eichmann met his friend and subordinate Hauptsturmführer Wisliceny. On that occasion Eichmann said that the feeling of having killed five million Jews gave him so much satisfaction that he would jump laughingly into his grave.[36] But Eichmann did not jump; when the war ended, he disappeared without a trace. He was seized fifteen years later by Israel agents in Argentina.[37]

On the Italian-Swiss frontier, just before the collapse, the German Ambassador to Italy, Rudolf Rahn, was unable to get into Switzerland. As he stood in the snow, he thought about the Jews: "Are we now going to share the fate of this unfortunate nation? Will we be dispersed in all directions, to give of our tenacity and ability to the welfare of other nations — only to provoke their resistance? Shall Germans too be fated to be at home in every place and welcome in none?"[38]

While his followers were scurrying like rats in the narrowing grip of the Allied armies, the supreme architect of the destruction of the Jews, Adolf Hitler, remained in Berlin, where in the early morning hours of April 29, 1945,

30. Testimony by Höss, *Trial of the Major War Criminals*, vol. XI, p. 407.

31. Affidavit by Bachmann, April 11, 1946, Kaltenbrunner-5. For other discussions between International Red Cross officials and Kaltenbrunner, see: Affidavit by International Red Cross President Carl Burckhardt, April 17, 1946, Kaltenbrunner-3; and Affidavit by International Red Cross Delegate Dr. Hans E. A. Meyer, April 11, 1946, Kaltenbrunner-4.

32. Affidavit by Frank, March 29, 1946, NO-1211.

33. Interrogation of Wied, July 21, 1945, G-215.

34. Affidavit by Höss, March 14, 1946, NO-1210.

35. Affidavit by Höttl, November 26, 1945, PS-2738.

36. Affidavit by Wisliceny, November 29, 1945, *Conspiracy and Aggression*, VIII, 610.

37. "Israelis Confirm Kidnapping Nazi," *New York Times*, June 7, 1960, pp. 1–2.

38. Rahn, *Ruheloses Leben*, pp. 292–93.

he wrote his political testament. In this legacy he said:

> It is untrue that I or anyone else in Germany wanted the war in 1939. It was desired and instigated exclusively by those international statesmen who were either of Jewish descent or worked for Jewish interests. I have made too many offers for the control and limitation of armaments – which posterity will not for all time be able to disregard – for the responsibility for the outbreak of this war to be laid on me. I have, further, never wished that after the first fatal world war a second against England, or even America, should break out. Centuries will pass away, but out of the ruins of our towns and monuments the hatred against those finally responsible, whom we have to thank for everything, international Jewry and its helpers, will grow. . . .
>
> I also made it quite plain that if the nations of Europe were once more to be regarded as mere chattel to be bought and sold by these international conspirators in money and finance, then that race, Jewry, which is the real criminal of this murderous struggle, will be saddled with the responsibility. Furthermore, I left no one in doubt that this time not only would millions of children of Europe's Aryan peoples die of hunger, not only would millions of grown men suffer death, and not only would hundreds of thousands of women and children be burned and bombed to death in the cities – but also the real criminal would have to atone for his guilt, even if by more humane means.
>
> After six years of war, which in spite of all setbacks will go down one day in history as the most glorious and valiant demonstration of a nation's life purpose, I cannot forsake the city which is the capital of this Reich. As the forces are too small to make any further stand against the enemy attack at this place and our resistance is gradually being weakened by men who are as deluded as they are lacking in initiative, I should like, by remaining in this town, to share my fate with those, the millions of others, who have also taken it upon themselves to do so. Moreover, I do not wish to fall into the hands of an enemy who requires a new spectacle organized by the Jews for the amusement of their hysterical masses.
>
> I have decided therefore to remain in Berlin and there of my own free will to choose death at the moment when I believe the position of the Führer and Chancellor itself can no longer be held.[39]

39. Political testament by Hitler, April 29, 1945, PS-3569.

CONCLUSION

X / *Reflections*

1 / The Perpetrators

The Germans killed five million Jews. A process of such magnitude does not come from the void; to be brought to a conclusion in such dimensions an administrative undertaking must have meaning to its perpetrators. To Adolf Hitler and his followers the destruction of the Jews had meaning. To these men, the act was worthwhile in itself. It could not be questioned. It had to be done. When half of Europe lay conquered at Germany's feet, the uniqueness of the opportunity became compelling. The chance could not be missed. At that moment the German bureaucrat beckoned to his Faustian fate. The scope of human experience was to be widened as never before. Inevitably, at this point the German machine of destruction had to attempt the ultimate, for when a generation seeks to accomplish more than its scientific and artistic heritage has equipped it for, its path to fulfilment lies only in destruction. The process of creation is tedious and long; destruction alone is both swift and lasting.

Let us point out at once that the Germans have not been the only ones in history who have had a reason to embark upon a destructive course of action. When we examine the world historical scene, we may note that many times, in many countries, bureaucracies have launched the opening phases of a destruction process. Even now, in the Union of South Africa and elsewhere specialists are selecting, exploiting, and concentrating new victims. Very often, seemingly harmless bureaucratic activities – such as the definition of a particular group and the exclusion of its members from office – contain the seeds of administrative continuity. Potentially, these measures are steppingstones to a killing operation, but as a rule insurmountable barriers from without and within arrest and disrupt the destructive development. Externally, the opposition of the victims may bring the process to a halt; internally, administrative and psychological obstacles may bar the way. The discriminatory systems of many countries are the leftovers of such disrupted destruction processes.

The German destruction of the Jews was not interrupted. That is its crucial, decisive characteristic. At the threshold of the killing phase the flow of administrative measures continued unchecked. Technocratic and moral obstacles were overcome. An unprecedented killing operation was inaugurated, and with the beginning of this operation the Germans demonstrated once and for all how quickly even large groups, numbering in the millions, could be annihilated.

How was this done?

The Destructive Expansion

The German destructive effort may be likened to a three-dimensional structure which was expanding in all three directions. In one direction we can see an alignment of agency after agency in a machinery of destruction. In another direction we note the development, step by step, of the destruction process. In the third we can observe an attempt to set up multiple processes aimed at new victims and pointing to a destruction, group by group, of all human beings within the German reach.

Let us examine first the horizontal expansion at the base: the growth of the machinery of destruction. We know that as the process unfolded, its requirements became more complex and its fulfilment involved an ever larger number of agencies, party offices, business enterprises, and military commands. The destruction of the Jews was a total process, comparable in its diversity to a modern war, a mobilization, or a national reconstruction.

An administrative process of such range cannot be carried out by a single agency, even if it is a trained and specialized body like the Gestapo or a commissariat for Jewish affairs, for when a process cuts into every phase of human life, it must ultimately feed upon the resources of the entire organized community. That is why we found among the perpetrators the highly differentiated technicians of the armament inspectorates, the remote officials of the Postal Ministry, and – in the all-important operation of furnishing records for determination of descent – the membership of an aloof and withdrawn Christian clergy. The machinery of destruction, then, was structurally no different from organized German society as a whole; the difference was only one of function. The machinery of destruction *was* the organized community in one of its special roles.

As the apparatus expanded, its potential increased – the wider the base, the farther the reach. When the machine was finished, so was the process. But now we may ask: What determined the order of involvement? What determined the sequence of steps? We know that the bureaucracy had no master plan, no basic blueprint, no clear-cut view even of its actions. How, then, was the process regulated? What was the key to the operation?

A destruction process has an inherent pattern. There is only one way in which a scattered group can effectively be destroyed. Three steps are organic in the operation:

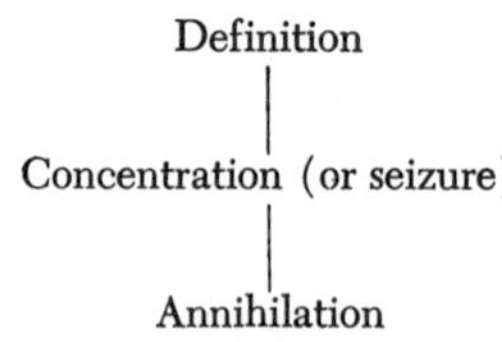

This is the invariant structure of the basic process, for no group can be killed without a concentration or seizure of the victims, and no victims can be segregated before the perpetrator knows who belongs to the group.

There are, of course, additional steps in a modern destructive undertaking. These added steps are not required for the annihilation of the victim, but they are dictated by considerations of cost and economy. These are expropriations. In the destruction of the Jews expropriatory measures were introduced after every organic step. Thus dismissals and Aryanizations came after the definition; exploitation and starvation measures followed concentration; and the confiscation of personal belongings was incidental to the killing operation. In its completed form a destruction process in a modern society will consequently be structured as shown in the accompanying chart.

The sequence of steps in a destruction process is thus determined. If there is an attempt to inflict maximum injury upon a group of people, it is therefore inevitable that a bureaucracy – no matter how decentralized its apparatus or how unplanned its activities – should push its victims through these stages.

This is a twofold destructive expansion: the growth of the machine of destruction and the development of the destruction process. Today we know of a destructive expansion upon still another plane: as the machine was thrown into high gear and as the process accelerated toward its goal, German hostility became more generalized. The Jewish target became too narrow. More targets had to be added. This development is of the utmost importance, for it casts a revealing light upon the perpetrators' fundamental aim.

If a group seeks merely the destruction of hostile institutions, the limit of its most drastic action would be drawn with the complete destruction of the bearers of the institutions. The Germans, however, did not draw the line with the destruction of Jewry. They attacked still other victims, some of whom were thought to be like Jews, some of whom were quite unlike Jews, and some of whom were Germans. The Nazi destruction process was, in short, not aimed at institutions; it was aimed at people. The Jews were only the first victims of the German bureaucracy; they were only the first caught in its path. That they should have been chosen first is not accidental – historical precedents, both administrative and conceptual, determined the selection of the people which for centuries had been the standby victim of recurring destructions. No other group could fill this role so well. None was so vulnerable. But the choice could not be confined to the Jews. Three illustrations will make this more clear.

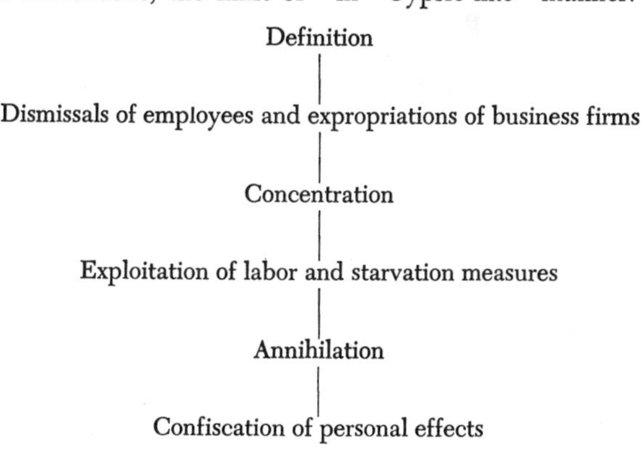

Example I. The destruction process engulfed a group which was classified as a parasitical people leading a parasitical life: the Gypsies.[1] There were 34,000 to 40,000 Gypsies in the Reich. In accordance with a Himmler directive the Criminal Police were empowered to seize all persons who looked like Gypsies or who wandered around in "Gypsie-like" manner. Those who were seized were classified as follows:

- Z — Full Gypsy (Zigeuner)
- ZM+ — Gypsy *Mischling*, predominantly Gypsy
- ZM — Gypsy *Mischling* with equal Gypsy and German "bloodshares" (*Blutsanteile*)
- ZM– — Gypsy *Mischling*, predominantly German
- NZ — Free of Gypsy blood (*Nicht Zigeuner*)

1. In the past the Gypsies had been linked to the Jews in popular belief as well as scholarly investigation. A seventeenth-century German writer, Johann Christof Wagenseil, wrote a thesis to prove that "the very first Gypsies were Jews who stemmed from Germany [*die allerersten Ziegeiner sind aus Teutschland gebürtige Juden gewesen*]." Wagenseil, *Der Meister-Singer Holdseligen Kunst* (in the introduction), printed 1697. The Nazis were not so sure of the Gypsy origins; however, it was thought that there was some racial affinity to the Jews. Two agencies were engaged in research on the subject: the *Reichszentrale zur Bekämpfung des Zigeunerwesens* and *Rassen-hygienische Forschungsstelle* of the *Reichsgesundheitsamt.* H. Küppers, "Die Beschäftigung von Zigeunern," *Reichsarbeitsblatt,* V (March 25, 1942), 177, reprinted in *Die Judenfrage* (*Vertrauliche Beilage*), April 15, 1942, pp. 30–31.

The victims in the first three categories were subjected to special wage regulations, taxes, and movement restrictions. Special provisions were made for "privileged Gypsy mixed marriages," etc.[2] In the 1940's the Germans went one step further: mobile units of the Security Police in Russia killed roving Gypsies;[3] the military commander in Serbia concentrated Gypsies and shot them;[4] and in Auschwitz several thousand Gypsies were gassed.[5]

Example II. The Poles in the territories incorporated by the Reich were in a rather precarious position. It had been planned to shove them into the *Generalgouvernement,* while the incorporated provinces to the west were to have become purely German. But that program, like the forced emigration of the Jews from Europe, collapsed. In the back of some people's minds a "territorial solution" now loomed for these Poles. On May 27, 1941, an interministerial conference took place under the chairmanship of Staatssekretär Conti of the Interior Ministry. The subject of discussion was the reduction of the Polish population in the incorporated territories. The following proposals were entertained: (1) no Pole to be allowed to marry before the age of twenty-five; (2) no permission to marry to be granted unless the marriage was economically sound; (3) a tax on illegitimate births; (4) sterilization following illegitimate birth; (5) no tax exemptions for dependants; and (6) permission to submit to abortion to be granted upon application of the expectant mother.[6]

One year later, on May 1, 1942, Gauleiter Greiser of the incorporated Wartheland reported to Himmler that the "special treatment" of 100,000 Jews in his *Gau* would be completed in another two or three months. Greiser then proceeded in the same paragraph to request Himmler's permission for the use of the experienced *(eingearbeiteten) Sonderkommando* at Kulmhof in order to liberate the *Gau* from still another danger which threatened "with each passing week to assume catastrophic proportions." Greiser had in his province 35,000 tubercular Poles. He wanted to kill them.[7] The suggestion was passed on to health expert Blome (Conti's deputy) who wanted to refer the matter to Hitler. Months passed without a decision. Finally Greiser expressed his disappointment to Himmler. "I for my person do not believe that the Führer has to be bothered with this question again, especially since he told me only during our last conversation, with reference to the Jews, that I may deal with those in any way I pleased."[8]

Example III. In consequence of an agreement between Himmler and Justice Minister Thierack, so-called asocials were transferred from prisons to concentration camps. On November 16,

2. Küppers in *Reichsarbeitsblatt,* V, 177. Circular decree by Sauckel, June 24, 1942, in *Ministerialblatt des Reichs- und Preussischen Ministeriums des Innern,* July 22, 1942, p. 1488.

3. See p. 241n.

4. See pp. 438, 439–40, 441n., 442.

5. Lengyel, *Five Chimneys,* pp. 68, 112–13, 121. The Gypsies had been brought to Auschwitz from the Reich-Protektorat area, Poland, France, and Hungary. A Gypsy transport was also brought to Lodz. See pp. 142–44. Gypsies were concentrated in a number of camps. Note reference to Lackenbach (Austria) in letter by Deputy Gauleiter Gerland of Niederdonau to Himmler, August 24, 1942, NO-39. In the Orleans area (France), Jaregeau had 600 Gypsies. Oberstabsarzt Sonntag to *Chef, Militärbezirk A* (Glt. von der Lippe), October 2, 1942, NOKW-1516. In general, see also Dora E. Yates, "Hitler and the Gypsies – The Fate of Europe's Oldest Aryans," *Commentary,* November, 1949, pp. 455–59.

6. Reich Chancellery memorandum, May 27, 1941, NG-844.

7. Greiser to Himmler, May 1, 1942, NO-246. Greiser was also *Reichsstatthalter*.

8. Greiser to Himmler, November 21, 1942, NO-249. The Poles were ultimately spared.

1944, after the transfer of the "asocials" had largely been completed, the judiciary met to discuss a weird subject: ugliness. The phrase on the agenda was "gallery of outwardly asocial prisoners [*Museum äusserlich asozialer Gefangener*]." The summary of that conference states:

> During various visits to the penitentiaries, prisoners have always been observed who – because of their bodily characteristics – hardly deserve the designation human [*Mensch*]; they look like miscarriages of hell [*Missgeburten der Hölle*]. Such prisoners should be photographed. It is planned that they too shall be eliminated [*auszuschalten*]. Crime and sentence are irrelevant. Only such photographs should be submitted which clearly show the deformity.[9]

The Obstacles

We have talked so far about a destructive expansion which is unparalleled in history. An entire bureaucratic network was involved in these operations; a destruction process was brought to its final conclusion; and a veritable target series was established in a first attempt at unlimited destruction. The German bureaucracy, however, did not always move with unencumbered ease. From time to time barriers appeared on the horizon and caused momentary pauses. Most of these stoppages were occasioned by those ordinary difficulties which are encountered by every bureaucracy in every administrative operation: procurement difficulties, shortages, mixups, misunderstandings, and all the other annoyances of the daily bureaucratic process. We shall not be concerned with these occurrences here. But some of the hesitations and interruptions were the products of extraordinary administrative and psychological obstacles. These blocks were peculiar to the destruction process alone, and they must therefore claim our special attention.

Administrative Problems. – The destruction of the Jews was not a gainful operation. It imposed a strain upon the administrative machine and its facilities. In a wider sense it became a burden which rested upon Germany as a whole.

One of the most striking facts about the German apparatus was the sparseness of its personnel, particularly in those regions outside the Reich where most of the victims had to be destroyed. Moreover, that limited manpower was preoccupied with a bewildering variety of administrative undertakings; upon close examination the machinery of destruction turns out to have been a loose organization of part-timers. There were at most a handful of bureaucrats who could devote all their time to anti-Jewish activities. There were the "experts" on Jewish affairs in the ministries, the mobile killing units of the RSHA, the commanders of the killing centers. But even an expert like Eichmann had two jobs: the deportation of Jews and the resettlement of ethnic Germans; the mobile killing units had to shoot Jews, Gypsies, commissars, and partisans alike; while a camp commander like Höss was host to an industrial concentration next to his gas chambers.

In the totality of the administrative process the destruction of the Jews presented itself as an additional task to a bureaucratic machine already overburdened and strained to the utmost by war preparations and by war itself. To grasp this fact, we need think only of the railroads or of the armies which moved east into Russia.[10] The German

9. *Generalstaatsanwalt* (chief prosecutor), *Oberlandesgericht Bamberg,* to Generalstaatsanwalt Helm in Munich, November 29, 1944, enclosing summary of conference held under the chairmanship of Ministerialdirektor Engert on November 16, 1944, NG-1546.

10. "In the Reich only the most vitally important transports are run." Präsident Emrich in traffic conference held on December

administration, however, was not deterred by the pressures of other assignments; it never resorted to pretenses, like the Italians, it never took token measures, like the Hungarians, it never procrastinated, like the Bulgarians. The German bureaucrats worked efficiently, in haste, and with a sense of urgency. Unlike their collaborators, the Germans never did the minimum. They always did the maximum.

Indeed, there were moments when an agency's eagerness to participate in the decision-making led to bureaucratic competition and rivalry. Such a contest was in the offing when Unterstaatssekretär Luther concluded an agreement with the RSHA to preserve the Foreign Office's power to negotiate with Axis satellites in Jewish matters.[11] Again, within the SS itself, a jealous struggle was waged between two technocrats of destruction, Obersturmbannführer Höss and Kriminalkommissar Wirth, over the replacement of carbon monoxide with Zyklon B in the killing centers.[12] We have observed this bureaucratic warfare also in the attempt of the judiciary to conserve its jurisdiction in Jewish affairs. When that attempt was finally given up, Justice Minister Thierack wrote to his friend Bormann:

> I intend to turn over criminal jurisdiction against Poles, Russians, Jews, and Gypsies to the *Reichsführer-SS*. In doing so, I base myself on the principle that the administration of justice can make only a small contribution to the extermination of these peoples.[13]

This letter reveals an almost melancholy tone. The judiciary had done its utmost; it was no longer needed.

The bureaucrats did not spare themselves; neither could they spare the economy. Just how expensive was the destruction of the Jews? What were the effects of this cost? Table 88 reveals the financial aspects of the operations.[14]

Upon analysis of Table 88, we observe two important trends: with the progress of the destruction process, gains declined; on the other hand, expenditures tended to increase. Looking at the table horizontally, we thereupon discover that in the preliminary phase (above the dividing line) financial gains, public or private, far outweighed expenses, but that in the killing phase (below the dividing line) receipts no longer balanced losses. Let us examine the cost of this killing phase a little more closely.

Receipts (last three items in the left column) were meager. This is explained by the fact that in occupied and satellite territories the Germans did not engage in extensive confiscations. In the interest of a "final solution" in these areas the German perpetrators had to leave most of the Jewish property to their non-German collaborators.[15]

Losses, however, were high. How do we explain those figures? Direct expenditures (here estimated in the hundreds of millions) were comparatively small. They represent a remarkable attempt at economizing. We have seen how sparingly personnel were used, both in the killing units and in the killing centers. The deportation trains (*Sonderzüge*) were made up of freight cars, and several thousand Jews could be transported in one train. The killing centers were extraordinarily cheap, notwithstanding Speer's complaint that

9, 1942, in Paris; summary, dated December 12, 1942, in Wi/I 2.10. As for the military in Russia, see chapter on mobile killing operations, *passim*.

11. See pp. 289–90.

12. See pp. 571–72.

13. See pp. 295–96.

14. Aryanization differentials, Reich property tax, and confiscations under the 11th Ordinance listed in letter from *Restverwaltung des ehemaligen Reichsfinanzministeriums* to Allied Control Commission, November 14, 1946, NG-4906. For other statistics, see this book, *passim*.

15. See p. 354.

Himmler was using scarce building materials too extravagantly. The installations were built with camp labor, and the inmates were housed in huge barracks with no light and no modern toilet facilities. The investment in gas chambers and ovens was not very great, either. Why all this economizing? The answer is simple. In all these cases savings did not reduce efficiency; they might even have promoted the smooth implementation of bureaucratic measures. The destruction process was oriented not to cost but to efficiency. Not money but time was of the essence.

This point is even more sharply illustrated when we examine the next two items. The razing of the Warsaw ghetto ruins after the battle of April–May, 1943, was a Himmler project for which the Finance Ministry received a bill in the amount of 150,000,000 reichsmark.[16] Himmler felt that a park should obliterate the site of the ghetto, lest Warsaw grow back to its former size.

The last item in the expense column – the loss of Jewish war production – is a glaring illustration of the triumph of speed over cost. Himmler never made any pretense that for him the destruction of the Jews had priority even over armaments. When he was overwhelmed with arguments in favor of the war effort, Himmler had only this reply: "The argument of war production, which nowadays in Germany is the favorite reason for opposing anything at all, I do not recognize in the

TABLE 88 / *The Cost of Destroying the Jews*

RECEIPTS, GAINS, SAVINGS	EXPENDITURES AND LOSSES
Net profits to industry from purchase and liquidations of Jewish enterprises: ca. one-fourth to one-half of value of Jewish business property in Reich-Protektorat area. These profits probably amounted to billions of reichsmark.	Loss of markets abroad in consequence of buyers' resistance and boycott: no estimates.
Aryanization differentials paid by companies to Reich: 49,000,000 reichsmark.	
Reich Flight Tax: 900,000,000 reichsmark.	
Reich Property Tax (fine): 1,127,000,000 reichsmark.	
Wage differentials and other industry savings as result of employment of Jewish labor: probably in tens of millions.	
Wage differentials, special income tax, and other wage savings accruing to Reich: probably in tens of millions.	Direct expenditures for *a.* personnel and overhead (prior to killing phase)
Confiscations under the eleventh ordinance (securities and bonds): 186,000,000 reichsmark.	*b.* personnel and overhead (in killing operations) *c.* Transport *d.* Camp installations (in hundreds of millions)
Confiscations under the eleventh ordinance and other measures (not including securities and bonds): 592,000,000 reichsmark.	Extraordinary direct expense for razing of Warsaw ghetto: 150,000,000 reichsmark.
Miscellaneous confiscations not booked by Finance Ministry in above figures: possibly hundreds of millions.	Loss of Jewish production in consequence of the "final solution": ca. 3,000,000,000 reichsmark.

first place."[17] In the measured language of the Ministry for Eastern Occupied Territories, the priority of the destruction process was phrased as follows: "Economic questions should not be considered in the solution of the Jewish question."[18] Let us now explore the consequences entailed by the loss of the Jewish labor force.

The war economy lost the aggregate value of those products which two or three million workers in Germany and in the occupied countries could produce in two or three years. This loss was total because the destruction process had removed the Jewish labor force without replacement from going concerns. This does not imply that in individual plants or warehouses Jews were not replaced; it does mean that in the total production picture the loss of Jewish labor could never be made up, in spite of all the labor recruitment drives by Plenipotentiary for Labor Allocation Sauckel. We know that by 1944 his requirements for more workers had reached a total of not less than 4,000,000.

What was the value of that lost production? In military terms the loss cannot be calculated, but in monetary terms it is possible to make some estimates. Economy Minister Funk estimated after the war that the total value of war production in Germany, from 1941 through 1943, was 260 billion reichsmark. The amount produced in the occupied territories he estimated (for the same period) at 90 billion marks.[19] If we consider that in Germany about 0.5 per cent of the labor force engaged in war production was Jewish, and that in the occupied territories about 2 per cent were Jews, the value of Jewish war production lost is approximately 3 billion reichsmark.

16. See p. 327.

17. In his pronouncements, *passim*.

18. See p. 247.

19. Testimony by Funk, *Trial of the Major War Criminals,* XIII, 129–30.

This figure swamps the entire income derived from the destruction process after the "final solution" had started, and it proves that whenever it was not efficient to be thrifty, the implementation of the operations could approach extravagance.

Psychological Problems.—The most important problems of the destruction process were not administrative but psychological. The very conception of the drastic "final solution" was dependent on the ability of the perpetrators to cope with weighty psychological obstacles and impediments. The psychological blocks differed from the administrative difficulties in one important respect: an administrative problem could be solved and eliminated; the psychological difficulties had to be dealt with continuously. They were held in check but never removed. Commanders in the field were ever watchful for symptoms of psychological disintegration. In the fall of 1941 Higher SS and Police Leader Russia Center von dem Bach shook Himmler with the remark:

> Look at the eyes of the men of this *Kommando,* how deeply shaken they are. These men are finished [*fertig*] for the rest of their lives. What kind of followers are we training here? Either neurotics or savages [*Entweder Nervenkranke oder Rohlinge*]![20]

Von dem Bach was not only an important participant in killing operations. He was also an acute observer. With this remark he pointed to the basic psychological problem of the German bureaucracy: the German administration had to make determined efforts to prevent the breakdown of its men into either "savages" or "neurotics." That was essentially a dual task – one part disciplinary, the other moral.

The disciplinary problem was understood clearly. The bureaucrats were

20. See p. 218.

fully aware of the dangers of plundering, torture, orgies, and atrocities. Such behavior was first of all wasteful from an administrative point of view, for the destruction process was an organized undertaking which had room only for organized tasks. Moreover, "excesses" attracted attention to aspects of the destruction process which had to remain secret. Such were the activities of Brigadeführer Dirlewanger, whose rumored attempts to make human soap drew the attention of the public to the killing centers.

Indeed, atrocities could bring the entire "noble" work into disrepute. What was wasteful administratively was dangerous psychologically. Loose behavior was an abuse of the machine, and a debauched administration could disintegrate. That was why the German administration had a certain preference for quick, blow-type *(schlagartige)* action. Maximum destructive effect was to be achieved with minimum destructive effort. The personnel of the machinery of destruction were not supposed to look to the right or to the left; they were not allowed to have either personal motives or personal gains. An elaborate discipline was introduced into the machine of destruction.

The first and most important rule of conduct of this discipline was the principle that all Jewish property belonged to the Reich. So far as Himmler was concerned, the enforcement of that rule was a success. In 1943 he told his Gruppenführer:

> The riches which they [the Jews] owned we have taken from them. I have given strict orders, which Obergruppenführer Pohl has carried out, that this wealth should naturally [*selbstverständlich*] be delivered to the Reich. We have taken nothing. Individuals who have transgressed are being punished in accordance with an order which I gave in the beginning and which threatened that anyone who takes just one mark is a condemned man. A number of SS men – not many – have transgressed against that order, and they will be condemned to death mercilessly. We had the moral right vis-à-vis *our* people to annihilate [*umzubringen*] *this* people which wanted to annihilate us. But we have no right to take a single fur, a single watch, a single mark, a single cigarette, or anything whatever. We don't want in the end, just because we have exterminated a germ, to be infected by that germ and die from it. I will not stand by while a slight infection forms. Whenever such an infected spot appears, we will burn it out. But on the whole we can say that we have fulfilled this heavy task with love for our people, and we have not been damaged in the innermost of our being, our soul, our character.[21]

There is, of course, considerable evidence that more than a few individuals "transgressed" against the discipline of the destruction process. No estimate can be formed of the extent to which transport *Kommandos,* killing units, the ghetto and killing center personnel, and even *Kommando* 1005 – the grave-destruction *Kommando* – filled their pockets with the belongings of the dead. Moreover, we should note that Himmler's rule dealt only with *unauthorized* takings by participating personnel in the field. It did not deal with *authorized* distributions to the participants.

The essense of corruption is to reward people on the basis of their proximity to the loot – in a corrupt system, the tax collectors become rich. In the course of the destruction process many distributions were made to the closest participants. We need remind ourselves only of the Finance Ministry's appropriation of fine furniture during the deportations of Jews from Germany, the distribution of better apartments to civil servants, the cuts taken by the railways, SS and Police, and

21. Speech by Himmler at *Gruppenführer* meeting at Poznan, October 4, 1943, PS-1919.

postal service in the allocation of the furniture of the Dutch, Belgian, and French Jews, the "gifts" of watches and "Christmas presents" to SS-men and their families. The destruction process had its own built-in corruption. Only unauthorized corruption was forbidden.

The second way in which the Germans sought to avoid damage to "the soul" was in the prohibition of unauthorized killings. A sharp line was drawn between killings pursuant to order and killings induced by desire. In the former case a man was thought to have overcome the "weaknesses" of "Christian morality;"[22] in the latter case he was overcome by his baseness. That was why in the occupied USSR both the army and the civil administration sought to restrain their personnel from joining the shooting parties on the killing sites.

Perhaps the best illustration of the official attitude is to be found in an advisory opinion by a judge on Himmler's Personal Staff, Obersturmbannführer Bender. Bender dealt with procedure to be followed in the case of unauthorized killings of Jews by SS personnel. He concluded that if purely political motives prompted the killing, if the act was an expression of idealism, no punishment was necessary unless the maintenance of order required disciplinary action or prosecution. However, if selfish, sadistic, or sexual motives were found, punishment was to be imposed for murder or for manslaughter, in accordance with the facts.[23]

The German disciplinary system is most discernible in the mode of the killing operation. At the conclusion of the destruction process Hitler remarked in his testament that the Jewish "criminals" had "atoned" for their "guilt" by "humane means."[24] The "humaneness" of the destruction process was an important factor in its success. It must be emphasized, of course, that this "humaneness" was evolved not for the benefit of the victims but for the welfare of the perpetrators. Time and again, attempts were made to reduce opportunities for "excesses" and *Schweinereien* of all sorts. Much research was expended for the development of devices and methods which arrested propensities for uncontrolled behavior and which lightened, at the same time, the crushing psychological burden on the killers. The construction of gas vans and of gas chambers, the employment of Ukrainian, Lithuanian, and Latvian auxiliaries to kill Jewish women and children, the use of Jews for the burial and burning of bodies – all these were efforts in the same direction. Efficiency was the real aim of all this "humaneness."

So far as Himmler was concerned, his SS and Police had weathered the destruction process. In October, 1943, when he addressed his top commanders, he said to them:

> Most of you know what it means when 100 corpses lie there, or when 500 corpses lie there, or when 1000 corpses lie there. To have gone through this and – apart from a few exceptions caused by human weakness – to have remained decent, that has made us great. That is a page of glory in our history which has never been written and which is never to be written. . . .[25]

However, the descent into savagery was not nearly so important a factor in the destruction process as the feeling of growing uneasiness that pervaded the bureaucracy from the lowest strata to the highest. That uneasiness was the product of moral scruples – the lingering effect of two thousand years

22. See p. 603.

23. Memorandum by OStubaf. Bender, October 22, 1942, NO-1744.

24. See p. 635.

25. Himmler speech, October 4, 1943, PS-1919.

of Western morality and ethics. A Western bureaucracy had never before faced such a chasm between moral precepts and administrative action; an administrative machine had never been burdened with such a drastic task. In a sense, the task of destroying the Jews put the German bureaucracy to a supreme test. The German technocrats solved also that problem and passed also this test.

To grasp the full significance of what these men did, we have to understand that we are not dealing with individuals who had their own separate moral standards. The bureaucrats who were drawn into the destruction process were not different in their moral makeup from the rest of the population. The German perpetrator was not a special kind of German. What we have to say here about his morality applies not to him specially but to Germany as a whole. How do we know this?

We know that the very nature of administrative planning, of the jurisdictional structure, and of the budgetary system precluded the special selection and special training of personnel. Even the killing units and the killing centers did not obtain professional killers. Every lawyer in the RSHA was presumed to be suitable for leadership in the mobile killing units; every finance expert of the WVHA was considered a natural choice for service in a death camp. In other words, all necessary operations were accomplished with whatever personnel were at hand. However one may wish to draw the line of active participation, the machinery of destruction was a remarkable cross-section of the German population. Every profession, every skill, and every social status was represented in it. We know that in a totalitarian state the formation of an opposition movement outside the bureaucracy is next to impossible; however, if there is very serious opposition in the population, if there are insurmountable psychological obstacles to a course of action, such impediments reveal themselves *within* the bureaucratic apparatus. We know what such barriers will do, for they emerged clearly in the Italian Fascist state. Again and again the Italian generals and consuls, prefects and police inspectors, refused to co-operate in the deportations. The destruction process in Italy and the Italian-controlled areas was carried out against unremitting Italian opposition. No such opposition is to be found in the German area. No obstruction stopped the German machine of destruction. No moral problem proved insurmountable. When all participating personnel were put to the test, there were very few lingerers and almost no deserters. The old moral order did not break through anywhere along the line. That is a phenomenon of the greatest magnitude.

Just how did the German bureaucracy overcome its moral scruples? We know that it was something of a struggle; we know also that the struggle was won only with the employment of the most complex psychological tools fashioned during centuries of German cultural development. Fundamentally, the psychological defense arsenal consisted of two parts: the repressive mechanism and the system of rationalizations.

First of all, the bureaucracy wanted to hide its deeds, it wanted to conceal the destruction process, not only from all outsiders but also from the censuring gaze of its own conscience. The repression proceeded through five stages. The first was secrecy.

As we might expect, every effort was made to hide the ultimate aim of the destruction process from Axis partners and from the Jews. Inquiries such as Hungarian Prime Minister Kallay put to the Foreign Office about the disappearance of European Jewry,[26] or questions which foreign journalists in Kiev asked army authorities about mass shootings,[27] could obviously not be answered. Rumors which could spread like wildfire had to be smothered. "Plastic" evidence, such as "souvenir" photographs of killings, mass graves, and the wounded Jews who had risen from their graves, had to be destroyed.[28] All these efforts were an administrative necessity. However, beyond that, they were necessary also for psychological reasons. The extreme care with which the machinery of destruction, and particularly the SS and Police, guarded the secrecy of its operations betrayed uncertainty, worry, and anxiety. In May, 1944, the RSHA complained to the Justice Ministry that the *Landgericht* in Vienna was making too many inquiries to elicit the whereabouts of deported Jews for the purpose of rendering decisions in proceedings involving proof of descent (*Abstammungsverfahren*). The *Landgericht* had been told repeatedly, said the complaint, that no information could be given about deportees, but the court had persisted in making inquiries. Quite apart from the fact that the "Jews" (that is, the persons seeking clarification of their status) had been given plenty of time to clear questions about their descent, these people were only trying to hide their ancestry, anyway, in order to remove themselves from the effect of "Security Police measures" (*sicherheitspolizeiliche Massnahmen*). For these reasons, and because of more pressing war work, the Security Police could not furnish replies, etc. etc.[29]

Thus the first stage in the repression was to shut off the supply of information from all those who did not have to know it. Whoever did not participate was not supposed to know. The second stage was to make sure that whoever knew would participate.

There was nothing so irksome as the realization that someone was watching over one's shoulder, that someone would be free to talk and accuse because he was not himself involved. This fear was the origin of what Leo Alexander has called the "blood kit,"[30] the irresistible force that drew every official "observer" into the destruction process. The "blood kit" explains why so many office chiefs of the RSHA were assigned to mobile killing units and why staff officers with the killing units were ordered to participate in the killing operations.[31] The "blood kit" also explains why Unterstaatssekretär Luther of the Foreign Office's *Abteilung Deutschland* insisted that the Political Division countersign all instructions to embassies and legations for the deportation of Jews.[32] Finally, the "blood kit" explains the significant words spoken by Generalgouverneur Frank at the conclusion of a police conference in Krakow:

> We want to remember that we are, all of us assembled here, on Mr. Roosevelt's war-criminals list. I have the honor of occupying first place on that list. We are therefore, so to speak, accomplices in a world-historical sense.[33]

The third stage in the process of repression was the prohibition of criticism. Public protests by outsiders were extremely rare; the criticisms were expressed, if at all, in mutterings on the rumor circuit. It is sometimes hard, even to distinguish between expressions of sensationalism and real criticism, for

26. See p. 522.
27. See p. 212.
28. See pp. 246, 249–50.
29. RSHA to Justice Ministry, May 3, 1944, NG-900.

30. Leo Alexander, "War Crimes and Their Motivation," *Journal of Criminal Law and Criminology*, XXXIX (September–October, 1948), 298–326.
31. See p. 215.
32. See p. 350.
33. See p. 332.

often the two were mixed. One example of such mixed reactions is to be found in the circulation of rumors in Germany about the mobile killing operations in Russia. The Party Chancellery, in confidential instructions to its regional machinery, attempted to combat these rumors. Most of the reports, the chancellery stated, were "distorted" and "exaggerated." "It is conceivable," the circular continued, "that not all of our people – especially people who have no conception of the Bolshevik terror – can understand sufficiently the necessity for these measures." In their very nature, "these problems," which were sometimes "very difficult," could be solved "in the interest of the security of our people" only with "ruthless severity."[34]

In the German documents we found a singular example of a genuine public protest: A Catholic priest named Lichtenberg, prayed for the Jews in open services at St. Hedwig's Cathedral in Berlin. He prayed not only for baptized Jews but for all the Jewish victims. Placed in custody, he pronounced himself a foe of National Socialism and declared that he wanted to share the fate of the Jews in the East, in order to pray for them there. Released from prison, Lichtenberg died on the way to a concentration camp.[35]

Within the bureaucracy we find a few more examples of criticism, though again it was very seldom outspoken protest. Of course, it was permissible to criticize measures from the viewpoint of German welfare. We have seen the unbelievable amount of discussion about the *Mischlinge* and Jews in mixed marriages – that is, persons against whom action could not be taken without hurting Germans. Again, we have noted the voluminous correspondence, dealing with the adverse effects of anti-Jewish measures on the war effort. Once in a while it was permissible even to mention the harmful psychological effects of killings on the perpetrators, but a sharp line was drawn between such criticisms and the implication that the destruction process itself was intrinsically wrong.

A Director of the Reichsbank, Wilhelm, overstepped the line when he cautioned his chief, Puhl, not to visit concentration camps and when he announced his refusal to participate in the distribution of Jewish belongings with the words: "The Reichsbank is not a dealer in second-hand goods."[36] Generalkommissar Kube of White Russia violated the injunction against moral condemnations by making accusations against the KdS in White Russia, Strauch. Kube implied that Jews – at least those Jews who had come from Germany ("from our own cultural level") – were human beings and that Strauch and his killers were maniacs and sadists who had satisfied their sexual lust during shootings. Strauch did not take kindly to such criticism. In a complaint against Kube he wrote that "it was regrettable that we, in addition to having to perform this nasty job, were also made the target of mudslinging."[37] In the Interior Ministry the expert on Jewish affairs, Ministrialrat Lösener, was disturbed by reports of killings which had occurred in Riga; he began to put questions to his chief, Staatssekretär Stuckart, and requested a transfer. After a while a colleague asked Lösener to stop pestering the Staatssekretär, for Stuckart's position was difficult enough.[38]

On the highest level, the following story was told by Gauleiter Schirach's secretary: While Schirach's wife was staying in a hotel in Amsterdam, she watched a roundup of Jews at night.

34. See p. 300.
35. See pp. 299–300.
36. See p. 617.
37. See p. 253.
38. Affidavit by Lösener, February 24, 1948, NG-1944-A.

The Jewish women "screamed terribly." Mrs. Schirach's nerves were so much on edge that she decided to tell her husband about it. The *Gauleiter* advised her to tell the story to Hitler himself, since the Führer would not tolerate such "abuses" (*Missstände*). During their next visit to Hitler Mrs. Schirach told the story. Hitler listened "ungraciously," interrupting several times and telling her not to be so sentimental. Everyone present found the exchange between Hitler and Mrs. Schirach "very embarrassing" (*äusserst peinlich*). The conversation broke down, no one spoke, and Mr. and Mrs. Schirach left the room. The Schirachs departed the next day without saying good-bye.[39]

In its fourth stage the repressive mechanism eliminated the destruction process as a subject of social conversation. Among the closest participants it was considered bad form to talk about the killings. This is what Himmler had to say on the subject in his speech of October 4, 1943:

> I want to mention here very candidly a particularly difficult chapter. Among us it should be mentioned once, quite openly, but in public we will never talk about it. Just as little as we hesitated on June 30, 1934, to do our duty and to put comrades who had transgressed [the brown shirts] to the wall, so little have we talked about it and will ever talk about it. It was with us, thank God, an inborn gift of tactfulness, that we have never conversed about this matter, never spoken about it. Every one of us was horrified, and yet every one of us knew that we would do it again if it were ordered and if it were necessary.
>
> I am referring to the evacuation of the Jews, to the extermination of the Jewish people. . . .[40]

This, then, was the reason why that particular "page of glory" was never to be written. There are some things that can be done only so long as they are not discussed, for once they are discussed they can no longer be done.

We know, of course, that among those who were not quite so close to the killing operations the sensations of the destruction process were irresistible. The rumor network was spread all over Axis Europe. One Foreign Office official stationed in Rome mentions that he discussed details of the killings with at least thirty of his colleagues.[41] But the urge to talk was not so deep in men who were heavily involved in the destruction process. Höss, the Auschwitz commander, says that he never spoke about his job even to his wife. She found out about what he was doing because of an inadvertent remark by a family friend, Gauleiter Bracht.[42] The Treblinka guard, Hirtreiter, never spoke of his task at all.[43]

The fifth and final stage of the repressing process was to omit mention of "killings" or "killing installations" even in the secret correspondence in which such operations had to be reported. The reader of these reports is immediately struck by their camouflage vocabulary: *Endlösung der Judenfrage* ("final solution of the Jewish question"), *Lösungsmöglichkeiten* ("solution possibilities"), *Sonderbehandlung* (or SB—"special treatment"), *Evakuierung* ("evacuation"), *Aussiedlung* (same), *Umsiedlung* (same), *Spezialeinrichtungen* ("special installations"), *durchgeschleusst* ("dragged through"), and many others.

There is one exchange of correspond-

39. Affidavit by Maria Höpken, January 19, 1946, Schirach-3. Affiant was not a witness but claims that the identical story was told to her on separate occasions by Schirach and his wife.

40. Himmler speech, October 4, 1943, PS-1919.

41. Affidavit by Vortragender Legationsrat Dr. Ulrich Dörtenbach, May 13, 1947, NG-1535.

42. See pp. 621–22.

43. See p. 622.

ence in which knowing officials carried the game of pretense to the point of distortion and outright falsification: In 1943 the Foreign Office inquired whether it would be possible to exchange 30,000 Baltic and White Russian Jews for Reich Germans in Allied countries. The Foreign Office representative in Riga replied that he had discussed the matter with the Security Police commander in charge; the BdS had felt that the "interned" Jews could not be sent away for "weighty Security Police reasons." As was known (*bekanntlich*), a large number of Jews had been "done away with" in "spontaneous actions." In some places these actions had resulted in "almost total extermination" (*fast völlige Ausmerzung*). A removal of the remaining Jews would therefore give rise to "anti-German atrocity propaganda," etc.[44] Thus even in 1943 an internal secret letter could claim that the Jews in the East had all been victims of pogroms.

A particularly revealing example of disassociation may also be found in a private letter written by a sergeant of the Rural Police to a police general. The sergeant, at the head of 23 German gendarmes and 500 Ukrainian auxiliary policemen, had killed masses of Jews in the Kamenets Podolski area. These are excerpts from his letter.

> Naturally we are cleaning up considerably, especially among the Jews. . . .
>
> I have a cozy apartment in a former children's asylum. One bedroom and a living room with all of the accessories. Practically nothing is missing. Naturally, the wife and the children. You will understand me. My Dieter and the little Liese write often, after their fashion. One could weep sometimes. It is not good to be a friend of children as I was. I hope that the war, and with it the time of service in the East, soon ends.[45]

The process of repression was continuous, but it was never completed. The killing of the Jews could not be hidden completely, either from the outside world or from the inner self; therefore the bureaucracy was not spared an open encounter with its conscience. It had to pit argument against argument and philosophy against philosophy. Laboriously, and with great effort, the bureaucracy had to justify its activities.

Psychological justification is called rationalization. The Germans employed two kinds of rationalizations. The first was an attempt to justify the destruction process as a whole; it was designed to explain why the Jews had to be destroyed. It was focused on the Jew. The other explanations served only to justify individual participation in the destruction process: a signature on a piece of paper or the squeeze of a trigger. They were focused entirely on the perpetrator. Let us consider first the broad rationalizations which encompassed the whole destruction process. In the formation of these justifications old conceptions about the Jew – reinforced and expanded by new propaganda – played an important role. Precisely how did German propaganda function in this process?

The Germans had two kinds of propaganda. One was designed to produce action. It exhorted people to do things, for instance, to come to a mass meeting, to boycott Jewish goods, or to kill Jews. This type of propaganda – the command propaganda – does not concern us here since it was confined, on the whole, to the incitement of boycotts and pogroms, the so-called *Einzelaktionen*. But the Germans also engaged in a campaign which consisted of a series of statements, for example, allegations which implied that the Jew was bad. This propaganda

44. Windecker to Foreign Office, April 5, 1943, NG-2652.

45. Meister der Gendarmerie Fritz Jacob to OGruf. Rudolf Querner, May 5, 1942, NO-5654.

had a very important place in the arsenal of psychological defense mechanisms.

The function of declarative propaganda is to act as a storehouse which may be drawn upon according to need. The statement "the Jew is bad" is taken from the storehouse and is converted in the perpetrator's mind into a complete rationalization: "I kill the Jew because the Jew is bad." To understand the function of this propaganda is to realize why it was continued until the very end of the war, and, surreptitiously, even after the end of the war. Propaganda was needed to combat doubts and guilt feelings wherever they arose — whether inside or outside the bureaucracy — and whenever they arose — before or after the perpetration of the acts.

In fact, we find that in April, 1943, after the deportations of the Jews from the Reich had largely been completed, the press was ordered to deal with the Jewish question continuously and without letup.[46] In order to build up a storehouse the propaganda had to be turned out on a huge scale. "Research institutes" were formed,[47] doctoral dissertations were written,[48] and volumes of propaganda literature were printed by every conceivable agency. At times this activity even led to bureaucratic competition. Thus Unterstaatssekretär Luther of the Foreign Office had to assure Obergruppenführer Berger of the SS-Main Office that the Foreign Office's pamphlet *Das russische Tor ist aufgestossen* ("*The Russian Gate is Thrown Open*") in no way competed with Berger's masterpiece *Der Untermensch* ("*The Subhuman*").[49]

What did all this propaganda accomplish? How was the Jew portrayed in this unending flow of leaflets and pamphlets, books and speeches? How did the propaganda image of the Jew serve to justify the destruction process?

First of all, the Germans drew a picture of an international Jewry ruling the world and plotting the destruction of Germany and German life. "If international-finance Jewry," said Adolf Hitler in 1939, "inside and outside of Europe should succeed in plunging the nations into another world war, then the result will not be the Bolshevization of the earth and, with it, the victory of the Jews, but the annihilation of the Jewish race in Europe."[50] In 1944 Himmler said to his commanders: "This was the most frightening order which an organization could receive — the order to solve the Jewish question," but if the Jews had still been in the rear, the front line could not have been held, and if any of the commanders were moved to pity, they had only to think of the bombing terror, "which after all is organized in the last analysis by the Jews."[51]

The theory of world Jewish rule and of the incessant Jewish plot against the German people penetrated into all offices. It became interwoven with foreign policy and sometimes led to preposterous results. Thus the conviction grew that foreign statesmen who were not very friendly toward Germany were Jews, part-Jews, married to Jews, or somehow dominated by Jews. Streicher did not hesitate to state publicly that he had it on good Italian authority that the Pope had Jewish blood.[52] Similarly, Staatssekretär Weiz-

46. Instructions by Reich Press Chief, April 29, 1943, NG-4705.

47. Notably, the Institut zur Erforschung der Judenfrage in Frankfurt, under Dr. Klaus Schickert. Steengracht to Rosenberg, January 22, 1944, NG-1689.

48. Dr. Hans Praesent, "Neuere deutsche Doktorarbeiten über das Judentum," *Die Judenfrage,* November 15, 1943, pp. 351–53.

49. Luther to Berger, June 22, 1942, NG-3304.

50. See p. 257.

51. Himmler speech, June 21, 1944, NG-4977.

säcker of the Foreign Office once questioned the British chargé d'affaires about the percentage of "Aryan" blood in Mr. Rublee, an American on a mission in behalf of refugees.[53]

This type of reasoning was also applied in reverse. If a power was friendly, it was believed to be free of Jewish rule. In March, 1940, after Ribbentrop had succeeded in establishing friendly relations with Russia, he assured Mussolini and Ciano that Stalin had given up the idea of world revolution. The Soviet administration had been purged of Jews. Even Kaganovich (the Jewish Politbureau member) looked rather like a Georgian.[54]

The claim of Jewish world rule was to be established irrefutably in a show trial. Toward the end of 1941 the Propaganda Ministry, the Foreign Office, and the Justice Ministry laid plans for the trial of Herschel Grynzpan, the man who had assassinated a German Embassy official (vom Rath) in Paris in 1938.[55] The trial was to prove that Grynzpan's deed was part of a "fundamental plan by international Jewry to drive the world into a war with National Socialist Germany,"[56] but it was never held, because the Justice Ministry in its eagerness had made the fatal mistake of adding homosexuality to the indictment. At the last moment, it was feared that Grynzpan might reveal "the alleged homosexual relations of Gesandtschaftsrat vom Rath." And so the whole scheme was dropped.[57]

When Germany began to lose the war at Stalingrad, the propaganda machine sought to make up in sheer volume of endless repetition for the "proof" it had failed to obtain in the ill-fated Grynzpan trial. The Jew was now the principal foe, the creator of capitalism and Communism, the sinister force behind the entire Allied war effort, the organizer of the "terror raids," and, finally, the all-powerful enemy capable of wiping Germany off the map. By February 5, 1943, the press had to be cautioned not to "overestimate the power of the Jews."[58] On the same day, however, the following instructions were issued:

> Stress: If we lose this war, we do not fall into the hands of some other states but will all be annihilated by world Jewry. Jewry firmly decided [*fest entschlossen*] to exterminate all Germans. International law and international custom will be no protection against the Jewish will for total annihilation [*totaler Vernichtungswille der Juden*].[59]

52. Memorandum by Ribbentrop, November 18, 1938, on the Italian protest in the Streicher affair, *Documents on German Foreign Policy 1918–1945,* Ser. D, IV, 524–25. The pontiff in question was the "temperamental Pope," Pius XI, not the "diplomatic Pope," Pius XII.

53. Weizsäcker to Wörmann, Dg. Pol., trade and legal divisions, *Referat Deutschland* (Aschmann), November 7, 1938, NG-4686. The British diplomat replied that he didn't think Rublee had any Jewish blood.

54. Summary of conference between Ribbentrop, Mussolini, and Ciano, May 10, 1940, PS-2835.

55. Ministerialrat Diewerge (Propaganda Ministry) to Gesandter Dr. Krümmer (Foreign Office), December 22, 1941, NG-971. Krümmer to Foreign Office press division, January 2, 1942, NG-971. Summary of interministerial conference, January 23, 1942, NG-973. Rintelen to Weizsäcker, April 5, 1942, NG-179. Krümmer via Luther to Weizsäcker, April 7, 1942, NG-179. Schlegelberger to Göbbels, April 10, 1942, NG-973. Memorandum by Diewerge, April 11, 1942, NG-971.

56. Rintelen to Weizsäcker, quoting Ribbentrop's views, April 2, 1942, NG-179.

57. Summary of Grynzpan conference, January 23, 1942, NG-973. Louis P. Lochner (ed.), *The Goebbels Diaries,* entries for February 11, 1942, and April 5, 1942, pp. 78, 161. After the trial was dropped, Grynzpan was kept "on ice." He was discovered in 1957, living quietly in Paris. Kurt R. Grossmann, "Herschel Gruenspan lebt!" *Aufbau* (New York), May 10, 1957, pp. 1, 5–6.

58. *Zeitschriften Dienst* (Propaganda Ministry), February 5, 1943, NG-4715.

59. *Deutscher Wochendienst,* February 5, 1943, NG-4714.

How was this theory applied to justify specific operations? The "Jewish conspiracy" was used over and over again. We find the theory in the correspondence of the German Foreign Office, which pressed for deportations in Axis countries on the ground that the Jews were a security risk.[60] The Jews were the spies, the enemy agents. They could not be permitted to stay in coastal areas because in the event of Allied landings they would attack the defending garrisons from the rear. The Jews were the inciters of revolt; that was why they had to be deported from Slovakia in 1944. The Jews were the organizers of the partisan war, the "middle men" between the Red Army and the partisan field command; that was why they could not be permitted to remain alive in partisan-threatened areas. The Jews were the saboteurs and assassins; that was why the army chose them as hostages in Russia, Serbia, and France.[61] The Jews were plotting the destruction of Germany; and that was why they had to be destroyed. In Himmler's words: "We had the moral right vis-à-vis our people to annihilate this people which wanted to annihilate us." In the minds of the perpetrators, therefore, this theory turned the destruction process into a kind of preventive war.

However, the Jews were portrayed not only as a world conspiracy but also as a criminal people. This is the definition of the Jews, as furnished in instructions to the German press:

> Stress: In the case of the Jews there are not merely a few criminals (as in every other people), but all of Jewry rose from criminal roots, and in its very nature it is criminal. The Jews are no people like other people, but a pseudo-people welded together by hereditary criminality [*eine zu einem Scheinvolk zusammengeschlossene Erbkriminalität*]. . . . The annihilation of Jewry is no loss to humanity, but just as useful as capital punishment or protective custody against other criminals.[62]

And this is what Streicher had to say:

> Look at the path which the Jewish people has traversed for millenia: Everywhere murder; everywhere mass murder![63]

A Nazi researcher, Helmut Schramm, collected all the legends of Jewish ritual murder.[64] The book was an immediate success with Himmler. "Of the book *The Jewish Ritual Murders*," he wrote to Kaltenbrunner, "I have ordered a large number. I am distributing it down to *Standartenführer* [SS-colonel]. I am sending you several hundred copies so that you can distribute them to your *Einsatzkommandos*, and above all to the men who are busy with the Jewish question."[65] *The Ritual Murders* was a collection of stories about alleged tortures of Christian children. Actually, hundreds of thousands of Jewish children were being killed in the destruction process. Perhaps, that is why *The Ritual Murders* became so important. In fact, Himmler was so enthusiastic about the book that he ordered Kaltenbrunner to start investigations of "ritual murders" in Roumania, Hungary, and Bulgaria; he also suggested that Security Police people be put to work tracing British court records and police descriptions of missing children, "so that we can report in our radio broadcasts to Eng-

60. See pp. 415, 548.

61. See pp. 198, 436-41, 404.

62. *Deutscher Wochendienst*, April 2, 1943, NG-4713.

63. Speech by Streicher during dedication of Wilhelm Gustloff Bridge in Nuremburg, September, 1937, M-4. Gustloff, the AO *Landesgruppenleiter* in Switzerland, had been assassinated by a Jew.

64. Helmut Schramm, *Der jüdische Ritualmord – Eine historische Untersuchung* (Berlin, 1943).

65. Himmler to Kaltenbrunner, May 19, 1943, NG-4589.

land that in the town of XY a child is missing and that it is probably another case of Jewish ritual murder."[66]

How the theory of Jewish criminality was applied in practice may be seen in the choice of some of the expressions in the reports of killing operations, such as the term "execution" (in German, *hingerichtet, exekutiert, Vollzugstätigkeit*). In correspondence dealing with the administration of the personal belongings taken from dead Jews, the WVHA used the cover designation "utilization of the property of the Jewish thieves [*Verwertung des jüdischen Hehler- und Diebesgutes*]."[67]

A very striking example of how the theory invaded German thinking is furnished in the format of portions of two reports by the army's Secret Field Police in occupied Russia:[68]

Punishable offenses by members of the population:	
Espionage	1
Theft of ammunition	1
Suspected Jews (*Judenverdacht*)	3
Moving about with arms (*Freischärlerei*)	11
Theft	2
Jews	2

In the culmination of this theory to *be* a Jew was a punishable offense (*strafbare Handlung*); thus it was the function of the rationalization of criminality to turn the destruction process into a kind of judicial proceeding.

There was a third rationalization which was focused on the Jew: the conception of the Jew as a lower form of life. Generalgouverneur Frank was given to the use of such phrases as "Jews and lice." In a speech delivered on December 19, 1940, he pointed out that relatives of military personnel surely were sympathizing with men stationed in Poland, a country "which is so full of lice and Jews." But the situation was not so bad, he continued, though of course he could not rid the country of all lice and Jews in a year.[69] On July 19, 1943, the chief of the *Generalgouvernement* Health Division reported during a meeting that the typhus epidemic was subsiding. Frank remarked in this connection that the "removal" (*Beseitigung*) of the "Jewish element" had undoubtedly contributed to better health (*Gesundung*) in Europe. He meant this not only in the literal sense but also politically: the re-establishment of sound living conditions (*gesunder Lebensverhältnisse*) on the European continent.[70]

In a similar vein Foreign Office Press Chief Schmidt once declared during a visit to Slovakia, "The Jewish question is no question of humanity, and it is no question of religion; it is solely a question of political hygiene" (*eine Frage der politischen Hygiene*).[71]

In the terminology of the killing operations the conception of Jews as vermin is again quite noticeable. Dr. Stahlecker, the commander of *Einsatzgruppe A,* called the pogroms conducted by the Lithuanians "self-cleansing actions" (*Selbstreiningungsaktionen*). In another report we find the phrase "cleansing-of-Jews actions" (*Judensäuberungsaktionen*). Himmler spoke of "extermination" (*Ausrottung*). Many times, the bureaucracy used the word *Entjudung;* this expression, which was used not only in connection with killings but also with reference to Aryani-

66. *Ibid.*

67. See p. 614.

68. GFP Group 722 to 207th Security Division Ic, February 23, 1943, NOKW-2210. GFP Group 722 to 207th Security Division Ic, March 25, 1943, NOKW-2158.

69. Speech by Frank to men of guard battalion, December 19, 1940, Frank diary, PS-2233.

70. Summary of *Generalgouvernement* health conference, July 9, 1943, Frank diary, PS-2233.

71. See p. 471.

zations of property, means to *rid* something of Jews.[72] Again, we discover the term *judenrein*, which in exact translation means "clean of Jews." Finally, in the most drastic application of this theory, a German fumigation company, the Deutsche Gesellschaft für Schädlingsbekämpfung, was drawn into the killing operations by furnishing one of its lethal products for the gassing of a million Jews. Thus the destruction process was also turned into a "cleansing operation."

In addition to the rationalizations which were used to justify the whole undertaking as a war against "international Jewry," as a judicial proceeding against "Jewish criminality," or simply as a "hygienic" process against "Jewish vermin," there were also those rationalizations which were fashioned in order to enable the individual bureaucrat to justify his individual task in the destruction process. It must be kept in mind that most of the participants did not fire rifles at Jewish children or pour gas into gas chambers. A good many, of course, also had to perform these very "hard" tasks, but most of the administrators and most of the clerks did not see the final, drastic link in these measures of destruction.

Most bureaucrats composed memoranda, drew up blueprints, signed correspondence, talked on the telephone, and participated in conferences. They could destroy a whole people while sitting at their desks. Except for inspection tours, which were not obligatory, they never had to see "100 bodies lie there, or 500, or 1000." However, these men were not stupid; they realized the connection between their paper work and the heaps of corpses in the East. And they realized, also, the shortcomings of those rationalizations which placed all evil on the Jew and all good on the German. That was why they were compelled to justify their individual activities. Their justifications contain the implicit admission that the paper work was to go on, regardless of the actual plans of world Jewry and regardless of the actual behavior of the Jews who were about to be killed. We can divide the rationalizations focused on the perpetrator into five categories.

The first rationalization was the oldest, the simplest, and therefore the most effective: the doctrine of superior orders. First and foremost there was discipline. First and foremost there was duty. No matter what objections there might be, orders were given to be obeyed. A clear order was like absolution; armed with such an order, a perpetrator felt that he could pass his responsibility and his conscience upward. When Himmler addressed a killing party in Minsk, he told his men that they need not worry. Their consciences were in no way impaired, for they were soldiers who had to carry out every order unconditionally.[73]

Every bureaucrat knows, of course, that open defiance of orders is serious business, but he also knows that there are many ingenious ways of evading orders. In fact, the opportunities for evasion and hesitation increase as one ascends in the hierarchy. Even in Nazi Germany orders were disobeyed, and they were disobeyed even in Jewish matters. We have mentioned the statement of Reichsbankdirektor Wilhelm, who would not participate in the distribution of "second-hand goods." Nothing happened to him. A member of the RSHA, Sturmbannführer Hartl, simply refused to take over an *Einsatzkommando* in Russia. Nothing happened to this man, either.[74] Even Generalkommissar Kube, who had actually

72. Compare *Entlausung* ("ridding of lice") and *Entwesung* ("ridding of vermin," or "fumigation").

73. See pp. 218–19.

74. Affidavit by Albert Hartl, October 9, 1947, NO-5384.

frustrated a killing operation in Minsk and who had otherwise expressed himself in strong language, was only warned.

The bureaucrat clung to his orders not so much because he feared his superior (with whom he was often on good terms) but because he feared his own conscience. The many requests for "authorization" – whether for permission to mark Jews with a star or to kill them – demonstrate the true nature of these orders. When they did not exist, the bureaucrats had to invent them.

The second rationalization was the administrator's insistence that he did not act out of personal vindictiveness. In the mind of the bureaucrat duty was an assigned path; it was his "fate." The German bureaucrat made a sharp distinction between duty and personal feelings; he insisted that he did not "hate" Jews, and sometimes he even went out of his way to perform "good deeds" for Jewish friends and acquaintances. When the trials of war criminals started, there was hardly a defendant who could not produce evidence that he had helped some half-Jewish physics professor, or that he had used his influence to permit a Jewish symphony conductor to conduct a little while longer, or that he had intervened on behalf of some couple in mixed marriage in connection with an apartment. While these courtesies were petty in comparison with the destructive conceptions which these men were implementing concurrently, the "good deeds" performed an important psychological function. They separated "duty" from personal feelings. They preserved a sense of "decency." The destroyer of the Jews was no "anti-Semite."

Staatssekretär Keppler of the Office of the Four-Year Plan was interrogated after the war as follows:

QUESTION [by Dr. Kempner of the prosecuting staff]: Tell me, Mr. Keppler, why were you so terribly against the Jews? Did you know the Jews?

ANSWER: I had nothing against the Jews.

QUESTION: I am asking for the reason. You were no friend of the Jews?

ANSWER: Jews came to me. Warburg invited me. Later Jews looked me up in the Reich Chancellery and asked me to join the board of directors of the Deutsche Bank.

QUESTION: When were you supposed to join the board of directors?

ANSWER: I didn't want to; it was in 1934, they wanted to give me a written assurance that I would be a director in half a year. If I had been such a hater of Jews, they would not have approached me.

QUESTION: But you transferred capital from Jews into Aryan hands

ANSWER: Not often. I know the one case of Simson-Suhl. Also the Skoda-Wetzler Works in Vienna. But it turned out that was no Jewish enterprise.

Keppler was then asked whether he had not favored the "disappearance" of the Jews from Germany. The Staatssekretär fell back on Warburg, with whom he had once had an "interesting discussion." The interrogator broke in with the remark that "now we do not want to talk about anti-Semitism but about the final solution of the Jewish question." In that connection, Keppler was asked whether he had heard of Lublin. The *Staatssekretär* admitted hesitantly that he had heard of Lublin and offered the explanation that he was "deeply touched by this matter" (*dass mich das furchtbar peinlich berührt*). What did Keppler do when he was touched like this? "It was very unpleasant for me, but after all it was not even in my sphere of jurisdiction."[75]

Another defendant in a war-crimes trial, the former commander in Norway, Generaloberst von Falkenhorst, offered the following explanation for his order to remove Jews from Soviet prisoner-of-war battalions in his area. Falkenhorst pointed out that, to begin with, there were no Jews among these prisoners, for the selection had already taken place in Germany (i.e., the Jewish prisoners had already been shot as they were shuttled through the Reich). The order was consequently "entirely superfluous and might just as well not have been included. It was thoughtlessly included by the officer of my staff who was working on it, from the instructions sent to us, and I overlooked it." The general then continued:

> For the rest it may be inferred from this that the Jewish question played as infamous a part in Norway as elsewhere, and that I and the Army were supposed to have been particularly anti-semitic.
>
> Against this suspicion I can only adduce the following: First, that in Scandinavian countries there are only very few Jews. These few are hardly ever in evidence. The sum total in Norway was only about 350. [Actual figure: 2000.] A negligible number among two or three million·Norwegians. These [Jews] were collected by [Reichskommissar] Terboven and according to orders despatched to Germany by steamship. In this manner the Jewish problem in Norway was practically solved [i.e., by deportation to Auschwitz].
>
> As regards myself, I made at this time an application to Terboven at the request of the Swedish Consul, General Westring, in Oslo, who did not much like visiting Terboven, for the release of a Jew of Swedish nationality and of his family with permission to leave the country, gladly and, as a matter of course, fulfilling the Consul's wish to facilitate the return of these people to Stockholm.
>
> If I had been a rabid anti-semite I could, without further ado, have refused this request, for the matter did not concern me in the slightest.
>
> On the one hand, however, I wanted to help the Swedish Consul, and, on the other hand, I have nothing against the Jews. I have read and heard their writings and compositions with interest, and their achievements in the field of science are worthy of the highest respect. I have met many fine and honorable people among them.[76]

How widespread the practice of "good deeds" must have been may be gauged from the following remark by Heinrich Himmler:

> And then they come, our 80,000,000 good Germans, and each one has his decent Jew. It is clear, the others are swine [*Schweine*], but this one is a first-class Jew. Of all those who speak thus, no one has seen it, no one has gone through it.[77]

But even if Himmler regarded these interventions as expressions of misplaced humanity, they were necessary tools in the attempt to crystallize one of the important justifications for bureaucratic action – duty. Only after a man had done "everything humanly possible" could he devote himself to his destructive activity in peace.

The third justification was the rationalization that one's own activity was not criminal, that the next fellow's action was the criminal act. The Ministerialrat who was signing papers could console himself with the thought that he did not do the shooting. But that was not enough. He had to be sure that *if* he were ordered to shoot, he would not follow orders but would draw the line right then and there.

The following exchange took place during a war-crimes trial. A Foreign Office official, Albrecht von Kessel, was asked by defense counsel (Dr. Becker) to explain the meaning of "final solution."

> ANSWER: This expression "final solution" was used with various meanings. In

75. Interrogation by Kempner of Keppler, August 20, 1947, NG-3041.

76. Affidavit by von Falkenhorst, July 6, 1946, in *Trial of Nikolaus von Falkenhorst* (London, 1949), p. 25.

77. Speech by Himmler, October 4, 1943, PS-1919.

1936 "final solution" meant merely that all Jews should leave Germany. And, of course, it was true that they were to be robbed; that wasn't very nice, but it wasn't criminal.

JUDGE MAGUIRE: Was that an accurate translation?

DR. BECKER: I did not check on the translation. Please repeat the sentence.

ANSWER: I said it was not criminal; it was not nice, but it was not criminal. That is what I said. One didn't want to take their life; one merely wanted to take money away from them. That was all.[78]

The most important characteristic of this dividing line was that it could be *shifted* when the need arose. To illlustrate: Once there was a Protestant pastor by the name of Ernst Biberstein. After several years of ministering to his congregation, he moved into the Church Ministry; from that agency he came to another office which was also interested in church matters – the Reich Security Main Office. That agency assigned him to head a local Gestapo office. Finally he became the chief of *Einsatzkommando* 6 in southern Russia. As commander of the *Kommando*, Biberstein killed two or three thousand people. These people, in his opinion, had forfeited the right to live under the rules of war. Asked if there were Jews among his victims, he replied: "It is very difficult to determine that. Also, I was told at that time that wherever there were Armenians, there were not so many Jews."[79] To Biberstein the moral dividing line was like the receding horizon. He walked toward it, but he could never reach it.

Among the participants in the destruction process there were very few who did not shift the line when they had to cross the threshold. One reason why the person of Generalkommissar Kube is so important is that he had a firm line beyond which he could not pass. The line was arbitrary, and very advanced. He sacrificed the Russian Jews and fought desperately only for the German Jews in his area. But the line was fixed. It was not movable, it was not imaginary, it was not self-deceptive. We have indicated that the destruction process was autonomous, that it could not be stopped internally; the adjustable moral standard was one of the principal tools in the maintenance of this autonomy.

There was a fourth rationalization which implicitly took cognizance of the fact that all shifting lines are unreal. It was a rationalization of more sophisticated people and was built on simple premise. No man alone can build a bridge. No man alone can destroy the Jews. The participant in the destruction process was always in company. Among his superiors he could always find those who were doing more than he; among his subordinates he could always find those who were ready to take his place. No matter where he looked, he was one among thousands. His own importance was diminished, and he felt that he was replaceable, perhaps even dispensable.

In such reflective moments the bureaucrat quieted his conscience with the thought that he was part of a tide and that there was very little a drop of water could do in such a wave. When Werner von Tippelskirch, a Foreign Office official, was interrogated after the war, he pointed out that he had never protested against the killing of Jews in Russia because he had been "powerless." His superiors, Erdmannsdorff, Wörmann, and Weizsäcker, had also been "powerless." All of them had waited for a "change of regime." Asked by Prosecutor Kempner whether it was right to wait for a change of regime "and in the meantime send thousands of people to their

78. Testimony by Albrecht von Kessel, Case No. 11, tr. pp. 9514–15.

79. Interrogation of Biberstein, June 29, 1947, NO-4997.

death," von Tippelskirch replied, "A difficult question."[80]

The fifth rationalization was the most sophisticated of all. It was also a last-ditch psychological defense, suited particularly to those who saw through the self-deception of superior orders, impersonal duty, the shifting moral standard, and the argument of powerlessness. It was a rationalization also for those whose drastic activity or high position placed them out of reach of orders, duty, moral dividing lines, and helplessness. It was the jungle theory.

Oswald Spengler once explained this theory in the following words: "War is the primeval policy of all living things, and this to the extent that in the deepest sense combat and life are identical, for when the will to fight is extinguished, so is life itself."[81] Himmler remembered this theory when he addressed the mobile killing personnel at Minsk. He told them to look at nature: wherever they would look, they would find combat. They would find it among animals and among plants. Whoever tired of the fight went under.[82]

From this philosophy Hitler himself drew strength in moments of meditation. Once at the dinner table, when he thought about the destruction of the Jews, he remarked with stark simplicity: "One must not have mercy with people who are determined by fate to perish [*Man dürfe kein Mitleid mit Leuten haben, denen das Schicksal bestimmt habe, zugrunde zu gehen*]."[83]

2 / The Victims

So far we have pointed out how the Germans overcame their administrative and psychological obstacles; we have dealt with the internal problems of the bureaucratic machine. But the internal technocratic and moral conflicts do not fully explain what happened. In a destruction process the perpetrators do not play the only role; the process is shaped by the victims, too. It is the *interaction* of perpetrators and victims that is "fate." We must therefore discuss the reactions of the Jewish community and analyze the role of the Jews in their own destruction.

When confronted by force, a group can react in five ways: by resistance, by an attempt to alleviate or nullify the threat (the undoing reaction), by evasion, by paralysis, or by compliance. Let us consider each in turn.

The reaction pattern of the Jews is characterized by almost complete lack of resistance. In marked contrast to German propaganda, the documentary evidence of Jewish resistance, overt or submerged, is very slight. On a European-wide scale the Jews had no resistance organization, no blueprint for armed action, no plan even for psychological warfare. They were completely unprepared. In the words of Anti-Partisan Chief and Higher SS and Police Leader Russia Center von dem Bach, who observed the Jews and killed them from 1941 to the end:

> Thus the misfortune came about. . . . I am the only living witness but I must say the truth. Contrary to the opinion of the National Socialists that the Jews were a highly organized group, the appalling fact was that they had no organization whatsoever. The mass of the Jewish people were taken completely by surprise. They did not know at all what to do; they had no directives or slogans as to how they should act. That is the greatest lie of anti-Semitism because it gives the lie to the

80. Interrogation by Kempner of Werner von Tippelskirch, August 29, 1947, NG-2801.

81. Oswald Spengler, *Der Untergang des Abendlandes* (Munich, 1923), II, 545–46.

82. See p. 219.

83. Henry Picker (ed.), *Hitler's Tischgespräche im Führerhauptquartier 1941–1942* (Bonn, 1951), entry for April 2, 1942, p. 227. The entries are summaries by Picker of "Hitler's remarks at the dinner table."

old slogan that the Jews are conspiring to dominate the world and that they are so highly organized. In reality they had no organization of their own at all, not even an information service. If they had had some sort of organization, these people could have been saved by the millions; but instead they were taken completely by surprise. Never before has a people gone as unsuspectingly to its disaster. Nothing was prepared. Absolutely nothing. It was not so, as the anti-Semites say, that they were friendly to the Soviets. That is the most appalling misconception of all. The Jews in the old Poland, who were never communistic in their sympathies, were, throughout the area of the river Bug eastward, more afraid of Bolshevism than of the Nazis. This was insanity. They could have been saved. There were people among them who had much to lose, business people; they didn't want to leave. In addition there was love of home and their old experience with pogroms in Russia. After the first anti-Jewish actions of the Germans, they thought now the wave was over and so they walked back to their undoing.[1]

The Jews were not oriented toward resistance. They took up resistance only in a few cases, locally, and at the last moment. Measured in German casualties, Jewish armed opposition shrinks into insignificance. The most important engagement was fought in the Warsaw ghetto (16 dead and 85 wounded on the German side, including collaborators).[2] In Galicia sporadic resistance resulted in some losses to SS and Police Leader Katzmann (8 dead, 12 wounded).[3] In addition, there were clashes between Jewish partisans and German forces in other parts of the East, and occasional acts of resistance by small groups and individuals in the ghettos and killing centers. It is doubtful that the Germans and their collaborators lost more than a few hundred men, dead and wounded, in the course of the destruction process. The number of men who dropped out because of disease, nervous breakdowns, or court martial proceedings was probably greater. The Jewish resistance effort could not seriously impede or retard the progress of destructive operations: The Germans brushed that resistance aside as a minor obstacle, and in the totality of the destruction process it was of no consequence.

The second reaction was the attempt to avert the full force of the German destructive measures. This attempt was carried out in three forms. One was the petition – the appeal. By appealing, the Jews sought to transfer the struggle from a physical to an intellectual and moral plane. If only the fate of the Jews could be resolved with arguments rather than with physical resources and physical combat – so Jewry reasoned – there would be nothing to fear. In a petition by Rabbi Kaplan to French Commissioner Xavier Vallat this Jewish mentality becomes absolutely clear. Among other things, the Rabbi pointed out that a pagan or an atheist had the right to defame Judaism, but in the case of a Christian, did not such an attitude appear "spiritually illogical as well as ungrateful?" To prove his point, Kaplan supplied many learned quotations.[4] The letter is as though it were not written in the twentieth century. It is reminiscent of the time toward the close of the Middle Ages when Jewish rabbis used to dispute with representatives of the Church over the relative merits of the two religions.

Yet in various forms, some more eloquent than others, the Jews appealed and petitioned wherever and whenever

1. Von dem Bach made this statement to Leo Alexander, who quoted it in his article "War Crimes and Their Motivation," *Journal of Criminal Law and Criminology,* XXXIX, 315.

2. See p. 326.

3. See pp. 317, 327.

4. See pp. 398–99.

the threat of concentration and deportation struck them: in the Reich, in Poland, in Russia, in France, in the Balkan countries, and in Hungary.[5] Everywhere the Jews pitted words against rifles, dialectics against force, and everywhere they lost. The reliance upon petitions became so great that internal struggles developed over the formulation and timing of the appeals.

When the petition system is unsuccessful, when an appeal fails to save the whole group, there is a tendency to appeal for part of the group. In the minds of the drafters, these appeals therefore become life-and-death matters. Whoever is excluded is given up. We may cite as an example the conflict in the Vienna Jewish community over the petitioning for exemptions from deportations. At the end of 1941, when the community organization (*Kultusgemeinde*) made an "agreement" with the Gestapo about "exempt" categories, the head of the Jewish war invalids, who had been left out of the "negotiations," accused the deportation expert of the *Kultusgemeinde* of "sacrificing" the disabled veterans.[6] Later on, when the war invalids were pressed to the wall, the leaders of the veterans' organization discussed the advisability of presenting an independent petition. One of the war-invalid chiefs remarked, "Fundamentally, I am of the opinion that we cannot afford a war with the *Kultusgemeinde*." Another commented: "The *Hauptsturmführer* will say to himself 'These are Jews, and those are Jews. Let them fight among themselves. Why should I worry about that?' He [the *SS-Hauptsturmführer*] will eventually drop us in this matter [*Er wird uns in dieser Frage eventuell fallen lassen*]." Thereupon the head of the war veterans said, "My answer is that in such an eventuality it will be time to disband our organization."[7]

5. See pp. 280, 150, 248, 398–99, 400, 481, 494–95, 503, 541–42.

Sometimes the Jews appealed not with words but with personal gifts; they attempted to bribe individual Germans. But these attempts were also largely unsuccessful: the German officials accepted the gifts but these Germans were not bought.[8] Even the few Jewish girls who offered themselves to policemen on the eve of ghetto-clearing operations were killed on the next day.[9] The bribery *did* worry Himmler, but it had no effect on the progress of the operations.

There was a second way in which the Jews tried to avert disaster: by judicious compliance with orders, and sometimes by anticipatory compliance with orders not yet issued. The most conspicuous example of anticipatory compliance was the decision of the Jewish community leaders in Poland to organize a forced labor system.[10] Another anticipatory move was made by the Jewish leadership in Kislovodsk (Caucasus), where, in full awareness of the German threat, the *Judenrat* confiscated all Jewish valuables – including gold, silver, carpets, and clothing – and handed the property to the German commander.[11] A third example of anticipatory compliance may be found in the minutes of a discussion held in the Shavel *Judenrat* (in Latvia) on March 24, 1943. The *Judenrat* had been asked three times whether any births had occurred in the ghetto, and each time it had denied that there were any births. Now, however, the Jewish leadership was confronted with twenty pregnancies. It decided to use persuasion and, if need be, threats on the women to submit to abortions. One woman was in her eighth month; the *Judenrat* decided that in this case a

6. See pp. 279–80.
7. See pp. 281–82.
8. See pp. 162, 529.
9. See pp. 248–49.
10. See p. 163.
11. Protocol by Prof. P. A. Ostankov and others, July 5, 1943, USSR-1 A (2-4).

doctor would induce premature birth and that a nurse would kill the child. (A doctor objected to doing the job himself.) The nurse would be told to proceed in such a way that she would not know the nature of her act.[12]

In one respect this Jewish co-operation created administrative problems within the machinery of destruction. The zeal with which the Jews applied themselves to the German war effort accentuated the differences of interests which paired industry and the armament inspectorates against the SS and Police, but these differences were ultimately resolved to the disadvantage of the Jews. And insofar as the Jews co-operated in other ways, the attempts at forestalling not only availed nothing but actually fitted into German plans. Playing into German hands, they speeded the process of destruction.

The third alleviation attempt may be noted in the system of relief and salvage, from the elaborate social services of the ghetto communities to the primitive "organization" in the killing centers.[13] The relief system was basically the product of a calculation of time, the hope or expectation that the liberation would come before the destruction process could consume itself. We know, simply by counting the relative handful of survivors, that this attempt failed also.

The basic reactions to force are fundamentally different from each other. Resistance is opposition to the perpetrator. Nullification or alleviation is opposition to the administrative enactment. In the third reaction, evasion, the victim tries to remove himself from the effects of force by fleeing or hiding. The phenomenon of flight is most difficult to analyze. We know that the emigration of approximately 350,000 Jews from Germany and German-occupied Czechoslovakia before the war was forced. In many cases the emigrating Jews had been deprived of their livelihood, and they reacted to the consequences of anti-Jewish measures rather than in anticipation of disaster. The flight of the Belgian and Parisian Jews in 1940 and the evacuation of Soviet Jews a year later was compounded with mass migrations of non-Jews. Here again, the flight was not a pure reaction to the threat of the destruction process but also a reaction to the war. We know that only a few thousand Jews escaped from the ghettos of Poland and Russia, that only a few hundred Jews hid out in the large cities of Berlin, Vienna, and Warsaw, that only a handful of Jews escaped from camps. Von dem Bach mentions that in Russia there was an unguarded escape route to the Pripet Marshes, but few Jews availed themselves of the opportunity.[14] In the main, the Jews looked upon flight with a sense of futility; the great majority of those who did not escape early did not escape at all.

There were instances when in the mind of the victim, the difficulties of resistance, undoing, or evasion were just as great as the problems of automatic compliance; in such instances the futility of all alternatives became utterly clear, and the victim was paralyzed. Paralysis occurred only in moments of crisis. During ghetto-clearing operations many Jewish families were unable to fight, unable to petition, unable to flee, and also unable to move to the concentration point to get it over with. They waited for the raiding parties in their homes, frozen and helpless. Sometimes the same paralytic reaction

12. Minutes of the Shavel *Judenrat,* March 24, 1943, found by the Red Army and turned over to the Soviet Extraordinary State Commission, in Jewish Black Book Committee, *The Black Book* (New York, 1946), pp. 331–33.

13. To "organize" in a camp meant to take a bit of food or some item of clothing wherever it could be found.

14. Statement by von dem Bach in *Aufbau* (New York), September 6, 1946, p. 40.

struck Jews who walked up to a killing site and for the first time gazed into a mass grave half-filled with the bloodied corpses of those who had preceded them.

The fifth reaction was automatic compliance. Much has been said and much has been written about the *Judenräte,* the informers, the Jewish police, the *Kapos* – in short, all those persons who deliberately and as a matter of policy co-operated with the Germans. But these collaborators do not interest us so much as the masses of Jews who reacted to every German order by complying with it automatically. To understand the administrative significance of this compliance, we have to see the destruction process as a composite of two kinds of German measures: those which perpetrated something upon the Jews and involved only action by Germans, such as the drafting of decrees, the running of deportation trains, shooting, or gassing, and those which required the Jews to do something, for instance, the decrees or orders requiring them to register their property, obtain identification papers, report at a designated place for labor or deportation or shooting, submit lists of persons, pay fines, deliver up property, publish German instructions, dig their own graves, and so on. The successful execution of these latter measures depended on action by the Jews. Only when one realizes how large a part of the destruction process consisted of the fulfilment of these measures can one begin to appraise the role of the Jews in their own destruction.

If, therefore, we look at the whole Jewish reaction pattern, we notice that in its two salient features it is an attempt to avert action and, failing that, automatic compliance with orders. Why is this so? Why did the Jews act in this way? The Jews attempted to tame the Germans as one would attempt to tame a wild beast. They avoided "provocations" and complied instantly with decrees and orders. They hoped that somehow the German drive would spend itself.

This hope was founded on a two-thousand-year-old experience. In exile the Jews had always been in a minority; they had always been in danger; but they had learned that they could avert danger and survive destruction by placating and appeasing their enemies. Even in ancient Persia an appeal by Queen Esther was more effective than the mobilization of an army. Armed resistance in the face of overwhelming force could end only in disaster.

Thus, over a period of centuries the Jews had learned that in order to survive they had to refrain from resistance. Time and again they were attacked; they endured the Crusades, the Cossack uprisings, and the Czarist persecution. There were many casualties in these times of stress, but always the Jewish community emerged once again like a rock from a receding tidal wave. The Jews had never really been annihilated. After surveying the damage, the survivors had always proclaimed in affirmation of their strategy the triumphant slogan, "The Jewish people lives [*Am Yisrael Chaj*]." This experience was so ingrained in the Jewish consciousness as to achieve the force of law. The Jewish people could not be annihilated.

Only in 1941, 1942, and 1943 did the Jewish leadership realize that, unlike the pogroms of past centuries, the modern machine-like destruction process would engulf European Jewry. But the realization came too late. A two-thousand-year-old lesson could not be unlearned; the Jews could not make the switch. They were helpless.

Let us not suppose, however, that compliance was easy. If it was difficult for the Germans to kill, it was harder still for the Jews to die. Compliance is a course of action which becomes increasingly drastic in a destruction process. It is one thing to comply with an order to register property but quite another to obey orders in front of a grave. The two actions *are* part of the same habit – the Jews who registered their property were also the ones who lined up to be killed. The Jews who lined up on a killing site were the ones who had registered their property. Yet these two activities are very different in their effects. Submission is altogether more burdensome in its last stages than in its beginning, for as one goes on, more and more is lost. Finally, in the supreme moment of crisis the primeval tendency to resist aggression breaks to the surface; resistance then becomes an obstacle to compliance, just as compliance is an obstacle to resistance. In the Jewish case the cooperation reaction was the stronger one until the end. The Jews consequently dealt with their resistance in much the same way as the Germans dealt with their consciences.

The major obstructions faced by the Jews in their course of submission were never physical ones. No major administrative encumbrances were encountered by the surrendering victims. Only a resistance organization with sufficient power to interfere with surrender can erect such obstructions. This kind of resistance organization could not be formed, and this kind of organized resistance could therefore not occur. However, there were significant psychological blocks on the path to capitulation, blocks which revealed themselves clearly in the victims' repressions and rationalizations.

People do not easily accept the fact that they are going to be killed; if they have the know-how to resist, they will defend themselves as best they can. If, on the other hand, they have unlearned the art of resistance, they will repress their knowledge of the true situation and will attempt to go on as though life could not change. The Jews could not resist. In complying with German orders they therefore tried, to the utmost of their ability, to ignore all evidence of danger and to forget all intimation of death. They pretended that nothing unusual was happening to them, and that belief became so crucial that they did anything to perpetuate it.

One is struck by the fact that the Germans repeatedly employed very crude deceptions and ruses. The Jews were bluffed with "registrations" and "resettlements," with "baths" and "inhalations." At each stage of the destruction process the victims thought that they were going through the last stage. And so it appears that one of the most gigantic hoaxes in world history was perpetrated on five million people noted for their intellect. But were these people really fooled? Or did they deliberately fool themselves?

We have evidence that even in the absence of misleading promises the Jewish victims managed to repress their awareness of catastrophe and to substitute for that knowledge a mere illusion. In survivors' accounts we find long descriptions of the elaborate educational programs for the children, and one survivor tells us that in the closing days of the Kaunas ghetto the slogan of the victims was "life for an hour is also life [*A sho gelebt is oich gelebt*]."[15]

The Jews, in short, did not always have to be deceived; they were capable of deceiving themselves; the Jewish repressive mechanism could work independently and automatically. In the minutes of the Vienna Jewish war invalids' conferences we discover the same significant absence of direct references to death and killing centers that we have already noted in German correspondence. The Jewish documents abound with such roundabout expres-

15. Samuel Gringauz, "The Ghetto as an Experiment in Jewish Social Organization," *Jewish Social Studies*, XI (1949), 17.

sions as "favored transport" (meaning Theresienstadt transport), "I see black," "to tempt fate," "final act of the drama," etc.[16] The direct word is lacking.

Moreover, the attempt to repress unbearable thoughts was characteristic not only of the ghetto community but of the killing center itself. In Auschwitz the inmates employed a special terminology of their own for killing operations: a crematory was called a "bakery"; a man who could no longer work – and who was therefore destined for the gas chamber – was designated a "Moslem"; and the depot holding the belongings of the gassed was named "Canada."[17] These, it must be emphasized, are not Nazi terms; they are expressions by the victims. They are the counterparts of the Nazi vocabulary, and, like the German euphemisms, they were designed to blot out visions of death.

There were moments, of course, when the issue could not be evaded, when forgetting was no longer effective. In such moments of crisis the victims, like the perpetrators, resorted to rationalizations. The Jews, too, had to justify their actions. It is interesting to note how the two principal rationalizations emerged directly from the repressive pattern.

The Germans were notably successful in deporting Jews by stages, for always those who remained behind could reason that it was necessary to sacrifice the few in order to save the many. The operation of that psychology may be observed in the Vienna Jewish community, which concluded a deportation "agreement" with the Gestapo, with the "understanding" that six categories of Jews would not be deported.[18] Again, the Warsaw ghetto Jews argued in favor of co-operation and against resistance on the ground that the Germans would deport sixty thousand Jews but not hundreds of thousands.[19] The bisection phenomenon occurred also in Salonika, where the Jewish leadership co-operated with the German deportation agencies upon the assurance that only "Communist" elements from the poor sections would be deported, while the "middle class" would be left alone.[20] That fatal arithmetic was also applied in Vilna, where *Judenrat* chief Gens declared: "With a hundred victims I save a thousand people. With a thousand I save ten thousand."[21]

In situations where compliance with death orders could no longer be rationalized as a life-saving measure there was still one more justification: the argument that with rigid, instantaneous compliance unnecessary suffering was eliminated, unnecessary pain avoided, the necessary torture reduced. The entire Jewish community, and particularly the Jewish leadership, now concentrated all its efforts in one direction – to make the ordeal bearable, to make death easy.

This effort is reflected in the letter which the Jewish Council in Budapest sent to the Hungarian Interior Minister on the eve of the deportations: "We emphatically declare that we do not seek this audience in order to lodge complaints about the merit of the measures adopted, but merely ask that they be carried out in a humane spirit."[22]

The effort is also illustrated in the following statement, which the chief of the Reich Association of the Jews in

16. See pp. 278–82.

17. On "bakery," see Lengyel, *Five Chimneys,* p. 22. On "Moslem" (*Muselmann*), see report by commander's office, Auschwitz III, May 5, 1944, NI-11019. On "Canada," see Sehn, "Oswiecim," in *German Crimes in Poland,* p. 41.

18. See pp. 279–80.

19. See pp. 318–20.

20. See pp. 445–46.

21. Philip Friedman, "Two 'Saviors' Who Failed," *Commentary,* December, 1958, p. 487.

22. See pp. 541–42.

Germany, Rabbi Leo Baeck, made after the war:

> I made it a principle to accept no appointments from the Nazis and to do nothing which might help them. But later, when the question arose whether Jewish orderlies should help pick up Jews for deportation, I took the position that it would be better for them to do it, because they could at least be more gentle and helpful than the Gestapo and make the ordeal easier. It was scarcely in our power to oppose the order effectively.[23]

When Baeck was in Theresienstadt, an engineer who had escaped from Auschwitz informed him about the gassings. Baeck decided not to pass on this information to anyone in the ghetto city because "living in the expectation of death by gassing would only be the harder."[24]

The supreme test of the compliance reaction came in front of the grave; yet here, too, the Jews managed to console themselves. From one of the numerous German eyewitness reports comes the following typical passage:

> The father was holding the hand of a boy about ten years old and was speaking to him softly; the boy was fighting his tears. The father pointed to the sky, stroked his head, and seemed to explain something to him. . . . I remember a girl, slim and with black hair, who passed close to me, pointed to herself, and said, "Twenty-three". . . . The people, completely naked, went down some steps which were cut in the clay wall of the pit and clambered over the heads of the people lying there, to the place where the SS-man directed them. Then they lay down in front of the dead or injured people; some caressed those who were still alive and spoke to them in a low voice. Then I heard a series of shots.[25]

The German annihilation of the European Jews was the world's first completed destruction process. For the first time in the history of Western civilization the perpetrators had overcome all administrative and moral obstacles to a killing operation. For the first time, also, the Jewish victims – caught in the strait jacket of their history – plunged themselves physically and psychologically into catastrophe. The destruction of the Jews was thus no accident. When in the early days of 1933 the first civil servant wrote the first definition of a "non-Aryan" into a civil service ordinance, the fate of European Jewry was sealed.

23. Leo Baeck in Eric H. Boehm (ed.), *We Survived* (New Haven, 1949), p. 288.

24. *Ibid.*, pp. 292–93.

25. Affidavit by Hermann Friedrich Graebe, November 10, 1945, PS-2992.

XI / *Consequences*

We have seen now how the Jews of Europe were destroyed; we have reconstructed, step by step, a history of their death. But our task is not completed with that analysis. The destruction process resulted in something more: It changed the lives of many who were not its victims. It was felt throughout the world. The impact of this operation is reflected in disturbances which it caused within three distinct groups. The first of these was the Jewish community; the second was the postwar population of Germany; the third was an alignment of bystanders, in the foreground of which stood the leadership of the wartime Allies.

For the Jews the destruction process engendered both physical and psychic upheavals. Physically, the dimensions of Jewish population, its distribution, and even its character underwent a permanent change. The statistics in Table 89 reveal in rough outline what happened. First of all, world Jewry lost one-third of its number; it declined from an all-time high of more than 16,000,000 people to about 11,000,000. In the second place, the geographic concentration of the population loss altered the distribution of the Jews. Before the rise of the Nazi regime, the bulk of Jewish population, wealth, and power was centered in Europe. When Germany was smashed, nearly half the world's Jews were living in the United States, and most of the Jewish wealth was located there. In that country, too, were henceforth to be found many of the decisive voices in world Jewish affairs. The third major change has only just begun: Before the war eastern and western Jewry supplied the main impetus to action in the Jewish community, and the masses of Jews in the Moslem lands were inert and forgotten. Now the Arab Jews will increasingly be drawn into Jewish history; they must supply the replacement for the European Jews who have been killed.

TABLE 89 / *The Jewish Population Loss 1939–45**

	1939	1945
Austria	60,000	7,000
Belgium	90,000	40,000
Bulgaria	50,000	47,000
Czechoslovakia	315,000	44,000
Denmark	6,500	5,500
France	270,000	200,000
Germany	240,000	80,000
Greece	74,000	12,000
Hungary	400,000	200,000
Italy	50,000	33,000
Luxembourg	3,000	1,000
Netherlands	140,000	20,000
Norway	2,000	1,000
Poland	3,350,000	50,000
Roumania	800,000	430,000
USSR	3,020,000	2,600,000
Estonia	4,500	
Latvia	95,000	
Lithuania	145,000	
Yugoslavia	75,000	12,000

*The statistics for 1939 refer to prewar borders, and postwar frontiers have been used for 1945. The figure of 80,000 for Germany includes 60,000 displaced persons; the estimate of 2,600,000 for the USSR comprises about 300,000 refugees, deportees, and survivors from newly acquired territories.

For other compilations, see: *Report of the Anglo-American Committee of Enquiry regarding the problems of European Jewry and Palestine* (London, 1946), Cmd. 6808, pp. 58–59. Institute of Jewish Affairs, "Statistics of Jewish Casualties during Axis Domination" (mimeographed; New York, 1945). American Jewish Committee, *American Jewish Year Book* (New York), XLVIII (1946–47), 606–9; L (1948–49), 697; LI (1950), 246–47.

Because the destruction of the Jews was accomplished in blood, the altered appearance of the Jewish community is its most striking consequence; yet in a sense that alteration was bound to come in any case. To the demographers the catastrophe was but a rapid acceleration of a long-range trend which had had its beginnings a half-century before. Already, then, European Jewry was approaching its decline; the American Jews were preparing to seize the reins; and both these groups were nearing the day when they could no longer replenish themselves.[1] It is thus not so unlikely that the profoundest changes have not been physical ones.

In brief, it is not *what* the Jews lost, but *how* they lost it that might well prove to be the most disturbing factor in Jewish life. The Jews were not prepared for the events of 1933 to 1945, and when the least expected became the overwhelming truth, it brought about a deep transformation in Jewish attitudes and thought. There has been a complication of relations between Jewry and the outside world; a lasting estrangement has grown into the centuries-old relationship with Germany; and ancient bonds of trust and dependence have been broken within the Jewish community itself.

The effect of the German destruction process on the position of Jewry within Christianity has been twofold: the Jews have been forced into a reappraisal of the past, and they have simultaneously developed apprehensions about the future.

Throughout the Second World War the Jewish people adopted the Allied cause as their own; they shut out many thoughts of their disaster and helped achieve the final victory. The Allied powers, however, did not think of the Jews. The Allied nations who were at war with Germany did not come to the aid of Germany's victims. The Jews of Europe had no allies. In its gravest hour Jewry stood alone, and the realization of that desertion came as a shock to Jewish leaders all over the world.

In the United States the principal Jewish organizations had gotten together in 1943 to form the American Jewish Conference, which soon became a forum for many disappointed voices. At the second session in New York, December 3–5, 1944, Dr. Joseph Tenenbaum of the American Jewish Congress made the following remarks:

> Let us not rely on others to defend our interests. When Japan was accused of using gas against the Chinese, there was a solemn warning by the President of the United States who threatened to retaliate with gas warfare on the Japanese. Millions of Jews were suffocated in the lethal gas chambers, but nobody even threatened the Germans with retaliation – there was no threat to gas their cities. Jews must stop being the expendables among the nations. . . .[2]

The third session of the Jewish Conference was permeated with the theme of disappointment. Speaker after speaker rose to explain that the Jews had been abandoned, forgotten, left alone, betrayed. Professor Hayim Fineman of the Labor Zionist bloc had this to say:

> In terms of comparative statistics, the number of Jews destroyed in what was Hitler's Europe totals twenty-two times the number of Americans who fell in battle. What renders the situation so horrifying is the fact that this tragedy was not unavoidable. Many of those who are dead might have been alive were it not for the refusal and delays by our own State Department, by the International Red Cross, the War Refugee Board, and other agencies to take immediate measures.[3]

1. Felix A. Theilhaber, *Der Untergang der deutschen Juden* (Munich, 1911). L. Hersh, "The Downward Trend of Jewish Population," *Commentary,* February, 1949, pp. 185–91. Mortimer Spiegelman (Metropolitan Life Insurance Company), "The Reproductivity of Jews in Canada, 1940–1942," *Population Studies,* IV (December, 1950), 299–313.

2. Verbatim remarks by Tenenbaum in Alexander S. Kohanski (ed.), *The American Jewish Conference, Proceedings of the Second Session, December 3–5, 1944* (New York, 1945), p. 71.

3. Verbatim remarks by Fineman in Ruth Hershman (ed.), *The American Jewish Con-*

From Germany a survivor, the president of the liberated Jews in the American zone, Dr. Zalman Grinberg, came to the conference to add the following remarks:

> Ladies and gentlemen: I realize that we are living in a cynical world. I am aware of the fact that humanity is accustomed to brutality. [But] I myself would never have believed that the civilized world of the twentieth century could be so unmoved by the decimation of the Jewish people in Europe. I am forced to believe that it is only because these things happened to the Jewish people and not to another people.[4]

In speech after speech, we may thus discern the theme that the Allied leaders had not merely been callous but that they had reserved their callousness for the Jews. That accusation reflected a deep-seated anxiety in the Jewish ranks. It was the unverbalized fear that the Allies secretly approved of what the Germans had done and that, under given circumstances, they might even repeat the experiment.

In articulate circles this fear sometimes rises to the surface. Thus in the Zionist publication, the *Jewish Forum*, one Edwin M. Sears wrote an article under the title "Was Hitler Right?"[5] Sears viewed the Jewish position in the United States as one of life and death. Jewish security, he said, depended on an equilibrium of opposing forces. The Jewish defense agencies, instead of concerning themselves with parlor anti-Semitism and rabble-rousing statistics, were to watch this delicate balance which was already shifting the wrong way. Already a question was shaping up "which may well become the crucial question for American Jewry. The question is was Hitler right?" Already some Americans considered that the struggle with Germany was a mistake. "Regret may turn into admiration, and admiration into acceptance. Acceptance would mean U.S. Jewry's zero hour."[6]

While Jewry's relationship to the world at large has been undermined by a feeling of uncertainty about the future, the Jewish attitude toward Germany is complicated by the certainty of the past. We know by now what the Germans have done to the Jews: the destruction process wiped out, on a world-wide basis, one Jew in every three. Few nations and few religions have ever suffered a comparable loss. But the shedding of this Jewish blood is not the whole extent of the grievance; there is an aggravating factor in the German methodology. This was not merely an annihilation of five million people who were Jews. It was a killing of Jewry that reached a total of more than five million. The living know that the Jews of Europe were brought to death deliberately, that women, girls, and children died in that operation like cattle. What, then, is the Jewish feeling toward Germany?

Two important centers of response have developed in the international Jewish community: one on the continents of America and Europe, the other in Israel. American Jewry is not prone to take measures against the Germans. The American Jews do business with Germany; they import German goods; they design German products for American consumption; they sponsor German artists in the United States.[7] There is no mass revenge. Occasionally, solitary figures like Henry

---

ference, Proceedings of the Third Session, February 17–19, 1946 (New York, 1946), p. 47.

4. Verbatim remarks by Grinberg, *ibid.*, p. 148.

5. *Jewish Forum*, XXIV (April–May, 1951), pp. 69, 71, 87–90.

6. Not long after the appearance of this article, Jewish Communists were speaking in even crasser terms. See Jack Greenstein, "Rise of an American Judenrat," *Jewish Life*, April, 1952, pp. 9–11.

Morgenthau, Bernard Baruch, and Walter Winchell stood up to fight a losing battle against the emerging *rapprochement*,[8] but they were alone. The entire Jewish tradition hampers the development of a general hostility pattern. In the Jewish religion revenge is a task relegated to God. The Jewish community tends to frustrate every impetus to strike out in anguish. Anger is regarded as provocative in the sense that it may invite further hurt. It may also be dangerous, for it may exhaust the "good will" of the countries in which the Jewish people live. Thus American Jews must look at Germany through "American eyes," Canadian Jews must view it through "Canadian eyes," British Jews through "British eyes," and so on. However, this kind of looking is not accomplished so easily. The business-as-usual policy demands a certain amount of forgetting, and it requires, in addition, a good deal of rationalizing.

The repressive mechanism appears in many forms. Here is one example, from a spokesman of the American Council for Judaism, whose eyes were almost completely shut during the passage of events. The paragraph was written in 1945:

> The indomitable faith of some Jews in that better future is apparent in the latest reports from occupied Berlin in July of 1945. Six thousand Jews have been found among the *survivors of the rubbled capital*. They are preparing to build their lives again in their homeland and "are preparing living quarters for thousands expected to return from Theresienstadt" and other concentration camps.
>
> But "official" Jews, insisting on proving that there is a "Jewish" people, will not leave them in peace.[9]

In addition to those who would not see, there are those who do not wish to be reminded. The following passage was written by Dr. Samuel H. Flowerman (Department of Scientific Research, American Jewish Committee) in an introduction of a book dealing with pre-Nazi anti-Jewish propaganda in Germany:

> *Rehearsal for Destruction* is not another recital of Nazi horrors. I think people in western democracies are surfeited with these horrible tales; the human organism seeks protection against such continued barrages of sadism and their hidden connotations of "collective" guilt. Paul Massing has eschewed the macabre aspects of Nazi antisemitism.[10]

---

7. One of the most conspicuous distributors of German consumer goods is R. H. Macy & Co. Macy's set the pattern for other Jewish department stores. One of the most important designers in German service is Raymond Loewy. The chief importer of German artistic talent is S. Hurok.

8. See Morgenthau's *Germany Is Our Problem* (New York and London, 1945). On Baruch, see his testimony before Senate Military Affairs Committee in hearings on elimination of German resources for war, 79th Cong., 1st sess., 1945, Pt. I, pp. 1–28. Some organizations, too, are involved in reminding and warning activities. Chief among them is the Society for the Prevention of World War III. The Jewish War Veterans, American Jewish Congress, and Anti-Defamation League have confined themselves on the whole to protesting the arrival of German artists, etc.

9. Elmer Berger, *The Jewish Dilemma* (New York, 1945), p. 228. Italics added.

10. Introduction by Samuel Flowerman in Paul Massing, *Rehearsal for Destruction* (New York, 1949). It should be noted that while many monuments are erected by Jewry in memory of the dead, there are few attempts to inquire into the actual killings. There is a large postwar literature describing the extinct communities, but few works deal with the extinction process itself. When German reparation funds became available for catastrophe research, the two receiving organizations, Yad Vashem in Jerusalem and the YIVO Institute for Jewish Research in New York, concluded an agreement on January 5, 1954, to set up three divisions: (1) bibliography, (2) archives (both in New York) and (3) *Pinkas Hakehilot* (annuals of destroyed Jewish communities; in Jerusalem). *American Political Science Review*, June, 1956, p. 615.

Repressions are not always effective, for there are always moments of reminder. Hence the Jews must rationalize too; they must find some justification for the rapid – almost hurried – normalization of their relations with Germany. The most common rationalization for that process is the argument of the "good Germans" and the "bad Germans." In this vein, the following reasoning was applied by a Zionist in support of reparation negotiations with the Adenauer government:

> The question is, were the majority of the Germans Nazis? Are all Germans responsible for Dachau and Oswiecim, for the torture cells and gas furnaces of the Hitler regime? My answer is emphatically, No. . . .
>
> At no time before Hindenburg appointed Hitler as Chancellor had the Nazi party received a majority of the German vote. . . .
>
> From 1933 to 1945, over two million Germians [*sic*] went through Hitler's concentration camps. This was their only way to demonstrate their opposition to Hitlerism.[11]

On the same track the organ of the Jewish community in Communist Budapest, *Uj Elet*, stated in a front-page editorial:

> It is impossible to correct injustice by injustice. *It would be a grave injustice, and the debasement of humanism if we charged the things that occurred in Germany to the German people.* . . . Modern sociology does not recognize guilty nations. There are no guilty nations, only guilty classes and ruling classes. . . .
>
> For this reason *all those who confuse hatred for fascism with hatred for the German people are on a very wrong and dangerous path.* . . .
>
> On this ground, we have faith in the new Democratic Eastern Germany in which Generalissimo Stalin, our own saviour, has also put his faith. . . .
>
> *From now on, we are no longer going to speak about hatred for the Germans.* A passion of this kind would lead us dangerously astray. *The German working people are just as good allies of the toilers of the world as any other people.*[12]

Closely allied to the "good Germans–bad Germans" rationalization is the notion of "good Jews–bad Jews." Thus a professor of the social sciences, writing in an American Jewish monthly, charges: "The anti-Germans have utilized allegations of 'the German danger' to justify notions as cruel and crazy as the Morgenthau plan."[13] In the more succinct language of Mathias Rakosi, the Jewish leader of the Hungarian Communists, there are "Jewish Fascists" too.[14]

The good-bad rationalization is in one sense incomplete: it leaves unsettled the problem of what should be done with the "bad" Germans. How should they be defined? What treatment should be meted out to them? Should they perhaps be destroyed? The Jews have answers to these questions also. Thus the publication of the National Conference of Christians and Jews notes that

> Dr. David Levy, clinical professor of psychiatry at Columbia, found that anti-Nazis in Germany had travelled and read more than anti-Semitic Nazis.

The evaluation and study of all the materials to be gathered was envisaged as a task for future generations.

11. Joseph Dunner, "Appeal to Reason," *Congress Weekly*, January 28, 1952, pp. 5–7.

12. Editorial in *Uj Elet* (Budapest), October 20, 1949, as cited by Eugene Duschinsky, "Hungary," in Peter Meyer *et al.*, *The Jews in the Soviet Satellites* (Syracuse, 1953), pp. 468–69. Italics in text.

13. David Riesman, "The 'Militant' Fight against Anti-Semitism," *Commentary*, January, 1951, pp. 12–13.

14. The remark was made before the Communist seizure of power in Hungary, in the presence of Hungarian President Tildy. Ferenc Nagy (former Prime Minister of postwar Hungary), *The Struggle behind the Iron Curtain* (New York, 1948), pp. 320–23.

> Anti-Nazis had lived in a less disciplined childhood, received more affection from parents. Perhaps most important, many of them recalled that their liberal outlook began in their teens when they heard a grown-up question the omnipotence of the Kaiser and the ruling class. Prejudiced persons suffer from "mental constriction," a narrowmindedness that prevents them from finding solutions, even to arithmetic problems.[15]

We may understand, therefore, the extensive Jewish preoccupation with German re-education and rehabilitation.[16] The "environment" is to be changed; the "bad" Germans are to be made "good"; in the end there is to be "peace." As Rabbi Leo Baeck put it: "In the name of God's command and man's future, this peace should finally be concluded. Two nations, both with one destiny, cannot forever turn their backs to each other and pass each other by."[17]

Let us not mistake the tenor of the Jewish repressions and rationalizations: these distortions are evidence of deep-rooted disturbances. It is safe to conclude that the more absurd the arguments appear to be, the greater must have been the effort to contain and smother the inner revolt. Indeed, the Jews of the Western world have sought outlets for their hostility elsewhere. They found such an outlet in the enemies of Israel.

The reaction of displaced hostility is not uncommon in the annals of individual and mass behavior. Here it was almost inevitable. Israel is Jewry's great consolation. It is a vast "undoing" achievement – one of the greatest in all history. Even while the Jews of Europe were being slaughtered, the delegates to the first session of the American Jewish Conference were turning their thoughts to the future state.

Their thoughts were expressed to some extent in a speech delivered by Dr. Israel Goldstein of the General Zionists during the rescue symposium: "For all our rivers of tears and oceans of blood, for our broken lives and devastated homes, for all our gutted synagogues and desecrated scrolls, for all our slain youths and spoliated maidens, for all our agony and for all the martyrdom of these black years, we shall be consoled when in Eretz Israel, reestablished as a Jewish Commonwealth, land of our sunrise, and in every land where the dispersed of Israel dwell, the sun of freedom will rise," etc. etc.[18] From this came the great concentration of fury upon England and, to a lesser extent, the Arab countries after the war. In the years 1945 to 1949, England was Jewry's primary enemy. The English, and the Arabs, moved into this position because in seeking to frustrate the establishment of a Jewish homeland, they were reopening wounds that only Israel could heal.

Significantly, the creation of the state of Israel resulted in the development of conditions under which Jews could express themselves in larger numbers and in much stronger terms as Germany's enemies than anywhere else. For a while at least, Israel kept its distance from Germany. No diplomatic representatives were exchanged.[19] Germans could not easily visit Israel, and the German language, as well as German

15. *Conference,* spring, 1949, p. 5.

16. The National Conference of Christians and Jews alone has sunk hundreds of thousands of dollars into its operations in Germany. These operations were subsidized by the American military government. *Ibid.*, pp. 15, 12.

17. Leo Baeck, "Israel und das deutsche Volk," *Merkur* (Stuttgart), October, 1952, p. 911.

18. Alexander S. Kohanski (ed.), *The American Jewish Conference – Its Organization and Proceedings of the First Session, August 29 to September 2, 1943* (New York, 1944), pp. 80–81.

music, was barred from public performances there.[20]

Two factors were chiefly responsible for the emergence of these reactions: One was the concentration of survivors in Israel — every seventh inhabitant of Israel was incarcerated in a German concentration camp; every third Israeli lost one or more relatives in the destruction process.[21] The second cause lay in the very fact of Israel's independence. The Jews of the Western and Soviet spheres were — willingly or unwillingly — a part of the countries in which they lived. The Jews in Israel had acquired a state of their own. They were not forever dependent upon "protection"; they did not have to guard constantly against a depletion of the reservoir of Christian good will; they no longer had to bury their feelings. There was no longer any need to rationalize impotence with forgiveness.

We have dealt at some length with Jewry's reactions to the world at large and to Germany in particular. We shall say little about the third great consequence of the catastrophe upon the psychological disposition of the Jews: the formation of barriers within Jewry itself. Over the centuries the dispersion of the Jews had a functional significance; whenever some part of the Jewish community was under attack, it depended upon help from other Jews. In the period of the Nazi regime that dependence broke down. Help did not come. Henceforth an insider could not reflect deeply about his fate without coming to the conclusion that the outsider had not done his all. "They were outside, we were inside. They were not immediately affected, we were the victims. They moralized, we feared death. They had sympathy for us and believed themselves to be powerless; we wanted to live and believed rescue *had* to be possible."[22] The Jewish catastrophe was attended by a *twofold* paralysis: the Jews inside could not break out; the Jews outside could not break in.

What about the Germans? What was their reaction? The complex of German postwar responses was in the first instance a continuation and extension of the wartime psychic defense mechanisms. The language of forgetting and justification was hardly changed. We may note only that, as the destruction process recedes into the background, the intensity of the reactions is lessening; i.e., the repressions and rationalizations are gradually fulfilling their psychological function. Let us look at some examples of these adjustments.

The postwar campaign to bury the past was actually launched on March 21, 1945, by Heinrich Himmler, when in a letter to his Swedish masseur he dismissed the entire destruction of the European Jews as "senseless" (*eine Unvernunft*). In that letter he demanded that both sides ignore "all their differences" and disregard the "bloodiest wounds." The time had come for "wisdom and logic," "the human heart and the will to help."[23]

19. An Israel mission was sent to West Germany for the purpose of selecting goods for shipment as reparations to Israel. Israel itself received no German mission. The Israel attitude toward Germany in international organizations is summarized by a study group of the Hebrew University of Jerusalem in *Israel and the United Nations* (New York, 1956), pp. 176, 198.

20. "Israel Backs Ban on Use of the German Language," *New York Times*, January 2, 1951, p. 4. "Israel Philharmonic Drops 'Eulenspiegel,'" *ibid.*, December 9, 1952, p. 42.

21. Statement by Dr. Uri Naor, director, information division, Israel Mission in Cologne, in *Aufbau* (New York), July 15, 1955, p. 15.

22. Dr. Rezsö Kastner, "Der Bericht des jüdischen Rettungskomitees aus Budapest 1942–1945" (mimeographed), pp. 88–89. In March, 1957, Kastner was killed by assassins in Tel Aviv for his activities in Budapest. Gershon Swet, "Rudolf Kastners Ermordung," *Aufbau* (New York), March 22, 1957, pp. 1, 4. Criticism, let alone violence, directed at surviving leaders is rare.

Himmler's demand has been echoed time and again.[24] A little difficulty remains, however, in stowing away the "prank." With the onset of the collapse the Germans lost hold of the machinery of government; they were now confronted with comment from without and reminders from within. The external problem was ultimately solved by deliveries of goods. When, in 1951, the new West German government offered to pay reparations to the Jews, it was buying silence.[25]

The internal situation was more complex. Within the German community itself the annihilation of the Jews was bound up with countless recollections of the Nazi regime and of the war. Hence the efforts at distortion have not ceased; the dead Jews show up in statistics as dead Germans and dead Poles.[26] One newspaper called the figure of 6,000,000 deaths "exaggerated" and proposed 1,000,000 as a "fair estimate."[27] Another publication, explaining that the Jews were racially weaker than Aryans, attributed the deaths to the hardships of warfare.[28] According to the sophisticated SS investigator Hauptsturmführer Dr. Morgen, the Jews destroyed themselves – completely, and almost without any outside help.[29] In a similar vein, the historian Sturmbannführer Dr. Höttl pointed out that the very first commander of the SS, Emil Maurice, was a "*Mischling* of the second degree." Höttl is practically certain that Himmler too had a Jewish relative. The RSHA chief Heydrich was such a bitter enemy of the Jews because they formed at least "a part of his ancestry."[30]

Even these distortions have not done the entire job. We may also observe erasures of a more familiar kind: the Jewish graveyards in Germany, constant reminders of a community that is now gone, are repeatedly targets of vandalistic destruction.[31]

In a sense, it is harder to destroy the dead than to kill the living. The living were killed quickly, the dead Jews

23. Himmler to Kersten, March 21, 1945, in Alexander Weissberg, *Die Geschichte von Joel Brand* (Cologne-Berlin, 1956), annex.

24. West German President Heuss used similar language six years later when he spoke of the "courage to love" (*Mut zur Liebe*). Interview of Heuss by Manfred George, *Aufbau* (New York), July 20, 1951, p. 2.

25. Text of the reparations agreement in State of Israel/Ministry for Foreign Affairs, *Documents Relating to the Agreement between the Government of Israel and the Government of the Federal Republic of Germany* (Jerusalem, 1953). Significantly, the agreement contains no addition of the dead. It is based instead on the number of survivors. Payment is thus determined not by the extent of the Jewish loss but by the cost of rebuilding the lives of those who remained.

26. See compilation by German Federal Government/Press and Information Office, *Germany Reports,* 1953, pp. 101–3.

27. "Escaped Nazi Gets Bonn Deputy's Aid," *New York Times,* January 11, 1953, p. 12.

28. Cited by Norbert Muhlen, *The Return of Germany* (Chicago, 1953), p. 157n.

29. Affidavit by Dr. Konrad Morgen, July 13, 1946, SS(A)-65.

30. Walter Hagen (alias Höttl), *Die Geheime Front* (Zürich, 1950), pp. 20–39. Höttl speculates that Heydrich may have been as much as a three-quarter Jew. Presumably not even the last quarter was entirely German, for Höttl endowed Heydrich also with a "slight Mongoloid touch" (*einen schwachen mongolischen Einschlag*).

31. Jack Raymond, "Germans Defacing Jewish Cemeteries," *New York Times,* May 14, 1950, p. 6. Also, *Aufbau* (New York), June 30, 1950, p. 3; July 14, 1950, pp. 20, 22; September 1, 1950, p. 3; November 2, 1951, p. 32; May 2, 1954, p. 26. There are 1700 Jewish cemeteries in West Germany; the leftover Jewish community is not in a position to care for them. The Interior Ministry was prevailed upon to assume financial responsibility for the upkeep of the graveyards. However, the exercise of this responsibility required a new law, since the supervision of "cultural" matters is normally a prerogative of the provinces. A report issued in 1956 stated that "this law is being prepared quietly in order to avoid unnecessary public debate." Hans Wallenberg, *Report on Democratic Institutions in Germany* (New York, 1956), p. 52.

linger on. And when memories of the act break through all repressive layers, the old rationalizations are expounded anew. As before, there are explanations focused on the victim as well as justifications centered on the perpetrator; however, the nature of postwar pressures has effected a redistribution of emphasis. There is not as much repetition of remarks about the Jews but all the more elaboration of testimony and argumentation designed to relieve the German bureaucrat of his responsibility.

We are familiar by now with the anti-Jewish conceptions which have been stockpiled in Germany for hundreds of years. Despite all the postwar Allied controls, despite "re-education" and "democratization," the Germans could not easily discard these ideas. Let us take the notion of Jewish world rule and world Jewish hostility to the German nation.

During the height of the fighting German propaganda had stressed that Jewry was directing the Allied war, and after Germany went down to defeat, the impression was strong that the Jews were guiding the Western governments in matters affecting the Allied occupation. When West German Chancellor Adenauer was ready to begin sovereignty negotiations in the United States, his advisors believed that the "success" of his mission "would depend in large measure on the attitude of Jewish groups toward him." Thus the offer to pay reparations was made also with a view to buying Jewish good will.[32]

In addition to that diluted theory of Jewish world rule, there are occasional but noteworthy references to Jewish "criminality." Within the Bavarian-Tyrolian region there have been recurring allegations of criminality in their crassest form: the Jews are still accused of ritual murder. Here are three examples.

1. In the Bavarian town of Memmingen a housewife, Frau Grammel, approached a lawyer with a complaint that her four-year-old son had been invited on Easter by a tenant, Gutfreund, to a party. The child had returned from Gutfreund's room "drunk." The vein of the child's left arm had been punctured; either the boy had been given an injection or his arm had been used to draw blood. Frau Grammel's lawyer, Dr. Heinrich Arnold, wrote down the charges along with the explanation that it was an "old Jewish custom" to add a drop of blood to the Easter pastry. In substantiation Dr. Arnold produced as his source Gauleiter Streicher's paper, *Der Stürmer*.[33]

2. In Munich a report was received that a child's hand had been found outside the city. Four women, the Frauen Aumer, Böttger, Holzapfel, and Schachtner, thereupon spread the rumor that "the Jews" had killed the child.[34]

32. Jack Raymond, "Bonn Delay Seen on Claim Payment," *New York Times*, October 14, 1951, p. 29. In Austria field representatives of Jewry were believed to be lurking in every American occupation office. When the U.S. High Commissioner in Vienna, Donnelly, refused at an Allied Control Council meeting to give unconditional approval to an Austrian amnesty measure for the benefit of wartime Nazis, on the ground that the Austrian government was proposing to indemnify ex-Nazis before giving consideration to the victims of Nazism, the chairman of the People's Party and later Chancellor of Austria, Julius Raab, resorted to an attack upon "certain emigrants" in the office of the High Commissioner. John MacCormac, "Vienna is Critical of U.S. 'Emigrants,'" *New York Times*, June 8, 1952, p. 14. No such "emigrants" were serving in the High Commissioner's office. "Es geht schon wieder los in Wien," *Aufbau* (New York), June 13, 1952, p. 4. "Die Wiener Hetze gegen 'US-Emigranten,'" *ibid.*, June 20, 1952, p. 9.

33. "Ritualmordschwindel in Memmingen," *ibid.*, April 1, 1949, p. 3.

34. "Ritualmordschwindel in München," *ibid.*, September 9, 1949, p. 7.

3. The Tyrolean village of Rinn was the scene of annual pilgrimages by busloads and trainloads of schoolboys sent by the Catholic Church to view a group of stone figures which portray the alleged ritual murder of a Christian boy by Jewish travelers who passed through the village on July 12, 1462. When the French High Commissioner and the chairman of an organization of Jewish camp survivors protested against this "commemoration" to the Catholic Church, Bishop Rusch of Innsbruck wrote to Cardinal Innitzer of Austria that "the Jewish letter goes much too far when it seeks to establish that Jews have never done such things at all." Cardinal Innitzer forwarded this reply without comment to the Jewish leader and the French High Commissioner.[35]

The postwar rationalization pattern is characterized not only by vestiges of Jewish "world rule" and "criminality"; the immediate postwar situation lent itself also to the maintenance and sharpening of conceptions about Jewish "parasitism." The occasion for the resurgence of such thinking was a concentration of Jewish survivors on German soil. These survivors did not wish to remain in Germany and they did not wish to contribute to German recovery. In German thinking these people were therefore useless. They were superfluous. They were the survivors of the "cleansing process." In August, 1949, a letter received by the *Süddeutsche Zeitung* in Munich portrayed the Jews as "bloodsuckers" *(Blutsauger)*. The letter was immediately published.[36]

The ancient rationalizations have not passed from the scene. At a time when the whole German nation was gagged by an Allied regime committed to the rooting out of Nazism and its tenets, enough was brought out publicly to reveal a persisting need for assurance that the Jews deserved to be destroyed.

More important, however, than the half-submerged attempts to indict the victims was the open campaign to absolve the perpetrators. Since it was hard to contradict the evidence produced against these men, one of the principal methods of absolution was to drag everyone into the picture as an accomplice. Such was the exchange which took place on April 18, 1946, before an international court, between a German defense counsel and former Generalgouverneur Frank:

> Dr. Seidl: Did you ever participate in the annihilation of the Jews?
>
> Frank: I say "yes;" and the reason why I say "yes" is because, having lived through 5 months of this trial, and particularly after having heard the testimony of the witness Hoess, my conscience does not allow me to throw the responsibility solely on these minor people. I myself have never installed an extermination camp for Jews, or promoted the existence of such camps; but if Adolf Hitler personally laid that dreadful responsibility on his people, then it is mine too, for we have fought Jewry for years; and we have indulged in the most horrible utterances – my own diary bears witness against me. Therefore, it is no more than my duty to answer your question with "yes." A thousand years will pass and still this

35. S. Wiesenthal, "Tiroler Ritualmord-Märchen – und die Kirche ändert nichts daran," *ibid.*, May 11, 1950, p. 40. Wiesenthal was chairman of the Jüdischer KZ-Verband. The controversy was continued for years. See "Tiroler Ritualmord-Spiele – Neue Kontroverse um den Bischof Rusch," *ibid.*, June 10, 1955, p. 5. Postwar ritual murder legends also emerged in Hungary, where Jews were reported to have killed Christian children to make them into sausages. Nagy, *The Struggle behind the Iron Curtain*, pp. 246–48. Eugene Duschinsky, "Hungary," in Meyer *et al.*, *The Jews in the Soviet Satellites*, pp. 419–20, 423–25.

36. After the publication of the letter about five hundred Jews marched along the Möhlstrasse in protest. The German police opened fire upon them. "Der Skandal von München: Antisemitismus wird erlaubt – Auf Juden wird geschossen," *Aufbau* (New York), August 19, 1949, pp. 1–2.

guilt of Germany will not have been erased.[37]

To Frank the destruction of the Jews was an act of world-historical proportions, both terrifying and grandiose. He saw himself as a major participant in this act, but if he were called upon to answer for that participation, Germany as a whole had to share his guilt.

The challenge which Frank had hurled at the tribunal could be broadened still more. In fact, a German theologian was to make that attempt. Late in 1945 a number of Lutheran churchmen met at Stuttgart and issued a declaration which read in part as follows:

> The council of the Evangelical Church in Germany welcomes to its meeting of October 18 and 19, 1945, the representatives of the Ecumenical Council of Churches.
>
> We are all the more grateful for this visit because we realize that we are bound to our people not only in a community of suffering but also in a solidarity of guilt. With heavy pain we say: Through us, unending misfortune was brought to many countries and nations.

Among the signers of this declaration were such church dignitaries as Wurm, Niemöller, and Asmussen. When the Catholic Church objected to the guilt formulation, Asmussen explained that he could understand the objection in the sense that

> nobody may maintain that the guilt which Adolf Hitler and his tribunes have shouldered upon themselves may be collected from the entire German people. No international tribunal has the right before God and man to do a thing like that. So far as that is concerned, there can be no talk of collective guilt.
>
> With weighty emphasis we must, however, stress the right of God to pursue those secret connections which link Hitler's guilt and mine. If the danger of misunderstanding were not so great, I should add that God is in a position, and in my opinion willing, to shed light upon those connections which link the murders of Heinrich Himmler and the attitude of an ordinary American citizen. For there can be no doubt about this: Although every man is responsible for his own deeds, as certain that mankind is one kind is the certainty that this guilt is anchored forever in all mankind. In Adam we have all died.[38]

The theologian Asmussen transformed a collective guilt into a universal one. In his explanatory hands guilt became indistinguishable from life itself.

There is a vast difference between actual performance and a potential for action. No words of generality, no theological argumentation, can obliterate the fact that Germans had reached out farther in the range of destruction than any other nation on earth. The destruction of the Jews will carry through history the trademark of Nazi Germany. Yet we must not dismiss Asmussen, for he pointed to the basic problem in the Allied stand: massive inaction becomes conspicuous; it is an act in itself.

What was the basis of the Allied response? To understand that reaction – whether in the West or in the East – we have to focus primarily upon the reason for which the Allied coalition fought its war. The Allies had been challenged. Now they wanted above all to win that struggle. Their effort to emerge victorious included neither an aim to destroy any segment of the German population nor a plan to save any part of Germany's victims. The postwar punishment of perpetrators was largely a consequence of afterthoughts. The liberation of the survivors was al-

37. Testimony by Frank, *Trial of the Major War Criminals,* XII, 13.

38. Dr. Hans Asmussen, "Die Stuttgarter Erklärung," *Die Wandlung* (Heidelberg), 1948, pp. 17–27.

most entirely a by-product of victory. We may note, therefore, that, on the one hand, the Allies could harmonize with their war effort all sorts of denunciations of the Germans but that, on the other hand, there was no disposition to deviate from military goals for the deliverance of the Jews. In that sense the destruction of the Jews presented itself as a problem with which the Allies could not effectively deal.

During the war the rescue of dying Jewry interfered with the doctrine of victory first; after the war the rectifications in favor of Jewry conflicted with the attempts which both East and West were carrying on to woo the occupied German power sphere. Thus there developed from the beginning an ambiguity in the Allied position; the condemnations of persecution, the freedom propaganda, the expressions of sympathy for the oppressed, were hedged in by reservations which preserved more basic Allied interests. These reservations were responsible for the functional blindness which afflicted the Allies during decisive moments of the Jewish catastrophe, and for some strange imputations which were levied against Jewry thereafter.

The repressive pattern manifested itself primarily in a refusal to recognize either the special character of German action or the special identity of the Jewish victims. Examples of the obscuration of the German destruction process are the periods of total silence, extending particularly from 1941 through 1942; the subsequent generality of language, such as the profuse but exclusive employment in the three-power Moscow Declaration of descriptive terms on the order of "brutalities," "atrocities," "massacres," "mass executions," and "monstrous crimes;"[39] the constant emphasis in the literature and in speeches upon "concentration camps," often including the epitomization of Dachau and Buchenwald but rarely embracing any mention of Auschwitz, let alone the faraway camps of Treblinka and Sobibor or Belzec; the tendency in public statements to link the Jewish fate with the fate of other peoples, such as the reference in a declaration by President Roosevelt to "the deportation of Jews to their death in Poland or Norwegians and French to their death in Germany;"[40] and finally the lawyers' invocation of the "act of state" doctrine to show that at least some of the German measures against Jewry were nothing special – they were "acts of government" by the "authorities of the German state"[41] or at worst "governmental persecution . . . under the municipal law of another state."[42]

Closely linked to that obliteration of the German destruction process is the disappearance of the Jewish victim. In the one case the annihilation phase is not fully recognized; in the other it descends upon an amorphous group of people. The aforementioned Moscow Declaration, which bears the heavy imprint of Churchill's hand and which also carries the signatures of Roosevelt and Stalin, managed to omit any reference to the Jewish disaster. This document, drafted in October, 1943, contains the public warning that "Germans who take part in the wholesale shooting of Italian officers or in the execution of French, Dutch, Belgian or

39. Statement signed by Roosevelt, Churchill, and Stalin, released to the press by the Department of State, November 1, 1943, in report by Justice Jackson to the President on *International Conference on Military Trials*, Department of State Publication 3080, 1949, pp. 11–12.

40. Statement by the President, released to the press by the White House, March 24, 1944, *ibid.*, pp. 12–13.

41. Justice Jackson in *International Conference on Military Trials*, p. 333.

42. Judge Learned Hand in Bernstein v. Van Heygen Freres Societe Anonyme (1947), 163 F 2d 246.

Norwegian hostages or of Cretan peasants, or who have shared in slaughters inflicted on the people of Poland or in the territories of the Soviet Union which are now being swept clear of the enemy, will know that they will be brought back to the scene of their crimes and judged on the spot by the peoples whom they have outraged."[43]

What happened to the Jews in this declaration? The Jews are among the "French hostages"; they are a component part of the "people of Poland"; they are lost in the "territories of the Soviet Union." The Western and Soviet governments alike were able to take from the Jews their special identity by the simple device of switching classifications. Thus the Jews of German nationality became Germans, the Jews of Polish nationality were converted into Poles, the Jews of Hungarian nationality into Hungarians, and so on.[44]

Some of the most fantastic legal consequences flowed from this legalistic interplay. For example, in 1942 Home Secretary Morrison replied to an inquiry by a member of Parliament that Jews in England who were rendered stateless by German decree would still be treated as German nationals, because the United Kingdom government did not recognize the competence of an enemy state in time of war to deprive its citizens of their nationality. In Berlin the Foreign Office legal expert Albrecht read about this development in a Transocean news report and wrote, "Good."[45] Again, in 1944 British military authorities in Belgium interned about 2000 Jews as "enemy aliens." When Sidney Silverman, M.P., intervened with the Earl of Halifax in Washington, he was told that the measure was dictated by "military necessity."[46] In the Soviet Union prominent Jews about to be purged had to expect as a matter of course to be accused of "spying" for the Germans.[47] Some 15,000 Hungarian Jewish forced laborers taken

43. Statement by Roosevelt, Churchill, and Stalin, in *International Conference on Military Trials*, pp. 11–12.

44. In the United States the Office of War Information as a matter of policy refrained from mentioning Jews as a special group of victims. Verbatim statement by Dr. Leon A. Kubowitsky (World Jewish Congress) in Kohanski, *American Jewish Conference, First Session*, p. 119. The OWI was headed by Elmer Davis. The domestic branch was under Gardner Cowles, policy and development under Archibald MacLeish, the overseas branch under Robert Sherwood.

45. Transocean report, dated July 31, 1942, with notation by Albrecht, NG-2111.

46. Dr. Maurice L. Perlzweig (chairman, British section of World Jewish Congress) in Kohanski, *American Jewish Conference, Second Session*, p. 214. The treatment of denationalized Jews in British, South African, American, French, and Swiss courts is discussed by H. Lauterpacht in "The Nationality of Denationalized Persons," *Jewish Year Book of International Law* (1948), pp. 164–85. Article 44 of the Geneva Convention of 1949 on Civilian Persons in War states that a belligerent in its own territory shall not treat as enemy aliens "refugees who do not, in fact, enjoy the protection of any government." Department of State Publication 3938, 1950.

47. See, for example, the case of the Red Army generals in W. G. Krivitsky, *In Stalin's Secret Service* (New York and London, 1939), p. 212. The author was chief of Red Army intelligence in western Europe. Also, the case of Wiktor Alter and H. Ehrlich, Jewish Socialists from Poland, shot in the USSR after organizing an international Jewish anti-Fascist committee, on the ground that they had appealed to the Soviet armies "to conclude an immediate peace with Germany." Bogomolov (Soviet Ambassador in London) to Raczinski (Polish Foreign Minister), March 31, 1943, in Government of Poland/Polish Embassy in London, *Polish-Soviet Relations 1918–1943*, p. 180, and preceding correspondence on pp. 178-79. During the period 1940–41 the Soviets also practiced the deportation of unwanted Jews of German nationality to German or German-occupied territory. Victor Kravchenko, *I Chose Freedom* (New York, 1946), pp. 210, 217, 264. Alexander Weissberg, *The Accused* (New York, 1951), pp. 501–5. On the approach of an American court toward the extradition of a Jew to Germany, see In re Normano (1934), 7 F. Supp. 329.

by the Red Army on the eastern front did not return home. They remained in captivity as "prisoners of war."[48]

The Allied governments always knew that they could be charged with a shortage of action in the case of the Jewish catastrophe. They therefore sought to alter the historical picture before them and to substitute a falsity for the fact. The Jews were no longer suffering a catastrophe; the catastrophe was not happening to the Jews. Through the years these distortions have resisted revelation and proof, and they remain in the Allied approach to a range of Jewish claims, the first line of defense.

In the wake of the destruction process there have also been statements which imply that the Jews had brought their fate upon themselves. These statements have a significance of their own, for they indicate an acceptance of the German position, an identification with the perpetrator, and thus also an incorporation of his ideas and thinking. The most conspicuous example of such propaganda is the Soviet drive of 1952–53 against Jewish "cosmopolitans," "doctor criminals," and "bandit scum."[49] In the West the characterizations of Jewry have been more subdued. Thus the comment: "Hitler . . . was carrying out a policy of putting the Jews where they wouldn't bother the rest of the world."[50] Right after the end of hostilities, we find also the notion that during the war the Jews had been "kicked around" but that "since the war, the situation has changed and the Jews are now on top and the other fellow is beaten down."[51]

In fact, the development of a postwar policy was completely in the hands of the Allies. From the moment of the German collapse to the resurgence of German power, the Allies were on top.

48. The figure is given by the Anglo-American Committee of Enquiry in its report of April, 1946, Cmd. 6808, p. 59. A somewhat higher estimate is supplied by Duschinsky, "Hungary," in Meyer *et al., The Jews in the Soviet Satellites,* pp. 392–95.

49. See, in general, *New York Times Index* for these years. Although linking its epitaphs with Jews and Jewish names, *Pravda* rejected even at the height of the drive the "zoological racism of the Hitlerites." *New York Times,* January 16, 1953, p. 3. At that very time Prime Minister Churchill in an unguarded moment accused a Jewish member of the opposition of "cosmopolitanism and internationalism." Raymond Daniell "Churchill Stirs Commons by Impugning Shinwell Patriotism," *ibid.,* December 4, 1952, pp. 1, 5. Before Churchill's resumption of the Prime Ministership, Shinwell had served as Minister of Defense in the Labor government.

50. From the paper of an American college student, 1956.

51. From a letter by President Truman to displaced persons expert Edwin Pauly, end of 1945, as quoted by Josiah E. DuBois Jr., *The Devil's Chemists* (Boston, 1952), p. 200. Let it be stressed that occasional rationalizations invoked for a policy of passivity are very different from organized vilifications that presage a totally dissimilar goal. For a while the United States had a small replica of the Nazi movement: the National Renaissance Party, headed by James Madole. It claimed, as the Nazis did, that the Jews were the creators of both capitalism and Communism. See House of Representatives/Committee on Un-American Activities, *Preliminary Report on Neo-Fascist and Hate Groups,* December 17, 1954. In Canada there was a group which held that Jewry is responsible for Nazism as well as Communism. See British Israel Association, *The Battle Is the Lord's* (Vancouver, B.C., undated).

More recently, an American Nazi party under Lincoln Rockwell hailed Adolf Hitler as the "gift of an inscrutable Providence." The party program proposes to "execute" Jews proved to have taken part in Marxist or Zionist "treason" plots. All "disloyal" Jews would be removed from positions, and debts owed to Jews by non-Jews would be cancelled should there be evidence of "unfair or immoral business methods." The "rare honest Jews" would be protected from popular "wrath," while a "scientific study" would determine "if the Jewish virus is a matter of environment and can be eliminated by education and training, or if some other method must be developed to render Jews harmless to Society." Letter by Seth D. Ryan (National Secretary) to Daniel J. Scheans, March 13, 1961, with enclosed party program, through the courtesy of Mr. Scheans.

They alone were in a position to determine what was to be done to the perpetrators and what was to be done for the victims. The reaction to the perpetrators reached its culmination in a series of trials. Action in behalf of the victims was evolved in two consecutive phases, the rescue of survivors and the salvage of their property.

1 / The Trials

The Allied leaders began to think about the postwar treatment of their Axis opponents in the fall of 1943. At that time thinking was confined to the possible proceedings against the top strata of the Axis leadership. These men — central targets of Allied resentment — were to suffer death. The only question open for consideration was the method of implementation: summary execution or execution after trial.

During the Moscow Conference on War Criminals in October, 1943, American Secretary of State Hull declared himself in favor of a "drumhead court-martial." He did not see why the Axis "outlaws" should have the benefit of a "fancy trial." The Soviet delegation agreed with "loud exclamations of approval." British Foreign Secretary Eden dissented; he thought that "all the legal forms" should be observed.[1]

Much later a law-and-order movement began in the U.S. War Department under Secretary Stimson and Assistant Secretary McCloy. Although President Roosevelt personally favored shooting, he appointed one of his assistants, Judge Samuel Rosenman, to "study the question for him." On January 18, 1945, Stimson, Rosenman, and Attorney General Biddle agreed that legal action should be taken.[2]

The Soviets, in the meantime, also veered to a policy of trial. A surprised Churchill reported to Roosevelt on October 22, 1944, that Stalin had suddenly adopted an "ultra-respectable line" — the Soviet dictator felt that the world might draw the wrong conclusions from a summary procedure.[3]

When both the Americans and the Russians had switched their positions, the British turned too. They were now *against* a trial. In a lengthy *aide-memoire* handed by Sir Alexander Cadogan to Judge Rosenman on April 23, 1945, the British official recorded his anxiety that the whole procedure would be regarded as a "put-up job," that it would be "exceedingly long," and that in the confusion attending an amalgamation of Russian, American, and British ideas the defense might even score some "unexpected point."[4]

The British reluctance to try the prospective defendants before executing them was soon overcome by American arguments,[5] and in the following summer months representatives of the United States, Great Britain, and Russia met in London to draw up a charter for an international military tribunal that would try those "major criminals" whose offenses had no particular geographic localization and who, in the words of the wartime Moscow Declaration, were to be "punished by joint decision of the Governments of the Al-

1. Cordell Hull, *The Memoirs of Cordell Hull* (New York, 1948), II, 1289–91.

2. Henry Stimson and McGeorge Bundy, *On Active Service in Peace and War* (New York, 1948), pp. 584–86. The Stimson movement was in response to a Morgenthau proposal for summary shooting. The full text of the Morgenthau plan has not been published. In his book, *Germany Is Our Problem,* Morgenthau does not even make passing reference to the treatment of the German perpetrators.

3. Churchill to Roosevelt, October 22, 1944, in Winston S. Churchill, "The Second World War," Vol. VI: *Triumph and Tragedy* (Boston, 1953), p. 240.

4. Cadogan to Rosenman, April 23, 1945, in *International Conference on Military Trials,* pp. 18–20. Cadogan was Permanent Undersecretary in the Foreign Office.

5. See American memorandum of April 30, 1945, *ibid.,* pp. 28–38, 39n.

lies."[6] The chief problem now was to define what was meant by "offenses." The prospective "major criminals" were responsible for many deeds across the lands of Europe. How, in that context, were the four delegations going to handle the destruction of the European Jews?

For a period of two years preceding the Charter Conference in London, the Jewish leadership in the United States had been concerning itself precisely with that question. To the Jews the problem of definition was paramount. An interim commission established during the first session of the American Jewish Conference in 1943 stated succinctly that the trials were "not a matter of vengeance or of punishment of the guilty in the ordinary sense"; they were a matter of "practical" import. The non-punishment of the Germans for their crimes against an entire people, said the commission, would "signify the acquiescence of the democratic nations in the act of Jewish extermination."

Already there were disquieting reports from German-occupied territories of "infection" with the anti-Jewish "virus." That "infection" had to be expunged, and a "warning" would have to be issued to "other countries, on other continents, that are trying to introduce the Nazi racial theories and methods in public life." The commission therefore recommended to the State Department that annihilation of a people, including all acts whereby this aim was sought to be accomplished before and during the war, in Axis territories and occupied areas, be made a punishable crime.[7]

In London the conferees considered three kinds of offenses. The first of these was "crimes against peace." To the American and British delegations, this was the "essence" of their complaint.[8] The American chief representative, Justice Jackson, was particularly concerned with that charge. As Attorney General of the United States in 1940, Jackson had advised President Roosevelt that the United States would not be violating its obligations as a neutral by extending aid to the Allies; now Jackson was determined to show that the United States had not done an illegal thing. He wanted to justify American action on the ground that German aggression had violated everybody's rights. Here in London he wanted to establish German responsibility in the only way that was still open to him: by declaring the planners of aggression personally culpable for their deeds.[9] No conceivable accusation could have been more remotely applicable to anti-Jewish acts, and in a sense no indictment could have done more to overshadow and obscure them.

The second charge was of primary interest to the Russians and French. It dealt with war crimes. In its final form that category of offenses was defined to

> include, but not be limited to, murder, ill-treatment or deportation to slave labor or for any other purpose *of civilian population of or on occupied territory,* murder or ill-treatment of prisoners of war or persons on the seas, killing of hostages, plunder of public or private property, wanton destruction of cities, towns or villages, or devastation not justified by military necessity.[10]

6. *Ibid.*, p. 22n.

7. Report of the Commission on Post-War in American Jewish Conference, *Report of Interim Committee* (New York, 1944), pp. 90–91, 98–99, 106, 123–25.

8. Statement by Sir David Maxwell Fyfe in verbatim minutes of London Conference, *International Conference on Military Trials*, p. 305.

9. Jackson to President Truman, June 6, 1945, *ibid.*, pp. 42–52. Jackson in verbatim minutes of London Conference, *ibid.*, pp. 299, 383–85.

10. Text of charter, August 8, 1945, *ibid.*, p. 423. Italics added.

War crimes have long been recognized as punishable under international law, and any definition of them would have covered the vast majority of German actions against the Jews. The very extent of the destruction process, its geographic range and administrative thoroughness, had trapped the perpetrators in the vise of this law. The killing of the Jews in the guise of anti-partisan operations was a war crime; the shooting of Jewish Red Army men in a German *Stalag* was a war crime; the gassing of Reich Jews on Polish soil at Auschwitz was a war crime. Under the traditional law of war almost the entire destruction process between 1939 and 1945 consisted of acts for which the perpetrators could be condemned, and for many of these acts they could be condemned to death. Yet there remained important segments of German activity to which the law of war could not apply. It did not automatically cover anti-Jewish measures wholly performed within Axis territories, nor did it reach the prewar decrees.

The four delegations though satisfied themselves, had not yet solved the problem for the Jews. In the first place, the two categories of offenses did not embrace everything the Germans had done. Conceivably, some of the "major criminals" might even escape conviction for their acts. At the same time, no special deterrent had been erected to prevent "other countries, on other continents," from introducing a destructive regime into their public life; the destruction of a minority on home territory was still legal, even when carried to an extreme. Confronting this situation, the Anglo-American delegates were faced with a dilemma: they wanted to remove the limitation upon the jurisdiction of the proposed tribunal,[11] they wanted to get Streicher,[12] but in *this* sphere of human activity they did not want to make new law.

In attempting to resolve the issue, the Anglo-American representatives set up a series of acts which could be recognized as criminal if they were a part or a product of the "conspiracy" to commit an aggression or a war crime. In short, this was not an independent category of offenses; it had to have a connection either with preparing for an illegal war or with fighting a war illegally. The chief of the British delegation, Sir David Maxwell Fyfe, explained the matter this way:

> The preparation would in my view include such acts as the terrorization and murder of their own Jewish population in order to prepare for war; that is, preparatory acts inside the Reich in order to regiment the State for aggression and regimentation. This would be important politically for us because the ill-treatment of the Jews has shocked the conscience of our people and, I am sure, of the other United Nations; but we should consider it at some stage, and I thought it was covered by this act in the preparation of this design. I just wanted to make it clear that we had this in mind because I have been approached by various Jewish organizations and should like to satisfy them if possible. I have in mind only such general treatment of the Jews as showed itself as part of the general plan of aggression.[13]

Justice Jackson, concurring in this view, pointed out in unmistakable language why there could be no other basis for jurisdiction:

> It has been a general principle from time immemorial that the internal affairs of another government are not

11. See note submitted by Jackson to other delegations, *ibid.*, p. 394.

12. Statement by Sir David Maxwell Fyfe, *ibid.*, p. 301.

13. Statement by Sir David Maxwell Fyfe in verbatim minutes of London Conference, *ibid.*, p. 329. See also his statement on p. 361. Sir David was Attorney General in the Conservative government.

ordinarily our business; that is to say, the way Germany treats its inhabitants, or any other country treats its inhabitants, is not our affair any more than it is the affair of some other government to interpose itself in our problems. . . . We have some regrettable circumstances at times in our own country in which minorities are unfairly treated. We think that it is justifiable that we interfere or attempt to bring retribution to individuals or to states only because the concentration camps and the deportations were in pursuance of a common plan or enterprise of making an unjust war in which we became involved. We see no other basis on which we are justified in reaching the atrocities which were committed inside Germany, under German law, or even in violation of German law, by authorities of the German state.[14]

After fifteen drafts the tribunal was therefore invested with power to try defendants for

> Crimes against humanity: namely, murder, extermination, enslavement, deportation, and other inhumane acts committed against any civilian population, before or during the war, or persecutions on political, racial or religious grounds in execution of or in connection with any crime within the jurisdiction of the Tribunal, whether or not in violation of the domestic law of the country where perpetrated.[15]

The London delegates were unwilling to recognize the destruction of European Jewry as a crime *sui generis;* in the end they were not even able to cover the prewar anti-Jewish decrees under the count of aggression. During the trial the prosecution failed completely to establish any connection between these decrees and the "conspiracy" to make war.[16] The "crimes against humanity" were deadwood.

14. Justice Jackson in verbatim minutes, *ibid.*, pp. 331, 333. Also, Jackson to Truman, June 6, 1945, *ibid.*, pp. 48, 50–51. The first American draft, prepared by representatives of the State, War, and Justice Departments in conference with Justice Jackson, referred specifically to acts which were unconnected with any other crime but which were in "violation of the domestic law of any Axis power." Narrowly construed, only "excesses" would have been covered by such a provision. More controversial would have been the contention that in German constitutional law the Hitler regime rested entirely upon illegal foundations. For a discussion of the latter point, see testimony by Prof. Herman Jahrreis, Case No. 3, tr. pp. 4253 ff. Jahrreis makes a distinction between "illegality" and "illegitimacy." Overriding was the viewpoint, expressed by Secretary of War Stimson in a memorandum dated September 9, 1944, that not even "excesses" could be dealt with by an "external court." Stimson, *On Active Service,* p. 585.

15. Text of agreement and charter, August 8, 1945, signed by Justice Robert Jackson for the United States, Judge Robert Falco for France, Lord Chancellor Jowitt for Great Britain, and Maj. Gen. Nikitchenko and Prof. A. Trainin for the USSR, with protocol containing correction, dated October 6, 1945, *International Conference on Military Trials,* pp. 423, 429.

16. Judgment of the International Military Tribunal at Nuremberg, *Trial of the Major War Criminals,* XXII, p. 498. The French delegation had suggested that persecutions be defined as an independent crime. See French draft and explanation by Prof. André Gros in *International Conference on Military Trials,* pp. 293, 360. The French government had already proposed during the killing of the Armenians in World War I that in view of these "crimes of Turkey against humanity," the Allied governments should announce publicly that all members of the Ottoman government and those of their agents who were implicated in the massacres would be held personally responsible for their acts. See American Ambassador in France (Sharp) to Secretary of State, May 28, 1915, enclosing French note of May 24, *Foreign Relations of the United States, 1915, Suppl.*, p. 981. The warning was duly delivered by the American Ambassador in Constantinople. Morgenthau to Secretary of State, June 18, 1915, *ibid.*, p. 982. French Delegate Gros did not think that the prosecution would be able to prove that the anti-Jewish persecutions had been inflicted in pursuit of aggression. Statement by Gros, *International Conference on Military Trials,* p. 361. The Soviet delegates were indifferent to the entire issue. They were preoccupied with procedural problems

About two months after the conclusion of the agreement the trial began in Nuremberg before an international military tribunal.[17] Most of the defendants, most of the exhibits, and most of the witnesses were produced by the Americans.[18] The chief defendant was Göring. From the party the prosecution had selected Hess, Ley, and Streicher. The ministers included Schacht, Funk, Frick, Ribbentrop, and von Papen. There were two ranking officials of the central bureaucracy: Kaltenbrunner of the RSHA and Ministerialdirektor Fritzsche of the Propaganda Ministry. The armament and labor mobilization machinery was represented by Speer and Sauckel. In the military the choice had fallen upon Keitel and Jodl, as well as Räder and Doenitz. In addition, there were five territorial chiefs: von Schirach (Vienna), von Neurath (Protektorat), Frank (*Generalgouvernement*), Rosenberg (Eastern Territories), and Seyss-Inquart (Netherlands).[19]

Although the selection of the defendants betrayed a definite emphasis upon the charge of aggression, the great bulk of them had been heavily implicated in actions against the Jews. There was no longer any way of hiding these actions. Too many copies had been made of too many reports, and in the closing phase of the war they could not be destroyed in time. Now this secret correspondence was introduced, item by item, to the judges.[20] "My own diary bears witness against me," said Frank, as he surveyed the situation and saw that he was doomed.[21] The crushing written evidence was reinforced by oral testimony from former subordinates of the defendants, such as Staatssekretäre Buhler and Steengracht and SS men Ohlendorf, Wisliceny, Höttl, Höss, and Pohl. The sight of these men provoked consternation in the defense, and when Himmler's own favored general, Obergruppenführer von dem Bach-Zelewski, testified for the prosecution, the prisoners were unanimous in calling him a *Schwein*.[22]

The defense did not have much to expect. Its arguments were desperate. Notwithstanding their high positions in the machinery of destruction, the accused claimed ignorance: they did not

such as the location of the proposed tribunal, etc. The principal Soviet delegate, Maj. Gen. Nikitchenko, took the view that the "chief war criminals" had "already been convicted" and that their "conviction" had already been "announced" by the Moscow declaration. See his statement in verbatim minutes, *ibid.*, pp. 104–5.

17. The judges, as well as the prosecutors, were drawn from the four powers. Nikitchenko now sat on the bench.

18. Statement by Jackson, *International Conference on Military Trials*, p. 343. On Soviet unpreparedness, see statement by Nikitchenko, *ibid.*, p. 213.

19. Indictment in *Trial of the Major War Criminals*, I, 68–79. Industry was to have been represented by Gustav Krupp von Bohlen and Halbach. He was judged too ill to stand trial.

20. The prosecution had assembled for the tribunal the following document series: EC, L, M, PS, R, RF, UK, and USSR.

21. Testimony by Frank, *Trial of the Major War Criminals*, XII, 13. Rudolf Hess complained that everybody was looking at him with "strange, glassy eyes." Testimony by Hess, *ibid.*, XXII, 370–71. The German Labor Front leader Ley committed suicide; he left a note in which he explained that he had a new solution to the Jewish problem. To remove the suspicion that he was advancing the solution for personal reasons, he had decided to kill himself. The Nazis, said Ley, had gone too far. "This is no criticism of my dead Führer," he continued, for the Führer "is too great and too noble to be tainted by a passing mistake." Ley was now worried that the triumphant Jews would go too far. That would be the same mistake. His plan consisted of a "conciliation" in which the returning Jews and the old anti-Semites would form a committee to make peace. Suicide statement by Dr. Ley found in his cell, October 25, 1945, after discovery of the body, in *Nazi Conspiracy and Aggression*, VII, 740–48.

22. Off-the-record comments recorded by the prison psychologist G. M. Gilbert in his *Nuremberg Diary* (New York, 1947), pp. 113–14.

know that Jewry was being annihilated. Von Schirach knew nothing.[23] Funk knew nothing.[24] Keitel knew nothing.[25] Jodl knew nothing.[26] Kaltenbrunner knew nothing.[27] Insofar as any of them had taken part in the destruction process, that participation was innocent. No one except Streicher blamed the Jews anymore. (Streicher, after getting into an argument with his own defense counsel, would not relinquish his assertion that the Jews were practicing ritual murder.)[28] Yet all the defendants had an excuse for their behavior: they acted under orders, and the man who gave the orders was Adolf Hitler.

How could one man give so many orders to so many people? "The Führer," explained Streicher, "had such a power of hypnotic suggestion that the entire people believed in him."[29] Why, then, could no one petition to Hitler? Answer: "The Führer could not be influenced."[30] Streicher's explanation was couched in psychological terms. Speer enlarged upon the theory in the language of engineering. To him, the totalitarian state was like a telephone exchange; it could be served and dominated by a single will. Earlier dictators had needed highly qualified assistants, but modern technology had dispensed with them. The communication system had "mechanized" subordinate leadership and had made it into an "uncritical recipient of orders."[31]

The defendants had not meant to harm the Jews. Schacht was trying to help them emigrate.[32] Streicher was a Zionist.[33] Von Schirach believed that the deportations from Vienna to Poland were "really in the interests of Jewry."[34]

Above all, the defendants were not alone in their deed; they had merely been singled out. Fritzsche felt that he was a stand-in for Goebbels.[35] Kaltenbrunner asserted that he had taken the place of the *Reichsführer-SS;* he was completely innocent. The guilty ones were the dead Himmler, the assassinated Heydrich, and the missing Müller. The line of command was really Himmler-Müller-Eichmann. Kaltenbrunner had nothing to do with the Jews.[36] Von Schirach, somewhat like Kaltenbrunner, was prone to ascribe exclusive responsibility to subordinates.[37] Hess reminded the tribunal that the Nazis were not the first to have established concentration camps – the British had erected them during the war with the Boers.[38] When Streicher was asked whether any publication other than his *Stürmer* had treated the Jewish question in an anti-Semitic way, he replied:

> Anti-Semitic publications have existed in Germany for centuries. A book I had, written by Dr. Martin Luther, was, for instance, confiscated. Dr. Martin Luther would very probably sit in

23. Testimony by von Schirach, *Trial of the Major War Criminals,* XIV, 487.
24. Testimony by Funk, *ibid.,* XXII, 387
25. Testimony by Keitel, *ibid.,* XI, 594.
26. Testimony by Jodl, *ibid.,* XV, 295, 331–33.
27. Testimony by Kaltenbrunner, *ibid.,* XI, 275. Also, comments by Doenitz, Keitel, and Ribbentrop in prison, Gilbert, *Nuremberg Diary,* pp. 45–46.
28. Testimony by Streicher, *Trial of the Major War Criminals,* XII, 306–7, 336–37.
29. Testimony by Streicher, *ibid.,* p. 322.
30. *Ibid.,* p. 324.
31. Testimony by Speer, *ibid.,* XXII, 406.
32. Testimony by Schacht, *ibid.,* p. 389.
33. Testimony by Streicher, *ibid,* XII, 384.
34. Testimony by von Schirach, *ibid.,* XIV, 431, 508–10.
35. Final plea by defense counsel Dr. Fritz, *ibid.,* XIX, 350.
36. Testimony by Kaltenbrunner, *ibid.,* XXII, 378–81. Argument by Dr. Gawlik (defense counsel for the SD), *ibid.,* pp. 36–40, particularly p. 39.
37. Testimony by von Schirach on deportations in 1941 and arrival of Hungarian Jews in 1944, *ibid.,* XIV, 416–17, 511. The subordinates involved were Dr. Dellbrügge and RR Dr. Fischer.
38. Testimony by Hess, *ibid.,* XXII, 371.

> the defendants' dock today, if this book had been taken into consideration by the Prosecution. In the book *The Jews and Their Lies,* Dr. Martin Luther writes that the Jews are a serpent's brood and one should burn down their synagogues and destroy them. . . .[39]

In constructing their defense, the accused were evidently reaching beyond the tribunal to address the whole world. Even so, they knew that they could not ward off the end.

The trial ended on October 1, 1946. The sentences imposed by the judges, and the extent to which the destruction of the Jews was noted in the judgment may be seen in Table 90.[40]

TABLE 90 / *Judgments of the International Military Tribunal*

DEFENDANT	SENTENCE	CONVICTED OF CRIMES AGAINST HUMANITY	ANTI-JEWISH ACTION AN APPARENT FACTOR IN CONVICTION
Göring	death	X	X
Hess	life		
Streicher	death	X	X
Schacht	free		
Funk	life	X	X
Frick	death	X	X
Ribbentrop	death	X	X
Von Papen	free		
Kaltenbrunner	death	X	X
Fritzsche	free		
Speer	20 years	X	
Sauckel	death	X	
Keitel	death	X	
Jodl	death	X	
Raeder	life		
Doenitz	10 years		
Von Schirach	20 years	X	X
Von Neurath	15 years	X	X
Frank	death	X	X
Rosenberg	death	X	X
Seyss-Inquart	death	X	X

The pattern of sentences contained a few anomalies. Schacht could not be convicted of crimes against humanity because his administration of the expropriatory exchange controls took place entirely before the war. Von Neurath, on the other hand, could not escape punishment for his enforcement of anti-Jewish measures in Prague because the tribunal was acting under the assumption that the Protektorat, as a territory with international personality (i.e., autonomy), had been under military occupation.[41]

Stranger still is the contrast between Streicher's conviction and Fritzsche's acquittal: Streicher was hanged because of his "incitement to murder and extermination at the time when Jews in the East were being killed";[42] Fritzsche was allowed to go free because he "did not urge persecution or extermination of Jews." Though that subtle dispenser of rationalizations had broadcast that the war had been caused by Jews and that their fate had turned out "as unpleasant as the Führer predicted," the tribunal still felt that he had not been "aware" of what was happening to them.[43] Even here in Nuremberg the tribunal was safeguarding the freedom to engage in declaratory propaganda.[44]

Before the establishment of the first tribunal in Nuremberg the principal difficulty was the formulation of an indictment which would spell out *why*

39. Testimony by Streicher, *ibid.*, XII 318.

40. Judgment, *ibid.*, XXII, 524–89. The Soviet judge, Nikitchenko, was of the opinion that Schacht, von Papen, and Fritzsche should have been convicted and that Hess should have been sentenced to death. He did not dissent from the other sentences. *Ibid.*, p. 589.

41. Judgment, *ibid.*, p. 581.

42. Judgment, *ibid.*, p. 549.

43. Judgment, *ibid.*, p. 584.

44. With regard to the other sentences, we should note that the judges were not in possession of Speer's full record. They did not know, for instance, of his connection with "primitive construction" in Auschwitz and other concentration camps. See pp. 597–98. In the case of Göring, Funk, Frick, Ribbentrop, von Neurath, Rosenberg, and Seyss-Inquart, the evidence was almost overwhelming. Yet all of these defendants were convicted also of aggression, and now it is no longer clear which charge was most decisive in determining their sentence.

the accused were being tried. When the prosecution of "lesser" personalities was brought into focus, the primary consideration became the question of *who* was to be charged. Whereas the qualitative issue was fought out mainly between the Allies, the quantitative problem concerned also a large number of Germans who waited in uncertainty for their fate.

The high point of Allied sentiment for massive punitive measures was reached in the spring of 1945 with the widespread publication of detailed accounts of wartime German activities. Thus in May, 1945, the editor of the *St. Louis Post-Dispatch,* Joseph Pulitzer, addressing the Society for the Prevention of World War III in Carnegie Hall, urged the shooting of 1,500,000 Nazis. He was joined by Representative Dewey Short of Missouri, who demanded mass executions of SS men and the OKW.[45]

Yet the counter-currents and counter-pressures against such a program were building up even before its beginning. On June 15, 1944, a commission of the Federal Council of Churches of Christ in America had declared that, while the punishment of "those most responsible" for the "systematic extermination of the Jews of Europe" was an "elementary demand of justice," such punishment had to be limited to men whose responsibility was "central" and could not extend, for example, to "soldiers who were implicated because they carried out orders."[46] Among the Jews themselves there was little eagerness for mass trials. In all the sessions of the American Jewish Conference and its interim committees, no proposal was put forward for the trial of any specific individual or category of individuals, save one: the ex-Mufti of Jerusalem.[47] The restraining influences could thus prevail. No significant group in the Allied world set out to achieve large-scale revenge.

The prosecution of the "lesser" offenders became essentially a process of elimination, and in that process basic attitudes in the ranks of the Allies came to the fore once again. The Americans were most persistent in reaching the lower strata of German leadership; the British limped along; and for the Russians the show was already almost over.

On April 26, 1945, the American Joint Chiefs of Staff sent a directive to the U.S. commander subjecting the following ten groups to automatic arrest:[48]

1. Party officials down to *Ortsgruppenleiter*
2. Gestapo and SD
3. *Waffen-SS* down to lowest noncommissioned rank (*USchaf.*)
4. General Staff officers
5. Police officers down to *Oberleutnant*
6. SA to lowest commissioned rank (*Stuf.*)
7. Ministers and leading civil servants as well as territorial officials down to *Bürgermeister* in the Reich and civil and military town commanders in occupied territories
8. Nazis and Nazi sympathizers in industry and commerce
9. Judges and prosecutors of special courts
10. Allied traitors

45. "Urges Execution of 1,500,000 Nazis," *New York Times,* May 23, 1945, p. 11.

46. Declaration of Federal Council of Churches, cited in American Jewish Conference, *Report of the Interim Committee,* pp. 104–5.

47. Hershman, *American Jewish Conference, Third Session,* p. 236. During the first conference Dr. DeSola Pool of the General Zionists went so far as to oppose the arrest of Germans who had acted under "compulsion." He preferred a resolution which would have urged the detention only of those who had given orders or who had committed acts of their own accord. Kohanski, *American Jewish Conference. First Session,* pp. 198–99, 203–4.

48. J.C.S. Directive 1067/6 to Commander-in-Chief of U.S. Forces of Occupation, April 26, 1945, in report of U.S. Military Governor, *Denazification,* 1948, pp. 14–16.

The automatic detainees were the chief suspects, and the most important among them faced trial by Allied military tribunals. Those Germans and their foreign collaborators whose activities had been confined to an occupied territory could expect to be charged on the soil of the country where they had committed their offense. The rest were to be channeled to German courts.

The trial of such masses posed special difficulties, since there was not enough evidence to form a complete picture of what each individual had done. Too many German documents had been destroyed, and too few made specific mention of people in the lower ranks. The American delegation at the London conference therefore hit upon the solution of accusing, along with the chief defendants, the organizations which they had led. If, after proof, an organization was declared criminal by the tribunal, all subsequent proceedings in individual cases could be confined to the sole question of membership.[49] Interestingly enough, the Soviet delegation did not quite see the need for the two-stage procedure. "The question of what the Gestapo really is," remarked Professor Trainin, "is perfectly well known to all countries." To this Jackson replied, "You don't want to depend on American judges to know all about the Gestapo."[50]

The prosecution asked for declarations of criminality against six organizations; the tribunal admitted only three and, in doing so, set limitations upon subsequent convictions by making them applicable only to those of the accused who had served in certain positions, at certain times, under certain conditions (see Table 91).[51] The tribunal's thinking in choosing these limits is not without interest: the lack of all-inclusiveness was based on the notion that "mass punishments should be avoided."

TABLE 91 / *Criminal Membership in Organizations*

	Position	Time	Condition	Recommended Maximum Penalty (under the Denazification Law of the American Zone)
Party	Upper echelons only	September 1, 1939 or after	Voluntary membership with knowledge of criminal purpose of the party	10 years
Gestapo and SD	All echelons except clerks, stenographers, janitors, etc.	September 1, 1939 or after	Knowledge of criminal purpose of the Gestapo and SD	10 years
SS	All echelons	September 1, 1939 or after	Voluntary membership with knowledge of criminal purpose of the SS	*Waffen*-SS officers to *Sturmbannführer*, 10 years *Waffen*-SS below that rank: 5 years

The membership date of September 1, 1939, or after, was decisive because it was founded on the ruling that crimes against humanity could not have been committed before the war; the conditions of participation were included in obedience to the principle that "criminal guilt is personal."[52] Three organizations were not declared criminal: the SA, because its activities after the outbreak of war were too insignificant; the Cabinet, because it was too small; and the "High Command and General Staff," because the definition given to that group by the prosecution comprised only a handful of generals. The prosecution had failed altogether to reach down into the civil service and into the officers' corps.[53]

The top strata were tried by Allied military tribunals, particularly in the American and British zones. By August, 1946, the American Subsequent Proceedings Division, headed by Brigadier General Telford Taylor, had compiled a trial list of close to 5000 names. That list had to be cut down because of "time, staff, and money," and in the reduction process an attempt was made to achieve "balance" with respect to types of offenses and occupations of offenders. In the end the bottom line was sometimes drawn by "the size of the defendants' dock in the particular courtroom which was to be used." Fewer than 200 men were brought into the courtrooms.[54] However, these defendants had not been minor cogs in the destructive machine; they were its central core, and the evidence amassed against them was so great that for the trial of most of them, there was little need to rely upon membership in criminal organizations to secure convictions.[55]

The 185 accused were divided into twelve groups for arraignment. The first case was brought against the medical doctors. In the second the sole defendant was Generalfeldmarschall Milch. The third group consisted of Schlegelberger and his associates in the judiciary. The fourth was Pohl and the bureaucracy of the concentration camps. In the fifth case the defendants were the industrialists of the Flick combine. In the sixth, they came from I. G. Farben. The seventh case involved the

49. American memorandum, April 30, 1945, presented at San Francisco and in London, *International Conference on Military Trials*, pp. 32–33. Jackson to Truman, June 6, 1945, *ibid.*, pp. 47–48. Compare this proposal with the Smith Act, 54 Stat. 671, promulgated in 1940 when Jackson was Attorney General.

50. *International Conference on Military Trials*, pp. 241–42.

51. Judgment, *Trial of the Major War Criminals*, XXII, 498–517.

52. *Ibid.*, p. 500. Not spelled out was the question of who had the burden of proof with respect to defendants' knowledge. In subsequent proceedings the burden was divided, in that knowledge was presumed after the prosecution had established certain facts. The tribunal ruled that *all* members of the Gestapo and SD had joined these organizations voluntarily. *Ibid.*, p. 503. In the case of the party and the SS, the voluntary character of membership was left to be established in each individual case.

53. *Ibid.*, pp. 517–23. In this connection, note that the RSHA was covered only in Offices III, IV, VI, and VII. The *Kripo*, because of its regular law-enforcement functions, was not even charged.

54. Brig. Gen. Telford Taylor (chief counsel for war crimes), *Final Report to the Secretary of the Army on the Nuremberg War Crimes Trials under Control Council Law No. 10* (Washington, D.C., 1949), pp. 50–51, 54–55, 73, 85, 91. The control council, as the four-power governing body of Germany sitting in Berlin, authorized the trials to be held in the four zones. Though the nationality of the judges in the subsequent proceedings at Nuremberg was American, the tribunals were therefore international.

55. Although there were ten times as many defendants in the subsequent proceedings as in the original trial, there was ten times as much evidence. The documents collected by the American prosecution for these trials were divided into four series; NG (governmental, i.e., ministerial materials), NI (industry), NO (Nazi organizations, particularly the SS), and NOKW (armed forces).

generals of the Southeast. Next came the RuSHA case. For the ninth the choice had fallen upon Ohlendorf and other officers of the *Einsatzgruppen*. The tenth case was directed against Krupp. In the eleventh case the chief defendants were Weizsäcker, Wörmann, Hencke, Lammers, Stuckart, von Krosigk, Berger, Schellenberg, and Rasche. The twelfth case engulfed the generals who had invaded Russia.

As the indictment drew nearer, the bureaucrats of destruction were seized with anxiety and depression, self-torture and visions of death. There were some who felt doomed because they knew they were guilty; there were others who believed themselves guilty only because they thought they were doomed. Among the self-accusers two prisoners, the Interior Ministry's Conti and former Food Minister Backe, did not wait for a trial – the sudden revelation of the irrepressible past was too much for them. Conti left a note in which he explained that he was taking his life because he had lied during an interrogation under oath. In this lie, he had tried to cover up his knowledge of medical experiments.[56] Backe was brooding in his cell about the effects of his wartime rationing decrees upon the lives of people in the concentration camps. He excused himself by saying that he had been ignorant and overburdened and that an eye disease had prevented him from reading every paper that he had signed. Writing to a German journalist and former inmate of Buchenwald, Eugen Kogon, Backe asked for forgiveness; then he killed himself.[57]

Edmund Veesenmayer too thought that there was no escape. He had in fact surrendered "voluntarily." Yet his reasons did not imply any wavering or doubt; he did not accuse himself. "If I am not here," he said, "others will be held responsible."[58] When prosecutor Kempner asked him what he thought about the trail, Veesenmayer said: "As main defendant I am your enemy, the type which must be eliminated. I do not know it otherwise. I am a criminal who must be exterminated." To this the Jewish prosecutor replied: "What you are is to be clarified before the American Tribunal."[59]

Notwithstanding the heavy sense of hopelessness in the Nuremberg prison, a force of 206 defense attorneys prepared for all-out battle. One hundred and thirty-six of these lawyers had been party members; ten had been in the SS; one, Dr. Rudolf Dix, was a former president of the German Bar Association; another, Dr. Ernst Achenbach, had been a deportation expert in the Paris Embassy.[60] There was no disposition in that group to hold back any argument. The old arsenal was emptied to exhaustion. All the defendants had been ignorant; all had carried out orders. Everyone was being discriminated against by being selected as a defendant. No one was a criminal. Even Blobel of the Kiev massacre was "decent at heart."[61]

The accused were, without exception, so kindly disposed toward their victims that Weizsäcker's lawyer, Dr. Becker, began to feel a little crowded.

56. Dr. Leonardo Conti to interrogating officer, undated, NO-3061.

57. Text of letter by Backe in Eugen Kogon, "Politik der Versöhnung," *Frankfurter Hefte*, April, 1948, pp. 323–24. Kogon did not identify Backe by name. He forgave him. There were four suicides *after* indictment: Westphal, Böhme, Haussmann, and von Blaskowitz. Four other defendants were too ill to be tried. Taylor, *Final Report*, p. 91.

58. Interrogation by Kempner of Veesenmayer, August 20, 1947, NG-2905.

59. Interrogation by Kempner of Veesenmayer, November 1, 1947, NG-3691.

60. Taylor, *Final Report*, pp. 47–48. Defense lawyers were paid by the American government, received cheap meals, free cigarettes, etc. *Ibid.*, p. 49.

61. Statement by his counsel, Dr. Heim, Case No. 9, tr. pp. 339–41.

In a moment of irritation he was moved to remark: "Everybody has saved the few survivors; nobody has killed the many dead [*Jeder hat die wenigen Geretteten gerettet, keiner hat die vielen Toten umgebracht*]."[62] Blame was passed upward, downward, and sideways. And for teeth-puller Pook, who had salvaged the gold from the mouths of the gassed, counsel Dr. Ratz had a unique defense: "The corpse has no more rights of any sort, but no one has any right to the corpse either. The body, so to speak, from a legal point of view, floats between heaven and earth."[63]

However, the most significant element in the defense array was the return to the attack. That return was pronounced most clearly in *United States* v. *Ohlendorf*, by the chief defendant himself. Ohlendorf maintained that the Jews *had* to be destroyed. Even if they had not actually started the war, they had now been attacked, and after such an assault one could expect from them only the most dangerous reactions. Asked by prosecutor Heath what had happened to the Jewish children, Ohlendorf replied, "They were to be killed just like their parents." Questioned about the reason for such relentlessness, he said, "I believe that it is very simple to explain if one starts from the fact that this order did not only try to achieve security but also permanent security because the children would grow up, and surely, being the children of parents who had been killed, they would constitute a danger no smaller than that of their parents." Then he added, "I have seen very many children killed in this war through air attacks, for the security of other nations."[64]

The judges in Nuremberg were established American lawyers. They had not come to exonerate or to convict. They were impressed with their task, and they approached it with much experience in the law and little anticipation of the facts. That is not to say that they were immune to outside pressures. On the first day of the I. G. Farben trial Judge James Morris remarked to Prosecutor Josiah DuBois at luncheon: "We have to worry about the Russians now; it wouldn't surprise me if they overran the courtroom before we get through."[65] Indeed, Chief Prosecutor Taylor was prompted to remark in his final report that on the whole "the sentences became lighter as time went on."[66]

There were variations from case to case which reflected more fundamental influences. The most stringent judgments were handed down in the SS cases, where the judges perceived murder in its most direct and unmitigated form. Three of these cases — the trials of the doctors, the *Einsatzgruppen* leaders, and the concentration camp administrators — were the only ones which resulted in death sentences.[67] Several defendants in the judiciary were imprisoned for life.[68] A sickening feeling had overcome the tribunal as it glanced upon the defendants who had once been judges themselves, and the court gave vent to this feeling in the statement that "the prostitution of a judicial system for the accomplishment of criminal ends involves an evil to the state which is not found in frank

62. Statement by Becker, Case No. 11, German tr. p. 26789.

63. Statement by Ratz, Case No. 4, tr. p. 7902.

64. Testimony by Ohlendorf, Case No. 9, *Trials of War Criminals*, IV, 356–58. Also, legal opinion by Dr. Reinhard Maurach. Ohlendorf-38. Phosphorus bombs, blockbusters, and atomic bombs were hurled as constant reminders by the defense at the tribunals.

65. DuBois, *The Devil's Chemists*, p. 95.

66. Taylor, *Final Report*, p. 92.

67. Originally, seven in the doctors' case, four in the Pohl case, and fourteen in the Ohlendorf case. For details, see pp. 704–15.

68. Klemm, Oeschey, Rothaug, and Schlegelberger.

atrocities which do not sully judicial robes."[69] In the military, too, several defendants were sentenced to life imprisonment.[70] The bureaucracy fared better, with a maximum of twenty years.[71] Among the industrialists only Alfried Krupp and two of his associates received as much as twelve years in prison. In the I. G. Farben case five defendants were convicted for their participation in I. G. Auschwitz; two of them, Dürrfeldt and Ambros, were handed eight years; Ter Meer got seven; Krauch and Bütefisch, six.[72] In the Flick case no defendant was convicted for anti-Jewish actions – the Petschek Aryanizations were not crimes against humanity.[73]

When judgments were rendered in all twelve cases of the subsequent Nuremberg proceedings, thirty-five defendants were declared not guilty, ninety-seven received prison terms ranging from time served to twenty-five years, twenty were imprisoned for life, and twenty-five were condemned to death. Considering the difficulties facing the accusers, the American prosecution had scored no minor success. However, as soon as the judgments were written, the reduction process began.

In the concentration camp case the tribunal itself reduced four sentences;[74] then the military governor, General Clay, commuted another;[75] and finally, a special clemency board arrived from the United States to review all the decisions for the High Commissioner.[76] The Clemency Board consisted of three officials: David W. Peck, Presiding Judge, Appellate Division, First Department, New York Supreme Court, chairman; Frederick A. Moran, chairman, New York Board of Parole; and Brigadier General Conrad E. Snow, Assistant Legal Adviser, Department of State. The board began its work in April, 1950. Although the members felt themselves "bound" by the facts in the judgments, the defense was allowed to introduce "new evidence" and to present old arguments.[77] The board then did four things: It recommended a downward revision of individual sentences on the basis of the newly acquired testimony.[78] It urged that var-

69. Judgment, Case No. 3, tr. pp. 10793–94.

70. Milch, List, Kuntze, Warlimont, and Reinecke.

71. Lammers and Veesenmayer.

72. Judge Hebert in a dissent said that three other defendants should have been held guilty on the Auschwitz charge. No defendants were found guilty for the supply of poison gas to the camp. The eight-year sentences were the maximum pronounced in the case. One judge had remarked privately during the proceedings that there were "too many Jews on the prosecution." DuBois, *The Devil's Chemists*, pp. 182–93. Two Jews served on the I. G. Farben trial team. *Ibid.*

73. Judgment, Case No. 5, *Trials of War Criminals*, VI, 1212–16.

74. Georg Lörner, Kiefer, Fanslau, Bobermin.

75. Sommer.

76. A High Commissioner, responsible to the State Department, replaced the military governor and took over from him responsibility and control over convicted war criminals. Executive Order 10062 of June 6, 1949, and Executive Order 10144 of July 21, 1950, in *Trials of War Criminals*, XV, 1154–56.

77. None of these materials were published, but their impact can broadly be gauged from the following paragraph in which the board gave its description of the anti-Jewish destruction process: "The elimination of Jews, occasionally by deportation, but generally by outright slaughter. This organized business of murder was centered in SS groups which accompanied the army for the purpose of eliminating the Jews, Gypsies, and all those even suspected of being partisans. No less than 2 million defenseless human beings were killed in this operation." Report of Advisory Board on Clemency for War Criminals (signed Peck, Moran, and Snow) to High Commissioner McCloy, August 28, 1950, *ibid.*, p. 1159.

78. In the main it would appear that these German appellants succeeded in convincing the board that their position had been more "remote" and also more difficult than the tribunals had assumed. *Ibid.*, pp. 1163–64. Statement and announcement of decisions by McCloy, January 31, 1951, *ibid.*, pp. 1176–91,

iations in sentences for similar offenses be resolved in favor of the most lenient treatment.[79] Insofar as imprisonment before and during trial had not been counted, such confinement was to be deducted now.[80] The board asked, finally, that the time credited to prisoners for "good behavior" be increased from five days to ten per month, thus cutting the reduced sentences by a third.[81]

High Commissioner McCloy was under considerable pressure not merely to accept these recommendations but to go beyond them.[82] "With difficulty" he commuted several more death sentences on his own.[83] When he announced his decisions on January 31, 1951, the 142 convicted defendants had shrunk to less than half: 77 were free, 50 were still imprisoned, one had been sent to Belgium,[84] the seven condemned in the doctors' case had already been hanged, and five remained under sentence of death. Among the freed were *all* the convicted industrialists. As the I. G.'s Ter Meer walked out of jail, he remarked to his entourage, "Now that they have Korea on their hands, the Americans are a lot more friendly."[85]

The prisons still held a number of generals who had been granted no reductions, and Chancellor Adenauer's military advisors lost no time in pointing out that this lack of clemency rested as a "heavy psychological burden" upon Germany's effort to rearm (*eine schwere psychologische Belastung des Wiederbewaffnungsproblems*).[86] The five who faced death included the now solitary figure of Pohl and four *Einsatzgruppen* leaders: Blobel, Braune, Naumann, and Ohlendorf. Though the sentences of these men had been reviewed again and again, the pressures for commutation did not abate. Bishop Johannes Neuhäusler declared that it would have been more "humane" to have decided quickly and then to have quickly carried out the decision.[87] In his prison cell Ohlendorf himself dic-

passim. The individual recommendations of the board were not published.

79. See particularly the evening-out of the sentences in the industrial cases to effect release of the Krupp defendants. Decisions by McCloy, January 31, 1951, *ibid.*, pp. 1187–88.

80. *Ibid.*, p. 1180. This recommendation affected the prison sentences in the SS cases.

81. *Ibid.*, p. 1180.

82. See summary by Arthur Krock of the minutes of a meeting held on January 9, 1951, between McCloy and a German delegation consisting of Hermann Ehlers (President of the *Bundestag*), Heinrich Höfler (Free Democrat), Carlo Schmid (Social Democrat), Jakob Altmeier (a Jew), Hans van Merkatz (German Party), and Franz Josef Strauss (Christian Democrat – Bavarian wing). "In the Nation," *New York Times*, April 26, 1951, p. 28. One German periodical explained that "automatic sympathies" were accruing to many a defendant because of the "composition" of the prosecution. "Die Juden," *Die Gegenwart*, September 1, 1949, pp. 5–6.

83. Decisions by McCloy in *Einsatzgruppen* case, *Trials of War Criminals*, XV, 1185–87.

84. Strauch.

85. "Flick, Dietrich, among 19 Nazi Criminals Freed from Jail after Serving 5 Years," *New York Times*, August 26, 1950, p. 7.

86. "Von 28 Todeskandidaten wurden 21 begnadigt," *Süddeutsche Zeitung* (Munich), February 1, 1952, pp. 1–2.

87. "Um die Landsberger Entscheidung," *ibid.*, February 2, 1951, p. 1. In appeals to the United States federal courts the defense argued that the German constitution of 1949 had abolished the death penalty and that in view of Allied recognition of Germany's new independence in 1951, the sentences could no longer be carried into effect. The appeals failed, not because the U.S. military tribunals had derived their powers from an international agreement and not because jurisdiction over war criminals was reserved by the Allies, but on the ground that the district judge had received no official certification that the state of war was over and so long as war continued, nonresident enemy aliens could not obtain relief in a federal court. Memorandum of the District Court of Columbia, May 29, 1951, and Supreme Court denial of ceritorari in *Trials of War Criminals*, XV, 1192–98.

tated a statement in which he protested his innocence, declaring that he had tried to rescind the Himmler order; that he had commanded the smallest *Einsatzgruppe;* that of thousands of *Einsatz* personnel only thirty-three had been tried and only fourteen condemned to death, and that, therefore, he was a martyr.[88] High Commissioner McCloy gave way no more. As one of the captains of the law-and-order movement in 1944, he could not scuttle the trials in 1951. To the accompaniment of the protests of Vice Chancellor Franz Blücher and a chorus of voices in the German press, the five were hanged on June 7.[89]

What was happening in Nuremberg was duplicated on a smaller scale in the British zone. Among the defendants in the British trials were a number of SS men in the Auschwitz-Belsen group, three members of the TESTA firm which had supplied Auschwitz with poison gas, and an assortment of generals from various theaters of war. The British military courts, unlike the American tribunals, were staffed with military men, and defense counsel too were British officers. The proceedings were handled with a certain amount of dispatch. From the SS group eleven were sent to the gallows – notable among the condemned were Krämer, Klein, Hössler, and Irma Grese.[90] The Zyklon B supplier, Dr. Bruno Tesch, was also hanged.[91] The generals, on the other hand, were not tried immediately, and that delay led to different results. Von Rundstedt and Strauss were freed as unfit to stand trial.[92] Von Brauchitsch died before indictment.[93] Kesselring was condemned to death, but his sentence was commuted to life and then reduced to twenty-one years. Released on medical parole and granted clemency in expectation that he would die, he resumed an active life in 1952.[94] In December, 1949, von Manstein was sentenced to eighteen years. Two months thereafter, his sentence was reduced to twelve years, and by 1952 he too was free.[95]

Once the British had joined their American partners in going to court; now they followed the Americans in opening the prison doors. In February, 1952, both powers agreed with the new Germany to establish a tripartite clemency board to review once more the sentences of the imprisoned war criminals.[96] When the board began its work in 1955, the number of anti-Jewish perpetrators still filling the American and British jails had shrunk to about two dozen.[97]

88. Text of Ohlendorf statement, January 19, 1951, in *Neues Abendland* (Augsburg), March, 1951, pp. 133–34.

89. Drew Middleton, "Germans Condemn U. S. on Executions," *New York Times*, June 8, 1951, p. 5.

90. *Law Reports of Trials of War Criminals* (London, 1947), II, 153–54. The royal warrant under which the judges sat limited their jurisdiction to crimes against Allied nationals. In one of the affidavits against an SS guard, it was alleged that he had shot a girl deported from Hungary to Bergen-Belsen. The defense objected on jurisdictional grounds. The prosecutor answered that, by that time, the Hungarians had "come to the Allied side," and that therefore they were "at least some form of Allies," though he did not know "to what extent." The defendant, Egersdorf, was pronounced not guilty. *Ibid.*, pp. 150, 153. The British judgments were not accompanied by reasoning.

91. *Ibid.*, I, 102. His *Prokurist*, Karl Weinbacher, suffered the same fate.

92. "British to Free von Rundstedt and Strauss," *New York Times*, May 6, 1949, p. 4. "Poles Question Britain on Nazis," *ibid.*, May 20, 1949, p. 14.

93. "Brauchitsch Dies of Heart Attack," *ibid.*, October 20, 1948, p. 7.

94. Alistair Horne, *Return to Power* (New York, 1956), p. 52.

95. *Ibid.*

96. "Adenauer Explains Board," *New York Times*, February 21, 1952, p. 6.

97. In March, 1954, the United States had decided to discontinue announcements of releases. "War Criminals Policy Is Changed by U.S.," *ibid.*, March 26, 1954, p. 5.

Although the proceedings before the military tribunals of the American and British zones were in the focus of world attention, a few major participants in the destruction of the Jews met their fate outside of Germany in foreign courts. Here we must distinguish between the foreign collaborators, who had to answer not so much for murder as for treason, and the Germans who under the Moscow Declaration were sent back to the countries "in which their abominable deeds were done." Among the collaborators who died by the hand of the executioner were Laval of France, President Tiso of Slovakia, Bagrianov of Bulgaria, the two Antonescus of Roumania, and Sztojay of Hungary. The captured and extradited Germans encountered varied treatment, depending not only on what they had done but also on when and where they were drawn to account. Table 92 reveals some of the contrasts in the disposition of these cases to 1955.[98]

Table 92 / *National Trials – West and East*

By the Netherlands: Rauter	Executed	by Czechoslovakia:	K. H. Frank Ludin Wisliceny
	Executed	by Poland:	Bühler Greiser Stroop Höss
	Executed	by Yugoslavia:	Kasche Löhr
	Executed	by Russia:	Jeckeln
by Denmark: Best by Belgium: Falkenhausen by France: Abetz	Freed	by Russia:	Clauberg

When Clauberg returned from Russia to Germany in October, 1951, he had the first opportunity in ten years to tell interviewing reporters that just prior to his capture he had perfected his sterilization method after all. The new method consisted of a simple injection, and he was now looking forward to its application, albeit only in "special cases."[99]

Those Germans who were not tried as war criminals by an Allied or foreign tribunal did not have so much to fear. They were left to German jurisdiction. Two kinds of proceedings evolved within the German sphere: one, denazification, was prescribed by the Allied occupation authorities; the other, trial in the regular criminal courts, depended upon German initiative. The denazification laws were based on the principle of automatic conviction. If we examine the design of the law enacted by the German *Länder* in the American zone, we may observe that it provided for the classification of the accused into five categories: major offenders, offenders, lesser offenders, followers, and the exonerated group. Inclusion in the first two categories was to be determined in the first instance by the defendant's former position. The positions enumerated in the law were taken from Control Council Directive No. 24, which was binding on the German authorities (see excerpts in Table 93).

98. For details, see pp. 704–15.

99. "Nazi Camp Doctor Back in Germany," *New York Times*, October 18, 1955, p. 10. "Doctor Who Sterilized Women for Nazis Still Proud of His Work," *New York Post*, October 18, 1955, p. 3.

TABLE 93 / *Classification of Major Offenders and Offenders*

CLASS I (PRESUMPTIVE MAJOR OFFENDERS)	CLASS II (PRESUMPTIVE OFFENDERS)
RSHA executive officials	Other RSHA personnel
GFP to *Feldpolizeidirektoren*	Other GFP and all *Abwehr*
All Gestapo, as well as executives of *Kripo(leit)stellen*	Other *Kripo* down to *Kriminalkommissar*
Generals and colonels of police	All *police* officers with *Einsatzgruppen* and *Einsatzkommandos,* as well as other police officers promoted after January 30, 1933, or in office after December 31, 1937
NSDAP officials down to *Amtsleiter* of *Kreisleitungen*	Members of *Institut zur Erforschung der Judenfrage*
Waffen-SS to *Sturmbannführer*	All other *Waffen-SS*
Ministers and bureaucrats to *Oberpräsidenten, Generalkommissare,* and *Ministerialdirektoren,* as well as *Ministerialräte* in newly created offices	*Regierungspräsidenten, Oberfinanzpräsidenten,* Labor Trustees, and Foreign Office officials down to consul
General Staff officers in OKW, OKH, OKM, or OKL on or after February 4, 1938	Other General Staff officers on or after February 4, 1938
Chiefs of military or civil administration in occupied territories	Town commanders
Chairman, presidents, and deputies of Reich and *Gau* Chambers of Commerce, of Reich groups and Reich associations	Executives of lower Chambers of Commerce, main rings, special rings, main committees, special committees and executives of Reich groups and associations, as well as all managers who belonged to the party
Judges and prosecutors of special courts, party courts, and SS courts, presidents of administrative courts, presidents of *Oberlandesgerichte* appointed after December 31, 1938, and prosecutors of *Oberlandesgerichte* appointed after March 31, 1933	Presidents and prosecutors of *Landgerichte*

With regard to possible classification as lesser offenders, the law provided for "careful special investigation" of persons who had been involved in Aryanizations and of officials who had served in military or civilian capacity in occupied areas. On the other hand, special consideration was to be given to *all* respondents for resignation from the party, "resistance," regular church attendance, good deeds, subjection to "persecution," and in the case of those born after January 1, 1919, "youth."[100] The meaning of these special considerations is clearly visible in the divergence between the charges which the prosecutors were required to make on the basis of the defendant's former position and the findings by the trial judges. The figures in Table 94 are cumulative for the American zone (minus Bremen and Berlin) to March

100. Law for Liberation from National Socialism and Militarism, by the Land Governments for Bavaria, Greater Hesse, and Württemberg-Baden, March 5, 1946, with annotations by U.S. military government in report of the military governor on *Denazification* (Cumulative Review), April, 1948, pp. 52–97.

TABLE 94 / *Denazification Statistics in the U.S. Zone*

	MANDATORY CHARGES	FINDINGS BY TRIAL JUDGES					
		Major Offenders	Offenders	Lesser Offenders	Followers	Exonerated	Proceedings Quashed
Major offenders	2,548	447	1,139	714	170	50	28
Offenders	59,192	54	4,268	14,402	29,761	1,989	8,718
Lesser offenders	41,554	0	131	6,795	26,521	2,949	5,613

31, 1947.[101] The penalties provided by the law for the first four classifications may be summarized as follows:[102]

Major offenders (mandatory sanctions):
- Two to ten years in a labor camp, with possible credit for internment after May 8, 1945, and with allowance for disability
- Confiscation of all property save necessities
- Ten-year prohibition of every activity except ordinary labor
- Prohibition to hold public office
- Loss of claims for pensions
- Restrictions on housing and residence

Offenders:
- Up to five years in a labor camp or assignment to special labor
- Confiscation of property in whole or part
- Five-year prohibition of every activity except ordinary labor
- Prohibition to hold public office
- Loss of claims for pensions
- Restrictions on housing and residence

Lesser offenders:
- Fines
- Confiscation of property acquired by political means, especially Aryanization and blocking of other property values
- Probationary prohibition of every activity except ordinary labor

Followers:
- Fines to 2000 reichsmark

Statistically, the sanctions imposed by mid-1949 revealed the following picture:[103]

Registrants	13,199,800
Charged	3,445,100
Amnestied without trial	2,489,700
Fines	569,600
Employment restrictions	124,400
Ineligibility for public office	23,100
Property confiscations	25,900
Special labor without imprisonment	30,500
Assignments to labor camps	9,600
Assignees still serving sentences	300

In a sense, the most significant figure in this tabulation is the last one. After four years only 300 persons were still in labor camps under sentences imposed by the denazification tribunals.

Denazification in all the occupation zones did not do much to those who had once staffed the machinery of destruction.[104] Hinrich Lohse, once

101. *Ibid.*, p. 5. Statistics do not show downward classifications by review tribunals.

102. *Ibid.*, pp. 59–63.

103. Report of military governor, July, 1949, *Statistical Annex* (Final Issue), p. 280. In many cases more than one sanction was imposed on the same individual. The amnesties were enacted because military government was in a hurry to conclude the program. See the *Denazification* report (Cumulative Review) and John H. Herz, "The Fiasco of Denazification in Germany," *Political Science Quarterly*, LXIII (1948), 569–94.

104. In terms of administrative design the British denazification decrees differed from the American in only two major respects: there was no total registration (charges were largely confined to the 27,000 persons under automatic arrest), and the program was discontinued in January, 1948, except for mem-

Reichskommissar of the *Ostland,* received the maximum of ten years; released in 1951 because of health, he was awarded a pension.[105] The former chief of the Main Trusteeship Office East, Dr. Max Winkler, was exonerated.[106] Ex-Staatssekretär Stuckart of the Interior Ministry, gravely ill, was sentenced in the eleventh case to time served, on the ground that any confinement would be tantamount to a death penalty. Brought before a denazification tribunal after his release, he was classified as a follower and fined 500 marks, payable upon receipt of a pension. Shortly thereafter he was killed in a crash of an automobile.[107] Obergruppenführer Wolff, who had headed Himmler's Personal Staff, was extradited by the Americans to the British zone to be tried there for his crimes.[108] Placed before a denazification court instead, he was sentenced to four years with credit for previous confinement; then informed by the presiding judge that he could leave "in clean and unstained dress" (*mit reinem und fleckenlosem Kleid*), he walked out of the courtroom with a radiant face, while his lawyer angrily demanded exoneration.[109]

There was one more hurdle confronting the former perpetrators: the Allies had also empowered the ordinary German courts to try cases involving war crimes. But, judging from its results, that punitive expedition assumed only the slightest proportions. The former Jewish expert of the Foreign Office, Legationsrat Rademacher, was sentenced to three years and five months; after his conviction, he skipped bail and disappeared, probably to South America.[110] Gerard Peters of DEGUSSA, whose Zyklon B had killed 1,000,000 Jews in Auschwitz, got five years. The defense succeeded in obtaining another trial, but drew a six-year sentence. Trying again in 1955 before another tribunal, Peters was declared not guilty – this time the prosecution had left its evidence at home.[111] Proceedings begun against Leibbrandt of the East Ministry and Generalkommissar Frauenfeld (Melitopol) were dropped.[112] Obersturmbannführer Dr. Schäfer (BdS Serbia of Semlin fame) had received twenty-one months from a denazification tribunal. Tried afterwards for his Serbian activities, he was declared to be a "basically clean and decent man," and sentenced to another six and a half years.[113] Obergruppenführer von dem Bach, who had served as Higher SS and Police Leader Russia Center as well as chief of the anti-partisan units, had been a prosecution witness at Nuremberg. Escaping extradition to Russia, he was sentenced by a denazification court to ten years of house arrest.[114] Fretting in his home

bers of criminal organizations. *Denazification Report* (Cumulative Review), pp. 12–13, 138–55.

105. Gerald Reitlinger, *The Final Solution* (New York, 1953), p. 512.

106. "Ein grosser Hehler des Nazi-Regimes entlastet," *Aufbau* (New York), August 26, 1949, p. 5.

107. "Himmler's Stellvertreter tötlich verunglückt," *ibid.,* December 11, 1953, p. 4.

108. Taylor, *Final Report,* p. 78.

109. "Sie gehen mit fleckenlosem Kleid," *Aufbau* (New York), July 1, 1949, p. 4. The above-cited cases were all decided in the British zone.

110. "Germans Jail Nazi Aide," *New York Times,* March 18, 1952, p. 4. "Neuer Haftbefehl gegen Rademacher," *Aufbau* (New York), September 26, 1952, p. 1.

111. "Gemütliches Deutschland," *ibid.,* March 30, 1951, p. 10. Kurt R. Grossmann, "Kronzeuge aus dem Grabe," *ibid.,* May 6, 1955, pp. 1–2, and Grossmann, "Der Freispruch im Blausäureprozess," *ibid.,* June 10, 1955, p. 3.

112. "Judenmörder laufen frei herum," *ibid.,* December 8, 1950, p. 3. "Haftentlassung Frauenfelds," *ibid.,* February 27, 1953, p. 3.

113. "Gestapo-Leiter der Judenvernichtung angeklagt," *ibid.,* September 19, 1952, p. 3. Horne, *Return to Power,* pp. 55–56.

114. Reitlinger, *The Final Solution,* p. 505.

and thinking about his past, the tortured *Obergruppenführer* denounced himself for mass murder.[115] An investigation was begun[116] but was apparently never finished.

The German drive against the perpetrators of destruction failed because there was so much sympathy for these men.[117] Everywhere the convicted and exonerated alike resumed their careers. The businessmen were the quickest to extricate themselves from their past. Friedrich Flick established a new holding company with investments in France and Belgium;[118] Krupp regained control of an industrial empire;[119] the former rulers of I. G. Farben and I. G. Auschwitz – Ambros, Bütefisch, Dürrfeld, and Ter Meer – were all elected to boards of directors of new concerns.[120] Outside of business the ex-perpetrators registered progress too. Many retired with pensions.[121] Some, like Achenbach and Best, entered right-wing politics.[122] Leibbrandt's former deputy, Bräutigam, obtained a position in the new Foreign Office's Eastern Division.[123] The old Foreign Office's northern expert, von Grundherr, became the federal envoy to Greece.[124] Ribbentrop's informant on *Einsatzgruppen* operations, Gustav Hilger, went to the United States.[125] The Interior Ministry's Hans Globke, who had once bestowed upon all of Reich Jewry the middle names "Israel" and "Sara," found in postwar Germany unparalleled opportunities for a new official life. Starting as City Treasurer of Aachen, he was subsequently appointed as *Ministerialdirektor* to the Chancellor's Office, and since 1953 has stood as *Staatssekretär* at Adenauer's side.[126]

In our account of the fate of the men who were in the destructive machine, we have omitted many names; the list below contains the names of a few.[127] For the great bulk of the per-

115. "Selbstanzeige wegen Massenmordes," *Aufbau* (New York), April 18, 1952, p. 11.

116. "Zeugen gesucht," *ibid.*, February 13, 1953, p. 32.

117. Alistair Horne uncovered some figures which showed that the German courts had tried 2058 cases involving war crimes in 1950 and 1951. Only 96 defendants received sentences of more than two years. Horne, *Return to Power,* p. 57. In Austria denazification proceedings and war-crimes trials were combined under the jurisdiction of People's Courts. Up to October 31, 1947, the Austrians had tried 7144 cases with the following results:

Acquittals	1,709
Imprisonment to 1 year	1,295
Imprisonment 1 to 5 years (*sic*)	3,948
Imprisonment 10 to 20 years	135
Imprisonment for life	21
Death sentences	36

Report of U.S. High Commissioner (Lt. Gen. Geoffrey Keyes) to Joint Chiefs of Staff, *Military Government Austria,* for November, 1947, pp. 145–46.

118. "Ex-Nazi Invests in Belgian Steel," *New York Times,* April 12, 1956, p. 5.

119. "Allies Decontrol Krupp Industries," *ibid.*, March 5, 1953, p. 5.

120. "Strafentlassene machen Karriere," *Aufbau* (New York), July 29, 1955, p. 23.

121. In 1958, pensions were paid to approximately 1550 generals or their widows, 2000 ranking civil servants (to Ministerialräte) or widows. Konrad Wille, "Pension eines Generalfeldmarschalls: 2500 D-Mark," *ibid.*, March 7, 1958, pp. 1–2.

122. "German Quits Unit Wooing Ex-Nazis," *New York Times,* November 29, 1952, p. 5. "Free Democrats in Adenauer Bloc Begin a Purge of Nazi Members," *ibid.*, April 27, 1953, p. 13.

123. Arnold Künzli, "Renazifizierung der Bundesrepublik," *Aufbau* (New York), June 1, 1956, p. 3.

124. "Ribbentrop-Mann nach Athen," *ibid.*, December 22, 1950, p. 7. He applied for retirement in May, 1952. "Säuberung in Bonn," *ibid.*, July 25, 1952, pp. 1, 26.

125. See Washington telephone directory.

126. Erwin Holst, "Von Globke und Genossen," *Aufbau* (New York), December 29, 1950, p. 5. "Adenauer Names New Aide," *New York Times,* October 28, 1953, p. 15.

127. Compiled from United Nations War Crimes Commission, *History of the United Nations War Crimes Commission* (London, 1948); *Trials of War Criminals; Law Reports of Trials of War Criminals*; a High Commissioner's report on the fate of Nazi ministers and party leaders; GenSt-8; *Aufbau* (*passim*); the *New York Times* (*passim*); Höttl's

petrators there is no report. We know that some are in Spain and Argentina; others are in the Arab Middle East; a few have probably found refuge in Italian monasteries; many more are undoubtedly hiding at home; but most of them have simply been by-passed. By the law they had not lived. By the law they did not die.

Abetz, Otto (Ambassador in Paris): Sentenced in France to twenty years. Released, 1954. Burned to death in auto collision, 1958.

Altstötter, Josef (Justice Ministry): Sentenced by U.S. military tribunal to five years for membership in criminal organization.

Ambros, Otto (I. G. Farben): Sentenced by U.S. military tribunal to eight years. Aufsichtsrat, Bergwerkgesellschaft Hibernia; Aufsichtsrat, Süddeutsche Kalkstickstoffwerke; Aufsichtsrat, Grünzweig und Hartmann, 1955.

Antonescu, Ion (Marshal): Executed in Roumania, 1946.

Antonescu, Mihai: Executed in Roumania, 1946.

Artukovic, Andrija (Croat Interior Minister): Entered U.S. as "visitor" in July, 1948. Deportation proceedings before federal district court in Los Angeles failed, 1959.

Bach, Erich von dem (Higher SS and Police Leader Russia Center, and Chief of Anti-Partisan Units): Sentenced by denazification court to ten years of house arrest. Denounced himself for mass murder, 1952. Sentenced by German court in Nuremberg to three and one-half years for participation in 1934 purge, February, 1961.

Backe, Herbert (Acting Food Minister): Suicide, 1947.

Baer, Richard (Commander of Auschwitz I): Arrested near Hamburg in December, 1960, after the posting of a reward for his capture.

Baier, Hans (WVHA): Sentenced by U.S. military tribunal to ten years.

Baky, Laszlo (Hungarian Interior Ministry): Executed in Hungary, 1946.

Bardossy, Laszlo (Hungarian Prime Minister): Executed in Hungary, 1946.

Bargen, Werner von (Foreign Office Representative in Belgium): Minister for Special Purposes in new Foreign Office, March, 1952. Declared by *Bundestag* committee as unfit for service because of past activities, July, 1952. Federal Ambassador to Iraq, November, 1960.

Beckerle, Adolf Heinz (Police President of Frankfurt and German Minister to Bulgaria): Arrested in West Germany upon apprehension of Eichmann by Israel, 1960.

Bene, Otto (Foreign Office Representative in Holland): Reported in new Foreign Office, 1952.

Berger, Gottlob (SS-Main Office): Sentenced by U.S. military tribunal to twenty-five years. Sentence reduced by Clemency Board to ten years.

Best, Werner (Plenipotenitary in Denmark): Condemned to death in Denmark. Sentence commuted to five years. Released, 1951.

Biberstein, Ernst (*Einsatzgruppe C*): Condemned to death by U.S. military tribunal. Sentence commuted to life by Clemency Board.

Biebow, Hans (Lodz ghetto administration): Condemned to death in Poland and executed, 1947.

Blankenberg, Werner (Führer Chancellery): Missing.

Blobel, Paul (*Einsatzgruppe C*): Condemned to death by U.S. military tribunal and executed, 1951.

Blome, Kurt (Party Main Office Health): Acquitted by U.S. military tribunal.

Blume, Walter (*Einsatzgruppe B*): Condemned to death by U.S. military

---

Geheime Front; Levai's *Martyrdom of Hungarian Jewry;* and Reitlinger's *Final Solution.*

tribunal. Sentence commuted to life by Clemency Board.

Bobermin, Hans (WVHA): Sentenced by U.S. military tribunal to twenty years. Sentence reduced by the tribunal to fifteen years. Freed by Clemency Board, 1951.

Bock, Fedor von (Commander, Army Group Center): Retired, 1942. Reported killed in air raid, 1945.

Böhme, Franz (Military Commander, Serbia): Committed suicide after indictment by U.S. prosecution in Nuremberg.

Bormann, Martin (Party Chancellery): Believed killed in Battle of Berlin, 1945.

Böttcher, Herbert (SS and Police Leader, Radom): Extradited from British zone in Germany to Poland, 1947. Hanged, 1950.

Bouhler, Philipp (Führer Chancellery): Suicide, 1945.

Bousquet, René (Secretary General of Police, France): Secretary General of the Bank of Indo-China, Paris, 1952.

Bracht, Fritz (*Gauleiter,* Upper Silesia): Missing.

Brack, Viktor (Führer Chancellery): Condemned to death by U.S. military tribunal and executed, 1948.

Brandt, Karl (Plenipotentiary for Health): Condemned to death by U.S. military tribunal and executed, 1948.

Brandt, Rudolf (Secretary of Heinrich Himmler): Condemned to death by U.S. military tribunal and executed, 1948.

Brauchitsch, Walter von (Commander-in-chief of the army): Died in British army hospital waiting for trial, 1948.

Braune, Werner (*Einsatzgruppe D*): Condemned to death by U.S. military tribunal and executed, 1951.

Bräutigam, Otto (East Ministry): Foreign Office, 1956.

Brizgys, Vincent (Auxiliary Bishop of Kaunas): In the United States.

Brunner, Alois (SS deportation expert in Salonika, France, and Slovakia): Missing.

Buhler, Joseph (*Generalgouvernement*): Condemned to death in Poland and executed, 1948.

Bütefisch, Heinrich (I. G. Farben): Sentenced by U.S. military tribunal to six years. Aufsichtsrat, Deutsche Gasolin A. G., Berlin; Aufsichtsrat, Feldmühle, Papier- und Zellstoffwerke, Düsseldorf; Director, Technical Committee of Experts, International Convention of Nitrogen Industry, 1955.

Calotescu, Corneliu (Governor, Bukovina): Condemned to death in Roumania. Indefinite stay granted by King Mihai upon petition from Prime Minister Groza and Justice Minister Patrascu.

Catlos, Josef (Slovak War Minister): Deserted to insurgent territory, 1944. Reported "liquidated" by Soviets.

Clauberg, Carl (Medical experimenter, Auschwitz): Released by Soviets, 1955. Died of apoplexy while waiting for trial in Kiel, 1957.

Daluege, Kurt (ORPO and Protektorat): Executed in Czechoslovakia, 1946.

Dannecker, Theodor (SS deportation expert, France and Bulgaria): Missing.

Dirlewanger (Dirlewanger Brigade): Reported in Cairo, 1952.

Dollmann (SS and Police, Rome): Arrested in Lugano, Switzerland, and deported to unspecified country, 1952.

Dorpmüller, Julius (Transport Minister): Retained by occupation forces. Died, July, 1945.

Dürrfeld, Walter (I. G. Auschwitz): Sentenced by U.S. military tribunal to eight years. Vorstand, Scholven-Chemie A. G. Gelsenkirchen, 1955.

Eichmann, Adolf (RSHA): Escaped, unrecognized, from internment camp in American zone, 1946. Apprehended by Israel agents in Argentina and flown to Israel for trial, May, 1960.

Eirenschmalz, Franz (WVHA): Condemned to death by U.S. military tribunal. Sentence commuted by Clemency Board to nine years.

Endre, Laszlo (Hungarian Interior Ministry): Executed in Hungary, 1946.

Falkenhausen, Alexander von (Military Commander, Belgium): Sentenced in Belgium to twelve years. Released, 1951.

Fanslau, Heinz (WVHA): Sentenced by U.S. military tribunal to twenty-five years. Sentence reduced by the tribunal to twenty years, further reduced by Clemency Board to fifteen years.

Fellgiebel, Erich (OKW): Purged and executed, 1944.

Felmy, Helmut (LXVIII Corps, South Greece): Sentenced by U.S. military tribunal to fifteen years, but not for anti-Jewish acts. Sentence reduced by Clemency Board to ten years. Released, 1952.

Fendler, Lothar (*Einsatzgruppe C*): Sentenced by U.S. military tribunal to ten years. Sentence reduced by Clemency Board to eight years.

Ferenczy, Laszlo (Hungarian *Gendarmerie*): Executed in Hungary, 1946.

Filov, Bogdan (Bulgarian Prime Minister): Executed in Bulgaria, 1945.

Fischer, Ludwig (*Gouverneur*, Warsaw): Executed in Poland, 1947.

Flick, Friedrich (Mitteldeutsche Stahlwerke): Sentenced by U.S. military tribunal to seven years, but not for anti-Jewish acts.

Forster, Albert (*Gauleiter*, Danzig–West Prussia): Executed in Poland, 1948.

Frank, August (WVHA): Sentenced by U.S. military tribunal to life. Sentence reduced by Clemency Board to fifteen years.

Frank, Hans (*Generalgouverneur*): Sentenced to death by International Military Tribunal and hanged, 1946.

Frank, Karl-Hermann (Protektorat): Executed in Czechoslovakia, 1947.

Frauenfeld, Alfred (*Generalkommissar*, Melitopol): Arrested for neo-Nazi activities and freed after investigation by German court, 1953.

Freisler, Roland (Justice Ministry): Reported killed in air raid, 1944.

Frick, Wilhelm (Interior Minister and *Reichsprotektor*): Sentenced to death by International Military Tribunal and hanged, 1946.

Funk, Walter (Economy Minister): Sentenced to life by International Military Tribunal. Released for reasons of health, 1957. Died, 1960.

Fünten, Ferdinand aus der (Central Office for Jewish Emigration in Holland): Condemned to death in Holland. Sentence commuted to life after reported intervention by Adenauer, 1951.

Ganzenmüller, Theodor (Transport Ministry): Reportedly retired.

Gebhardt, Karl (Chief clinician, SS): Condemned to death by U.S. Military Tribunal and executed, 1948.

Gemecke, Konrad (Commander of Westerbork): Reportedly living in Düsseldorf, February, 1960.

Genzken, Karl (Medical service, SS): Sentenced by U.S. military tribunal to life. Sentenced reduced by Clemency Board to twenty years. Fined by West Berlin denazification court, 1955.

Globke, Hans (Interior Ministry): *Ministerialdirektor*, Chancellor's Office, 1950; *Staatssekretär*, 1953.

Globocnik, Odilo (SS and Police Leader, Lublin): Suicide, 1945.

Glücks, Richard (WVHA): Reported by Höss to have been delivered, "half dead", to naval hospital in Flensburg just before surrender. Subsequently missing.

Göbbels, Paul Josef (Propaganda Minister and *Gauleiter* of Berlin): Suicide in Berlin, 1945.

Goldschmidt, Theo (DEGESCH): Aufsichtsrat, Farbenfabriken Bayer A. G., Leverkusen, 1951.

Göring, Hermann: Condemned to death by International Military Tribunal. Committed suicide before execution, 1946.

Grawitz, Ernst (Reich Physician, SS): Suicide, 1945.

Greifelt, Ulrich (Staff Main Office): Sentenced by U.S. military tribunal to life. Died, 1949.

Greiser, Artur (*Gauleiter*, Wartheland): Executed in Poland, 1946.

Grese, Irma (Auschwitz administration): Condemned to death by British court and executed, 1945.

Grundherr, Werner von (Foreign Office): Federal Ambassador to Greece, 1952. Forced into retirement upon investigation by *Bundestag* committee during the same year.

Guderian, Heinz (Commander of Panzer Group 3, Russia Center, and Chief of General Staff): Retired.

Günther, Rolf (RSHA): Missing, believed dead.

Haberland, Ulrich (I. G. Farben): Vorstand, Farbenfabriken Bayer A. G., Leverkusen, 1951.

Haensch, Walter (*Einsatzgruppe C*): Condemned to death by U.S. military tribunal. Sentence commuted to fifteen years by Clemency Board.

Halder, Franz (Chief of General Staff): Indicted as major offender before Bavarian denazification court. Exonerated, 1948.

Handloser, Siegfried (Chief, Armed Forces Medical Service): Sentenced by U. S. military tribunal to life. Sentence reduced by Clemency Board to twenty years.

Hartjenstein, Fritz (Auschwitz administration): Sentenced by British court to life, upon charge involving no acts at Auschwitz.

Heinburg, Kurt (Foreign Office): *Bundestag* committee on record against retention in new Foreign Office, 1952.

Heydrich, Reinhardt (RSHA and *Reichsprotektor*): Assassinated in Prague, 1942.

Hildebrandt, Richard (Higher SS and Police Leader. Danzig, and chief, RuSHA): Sentenced by the U.S. military tribunal to twenty-five years. Reportedly free, 1955.

Hilger, Gustav (Foreign Office): In the United States.

Himmler, Heinrich: Committed suicide upon capture, 1945.

Hindenburg, Oskar von (Commander of PW camps, East Prussia): Fined by denazification court. Died, 1960.

Hitler, Adolf: Suicide, April 30, 1945.

Höfle, Hans (Office of the SS and Police Leader, Lublin): Reported under arrest in Salzburg, Austria, January, 1961.

Höfle, Hermann (Higher SS and Police Leader, Slovakia): Condemned to death in Czechoslovakia, 1948.

Hofmann, Otto (RuSHA): Sentenced by U.S. military tribunal to twenty-five years. Sentence reduced by Clemency Board to fifteen years.

Hohberg, Hans (WVHA): Sentenced by U.S. military tribunal to ten years. Sentence reduced by Clemency Board to time served, 1951.

Höppner, Erich (Commander of Fourth Panzer Army, Army Group North): Purged and executed, 1944.

Höss, Rudolf (Commander of Auschwitz): Condemned to death in Poland and executed, 1947.

Hössler, Franz (Auschwitz administration): Condemned to death by British court and executed, 1945.

Hoth, Hermann (Commander of Panzer Group 3, Army Group Center, and commander of Seventeenth Army, Army Group South): Sentenced by U.S. military tribunal to fifteen years.

Höttl, Wilhelm (RSHA): In conference with Raab on Nazi vote in Austria, 1949. Arrested in Vienna by U.S. military in connection with Communist espionage, 1953.

Houdremont, Eduard (Krupp Essen): Sentenced by U.S. military tribunal to ten years. Sentence reduced by Clemency Board to time served, 1951.

Hoven, Waldemar (Camp doctor,

Buchenwald): Condemned to death by U.S. military tribunal and executed, 1948.

Hunsche, Otto (RSHA): Apprehended in Frankfurt, 1957. Tried twice and finally acquitted. Active as practicing attorney.

Ihn, Max Otto (Krupp personnel): Sentenced by U.S. military tribunal to nine years. Sentence reduced by Clemency Board to time served, 1951.

Ilgner, Max (I. G. Farben): Sentenced by U.S. military tribunal to three years, but not for anti-Jewish acts. Vorsitz, Vorstand des Freundeskreises der internationalen Gesellschaft für christlichen Aufbau, 1955.

Imredy, Bela (Hungarian Economy Minister): Executed in Hungary, 1946.

Isopescu, Modest (Golta Prefecture, Transnistria): Condemned to death in Roumania. Indefinite stay granted by King Mihai upon petition from Prime Minister Groza and Justice Minister Patranascu.

Jarosz, Andor (Hungarian Interior Minister): Executed in Hungary, 1946.

Jeckeln, Friedrich (Higher SS and Police Leader, *Ostland*): Executed in USSR, 1946.

Jodl, Alfred (OKW): Sentenced to death by International Military Tribunal and hanged, 1946.

Jost, Heinz (Commander of *Einsatzgruppe A*): Sentenced by U.S. military tribunal to life. Sentence reduced by Clemency Board to ten years. Fined 15,000 marks by West Berlin denazification court, 1959.

Kaltenbrunner, Ernst (RSHA): Sentenced to death by International Military Tribunal and hanged, 1946.

Kammler, Hans (WVHA): Reportedly a suicide, 1945.

Kappler, Herbert (SS and Police, Rome): Sentenced by Italian military court to life.

Kasche, Siegfried (Minister to Croatia): Executed in Yugoslavia, 1947.

Katzmann, Fritz (SS and Police Leader, Galicia): Died in Darmstadt, 1957.

Kehrl, Hans (Economy Ministry and Armament Ministry): Sentenced by U.S. military tribunal to fifteen years. Sentence reduced by Clemency Board to time served, 1951.

Keitel, Wilhelm (OKW): Sentenced to death by International Military Tribunal and hanged, 1946.

Keppler, Wilhelm (Foreign Office): Sentenced by U.S. military tribunal to ten years. Sentence reduced by Clemency Board to time served, 1951.

Kesselring, Albert (Commander-in-chief, South): Condemned to death by British court. Sentence commuted to life, and subsequently reduced to twenty-one years. Released, 1952.

Kiefer, Max (WVHA): Sentenced by U.S. military tribunal to life. Sentence reduced by the tribunal to twenty years, and further reduced by Clemency Board to time served, 1951.

Killinger, Manfred von (Minister to Roumania): Suicide in Bucharest, 1944.

Klein, Fritz (Auschwitz Camp Doctor): Condemned to death by British Court and executed, 1945.

Kleist, Ewald von (Panzer Group 1, Army Group South): Extradited from Yugoslavia to USSR in 1949. Reportedly died there in 1954.

Klemm, Herbert (Justice Ministry): Sentenced by U.S. military tribunal to life. Sentence reduced by Clemency Board to 20 years.

Klingelhöfer, Waldemar (*Vorkommando Moskau*): Condemned to death by U.S. military tribunal. Sentence commuted to life by Clemency Board.

Klingenfuss, Karl Otto (Foreign Office): Wanted in American zone, but not extradited from Konstanz, 1949. Working as translator, 1950. Reported in Argentina, 1951. West German request for extradition from Argentina reported turned down, 1958.

Klopfer, Gerhard (Party Chancellery): Reported at liberty, 1960.

Kluge, Guenthern von (Commander of Army Group Center): Suicide, 1944.

Knochen, Helmut (BdS France): Condemned to death in France, 1954. Sentence commuted to life, 1958.

Koch, Erich (*Reichskommissar* Ukraine): Seized by British, 1949. Extradited to Poland, 1950. Brought to trial in 1958 and condemned to death in 1959. Execution postponed indefinitely because of continuing illness.

Koppe, Wilhelm (Higher SS and Police Leader, Wartheland and *Generalgouvernement*): Director, chocolate factory in Bonn. Arrested 1960.

Körner, Paul (Office of Four-Year Plan): Sentenced by U.S. military tribunal to fifteen years. Sentence reduced by Clemency Board to time served, 1951. Pensioned.

Korschan, Heinrich Leo (Krupp Markstädt): Sentenced by U.S. military tribunal to six years. Sentence reduced by Clemency Board to time served, 1951.

Kramer, Josef (Commander of Auschwitz II and commander of Bergen-Belsen): Condemned to death by British court and executed, 1945.

Krauch, Carl (General Plenipotentiary Chemical Industry): Sentenced by U.S. military tribunal to six years.

Krebs, Friedrich (*Oberbürgermeister* of Frankfurt): Elected to City Council on the ticket of the German Party, 1952.

Kritzinger, Friedrich Wilhelm (Reich Chancellery): Died at liberty after severe illness.

Krosigk, Schwerin von (Finance Minister): Sentenced by U.S. military tribunal to ten years. Sentence reduced by Clemency Board to time served, 1951.

Krüger, Friedrich (Higher SS and Police Leader, *Generalgouvernement*): Reportedly killed in action, May, 1945.

Krumey, Hermann (*Einsatzkommando Eichmann*): Pronounced lesser offender by denazification court, 1948. Rearrested in Waldeck near Frankfurt upon Austrian allegation of extortion against Hungarian Jews, April, 1957. Released without bail; active in right-wing politics and as drugstore owner, November, 1957. Reported under arrest again, April, 1958.

Krupp, Alfried: Sentenced by U.S. military tribunal to twelve years and deprivation of property. Sentence reduced by Clemency Board to time served and restoration of assets.

Kube, Wilhelm (*Generalkommissar*, White Russia): Assassinated, 1943.

Küchler, Georg von (Commander of Eighteenth Army and commander of Army Group North): Sentenced by U.S. military tribunal to twenty years. Sentence reduced by Clemency Board to twelve years because of defendant's age.

Kuntze, Walter (Commander-in-chief, Southeast): Sentenced by U.S. military tribunal to life.

Kvaternik, Eugen (Croat Interior Ministry): Reported in Argentina, 1950.

Kvaternik, Slavko (Croat Defense Minister): Executed in Yugoslavia, 1946.

Lages, Willy (Security Police and SD, Amsterdam): Condemned to death in Holland, 1949. Sentence commuted to life, 1952.

Lammers, Hans Heinrich (Reich Chancellery): Sentenced by U.S. military tribunal to twenty years. Sentence reduced by Clemency Board to ten years. Released, 1952.

Landfried, Friedrich (Economy Ministry): Released from custody because of mental condition. Pensioned. Died, 1953.

Lange, Otto (KdS, Latvia): Reported escaped from British detention, 1949, to Buenos Aires.

Lanz, Hubert (XXII Corps, Greece and Hungary): Sentenced by U.S. military tribunal to twelve years, but not for anti-Jewish acts. Sentence reduced by Clemency Board to time served, 1951.

Laval, Pierre (Premier of France): Executed in France, 1945.

Leeb, Wilhelm von (Commander, Army Group North): Sentenced by U.S. military tribunal to three years, but not for anti-Jewish acts.

Leibbrandt, Georg (East Ministry): Proceedings before German court in Nuremberg discontinued, 1950.

Liebehenschel, Arthur (Commander of Auschwitz): Condemned to death in Poland and executed, 1948.

Lindow, Kurt (RSHA): Arrested by German authorities, 1950, but apparently not brought to trial.

List, Wilhelm (Wehrmacht commander, Southeast): Sentenced by U.S. military tribunal to life. Released on medical parole, 1951.

Löhr, Alexander (Army Group E, Southeast): Executed in Yugoslavia, 1945.

Lohse, Hinrich (*Reichskommissar, Ostland*): Sentenced by denazification court to ten years. Released because of ill health, 1951.

Lorenz, Werner (VOMI): Sentenced by U.S. military tribunal to twenty years. Sentence reduced by Clemency Board to fifteen years.

Lorkovic (Croat Foreign Minister): Purged and executed by Croat government, 1944.

Lörner, Georg (WVHA): Condemned to death by U.S. military tribunal. Sentence commuted by the tribunal to life, further reduced by Clemency Board to fifteen years. Upon release, acquitted by Bavarian denazification court, 1954.

Lörner, Hans (WVHA): Sentenced by U.S. military tribunal to ten years. Sentence reduced by Clemency Board to time served, 1951.

Lösener, Bernard (Interior Ministry): Oberfinanzdirektor, Cologne. Died 1952.

Löser, Ewald (Krupp): Sentenced by U.S. military tribunal to seven years. Sentence reduced by Clemency Board to time served, 1951.

Ludin, Hans Elard (Minister to Slovakia): Condemned to death in Czechoslovakia, 1946.

Luther, Martin (Foreign Office): Purged. Died in concentration camp.

Mach, Sano (Slovak Interior Minister): Sentenced in Czechoslovakia to thirty years.

Mackensen, Eberhard von (Commander in Rome): Condemned to death by British court. Released, 1952.

Manstein, Erich von (Commander, Eleventh Army): Sentenced by British court to eighteen years. Sentence reduced to twelve years. Released, 1952. Informal consultant to West German Defense Ministry during subsequent years.

Mengele, Josef (Camp doctor, Auschwitz): West German requests for extradition from Argentina, 1959 and 1960, without success. Subsequently reported hiding in Brazil and Argentina.

Merten, Max (Chief of military administration, Salonika): Active as attorney after the war. Returned to Greece as representative of travel bureau. Arrested there and sentenced to tweny-five years, 1959. Released before conclusion of indemnification agreement between West Germany and Greece during the same year.

Meyer, Alfred (East Ministry): Suicide, 1945.

Milch, Eberhard (Air Force and *Jägerstab*): Sentenced by U.S. military tribunal to life. Sentence reduced by Clemency Board to fifteen years.

Mrugowsky, Joachim (Chief, Hygienic Institute, SS): Condemned to death by U.S. military tribunal and executed, 1948.

Müller, Erich (Krupp Artillery Construction): Sentenced by U.S. military tribunal to twelve years. Sentence reduced by Clemency Board to time served, 1951.

Müller, Heinrich (RSHA): Missing.

Mummenthey, Karl (WVHA): Sentenced by U.S. military tribunal to life. Sentence reduced by Clemency Board to twenty years.

Naumann, Erich (Commander of *Einsatzgruppe B*): Condemned to death by U.S. military tribunal and executed, 1951.

Nebe, Artur (RSHA): Reported purged and executed, 1944–45.

Nedic, Milan (Chief of Serb government): Suicide.

Neubacher, Hermann (Mayor of Vienna and Economic Plenipotentiary, Southeast): Sentenced in Yugoslavia to twenty years of hard labor; amnestied after seven years. With Austrian Airlines, 1958. Died, 1960.

Neurath, Constantin von (Foreign Minister and *Reichsprotektor*): Sentenced by International Military Tribunal to fifteen years. Released, 1954.

Nosske, Gustav (*Einsatzgruppe D*): Sentenced by U.S. military tribunal to life. Sentence reduced by Clemency Board to ten years.

Novak, Franz (RSHA): Arrested in Vienna, January, 1961, within hours after broadcast of DM 10,000 reward offered by State Prosecutor in Frankfurt.

Oberg, Karl Albrecht (SS and Police Leader, Galicia, and Higher SS and Police Leader, France): Condemned to death in France, 1954. Sentence commuted to life, 1958.

Ohlendorf, Otto (Commander of *Einsatzgruppe D*): Condemned to death by U.S. military tribunal and executed, 1951.

Ott, Adolf (*Einsatzgruppe B*): Condemned to death by U.S. military tribunal. Sentence commuted to life by Clemency Board.

Panzinger, Friedrich (RSHA): Released from Soviet captivity, 1955. Collapsed and died in Munich apartment upon arrest by German police, 1959.

Pavelic, Ante (Chief of Croat state): In Argentina until 1957. Died in Madrid, 1959.

Pemsel, Max Joseph (Chief of staff to commanding general in Serbia): Commander, Military District IV, West German Army, during middle 1950's.

Pfannenstiel (Professor, Marburg an der Lahn): Investigation begun by German authorities in Marburg, 1950. Apparently no trial.

Pleiger, Paul (Hermann Göring Works): Sentenced by U.S. military tribunal to fifteen years. Sentence reduced by Clemency Board to nine years.

Pohl, Oswald (WVHA): Condemned to death by U.S. military tribunal and executed, 1951.

Pokorny, Adolf (Author of sterilization plan): Acquitted by U.S. military tribunal.

Pook, Hermann (WVHA): Sentenced by U.S. military tribunal to five years. Sentence reduced by Clemency Board to time served, 1951.

Pradel, Johannes (RSHA): Police officer in Hannover. Arrested there, January, 1961.

Prützmann, Hans (Higher SS and police leader, Ukraine): Suicide, 1945.

Puhl, Emil (Reichsbank): Sentenced by U.S. military tribunal to five years.

Rademacher, Karl (Foreign Office): Arrested by German authorities, 1949. With REEMTSA cigarette concern, 1950. Sentenced by German court to three years, March, 1952. Skipped bail, August, 1952. Believed in South America, September, 1952. Reported by *Bundestag* Deputy Arndt to be in Egypt, 1959.

Radetzky, Waldemar von (*Einsatzgruppe B*): Sentenced by U.S. military tribunal to twenty years. Sentence reduced by Clemency Board to time served, 1951.

Rahn, Rudolf (On Foreign Office mission in France, Foreign Office Representative in North Africa, Ambassador to Italy): denazified, 1950.

Rasch, Otto (Commander of *Einsatzgruppe C*): Indicted before U.S. military tribunal. Too ill to be tried.

Rasche, Karl (Dresdner Bank): Sentenced by U.S. military tribunal to seven years. Released, 1950.

Rascher, Sigmund (Medical experimenter, Dachau): Purged. Rumored shot in Dachau, 1945.

Rauter, Hans Albin (Higher SS and Police Leader, Holland): Condemned to death in Holland and executed, 1949.

Reichenau, Walter von (Commander Sixth Army, and commander, Army Group South): Died, 1942.

Reinecke, Hermann (OKW): Sentenced by U.S. military tribunal to life.

Reinhardt, Hans (Commander, Panzer Group 3, Army Group Center, and commander, Third Panzer Army): Sentenced by U.S. military tribunal to fifteen years.

Rendulic, Lothar (Commander, 52d Infantry Division, Russian front): Sentenced by U.S. military tribunal to twenty years. Sentence reduced by Clemency Board to ten years. Released, 1952.

Ribbentrop, Joachim (Foreign Minister): Sentenced to death by International Military Tribunal and hanged, 1946.

Richter, Gustav (SS deportation expert in Roumania): In Stuttgart, 1959.

Ritter, Karl (Foreign Office): Sentenced by U.S. military tribunal to four years, but not for anti-Jewish acts.

Roques, Karl von (Commander, Rear Area Army Group South): Sentenced by U.S. military tribunal to twenty years. Died, 1949.

Rose, Gerhard (Robert Koch Institute/Division of Tropical Medicine): Sentenced by U.S. military tribunal to life. Sentence reduced by Clemency Board to fifteen years.

Rosenberg, Alfred (East Minister): Sentenced to death by International Military Tribunal and hanged, 1946.

Rothaug, Oswald (Judiciary): Sentenced by U.S. military tribunal to life. Sentence reduced by Clemency Board to twenty years. Pensioned.

Rothenberger, Curt (Justice Ministry): Sentenced by U.S. military tribunal to seven years. Pensioned.

Röthke, Heinz (SS deportation expert in France): Missing.

Ruehl, Felix (*Einsatzgruppe D*): Sentenced by U.S. military tribunal to ten years. Sentence reduced by Clemency Board to time served.

Rundstedt, Karl von (Commander, Army Group South): Held in British zone for trial, 1948. Pronounced too sick to be tried, 1949. Subsequently freed, and retired with pension of ca. 2000 marks per month, 1951. Died, 1953.

Rust, Bernard (Education Minister): Suicide, 1944.

Salmuth, Hans von (Commander, XXX Corps, Eleventh Army, and commander, Second Army, Army Group Center): Sentenced by U.S. military tribunal to twenty years. Sentence reduced by Clemency Board to twelve years.

Sandberger, Martin (*Einsatzgruppe A*): Condemned to death by U.S. military tribunal. Sentence commuted to life by Clemency Board.

Sauckel, Fritz (Labor Plenipotentiary): Sentenced to death by International Military Tribunal and hanged, 1946.

Schacht, Hjalmar (Reichsbank): Acquitted by International Military Tribunal, 1946. Stopped during international flight at Lydda, Israel, and strolled in air terminal unmolested, 1951.

Schäfer, Emanuel (BdS, Serbia): Sentenced by denazification court to one year, nine months. Subsequently sentenced by German criminal court to an additional six years, six months.

Scheide, Rudolf (WVHA): Acquitted by U.S. military tribunal.

Schellenberg, Walter (RSHA): Sentenced by U.S. military tribunal to six years, but not for anti-Jewish acts. Released before serving sentence. Died in Italy, 1952.

Schirach, Baldur von (*Reichsstatthalter* of Vienna): Sentenced by International Military Tribunal to twenty years.

Schlegelberger, Franz (Justice Ministry): Sentenced by U.S. military tribunal to life. Released on medical probation upon recommendation of Clemency Board, 1951.

Schmitz, Hermann (I. G. Farben): Sentenced by U.S. military tribunal to four years, but not for anti-Jewish acts. Chairman of Aufsichtsrat, Rheinische Stahlwerke, 1955.

Schnitzler, Georg von (I. G. Farben): Sentenced by U.S. military tribunal to five years.

Schobert, Ritter von (Commander, Eleventh Army). Killed in action, 1941.

Schöngarth, Karl (BdS *Generalgouvernement* and BdS Holland): Condemned to death by British court, 1946.

Schreiber, Walter (Army Medical Service): Under 180-day contract with Air Force School of Aviation Medicine at Randolph Field, San Antonio, Texas. Upon contract expiration, dropped by Secretary Thomas K. Finletter because of charges in regard to medical experiments by Boston group of doctors, 1952.

Schröder, Oskar (Air Force Medical Service): Sentenced by U.S. military tribunal to life. Sentence reduced by Clemency Board to fifteen years.

Schubert, Heinz Hermann (*Einsatzgruppe D*): Condemned to death by U.S. military tribunal. Sentence commuted by Clemency Board to ten years.

Schulz, Erwin (*Einsatzgruppe C*): Sentenced by U.S. military tribunal to twenty years. Sentence reduced by Clemency Board to fifteen years.

Seibert, Willi (*Einsatzgruppe D*): Condemned to death by U.S. military tribunal. Sentence commuted by Clemency Board to fifteen years.

Seidl, Siegfried (Commander of Theresienstadt): Condemned to death by Austrian court, 1946.

Seyss-Inquart, Artur (*Reichskommissar,* Holland): Sentenced to death by International Military Tribunal and hanged, 1946.

Sievers, Wolfram (Ahnenerbe): Condemned to death by U.S. military tribunal and executed, 1948.

Simon, Gustav (Chief of Civil Administration, Luxembourg): Arrested in 1945. Suicide.

Six, Franz (*Vorkommando Moskau*): Sentenced by U.S. military tribunal to twenty years. Sentence reduced by Clemency Board to ten years. Released, 1952. Agent for Porsche motorcars.

Sollmann, Max (Lebensborn): Sentenced by U.S. military tribunal to time served for membership in criminal organization.

Sommer, Karl (WVHA): Condemned to death by U.S. military tribunal. Sentence commuted to life by Military Governor, further reduced by Clemency Board to twenty years.

Speer, Albert (Armament Minister): Sentenced by International Military Tribunal to twenty years, 1946.

Speidel, Wilhelm (Military commander, Greece): Sentenced by U.S. military tribunal to twenty years, but not for anti-Jewish acts. Sentence reduced by Clemency Board to time served, 1951.

Sporrenberg (SS and Police Leader, Lublin): Condemned to death in Poland, 1950.

Stahlecker, Franz Walter (Commander of *Einsatzgruppe A*): Killed in action, 1942.

Steengracht von Moyland, Adolf (Foreign Office): Sentenced by U.S. military tribunal to seven years. Sentence reduced by the tribunal to five years by removing conviction for aggression. Released, 1950.

Steimle, Eugen (*Einsatzgruppe B*): Condemned to death by U.S. military tribunal. Sentence commuted by Clemency Board to twenty years.

Steinbrinck, Otto (Mitteldeutsche Stahlwerke): Sentenced by U.S. military tribunal to five years, but not for anti-Jewish acts.

Strauch, Eduard (*Einsatzgruppe A*): Condemned to death by U.S. military tribunal. Extradited to Belgium and condemned to death again. Execution stayed because of defendant's insanity.

Strauss, Adolf (Commander, Ninth Army, Army Group Center): Held in British zone for trial, 1948. Pronounced too ill to be tried, 1949.

Streicher, Julius (Publisher, *Der Stürmer*): Sentenced to death by International Military Tribunal and hanged, 1946.

Stroop, Jürgen (SS and Police Leader, Warsaw): Condemned to death in Poland and executed, 1951.

Stuckart, Wilhelm (Interior Ministry): Sentenced by U.S. military tribunal to time served because of ill health. Fined 500 marks by denazification court. Killed in automobile accident, 1953.

Stülpnagel, Heinrich von (Commander, Seventeenth Army, and military commander, France): Purged and executed, 1944.

Stülpnagel, Otto von (Military commander, France): Committed suicide in French prison, 1948.

Szalasi, Ferenc (Hungarian Chief of State): Executed in Hungary, 1946.

Sztojay, Döme (Hungarian Prime Minister): Executed in Hungary, 1946.

Taubert, Eberhard (Propaganda Ministry): Volksbund für Frieden und Freiheit, 1955.

Ter Meer, Fritz (I. G. Farben): Sentenced by U.S. military tribunal to seven years. Released, 1950. Deputy Chairman, T. G. Goldschmidt A. G., Essen; Aufsichtsrat, Bankverein Westdeutschland A. G., Düsseldorf; Aufsichtsrat, Düsseldorfer Waggonfabrik, 1955.

Thadden, Eberhard von (Foreign Office): Indicted before German court in Nuremberg, 1948. Escaped to Cologne, where state attorney refused extradition, 1949 and 1950. Still in Cologne, 1953.

Thierack, Otto (Justice Minister): Suicide, 1946.

Thomas, Georg (OKW/Wi Rü): Purged and incarcerated in Buchenwald. "Liberated" there by Allies, 1945.

Thomas, Max (BdS Ukraine): Believed killed in action, 1944.

Tiso, Jozef (President of Slovakia): Shielded by Cardinal Faulhaber in Bavarian monastery, May, 1945. Caught by Americans and extradited to Czechoslovakia, November, 1945. Executed there, 1947.

Tschentscher, Erwin (WVHA): Sentenced by U.S. military tribunal to ten years. Sentence reduced by Clemency Board to time served, 1951.

Tuka, Vojtech (Slovak Prime Minister): Condemned to death in Czechoslovakia, 1946.

Turner, Harald (Office of military governor, Serbia): Condemned to death in Yugoslavia, 1947.

Vallat, Xavier (Anti-Jewish commissioner, France): Sentenced in France to ten years. Released by Justice Minister Rene Mayer, 1950.

Veesenmayer, Edmund (Minister to Hungary): Sentenced by U.S. military tribunal to twenty years. Sentence reduced by Clemency Board to ten years.

Volk, Leo (WVHA): Sentenced by U.S. military tribunal to ten years. Sentence reduced by Clemency Board to eight years.

Wächter, Otto (*Gouverneur* of Galicia): Died in Rome Monastery Maria dell' Anima under protection of Bishop Alois Hudal, 1949.

Wagner, Eduard (*Generalquartiermeister* of the Army): Purged and executed, 1945.

Wagner, Horst (Foreign Office): Arrest ordered by German authorities in 1949. Fled to Spain and then to Italy. Extradition proceedings in Italy commenced in 1953 and failed. Subsequently went back to Germany. Arrested after making application for pension, and released upon 80,000-mark bail, April, 1960.

Wagner, Robert (*Reichsstatthalter* of Baden and Chief of Civil Administration in Alsace): Executed in France, 1946.

Warlimont, Walter (OKW): Sentenced by U.S. military tribunal to life. Sentence reduced by Clemency Board to eighteen years.

Weichs, Maximilian von (Commander, Second Army, Army Group Center, and commander-in-chief, Southeast): Indicted before U.S. military tribunal. Too ill to be tried.

Weizsäcker, Ernst von (Foreign Office): Sentenced by U.S. military tribunal to seven years. Sentence reduced by the tribunal to five years by removing conviction for aggression. Released, 1950. Died, 1951.

Winkler, Max (Main Trusteeship Office East): Exonerated by denazification court, 1949. Died 1961.

Wisliceny, Dieter (SS deportation expert in Slovakia, Greece, and Hungary): Executed in Czechoslovakia, 1948.

Wöhler, Otto (Eleventh Army): Sentenced by U.S. military tribunal to eight years.

Wohlthat, Helmut (Office of the Four-Year Plan): Aufsichtsrat, Farbenfabriken Bayer A. G., 1951.

Wolff, Karl (Chief of Himmler's Personal Staff): Sentenced by denazification court to time served, 1949.

Wörmann, Ernst (Foreign Office): Sentenced by U.S. military tribunal to seven years. Sentence reduced by the tribunal to five years by removing conviction for aggression.

Wüster, Karl (I. G. Farben): Acquitted by U.S. military tribunal. Chairman, Badische Anilin and Sodafabrik, Ludwigshafen, 1951.

Zirpins, Walter (Criminal Police, Lodz): *Polizeidirektor* in Hannover. Arrested there, November, 1960.

2 / Rescue

The most effective rescue is that which is undertaken before the danger point has been reached. In the Jewish case this meant emigration before the outbreak of war. However, the prewar migration was limited by two decisive factors. The first of these was the inability of the European Jews to foresee the future. The second was the limitaion upon reception facilities for prospective emigrants. Most of the world's surface offered no economic base for a new productive life, and the two countries which historically had been the most feasible goals of Jewish emigration, the United States and Palestine, were saddled with entry restrictions.[1]

In the United States the maximum number of immigrants to be admitted in one year was fixed in accordance with the following formula:

$$\frac{\text{Yearly quota of admissible persons born in a given country}}{150{,}000} = \frac{\text{Population of U.S. in 1920 whose "national origin" was traced to such country}}{\text{Total population of European descent in U.S. in 1920}}$$

On April 28, 1938, the "national origin immigration quotas" were consequently distributed as follows:[2]

Great Britain	65,721
Germany (including Austria)	27,370
Eire	17,853
Poland	6,524
Italy	5,802
Sweden	3,314
Netherlands	3,153
France	3,086
Czechoslovakia	2,874
USSR	2,712
Norway	2,377
Switzerland	1,707
Belgium	1,304
Denmark	1,181
Hungary	869
Yugoslavia	845
Finland	569
Portugal	440
Lithuania	386
Roumania	377
All other states under the quota system	less than 300

Until 1939 the United States provided a ready haven for German- and Austrian-born Jews who wanted to emigrate and who had the money for train and ship fare. "In the State Department," said Secretary Hull, "we began to fill the German, Austrian, and later Czech immigration quotas almost entirely with Jews, and in addition we issued scores of thousands of visitors' visas to Jews in the hope that after coming to this country they would find refuge in other countries or could eventually be received here permanently."[3] Nevertheless, by 1939 the German quota was oversubscribed,[4] and the Polish-born Jews in the Reich-Protektorat area shared with the entire population of Poland a yearly quota of 6524.

The Jews were therefore dependent upon Palestine as well. Here, however, they encountered all the difficulties created by British Middle Eastern policy. The British were thinking not only about the Jews but also about the Arabs. In the event of war the support of the world Jewish community was assured in any case. The Jews could not choose sides; the Arabs could. That consideration was decisive.

The mandate which the British government had received from the League of Nations provided in Article 6 that "the Administration of Palestine, while ensuring that the rights and position of other sections of the population are not prejudiced, shall facilitate Jewish immigration under suitable conditions. . . ." That provision allowed for considerable interpretation. In 1922 the Colonial Secretary (Winston Churchill) interpreted the provision to hold that "this immigration cannot be so great in volume as to exceed whatever may be the economic capacity of the country at the time to absorb new arrivals. It is essential to ensure that the immigrants should not be a burden upon the people of Palestine as a whole, and that they should not deprive any section of the present population of their employment."[5]

In pursuance of this policy the British allowed unrestricted entry of so-called

1. See letter by Albrecht (Foreign Office Legal Division) on immigration laws in the United States, Canada, Brazil, Guatemala, El Salvador, Ecuador, Bolivia, South Africa, and Palestine, to Himmler, November 10, 1937, NG-3236.

2. Proclamation by the President, April 28, 1938, 8 USCA 211. In the case of quotas exceeding 300, no more than 10 per cent of the quota was to be exhausted in one month. *Ibid.* Not affected by the quota system were all immigrants born in American countries, further, the spouses or unmarried children of U.S. citizens, residents returning from temporary visits abroad, ministers of the church (including rabbis), professors, students, and women who had lost U.S. citizenship by reason of marriage. 8 USCA 204.

3. Cordell Hull, *Memoirs* (New York, 1948), II, 1538.

4. Hans Lamm, "Über die Innere und Äussere Entwicklung des Deutschen Judentums im Dritten Reich," (Erlangen, 1951) mimeographed, p. 218.

5. Cmd. 1700.

capitalists, that is, Jews who had a certain amount of money in pounds sterling. Workers, on the other hand, were no longer free to immigrate in unlimited numbers.[6] In May, 1939, the Colonial Office moved to bring the Jewish Palestine-bound refugee migration to a conclusion. In a statement of policy which has henceforth become known as the "White Paper," the British declared that "His Majesty's government do not read [their previous statements] as implying that the mandate requires them, for all time and in all circumstances, to facilitate the immigration of Jews into Palestine subject only to consideration of the country's economic capacity."

The time had come to take account also of the political situation. The Arab population was exhibiting "widespread . . . fear of indefinite Jewish immigration." Accordingly, Jewish immigration was to be permitted only for another five years, at the rate of 10,000 per year. In addition, "as a contribution to the solution of the Jewish refugee problem," 25,000 refugees were to be admitted as soon as the High Commissioner was satisfied that adequate provision for their maintenance was ensured.[7]

The year 1939 was thus a year of crisis. The number of Jews who were clamoring to get out was greater than the number whom the world was willing to receive. In the year before the war the Jews of the Reich-Protektorat area were seeking alternate places of refuge in far-off areas that offered little hope for work and subsistence. Many children were received in England. Thousands of families booked passage for Cuba, to wait there for quota entry into the United States. Many thousands clogged ships on the way to Japanese-occupied Shanghai. Tens of thousands went only as far as France, Belgium, and Holland, where most of them were overtaken by German armies in 1940. The total picture can no longer be assessed with accuracy, for the Jews went on from one country to the next. The following table is therefore only an approximate listing of the number of Jews arriving at final destinations:[8]

United States	155,000
Palestine	70,000
Other countries out of German reach	130,000
Countries overtaken by Germans	100,000

The breakdown by area of departure is approximately this:[9]

Reich	300,000
Austria	130,000
Bohemia-Moravia	25,000

Polish Jewry had no chance. The quota to the United States was oversubscribed, and movement to Palestine was no longer possible.[10] Emigration to places like Australia, South America, and the Union of South Africa, even if unrestricted, would have been too costly for the millions of poverty-stricken Polish Jews.[11]

6. See Albrecht to Himmler, November 10, 1937, NG-3236.

7. Palestine statement of policy presented by the Secretary of State for Colonies to Parliament in May, 1939. Cmd. 6019. The Permanent Mandates Commission of the League of Nations unanimously abstained from endorsing the White Paper. Four members of the commission held that the paper was inconsistent with the mandate. Three thought that it was not in accordance with the commission's previous interpretation of the mandate and that the Council should be consulted on whether a new interpretation was possible under the circumstances. The League Council never met to consider the issue.

8. American Joint Distribution Committee, *Reports* for 1939, 1940, and 1941. *American Jewish Year Book, 1950,* p. 75. Lamm, "Deutsches Judentum," pp. 209–45.

9. *Ibid.* Korherr to Himmler, April 19, 1943, NO-5193.

10. During 1936–39, Jewish emigration from Poland to Palestine accounted for about 9000 or 11 per cent of all arrivals. *Report of Anglo-American Committee,* 1946, Cmd. 6808, p. 51n.

With the onset of the war and the beginning of the "final solution of the Jewish question" in Europe, the problem of migration was fundamentally altered. Before the war the Jews made every attempt to hold on, and the Germans applied every pressure to effect a Jewish mass departure; by 1941 all the Jews of German-dominated Europe wanted to leave, but now the German machinery of destruction held them captive.

On the outside the issue between the world Jewish community and the Allied governments had sharpened. Before the war the Jews could argue only that emigration was necessary for the relief of misery, and the Allied position was correspondingly based on "absorptive capacities" and "political considerations." Now rescue had become for the Jews a matter of life and death. If the Nazi ring could not be sprung open and the Jews brought to a safe destination, they would die in mounting numbers as the catastrophe quickened. The British government and its helpers were not moved to drastic action by this situation. The old reasons for barring the Jews from Palestine were even stronger now, and the old arguments with respect to the political situation were reinforced with the war. Significantly, however, the dichotomy between the Jewish and Allied positions was not from the outset clearly visible. The Jews were slow to react to the challenge; and when the apparatus of Jewish organizations was finally activated in behalf of the victims in Europe, the Jewish leadership, already confronted with millions of dead, was prepared to do little more than save those who were already safe.

We have pointed out repeatedly that the Jews did not anticipate the "final solution." When they woke up to the facts, the disaster was already upon them. By the summer of 1942, however, the volume of deportations and killings had far surpassed the limits within which such an operation could be kept secret from the outside world. Hints, rumors, and reports began to accumulate in information-gathering agencies at widely scattered points.

On August 1, 1942, at a time when about 1,500,000 Jews were already dead, the chief of the Geneva office of the World Jewish Congress, Dr. Gerhardt Riegner, heard through a German industrialist "that a plan had been discussed in Hitler's headquarters for the extermination of all Jews in Nazi-occupied lands." Riegner sent the information via the American and British consulates to Rabbi Dr. Stephen Wise in the United States and M. P. Sidney Silverman in England. Silverman got the information, Wise did not. Silverman then transmitted the message to Rabbi Wise. The rabbi, who was American Jewry's most prominent leader, decided to carry the report to Undersecretary of State Welles. The Undersecretary asked him not to release the story until an attempt could be made to confirm it.[12]

The following three months were spent in checking the Riegner report. They were Jewry's bloodiest months. About one million Jews died during this period. The second sweep in Russia was in fullest swing; the Polish ghettos were being emptied out; from the western states and from the Reich itself dozens of transports were converging upon the killing centers. On October 5, 1942, the Jewish Telegraphic Agency reported that mass executions of thousands of

11. In the depression years 1931–1938 a total of 117,138 Jews left Poland. Bernard D. Weinryb, "Poland," in Meyer *et al., The Jews in the Soviet Satellites,* p. 211.

12. Stephen Wise, *Challenging Years* (New York, 1949), pp. 274–75. Henry Morgenthau, Jr., "The Morgenthau Diaries VI – The Refugee Run-Around," *Collier's,* November 1, 1947, pp. 22–23, 62, 65. Morgenthau was then U.S. Secretary of the Treasury. In 1942 the Treasury Department was not yet apprised of anything.

Jews of all ages, including women, were taking place from time to time. Systematic deportations were engulfing the Jews of Lodz. The Lodz Jews, said the telegraphic agency, "are poisoned by gas."[13]

In the meantime, the checking continued. Finally, in November, 1942, the American Legation in Berne transmitted to Washington four affidavits which confirmed Riegner's original report. Welles thereupon told Wise that the information could be made public.[14] On December 17, 1942, the Department of State joined the other Allied governments in a declaration entitled "German Policy of Extermination of the Jewish Race," which stated that the responsible perpetrators "shall not escape retribution."[15]

The Jewish leadership was now confronted with the facts; the issue was clear. What, then, did Jewry's leaders propose to do? On January 6, 1943, Henry Monsky, president of B'nai Brith, called a preliminary meeting of an American Jewish Conference. In his letter of invitation, which was sent to thirty-four Jewish organizations, he wrote:

> American Jewry, which will be required in large measure to assume the responsibility of representing the interests of our people at the Victory Peace Conference, must be ready to voice the judgment of American Jews along with that of other Jewish communities of the free countries with respect to the post-war status of Jews and the upbuilding of a Jewish Palestine.

In this letter no warning to the Germans is proposed, no scheme to put an end to the destruction process is suggested; the destruction of the European Jews is not even mentioned.[16] The European Jews are already given up, and all thoughts turn to postwar salvage. Clearly, the world-wide Jewish action machinery – the network of Jewish pressure groups – was at a standstill. Budgets were at a low point. The holocaust was unopposed. The paralysis was complete.

On January 21, 1943, Undersecretary of State Welles received Cable 482 from the Legation in Berne; the cable contained a message from Riegner reporting that Jews were being killed in Poland at the rate of 6000 a day and that Jews in Germany and Roumania were starving to death. Welles passed on the cable to Wise and instructed Minister Harrison to keep sending full reports from Switzerland. The Jewish organizations now seemed to be jolted. A mass meeting was held in Madison Square Garden, relief agencies doubled their efforts, and rescue schemes poured into Washington.[17]

The Jewish restlessness apparently disquieted the State Department, and the department took the position that

13. Jewish Telegraphic Agency, *Daily News Bulletin*, New York, October 6, 1942, p. 4, NI-12321.

14. Morgenthau in *Collier's*, November 1, 1947.

15. Department of State press release of December 17, 1942, in *International Conference on Military Trials*, pp. 9–10. For original British draft of declaration, together with U.S. and Soviet amendments, see correspondence, dated December 7–17, 1942, in *Foreign Relations 1942*, I, 66–70. Harold H. Tittmann, assistant to President Roosevelt's personal representative to Pope Pius XII, asked Cardinal Secretary of State Maglione whether there was not something the Holy See could do "along similar lines." The Cardinal replied that the Holy See was "unable to denounce publicly particular atrocities." It could only condemn atrocities in general. For the rest, "everything possible was being done privately to relieve the distress of the Jews." Tittmann report in telegram by Harrison (U.S. Minister in Switzerland) to Hull, December 26, 1942, *ibid.*, pp. 70–71.

16. Kohanski, *American Jewish Conference, First Session*, pp. 15, 319.

17. Morgenthau in *Collier's*, November 1, 1947. DuBois, *The Devil's Chemists*, pp. 184, 187. DuBois was then in the Foreign Funds Control Division of the Treasury Department.

the question had to be "explored." Some of its political experts then decided to suppress the flow of information. A cable, numbered 354, was dispatched under the signature of Undersecretary Welles to Harrison in Berne. It referred to "Your cable 482, January 21." The text then proceeded as follows:

> In the future we would suggest that you do not accept reports submitted to you to be transmitted to private persons in the United States unless such action is advisable because of extraordinary circumstances. Such private messages circumvent neutral countries' censorship and it is felt that by sending them we risk the possibility that steps would necessarily be taken by the neutral countries to curtail or forbid our means of communication for confidential official matter.[18]

The cable was initialed by four officers of the Foreign Service. The message was handled only by the European Division and the political adviser of the State Department; the Undersecretary is believed to have signed the document without full awareness of its contents.[19] It appears, then, that the career men were attempting to withhold the information not only from the Jewish community but also from the men who directed the affairs of the United States government.

In March, 1943, the British Foreign Secretary, Anthony Eden, arrived in Washington for conferences with American leaders. During one of these discussions the American Secretary of State Hull brought up the problem of rescuing the Jews, in the presence of President Roosevelt, Harry Hopkins, Undersecretary Welles, British Ambassador Halifax, and the Assistant Undersecretary of State in the British Foreign Office, William Strang. Hopkins' summary of that exchange of words was:

> Hull raised the question of the 60 or 70 thousand Jews that are in Bulgaria and are threatened with extermination unless we could get them out and, very urgently, pressed Eden for an answer to the problem. Eden replied that the whole problem of the Jews in Europe is very difficult and that we should move very cautiously about offering to take all Jews out of a country like Bulgaria. If we do that, then the Jews of the world will be wanting us to make similar offers in Poland and Germany. Hitler might well take us up on any such offer and there simply are not enough ships and means of transportation in the world to handle them.
>
> Eden said that the British were ready to take about 60 thousand more Jews to Palestine but the problem of transportation, even from Bulgaria to Palestine is extremely difficult. Furthermore, any such mass movement as that would be very dangerous to security because the Germans would be sure to attempt to put a number of their agents in the group. They have been pretty successful with this tech-

18. Text of cable 354, dated February 10, 1943, in Morgenthau, *Collier's,* November 1, 1947.

19. Josiah DuBois reports that "the 'political boys' had ordered that Treasury was not under any circumstances to have a copy." DuBois, *The Devil's Chemists,* p. 187. Neither Morgenthau nor DuBois believes that Welles signed the message with intent to suppress information about the Jewish catastrophe. The attitude of the European Division in Jewish matters appears to have been recorded before the end of 1941, upon receipt of a suggestion from the Turkish Minister in Bucharest that the Roumanian Jews be brought across Turkey to Palestine. Cavendish Cannon wrote at that time to the acting chief of the division (Atherton) and the adviser on political relations (Dunn) that no formal note should be sent to the British. The arguments against tackling the problem included, among others, "ships," the "Arab question," the possibility of "pressure for an asylum in the western hemisphere," and a possible request for similar treatment of the Jews in Hungary "and, by extension, all countries where there has been intense persecution." Memorandum by Cannon, November 12, 1941, *Foreign Relations 1941,* II, 875–76.

> nique both in getting their agents into North and South America.
>
> Eden said that the forthcoming conferences in Bermuda on the whole refugee problem must come to grips with this difficult situation.
>
> Eden said he hoped that on our side we would not make too extravagant promises which could not be delivered because of lack of shipping.[20]

During the following months two abortive rescue schemes were considered in London and Washington. The British government, through the Swiss Legation in Berlin, offered to accept 5000 Jewish children from the *Generalgouvernement* and the occupied eastern territories in Palestine. The German Foreign Office agreed to deliver the children to Britain in exchange for interned Germans. The British refused to release any Germans on the ground that the children were not nationals of the British Empire. That was where the matter rested.[21]

The second rescue scheme evolved when Undersecretary of State Welles cabled to Berne for more information about the destruction of the European Jews. In reply he received what appears to be the Antonescu plan for the release of some 60,000 Jews in exchange for money. The State Department experts were not enthusiastic about a ransoming attempt; they had to be worn down by the department's economic adviser Dr. Herbert Feis, the weighty intervention of the Treasury Department's Foreign Funds Control Division under John Pehle, and an appeal by Rabbi Wise to President Roosevelt himself. After eight months the State Department issued a license enabling Jewish organizations to deposit money to the credit of Axis officials in blocked accounts in Switzerland. The license was issued over the opposition of the British Foreign Office, which – in the words of a note delivered to the American Embassy in London by the British Ministry of Economic Warfare – was concerned with the "difficulties of disposing of any considerable number of Jews" in the event of their release from Axis Europe.[22]

The rescue effort was failing. Within the State Department there was disinclination to undertake large-scale action; within the Foreign Office there was fear of large-scale success; and within Axis Europe fewer and fewer Jews remained. The frustrations inherent in this situation finally resulted in an establishment of special rescue machinery in the American Jewish community and in the United States government itself.

From August 29 to September 2, 1943, the first session of the American Jewish Conference, which had been called seven months before, met in deliberation. The destruction of the European Jews was still not on its agenda. In the preliminary meeting only two substantive points had been drawn up for discussion: "rights and status of Jews in the post-war world" and "rights of the Jewish people with respect to Palestine." In the words of the B'nai Brith delegate David Blumberg, the purpose of the conference was the formulation of a program to be heeded "by the proper authorities after the war is over." Rabbi Dr. Stephen Wise, as delegate of the American Jewish Congress, then declared that the conference would have to deal immediately with the problem of rescuing European Jewry.

20. Memorandum by Hopkins on meeting between Roosevelt, Hopkins, Hull, Welles, Eden, Halifax, and Strang, on March 27, 1943, in Robert E. Sherwood, *Roosevelt and Hopkins* (New York, 1948), p. 717.

21. Wagner to Müller (RSHA), July 13, 1943, NG-4747. Wagner via *Staatssekretär* to Ribbentrop, July 21, 1943, NG-4786. Von Thadden to Wagner, April 29, 1944, NG-1794.

22. Morgenthau in *Collier's*, November 1, 1947. DuBois, *The Devil's Chemists*, pp. 185–88.

An observer, the chairman of the British section of the World Jewish Congress, Dr. Maurice L. Perlzweig, proposed that the conference urge the Allied nations to demand from the Axis the release of its Jewish victims and to proclaim the right of asylum for any Jews who should succeed in escaping. The conference thereupon adopted a resolution calling for a "solemn warning" to the Axis and the establishment of a "temporary asylum" for the Jews.[23] The delegates then adjourned and left the business of the conference in the hands of an interim committee which established, on October 24, 1943, a rescue commission.[24]

One of the commission's efforts was directed towards the creation of a parallel agency in the government. Such an agency was finally set up by executive order after considerable agitation in Congress and a "personal report" by Morgenthau to President Roosevelt on the State Department's conduct in the refugee question. The date of the executive order was January 22, 1944. The title of the agency was the War Refugee Board. Its membership consisted of the Secretaries of State, the Treasury, and War (Hull, Morgenthau, and Stimson); the executive director was John Pehle of the Treasury Department. The board maintained its own network of special representatives abroad.[25]

The rescue program had thus been centralized. A specific agency had been created for the task. That agency had centers for the receipt of information, means of communication, and powers of negotiation. Moreover, it could call upon private Jewish organizations for detailed knowledge, age-old experience, and – in the event of ransom possibilities – "quickly available funds."[26] The challenge came soon, for in the spring of 1944 Hungarian Jewry was threatened with destruction.

We have already seen what happened in Hungary: on March 19, 1944, the Hungarian government was overthrown, and the line to Auschwitz was cleared. For the Germans there was no further barrier; for Jewry there was no more protection. Between the Jews and the gas chambers there remained

23. Kohanski, *American Jewish Conference, First Session,* particularly pp. 15, 18–19, 25–26, 33, 73, 115–17, 127–30.

24. American Jewish Conference, *Report of Interim Committee,* November 1, 1944, pp. 13 ff.

25. The following is a list of the posts:
United Kingdom: Josiah E. DuBois, Jr., general counsel of the board, from the Treasury Department
Turkey: Ira A. Hirschmann, department store executive
Portugal: Dr. Robert C. Dexter, Unitarian Service Committee
Sweden: Iver C. Olsen, Treasury
Switzerland: Rowell McClelland, American Friends Service Committee
Italy: Leonard Ackerman, Treasury
Another post was established in North Africa. American Jewish Conference, *Report of Interim Committee,* 1944, pp. 19–22. Executive Director, War Refugee Board (William O'Dwyer), *Final Summary Report* (Washington, D.C., 1945), pp. 1–6. Morgenthau in *Collier's,* November 1, 1947. DuBois, *The Devil's Chemists,* pp. 15, 31, 188, 198.

26. The War Refugee Board collected a considerable amount of information. In April, 1944, two Slovak Jews escaped from Auschwitz and made their way to Switzerland. They brought with them many details about transport arrivals and gassings in the camp. Not clear is the date on which the statements were received, when they were transmitted to Washington, and what action was based on them. See affidavit by Pehle, November 13, 1947, NI-12545. Further, DuBois, *The Devil's Chemists,* pp. 183–84. Also, the report itself, published by the War Refugee Board in November, 1944, under the title, "The Extermination Camps of Auschwitz and Birkenau" (mimeographed). The War Refugee Board could not spend much money. Under the U.S. Constitution federal expenditures must be authorized by Congress; agencies established by congressional statute are usually provided with necessary funds, but the War Refugee Board was set up by the President in an executive order.

only a series of predetermined bureaucratic steps. However, the activation of these steps required a certain amount of preparation, and the Germans did not have very much time. They were losing the war. Every day the German position was becoming more difficult. The steady buildup of this destructive operation was the work of an administrative machine in which the bolts were already beginning to loosen. Everything therefore depended on the ability of outside forces to recognize these weaknesses and to immobilize the machine before it could deliver its blow.

The outside world was in a position to attempt a rescue effort on two levels, the physical and the psychological. Physical action could be implemented from the air. We have already noted that a Slovak official furnished to the Jewish Bratislava rescue committee the routes over which the Jews were to be carried to their death. That information was transmitted to Switzerland, but it brought no results. The railway junctions were not bombed. When the transports arrived in Auschwitz, no bombers appeared over the gas chambers. The opportunity was lost. The notion of stopping the killings by physical means apparently occurred to no one. The outside Jews were not accustomed to think about rescue in terms of physical force, and the outside Christians were not thinking about force for the purpose of rescue. The Hungarian Jews thus had to be saved with psychological methods alone.

We know that in the psychological sphere the Allies possessed a potent weapon. At a time when Hungary was gripped with the fear of Allied air raids, the Hungarian government was concentrating the Jews in cities of 10,000 people or more. Today one might easily question why no one thought then about the possible consequences of an Allied promise of immunity that would have been honored as long as the Jews remained in those cities. The answer appears to be that the Jews could not think in terms of "interfering" with the war effort, and the Allies on their part could not conceive of such a promise. They could no more take the Jews into account to refrain from bombing than they could think of Jews in planning their missions. The Allied bombers roared over Hungary at will, killing Hungarians and Jews alike.

The world outside was inert. The War Refugee Board and the Jewish offices at its service had posted a receiving organization at the perimeter of the destructive arena. There the rescuers waited for openings, opportunities, and offers. Incredibly enough, an offer was to come.

We have had previous occasion to note that on April 6 and 7, at a time when the German momentum in Hungary was approaching its climax, the Armaments Ministry secured from Hitler himself an authorization to remove 100,000 of the expected Jewish deportees from Auschwitz to construction projects which were then being planned by the Pursuit Planes Staff.[27] Two and a half weeks after this diversion had been authorized, Obersturmbannführer Eichmann called to his office in the Budapest Hotel Majestic a leader of the Jewish rescue committee in Hungary, Joel Brand.[28] Eichmann received Brand with words in the following vein:

> Do you know who I am? I have carried out the *Aktionen* in the Reich — in Poland — in Czechoslovakia. Now it is Hungary's turn. I let you come here to talk business with you. Before that I investigated you — and your people.

27. See pp. 599–600.

28. Except as indicated otherwise, the entire account of the Brand mission is taken from Alexander Weissberg, *Die Geschichte von Joel Brand* (Cologne-Berlin, 1956).

> Those from the Joint and those from the Agency.[29] And I have come to the conclusion that you still have resources. So I am ready to sell you – a million Jews. All of them I wouldn't sell you. That much money and goods you don't have. But a million – that will go. Goods for blood – blood for goods. You can gather up this million in countries which still have Jews. You can take it from Hungary. From Poland. From Austria. From Theresienstadt. From Auschwitz. From wherever you want. What do you want to save? Virile men? Grown women? Old people? Children? Sit down – and talk.

Brand was a careful negotiator. How was he to get goods, he asked, that the Germans could not confiscate on their own? Eichmann had the answer: Brand was to go abroad; he was to negotiate directly with the Allies and bring back a concrete offer. With these words Eichmann dismissed Brand, warning him in parting that the discussion was a Reich secret that no Hungarian was allowed to suspect.

Sometime in the beginning of May, following the railway conference in Vienna which determined the routing of the transports, Eichmann called Brand again. "Do you want a million Jews?" If so, Brand was to leave immediately for Istanbul. He was to bring back an offer to deliver trucks. "You deliver one truck for every hundred Jews. That is not much." The total would be 10,000 vehicles. The trucks had to be new and suitable for winter driving. "You can assure the Allies that these trucks will never be used in the West. They will be employed exclusively on the eastern front." In addition, the Germans would be pleased if the Allies would throw in a couple of thousand tons of tea, coffee, soap, and other useful items.

Cautiously, Brand replied: "Mr. Obersturmbannführer, I personally can believe that you will keep your word, but I do not possess ten thousand trucks. The people with whom I must negotiate in Istanbul will demand guarantees. Nobody is going to deliver ten thousand trucks in advance. What assurance can you offer that these million Jews will actually be freed?"

Eichmann thereupon gave a decisive answer. "You think we are all crooks. You hold *us* for what *you* are. Now I am going to prove to you that I trust you more than you trust me. When you come back from Istanbul and tell me that the offer has been accepted, I will dissolve Auschwitz and move 10 per cent of the promised million to the border. You take over the 100,000 Jews and deliver for them afterwards one thousand trucks. And then the deal will proceed step by step. For every hundred thousand Jews, a thousand trucks. You are getting away cheap."

Brand had to conceal his excitement. For the first time he saw a way out. If the verbal assurance could be given in time, the Jews could, without delivering a single truck, score a major breakthrough. To be sure, the Germans could change their conditions. So far they had made no concessions, but if Brand could return with a promise, the Germans could not kill so long as they wanted the trucks. Without blood, no merchandise.[30]

The rescue committee now telegraphed to Istanbul that Brand would be arriving there; the answer came quickly, "Joel should come, Chaim will be there." To the committee this could mean only that Chaim Weizmann himself, the president of the Executive of the Jewish Agency, would be on hand.

On May 15 Brand saw Eichmann for the last time. It was the day on which the deportations began. Eichmann

29. Reference here is to the American Jewish Joint Distribution Committee and the Jewish Agency for Palestine.

30. Brand did not know of the German plan to use up to 100,000 Jews for forced labor in any case.

warned Brand to return quickly. If the offer came in time, Auschwitz would be "blown up" (*dann sprenge ich Auschwitz in die Luft*), and the deportees now leaving Hungary would be the first to be sent to the border.

On the following day, Brand secured "full powers" from the *Zentralrat der Ungarischen Juden;* he also received a companion: a Jew who had served the *Abwehr,* Bandi Grosz. The two went to Vienna and, paying for their fare in dollars, left by special plane to Istanbul.

When Brand landed at the Istanbul airport, he made a disturbing discovery. The Jewish Agency had not processed an entry visa for him, and "Chaim" was not there. The man to whom Jerusalem had referred was not the agency's chief executive, Chaim Weizmann, but the chief of its Istanbul office, Chaim Barlasz, and that man was riding around in the city at the very moment of the plane's arrival to obtain a visa for Brand. Fortunately, Brand's counterintelligence companion, Grosz, had many connections in Istanbul. After a few telephone calls by Grosz, the two men were allowed to move into a hotel. There the Jewish Agency representatives were waiting for the emissaries.

Brand was angry and excited. "Comrades, do you realize what is involved? . . . We have to negotiate. . . . With whom can I negotiate? Do you have the power to make agreements . . . ? Twelve thousand people are hauled away every day . . . that is five hundred an hour. . . . Do they have to die because nobody from the Executive is here? . . . . I want to telegraph tomorrow that I have secured agreement. . . . Do you know what is involved, comrades? The Germans want to negotiate. The ground is burning under their feet. They feel the coming of the catastrophe. Eichmann has promised us an advance of a hundred thousand Jews. Do you know what this means? . . . I insist, comrades, that a man come here whom all the world knows. The Germans are observing us. They will know at once that Weizmann is here or Shertok. Even if you cannot accomplish anything concrete with the Allies while I am here, I can go back and tell Eichmann that the Agency has accepted. Then Auschwitz can be blown up. . . ."

To the representatives of the Jewish Agency the matter was not so simple. They could not be sure, they said, that a telegram sent to Jerusalem would arrive there without mutilation. No one had enough influence to obtain a plane. No representative of the War Refugee Board was on the scene. Brand wanted to reach Steinhardt, the American Ambassador in Ankara. "Steinhardt," he said, "is supposed to be a good Jew. And besides that, a good man." But no plane seat could be bought for a trip to Ankara. The hours began to pass, then the days. Brand, still waiting for someone to arrive in Istanbul, gave the Jewish Agency representatives some important data. "I gave the comrades an accurate plan of the Auschwitz concentration camp. I demanded the bombing of the gas chambers and crematories insofar as this was technically possible. I demanded diversions and air strikes against the junctions on the railway lines which led to Auschwitz. I gave our comrades accurate information about places where parachute troops could land, and I gave them a list of documents and other things that the parachutists absolutely had to have to get through. I named a number of addresses of reliable helpers on the roads to Budapest."

Brand had exhausted his mission, and it was exhausting him in turn. In repeated discussions with the Jewish Agency representatives he gained the distinct impression that they did not quite realize what was at stake. "They did not, as we did in Budapest, look daily at death."

As Brand waited for a reply, a number of unexpected things began to happen. For a few days he was in danger of deportation. The Turkish authorities had ordered his apprehension, together with Bandi Grosz, although the latter was a "director" of a Hungarian transport corporation engaged in discussion with the director of a Turkish state transport company. Why the deportation of Grosz? Already Brand suspected that the British were controlling the "main switch," but he dismissed the thought. "I could not believe," he states, "that England – this land which alone fought on while all other countries of Europe surrendered to despotism – that this England which we had admired as the inflexible fighter for freedom wanted simply to sacrifice us, the poorest and weakest of all the oppressed."

Soon, however, another curious situation arose. Moshe Shertok, the chief of the political department of the Jewish Agency, its second in command, was unable to obtain a visa to Turkey. The agency decided to bring Brand to Aleppo in British-occupied Syria; there Shertok was to meet him. On June 5, 1944, after fifteen fruitless days in Istanbul, Brand, with a British visa in his German passport, boarded the Taurus express train. When the train passed through Ankara, a representative of the Jewish Revisionists (*Irgun*), accompanied by an Orthodox Party man, got on to warn him that he was moving into a "trap." Shertok had not obtained a visa because the British wanted to lure Brand into British-controlled territory, where they could arrest him. Britain was in this matter no "ally" (*Die Engländer sind in dieser Frage nicht unsere Verbündeten*). They did not want his mission to succeed If he continued on his journey, he would never be able to return; he would be arrested.

Brand was confused. The train was about to pull out, and he decided to stay on it. On June 7, 1944, he arrived in Aleppo. A porter entered the compartment and took off Brand's luggage. Brand wanted to follow the porter when an Englishman in civilian clothes blocked his way.

"Mister Brand?"

"Oh, yes."

"This way, please."

Before Brand knew what was happening, two plainclothesmen had pushed him into a waiting jeep whose motor was already running. Brand tried to resist, but it was too late.

After two days of arrest the British brought Brand to a villa where Shertok was waiting. Shertok invited Brand to tell about his mission again. In the presence of the British, who were listening silently, Brand talked for ten to twelve hours. When the session was over, Shertok went into a huddle with the British representatives. Then he turned to Brand. "Dear Joel, I have to tell you something bitter now. You have to go south. The British demand it. I have done everything to change this decision, but it is a decision of the highest authorities. I could not alter it."

For a second Brand did not understand what had been said to him. When finally he caught on, he screamed: "Do you know what you are doing? That is simply murder! That is mass murder. If I don't return our best people will be slaughtered! My wife! My mother! My children will be first! You have to let me go! I have come here under a flag of truce. I have brought you a message. You can accept or reject, but you have no right to hold the messenger. . . . I am here as the messenger of a million people condemned to death. . . . What do you want from us? What do you want from me . . . ?"

Brand was brought to Cairo for exhaustive intelligence interrogations. He was henceforth a prisoner. Shertok, at the behest of Foreign Minister Eden, flew to London for more "discussions." The War Refugee Board's representative, Ira Hirschmann, chased after Brand in Istanbul and, not finding him there, moved on to Cairo. In Cairo the ranking British official, Deputy Minister of State Lord Moyne, tried to persuade Hirschmann to fly to London too. Hirschmann, a New York department store executive not given to diplomatic niceties, told Moyne that he would be ready to take orders from Eden whenever Moyne decided to follow the instructions of Secretary of State Hull. Finally Hirschmann managed to talk to Brand. By that time it was July.[31]

The almost impossible had happened. An incredible German offer had been met with the most unlikely refusal. There were to be no negotiations; there was to be no bombing. Not even the parachutists had been landed in the right places. Those Jewish volunteers from Palestine were dropped over military targets where most of them could die for England.[32]

By the beginning of July most of the Hungarian Jews were dead. The Jews of Budapest were waiting for their turn. They were saved at the last moment, when the Regent Horthy and the Sztojay government, wearied by the protests of neutral states and the Church and frightened by intercepted Anglo-American teletype messages containing among other things the Jewish requests for target bombings of Hungarian government offices as well as the names of seventy prominent officials, decided to stop the operation in its tracks. Two days after the deportations had come to a halt outside the Hungarian capital, Prime Minister Churchill wrote the following letter to Eden:

> There is no doubt that this is probably the greatest and most horrible crime ever committed in the whole history of the world, and it has been done by scientific machinery by nominally civilised men in the name of a great state and one of the leading races of Europe. It is quite clear that all concerned in this crime who may fall into our hands, including the people who only obeyed orders by carrying out the butcheries should be put to death after their association with the murders has been proved. . . . There should therefore, in my opinion, be no negotiations of any kind on this subject. Declarations should be made in public, so that everyone connected with it will be hunted down and put to death.[33]

This letter reveals a great deal about the British Prime Minister's thoughts. In these instructions Churchill was not particularly concerned with the safety of the Jews; he was worried about the reputation of the German nation. The culprits had disgraced their race.

The Jews continued to be gassed. Outside Hungary the operation was not over. The Jews were being deported from Italy; they were shipped out from the islands of Greece; they were hauled out of the ghetto of Lodz; they were thinned out in Theresienstadt; they were moved out of the Polish labor camps. In the fall came the turn of the remaining Slovakian Jews. Once more, ransom negotiators were sent out from Germany; this time the associate president of the Zionist Organization in

31. Ira A. Hirschmann, *Lifeline to a Promised Land* (New York, 1946), pp. 109–32.

32. Marie Syrkin, *Blessed Is the Match – The Story of Jewish Resistance* (Philadelphia, 1947), pp. 19–35. Veesenmayer to Ritter, July 8, 1944, NG-5616.

33. Churchill to Eden, July 11, 1944, in Winston S. Churchill, "The Second World War," Vol. VI: *Triumph and Tragedy* (Boston, 1953), p. 693.

Hungary, Kastner, accompanied by Standartenführer Becher, arrived in Switzerland. They too were negotiating with the wrong party. On the opposite side stood the president of the Jewish community in Switzerland, Saly Mayer. He disliked the negotiations and refused to promise the Germans anything.[34] If Saly Mayer reflected upon his negotiating tactics after the war, his only consolation must have been the circumstance that the SS and Police were determined to destroy the Slovak Jews in any case. The negotiators on the German side had not been the right party either.[35]

In Cairo Joel Brand remained in custody. His mission had failed, and his wife and children in Budapest had almost paid the penalty for the failure. He was constantly afraid that they might still have to pay, but the British would not let him go. He was now invited to clubs and hotels, more as an object of curiosity than a source of intelligence information. One day at the British-Egyptian Club Brand was engaged in conversation by a man who did not introduce himself but who, Brand believes, may have been Lord Moyne. The Englishman asked once more about the Eichmann offer and how many Jews were involved. Brand replied that the offer encompassed a million people. "But Mr. Brand," the British host exclaimed, "what shall I do with those million Jews? Where shall I put them?"[36] There were no longer a million; from the moment of Brand's departure from Budapest 500,000 Jews had been killed in the gas chambers of Auschwitz. The entire network of standby organizations had become a vast organization of bystanders.

By the beginning of 1945, five million Jews were dead. There were no more gassings. Auschwitz had been abandoned. But tens of thousands of Jews were still to die. During the shadow months of the Nazi regime Roswell McClelland of the War Refugee Board negotiated in Berne with Standartenführer Becher of the SS and Police for the amelioration of conditions in the camps. In the final weeks the International Red Cross also made itself felt; the Germans began to release thousands of Jews. The Allied armies found the remainder alive, dead, or dying in the camps.[37]

Up to May 8, 1945, the Jewish masses could not be rescued from catastrophe; now the survivors had to be saved from its consequences. On the conquered territory of the former German Reich, some tens of thousands of Jews clustered around the liberated concentration camps: Bergen-Belsen in the British zone, the Dachau complex in the American zone, Mauthausen in Austria.[38] Thousands of the worst cases among the camp survivors were taken to hospitals in Germany, Switzerland, and Sweden; other thousands began to trek back to Hungary and Poland in search of lost families. To the south and east the broken Jewish remnant communities formed a belt of restlessness, extending from the Balkans through Poland to the depths of Russia. The Hungarian-Roumanian area still contained a half-million Jews. Many

34. Dr. Rezsö Kasztner (Kastner), *Der Bericht des jüdischen Rettungskomitees aus Budapest*, pp. 91–99.

35. See pp. 472–73.

36. Weissberg, *Brand*, pp. 214–15. Lord Moyne was shortly thereafter assassinated by two *Irgunists*. Brand speculates that the conversation had been reported in Palestine and that the *Irgun* struck at Moyne in anguish. *Ibid.*, p. 216. Long afterwards, Eichmann said: "The plain fact was that there was no place on earth that would have been ready to accept the Jews, not even this one million." *Life*, December 5, 1960, p. 148.

37. See pp. 633–34. Kasztner, *Bericht*, pp. 112–13. War Refugee Board, *Final Report*, pp. 34, 43–45, 59.

38. Most of these camp inmates were Hungarian Jews. Other significant groups were deportees from Poland, Holland, Slovakia, and Lithuania.

were dispersed, most were destitute, and all were insecure.[39]

In Poland the scattered survivors found possessions and homes in other hands. Not a few of these Polish Jews, emerging from labor camps and out of hiding, were greeted with the query: "Still alive?"[40] These Jews, too, wanted to get out, but no door was opened to them. The United States still had its immigration quotas. (The total quotas allotted to *all* the people born in the eastern half of Europe could not exceed about 1500 a month.[41]) In Palestine the White Paper of 1939 had set a permissible immigration total of 75,000 Jews for a period of five years. When it was discovered in the autumn of 1943 that only 44,000 of these certificates had been used, the British government agreed to the utilization of the remaining 31,000 passes after 1944.[42] By the end of 1945 no certificates were left. From January 1, 1946, therefore, the British Labor government, under the severest pressure, allowed the Palestinian migration to continue at the rate of 1500 a month.[43] In short, the United States and Palestine together offered the Jews accommodation at the trickling rate of a few thousand month after month. For the hundreds of thousands of uprooted survivors the only prospect was a wait of years.

In Poland, Czechoslovakia, and Hungary many Jews chose not to wait; they decided to embark upon their journey, even if in the meantime they could not travel more than halfway. From Poland the exodus began through Czechoslovakia to the American zone in Germany.[44] From Hungary and even Roumania the Jews began to arrive in Austria.[45] By November, 1945, the flow was beginning to thicken, and thousands of refugees were spilling over into Italy.[46] These infiltrations were only an introduction. Under a Soviet-Polish agreement, all Jews and Poles in Soviet Russia who had been Polish citizens before September 19, 1939, were permitted to return to Poland;[47] over 150,000 Jews in Soviet Asia were affected by that agreement. From their Uzbek, Turkmen, Tadzhik, and Kazakh exiles the Jews now started to move westward to the new Polish frontier. Passing the gutted ghettos, they were sent on to the newly administered Polish territory to the west, where they could come into possession of abandoned German lands and homes. But the migrants from the Asian USSR did not stop in the Pomeranian-Silesian region; joining the survivors of Poland, they overflowed into the Western-occupied zones of Germany.[48]

The British authorities in Germany looked upon the influx of the Jews as a vast conspiracy to explode the immigration barriers to Palestine. Lieutenant General Sir Frederick Morgan, who served as chief of displaced persons operations in Germany for the United Nations Relief and Rehabilitation Administration (UNRRA), declared in an interview before newsmen that an unknown secret Jewish organization was behind the infiltration into Germany from the east, that these Jews were

39. See, particularly, Duschinsky, "Hungary," in Meyer *et al*, *The Jews in the Soviet Satellites,* pp. 373–489, and Nicolas Sylvain, "Rumania," *ibid.,* pp. 491–556.

40. Weinryb, "Poland," *ibid.,* p. 244.

41. See pp. 715–16.

42. *Report of Anglo-American Committee,* 1946, Cmd. 6808, pp. 65–66.

43. *Ibid.*

44. Weinryb, "Poland," in Meyer, *et al., The Jews in the Soviet Satellites,* pp. 254–57.

45. *Report of the Anglo-American Committee,* 1946, Cmd. 6808, pp. 48–49.

46. Transit to Italy was facilitated by the Jewish Brigade from Palestine, then stationed in the British zone of Austria, astride the route from Vienna to the Italian frontier. *Ibid.*

47. Weinryb, "Poland," in Meyer *et al., The Jews in the Soviet Satellites,* pp. 361–62.

48. *Ibid.,* pp. 362, 266–68.

"well dressed, well fed, rosy cheeked," and that they had "plenty of money." "They certainly do not look like persecuted people," he observed; and then, warning that the European Jews were "growing into a world force," he confided that they were all planning to leave Europe.[49]

The sentiments expressed by this general guided the British in their actions. The Jewish Brigade was withdrawn from Austria, and the frontier controls were tightened.[50] To the north, in Germany, the British denied admission to displaced persons camps in their zone to all persons who arrived there after June 30, 1946. The protests of Director General La Guardia of UNRRA to Prime Minister Attlee did not change the British decision in this matter.[51] Toward the end of 1946 the British government decided to adopt a compulsory labor law for residents of the displaced persons camps in the British zone of Germany. The UNRRA administration's protest that the law contained no safeguard for Jews and other ex-inmates of German concentration camps was entirely in vain.[52]

Blocked by the British, the Jews poured into the American zones. From January to April, 1946, the rate of entry was 3000 a month into the American zone of Germany and nearly 2000 into American-occupied Austria, including the Vienna area.[53] In April of that year the Jewish displaced persons population in Western-occupied Germany was 3000 in Berlin, 1600 in the French zone, 15,600 in the British zone, and 54,000 in the American zone; the comparable figures for Austria were 1000 in the British zone and 6500 in the American zone.[54] By the end of 1946 the number of displaced Jews in the Western zones of Germany and Austria had risen to about 204,000; the American area contained 183,600, or about 90 per cent of them.[55]

The concentration of so many displaced persons in the American zones prompted Senator Conolly to express the opinion that the United States was "the biggest sucker in the world" and that in Germany the Americans were "accepting people from all the other zones and feeding them."[56] Senator Conolly's remark indicated that, whereas the Palestine issue was dictating British actions, the cost of maintenance would become the chief prob-

49. "UNRRA Aide Scents Jews' Exodus Plot," *New York Times*, January 3, 1946, pp. 1, 3.

50. *Report of Anglo-American Committee*, 1946, Cmd., 6808, p. 48.

51. George Woodbridge (Chief Historian of UNRRA), *UNRRA – The History of the United Nations Relief and Rehabilitation Administration* (New York, 1950), II, 512.

52. *Ibid.*, p. 520.

53. German statistics from Jay B. Krane, chief, reports and analysis branch of UNRRA Central Headquarters for Germany, to Ira Hirschmann, special representative to the Director General of UNRRA, June 26, 1946, typewritten carbon copy of the original letter in UNRRA Central Headquarters for Germany, *Miscellaneous Documents*, 1945–47, Columbia Law Library. For monthly statistics of arrivals and departures of Jews in the American-held territory of Austria, from November, 1945, to August, 1949, see U.S. High Commissioner, *Civil Affairs Austria – Statistical Annex*, August, 1949, p. 11.

54. *Report of Anglo-American Committee*, 1946, Cmd., 6808, pp. 47–48. In Italy there were about 16,000. *Ibid.*, p. 58.

55. Testimony by Assistant Secretary of State John H. Hilldring, Hearings before Subcommittee on Immigration and Naturalization of the Committee on the Judiciary, House of Representatives, 80th Cong., 1st sess., June–July, 1947, pp. 124–25. The division between the two U.S. zones was: Germany 152,803; Austria 30,797. The Austrian figure is 6200 higher than the one in the statistical annex of the High Commissioner's report, August, 1949, p. 11. Hilldring's figure for the number of Jewish displaced persons in Italy on December 31, 1946, was 21,288.

56. Confidential report by George Meader, Chief Counsel, Special Senate Committee Investigating the National Defense Program, November 22, 1946, mimeographed, p. 8. The report was subsequently released.

lem in the American zones. Under Control Council Law No. 2, the care of displaced persons on German soil was a German responsibility. From 1946 on, however, the United States was guaranteeing to the Germans a minimum standard of living, and to make good that guarantee, the United States Army was spending in Germany over $500,000,000 a year under the budget heading "Government and Relief in Occupied Areas" (GARIOA). Insofar, therefore, as the German economy did not supply the needs of the displaced persons (and it supplied in the main only fringe services of an administrative character), the clothing and feeding of the DP's had to be financed from GARIOA. And while non-Jewish DP's were leaving the American zone to go back to their homes, more and more Jews arrived on the scene.[57]

Searching for a solution to this problem, War Department officials thought of ridding themselves of 70 per cent of their DP burden by closing the camps to all but persecutees. The plan failed when strong Catholic and Protestant groups protested to President Truman that the measure was an act of discrimination which would favor only the Jews.[58] The military authorities then considered the less novel solution of reducing the standards of upkeep, for both shelter and food.

The billeting problem was complicated by the arrivals of trainloads of German expellees from Czechoslovakia and Hungary. Although by an old military directive displaced persons were accorded priority over the German population in matters of housing,[59] the practice was often quite different. Thus a group of 300 Jews who were living in houses at the DP center in Fürth was ejected by military police in order to make room for a trainful of Germans who were waiting at a siding to move in.[60]

In June, 1946, the Third Army directed its three divisions that under no circumstances were substandard accommodations to be provided for persecutees.[61] Nevertheless, the great bulk of the Jews were forced to remain in the camps. Frequently, these camps were overcrowded. Some lacked basic facilities for heating, cooking, and washing. Family privacy could often be achieved only by partitioning the barracks with blankets swung across ropes.[62] In a somewhat similar vein, the clothing goal was met by a yearly issue of one complete set of clothes — sometimes a little "strange and worn."[63] The food allowance was fixed in calories, two-thirds of which came from bread and potatoes.[64] The UNRRA's

57. At the end of the war Jews constituted a negligible percentage among millions of DP's. By the end of 1946, 30 per cent of all DP's in camps of the American zone were Jews. The yearly budget for DP maintenance in that zone was calculated at $109,000,000. For each DP the cost was as follows: food $12 monthly ($13.20 for persecutees, including Jews); maintenance $5 monthly; initial outfit of clothing $49. Meader report, p. 47. The cost of maintaining the Jews was thus in the neighborhood of $33,000,000 per year.

Unlike Germany, Austria was a recipient of UNRRA aid, and from April 1, 1946, to December 1, 1946, UNRRA took responsibility for supplying the DP's. From January 1, 1947, to August 18, 1947, the American Army bore the cost. The army, however, spent only $10 per month. Headquarters, United States Forces in Austria, *A Review of Military Government,* September 1, 1947, p. 166. At that rate, the cost to the U.S. Army of supplying the Jewish DP's in Austria was approximately $2,500,000.

58. Krane to Hirschmann, June 26, 1946, UNRRA *Miscellaneous Documents.* Meader report, p. 43.

59. Louise W. Holborn, *The International Refugee Organization* (London, New York, and Toronto, 1956), p. 131, citing SHAEF memorandum of April 16, 1945.

60. Leo W. Schwarz, *The Redeemers* (New York, 1953), pp. 104–6.

61. Krane to Hirschmann, June 26, 1946, UNRRA *Miscellaneous Documents.*

62. Holborn, *The IRO,* pp. 218–19. Woodbridge, *UNRRA,* II, 500.

63. Woodbridge, *UNRRA,* II, 503.

historian Woodbridge states that "since the indigenous populations resented the giving of food to displaced persons," and "since the military authorities frequently sympathized with the indigenous populations . . . it required unremitting efforts by the UNRRA officials to keep their charges from starvation."[65]

Unlike the British, the Americans did not require the Jewish DP's to pay for their upkeep by donating their labor to the German economy.[66] "It is understandable," said Assistant Secretary of State Hilldring, that Jews "have no wish to work for or under the Germans."[67] Not all Americans, however, were so understanding. Chief Counsel of a special Senate committee investigating the defense program, George Meader, compared the Jews with the Balts. In contrast to the industrious Balts, he said, the Jews "do not desire to work, but expect to be cared for, and complain when things are not as well done as they think they should be. . . . It is very doubtful," he added, "that any country would desire these people as immigrants."[68]

By April, 1947, the War Department followed the British example by closing the gates to the camps. After April 21 no new arrival was allowed refuge in them.[69]

It should be pointed out that the military authorities in all zones of occupation undertook responsibility only for essential care and that on occasion there were lapses in the exercise even of this responsibility. To plug some of the gaps and to supply all the "supplementals," from additional food rations to schooling of children and training of adults, the resources of international organizations and private societies had to be brought into operation. Up to June 30, 1947, the international agency concerning itself with refugee matters was UNRRA. Since UNRRA had been created for the relief and rehabilitation of Allied nations only, a question arose immediately whether Jews who were stateless or who carried the nationality of an enemy or ex-enemy state should receive any aid at all.

The British government took the view that such Jews were not entitled to assistance. In a letter by Sir George Rendel to UNRRA's displaced persons division, the British delegate declared: "The fact that Jews can, as a race be identified by certain characteristics, and that political developments, and in particular the National Socialist racial doctrine, have given them peculiar problems of importance in international politics, are not sufficient reasons for treating 'Jews' as a separate national category."[70] The British objection was

64. *Ibid.*, pp. 503–4. From October, 1945, to August, 1946, the number of calories for Jewish DP's in Germany dropped from 2500 to 2200 in the U.S. zone and from 2170 to 1550 in the British zone. In the American zone of Austria, the drop was from 2400 (U.S. Army) to 1200 (UNRRA). *Ibid.*, p. 503. *Report of Anglo-American Committee*, 1946, Cmd. 6808, p. 49. The U.S. Army made additional allowance for persecuted persons (mostly Jews). In Germany that allowance was 200 calories (included in figures above). The British classified Jews by "nationality."

65. Woodbridge, *UNRRA*, II, 504.

66. Wages accruing from German employment could be paid only in reichsmark, which had no foreign exchange value and which could not even be used for purchasing in the rationed German market. The Americans could not benefit either. DP income was subject to German taxation, and savings were headed for devaluation.

67. Testimony by Maj. Gen. Hilldring in Hearings before Immigration Subcommittee, House Judiciary Committee, 80th Cong., 1st sess., June–July, 1947, pp. 126–27.

68. Meader report, pp. 45, 42.

69. Headquarters, United States Forces in Austria, *A Review of Military Government*, September 1, 1947, p. 165. Woodbridge, *UNRRA*, II, 512.

70. Text of British memorandum in UNRRA Standing Technical Sub-Committee on Displaced Persons for Europe, 9th meeting, August 11, 1944, TDP/E(44)38. Also,

overcome by an American-sponsored resolution which extended UNRRA's aid to all persons "who have been obliged to leave their country or place of origin or former residence or who have been deported therefrom, by action of the enemy, because of race, religion or activities in favor of the United Nations."[71]

When the International Refugee Organization assumed UNRRA's caretaking functions on July 1, 1947, it attempted to improve the accommodations, clothing, and food rations of the DP's.[73] Nevertheless, the combined rate of military and international spending was only enough to guarantee to the survivors continued life, and it fell to Jewish organizations to invest substantial sums for the innumerable needs of a completely rootless community.[74]

TABLE 95 / *UNRRA Aid to DP's*

		SUPERVISION OF CAMPS	SUPPLY OF ESSENTIAL FOOD, FUEL, AND CLOTHING
Germany:	American zone	All camps	$2,427,000 for food
	British zone	Most camps	
Austria		Less than half of camps	Complete for April–December, 1946
Italy		A few camps	Complete

The type of assistance rendered by UNRRA was in the main a rounding-out of essential care. Table 95 shows UNRRA's responsibility before its liquidation.[72]

Between 1945 and 1948 a quarter of a million Jews had become DP's. Ger-

British draft resolution on UNRRA operations in enemy or ex-enemy areas, September 12, 1944, UNRRA Council, 2d sess., Document 32.

71. Council Resolution No. 57, 2d sess., September, 1944, in Woodbridge, *UNRRA*, I, 135. The wording of the resolution was such that aid could not easily be given to post-hostility refugees. The UNRRA administration solved that problem by adopting the doctrine of "internal displacement"; that is, the "infiltrees" were covered because they were displaced from the moment they were forced to leave their homes by the Germans. Woodbridge, *UNRRA*, II, 509–10. The British restriction in respect of "nationality" would have deprived more than 20,000 Jews of UNRRA benefits. See chart of Jews receiving IRO assistance (by nationality), July 31, 1947, from Report of Special Subcommittee on Displaced Persons and the International Refugee Organization, House Foreign Affairs Committee, 80th Cong., 1st sess, 1947, p. 8, in Holborn, *The IRO*, p. 199. The IRO took over UNRRA's function in refugee matters on July 1, 1947.

72. Woodbridge, *UNRRA*, II, 491–92, 500 ff. Compilations of camps under UNRRA supervision in Holborn, *The IRO*, p. 236. On December 31, 1946, the division of the Jews in Austria was as follows:

UNRRA camps	9,833
Military camps	20,213

Testimony by Hilldring, Immigration Subcommittee, House Judiciary Committee, 80th Cong., 1st sess., June–July, p. 125. UNRRA had a $4-billion operation financed to the extent of 70 per cent by the United States. Expenditures for DP's were approximately $60,000,000. The Jewish share was about $15,000,000. See statistics in Woodbridge, *UNRRA*, III, 423, 428, 500, 506. Germany was not entitled to UNRRA aid. Austria and Italy received $135,513,200 and $418,222,100, respectively. *Ibid.*, p. 428.

73. Holborn, *The IRO*, pp. 218–38. Unlike UNRRA, the IRO was devoted entirely to refugees. Operating to the end of 1951, it spent $400,000,000. Expenditures, with overhead, for care of DP's was ca. $175,000,000. Care of Jewish DP's may have cost about $30,000,000. *Ibid.*, pp. 124, 199–200, 238.

74. The Jewish share of military-international spending probably exceeded $150,000,000. During the life of the IRO the principal Jewish relief organization (the Joint Distribution Committee) contributed

many had created these displaced Jews, but it took the whole world to prolong their displacement for years. The Jews were being dammed up: they were coming in a massive flow but could leave only in trickles. One of the small openings was an order by President Truman, dated December 22, 1945, that visas within the quota limits be distributed so far as possible to DP's of "all faiths, creeds and nationalities" in the American occupation zones.[75] Most other openings were smaller still. The war-torn countries of Europe were largely closed; the British Dominions were not anxious to receive masses of Jews, and the Jews themselves were more and more resolved to move to their national home. In 1946 the authorized migration to Palestine was beginning to be supplemented by small, crowded ships attempting to crash the British blockade. Several thousand Jews were landed. Sixteen thousand were intercepted and interned on the island of Cyprus. One ship, the "Exodus," was boarded, and its passengers were sent back to Germany. But in 1948 the British were ready to quit. When on May 15 of that year the Jewish state was established in Palestine, the log jam was finally broken.

One month after the mass movement of Jews to Israel got under way, the United States too opened its doors. Special legislation was required for the large-scale admission of the stranded DP's, and a skeptical Congress had debated such legislation for a year. The lawmakers' skepticism was reflected in the thinking of Texas Representative Gossett of the Immigration Subcommittee of the House. If the United States was going to follow humanitarian motives, he reasoned, why not admit Chinese, Indians, and all other suffering groups in unlimited numbers? Conversely, if economic considerations were going to be decisive, America could get better people than DP's. With regard to the Polish Jews, he was convinced of one thing: their rightful place was behind the Iron Curtain. "Somebody," he said, "has to fight communism in those countries, and are not some of these people equipped to do that?" Told about the pogroms, he asked Secretary of State Marshall, "But the thing that puzzles me is why there would be any persecution of Jews in Poland when half of the Polish Government are Jews?"[76]

The final outcome of the doubts and opposition was the passage of a compromise bill at the end of a long legislative day at two o'clock in the morning. The act excluded (with certain exceptions) all DP's who had arrived in Germany, Austria, or Italy after December 22, 1945. Of 202,000 DP's who were to be admitted between July 1, 1948, and June 30, 1950, 80,800 visas were to be set aside for Balts and 60,-600 for persons who were engaged in agricultural pursuits (Balts or others);

---

about $26,000,000 to the upkeep of Jewish DP's. Holborn, *The IRO*, pp. 148–49. The total Jewish contribution is considerably more.

75. Statement by Truman, December 22, 1945, and his letter of the same date to Secretaries of State and War, Attorney General, Surgeon General, and Director General of UNRRA, in *New York Times*, December 23, 1945, p. 10. With regard to the provision of the immigration law requiring immigrants to pay their own fare, the President authorized admission of DP's whose fare was advanced by private welfare organizations. *Ibid.*

British Labor Minister George Isaacs attempted to facilitate entry of DP's from the British zones to England. He was unsuccessful. The British government wanted only young unmarried people who could be put up in barracks and who would not complicate the housing situation. Testimony by Rabbi Philip S. Bernstein (adviser on Jewish DP's to General Clay), Immigration Subcommittee, House Judiciary Committee, 80th Cong., 1st sess., June–July, 1947, p. 241.

76. Remarks by Gossett in Hearings of Immigration Subcommittee, House Judiciary Committee, 80th Cong., 1st sess., June–July, 1947, pp. 237, 511.

on the other hand, the eligible DP's could be admitted without regard to quota limitation, in that 50 per cent of the quota of succeeding years could be mortgaged to reach the 202,000 total. Among the preferences prescribed for the selection of the 121,000 non-agricultural DP's, one category comprised clothing and garment workers.[77] Apart from that provision, the Jews had only one advantage: their organizations were well prepared. They could employ major resources to speed the processing of the DP's and to provide assurances of support for the period of their integration. That preparation paid off; during the two-year period about 40,000 Jewish DP's were admitted to United States shores.[78]

In the winter of 1949/50 hearings were resumed with a view to extending the Displaced Persons Act. The Jews were interested in three amendments: They wanted the removal of the cutoff date of December 22, 1945, in order that the later infiltrees could come into the United States; they asked that eligibility be granted to the Shanghai Jews; and they desired that clothing workers and agricultural workers be given equal chances in the preference scheme.

Let us point out that the Jews were not the only petitioners. Polish, Greek, and Italian interests were working too. Above all the German-American organizations were demanding major concessions. Though Senator Langer of North Dakota had secured one-half of the German-Austrian quotas from July, 1948, to June, 1950, for ethnic German refugees, the German-Americans were decidedly not satisfied. Testifying before a subcommittee of the Senate Judiciary Committee, Otto Hauser of American Relief for Germany, Inc., declared: "Thirty-three millions of German extraction demand the same rights under the immigration laws of the United States as are enjoyed by Americans of any other extraction."[79] Otto Durholz of the Committee for Christian Action in Central Europe argued that an exclusion of ethnic Germans would be "racist."[80] J. H. Meyer of the Steuben Society assured the Senators that the "co-racials" of the prospective immigrants in the United States were good hard-working farmers.[81]

Congressman Celler then came to testify before the Senate Committee. As chairman of the House Judiciary Committee, his influence was considerable. Now he found himself in a difficult position: he was a Jew. He had reason to suspect that ethnic Germans had participated out of proportion to their numbers in the destruction of the Jews; yet he did not wish to jeopardize the extension of the act. Resigning himself to a horse trading session, he said, "There are some good Volksdeutsche, there are some bad Volksdeutsche."[82] The Jews got their revisions; an additional 22,000 Jewish DP's were brought into the country. The German-American organizations secured authorization for the admission of an additional 54,744 ethnic German refugees.[83]

77. Displaced Persons Act, approved by the President on June 25, 1948, 62 Stat. 1009.

78. Statement by Lewis Neikrug, Director General of the Hebrew Immigrant Aid Society (HIAS), cited in report of special subcommittee of House Judiciary Committee on Displaced Persons in Europe and their Resettlement in the United States, 81st Cong., 2d sess., January 20, 1950, pp. 76, 80–81. Also, Senate Report No. 1237, January 25, 1950, United States Code Congressional Service, 81st Cong., 2d sess., No. 5, pp. 1337–43.

79. Testimony by Hauser, Hearings, Senate Judiciary Committee/Subcommittee on Amendments to the Displaced Persons Act, 81st Cong., 1st and 2nd sess., March 25, 1949–March 16, 1950, p. 187.

80. Testimony by Durholz, *ibid.*, p. 77.

81. Testimony by Meyer, *ibid.*, p. 161.

82. Testimony by Celler, *ibid.*, pp. 192–93.

83. The cutoff date was extended from December 22, 1945, to January 1, 1949, benefiting Jewish DP's and German expellees alike. A total of 4000 visas were authorized for DP's in China. Farm and clothing work-

In the final tally the quarter of a million Jewish DP's found their homes in the following places:[84]

Israel	142,000
United States	72,000
Canada	16,000
Belgium	8,000
France	2,000
Others	10,000
Total	250,000

It is noteworthy that before the war the United States received more than twice as many refugees as Palestine. After the war – in spite of the DP Act – that ratio was reversed.

Nor was this all. In the eastern countries the Jewish communities could no longer maintain themselves. The catastrophe had brought to Jewry rampant physical privation. In the immediate postwar years the principal American Jewish relief organization – the Joint Distribution Committee – gave aid to more than 300,000 Jews in Roumania and Hungary alone.[85] Tens of millions had to be spent to prevent disease, starvation, and death. The Roumanian-Hungarian area in particular was affected by another plague – deportations.

On September 1, 1949, a roundup struck the Transnistrian Jews. These people originally hailed from the Bukovinian-Bessarabian region; they had been deported east when Roumania expanded and transported west when the Roumanian line receded. Many reached old Roumania and began to settle there. But the Bukovinian-Bessarabian provinces had become Soviet territory, and the hounded remnants of Transnistria were claimed by the Soviet Union as its citizens. They disappeared by ship and rail behind the Soviet border.[86]

In February, 1952, Roumanian police launched a drive to relieve the "overpopulation of Bucharest" by deporting from the city a sizeable number of former shop owners and other "unproductive" people. The deportees, who included many Jews, were sent to the Danubian-Black Sea canal construction project and to further destinations within the USSR.[87] Shortly thereafter, Hungarian officials decided to solve their housing shortage in Budapest in an identical manner.[88] The Jews behind the Iron Curtain thus found themselves in an impossible position: the Communist Party looked upon them as exponents of capitalistic cosmopolitanism; within the population itself there was a

ers received preferences without specified numbers or percentages. The German-American organizations scored a number of successes: only the first 7000 ethnic German immigrants were chargeable to the German-Austrian quotas; the remainder was taken off the quotas of the respective countries of birth. Since IRO was paying for transportation of DP's only, the U.S. government transported the ethnic German refugees. See Displaced Persons Act Amendment, approved June 16, 1950, 64 Stat. 219. A total of about 64,000 Jews arrived in the United States under the DP Act and its amendments from July, 1948, to June, 1952. During the same period 53,448 ethnic Germans were admitted to the country. Final Report of Displaced Persons Commission, *The DP Story,* (Washington, D.C., 1952), pp. 248, 366.

84. For the period from July 1, 1947, to December 31, 1951, statistics of Jewish DP movements totaling 231,548 may be found in Holborn, *The IRO,* p. 440. Adjustments for the two years preceding IRO operations are approximations. IRO contributed, with overhead, more than $20,000,000 to the transportation of Jewish DP's. Jewish organizations covered the remaining costs.

85. Sylvain, "Rumania," in Meyer, *et al., The Jews in the Soviet Satellites,*" pp. 520–23, 543. Duschinsky, "Hungary," *ibid.,* pp. 407–8, 434, 464–66.

86. *American Jewish Year Book,* LII (1951), 351–52, from a report in the *Jewish Daily Forward* (New York), October 4, 1949.

87. Wolfgang Bretholz, "Tragödie in Bukarest," *Aufbau* (New York), April 18, 1952, pp. 1, 12. Sylvain, "Rumania," in Meyer *et al., The Jews in the Soviet Satellites,* p. 550.

88. Duschinsky, "Hungary," *ibid.,* pp. 471–82.

tendency to identify them with Communist rule. The eastern Jews therefore had only one escape: they had to move out.[89]

ter of a million Jews were hauled out of eastern Europe after the end of the DP migrations, between 1948 and 1957 (see Table 96).[93]

TABLE 96 / *Postwar Jewish Population Changes in Eastern Europe*

	SURVIVORS AND RETURNEES 1945–46	DP MIGRATION 1945–48	NEW MIGRATION 1948–57	DEPORTATIONS 1949–52	REMAINING 1957
Czechoslovakia	44,000	5,000	20,000	none	19,000
Poland	225,000	150,000	55,000	none	20,000
Roumania	430,000	40,000	95,000	50,000	245,000
Hungary	200,000	25,000	30,000	none	145,000
Bulgaria	47,000	none	40,000	none	7,000
Yugoslavia	12,000	none	5,000	none	7,000
Greece	12,000	none	5,000	none	7,000
Total	970,000	220,000	250,000	50,000	450,000

Mass emigration from eastern Europe was easiest in non-Communist Greece and in the neighboring states of Yugoslavia and Bulgaria. It was beset with obstacles, interruptions, and restrictions in the countries to the north, particularly in Roumania and Hungary. It could not even begin in Russia. In the overall view the obstructions were introduced because of economic considerations. The "necessary" Jews had to stay behind; the others had to leave at least some of their possessions. The emigrating Jews were subjected to heavy passport fees in Czechoslovakia.[90] Passage had to be booked for an exorbitant price on government ships in Roumania.[91] Dollar ransoms were paid to get 3000 Jews out of Hungary.[92] In spite of all these impediments, about a quar-

In the center of Europe the Jews of Germany and Austria in 1957 totaled 5 per cent of the number who had lived there in 1933. Germany still had 25,000, Austria about 10,000. These Jews no longer constituted a viable community; they were composed of survivors in mixed marriages, old people from Theresienstadt, DP's who had not moved on, and returnees from prewar emigration. In 1950, 13 per cent of the Jews in Germany were under eighteen.[94] The economy of the Jews in Germany was party marginal, party terminal. Roughly a third of them derived an income from business, professional fees, or employment. The business sector consisted of about 1800 shopkeepers and 100 owners of small manufactur-

89. A German who observed a number of Jews in the Soviet slave labor camp at Vorkuta remarked: "If the system lasts, they will stay in the camps for the rest of their lives; if it collapses they will go down with it." Joseph Scholmer, *Vorkuta* (New York, 1955), p. 116.

90. Meyer, "Czechoslovakia," in Meyer *et al., The Jews in the Soviet Satellites*, pp. 145–52. Also, A. Nissim, "Falls Dr. Fischl auftauchen sollte," *Aufbau* (New York), May 11, 1951, p. 7.

91. Sylvain, "Rumania," in Meyer *et al., The Jews in the Soviet Satellites*, pp. 548–50.

92. "Last Jews To Quit Red Hungary Sail," *New York Times*, November 18, 1953, p. 5. The price was $3,000,000.

93. Statistics of migrations from Meyer, Weinryb, Duschinsky, and Sylvain, *The Jews in the Soviet Satellites*, and subsequent reports. The costs of transportation were borne by the emigrants and the Jewish organizations. About 95 per cent of the new migration was directed to Israel. A number of the 17,000 Hungarian Jews who fled in 1956/57 were admitted under the parole provisions of the immigration law to the United States.

94. *American Jewish Year Book*, LII (1951), 316.

ing plants; most of these businessmen were DP's. The self-employed professionals also numbered about 100; most of them were lawyers. There were in the neighborhood of 3000 employees, including wage earners in Jewish establishments and the personnel of the Jewish community machinery. The remaining Jews were dependent upon pensions and indemnification payments, rent from restituted property, Jewish assistance, and government relief.[95]

More so than anywhere else, the Jews of western Europe have re-established their normal mode of existence, but one problem is peculiar to that region. Thousands of children who had been sheltered in convents and homes had become Jewish orphans in Christian custody, and the return of these children to the Jewish community was a slow and drawn-out process. Some were not returned at all. "It would thus seem," remarked a Jewish writer, "as if the Jewish people, after having lost 6 million souls through the savagery and sadism of Nazi paganism, will have to resign itself to the loss of another few thousand to the mercy of Christendom."[96]

3 / Salvage

If we were to survey the hurt inflicted by the Germans upon the Jews, we would have to consider the suffering and dying of the victims; we would have to measure the impact of these deaths upon those who were closest to the victims; we would have to think about the long-range effects of the entire destruction process upon Jewry as a whole. All this adds up to a vast, almost nonassessable loss. What, then, is to happen after such damage has been done? When ordinary justice prevails, there is an expectation of compensation for every wrong, and the bigger the injury, the greater will be the claim for payment. However, the postwar situation confronting the Jews was far from ordinary. They were in the midst of a cold war, and neither side was dependent on their support. Much that the Jews wanted had to be gotten in Germany, and Germany was the battleground itself.

In 1945 the demarcation line running through Germany split Europe in two. East and West carried out their separate policies in their respective areas. The Soviet policy was directed toward a maximum exploitation of the newly conquered zone, and during that exploitation stage the Jews were not recognized as a special group with special problems of their own. When East Germany was graduated to junior satellite status, the Jews, with Moscow's blessing, continued to be ignored. Now that the Soviets had had their meal, the Germans had to eat. For Jewry nothing was left except the principles of socialist equality.

The Western aim in Germany was wholly different from that of the Soviets. Though initially concerned with depriving Germany of its war industries and external assets, the Western coalition soon began to look upon the West German industrial complex as a potential bulwark against the Soviet Union. That consideration dictated the preservation and ultimately even the expansion of Germany's productive capacity. During the en-

95. Kurt R. Grossman, "Die Wirtschaftslage der Juden in Deutschland," *Aufbau* (New York), August 31, 1956, pp. 25, 37. For an earlier study, see Jack Hain, *Status of Jewish Workers and Employers in Post-War Germany,* Office of U.S. Military Government/ Manpower Division, Visiting Expert Series No. 10, August, 1949.

96. Israel Cohen, *Contemporary Jewry* (London, 1950), pp. 263–64. Also, Hildegard Level, "Return to Holland," *Congress Weekly,* January 2, 1950, pp. 9–11. Three cases of conversion and kidnapping aroused publicity in western Europe and America. The cases involve the Finaly brothers in France, Rebecca Melhado and Anneke H. Beekman in Holland. Anneke has disappeared. See *New York Times Index* and other papers, 1953–54.

suing buildup the United States and England rendered great assistance to the Germans. At the same time, nothing was to be shipped out of Germany that was needed for German recovery, and insofar as there were any significant exports of the least essential items, the accruing foreign credits were to be used only for the most essential imports. The claimants outside Germany's borders could thus be paid neither in goods nor in money. However, the Allied controls in their very nature were designed to guarantee an eventual German ability to make some payments abroad; consequently, the Allied authorities did not summarily dismiss the question of admitting claims advanced by the Jews.

From the very start the Jews asked only for three things: They insisted upon the restitution of all Aryanized and confiscated Jewish property; they wanted indemnification for survivors who had suffered damage and injury; and they claimed reparations for the rehabilitation of the displaced.[1] In all these demands the Jews were confining themselves to the needs of the victims who were still alive. For all those who had gone down with everything they had there was no further claim. Though European Jewry had for centuries been the fountainhead of all that mattered in Jewish life, the Jews of the world did not step forward now as its heirs in law. One might say that the Jewish organizations were reversing the inherent proportionality between infliction and adjustment: their claim was like a salvage operation in which recovery is inversely proportional to the depth of the loss. In a sense, the perpetrators were asked to pay for the incompleteness of their job. Yet even this bill was not paid in full.[2]

The Jews could expect their earliest success in the battle for restitution. However, this contest became at the very outset a struggle for two objectives: the return of property values to individual survivors and the recovery of assets which had no heirs. The first objective was much easier to achieve than the second. At that, the difficulties within the realm of individual restitution were already quite formidable. Some of these obstacles were the product of intrinsic factors; the others were the outcome of extraneous causes.

The inherent limitations in the individual procedure were threefold. In the first place, the restoration of a property right was feasible only to the extent that the object was identifiable; that is, it had to be something which could be spotted in the hands of a wrongful possessor. Little could be done, for example, to effect the return of movables which had long been articles in non-Jewish homes. Secondly, the restitution laws did not lend themselves to the re-creation of an asset which had disappeared, such as a liquidated business or a job which was no longer in existence. A third limitation was generally the repossession of something that had only been rented,

1. Dr. Chaim Weizmann (Jewish Agency for Palestine) to governments of United Kingdom, United States, USSR, and France, September 20, 1945, in Government of Israel/Ministry for Foreign Affairs, *Documents Relating to the Agreement between the Government of Israel and the Government of the Federal Republic of Germany* (Jerusalem, 1953), pp. 9–12. Statement of the American Jewish Conference on the German Peace Treaty, together with proposals for inclusion in the treaty, approved by the interim committee of the conference on January 22, 1947, and signed by Henry Monsky, chairman of the interim committee, and Louis Lipsky, chairman of the executive committee, in American Jewish Conference, *Nazi Germany's War against the Jews* (New York, 1947), pp. iii–xv. The conference proposals differed from those of the agency principally in their emphasis upon restitution and indemnification. While Weizmann demanded German contributions for resettlement in Palestine, the conference spoke only of "token" reparations.

2. In Jewish terminology the demands were "material claims." The Germans called their payments "amends" (*Wiedergutmachung*).

such as an apartment. Clearly, these were natural limits; the very idea of a restitution process did not encompass the solution of such problems. However, the Jews were also confronted with complications which did not have their root in the administrative characteristics of the operation, but which were the result of outside forces. These factors, which effectively blocked or impeded the return of tangible property, could be found primarily in eastern Europe and in occupied Germany.

Because of the communization of the East, the Jews could no longer count on the permanent recovery of agricultural land or industrial enterprises. In the former Axis states (Bulgaria, Roumania, and Hungary) Jewish property that had been acquired by the Germans was treated by the Soviets as a German asset; that is, it was now subject to Soviet acquisition as part of German reparations.[3] The Czechoslovak government looked upon all Jews who had held German or Hungarian nationality in 1930 as enemy aliens who were not entitled to the receipt of their former belongings.[4] On the whole, not much was returned to the Jews in the East. The meagerness of the results forced more and more Jews to the edge of departure, and the ensuing emigration nullified, in turn, much of what had already been granted.

In Germany the principal problem arose from the fact that most of the claimants were already outside the country. These prewar refugees did not merely want their property returned to them; they wanted to sell it and enjoy the proceeds. The goal was not to be attained without an uphill fight.

The anchor of Jewish hopes lay in an ancient Western commitment: a Western system of law could not ipso facto recognize changes brought about by contracts which had not been freely negotiated. The United States in particular took that position from the beginning. In the earliest directive from the Joint Chiefs of Staff, the U.S. zone commander was instructed to "impound and block" all "property which has been the subject of transfer under duress. . . ."[5] A long time elapsed, however, between the initial blocking of the "duress properties" and their ultimate restitution.

The drafting of a restitution law was tackled toward the end of 1946, and the law was proclaimed on November 10, 1947.[6] Its basic provisions, which in

3. Sylvain, "Rumania," in Meyer *et al.*, *The Jews in the Soviet Satellites*, p. 515. In Paris during the peace conference of June, 1946, the Jewish organizations had succeeded in inserting into the treaties with Roumania and Hungary provisions for the restoration of property rights. The Bulgarian Jewish community did not desire the insertion of such a clause in the peace treaty with Bulgaria. Israel Cohen, "Jewish Interests in the Peace Treaties," *Jewish Social Studies*, 1949, pp. 111–12. The USSR was undeterred by these treaty provisions, although it was a party to the treaties. The Soviet stand with regard to Aryanized property in German hands was duplicated in Austria. See report of an incident in Soviet Vienna by the U.S. High Commissioner, *Civil Affairs Austria*, August, 1949, pp. 54–55.

4. Meyer, "Czechoslovakia," in Meyer *et al.*, *The Jews in the Soviet Satellites*, pp. 78–84.

5. Par. 48*e* of Joint Chiefs of Staff Directive 1067/6, April 26, 1946, in Special Report of Military Governor, *Property Control in the U.S.-Occupied Area of Germany, 1945–1949*, July, 1949, pp. 46–47. Also, American Military Government Law No. 52 (revised text, July, 1945), *ibid.*, p. 39. Further, Par. 42*b* of Control Council Proclamation No. 2 on "Certain Additional Requirements Imposed on Germany," September 20, 1945, *ibid.*, p. 38.

6. American Military Government Law No. 59 on Restitution of Identifiable Property, November 10, 1947, together with implementary regulations, in Special Report of Military Governor, *Property Control 1945–1949*, pp. 72–83. During the drafting period the United States attempted two alternate approaches: (1) to bring about four-power agreement upon a restitution law for the whole of occupied Germany, and (2) to persuade the

substance were duplicated in British and French legislation as well as by a joint enactment for the three Western sectors of Berlin, dealt with "identifiable property," – i.e., in the main, business firms and real estate.[7] The holder of such property had to report it to the occupation authorities, and the original owner had to file claim with them. Recovery could be effected by agreement between claimant and possessor or by an order from a German restitution agency from which appeal could be taken, via German courts, to an American board of review.

Insofar as any asset was subject to restitution, the original transfer was deemed to be incomplete, and the claimant was given the option of finalizing the transaction or voiding it. In the first case the seller could treat the acquirer as a debtor, and demand the difference between the original purchase price and fair market value, with interest; in the second case the entitled owner could view the holder as a trustee, and recover the lost property together with accumulated profits by refunding the original purchase price, plus costs of reasonable maintenance.[8]

Since most of the claimants were no longer living in Germany, one might expect that a great many of them would rather have chosen ready money than the cumbersome route which – through refunding, repossession, and eventual sale – could theoretically lead to the same result. However, assuming even that the restitutor's money was ready, an added factor had been introduced into the picture: the currency reform of 1948. Under that law, old reichsmark were converted into new deutschmark at rates as drastic as ten to one. Insofar as any judgment allowed the holder to discharge his obligation at that rate (and such was a decision of the American board of review),[9] the simple path to restitution was virtually extinguished.

Fortunately for the claimant, the 10:1 conversion was applied to refunds too.[10] Yet this was no decisive change,

---

newly constituted German provincial governments to enact an acceptable measure in the U.S. zone. Both attempts failed. *Ibid.*, pp. 40–41, 44.

The following laws were enacted in the other zones: French Decree No. 120, November 10, 1947, *Amtsblatt des französischen Oberkommandos in Deutschland,* 1947, p. 1219. British Law No. 59, May 12, 1949, *Amtsblatt der Militärregierung Deutschland – Britisches Kontrollgebiet,* 1949, p. 1196. West Berlin Ordinance BK/0(49)180 (by the three Western powers jointly), July 26, 1949, *Verordnungsblatt für Gross-Berlin,* I, 221. In the Soviet zone the enactment of restitution laws was entrusted to German provincial authorities which, except in the case of Thuringia, did not even admit claims from absentee owners. In 1953, East Berlin declared all unclaimed Jewish property in control of the state to be "people's property." "Ost-Berlin macht jüdisches Eigentum zu Volkseigentum," *Aufbau* (New York), January 16, 1953, p. 1.

7. Generally speaking, three types of property were not recoverable under the provisions of the law: (1) All tangible personal property the value of which did not exceed RM 1000 at time of loss, (2) stock certificates, unless they represented ownership in a Jewish enterprise, and (3) discriminatory taxes, including "fines," emigration taxes, and the *Sozialausgleichsabgabe.* (In the case of real estate encumbered by such taxation, the encumbrance devolved upon the persecutee.)

8. Management costs generally could not exceed 50 per cent of net profits, and the restitutor was liable for profits that should have been made but for his wilful failure or neglect. Depreciation was subtracted from the refund; the costs of improvements were added to it.

9. Decision No. 147 by the U.S. Court of Restitution Appeals, reported by the American Federation of Jews from Central Europe, "Umstellung des Anspruches auf Nachzahlung," *Aufbau* (New York), February 22, 1952, p. 8.

10. Decision No. 15 by U.S. Court of Restitution Appeals, April 26, 1950, reported by Herman Muller of Federation of Central European Jews, "Wichtige Entscheidung des amerikanischen Rückerstattungsberufungsgerichts," *Aufbau* (New York), April 18, 1950, p. 22. Decision by Restitution Chamber of West Berlin Chancery Court (3 W. 1376/

for in that case the recoverable profits were decreased to 10 per cent as well. If the profits had been great, so was their reduction; if they had been few, so were the chances for a future sale. In this intricate mechanism the opportunities to achieve a fast recovery in full were few.[11]

When a claimant finally had his cash, he was confronted with still another difficulty: he had to exchange the money for the currency of the country in which he lived. At first this was impossible, but after a while the Allied authorities permitted the sale of the blocked accounts to non-German investors.[12] Such disposals involved losses of about 40 per cent.[13] With the improvement of the German trade position, the permissible uses of the funds were increased and the value of the sperrmark rapidly began to approximate that of the deutschmark itself. By the end of 1954 there was no longer a transfer problem.[14] In the interval, those who could least afford to wait had been forced to take the greatest loss.

Much Jewish property had remained on European soil, for which there were no living owners and no surviving heirs. Ordinarly, heirless property falls to the state, and, indeed, few of these assets were made available to the Jewish communities. In the East their restitution was almost negligible. Hungary turned over a few movables and several hundred buildings; Roumania supplied the Federation of Jewish Communities with old furs and old valuables; Czechoslovakia handed over to the Jewish community of Bohemia-Moravia the leftovers of Theresienstadt, amounting to about 60,000,000 crowns or $1,200,000.[15] Outside of the Communist sphere heirless-property laws were enacted during the first postwar years in Greece, Italy, and the Western zone of Trieste. In Western Germany the Allies found two kinds of assets: remnants of valuables which the Germans had hauled in from the Polish killing centers, and capital investments which had once belonged to Jews de-

---

50), reported by Lyonel J. Meyer, "Eine Entscheidung des Kammergerichts," and decision by British Board of Review (51/66) of May 30, 1951, reported by Federation of Central European Jews, "Rückgewähr des des Kaufpreises," *ibid.*, August 3, 1951, p. 6.

11. German industrial interests in the meantime fought for changes of the following order: (*a*) no restitution of property acquired before November 9, 1938; (*b*) admissibility of the plea of "good faith"; (*c*) conversion ratios favorable to the restitutor; (*d*) no interest payments on differentials; (*e*) no restitution of profits; (*f*) no liability for value diminution except in cases of gross neglect; (*g*) exclusive jurisdiction of German courts. The industrialists were basing their hopes on supposed wearying of the British and French, and a decline of the "influence of Jewish circles in America." Summary of meeting in the legal committee of the Industrial Associations/Commission for Restitution Questions, held on March 2, 1950, in Bonn, reprinted under the title "Neues Attentat auf die Wiedergutmachung," in *Aufbau* (New York), April 21, 1950, pp. 1–2. The German attempt did not succeed.

Jewish property "returned or compensated for" in the U.S. zone was estimated at DM 906,000,000 for the period to May, 1954. The program was three-fourths completed by that time. See Margaret Rupli Woodward, "Germany Makes Amends," *Department of State Bulletin*, XXXI (July 26, 1954), 128–29.

12. Initially, four types of investments were recognized: (*a*) the purchase of securities, (*b*) the acquisition of real estate, (*c*) construction and reconstruction, (*d*) credits and business participation. Advertisement for sperrmark by Hamburg-Bremen Steamship Agency, *Aufbau* (New York), May 18, 1951, p. 5. *Aufbau* carried dozens of ads for German sperrmark and Austrian sperrschillinge.

13. From mid-1951 to mid-1953, sperrmark rose from a low of 10c to roughly 14c. The deutschmark on the free market rose from about 19c to 23c.

14. When sperrmark were abolished in September of that year, the deutschmark was traded for 23.5 cents. "Keine Sperrmark mehr," *Aufbau* (New York), September 17, 1954, p. 1.

15. Cohen, *Contemporary Jewry*, pp. 259–60.

ported from the Reich. So far as the valuables were concerned, the Allies promptly decided to sell this haul for non-German currency and to turn over 90 per cent of the receipts to Jewish relief organizations for rehabilitation.[16] The sales were accomplished with due dispatch, but it was a small operation which netted only petty cash.[17]

The disposal of the immovable property which the dead Jews of Germany had owned promised somewhat greater results — but they were not to be achieved so easily. The Allies did recognize that the Jewish community in Germany was no longer large enough to make use of that property. Under the restitution laws, title to the assets was therefore granted to Jewish successor organizations for the benefit of surviving victims everywhere.[18] However, there was no time for the prolonged process of effecting recovery ten-thousand-fold. Pressed by survivors' needs, the organizations sold their claims to German provincial authorities for whatever the traffic could bear.[19] Since the proceeds had to be used all over the world, the successor organizations were then faced by the transfer problem; and once that obstacle had been overcome, a bitter struggle broke out over the right of refugee Jews from Germany to receive a special allocation.[20]

16. Paris Reparations Agreement, Part I, Art. 8-B (so-called non-monetary gold clause), January 14, 1946, *U.S. Treaties and Other International Acts Series*, No. 1655. Implementation agreement between the United States, Great Britain, France, Czechoslovakia, and Yugoslavia, June 14, 1946, *ibid.*, No. 1657. Report by H. W. Emerson, director, Intergovernmental Committee on Refugees, to Preparatory Commission of the International Refugee Organization, PREP/6, Geneva, February 13, 1947. Most of the gold was converted into bullion for sale to governments. Artistic items, including porcelain, rugs, etc., were sold at auction in New York. IRO/Public Information Office/Monthly Digest No. 3, November, 1947, pp. 7–8, 26–27.

17. Early in 1949 the proceeds amounted to $2,171,874, and the final figure was expected to total ca. $3,500,000. IRO/General Council, 2d sess., report by the Director General on the activities of the organization from July 1, 1948, GC/60, March 22, 1949, pp. 79–87.

18. The Jewish Restitution Successor Organization in the American zone, the Jewish Trust Corporation in the British and French zones, and both organizations in West Berlin.

19. Claims amounting to about 150,000,000 deutschmark in the American zone were thus reduced to less than half. Jack Raymond, "Jews' Claims Cut To Aid Restitution," *New York Times*, February 13, 1951, p. 11. Raymond, "Restitution Pact Made in Bavaria," *ibid.*, March 16, 1952, p. 12. "Erbloses jüdisches Eigentum in Berlin," *Aufbau* (New York), January 6, 1956, p. 9.

20. Rabbi Dr. Leo Baeck (president of the Council for the Protection of the Rights and Interests of Jews from Germany) to Monroe Goldwater (president, Jewish Restitution Successor Organization), March 24, 1954, *Aufbau* (New York), April 2, 1954, p. 2. Goldwater to Baeck, *ibid.*, April 23, 1954, p. 7. The successor organizations were also engaged in two other operations: the recovery of community property, and the collection of individual items in behalf of owners who had missed the deadline for filing their claims.

The Austrian restitution laws did not deal with heirless property. The four occupying powers consequently inserted a provision into Article 26 of the Austrian State Treaty, under which such assets were to be made available for the relief and rehabilitation of persecutees, with the qualification that Austria was not required to "make payments in foreign exchange or other transfers to foreign countries." State Treaty for the Re-Establishment of an Independent and Democratic Austria, signed on May 15, 1955, and entered into force on July 27, 1955, *U.S. Treaties and Other International Acts Series*, No. 3298. After signing the treaty, the Austrian government agreed to relinquish its hold over the assets for the benefit of surviving victims *resident* in Austria. "Entschädigung in Österreich geregelt," *Aufbau* (New York), July 15, 1955, p. 1.

Under the Paris reparations agreement, each signatory power was given title to German assets within its frontiers. The United States subsequently released that portion of its share which had belonged to Jews who had left no heirs. The portion, which was worth $3,000,000, was to be used for rehabilitation work within the United States. Amendment to the Trading with the Enemy

The restitution laws had been designed for the upper middle class; they covered the kind of property which was substantial enough to be preserved in identifiable form. For those who had never possessed such assets, there was as yet no remedy. The masses of the poorer Jews who had lost their relatives, their health, their liberty, and their economic prospects could not make use of restitution laws. These Jews could be served only by a money grant, and such payment had to be obtained out of the public funds of the country which was responsible for their misery: Germany. This was a much tougher proposition.

The occupying power which promised to take the initiative in the matter was once more the United States. When the restitution law was drafted in the American zone, the U.S. military government adopted the view "that persons who [had] suffered personal damage or injury through National Socialist persecution should receive indemnification in German currency."[21] In the course of the following two years, the lengthy process of pressure and drafting got under way. The pressure came from Jewish organizations; the drafting was done by the German *Länder* governments in the American-occupied territory. Towards the end of this development the military grew weary, the State Department seemed dubious, and the British Foreign Office expressed its opposition. At the last moment the High Commissioner designate, John J. McCloy, cast his lot for the Jews. As a result, a general claims law went into effect for the United States zone.[22]

The design of the law was to allow every persecutee to file a claim if he resided in the U.S. zone on January 1, 1947, or if he had emigrated from there before that time. The eligible claimants thus comprised postwar displaced persons as well as prewar refugees. The losses for which a claimant was covered included the killing of relatives who had given support to the victim, damage to health, deprivation of freedom, confiscation or destruction of property and capital, discriminatory exaction of taxes, the impairment of professional or economic advancement, and the curtailment of insurance payments and pensions. Except for the property losses, the law recognized injuries and damage without regard to the place where they had been inflicted, so long as they were the product of discriminatory action by the German state.[23]

The American - sponsored general claims law served as a model for similar legislation in the French zone and in

Act, August 23, 1954, 68 Stat. 767. The recipient of the funds was the Jewish Restitution Successor Organization. "JRSO empfängt jüdisches erbloses Eigentum in U.S.A.," *Aufbau* (New York), January 21, 1955, p. 9.

The Paris reparations agreement also provided that heirless assets in neutral countries be made available to persecutees. However, in the implementation agreement between the United States, Great Britain, France, Czechoslovakia, and Yugoslavia, the two Eastern signatories declared that they had not given up their claim to the forthcoming inheritances, "which, according to the provisions of international law, belong to their respective states." See Eli Ginzberg, "Reparation for Non-Repatriables," *Department of State Bulletin,* XV (July 14, 1946), 56, 76. Switzerland subsequently transferred to Poland all heirless property of Polish Jews. "Herrenloses Vermögen in der Schweiz," *Aufbau* (New York), March 3, 1950, p. 10. The provision for heirless assets in the neutral states appears to have remained a dead letter.

21. Military Government Regulation 23 2050/Directive on U.S. Objectives and Basic Policy in Germany, July 15, 1947, in Office of Military Government, *Property Control,* November, 1948, p. 21.

22. Jack Raymond, "McCloy, Reversing U.S. Position, Orders Payment to Nazis' Victims," *New York Times,* August 10, 1949, pp. 1, 14.

23. For a summary analysis, see Herman Muller, "Das Entschädigungsgesetz in der amerikanischen Zone," *Aufbau* (New York), August 19, 1949, pp. 5–6; August 26, 1949, p. 11; September 2, 1949, p. 16.

West Berlin.[24] The British, however, deserted from the American principle. In their zone a victim was barred from filing a claim if he was no longer a resident at the time of the enactment of the legislation. In short, compensation was granted, with few exceptions, only to German persecutees.[25]

After a while difficulties developed in the American zone with respect to the administration of the law. The administrators were German provincial authorities, and in Bavaria that authority was used in attempts to subvert and disrupt the indemnification process. The first attempt was a Bavarian implementation decree which simply eliminated the refugees.[26] With regard to the displaced persons, the Bavarians appeared to have another scheme: in the case of awards above $600, the law directed that one-half of the amount be paid in cash and that the rest fall due in 1954. The displaced persons who were in great need frequently sold the unpaid half of the claim for about 45 per cent of nominal value. The promissary notes were collected by banks such as the Bayrische Staatsbank, the Hypotheken- und Wechselbank, the Gemeindebank, the Vereinsbank, and Seiler and Company. Reportedly, these Bavarian banks had made an agreement with the Bavarian *Staatssekretär* for Finance, Dr. Richard Ringelmann, to resell the notes to the government for 62–65 per cent of value – in 1952.[27]

On March 9, 1951, the Bavarian administration pulled a minor coup. The Jewish president of the Indemnification Office, Philip Auerbach (an Auschwitz survivor), was dismissed from his office and placed under arrest to face a variety of charges, including the fraudulent use of the title "Doctor," the granting of credits without adequate guarantees, the deposit of private money as organization income in order to obtain a more favorable currency conversion rate, the receipt of kickbacks from a contractor charged with the renovation of a Jewish cemetery, and the processing of 111 claims of allegedly nonexistent persons. For weeks the Indemnification Office was closed while Munich police were looking for evidence.

At the trial Auerbach admitted his use of the title "Doctor" (he had been called by that title for so long that he finally adopted it). The court itself freed him from the principal charge of making payments to "dead souls." His conviction upon the remaining charges led to a sentence of two and one-half years in prison and $643 in fines. Stunned, Auerbach on a sickbed protested his innocence. Then he took his life.[28]

24. In the French zone each province enacted its own law: Baden on January 10, 1950, Württemberg-Hohenzollern on February 14, 1950, and Rheinland-Pfalz on May 22, 1950. For an analysis of the laws, which were substantially alike, see American Federation of Jews from Central Europe/United Restitution Office/Indemnification Section, "Entschädigungsgesetz in der französischen Zone," *Aufbau* (New York), June 23, 1950, p. 5. A West Berlin city ordinance was adopted on October 26, 1950. Walter Braun, "Berlins Entschädigungsgesetz für Naziopfer," *ibid.*, November 24, 1950, p. 9; December 1, 1950, p. 8.

25. "Protest gegen ein böswilliges Gesetz," *Aufbau* (New York), August 24, 1951, p. 15. The law under criticism was the newly passed measure in Nordrheinland-Westfalen.

26. For correspondence between the editor of *Aufbau* (Manfred George), Bavarian Indemnification Commissioner Philip Auerbach (Jewish survivor), and the office of the High Commissioner, see *Aufbau* (New York), December 30, 1949, pp. 2, 26; February 10, 1950, pp. 1–2. The decree, dated November 26, 1949, removed the eligibility of victims who had left Bavaria before January 1, 1947.

27. "Rings um den Fall Auerbach," *Aufbau* (New York), April 6, 1951, pp. 1–2.

28. "SPD drängt auf Klärung der Massnahmen gegen das Entschädigungsamt," *Süddeutsche Zeitung* (Munich), February 3/4, 1951, p. 2. "Bis jetzt 200 Fälschungen aufgedeckt," *ibid.*, February 5, 1951, p. 2. "Jewish Aides Guilty in Nazi Victim Fraud,"

The Jewish organizations were now prompted by a dual necessity to press for a West German indemnification law. They had to resolve the problem of inequality between the zones, and they had to have insurance against the Allied abdication of power. Only one measure could give the Jews both uniformity and continuation: an indemnification law enacted at the behest of the Allies by the new West German Parliament.

The organizational spokesmen made their views known to the State Department on September 27, 1951.[29] During the following months the Western Allies conducted negotiations with the West German government for the replacement of the occupation regime with a contractual relationship. The Jewish request was inserted as one of the chapters in the proposed settlement. The Germans accepted the provision. They did not have their freedom yet, they needed good will, and they could not very well proceed with the indemnification of German persecutees, let alone with the pensioning of Nazi perpetrators, without also recognizing the Jewish claim.[30]

The Federal Indemnification Law was enacted on September 19, 1953. Its basic framework was taken from the claims law in the American Zone. It superseded all the *Länder* laws; however, no victim could receive payment for the same thing twice, and the 730,000,000 deutschmark which had already been paid out were no longer a charge against West Germany.[31] While money was going to be appropriated by the federal government, the law required the aggregate of the *Länder* to match these appropriations, each *Land* making its contribution in proportion to its population.[32] That division of the burden was to make any revision in favor of the victims a difficult proposition politically, and it took nearly three years before some of the inadequacies of the law could be removed.[33] The following outline is designed to show how the law in its amended form categorized the eligible

New York Times, August 15, 1952, pp. 1, 3. Manfred George, "Exit Auerbach," *Aufbau* (New York), August 22, 1952, pp. 1-2. "Das grosse Echo auf Auerbachs Selbstmord," *ibid.*, August 29, 1952, pp. 7–8. See also running accounts in these papers, 1951–52.

29. The conference was attended by the following officials:

- Department of State: Henry A. Byrode, Geoffrey Lewis, George Baker
- Congress (representing a refugee district): Jacob K. Javits
- American Federation of Jews from Central Europe: Rudolf Callman, Herman Muller, Alfred Prager
- Axis Victims League: Bruno Weil, Fremont A. Higgins
- American Association of Former European Jurists: Julius B. Weigert

"Mindestforderungen für die Durchführung der Wiedergutmachung – Eine Konferenz im Department of State," *Aufbau* (New York), October 5, 1951, p. 28.

30. See chapter 4 of the Convention on the Settlement of Matters Arising out of the War and the Occupation, signed by the United States, Great Britain, France, and Germany on May 26, 1952, *U.S. Treaties and Other International Agreements* VI, Part 4, 4474–76. The detailed outline of the proposed federal law was agreed upon in Protocol No. 1, signed by Chancellor Adenauer for Germany and Dr. Nahum Goldman for the Conference on Jewish Material Claims against Germany, September 10, 1952, in Government of Israel/Ministry for Foreign Affairs, *Documents Relating to the Agreement between the Government of Israel and the Federal Republic of Germany* (Jerusalem, 1953), pp. 152–57.

31. The figure of 730,000,000 deutschmark is taken from "Wiedergutmachungs-Statistik 1957," *Aufbau* (New York), April 18, 1958, p. 17.

32. In the case of West Berlin the cost was to be borne by the federal government (60 per cent), the nine *Länder* (25 per cent), and the city itself (15 per cent).

33. See an analysis of counter-agitation from the Rheinland-Pfalz by Konrad Wille, "Es geht schon wieder los: Dunkle Machenschaften gegen Wiedergutmachung," *Aufbau* (New York), February 21, 1958, p. 17.

claimants and the losses for which a claim could be made.[34]

I. ELIGIBLE CLAIMANTS (general coverage)

Residents of West Germany or West Berlin on December 31, 1952 (mostly German political persecutees).

People who emigrated (or were deported) from an area which was German on December 31, 1937 (mostly Jewish refugees).

Nonrepatriable displaced persons who were housed in a camp in West Germany or West Berlin on January 1, 1947 (mostly Jewish survivors).

Admissible Claims for

Loss of Life caused by persecution, if claimant had been a wife or child of the deceased, or if claimant, as a dependent husband, parent, grandparent, or orphaned grandchild, had been deprived of support from the deceased.

Monthly payments to claimant equal to the pension which would have been granted if the deceased had held a German civil service rank commensurate with his economic or social status before his persecution, and if he had thereupon suffered accidental death on duty. Payments terminable upon achievement of reasonable self-support, or after remarriage in the case of a widower or widow, or at age seventeen in the case of a child. Lump-sum payment for the period from date of death to November 1, 1953, on the basis of the rate paid in November 1953.

Damage to Body and Health, including

Medical Costs: in accordance with rates established by the German government for its civil servants in the case of accidents.

Reduction of Income: provided that income was reduced by at least 25 per cent. The income was presumed to be that which claimant – on the basis of his economic and social status before his persecution – would have received in the German civil service on May 1, 1949.

Compensation from 15 per cent of the civil service salary (in the case of 25 per cent disability) to 70 per cent (in the case of total disability). Monthly payments, in accordance with prevailing salary rates, for the duration of the disability. Lump-sum payment for impairment to November 1, 1953, with reichsmark salaries converted into deutschmark at the rate of 10:2.

Re-education: to the extent that such training was conducive to an increase of income.

Loss of Freedom, including

Wearing of the star outside of a ghetto or camp (Reich, Protektorat, *Generalgouvernement,* Netherlands, Belgium, Luxembourg, France, Serbia, and Croatia).

Living in "illegality under degrading conditions" (hiding).

Incarceration in a ghetto (including Shanghai).

Incarceration in a camp (interpreted by some of the courts to include southern France and Italy during 1940–43, Hungary from September, 1942, and Transnistria after the Tighina agreement).

Individual arrest.

Lump-sum payment at the rate of 150 deutschmark for each month of deprivation of liberty.

Property Losses involving belongings which in the area of the Reich (borders of December 31, 1937) were

Destroyed

Damaged

34. Indemnification Law, September 18, 1953, BGBl I, 1387. Second Law (amendment), August 10, 1955, BGBl I, 506. Third Law (amendment), June 29, 1956, BGBl I, 559. For text of the law as amended in 1956, see *Bundesentschädigungsgesetz,* with introduction by Dr. H. G. van Dam (Düsseldorf-Benrath, 1956).

Lost, or
Abandoned because of emigration, deportation, or hiding.

Lump-sum payment of replacement value up to a maximum of 75,000 deutschmark for all property losses, provided that for loss of personal belongings, a persecutee could demand payment of 150 per cent of his yearly income of 1932, converted 1:1, up to a maximum of 5,000 deutschmark. Under the Federal Restitution Law of 1957, owners of articles confiscated by the Reich or one of its subdivisions were granted payment of replacement value, without maximum, plus 10 per cent for securities and 25 per cent for other objects.

Capital Losses involving capital which in the area of the Reich (borders of December 31, 1937) was diminished by at least 500 reichsmark because of

Boycott.
Liquidation.
Transfer of reichsmark into foreign currency with a loss of more than 20 per cent.
Emigration expenses.

Lump-sum payment, by converting reichsmark loss into deutschmark at the rate of 10:2, up to a maximum of 75,000 deutschmark for all capital losses, provided that emigration expenses were to be compensated up to a maximum of 5000 deutschmark.

Discriminatory Taxes to the Reich or any of its subdivisions, insofar as recovery was not effected through restitution laws.

Lump-sum payment at the rate of 10:2 without maximum, except that a persecutee who in the course of a restitution proceeding had paid an Aryanizer at the rate of 10:1 for removal of discriminatory tax encumbrances was now repaid at the same rate. Many claimants were unable to recover taxes under the Federal Indemnification Law because such suits were deemed to be actions for return of assets sufficiently "identifiable" to have been covered by the restitution laws. The difficulty was removed by the Federal Restitution Law, which provided, however, for a conversion rate of 10:1.

Impairment of Professional or Economic Advancement, in the case of

Entrepreneurs: provided that income was reduced by at least 25 per cent.

Payment in either:
Lump sum, for a period ending with the achievement of an "adequate standard of living" (in terms of a German civil service career) or at age 70, such sum to consist of a differential between actual earnings and 75 per cent of the salary earned by the equivalent civil servant at the end of such period, plus 20 per cent of that differential, with possible adjustments in favor of claimants in countries where the purchasing power of the local currency might be out of line with official exchange rates, up to a maximum of 40,000 deutschmark,
or:
at the election of a claimant who had no reasonable expectation of achieving an adequate living standard, monthly rates for life consisting of a differential between actual earnings (if any) and two-thirds of such pension as claimant would have received if he were a civil servant at the time of entry into force of the law, plus twelve monthly payments for the period preceding November 1, 1953, the maximum monthly payment not to exceed 600 deutschmark.

Private Employees.

Payment in lump sum only, calculated as above, except that employees covered by social security or pension could not receive the 20 per cent addition to their differential.

Public Servants (including university professors and employees of the Jewish community who were in office before 1933).

Lump sum payment consisting of a differential between pension received (if any) and three-fourths of the last full salary, for the period from date of dismissal or forced retirement to April 1, 1950, converted 10:2.

Students or Trainees

Lump sum payment up to a maximum of 10,000 deutschmark.

A persecutee who, in addition to a claim for impairment of advancement, won recognition of either a death claim or claim for damage to health, could receive the bigger award in full and the smaller award to the extent of 25 per cent.

Loss of Life Insurance Payments and Private Pensions (insofar as no satisfaction was received under the restitution laws)

In the case of holders of life insurance

Payment in lump sum or annuities — depending on the provisions of the policy — converted according to a rate applicable to the policy under the currency laws. If there were unpaid premiums, claimant had the option of having such premiums deducted from the award at the rate of 10:1, or of claiming such sums as he would have received under the terms of the policy for the money he had paid in. (Lump-sum indemnification in such cases was made at the rate of 10:2.) Maximum payment to claimant: 25,000 deutschmark.

In the case of pensioners

Payment in lump sum or annuities, as provided for in the pension, converted 10:2. However, no annuities were granted for the period prior to November 1, 1952, and maximum payments to claimant and his survivors could not exceed 25,000 deutschmark.

II. Special Claimants (limited coverage)

A. Corporate persons (or their successors) who maintained their headquarters in West Germany or West Berlin on December 31, 1952, or who had removed their headquarters from an area which was German on December 31, 1937, because of persecution.

Admissible Claims for

Property and Capital Losses: Payments as above, except that in the case of religious organizations or their successors, the maximum could be exceeded.

B. Persons who, because of persecution, lost real estate in the area of West Germany or West Berlin.

Admissible Claims for

Property Losses: Payments as above.

C. Persons who, because of their nationality, suffered permanent impairment of their health (mainly as a result of medical experiments).

Admissible Claims for

Damage to Health: Monthly payments, depending on disability, from 100 to 200 deutschmark.

D. Heirs of persons who died as result of persecution before December 31, 1952, and whose last residence was in West Germany or West Berlin.

Admissible Claims for

Death of the Persecutee: Payments as above, provided that the requirements of the claim were fulfilled as above.

E. Persons who had lived in an area from which Germans were expelled after the war (principally Czechoslovakia and western Poland) and who could be considered German by reason of language or culture.

Admissible Claims for

Death of another person in the same category: Conditions and payments as above, but no payment was granted for periods to January 1, 1949.

Damage to Health: Payments as above.

Loss of Freedom: Payments as above.

Discriminatory Taxes: Lump-sum payment at the rate of 100:6.5, up to a maximum of 9750 deutschmark.

Impairment of Advancement: Payments as above, except that the maximum of the lump-sum payment was fixed at only 10,000 deutschmark, and maximum monthly payments were limited to 200 deutschmark.

F. Persons who had lost or changed their nationality (other than Austrian) and who were resident in some country other than Israel.

Admissible Claims (only in cases of non-support from any public agency) for

Death of another person in the same category: Conditions and payments as above, but no payment was granted for periods to January 1, 1949.

Damage to Health: Payments substantially as above, except that no payment was granted for periods of disability prior to January 1, 1949, or for retraining.

Loss of Freedom: Payments as above.

G. Persons who had lost or changed their nationality (other than Austrian) and who were resident in Israel.

Admissible Claims (only in cases of non-support from any public agency) for

Death of another person in the same category: Conditions and monthly payments as above, except that no lump-sum payment was granted at all.

Loss of Freedom: Payments as above.

The Federal Indemnification Law contained a double compromise: (1) it did not cover all the surviving victims; (2) it did not provide full indemnification for those whom it covered.

The first set of restrictions was the more serious. The definition of eligibility omitted Jewish survivors in northern Europe, the West, the Balkans, and the East. In fact, the Jewish claimants comprised in the main only refugees from Germany and the nonrepatriable displaced persons who had passed through camps on German soil.[35] Even that comparatively narrow category was not recognized in full: There was no compensation for the Austrian Jews. The West Germans felt that the Austrians had been sufficiently active partners in the Nazi destruction process to share in the payment for its effects. The Austrians on their part contended that as an "occupied" nation they were not responsible for anything that might have transpired with their co-operation. Caught between these irreconcilable positions, the Jews of Austria finally accepted a Viennese offer of a few crumbs.[36]

35. The Jews from eastern Europe who were landed directly in Israel were allowed payments only for death and loss of freedom. That provision did not cover the Polish Jews who had fled to the interior of the USSR with the Red Army.

36. In 1955 the Vienna government agreed after long negotiations and much unfavorable publicity to grant lump-sum payments to victims living abroad who had been Austrian citizens, or who had resided in Austria during the entire decade from 1928 to 1938. A total of 550,000,000 schillinge, or $21,000,000, was made available for expenditure over a period of ten years. Indemnification was granted for: (*a*) loss of earning capacity due to impairment of health (S. 10,000 to a maximum of S. 30,000, or $385 to $1,155); (*b*) total disability caused by persecution (S. 30,000, plus S. 10,000 if the disability was incurred as a result of at least six months of harsh imprisonment); (*c*) persecution in general, to the extent that funds permitted, with priority for elderly victims in need (up to S. 20,000). "Das Wiener Entschädigungs-Abkommen," *Aufbau* (New York), July 22, 1955, pp. 1, 4. "Österreichischer Hilfsfonds," *ibid.*, November 2, 1956, p. 6.

Under Article 26 of the Austrian State Treaty, the Austrian Government was obligated to indemnify persecutees for property losses incurred in Austria. After an exchange of notes with Great Britain and the United States in 1959, the Austrian Parliament authorized $6,000,000 for this purpose. The law, passed in March, 1961, covered only

The second drawback — the extent of compensation — concerned those who were eligible claimants. Here we find limitation placed upon limitation. From a somewhat restricted coverage of losses and injuries, the lawmakers had proceeded to establish substantive conditions for giving effect to the coverage, and that effect was modified in turn by major restrictions on payments.

To begin with, the law did not recognize every kind of loss. There was no recognition of sheer torment and chagrin. No provision of the law authorized payments for suffering as such. For the pure hurt inflicted by the German state there was no remedy at all. Recovery for pain could be effected only in the regular courts — and from private defendants. Similarly, the law authorized no compensation for forced labor, nor could anyone who had once been compelled to work for a public agency now find satisfaction under any law. However, those who had been detailed to private firms could sue those corporations under the civil code in the regular courts. One ex-employee of I. G. Auschwitz thus won 10,000 deutschmark in a suit. The liquidators of the I. G. Farben concern, fearing a cascade of such actions, thereupon moved quickly to effect a settlement with a Jewish claims conference for 27,000,000 deutschmark.[37]

While the indemnification law did recognize a wide variety of losses, it made the recognition of many of them conditional. We have seen the condition of a minimum: the property losses had to amount to at least 500 reichsmark; transfer losses had to reach at least 20 per cent; reduction of income at least 25 per cent. There was also a condition with regard to the place of the damage. Property and capital losses, regardless of size, were not indemnifiable if they had occurred outside of the borders of 1937. A host of additional conditions were interpolated in the course of interpretation with the effect of blocking awards until final rulings could be obtained. Examples of such complications were questions of the following order: Was a place a ghetto if it had no walls?[38] Was a claimant a persecutee if his captors

---

bank deposits, notes, cash, confiscated mortgage payments, and discriminatory taxes. It adjusted for currency revaluation and provided for maximum payments. "Zwei Gesetze," *ibid.*, March 31, 1961, p. 25.

At the same time, the Austrians passed another law providing compensation for wearing the star, reduction of earning capacity, and interruption of education. However, the entry into force of the law was made conditional upon a financing agreement with West Germany. *Ibid.*

Survivors in East Germany could receive indemnification only at age 60 in the case of men or at age 55 in the case of women. Maximum payments were DM (East) 480 per month. Bruno Weil, "Vereinigung und Wiedergutmachung," *ibid.*, October 21, 1955, p. 11.

37. Agreement signed by Dr. Fritz Brinckmann and Dr. Walter Schmidt (liquidators for the I. G.) and Dr. Ernst Katzenstein (for the Conference on Jewish Material Claims against Germany, Inc.), February 6, 1957. Also, letter by Brinckmann and Schmidt to the stockholders, February, 1957. Photostatic copies through the courtesy of Mr. Frank Petschek. The agreement covered Buna IV, Heydebreck, Fürstengrube, and Janinagrube. The number of Jewish claimants was estimated at 3400. An additional 3,000,000 deutschmark was made available for non-Jewish slave laborers who qualified as "persecutees."

Following the passage of a federal law which placed a time limit on wartime claims against private German firms, ex-inmates who had slaved for the AEG, Brabag, Heinkel, Holzmann, Krupp, Moll, Rheinmetall Borsig, Siemens-Schuckert, Telefunken, and other companies formed a committee of former Jewish slave laborers in Germany to expedite matters. "Ein Komitee früherer jüdischer Zwangsarbeiter," *Aufbau* (New York), December 13, 1957, p. 2. In 1959 the claims conference made a settlement with Krupp in the amount of 6 million–10 million deutschmark, assuming 1200 to 2000 claimants. "Friedrich Krupp will Sklavenarbeiter entschädigen," *ibid.*, January 1, 1960, p. 1.

were not Germans?[39] Could an award be granted for damage to health if the illness was a neurosis?[40]

Finally, we may mention the limitations on payment. These limitations were manifested through (1) the insertion of ceilings on amounts, (2) arbitrary conversion, (3) failure to compensate for delay, and (4) the provisions for the contingency of the claimant's death. Maximum amounts were fixed in the case of income reductions by "assimilation" with the German civil service,[41] and in the case of property losses by outright figures.[42] Arbitrary conversions were applied in many claims which were founded on damage that was measured in reichsmark. (Here we may think of the claims for disability, capital losses, discriminatory taxes, and lost pensions.) The reichsmark amounts in such instances were converted for lump-sum payment into deutschmark at the rate of 10:2 or less – i.e., for a 100,000 reichsmark loss, 20,000 deutschmark.

For a long time, that situation was particularly aggravated for claimants in the United States: for every 4.2 deutschmark they could receive one dollar; yet that dollar on the receiving end was not the equivalent in purchasing power of 4.2 deutschmark in Germany. Not until 1960 did the German courts adopt realistic exchange rates for American claimants.[43]

Next we may consider the problem of delay. The basic correction for delay in payment is interest, but the indemnification legislation provided for no interest payments aside from limited allowances in the case of articles confiscated by the Reich. More serious still was the provision for the event that the claimant died. During the mid-1950's the claimants were dying at the rate of 5–6 per cent per year.[44] With the death of a claimant, all monthly payments lapsed. For the contingency that a lump-sum payment had not yet been granted, there was a threefold regulation:[45]

38. Kurt R. Grossmann, "Sabotage der Wiedergutmachung – Der Fall des 'nicht abgeriegelten Ghettos'" (Przemysalny), *Aufbau* (New York), September 30, 1955, p. 5.

39. Extraordinary difficulties were encountered in this connection by claimants from Roumania. See R. M. W. Kempner, "Entschädigung für Juden aus Rumänien vorläufig gestoppt," *Aufbau* (New York), July 19, 1957, pp. 5–6. Herman Muller, "Entschädigung für Juden aus Rumänien," *ibid.*, August 9, 1957, p. 13. Bukowiner Freunde, "Entschädigungs-Ansprüche der Bukowinaer Juden," *ibid.*, March 7, 1958, p. 6.

40. Richard Dyck, "Die Neurosen in der Wiedergutmachung," *Aufbau* (New York), March 7, 1958, p. 15; March 21, 1958, pp. 19–20; April 4, 1958, p. 16, with comments by Dr. Hans Strauss in the issue of April 18, 1958, p. 18.

41. The prewar economic and social status was to be considered in the assimilation procedure. However, in the case of death and health claims, social status was not to be used to the detriment of the claimant. See Par. 11 of the 1st Implementation Decree (death claims) and Par. 14 of the 2d Implementation Decree (health claims) in H. G. van Dam, *Durchführungsverordnungen zum Bundesentschädigungsgesetz* (Düsseldorf, 1957), pp. 27, 39.

42. The Federal Restitution Law of 1957 did allow actions without maximum. The law provided, however, for a total expenditure of not more than 1,500,000,000 deutschmark. Insofar as the allowable claims were to exceed that sum, the built-in safety provisions of the law stipulated in effect that awards to the extent of 10,000 deutschmark be paid in full, that determinations between that figure and 100,000 deutschmark be largely satisfied, and that larger amounts be reduced in rough proportion to the remaining funds. The wind-up of the program was projected for the early 1960's.

43. Robert Held, "Zweierlei Mass," *Aufbau* (New York), October 18, 1957, p. 18. Robert Kempner, "Neuer Wiedergutmachungs-Entscheid," *ibid.*, March 11, 1960, p. 1. Walter Peters, "Zum Streit um die Kaufkraft," *ibid.*, March 18, 1960, p. 33. Robert O. Held, "Lösung des Kaufkraft-Problems?" *ibid.*, March 31, 1961, p. 25.

44. Kurt Grossmann, "Pläne zur Finanzierung des Lastenausgleichs," *Aufbau* (New York), February 21, 1958, p. 17.

1. The law admitted as claimants all heirs of victims whose last residence had been West Germany or West Berlin and who had died at any time before December 31, 1952.

2. Insofar as an otherwise fully eligible claimant had died before adjudication, the payments for property, capital, and tax losses could be claimed by any heir; the award of payments for other losses was restricted to heirs in the immediate family.

3. In the event that a special claimant from an expellee area had died before a decision had been reached, payments for discriminatory taxes were granted only to heirs in the immediate family; and in the event that a special claimant in the nationality category had died before an award, the payments for death were disallowed altogether.

After the first few years of indemnification legislation, its eventual cost was estimated at ca. 18,000,000,000 deutschmark (about $4,300,000,000).[46] Not all of this money was going to be paid to the Jews. Although the German machine of destruction had struck out much more heavily at Jewish victims than at German persecutees, that ratio was not going to be reflected in the payments, for the number of survivors was relatively greater in the German group, and the recognition of Germans as eligible claimants was somewhat more complete.[47] The initial statistics also revealed something about the distribution of payments, by cause. This was the rank order (not including the satisfaction of claims under the Federal Restitution Law): the largest amount was for loss of freedom, followed by losses of economic advancement, property, capital, tax money, and health, down to payments for loss of life.[48] The Jews were getting the smallest amount for what had been their greatest loss.

If we could imagine for a moment a restitution - indemnification program which would have given to every victim the fullest possible coverage, we would see before us a financial foundation upon which the lives of the survivors could have been rebuilt. As things were, the program contained many gaps, and the necessary foundation for a complete reconstruction did not exist. Actually, an important part of the rehabilitation cost rested upon the Jewish community and the individual survivor himself. That portion which was borne by the community in Israel and

45. If there was no will, heirs-in-law were not excluded, but in no case was payment made to a foreign state. A victim who was missing after the war was presumed to have died on May 8, 1945, unless there was evidence to support an earlier date.

46. Up to March 31, 1958, ca. 4,500,000,000 deutschmark had been paid out under the provincial and federal laws. The windup was expected to require another five years, with an annual allocation of about 1,300,000,000 deutschmark each by the federal government and the *Länder*. Many monthly payments were going to be made thereafter. "Totalschätzungen für Entschädigungen verfrüht," *Aufbau* (New York), March 28, 1958, p. 5.

47. Between October 1, 1953, and December 31, 1959, payments to claimants abroad (Jews and a handful of German political refugees) totaled 4,450,000,000 deutschmark, while the amount received by residents in Germany (Germans and a handful of Jewish survivors) was 1,977,000,000 deutschmark. German Federal Government/Press and Information Office, *Bulletin*, June 14, 1960, "The Restitution Programme," pp. 4–5. The principal categories among the German claimants included: (*a*) political ex-inmates (other than purged Nazis) of concentration camps, (*b*) civil servants and artists who had lost their positions for political reasons, (*c*) persons sterilized on "eugenic" grounds and dependent heirs of persons killed in the course of the "euthanasia" program (hardship payments only, as determined by the indemnification offices). The principal group of German ineligibles consisted necessarily of persecutees in all of the above categories who were living in East Germany.

48. Statistics up to December 1, 1956, in "Geht es mit der Entschädigung wirklich vorwärts?" *Aufbau* (New York), March 29, 1957, p. 11.

elsewhere became the cause of a special claim: the "reparations."

The Jews had to obtain their reparations through the use of two separate channels: first, the allocation of a share from Allied takings after the war, and second, direct negotiations with the West Germans themselves. Let us say at once that the first operation did not yield very much.

The Allied reparations plan envisaged a broad division between East and West, and a further subdivision among the western countries. Russia was to satisfy its own requirements and those of Poland from three sources: removals in its occupied territory, deliveries from the Western zones, and the acquisition of German external assets in the former Axis satellites of Hungary, Roumania, and Bulgaria. Since the Soviets were primarily interested in hard economic gain, it is hardly necessary to add that the Jewish community received nothing in the Eastern area.[49]

The Western reparations policy was based more on a containment of the German war potential than on an exploitation of available spoils. Accordingly, the Western powers concentrated their attention upon shipping, heavy industry, and German external assets in Allied and neutral states. At the Paris Reparations Conference the United States proposed that a small part of the enemy assets in neutral countries be allocated to nonrepatriable displaced persons. The sum agreed upon was $25,000,000. Under a subsequent agreement the money was to be made available by the Allied governments as a priority on the proceeds of the liquidation of the German property in the neutral countries, and 90 per cent of the funds were to be devoted to Jewish rehabilitation.[50]

The administering authority of the $25,000,000 was to be the International Refugee Organization. When the Preparatory Commission of the IRO discussed the use of the money in February, 1947, the representative of the United Kingdom, Sir George Rendel, questioned the allocation of 90 per cent of the proceeds to Jewish organizations. The Jews, he said, now constituted less than 10 per cent of the refugees. No class of refugee, said Sir George, should be excluded from the utmost help that international action could give.[51]

In the meantime, there were as yet no funds. The first payment was made by Sweden, not from German assets but out of its own treasury. That sum amounted to 50,000,000 kroner.[52] Switzerland followed with 20,000,000 Swiss francs. The dollar equivalent of these two amounts was approximately $18,500,000, and that was all the reparations money received by IRO for re-

49. An exception was the abandoned German property made available by the Poles to Jewish repatriates from Siberia. The Jews soon left. It should be pointed out that the Jewish needs which were now unrecognized stemmed from Jewish losses which the Soviets had not forgotten to figure in for their justification of reparations claims. The Jewish dead from territories bounded by the postwar USSR and Poland numbered 4 million.

50. See Ginzberg, "Reparation for Non-Repatriables," pp. 56, 76. The author, professor of economics at Columbia University, was the U.S. representative at the five-power conference of June 14, 1946.

51. Summary records (mimeographed), PREP/SR/6, February 15, 1947.

52. Accord between the United States, France, the United Kingdom, and Sweden, signed on July 18, 1946, entered into force March 28, 1947, 61 Stat., Part 3, 3191; *Treaties and Other International Acts Series,* No. 1657. IRO/Public Information Office, Monthly Digest No. 3, November, 1947, pp. 26–27. The agreement specified that the German assets be used exclusively to satisfy Swedish claims and for the purchase of commodities essential to the German economy, that German owners be indemnified in German money, and that Germany be required to confirm the transfers.

settlement purposes during its lifetime.[53]

Years afterwards the new state of Israel, staggering under the influx of the survivors, turned its attention to the reparations question.[54] On March 12, 1951, the Israel government dispatched identical notes to Washington, London, Paris, and Moscow, to ask for the help of the four occupying powers in securing from the two German republics reparations equal to the cost of the absorption and rehabilitation of 500,000 victims in Israel. That cost was $1,500,000.[55] The three Western governments replied that they were precluded by the terms of the Paris reparations agreement from asserting, either on their own behalf or on behalf of other states, further reparations demands on Germany.[56] The Soviet Union did not bother to reply.

The stage was now set for a gesture from the government in Bonn. The West Germans could no longer sidestep the problem. They had been endowed with freedom of action; yet it was precisely this freedom that compelled them to act. Much that was recessed and remote came to the foreground now. At this moment, particularly, the inner disturbance could not be removed without an outer settlement; at this moment, too, there was much German concern with possible Jewish opposition to the re-establishment of Germany as a power in the world. At the same time it was realized that the Jewish figure, somewhat reduced in total and greatly spread out in years, would not constitute Germany's heaviest burden. Accordingly, on September 27, 1951, Chancellor Adenauer declared before the German Parliament that, in view of the terrible crimes which in another epoch had been committed in the name of the German people, the federal government was ready to settle with representatives of Jewry and of Israel the problem of material amends.[57]

The representatives of Jewry were quick to accept the Chancellor's invitation. In October, 1951, twenty Jewish organizations formed the Conference on Jewish Material Claims against Germany, Inc., in order to request the payment of $500,000,000 for the rehabilitation of Jewish victims outside Israel.[58]

In Israel the decision to dispatch emissaries of the Jewish state to a conference with German officials was not

53. IRO/General Council, 2d sess., report by the Director General, GC/60, March 22, 1949, pp. 79–87. Disbursements as of December 30, 1948, totaled $13,867,359, including $4,636,344 to the Joint Distribution Committee, $9,019,392 to the Jewish Agency, and $211,623 to non-Jewish organizations. *Ibid.* In England £250,000 (or $700,000) from confiscated German assets were allotted to victims there through a "Nazi Victims Relief Trust." "Britischer Hilfsfonds für Naziopfer," *Aufbau* (New York), November 15, 1957, p. 19.

54. Thus, in 1950, German investments in Israel were impounded as security for the collection of future reparations. The assets, which did not include certain properties of the Church, were worth about $9,000,000. Most of the owners had been deported by the British to Australia during the war. *Congress Weekly* (New York), January 30, 1950, p. 2. Haim Cohn (Attorney General of Israel), "The New Law in the Country of the Law," *United Nations World*, September, 1950, pp. 62–63.

55. Israel note to the four occupying powers, March 21, 1951, Government of Israel/Ministry for Foreign Affairs, *Documents Relating to the Agreement between the Government of Israel and the Government of the Federal Republic of Germany* (Jerusalem, 1953), pp. 20–24. The figure of 500,000 included prewar refugees as well as anticipated arrivals.

56. Notes by the United States, the United Kingdom, and France to Israel, July 5, 1951, *ibid.*, pp. 34–41.

57. Declaration by Adenauer before Parliament, September 27, 1951, *ibid.*, pp. 42–43.

58. Resolution by the Conference on Jewish Material Claims, October 26, 1951, *ibid.*, pp. 46–47.

so easy to make. After Chancellor Adenauer indicated a willingness to accept the Israel figures as a basis of discussion, Prime Minister Ben-Gurion submitted the question to Parliament,[59] and the legislature consented by a narrow margin.[60] The figure of Israel's claim against West Germany was $1,000,000,000.

The negotiations began at The Hague in the Netherlands on March 21, 1952. The delegations were headed by the following specially chosen men:

West Germany: Prof. Franz Josef Böhm, Rector of Frankfurt University; Dr. Otto Küster, lawyer
Claims Conference: Moses A. Leavitt
Israel: Dr. A. F. Shinnar, Foreign Office; Dr. Giora Josephtal, Jewish Agency

The official language of the meetings was English.[61]

The $500,000,000 figure of the Claims Conference was reduced by the Germans to 500,000,000 deutschmark. Ten per cent of that amount was to be made available by the federal government for aid to converts; the other 450,000,000 deutschmark ($107,000,000) was to be received by the Claims Conference, over a period of ten years, for relief, rehabilitation, and resettlement of Jewish victims in all parts of the world.[62]

When the Israelis submitted their total of $1,000,000,000 (representing West Germany's expected contribution to Israel's $1,500,000,000 absorption cost), the German delegates asked some twenty-five questions about the basis of the claim. They wanted to know whether the emigration of fugitives from eastern Europe was not the result of Communist rather than Nazi measures; they questioned the estimate of $3000 for resettlement cost per person.[63] Following that questioning, they presented a round figure of their own. The $1,000,000,000, or 4,300,000,000 deutschmark, were scaled down to 3,000,000,000 deutschmark, or $715,-000,000. The Germans then declared that because of their country's current economic and financial position they

59. Adenauer to Dr. Nahum Goldmann (chairman of Claims Conference), December 6, 1951, *Documents Relating to the Agreement,* p. 57. Statement by Ben-Gurion in Knesset (Israel's one-house legislature), January 7, 1952, *ibid.,* pp. 57-60.

60. The vote was 61 to 50, with five abstentions and four absences. To the right of center, the *Herut* Party and General Zionists were in basic opposition. The left (consisting of the pro-Soviet *Mapam* and the Communists) voted against negotiations in reflection of the attitude of the USSR. The majority in the center included a few votes of Arab deputies. See Dana Adams Schmidt, "Foes of Bonn Talks Lose Israeli Vote," *New York Times,* January 10, 1952, p. 14. Also, advertisement by Zionist-Revisionists of America (*Herut*), *ibid.,* January 6, 1952, p. 15.

61. Michael Hoffman, "Bonn Assures Jews on Reparation Aim," *New York Times,* March 22, 1952, p. 5. On Böhm, see "Der Unterhändler," *Aufbau* (New York), February 8, 1952, p. 5. On Küster (a former indemnification commissioner in Württemberg-Baden), see Albion Ross, "Slave Laborers Find a Champion," *New York Times,* March 6, 1955, p. 9.

62. "Bonn Makes Jews $107,000,000 Offer," *New York Times,* June 17, 1952, p. 3. Protocol No. 2 between West Germany and the Claims Conference, signed at Luxembourg on September 10, 1952, by Adenauer and Goldmann, *Documents Relating to the Agreement,* pp. 161–63. Under the agreement the deutschmark accruing to the Claims Conference were paid to Israel, which was to make available the funds in the required currencies. During the first year of its operations, the Claims Conference spent $8,705,000 in fifteen countries. Of that amount, over $7,000,000 was spent for direct relief, $900,000 was allocated for "cultural reconstruction" (grants to scholars with emphasis on catastrophe research), and $800,000 was given to the United Restitution Office, a legal agency which processed indemnification claims of eligible Jewish victims – probably the largest legal aid society in the world. "100,000 Naziopfer profitieren von den deutschen Reparationen," *Aufbau* (New York), October 15, 1954, p. 17.

63. "Bonn and Israelis Push Claims Talks," *New York Times,* April 1, 1952, p. 13.

could not even guarantee the payment of that sum.[64]

The complicating factor in the situation was a concurrent conference in London, between thirty states (representing private holders of prewar German public bonds) and the West German government, over the settlement of Germany's external debts. The leader of the German delegation in London, Hermann J. Abs (Deutsche Bank), had agreed with Professor Böhm of the Hague delegation that no commitments were to be made until it was possible to assess Bonn's total obligation.[65] When the Israelis were confronted with this impasse, Israel's Parliament voted to break off the negotiations.[66]

Following the action by the Israelis, Böhm reworked his agreement with Abs in order to be able to resume the talks, but he found an unrelenting opponent in Finance Minister Schäffer. The theory that there was only one pot from which to pay had become a basic pre-condition in Bonn, and at that moment Germany's foreign credit was considered a little more important than Germany's moral debt. At a Cabinet meeting in mid-May, Adenauer apparently sided with Schäffer. Böhm and Küster thereupon pulled an unexpected punch: they resigned. In their statement of resignation these independent men charged their government with insincerity.[67]

Faced with the necessity of retrieving its position, the Federal government now tried something else. Hermann Abs informally approached Israeli aides in London and suggested a down payment of deliveries amounting to 1,000,000,000 deutschmark (ca. $250,-000,000) over a period of three years, the balance to be settled later. He was refused.[68] The Germans then made their "binding offer" of $715,000,000.[69] That offer was accepted.

Under the terms of the agreement the obligation was to be discharged in the course of the ten years following exchange of ratifications. The federal government was to deposit the money in the agreed installments at the Bank Deutscher Länder. An Israel mission, with diplomatic status, was empowered to draw upon the account for the purchase of steel, machines, chemicals, and a variety of other capital goods.[70]

After the document had been signed, the Israelis awaited the approval of Bonn before doing anything. The Ger-

64. Statement by German delegation, April 5, 1952, *Documents Relating to the Agreement,* p. 82.

65. "Bonn-Jewish Talk at Crucial Stage," *New York Times,* April 3, 1952, p. 5.

66. Decision of the Knesset, May 6, 1952, *Documents Relating to the Agreement,* p. 90.

67. "Top Germans Quit in Israel Fund Lag," *New York Times,* May 20, 1952, pp. 1, 11.

68. "New Bonn Feeler to Israel Spurned," *ibid.,* June 1, 1952, p. 9.

69. "Bonn, Jews Reach New Parley Basis," *ibid.,* June 11, 1952, p. 7.

70. Text of agreement (with exchange of letters) signed at Luxembourg on September 10, 1952, by Sharett (Shertok) and Adenauer, in *Documents Relating to the Agreement,* pp. 125–51. Certain items (such as oil) could be purchased with German-held balances in foreign markets, and special consideration was to be given by Israel to industries of West Berlin. No discrimination was to be exercised by the federal government against Israel in the event of any restrictions upon exports, and no commodities obtained by Israel were to be re-exported to any third state. Clauses calling for re-negotiation were included to provide for the possibility of economic inability to pay, or of inflation. Israel agreed not to advance any further claim against West Germany, and, subsequent to the entry into force of the treaty, negotiations were begun in Rome between Israel, West Germany, and Australia, for the return to the Palestine Germans of the money obtained by Israel from the sale of their assets. "Templer fordern Wiedergutmachung von Israel," *Aufbau* (New York), January 22, 1954, p. 17. Of interest too was Israel's immediate offer to release ca. $15,000,000 in bank deposits belonging to Arab refugees. "Israel Will Free Arabs' Bank Funds," *New York Times,* October 10, 1952, pp. 1, 3.

man Parliament was taking its time. A number of German industrialists were worried about the loss of the Arab market,[71] while German shipping interests were protesting the absence of a stipulation extending some business to their flag.[72] At last the approval came, over the opposition of a coalition of elements from the extreme left and extreme right wings.[73] The Israel Cabinet then ratified the instrument without submitting it to the legislature for another vote.[74]

In the years that followed the exchange of ratifications, West Germany was able to discover that, due to its steadily growing economic output, the burden of the payments was shrinking into insignificance. By 1958 the reparations amounted to less than 1 per cent of the federal budget and only about 0.2 per cent of the gross national product. However, this agreement was not merely the adjustment of a claim; it was also the conclusion of a peace.

That aspect of the settlement was to produce some unexpected psychological repercussions. After a while it became clear that the Germans were engaging in strange behavior – they were praising the Jews. In countless articles and editorials, in mass demonstrations at Bergen-Belsen, in vast and silent attendance at the performance of a play whose simple lines were taken from the diary of a dead Jewish girl, Germans were paying homage to the massacred Jews and to living Jewry everywhere. The contrast between that spectacle and all that had preceded it was so strong that observers were struck by something uncanny in the demonstration.[75] It seemed almost that the Germans were going a little too far. This was not mere repentance; like their ancient Teutonic ancestors, the Germans were deifying the slain.

The West German decision to make peace with Israel placed the East Germans in an awkward position. At one point, in fact, an East German spokesman, caught at a press conference in West Germany, found himself speaking about the possibility of negotiations with Israel.[76] To be sure, that willingness was soon withdrawn; at the end of 1953, Albert Norden of the East German government declared before a press gathering in Soviet-controlled territory that Israel had no right to reparations, since it was a military base of the United States and not the legal successor of millions of Jewish victims of Nazi tyranny. In the event of a peace conference East Germany was not going to recognize West Germany's commitment.[77]

71. The Bonn government offered the Arabs $95,000,000 in credits, but Cairo wanted ten times as much. M. S. Handler, "Bundesrat in Bonn Gets Israeli Pact," *New York Times,* February 14, 1953, p. 3. The Free Democrats suggested that the reparations be administered by the United Nations and that a part of the funds be diverted for Arab refugees. "German-Arab Plan Drawn," *ibid.,* November 14, 1952, p. 8. For a while some of the industrialists were also talking about a "vendors' strike," i.e., a refusal to make deliveries to Israel. "Israel Will Press Bonn on Payments," *ibid.,* January 6, 1953, p. 12.

72. "Vertrag Bonn–Tel Aviv vor dem deutschen Parlament," *Aufbau* (New York), February 27, 1953, p. 1. Israel's government thereupon lifted the ban on German shipping in its ports. "Die Israel-Regierung hebt den Boykott der deutschen Flagge auf," *ibid.,* March 6, 1953, p. 1.

73. For an analysis of the vote in the Bundestag (lower house), see Kurt R. Grossmann, "Ratifiziert!" *ibid.,* March 27, 1953, pp. 1–2.

74. Dana Adams Schmidt, "Tel Aviv Ratifies Reparations Pact," *New York Times,* March 23, 1953, p. 12. Ratifications were exchanged on March 27, 1953, in New York.

75. See Alfred Werner, "Germany's New Flagellants," *American Scholar,* Spring, 1958, pp. 169–78. Also, William S. Schlamm, *Die Grenzen des Wunders* (Zurich, 1959), pp. 62–73, particularly pp. 63–65.

76. "Israelis Welcome East German Bid," *New York Times,* September 22, 1952, p. 5. The speaker was East German Agriculture Minister Goldenbaum.

For the Jewish community the satisfaction of its claims meant the abandonment of a host of reservations which it had hitherto retained in its dealings with Germany. Outside of Israel the channels of trade were cleared almost immediately;[78] in Israel itself, restrictions were thrown aside one by one. Even while negotiations were still in progress, the Tel Aviv–Jaffa Chamber of Commerce was faced with the question of what to do in respect to member firms who were assuming the representation of German companies in violation of the boycott.[79] In 1953 the Israel government lifted its ban on the registration of German patents and trademarks.[80] A few years later German travel bureaus were booking tourists for visits to Israel, and a five-man German industrial delegation left for Israel to examine the opportunities for investments there.[81] In 1957 the West German Foreign Minister, Heinrich von Brentano, declared in answer to a question whether any power had been approached to bring about an establishment of German-Israeli diplomatic relations:

> No steps have been taken to establish diplomatic relations with Israel in the near future. When we arrive at such a decision, there will be no need for a third power as an intermediary. Our relations with Israel are so unequivocal and good that, in my opinion, only direct talks between Israel and the Federal Republic will be required in order to put them on a formal basis as soon as both of us shall consider the moment appropriate.[82]

77. "Ostdeutschland lehnt offiziell Wiedergutmachung ab," *Aufbau* (New York), January 1, 1955, p. 11.

78. See the comment on the spur of German diamond exports, "Diamond Industry in Germany Grows," *New York Times*, February 21, 1952, p. 43. On the interesting development in which Jewish public relations experts were enlisted in the drive for recovery of German assets in the United States, see William Harlan Hale and Charles Clift, "Enemy Assets – The $500,000,000 Question," *Reporter*, June 14, 1956, pp. 8–15.

79. "Um die Vertretung deutscher Firmen in Israel," *Aufbau* (New York), April 25, 1952, p. 8.

80. "Wieder deutsche Patente in Israel," *ibid.*, June 26, 1953, p. 31.

81. Kurt R. Grossmann, "Deutsch-israelische Annäherung wächst," *ibid.*, June 21, 1957, p. 1.

82. *News from the German Embassy* (Washington, D.C.), June 24, 1957, p. 3.

XII / *Implications*

As time passes on, the destruction of the European Jews will recede into the background. Its most immediate consequences are almost over, and whatever developments may henceforth be traced to the catastrophe will be consequences of consequences, more and more remote. Already the Nazi outburst has become historical. But this is a strange page in history. Few events of modern times were so filled with unpredicted action and unsuspected death. A primordial impulse had suddenly surfaced among the Western nations; it had been unfettered through their machines. From this moment, fundamental assumptions about our civilization have no longer stood unchallenged, for while the occurrence is past, the phenomenon remains.

Before the emergence of the twentieth century and its technology, a destructive mind could not play in fantasy with the thoughts that the Nazis were to translate into action. The administrator of earlier centuries did not have the tools. He did not possess the network of communications; he did not dispose over rapid small arms fire and quick-working poison gases. The bureaucrat of tomorrow would not have these problems; already, he is better equipped than the German Nazis were. Killing is not as difficult as it used to be. The modern administrative apparatus has facilities for rapid, concerted movements and for efficient massive killings. These devices not only trap a larger number of victims; they also require a greater degree of specialization, and with that division of labor the moral burden too is fragmented among the participants. The perpetrator can now kill his victims without touching them, without hearing them, without seeing them. He may feel sure of his success and safe from its repercussions. This ever growing capacity for destruction cannot be arrested anywhere.

In the first chapter we saw how the Nazis had built upon the experiences of the past. Now there are means which will allow still others to seize upon the Nazi experience, so that it in turn may yet become a precedent for the future. This is an unsettling thought. It bothers possessors of the new potential. It disturbs some of the carriers of the new vulnerability. For now the long-established discriminations of Christianity and the long-practiced appeals of the Jews have acquired implications that did not exist before. Standing alone, the old ways may seem harmless enough. In the framework of the Nazi model the mildest exclusions are threatening links in an incomplete chain of destruction, while the repeated appeals are commitments to a course of action which in the extreme situation can lead to an all-encompassing doom.

With the recognition of the latent danger in habitual actions and traditional thinking, there has been an almost involuntary shift from the old position. But this reorientation has had its limits. Within the United States and the USSR the limits have been drawn in characteristically contrasting patterns. The Americans have moved to abrogate the physical barriers, but there is little interference when hostile words are uttered. The Soviets have dealt with the verbal issue, but they have not removed their administrative bars.

In American society a steady demolition of the discriminatory structure has been under way for decades. Long before World War II the New World was faced with the irreconcilability of its claims of equality with the facts of discrimination.[1] Now a catalyst was introduced into the picture. In the words of President Truman, "Hitler's persecution of the Jews did much to awaken Americans to the dangerous extremes to which prejudice can be carried if allowed to control government actions."[2] With uncommon perception, the President saw that the retention in mid-twentieth century of discriminatory barriers signified the maintenance of a springboard, and the preservation of a target, for destruction. Such a position could no longer be retained.

Since the American entry into the war, the dismantlement of the barriers has become an object of measures by all levels of government. Federal action has been designed to eliminate the involvement in discrimination of government itself: thus the Congressional legislation to guarantee to all the people the right to vote, the executive order for the desegregation of the armed forces, the executive orders requiring companies under contract with federal agencies to refrain from discrimination in employment, the Supreme Court decisions aimed at desegregating the public schools, and the ruling by the same tribunal that no court of any state may enforce a clause of a contract which prohibits the purchaser of a house to resell the property to a member of a minority group.

On state and local levels, laws are aimed primarily at discrimination in the private sector. The most important of them are the fair employment practices acts (or prohibitions of discrimination in private employment), laws against exclusions in private schools, laws forbidding restrictions in the renting of apartments, and public accommodation laws which make criminal the refusal to serve customers in hotels, restaurants, etc., because of race or creed.[3]

Two reactions have manifested themselves during the continuing retrenchment: there is little effort to recapture bastions that have been given up; at the same time, each new penetration encounters greater and greater resistance. As the rollback proceeds, minorities must be integrated in countless ways. The retreat is an absorption process. Structurally, that phenomenon is an exact inversion of the destruction process which the Germans had brought to perfection (see Table 97). The two processes are reversible.

There is, however, one crucial difference between them. Absorption is far more easily converted into destruction than destruction into absorption. The destruction process can descend upon its victims with lightning speed; absorption progresses from generation to generation. The destruction process had a tendency to accelerate in its final steps; absorption slows down as it reaches toward its goal. In the last analysis, total integration requires complete acceptance. So long as that acceptance is withheld from a group of people, those people will live more or less peacefully in a state of equilibrium between ultimate incorporation and final annihilation.

While the Americans have given ground in the administrative sphere, there has been no yielding on the psychological front. During the drafting of the Genocide Convention the American delegate went so far as to object to the inclusion of a provision

1. See Gunnar Myrdal, *An American Dilemma* (New York and London, 1944), I, xli–lv.

2. Harry S. Truman, *Memoirs* (Garden City, 1956), II, 184.

3. See Jack Greenberg, *Race Relations and American Law* (New York, 1959), as well as the annual and special reports of the U.S. Commission on Civil Rights, from 1959.

which was aimed at "direct incitement" to destruction. He expressed fears that such a prohibition would infringe upon the freedom of the press.[4] Moreover, there is a general reluctance in Congress and the state legislatures to enact any kind of group libel law. The American people have retained their freedom to rationalize. In fact, they have discovered a new set of rationalizations specially suited for an interruption of the integration campaign. Thus the minorities of the country do not "wish" to be integrated; they do not "wish" to mingle with the majority. Even if they should, an American can admit today that he is biased. He cannot "help" that feeling because it has been "instilled" in him in his early youth. The task of liberalization has accordingly been handed to the next generation. One cannot "legislate against prejudice."

TABLE 97 / *The Absorption and Destruction Processes*

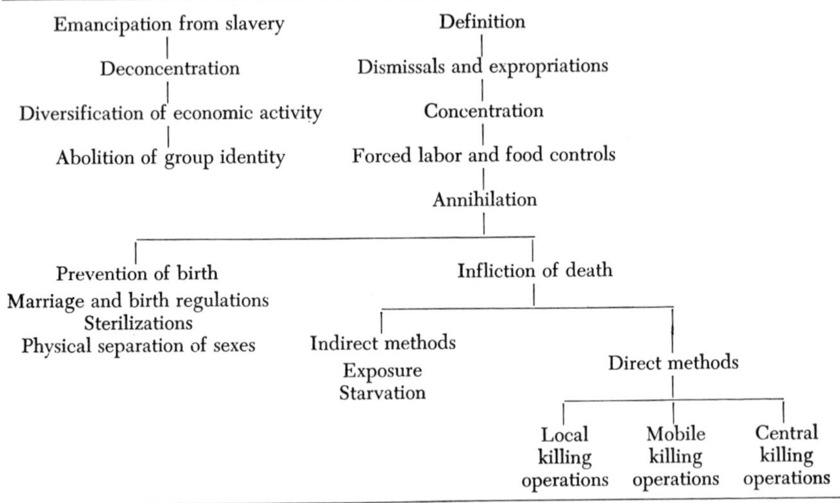

In contradistinction to the United States, the Soviets have not hesitated to restrict the freedom of verbal expression. In the Soviet Union it is a crime to insult the Jews. The same is now true in the satellites.[5] Moreover, during the deliberations in the United Nations Legal Committee on the Genocide Convention, the Soviet delegate invited all the prospective High Contracting Parties to enact "necessary legislative measures" which would outlaw "all forms of public propaganda (press, radio, cinema, etc.) aimed at inciting racial, national or religious enmities."[6] At the same time, however, there appears to be no end in the USSR to bureaucratic discrimination. Since World War II there have been quota

4. Summary of remarks by John Maktos in General Assembly/Legal Committee, *Official Records*, October–December, 1948, pp. 213–14, 224/26. Maktos was supported by Great Britain. Compare with the decision by the U.S. Supreme Court in *Terminiello* v. *Chicago*, 337 US 1 (1949).

5. See Israel Cohen, *Contemporary Jewry* (London, 1950), pp. 291–93.

6. Amendment by USSR, October 9, 1948, UN Doc. A/C.6/215/Rev. 1. The amendment was rejected. In general discussion of the proposal the Russians had the support of France.

restrictions in universities, expulsions of Jews from Party committees down to *Rayon* level, rejections of Jewish applications for positions in the bureaucracy, and nonpromotions of Jews – along with other "unreliable" nationalities – above the rank of junior lieutenant in the Red Army.[7] In administrative matters the Soviets have acknowledged no special problem.

The uneasiness which has been felt by potential perpetrators is not nearly as great as that which is borne by some of the potential victims. Today no group of people is more keenly aware of the increased range of destructive possibilities than the sensitized community of the Jews. Hence we might well ask how the Jewish community has approached its newest challenge. In history we are accustomed to think that new forms of attack will bring out new methods of defense; however, there is usually a lag between the two. The Jews are now in the midst of just such a lag. There has been no radical change in the Jewish position. The Jewish leadership has been retained. Its thinking has been perpetuated. In all the postwar Jewish activities we can see only an intensification of Jewry's two traditional reactions, the appeal and the tendency to flight.

The Jewish appeal has become more total. It is no longer a request for a Jewish privilege but a demand for universal rights. It seeks admission not only for Jews but for all sufferers of discrimination. The Jewish community no longer wants a private assurance but legal rules and established practice on a national and international scale. The Jews seek to perfect their position in society by perfecting the society in which they live.[8]

In the United States one of the chief contributors to the new course was a lawyer, Alexander Pekelis. Partly as a consequence of his efforts, the American Jewish Congress established a "Commission on Law and Social Action" which since 1945 has fought, law in hand, battle after battle in the American courts.[9]

On an international basis a campaign started almost single-handedly by Raphael Lemkin resulted in the writing of a convention which is directed at persons who are committing acts with intent to destroy, in whole or in part, a national, ethnic, racial, or religious group. The convention obligates each member state that may be the scene of these acts to try such persons for their offense. Should there be no trial, or should a government be involved itself, any contracting party may submit the case to the International Court of Justice.[10] The text of the document

7. See U.S. Department of State/Office of Intelligence Research/External Research Staff, *The Soviet Union As Reported by Former Soviet Citizens,* Interim Reports 1–16, 1951–55, *passim.* Also, Joseph Scholmer, *Vorkuta* (New York, 1955), pp. 104–20. For a discussion of the Jewish position in the USSR up to 1951, see Solomon M. Schwarz, *The Jews in the Soviet Union* (Syracuse, 1951). Roumania and Hungary, through the introduction of forced labor, appear to have dealt more harshly with their Jewish population. See Peter Meyer *et al., The Jews in the Soviet Satellites* (Syracuse, 1953). Anti-Jewish machinations of the Stalinist faction in Poland are described by Lucjan Blit in "Poland and the Jewish Remnant," *Commentary,* March, 1957, pp. 215–21.

8. See David W. Petegorsky, *On Combating Racism* (New York, 1948).

9. The commission was established on November 29, 1945, after the submission of a memorandum by Will Maslow and Alexander Pekelis on August 1, 1945. Albert Churchill Ettinger, "Socio-Economic Ideological Change in the American Jewish Congress and the National Association for the Advancement of Colored People," 1950, unpublished.

10. See the text of the Genocide Convention, adopted by the General Assembly on December 9, 1948, and opened for signature and ratification or accession, in U.N. Press Release PGA/100, Part VII, pp. 12–16. The term "genocide" was coined by Lemkin. See his *Axis Rule in Occupied Europe* (Washington, 1944), pp. 79–95.

reads almost as though there were a determination to root out the scourge.

However, the acceptance of the convention by a majority of all countries around the globe does not imply that each accepting state has admitted the possibility of destructive action by its government against some minority group. If there is any implication, it is rather the propensity of each state to accuse some other signatory of that possibility. Such was the attempt of the United States to insert a provision against the destruction of "economic groups" and the attempted inclusion by the USSR of a declaration in the preamble that "genocide is organically bound up with fascism-nazism and other similar race 'theories.'"[11] In the end the United States did not ratify that treaty, and the Soviets accepted it only with the reservation that they would not be answerable for their actions to the International Court.[12] Thus the two most powerful states in the world would not even pay unqualified lip service to a convention whose manifest aim is the frustration of another catastrophe.

The Jewish attempt to constrain the potential perpetrator in a complex system of legal bounds is supplemented by parallel action in the propagandistic field. The propaganda deals with the cost which would be incurred in a destructive upheaval. That, to be sure, is an old message, but its emphasis has changed. In the past the Jews have talked about their usefulness and indispensability. Now there are hints of the actual damage which destruction must invariably cause outside the initial target group. Even in its early stages the attack will engulf other races and other nationalities.[13] With the onset of drastic action, psychically crippling effects will leave their mark on the slaughterers.[14] When, finally, a society runs amuck in limitless destruction, no one will be safe. "It is one of the laws of psychology, which is in harmony also with more general physiological principles, that destructive urges of great magnitude and depth and destructive concepts arising therefrom cannot remain limited or focused but must inevitably spread and be directed against one's own group and ultimately against the self."[15]

Along with a strengthened appeal,

11. U.S. amendment of October 4, 1948, U.N. Doc. A/C.6/214. Soviet amendment of November 18, 1948, U.N. Doc. A/C.6/273. Neither amendment was adopted.

12. Fear was expressed before the U.S. Senate Foreign Relations Committee that, under Article 6 of the U.S. Constitution, the convention as "supreme law of the land" would be invoked by minority groups before the courts to strike down discriminatory laws of various state and local jurisdictions. See testimony by George A. Finch (American Bar Association) in Hearings on the Genocide Convention in Subcommittee of the Senate Committee on Foreign Relations, 81st Cong., 2d sess., January 23–February 9, 1950, p. 217. Also, replies and explanations by Adrian Fisher (legal adviser, Department of State), *ibid.*, pp. 263–64. Text of Soviet reservation in *American Journal of International Law,* XLV supp., 11–14.

13. Note the implications in T. W. Adorno, Else Frenkel-Brunswick, Daniel Levinson, and R. Nevitt Sanford, *The Authoritarian Personality* (New York, 1950), p. 45. Characteristic is this jingle by Edward James Smythe, executive chairman of a paper organization called the Protestant War Veterans:

> God Bless America
> The Jews own it
> The Catholics run it
> The Negroes enjoy it
> The Protestants founded it
> But
> The Communists will destroy it

Ralph Lord Roy, *Apostles of Discord* (Boston, 1953), pp. 171–73.

14. Leon Poliakov, *Harvest of Hate* (New York, 1954), pp. 286–88.

15. Leo Alexander, "War Crimes – Their Social-Psychological Aspects," *American Journal of Psychiatry,* CV, 172. Also, his "Destructive and Self-Destructive Trends in Criminalized Society," *Journal of Criminal Law and Criminology,* January–February, 1949, XXXIX, 559.

the Jews have developed to a greater extent than before their mechanism of flight. The perfection of this system has involved the Jewish community in far-flung activities. An attempt has been made to establish an international right of escape. Thus the provisions of the Universal Declaration of Human Rights:

> Everyone has the right to leave any country, including his own. . . .
> Everyone has the right to seek and to enjoy in other countries asylum from persecution. . . .[16]

To make sure that no movement would flounder in midstream, the Jews have been clearing the way. A veritable escape apparatus has been built. A place of refuge has been established in Israel.[17] Fund-raising organizations capable of financing major migrations are operating on a permanent basis. Danger areas have been charted on the map, and the relaxation of exit restrictions in such areas can be followed by instantaneous evacuations.[18]

Since the end of the Jewish catastrophe, basic decisions have been made about the future. In the Christian world the remaining alternatives are gradually moving toward polar ends. After two thousand years there is no defensible middle ground. The ancient compromise, with all its contradictions, is weakening day by day. To the Jewish community that growing dichotomy conveys unique opportunities and unprecedented vulnerabilities. Jewry is faced with ultimate weapons. It has no deterrent. The Jews can live more freely now. They can also die more quickly. The summit is within sight. An abyss has opened below.

16. Universal Declaration of Human Rights, adopted by the General Assembly on December 10, 1948, U.N. Press Release PGA/100, Part IV, pp. 11–16. The United Nations established under the Economic and Social Council a Commission on Human Rights. This commission has a Subcommission on the Prevention of Discrimination and Protection of Minorities. In 1958 the United States delegate in the subcommission, Judge Philip Halpern, was able to win unanimous support (including the vote of the delegate of the USSR) for his resolution that the subcommission study for its next report the subject of emigration. Verbatim text of press conference by J. Halpern, February 7, 1958, issued by U.S. Mission to United Nations (mimeographed).

17. Under Israel law all Jews are eligible to migrate into the country, and no extradition treaty may be made for the return of any Jewish escapee.

18. This development has not been produced without a certain degree of internal resistance. There is an isolationist movement among the Jews which seeks to cut itself off from all fortunes of Jewish communities abroad. It is characterized by a reluctance to participate in international Jewish projects, repeated denunciations of Zionism, and frequent declarations of loyalty and undivided allegiance to the country of permanent residence.

APPENDIXES

Appendix I / *Civil Service Ranks*

Rank	Administrative Unit
Reichsminister *Staatssekretär*	*Reichsministerium*
Unterstaatssekretär *Ministerialdirektor*	*Abteilung*
Ministerialdirigent	*Unterabteilung* or *Amt* or *Amtsgruppe*
Ministerialrat *Oberregierungsrat* *Regierungsrat* *Botschaftsrat* (Foreign Office) *Gesandtschaftsrat* (Foreign Office) *Legationsrat* (Foreign Office) *Amtsrat*	*Referat*

See Arnold Brecht, *The Art and Technique of Administration in German Ministries* (Cambridge, 1940), pp. 171–85. The *Referent* (level of *Referat*) was usually an expert. Most first drafts of decrees were prepared by *Referenten*. See Brecht, *ibid.*, pp. 179–82. For complete classifications, by salary, see the following decrees: December 16, 1927, RGBl I, 349; March 19, 1937, RGBl I, 342; March 30, 1943, RGBl I, 189.

Appendix II / *SS and Army Ranks*

SS	German Army	U.S. Army
Untersturmführer	*Leutnant*	Second lieutenant
Obersturmführer	*Oberleutnant*	First lieutenant
Hauptsturmführer	*Hauptmann*	Captain
Sturmbannführer	*Major*	Major
Obersturmbannführer	*Oberstleutnant*	Lieutenant colonel
Standartenführer	*Oberst*	Colonel
Oberführer		
Brigadeführer	*Generalmajor*	Brigadier general
Gruppenführer	*Generalleutnant*	Major general
Obergruppenführer	*General der Infanterie, Artillerie,* etc.	Lieutenant general
Oberst-Gruppenführer	*Generaloberst*	General
Reichsführer	*Generalfeldmarschall*	General of the army

Appendix III / Statistics on Jewish Dead

Statistical Recapitulation of Jewish Dead (by operation)

Area of mobile killing operations			1,400,000
Tabulated dead		900,000	
Untabulated dead		500,000	
Unreported by *Einsatzgruppen*	150,000?		
Higher SS and Police Leaders and BdS GG	100,000		
Army killings, PW killings, and operations by anti-partisan units	100,000		
Ghetto dead	100,000?		
Death of fleeing Jews	50,000?		
Area of deportations			3,700,000
Killed in camps (including Transnistria)		3,000,000	
Ghetto and aggravated deaths		700,000	
Total			5,100,000

*Statistical Recapitulation of Jewish Dead (by territory)**

250,000	Reich-Protektorat area		250,000
	USSR		700,000
3,900,000	Baltic states		200,000
	Poland		3,000,000
	Mobile operations	500,000	
	Ghetto dead	550,000	
	Killed in camps	1,950,000	
	North	(less than a thousand)	
200,000	The Low Countries		130,000
	France and Italy		70,000
	Yugoslavia		60,000
	Greece and Rhodes		60,000
750,000	Slovakia		60,000
	Roumania		270,000
	Hungary and Carpatho-Ukraine		300,000
5,100,000	Total		5,100,000

*Borders refer to August, 1939.

Appendix IV / *Notation on Sources*

Documents

In the main, German documents have been cited only by series and number. The following is a key to the various document series referred to in the notes.

1. Nuremberg documents: (Reasonably complete collections of mimeographed copies may be found in major depository libraries such as the Library of Congress and the Columbia Law Library.)

EC	PS
L	R
M	RF
NG	SA
NI	SS
NO	UK
NOKW	USSR

All documents beginning with the name of a defendant, for instance, Funk-13, Speer-10, etc.

A number of the documents (other than NG, NI, NO and NOKW) may be consulted in two publications:

International Military Tribunal, *Trial of the Major War Criminals* (Nuremberg, 1947–49), 42 vols. (in German).

Office of United States Counsel for Prosecution of Axis Criminality, *Nazi Conspiracy and Aggression* (Washington, D.C., 1946–48), 8 vols. and 2 supp. (in translation).

Some of the documents used in Nuremberg subsequent trials (including NG, NI, NO, and NOKW) are printed in:

Nuernberg Military Tribunals, *Trials of War Criminals* (Washington, D.C., 1947–49), 15 vols. (in translation).

Mimeographed transcripts of the Nuremberg trials are located in depository libraries. A complete transcript of the trial before the International Military Tribunal is included in the *Trial of the Major War Criminals;* excerpts from the transcripts of the subsequent proceedings are reproduced in the *Trials of War Criminals.*

2. Original documents in the YIVO Institute, 1048 Fifth Avenue, New York City:

G, Occ, the Ghetto Collections (documents of the Jewish councils of Lodz, Warsaw, and Vilna, mostly in Yiddish).

3. Original documents in the Federal Records Center, Alexandria, Virginia, declassified for public use, and cited with the permission of the Adjutant General, United States Army:

EAP
H
OKW
Wi

4. The Himmler Files in the Manuscript Division of the Library of Congress. The files contain the correspondence of the *Reichsführer-SS/Persönlicher Stab.*

5. Document collections available to the American public only in printed form.

Akten zur Deutschen Auswärtigen Politik 1918–1945, containing the German Foreign Office correspondence; volumes dealing with the period 1933–41 have been published so far by the governments of the United States, Great Britain, and France.

Dokumenty i Materialy, containing correspondence of German agencies in Poland, and published by the Jewish Historical Commission in Poland; three volumes, available in the YIVO Institute.

Leon Poliakov (ed.) (Centre de Documentation), *La Condition des Juifs en France sous l'occupation italienne* (Paris, 1946).

Laws, statutes, etc.

The principal source of German law was the *Reichsgesetzblatt* (RGBl). In addition, central ministries and regional authorities in areas outside the Reich published ordinances in gazettes of their own. Examples of ministerial gazettes are the *Reichsarbeitsblatt* of the Labor Ministry and the *Ministerial-Blatt* of the Interior Ministry. Examples of territorial gazettes published in occupied territory are the *Verordnungsblatt des Reichsprotektors in Böhmen und Mähren* and the *Verordnungsblatt des Generalgouverneurs.* Large collections of these decrees may be found in the Columbia Law Library and in the Foreign Law Division of the Library of Congress.

Readers may also be interested in consulting commentaries by German bureaucrats. These commentaries are authoritative insofar as they were prepared by the same people who had drafted the decrees. Examples of such works are Stuckart's *Rassenpflege* and Oermann's *Sozialausgleichsabgabe*.

Newspapers and periodicals

Two newspapers published in German-occupied territories contain an extraordinary amount of information about Jewish matters. The papers are the *Krakauer Zeitung* (published in identical editions in Krakow and Warsaw) and the *Donauzeitung* (published in Belgrade). They are available in the Newspaper Division of the Library of Congress.

One Nazi periodical was devoted entirely to Jewish affairs: *Die Judenfrage*. Its confidential annex (*Vertrauliche Beilage*) contains interesting information about anti-Jewish action in Germany and other countries. *Die Judenfrage* may be consulted in the Library of Congress and the YIVO Institute.

The Jewish communities in Berlin, Vienna, and Prague published separate editions of the *Jüdisches Nachrichtenblatt*. The counterpart of that paper in Poland was the *Gazeta Zydowska*. Copies of the Jewish ghetto press are on deposit in the YIVO Institute.

Accounts by survivors

The number of titles in this category numbers in the tens of thousands. An exhaustive compilation of the entire catastrophe literature was under preparation by the late Dr. Philip Friedman of Columbia University and the YIVO Institute.

Postscript

Six years have passed since the original publication of this book. More documents have become available during that time. The great majority of them add to those passages which are already the most detailed. They do not fill major gaps nor do they alter important conclusions.

We have obtained, for example, an exact count of Jews deported from Italy, and we now know the precise number of guards killed in the Sobibor revolt. We can draw upon new sources on the naval deportations of several hundred Jews from Norway, and we have a day-by-day record of the convulsions in Hungary.

On the other hand, occurrences which could only be surmised when this book first went to press are largely still unknown. What has come to light about them is fragmentary and incomplete. To be sure, these fragments are markers in uncharted territory; unlike the accretions to known domains, they are indications of developments yet to be explored. Three samples of such items are listed below. One is taken from the earliest phase of the destruction process, the second is a highlight of its climax, the third is a revelation from its end.

Example I. One of our difficult problems is to understand how the German bureaucracy started its work, how its very first moves were made. To comprehend these beginnings is to have insight into some of the motivations and predispositions which gave rise to the whole undertaking. We could always assume that the administrative apparatus was ready to act, that it did not have to be told what to do. Yet, we did not have much evidence about actual conceptualizations in the bureaucratic ranks as the process began. Now, through the courtesy of an East German ambassador, Professor Stefan Heymann, we may cite such a document from the archives of East Berlin. It is a directive, drafted by an expert in the Prussian Interior Ministry with a text that seems almost innocuous.

The subject of the directive was names. Part VI was entitled "Jew names" (Judennamen). It was not dishonorable, the directive stated, for a Jew to carry a Jewish name. The regional offices were consequently instructed not to grant name changes to persons who wished to conceal their Jewish origins. Neither conversion to Christianity nor anti-Semitic "currents" were grounds for such action. Only those applicants who had "offensive" Jewish names (like Itzig or Schmul) or repulsive names (such as Totenkopf or Nachtschweiss) might obtain relief in the same way as Germans who were afflicted with offensive names of German origin. But the Jews would have to adopt a name similar to the one they wanted to drop (Issen or Schmal), or the name of some relative or a fantasy name. They were not to be given a name which was circulating in the general population.

The directive, which was marked "not for publication," was written by Dr. Hans Globke, a man who rose to high rank in the civil service during and after the Nazi regime. It was issued on December 23, 1932, five weeks *before* Adolf Hitler became Chancellor of the German Reich.

Example II. One of the agencies heavily involved in the physical destruction of the Jews was the administration of the German railways. Trains brought more than half of the victims to their death. The men who organized the transports and shoved them to the very gates of the gas chambers were members of one of the largest bureaucracies in Germany. Yet, documents of the railroads are few and far between. The Jewish Historical Commission of Warsaw discovered one of the more revealing ones. It is a bill, presented May 19, 1942, by a railway man in Lodz to the Gestapo in that city, for payment of 32,429 Reichsmark and 35 Pfennige at the ticket window of the railway station, following the dispatch of 10,993 Jews in twelve "special trains" (*abgefertigten Juden-Sonderzüge*) to the vicinity of the nearby killing center of Kulmhof. For the 155 guards, the railway demanded 868 Reichsmark round-trip fare.

Example III. As yet, we know less than we might wish about events outside the destructive arena, particularly in allied capitals where the killing of the Jews was watched from afar. In their letters and memoirs the allied leaders appear to have omitted the Jews more often than they mentioned them. But one of the more important communications from an allied government is now available. It was introduced in the Eichmann trial, and a copy was sent to me in a folder from the Weizmann Institute through the kindness of the Prime Minister's Office in Jerusalem.

During the deportations of the Hungarian Jews in 1944, Chaim Weizmann transmitted two Jewish requests to Foreign Secretary Eden to bomb gassing installations and railway lines at Birkenau in Auschwitz where, in the twilight hours of the Nazi regime, several hundred thousand Jews were being killed. The answer was not immediate. It came on September 1, 1944, and its text in full is as follows:

> My dear Dr. Weizmann,
>
> You will remember that on the 6th of July you discussed with the Foreign Secretary the camp at Birkenau in Upper Silesia, and the atrocities that were being committed there by Germans against Hungarian and other Jews. You enquired whether any steps could be taken to put a stop to, or even to mitigate, these massacres, and you suggested that something might be achieved by bombing the camps, and also, if it was possible, the railway lines leading to them.
>
> As he promised, Mr. Eden immediately put the proposal to the Secretary of State for Air. The matter received the most careful consideration of the Air Staff, but I am sorry to have to tell you that, in view of the very great technical difficulties involved, we have no option but to refrain from pursuing the proposal in present circumstances.
>
> I realise that this decision will prove a disappointment to you, but you may feel fully assured that the matter was most thoroughly investigated.
>
> Yours sincerely,
> Richard Law

Documents like these are nuclei of information about happenings which were heretofore unseen. We shall never know the whole story, but we shall reduce our ignorance as relentlessly as once these events were pressed.

INDEX